Southwest

Rob Rachowiecki

LONELY PLANET PUBLICATIONS
Melbourne • Oakland • London • Paris

Southwest

2nd edition

Published by
    Lonely Planet Publications
    Head Office: PO Box 617, Hawthorn, Vic 3122, Australia
    Branches: 150 Linden St, Oakland, CA 94607, USA
                    10A Spring Place, London NW5 3BH, UK
                    1 rue du Dahomey, 75011 Paris, France

Printed by
    The Bookmaker Pty Ltd
    Printed in China

Photographs by
    Front cover: Ralph Lee Hopkins/Wilderland Images, saguaro cactus in the desert

Lee Foster	Ralph Lee Hopkins	Chuck Place
Rick Gerharter	Bonnie Kamin	Rob Rachowiecki
Kim Grant	Maria Massolo	Stephen Trimble
Kim Hammar	Ann Neet	Tony Wheeler

First Published
    November 1995

This Edition
    March 1999

Although the author and publisher have tried to make the information as accurate as possible, they accept no responsibility for any loss, injury or inconvenience sustained by any person using this book.

ISBN 0 86442 539 2

text & maps © Lonely Planet 1999
photos © photographers as indicated 1999
climate chart compiled from information supplied by Patrick J Tyson, © Patrick J Tyson, 1999

FROM THE AUTHORS
Rob Rachowiecki

Rob was born in London and became an avid traveler as a teenager. He has visited places as diverse as Greenland and Thailand and is the author of Lonely Planet's guides to Ecuador, Peru and Costa Rica. Rob is an active member of the Society of American Travel Writers. Since 1989, he has lived in Tucson, Arizona, with his wife, Cathy, and children, Julia, Alison and David. He finds Tucson to be an ideal base from which to explore what he considers to be the most beautiful region of the USA.

Dedication To my son, David, who is the coolest dude I know.

Thanks I thank the staffers at chambers of commerce throughout the Southwest who provided town maps and useful information. Rangers and officials at all federal and state parks were unfailingly helpful with updating; Russ Bodnar at Chaco Canyon was especially helpful with his interpretation of that site. Mrs Ina McAteer's 2nd grade class (with my daughter Alison) allowed me to tag along on their field trip to Tombstone. I enjoyed seeing that town through the eyes of eight-year-olds!

Many readers of the 1st edition sent in suggestions and updates – their names are listed at the back of this book. I really do appreciate all of your input. I thank the several editors (especially Ben Greensfelder) and cartographers (especially Henia Miedzinski) who worked so hard to make this 2nd edition a great improvement over the 1st.

I especially thank my family for enabling me to travel for many weeks to update this book, and for being unfailingly supportive of my work. I love you.

Jennifer Rasin Denniston

Jennifer began traveling independently as a teenager, and by age 21 had visited Africa, Australia, Europe, Vietnam, Japan and China. Although born and raised in the Midwest, she lived several years in Albuquerque and calls New Mexico home. When she is not researching or writing on the Southwest for Lonely Planet, Jennifer is studying the American West and visual culture as an American Studies PhD candidate at the University of Iowa. She is joined in Iowa City and in her roving explorations of the United States by her husband, Rhawn, and their golden retriever, Cyril.

Thanks Thanks to Rob for his support, guidance and patience; to Ben for his help; and to the cartographers at Lonely Planet. To my husband, whose offhanded comment on a plane encouraged me to follow my passion, simply thank you.

FROM THE PUBLISHER

This book was produced in Lonely Planet's Oakland, California, office. The numerous maps were drawn by Henia Miedzinski, Tim Lohnes and Andy Rebold, each of whom oversaw the mapping at a different stage of the project. Also working on maps were Tracey Croom, Amy Dennis, Dion Good, Guphy, Patrick Huerta, Margaret Livingston, Kimra McAfee, Chris Whinihan and Bart Wright. Alex Guilbert supervised the mapping crew.

The book was taken through production by Ben Greensfelder, with much support from Kate Hoffman and Suki Gear. Copy editing was done by Suki and Ben, Jeff Campbell and Julie Connery. Proofreaders were Julie, Suki, Joslyn Leve and Ben. Joslyn also provided invaluable help checking maps, facts and more details. Ben and Suki indexed the book. Layout was done by Wendy Yanagihara, Emily Douglas and Richard Wilson. The cover was designed by Rini Keagy and Hugh D'Andrade, and the illustrations were drawn by Hayden Foell, Hugh, John Fadeff, Jim Swanson and Jacques Talbot.

The Southeastern Colorado chapter was drawn from material written by the ever-conscientious Nicko Goncharoff for Lonely Planet's *Rocky Mountains*; the Las Vegas chapter was written by Scott McNeely for Lonely Planet's *USA*.

Warning & Request

Things change – prices go up, schedules change, good places go bad and bad places go bankrupt – nothing stays the same. So, if you find things better or worse, recently opened or long since closed, please tell us and help make the next edition even more accurate and useful.

We value all of the feedback we receive from travelers. A small team reads and acknowledges every letter, postcard and email, and ensures that every morsel of information finds its way to the appropriate authors, editors and publishers. All readers who write to us will find their names in the next edition of the appropriate guide and will also receive a free subscription to our quarterly newsletter, *Planet Talk*. The very best contributions will be rewarded with a free Lonely Planet guide.

Excerpts from your correspondence may appear in new editions of this guide, in *Planet Talk* or in the Postcards section of our website – so please let us know if you don't want your letter published or your name acknowledged.

Thanks

Many thanks to the travelers who used the last edition and wrote to us with helpful hints, useful advice and interesting anecdotes. Your names appear in the back of the book.

Contents

INTRODUCTION **15**

FACTS ABOUT THE SOUTHWEST **17**

History 17	Flora & Fauna 35	Arts 43
Geography 27	Government & Politics 40	Religion 45
Geology 28	Economy 42	Language 46
Climate 31	Population 42	
Ecology & Environment 32	People 43	

FACTS FOR THE VISITOR **47**

Planning 47	Electricity 61	Emergency 72
Tourist Offices 48	Weights & Measures 61	Legal Matters 72
Visas & Documents 48	Laundry 62	Business Hours & Holidays . . 73
Embassies 50	Recycling 62	Cultural Events 73
Customs 51	Toilets 62	Special Events 74
Money 51	Health 62	Work 77
Post & Communications 54	Women Travelers 65	Accommodations 78
Internet Resources 56	Gay & Lesbian Travelers 66	Food 84
Books 57	Disabled Travelers 67	Drinks 86
Newspapers 60	Senior Travelers 68	Entertainment 87
Radio & TV 60	Travel with Children 68	Spectator Sports 87
Photography & Video 61	Useful Organizations 68	Shopping 88
Time 61	Dangers & Annoyances 70	

OUTDOOR ACTIVITIES **91**

Hiking & Backpacking 91	Downhill Skiing &	Rock Climbing 99
Bicycling & Mountain Biking . 95	Snowboarding 97	Hot-Air Ballooning 99
River Running 96	Other Winter Activities 98	Rockhounding 100
Boating 96	Bird Watching 99	Jeep Touring 100
Fishing 97	Horseback Riding 99	Golf 100

GETTING THERE & AWAY **101**

Air 101	Organized Tours 109	Departure Taxes 110
Land 107		

GETTING AROUND **111**

Air 111	Car 112	Local Transport 116
Bus 111	Bicycle 115	Organized Tours 116
Train 112	Hitchhiking 115	

FACTS ABOUT UTAH ... 118

SALT LAKE CITY ... 123

History ... 123
Orientation ... 124
Information ... 126
Downtown ... 128
Around Downtown ... 133
Outside The City ... 136
Activities ... 138
Organized Tours ... 142
Special Events ... 143
Places to Stay ... 143
Places to Eat ... 149
Entertainment ... 155
Spectator Sports ... 156
Shopping ... 157
Getting There & Away ... 157
Getting Around ... 158

WASATCH MOUNTAINS REGION ... 159

Antelope Island State Park ... 159
Ogden ... 161
Ogden-Area Ski Resorts ... 169
Willard Bay State Park ... 170
Ogden to Park City ... 170
Park City ... 171
Heber City & Midway Area ... 182
Around Heber City ... 185
Provo ... 187
Around Provo ... 194

NORTHERN UTAH ... 196

**Brigham City & the
  Northwest Corner ... 196**
Brigham City ... 196
Tremonton ... 200
Golden Spike National
  Historic Site ... 200
Around Golden Spike
  National Historic Site ... 201
The Northwestern Mountains 202
Bridgerland ... 202
Logan ... 202
Around Logan ... 207
Logan Canyon Scenic Drive ... 208
Beaver Mountain Ski Area ... 209
Garden City & Bear Lake ... 209
South of Bear Lake ... 211

NORTHEASTERN UTAH ... 212

Mirror Lake Highway
  (Hwy 150) ... 212
Strawberry Reservoir Area ... 212
Uinta Mountains ... 214
Duchesne & Around ... 215
Roosevelt & Around ... 216
Uintah & Ouray Indian
  Reservation ... 218
Vernal ... 218
Around Vernal ... 222
Flaming Gorge National
  Recreation Area ... 223
Dinosaur National
  Monument ... 228

WESTERN UTAH ... 231

Wendover ... 231
Bonneville Salt Flats ... 233
Tooele ... 234
Around Tooele ... 235
Pony Express Trail ... 236
Eureka ... 238
Little Sahara Recreation Area 238
Delta ... 239
Around Delta ... 240
Great Basin National Park
  (Nevada) ... 240
Hwy 21 ... 241

CENTRAL UTAH ... 243

Central I-15 Corridor ... 244
Payson ... 244
Nephi & Around ... 245
Fillmore & Around ... 246
Central Hwy 89 Corridor ... 248
Skyline Drive ... 248
Fairview ... 248
Mt Pleasant ... 249
Spring City ... 250
Ephraim ... 250
Manti ... 251
Gunnison ... 252
Salina ... 252
Richfield ... 253
Monroe ... 255
Fremont Indian State Park ... 256
Marysvale ... 256
**East of the Wasatch
  Plateau ... 256**
Helper ... 257
Scofield State Park ... 258
Price ... 258
Wellington ... 261
Huntington & Around ... 262
Castle Dale & Around ... 262
Ferron ... 264

SOUTHWESTERN UTAH 265

I-15 Corridor &
   Zion National Park 265
Beaver 266
East of Beaver 269
Parowan 270
Brian Head 272
Cedar Breaks National
   Monument 273
Cedar City 274
Hwy 14 East of Cedar City . . 279
St George 279
Around St George 287
Hurricane 289
Grafton Ghost Town &
   Rockville 290

Springdale 290
Zion National Park 293
Southern Hwy 89 Corridor . 299
Junction, Circleville
   & Around 299
Panguitch 300
Panguitch Lake 302
Hatch 303
Glendale 304
Orderville & Mt Carmel
   Junction 304
Coral Pink Sand Dunes State
   Park 304
Kanab 305

Bryce Canyon to
   Capitol Reef 308
Bryce Canyon National Park . 308
Kodachrome Basin
   State Park 313
Escalante & Around 313
Grand Staircase-Escalante
   National Monument 314
Boulder 318
Torrey Area 318
Loa & Fish Lake 320
Capitol Reef National Park . . 321
Caineville 325

SOUTHEASTERN UTAH 326

Green River & Around 326
Green River 327
Thompson & Sego Canyon . . 330
San Rafael Desert & Reef . . . 330
Goblin Valley State Park 331
Hanksville 331
Henry Mountains 331
Arches National Park
   to Blanding 332
Arches National Park 332

Dead Horse Point State Park . 337
Canyonlands National Park . . 337
Moab 343
Newspaper Rock Park 353
Monticello 353
Blanding 355
Around Four Corners 357
Natural Bridges National
   Monument 357
Fry Canyon 358

Hwy 261 – The Moki Dugway
   Backway 358
Mexican Hat &
   Monument Valley 359
Glen Canyon National
   Recreation Area 360
Bluff 360
Hovenweep National
   Monument 362

NEVADA

LAS VEGAS, NEVADA 366

Around Las Vegas 371

ARIZONA

FACTS ABOUT ARIZONA 374

PHOENIX 381

History 381
Orientation 383
Information 384
Central Phoenix 388
Outer Phoenix 391
Scottsdale 392
Tempe 394

Mesa 395
Suburban Phoenix 397
Suburban Parks 398
Activities 399
Organized Tours 401
Special Events 401
Places to Stay 402

Places to Eat 410
Entertainment 415
Spectator Sports 416
Shopping 417
Getting There & Away 418
Getting Around 418

GRAND CANYON & LAKE POWELL 420

South of the
Colorado River 422
Grand Canyon National
Park – South Rim 422
Tusayan 438
Valle 441
Hualapai Indian Reservation . 441
Havasupai Indian
Reservation 443

Cameron & Around 444
The Arizona Strip 445
Marble Canyon &
Lees Ferry Area 445
Jacob Lake Area 446
Grand Canyon National
Park – North Rim 448
Fredonia 451
Around Fredonia 451

Lake Powell Area 452
Page 452
Glen Canyon National
Recreation Area 457
Rainbow Bridge
National Monument 461

WESTERN ARIZONA 463

Northwestern Arizona 463
Kingman 465
Route 66 469
Chloride 470
Lake Mead National
Recreation Area (NRA) . . 471
Bullhead City & Laughlin . . . 475
Havasu National
Wildlife Refuge 478

Lake Havasu City 478
Parker 484
Quartzsite 486
Salome 487
Alamo Lake State Park 488
The Lower Colorado 488
Kofa National Wildlife
Refuge 488

Cibola National Wildlife
Refuge 489
Imperial National Wildlife
Refuge 489
Yuma 489
Cabeza Prieta National
Wildlife Refuge 498
Gila Bend 498

CENTRAL ARIZONA 500

Wickenburg 500
Prescott 505
Jerome 514
Cottonwood 517

Camp Verde & Around 520
Sedona 522
Flagstaff 536
Around Flagstaff 551

Williams 555
Ash Fork 561
Seligman 562

NORTHEASTERN ARIZONA 563

The I-40 Corridor 564
Winslow 564
Holbrook 567
Petrified Forest National
Park 570
Navajo Indian Reservation 571
Window Rock 575
Hubbell Trading Post
National Historic Site 577

Canyon De Chelly
National Monument 577
Tsaile 580
Four Corners Monument
Navajo Tribal Park 580
Tes Nez Iah 580
Kayenta 580
Monument Valley Navajo
Tribal Park 581
Navajo National Monument . 582

Shonto 583
Tuba City 583
Hopi Indian Reservation . . 583
Orientation 584
Keams Canyon 585
First Mesa 585
Second Mesa 587
Third Mesa 587

EAST-CENTRAL ARIZONA 588

Payson & Around 589
Scenic Hwy 260 593
Show Low 594
Pinetop-Lakeside 597
White Mountain Apache
Indian Reservation 601
Greer 603

Springerville & Eagar 604
Lyman Lake State Park 608
St Johns 608
Coronado Trail Scenic Road . 608
Alpine 609
Clifton & Morenci 610
Safford 611

San Carlos Apache Indian
Reservation 614
Globe 615
Around Globe 618
The Apache Trail 618

TUCSON & SOUTHERN ARIZONA 621

Tucson **622**
History................... 623
Orientation............... 624
Information............... 625
Downtown Tucson 628
University of Arizona 630
Beyond Downtown 632
Activities................. 633
Organized Tours 637
Special Events............. 637
Places to Stay 638
Places to Eat 643
Entertainment 648

Spectator Sports 650
Shopping 650
Getting There & Away 651
Getting Around 651
Around Tucson 652
Saguaro National Park...... 654
Between Tucson &
   Phoenix.............. 656
Picacho Peak State Park 656
Casa Grande Area 657
West of Tucson 658
Buenos Aires National
   Wildlife Refuge Loop.... 658

Tohono O'odham Indian
   Reservation............ 659
Kitt Peak National Optical
   Observatory........... 660
Organ Pipe Cactus National
   Monument............. 660
Lukeville & Sonoita (Sonora) 661
Ajo...................... 661
South of Tucson......... 662
Green Valley & Around 662
Tubac & Around 664
Nogales & Around 665
Patagonia & Sonoita 668

SOUTHEASTERN ARIZONA 672

Benson................... 673
Around Benson 674
Sierra Vista 675
Around Sierra Vista........ 678

Tombstone............... 680
Bisbee Area.............. 684
Douglas & Around 689
Willcox 691

Around Willcox........... 694
Chiricahua Mountains &
   Chiricahua National
   Monument............. 695

COLORADO

SOUTHWESTERN COLORADO 700

Cortez 700
Around Cortez........... 703

Mesa Verde National Park .. 707
Mancos 713

Dolores 713

NEW MEXICO

FACTS ABOUT NEW MEXICO...................................... 716

ALBUQUERQUE... 723

History................... 723
Orientation............... 724
Information 725
Old Town Area 725
Downtown Area 727
University of New Mexico
   (UNM) Area 728

Metropolitan Albuquerque .. 729
Activities................. 731
Organized Tours 732
Special Events............. 732
Places to Stay 733
Places to Eat 738
Entertainment 741

Spectator Sports 744
Shopping 744
Getting There & Away 744
Getting Around 745
North of Albuquerque...... 745
East & South of Albuquerque 748

SANTA FE & TAOS... 752

Santa Fe................. 753
Around Santa Fe 776
Santa Fe to Española....... 777
Española & Around........ 779
Española to Taos.......... 781

Taos..................... 784
The Enchanted Circle 802
Questa 803
Wild Rivers National
   Recreation Area 803

Red River................ 803
Eagle Nest 806
Angel Fire 806

NORTHWESTERN NEW MEXICO 808

The Farmington Area 808
Farmington 809
Around Farmington 816
Aztec 816
Bloomfield 819
Navajo Dam & Navajo Lake
State Park 820
Chaco Culture National
Historical Park 821
Jicarilla Apache Indian
Reservation 822
Chama to Española 823
Chama 824

Tierra Amarilla & Around . . . 828
Carson National Forest 828
Abiquiu & Around 829
Pajarito Plateau &
Jemez Mountains 830
Los Alamos 831
White Rock 835
Bandelier National
Monument 835
Jemez Springs & Around . . . 836
Cuba 838
Zia Pueblo 839
Santa Ana Pueblo 839

I-40 Corridor West of
Albuquerque 839
Laguna Pueblo 840
Acoma Pueblo 840
Grants & Around 841
El Malpais National
Monument 844
El Morro National
Monument 845
Zuni Pueblo 846
Gallup 847

NORTHEASTERN NEW MEXICO 854

I-40 Corridor East of
Albuquerque 855
Santa Rosa 855
Vaughn 857
Tucumcari 858
Around Tucumcari 861
Las Vegas to Colorado . . . 862

Las Vegas 862
Around Las Vegas 866
Mora & Around 867
Springer & Around 868
Cimarron 869
Around Cimarron 871
Raton 871

Around Raton 875
The Northeast Corner 876
Capulin Volcano National
Monument 876
Clayton 877
Around Clayton 879

SOUTHWESTERN NEW MEXICO 880

Socorro 880
Around Socorro 885
Socorro to Quemado 885
Truth or Consequences 886
Around Truth Or
Consequences 889

Hatch 891
Las Cruces 891
Around Las Cruces 900
Deming 901
Around Deming 904
Pancho Villa State Park 905

Silver City 905
North of Silver City 910
East of Silver City 912
Silver City to Reserve 912
Lordsburg & Around 913
The Southwest Corner 915

SOUTHEASTERN NEW MEXICO 917

White Sands National
Monument 917
Alamogordo 918
Around Alamogordo 923
Carrizozo 923
West of Carrizozo 924
North of Carrizozo 924
Cloudcroft 924
Mescalero Apache Indian
Reservation 928

Ruidoso 929
Smokey Bear Historical
State Park 937
Lincoln 938
Roswell 939
Around Roswell 945
Artesia 945
Carlsbad 947
White's City 952

Carlsbad Caverns
National Park 953
Guadalupe Mountains 956
Hobbs 957
Lovington 961
Portales 962
Clovis 965
Fort Sumner 969

APPENDIX: WEBSITE DIRECTORY 972

INDEX 974

Maps 974   Text 975   Sidebars 984

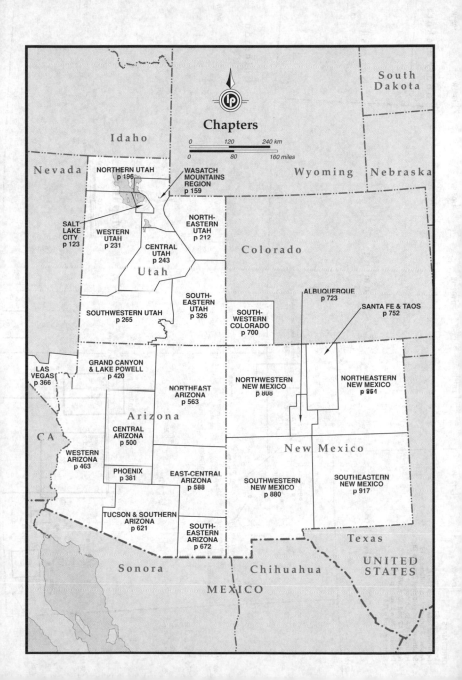

Chapters

NORTHERN UTAH p 196

WASATCH MOUNTAINS REGION p 159

SALT LAKE CITY p 123

WESTERN UTAH p 231

NORTH-EASTERN UTAH p 212

CENTRAL UTAH p 243

SOUTHWESTERN UTAH p 265

SOUTH-EASTERN UTAH p 326

SOUTH-WESTERN COLORADO p 700

ALBUQUERQUE p 723

SANTA FE & TAOS p 752

LAS VEGAS p 366

GRAND CANYON & LAKE POWELL p 420

NORTHEAST ARIZONA p 563

NORTHWESTERN NEW MEXICO p 808

NORTHEASTERN NEW MEXICO p 854

CENTRAL ARIZONA p 500

WESTERN ARIZONA p 463

PHOENIX p 381

EAST-CENTRAL ARIZONA p 588

TUCSON & SOUTHERN ARIZONA p 621

SOUTH-EASTERN ARIZONA p 672

SOUTHWESTERN NEW MEXICO p 880

SOUTHEASTERN NEW MEXICO p 917

Idaho

South Dakota

Nevada

Wyoming

Nebraska

Colorado

Utah

Arizona

New Mexico

CA

Sonora

Chihuahua

Texas

UNITED STATES

MEXICO

0   120   240 km
0   80   160 miles

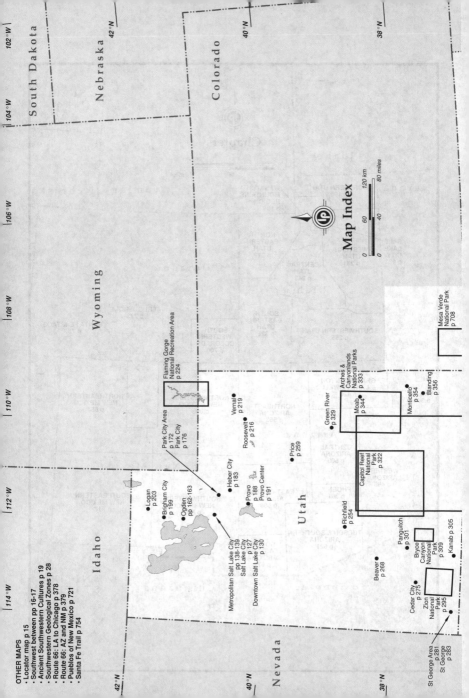

OTHER MAPS
- Locator map p 15
- Southwest between pp 16-17
- Ancient Southwestern Cultures p 19
- Southwestern Geological Zones p 28
- Route 66: LA to Chicago p 378
- Route 66: AZ and NM p 379
- Pueblos of New Mexico p 721
- Santa Fe Trail p 754

South Dakota

Nebraska

Colorado

Wyoming

Idaho

Utah

Nevada

Map Index

0   60   120 km

0   40   80 miles

Flaming Gorge
National Recreation Area
p 224

Park City Area
p 172
Park City
p 176

Logan
p 203

Brigham City
p 199

Ogden
pp 162-163

Metropolitan Salt Lake City
pp 138-139
Salt Lake City
p 127
Downtown Salt Lake City
p 130

Vernal
p 219

Roosevelt
p 216

Heber City
p 183

Provo
p 188
Provo Center
p 191

Price
p 259

Green River
p 329

Arches &
Canyonlands
National Parks
p 333

Moab
p 344

Monticello
p 354

Blanding
p 356

Mesa Verde
National Park
p 708

Richfield
p 254

Capitol Reef
National Park
p 322

Panguitch
p 301

Bryce
Canyon
National
Park
p 309

Kanab p 305

Beaver
p 268

Cedar City
p 275

Zion
National
Park
p 295

St George Area
p 281
St George
p 283

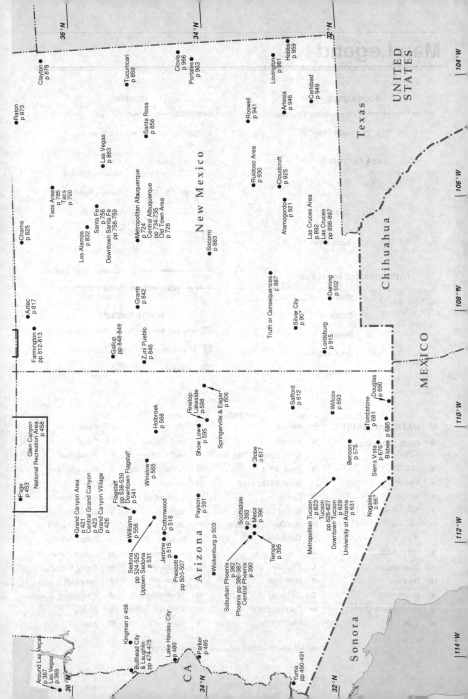

Map Legend

Around Las Vegas
p 367
Las Vegas
p 369

Kingman p 456

Bullhead City
& Laughlin
pp 474-475

Lake Havasu City
p 480

Parker
p 485

Page
p 453

Glen Canyon
National Recreation Area
p 458

Grand Canyon Area
p 421
Central Grand Canyon
p 423
Grand Canyon Village
p 426

Williams
p 556

Sedona
pp 524-525
Uptown Sedona
p 531

Jerome
p 515

Cottonwood
p 518

Prescott
pp 503-507

Wickenburg p 503

Suburban Phoenix
p 382
Phoenix pp 386-387
Central Phoenix
p 390

Scottsdale
p 393

Mesa
p 39E

Tempe
p 395

Payson
p 591

Globe
p 617

Winslow
p 565

Holbrook
p 568

Show Low
p 595

Finetop-
Lakeside
p 598

Springerville & Eagar
p 606

Safford
p 612

Willcox
p 693

Benson
p 575

Tombstone
p 681

Metropolitan Tucson
p 623
Tucson
pp 606-627
Downtown Tucson
p 629
University of Arizona
p 631

Sierra V'sta
p 676

Bisbee p 685

Douglas
p 690

Nogales
p 667

Yuma
pp 490-491

Arizona

Sonora

MEXICO

Page
p 453

Farmington
pp 812-813

Aztec
p 817

Gallup
pp 848-849

Zuni Pueblo
p 846

Grants
p 842

Chama
p 825

Los Alamos
p 832

Taos Area
p 785
Taos
p 790

Santa Fe
p 756
Downtown Santa Fe
pp 758-759

Metropolitan Albuquerque
p 724
Central Albuquerque
pp 734-735
Old Town Area
p 726

Socorro
p 883

Truth or Consequences
p 887

Silver City
p 907

Lordsburg
p 915

Deming
p 902

Las Cruces Area
p 892
Las Cruces
pp 896-897

Alamogordo
p 921

Cloudcroft
p 925

Ruidoso Area
p 930

Raton
p 873

Clayton
p 878

Tucumcari
p 859

Santa Rosa
p 856

Las Vegas
p 863

Roswell
p 941

Artesia
p 946

Carlsbad
p 949

Clovis
p 966

Portales
p 963

Lovington
p 961

Hobbs
p 959

New Mexico

Chihuahua

Texas

UNITED
STATES

MEXICO

Map Legend

BOUNDARIES

— · · — · · — · · — International Boundary

— · · — · · — · · — State Boundary

AREA FEATURES

Park

Forest

Indian Lands

HYDROGRAPHIC FEATURES

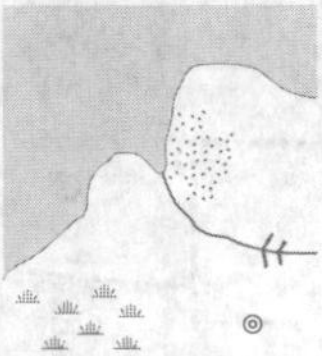

Water

Coastline

Beach

River, Waterfall

Swamp, Spring

ROUTES

Freeway

Toll Freeway

Primary Road

Secondary Road

Tertiary Road

Unpaved Road

Trail

Ferry Route

Railway, Train Station

Mass Transit Line & Station

ROUTE SHIELDS

90 Interstate Freeway   **10** State Highway

MEX 66 Mexican Highway   **229** County Road

84 US Highway   **USFS 604** US Forest Service Road

SYMBOLS

✪ **NATIONAL CAPITAL**	✈ Airfield	❖ Garden
◉ **State, Provincial Capital**	✕ Airport	☗ Gas Station
● **LARGE CITY**	∴ Archaeological Site, Ruins	⌐ Golf Course
● **Medium City**	⑤ Bank, ATM	◎ Hospital, Clinic
● Small City	◱ Baseball Diamond	❶ Information
● Town, Village	⚐ Beach	☖ Lighthouse
○ Point of Interest	⚓ Border Crossing	✳ Lookout
	◒ Bus Depot, Bus Stop	⚒ Mine
■ Hotel, B&B	⊞ Cathedral	⚑ Mission
⚐ Campground	⌒ Cave	⚑ Monument
⊕ RV Park	† Church	▲ Mountain
▼ Restaurant	⬟ Dive Site	⚏ Museum
⬤ Bar (Place to Drink)	◌ Embassy	⚎ Observatory
⚏ Cafe	⚑ Fish Hatchery	← One-Way Street
	⋋ Foot Bridge	▲ Park

ⓟ Parking
) (Pass
⌐ Picnic Area
★ Police Station
⚌ Pool
✉ Post Office
❖ Shopping Mall
⚐ Skiing (Alpine)
⚐ Skiing (Nordic)
⛫ Stately Home
▣ Tomb, Mausoleum
⚐ Trailhead
◢ Windsurfing
⚐ Winery
⚐ Zoo

Note: Not all symbols displayed above appear in this book.

Introduction

Mention the Southwest and distinct images leap to mind: thick arms of the saguaro cactus, towering red-rock outcrops of Monument Valley, howling coyotes, stunning ancient Indian sites tucked against cliffs, the changing colors of the Grand Canyon. Deserts, grasslands, mountain ranges and high mesas and plateaus are all engulfed in the vast sky. Yet, more than a magnificent geographical terrain, the Southwest also exists as a cultural phenomenon.

The first people in the region were the ancestors of today's Native Americans. Archaeologists have excavated fragments of their villages, hunting sites and irrigation ditches, and have found petroglyphs and pictographs – many of which can been seen in protected national monuments and in museums. Today's Southwestern tribes – the Navajo, Apache, Pueblo and Tohono O'odham, among others – relate oral histories that shed light on their ancestors, and their vibrant cultures and languages reveal traces of their forebears.

The first Europeans in the region were Spanish conquistadors and missionaries searching for gold, land, slaves and converts. But the Indian tribes had no gold and held land communally. They rebelled against forced labor and resented the new religion. After centuries of overt and covert resistance, many tribes succeeded in maintaining their own cultural identity, and learned the lessons they would rely on when they confronted the next wave of newcomers – the Anglo Americans.

After Mexico won its independence from Spain, the USA was quick to fight for the new territory. After the Mexican War of 1846 to 1847, the USA assumed control over what was to be called the New Mexico Territory, which included most of Arizona and New Mexico. Traders continued to travel west from Missouri to New Mexico along the Santa Fe Trail, but the best route to California lay south of the territorial border. In 1853 the Gadsden Purchase brought southern Arizona into US hands. The government soon sent troops to 'clear' the lands of the Native Americans, establishing massive reservations that still cover large parts of the Southwest.

Meanwhile to the north, members of a new Christian sect, the Church of Jesus Christ of Latter-Day Saints (LDS), had

reached the Great Salt Lake, where their leader, Brigham Young, announced 'this is the place' where they would settle. Under Young's orders, small bands of Mormons, as LDS members were called, established communities throughout what is now Utah. The progeny of those pioneers still form the majority in most Utah towns.

These three groups – the Native American, Hispanic and the Anglo American – live side by side today, and while the three have assimilated aspects of each other's cultures, they remain distinct. The large cities of Phoenix, Tucson, Santa Fe and Albuquerque all have districts where one culture or another is more prevalent, and many smaller towns still reflect the ethnicity of their founders in their residents and architecture. In Salt Lake City, the Mormon influence is still strong, but even

there economic growth has lured newcomers of various races and religions.

As you raft through the Grand Canyon on the Colorado River or mountain bike on slickrock trails outside Moab, watch for the evidence of other eras: lacy fossils of sea creatures, footprints of dinosaurs, pottery shards and rusting mining rigs. As you hike through Canyon de Chelly or Monument Valley, contemplate the peaceful life of the Indians disrupted by the Spaniards and US Cavalry. When you drive in the warmth of your car to ski slopes covered in Utah's world-famous snow, imagine Mormon pioneers digging their wagons out of those deep drifts. A visit to any Indian reservation affords perhaps the finest contrast of traditions: the US flag flies over most powwows, and you may catch sight of a ceremonial dancer slipping on Ray-Ban sunglasses.

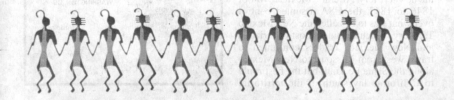

KIM GRANT

RALPH LEE HOPKINS

RALPH LEE HOPKINS

RICK GERHARTER

ROB RACHOWIECKI

RALPH LEE HOPKINS

Top Left: Saguaro cactus in bloom
Middle Left: Balsamroot
Bottom Left: Saguaro cacti, found only in southern Arizona and northern Mexico

Top Right: Hedgehog cactus
Middle Right: Barrel cacti
Bottom Right: Desert paintbrush and yucca

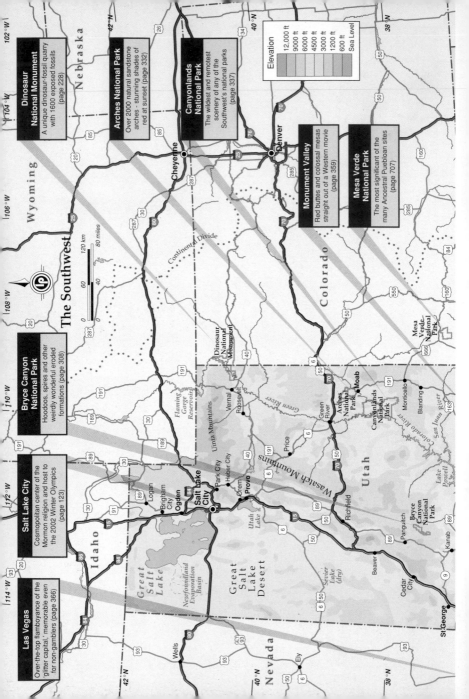

The Southwest

Las Vegas
Over-the-top flamboyance of the 'glitter capital', memorable even for non-gamblers (page 366)

Salt Lake City
Cosmopolitan center of the Mormon religion and host to the 2002 Winter Olympics (page 123)

Bryce Canyon National Park
Hoodoos, spires and other weirdly wonderful eroded formations (page 308)

Dinosaur National Monument
A unique dinosaur-fossil quarry with 1600 exposed fossils (page 228)

Arches National Park
Over 2000 natural sandstone arches - stunning shades of red at sunset (page 332)

Canyonlands National Park
The wildest and remotest scenery of any of the Southwest's national parks (page 337)

Monument Valley
Red buttes and colossal mesas straight out of a Western movie (page 359)

Mesa Verde National Park
The most significant of the many Ancestral Puebloan sites (page 707)

Elevation

	12,000 ft
	9000 ft
	6000 ft
	4500 ft
	3000 ft
	1200 ft
	600 ft
	Sea Level

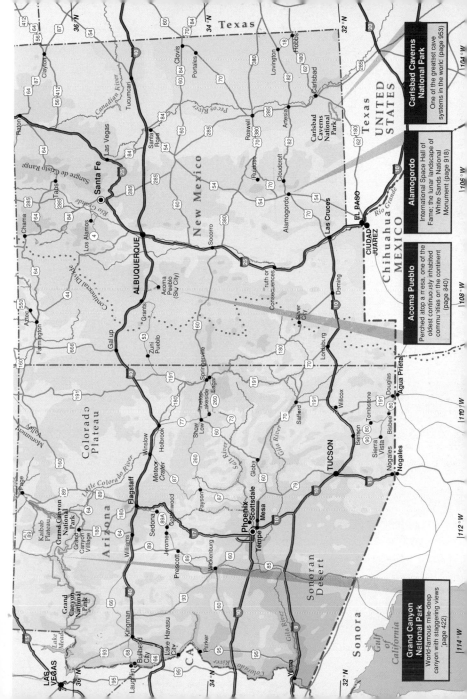

Grand Canyon National Park
World-famous mile-deep canyon with staggering views (page 422)

Acoma Pueblo
Perched atop a mesa, one of the oldest continuously inhabited communities on the continent (page 340)

Alamogordo
International Space Hall of Fame; the lunar landscape of White Sands National Monument (page 918)

Carlsbad Caverns National Park
One of the greatest cave systems in the world (page 953)

STEPHEN TRIMBLE

CHUCK PLACE

BONNIE KAMIN

LEE FOSTER

CHUCK PLACE

Top Left: Navajo concha belt & Ganado rug, c.1900
Bottom Left: Basket weaving

Top Right: Hopi long-billed kachinas
Middle Right: Turquoise earrings
Bottom Right: Navajo whirling log sandpainting

Facts about the Southwest

HISTORY

The First Americans

The history of the sun-baked Southwest begins not with sun but with ice. For it was during the last ice age, roughly 25,000 years ago, that the first people reached the North American continent from Asia by way of the Bering Strait. These first Americans were hardy nomadic hunters who, armed with little more than pointed sticks and the courage born of hunger, pursued Ice Age mammals such as mammoths, cave bears and giant sloths.

As the climate began to warm, the glaciers that had covered much of North America receded and the nomads began to move south. It is not known when the first people appeared in the canyons and plateaus of the Southwest. In fact, until the late 1920s, archaeologists believed that the continent had been inhabited for a mere 4000 years. Then workers in the New Mexico towns of Folsom and Clovis began studying stone spear points fashioned by Paleolithic hunters. They found these artifacts embedded in the bones of extinct large mammals that were dated to over 11,000 years ago. This is the earliest current evidence of the first inhabitants of the Southwest, although people may have populated the area before then. By the time of the Clovis hunters, people had spread from Asia and Alaska throughout most of North, Central and South America.

Even though the above scenario is a widely accepted one, there are other descriptions of the arrival of the first Americans. Some archaeologists claim that people crossed from Asia perhaps 35,000 or more years ago, while others suggest no more than 15,000. Indian oral histories offer various other scenarios. One cosmic origin myth describes how the first arrivals, four men and three women, came from the Man Carrier (an Indian name for the Big Dipper constellation) 50,000 years ago. There are many other tribal beliefs.

Theories on the descent of Native Americans from East Asians point to various similar features, including the two groups' dentition patterns. Native Americans and East Asians have a pronounced curved shape (termed shovel-shaped by anthropologists) on the backs, fronts or both sides of their incisor teeth, while people of European, African and West Asian heritage have almost flat incisor surfaces. (Check your teeth to see if you can support this evidence.)

Soon after the end of the last ice age, the large game mammals abruptly became extinct, and people began hunting the smaller animals we know today, such as deer and rabbits. They used a throwing device called an *atlatl* to propel hunting spears, and also built simple traps.

In addition, the gathering of wild food crops (berries, seeds, roots and fruits) bolstered their diet and became as important as hunting. Baskets were used to collect food, and stone metates were developed to grind hard seeds and roots. Some baskets were so tightly woven that they held water and could even be used for cooking when heated stones were dropped into the water. Archaeological sites in or near Cochise County in southeastern Arizona have yielded the remains of basket and stone cooking implements, and thus the Southwestern hunter-gatherers of this early period (approximately 7000 BC to 500 BC) have been named the Cochise people.

After about 3000 BC, contacts with early farmers from farther south (in what is now central Mexico) led to the beginnings of agriculture in the Southwest. The first crops were minor additions to the Cochise people's diets, and they continued their nomadic hunter-gatherer lifestyles. Eventually, people started reusing the same plots of land for their crops and spending more

17

time in these areas. Primitive corn was one of the first crops. By about 500 BC, beans and squash were also being cultivated, and cotton followed not long afterward. Finally, around 300 BC to 100 AD, distinct groups began to settle in semipermanent villages in the Southwest.

Ancient Southwestern Cultures

Most archaeologists agree that, by about 100 AD, three dominant cultures were emerging in the Southwest: the Hohokam of the desert, the Mogollon of the central mountains and valleys, and the Ancestral Puebloan (formerly referred to as the Anasazi) of the northern plateaus. In addition, several other groups were either blendings of or offshoots from the three main cultures – these smaller groups are still the subject of controversy among archaeologists. Examples are the Hakataya, Fremont, Salado and Sinagua traditions.

These groups are all discussed below, but there is still debate and disagreement about these matters. Clearly, neither the three dominant cultures nor the smaller ones existed in isolation, and much blending and fusion of lifestyles took place. By the mid-15th century, and earlier in some cases, most of these cultures had disappeared, their villages abandoned. The reasons for this are unclear, although many theories have been suggested. Most likely it was a combination of factors including a devastating drought near the end of the 12th century, climate changes, overhunting, soil erosion, disease and the arrival of new groups.

Hohokam This culture existed in the southern and central deserts of Arizona from about 300 BC to 1450 AD. These people created an advanced irrigation system based on the Gila, Salt and Verde Rivers and became extremely well adapted to desert life. Apart from farming, they collected wild desert food such as the fruit of the giant saguaro cactus and the beans of the mesquite tree – a practice that can still be observed today among desert Indians such as the Tohono O'odham tribe.

The irrigation system was quite incredible. Using stone tools the people dug many miles of canals, some of which were 15 feet deep and twice as wide.

The people lived in simple shelters of mud or sticks over a shallow depression in the earth. As time passed, this culture developed low earthen pyramids, which may have been temples, and sunken ball courts with earthen walls in which games were played. These features clearly point to the Hohokam connection with the cultures of Mexico and Guatemala. The dead were cremated, and so archaeologists today can learn comparatively little by excavating burial sites. A rich heritage of pottery, however, attests to Hohokam artistry, and their ceramics and other artifacts can be seen in such places as the Arizona State Museum in Tucson, Arizona. Hohokam sites can be visited in the Pueblo Grande Museum and Cultural Park, Phoenix, Arizona, and the Casa Grande National Monument, between Phoenix and Tucson.

Around the middle of the 15th century, the Hohokam disappeared. Why? We don't know. Today's Pima and Tohono O'odham, (formerly called Papago) Indians appear to be descended from the Hohokam, but the links are not clear. This is but one of the many mysteries that make the Southwest a fascinating place to travel in.

Mogollon The Mogollon (pronounced 'muggy-un' or 'mo-guh-YOHN') Culture is named after the mountains of the same name in western New Mexico and the Mogollon Rim in eastern Arizona. The region south of these mountainous areas as far as the Mexican border and east to the Llano Estacado flatlands of eastern New Mexico was the province of the Mogollon Culture, which existed here from about 200 BC to 1450 AD.

The Mogollon people settled in small communities, often elevated on an isolated mesa or ridge top. Their houses were simple pit dwellings. They did some farming, but depended more on hunting and foraging than did their contemporaries of other cultures. As the Mogollon people

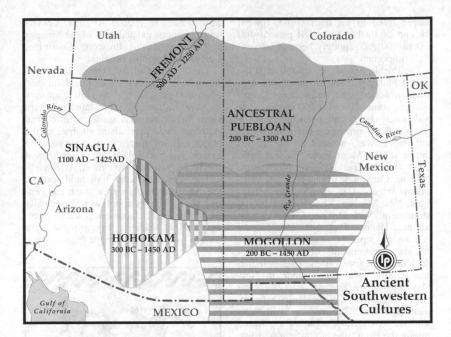

Utah

Nevada

Colorado

OK

FREMONT
500 AD – 1250 AD

Colorado River

ANCESTRAL
PUEBLOAN
200 BC – 1300 AD

Canadian River

SINAGUA
1100 AD – 1425AD

New
Mexico

Texas

CA

Arizona

Rio Grande

HOHOKAM
300 BC – 1450 AD

MOGOLLON
200 BC – 1450 AD

Gulf of
California

MEXICO

Ancient
Southwestern
Cultures

developed, their villages grew bigger and often featured a *kiva* (a circular, underground chamber used for ceremonies and other purposes).

As time progressed, the Mogollon people began to depend on farming to a greater extent. There are many signs that by about the 13th or 14th century the Mogollon were being peacefully incorporated into the Ancestral Puebloan groups from the north. The beautiful black-on-white Mimbres pottery (from the Mimbres River area in southwestern New Mexico) has distinctive animal and human figures executed in a geometric style reminiscent of Puebloan ware. The Gila Cliff Dwellings National Monument, near the Mimbres area, is a late Mogollon site with Puebloan features. In fact, most of today's Pueblo Indians trace their ancestry to the Mogollon or Ancestral Puebloan Culture.

Ancestral Puebloan These people inhabited the Colorado Plateau (also called the Four Corners area) which comprises northeastern Arizona, northwestern New Mexico, southwestern Colorado and southeastern Utah). This culture left us by far the richest heritage of archaeological sites and ancient settlements which are still inhabited in the Southwest. Until recently, this culture was called the 'Anasazi,' which is a Navajo term meaning 'enemy ancestors.' The Navajo, however, were late arrivals on the scene (see Later Cultures, below) and modern Pueblo people prefer the term Ancestral Puebloan, which is more accurate and is used in this book. Texts written prior to the late 1990s (including the first edition of this book) all used Anasazi.

Like the Hohokam and Mogollon Cultures, the earliest Ancestral Puebloans were hunter-gatherers who slowly brought farming into their repertoire of methods of obtaining food. They gathered food in baskets, and the excellence of their basket weaving has led archaeologists to refer to these as the Basket Maker periods. The people lived in pit houses and, toward the end of Basket Maker III period (400 AD to 700 AD), pottery became increasingly important.

The Pueblo periods, which followed the Basket Maker periods, saw much development in pottery and architecture. Larger villages, some with over 100 rooms, were built, many (but not all) of them in shallow caves under overhanging cliffs. Important and impressive Ancestral Puebloan sites can be seen at Mesa Verde National Park, Colorado; Navajo National Monument, Arizona; Canyon de Chelly National Monument, Arizona; Bandelier National Monument, New Mexico; Aztec Ruins National Monument, New Mexico; Chaco Culture National Historic Park, New Mexico; and in many other places.

Today, descendants of the Ancestral Puebloans are found in the Pueblo Indian groups along the Rio Grande in New Mexico, and in the Acoma, Zuni and Laguna Pueblos of New Mexico's northwestern corner. The most ancient links with the Ancestral Puebloans are found among the Hopi tribe of northern Arizona. Here, perched on a mesa top, the village of Old Oraibi has been inhabited since the 1100s, the oldest continuously inhabited settlement in North America. The living pueblos at Acoma and Taos in northwestern New Mexico may be as old.

By about 1450 AD, the Hohokam had mysteriously disappeared and the Mogollon people had been more or less incorporated into the Ancestral Puebloans, who themselves began to leave many of their ancient pueblos in the 1400s and, by the 1500s, had mainly moved to the pueblos now found along the Rio Grande.

Smaller Groups The Hakataya is the term given to several small groups who once lived in western and central Arizona and were contemporaries of the Ancestral Puebloans. The best known of these groups is the Sinagua, who left a variety of interesting and attractive sites such as those at the Montezuma Castle, Tuzigoot, Walnut Canyon and Wupatki National

Monuments in central Arizona. Lesser-known groups existed west of the Sinagua and included the Prescott, Cohonina, Cerbat and Laquish peoples.

The Salado Culture exhibits influences from both the Ancestral Puebloan and Mogollon peoples, and the culture appears to have influenced some late Hohokam sites. Salado remains are found in central Arizona, in an area where all three of the major cultural groups overlapped to some extent. The best Salado site can be seen at the Tonto National Monument, Arizona.

The Fremont Culture took hold north of the Ancestral Puebloan, in south and central Utah. The Fremont were marginally related to the Puebloan but possessed several distinct features. Among these are a unique form of pottery made from a coarse

Petroglyphs
Throughout the Southwest, rocks, boulders and cliffs may be darkened with a blue-black layer called desert varnish. The dark color is caused by iron and manganese oxides that leach out of the rock over many centuries, leaving a thin and slightly shiny polish that sometimes streaks cliffs from top to bottom. Ancient Indians chipped away the varnish to expose the lighter rock beneath, thus creating the rock art known as petroglyphs. ■

sand/clay mixture and a greater reliance on hunting. A good place to see artifacts from this culture is in Fremont Indian State Park, Utah.

Later Cultures

The cultures described above can generally be traced back in the Southwest for two millennia or longer. Many of the tribes living in the Southwest today, however, are comparatively recent arrivals. Nomadic bands of Indians from two distinct language groups, the Shoshonean and the Athapaskan, straggled into the Southwest from the north between about 1300 AD and 1600 AD.

Shoshonean tribes found in the Southwest today live mainly in Utah and make up only a small part of the population. They include the Shoshone in northern Utah (and into Idaho and Wyoming), Utes in central and eastern Utah (and into Colorado), Goshutes in western Utah (and into Nevada) and Southern Paiutes in southwestern Utah (and into Nevada and Arizona).

The Navajo and a variety of Apache tribes are of Athapaskan descent; they now make up a substantial part of Arizona's and New Mexico's populations. The Navajos moved into the Four Corners area, especially the northeastern part of Arizona. The Apaches consisted of several distinct groups, of which the most important were the Jicarilla Apaches in the north-central mountains of New Mexico, the Mescalero Apaches in New Mexico's south-central mountains and various other groups, together referred to as the Western Apaches, in southeastern Arizona.

These late arrivals did not conquer the Pueblo and Hopi descendants of the Ancestral Puebloans but rather coexisted with them. Certainly, there were occasional skirmishes and raids, but generally the Pueblo peoples took advantage of the hunting skills of the newcomers, while the Apache and Navajo learned about pottery, weaving and agriculture from the Pueblo tribes. Then the Europeans arrived in the Southwest, bringing a lifestyle completely foreign to the Native Americans. Mother Earth and Father Sky, bows and arrows, ritual dances and sweatlodges, foot travel, spiritual oneness with the land – all these were to be challenged by the new concepts of Christ and conquest, gunpowder and sword, European civilization and education, horses, and a grasping desire for land.

The Spaniards

For the next three centuries, it was the Spanish who wrought the greatest changes in the region. Most of what is now Arizona and New Mexico became a Spanish colony and, much later, part of Mexico. It was not until the 1840s that the Southwest became part of the USA. Utah, however, remained almost unexplored by Europeans until the arrival of the Mormons in the 19th century.

After brief incursions into the Southwest by small Spanish groups in 1536 and 1539, a major expedition was launched in 1540 under the leadership of Francisco Vásquez de Coronado. He set off from Mexico City with 336 Europeans, 1000 Indians and 1100 pack and riding animals. The expedition's goal was the fabled, immensely rich 'Seven Cities of Cibola.'

For two years, they traveled through Arizona, New Mexico and as far east as Kansas, but instead of gold and precious gems, the expedition found Indian pueblos of mud bricks. Some of the leaders took contingents to explore the Hopi mesas and the Grand Canyon, among other areas. During the harsh winters, the expedition expropriated some of the pueblos for its own use, burned one, and killed dozens of Indians. This ferocity was to prove typical of the behavior of many of the Europeans who were yet to come. Finally, the expedition returned home, penniless and broken. Coronado had failed to become rich or find the fabled cities and, for the next 50 years, Spanish exploration focused on areas outside the Southwest.

The dreams of fabulously rich cities were revived periodically by small groups making minor forays, especially along the Rio Grande. Then, in 1598, a large force of 400 European men and an unknown number of Indians, women and children, accompanied by a reputed 7000 head of various livestock and 83 oxcarts, headed north from Mexico and up the Rio Grande. Their leader was a fortune-seeker named Juan de Oñate, a Spaniard born in Mexico whose deceased wife had been a descendant of both the conquistador Hernán Cortés and the Aztec emperor, Moctezuma. Oñate was accompanied by his 12-year-old son and two of his nephews.

Near what is now El Paso, the Texan city by the tri-border of Texas, New Mexico and Mexico, Oñate stopped. He called the land to the north New Mexico, claimed it for Spain and became governor of this land. Then he headed north and, as the Rio Grande began to swing westward, he continued north through the dry and inhospitable desert that became named *Jornada del Muerto* or the 'Journey of the Dead.' (This is where the USA chose to detonate the first nuclear bomb, which gives you an idea of how desolate this Jornada del Muerto is.)

After a desperate journey, Oñate reached San Juan Pueblo near the confluence of the Rio Chama and Rio Grande. After a brief stop there, he crossed the Rio Grande and set up the first capital of New Mexico, San Gabriel. Apart from some church ruins, nothing remains of San Gabriel today. This route along the Rio Grande and Jornada del Muerto became known as *El Camino Real* (the royal road) and was the standard trail linking Mexico with northern New Mexico. For most of the 17th century, there was little European exploration of other parts of the Southwest.

During the Spaniards' first few years in northern New Mexico, they tried to subdue the pueblos, which led to much bloodshed. The fighting started in Acoma Pueblo, when a Spanish contingent of 30 men led by Juan de Zaldívar, one of Oñate's nephews, demanded payment of taxes in the form of food. The Indians of Acoma responded by killing Zaldívar and about half of his force. Oñate then sent 70 soldiers led by his other nephew, Vicente de Zaldívar, to punish the inhabitants of Acoma. This was accomplished with the

Spaniards' usual ruthlessness: several hundred Indians were killed, and hundreds more were taken prisoner and subjected to punishments such as amputation of a foot or slavery. By 1601, three other pueblos were ransacked and many hundreds of Indians were killed or enslaved.

Meanwhile, San Gabriel fared poorly as the capital of New Mexico. Tense relations with the Indians, poor harvests, harsh weather and accusations of Oñate's cruelty led to many desertions among the colonizers. By 1608, Oñate had been recalled to Mexico and, on the journey south, lost his son to an attack by Indians. When he arrived, he was stripped of his governorship.

A new governor, Pedro de Peralta, was sent north to found a new capital, which he did in 1609. This was Santa Fe, and it remains the capital of New Mexico today, the oldest capital in what is now the USA. In 1610, Peralta built the Palace of the Governors on the Plaza in Santa Fe – the oldest non-Indian building in the USA still in use today. (The first British colony was founded in Jamestown, Virginia, in 1607. The second British colony was founded in 1620 at Plymouth, Massachusetts, by the famous Pilgrims.)

A steady trickle of colonists, accompanied by soldiers and Franciscan priests, moved from Mexico to the Santa Fe area over the next 50 years. Their aim was to settle and farm the land and bring the Indians into the Catholic Church. Most of the Pueblo groups had little interest in being converted, although some blended Catholicism with their own beliefs. Neither were the Indians much inclined to help the Spanish build churches in their pueblos nor to work for the new colonists. For the most part, the Spanish treated the recalcitrant Pueblo people brutally at any sign of resistance: imprisonment, beatings, torture and executions were common.

A particularly destructive Spanish campaign in 1675 was aimed at destroying the Pueblo kivas and powerful ceremonial objects such as prayer sticks and kachina dolls. The horrified Indians tried to protect their heritage but were punished harshly.

This was the last straw for them. In 1680, the united northern Pueblos rose up in the 'Pueblo Revolt' and succeeded in driving some 2400 Spaniards back down the Rio Grande to El Paso. The Pueblo people took over Santa Fe's Palace of the Governors and held it until 1692.

The northern Pueblo people were a mix of many different tribes, languages and beliefs, so they didn't remain united for very long. In 1692, the Spaniards, led by Diego de Vargas, again took over Santa Fe and, over the succeeding years, subdued all the pueblos in the area. During the 18th century, the colony grew slowly but steadily, and the Spaniards lived uneasily but relatively peacefully alongside the Pueblo peoples.

Meanwhile, less brutal incursions were being made into Arizona by the Jesuit priest Eusebio Kino, who has garnered almost mythical status as the bringer of God to what is now (mainly) southern Arizona. He began his travels in Mexico in 1687 and spent over two decades in the Arizona-Sonora area. His approach to being a missionary was, certainly by the standards of the day, humane, and this, at least, distinguished him from many of his contemporaries. He established missions at Tumacacori and San Xavier del Bac (both between Tucson and the Mexican border); these sites can be visited today, although the present buildings were erected about a century after Kino was there.

After Kino's departure, conditions for the Indians in what is now Arizona deteriorated and led to the short-lived Pima Revolt of 1751 and the Yuma Massacre of 1781, when the Yumans killed colonizers in their area.

Throughout the Southwest, Apaches, Comanches, Navajos and Hopis were alternately fighting with one another or with the Spaniards, and it was this warfare that limited further Spanish expansion in the area during the 18th century.

In an attempt to link Santa Fe with the newly established port of San Francisco and to avoid Indian raids, the Spanish priests Francisco Atanasio Domínguez and Silvestre Vélez de Escalante led a small group of explorers into what is now Utah, but they were turned back by the rugged and arid terrain. The 1776 Domínguez-Escalante expedition was the first to survey Utah, but no attempt was made to settle there.

Although the historically important events outlined above provide a sketch of Hispanic-Indian relations during the 16th to the 18th century, one crucial point has not been discussed. The Europeans brought with them diseases to which the Indians had no resistance and which caused terrible epidemics within the tribes. By some accounts, 80% of Native Americans died from disease in the 16th century, and the history of North America may have been very different if epidemics had not taken such a terrible toll.

The Anglos

In 1803, the Louisiana Purchase resulted in the USA's acquiring a huge tract of land – stretching from Louisiana to the Rocky Mountains – from the French, doubling the size of the young country. The Spanish colonies of the Southwest now abutted, for the first time, US territory, and the two countries maintained an uneasy peace.

During the winter of 1806-1807, a small contingent of US soldiers led by Lieutenant Zebulon Montgomery Pike reached the upper Rio Grande and were taken by Spanish soldiers to Santa Fe for lengthy interrogation before being allowed to return to the USA. In 1810, Pike published a book about his experiences. He described New Mexican life, including details of the high cost of merchandise in Santa Fe because of the great distances from the rest of New Mexico. This induced several groups of US traders and entrepreneurs to make the difficult journey to Santa Fe with trade goods, but the Spanish repudiated their efforts, jailing the Americans and confiscating their goods.

This situation changed in 1821, when Mexico became independent from Spain. The next party of US traders who arrived in Santa Fe were welcomed by the newly independent Mexicans, and a major trade route was established. This was the famous Santa Fe Trail between Missouri and Santa Fe, a trail traversed by thousands of people until the coming of the railway in 1879.

Politically, the Southwest had changed, but the reality was that, for a couple of decades, life continued much as before. The Spanish soldiers and missionaries left and were replaced by a Mexican army. Santa Fe grew and thrived, but the Hispanic inhabitants continued to be hampered by raiding Indians, especially Apaches and Comanches (a nomadic prairie tribe known for their skills in buffalo hunting and horseback riding). Few Anglos (as the non-Hispanic whites from the USA were called) ventured beyond the Santa Fe Trail. Some who did were the 'mountain men' – hunters and trappers who explored all over the West. These men were the first Europeans to explore Utah since the Domínguez-Escalante expedition in 1776.

In 1846, the USA declared war on Mexico, and two years later, Mexico gave up all the land between Texas and the Pacific. The border more or less followed the present one, with the exception of 30,000 sq miles in southern Arizona and New Mexico, which the USA bought from the Mexicans in 1853 in what was to become known as the 'Gadsden Purchase.' The Mormons, led by Brigham Young, founded Salt Lake City, still technically part of Mexico, in 1847. A Mormon battalion was sent to help US forces in the Mexican War effort, although it saw no action.

The Territory Years
After the Mexican War, most of present-day Arizona and New Mexico became the New Mexico Territory of the United States, while most of Utah and Nevada became the Utah Territory. It was not until 1861 that Nevada became a separate territory, and in 1863 Arizona became a separate territory.

Territories differed from states in that they were not allowed to elect their own senators and representatives to the US Congress in Washington, DC. Territories were headed by an elected governor, who had little real power in the nation's capital.

Utah's territorial capital was briefly in Fillmore but was relocated to Salt Lake City in 1858, where it has remained. Arizona's first capital was Prescott, but was moved quickly to Tucson in 1867, returned to Prescott in 1877 and finally moved to the present location, Phoenix, in 1889. New Mexico's capital has been Santa Fe since its foundation in 1609. Statehood came first to Utah in 1896, and much later to New Mexico and Arizona in 1912.

The history of the Southwest during the territory years and the gaining of statehood is complex and colorful. It is beyond the scope of this book to probe deeply into it, and readers are directed to the Books section in Facts for the Visitor for suggestions for further study. Also see the Recent History sections beginning each state. Following are overviews of some of the more important historical topics.

Indian Wars & Reservations The Americans settled the new territories much more aggressively than the Spaniards had. For decades, US forces had pushed west across the continent, killing or forcibly moving whole tribes of Indians who were in their way. This continued in the Southwest as the West was 'won.'

The best-known incident was the forceful relocation of many Navajos in 1864. US forces, led by Kit Carson, destroyed Navajo fields, orchards and houses and forced the people into surrendering or withdrawing into remote parts of the Canyon de Chelly in Arizona. Eventually, they were starved out and a total of about 9000 Navajos were rounded up and marched 400 miles east to a camp at Bosque Redondo, near Fort Sumner in New Mexico. Hundreds of Indians died from sickness, starvation or gunshot along the way. The Navajos call this 'The Long Walk,' and it remains an important part of their history.

Life at Bosque Redondo was harsh with inadequate resources for 9000 people; over 2000 Navajos died. Even from the Anglo point of view, this relocation was not working and, after four years, the surviving Navajos were allowed to return to their lands in northeastern Arizona and allotted over 5000 sq miles for their reservation. Since the 1868 treaty, the reservation has grown to encompass over 20,000 sq miles in Arizona, New Mexico and Utah; it is the largest in the USA and the Navajo people are the largest tribe.

Every one of the many tribes in the Southwest resisted the westward growth of the USA to a greater or lesser extent.

The last serious conflicts were between US troops and Apaches. This was partly because raiding was the essential and honorable path to manhood for Apaches. Any young Apache man had to demonstrate raiding skills in order to marry well, and then to provide for his extended family and to be considered a leader. As the US forces and settlers moved into Apache land, they became obvious targets for the raids that were part of the Apache way of life. These continued under the leadership of Mangas Coloradas, Cochise, Victorio and, finally, Geronimo, who surrendered in 1886 after being promised that he and the Apaches would be imprisoned for two years and then allowed to return to their homeland. As with many promises made during these years, this one, too, was broken. The Apaches spent 27 years as prisoners of war.

By the time of Geronimo's surrender, there were many Indian reservations in the Southwest, each belonging to one or sometimes a few tribes. Although the wars were over, Indian people continued to be treated like second-class citizens for many decades. Non-Indians used legal loopholes and technicalities to take over reservation land. Many children were removed from reservations and shipped off to boarding schools where they were taught in English and punished for speaking their own languages or behaving 'like Indians' – this practice continued into the 1930s. Older Indians were encouraged to lose their culture and customs. Despite the history of cultural oppression, Indians today still practice spiritual customs and other beliefs that predate US expansion. Many native languages are still spoken, and a majority of Navajos learn their tribal language before English.

Indians fought alongside Americans in WWI but were not extended US citizenship until 1924 and were not given voting rights until 1948 in Arizona and New Mexico, and 1957 in Utah. Most tribes have their own governments and laws that are applicable to people living on or visiting their reservations. Federal laws are also applicable to reservations, but normally state and other local laws do not apply.

WWII prompted the first large exodus of Indians from the reservations; they went to join the US war effort. One of the most famous units was the Navajo Code Talkers – 420 Navajo marines who used a code based on their language for vital messages in the Pacific arena. This code was never broken by the Japanese. Today, the surviving code talkers are among the most revered of Navajo elders and are often honored in public events.

Currently, about half of US Indians live off reservations, but many of these maintain strong ties with their tribes.

Transportation The history of the Southwest during the 19th century is strongly linked to the development of transportation in the region. During early territorial days, movement of goods and people from the East to the Southwest was very slow. Horses, mule trains and stagecoaches were state-of-the-art transportation in those days.

Major trails included the Santa Fe Trail, which linked Missouri with Santa Fe from the 1820s to the 1870s, and the Old Spanish Trail, from Santa Fe into central Utah and across Nevada to Los Angeles, California. Regular stagecoach services along the Santa Fe Trail began in 1849.

The Mormon Trail reached Salt Lake City in 1847. In succeeding years, thousands of Mormon settlers followed this route, many pulling their possessions for hundreds of miles in handcarts.

The Butterfield Overland Mail Company opened in 1858 and linked St Louis, Missouri, with San Francisco, California, via southwestern New Mexico, Tucson and Yuma. Butterfield offered two stagecoaches a week that completed the journey in 25 days – an incredibly exhausting trip.

Cattle trails, along which cowhands drove many thousands of head of cattle, letting them feed as they went, sprang up in the 1860s and 1870s; among these, the most important were the Goodnight-Loving Trail for moving cattle from Texas through eastern New Mexico into Colorado, and the Chisholm Trail, which branched off from the Goodnight-Loving Trail near Roswell, New Mexico, and directed cattle west into Arizona. Clearly, ranching was already important business; it has remained so to this day.

More people arrived with the advent of the railroads. The first transcontinental line was completed in northern Utah in 1869 and led to an influx of non-Mormons into Utah. The Atchison, Topeka and Santa Fe Railroad reached Santa Fe in 1879, linking that city with the east. Meanwhile, the Southern Pacific Railroad had been pushed inland from Los Angeles through Yuma and Tucson as far as Deming, New Mexico. A few years later, this was linked up to the Santa Fe line. The Atlantic and Pacific Railroad, built in 1883, went from near Albuquerque across northern Arizona to Los Angeles.

The arrival of more people and resources via the railroad led to further exploration of the land, and the frequent discovery of mineral deposits. The 1870s and 1880s saw the foundation of many mining towns; some of these are now ghost towns, while others (for example Tombstone and Silver City) remain active today. Gold, copper and silver mining all boomed, although silver mining busted suddenly with the crash of 1893. Mining, particularly for copper, continues to be an significant part of the Southwest's economy today.

The Wild West Desperate tales of gunslingers and cattle rustlers, outlaws and train robbers, are all part of the legend of the Wild West. The good guys and the bad guys were designations often in flux – a tough outlaw in one state might become a sheriff in another. New mining towns, mushrooming overnight near the richest mines, often had more saloons and bordellos than any other kind of building. Newly rich miners would come into town to brawl, drink and gamble, sometimes being fleeced by professional cardsharps. It was no surprise that law and order was practically nonexistent in many parts of the Southwest during the latter part of the 19th century.

Some of the most legendary figures in the Southwest include Billy the Kid and Sheriff Pat Garrett, who were involved in the infamous Lincoln County War in New Mexico in the late 1870s. Billy the Kid reputedly shot and killed over 20 men in a brief career as a gunslinger – he himself was shot and killed by Garrett at the tender age of 21. In 1881, Wyatt Earp, along with his brothers Virgil and Morgan and Doc Holliday, shot dead Billy Clanton and the McLaury brothers in a blazing gunfight at the OK Corral in Tombstone, Arizona – the whole thing took less than a minute. Both sides accused the other of cattle rustling, but the real story will never be told. Today, reenactments of the gunfight take place regularly in Tombstone.

In fact, reenactments are the closest you'll get to those lawless frontier days, and several towns have them during various festivals. Old Tucson Movie Studios outside of Tucson is as good a place as any to see some Wild West action. One chilling event that you won't see reenacted is the hanging of notorious train robber Black Jack Ketchum in Clayton in 1901 – an error by the hangman caused Ketchum to literally lose his head. Other names inextricably linked with the Southwest are Butch Cassidy and the Sundance Kid, who roamed over much of Utah and other parts of the West. Cassidy was a Mormon, and during the 1890s he and his Wild Bunch gang robbed banks and trains, but he never killed anyone.

By the turn of the 19th century, some semblance of law and order had arrived in the Southwest, and the days of gunslingers were over.

GEOGRAPHY

Travelers will find that vast canyons and steep bluffs, buttes, mesas and mountains often make it difficult to get from here to there. Although the varied topography may hinder travel, it is also one of the attractions that lure travelers to the region in the first place. The scenery is literally breathtaking.

The central part of the Southwest is the Colorado Plateau, which covers most of northern Arizona, southeastern Utah, northwestern New Mexico and southwestern Colorado. The center of the Colorado Plateau is often called the Four Corners region, because all four of these states share a common boundary point at Four Corners, the only place where four US states meet. Much of this area is part of the Navajo Indian Reservation, the largest in the USA, and the Hopi Indian Reservation.

The Colorado Plateau is actually a series of plateaus between 5000 and 8000 feet in elevation. They are separated by deep canyons, among them the world-famous Grand Canyon. The plateaus are not flat but rather are topped by distinctive buttes, mesas and other topographical features that give the landscape its Southwestern character. Erosion has played with these features, resulting in natural arches, bridges, spires and towers. These, combined with the canyons, led to the foundation of the region's many national parks and other scenic sites.

The Colorado Plateau is more or less surrounded by mountainous regions. Southwest of the plateau, Arizona's terrain drops in a rugged cliff called the Mogollon Rim, which is as high as 2000 feet in some places and stretches about a third of the way across that state. Beyond lies a broad belt of mountain ranges, getting progressively lower to the southwest.

The southwestern and south-central parts of Arizona belong to the desert Basin and Range province. Flat desert basins alternate with mountain ranges, many topped by forests and almost all running north to south. It's in these arid basins that Arizona's major cities, Phoenix and Tucson, are found, supported by massive irrigation projects from the Colorado, Gila and Salt Rivers. This is part of the **Arizona-Sonora Desert**.

Basin and Range country continues northwest into Nevada and swings back into Utah. In Utah, northwest of the Colorado Plateau, the Basin and Range province forms part of the **Great Basin Desert**. Where the Great Basin Desert abuts the Wasatch Mountains (part of the Rocky Mountain Region) in north-central Utah lies a fertile valley where Salt Lake City and other important Utah towns are found. The northeastern corner of Utah pertains more to the Rocky Mountains than to the Southwestern deserts. This region includes the unusual Uinta Mountains, one of the few US mountain ranges that trends from west to east, and the largest of those that do so in the lower 48 states.

Southeast of the Colorado Plateau, heading into New Mexico, the traveler again encounters the Rocky Mountains, whose Continental Divide snakes through the western part of the state. The Southwest's highest peaks belong to the Rocky Mountains in north-central New Mexico, including Wheeler Peak at 13,161 feet. These highland areas are home to many of the state's inhabitants today, as they were in earlier centuries for the Ancestral Puebloans. New Mexico's biggest city, Albuquerque, is on the edge of the Rockies, and the state capital of Santa Fe is, at 6950 feet, easily the highest capital in the nation.

Farther south, the Rockies are split by New Mexico's most important river valley, that of the Rio Grande. To the west is the beginning of the Basin and Range province.

East of the Continental Divide are the high plains of the 'Llano Estacado,' the westernmost parts of the Great Plains.

About a third of New Mexico falls into this area, which is mainly pancake-flat ranching country, with some oil production in the south. This area is watered by the Pecos River and the recently discovered Ogallala Aquifer.

By way of comparison, the Southwest lies within about the same latitudes as Spain, Greece, Turkey, and northern China and Japan.

GEOLOGY

The Southwest owes its unusual and dramatic landscape to the interaction of two processes: large-scale forces that have stretched the earth's crust, uplifted mountain ranges, and erupted volcanoes; and less powerful forces responsible for eroding the rocks away. It's not difficult to visualize wind and rain slowly wearing down hillsides and carrying away loose sediment. Harder to grasp are the movements of the crust, called plate tectonics, that have pushed and pulled the Southwest into a variety of geologic provinces including the Basin and Range, Colorado Plateau, Rocky Mountains, and Rio Grande Rift. The basic idea behind plate tectonics (also referred to as continental drift), is that the crust is divided into a dozen or so large pieces (plus several smaller ones), called *plates*, that fit together like a jigsaw puzzle but move independently of one another. Although the plates travel at only millimeters per year, collisions between them fold and buckle their edges; their interiors, meanwhile, remain largely untouched. As a result, mountains, volcanoes and earthquakes are generally found along plate boundaries while the centers of continents, far removed from this activity, are worn flat by millions of years of erosion.

In order to discuss the sequence of events that led to present-day Arizona, New Mexico and Utah, it is first necessary to know something about geologic time. When the earth formed approximately 4.6 billion years ago, it was very different from

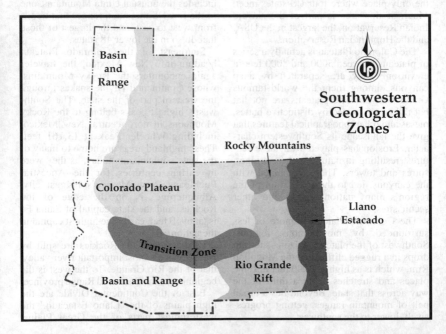

Southwestern Geological Zones

Basin and Range

Rocky Mountains

Colorado Plateau

Llano Estacado

Transition Zone

Basin and Range

Rio Grande Rift

the way we see it today. Bacteria and other primitive creatures arrived early in the earth's history, but not much else existed until around 570 million years ago. The appearance of numerous fossils in the geologic record marks the beginning of the **Paleozoic** (ancient life) **Era**, the oldest segment of which is the **Cambrian Period**. This rapid evolution of marine invertebrate animals has been named the Cambrian Explosion; earth's four-billion-year history prior to this event is lumped together as the **Precambrian Era**. The **Mesozoic** (middle life) **Era** began approximately 245 million years ago with the appearance of dinosaurs and ended 65 million years ago with their sudden extinction (when a large meteorite slammed into the Yucatan Peninsula). The **Cenozoic** (recent life) **Era** witnessed the proliferation of mammals.

Because little evidence remains exposed today, we know only the highlights of the Southwest's earliest geologic history. During the Precambrian Era, approximately 1.7 billion years ago, what is now the Southwest formed the western edge of the North American continent (tectonic plates would later mash themselves onto western North America, extending it to the west). Tectonic plates crashed against North America, buckling the crust, raising mountain ranges the size of the Himalayas, erupting huge volumes of volcanic ash and lava, and producing molten magma deep in the earth that rose into the crust and cooled to form large bodies of granite. Millions of years later, sea levels rose and flooded the region, depositing thick sequences of marine sediments that formed shales, siltstones and sandstones.

Then, about 1.4 billion years ago, numerous granite bodies again intruded into the crust during a new round of mountain-building. As the Precambrian came to an end, the seas gradually withdrew, and for hundreds of millions of years the region was slowly beveled by erosion. Now called the **Great Unconformity**, this erosion removed over one billion years of geologic history from much of the Southwest.

At the start of the Paleozoic, North America was joined with Europe, Asia, Africa and Antarctica into a supercontinent named **Pangaea**. Early in the Cambrian, a sea advanced across western Pangaea and began depositing another thick sequence of sediments. As the Paleozoic progressed, sea levels rose and fell, alternating fossil-rich marine rocks with continental deposits that formed on floodplains and in deltas. In what is now the Colorado Plateau, these seas laid down horizontal layers of sandstone and limestone exposed so spectacularly today in the walls of the Grand Canyon. During the late Paleozoic, about 200 million years later, mountains rose in north-central New Mexico – ancestors of today's Rocky Mountains. At about the same time, southern New Mexico lay under a shallow, tropical sea teeming with life, including a large barrier reef that would later host Carlsbad Caverns.

During the early Mesozoic, much of the Southwest may have looked somewhat like northern Egypt: floodplains and deltas surrounded by vast expanses of desert. Rising mountains in the west shut off moisture from the ocean while mountains in central and eastern Arizona collected what rain did fall and channeled it toward the west. However, the climate become more humid as the Mesozoic progressed; meandering rivers dissected floodplains and swamps filled lowlands – an ideal climate for dinosaurs. Fossil remains of *Coelophysis*, the earliest known dinosaur, tell us that they roamed the Southwest from the start of the Mesozoic, and *Seismosaurus*, the largest dinosaur ever discovered, shook New Mexican ground.

The final segment of the Mesozoic, named the **Cretaceous Period**, was a busy time in the Southwest. The ocean swept in once again, forming a long, north-south trending sea called the Cretaceous Seaway, which extended as far north as Canada. At about the same time, a series of tectonic microplates began crunching into the western coast of North America, folding and shortening the crust by up to 60 miles, and uplifting Utah's Sevier

Mountains. Meanwhile, North America had broken away from Europe and begun drifting west. The resulting gap between the continents formed the Atlantic Ocean. As North America moved, it rode roughly over a piece of crust known as the East Pacific plate. This collision, named the **Laramide Orogeny**, resulted in the birth of the modern Rocky Mountains (their predecessors having long since eroded away), uplifted the Colorado Plateau and led to another round of volcanic eruptions throughout the Southwest. In Arizona, magma rich in precious metals intruded into the crust. Circulating groundwater then concentrated this gold, silver and copper into valuable veins.

The Cenozoic has been a geologically complex era. Uplift of the Rockies continued well into the Cenozoic leading to powerful volcanic eruptions in Utah around 40 million years ago. About 10 million years later, an unusual event began: in contrast to the compression that uplifted the Rockies, the crust began to stretch to the east and west. In response to this pulling, the crust cracked along two long parallel fractures that extended from Colorado through New Mexico and into Texas. As the stretching continued, the area that lay between these two faults dropped down and the rocks on either side tilted outward; this was the beginning of the **Rio Grande Rift**. East of the rift, tilted blocks of crust formed a series of mountain ranges that helped channel the Rio Grande river. Magma rose quickly and easily along the rift's fractures and erupted in a chain of volcanoes. East from the mountains that flank the Rio Grande Rift, the ground is quite flat, with most of the relief due to erosion by the Pecos and Canadian Rivers, a small number of sinkholes and a scattering of early and late Cenozoic volcanoes. This is the **Llano Estacado** – the western edge of North America's stable interior. Largely unaffected by the tectonic activity that pushed and pulled the crust farther to the west, the rocks here remain horizontal, just as they were originally deposited.

Between 15 and 8 million years ago, the crust throughout western Arizona, western Utah, and southern New Mexico began stretching as well. And just as in the Rio Grande Rift, cracks in the crust formed long, linear north-south trending mountains (ranges) and valleys (basins). This geologic province, called the **Basin and Range**, forms one of the most distinctive of Southwestern landscapes. By the time it finished, rifting had thinned and extended the crust approximately 50 miles to the east and west. Separating the Basin and Range from the Colorado Plateau is a northwest/southeast band of mountains, called the **Central Highlands**, that crosscuts Arizona and western New Mexico. Also called the Transition Zone, this area shares the northeast-southwest mountains and valleys of the Basin and Range with the flat-lying sedimentary rocks of the Colorado Plateau. Uplifted by the Laramide Orogeny and stretched with the Basin and Range, the Central Highlands were also intruded by granite several times in the early Cenozoic. In Utah, runoff from the rising Rockies fed large lakes that teemed with alligators, fish, and turtles, many of which are well preserved as fossils in the **Green River Formation**.

Although some rifting, volcanism and uplift have occurred within the last few million years, wind and rain have played a more important role in sculpting most of the modern Southwestern landscape. Much of the Southwest is desert today, but climate has fluctuated a great deal throughout the Cenozoic. Evidence of wetter times includes massive amounts of sediment, often thousands of meters thick, that were shed off of mountain ranges and carried into adjacent valleys by a network of streams. Changing climate is also recorded in the dry lake basins scattered throughout the Southwest. By 20,000 years ago, massive glaciers, some over a mile thick, had moved south from Canada into the upper Midwest. As a result, the jet stream, which today flows west to east across the northwestern US, was split in two, one arm going farther north and the other swinging south to cross over the Southwest. This southern jet stream carried moisture-laden air from the Pacific, increasing cloud cover and precipitation. Isolated basins filled and finally overflowed, merging together into **Lake Bonneville**, the Great Salt Lake's ancestor, which once covered 20,000 sq miles. Around 10,000 years ago, the glaciers retreated, returning the jet stream to its normal route and the area to desert.

Weathering and erosion beautify the landscape by carving flat-lying rocks into plateaus, mesas, buttes and spires. In areas with tilted strata, hills develop sharp ridgetops called hogbacks and cuestas. Sandstone is occasionally sculpted into natural bridges and arches, some of the most dramatic examples of which include Utah's Canyonlands and Arches National Parks. Erosion has also exposed the plumbing of ancient volcanoes, called volcanic necks, such as Shiprock in northwestern New Mexico. Rainwater reacts with chemical elements in some rocks to produce a wide range of colors, making the Southwest one of North America's most visually stunning landscapes. Iron and manganese oxides rust to red, pink, yellow and purple; unrusted iron oxides may look blue or green. In addition, black lavas, tan volcanic ash and white limestones are often painted with patches of orange, green and brown lichens. These areas are popularly called painted deserts.

CLIMATE

The Southwest conjures up images of searing desert heat, and this is certainly true in many parts of the region (see the charts on the following page). An excellent rule of thumb, however, is to gauge the climate by the altitude. The lower you are, the hotter and drier it will be. As you climb, temperatures drop about 3° to 5°F for every 1000 feet of elevation gain.

The southwestern and south-central parts of Arizona are below 3000 feet in elevation and are often the hottest places in the USA. High temperatures exceed 100°F for weeks on end and go over 120°F several times each year. The humidity is low, however, and evaporation helps to cool the body. As the locals say, 'It's a dry heat.' Dry air does not hold heat like humid air does, and so nighttime temperatures drop by 20° or 30°F, or even more. Winter temperatures occasionally will drop below freezing but only for a few hours. Yuma, at just 138 feet elevation in the southwestern corner of Arizona, averages about 2 inches of rain a year, making it the driest part of the region covered in this book. The rest of Arizona is higher and cooler, and the state has an average elevation of 4100 feet.

Almost 90% of New Mexico is over 4000 feet, with the exception being the lower Rio Grande and Pecos River valleys, which are the hottest parts of the state. The average elevation of New Mexico is 5700 feet, rather higher and slightly cooler than the 5000 feet at Albuquerque. Utah is generally higher and cooler still, with an average elevation of 6100 feet (the third highest state in the USA). The far southwestern corner of Utah is the lowest and hottest part of that state.

Over 90% of the Southwest receives well under 20 inches of precipitation annually and about 30% receives less than 10 inches a year. In the driest areas of southwestern Arizona, almost no rain falls from April to June. The highest rainfall here is during the monsoons of July and August, but then rains tend to be brief, with heavy downpours falling mainly in the afternoon. In the less dry areas, it can rain at any time, but even so, few areas have more than five wet days in any month.

The areas of greatest precipitation – over 20 inches – are mostly in the high mountains of central Arizona, the Wasatch and Uinta Mountains of northern Utah and the mountains north of Albuquerque in New Mexico. These areas receive the most snowfall in winter and have excellent skiing.

Conditions can be extreme, and every year people die from such causes as lightning, dehydration and flash floods. See Dangers & Annoyances in the Facts for the Visitor chapter, and the Flash Floods sidebar in the Outdoor Activities chapter for more information on such conditions.

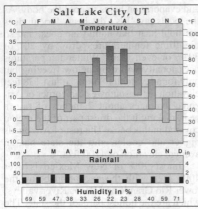

Salt Lake City, UT

Temperature

Rainfall

Humidity in %
69 59 47 38 33 26 22 23 28 40 59 71

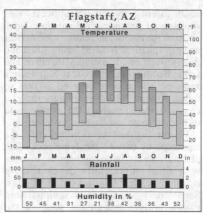

Flagstaff, AZ

Temperature

Rainfall

Humidity in %
50 45 41 31 27 21 38 42 36 36 43 52

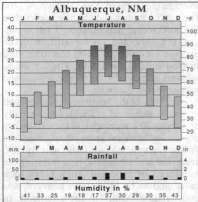

Albuquerque, NM

Temperature

Rainfall

Humidity in %
41 33 25 19 18 17 27 30 29 30 35 43

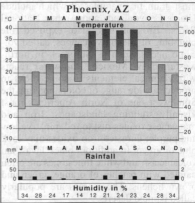

Phoenix, AZ

Temperature

Rainfall

Humidity in %
34 28 24 17 14 12 21 24 23 24 28 34

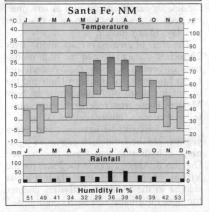

Santa Fe, NM

Temperature

Rainfall

Humidity in %
51 49 41 34 32 29 36 38 40 39 42 53

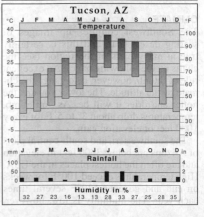

Tucson, AZ

Temperature

Rainfall

Humidity in %
32 27 23 16 13 13 28 33 27 25 28 35

ECOLOGY & ENVIRONMENT

The present ecology and environment of the arid Southwest are closely linked with the history of modern settlement and the accompanying development of water use. The most important river in the region is the Colorado River, which, at 1450 miles in length, is the ninth longest in North America. The Rio Grande, at 1900 miles, is longer but has less water. Other important rivers are the Salt, Gila, Green and Little Colorado, all tributaries of the Colorado, and the Pecos River.

The climate, dry for months and then subject to sudden storms of very heavy rain, made the rivers difficult to control for early settlers. Reduced to a trickle or drying completely during the dry months, rivers could change into tremendous torrents in a matter of hours after a monsoon storm. Interestingly enough, the ancient Hohokam people had learned how to irrigate large parts of central and southern Arizona, but their system is long forgotten and silted up.

From the 1870s until the early 1900s, Mormon pioneers along the Little Colorado River, ranchers along the Salt and Pecos Rivers and settlers along river valleys throughout the Southwest built makeshift dams in attempts to control and divert the waters for irrigation. Time after time, floods would sweep away the dams and they would be rebuilt. In 1905, a huge flood along the lower Colorado River resulted in a permanent alteration of its course.

At the time, it was clear that something needed to be done to control the rivers, and so the Reclamation Act of 1902 was passed, which led to the building of huge federally funded dams, constructed to resist even the wildest of floods. The first was the Theodore Roosevelt Dam on the Salt River, completed in 1911, soon followed by the Strawberry River Dam in Utah in 1913, the Rio Grande's Elephant Butte Dam in 1916 and the Coolidge Dam, finished in 1929 on the Gila River.

There were constant disagreements and rancorous debates within each state as to who should be allowed to use the water of these rivers. Colorado River water rights, however, were a much bigger matter – seven different states had claims to the water. In 1922, US secretary of commerce (later president) Herbert Hoover brought the states together in the Colorado River Compact and engineered a scheme to divide up the water rights, with California getting the largest share.

Disagreements continued, however, with Arizona refusing to ratify the compact until 1944. Despite this, the 1922 compact laid the groundwork for a series of major dams on the Colorado River, particularly the Hoover Dam, built between 1931 and 1936, then the largest ever built and still the second highest in the USA. Hoover Dam's reservoir, Lake Mead, has the largest capacity in the USA, followed closely by Lake Powell, which was formed in 1966 by the construction of Glen Canyon Dam, also on the Colorado River.

Despite this seeming bounty of water created by modern technology, there were and are many water problems, not the least of which were ethical ones – the huge lakes formed by the dams flooded canyons containing hundreds of ancient Indian sites that are now lost. Technical problems have included the inaccurate measurement of water flow by early gauges; it is now thought that the original estimates of available water were 20% too high. Other technical problems include what to do with the silt that drops out of the water when it comes to a halt behind a dam (see the Lake Powell sidebar). And some problems have no solution – dams built to withstand the biggest floods can do nothing when there is a drought, as has occurred during several years of the last decade.

Nevertheless, water has become available in the Southwest and, with it, towns have grown. More water means more people who need more water still – a vicious cycle that has reached crisis proportions. Phoenix is a noteworthy example. Founded in 1870, the city had 5,500 inhabitants in 1900 and has over 1 million today, the ninth largest in the country. Combined with adjoining towns, 2.5 million people live in the metropolis.

There is simply not enough water to continue supplying all these people.

Recent additions to the Southwest's water supply are underground water reserves, or aquifers, which have been discovered in west-central Arizona, southwestern Utah and elsewhere. The most important of these is the Ogallala Aquifer of the Great Plains, which provides water for large parts of New Mexico and five other plains states.

These aquifers are being 'mined' – in other words, water is being extracted from them at a faster rate than it can naturally be replenished. Recent legislative action is attempting to halt this exploitation to avoid losing the aquifers by early in the 21st century. Southwesterners can only hope that this will be successful. Providing water to the ever-growing population of the Southwest remains the region's most serious problem, and some groups have been eyeing rivers as far away as the Pacific Northwest and Canada as possible sources of water.

It is not only the city dwellers with their daily showers and water-thirsty golf courses (almost 150 in the Phoenix area alone), but also rural inhabitants who have played a part in making water issues the Southwest's major ecological concern. Agriculture requires a huge volume of water for irrigation. Before the building of dams irrigation was limited, but water can now reach extensive areas. In the 1990s, the Central Arizona Project (CAP) enabled Tucson and southeastern Arizona to receive water from the Colorado River. Much of this is used for agricultural purposes, partly because the quality of the water for drinking purposes has been questionable.

Draining Lake Powell?

In Lake Powell, formed by Glen Canyon Dam on the Colorado River, 90% of the river sediment settles behind the dam, leaving the river below the dam lacking in nutrients and unable to properly support native fish, amphibians and other organisms. The silt has also been shown to contain heavy metals that, as they build up, will eventually harm or kill fish and other wildlife in the lake. The lake attracts boaters, which also leads to pollution. The Glen Canyon Institute, an environmental think tank, estimates that the amount of oil left in the lake by recreational users every four years is equivalent to the oil leaked in the Exxon Valdez disaster. River runners on the Colorado have noted that beaches that used to be formed along the river by annual floods are now slowly washing away as the flooding has become regulated by the dam. And water-use advocates say that more than a billion cubic meters of water are lost annually from the lake due to evaporation and seepage.

These factors have given rise to some serious concerns about the negative environmental aspects of massive dams. While the problems are still not devastating (Lake Powell is a recent phenomenon – it took 17 years to fill after the dam was completed in 1963), there is a real fear that a few decades from now the whole river ecosystem will be irreversibly damaged, having suffered pollution, the removal of beaches and losses of native species. One solution that has been receiving recent publicity is draining the lake – a massive though feasible undertaking. Organizations such as the Glen Canyon Institute and the Sierra Club believe that this proposal makes sense.

Will the lake be drained? Probably not for many years, if ever. The vast economic importance of the dam as a source of electric power for most of southern Utah and parts of Arizona and Colorado, and as a source of tourism revenue (with well over 2 million annual visitors) will make it a long uphill battle against legitimate concerns. However, the fact that the issue is being seriously discussed means that it may eventually happen. ∎

Water use for crop agriculture has contributed to environmental problems but cattle ranching is also a concern. Many federal lands are leased inexpensively to ranchers to graze cattle. This can result in severe degradation of riparian areas when cattle trample the edges of streams in efforts to find water. This trampling does not allow plants to grow and deteriorates the banks so that they are washed away. Over 90% of riparian habitats have disappeared in Arizona over the past century. Although questionable ranching and agricultural practices have led to environmental deterioration, some ranchers are figuring out more sustainable techniques. The Malpais Borderlands Group, with about 25 environmentally minded ranchers on the southern New Mexican-Arizona border, has pushed for sound ranching techniques in this area. They are led by William McDonald, a fifth-generation rancher from Douglas, Arizona, who won major recognition with a MacArthur Foundation Genius Award in 1998.

One of the few remaining riparian areas is along the San Pedro River in southeastern Arizona, with a phenomenal diversity of species. Almost half of the birds in North America have been recorded here (which is partly why southeastern Arizona is considered one of the premier birding regions in the continent), as well as large numbers of amphibians, reptiles, mammals and other wildlife. Despite being protected as a BLM Conservation Area, parts of the San Pedro dry up during certain times of year, and the water levels are dropping annually, due mainly to burgeoning growth in the nearby towns of Sierra Vista and the adjoining military base of Fort Huachuca.

Although water use and agriculture are among the major ecological and environmental concerns, the mining industry also plays a dangerously controversial role. Huge copper mines scar the earth's surface (the Bingham Canyon mine near Salt Lake City is proudly called 'the biggest hole on earth') and strip-mining for coal is also a contentious issue. Uranium mines in the Moab area have become unproductive, but their debris (known as tailings) continues to pollute the environment long after mines go out of business. The Atlas site near Moab causes the worst of the nation's uranium tailings pollution, with almost 11 million gallons of pollutants annually leaking out of the tailings into the Colorado River.

Perhaps the most contentious mining issue at this time is what to do with all the radioactive waste left as a legacy of the Cold War. One solution, which has been two decades in the making, is to bury it deep underground in the Waste Isolation Pilot Plant (see the Hazard, Boon or Both? sidebar in Southeastern New Mexico). Unfortunately, even if this scheme succeeds, it will only take care of a tiny fraction of the nation's nuclear waste.

FLORA & FAUNA

The wildlife of the Southwest is unique and fascinating, and much of it can easily be seen and experienced. Forests of the giant saguaro cactus cover many slopes of southern Arizona. The roadrunner, the state bird of New Mexico, and the coyote, the wily trickster of Navajo legend, are often seen darting across the highways or skulking off the road. Vultures wheel through the air, poisonous lizards and venomous snakes are occasionally glimpsed, tarantulas and scorpions scuttle along the ground and jackrabbits bound along with prodigious leaps. Southeastern Arizona is a mecca for birders, with 16 species of hummingbirds recorded (eight are commonly seen). This area also has many other exotic species and people fly thousands of miles to record an unusual bird here.

Clearly, there is plenty of life in this desert – the question is, which desert? What was once called the Great Southwestern Desert by early travelers is now divided into four different deserts. Each has a characteristic flora, fauna, climate and physical geography to distinguish it from the others, although some features are common to all four deserts as well as other areas. In addition, highland regions in all three Southwestern states and the plains of eastern New Mexico also have distinct ecological regions with unique plants and animals.

A brief overview of these regions introduces you to the diversity of plants and animals in the Southwest. Note that many of the species mentioned below are found, to a greater or lesser extent, in areas other than those under which they are mentioned.

For information about poisonous creatures (snakes, spiders, scorpions, etc) see the sections on Health and Dangers & Annoyances in Facts for the Visitor.

The Arizona-Sonora Desert

This area covers most of southern Arizona and much of the northern part of Mexico's state of Sonora, most of Baja California, and the southeastern corner of California. It is a subtropical desert with two distinct wet seasons: the summer monsoons and the winter rains. Generally low-lying and extremely hot, it has a greater diversity of wildlife than the other deserts. This is partly because the rainfall pattern allows for two flowering seasons and also because tropical regions have many more species than do temperate ones. The spring flowering season, in particular, can sometimes be incredibly spectacular, though shortlived. If winter rainfall and temperature are just right, yellow, orange, blue, violet and pink flowers bloom by the millions.

More than any other region, the Arizona-Sonora Desert is characterized by cacti, especially by the giant saguaro cactus that is found in southern Arizona but nowhere else in the USA. These huge columnar cacti with their uplifted arms are part of almost everyone's image of the Southwest. The organ-pipe cactus and the senita cactus are other giants found in southern Arizona near the Mexican border. Dozens of other species are here too: prickly pear, barrel, fishhook, hedgehog and teddybear cholla are the most typical cacti of this desert.

The Arizona-Sonora Desert also has the greatest variety of trees, which tend to be short and spiny with small leaves. The Arizona state tree, the blue paloverde, as well as the yellow and Mexican paloverdes are

common here. *Paloverde* is Spanish for 'green stick' and refers to the color of the bark, which is capable of photosynthesizing. The ironwood, a tree with very dense wood that sinks in water, is also typical of this desert. Mesquite trees are common but not confined to this region.

Animals are easily seen, especially many species of lizards and, sometimes, several snake species including various rattlesnakes and the highly venomous Arizona coral snake. Commonly seen mammals are coyotes, several species of rabbits and various species of ground, rock and antelope squirrels. (These mammals are common throughout most of the Southwest.) Birds include the quaint Gambel's quail, with its question-mark-shaped head plume, the roadrunner and the ubiquitous cactus wren.

The superb Arizona-Sonora Desert Museum in Tucson provides visitors with an excellent introduction to this region.

The Chihuahua Desert

This desert is found in southern New Mexico, western Texas, the extreme southeastern corner of Arizona and the Mexican state of Chihuahua. Although at a similar latitude to the Arizona-Sonora Desert, it lies at a generally higher elevation and is therefore cooler. On average, more rain falls in summer, and most flowers bloom in late summer and early fall.

The desert's most striking plants are agaves and yuccas. The agaves, of which there are several species (some found in the other desert regions), have a rosette of large, tough, spiny swordlike leaves out of which shoots an amazing flowering stalk, often reaching as high as 15 feet, and covered with thousands of tiny flowers. This stalk can grow as much as a foot a day and the energy required to produce this huge reproductive body is so great that it is a one-time occurrence. After flowering for a few weeks, the plant dies.

Some yuccas resemble agaves with rosettes of tough leaves and tall flower stalks; others are more shrublike. Unlike the agave, however, the yucca flowers annually. There are some 15 species of

Packrats – Today's Pest, Yesterday's Historian

Packrats (or, more properly, woodrats, genus *Neotoma*) are large rodents, related to mice, that have an incredible ability to dig and burrow through the hard desert soil. The nickname packrat arose out of their habit of collecting and hoarding almost anything in large and often inaccessible nests. Plants and pennies, bones and bottle caps are all collectibles for the packrat. Tales abound in the Southwest of packrats ruining air-conditioning systems or collapsing patios with their endeavors. I once left a refrigerator in storage for six months and returned to find a packrat nest inside and the wiring stripped away.

The dry conditions of the Southwest preserve packrat nests remarkably well. Scientists have discovered nests thousands of years old. Microscopic scrutiny of the contents has revealed much about the ancient history of the region. Plant materials found inside the nests show that the environment was much wetter and greener when the first people arrived in the Southwest, at least 11,000 years ago. ■

yucca in the Southwest; the soaptree yucca is New Mexico's state flower. The flowers are pollinated at night by yucca moths, which lay their eggs inside the flowers. The moth larvae then feed on the developing fruit and thus both plant and animal benefit. The most interesting aspect of this mutualism is that each species of yucca is pollinated by its own species of yucca moth that has coevolved with it.

Creosote bush dominates the ground cover of the Chihuahua Desert, and is found in the Arizona-Sonora and Mojave Deserts as well. Although this low, straggly bush is not much to look at, it produces complex oils and resins that make it taste bad to most animals. When it rains, these chemicals are released and give the air a characteristically astringent but not unpleasant smell.

The ocotillo is a common plant of both the Chihuahua and Arizona-Sonora Deserts. During dry months, this plant looks like a bunch of skinny, spiny stems that become covered by many tiny green leaves after rain. They are tipped by clusters of small, bright red flowers.

Both the Chihuahua and Arizona-Sonora Deserts are home to mammals that are typical of Mexico but not frequently seen by visitors to the USA. If you enjoy hiking and backcountry camping, you may well see javelina or coati. Javelinas, also called collared peccaries, are pig-like mammals that travel in small groups or occasionally herds of up to 60, feeding on cacti and making quiet grunting sounds. They are most easily seen in early morning or late afternoon. If you're lucky, you might catch sight of them in the suburbs of towns. Coatis are members of the raccoon family and live primarily in subtropical regions of Central and South America. They have made inroads northward and are sighted fairly often both in the deserts and in the mountains as far as the Mogollon Rim in Arizona.

One of the best places to learn more about this area's biology is the Living Desert State Park in Carlsbad, New Mexico.

The Mojave Desert

This desert covers parts of southern Nevada, southeastern California, northwestern Arizona and the extreme southeast of Utah, and so only a small portion falls within the area covered by this book. The Mojave is the smallest, driest and hottest of the country's deserts, and it is also thought of as a transition desert between the Arizona-Sonora and Great Basin Deserts.

Much of this desert is low-lying, and in fact it includes the lowest point – 282 feet below sea level – in the Western Hemisphere: California's Death Valley. The low areas, usually the hottest and driest, are characterized by widely spread shrubby

Cacti of the Southwest

My mother always had a couple of small cacti surviving desperately in tiny pots on the sunless windowsills of our suburban London house. I'll never forget the spring day when one of those hopelessly decrepit specimens suddenly burst into a florid bloom, exotically overwhelming all the surrounding houseplants. And exotic it certainly was – every one of the world's over 2000 species of cactus is native to the Americas.

Researchers cannot agree on exact numbers, but over 100 of the approximately 2000 species of cactus are found in the Southwest and are superbly adapted to survival in these arid environments. The succulent pads that form the body of the plant are actually modified stems, and their waxy 'skin' helps retard moisture loss. The leaves, which in other plants normally allow a lot of water to escape through transpiration, have been modified into spines that not only lose little moisture, but also protect the plant against herbivores looking for water. Evaporation is further reduced by the plant keeping its pores closed during the day and open only at night. These remarkable plants are further enhanced by their often splendid flowers.

Identification It is fairly easy to identify at least the six most common types of Southwestern cactus. The six types are prickly pear, pincushion, cholla, giant columnar, barrel and hedgehog cacti.

Prickly pears are often of the genus *Opuntia* and are distinguished by the flattened cross-section of their pads. If the pads are cylindrical, read on.

Pincushion cacti, often of the genus *Mammilaria*, are small and cylindrical in cross-section, and don't have ribs running from top to bottom. Spine clusters grow out of nipple-like bumps on the stems – hence the scientific name. Many species have hooked spines.

Cholla (CHOY-uh) cacti are also cylindrical and lack ribs, but are much taller and have branches. Like the prickly pears, they belong to the genus *Opuntia*. They can range from pencil chollas, with extremely thin branches; to teddybear chollas, which look warm and

vegetation or empty sand dunes and dry lakebeds. In Arizona and Utah the elevations are higher and the dominant plants are the eerie Joshua trees. These 30- to 40-foot-high plants, which are believed to live as long as 1000 years, are the largest species of yucca and are members of the lily family.

After the right amount of rainfall in winter, when it rains the most, spring can bring a carpet of about 250 species of flowers, of which 80% are endemic to the Mojave Desert. Cacti are quite common, although they are generally smaller than the ones of the Arizona-Sonora Desert. Creosote bushes are also seen in great and odorous quantities. Large numbers of lizards and desert birds are also present.

The Great Basin Desert

This is the continent's most northerly desert, covering most of Nevada, western Utah and the Colorado Plateau, and stretching on into Idaho and Oregon. The name 'Great Basin' paints something of an unclear picture; this region within the Basin and Range province contains many basins. The name derives from the fact that the Great Basin is an area of interior drainage, where most of the waterways drain into desert flats, not into the sea.

This is generally a high desert, with most of the basins at over 4000 feet. The high latitude and elevation make this a cooler desert than the others, and also one that has less wildlife. There are few of the cacti, agaves and yuccas that are so noticeable in the hot deserts, and those that are present tend to be small. Instead, miles of low, rather nondescript shrubs such as saltbrush and sagebrush cover the ground.

Here, the big sagebrush, which can reach over 6 feet in height, replaces the

fuzzy but have wickedly barbed spines; to large jumping chollas, which have fruits hanging in loose chains. Brushing a jumping cholla lightly often results in part of the chain becoming attached to your body – almost as if it had jumped onto you. Jumping chollas often grow in thick stands. The chollas have some of the sharpest and most difficult to remove spines – if you are stuck, it may be easier to cut the spines with scissors and then remove them one by one with tweezers.

The remaining three main types are all cylindrical in cross-section and ribbed. If they are also very tall (from 15 to 50 feet high), they are giant columnar cacti and most likely to be a saguaro cactus *(Cereus giganteus)*, which has branches high off the ground (and is found only in southern Arizona and northern Mexico). In a few places in southern Arizona, you might see large cacti branching from the ground. These are either organ-pipe or senita cacti. (Organ-pipes have 10 or more ribs, and lack the white or gray hairs of the senita. You can see them at Organ Pipe Cactus National Monument.) There are many more species of columnar cacti across the border in Mexico.

Finally, smaller cylindrical cacti with ribs are likely to be hedgehog or barrel cacti. Hedgehog cacti, often of the genus *Echinocereus*, are small, with the main pad less than 4 inches in diameter. When they bloom, the flowers grow from the sides. Barrel cacti, often of the genus *Ferocactus*, are over 5 inches in diameter and their flowers grow from the top. The largest examples can grow to 10 feet in height, although this is unusual.

All six types are commonly found in southern Arizona. The other Southwestern deserts lack the giant columnar cacti. The Great Basin Desert tends to have just the smaller species.

Protection Cacti are legally protected. You need a permit to collect any kind of cactus from the wild. It is also illegal to damage or destroy a cactus. A famous (and true) story you may hear is of a man who was shooting at a saguaro from close range. One of the huge arms of the cactus toppled over and killed him. ■

creosote of the hot desert. It is very wide-spread in the Great Basin Desert and, like creosote, has volatile oils to make it less appetizing to potential herbivores. It also gives off a pleasantly pungent odor after rain or when crushed. (This sagebrush is no relation to the sage herb used in cooking.) So pervasive is the big sagebrush that, in some areas, it provides 70% of the ground cover and an astonishing 90% of the plant biomass.

Generally, wildlife is either scarce or hard to observe. A bird that is closely associated with big sagebrush is the sage grouse, which eats twice as much of this plant as all its other food combined. Males make a resonant booming call and dance around in specific places (called leks) to attract females during the early spring breeding season, when they are the most easy to observe. Various other birds associ-

ated with big sagebrush (sage sparrow, sage thrasher) are small, secretive and hard to spot.

Raptors are seen fairly often, particularly red-tailed hawks and kestrels. They feed on lizards and snakes which, although less common than in other deserts, are still numerous. Otherwise, rabbits are the most likely animals to catch your eye. If you're lucky, though, you never know what you may run into (or over if you're not careful). My best sighting of a badger was in the Great Basin Desert, and you may see pronghorns browsing among the sagebrush.

Grasslands

Grasslands once covered extensive areas of the Southwest, particularly in the river basins of Arizona and New Mexico. Millions of head of cattle and sheep were introduced into these fine grazing areas in the 1870s and 1880s. The animals over-grazed the grasslands, and many of these areas quickly became extensions of the deserts. Today, the grassland areas are found in eastern New Mexico, especially in the northeastern part of the state. Here, the observant traveler can spot small herds of pronghorn grazing. The pronghorn is also known as the pronghorn antelope because of its small forked horns and graceful body, but it is unrelated to the antelopes of Africa and Asia.

Higher Life Zones

As you climb into the mountain ranges, you'll pass plants and animals recalling the northern parts of the continent. A very rough rule of thumb is that a 1000-foot elevation gain is equivalent to a drive of several hundred miles to the north; in other words, the vegetation of the Southwest's high mountains is comparable to that of Canada.

Biologists divide the elevations of the mountains into a series of life zones that, despite being somewhat arbitrary and imprecise in regards to their altitude, are useful tools for making sense of the sudden and bewildering changes in flora and the associated fauna. The following is a popular zonation.

The lower elevations (below 4500 feet) are called the Lower Sonoran Zone, followed by the Upper Sonoran Zone (4500 to 6500 feet). These encompass most of the deserts discussed above. The Upper Sonoran Zone also supports evergreen trees such as small junipers and the piñon pine.

The Transition Zone (6500 to 8000 feet) falls between the desert basins and the high mountains. Much of the Colorado Plateau appears to be in this zone, although many biologists include it in the Great Basin Desert. The most notable vegetation is the ponderosa pine, of which there are large stands, especially in New Mexico, where it is extensively logged. The cacti, agaves, yuccas, creosote and sagebrush of lower elevations are no longer common in this zone. Other plants found here are Gambel's oak and various shrubs. There are fewer species of reptiles, but squirrels and chipmunks are common. Black bears and mountain lions live here, but you are unlikely to see them. White-tailed deer are more often sighted, and in some places, you may see elk.

From about 8000 to 9500 feet, the predominant trees are Douglas firs and aspens in what is called the Canadian Zone (also called the Montane Forest Zone). Other trees include white fir and juniper, and the shading of these thick forests precludes the growth of many other plants. From 9500 to 11,500 feet, in the Hudsonian Zone (also called Subalpine Forest Zone), other conifers tend to predominate, including Engelmann spruce, subalpine fir and bristlecone pine, among others. This zone receives very heavy snow in winter, and few mammals are found here outside of the summer months. The tree line begins at about 11,500 feet, and the zone above the tree line is called the Alpine Zone. There are only a few areas in the Southwest that reach these elevations, which are characterized by small tundra-like plants.

GOVERNMENT & POLITICS

The USA has a republican form of government, which is popularly defined as government 'of the people, by the people and for the people.' The US Constitution, ratified in 1789 and amended 26 times since then, provides the fundamental laws for the running of the national government and the relations between the national and state governments.

US citizens over the age of 18 are eligible to vote (criminals may lose this right, depending on their crime). Elections are hotly contested, and politicians and parties spend many millions of dollars on political campaigns that can become very acrimonious. Despite this, barely half of the eligible voters cast ballots in recent elections.

There are two main political parties – the Republicans (called the GOP for Grand Old Party) and the Democrats. Independent politicians occasionally provide a third choice. Other parties do exist, but they are too small to play a significant part in government. Traditionally, Republicans are conservative, and Democrats are liberal. Often, the President and his Cabinet are of one party while Congress has a majority of the opposing party.

Insofar as generalizations can be made, Republicans favor cutting taxes; shrinking nationally funded (federal) programs of health care, education, welfare and so forth; and minimizing or eliminating national funding for items such as arts programs and abortion. Republicans believe such programs are better handled at the state level. Democrats prefer higher taxation and more federal funding of these programs. However, Republicans support spending a larger proportion of the federal budget on the military than do Democrats.

National Government

The government has three branches: the legislative branch makes the laws of the land, the executive branch executes (carries out) these laws, and the judicial branch studies and interprets both the Constitution and the laws.

The legislative branch is made up of the bicameral Congress, which is composed of the Senate and the House of Representatives. The 100-member Senate has two senators from each of the 50 states, while the 435-member House has one or more members from each state, depending on the size of each state's population. States are constitutionally equal, and so those with small populations are overrepresented in the Senate, but this influence is diluted in the House. Senators are elected for six years, and representatives are elected for two.

The fact that two parties with opposing views are both strongly represented in Congress means that it is sometimes difficult to pass laws that are seen as beneficial to the country by one party but not by the other.

The executive branch consists of the President, the Cabinet and various assistants. The 14 members of the President's Cabinet are each appointed by the President but must be approved by the Senate.

The President has the power to veto the laws passed by Congress, although a law can still be passed if two-thirds of the members vote for it the second time, overriding the President's veto.

The judicial branch is headed by the Supreme Court, which consists of nine justices who are appointed for life by the President and approved by the Senate.

The President, whose term is four years, is chosen by an Electoral College consisting of a number of individual electors from each state equivalent to its number of senators and representatives, who vote in accordance with the popular vote within their state. To be elected president a candidate must obtain a majority of 270 of the total 538 electoral votes (the District of Columbia has no voting representatives in Congress, but nevertheless has three electoral votes). The President may serve only two terms. The 104th Congress (1995 to 1997), had a Republican majority in both houses, the first time they have had such a majority since WWII.

State Government

Each of the 50 states has its own government, run along similar lines to the national government with some differences, mainly regarding how long an elected representative remains in office. The head of the executive branch of state government is the governor, and the bicameral legislature consists of a senate and a house delegation.

National (federal) laws apply to all states, although there are often conflicts between federal and state interests. In addition, each state enacts its own laws that visitors should be aware of. States have different laws about driving, alcohol use and taxes, which are discussed in Facts for the Visitor.

Traditionally, most Western states (including those in the Southwest) support the Republican party. Utah and Arizona are generally conservative, New Mexico is more middle-of-the-road. In a land where water is a scarce resource and the population is increasing more rapidly than in the country as a whole, it is not surprising that the most contentious issues in the region concern water and land use.

ECONOMY

Traditionally, mining and agriculture (especially ranching) have been the backbone of the Southwest's economy. Ranching, of course, is more than just a meat and dairy industry – it is a way of life, a tradition. *Gunsmoke* reruns on TV, cowboys riding into purple sage sunsets, rodeos, roundups, lassos and wide open plains, are all part of the psyche of the American West. Traditions die hard, and although ranching today is a far cry from the rough-and-tumble 19th century, it still sparks the interest of many visitors who stay on 'dude ranches' or take part in cowboy-led horse packing trips.

Mining and ranching were major factors in the settling of the Wild West. Laws were enacted in the 19th century to regulate these industries, and some are still in force today. Recent moves to modernize this legislation have met with strong resistance from the industries involved. Miners and ranchers consider the old laws to be reasonable; others find that current concerns about fair price for the use of public lands, conservation, water quality and pollution necessitate a modernization of the laws. One of the most contentious issues is that of ranchers' traditional rights to graze on public land for which they pay only a small fraction of the current cost of a grazing lease on private land.

In modern times, manufacturing, tourism, government and service industries have become increasingly important sectors in the Southwest's economy.

POPULATION

The US Census Bureau takes a census of the population every 10 years. The last census was in April 1990, and the figures given below are estimates for 1996. Persons are asked to classify their race by choosing the one with which they most closely identify. Five main race categories are listed: white, black, Native American, Asian or Pacific Islander, and other. In addition, persons may also identify themselves as Hispanic, but this is not considered a race category because Hispanic people can be of any race.

The populations of the Southwestern states are shown in the table, and figures for the USA are given for comparative purposes.

The table demonstrates that New Mexico and Arizona have a rich Hispanic heritage. These states also have large populations of Native Americans, over half of which are Navajo. Other tribes include various Apache groups, Havasupai, Hopi, Hualapai, various Pueblo tribes, Tohono O'odham,

US Census Figures

(1996 estimates for population; 1990 figures for ethnic distribution)

State	White	Black	Native American	Asian or Pacific Islander	Other	Hispanic
USA 265,283,783	80.3%	12.1%	0.8%	2.9%	3.9%	9%
Arizona 4,428,068	80.8%	3%	5.6%	1.5%	9.1%	18.8%
New Mexico 1,713,407	75.6%	2%	8.9%	0.9%	12.6%	38.2%
Utah 2,000,494	93.8%	0.7%	1.4%	1.9%	2.2%	4.9%

Ute and a host of smaller groups. Arizona and New Mexico have the third and fourth largest Native American populations of the 50 states (Oklahoma and California have the largest). The Southwest's black population, on the other hand, is very small, as is the Asian/Pacific Islander group. Utah, with its strong Mormon heritage, is very predominantly white.

The Southwestern states are sparsely populated. Arizona's comparatively high population density is skewed by the presence of the greater Phoenix metropolitan area, which accounts for over half of the state's inhabitants. Similarly, the Salt Lake City region accounts for over half of Utah's population. The Southwest is one of the fastest-growing regions in the USA, with the warm weather attracting large numbers of retirees. From 1990 to 1996, Arizona's population grew by 20.8%, Utah's by 16.1% and New Mexico's by 13.1%, compared to 6.7% for the nation as a whole. Since 1940, Arizona's population has increased almost ninefold – one of the greatest increases of any state.

PEOPLE

The Southwest is commonly perceived as having a tricultural mix of Indian, Hispanic and Anglo cultures. Only in northwestern and north-central New Mexico can you see clear evidence of all three cultures – ancient Indian pueblos, historic Hispanic churches and Anglo atomic bomb laboratories coexist in an intricate and unique alliance.

In the rest of the Southwest, all three cultures make their mark in differing degrees depending on the region. The Indians predominantly live in the Four Corners area, especially the Navajo and Hopi Reservations of northeastern Arizona, and in the pueblos of northwestern New Mexico. There are also the large Apache reservations in mountainous eastern Arizona and the Tohono O'odham Reservation in the desert south of Arizona as well as a scattering of smaller reservations elsewhere in the region. With the exception of the pueblo areas, none of these places can be

considered tricultural! However, reservation culture is definitely bicultural – Indian and Anglo – in most respects.

New Mexico has the highest proportion of Hispanic people, with the Rio Grande Valley and Santa Fe being historically the center of that culture. Southern Arizona, too, has much Hispanic influence, as can be seen by the huge number of Mexican restaurants in Tucson and the fact that telephone directories and government documents have Spanish sections or translations. Architecture in parts of southern Arizona, and especially along the Rio Grande and in Santa Fe, is an attractive blend of Hispanic and Indian styles.

Anglos dominate the scene in most of Mormon Utah and in the fast-growing cities of Arizona, particularly the Phoenix metropolitan area and the towns along the Colorado River in western Arizona. In rural areas of the Southwest, many off-reservation ranches and mines are Anglo-owned, although workers may be Hispanic or Indian.

But the Southwest's unique flavor does not stem simply from its triculturalism. That must be combined with the land and climate – beautifully desolate, splendidly harsh, incredibly varied and rarely forgiving. People's survival in these extreme conditions has shaped what may be perceived as the culture of the Southwest.

ARTS

New Mexico and Utah both have symphony orchestras – at Albuquerque and Salt Lake City respectively – and Phoenix and Tucson have their own symphony orchestras. Major opera companies in the Southwest include the Arizona Opera Company, which performs in Tucson and Phoenix; the Santa Fe Opera; and the Utah Opera in Salt Lake City. The famous Mormon Tabernacle Choir has performed in weekly radio broadcasts since 1929. Notable dance companies include Ballet Arizona in Phoenix; Ballet West and the Repertory Dance Theater in Salt Lake City; and the Maria Benitez Teatro Flamenco in Santa Fe. Every city of any size has

Native American Dance & Music

Swirling dancers bedecked in headdresses and facepaint, wearing intricately beaded clothing and stomping in time to a circle of drummers – this spectacle is one that many travelers to the region want to see. Here are suggestions on how to best enjoy the various dances that are held many times throughout the year all over the Southwest.

From the visitor's point of view, Native American dances can be grouped into three categories, although there is certainly overlap between them.

Religious First, there are the ceremonial or ritual religious dances that take place on Indian reservations at traditionally specified times of the year. Some of these are celebratory occasions that mark stages of life (for instance, a girl's puberty rite), and others, such as rain dances, revere specific gods. Precise dates and locations vary from year to year and are often not known until a few weeks before the event. Because of the strong religious and traditional motive, access to ceremonial dances is usually strictly controlled.

Some ceremonials are open to the public, but photography or recording of any kind is completely prohibited. It is important for tourists to respect this rule. Occasionally, a tourist might try to sneak a quick and unobtrusive photo – in this case, a tribal policeman may confiscate the camera, or an irate tribal elder may simply grab the camera and hurl it over the nearest cliff! Other rules for watching ceremonial dances are refraining from applauding and asking many questions, following instructions about where to stand or sit, wearing appropriate clothing (no shorts or tank tops) and generally behaving in a quiet and respectful way. Alcohol is not permitted during dances or anywhere on most Indian reservations. Increasing numbers of ceremonial dances are being closed to the general public because the Indians are fed up with non-Indians' behavior.

For details of which dances are performed when, contact the tribal offices listed in the relevant parts of the text.

Social Social dances can be very traditional or relatively modern, and are danced for competition, display, to tell a story, as an honor, or just for fun and getting together with other families, clans or tribes. The dancers are accompanied by drum groups and singers. Usually, songs are in one of the Native American languages, or they are vocables (songs made up of sounds that are not words). An emcee calls each dance, often with an inside joke or two, and usually at least some of the dances are called in English, especially the intertribals, when anyone, including members of the tourist tribe, can go out and dance.

For visitors, these are the best kind of dances because you can enjoy them, participate if you wish, and let go of your worries about interfering in a religious ceremony. Social dances occur throughout the Southwest during powwows or at various festivities with names like 'Indian Days.' They also occur during fairs, rodeos and other gatherings in Indian reservations. Details are given under the appropriate places in the text.

Often, a small admission fee is charged; Indian food, arts and crafts, and cassettes or CDs are sold; and photography may be permitted. Photographers can usually take general pictures of the festivities but should always ask permission to take photographs of individuals. A small tip may be requested in this case.

Performances The third category of dances is purely performance dancing, where you sit in a theater (often outdoors) and watch. These dances are usually of the social kind and are very colorful. It's performance art, but it's also authentic – the dancers don't just make up non-Indian dances for tourists! One of the best places to see dance performances is during the summer at Red Rock State Park just outside of Gallup, New Mexico. ■

many theaters, art galleries and museums. Performers from all over the world are regularly hosted in venues of major Southwestern cities – you can hear and see anything from Japanese kodo drummers to Ukrainian folk dancers.

In addition, strong Hispanic and Native American influences have helped create a distinctive local arts scene. Much of this Southwestern aesthetic is evident in the region's pottery, paintings, weavings, jewelry, sculpture, woodcarving and leatherworking. Southwestern art can be very traditional or cutting-edge contemporary.

Perhaps the region's most famous artist is Georgia O'Keeffe (1887-1986), whose Southwestern landscapes and motifs are found in major museums throughout the world. Also highly regarded is the Navajo artist RC Gorman (born 1932), whose sculptures and paintings of Navajo women are becoming increasingly famous worldwide. Gorman has made his home in Taos for many years. Both Taos and nearby Santa Fe have large and active communities of artists and are considered seminal places in the development of Southwestern art.

Many visitors are anxious to see Native American art. The Southwest certainly has a wide variety: Navajo rugs, Hopi kachina dolls, Zuni silverware, Tohono O'odham basketry and Pueblo pottery are some of the best known. Maria Martinez (1887-1980) of the San Ildefonso Pueblo led a revival of traditional pottery making during the 1920s; her 'black on black' pots are considered some of the finest ever made and are now worth thousands of dollars. Excellent examples of Southwestern Native American art can be seen in many museums, of which the Heard Museum in Phoenix is one of the best.

Contemporary Native American art is eminently buyable, and both traditional and modern work is available in hundreds of galleries throughout the region.

The Southwest's music scene, too, has its Hispanic and Native American influences. Of course, you can hear anything from jazz to hip-hop in the major cities, but you can also catch *mariachis* (Mexican street bands typically dressed in dark, ornately sequined, body-hugging costumes and playing predominantly brass instruments and guitars), especially in the towns close to the Mexican border. Native American dances and music are performed throughout the Southwest. A couple of noteworthy musicians are Carlos R Nakai and Perry Silver Bird, both flute players. Nakai is a Navajo-Ute who has played his traditional cedar flute with a variety of musicians, ranging from his own ethnic jazz ensemble, called Jackalope, to the Tucson Symphony Orchestra.

See the Books section in Facts for the Visitor for information on Southwestern authors and literature.

RELIGION

The US Constitution mandates separation of church and state, and tolerance is the norm. However, issues like prayer in public schools and abortion have brought theological issues onto the secular stage. Nominal allegiance is more widespread than church attendance, but many churchgoers are extremely devout.

The USA is predominantly Christian – one source claims that 85% of the population professes some kind of Christianity (approximately 40% Roman Catholic, 40% Protestant and 20% other denominations). Over 9% are nonreligious or atheists, 2.5% are Jewish and the remaining 3.5% are a diverse mix of other beliefs. Other sources give figures of 55.1% Christian (of which over 60% are Protestant) and 2.1% Jewish. These figures are probably both 'right' – it depends on the definition of how religious a person has to be.

The overall picture in the Southwest is that Christians make up the religious majority, with Catholics having the numerical edge in New Mexico and Mormons being by far the majority in Utah. New Mexico and Utah have very few Jews, while Arizona's Jewish population is about the national average.

The oldest religions in North America are those of Native American tribes, though they have changed much since contact with

Europeans. Some, like the Native American Church, which uses hallucinatory peyote buttons as a sacrament, are in part pan-Indian responses to encroachment by the politically dominant culture imposed on them.

Various Native American religions are closely followed by tens of thousands of people. In any discussion of Indian religious beliefs, several points are worth bearing in mind. First, different tribes often have very different creation stories, rituals and practices, which means that there are dozens of unique and carefully prescribed spiritual ways of life. Second, Indians usually maintain a strict sense of privacy about their most important ceremonies and thus books written by even the most respected anthropologists usually contain some inaccuracies when describing Indian religion. Third, the Indian ways are beliefs that Indians feel and know essentially because they are Indians – it's not something that non-Indians can properly understand or convert to.

Travelers will find that members of almost every religion, belief, faith or sect can be found in major cities. Even small towns have several religious groups to choose from. For further information, look in the telephone yellow pages under Churches, Mosques or Synagogues.

LANGUAGE

Although American English is spoken throughout the USA, there are regional variations. According to the most recent census, 35.5% of New Mexico's population (over the age of five) speaks a language other than English at home – this is the highest percentage of any state (compare this to the USA as a whole with 13.8%). In Arizona, 20.8% speak a language other than English at home, but in Utah it's only 7.8%. In New Mexico and Arizona, the languages spoken at home (other than English) are usually Spanish or one of numerous Indian languages.

For the traveler, however, this is not of major concern. Almost every Mexican restaurant or Native American art gallery will have English-speaking staff, and you don't need to brush up on your Spanish or learn Navajo. If you are interested in hearing speech or music in these languages, you'll find plenty of Spanish-speaking radio stations in the southern parts of New Mexico and Arizona, many broadcasting from Mexico. In the Four Corners area, KTTN radio station, broadcasting out of Window Rock on 660 AM, has many programs in Navajo. One word you might hear frequently in this area is the Navajo greeting ya'at'eeh.

Visitors to Indian reservations should bear in mind that silence is almost like a statement. If you say something to an Indian and are met by silence, this doesn't indicate that the person you are talking to is ignoring you. Indians speak their minds when they disagree with the speaker and may remain silent when they agree with the speaker or have no special opinion. This can be strange to non-Indians who are used to interjecting 'uh huh' and 'really' after almost every sentence they hear.

Finally, visitors to the major national parks will often find introductory brochures printed in Spanish, German, French or Japanese. Although speakers of the last three languages are among the most frequent foreign visitors to the Southwest, they will find that few Americans here speak these languages.

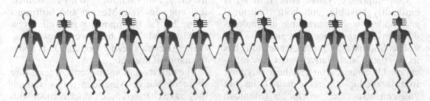

Facts for the Visitor

PLANNING
When to Go
The best season to visit the Southwest is January to December.

In northern Arizona, New Mexico and Utah, summer is the high season, coinciding with school vacations in both North America and Europe. Traditionally, Memorial Day weekend (end of May) to Labor Day weekend (beginning of September) is the vacation season, and you can expect higher prices and more crowds except in hot southern Arizona, where luxury resorts cut their prices in half.

Winter visitors flock to the highlands for great skiing. Utah especially has world-class skiing, but New Mexico and Arizona also have good ski areas. If you don't like the idea of hurtling down snow-covered mountains, head down to southern Arizona. Hotels in Phoenix, Tucson and other southern Arizona towns consider winter (Christmas to May) their high (and more expensive) season. While the rest of the country is buried under snowdrifts, southern Arizonans enjoy T-shirt weather (you might need a sweater some days, but you won't need a down jacket).

I enjoy the spring and fall when there are fewer people, but some services may not be available then.

Maps
Free state maps are available from state tourist information offices and welcome centers. Members of the American Automobile Association (AAA) and its foreign affiliates (see Useful Organizations later in this chapter) can receive free state maps from AAA offices. Ask about their recommended *Indian Country* map, which covers the Four Corners area in excellent detail. The AAA also has maps of major cities. AAA maps are available to nonmembers for a few dollars. City maps are often pro-

vided by chambers of commerce for free or at nominal cost.

National park maps are free at each park after you pay the entrance fee. US Forest Service (USFS) ranger stations sell maps of their national forest for $4.

Topographic maps published by the US Geological Survey (USGS) are available at their Map and Book Sales, Denver, CO 80225 (☎ 303-236-7477). A list of maps is available upon request. Many camping stores, US National Park visitor centers and USFS ranger stations sell USGS maps of their immediate area. Maps with a scale of 1:62,500 (approximately 1 inch = 1 mile) or 1:24,000 are ideal for backcountry use. Map specialty stores carry maps for the whole country.

The DeLorme Mapping series publishes individual state atlases for Arizona and Utah that contain detailed topographic and highway maps at a scale of 1:250,000, as well as listings of campgrounds, historic sites, parks, natural features and even scenic drives. Available in good bookstores, these maps are especially useful off the main highways and cost about $20 each. New Mexico is covered by the *New Mexico Road & Recreation Atlas* from Benchmark Maps.

What to Bring
The Southwest generally has a casual attitude, and people's clothing reflects that. Clean jeans and cowboy boots are seen in symphony halls and good restaurants, although you can certainly dress up if you want. Very few restaurants expect men to wear ties and, in those, a bola tie is fine. (A bola tie is a leather cord fastened with a semiprecious stone and/or metal clasp; it is Arizona's state neckwear.) Utah, with its Mormon influence, appears to be the most formal, but even here, clean casual attire is just fine.

Your clothing will depend on season and elevation. Southern Arizonans wear shorts and T-shirts all summer long, but if you are heading into the highlands, you'll need some warmer clothes for the evening, even in midsummer. The climate charts in this book will help you decide.

Beware of the extreme sunshine. For much of the year, severe sunburn is a real possibility, so bring plenty of sunblock or wear light, long pants or skirts and long-sleeved shirts. A broad-brimmed hat and sunglasses are important, too. Bring a water bottle if you plan on doing any walking outside of towns; the heat will dehydrate you very quickly. Don't forget prescription medicines, spare contact lenses or glasses, and copies of your pre-scriptions.

If you are staying in the cheapest motels, a travel alarm clock is useful. (Wake-up calls can be arranged in better hotels.) Some travelers bring a small immersion heater and a cup to heat up water for instant coffee or soup in their room.

If you forget something, you can usually buy it without much hassle in any city or larger town.

TOURIST OFFICES
Many towns don't have tourist offices per se – this function is often performed by the local chambers of commerce. They can provide local information about what to see and where to stay, but their degree of use-fulness is far from uniform. The reference sections of libraries are also useful sources of local information.

State Tourist Offices
State tourist offices can send you informa-tive, colorful brochures about their states' main attractions. These free brochures are updated annually and contain addresses and telephone numbers of chambers of commerce, hotel lists and other useful information. State tourist offices may be able to answer specific questions or refer you to the appropriate office. The Utah Travel Council also publishes an annual *Ski Utah* brochure with detailed informa-tion about each ski area. These brochures are available in many chambers of com-merce and tourist offices, including the state tourist offices listed below.

Arizona Office of Tourism
    2702 N 3rd, Suite 4015, Phoenix, AZ 85004
    (☎ 602-230-7733, 800-842-8257, fax 602-
    240-5475)
New Mexico Department of Tourism
    491 Old Santa Fe Trail, Santa Fe, NM 87503
    (☎ 505-827-7400, 800-545-2040, 800-733-
    6396)
Utah Travel Council
    Council Hall/Capitol Hill, Salt Lake City,
    UT 84114 (☎ 801-538-1030, 800-200-1160,
    fax 801-538-1399)

Tourist Offices Abroad
The USA currently has no government affiliated tourist offices in other countries. Contact a travel agency for information.

VISAS & DOCUMENTS
Passports & Visas
Canadians must have proper proof of Cana-dian citizenship, such as a citizenship card with photo ID or a passport. Visitors from other countries must have a valid passport and many visitors also require a US visa.

However, there is a reciprocal visa-waiver program in which citizens of cer-tain countries may enter the USA for stays of 90 days or less with a passport but without first obtaining a US visa. Currently these countries are Andorra, Argentina, Australia, Austria, Belgium, Brunei, Den-mark, Finland, France, Germany, Iceland, Ireland, Italy, Japan, Liechtenstein, Lux-embourg, Monaco, The Netherlands, New Zealand, Norway, San Marino, Slovenia, Spain, Sweden, Switzerland, and the United Kingdom. Under this program you must have a roundtrip ticket that is non-refundable in the USA, and you will not be allowed to extend your stay beyond 90 days.

Other travelers will need to obtain a visa from a US consulate or embassy. In most countries the process can be done by mail.

Your passport should be valid for at least six months longer than your intended stay in the USA and you'll need to submit a recent photo 1½ inches square (37mm x

HIV & Entering the USA

Everyone entering the USA who isn't a US citizen is subject to the authority of the Immigration & Naturalization Service (INS). The INS can keep someone from entering or staying in the USA by excluding or deporting them. This is especially relevant to travelers with HIV (human immunodeficiency virus). Though being HIV-positive is not grounds for deportation, it is a 'ground of exclusion' and the INS can invoke it to refuse admission.

Although the INS doesn't test people for HIV at customs, it may try to exclude anyone who answers yes to this question on the non-immigrant visa application form: 'Have you ever been afflicted with a communicable disease of public health significance?' INS officials may also stop people if they seem sick, are carrying AIDS/HIV medicine or, sadly, if the officer happens to think the person 'looks gay,' though sexual orientation is not legally a ground of exclusion.

It's imperative that visitors know and assert their rights. Immigrants and visitors who may face exclusion should discuss their rights and options with a trained immigration advocate before applying for a visa. For legal immigration information and referrals to immigration advocates, contact the National Immigration Project of the National Lawyers Guild (☎ 617-227-9727), 14 Beacon St, Suite 602, Boston, MA 02108; or Immigrant HIV Assistance Project, Bar Association of San Francisco (☎ 415-782-8995), 465 California St, Suite 1100, San Francisco, CA 94104. ■

37mm) with the application. Documents of financial stability and/or guarantees from a US resident are sometimes required, particularly for those from Third World countries.

Visa applicants may be required to 'demonstrate binding obligations' that will ensure their return to their countries. Because of this requirement, those planning to travel through other countries before arriving in the USA are generally better off applying for their US visa while they are still in their home country – rather than while on the road.

The validity period for US visitor visas depends on what country you're from. The length of time you'll be allowed to stay in the USA is ultimately determined by US immigration authorities at the port of entry.

Incidentally, the infamous prohibition against issuing visas to people who 'have been members of communist organizations' has been dropped. An anachronism of the Cold War, it still appears on the visa applications although most consular offices have penned a line through the item.

The US State Department has a Visa Services webpage that contains a good deal of information on various kinds of visas: http://travel.state.gov/visa_services.html. It also includes a list of embassy phone and fax numbers and addresses.

Although Canadians do not need their passports to visit the US, they and US citizens may want to bring them along to the Southwest, in the event they're tempted to extend their travels into Mexico or beyond. All visitors should bring their driver's license and any health-insurance or travel-insurance cards.

You'll need a picture ID to show that you are over 21 to buy alcohol or gain admission to bars or clubs (make sure your driver's license has a photo on it, or else get some other form of ID).

For information on work visas and employment in the US, see Work later in this chapter.

Visa Extensions & Re-Entry

If you want, need or hope to stay in the USA longer than the date stamped on your passport, go to the local Immigration & Naturalization Service (INS) office (to locate the nearest office, look in the blue section of the local white pages telephone directory under 'US Government' or call ☎ 800-755-0777) *before* the stamped date to apply for an extension. Anytime after that will usually lead to an unamusing conversation with an INS official who will assume you want to work illegally. If you find yourself in that situation, it's a good idea to bring a US citizen with you to vouch for your character. It's also a good idea to have some verification that you have enough money to support yourself.

Photocopies
It's a good idea to make a couple of photocopies of all your travel documents including airline tickets, your passport and international ID. Keep one copy separate from the originals and use the other to carry around instead of the originals. There's nothing worse than losing your identity on a trip.

Travel Insurance
No matter how you're traveling, make sure you take out travel insurance. This should cover you not only for medical expenses and luggage theft or loss, but also for cancellations or delays in your travel arrangements, and everyone should be covered for the worst possible case, such as an accident that requires hospital treatment and a flight home. Coverage depends on your insurance and type of ticket, so ask both your insurer and your ticket-issuing agency to explain the finer points. STA Travel and Council Travel offer travel insurance options at reasonable prices. Ticket loss is also covered by travel insurance. Make sure you have a separate record of all your ticket details – or better still, a photocopy of it. Also make a copy of your policy, in case the original is lost.

Buy travel insurance as early as possible. If you buy it the week before you fly, you may find, for instance, that you're not covered for delays to your flight caused by strikes or other industrial action that may have been in force before you took out the insurance.

Insurance may seem very expensive – but it's nowhere near the cost of a medical emergency in the USA.

International Driving Permit
An International Driving Permit is a useful accessory for foreign visitors in the USA. Local traffic police are more likely to accept it as valid identification than an unfamiliar document from another country. Your national automobile association can provide one for a nominal fee. They're usually valid for one year.

Automobile Association Membership Cards
If you plan on doing a lot of driving in the USA, it would be beneficial to join your national automobile association. See Useful Organizations later in this chapter for more information.

Hostel Card
Most hostels in the USA are members of Hostelling International/American Youth Hostel (HI/AYH). HI is managed by the International Youth Hostel Federation (IYHF). You can purchase membership on the spot when checking in, although it's probably advisable to purchase it before you leave home.

Student Card
If you're a student, get an international student ID or bring along a school or university ID card to take advantage of the discounts available to students.

Seniors' Cards
All people over the age of 65 get discounts throughout the USA. All you need is ID with proof of age. In some cases, people over 60 or 62 are considered seniors, so ask. There are organizations such as the AARP (see Senior Travelers later in this chapter) that offer membership cards for further discounts and extend coverage to citizens of other countries.

EMBASSIES
US Embassies & Consulates
US diplomatic offices abroad include the following:

Australia
    21 Moonah Place, Yarralumla ACT 2600

(☎ 2-6214-5600)
Level 59 MLC Centre 19-29 Martin Place,
Sydney NSW 2000 (☎ 2-9373-9200)
553 St Kilda Rd, Melbourne, Victoria
(☎ 3-9526-5900)
Canada
100 Wellington St, Ottawa, Ontario K1P
5T1 (☎ 613-238-5335)
1095 W Pender St, Vancouver, BC V6E
2M6 (☎ 604-685-4311)
1155 rue St-Alexandre, Montreal, Quebec
(☎ 514-398-9695)
France
2 rue Saint Florentin, 75001 Paris
(☎ 01 42 96 12 02)
Germany
Deichmanns Aue 29, 53170 Bonn
(☎ 228-33-91)
Ireland
42 Elgin Rd, Ballsbridge, Dublin
(☎ 1-687-122)
Israel
71 Hayarkon St, Tel Aviv (☎ 3-517-4338)
Japan
10-5 Akasaka 1-chome, Minato-ku, Tokyo
107 (☎ 3-3224-5000)
Netherlands
Lange Voorhout 102, 2514 EJ, The Hague
(☎ 70-310-9209)
Museumplein 19, 1071 DJ Amsterdam
(☎ 20-310-9209)
New Zealand
29 Fitzherbert Terrace, Thorndon, Wellington
(☎ 4-722-068)
Norway
Drammensveien 18, 0244 Oslo
(☎ 22-44-85-50)
Sweden
Strandvagen 101, S-115 89 Stockholm
(☎ 8-783-5300)
Switzerland
Jubilaeumsstrasse 93, 3005 Bern
(☎ 31-357-70-11)
United Kingdom
5 Upper Grosvenor St, London W1
(☎ 0171-499-9000)
3 Regent Terrace, Edinburgh EH7 5BW
(☎ 31-556-8315)
Queens House, 14 Queen St, Belfast BT1
6EQ (☎ 232-328-239)

Foreign Embassies & Consulates

Most nations' main consuls or embassies are in Washington, DC. To find the telephone number of your embassy or consul,

call Washington, DC, directory assistance (☎ 202-555-1212).

There are a few foreign consular offices in the Southwest. Albuquerque has Mexican and German consuls; Salt Lake City has Mexican, Guatemalan, New Zealand, Swiss, French, Norwegian and Italian consuls; Phoenix has Mexican, Dutch, French, Swedish and Swiss consuls; and Tucson has a Mexican consul. These lists change often and are found in the yellow pages of telephone directories under 'Consulates.' The UK has a consul in Los Angeles (☎ 310-477-3322).

CUSTOMS

US Customs allows each person over the age of 21 to bring 1 liter of liquor and 200 cigarettes duty-free into the USA. US citizens are allowed to import, duty-free, $400 worth of gifts from abroad, and non-US citizens are allowed to bring in $100 worth. Should you be carrying more than $10,000 in US and foreign cash, traveler's checks, money orders or the like, you need to declare the excess amount. There is no legal restriction on the amount that may be imported, but undeclared sums in excess of $10,000 may be subject to confiscation. Agricultural inspection stations at the Arizona-California border may ask you to surrender fruit when entering California, in an attempt to halt the spread of pests associated with the fruit.

MONEY
Currency & Exchange Rates

The US dollar ($) is divided into 100 cents (¢). Coins come in the following denominations, with these names and descriptions:

1¢ – penny, copper colored
5¢ – nickel, fat and silver colored
10¢ – dime, the smallest coin, thin and silver colored
25¢ – quarter, silver colored with rough edges
50¢ – half-dollar, larger than a quarter and silver colored, with a profile of John F Kennedy
$1 – dollar, comes in one of two coins, neither as common as the dollar bill: a large, silver-colored coin with a profile of

Dwight D Eisenhower (often called a silver dollar), or almost quarter-size, with a profile of Susan B Anthony (called the Susan B Anthony Dollar)

You are unlikely to see either the half-dollar or dollar coins, unless you go gambling and play the slots, or get them as change from ticket and stamp machines. Be aware that they look similar to quarters.

Bills – paper currency – are confusing to many foreign visitors. They are all the same size and color, regardless of denomination. Be careful to check the denomination in the corners of the bills so you don't pay the wrong amount or receive the wrong amount in change. Bills come in denominations of $1, $2 (rare), $5, $10, $20, $50 and $100. Many places won't accept bills larger than $20, so if you are going out, break large bills at your hotel or a bank.

In 1996, the US Treasury began redesigning the bills to thwart counterfeiters, starting with the $100 bill and proceeding down through the valuations, one bill each year. Old-design currency remains valid during the process. If you receive one of the new $100 bills, which have large, off-center portraits, unlike the other US bills, see if you agree with many who insist that Ben Franklin looks flatulent.

At press time, exchange rates were:

Australia	A$1	=	US$0.59
Canada	C$1	=	US$0.66
Euro	1	=	US$1.16
France	FF1	=	US$0.17
Germany	DM1	=	US$0.55
Hong Kong	HK$10	=	US$0.12
Japan	¥132	=	US$1
New Zealand	NZ$1	=	US$0.51
United Kingdom	UK£1	=	US$1.67

What to Carry

Cash & Traveler's Checks Though carrying cash is more risky, it's still a good idea to travel with some for the convenience; it's useful for tips and some smaller places may not accept credit cards or traveler's checks. Traveler's checks offer greater protection from theft or loss and in many places can be used as cash. American Express and Thomas Cook are widely accepted and have efficient replacement policies.

Keeping a record of the check numbers and the checks you have used is vital to replace lost checks. Keep this record separate from the checks themselves.

You'll save yourself trouble and expense if you buy traveler's checks in US dollars. The savings you *might* make on exchange rates by carrying traveler's checks in a foreign currency don't make up for the hassle of exchanging them at banks and other facilities. Restaurants, hotels and most stores accept US-dollar traveler's checks as if they were cash, so if you're carrying traveler's checks in US dollars, the odds are you'll rarely have to use a bank or pay an exchange fee.

Take large denomination checks. It's only toward the end of a stay that you may want to change a small check so that you aren't left with too much local currency.

Credit & Debit Cards Major credit and charge cards are widely accepted by car-rental agencies and most hotels, restaurants, gas stations, shops and larger grocery stores. Many recreational and tourist activities can also be paid for by credit card. The most commonly accepted cards are Visa, MasterCard and, to a lesser extent, American Express.

It's difficult to perform certain transactions without a credit card. Ticket buying services, for instance, won't reserve tickets over the phone unless you offer a credit card number, and it's virtually impossible to rent a car without a credit card.

Places that accept Visa and MasterCard are also likely to accept debit cards. Unlike a credit card, a debit card deducts payment directly from the user's savings account. Sometimes a minimal fee is charged for the transaction. Check with your bank to confirm that your debit card will be accepted in other states; debit cards from large commercial banks can often be used worldwide. Check with your bank or credit card company about which toll-free number you should call if you need to report a card lost or stolen.

Changing Money

Some banks exchange cash or traveler's checks in major foreign currencies, though banks in outlying areas do this infrequently and it may take them some time. It's easier to exchange foreign currency in larger cities. Additionally, Thomas Cook, American Express and exchange windows in international airports offer exchange (although you'll get a better rate at a bank).

Automated Teller Machines (ATMs)

ATMs are another plastic alternative. Most banks have these machines which are usually open 24 hours a day. There are various ATM networks and most banks are affiliated with several. Some of the most common are Cirrus, Plus, Star and Interlink. For a nominal service charge, you can withdraw cash from an ATM using a credit or debit card. Credit card companies usually charge a 2% fee ($2 minimum), but cards linked to your personal checking account usually give fee-free cash advances from any branch of your bank. Check with your bank or credit card company for exact information.

You'll also find ATMs at most airports, shopping malls and some grocery or convenience stores. A reader writes that their British credit card didn't work in US ATMs; ask your bank about this before leaving home.

Security

Be cautious – but not paranoid – about carrying money. If your hotel or hostel has a safe, keep your valuables and excess cash in it. It's best not to display large amounts of cash in public. A money belt worn under your clothes is a good place to carry excess currency when you're on the move or otherwise unable to stash it in a safe. Avoid carrying your wallet in a back pocket of your pants. This is a prime target for pickpockets, as are handbags and the outside pockets of day packs and fanny packs (bum bags). See Dangers & Annoyances later in this chapter.

Costs

The highest cost of traveling around the Southwest is likely to be transportation. The best way to get around is by car, because intercity buses, trains and planes are not very cheap, nor do they go to the out-of-the-way places. Car rental is available in most towns of any size, and rates can be as cheap as $100 a week for the smallest (subcompact) cars – these are off-season rates. More often, though, rentals begin around $140 for a week. A midsize car is about $40 more and jeeps or 4WD vehicles can be as high as $90 a day. Insurance, if you are not already covered by a credit card or personal insurance policy, is usually another $7 to $12 a day. Gas (petrol) is cheap, ranging from about $1 to $1.70 for a US gallon, depending on the location, grade of fuel and international economic factors.

For more information on rentals and purchasing a car, see the Getting Around chapter.

If you are on a very tight budget, you can camp for free on public lands in many places and cook for yourself. Maintained campgrounds range from about $6 for basic places with cooking grills and pit toilets to over $20 for some full-service campgrounds with RV (recreational vehicle) hookups.

Youth hostels are few and charge around $10 to $14 per person. Cheap and basic motels for about $20 a double are often a better deal for budget travelers. Some towns, for example Gallup, Tucumcari and Flagstaff, are known for their motel strips full of places advertising rooms for about $20. Most other towns have basic motels beginning in the mid-$20s for a double room and going on up from there.

Travelers looking for more than a basic room can find satisfactory midrange accommodations for $40 to $80 a double in most places, and some towns have luxury hotels with rooms over $100. There are also world-class resorts and dude ranches where you can pay over $200 a day. Some towns in the Southwest are relatively expensive – Sedona, Santa Fe and Taos are among these. Lodges in national parks are also pricey – there is a high demand for these rooms, which start at about $80. B&Bs (Bed & Breakfasts) are not for budget travelers; they start at about $50 for a double, but most are in the $70 to $140 range. There is more information about accommodations later in this chapter.

Meals also vary tremendously in price. All but the tiniest towns will have one of the ubiquitous fast-food restaurants where you can get a large hamburger, soft drink and french fries for about $3 or $4. Many towns have all-you-can-eat restaurants where the starving budget traveler can fill up for about $5 or $6. This is eating to live, not living to eat! But penurious travelers needn't be limited to junk food or unappetizing selections of all-you-can-eat buffets. Mexican restaurants abound in the Southwest and offer great meals for under $10, and a large pizza – enough for two – can be had for $10 and up. You can eat very well any night in any town for under $25 per person for a complete meal with wine. If you are looking for a splurge, bigger cities have first-class restaurants where you can spend $100 or more on dinner for two. More details on food are given later in this chapter.

Entrance into National Park Service (NPS) areas (parks, monuments, historical sites) costs $4 to $20 a vehicle (whether there are six people or just a driver), and this is valid for seven days with in-and-out privileges. Some less frequently visited NPS areas are free. If you plan on visiting several national parks, you can obtain money-saving passes – see the NPS section under Useful Organizations, later in this chapter.

First-run movies are usually $6 or $7, but you can pay under $2 in budget theaters showing movies that have been out for a few months. A 12-oz bottle of domestic beer can range from $1.50 to $3 in a bar or restaurant. A six-pack of domestic beers costs $3 to $5 in the supermarket, while a six-pack of soft drinks is about $2, depending on the brand. A cup of coffee is usually 50¢ to $1. Museums can range from free to as much as $8 to visit.

Tipping

Tipping is expected in restaurants and better hotels, as well as by taxi drivers, hairdressers and baggage carriers. In restaurants and bars, wait staff are paid minimal wages and rely upon tips for their livelihoods. Tip 15% unless the service is terrible (in which case a complaint to the manager is warranted) or up to 20% if the service is great. Don't tip in fast-food, take-out or buffet-style restaurants where you serve yourself.

Taxi drivers expect 10% to 15% and hairdressers get 15% if their service is satisfactory. Baggage carriers (skycaps in airports, bellboys in hotels) receive $1 for the first bag and 50¢ for each additional bag carried, or more if they go a long way. In better hotels, housekeeping staff get $1 or $2 a day, and parking valets get $1 or $2 upon delivering your car.

Taxes

Almost everything you pay for in the USA is taxed. Occasionally, the tax is included in the advertised price (eg, gas, drinks in a bar, or museum or theater entrance tickets). Transportation (taxi, bus, train and plane tickets) taxes are usually included in the advertised price. Airport taxes are added to the ticket price, not paid at the airport. Restaurant meals and drinks, motel rooms and most other purchases are taxed, and this is added to the advertised cost.

Tax rates are bewildering. For meals, rooms and other purchases, there are both state and local (city or county) taxes as well as lodging, restaurant and car rental taxes, so as you travel around the region, you'll pay different taxes in every town. Basic state sales taxes are 5% in Utah, 5.75% in New Mexico and 6.75% in Arizona, but most restaurants add 6% to 8% to the bill, most hotels add 10% to 14%, and most car rental companies add 7% to 13%. The prices given in this book do not reflect local taxes.

POST & COMMUNICATIONS
Postal Rates

Postage rates increase every few years. At the time of this writing, 1st-class mail within the USA cost 32¢ for letters up to 1 ounce (23¢ for each additional ounce) and 20¢ for postcards.

International airmail rates (except to Canada and Mexico) are 60¢ for a half-ounce letter, $1 for a 1-ounce letter and 40¢ for each additional half ounce. International postcard rates are 50¢. Letters to Canada are 46¢ for a half-ounce letter, 52¢ for a 1-ounce letter and 40¢ for a postcard. Letters to Mexico are 40¢ for a half-ounce letter, 46¢ for a 1-ounce letter and 35¢ for a postcard. Aerogrammes are 50¢.

The cost for parcels airmailed anywhere within the USA is $3 for 2 pounds or less, increasing by $1 per pound up to $6 for 5 pounds. For heavier items, rates differ according to the distance mailed. Books, periodicals and computer disks can be sent by a cheaper 4th-class rate.

Sending Mail

If you have the correct postage, you can drop your mail into any blue mailbox. However, to send a package 16 ounces or larger, you must bring it to a post office. If you need to buy stamps or weigh your mail, go to the nearest post office. The address of each town's main post office is given in the text. In addition, larger towns have branch post offices and post office centers in some supermarkets and drugstores. For the address of the nearest, call the main post office listed under 'Postal Service' in the blue US Government section of the white pages telephone directory, or call the United States Postal Service at ☎ 800-275-8777.

Usually, post offices in main towns are open from 8 am to 5 pm, Monday to Friday and 8 am to 3 pm on Saturday, but it all depends on the branch so call first. If the branch has a local phone number, it is given in the text. Otherwise, call USPS at the toll-free number listed above.

Receiving Mail

You can have mail sent to you care of General Delivery at any post office that has its own 5-digit zip (postal) code. Mail is usually held for 10 days before it's returned to the

sender; you might request your correspondents to write 'hold for arrival' on their letters. Mail should be addressed like this:

Lucy Chang
c/o General Delivery
Caballo, NM 87931

Alternatively, you can have mail sent to the local American Express or Thomas Cook representative, both of which provide mail service for their customers.

Telephone

All phone numbers within the USA consist of a three-digit area code followed by a seven-digit local number. If you are calling locally, just dial the seven-digit number. If you are calling long distance, dial 1 + the three-digit area code + the seven-digit number. If you're calling from abroad, the international country code for the USA is '1.'

For local directory assistance dial ☎ 411. For directory assistance outside your area code, dial 1 + the three-digit area code of the place you want to call + 555-1212. Area codes for places outside the region are listed in telephone directories. If you aren't sure of the area code of the place you want to call, try 1 + 411, which can give you numbers nationwide from many phones in the Southwest. Directory assistance calls cost up to 85¢.

Due to skyrocketing demand for phone numbers (for faxes, cellular phones, etc), many areas are being divided into multiple new area codes. These changes are not reflected in older phone books. Operators can help in these cases.

The 800 or 888 area code is designated for toll-free numbers within the USA, and these sometimes work from Canada as well. These calls are free (unless you are dialing locally, in which case the toll-free number is not available). If a toll-free number has changed, call ☎ 800-555-1212 and request the company's new number.

The 900 area precedes numbers for which the caller pays a premium rate.

These phone numbers are often associated with sleazy operations – a smorgasbord of phone sex at $2.99 a minute is one of many offerings.

Rates Local calls usually cost 25¢ at pay phones, but watch out for occasional private phones that may charge more. Many middle and top-end hotels add a service charge of 50¢ to $1 for local calls made from a room phone and also have hefty surcharges for long-distance calls. Public pay phones, found in many hotel lobbies, are cheaper. You can pump in quarters, use a phone card or make collect calls from pay phones. A new long-distance alternative is phone debit cards, which allow purchasers to pay $5, $10, $20 or $50 in advance, with access through an 800 number.

When using phone credit cards, be aware of people watching you in public places such as airports. Thieves can memorize numbers and use them to make numerous international calls. Shield telephones with your body when dialing card numbers.

Long-distance rates vary depending on the destination and which telephone company you use – call the operator (0) for rates information. Don't ask the operator to put your call through, however, because operator-assisted calls are much more expensive than direct-dial calls. Generally, nights (11 pm to 8 am), all day Saturday and from 8 am to 5 pm Sunday are the cheapest (60% discount) times to call. A 35% discount applies in the evenings from 5 to 11 pm Sunday to Friday. Daytime calls (8 am to 5 pm Monday to Friday) are full-price calls within the USA.

International Calls To make an international call direct, dial 011, then the country code, followed by the area code and the phone number. You may need to wait as long as 45 seconds for the ringing to start. International rates vary depending on the time of day, telephone company used and the destination. Call the operator (0) for rates. The first minute is always more expensive than the following extra minutes.

Fax
Fax machines are easy to find in the USA, at shipping companies like Mail Boxes Etc, photocopy stores and hotel business service centers, but be prepared to pay high prices (over $1 a page).

INTERNET RESOURCES
Email
Email is quickly becoming a preferred method of communication; however, unless you have a laptop and modem, it's still a hassle to get online while on the road. Hotel business service centers may provide connections, and trendy restaurants and cafes sometimes offer Internet service as well. Note that some 'modern' hotel telephone systems don't have the capability of letting you hook up a modem in your room, though increasing numbers do have this capability and most probably will have by early in the 21st century. I've also found that I can connect my modem to the phone line in most budget 'mom-and-pop' motels.

Websites
Thousands of Southwestern businesses and other organizations have websites (see the Website Directory appendix). Good starting points for travelers are websites sponsored by state travel organizations. These have links to hundreds of other websites featuring anything from cities to hotels to ski resorts.

Arizona Office of Tourism
    www.arizonaguide.com
New Mexico Department of Tourism
    www.newmexico.org
Utah Travel Council
    www.utah.com

Don't forget to add 'http://' to the beginning of the URLs given throughout this book.

My main criticism of many of these links is that it can be over a year between updates, so despite the seeming immediacy of the Internet, the information on it is often out of date. Always check the date of the last site update.

The National Park Service has a website with links to sites for every park and monument at www.nps.gov.

The NPS links are among the best for useful and accurate information, updated every few months in many cases.

BOOKS

Many thousands of books have been written about the Southwest, and I can introduce only a few. Many of these, however, have comprehensive indexes that will lead you as far as you want to go. Most are updated periodically; check that you are getting the most recent edition.

Regional Overviews

Compass American Guides publishes *Arizona* by Larry Cheek, *New Mexico* by Nancy Harbert and *Utah* by Tom & Gayen Wharton. Each is well illustrated with both old and new photos and drawings and gives great background information. Their travel information for hotels and restaurants is limited to a few pages of brief listings. Beautiful photographs and standard background essays are the hallmark of the Insight Guides Series – their *American Southwest* book is no exception.

Great photos and insightful essays by some of the region's best writers are found in *Arizona, the Land and the People*, edited by Tom Miller. Detailed writings about many aspects of New Mexico appear in *New Mexico: A New Guide to the Colorful State* by L Chilton et al. Neither offers hotel or restaurant information.

Archaeology & History

Those Who Came Before by Robert H & Florence C Lister is my favorite source of readable information about the prehistory of the Southwest and about the archaeological sites of the national parks and monuments of this area. It is extensively indexed.

Indians of the American Southwest by Steven L Walker is a slim, large-format book with introductory essays to the ancient inhabitants of the area, illustrated by some

of the Southwest's premier photographers. An expanded version by the same author is *The Southwest: A Pictorial History of the Land and Its People*.

The best general history is *The Southwest* by David Lavender. It has a detailed (if dated) index. *The Smithsonian Guide to Historic America – The Desert States* by Michael S Durham is a beautifully illustrated guide to the historic sites of the region.

New Mexico by Calvin A and Susan A Roberts is probably the best book on that state's history through the early 1980s. *Utah – A Bicentennial History* by Charles S Peterson covers the period till 1976. *Arizona: A History* by Thomas E Sheridan covers the area from prehistoric times through the early 1990s.

Geology

Basin and Range by John McPhee is as much a journey as a popular geological text. It covers Nevada as well as Utah, and is a recommended read.

Roadside Geology of Arizona, *Roadside Geology of New Mexico* and *Roadside Geology of Utah*, all by Halka Chronic, are good guides for the curious non-geologist. They describe the geology along major roads and are well illustrated. *Geology of Utah* by William L Stokes and *Geology of Arizona* by Dale Nations and Edmund Stump are more technical overviews of those states' geologies.

Useful and readable geology books about the national parks include *A Guide to Grand Canyon Geology along the Bright Angel Trail* by Dave Thayer. This will take you back 2 billion years in time as you descend to the bottom of the Grand Canyon. Another choice is *The Sculpturing of Zion – With Road Guide to the Geology of Zion National Park* by Wayne L Hamilton. An introduction for the nonspecialist is *The Colorado Plateau: A Geologic History* by Donald L Baars.

Natural History

A tremendous variety of books will help you identify Southwestern plants and animals, tell you where you can see them and give you insight into their biology.

The Peterson Field Guide Series has almost 40 excellent books including *A Field Guide to the Mammals* by William H Burt and Richard P Grossenheider, *Western Birds* by Roger Tory Peterson, *Western Reptiles and Amphibians* by Robert C Stebbins, *Western Butterflies* by Tilden & Smith and *Southwestern and Texas Wildflowers* by Niehaus, Ripper & Savage.

An excellent series of pocket books published by the Southwest Parks & Monuments Association in Tucson helps you identify the region's plants. Titles include *Flowers of the Southwest Deserts* by Natt N Dodge & Jeanne R Janish, *Flowers of the Southwest Mountains* by Leslie P Arnberger & Janish, *Flowers of the Southwest Mesas* by Pauline M Patraw & Janish, and *Shrubs and Trees of the Southwestern Uplands* by Francis H Elmore & Janish. Also from this publisher is *Mammals of the Southwest Deserts* by George Olin & Dale Thompson, which is less a field guide and more a description of the mammals, illustrated with full-page drawings.

There are numerous other field guides. The series of *Audubon Society Field Guides* covers birds, plants and animals, arranged by color and using photos – a departure from the standard field guides, which are arranged in biological sequence and are illustrated by color paintings. The Audubon Society Nature Guide *Deserts* by James A MacMahon gives a fine overview of all four Southwestern deserts, as well as being a field guide to the most important plants and animals of those regions. The *Golden Field Guide* series (Western Publishing Company) is known for its simple approach and is often preferred by beginners. The National Geographic Society's *Field Guide to the Birds of North America* is well done and one of the most detailed.

Birders may want to supplement their field guides with *Birds in Southeastern Arizona* by William A Davis & Stephen M Russell, which describes the seasonal distribution and abundance of birds in

what is one of the premier birding 'hot spots' in the country, and gives directions on how to travel to scores of the best birding areas.

Utah Wildlife Viewing Guide by Jim Cole, *Arizona Wildlife Viewing Guide* by John N Carr and *New Mexico Wildlife Viewing Guide* by Jane S MacCarter list scores of places to see wildlife. Access information and descriptions of the probability of seeing the most important species at specific sites are given.

Several excellent books about Southwestern natural history are designed to be read rather than used as field guides. I recommend all of the following. *The Great Southwestern Nature Factbook* by Susan J Tweit is full of interesting details about everything from Gila monsters to the Grand Canyon. *The Desert Year* by Joseph Wood Krutch is a classic account of nature in the Sonoran desert. More detailed are John Alcock's excellent and very readable *Sonoran Desert Spring* and *Sonoran Desert Summer*. *Gathering the Desert* by Gary Paul Nabhan describes in splendid and fascinating detail 12 desert plants and their importance to Native Americans.

Ann Zwinger writes eloquently in *The Mysterious Lands: A Naturalist Explores the Four Great Deserts of the Southwest*. Her *Run, River, Run: A Naturalist's Journey down One of the Great Rivers of the American West* describes her journey down the Green River from its headwaters in Wyoming to its confluence with the Colorado River in southeastern Utah. And her *Wind in the Rock* explores the natural history of the Four Corners region.

Native Americans

The best introduction for the serious student is the 20-volume *Handbook of North American Indians* (Smithsonian Institution). The volumes that cover this region are *Volume 9: Southwest* and *Volume 10: Southwest* edited by Alfonso Ortiz, and *Volume 11: Great Basin* edited by Warren L D'Azevedo.

An even better introduction for the generalist is *The People: Indians of the South-*

west by Stephen Trimble. The author traveled among the area's many tribes, photographing and interviewing them for almost a decade. Much of the book is in the words of the Indians themselves – a remarkable and satisfying work. The excellent 14-page annotated bibliography will lead you to many other books.

Some introductions to Southwestern Indian arts and crafts include *Navajo Rugs: How to Find, Evaluate, Buy and Care for Them* by Don Dedera; *Hopi Kachinas: The Complete Guide to Collecting Kachina Dolls* by Barton Wright; and *Hopi Silver: A Brief History of Hopi Silversmithing* by Margaret Wright.

Native Roads by Fran Kosik is subtitled 'The Complete Motoring Guide to the Navajo and Hopi Nations' and does an excellent job describing the history and native cultures to be experienced along the highways through and around these reservations.

Native American writers are mentioned in the section on fiction.

Fiction

It comes as some surprise that one of the earliest novels about the Southwest is Arthur Conan Doyle's first Sherlock Holmes mystery, *A Study in Scarlet* (1887). Half the book is set in the 'Alkali Plains' of Mormon Utah. Another surprise is that the author of *Ben Hur* (1880) was New Mexico Governor Lew Wallace. Other early novels of note include Zane Grey's westerns, of which *Riders of the Purple Sage* (1912) is the best known. Grey spent years living in Arizona. *Death Comes for the Archbishop* (1927) by Willa Cather is a novel based on the life of Bishop Jean Baptiste Lamy, who was the first archbishop of Santa Fe. It gives insights into New Mexican life during territorial days. Oliver La Farge won a Pulitzer prize for his *Laughing Boy* (1929), a somewhat romantic portrayal of Navajo life.

House Made of Dawn (1969) won Native American novelist and poet N Scott Momaday a Pulitzer prize. His theme of a Pueblo Indian's struggle to return physically and spiritually to his home after fighting in WWII is echoed in another superb book, *Ceremony* by Leslie Marmon Silko (1977). Silko, herself a Pueblo Indian, is one of the best Southwestern novelists. Other critically acclaimed novels by Silko include *Almanac of the Dead* and *Storyteller*.

Tony Hillerman, an Anglo, writes award-winning mystery novels that take place on the Navajo, Hopi and Zuni Reservations. Even Indians find his writing to be true to life. Following the adventures of Navajo policemen Jim Chee and Joe Leaphorn is a lot of fun, particularly when you are driving around the reservations of the Four Corners area. Hillerman's first mystery novel was *The Blessing Way* (1970), and he has written over a dozen since then.

The Monkey Wrench Gang by Edward Abbey (1975) is hugely fun to read, which is more than can be said of many classic novels, and this one certainly is a classic. It's a fictional and comic account of real people who become 'eco-warriors' – their plan is to blow up Glen Canyon Dam before it floods Glen Canyon. You don't have to believe in industrial sabotage to enjoy this book – or any of his others. *The Milagro Beanfield War* by John Nichols (1974) tells the story of bean growers trying to protect their New Mexican lands against developers. It's a good book, and a good movie, too (directed by Robert Redford).

My favorite recent Southwestern novelist is Barbara Kingsolver, whose novels are superb portrayals of people living in the Southwest. *The Bean Trees* (1988) echoes the author's own life – a young woman from rural Kentucky moves to Tucson. *Animal Dreams* (1990) gives wonderful insights into the lives of people from a small Hispanic village near the Arizona-New Mexico border and from an Indian pueblo. Don't miss these books.

Outdoor Activities

Books dealing with this subject are listed under the appropriate headings in the Outdoor Activities chapter.

Author Picks

The first book I remember reading about the Southwest was *Desert Solitaire: Season in the Wilderness* by Edward Abbey. I read it in 1974 during my first visit to the Southwest, and it has remained one of my favorite books. It describes the author's job as a park ranger in Arches National Park in the 1950s, when the park was still a monument reached by a dirt road and locals easily outnumbered tourists in nearby Moab. Abbey shares his philosophy and passions about the desert, the mismanagement of the Southwest, and the problems of mass tourism – which he foresaw with striking clarity. This book is a classic.

Other important books are *Grizzly Years: In Search of the American Wilderness* by Doug Peacock. The author was a friend of Edward Abbey's (one of the Monkey Wrench Gang members was based on Peacock) and is one of the world's experts on grizzly bears. Although much of the action takes place in the northern Rockies, with Vietnam flashbacks, the narrative occasionally returns to Tucson, where the author lives. Another Abbey protégé is Charles Bowden, who wrote eloquent essays about Arizona in *Blue Desert* and *Frog Mountain Blues*. Other insightful essays on the Southwest are found in *The Telling Distance* by Bruce Berger.

Also consider reading *Cadillac Desert: The American West and Its Disappearing Water* by Marc Reisner, which is a thorough account of how the exploding populations of Western states have utilized every possible drop of available water. *The Man Who Walked Through Time* by Colin Fletcher tells the story of the author's many weeks backpacking the length of the Grand Canyon – the first account of such a trip.

NEWSPAPERS

There are over 1500 daily newspapers published in the USA. Those with the highest circulation include the *Wall Street Journal* (with an emphasis on financial and business news), *USA Today* (general US and world news), the *New York Times* and the *Los Angeles Times*, which are all available in main cities.

Major Southwestern newspapers are published in Salt Lake City, Albuquerque, Phoenix and Tucson – see those cities for details. These papers are generally available in many other towns in their respective states.

RADIO & TV

All rental cars have radios. Most stations have a range of less than 100 miles, so you'll have to keep changing stations as you drive. In the southern parts of the region, stations broadcasting from Mexico (in Spanish) can easily be picked up. In and near major cities, you have scores of stations to choose from with a wide variety of music and entertainment. In rural areas, be prepared for a predominance of country & western music, Christian programming, local news and 'talk radio.'

There are many talk radio stations, especially on the AM dial, and they have gained much popularity. They can be entertaining, but don't believe most of what you hear. As Bill Watterson's cartoon character Calvin describes it: 'I'll spout simplistic opinions for hours on end, ridicule anyone who disagrees with me, and generally foster divisiveness, cynicism, and a lower level of public dialog!'

National Public Radio features a more level-headed approach to news, discussion, music and more. NPR normally broadcasts on the lower end of the FM dial.

All the major TV networks have affiliated stations throughout the USA. These include ABC, CBS, NBC, FOX (all commercial stations) and PBS (noncommercial and, to my taste, the best of the lot). Cable News Network (CNN), a cable channel, provides continuous news coverage. There are many other cable stations such as ESPN (sports), HBO (mainly movies) and the Weather Channel. Almost all hotel rooms have TVs (most with cable), but many B&Bs do not.

PHOTOGRAPHY & VIDEO
Film & Equipment

Print film for amateur photography is widely available at supermarkets and discount drugstores throughout the Southwest. Color print film has a greater latitude than color slide film; this means that print film can handle a wider range of light and shadow than slide film. However, slide film, particularly the slower speeds (under 100 ASA), has better resolution than print film. Like B&W film, the availability of slide film outside of major cities is rare or at inflated prices when found.

Film can be damaged by excessive heat, so don't leave your camera and film in the car on a hot summer's day and avoid placing your camera on the dashboard while you are driving.

It's worth carrying a spare battery for your camera to avoid disappointment when your camera dies in the middle of nowhere. If you're buying a new camera for your trip, do so several weeks before you leave and practice using it.

Drugstores are a good place to get your film cheaply processed. If it's dropped off by noon, you can usually pick it up the next day. A roll of 100 ASA 35mm color film with 24 exposures will cost about $6 to get processed.

If you want your pictures right away, you can find one-hour processing services in the yellow pages under 'Photo Processing.' Be prepared to pay dearly; prices start at around $11. Many one-hour photo finishers operate in the larger cities, and a few can be found near tourist attractions.

Video Systems

Overseas visitors who are thinking of purchasing videos should remember that the USA uses the National Television System Committee (NTSC) color TV standard, which is not compatible with other standards (PAL or SECAM) used in Africa, Europe, Asia and Australasia unless converted.

Photographing People & Places

Most Indian reservations have photography restrictions. In some, no photography of any kind is allowed. In others, you need to buy a tribal camera permit. Photographing Indians is either not allowed or allowed only with permission, and then a tip is expected. More details are given in appropriate parts of the text.

Airport Security

All passengers on flights have to pass their luggage through X-ray machines. Most technology as it is today doesn't jeopardize lower-speed film, but this is changing, and it's best to carry film and cameras with you and ask the X-ray inspector to visually check your camera and film.

TIME

The Southwest is on Mountain Time, which is seven hours behind Greenwich Mean Time. Daylight-saving time begins on the first Sunday in April, when clocks are put forward one hour, and ends on the last Sunday in October, when the clocks are turned back one hour.

Arizona does not use daylight-saving time, and so during that period it is eight hours behind Greenwich Mean Time and one hour behind the rest of the Southwest. The Navajo Indian Reservation, most of which lies in Arizona, does use daylight-saving time, but the small Hopi Indian Reservation, which lies surrounded by the Navajo Indian Reservation, doesn't.

ELECTRICITY

The entire USA uses 110 V and 60 cycles and the plugs have two (flat) or three (two flat, one round) pins. Plugs with three pins don't fit into a two-hole socket, but adapters are easy to buy.

WEIGHTS & MEASURES

Distances are in feet (ft), yards (yds) and miles (m or mi). Three feet equal 1 yard; 1760 yards or 5280 feet equal 1 mile (1.61 kilometers). In southern Arizona and New Mexico, distances are also marked in kilometers to aid Mexican drivers on trips into the USA.

Dry weights are in ounces (oz), pounds (lbs) and tons (16 ounces are one pound;

2000 pounds are one ton), but liquid measures differ from dry measures. One pint equals 16 fluid ounces; 2 pints equal 1 quart, a common measure for liquids like milk, which is also sold in gallons (4 quarts). Gasoline is dispensed in US gallons, about 20% less than Imperial gallons. Pints and quarts are also 20% less than Imperial ones. There is a conversion chart on the inside back cover of this book.

LAUNDRY

There are self-service, coin-operated laundry facilities in most towns of any size and in better campgrounds and some hotels. Washing a load costs about $1 and drying it another $1. Some laundries have vending machines that sell one-load packets of detergent; others have attendants who will wash, dry and fold your clothes for you for an additional charge. To find a laundry, look under 'Laundries' or 'Laundries – Self-Service' in the yellow pages of the telephone directory. Dry cleaners are listed under 'Laundries' or 'Cleaners.'

RECYCLING

Traveling by car seems to generate large numbers of cans and bottles, which can be recycled in the recycling centers listed in larger towns. Plastic and glass bottles, aluminum and tin cans, and newspapers are usually accepted. Some campgrounds, many city, state and national parks and a few roadside rest areas also have recycling bins next to the trash bins. Take advantage of them!

Better than recycling is to reduce your use of these products. Many gas stations and convenience stores sell large plastic insulated cups with lids that are inexpensive and ideal for hot and cold drinks. Refills are usually substantially cheaper.

TOILETS

Public toilets are normally free and found in shopping malls and parks. People often use the facilities in restaurants and gas stations when necessary. Toilets are commonly called bathrooms or restrooms.

HEALTH

Generally speaking, the USA is a healthy place to visit and the country is well-served by hospitals. However, because of the high cost of health care, international travelers should take out comprehensive travel insurance (see below) before they leave.

Predeparture Preparations

Health Insurance A travel insurance policy to cover medical problems (as well as theft or loss) is recommended. Even the most cursory visit to a doctor will cost around $50, and hospitalization for two days may cost more than your entire vacation. Get insurance!

Policies vary significantly and your travel agent will have recommendations. International student travel policies handled by STA Travel or other student travel organizations are usually a good value. Some policies offer lower and higher medical expenses options. The higher one is for countries like the USA with extremely high medical costs. Check the small print.

Some policies specifically exclude 'dangerous activities' like motorcycling. Some policies pay doctors or hospitals directly. Others reimburse you after you pay, in which case keep *all* documentation. Some policies require a collect (reverse charge) call for an immediate assessment of your problem. Few policies cover emergency evacuations, body repatriation or flights home requiring two or three seats to stretch out on. This may require a separate policy.

Medical Kit It's useful to carry a small, straightforward medical kit. This might include:

Aspirin, acetaminophen or panadol, for pain or fever
Antihistamine (such as Benadryl), as a decongestant, to ease itching from allergies, insect bites and stings or to help prevent motion sickness
Antibiotics (by prescription only) if traveling away from medical facilities (eg, several days of river-running or backpacking)
Bismuth subsalicylate solution (Pepto-Bismol), Imodium or Lomotil, for stomach upsets

Rehydration mixture, for severe diarrhea, if you're traveling with children away from medical facilities

Antiseptic, mercurochrome and antibiotic powder or similar 'dry' spray, for cuts and grazes

Bandages and Band-aids (Elastoplasts) or similar dressings

Scissors, tweezers and a medical thermometer

Insect repellent, sun-screen, lip balm and water purification tablets

Health Preparations Before leaving on a long trip, get a dental checkup and ensure immunizations are up-to-date. Take spare glasses and your prescription. New spectacles are made for under $100 (except for difficult prescriptions or better frames). Take an adequate supply of necessary medications and bring a prescription in case you lose your supply.

Water
I drink tap water everywhere in the Southwest, though it can cause mild stomach upsets if you are not accustomed to it. Bottled drinking water, carbonated or noncarbonated, is widely available. Water from rivers is almost always contaminated.

Everyday Health
Normal body temperature is 98.6°F or 37°C; more than 2°C or 4°F higher indicates a 'high' fever. Normal adult pulse rate is 60 to 80 beats per minute (children 80 to 100, babies 100 to 140). Between 12 and 20 breaths/minute is normal for adults and older children (up to 30 for younger children, 40 for babies). People with high fever or serious respiratory illness breathe more quickly.

Travel- & Climate-Related Problems
Sunburn In the desert or at high altitude you can get sunburned in an hour, even through cloud cover. Use a sunscreen (protection factor 30+) and take extra care to cover areas not normally exposed to sun.

Heat Exhaustion Dehydration or salt deficiency can cause heat exhaustion. Take time to acclimatize to high temperatures

and ensure you get enough liquids. Salt deficiency is characterized by fatigue, lethargy, headaches, giddiness and muscle cramps. Salt tablets may help. Vomiting or diarrhea can also deplete your liquid and salt levels. Anhydrotic heat exhaustion, caused by the inability to sweat, is quite rare. Unlike other forms of heat exhaustion, it may strike people who have been in a hot climate for some time, rather than newcomers. Always use water bottles on long trips. Four quarts per person per day is recommended if hiking. It's a good idea to carry jugs of drinking water in your car in case it should break down.

Heat Stroke Long, continuous periods of exposure to high temperatures can lead to this serious, sometimes fatal, condition, which occurs when the body's heat-regulating mechanism breaks down and body temperature rises to dangerous levels. Avoid excessive alcohol intake or strenuous activity when you first arrive in a hot climate.

Symptoms include feeling unwell, lack of perspiration, and a high body temperature. Hospitalization is essential for extreme cases, but meanwhile get out of the sun, remove clothing, cover with a wet sheet or towel, and fan continually.

Hypothermia Skiers and winter hikers will find that temperatures in the mountains or desert can quickly drop to below freezing, or a sudden soaking and high winds can lower your body temperature rapidly. Travel with a partner whenever possible.

Seek shelter when bad weather is unavoidable. Woolen clothing and synthetics, which retain warmth even when wet, are superior to cottons. Carry a good-quality sleeping bag and high-energy, easily digestible snacks like chocolate or dried fruit.

Get hypothermia victims out of bad weather and put on dry, warm clothing. Give hot liquids (not alcohol) and high-calorie, easily digestible food. In advanced stages place victims in warm sleeping bags and get in with them. Do not rub victims.

Fungal Infections Fungal infections occur with greater frequency in hot weather. Minimize them by wearing loose, comfortable clothes, avoiding artificial fibers, washing frequently and drying carefully. If you are infected, wash the area daily with a disinfectant or medicated soap and water, rinse and dry well. Apply antifungal powder, air the infected area when possible, wash towels and underwear in hot water and change them often.

Altitude Sickness This can happen when ascending too quickly to high altitude, such as driving up to a ski resort. Lack of oxygen at high elevations causes headaches, nausea, shortness of breath, physical weakness and other symptoms that can be fatal (though rarely at Southwestern elevations). Most people recover within a day or two. If symptoms persist, descent to lower elevations is the only effective remedy. For mild cases, aspirin (or similar) will relieve symptoms until the body adapts. Avoid smoking, alcohol, sedatives, eating heavily or exercising strenuously. Drink extra fluids. Ascend slowly where possible and sleep at lower altitudes than those reached during the day.

Motion Sickness Eating lightly before and during a trip reduces the chances of motion sickness. Those prone to motion sickness should find a place that minimizes disturbance: near the wing on aircraft, near the center on buses. Fresh air usually helps; reading or cigarette smoke don't. Commercial antimotion sickness preparations, which can cause drowsiness, should be taken before the trip commences; when you're feeling sick, it's too late. Ginger, a natural preventative, is available in capsule form.

Jet Lag This is experienced when a person flies across more than three time zones. It occurs because many body functions (temperature, pulse rate and emptying of the bladder and bowels) are regulated by internal 24-hour cycles (circadian rhythms). During jet lag, our bodies are adjusting to the 'new time' of our destination, and we may experience fatigue, disorientation, insomnia, anxiety, impaired concentration and loss of appetite. These effects usually disappear within three days of arrival.

To minimize jet lag, rest well on the days prior to departure. Select flight schedules that minimize sleep deprivation; arrive late in the day and sleep after you arrive. For very long flights, arrange a stopover. Avoid excessive eating, alcohol and smoking on flights. Drink plenty of juice or water. Wear comfortable loose clothing.

Infectious Diseases
Diarrhea Changes in water or food can cause the runs; diarrhea from contaminated food or water (uncommon in the USA) is more serious. Use bottled water if you are susceptible, and never drink from streams or lakes.

Despite precautions you may still have a mild bout of travelers' diarrhea, but this is rarely serious. Dehydration is the main danger, particularly for children, where dehydration can occur quite quickly. Fluid replacement is important. Weak black tea with a little sugar, soda water or soft drinks allowed to go flat and diluted 50% with water are all good. With severe diarrhea, a rehydrating solution is necessary to replace minerals and salts. Commercially available ORS (oral rehydration salts) are useful.

Lomotil or Imodium relieve the symptoms, but do not cure the problem. Only use them if absolutely necessary – eg, if you *must* travel.

Giardiasis Also called Giardia, this intestinal parasite is present in apparently pristine backcountry streams. Giardia can appear weeks after drinking contaminated water; symptoms may recur repeatedly, disappearing for a few days and then returning.

Symptoms are stomach cramps, nausea, bloated stomach, watery, foul-smelling diarrhea and frequent gas. Tinidazole

(Fasigyn) or metronidazole (Flagyl) are the recommended drugs; antibiotics are useless.

HIV/AIDS Any exposure to blood, blood products or bodily fluids may put an individual at risk for HIV. Infection can come from practicing unprotected sex or sharing contaminated needles. Apart from abstinence, the most effective preventative is to practice safe sex using condoms. It is impossible to detect the HIV-positive status of an otherwise healthy-looking person without a blood test.

A good resource for help and information is the US Centers for Disease Control AIDS hotline (☎ 800-342-2437).

Cuts, Bites & Stings
Cuts & Scratches Skin punctures can become infected in hot climates and may be difficult to heal. Treat cuts with an antiseptic such as Betadine. Where possible avoid bandages and Band-Aids, which can keep wounds wet.

Bites & Stings Bee and wasp stings are usually painful rather than dangerous. Calamine lotion gives relief, and ice packs reduce pain and swelling.

Some spiders have dangerous bites, and scorpion stings are very painful, but both are rarely fatal. Avoid bites by not using bare hands to turn over rocks or pieces of wood.

Bites from snakes do not cause instantaneous death, and antivenins are usually available. Seek medical help. The Arizona Poison Control System reports that half of reported snake bites result from people picking up the snake, either out of bravado or mistakenly assuming that the animal was dead. Keep a healthy distance away from snakes and watch where you step.

If you are bitten or stung, call Poison Control (see below). After snake bite, avoid slashing and sucking the wound, avoid tight tourniquets (a light constricting band above the bite can help), avoid ice, keep the affected area below the level of the heart and move it as little as possible. Don't ingest alcohol or drugs. Stay calm and get to a medical facility promptly.

There are no special first-aid techniques for spider or scorpion injuries. A black widow spider bite may be barely noticeable, but their venom can be dangerous. Conenose bug bites may also require medical assistance. Bites from a centipede, bee, wasp or ant bites may be relieved by application of ice (but don't use ice for the other critters mentioned above).

If you are hiking away from help, and you are bitten or stung, hike out and get help, particularly in the case of snake and spider bites. Often, reactions are delayed for up to 12 hours and you can hike out before then. Hiking with a companion is recommended. Also see Dangers & Annoyances later in this chapter.

Poison Control Centers These are staffed 24 hours a day and advise about bites, stings and ingested poisons of all kinds. If you have trouble reaching one, dial 911 or 0.

Arizona: Phoenix, ☎ 602-253-3334; Tucson, ☎ 520-626-6016; the rest of Arizona, ☎ 800-362-0101

New Mexico: Albuquerque, ☎ 505-843-2551; the rest of New Mexico, ☎ 800-432-6866

Utah: Salt Lake City, ☎ 801-581-2151; the rest of Utah, ☎ 800-456-7707

WOMEN TRAVELERS
Women often face different situations when traveling than men do. If you are a woman traveler, especially traveling alone, it's a good idea to travel with a little extra awareness of your surroundings.

The USA is such a diverse and varied country that it's impossible to give advice that will fit every place and every situation. People are generally friendly and happy to help travelers, and you will probably have a wonderful time unmarred by dangerous encounters. Consider the following suggestions, however, which should reduce your chances of problems. The best advice is to trust your instincts.

In general, exercise more vigilance in large cities than in rural areas. Try to avoid the 'bad' or unsafe neighborhoods or districts; if you must go into or through these areas, use a private vehicle (car or taxi). It's more dangerous at night, but in the worst areas crime can occur even in the daytime. If you are unsure which areas are considered unsafe, ask at your hotel or telephone the tourist office for advice. Tourist maps can sometimes be deceiving, compressing areas that are not tourist attractions and making the distances look shorter than they are.

While there is less to beware of in rural areas, women may still be harassed by men unaccustomed to seeing women traveling solo. Try to avoid hiking or camping alone, especially in unfamiliar places. Use the 'buddy system,' not only for protection from other humans, but also for aid in case of unexpected falls or other injuries, or encounters with rattlesnakes, bears or other potentially dangerous wildlife.

Women must recognize the extra threat of rape, which is a problem not only in urban but also in rural areas, albeit to a lesser degree. The best way to deal with this threat is to avoid putting yourself in vulnerable situations. Conducting yourself in a common-sense manner will help you to avoid most problems. For example, you're more vulnerable if you've been drinking or using drugs than if you're sober; you're more vulnerable alone than if you're with company; and you're more vulnerable in a high-crime urban area than in a 'better' district.

If, despite all precautions, you are assaulted, call the police; in any emergency, telephoning 911 will connect you with the emergency operator. In some rural areas where 911 is not active, dial '0' for the operator. Cities and larger towns have rape crisis centers and women's shelters that provide help and support; these are listed in the telephone directory, or the police can refer you to them.

Men may interpret a woman drinking alone in a bar as a bid for male company, whether you intend it that way or not. If you

don't want the company, most men will respect a firm but polite 'no thank you.'

Don't hitchhike alone, and don't pick up hitchhikers if driving alone. If you're driving long distances, it's a good idea to have a premade sign to signal for help if you get stuck on a road. At night avoid getting out of your car to flag down help; turn on your hazard lights and wait for the police to arrive. Be extra careful at night on public transit, and remember to check the times of the last bus or train before you go out at night.

To deal with potential dangers, many women protect themselves with a whistle, mace, cayenne pepper spray or some self-defense training. If you do decide to purchase a spray, contact a police station to find out about regulations and training classes. Laws regarding sprays vary from state to state and town to town, so be informed based on your destination. It is a federal offense to carry defensive sprays on airplanes.

The headquarters for the National Organization for Women (NOW; ☎ 202-331-0066), 1000 16th St NW, Suite 700, Washington, DC 20036, is a good resource for any woman-related information and can refer you to state and local chapters. Planned Parenthood (☎ 212-541-7800), 810 7th Ave, New York, NY 10019, can refer you to clinics throughout the country and offer advice on medical issues. Check the yellow pages under 'Women's Organizations & Services' for local resources.

GAY & LESBIAN TRAVELERS

There are gay people throughout the USA, but by far the most established gay communities are in the major cities, especially on the west and east coasts. In major coastal cities it is easier for gay men and women to live their lives with a certain amount of openness. As you travel into the middle of the country, it is much harder to be open about your sexual orientation, and many gays are still in the closet. This matches the prevailing attitude of the country, which prefers that gay people are neither seen nor heard. Gay travelers should be careful, *especially* in the predominantly rural areas – holding hands might get you bashed.

A couple of good national guidebooks are *Women's Traveller*, providing listings for lesbians, and *Damron's Address Book* for men, both published by the Damron Company (☎ 800-462-6654, 415-255-0404), PO Box 422458, San Francisco, CA 94142-2458. Ferrari's *Places for Women* and *Places for Men* are also useful, as are guides to specific cities. These can be found at any good bookstore.

Another good resource is the Gay Yellow Pages (☎ 212-674-0120), PO Box 533, Village Station, NY 10014-0533, which has a national edition as well as regional editions.

National resource numbers include the National AIDS/HIV Hotline (☎ 800-342-2437) and the National Gay/Lesbian Task Force (☎ 202-332-6483 in Washington, DC).

In the Southwest, there are few gay organizations compared to coastal cities. They are listed under Gay & Lesbian Organizations in the yellow pages of major cities' telephone directories. The most active gay community is in the Phoenix area, which is hardly surprising when you consider that the Phoenix urban area has a far larger population than either of the states of Utah or New Mexico. Utah, conservative and Mormon, has almost no gay life outside of a few contacts in Salt Lake City.

DISABLED TRAVELERS

Travel within the USA is becoming easier for people with disabilities. Public buildings (including hotels, restaurants, theaters and museums) are now required by law to be wheelchair accessible and to have available restroom facilities. Public transportation services (buses, trains and taxis) must be made accessible to all, including those in wheelchairs, and telephone companies are required to provide relay operators for the hearing impaired. Many banks now provide ATM instructions in Braille, and you will find audible crossing signals as well as dropped curbs at busier roadway intersections.

Larger private and chain hotels (see Accommodations, later in this chapter, for listings) have suites for disabled guests. Main car rental agencies offer hand-controlled models at no extra charge. All major airlines, Greyhound buses and Amtrak trains allow service animals to accompany passengers and frequently sell two-for-one packages when attendants of seriously disabled passengers are required. Airlines also provide assistance for connecting, boarding and deplaning the flight – just ask for assistance when making your reservation. (Note: airlines must accept wheelchairs as checked baggage and have an onboard chair available, though some advance notice may be required on smaller aircraft.) Of course, the more populous the area, the greater the likelihood of facilities for the disabled, so it's important to call ahead to see what is available. The National Park Service (see Useful Organizations, below) issues free Golden Access passes for disabled travelers.

There are a number of organizations that specialize in the travel needs of disabled travelers:

Access-Able Travel Source
  Has an excellent website with many links. PO Box 1796, Wheat Ridge, CO 80034 (☎ 303-232-2979, fax 239-8486; www.access-able.com)
Mobility International USA (MIUSA)/National Clearinghouse on Disability & Exchange (NCDE)
  These organizations primarily run educational exchange programs, both in the USA and overseas. PO Box 10767, Eugene, OR 97440 (☎ 541-343-1284, fax 541-343-6812, info@miusa.org; www.miusa.org)
Moss Rehabilitation Hospital's Travel Information Service
  (☎ 215-456-9600, TTY 456-9602)
National Spinal Cord Injury Association
  Publishes free fact sheet number 15 (Travel After Spinal Cord Injury) with useful tips and a resources list. 8300 Colesville Rd, Suite 551, Silver Springs, MD 20910 (☎ 301-588-6959, 800-962-9629)
Society for the Advancement of Travel for the Handicapped (SATH)
  347 Fifth Ave No 610, New York, NY 10016 (☎ 212-447-7284, fax 725-8253, sathtravel@aol.com)

Travelin' Talk
An international network of people providing assistance to disabled travelers. P.O. Box 3534, Clarksville, TN 37047 (☎ 615-552-6670, fax 552-1182, trvlntlk@aol.com)

Twin Peaks Press
Publishes handbooks for disabled travelers. PO Box 129, Vancouver, WA 98666 (☎ 360-694-2462, 800-637-2256)

SENIOR TRAVELERS

When retirement leaves the time clock behind and the myriad 'senior' discounts begin to apply, the prospect of rediscovering the USA elicits a magnetic draw for foreigners and the native-born alike. Though the age when the benefits begin varies with the attraction, travelers from 50 years and up can expect to receive cut rates and benefits unknown to (and the envy of) their younger fellows. Be sure to inquire about such rates at hotels, museums and restaurants.

The National Park Service (see Useful Organizations, below) issues Golden Age Passports that cut costs greatly for seniors.

Some national advocacy groups that can help in planning your travels include the following:

American Association of Retired Persons
AARP (☎ 800-424-3410; www.aarp.org), 3200 E Carson St, Lakewood, CA 90712 (membership), is an advocacy group for Americans 50 years and older and is a good resource for travel bargains. US residents can get one-year/three-year memberships for $8/20. Citizens of other countries can get same memberships for $10/24.

Elderhostel
This organization (☎ 617-426-8056), 75 Federal St, Boston, MA 02110-1941, is a nonprofit organization that offers seniors the opportunity to attend academic college courses throughout the USA and Canada. The programs last one to three weeks and include meals and accommodations. They are open to people 55 years and older and their companions.

Grand Circle Travel
This group offers escorted tours and travel information in a variety of formats and distributes a free useful booklet, *Going Abroad: 101 Tips for Mature Travelers*. Contact them at 347 Congress St, Boston, MA 02210 (☎ 617-350-7500, 800-350-7500; www.gct/gcc.com).

TRAVEL WITH CHILDREN

Children receive discounts on many things in the USA, ranging from motel stays to museum admissions. The definition of a child varies widely – some places count anyone under 18 eligible for children's discounts while other places only include children under six.

Many hotels and motels allow children to share a room with their parents for free or for a modest fee, though B&Bs rarely do and some don't allow children at all. More expensive hotels can arrange babysitting services or have 'kids' clubs' for younger children. Restaurants offer inexpensive children's menus with a limited selection of kid-friendly foods at cheap prices only for patrons under 12 or 10 years of age.

Airlines do discount children's tickets, but I have found that they are often more expensive than the cheapest APEX adult tickets. Most buses and tours have discounted children's prices, though the discounts are not always very big. Car rental companies provide infant seats for their cars on request.

Various children's activities are mentioned in appropriate places in the text. For information on enjoying travel with the young ones, read *Travel With Children* by Lonely Planet cofounder Maureen Wheeler.

USEFUL ORGANIZATIONS
American Automobile Association (AAA)

The AAA, with offices in all major cities and many smaller towns, provides useful information, free maps and routine road services like tire repair, towing (free within a limited radius) and locksmith service to its members. The membership card can often be used to obtain car rental and sightseeing admission discounts. Members of AAA's foreign affiliates, like the Automobile Association in the UK, are entitled to the same services; for others, the basic membership fee ranges from $39 to $41 per year, plus a one-time initiation fee of $17 (still an excellent investment for the maps alone, even for nonmotorists). Its nationwide toll-free roadside assistance number is ☎ 800-222-4357 (800-AAA-HELP).

National Park Service (NPS)
The NPS, part of the Department of the Interior, administers national parks, monuments, historic sites and a few other areas. Visitors can often camp and hike in the bigger areas, but hunting and commercial activities like logging are prohibited in these protected sites. All have visitor centers with information (exhibits, films, park ranger talks, etc) about why that particular site has been preserved for posterity.

National parks surround spectacular natural features and cover hundreds of square miles. The many Southwestern NPS sites (including the famous Grand Canyon, Zion, Arches and Canyonlands National Parks) are fully described in detail in the text. National park campground and reservations information can be obtained by calling ☎ 800-365-2267 or writing to the National Park Service Public Inquiry, Department of the Interior, 18th and C Sts NW, Washington, DC 20013. Lodges within parks, and motels and campgrounds near them, are privately owned. Details are given in the text.

Most NPS areas charge entrance fees, valid for seven days, of $4 to $10 per vehicle (usually half-price for walk-in or biking visitors). Extremely popular parks, like the Grand Canyon, charge $20. A few are free, and some don't collect entrance fees during periods of low visitation (usually late fall to early spring). Additional fees are charged for camping and some other activities, depending on each park.

Golden Passports Golden Eagle Passports cost $50 annually and offer one-year entry into all national parks to the holder (and anyone in the holder's car). You can buy one at any NPS fee-area, and it is valid immediately, so you can use it for your first visit to any national park and all visits to all NPS sites for the next year – a great deal! The passes are not transferable, and pass-holders may be asked for a picture ID.

Golden Age Passports cost $10 and allow permanent US residents 62 years and older unlimited free entry to all NPS sites, plus 50% discounts on camping and other fees.

Golden Access Passports are free and give free admission to US residents who are legally blind or permanently disabled.

US Forest Service (USFS)
The USFS is part of the Department of Agriculture. National forests are less protected than parks, allowing commercial exploitation in some areas (usually logging or privately owned recreational facilities). Forests are multi-use, with recreational activities such as hunting, fishing, snowmobiling, 4WD use and mountain biking permitted in many areas, unlike the NPS parks, where these activities are infrequently permitted. There are many forest campgrounds, which vary from simple sites with a fire ring and a pit toilet but no water to campgrounds with showers and sometimes limited RV hookups. Most sites are $6 to $12; a few without water are free.

Entrance into national forests is often free, although in 1997 a new experimental program was introduced by which some of the most popular roads through the forest cost $2 to $5 (per vehicle) to drive through. These fees were normally valid for several days and Golden Passports were accepted in some, but not all, cases. This fee-collecting program is expected to go through various changes over the next few years.

Current information about national forests can be obtained from ranger stations, which are listed in the text. National forest campground and reservation information can be obtained by calling ☎ 800-280-2267 (280-CAMP). General forest information is also available from the following:

National Forests Southwestern Region Public Affairs Office, 517 Gold Ave NW, Albuquerque, NM 87102 (☎ 505-842-3292). This office covers Arizona as well.
National Forests Intermountain Region, 324 25th St, Ogden, UT 84401 (☎ 801-625-5605)

Bureau of Land Management (BLM)
The BLM, within the Department of the Interior, manages public use of many federal lands outside of the parks and forests. This includes grazing and mining leases as well as recreational uses. They may offer no-frills camping, often in untouched settings. Entrance fees are charged for a small number of BLM sites, and Golden Passports may be valid in some cases. Regional information offices are found in each state capital:

222 N Central Ave, Phoenix, AZ 85004-2203 (☎ 602-417-9200, 602-417-9503)
1474 Rodeo Rd, Santa Fe, NM 87505-5630 (☎ 505-438-7400)
324 S State, Salt Lake City, UT 84111-2397 (☎ 801-539-4001)

State Fish & Game Departments
Unlike the above organizations, the Fish & Game departments are run by state governments. Information about seasons, licenses and other regulations is available from the following agencies:

Arizona Game & Fish Department
    2222 W Greenway Rd, Phoenix, AZ 85023-4313 (☎ 602-942-3000)
New Mexico Game & Fish Department
    Villagra Building, State Capitol, Santa Fe, NM 87503-0001 (☎ 505-827-7911)
Utah Wildlife Resources Division
    1594 W North Temple, Salt Lake City, UT 84114-6301 (☎ 801-596-8660)

DANGERS & ANNOYANCES
Crime
The cities of the Southwest generally have lower levels of violent crime than the larger, better known cities such as Wash-ington, DC, New York and Los Angeles. Nevertheless, violent crime is certainly present, and you should take the usual precautions, especially in the cities.

Always lock cars and put valuables out of sight, whether leaving the car for a few minutes or for longer, and whether you are in towns or in the remote backcountry. Rent a car with a lockable trunk. If your car is bumped from behind by another vehicle, it is best to keep going to a well-lit area, service station or even a police station.

Be aware of your surroundings and who may be watching you. Avoid walking dimly lit streets at night, particularly if you are alone. Walk purposefully. Exercise particular caution in large parking lots or parking structures at night. Avoid unnecessary displays of money or jewelry. Split up your money and credit cards to avoid losing everything, and try to use ATM machines in well-trafficked areas.

In hotels, don't leave valuables lying around your room. Use safety deposit boxes or at least place valuables in a locked bag. Don't open your door to strangers – check the peephole or call the front desk if unexpected people are trying to enter.

Weather
Summer storms can be dangerous in the Southwest. Lightning is common and you should avoid being in the open, especially on canyon rims or hilltops, or next to tall or metallic objects.

During heavy rain, flash floods occur regularly. A normally dry river bed can become a raging torrent in minutes, strong enough to sweep a person, or even a vehicle, away. Please see the sidebar on Flash Floods in the Outdoor Activities chapter for more information.

The Southwest is very dry, and people die of dehydration every year. Dehydration occurs rapidly in 100°F weather. Tourists on short day hikes have become disoriented and lost – what starts off as an hour or two of hiking can turn into a fatal accident without water. Don't attempt any hike, however short, without carrying plenty of water. A minimum of four quarts per person per day is needed in the summer. Also remember to carry containers of water in the car, in case you break down on a rural road.

Dust storms are brief but can be temporarily blinding. If caught in a dust storm while driving, pull over as far to the side of the road as you can and wait it out. It shouldn't take more than a few minutes to blow over.

Wildlife Big & Small

Drivers should watch for livestock on highways, especially on Indian reservations, which are generally unfenced, and in areas signed as 'Open Rangelands' or words to that effect. Hitting a cow (or a deer) at 65 mph can total your car and kill the animal, and it might kill you as well.

Despite the large numbers of snakes, spiders, scorpions and other venomous creatures in the Southwest, fatalities are very rare. This is partly because these animals tend to avoid humans and partly because their venom is designed to kill small animals rather than big ones like ourselves. If you are bitten or stung by one of these critters, refer to the Health section under Cuts, Bites & Stings.

The descriptions below are more for interest than because large numbers of readers are likely to be bitten. Note that most of these animals can be found in urban as well as rural areas.

Snakes When hiking, watch where you are stepping, particularly on hot summer afternoons and evenings when rattlesnakes like to bask in the middle of the trail. They are also often active at night. There are many species of rattler, most easily identified by the 'rattle' of scales at the tip of the tail. These emit a rapid rattling sound when the snake is disturbed. The rattle is made of brittle material and can break off, and baby rattlesnakes are born without rattles, but with venom. So don't rely solely on the rattles to identify the snake. Most rattlesnakes have roughly diamond-shaped patterns along their backs and vary in length from two to six feet. They are found all over the western USA. If you are bitten, you will experience rapid swelling, very severe pain and possible temporary paralysis, but rarely do victims die. Antivenin is available in Southwestern hospitals.

Rarer than the rattlesnake, but much more poisonous, is the Arizona coral snake, found from central Arizona to southwestern New Mexico. This small snake, usually 13 to 21 inches in length, is easily identified by a pattern of glossy bands – wide black, narrow yellow, wide red, narrow yellow – repeated along its length. This snake tends to burrow underground and emerge after warm night rains. It is unlikely that you will see one. Few people have been bitten, but of those victims, some have required hospitalization. Antivenin is available.

Spiders The most dangerous spider in the area is the black widow, a species that has gained notoriety because the venomous female eats her mate after sex. The female has a small, round body marked with a red hourglass shape under its abdomen. She makes very messy webs, so avoid these, as the widow will bite if harassed. Bites are very painful but rarely fatal, except in young children. Antivenin is available.

The brown spider, of which there are several species, occasionally hides in closets and may bite when you put on some clothing in which it is hiding. The bite may become large and painful and flu-like symptoms are reported, but long-term problems are unlikely.

The large (up to six inches in diameter) and hairy tarantula looks much worse than it is – it bites very rarely and usually only when roughly handled. The bite is not very serious, although it is temporarily quite painful. There are over a dozen species in the Southwest.

Gila Monster This is one of only two venomous lizards in the world. It is found in most of Arizona except the northeastern plateau, and it also dwells in extreme southwestern Utah and southwestern New Mexico. This large and slow lizard, which can reach two feet in length, has a bizarre, multicolored, beaded appearance. Although a bite could be fatal, it's very hard to get bitten. You pretty much have to pick the monster up and force-feed it your finger. There have been no fatalities in the last several years. Gila monsters are legally protected and should not be handled.

Scorpions About 20 species of scorpions are found throughout the Southwest. They spend their days under rocks or woodpiles, so use caution when handling these. The long stinger curving up and around the back is characteristic of these animals. The stings can be very painful but are almost never fatal; again, small children are at highest risk.

Other Creatures
Centipedes bite occasionally, resulting in a painfully inflamed wound that lasts for about a day. Bees and wasps deliver sharp and painful stings, which may cause severe reactions if you are allergic to these. Some ants may also give painful stings. Conenose bugs (also called kissing or assassin bugs) are from one-half to 1 inch long and have elongated heads. The winged bodies are oval and brown or black with lighter markings (sometimes orange) around the edges. Bites are painful and can result in severe allergic reactions.

EMERGENCY
If you need any kind of emergency assistance, such as police, ambulance or fire station, call 911. This is a free call from any phone. A few rural phones might not have this service, in which case dial 0 for the operator and ask for emergency assistance.

LEGAL MATTERS
If you are stopped by the police for any reason, remember that there is no system of paying fines on the spot. For traffic offenses, the police officer will explain your options to you. Attempting to pay the fine to the officer is frowned upon at best and may lead to a charge of bribery to compound your troubles.

If you are arrested for more serious offenses, you are allowed to remain silent and are presumed innocent until proven guilty. Apart from identifying yourself, there is no legal reason to speak to a police officer if you don't wish to. All persons who are arrested are legally allowed (and given) the right to make one phone call. If you don't have a lawyer or family member to help you, call your embassy. The police will give you the number upon request.

Driving & Drinking Laws
Each state has its own laws, and what may be legal in one state may be illegal in others.

Some general rules are that you must be at least 16 years of age to drive (older in some states). Speed limits are normally 55 to 75 mph on interstates and freeways. You can drive up to 5 mph over the limit without much likelihood of being pulled over, but if you're doing 10 mph over the limit, you'll be caught sooner or later. Speed limits on other highways are 60 mph or less, and in cities they can vary from 25 to 45 mph. Watch for school zones, which can be as low as 15 mph during school hours – these limits are strictly enforced. Seat belts must be worn in most states. Motorcyclists must wear helmets.

The drinking age is 21 and you need a photo ID to prove your age. You could incur stiff fines, jail time and penalties if you are caught driving under the influence of alcohol. During festive holidays and special events, road blocks are sometimes set up to deter drunk drivers. See also Driving & Drinking Laws in the Introduction to each state.

For more information on other car-related topics, see the Getting Around chapter.

BUSINESS HOURS & HOLIDAYS

Generally speaking, business hours are from 9 am to 5 pm, but there are certainly no hard and fast rules. In large cities, a few supermarkets, restaurants and the main post office lobby are open 24 hours a day. Shops are usually open from 9 or 10 am to 5 or 6 pm, but they are often open until 9 pm in shopping malls, except on Sunday, when hours are noon to 5 pm. Post offices are open from 8 am to 4 or 5:30 pm Monday to Friday, and some are open from 8 am to 3 pm on Saturday. Banks are usually open from either 9 or 10 am to 5 or 6 pm Monday to Friday. A few banks are open from 9 am to 2 or 4 pm on Saturday. Call individual banks for exact hours.

National public holidays are celebrated throughout the USA. Banks, schools and government offices (including post offices) are closed and transportation, some museums and other services are on a Sunday schedule. Holidays falling on a Sunday are usually observed on the following Monday.

New Year's Day, January 1
Martin Luther King, Jr, Day, 3rd Monday in January
Presidents' Day, 3rd Monday in February
Easter, a Sunday in late March or April
Memorial Day, last Monday in May (honors the war dead; the unofficial beginning of the summer tourist season)
Independence Day, July 4
Labor Day, 1st Monday in September (honors working people; the unofficial end of the summer tourist season)
Columbus Day, 2nd Monday in October (a federal holiday, though celebrating Columbus' 'discovery' of America has become controversial)
Veterans Day, November 11
Thanksgiving, 4th Thursday in November
Christmas Day, December 25

CULTURAL EVENTS

The USA is always ready to call a day an event. Retailers remind the masses of coming events with huge advertising binges running for months before the actual day. In larger cities with diverse cultures, traditional holidays of other countries are also celebrated with as much, if not more, fanfare. Some of these are also public holidays (see above) and therefore banks, schools and government buildings are closed.

Valentine's Day, February 14. No one knows why St Valentine is associated with romance in the USA, but this is the day of roses, sappy greeting cards and packed restaurants.
St Patrick's Day, March 17. The Irish patron saint is honored by those who feel the Irish in their blood: folks wear green, stores sell green bread, bars serve green beer and towns and cities put on frolicking parades of marching bands and community groups.
Easter, a moveable feast. This Christian holiday is accompanied by secular rituals of painting eggs, eating chocolate eggs and searching for plastic eggs hidden by the 'Easter bunny.' Travel during this weekend is usually expensive and crowded. Incidentally, Good Friday is not a public holiday and often goes unnoticed. *Passover*, date depends on the Jewish calendar. Jewish families gather for a symbolic seder dinner to remember God's deliverance of the ancient Hebrews from bondage in Egypt.
Cinco de Mayo, May 5. This is the anniversary of Mexico's 1862 victory over the French in the Battle of Puebla. There are often parades, and everyone eats lots of Mexican food and drinks margaritas. *Mothers Day*, third Sunday of May. This 'Hallmark holiday' is marked by lots of cards, flowers and busy restaurants.
Fathers Day, third Sunday of June. Same idea, different parent.
Independence Day, July 4. American independence from Britain is celebrated by flying flags, lighting barbecues, parading in the streets and igniting public fireworks displays.
Halloween, October 31. Kids dress in costumes and, in safer neighborhoods, go 'trick-or-treating' for candy. Some adults go to parties to act out their alter egos.
Day of the Dead, November 2. A traditional Mexican celebration for families to honor dead relatives; often, breads and sweets are made resembling skeletons, skulls and such. *Election Day*, second Tuesday of November. US

citizens perform their patriotic duty and vote. *Thanksgiving*, last Thursday of November. This important family gathering is celebrated with a bounty of food (traditionally a turkey dinner with fall harvest vegetables) and (more recently) American football games on TV. The following day is considered the biggest shopping day of the year (I recommend you avoid stores).

Chanukah – generally, it's sometime in December. This is an eight-day Jewish holiday commemorating the victory of the Maccabees over the armies of Syria and the rededication of their temple in Jerusalem. The date of Chanukah changes year to year, as it's tied to Kislev 25 to Tevet 2 in the Hebrew calendar, a nonlunar system. *Christmas*, December 25. Christmas eve is as much of an event as the day itself, with church services, caroling in the streets, people cruising neighborhoods looking for the best light displays and stores full of procrastinators. *Kwanzaa*, begins December 26. A seven-day traditional African-American harvest celebration. Families join together for a feast and practice seven different principles corresponding to the seven days of celebration.

SPECIAL EVENTS

From highbrow arts festivals to down-home country fairs, from American Indian ceremonials to chile-cooking competitions, from duck races to hot-air balloon ascents, the Southwest has literally hundreds of holidays, festivals and sporting events. Entire books have been written describing Southwestern festivals – only a selection of the most important or unusual events can be given below.

As dates for many events vary slightly from year to year, it's best to check local papers or chambers of commerce for precise dates.

January

Various Dances are held on January 1 and 6 at most Indian pueblos in New Mexico. The *Sundance Film Festival* takes place the second half of January in Park City, Utah. *Animal Dances* are held on the evening of January 22 and throughout the next day in San Ildefonso Pueblo, New Mexico.

Visitors' Etiquette in Pueblos & on Reservations

Indian pueblos and reservations are governed by both federal and tribal law. Each tribe is independent, and visitors should be aware that what is permitted on one reservation may be banned on another. Language, customs and religious ceremonies differ from one reservation to the next. Many Indians prefer to speak their own language, and some don't speak English. Privacy is cherished, both on an individual and community level. Visitors to pueblos and reservations are generally welcome, but they should behave in an appropriately courteous and respectful manner. Tribal rules are often clearly posted at the entrance to each reservation, but here are a few guidelines.

Photography & Other Recording Many tribes ban all forms of recording be it photography, videotaping, audiotaping or drawing. Others permit these activities in certain areas only if you pay the appropriate fee. If you wish to photograph a person, do so only after obtaining his or her permission. This also holds true for children. A posing tip is usually expected. Photographers who disregard these rules can expect tribal police officers to confiscate their cameras and then escort them off the reservation.

Private Property Do not walk into houses or climb onto roofs unless invited. Do not climb on ruins. Kivas are always off-limits to visitors. Do not remove any kind of artifact. Off-road travel (foot, horse or vehicle) is not allowed without a permit.

Verbal Communication It is considered polite to listen without comment, particularly when an elder is speaking. Silent listening does not mean that the listener is ignoring the speaker; to the contrary, intent listening is considered respectful. Be prepared for long

February

The *Quartzsite Gem & Mineral Show and Swap Meet*, held in late January to mid-February in Quartzsite, Arizona, draws thousands of gem fans to this small town – be prepared to camp. *Candelaria Day*, February 2, brings ceremonial dances to Santo Domingo, San Felipe and Acoma Pueblos, New Mexico. The *Tucson Gem & Mineral Show*, held during the first two weeks in Tucson, Arizona, is one of the biggest in the country. The *Tubac Festival of the Arts*, which occurs in early February in Tubac, Arizona, is one of the state's most important arts and crafts festivals. *O'odham Tash*, held at Casa Grande, Arizona, in mid-February, involves major Indian festivities – dances, a rodeo, a parade, food and arts and crafts. *La Fiesta de los Vaqueros*, celebrated from the last Thursday to Sunday of February in Tucson, Arizona, begins with the world's largest nonmotorized parade, followed by a rodeo and other cowboy events – even the city's schools close for the last two days of what is locally called 'Rodeo Week.'

March

Wa:k Powwow Conference, hosted in early March by the Tohono O'odham tribe in San Xavier del Bac Mission, near Tucson, Arizona, is attended by members of many Southwestern Indian tribes. Highlights include several days of dances, singing, food and other entertainment. *Easter* is celebrated with masses, races, dances and parades in many Indian pueblos and at the Indian Pueblo Cultural Center in Albuquerque, New Mexico.

April

Albuquerque Founder's Day, April 23 (New Mexico), involves a parade and street fair in Albuquerque's Old Town Plaza during the third or fourth weekend. *American Indian Week*, the week around the Gathering of Nations Powwow (see below), includes lectures, audiovisual presentations, dances and art displays that celebrate Indian traditions. Events are held at the Indian Pueblo Cultural Center in Albuquerque. *Gathering of Nations Powwow*, a weekend in late April (or early May), consists of a Miss Indian World contest, dances and arts and crafts at the University of New Mexico Arena in Albuquerque. The *Annual Square Dance Festival*, held three days (Friday to Sunday) over the third or fourth weekend, includes workshops, performances and public dances (spectators welcome) at Red Rock State Park, Gallup, New Mexico.

silences in the middle of conversations; such silences often indicate that a topic is under serious consideration.

Ceremonials & Powwows These are either open to the public or exclusively for tribal members. Ceremonials are religious events. Applauding, chatting, asking questions or trying to talk to the performers is rude. Photography and other recording are rarely permitted. While powwows also hold spiritual significance, they are usually more informal. Many ceremonials and powwows don't have a fixed date and are arranged a couple of weeks ahead of time. The tribal office can inform you of upcoming events.

Clothing Modest dress is customary. Especially when watching ceremonials, you should dress conservatively. Halter or tank tops and miniskirts or short shorts are inappropriate.

Alcohol Most reservations ban the sale or use of alcohol. The Apache reservations are notable exceptions. Drugs are banned on all reservations.

Eating There are few restaurants. Especially during public ceremonials, visitors may be invited into a house for a meal. Courteous behavior includes enjoying the food (of course!) but not lingering at the table after your meal, because others are waiting. Tipping is not customary.

Recreation Activities such as backpacking, camping, fishing and hunting require tribal permits. On Indian lands, state fishing or hunting licenses are not valid. ■

May

San Felipe Day, May 1, is celebrated with dances at San Felipe and other pueblos in New Mexico. *Santa Cruz Day*, May 3, is celebrated with dances at Cochiti and Taos Pueblos, New Mexico. *T & C Fiesta*, on the first weekend in May, has taken place annually for half a century in Truth or Consequences, New Mexico. It features an old-time fiddlers contest as well as a rodeo, parade and street booths. The *Tularosa Rose Festival*, held over the first weekend in May in Tularosa, New Mexico, features music, arts, crafts and food as well as roses. *Cinco de Mayo*, May 5, is a Mexican holiday that is celebrated in many Southwestern towns, especially those with a strong Hispanic heritage. Parades, dances, music, arts and crafts, street fairs and Mexican food are the order of the day. *Golden Spike Anniversary*, May 10, is remembered with a reenactment of the joining of the first east-to-west railroad in 1869. It takes place in Golden Spike National Historic Site, Utah.

June

The *Billy the Kid Tombstone Race* is held in mid-June at Fort Sumner, New Mexico. *St Anthony's Day*, June 13; *San Juan Day*, June 24; and *St Peter's and St Paul's Day*, June 29, are celebrated with dances and other events at several Indian pueblos and villages in New Mexico. The *Utah Arts Festival* is held in late June in Salt Lake City, Utah. Various summer-long *Arts Festivals* occur in Flagstaff, Arizona. The *Mormon Miracle Pageant* is held in June or July in Manti, Utah.

July

The *Utah Shakespearean Festival*, from late June through late August, takes place in Cedar City, Utah. The *Ute Indian Powwow*, dates vary, happens in Fort Duchesne, Utah. *Fourth of July* is celebrated in most Southwestern towns with a variety of events, including races, rodeos, arts and crafts fairs, ceremonial Indian dances, pageants, music festivals, pancake breakfasts, barbecues, picnics and country & western dancing. These are in addition to parades and fireworks. *Days of '47* (also called Pioneer Days), two weeks up to July 24, celebrates the arrival of pioneering Mormon leader Brigham Young on July 24, 1847. It's celebrated in Salt Lake City and other towns in Utah. *Santiago and Santa Ana Days*, July 25 and 26, are celebrated with dances at several Indian pueblos and a big traditional fiesta in Taos, New Mexico. *Spanish Market*, held during the last weekend, includes arts and crafts and entertainment in the Plaza in Santa Fe, New Mexico. The *Ruidoso Art Festival*, over the last weekend, showcases arts and crafts of a high standard in Ruidoso, New Mexico. The *Festival of the American West* takes place late July/early August in Logan, Utah.

August

Park City Arts Festival is held the first weekend in Park City, Utah. *Old Lincoln Days*, the first weekend, includes the Last Escape of Billy the Kid pageant in Lincoln, New Mexico. The huge *Inter-Tribal Indian Ceremonial*, during the second week, draws members of dozens of tribes and includes rodeos, dances, powwows, parades, races, food, arts and crafts and much more. It's held in Red Rock State Park, Gallup, New Mexico. *San Lorenzo Day*, August 10, is celebrated with dances at Acoma, Laguna and Picuris Pueblos, New Mexico. The *Indian Market*, on the third weekend, offers a chance to buy high-quality Indian arts and crafts. It has occurred annually since 1922 in Santa Fe, New Mexico. The *Great American Duck Races* are held on the third or fourth weekend in Deming, New Mexico.

September

Peach Days, on the first weekend, celebrates the local harvest in Brigham City, Utah. *Fiesta de Santa Fe*, held on the first (occasionally second) weekend in Santa Fe, New Mexico, is one of the oldest annual fiestas in the country. *Navajo Nation Fair*, held mid-September in Window Rock, Arizona, is the largest Indian fair in the country and offers a rodeo, parade, dances, songs, arts and crafts, food and more. The *New Mexico State Fair and Rodeo*, held for two weeks mid-month in Albuquerque, ranks as one of the largest state fairs in the USA. The *Utah State Fair* is celebrated in mid-September in Salt Lake City, Utah. *Old Taos Trade Fair*, on the fourth weekend in Taos, New Mexico, celebrates life in the 1820s at Martínez Hacienda. *Taos Fall Arts Festival* takes place in late September to early October in Taos, New Mexico.

October

The *Whole Enchilada Festival*, which takes place the first weekend in Las Cruces, New Mexico, showcases the world's biggest enchilada. Other draws include local food, entertainment, arts and crafts and races. The *Arizona State Fair* is held the last two weeks in Phoenix, Arizona. *All Hallows Day* and *All Saints' Day*, on October 31 and November 1, are celebrated with ceremonies and dances at most Indian pueblos in New Mexico.

November

San Diego Day, on November 12, involves ceremonial dances at Tesuque and Jemez Pueblos,

New Mexico. *Christmas Lighting of Temple Square* takes place the last weekend in Salt Lake City, Utah.

December

Fiesta of Our Lady of Guadalupe, December 10 to 12, is celebrated with traditional dances and a pilgrimage in Tortugas, Las Cruces, New Mexico. *Christmas* festivities occur all month, including Nativity pageants and festivals of lights in many Southwestern towns.

Sporting Events

From football to rodeos to mountain-bike races, the Southwest has many sporting events.

January

The *Fiesta Bowl*, January 1, in Tempe, Arizona, is a major post-season college football game. The *Utah Winter Games* are held throughout the state over the first two weeks. The *Tucson Open*, held in mid-January in Tucson, Arizona, is a men's PGA (Professional Golfer's Association) tournament. The *Phoenix Open*, held in late January in Scottsdale, Arizona, is a men's PGA tournament.

February

The *Mount Taylor Winter Quadrathlon*, no fixed date, invites teams of one to four athletes to compete in bicycling, running, cross-country skiing and snowshoeing near Grants, New Mexico. The *Chama Chili Classic*, over President's Day weekend, consists of cross-country ski races near Chama, New Mexico.

March

The *Tucson Open*, held in mid-March in Tucson, Arizona, and the *Turquoise Classic*, held in Phoenix, Arizona, in late March, are women's PGA tournaments. *Jeep Safari* takes place over Easter Week in Moab, Utah.

May

The *Great Rio Grande Raft Race*, held in mid-May in Albuquerque, New Mexico, features homemade boats as well as more conventional canoes, kayaks and rafts.

June

Tour of the Gila, around the second weekend, is a premier bicycle stage race that takes place in Silver City, New Mexico. The *Utah Summer Games* are held in late June in Cedar City, Utah. The *Annual PRCA and WRPA Rodeo* is hosted the fourth weekend in Raton, New Mexico.

July

Frontier Days, held during the first week in Prescott, Arizona, hosts one of the world's oldest professional rodeos plus other entertainment.

August

The *Connie Mack World Series Baseball Tournament*, during mid-August in Farmington, New Mexico, has the country's best amateur teams competing. *Payson Rodeo*, the world's other oldest rodeo, is held in mid-August in Payson, Arizona. Expect to see plenty of top-ranking cowboys. *Bonneville Nationals Speed Week* takes place near the third week in Bonneville Salt Flats, Utah.

September

All American Futurity, on Labor Day in Ruidoso Downs, New Mexico, is a quarter-horse race worth $2 million.

October

The *International Balloon Fiesta*, held the second week in Albuquerque, New Mexico, is the biggest gathering of hot-air balloons in the world. The *World Senior Games* are held in mid-October in St George, Utah. The *Fat Tire Festival*, sometime in late October, includes mountain-bike races in and around Moab, Utah.

November

Many *ski resorts* open in late November.

December

The *Red Rock Balloon Rally* takes place the first weekend in Red Rock State Park, Gallup, New Mexico.

WORK

Seasonal work is possible in national parks and other tourist sites, especially ski areas; for information, contact park concessionaires or local chambers of commerce.

If you're coming from abroad and want to work in the USA, you need to apply for a work visa from the US embassy in your home country before you leave. The type of visa varies depending on how long you're staying and the kind of work you plan to do. Generally, you need either a J-1 visa, which you can obtain by joining a visitor-exchange program, or an H-2B visa, which you get when being sponsored by a US employer. The latter is not easy to

Rodeo: A Western Ritual

Rodeo, from the Spanish word meaning roundup, began with the cowboys of the Old West. As they used to say, 'There was never a horse that couldn't be rode – and never a rider that couldn't be throwed.' Naturally, cowboys riding half-wild horses eventually competed to determine who was the best. The speed with which they could rope a calf also became a competitive skill.

Rodeo as we know it today began in the 1880s. The first rodeo to offer prize money was held in Texas in 1883, and the first to begin charging admission to the event was in Prescott, Arizona, in 1888. Since then, rodeo has developed into both a spectator and professional sport under the auspices of the Professional Rodeo Cowboys Association (PRCA). Despite rodeo's recognition as a professional sport, very few cowboys earn anywhere near as much as other professional athletes.

For the first-time spectator, the action is full of thrills and spills but may be a little hard to understand. Within the arena, the main participants are cowboys and cowgirls, judges (who are usually retired rodeo competitors) and clowns. Although the clowns perform amusing stunts, their function is to help out the cowboys when they get into trouble. During the bull riding, they are particularly important if a cowboy gets thrown. Then clowns immediately rush in front of the bull to distract the animal, while the winded cowboy struggles out of the arena.

While men are the main contenders in a rodeo, women also compete, mainly in barrel racing, team roping and calf roping.

Each rodeo follows the same pattern, and once you know a few pointers, it all begins to make sense. The first order of the day is the grand entry, during which all contestants, clowns and officials parade their horses around the arena, raise the US flag and sing the national anthem. The rodeo then begins, and usually includes seven events, which are often in the following order.

Bareback Bronc Riding A rider must stay on a randomly assigned bucking bronco (a wild horse) for eight seconds. This might not seem long from a comfortable seat in the stands, but from the back of a horse it can seem like an eternity. The cowboy holds on with one hand to a handle strapped around the horse just behind its shoulders. His other hand is allowed to touch nothing but air; otherwise he's disqualified. His spurs must be up at the height of the horse's shoulders when the front hooves hit the ground on the first jump out of the chute, and he must keep spurring the horse during the ride. Two judges give up to 25 points to each the horse and the rider, for a maximum possible total of 100. A good ride is one in which the horse bucks wildly and the rider stays on with style – a score of over 70 is good.

Calf Roping This is a timed event. A calf races out of a chute, followed closely by a mounted cowboy with a rope loop. The cowboy ropes the calf (usually by throwing the loop over its head, although a leg catch is legal), hooks the rope to the saddle horn, and

obtain (since the employer has to prove that no US citizen or permanent resident is available to do the job); the former is issued mostly to students for work in summer camps or as au pairs.

ACCOMMODATIONS

The Southwest has a comprehensive range of accommodations, including free camping, developed campsites for tents and RVs, youth hostels, cheap and mid-priced motels, B&Bs, expensive hotels, guest ranches and luxury resorts. For information on lodging taxes, see Taxes earlier in this chapter.

Camping

Public Campgrounds These are on public lands such as in national forests, state and national parks and BLM land. Although the

dismounts, keeping the rope tight all the way to the calf. Watch the horse as the cowboy goes to the calf. A well-trained horse will stand still and hold the rope taut to make the cowboy's job less difficult. When he reaches the calf, the cowboy throws the animal down, ties three of its legs together with a 6-foot-long 'piggin string' and throws up his hands to show he's done. A good roper can do the whole thing in under eight seconds.

Saddle-Bronc Riding This has similar rules to the bareback event and is scored the same way. In addition to starting with the spurs up above the horse's shoulders and keeping one hand in the air, the cowboy must keep both feet in the stirrups. Dismounting from the saddle of a bucking bronco is not easy – watch the two pickup men riding alongside to help the contestant off. This demands almost as much skill as the event itself.

Steer Wrestling In this event (also called bull-dogging), a steer that may weigh as much as 700 pounds runs out of a chute, tripping a barrier line, which is the signal for two cowboys to pursue the animal. One cowboy – the hazer – tries to keep the steer running in a straight line, while the other cowboy – the wrestler – rides alongside the steer and jumps off his horse trying to grip the steer's head and horns – this at speeds approaching 40 miles per hour! The wrestler must then wrestle the steer to the ground. The best cowboys can accomplish this in under five seconds.

Barrel Racing Three large barrels are set up in a triangle, and the rider must race around them in a cloverleaf pattern. The turns are incredibly tight, and the racer must come out of them at full speed to do well. There's a five-second penalty for tipping over a barrel. Good times are around 15 to 17 seconds.

Team Roping A team of two horseback ropers pursues a steer running out of the chute. The first roper must catch the steer by the head or horns and then wrap the rope around the saddle horn. The second team member then lassos the steer's two rear legs in one throw. Good times are under seven seconds.

Bull Riding Riding a bucking and spinning 2000-pound bull is wilder and more dangerous than bronc riding, and it is often the crowd's favorite event. Using one heavily gloved hand, the cowboy holds on to a rope that is wrapped around the bull. And that's it – nothing else to hold on to, and no other rules apart from staying on for eight seconds and not touching the bull with your free hand. Scoring is the same as for bronc riding.

Books For a full overview on rodeo, consult Kristine Fredriksson's *American Rodeo from Buffalo Bill to Big Business*, Clifford P Westermeier's *Man, Beast, Dust: The Story of Rodeo*, Teresa Jordan's *Cowgirls: Women of the American West* and Mary Lou LeCompte's *Cowgirls of the Rodeo: Pioneer Professional Athletes*. ■

land is government-owned, campgrounds on public lands are increasingly being managed by private concessionaires.

Free dispersed camping (meaning you can camp almost anywhere) is permitted in many public backcountry areas in national forests and BLM lands, less so in national parks. Sometimes you can camp right from your car along a dirt road, and sometimes you can backpack your gear in. Informa-

tion on where camping is permitted and detailed maps are available from many local ranger stations (addresses and telephone numbers are given in the text) and may be posted along the road. Sometimes a camping permit is required. The less-developed sites are often on a first-come, first-served basis, and can fill up on Friday nights. More developed areas may accept or require reservations.

Camping in an undeveloped area, whether from your car or backpacking, entails basic responsibility. Choose a campsite at least 100 yards from water, and wash up at camp, not in the stream. Dig a 6-inch-deep hole to bury your shit in, and burn your toilet paper (unless fires are prohibited because of high forest-fire danger). Carry out all trash. Use a portable charcoal grill or camping stove; don't build new fires. If there already is a fire ring, use only dead and down wood or wood you have carried in yourself. Leave the campsite as you found it.

Developed areas usually have toilets, drinking water, fire pits (or charcoal grills) and picnic benches. Some don't have drinking water. At any rate, it is always a good idea to have a few gallons of water with you if you are going to be out in the boonies. These basic campgrounds usually cost about $7 to $12 a night. More developed areas may have showers or recreational vehicle (RV) hookups. These may cost more.

Costs given in the text for public campgrounds are per site. A site is normally for up to six people (or one vehicle). If there are more of you, you'll need two sites. Public campgrounds often have seven- or 14-night limits.

Private Campgrounds These are on private property and are usually close to or in towns. Most are designed with recreational vehicles (RVs) in mind; tenters can camp but fees are several dollars higher than in public campgrounds. Also, fees given in the text are for two people per site. There is usually a charge of $1 to $3 per extra person and state and city taxes apply. However, they may offer discounts for week or month stays. Private campgrounds often have many facilities lacking in public ones. These include hot showers, a coin laundry, a swimming pool, full RV hookups, a games area, a playground and a convenience store. Kampgrounds of America (KOA) (☎ 406-248-7444, !camping@attmail.com; www .KOAkampgrounds.com) is a national network of private campgrounds. You can get its annual directory of sites by calling, or by writing: KOA, PO Box 30558, Billings, MT 59114-0558.

Hostels

The US hostel network is less widespread than in Canada, the UK, Europe and Australia, and is predominately in the north and coastal parts of the country. Not all hostels are affiliated with Hostelling International/ American Youth Hostels (HI/AYH). Those that are offer discounts to HI/AYH members and allow nonmembers to stay for $3 more. Dormitory beds cost about $10 to $14 per person a night. Rooms are in the $20s for one or two people, sometimes more. Annual membership is $25 for 18- to 54-year-olds, $10 for youths and $15 for seniors.

HI/AYH hostels expect you to rent or carry a sleeping sheet or sleeping bag to keep the beds clean. Dormitories are segregated by sex and curfews may exist. Kitchen and laundry privileges are usually available in return for light housekeeping duties. Information and advertising boards, TV rooms and lounge areas are common. Alcohol may be banned.

Reservations are advised during the high season, when there may be a three-night limit. Get further information from HI/ AYH (☎ 202-783-6161, fax 202-783-6171, hiayhserve@hiayh.org; www.hiayh.org), 733 15th St NW, Suite 840, Washington, DC 20005, or use their code-based reservation service at ☎ 800-909-4776 (you need the access code for the hostels to use this service, available from any HI/AYH office or listed in their handbook).

Independent hostels have comparable rates and conditions to HI/AYH hostels and may sometimes be better. They often have a few private single/double rooms available, sometimes with private bathrooms. Kitchen, laundry, notice board and TV facilities are available. *The Hostel Handbook* by Jim Williams is a 66-page listing of all hostels. It is available for $5, payable to the author at 722 St Nicholas Ave, New York, NY 10031 (☎ 212-926-7030, infohostel@aol.com). The Internet Guide to Hostelling (www.hostels.com) lists hostels throughout the world.

B&Bs

If you've only experienced B&Bs (Bed & Breakfasts) in Britain, then you're probably in for a surprise when you stay at US B&Bs. B&Bs all have breakfast included in their prices, but similarities stop there. A few establishments, with rooms in the $40s, may have clean but unexciting rooms with a shared bathroom. Most B&Bs are pricier and have rooms with private baths and, perhaps, amenities such as fireplaces, balconies and dining rooms with enticingly delicious breakfasts. Other places may be in historical buildings, quaint country houses or luxurious urban homes.

Many B&Bs fall in the $60 to $100 price range, but some go over $100. The best are distinguished by a friendly attention to detail by owner/hosts who can provide you with local information, contacts and a host of other amenities. One place I stayed in whipped up a homemade chocolate birthday cake for my wife – no extra charge. Another might dig out a bike for you to ride or lend you a pair of binoculars for a birdwatching trip. B&B hosts should, and usually do, lend a personal touch to your stay.

Most B&Bs in this book are fairly well established, but some may come and go quickly or are only seasonal, so call ahead to make sure the inn is still in operation; check the local chamber of commerce for new B&Bs that might have opened. Most B&Bs prefer reservations over walk-in customers, and many don't accept children, pets or smokers.

Hotels

The cheapest motel rooms are around $20 for a double, which is, perhaps, why there are few hostels in the Southwest and more in the coastal cities, where cheap motels are harder to find.

Motel and hotel prices vary tremendously in price from season to season. A hotel charging $40 for a double in the high season may drop to $25 in the low and may raise its rates to $55 for a special event when the town is overflowing. A $220-a-night luxury resort may offer special weekend packages for $79 in the low season. So be aware that the prices in this book are only an approximate guideline at best. Also, be prepared to add room tax to prices. Rates given are usually for one or two people; extra people are charged anywhere between $3 and $10 per person.

Although high seasons and special events (when prices may rise) are indicated in the text, you never know when something out of the ordinary may happen to ruin your plans. I pulled into St George, Utah, one afternoon when nothing much was supposed to be happening and found almost every hotel full and the remainder overpriced, all due to an Amway convention that had taken over several hundred rooms.

Children are often allowed to stay free with their parents, but rules vary. Some hotels allow free stays for children under 18, others allow only children under 12 and others may charge a few dollars per child. Call and inquire if traveling with a family.

The prices advertised by hotels are called 'rack rates' and are not written in stone. If you simply ask about any specials that might apply, you can often save quite a bit of money. Booking through a travel agent also saves you quite a bit of money as well. Members of AARP and AAA can qualify for a 'corporate' rate at several hotel chains.

Making phone calls directly from your hotel room is usually very expensive. Hotels charge around 75¢ for local calls vs 25¢ at a pay phone (though many motels allow free local calls). Long-distance rates may be inflated 100% to 200%!

Budget Motels Motels with $20 rooms are found especially in small towns on major highways and in the motel strips of some larger towns. A quick drive through one of these will yield a selection of neon-lit signs such as '$19.95 for Two.' Take your pick. A few towns that may currently be experiencing great popularity just won't have rock-bottom budget motels. These towns include Santa Fe, Taos, Moab and Sedona, where a room close to $40 is rock-bottom budget. Therefore, what I may call a bottom-end motel in one town may pass for a middle hotel in another. Utah, on the whole, has budget rooms starting in the mid $20s rather than around $20.

I list cheap and very basic motels as information for budget travelers, not because the rooms are anything special. They're often not! Rooms are usually small, beds may be soft or saggy, but the sheets are usually clean. A minimal level of cleanliness is maintained, but expect scuffed walls, atrocious decor, old furniture and strange noises from your shower. Even these places, however, normally have a private shower and toilet and a TV in each room. Most have air-conditioning and heat. Some of even the cheapest motels may advertise kitchenettes. These may cost a few dollars more but give you the chance to cook a simple meal for yourself if you are fed up with restaurants. Kitchenettes vary from a two-ring burner to a spiffy little minikitchen and may or may not have utensils. If you plan on doing a lot of kitchenette cooking, carry your own set.

In smaller towns, I find cheap rooms to be acceptable 'mom-and-pop' type places, but in larger towns, the cheap motels may be in the least salubrious areas. Don't leave valuables out in your car and exercise caution. However, I've spent several months of nights in rock-bottom hotels and have never had serious problems. Budget travelers shouldn't shun these $20-a-night cheapies. Many readers may be thinking, 'Saggy beds? Strange shower noises? Twenty bucks? This guy's gotta be kidding!' Well, no, I'm not. These accommodations are out there for those who want them, but there are plenty of nicer places. Read on!

Motel & Hotel Chains There are many motel and hotel chains in the USA. These maintain a certain level of quality and style throughout the chain. It's partially true that 'If you've stayed in one, you've stayed in them all!' but, depending on location, there are certainly individual variations in both standards and, especially, prices. Some travelers like a particular chain and stay there repeatedly, generally receiving the level of comfort they've come to expect. These travelers should investigate the chain's frequent-guest program – discounts and guaranteed reservations are offered to faithful guests.

The cheapest national chain is Motel 6, and they are a fair value. Rooms are small and very bland, but the beds are usually OK, every room has a shower, table, TV and phone (local calls are free), free coffee is offered in the mornings and most properties have a swimming pool. Rooms start in the high $20s for a single in smaller towns, in the $30s and $40s in larger towns. They usually charge a flat $6 for each extra person.

Several motel chains compete with one another at the next price level, with rooms starting in the $30s in the smaller towns or in the $40s and $50s in larger or more popular places. The main difference between these chains and Motel 6 is that the rooms are larger. Beds are always reliably firm, decor may be a little more attractive, a 24-hour desk is often available and little extras like a light continental breakfast, cable or rental movies, a refrigerator, or a bathtub with your shower may be offered. If these sorts of things are worth

Gas, Food, Lodging

When coming into a city on the highway you often see signs that say 'Gas Food Lodging' followed by something like 'Next Three Exits.' Many times these exits will lead you to strips of chain motels, fast-food restaurants and gas stations with small grocery stores; they don't necessarily lead to the city center. If you just want a bite to eat, a few hours of sleep, and a quick hop back onto the road, these establishments provide a cheap alternative to downtown and a bit of true Americana. ■

an extra $10 or $15 a night, then you'll be happy with the Super 8 Motels, Days Inn or Econo Lodge and the less-common Budget Host motels. Not all of these have pools, however – Super 8 Motels frequently lack a pool.

Stepping up to chains with rooms in the $45 to $90 range (depending on location), you'll find noticeably nicer rooms; cafes, restaurants or bars may be on the premises or adjacent to them; and the swimming pool may be indoors with a spa or exercise room also available. The Best Western chain consistently has properties in almost every town of any size and offers good rooms in this price range. Often they are the best available in a given town. Less widespread but also good are the Comfort Inns, Sleep Inns and Fairfields by Marriott. Both the Holiday Inn and Ramada Inn chains now have midpriced 'Express' hotels that are comparable to the Best Westerns and Comfort Inns. Rodeway Inns fall at the lower end of this category.

Private Hotels There are, of course, non-chain establishments in these price ranges. Some of them are funky historical hotels, full of turn-of-the-century furniture. Others are privately run establishments that just don't want to be a part of a chain. In smaller towns, complexes of cabins are available – these often come complete with fireplace, kitchen and an outdoor area with trees and maybe a stream a few steps away.

Another choice is self-contained condo-units, which are apartments (flats) with kitchen and laundry facilities. They often have two or more bedrooms, and are designed for longer stays for groups or families. These places don't always have hotel services such as daily maids.

Top-End Hotels Full-service hotels, with bellhops and doormen, restaurants and bars, exercise rooms and saunas, room service and concierge, are found in the main cities almost exclusively. If you feel like it, splurge on one when you hit the big urban areas because they are otherwise few and far between.

Lodges
In national parks, you can either camp or stay in park lodges operated as concessions. Lodges are often rustic-looking but are usually quite comfortable inside. Restaurants are on the premises, and tour services are often available. National park lodges are not cheap, with most rooms going for around $100 or more for a double during the high season, but they are your only option if you want to stay inside the park without camping. A lot of people want to do that, so many lodges are fully booked months in advance. Want a room the day after tomorrow? Call anyway – you might be very lucky and hit on a cancellation. But your best bet for national park lodges, especially in the high season, is to make reservations months ahead.

Resorts & Guest Ranches
Luxury resorts and dude ranches really require a stay of several days to be appreciated and are often destinations in themselves. Guests at a luxury resort can start the day with a round of golf, then continue with a choice of tennis, massage, horseback riding, shopping, beauty treatments, swimming, sunbathing, hot tubbing, drinking and dancing. Guest ranches are even more like 'whole vacations,' with busy schedules of horseback riding and maybe cattle roundups, rodeo lessons, cookouts and other Western activities. Ranches in the desert lowlands may close in summer, while those in the mountains may close in winter or convert into skiing centers.

There is decent skiing in all three Southwestern states, with Utah definitely offering the best. Skiing resorts may charge $200 or more for a condo in mid-season; prices drop to less than half in the snowless summer.

Reservations
The cheapest bottom-end places may not accept reservations, but at least you can call them and see if they have a room, which they'll often hold for an hour or two.

Chain hotels take reservations days or months ahead. Normally, you have to give a credit card number to hold the room. If you don't show and don't call to cancel, you will be charged the first night's rental. Cancellation policies vary – some let you cancel at no charge 24 hours or 72 hours in advance; others are less forgiving. Find out about cancellation penalties when you book. Also make sure to let the hotel know if you plan on a late arrival – many motels will rent your room if you haven't arrived or called by 6 pm. Chains often have a toll-free reservation number or website (see below), but their central reservation system might not be aware of local special discounts. Booking ahead, however, gives you the peace of mind of a guaranteed room when you arrive.

Some places, especially B&Bs and some cabins, won't accept credit cards and want a check as a deposit before they'll reserve a room.

Motel Chains The chains with widespread representation in the Southwest are listed below. US chains with very few hotels in the Southwest are excluded.

Best Western	☎ 800-528-1234
www.bestwestern.com	
Budget Host	☎ 800-283-4678
www.budgethost.com	
Comfort Inn	☎ 800-228-5150
www.comfortinn.com	
Days Inn	☎ 800-329-7466
www.daysinn.com	
Econo Lodge	☎ 800-553-2666
www.econolodge.com	
Fairfield Inn by Marriott	☎ 800-228-2800
www.fairfieldinn.com	
Holiday Inn	☎ 800-465-4329
www.holiday-inn.com	
Howard Johnson	☎ 800-654-2000
www.hojo.com	
Motel 6	☎ 800-466-8356
Ramada Inn	☎ 800-272-6232
www.ramada.com	
Quality Inn	☎ 800-228-5151
www.qualityinn.com	
Sleep Inn	☎ 800-753-3746
www.sleepinn.com	
Super 8 Motel	☎ 800-800-8000
www.super8motels.com	
Travelodge	☎ 800-578-7878
www.travelodge.com	

FOOD

Whatever your eating preference, you'll be able to find it in the Southwest. From fast food to fancy French, it's all here.

This book's restaurant listings provide a good cross-section of possibilities for everybody. I don't stick to just the best, prize-winning places. I also list 24-hour restaurants (the food is basic but quite acceptable, especially if you need a 4 am breakfast or arrive late in town), all-you-can-eat joints for starving students on a tight budget, family restaurants with bland inexpensive American food, funky local places where townsfolk gather for breakfast, ice-cream parlors, restaurants with an interesting history and, of course, the various ethnic, Mexican, nouvelle Southwestern and uptown possibilities. I don't mention fast-food places, but you can count on every town having one or more, usually on the main drag, their neon-lit logos visible from many blocks away.

The predominant pleasure, for me at least, is Mexican (or New Mexican) cooking. Many authentic, inexpensive restaurants serve delicious Mexican fare. In small towns, your best choice is often between Mexican and American food – only in the bigger cities and resort areas will you find large varieties of ethnic dining and fine Continental cuisine. Here, I discuss only Southwestern food, but rest assured that you can eat Italian, Greek, Chinese, Thai, Indian, French, Japanese and less obvious ethnic choices such as Guatemalan, Russian or Hungarian. These other options are listed in the text.

Mexican food is often hot and spicy, but it doesn't have to be. If you don't like spicy food, go easy on the salsa and you'll find plenty to choose from (see the glossary below). There are distinct regional variations. In Arizona, Mexican food is of the Sonoran type, with dishes like *carne seca* being a specialty. Meals are usually served with refried beans, rice and flour or corn tortillas, and the chiles used are relatively mild. Tucsonans call their home the 'Mexican food capital of the universe,' which, although hotly contested by a few other towns, is a statement with some ring of truth to it.

New Mexican food is different from, but reminiscent of, Mexican food. Tortillas may be made from blue corn, pinto beans are served whole instead of refried, and *pozole* may replace rice. Chiles are used not so much as part of a condiment (like salsa) but more as an essential ingredient in almost every dish. Some can be eye-wateringly hot – ask your waiter for advice if you want a mild meal. One dish that is more likely to be found here than in other parts of the Southwest is *carne adobada*.

And then, of course, there's *nouvelle* Southwestern cuisine, an eclectic mix of Mexican and Continental (especially French) traditions that began to flourish in the 1970s. This is your chance to try innovative combinations such as chiles stuffed with lobster or barbecued duck tacos. But don't expect any bargains here. Mexican and New Mexican cooking is usually inexpensive; tack on nouvelle and you'll pay big bucks for your gourmet meal.

What about non-nouvelle Southwestern cooking? Head into one of the many steak houses and get a juicy slab of beef with a baked potato and beans. There won't be much here for a vegetarian dining companion.

Native American food is not readily available in restaurants. More often, you'll be able to sample it from food stands at state fairs, powwows, rodeos and other outdoor events in the region. The variety is quite limited. The most popular is fry bread (deep-fried cakes of flattened dough), which may be topped with honey or other delights. Navajo tacos are fry bread topped with a combination of beans, cheese, tomato, lettuce, onion or chile – and sometimes with ground beef.

Generally speaking, Arizona and New Mexico have the most Mexican and nouvelle Southwestern restaurants. Utah doesn't have a tradition of Mexican-influenced food. Here, the influence is mainly Mormon – good, old-fashioned American food like chicken, steak, potatoes and vegetables, homemade pies and ice cream. Salt Lake City, of course, is large and cosmopolitan enough to have a good range of ethnic restaurants.

Southwestern Food Glossary

The items listed below have regional variations – if you like Mexican food, part of the fun of traveling around the Southwest will be figuring out the variations.

burrito (or *burro*) – a soft flour tortilla folded around a choice of chicken, beef, chile, bean or cheese filling. A breakfast burrito is stuffed with scrambled eggs, potatoes and ham. (A burro is a large burrito.)

carne adobada – pork chunks marinated in spicy chile and herb sauce, then baked.

carne seca – beef that has been dried in the sun before cooking.

chile relleno – chile stuffed with cheese and deep-fried in a light batter.

chimichanga – a burrito that is deep-fried to make the tortilla crisp.

enchilada – a rolled corn tortilla stuffed with a choice of sour cream and cheese, beans, beef or chicken, and smothered with a red (or green) chile sauce and melted cheese.

fajitas – marinated beef or chicken strips, grilled with onions and bell peppers, and served with tortillas, salsa, beans and guacamole.

flauta – similar to a burrito but smaller and tightly rolled rather than folded, and then fried.

guacamole – mashed avocado seasoned with lime juice and cilantro, and optionally spiced with chopped chiles and other condiments.

huevos rancheros – fried eggs on a soft tortilla, covered with chile sauce and melted cheese, and served with beans.

menudo – spicy tripe soup – a hangover remedy.

mole – a mildly spicy, dark sauce of chiles flavored with a hint of chocolate, usually served with chicken.

nachos – tortilla chips covered with melted cheese and other toppings.

pozole – a corn stew (similar to hominy in other states). This may be spicy and have meat.

refried beans – a thick paste of mashed, cooked pinto beans fried with lard.

salsa – a cold dip or sauce of chopped chiles, pureed tomatoes, onions and other herbs and spices.

sopaipilla – deep-fried puff pastry served with honey as a dessert.

taco – a crispy, fried tortilla, folded in half and stuffed with a combination of beans, ground beef, chiles, onions, tomatoes, lettuce, grated cheese and guacamole.

tamale – slightly sweet corn dough *(masa)* stuffed with a choice of pork, beef, chicken, chile or olives (or nothing) and wrapped in a corn husk before being steamed.

tortilla – a pancake made of unleavened wheat or corn flour. They stay soft when baked, become crisp when fried, and form the basis of most Mexican dishes. Small pieces, deep-fried, become the crispy tortilla chips served with salsa as an appetizer (often at no extra cost) in many Mexican restaurants.

tostada – a flat (ie, open-faced) taco.

Meals

Usually served between about 6 and 10 am, standard American breakfasts are large and filling, often including eggs or an omelet, bacon, sausage or ham, fried potatoes, toast with butter and jam and coffee or tea. Continental breakfasts are often pale imitations of their European counterparts and can be as simple as coffee with toast or a donut. Some hotels include a continental breakfast in their rates, but don't expect anything fancy in most of them.

Lunch is available between 11 am and 2 pm. One strategy for enjoying good restaurants on a budget is to frequent them for lunch, when inexpensive fixed-price specials are common. Many towns have American or ethnic restaurants (particularly Chinese and Indian) with all-you-can-eat buffet lunches for about $5 – a good deal for the impecunious.

Dinners, served anytime between about 5 and 10 pm, are more expensive but often very reasonably priced, and portions are usually large. Specials may also be available, but they will usually be more expensive than lunch specials. Some of the better restaurants require reservations.

DRINKS
Nonalcoholic

Restaurants provide customers with free ice water (tap water is safe to drink). All the usual flavors of soft drinks are available, although you may be asked to accept Coke instead of Pepsi and vice versa. Many restaurants offer milk or juices; a

few have a wide variety of fruit juices. British travelers should remember that 'lemonade' is a lemon-sugar-ice water mix rather than the carbonated variety. (If you want the fizzy kind, ask for a Sprite or Seven-Up, mate.)

Coffee is served much more often than tea. Most restaurants offer several free coffee refills to customers eating a meal. Drinkers of English-style tea will be disappointed. Tea is usually a cup of hot water with a tea bag next to it – milk is not normally added but a slice of lemon often is. Herb teas are offered in better restaurants and coffee shops.

Alcoholic

The laws for obtaining alcoholic drinks vary from state to state and are outlined in the introductions to each state.

Bland and boring 'name brand' domestic beers are available everywhere alcohol is sold. Most stores, restaurants and bars also offer much tastier but lesser known local brews, some of which I mention in the text. These may cost more than a Bud, but I think they are worth it. Imported beers are also easily available and, although a little more expensive, offer a wider choice of flavors than domestic brands. Mexican beers, of course, are easy to find everywhere, but UK, European, Canadian and Australian brews are also common.

Wine drinkers will find that Californian wines compete well with their European and Australian counterparts. For those interested in experimenting, there are little-known wineries in Arizona and New Mexico. A few of these may offer tours and wine tasting and are mentioned in the text.

Alcohol & Drinking Age

In all three states, persons under the age of 21 (minors) are prohibited from consuming alcohol. Carry a driver's license or passport as proof of age to enter a bar, order alcohol at a restaurant or buy alcohol. Servers have the right to ask to see your ID and may refuse service without it. Minors are not allowed in bars and pubs, even to order nonalcoholic beverages. Unfortunately, this means that most dance clubs are also off-limits to minors, although a few clubs have solved the under-age problem with a segregated drinking area. Minors are, however, welcome in the dining areas of restaurants where alcohol is served.

ENTERTAINMENT
Cinemas
The drive-in cinema that was once part of US culture is now a thing of the past. Today, just about every town of any size has multiscreen cinemas showing a variety of first-run Hollywood flicks on two to eight screens. Only the bigger towns have one or two cinemas screening foreign, alternative or underground films.

Bars
In small Southwestern towns, a bar might be the best place in town to have a beer, meet some locals, shoot a game of pool or listen to a country & western band. Patrons usually take an interest upon hearing a foreign accent, so if you have one, this is a good opportunity to meet people. Bars in bigger towns offer anything from big TV screens showing sporting events to live music of various genres.

Theater & Performances
The main cultural centers are mentioned under Arts in the Facts about the Southwest chapter. In addition, smaller towns may have local amateur theatrical performances. These include Indian pageants, Mormon pageants, vaudeville shows with audience participation (boo the villain, cheer the hero), mystery crime weekends (where a hotel becomes the scene of a hideous 'crime' and guests are both suspects and sleuths) as well as standard dramatic performances.

SPECTATOR SPORTS
Sports in the USA developed separately from the rest of the world, and baseball (with its clone, softball), American football and basketball dominate the sports scene, both for spectators and participants. Football and basketball, in particular, are

quite popular. Both are sponsored by high schools and universities, which gives them a community foundation that reinforces their popularity. Basketball has the additional advantages of needing only limited space and equipment, making it a popular pastime among inner-city residents. Soccer has made limited inroads, and remains a relatively minor diversion.

The Southwest has a few nationally ranked teams playing the big three US professional sports. Tickets for these events are very hard to get, although you might be lucky. Scalpers sell overpriced tickets outside the stadiums before a game. The only Southwestern major league football team is the Arizona Cardinals of Phoenix. A new major league baseball team, the Arizona Diamondbacks of Phoenix, joined the league in 1998. Several major league baseball teams come from the wintry north in February and March for training seasons in the warm climate of Arizona (see sidebar).

Professional basketball is better represented with the Phoenix Suns (men) and Phoenix Mercury (women) and the Utah Jazz (out of Salt Lake City). College basketball is always popular – fans seem to enjoy watching the students as much as the pros. Currently, the University of Arizona Wildcats (from Tucson) are the highest ranked Southwestern team, consistently placing among the top 25 college teams in the nation; they won the national college championship in 1997.

Rodeo is popular in the Southwest – after all, rodeo as a paying spectator sport started here. From late spring to early fall, there are rodeos almost every week somewhere in the Southwest. Rodeo circuits sponsored by the Professional Rodeo Cowboy Association (PRCA) draw competitors from many western states.

Phoenix, as befits the Southwest's biggest city, has several other professional spectator sports including two ice hockey teams (a surprise in the desert!) – the Coyotes and the Roadrunners – as well as horse, greyhound and car racing tracks. Golf tournaments, bicycle races and other events are listed in the Sports section under Special Events.

Last, but by no means least, are winter spectator sports. Salt Lake City will be hosting the 2002 Winter Olympics (see sidebar).

SHOPPING

The main items of interest to travelers are Indian, Hispanic and Southwestern arts and crafts. Often, the dividing line between traditional tribal or Hispanic crafts and Southwestern art is a hazy one, with the latter often being heavily influenced by the former. Tribal crafts, too, have changed somewhat in response to what travelers want to buy.

Buying Indian crafts on reservations, directly from the makers, is often substantially cheaper than buying in off-reservation

gift shops. However, the latter afford the buyer a much greater selection and, in the best stores, knowledgeable sales staff who have chosen only the finest quality work and can tell you about it. Buying from roadside stands in reservations can be fun, and you know that you are avoiding the middleman, but it's definitely a case of 'buyer beware' – the quality will vary tremendously.

Various tribes are especially known for particular crafts, though, again, there is much overlap between them. Just about all of them make beautiful jewelry, for example. Navajo weavings are highly sought after (see sidebars 'Navajo Weaving' in the Northeastern Arizona chapter and 'Rug Auction' in Northwestern New Mexico). The Hopis are famed for their kachinas (see that sidebar in Northeastern Arizona). The Zuni are accomplished silversmiths and make wonderful

---

Major League Baseball Spring Training: Cactus League

Before the start of each season, major league baseball teams spend March in Arizona and Florida auditioning new players, practicing and playing games. Although for established players spring training is only a chance to get back into shape, for fans it is a unique opportunity to see big leaguers in small, intimate parks.

Eight teams play spring training baseball in southern Arizona's Cactus League: the Anaheim Angels, Chicago Cubs, Colorado Rockies, Milwaukee Brewers, Oakland Athletics, San Diego Padres, San Francisco Giants and Seattle Mariners. The Chicago White Sox and the newly formed Arizona Diamondbacks were added in 1998. The remaining teams belong to Florida's Grapefruit League. The Cleveland Indians originated the Cactus League in 1947, but eventually left for Florida in 1993; the Chicago Cubs, on the other hand, have spent spring in Arizona since 1952.

In contrast to regular season games, Cactus League games are relaxed and unofficial, tickets are about half the price, and there aren't any bad seats or long lines. The baseball parks are quite small, with attendance averaging 8000, in contrast to the 30,000-plus crowds commonly encountered at teams' hometown stadiums. This brings players into close range, and many are willing to sign autographs, pose for photographs and talk with fans. The intimacy of the parks adds another dimension to the game – sound; fans can actually hear players sliding into home and talking to each other on the field, and the umpire calling strikes and balls. Players are most accessible during team practices, which begin in mid-February and are free and open to the public.

A recent increase in the popularity of spring training has driven up ticket prices slightly; tickets range from $6 to $14 for stadium seats, but open lawn seating is often available for $4. While the attendance at each game is often near capacity, you can usually get tickets at the box office before each game, and scalping, an adjunct sport, is legal more than 200 feet from the ballpark. For schedules and advance ticket information, call the Phoenix Chamber of Commerce at ☎ 520-827-4700, ext 3019, or 800-283-6372, or call each team's box office beginning January 1. – *Rhawn Denniston*

Gearing Up for 2002

Since 1966, Salt Lake City has put in bids to host the Winter Olympics. The city's persistence has been rewarded with the 2002 Winter Olympic Games. At press time, the city was still involved in major reconstruction and maintenance projects on downtown streets and interstates that cross through town, causing delays and detours to locals and visitors alike, so prepare for this if visiting in the years prior to the games.

Although Salt Lake City is the host, many of the events will be held in several surrounding towns, particularly Park City, which is the US Olympic Team's headquarters. Here, the new Utah Winter Sports Park will be able to accommodate 20,000 spectators for the bobsled, luge and ski-jumping events (see Park City, in the Wasatch Mountains Region chapter, for information about how the public can try these facilities). Park City Mountain Resort will have the giant slalom and snowboard events, and the Deer Valley Resort will be the site of the slalom, freestyle and mogul skiing competitions.

In Salt Lake City itself, the 15,000-seat Delta Center will host the ice hockey games and figure skating. Curling will be held at the Cottonwood Heights Ice Arena, in the southeastern suburbs, where 2000 spectators can be accommodated. In the southwestern suburb of Kearns, the open-air Oquirrh Park Skating Oval will be enclosed by the year 2000 and will have a capacity of 6000 spectators for the speed-skating events.

Near Ogden, north of Salt Lake City, the Snowbasin Ski Area will have room for 36,000 spectators watching the giant slalom and super g racing.

Soldier Hollow, in Wasatch State Park near Heber City, will be the busiest venue during the Olympic Winter Games as the scene for 16 events, including 6 for biathlon, 10 for cross-country skiing and 2 for the skiing portions of Nordic combined.

While 2002 is still a ways off, hotels are already taking reservations and construction of facilities will continue. The Games will be held from February 8 to 24 and tickets will go on sale about a year before that. At press time, there was no information on ticket sales, though tickets are estimated to range in price from $25 for high-capacity events, like cross-country, to $300 for the opening and closing ceremonies and good seats at ice hockey. Average prices will be $50 and it is estimated that 1.7 million tickets will be available for all the events combined. Ticket prices will include shuttle buses for spectators. For more information contact the Salt Lake Olympic Organizing Committee (☎ 801-322-2002), 215 S State St, No 2002, Salt Lake City, UT 84111, or the Salt Lake City Convention & Visitors Bureau (☎ 801-521-2822, fax 801-355-9323, slcvb@saltlake.org), 90 S West Temple, Salt Lake City, UT 84101. The Olympic Organizing Committee has a detailed website at www.slc2002.org. ■

fetishes (see the Zuni Art sidebar in the Zuni Pueblo section of Northwestern New Mexico). Most of the New Mexican pueblos produce distinctive ceramics and pots, which vary from tribe to tribe. The Tohono O'odham of southern Arizona and the Jicarilla Apache of northwestern New Mexico are both famed for their intricate basketwork, which requires many days of labor and is therefore not cheap.

Hispanic art includes religious paintings and altarpieces called *retablos*, brightly painted handmade wooden furniture, metal work (especially tin, copper and wrought iron) and fine art such as paintings and sculptures.

Off the reservations, gift shops and trading posts in all the major and many of the smaller cities have good selections of Indian and Hispanic crafts and their spinoff, Southwestern Art. This can vary from tacky to breathtaking, from purely utilitarian to completely decorative. Themes include Southwestern wildlife and plants (cacti in Arizona, chile peppers in New Mexico), the landscape, Native American people and their legends, cowboy art (especially bronzes and oil paintings) and much more. Towns renowned for art galleries include Scottsdale, Sedona, Tubac and Bisbee in Arizona, Santa Fe and Taos in New Mexico, and (to a lesser extent) Moab in Utah. However, every town will have Southwestern art galleries – see the Shopping sections throughout the book.

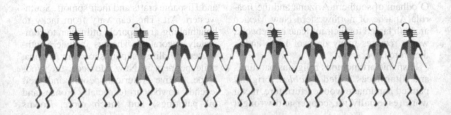

Outdoor Activities

For many of the millions of people who visit the Southwest, especially for the first time, the sheer scale and grandeur of the scenery viewed from vehicle windows and scenic overlooks is reward enough in itself. Locals, however, know that the Southwest offers a multitude of world-class outdoor activities, some of which, such as skiing or boating, may not be the first thing that comes to mind when one thinks about desert states. This chapter highlights the myriad outdoor activities possible in the Southwest.

General Books & Resources

Of the thousands of books about hiking, climbing, river running, canyoneering, bicycling and other activities in the Southwest, I mention some general ones in this chapter. Books about a specific place are mentioned in the appropriate parts of the text. Most of the books have extensive bibliographies. Outdoor equipment stores as well as bookstores will have many of these and other books.

Adventuring in Arizona by John Annerino gives a selection of hikes, car tours, river expeditions, climbs and canyoneering adventures all around the state. *Utah's National Parks: Hiking, Camping and Vacationing in Utah's Canyon Country* by Ron Adkison is a thorough and useful book with good historical background text.

Many outdoor activities are described on the Internet. One of the most wide-ranging sites is Great Outdoors Recreation Pages at www.gorp.com. For information about activities and permits in national parks, browse the National Park Service website at www.nps.gov (with links to every park). Other lands are managed by the US Forest Service, Bureau of Land Management (BLM) and state wildlife and fisheries departments. The Federal Government has a website – www.recreation.gov with detailed information about fed-

erally owned public lands, including forests and BLM areas. See Useful Organizations (in Facts for the Visitor) for more details.

HIKING & BACKPACKING

If you have transportation, you can find perfect hiking and backpacking at any time of year. When highland trails are blanketed in snow, southern Arizona delights in balmy weather, and when temperatures hit the hundreds during Phoenix summers, cooler mountain trails beckon. Utah and New Mexico are generally higher in elevation than southern Arizona. Parts of those states, however, such as the parks near St George in southwestern Utah, offer pleasant hiking possibilities even in mid-winter. Of course, hardy and experienced backpackers can don cross-country skis or snowshoes and head out into the mountains in winter as well.

Planning

Perhaps the most attractive backpacking trip for many visitors is the descent into the Grand Canyon. This trip in particular requires careful advance planning because the number of backpackers is limited by the number of campsites available. Reservations are essential for most months of the year and details are given in the Grand Canyon chapter. Backpacking in Canyonlands National Park is also by reservation in the busy spring and fall months. Visitors without reservations may want to consider the less heavily used Bryce Canyon National Park for a backpacking trip in canyon country during the spring to fall months.

Visitors can also hike and backpack in many other public areas, especially in national forests, BLM lands and state parks. Addresses and phone numbers of individual state parks and USFS or BLM ranger stations are given in the text. These places are less famous than the national parks and usually there is no problem with just showing up and going backpacking. These areas are generally less restricted for wilderness camping than the national parks.

Books

Hiking the Southwest by Dave Ganci covers hikes in Arizona, New Mexico and west Texas. For suggestions about hiking the desert as safely and comfortably as possible, read Ganci's *Desert Hiking* and *Desert Survival.* Falcon Press publishes a series of hiking guides including *The Hiker's Guide to Arizona* by Stewart Aitchison and Bruce Grubbs, *The Hiker's Guide to New Mexico* by Laurence Parent, and *The Hiker's Guide to Utah* by Dave Hall. *Arizona Trails: 100 Hikes in Canyon and Sierra* by David Mazel is also good. There are hundreds of books about smaller areas, covering one national park or mountain range, for example. The best are mentioned in the text.

Maps

A good map is essential for any hiking trip. NPS visitor centers and USFS ranger stations usually stock topographical maps that cost from $2 to $6. Apart from these, local bookstores and outdoor equipment stores often sell maps. There are many free planning maps available from the national parks that may not be adequate for the trip itself.

Longer hikes require two types of maps: USGS quadrangles and USFS maps. To order a map index and price list, contact the US Geological Survey, PO Box 25286, Denver, CO 80225. For general information on maps, see the Facts for the Visitor chapter; for information regarding specific maps of forests, wilderness areas or national parks, see the appropriate geographic entry.

Minimizing Your Impact

Backcountry areas are composed of fragile environments and cannot support an inundation of human activity, especially any insensitive and careless activity. A new code of backcountry ethics is evolving to deal with the growing numbers of people in the wilderness. Most conservation organizations and hikers' manuals have their own set of backcountry codes, all of which outline the same important principles: minimizing the impact on the land, leaving no trace and taking nothing but photographs and memories. To avoid erosion and, in many desert areas, damage to the cryptobiotic crust (see the sidebar 'The Desert's Delicate Skin' in Southeastern Utah), stay on the main trail.

Wilderness Camping

Camping in undeveloped areas is rewarding for its peacefulness but raises special concerns. Take care to ensure that the area you choose can comfortably support your presence, and leave the surroundings in at least as good condition as when you arrived. The following list of guidelines should help:

- Camp below timberline, since alpine areas are generally more fragile. Good campsites are found, not made. Altering a site shouldn't be necessary.
- Camp at least 200 feet (70 adult steps) away from the nearest lake, river or stream.
- Bury human waste in cat holes dug 6 to 8 inches deep, at least 200 feet from water, camp or trails. The salt and minerals in urine attract deer; use a tent-bottle (funnel attachments are available for women) if you are prone to middle-of-the-night calls by Mother Nature. Camouflage the cat hole when finished.
- Use soaps and detergents sparingly or not at all, and never allow these things to enter streams or lakes. When washing yourself (a backcountry luxury, not necessity), lather up (with biodegradable soap) and rinse yourself with cans of water 200 feet away from your water source. Scatter dishwater after removing all food particles.
- Some folks recommend carrying a lightweight stove for cooking and using a lantern instead of a campfire.
- If a fire is allowed and appropriate, dig out the native topsoil and build a fire in the hole. Gather sticks no larger than an adult's wrist from the ground. Do not snap branches off live,

dead, or downed trees. Pour wastewater from meals around the perimeter of the campfire to prevent the fire from spreading, and thoroughly douse it before leaving or going to bed.

- Burn cans to remove odors, then take them from the ashes and pack them out.

- Pack out what you pack in, including all trash. Make an effort to carry out trash left by others, as well.

Safety

The major forces to be reckoned with while hiking and camping are the weather (which is uncontrollable) and your own frame of mind. Be prepared for unpredictable weather, such as heavy downpours that can cause deadly flash floods (see sidebar). In the Southwest, the most frequent weather problem is the heat. A gallon of water per person per day is the recommended minimum in hot weather; more if you are working up a real sweat. This will have to be carried in waterless areas. Sun protection (brimmed hats, dark glasses and sunblock)

are all basic parts of a desert hiker's equipment. A positive attitude is helpful in any situation. If a hot shower, comfortable mattress, and clean clothes are essential to your well-being, don't head out into the wilderness for five days – stick to day hikes.

The most stringent safety measures suggest never hiking alone, but solo travelers should not be discouraged, especially if they value solitude. The important thing is to always let someone know where you are going and how long you plan to be gone. Use sign-in boards at trailheads or ranger stations. Travelers looking for hiking companions can inquire or post notices at ranger stations, outdoors stores, campgrounds, and youth hostels.

People with little hiking or backpacking experience should not attempt to do too much too soon or they might end up being nonhikers for the wrong reasons. Know your limitations, know the route you are planning to take and pace yourself accordingly. Remember, there is absolutely nothing

Flash Floods – A Deadly Danger in the Desert

A flash flood can occur when a very large amount of rain falls suddenly and quickly. This is most common in the Southwest during the 'monsoon months' of mid-July to early September, although heavy precipitation in late winter can also cause these floods. They occur with little warning and reach a raging peak in a matter of minutes. Rainfall occurring miles away is funneled into a normally dry wash or canyon from the surrounding mountains, and a wall of water several feet high can appear seemingly out of nowhere. There are few warning signs – perhaps some distant rain clouds – and if you see a flash flood coming, the only recommendation is to reach higher ground as quickly as possible.

A swiftly moving wall of water is much stronger than it appears. At only a foot high, it will easily knock over a strong adult. A 2-foot-high flood sweeps away vehicles. Floods carry a battering mixture of rocks and trees and can be extremely dangerous. August 1997 was a particularly bad month for flash floods. One event, in Antelope Canyon on the Arizona/Utah border, killed 11 hikers. Another, near Kingman, Arizona, was strong enough to derail an Amtrak passenger train. In a third, several hundred locals and visitors were evacuated by helicopter from the village of Supai in the Havasupai Indian Reservation. The following September, a Capitol Reef National Park ranger had his pickup truck swept away and completely submerged in a flood (the ranger jumped out in time). There were many other flash floods during this period.

Especially during the monsoon season, heed local warnings and weather forecasts, and avoid camping in sandy washes and canyon bottoms – the likeliest spots for flash floods. Campers and hikers are not the only victims; every year foolhardy drivers attempt to drive across flooded roads and are swept away. Flash floods usually subside fairly quickly. A road that is closed will often be passable later on the same day. ■

The Arizona Trail

Proposed by Flagstaff hiker and teacher Dale Shelwater in the mid 1980s, this 750-mile trail running from the Mexican border to the Utah state line is finally becoming a reality. About 400 miles of the trail have been completed and almost 200 more are open, though some work such as signing remains to be done. The rest is being planned, and it is hoped that the entire trail will be finished and signed by the year 2000.

Meanwhile, those parts of the trail that are open are quite an adventure because no trail guide, as such, exists. Bits and pieces of the trail are described in various hiking books, but the best single source of information is the Arizona Trail Association (☎ 602-252-4794, ata@aztrail.org, www.primenet.com/~aztrail/), PO Box 36736, Phoenix, AZ 85067. There are 44 sections of trail, each with a trailhead that can be reached by vehicle, and the ATA has planning maps and information sheets about those sections that are open.

The trail varies from desert to pine forest and from canyon to mountain. (A side trail reaches Arizona's highest point, Humphreys Peak, 12,633 feet.) Depending on the time of year, there is always a part of the trail where weather conditions are ideal for hiking. Parts of the trail, such as crossing the Grand Canyon via the Bright Angel and North Kaibab Trail, can be quite busy and require advance permits, while other areas are remote and lightly traveled, and don't require a permit. There's something for everyone. ∎

wrong with turning back or not going as far as you originally planned. Beginners should refer to one of the many books available about how to go backpacking. Chris Camden's *Backpacker's Handbook* is a beefy collection of tips for the trail. More candid is *A Hiker's Companion*, by Cindy Ross and Todd Gladfelter, who hiked 12,000 miles before sitting down to write. *How to Shit in the Woods* is Kathleen Meyer's explicit, comic and useful manual on wilderness 'toilet' training for adults.

Canyoneering

At its simplest, canyoneering is visiting canyons under your own power. A canyoneer's adventures can vary from a pleasant day hike to a multi-day walking excursion stretching the length of a canyon. Longer trips may involve rock climbing with ropes, swimming across pools and down waterfalls, and camping; many experienced canyoneers bring inflatable mattresses to float their backpacks on as well as to sleep on. Some canyon areas designated as 'wilderness' are very remote, as no development is allowed. Canyoneers must reach the edges of these areas by dirt roads and then continue on foot over poor or barely existent trails to canyon bottoms.

Arizona, the Grand Canyon State, along with its northern neighbor Utah, provides some of the best canyoneering anywhere. The first canyoneers in the huge gashes of the Colorado Plateau were Native Americans, whose abandoned cliff-dwellings and artifacts mark their passage. Adventurers and explorers in the 19th and 20th centuries sought to unravel the many secrets of the canyons. The most famous was John Wesley Powell, the one-armed geologist who led the first boat descent of the Colorado River.

Today the Grand Canyon is the most popular place for canyoneering, with thousands of hikers descending from the rim every year. Many other canyons, however, are more difficult to access and provide uncrowded and equally scenic challenges. One of the most remote and lovely areas is the rarely visited **Sycamore Canyon Wilderness**, about 16 miles due west of the heavily traveled Oak Creek Canyon near Sedona. It takes three days to hike, scramble and wade the canyon's 25-mile length; Coconino National Forest rangers in Sedona or Flagstaff can provide information. In the same forest, the **Wet Beaver Creek Wilderness** (east of Camp Verde) provides an even more challenging three-day canyoneering adventure; you'll need to swim through more than 20 ponds, so be sure to bring a flotation device.

Then there are the slot canyons, hundreds of feet deep and only a few feet wide. These must be negotiated during dry months, because summer monsoon rains can cause deadly flash floods that may raise the height of the river by many feet in mere minutes. Always check with the appropriate rangers for weather and safety information. The **Paria Canyon**, a tributary of the Colorado River on the Arizona-Utah border, includes the amazing Buckskin Gulch, a stretch of canyon 12 miles long, hundreds of feet deep and only 15 feet wide for most of its length.

Adventures in these and other canyons are described in Annerino's *Adventuring in Arizona*. One of the greatest canyoneering challenges, however, is to get topo maps and set out on your own to explore side canyons of the better-known areas, or to find new canyons that aren't described in guidebooks.

BICYCLING & MOUNTAIN BIKING
As with hiking and backpacking, perfect cycling weather can be found at any time of year if you travel to different parts of the Southwest. Southern Arizona is a perfect winter destination, and Tucson is considered a bicycle-friendly city with many bike lanes and some parks with bike trails. In spring and fall, Moab in southeastern Utah is an incredibly popular destination for mountain bikers wanting to spin their wheels on the many scenic slickrock trails in that area. In the searing heat of summer, the high elevations around Brian Head in southwestern Utah attract an increasing number of bikers looking for a scenic destination that beats the heat. More details about these places are given in the text.

Local bike shops in all major and many minor cities rent bikes and provide local maps and information. Bicycle shops are listed in the text. Most bicycle rentals automatically come with a helmet. State and city visitor information offices and chambers of commerce often have brochures about trails in their areas.

Books
Mountain Bike Rides of the West by Dennis Coello details 20 classic tours of which a dozen are in the Southwest. Also look for *Bicycle Touring Arizona* and *Bicycle Touring Utah* from the same author. Also see *Mountain Biking in Northern New Mexico* by Craig Martin, *The Mountain Bikers Guide to Arizona* by Sarah Bennett and *The Mountain Bikers Guide to Utah* by Gregg Bromka.

Transporting Your Bike
Bicycles can be transported by air. You *can* disassemble them and put them in a bike bag or box, but it's much easier simply to wheel your bike to the check-in desk, where it should be treated as a piece of baggage, although airlines often charge an additional

fee. You may have to remove the pedals and front tire so that it takes up less space in the aircraft's hold. Check any regulations or restrictions on the transportation of bicycles with the airline well in advance, preferably before you pay for your ticket. Remember that while some airlines welcome bicycles, others consider them a nuisance and do everything possible to discourage them.

You can also take bicycles on Greyhound buses and Amtrak trains, but again, check with them in advance. For full protection bicycles must be boxed.

Bikes are often allowed on metropolitan public transportation, but the number of buses or other types of transport able to accommodate bikes may be limited. Call the local transit authorities for information.

Safety

On the road, bicyclists are generally treated courteously by motorists. You may, though, encounter the occasional careless one who passes too closely or too fast (or both). Helmets should always be worn to reduce the risk of head injury; in most states they are required by law. Always keep at least one hand on the handlebars. Stay close to the edge of roads and don't wear anything, such as headphones, that can reduce your ability to hear. Bicyclists should always lock their bicycles securely and be cautious about leaving bags on the bike, particularly in larger towns or more touristed locations.

Bicyclists should carry at least a gallon of water and refill bottles at every opportunity. Dehydration is a major problem in the arid Southwest.

Laws & Regulations

Cycling has increased in popularity so much in recent years that concerns have risen over damage to the environment, especially from unchecked mountain biking. Know your environment and regulations before you ride.

Bikes are restricted from entering wilderness areas and some designated trails but may otherwise ride in NPS sites, state parks, national and state forests and BLM single-track trails. In many NPS sites, there are no bicycle trails and cyclists are limited to paved roads only. In other areas, off-road trails are shared with other users. Trail etiquette requires that cyclists yield to horses and hikers.

Bikes aren't allowed on interstate highways (with a few exceptions). In cities, obey traffic lights and signs and other road rules; yield to pedestrians; in downtown areas don't ride on the sidewalk unless there's a sign saying otherwise and don't ride two abreast unless in a cycle lane or path.

RIVER RUNNING

Although it is possible to run rivers privately, most visitors who want to go rafting will take a guided tour. Many companies run the Colorado River through the Grand Canyon – they are listed in that chapter. Most of these companies offer other rafting options on several other rivers in the Southwest and beyond. Not all rafting trips have to be white-water; many companies run scenic float trips. Trips through the Grand Canyon are multi-day affairs with camping on beaches. For half-day and one-day trips on the Colorado River in and beyond Canyonlands National Park, the Moab area has many companies, most of which do multi-day trips as well. See the Grand Canyon chapter and Moab for details. Other recommended river-running options include the Green and Yampa Rivers out of Vernal (see Northwestern Utah) and the Rio Grande out of Santa Fe and Taos.

Books

Rivers of the Southwest: A Boater's Guide to the Rivers of Colorado, New Mexico, Arizona and Utah by Fletcher Anderson and Ann Hopkinson (Pruett Publishing, 1987) is an introduction. There are several books about individual rivers.

BOATING

Despite its desert location, Arizona reputedly has more boats per capita than any other state. The main reason for this is the region's many dams, which form huge artificial lakes providing boaters with relief from summer heat. In addition, the rivers suitable for rafting are also often suitable for kayaking or canoeing, and many of the companies at the Grand Canyon and in Moab, Vernal, Santa Fe and Taos will either arrange guided kayaking or canoeing excursions or rent you the equipment and tell you where to go (this latter option is not available in the Grand Canyon where noncommercial private trips must be booked many years in advance). If you have a kayak or canoe with you, the visitor centers or chambers of commerce in those towns and others with access to water have information about good put-in spots.

Arizona's 'West Coast' is a series of dammed lakes on the lower Colorado River on the California/Arizona state line. These lakes are described in detail in the Western Arizona chapter. This is the lowest and hottest part of the Southwest and the lakes are thronged with boaters for much of the year. You can rent canoes, fishing boats, speed boats, water-skiing boats, jet skis and windsurfers at the marinas on those lakes. On the biggest lakes, especially Lake Powell in the Glen Canyon National Recreation Area and Lakes Mead and Mojave in the Lake Mead National Recreation Area, you can also rent houseboats that will sleep from six to 12 people and allow you to explore remote areas that are hard to reach on foot. Many smaller lakes throughout the Southwest offer at least basic fishing and rowing boat rentals. Details are given in the text.

Safety

The many lakes and marinas offer boat-rental opportunities to the general public, but many folks are not very knowledgeable about watercraft. Accidents, sometimes fatal, do happen. The main contributing factors to accidents include alcohol and speed – two things that don't mix. You should take the same precautions with alcohol as when you are driving a car. Have a designated sober person to pilot the boat if you are having a party. Check local regulations about speed limits – in some places you should not leave a wake. This not only limits your speed but also cuts down on erosion of the banks caused by waves.

Always use lifejackets, even if you know how to swim. If you have an accident, a bump on the head can render your swimming skills useless.

FISHING

The many popular boating lakes also give rise to excellent fishing. Frequent species caught in lakes include bass (striped, large-mouth and smallmouth), bluegill, catfish, crappie and walleye while river anglers go for a variety of trout and salmon. Fish hatcheries are used to stock many lakes and rivers and Southwestern fishing compares favorably with any landlocked area in the contiguous USA. Bass fishing is especially good and San Carlos Lake in Arizona and Elephant Butte Lake in New Mexico are two of the best bass-fishing lakes in the country. Although you can eat what you catch, you should check locally about limits in number and size as well as for possible health problems in some places. Many anglers practice 'catch and release.'

Fishing is regulated by the individual states rather than by the federal government and anglers require a state license for each state that they fish in. The exception is on Indian reservations, where tribal permits are normally required. Licenses are widely available from the Fish & Game departments of each state, as well as from numerous outdoor outfitting stores and guide services, and often in gas stations, marinas and state or national parks on or near good lakes and rivers. The cost of licenses varies from about $10 to $50 depending on how many days you want to fish (normally, licenses are available for one day, one year, and various intermediate lengths like a week or a season). Residents of each state get substantial discounts. In some federal areas, additional permits that cost a few dollars may be required, such as 'Habitat Improvement Stamps.'

DOWNHILL SKIING & SNOWBOARDING

Southwestern mountain ranges have numerous resorts offering great opportunities for skiing as well as other snow-related sports. Facilities range from day-only ski areas to resorts that are self-contained mini-cities, from gentle slopes for the learner to trails that challenge the most expert skier.

Snowboarding has swept the nation's ski culture and taken on a following of its own. Many Southwestern ski areas are developing half-pipes, renting the necessary equipment in ski shops and offering introductory lessons. Most at least permit snowboarding (Taos is a notable exception). Snowboarders stand sideways, strapped to a board 4 or 5 feet long, to cruise down the mountains. The motion is comparable to surfing or skateboarding rather than skiing.

The best skiing is undoubtedly in Utah, which boasts 'The Greatest Snow on Earth.' It's good enough that Salt Lake City and nearby towns will host the 2002 Winter Olympics. Pick up a free copy of the *Utah Winter Vacation Planner* for details of the 14 main areas, most of which are near Salt Lake City or in the Wasatch Mountains.

The skiing in New Mexico, especially in the mountains of northern New Mexico and Ski Apache near Ruidoso, is generally pretty good. Taos is considered the best area for its challenging runs and low-key atmosphere.

Arizona has four ski areas, with Snowbowl near Flagstaff and Sunrise on the White Mountain Apache Reservation near Pinetop-Lakeside considered the best. There's also a small area in Williams. Mt Lemmon near Tucson is the southernmost ski area in the USA. Snow conditions in Arizona are more variable than in other states.

Planning

The skiing season lasts from about late November to early April, depending on the area (some have shorter seasons). State tourist offices have information on resorts (Utah's *Winter Vacation Planner* is especially good), and travel agents can arrange full-package tours that include transport and accommodations. Many of the resorts are close to towns so it's quite feasible to travel on your own to the slopes for the day and return to town at night. If you have travel insurance make sure that it covers you for winter sports.

Ski areas are often well equipped with accommodations, eateries, shops, entertainment venues, child-care facilities (both on and off the mountain) and transport. In fact, it's possible to stay a week at some of the bigger places without leaving the slopes.

Equipment rentals are available at or near even the smallest ski areas, though renting equipment in a nearby town can be cheaper if you can transport it to the slopes.

For information on skiing nationally contact the US Recreational Ski Association (☎ /fax 209-539-6332), PO Box 397, Springville, CA 93265. Recreational programs for handicapped people are offered by Disabled Sports USA (☎ 301-217-0960, fax 301-217-0968, TDD 301-217-0963, www.nas.com/~dsusa), 451 Hungerford Dr, Suite 100, Rockville, MD 20850. They have state branches across the country. Skiers 70 years of age and over can contact the 70+ Ski Club (☎ 518-346-5505, fax 518-346-5248, RTL70plus@aol.com), 1633 Albany St, Schenectady, NY 12304.

In the recommended *Skiing America* (World Leisure Corporation, Hampstead, NH), Charles Leocha has compiled facts and figures about the USA's big ski resorts. *Ski* and *Skiing* are year-round magazines available in most newsstands, airports and sporting-goods stores. *Snow Country* magazine ranks ski resorts in the US using criteria that include terrain, ski school, nightlife, lodging and dining.

Ski Schools

Visitors planning on taking lessons should rent equipment on the mountain since the price of a lesson usually includes equipment rentals, with no discount for having your own gear. Children's ski schools are popular places to stash the kids for a day, offering lessons, day-care facilities and providing lunch.

OTHER WINTER ACTIVITIES

Both cross-country skiing and snowmobiling are popular, and often conflict with one another. Anywhere that there is substantial snowfall, you'll find groomed tracks designed for both activities, and equipment rental readily available. Snowshoeing is another activity for which equipment rental is available in higher areas with lots of snow.

Lakes often freeze hard in the mountains, where both ice-skating and ice fishing are possible. Ice-skating is also featured in various towns with ice-skating rinks including, surprisingly, Tucson, Arizona, where a year-round indoor ice-skating rink remains open even when summer temperatures soar into the 100s°F.

Park City, Utah, the headquarters of the US Olympic ski team, is also one of the few places where you can try the Olympic sports of ski jumping, bobsledding and luge – details are given in the text.

BIRD WATCHING

The Southwest has a great variety of different habitats, which leads to many different species of birds. Southeastern Arizona, in particular, has great avian biodiversity with species from Mexico flying in to add to the many birds found in the deserts, mountains, forests and riparian zones of that area. This attracts avid birders from around the world. The Tucson Audubon Society is a great resource for this area. More information can be found in the Tucson & Southern Arizona and Southeastern Arizona chapters.

HORSEBACK RIDING

Cowboys and Indians, the Pony Express, stagecoaches, cattle drives and rodeo riding – horse legends are legion in the Southwest. This continues to the present day with Bob Baffert, the horse trainer from Nogales, Arizona, whose *Real Quiet* won the Kentucky Derby and Preakness Stakes of the USA's leading 'Triple Crown' horseraces in 1998 and came in second (literally by a nose) in the third race, the Belmont Stakes. (This was the closest that a horse has come to winning the 'Triple Crown' since 1978.)

OK. You probably aren't looking at winning the Derby, but horseback riding is a popular attraction in the Southwest. This ranges from one-hour rides for complete beginners (or experienced riders who just want to get on a horse again) to multi-night horsepacking trips with wranglers, cooks, guides and backcountry camping. Another possibility is staying at a ranch where the main activity is horseback riding on a daily basis, and the comforts of a bed and shower await at the end of the day.

Many towns have stables and offer horseback rides. In a few locations, such as on the South Rim of the Grand Canyon, only mules are available. During the winter, southern Arizonan towns such as Tucson, Phoenix and Wickenburg have delightful weather for riding. Wickenburg, especially, is known for its ranches. When the weather warms up, head up to Sedona and Pinetop-Lakeside in Arizona, Chama in New Mexico or Moab in Utah for horseback riding. More places are listed in the text.

ROCK CLIMBING

There are many rock-climbing areas, some of which have become quite famous, such as Mt Lemmon near Tucson and the Fischer Towers near Moab. Many of the red-rock national parks in southern Utah permit rock climbing. There is also good climbing in the Sedona area – in fact almost anywhere that there are mountains. Some cities, such as Flagstaff and Tucson, have indoor rock-climbing gyms where the public is welcome to practice for a small fee.

Outdoor equipment stores sell guidebooks, some for large areas and others covering a small local area. Some useful books include *Rock Climbing New Mexico & Texas* by Dennis R. Jackson, *Backcountry Rockclimbing: Southern Arizona* by Bob Kerry and *Wasatch Range: Classic Rock Climbs* by Stuart and Bret Ruckman.

HOT-AIR BALLOONING

Dozens of companies offer scenic hot-air balloon flights over many parts of the Southwest. Flights usually lift off in the calm morning air, drift for about an hour and finish with a traditional champagne brunch; costs are in the low $100s per person. Most companies can arrange flights on a day's notice, but flights may be canceled in windy weather and in summer.

Cities especially known for this activity include Albuquerque, with what may be the world's biggest hot-air ballooning festival held every October, as well as Tucson, Phoenix and Sedona in Arizona and Park City in Utah.

ROCKHOUNDING

Rockhounding – the searching for semi-precious or just plain pretty rocks, minerals and crystals – is a passion for some people in the Southwest. Tucson has an annual Gem & Mineral Show in February that is one of the biggest in the world. Also in Arizona, the area around Quartzsite is a famous gathering ground for hundreds of thousands of rockhounds and collectors during January and February.

Near Deming, New Mexico, Rockhound State Park is one of the few parks that not only permit collecting, but actually were established to allow rockhounds to search for their quarry. Most parks, such as the Petrified Forest National Park, famous for its fossilized wood specimens, do not permit any collecting at all, though there are plenty of shops in nearby Holbrook that legally sell samples. Very remote areas gaining a reputation among rockhounds include Hwy 21 in western Utah and the San Rafael Swell in central Utah.

JEEP TOURING

Taking to the backcountry in a 4WD vehicle, whether just for a half-day or equipped with camping gear, water and food for several days, is a popular activity. In some areas, such as Moab, numerous companies offer 4WD tours or rentals. Especially interesting in the Moab area is an extended 4WD camping trip in the remote reaches of Canyonlands National Park. Sedona is another good center for 4WD activities if you need to rent a vehicle.

Little Sahara Recreation Area in western Utah is especially designed for ORVs (off-road vehicles). The Skyline Drive in central Utah is a beautiful high-altitude drive for which 4WD is recommended. Canyon de Chelly in northeastern Arizona is famous for its Navajo-guided tours in 6WD vehicles – scenic and interesting.

You can drive on dirt roads in many federally owned lands, such as national forests and BLM areas. However, there are some restrictions and certain roads are periodically closed.

GOLF

Just about every sizeable town in the Southwest has a golf course, and the bigger cities have dozens of courses, many of which are listed in the text. In many desert areas, golf courses are viewed as a welcome green amenity but the greenness comes at a high price – it has to be irrigated. Conservationists decry the use of this most precious of desert resources for golf courses, but this hasn't stopped the development of this activity throughout the area.

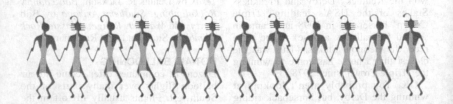

Getting There & Away

Most travelers arrive by air, bus or private vehicle. Train service is a little-used fourth option. The landlocked Southwest can't be reached by sea, but the lack of ports has been remedied somewhat by naming the Phoenix International Airport 'Sky Harbor.'

This chapter focuses on getting to the major transport hubs in the Southwest from the major US ports of entry and other parts of the world. Because of the proliferation of routes into and out of the USA and the complexity of air travel, much of this information is general. Be sure to read Travel Insurance in the Facts for the Visitor chapter for important information on that subject.

AIR

Unless you live in or near the Southwest, flying there and renting a car is the most time-efficient option. If time is not a problem, drive – and enjoy the rest of the country.

Airports

Sky Harbor Airport in Phoenix, Arizona, and McCarran in Las Vegas, Nevada, each with over 30 million passengers arriving or departing every year, are among the busiest international airports in the USA and are the region's most important. Despite this, most international visitors will probably arrive elsewhere in the US (eg, Los Angeles, Chicago, New York, Miami or Dallas/Fort Worth) and connect with flights to the Southwest.

The Salt Lake City (Utah) airport, with about half as many flights as Phoenix, is the third most important airport in the region, and the Albuquerque (New Mexico) and Tucson (Arizona) airports are fairly distant fourth and fifth places. The many other airports in the Southwest are small and used for regional transportation. More details are given under individual cities.

Denver International Airport (Colorado) is busier than Phoenix, and if you rent a car

in Denver, you can be in northeastern New Mexico in four hours. Los Angeles, busier than any of these, is an easy day's drive from western Arizona or southwestern Utah via Las Vegas. El Paso, Texas, a few miles from the New Mexico border, is a possible minor gateway.

Airlines

Phoenix is an important hub for America West and Southwest Airlines. Las Vegas is a hub for America West. (Continental Airlines shares these America West hubs.) Salt Lake City is a Delta hub, and Denver is a United Airlines hub. Many other major airlines fly into one or more of these cities. Reno Air flies between the Southwest and the West Coast. Mesa Air is a small local company with service between nine New Mexican towns and Dallas/Fort Worth, Texas.

US Domestic Airlines The main domestic airlines serving the Southwest include the following:

Alaska	☎ 800-426-0333
America West	☎ 800-235-9292
American	☎ 800-433-7300
Continental	☎ 800-523-3273
Delta	☎ 800-221-1212
Hawaiian	☎ 800-367-5320
Mesa Air	☎ 800-637-2247
Northwest	☎ 800-225-2525
Reno Air	☎ 800-736-6247
Southwest	☎ 800-435-9792
TWA	☎ 800-221-2000
United	☎ 800-241-6522
US Airways	☎ 800-428-4322

Major International Airlines Some US carriers have different numbers for their international desk:

Air Canada	☎ 800-776-3000
Air France	☎ 800-237-2747
Air New Zealand	☎ 800-262-1234
American	☎ 800-433 7300
British Airways	☎ 800-247-9297

101

Canadian	☎ 800-426-7000
Continental	☎ 800-231-0856
Delta	☎ 800-221-4141
Japan Air Lines	☎ 800-525-3663
KLM	☎ 800-374-7747
LTU	☎ 800-888-0200
Northwest	☎ 800-447-4747
Qantas Airways	☎ 800-227-4500
TWA	☎ 800-892-4141
United	☎ 800-538-2929
US Airways	☎ 800-622-1015

Buying Tickets

Your plane ticket may well be the single most expensive item in your budget, and buying it can be intimidating. It is always worth putting aside a few hours to research the current state of the market. Numerous airlines fly to the USA, and many fares are available – from straightforward roundtrip tickets to Round-the-World (RTW) tickets or Circle Pacific fares. So rather than just walking into the nearest travel agent or airline office, you should do a bit of research and shop around first. Start shopping for a ticket early – some of the cheapest tickets must be bought months in advance, and some popular flights sell out early. Look at the travel ads in newspapers and magazines, and watch for special offers. Don't be surprised if they're sold out when you contact the agents.

Fares within the USA are incredibly varied. An economy roundtrip ticket from Phoenix to the West Coast can cost under $100 or four times as much, and these disparities occur almost wherever you fly in the USA. The cheapest flights are often (but not always) those booked 21 days or more in advance and with a Saturday night stopover. Nothing determines fares more than demand, and when things are slow, airlines lower their fares to fill empty seats. Competition is stiff, and at any given time any of the airlines could have the cheapest fare.

The most expensive fares are those booked at the last minute; cheap standby fares are not normally offered. One-way tickets usually cost much more than half of a roundtrip ticket.

Once you have your ticket, write down its number, together with the flight number and other details, and keep the information somewhere separate. If the ticket is lost or stolen, this will help you get a replacement.

Remember to buy travel insurance as early as possible.

Discount Tickets The cheapest tickets are often nonrefundable and require an extra fee for changing your flight, so plan ahead carefully. Returning earlier, if there is space available when you show up, is often no problem, but postponing your return will incur penalties. Many insurance policies will cover this loss if you have to change your flight for emergency reasons.

Call travel agents advertising in travel sections of newspapers and magazines for bargains (airlines can supply information on routes and timetables; however, except at times of fare wars, they do not supply the cheapest tickets). Airlines often have competitive low-season, student and senior citizens' fares. Find out the fare, the route, the duration of the journey and any restrictions on the ticket. Student travel agencies found in many countries include Council Travel and STA. They not only provide cheap tickets to students, they often have some of the best deals for the general public as well.

STA Travel has a national toll-free number for the US, 800-781-4040, and offices in several cities, including the following:

7202 Melrose Ave, Los Angeles, CA 90046
☎ 213-934-8722

10 Downing St, New York, NY 10014
☎ 212-627-3111

51 Grant Ave, San Francisco, CA 94108
☎ 415-391-8407

Internet users may also find that booking tickets online can result in quite good rates, though discount travel agencies may be cheaper.

Courier flights (where you fly with only carry-on luggage, and provide a courier company with your checked luggage space) are possible from Europe, although they are not yet as well known or popular as they are from the USA to Europe. Look in the classifieds of Sunday newspapers or read a book on the subject. If you can manage with just carry-on luggage, these flights are by far the cheapest and are completely legal.

Seasons High season in the USA is mid-June to mid-September (summer) and the days around major holidays (Thanksgiving is one of the busiest times of year, and Christmas, New Year's, Easter, and Memorial Day and Labor Day weekends are all very busy with few cheap fares). The best rates for travel to and within the USA are found November through March (except for the holidays).

Special Fares for Foreign Visitors

Almost all domestic carriers offer Visit USA passes to non-US citizens. The passes are actually a book of coupons – each coupon equals a flight. Typically, the minimum number of coupons is three or four and the maximum is eight or ten, and they must be purchased in conjunction with an international airline ticket anywhere outside the USA except Canada and Mexico. Coupons cost anywhere from $100 to $160, depending on how many you buy. Most airlines require you to plan your itinerary in advance and to complete your flights within 60 days of arrival, but rules can vary between individual airlines. A few airlines may allow you to use coupons on standby, in which case call the airline a day or two before the flight and make a 'standby reservation.' Such a reservation gives you priority over all other travelers who just appear and hope to get on the flight the same day.

Round-the-World Tickets

Round-the-World (RTW) tickets have become very popular in the last few years. Airline RTW tickets are often real bargains and can work out to be no more expensive or even cheaper than an ordinary return

ticket. Prices start at about UK£850, A$1800 or US$1300. These are for 'short' routes such as Los Angeles, New York, London, Bangkok, Honolulu, Los Angeles. As soon as you start adding stops south of the equator, fares can go up to the US$2000 to $3000 range.

The official airline RTW tickets are usually put together by a combination of two airlines, and they permit you to fly anywhere you want on their route systems as long as you do not backtrack. Other restrictions are that you must usually book the first sector in advance and cancellation penalties apply. There may be restrictions on the number of stops permitted, and tickets are usually valid from 90 days up to a year. An alternative type of RTW ticket is one put together by a travel agent using a combination of discounted tickets.

Although most airlines restrict the number of sectors that can be flown within the USA and Canada to four, and some airlines black out a few heavily traveled routes (like Honolulu to Tokyo), stopovers are otherwise generally unlimited. In most cases a 14-day advance purchase is required. After the ticket is purchased, dates can be changed without penalty and tickets can be rewritten to add or delete stops for $50 each.

The majority of RTW tickets restrict you to just two airlines. For example, Qantas flies in conjunction with either American Airlines, British Airways, Delta Airlines, Northwest Airlines, Canadian Airlines, Air France or KLM. Canadian Airlines links up with Philippine Airlines, KLM or South African Airways, among others. Continental Airlines flies with either Malaysia Airlines, Singapore Airlines or Thai Airways. The possibilities go on and on. Your best bet is to find a travel agent that advertises or specializes in RTW tickets.

Circle Pacific Tickets

Circle Pacific tickets use a combination of airlines to circle the Pacific – combining Australia, New Zealand, North America and Asia. Rather than simply flying from point A to point B, these tickets allow you to swing through much of the Pacific Rim and eastern Asia taking in a variety of destinations – as long as you keep traveling in the same circular direction. Some of these Circle Pacific tickets even allow you to stop on the Atlantic; I recently saw one that included New York as one of the permitted destinations. As with RTW tickets, there are advance purchase restrictions and limits on how many stopovers you can take. These fares are likely to be around 15% cheaper than RTW tickets. Again, the best fares are found with agents who specialize in RTW tickets.

Getting Bumped

Airlines routinely overbook and count on some passengers canceling or not showing up. Occasionally, almost everybody does show up for a flight, and then some passengers must be 'bumped' onto another flight. Getting bumped can be a nuisance because you have to wait around for the next flight, but if you have a day's leeway, you can turn this to your advantage.

On oversold flights, the gate agent will first ask for volunteers to be bumped in return for a later flight plus compensation of the airline's choosing. (If there aren't enough volunteers, some passengers will be forced onto a later flight. Each airline has its own method of choosing which customers will be bumped.) When you check in at the airline counter, ask if the flight is full and if there may be a need for volunteers. Get your name on the list if you don't mind volunteering. Depending on how oversold the flight is, compensation can range from a discount voucher toward your next flight to a fully paid roundtrip ticket or even cash. Be sure to try and confirm a later flight so you don't get stuck in the airport on standby. If you have to spend the night, airlines frequently foot the hotel bill for their bumpees. You don't have to accept the airline's first offer and can haggle for a better deal.

However, be aware that, due to this same system, being just a little late for boarding could get you bumped with none of these benefits.

Baggage & Other Restrictions

On most domestic and international flights you are limited to two checked bags and two carry-ons, or three checked bags if you don't have a carry-on. There could be a charge if you bring more or if a bag exceeds the airline's size limits. Many but not all airlines will allow a bicycle or other specialized oversized items as checked luggage. It's best to check with the individual airline if you are worried about this. On some international flights the luggage allowance is based on weight, not size; again, check with the airline.

If your luggage is delayed upon arrival (which is rare), some airlines will give a cash advance to purchase necessities. If sporting equipment is misplaced, the airline may pay for rentals. Should the luggage be lost, it is important to submit a claim. The airline doesn't have to pay the full amount of the claim; rather, they can estimate the value of your lost items. It may take them anywhere from six weeks to three months to process the claim and pay you.

Smoking Smoking is prohibited on all domestic flights in the USA. Many international flights are following suit. The restriction applies to the passenger cabin and the lavatories but not the cockpit. Many airports in the USA also restrict smoking, but they compensate by having 'smoking rooms.'

Illegal Items Items that are illegal to take on a plane, either checked or as carry-on, include weapons, aerosols, tear gas and pepper spray, camp stoves with fuel and divers' tanks that are full. Matches should not be checked.

Travelers with Special Needs

If you have special needs of any sort – dietary restrictions, dependence on a wheelchair, responsibility for a baby, fear of flying – airports and airlines can be surprisingly helpful, but do let them know as soon as possible so that they can make arrangements accordingly. You should remind them when you reconfirm your booking (at least 72 hours before departure) and again when you check in at the airport. It may also be worth calling around before you make your booking to find out how the airlines will handle your particular needs.

Guide dogs for the blind often have to travel away from their owners in a specially pressurized baggage compartment with other animals, though smaller guide dogs may be admitted to the cabin. Guide dogs are not subject to quarantine as long as they have proof of being vaccinated against rabies.

Deaf travelers can ask for airport and inflight announcements to be written down for them. Most international airports can provide escorts from check-in desk to plane where needed, and there should be ramps, lifts, accessible toilets and reachable phones. Aircraft toilets, on the other hand, may present a problem; travelers should discuss this with the airline at an early stage.

Children under two travel for 10% of the standard fare (or free, on some airlines), as long as they don't occupy a seat. (They don't get a baggage allowance either.) 'Skycots' should be provided by the airline if requested in advance; these will take a child weighing up to about 22 pounds. Children between two and 12 can usually occupy a seat for half to two-thirds of the full fare, and do get a baggage allowance. Folding strollers can often be taken on as hand luggage; larger ones can be checked at the door of the aircraft and are returned to you when you land.

Canada
Travel CUTS (☎ 888-838-2887, 416-977-2185 in Toronto) has offices in all major cities. They have good deals for students and deal with the general public as well. The Toronto *Globe and Mail* and *Vancouver Sun* carry travel agents' ads.

Many connections between the Southwest and Canada are through Vancouver, BC. Both Phoenix and Salt Lake City have frequent and inexpensive flights to/from Vancouver, which is serviced by Air Canada and Canadian Airlines. Airlines

flying to the Southwest include Alaska Airlines, United and Delta.

The UK
Discount ticket agencies ('bucket shops') generally provide the cheapest fares from London. Agencies advertise in the classifieds of newspapers ranging from *The Times* to *Time Out*.

Most British travel agents are registered with the Association of British Travel Agents (ABTA). If you have purchased a ticket from an ABTA-registered agent who then goes out of business, ABTA will guarantee a refund or an alternative. Unregistered bucket shops are riskier but sometimes cheaper.

London is arguably the world's headquarters for bucket shops, which are well advertised and can usually beat published airline fares. Good, reliable agents for cheap tickets in the UK are Trailfinders (☎ 0171-937-5400), 194 Kensington High St, London, W8 7RG; Council Travel (☎ 0171-437-7767) 28a Poland St, London, W1, and STA Travel (☎ 0171-581-4132), 86 Old Brompton Rd, London SW7 3LQ. The Globetrotters Club (BCM Roving, London WC1N 3XX) publishes a newsletter called *Globe* that covers obscure destinations and can help you find traveling companions.

Most of the above will get you cheap fares connecting via various US cities. A nonstop flight from London to Phoenix is available on British Airways, but this popular route is more expensive than connecting flights. Several carriers fly nonstop to Los Angeles.

Continental Europe
There are no direct flights to the Southwest from Europe. Flying straight to the West Coast is quicker than transferring in a city such as New York or Chicago. Nonstop flights to Los Angeles are available from Amsterdam with Northwest and KLM; from Frankfurt with Delta, United and Lufthansa; from Paris with Air France and AOM; and from Rome with TWA and Delta. San Francisco has nonstop flights from Paris with United and Air France and

from Frankfurt with United and Lufthansa. These flights are the most convenient, but they usually cost more than flights with stops or connections.

European travelers will find that the cheapest flights from London may be about $200 cheaper than flights from European cities. You may want to give London a quick visit before heading over the Atlantic.

Council Travel has several locations in Paris, as well as in the French towns of Aix-en-Provence, Lyon and Nice. The main travel office in Paris is at 1, place de l'Odeon, 75006 (☎ 01 44 41 89 80). Other Council Travel offices include the following in Germany: Düsseldorf (☎ 211-36-30-30), at Graf Adolph Strasse 18, 42112 Düsseldorf, and Munich (☎ 089-39-50-22), Adalbert Strasse 32, 80799 München 40. STA Travel is at Berger Strasse 118, 60316 Frankfurt 1, Germany (☎ 4969-43-01-91, fax 4969-43-01-91). STA is also in another dozen German cities – call the Frankfurt office for details.

Australia & New Zealand

Flights to Los Angeles and/or San Francisco leave from Sydney, Melbourne, Cairns and Auckland.

STA Travel in Australia and New Zealand have many offices in the major cities. They sell tickets to everyone but have special deals for students and travelers under 30. Head offices are at STA Travel, 224 Faraday St, PO Box 75, Carlton South, Melbourne, VIC 3053, Australia (☎ 1800-360-960, 03-9207-5900, 9347-4711, 9347-6911, fax 9347-0547, 9347-0608), and STS, 10 High St, Auckland, New Zealand (☎ 09-309-9723, 309-0458, fax 309-9829). Flight Centres International are another major dealer in cheap air fares; check the travel agents' ads in the Yellow Pages and call around.

The cheapest tickets usually have a 21-day advance-purchase requirement, a minimum stay of seven days and a maximum stay of 60 days.

Asia

Hong Kong is the discount plane ticket capital of the region, but its bucket shops can be unreliable. Ask the advice of other travelers before buying a ticket. STA Travel, which is dependable, has branches in Hong Kong, Tokyo, Singapore, Bangkok and Kuala Lumpur. Council Travel, also reliable, has branches in Tokyo, Singapore and Bangkok. Many flights to the USA go via Honolulu, Hawaii.

Japan United Airlines has flights from Tokyo nonstop to Los Angeles and San Francisco as well as flights via Honolulu. Northwest and Japan Air Lines also have daily flights to the West Coast from Tokyo. There are also flights, some nonstop, from Osaka, Nagoya, Fukuoka and Sapporo.

Southeast Asia There are numerous airlines flying to the USA from Southeast Asia; bucket shops in places like Bangkok and Singapore should be able to come up with the best deals. Tickets to the US West Coast often allow a free stopover in Honolulu.

Mexico, Central & South America

Most flights from Central and South America to the Southwest go via Miami, New Orleans, Houston, Dallas/Fort Worth or Los Angeles. Most countries' international flag carriers and/or privatized airlines, as well as US airlines like United, American and Continental, serve these destinations from Latin America, with onward connections to cities in the Southwest.

America West has nonstop flights to Phoenix from Acapulco, Los Cabos, Mazatlán, Mexico City and Puerto Vallarta in Mexico. AeroMexico has nonstops to Tucson from Ciudad Obregón, Guaymas and Hermosillo.

Arriving in the USA

As you approach the USA, your flight's cabin crew will pass out customs and immigrations forms for you to complete.

You must complete customs and immigrations formalities at the airport where you first land, even if you are continuing immediately to another city. Choose the proper immigration line: US citizens/residents or non-US citizens. After immigration, recover your luggage in the customs area and proceed to an officer who will ask a few questions and perhaps check your luggage. Dogs trained to detect drugs, explosives and restricted food products might sniff your bags.

If you are continuing to another city, you must recheck your baggage. Airline representatives outside the customs area will assist you.

Leaving the USA
You should check in for international flights two hours early. During check-in procedures, you will be asked several questions for security reasons: whether you packed your own bags, whether anyone else has had access to them since you packed them and whether you have received any parcels to carry.

LAND
The Southwest is well served by several interstate freeways that connect with the rest of the USA. During the winter, however, even the interstates can be temporarily closed or slowed by snow. I-8 from San Diego and I-10 from Los Angeles into southern Arizona and southwestern New Mexico, continuing into Texas, are normally spared weather closures.

Bus
Greyhound (☎ 800-231-2222) is the main bus system in the USA, and it plays an important transportation role in the Southwest. Parts of New Mexico are served by the TNM&O (Texas, New Mexico & Oklahoma) bus line in conjunction with Greyhound. There are also a few minor regional bus lines, which are detailed in the text. These companies serve major cities and minor towns that happen to be on the routes between major cities. They don't serve places off the main routes, so you won't find buses (except tour buses) to most national parks or important, off-track tourist towns such as Moab. For this reason, traveling by car is definitely recommended as more convenient, although bus

services are described in the text if you don't have access to a car or prefer bus travel. Long-distance buses can get you to the region, and then you could rent a car.

Bus travel, of course, gives you the chance to see some of the countryside and talk to some of the inhabitants that car drivers might miss. Meal stops, usually in inexpensive and unexciting cafes, are made on long trips; you pay for your own food. Buses have on-board lavatories. Seats recline for sleeping. Smoking is not permitted aboard Greyhound buses. Because buses are so few, schedules are often inconvenient, fares are relatively high and bargain air fares can undercut buses on long-distance routes; in some cases, on shorter routes, it can be cheaper to rent a car than to ride the bus. However, very long distance bus trips are often available at bargain prices by purchasing or reserving tickets in advance. Bus terminals are often in poorer or more dangerous areas of town – take a cab to your hotel if you arrive after dark.

Bus Passes At the time of writing, Greyhound Ameripasses cost $199 for seven days, $299 for 15 days, $409 for 30 days and $599 for 60 days. Students and seniors receive discounts. These tickets can be bought in advance and use begins from the date of your first trip. You can get on and off at any Greyhound stop or terminal, and the Ameripass is available at every Greyhound terminal.

Foreign tourists and foreign students and lecturers (with their families) staying less than one year can buy International Ameripasses, which are about 20% cheaper. They also can buy a four-day Monday to Thursday pass. The International Ameripass is usually bought abroad at a travel agency, or it can be bought in the USA through the Greyhound International depot in New York City (☎ 212-971-0492, 800-246-8572) at 625 8th Ave at the Port Authority Subway level, open Monday to Friday from 9 am to 4:30 pm. New York Greyhound International accepts Master-Card and Visa, traveler's checks and cash, and allows purchases to be made by phone.

Those buying an International Ameripass must complete an affidavit and present a passport or visa (or waiver) to the appropriate Greyhound officials.

Train

The Amtrak train system crosses the south, central and northern part of the Southwest. The trains are used more as a means of getting to or through the area than for touring around the region. Amtrak has been losing money for decades, and the service, limited as it is, keeps getting cut back even further. European travelers cannot expect anything close to the rail service they are used to at home. Many trips leave only three times a week!

Train travel can be an experience in itself: meals on wheels, being rocked to sleep and, of course, splendid vistas from special carriages with large viewing windows. Sleeping cabins are available, ranging from inexpensive family cabins with bunks sleeping four to double cabins with private baths and hot showers. You can also sleep in your ordinary reclining seat. Dining and lounge cars serve meals, including alcoholic drinks; meals are included in the cost of tickets for the sleeping cabins. Long-distance trains provide entertainment such as movies (and cartoons for kids), bingo and other games. Smoking is not permitted on most routes; however, on some routes smoking is allowed in private rooms and in the lounge car during specific times.

The *Southwest Chief* has daily service between Chicago and Los Angeles via Kansas City, Albuquerque, Flagstaff and Kingman. There are daily *California Zephyr* trains between Chicago, Salt Lake City and San Francisco. The *Sunset Limited* train runs three times a week on the southern route from Los Angeles through Phoenix, Tucson and El Paso to New Orleans.

On some journeys, local guides get on the train to talk about the area you are going through; the Indian guides on the *Southwest Chief* train between Gallup and Albuquerque are particularly popular.

These run daily in the morning eastbound and in the evening westbound.

All tickets should be booked in advance. Amtrak arranges a variety of train-based tours and discounts. For further travel assistance, call Amtrak (☎ 800-872-7245, which works out to 800-USA-RAIL) or ask your travel agent. Note that most small train stations don't sell tickets; you have to book them with Amtrak over the phone. Some small stations have no porters or other facilities, and trains may stop there only if you have bought a ticket in advance.

For non-US citizens, Amtrak offers a variety of USA Rail Passes that must be purchased outside the US (check with a travel agent). Prices vary from high to low season:

Duration	Route	High/Low Season
15 day	national	$425/285
	west coast	$315/195
	east coast	$250/205
30 day	national	$535/375
	west coast	$310/260
	east coast	$395/255

Car

Foreign motorists and motorcyclists will need the vehicle's registration papers, liability insurance and an international driver's permit in addition to their domestic license. Canadian and Mexican driver's licenses are accepted.

For information on buying or renting a car, see the Getting Around chapter.

Drive-Aways Drive-aways are a cheap way to get to the Southwest if you like long-distance driving and meet eligibility requirements. In a typical drive-away, somebody might move from Boston to Phoenix, for example, and elect to fly rather than drive; he or she would then hire a drive-away agency to get the car to Phoenix. The agency will find a driver and take care of all necessary insurance and permits. If you happen to want to drive from Boston to Phoenix, have a valid driver's license and a clean driving record, you can apply to drive the car. Normally, you have to pay a small refundable deposit. You pay for the gas (though sometimes a gas allowance is given). You are allowed a set number of days to deliver the car – usually based on driving eight hours a day. You are also allowed a limited number of miles, based on the best route and allowing for reasonable side trips, so you can't just zigzag all over the country. There is usually a minimum-age requirement as well.

Drive-away companies often advertise in the classified sections of newspapers under 'Travel.' They are also listed in the yellow pages of telephone directories under 'Auto Transporters & Drive-away Companies.' A well-known company that has been providing this service since 1952 and has about 75 offices throughout the country is Auto Driveaway Co.

You need to be flexible about dates and destinations when you call. If you are going to a popular area, you may be able to leave within two days or less, or you may have to wait over a week before a car becomes available. The routes most easily available are coast to coast, although intermediate trips are certainly possible.

Shipping a Car or Motorcycle

In general, because good used cars are cheap in the USA and car rental is less expensive than in most countries, it is usually unnecessary to ship a car, but a surprising number of people take their own transport to the USA and beyond. Jonathon Hewat, who drove a VW Kombi around the world, wrote a book called *Overland and Beyond* (Roger Lascelles, UK), which is a worthwhile read for anyone contemplating such a trip.

Air-cargo planes do have size limits, but a normal car or even a Land Rover can fit. For motorcyclists, air is probably the easiest option; you may be able to get a special rate for air cargo if you are flying with the same airline. Start by asking the cargo departments of the airlines that fly to your destination. Travel agents can sometimes help as well.

ORGANIZED TOURS

Tours of the USA are so numerous that it would be impossible to attempt any kind of comprehensive listing; for overseas visitors, the most reliable sources of information on the constantly changing offerings are major international travel agents. Probably those of most interest to the general traveler are coach tours that visit the national parks and guest ranch excursions; for those with limited time, package tours can be an efficient and relatively inexpensive way to go.

A number of companies offer standard guided tours of the Southwest, usually by bus and including hotel accommodations. Any travel agent can tell you about these and arrange air, train or bus tickets to get you to the beginning of the tour.

Some more specialized tours include the following. Green Tortoise (☎ 415-956-7500, 800-867-8647, fax 415-956-4900), 494 Broadway, San Francisco, CA 94133, offers alternative bus transportation with stops at places like hot springs and national parks. Meals are cooperatively cooked, and you sleep on bunks on the bus or camp. This is not luxury travel, but it is fun and popular with young international travelers. The company's National Parks Loop from San Francisco is 16 days, eight of which are in Utah and northern Arizona. The cost is $499 plus $141 toward the food fund. The nine-day Grand Canyon trip from San Francisco spends seven days in northern Arizona and southern Utah – $329 plus $81 for the food fund. These trips run from June through September only. Green Tortoise also does coast-to-coast trips (Boston/New York to San Francisco) on three routes taking 10 to 14 days for from $299 plus $101 for food to $379 plus $111 for food.

Roundtrip van camping tours of the Southwest (and other areas of the country) are offered by TrekAmerica (☎ 973-983-1144, 800-221-0596, fax 973-983-8551, trekamnj@ix.netcom.com), PO Box 189, Rockaway, NJ 07866. In England, they are at TrekAmerica (☎ 0129-525-6777, fax 0129-525-7399, info@trekamerica .com), 4 Waterperry Court, Middleton Rd,

Banbury, Oxon OX16 8QG. These tours last from 10 days to five weeks (or longer by combining tours) and are designed for small, international groups (13 people maximum) of 18- to 38-year-olds. In addition, Footloose tours are offered for all ages over 16 and with an 11-person maximum. Tour prices vary with season, and July to September are the highest. Sample prices, including food and occasional hotel nights, range from $950 for a 10-day tour of the canyonlands of northern Arizona and southern Utah to $1700 for a five-week tour of the American West, of which about half is in the Southwest. Some side trips and cultural events (cowboy cookouts!) are included in the price, and participants help with cooking and camp chores.

Road Runner (☎ 617-984-1556, 800-873-5872, fax 617-984-2045, amadusa@attmail.com), 1050 Hancock St, Quincy, MA 02169, organizes one-, two- and three-week van trips in conjunction with Hostelling International to different parts of the USA and across the country. They also have offices in England (☎/fax 0189-251-2700, amaduk@attmail.com) at 64 Pleasant Ave, Tunbridge Wells, Kent TN1

1QY, and in 20 other countries. A partner of Roadrunner is AmeriCan Adventures (same addresses), which uses camping and a variety of motel, hostel, ranch and hotel accommodations. Their tours are among the least expensive, and most clients are in their 20s (18 years minimum, no maximum for the 'young-at-heart'). Maximum group sizes are 13 people.

Similar deals are available from Suntreks (☎ 707-523-1800, 800-786-8735, suntrek@suntrek.com), with representation in many countries. For reasons best known to them, they didn't want to disclose more details to me when I told them I was researching this book.

DEPARTURE TAXES

There's a $6 airport departure tax charged to all passengers bound for a foreign destination. However, this fee, as well as a $6.50 North American Free Trade Agreement (NAFTA) tax charged to passengers entering the USA from a foreign country, are normally included in the cost of tickets bought in the USA, although tickets purchased abroad may not have this included.

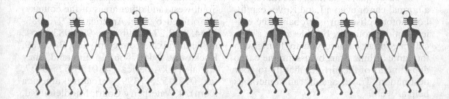

Getting Around

Once you reach the Southwest, traveling by car is generally considered the best way of getting around. A car will get you to rural areas not served by air, bus or train. However, you can use public transport to visit the towns and cities, then hire a car locally to get to places not served by public transport. This option is usually more expensive than just renting a car and driving yourself everywhere, but it can cut down on long-distance driving trips if you don't relish them.

AIR

Phoenix is the hub of America West Express, which serves small towns throughout Arizona, northwestern New Mexico and southwestern Colorado. Albuquerque is the hub of Mesa Air, which serves small towns throughout New Mexico. Salt Lake City is the hub for Delta Connection, serving St George, Cedar City and Vernal in Utah and some Colorado towns. These short-hop flights tend to be used mainly by local residents and businesspeople, and fares are not very cheap, but they are an option for tourists with money.

America West, Southwest and Delta are the main carriers linking Phoenix, Salt Lake City, Las Vegas, Tucson and Albuquerque. Reno Air links Tucson and Albuquerque with Las Vegas.

Regular fares on these routes can be expensive if you don't have advance booking, but fares can drop by about half if you are able to fly very early in the morning, late at night or on specific flights. Ask about special fares when making reservations.

If you are arriving from overseas or from another major airport in the USA, it is usually much cheaper to buy a through ticket to small airports as part of your fare rather than separately, unless your travel plans are so spontaneous as to preclude doing so.

Another alternative is an air pass, available from the major airlines that fly between the USA and Europe, Asia and Australia. Air passes are particularly valuable if you're flying between widely separated destinations. (See Special Fares for Foreign Visitors in Getting There & Away.)

Regional Carriers

America West,	
America West Express	☎ 800-235-9292
Delta, Delta Connection	☎ 800-221-1212
Mesa Air	☎ 800-637-2247
Reno Air	☎ 800-736-6247
Southwest Airlines	☎ 800-435-9792

BUS

Greyhound (☎ 800-231-2222 for fares and schedules, 800-822-2662 for customer service) is the main carrier in the Southwest. They run buses several times a day along major highways between large towns, only stopping at smaller towns that happen to be along the way. Greyhound has reduced or eliminated services to smaller rural communities it once served efficiently. In many small towns Greyhound no longer maintains terminals but merely stops at a given location, such as a grocery store parking lot. In these unlikely terminals, boarding passengers usually pay the driver with exact change. Buses have air conditioning, on-board lavatories and reclining seats. Smoking is not permitted on Greyhound buses. The buses do stop for meals, usually at fast-food restaurants or cafeteria-style truck stops.

Towns not on major routes are often served by local carriers. Greyhound usually has information about the local carriers – the name, phone number and, sometimes, fare and schedule information. Information about the many local bus companies is given in the text.

In New Mexico, a major carrier that serves or replaces Greyhound routes is TNM&O (Texas, New Mexico and Oklahoma) lines.

Buying Tickets

Tickets can be bought over the phone with a credit card (MasterCard, Visa or Discover) and mailed to you if purchased 10 days in advance, or they can be picked up at the terminal with proper identification. Greyhound terminals also accept American Express, traveler's checks and cash. Reservations are made with ticket purchases only.

Fares vary tremendously. Sometimes, but not always, you can get discounted tickets if you purchase them three, seven or 21 days in advance. Sometimes a roundtrip ticket costs twice the price of a one-way ticket; at other times roundtrips are cheaper than two one-ways. Special fares are sometimes offered (eg, 'Anywhere that Greyhound goes for $98 roundtrip' was a promotional offer available at the end of 1997). These details depend on where and when you are traveling, and they change from season to season. It's best to call Greyhound for current details.

Fares do not necessarily depend on the distance traveled. The 260-mile trip from Tucson to Flagstaff may cost almost the same as the 470-mile trip from Phoenix to Albuquerque (both about $40 to $50 without special discounts). Children's fares are half price for two- to 11-year-olds. Student discounts are available occasionally on specific routes during certain times of the year – in other words, call Greyhound. Student bus passes at a discount may be available for foreign students in their home country – ask your travel agent specializing in student travel.

For more details on bus passes, see the Getting There & Away chapter.

TRAIN

Amtrak (☎ 800-872-7245) has three main train routes through the Southwest. These run more or less east to west, and these parallel lines are not convenient for touring the region. Fares vary greatly, depending on different promotional fares and destinations. Reservations (the sooner made, the better the fare) can be held under your surname only; tickets can be purchased by credit card over the phone, from a travel agent or at an Amtrak depot.

If you want to take a train just for the ride, you'll find that a roundtrip ticket, when reserved in advance, is not much more than a one-way ticket. For example, the one-way fare from Flagstaff to Albuquerque is $85, and the roundtrip fare is $92. (Restrictions apply; mainly, no stopovers are allowed, except at your destination.) This particular route is interesting because an Indian Country Tour Guide narrates the section between Gallup and Albuquerque. The Getting There & Away chapter has more information on train routes and fares.

Apart from Amtrak, there are several lines that provide service using historic old steam trains and are mainly for sightseeing, although the Williams to Grand Canyon run is a destination in itself. These are detailed in the text under Williams, Benson, Cottonwood, Yuma and Chama.

CAR

The US highway system is very extensive, and since distances are great and buses can be infrequent, traveling by automobile is worth considering despite the expense. Officially, you must have an International or Inter-American Driving Permit to supplement your national or state driver's license, but US police are more likely to want to see your national, provincial or state driver's license.

Safety

Read the Dangers & Annoyances section in the Facts for the Visitor chapter for general safety rules regarding driving and traveling in the Southwest, and the Legal Matters section for information on drinking and driving laws.

Also bear in mind that Gallup, New Mexico, has built up an unfortunate reputation for careless and drunken driving. Hwy 666 north to Shiprock has an especially

A Crash Course

Accidents do happen – especially in such an auto-dependent country as the USA. It's important for a visitor to know the appropriate protocol when involved in a 'fender-bender.'

- *Don't try to drive away!* Remain at the scene of the accident; otherwise, you may spend some time in the local jail.
- Call the police (and an ambulance, if needed) immediately, and give the operator as much specific information as possible (your location, if there are any injuries, etc). The emergency phone number is 911.
- Get the other driver's name, address, driver's license number, license plate and insurance information. Be prepared to provide any documentation you have, such as your passport, international driver's license and insurance documents.
- Tell your story to the police carefully. Refrain from answering any questions until you feel comfortable doing so (with a lawyer present, if need be). That's your right under the law. The only insurance information you need to reveal is the name of your insurance carrier and your policy number.
- Always agree to an alcohol breathalyzer test. If you take the option not to, you'll almost certainly find your driving privileges automatically suspended.
- If you're driving a rental car, call the rental company promptly. ∎

high accident rate. New Mexico has one of the highest ratios of fatal car accidents to miles driven in the whole country. Be extra defensive while driving in the Southwest, especially in New Mexico.

Distances are great in the Southwest, and there are long stretches of road without gas stations. Running out of gas on a hot and desolate stretch of highway can be hazardous to your health, so pay close attention to signs that caution 'Next Gas 68 Miles.'

American Automobile Association

The American Automobile Association (AAA, or 'Triple A') has hundreds of offices throughout the USA and Canada. Annual membership varies from state to state but costs about $40 (plus a one-time initiation fee of about $20) for one driver and $20 for each additional driver in the same household. Reciprocal member services for residents of one state are available in all other states. Members of many similar foreign organizations also receive reciprocal member services.

AAA provides free and detailed state and city maps and will help you plan your trip. If you break down, get a flat tire, run

out of gas or have a dead battery, call their toll-free number (☎ 800-222-4357) and they will send out a reputable towing company at costs lower than if you had called the towing company yourself. They'll make minor repairs (changing a tire, jump-starting a car, etc) for free or tow you to the nearest repair shop. Normally, the first three miles of towing are free, or you can buy a more expensive membership with free towing up to 100 miles. Benefits apply when you are driving rented or borrowed cars as well. The AAA travel agency will also book car rentals, air tickets and hotel rooms at discount prices.

The main full-service offices in the Southwest are in Phoenix and Salt Lake City. Maps and many other services are available at the smaller branches in Tucson, Yuma, Albuquerque, Santa Fe, Las Cruces, Ogden and some other towns. Hours are 8:30 am to 5 pm, Monday to Friday. Emergency breakdown services are available 24 hours a day.

Rental

Major international rental agencies have offices throughout the region. To rent a car, you must have a valid driver's license, meet minimum age requirements (25 years in many cases, or an extra fee applies) and present a major credit card (some companies will accept a large cash deposit).

Exact details vary from city to city, company to company, and depend on the time of year, so call around. Also try calling some of the smaller, lesser known, local agencies, which are more likely to allow people under 25 to rent a car with no age surcharge. Very few companies will rent cars to drivers under 21, and those that do charge significantly higher rates.

Many rental agencies have bargain rates for weekend or week-long rentals, especially outside the peak summer season or in conjunction with airline tickets. Prices vary greatly in relation to the region, the season and the type or size of the car you'd like to rent. In the off-season, I have rented compact cars as cheaply as $89 a week, but rates of $129 to $169 a week are more common in the high season. Larger, more comfortable cars are available at higher rates. Taxes are extra and average around 10%. If you rent a car for a week and return it sooner, many rental companies will recalculate the rate you were charged at a daily rate, rather than prorate the weekly rate, and you may end up spending more than you were originally quoted.

If you want to rent a car for less than a week, daily rates will be more expensive: $30 a day is a good price but closer to $40 is not unusual. You can get discounts if you are a member of AAA or another travel club. Although $150 or more a week may seem high for travelers on a tight budget, if you split the rental between two or three (or squeeze in a fourth!), it works out much cheaper than going by bus.

Rates usually include unlimited mileage, but make sure they do. If there is a mileage charge, your costs will go up disconcertingly as you drive the long distances of the Southwest. You are expected to return the car to the same place where you picked it up. You can arrange to drop the car off elsewhere, but there is a large surcharge.

Be aware that the person who rents the car is the only legal driver, and in the event of an accident, only the legal driver is covered. However, when you rent the car, additional drivers may be signed on as legal drivers for a fee, usually $3 per day per person.

Basic liability insurance, which will cover damage you may cause to another vehicle, is required by law and comes with the price of renting the car. Liability insurance is also called third-party coverage.

Collision insurance, also called the Collision Damage Waiver (CDW) or Loss Damage Waiver, is optional; it covers the full value of the vehicle in case of an accident, except when caused by acts of nature or fire. For a midsized car the cost for this extra coverage is around $15 per day. You don't need to buy this waiver to rent the car, though you are responsible for covering the cost of repairs in the event of a collision, and so it is advisable to buy CDW unless you have some other kind of insurance.

Many credit cards will cover collision insurance if you rent for 15 days or less and charge the full cost of rental to your card. If you have collision insurance on your personal car insurance policy, this will often cover rented vehicles. The credit card will cover the large deductible. To find out if your credit card offers such a service, and the extent of the coverage, contact the credit card company.

Note that many rental agencies stipulate that damage a car suffers while being driven on unpaved roads is not covered by the insurance they offer. Check with the agent when you make your reservation. It never hurts to read the fine print when you get the contract, either.

Be aware that some major rental agencies no longer offer unlimited mileage in noncompetitive markets – this greatly increases the cost of renting a car.

The following companies rent cars throughout the Southwest. The large cities have the best selection of companies, cars and rates. You can rent subcompact to luxury cars, pickup trucks, 4WDs, vans or moving trucks. Smaller cities have less selection and often charge a little more. Small companies serving just one or two towns are not listed below.

Advantage	☎ 800-777-5500
Alamo	☎ 800-327-9633
Avis	☎ 800-831-2847
Budget	☎ 800-527-0700
Dollar	☎ 800-800-4000
Enterprise	☎ 800-736-8222
Hertz	☎ 800-654-3131
National	☎ 800-227-7368
Rent-A-Wreck	☎ 800-535-1391
Sears	☎ 800-527-0770
Thrifty	☎ 800-367-2277

Purchase

If you're spending several months in the USA, purchasing a car is worth considering, but buying one requires some research.

It's possible to purchase a working car in the USA for about $1500, but you can't expect to go too far before you'll need some repair work that could cost several hundred dollars or more. It doesn't hurt to spend more to get a quality vehicle. It's also worth spending $50 or so to have a mechanic check it for defects (some AAA offices have diagnostic centers where they can do this on the spot for its members and those of foreign affiliates).

You have to register your car with the Department of Motor Vehicles, which will cost several hundred dollars (less for an old cheap clunker, more for a new car), and buy insurance, which will be several hundred dollars for six months. You also have to allow time at the end of your trip to sell the car. Generally, it's more hassle than it's worth unless you are spending six months or more traveling in the USA.

Inspect the title (as the ownership document is called) carefully before purchasing the car; the owner's name that appears on the title must match the identification of the person selling you the car.

BICYCLE

Cycling is a cheap, convenient, healthy, environmentally sound and, above all, fun way of traveling. A note of caution: Before you leave home, go over your bike with a fine-toothed comb and fill your repair kit with every imaginable spare. You may not be able to buy that crucial gizmo for your machine when it breaks down somewhere in the back of beyond as the sun sets. Carry and use the toughest bicycle padlock you can get.

Bicycles can travel by air. You can take them apart and put them in a bike bag or box, but it's much easier simply to wheel your bike to the check-in desk, where it should be treated as a piece of baggage. You may have to remove the pedals and turn the handlebars sideways so that it takes up less space in the aircraft's hold; check all this with the airline well in advance, preferably before you pay for your ticket.

If you'd rather rent a bike when you get there, look under 'Bicycles – Rental' in the telephone directory yellow pages. There are several places to choose from in larger towns. In smaller towns, I mention bicycle rentals in the text. For a long-term rental, you might want to consider buying a new or used bike and then selling it back. Call around the bike stores in the town where you want to start from and explore these options.

Bicycles are generally prohibited on interstate highways. However, where a suitable frontage road or other alternative is lacking, bicyclists are permitted on some interstates. Call the local police to find out about this possibility. Note that some scenic areas have cycling restrictions.

HITCHHIKING

Hitching is never entirely safe in any country in the world. Travelers who decide to hitch should understand that they are taking a small but serious risk. You may not be able to identify the local rapist/murderer before you get into the vehicle. People who do choose to hitch will be safer if they travel in pairs and let someone know where they are planning to go. Ask the driver where he or she is going rather than telling the person where you want to go.

Hitching is illegal on the interstates, but you can stick out your thumb at the bottom of the on-ramp. Police routinely check hitchhikers' IDs, so be prepared for this. You may be asked to show the police some money to prove you aren't destitute. (The police won't continue to hassle you if you have an ID and act in a reasonable manner.) There used to be many hitchhikers on the road 20 years ago; now most of them have disappeared and hitchhiking is generally not recommended.

LOCAL TRANSPORT
There are no urban train systems in any Southwestern city.

Cities and many larger towns have local bus systems that will get you around. These generally run on very limited schedules on Sundays and at night. Telephone numbers of urban bus systems are given in the text.

Taxis will get you around, but they are not cheap. Expect to pay around $2 a mile, which makes them very expensive for long distances. Check the yellow pages under 'Taxi' for phone numbers and services. Drivers expect a tip of about 10% to 15% of the fare. In most cities, you have to telephone for a taxi, as there are few to hail on the streets.

ORGANIZED TOURS
Hundreds of companies offer a huge variety of tours of the Southwest. You can hike, camp, bike, run or float rivers, learn about archaeology, watch birds, go on photo workshops and take advantage of many more possibilities. Many companies are listed in the text under the appropriate towns or areas. Read the information on tours in the Getting There & Away chapter as well.

Utah

TONY WHEELER

Facts about Utah

Utah's world-famous red-rock scenery comprises an astonishing array of canyons, cliffs, mesas, buttes, plateaus, pinnacles, hoodoos, spires, towers, faults, uplifts, folds, bridges and arches, covering the land in a bewilderingly beautiful maze. Much of this land was not settled until recently. Today's roads through red-rock country remain winding and narrow, forcing travelers to cover large distances slowly.

Many visitors spend their time in the southern half of the state, where the majority of the national parks and monuments are. The northern half, however, offers an opportunity to explore the unique culture of the Mormons, based in attractive Salt Lake City. Just to the east of the city, the splendid Wasatch Mountains give access to forested hiking and camping in summer and wonderful skiing in winter. And northeastern Utah draws travelers with the lure of dinosaurs – you can watch workers in the process of excavating fossils and examine complete skeletons in various museums.

Utah is named after the Ute Indians, who roamed the area in small bands when the first whites arrived.

Recent History

Salt Lake City was founded by Mormon pioneers in 1847, marking the beginning of the modern era. The region was part of Mexico until 1848, after which it became part of the State of Deseret, which means 'honeybee' according to the *Book of Mormon*. In 1850 the name was changed to Utah Territory because non-Mormons objected to the religious implications of Deseret. Church leader Brigham Young (see The Mormon Church sidebar in the Salt Lake City chapter) was the first governor.

In the 1850s, several other Mormon towns were founded. The Ute Indians felt threatened by this expansion and in 1853 the Walker War ensued, so named for Ute

Chief Walkara. Although Walkara was defeated by the Mormons, the relations between the Utes and the Mormons were friendlier than Indian-white relations elsewhere. Brigham Young preferred trying to convert the Indians to Mormonism and coexisting with them rather than trying to wipe them out. The Utes were eventually settled on a reservation in the Uinta Mountains in 1872.

As Mormonism gained a solid foothold in Utah, the rest of the country began to have misgivings about this new power on the Western frontier. Anti-Mormon feelings were strong in the eastern USA, and the early Mormon practice of polygamy was particularly targeted.

The Mormons petitioned Congress for statehood six times, the first as far back as 1856, but these petitions were consistently rejected due to Mormon polygamy. The practice was outlawed by the US government in 1862, but the law was not enforced by the Mormons. Church leaders considered the practice protected by the First Amendment (which guarantees freedom of

Utah Trivia
Statehood: January 4, 1896 (45th state)
Area: 84,904 sq miles
(13th largest state)
Highest Point: Kings Peak (13,528 feet)
Lowest Point: Beaverdam Creek,
SW Utah (2000 feet)
Population (1996): 2,000,494
(34th most populous state)
Nickname: Beehive State
State Capital: Salt Lake City
State Motto: Industry
State Bird: California gull
State Mammal: Rocky Mountain elk
State Tree: Blue spruce
State Flower: Sego lily

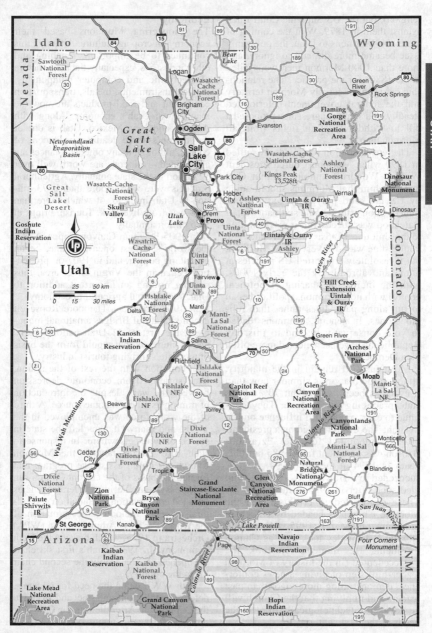

religion), but the US Supreme Court ruled against them in 1879. With the coming of more non-Mormons to Utah, the polygamy issue became more difficult to ignore, and more than 1000 Mormon men were jailed in the 1880s for the practice. The relationship between the largely Mormon territory and the federal government deteriorated steadily, and some congressmen proposed a bill to withdraw voting rights from all Mormon men.

The tense situation was suddenly settled in 1890 when Mormon Church President Wilford Woodruff announced that God had told him that Mormons should abide by US law, and polygamy was discontinued. Soon after, Utah's sixth attempt at statehood was successful; it was admitted to the Union in 1896 as the 45th state. The young state was still very much Mormon, but it resolutely supported US policies at home and abroad. By the early 1900s, with the increasing sharing of political control with non-Mormons, politics began to run along party lines rather than religious ones. In general, Mormons tended to vote conservatively, and to this day Republicans have been elected more often than Democrats.

Mormons still remain in the majority, although the margin is slimmer now than it ever has been, with about 70% of the state practicing the religion. They continue to exert a powerful influence on life in Utah. The Church is led by a president-prophet appointed for life. Ezra Taft Benson was president from 1985 until his death in 1994 at the age of 94. He was succeeded by Howard W Hunter, who died soon after in 1995 at the age of 87. These deaths led to criticism that the Mormon Church is headed by enfeebled old men. On March 1995, 84-year-old Gordon B Hinckley took over as Church president. He immediately took the unprecedented (in the history of Mormon leadership) step of giving a news conference, demonstrating more vigor than past leaders and implying that the Church will be advancing technologically to meet the needs of the 21st century.

Economy

The pioneering Mormons based their economy on crop agriculture. Although this continues to be important, ranching and other industries, especially the manufacture of electronic and computer components, medical instruments, metals, transportation equipment and food products are now the mainstay of Utah's economy. Along with Arizona and New Mexico, Utah is one of the nation's three leading producers of copper, although many other substances are also mined – minerals are worth well over $2 billion to the state annually. Agricultural products were worth more than $873 million to Utah in 1996, of which more than 74% was from livestock. Tourism brings in $3.6 billion annually.

In 1905 Brigham Canyon Copper Mine, the world's largest open-pit mine, began producing copper, and in 1907 oil production began in the Virgin River area, thus making mining an important addition to Utah's traditional agricultural economy.

In 1908 President Theodore Roosevelt declared Natural Bridges a national monument, the first of 11 Utah national parks and monuments that would form the basis of the state's thriving tourist industry.

In common with the rest of the nation, Utah suffered from economic depression between the wars, despite the introduction of mining as a new income source. A third of the work force was unemployed in the 1930s, and many Utahans left the state in search of work elsewhere. In response to such dire circumstances, the Mormon Church set up an assistance program that formed the basis of the current Church-run welfare system. Various federal agencies initiated conservation, reclamation and cultural projects, including the formation of the Works Progress Administration (WPA) Orchestra in 1935, which became the Utah Symphony. In 1938, Utah's first ski chair lift opened at Alta – only the second chair lift in the country.

With WWII came the need for minerals, defense installations and steel and an end to the Depression. After the war, the Cold War provided further economic boosts. In 1952, the discovery of uranium near Moab led to a uranium boom that went bust by the end of the decade and never fully recovered. (However, radioactive tailings still pose problems that the current government is grappling with.) Manufacturing began to play a larger role in the state's economy, and in 1956 a missile industry was established that continues to be important.

The development of these new industries attracted people back to Utah, and the population has almost quadrupled since the beginning of WWII. Most of the people settled along the Wasatch Front (the western slope facing Salt Lake City).

Recently, recreational tourism and technology, particularly in the computer and medical fields, have grown in importance. Opportunities to ski the 'greatest snow on earth' in winter and explore the national parks in summer support a year-round tourism industry. Provo has become the center of Utah's growing computer industry, and scientists at the University of Utah in Salt Lake City have pioneered medical and energy techniques of international significance, including the first artificial human heart implant in 1982. In 1989 scientists announced a successful nuclear fusion reaction, that, if it ever can be repeated on a large-scale basis, would solve the world's energy problems. Salt Lake City and nearby Park City will be host to the 2002 winter Olympic Games, which will boost the economy during that year.

Information

Telephone Salt Lake City and the surrounding areas use the 801 area code. This includes all of the counties of Salt Lake, Weber, Morgan, Davis and most of Utah County. Small sections of Box Elder, Tooele and Wasatch Counties also use the 801 area code. On March 22, 1998, the rest of Utah changed to the new 435 area code. For emergencies dial ☏ 911 or 0.

Time The state is on Mountain Time. When it is noon in Utah, it is 11 am on the West Coast, 2 pm on the East Coast, and 7 pm in London.

Street Layout Throughout Utah, towns and cities use the same street layout. It's easy, once you know the system. Learn it, for example, in Salt Lake City, and you'll be able to use it all over Utah. The system is more complicated to explain than it is to learn. Just go and use it – you'll soon get the hang of it.

Normally, there is a zero point in the town center, at the intersection of two major streets (one of which is often called Main St, and the other, more often than not, Center St). Addresses and street names radiate out from this zero point, rising by 100 with each city block. Thus an address of 500 South 400 East (**A** on the map below) will be at the intersection of 500 South St and 400 East St, or five blocks south and four blocks east of the zero point. The first cardinal point is usually abbreviated, but the second cardinal point is abbreviated less often – 500 S 400 East would be the most likely designation. (The 'St' is often dropped.) An address such as 270 S 300 East (**B**) is a building on 300 East St between 200 South and 300 South St.

Just to complicate things, there are areas where streets don't follow the same pattern, but the general numbering system

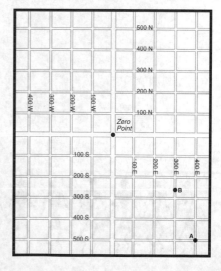

remains the same. 500 N 600 East will always be to the northeast of the zero point.

Note that a few maps might use 1st North, 2nd North etc, instead of 100 North, 200 North. It means the same thing.

Driving Laws You must be at least 16 years old to obtain a driver's license. Drivers and front-seat passengers are required to wear safety belts. Children under age eight must use child restraints. You must be over 16 to obtain a motorcycle license; motorcycle helmets are required for rider and passenger if they are under 18. The blood alcohol concentration over which you are legally considered drunk while driving is 0.08 (lower than the 0.10 of most other states). It is illegal to have an open container of alcohol in your car while driving.

Drinking Laws As in all of the USA, you must be 21 to buy a drink in a store, bar or restaurant. Beyond that, liquor laws in Utah differ noticeably from the rest of the country. Grocery stores can sell beer of not more than 3.2% alcohol content every day of the week. Stronger beer, wine and spirits are sold in state-run liquor stores (also called package stores) that are closed on Sundays. Hours on other days vary from town to town.

Lounges and taverns sell only 3.2% beer – stronger drinks are sold in 'private clubs.' Temporary visitor's membership to any private club costs $5 and is valid for two weeks. All members (including temporary ones) can invite in up to five guests. If you ask at the door of a private club, you can often get one of the staff or other patrons to invite you in as their guest.

Restaurants must have licenses to serve alcohol. Servers are not permitted to offer you a drink or even show you a menu with drinks unless you specifically ask for one. You must order food to buy a drink, but it can be just a snack shared between several people. You cannot buy two drinks for yourself at any one time, so 'doubles' or 'a shot and a chaser' aren't served. Alcohol is prohibited on Indian reservations.

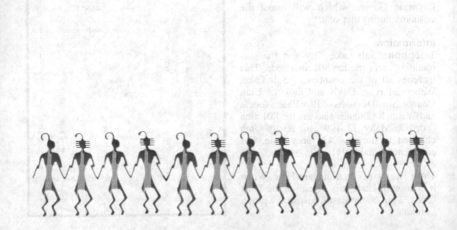

Salt Lake City

Salt Lake City, the capital of Utah, is by far the largest city in the state. It is also the headquarters of the Mormon Church. The Great Salt Lake and the impressive architecture and culture of the Mormon Church are the two most famous attractions for visitors. There is much more to see, however, not the least of which is the city's spectacular setting at the foot of the Wasatch Mountains. The mountains offer great recreational opportunities for the residents of the city; beautiful hiking in summer, lovely fall colors and some of the country's best skiing in winter and spring.

The population of Salt Lake City (popularly called Salt Lake), is a seemingly modest 171,000, but almost 1.5 million people live in the Salt Lake-Ogden-Provo metropolitan area – about three-quarters of the population of Utah. The city's elevation of 4330 feet ensures a relatively mild climate year-round, with summer highs occasionally rising into the 90°s F and winter highs usually staying above freezing.

HISTORY

The city's history is linked inextricably with the remarkable history of the Mormons (see The Mormon Church sidebar). Within a few weeks of the city's founding on July 24, 1847, the pioneers' numbers had swelled to 2000. Streets were built 132 feet wide, so that four oxen pulling a wagon could turn around. Each city block was 10 acres in size, which gave rise to a spaciousness that is still evident in downtown Salt Lake and in many other Utah towns founded by the Mormons.

In 1847, Great Salt Lake City ('Great' was dropped in 1868) was a long way from anywhere. The Mormon settlers had to be a self-reliant group to be able to survive. Times were hard for the first years, especially in 1848 when a late frost followed by a plague of grasshoppers threatened to wipe out the crops. What happened next is

still regarded as miraculous by the Mormons; a flock of gulls flew in, ate the grasshoppers and saved the remaining crop. (That is why Utah's official state bird is the California gull.)

By 1849, there were some 7500 Mormons in Salt Lake. The California gold rush of that year drew a flood of travelers and prospectors across the country and an estimated 25,000 people passed through the city during 1849-50. The Mormons seized the opportunity to sell food and lodging (at as high a price as the market could bear) and to buy much-needed supplies from the prospectors. The city flourished and by the mid-1850s about 60,000 Mormons had arrived.

In 1857, President Buchanan sent hundreds of troops to Salt Lake City to squash a supposed 'Mormon rebellion' and thus began the so-called Utah War. The army marched into the city in 1858, only to find it abandoned except for a few men with orders to burn the town to the ground if the soldiers tried to occupy it. The troops continued through the city and made camp 40 miles away at Camp Floyd, avoiding conflict altogether.

Salt Lake remained almost 100% Mormon until 1869, when the finishing of the transcontinental railway brought a flood of non-Mormons (which the Mormons called 'Gentiles') to northern Utah. By the late 1800s, only half of the inhabitants of Salt Lake were Mormons and today the figure is about 40% (though most other Utah cities are predominantly Mormon).

After polygamy was abolished by the Mormon Church, Salt Lake City was controlled by a Gentile government from 1890 to 1893. When Utah was granted statehood in 1896, Salt Lake City became the state capital. The magnificent capitol building was finished in 1915.

The history of the 20th century in Salt Lake City follows a similar pattern to that of many other US cities. A period of economic growth in the first decades of the century was followed by the Depression in the 1930s. The economy revitalized with WWII and industry blossomed. Then prices and production of minerals fell but a new economic mainstay was found: tourism and related industries that still play a vital part in Utah's economy. To maintain the integrity of downtown, shopping malls and renovation projects were developed, and the center remains vibrant.

New industries related to computer development and biomedicine are becoming important and the selection of Salt Lake for the 2002 Winter Olympics seems to ensure the continued success of this city.

ORIENTATION

Salt Lake City (as with most Mormon towns) is laid out in a spacious grid with

The Mormon Church
About 70% of Utah's population is Mormon, so it's worth learning a little about this religion.

History In the 1820s, Joseph Smith, a New York farmer, experienced a series of angelic visitations during which the word of God, in the form of writings on golden tablets, was revealed to him. During these visions, Smith was told that he was a prophet who would lead the Church. Smith translated the writings, which were written in some ancient but unknown language, using 'stone spectacles' provided by the angel Moroni. After Smith finished the translations, the golden tablets were taken away by the angel and neither the tablets nor the angel have been seen since.

Smith's translation, published in 1830 as the *Book of Mormon*, recounts the epic story of the supposed arrival of the first Americans from the Old World about 4000 years ago and of the teachings of Jesus Christ in America. Later that year, Smith founded the Church of Jesus Christ of Latter-day Saints (LDS), appointing himself the first president of the Church. Confronted with strong opposition to his new sect, he decided to leave New York with a small group of followers in 1831. They built their first church in Kirtland, Ohio, and some Mormons pushed on as far as Missouri. But confrontation continued; most citizens of Ohio and Missouri felt their way of life was being threatened by this strange new denomination, and the Mormons were continually harassed and persecuted. Within a few years, they had pushed on to Illinois, where they founded the Mormon community of Nauvoo.

Many non-Mormons opposed the Mormon newcomers, particularly their teachings of polygamy and religious superiority. Mormons were persecuted, attacked and killed, and in 1844 Joseph Smith and his brother Hyrum were murdered in a jail at Carthage, Illinois. Almost immediately Brigham Young (see illustration to right), the senior member of the LDS, became the second president.

In 1845, Church leaders decided to move farther west to find a place where they could build a peaceful community without being persecuted. The first group left in 1846, wintered in the plains of present-day Nebraska and arrived at the Great Salt Lake in July 1847. This was the place that Brigham Young had been looking for, remote and unwanted. A few days after their arrival, Brigham Young uttered the now-famous phrase 'This is the right place,' and Salt Lake City was founded, becoming the center of the Mormon faith.

Religion Church doctrine was originally derived from the *Book of Mormon*, and most of these original tenets remain integral to Mormon life today. Leadership is through the Church President and 12 elected laymen called the Twelve Apostles. Members are required to be strongly supportive of their families, and the families supportive of one another. A woman marries a man 'into eternity,' and all their relatives (including deceased ancestors) and offspring automatically become Mormons – hence, the Mormon interest in genealogy. Hard work, tithing (donating 10% of one's annual income) and a strict obedi-

streets aligned north-south or east-west. The most important block is Temple Square, bounded by N Temple, W Temple, S Temple and Main (formerly E Temple), all important downtown streets. N Temple, westbound, reaches the airport a convenient 6 miles from downtown.

There is a zero point at the intersection of S Temple and Main. S Temple runs east-west; Main runs north-south. Addresses are given from this zero point with 100 being equivalent to one city block (see the Downtown Salt Lake City map in this chapter, and Street Layout in Facts about Utah).

Heading south of S Temple, where much of Salt Lake City has grown, most streets are numbered: 100 South, 200 South, etc to 9000 South and beyond. The street at 100 W (or parallel to and one block west of Main) is W Temple, followed by 200 West, 300 West etc. Heading east, State St is at 100 East, followed by 200 East, 300 East etc.

ence to Church leaders are important. Smoking and drinking alcohol, tea or coffee are forbidden, because they do not promote a healthy or moral lifestyle. During the early decades of the Church, polygamy was encouraged, particularly within the upper ranks, but this practice was renounced in the 1890s (although isolated pockets of polygamists still exist in a few remote settlements).

The LDS has attracted large numbers of followers who like the strong sense of community, the healthy lifestyle and the fact that Mormons consider themselves God's chosen people. Mormons consider the LDS the one rightful Christian Church; they believe other Christian denominations are defective or corrupt.

The religion is practiced in public and in private. Public services, complete with hymns and sermons, are often held in tabernacles. Private ceremonies, including weddings and baptisms, are usually held in temples and are open only to practicing Mormons who vow to keep the secrets of the faith. Apparently, ceremonies performed in the temples require the attendees to wear special temple undergarments. Talking to non-Mormons about these 'secret ceremonies' leads to excommunication, and generally the Mormons are a close-mouthed bunch when questioned about these details. Temples are only open to non-Mormons when they are new and then only for a few weeks.

The LDS Church is very conservative. African American men were not allowed to become Church leaders until 1978. Women are still not allowed to take on leadership roles and, until 1990, had to pledge to obey their husbands. In Mormon schools and colleges, dress codes are very strict – no shorts or skirts above the knee, for example. Mormon men are not allowed to grow beards. The LDS Church is strongly supportive of the conservative Republican Party.

In recent decades, young adults have been performing voluntary missionary service to spread the faith around the world. Women, called Sisters during their service, spend 18 months, while the men, called Elders, spend two years. There are now over eight million Mormons worldwide, and the number is growing rapidly. ■

Heading north from S Temple, N Temple is 100 North, followed by 200 North, then 300 North and so on. Just to complicate things, there are areas where streets don't follow the same pattern, especially to the northeast part of the city, in the area called 'The Avenues' where there are Avenues from 1st Ave northward and streets from A St to U St eastward.

Two major interstates intersect at Salt Lake City. I-15 heads north-south and I-80 east-west. I-215 is a loop that skirts the city to the east, south and west. I-15 is being rebuilt during 1998/99 and some sections may be closed. Daily information is available at 888-463-6415 or at www.I15.com.

INFORMATION
Tourist Information Offices

Both city and state information are available in two interesting buildings, each worth a visit.

The Visitor Information Center (☎ 801-944-4240, 801-534-4974) and the Salt Lake Convention & Visitors Bureau (☎ 801-521-2822, fax 801-355-9323, slcvb@saltlake.org), 90 S West Temple, Salt Lake City, UT 84101, are both in the modern new Salt Palace Convention Center. Information center hours are 8 am to 5 pm (6 pm in summer) from Monday to Friday, 9 am to 5 pm on Saturday and 10 am to 5 pm on Sunday. The bureau publishes the useful *Salt Lake Visitors Guide*, which is free, and an abundance of other brochures and information is available. There is a gift shop with Utah souvenirs here and also several monumental art pieces (see sidebar).

Once a historic downtown building, the large, two-storied Council Hall was moved to Capitol Hill in 1960. It houses the Utah Tourism & Recreation Information Center (☎ 801-538-1467), Council Hall, Capitol Hill, Salt Lake City, UT 84114 (at the corner of 300 North and N State), open from 8 am to 5 pm, Monday to Friday, and from 10 am to 5 pm on some weekends. This is run by the Utah Travel Council (☎ 801-538-1030, 800-200-1160, fax 801-538-1399, www.utah.com), which pub-

Salt Palace Windmills & Tower

The most intriguing of several giant art installations at the Salt Palace is *Windmills and Tower*. Designed by Montana artist Patrick Zentz, the six large windmills on West Temple are electronically connected to the huge glass tower that forms the atrium to the Salt Palace. Inside the tower, marimba-like percussion instruments mounted high on the walls pick up the wind-generated electronic signals, creating odd and unpredictable patterns of sound within the tower (it doesn't work when there is no wind). Zentz has a reputation for creating massive machine-like sculptures with acoustical interpretations of events – in this case, wind patterns around the Salt Palace. It certainly makes a visit to the information center a futuristic experience! ■

lishes the helpful free *Utah Travel Guide*, available here and at the Visitor Information Center. It also provides limited information from the National Park Service (NPS), US Forest Service (USFS), Bureau of Land Management (BLM) and Utah State Parks.

Other Government Offices

The National Forest Service (USFS) (☎ 801-524-5030), 8th Floor, Federal Building, 125 S State, Salt Lake City, UT 84138, has maps and information about all of Utah's national forests. The local Salt Lake Ranger Station (☎ 801-943-1794), 6944 S 3000 East, has Wasatch-Cache National Forest information. Both are open 8 am to 4:30 pm Monday to Friday.

The US Geological Survey (☎ 801-975-3742), 222 W 2300 South (hard to find, call for directions), has the best selection of topographic and other maps in the Southwest. Hours are 8 am to 4 pm Monday to Friday.

The BLM (☎ 801-539-4001), 324 S State, has information about BLM lands. Their Western Deserts office (☎ 801-977-4300),

UTAH

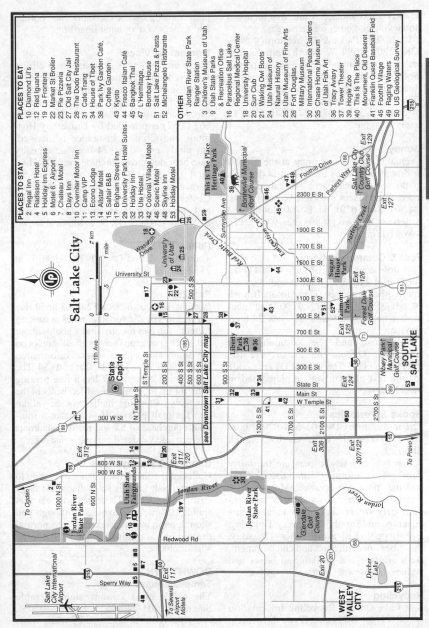

Salt Lake City

PLACES TO STAY

2 Regal Inn
4 Radisson Hotel
5 Holiday Inn Express
6 Motel 6 - Airport
7 Chateau Motel
8 Days Inn
10 Overniter Motor Inn
11 Camp VIP
13 Econo Lodge
14 Allstar Motel
15 Saltair B&B
17 Brigham Street Inn
29 University Park Hotel Suites
32 Holiday Inn
42 Colonial Village Motel
46 Scenic Motel
48 Skyline Inn
53 Holiday Motel

PLACES TO EAT

10 Diamond Lil's
12 Red Iguana
16 La Frontera
22 Market St Broiler
23 Pie Pizzeria
27 Old Salt City Jail
28 The Dodo Restaurant
31 Cafe Trang
34 House of Tibet
38 Park Ivy Garden Café,
   Coffee Garden
43 Kyoto
44 Fresco Italian Café
45 Bangkok Thai
47 L'Hermitage,
   Bombay House
51 Salt Lake Pizza & Pasta
52 Michelangelo Ristorante

OTHER

1 Jordan River State Park
   Ranger Station
3 Children's Museum of Utah
9 Utah State Parks
   & Recreation Office
16 Paracelsus Salt Lake
   Regional Medical Center
18 University Hospital
20 Sun Club
21 Waking Owl Boots
24 Utah Museum of
   Natural History
25 Utah Museum of Fine Arts
26 Fort Douglas,
   Military Museum
30 Chase Home Museum
   of Utah Folk Art
35 International Peace Gardens
36 Tracy Aviary
37 Tower Theater
39 Hogle Zoo
40 This Is The Place
   Monument, Old Deseret
41 Franklin Quest Baseball Field
45 Foothill Village
49 Raging Waters
50 US Geological Survey

2370 W 2300 South, has information about Bonneville and other western areas.

Utah State Parks & Recreation (☎ 801-538-7220), 1594 W North Temple, has park information and sells an annual permit ($60) valid for day use in all state parks. Hours are 8 am to 5 pm Monday to Friday. Camping reservations can also be made (☎ 801-322-3770, 800-322-3770) for a $5 reservation fee.

Money
Exchange foreign currency at the airport or downtown banks because it is difficult to do so in other parts of Utah. Downtown, good places are First Security Bank (☎ 801-246-5629), 41 E 100 South, and American Express (☎ 801-328-9733), 175 S West Temple.

Post & Communications
The downtown post office (☎ 801-978-3001) is at 230 W 200 South and there are many other branches. The Airport Branch (☎ 801-359-0075), 320 N 3700 West (near to, but not in the terminals), has 24-hour service.

Salt Lake and the Wasatch Front (including Ogden and Provo) use the (801) area code. The new (435) area code for the rest of Utah was implemented in March 1998.

Books & Periodicals
The main library (☎ 801-524-8200) is at 209 E 500 South. There are five branch libraries.

The two city newspapers are the fairly conservative morning *Salt Lake Tribune* and the more conservative, Mormon-run, afternoon *Deseret News*. Utah's independent *City Weekly* has good local events coverage and is published every Thursday. *Event*, published every other Thursday, describes upcoming arts and entertainment. Both are free and available in boxes and venues downtown.

Recycling
Salt Lake County Recycling Information (☎ 801-974-6902) can tell you the nearest place to drop off the cans, plastics, bottles and papers you've been hoarding.

Medical Services
There are dozens of hospitals and clinics scattered throughout the Salt Lake City Area. See the listings in the yellow pages under clinics, hospitals and physicians. Physician referral (☎ 801-581-2897, 800-662-0052) is provided by University Hospitals and Clinics. Insurance is advised. Hospitals providing 24-hour emergency care near downtown include the LDS Hospital (☎ 321-1100), 8th Ave at C St; Paracelsus Salt Lake Regional Medical Center (☎ 801-350-4111, 801-350-4631); and the University Hospital (☎ 801-581-2121, 801-581-2291), 50 N Medical Drive.

Police
The police station (☎ 801-799-3100) is at 315 E 200 South.

Parking
Parking downtown costs $2 to $5 in all-day parking lots or 25¢ for 30 minutes at parking meters. You can usually find a spot without too much problem. There is an all-day lot on the south side of the Visitor Information Center, 90 S West Temple, that costs $4. The information center itself has a free parking zone for up to 30 minutes. Merchants in the downtown shopping malls provide validation for mall parking if you make a minimum purchase of $5 and many restaurants also provide validated parking – just ask.

Dangers & Annoyances
Utah is not considered a dangerous state to visit and Salt Lake is safer than most large cities in the USA. There are no areas that should definitely be avoided, although you should, as in any city, exercise the normal precautions as outlined in the Facts for the Visitor chapter.

DOWNTOWN
Temple Square
The city's most famous sight, Temple Square (☎ 801-240-2534, 800-537-9703), is a 10-acre block enclosed by white walls

15 feet high. It is bounded by N Temple, W Temple, S Temple and Main. Within are some of the most important Mormon buildings, visitor centers, exhibits and tours. Even if you are not interested in the LDS (Mormon) religion, you'll find a visit worthwhile for the architecture and culture.

Enter either from S or N Temple. Near either entrance guides will advise you on where to go, what to see and how to hook up with a free **guided tour** led by Mormon missionaries. Tours leave several times an hour, last about 40 minutes and are available in several languages. Questions are welcome.

You are also free to walk around at your own pace; there are plenty of signs. The **South Visitor Center** (by the south entrance) houses paintings of church history and an exhibit about the *Book of Mormon*. Photos of the inside of the Temple (which non-Mormons cannot enter) are also on display. The **North Visitor Center** (by the north entrance) has many religious paintings and murals as well as a small theater with audiovisual presentations.

Temple Square is open daily from 9 am to 9 pm and from 8 am to 10 pm in the summer. Admission to the square, buildings and performances is free.

The Temple The most impressive building inside Temple Square is the 210-foot-high Temple; atop the tallest spire stands a golden statue of the angel Moroni who appeared to LDS founder Joseph Smith. Built between 1853 and 1893, the Temple was opened upon completion to all visitors for a few days and then closed to everybody except Mormons engaged in secret sacred ceremonies. (The practice of briefly opening a new temple to visitors and then closing it to all but worshipping Mormons still occurs whenever a new temple is completed.) When worshipers enter the building for these ceremonies, they are clothed entirely in white.

The Tabernacle You should make every effort to enter the Tabernacle, opposite the Temple, when the world-famous Mormon Tabernacle Choir is singing or an organ recital is being given. This domed building, constructed between 1863 and 1867, has stunning acoustics. Guides leading tours will demonstrate that you literally can hear a pin drop on the stage even when sitting in the back row of the tabernacle. The organ has 11,623 pipes, and 30-minute recitals are given at noon from Monday to Saturday and at 2 pm on Sunday. In summer, there are additional 2 pm recitals from Monday to Saturday. The Mormon Tabernacle Choir rehearses every Thursday at 8 pm and gives a live radio/TV broadcast at 9:30 am every Sunday (arrive by 9 am for seats). This radio broadcast, which has been airing continuously since 1929, is now heard all over the world. The Mormon Youth Chorus & Symphony rehearses at 7:30 pm on Tuesdays and Wednesdays. (Check times as there are occasional changes.)

Assembly Hall South of the Tabernacle lies Assembly Hall, built between 1877 and 1882. It houses a smaller organ. A concert series (☎ 801-240-3323) is performed here in summer and December, and on many weekends during the rest of the year. Outside Assembly Hall is the **Seagull Monument**, built in honor of the state bird (see History above for details).

Near Temple Square
The two blocks flanking Temple Square to the west and east have several other important Mormon buildings and monuments. The **Museum of Church History and Art** (☎ 801-240-3310), 45 N West Temple, has impressive exhibits of pioneer history and a large selection of fine art. A log cabin built in 1847 is nearby. Guided tours are available only by reservation a week in advance. Hours are 9 am to 9 pm, Monday to Friday, 10 am to 7 pm weekends and holidays and closed New Year's Day, Easter, Thanksgiving and Christmas. Admission is free.

Next door, at 35 N West Temple, is the **Family History Library** (see the Mormon Genealogy sidebar).

On Main at South Temple the **Brigham Young Monument** marks the median

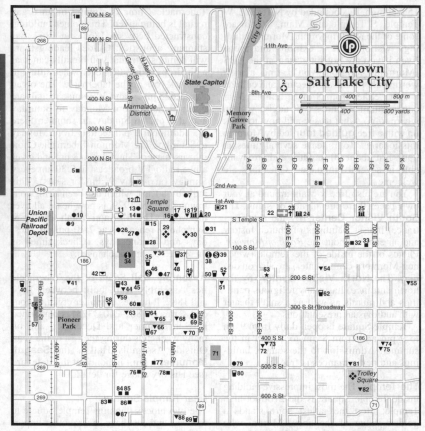

where the street numbering system for Salt Lake originates. East of the monument, at 15 E South Temple, stands the elaborate old Utah Hotel, which housed guests from 1911 until 1987 when it was converted into the **Joseph Smith Memorial Building** (☎ 801-240-1266). It is open 8 am to 10 pm Monday to Saturday (till 9 pm in winter) and has free tours of the sumptuously elegant old lobby, or walk around unguided. There is an observation deck on the 10th floor and a restaurant. The building houses a large-screen theater (☎ 801-240-4383) with several free daily screenings of the 53-minute long *Legacy* about the Mormons' historical journey west to Salt Lake. Also here is **FamilySearch** (see the Mormon Genealogy sidebar later in this chapter).

The 28-story **LDS Office Building** (☎ 801-240-1588), 50 E North Temple, the tallest building in Salt Lake City, is where the day-to-day running of the Church is coordinated. Free 30-minute tours begin in the lobby and go up to the 26th floor observation deck. Hours are 9 am to 4:30 pm, Monday to Friday, plus Saturday from Memorial Day to Labor Day.

PLACES TO STAY
1   Marmalade Inn
5   Royal Executive Inn
6   Travelodge - Temple Square
8   Avenues Youth Hostel
14 Best Western Salt Lake Plaza
15 The Inn at Temple Square
28 Marriott Hotel
32 Anton Boxrud B&B
33 Armstrong Mansion B&B
45 Shilo Inn
60 Peery Hotel
76 Travelodge - City Center
77 Deseret Inn
78 Little America Hotel
83 Super 8 Motel
84 Motel 6
85 Quality Inn - City Center
86 Best Western Olympus Hotel

PLACES TO EAT
18 Lion House Restaurant
36 Mikado
41 A Cup of Joe, Salt Lake Brewing Company
44 Pierpont Cantina
48 Lamb's Restaurant
49 Bad Ass Coffee Company
51 Cedars of Lebanon
52 Star of India
54 Oasis Café & Restaurant
55 Wild Oats Community Market
56 Rio Grande Cafe
58 Red Rock Brewing Company

59 Baci Trattoria
63 Squatter's Pub Brewery
65 New Yorker, Market Street Oyster Bar, Market Street Grill
66 Barking Frog Grill
68 Shogun
70 Baba Afghan
74 Chuck-A-Rama
75 Ruby River
72 Le Parisien
73 Salt Lake Roasting Company
81 Bill & Nada's Cafe
82 Old Spaghetti Factory, Desert Edge Brewery
88 Millcreek Coffee Roasters

OTHER
2   LDS Hospital
3   Pioneer Memorial Museum
4   Council Hall, Utah Tourism & Recreation Information Center
7   LDS Office Building
9   Delta Center
10 Triad Center
11 Greyhound Bus Depot
12 Museum of Church History & Art
13 Family History Library
16 Brigham Young Monument/Meridian Marker
17 Joseph Smith Memorial Building
19 Beehive House
20 Eagle Gate
21 Brigham Young's Grave
22 Cathedral of the Madeleine

23 First Presbyterian Church
24 Enos A Wall Mansion
25 Kearns Mansion
26 Abravanel Hall
27 Salt Lake Art Center
29 Crossroads Plaza
30 ZCMI Shopping Center
31 Hansen Planetarium
34 Salt Palace Convention Center, Visitor Information Center, Salt Lake Convention & Visitors Bureau
35 Dead Goat Saloon, DV8
37 Ashbury Pub
38 USFS Office
39 First Security Bank
40 Bricks Club
42 Post Office
43 The Library (bar)
46 American Express
47 Capitol Theater
50 Bar X
53 Police
57 Rio Grande Depot & Utah Historical Society
61 Sam Weller Books
62 Holy Cow
64 Zephyr
67 Port-O-Call
69 BLM Office
71 City & County Building
79 Library
80 Junior's Tavern
87 Brewvies
89 Ichabod's

The **Beehive House** (☎ 801-240-2671), 67 E South Temple, was built in 1854 for Brigham Young, who lived here until his death in 1877. At the time it was the most elegant house in Salt Lake City and it has been meticulously maintained with period furnishings and artwork. An ornate reception room, bedrooms, dining room, children's playroom (polygamist Young had at least 44 children!) and so forth can all be inspected. The name of the house derives from the hard-working qualities of bees; symbolic beehives appear on the roof and throughout the house. (Utah is nicknamed the Beehive State.) Free guided tours leave several times an hour from 9:30 am to 4:30 pm Monday to Saturday (extended to 6:30 pm on summer weekdays) and 10 am to 1 pm on Sundays and holidays.

Next door to the Beehive House is the **Lion House**, 63 E South Temple, which was built in 1855 as additional living space for Brigham Young's many wives. The building is closed to public touring but the Lion House Restaurant on the lower level is open for public dining (see the Historic Restaurants aside in Places to Eat, later in this chapter). At the intersection of State and S Temple, just east of the Beehive House, stands the impressively arching **Eagle Gate**, which was originally the entrance to Brigham Young's property. Walking the short block north on State St and turning east at 1st Ave brings you to

Brigham Young's Grave, where he and several family members are buried.

Hansen Planetarium

A good stop for stargazers of all ages, the Planetarium (☎ 801-538-2104), 15 S State, has a museum, gift shop and theater. Among the museum's two floors of exhibits, you can see a rock from the moon. Museum admission is free. Hours are 9:30 am to 9 pm Monday to Thursday, till midnight on Friday and Saturday and from noon to 5 pm on Sunday.

The domed theater offers a variety of astronomical (☎ 801-538-2098), laser/rock music (☎ 801-363-0559) and live performances costing from $4.50 to $7.50 for adults and $3.50 to $6 for children.

Salt Lake Art Center

Changing shows at the Art Center (☎ 801-328-4201), 20 S West Temple (on the north side of Salt Palace), cover the art spectrum, and classes, lectures, demonstrations, readings, discussions and performances are offered. Call to learn about upcoming events. Hours are 8 am to 5 pm, Tuesday to Saturday, till 9 pm on Friday and from 1 to 5 pm on Sunday. Admission is free but $2 donations are appreciated.

Utah Historical Society

Housed in the old Rio Grande Railroad Depot, the Historical Society (☎ 801-533-3500, 801-533-3501) is at 300 S Rio Grande (just west of 200 S 400 W). There are exhibits about local and state history, an excellent bookstore with regional books, and a research and historic photo library. Hours are 8 am to 5 pm from Monday to Friday and 10 am to 3 pm on Saturday. Admission is free.

South Temple

In addition to the buildings and monuments at adjoining Temple Square, many other interesting buildings line South Temple, originally called Brigham St and perhaps the most historic street in the state. The following is a selection.

The grand old **Union Pacific Railroad Depot**, 400 W South Temple, was completed in 1909. The Roman Catholic **Cathedral of the Madeleine** (☎ 801-328-8941), 331 E South Temple, has elaborate stained-glass windows and marble altars. The Gothic-style building, which dates from 1900, was renovated in 1992. The red-sandstone **First Presbyterian Church** (☎ 801-363-3889), 347 E South Temple, also has beautiful stained-

Mormon Genealogy

Genealogy is of great importance to the Mormons because they believe that all family members are united within the LDS Church and therefore ancestors and relatives can be baptized and saved. Mormons have amassed the world's most thorough genealogical collection and research facility in Salt Lake City's **Family History Library** (☎ 801-240-2331), 35 N West Temple, Salt Lake City, UT 84150, and also in the nearby **Joseph Smith Memorial Building** (☎ 801-240-1266), 14 E South Temple, as well as in numerous other facilities all over the United States, linked with the main library by computer. Non-Mormons are permitted to use the facilities to research their own roots.

In the Family History Library, an orientation center instructs visitors on how to use the facilities. Genealogical information is arranged by geographic location and then by date, so you should know in advance where your family came from. Library hours are 7:30 am to 6 pm on Monday, to 10 pm from Tuesday to Saturday. Admission is free. The 1st and 4th floors of the Joseph Smith Memorial Building house a powerful computer system, called FamilySearch, that has information on hundreds of millions of deceased people from around the world from 1500 AD onwards. Use is free and staff members can assist you. ∎

glass windows. The **Enos A Wall Mansion**, 411 E South Temple, which houses the LDS Business College, has an ornate turn-of-the-19th-century exterior. The **Kearns Mansion** (☎ 801-538-1005), 603 E South Temple, was built in 1902 by mining magnate and Utah senator Thomas Kearns. The lavish mansion became the official residence of the governor; a serious fire in December 1993 caused extensive damage, but the building was restored and reopened for tours in 1996. It remains the official residence of Utah's governor. Tours are offered on Tuesday and Thursday afternoons from April to November.

Pioneer Memorial Museum

This museum (☎ 801-538-1050), 300 N Main, is run by the Daughters of Utah Pioneers (DUP). You'll find many DUP museums and monuments as you travel around the state, but this is the organization's best museum. Four floors and 38 rooms are filled with carefully labeled and well-displayed historical memorabilia, painstakingly and proudly collected by the DUP. You can see old photographs and portraits, locks, crafts, furniture, toys, kitchen implements, clothing, firearms, walking sticks – you name it and you'll probably find it. An adjoining building contains pioneer wagons and farm machinery. Hours are 9 am to 5 pm, Monday to Saturday, year-round, and 1 to 5 pm Sundays from June to August. Admission is free. Tours are conducted several times a day and a short film is shown at 30-minute intervals.

Marmalade District

Just north of the Pioneer Memorial Museum and west of the State Capitol is an area of steep little streets angled away from the grid pattern of the city. The triangular area, bounded by 300 North to the south, 500 North to the north, Center to the east and Quince to the west, is a residential area with many late-19th-century buildings. Several streets are named after fruit-bearing trees planted in the area – hence the district's name. There are no particular houses to visit; just explore the area at your leisure.

Utah State Capitol

This impressive structure (☎ 801-538-3000, tour information 801-538-1563), stands at the north end of State on the appropriately named Capitol Hill. The impressive legislative building is modeled after the national Capitol in Washington, DC. The exterior is Utah granite topped by a shining copper dome. Inside the rooms are spacious and elegant; lined with huge columns, the walls are covered with murals of Utah's history. The beautifully landscaped gardens contain monuments of Chief Massasoit (a Wampanoag Indian who aided the Pilgrims in Massachusetts in the 1620s) on the south side and the Mormon Battalion on the southeast side. A stairway behind the latter monument leads to **Memory Grove**, where statues honor Utah veterans. The Grove, situated in **City Creek Canyon**, is open during daylight hours. It's a favorite spot for local walkers, runners and bicyclists.

From the Capitol grounds there are good views of the city. Across the street on the south side is **Council Hall**, originally built downtown in the 1860s as the city hall. The entire structure was moved to its present location in 1960 and now houses the Utah Tourism & Recreation Information Center (see Information, earlier in this chapter).

The Capitol is open daily from 8 am to 8 pm in the summer and 8 am to 6 pm during the rest of the year. Free tours depart every half hour from 9 am to 3:30 pm Monday to Friday and brochures detailing self-guided tours are available.

AROUND DOWNTOWN
University of Utah

The 'U of U' (☎ 801-581-6515), 2 miles east of downtown on 200 South, is the oldest and largest college in Utah and now provides for more than 30,000 students and faculty.

The **Utah Museum of Natural History** (☎ 801-581-4303) is on President's Circle, just east of 200 South and University. This fine two-story museum is small enough to visit in a couple of hours. Biology, geology, anthropology and the ever-popular paleontology (dinosaurs!) are featured. There is a gift shop. The museum is fun for children as well as adults. Hours are 9:30 am to 5:30 pm from Monday to Saturday, noon to 5 pm on Sunday; closed on major holidays. Admission is $3 for adults; $1.50 for three- to 12-year-olds and seniors. Parking outside is free if you ask for a pass inside the museum.

The **Utah Museum of Fine Arts** (☎ 801-581-7332) is just off S Campus Drive (the eastern extension of 400 South). Although small, the museum has exhibits from all over the world and from many periods. Changing shows are also featured. Hours are 10 am to 5 pm, Monday to Friday, 2 to 5 pm on weekends (closed on major holidays). Admission is free and there is metered parking outside.

The lovely **Arboretum** (☎ 801-581-4747) spreads out throughout the campus and beyond to **Red Butte Gardens**, east of the university along S Campus Drive. The 25-acre gardens and 4 miles of walking paths are open from 9 am to 8 pm daily from May to October and 10 am to 5 pm, Tuesday to Sunday, the rest of the year. Admission is $3; $2 for seniors and children.

Fort Douglas & Military Museum

Fort Douglas, just east of the university, was built in the 1860s and contains several impressive red-sandstone buildings. The Fort Douglas Military Museum (☎/fax 801-588-5188) has exhibits pertaining to Utah's military history and a self-guiding leaflet describing some of the historic buildings is available. (The fort is still in use and some sections are off-limits.) Museum hours are 10 am to noon and 1 to 4 pm from Tuesday to Saturday all year except during holiday weekends. Admission is free.

This Is The Place Heritage Park

This historic state park (☎ 801-584-8391), 2601 E Sunnyside Ave (eastern extension of 800 South), is for day use only. Picnicking in summer and cross-country skiing in winter are popular activities. This is the closest area to downtown where you can do some bird-watching and maybe see mule deer, raccoons or red foxes. The huge **This Is The Place Monument** looms over the park – it was dedicated in 1947 to mark the 100th

---

Kids' Stuff

Apart from the usual favorites like the zoo and natural history museum, Salt Lake offers several attractions especially for children.

Children's Museum of Utah Interactive exhibits at this museum (☎ 801-328-3383), 840 N 300 West, encourage children to 'work' as archaeologists, TV producers, surgeons, artists, pilots, performers and more. Other exhibits introduce children to the difficulties of physical handicaps. Hours are 9:30 am to 5 pm from Monday to Saturday (until 8 pm on Fridays). Admission is $3 for anyone over two.

Wheeler Historic Farm The farm (☎ 801-264-2212), 6351 S 900 East, dates from 1887. It used to be south of the city but now is surrounded by suburbs. The farm is worked in a traditional manner. City folks can see (and help at certain times, usually in the late afternoon) farmhands milk cows, churn milk into butter, feed animals or collect chicken eggs – an eye-opening experience for kids who have only seen eggs and milk on supermarket shelves! Hay rides and sleigh rides are offered. You can fish in the duck pond and tour the historic farmhouse and farm buildings where demonstrations are given. The farm is open daily from 9:30 am to 8 pm in summer, Monday to Saturday from 9:30 am to 5 pm in the spring and fall, and noon to 5 pm in winter. Admission is $2 for three- to 11-year-olds and $3 for older 'kids.'

Raging Waters If you're traveling with children who threaten to throw up if they have another museum or historic building inflicted upon them, cart them to Raging Waters

anniversary of the arrival of the Mormons. Three walls of the nearby visitor center are covered with murals depicting the Mormon odyssey and audio narration describes the events. Park hours are 8 am to 8 pm. The visitor center is open 10 am to 4:30 pm (or 6 pm in the summer). Admission to the visitor center, monument and park are free.

Within the park is **Old Deseret**, which is a living-history museum with actors in mid-19th-century clothes working among buildings typical of the early Mormon settlements. Some buildings are replicas; others are renovated originals, including Brigham Young's farmhouse.

Old Deseret is open daily from 10 am to 5 pm from Memorial Day to Labor Day only. Admission is $5 for 12- to 61-year-olds; $3 for seniors and children over two. In April, May, September and October, there is no acting but guided tours are offered for $2/1.

Hogle Zoo

The state zoo (☎ 801-582-1631), 2600 E Sunnyside Ave (opposite This Is The Place State Park), has the usual collection of animals from all over the world, well displayed in appropriate settings. There is a children's petting zoo and a miniature train ride ($1, summers only). The zoo is open daily (except New Year's Day and Christmas), 9 am to 6 pm from Memorial Day to Labor Day, 9 am to 4:30 pm the rest of the year. Admission is $5; $3 for children (four to 14) and seniors over 65, and you can stay for 90 minutes after closing time.

Liberty Park

This extensive park (☎ 801-972-7800) is bounded by 500 and 700 East, and 900 and 1300 South. During the summer you'll find a swimming pool, tennis courts, children's amusement park, playground, pond with rental boats, horseshoe pits and formal flower gardens.

The **Tracy Aviary** (☎ 801-322-2473, 801-596-8500) is in the southwest corner of Liberty Park. Bird lovers will enjoy wandering through the displays of hundreds of

---

(☎ 801-977-8300, 801-972-3300), 1700 S 1200 West, for a cool time. Youngsters of all ages can go wild on the world's first water roller coaster, bodysurf in a giant wave-making pool, splash down over 20 water slides (totaling 3000 feet) or simply swim in one of 10 heated pools, including a pool for small children. There are picnic areas and food concessions. From Memorial Day to Labor Day, the park is open 10:30 am to 8 pm Monday to Saturday and 10:30 am to 6:30 pm on Sunday. Admission is $13.95 for kids over 10, $9.95 for kids three to nine, and free for those two and under or 60 and over.

Amusement Centers Kids will head with glee to these fun centers, both of which include a video arcade, mini-golf, food and other attractions. The outdoor **Sports Park** (☎ 801-562-4444), 8695 S Sandy Pkwy at I-15 and 9000 South, also has seven baseball cages, five car-racing tracks and a winter ice-skating rink. Hours are noon to 10 pm on weekdays, noon to 11 pm on Saturdays and to 6 pm on Sundays. The indoor **Utah Fun Dome** (☎ 801-265-3866, 801-263-8769), 4998 S 360 West, has 30 bowling lanes, roller-skating, laser tag, a 70-foot bungee-jumping tower, a 3-D theater and rides. Hours are 4 to 10 pm Monday to Thursday, 4 to 11 pm Friday, 11 am to 1 am Saturday and noon to 8 pm Sunday, with weekday morning hours for bowling. Admission to both centers is free, but bring plenty of change and small bills for the attractions.

Outside the City Also read about the Lagoon Amusement Park (below) and the Seven Peaks Resort in Provo (in the Provo section of the Wasatch Mountains Region chapter). ■

birds from all over the world. Kids can feed the ducks. Hours are 9 am to 6 pm in summer and 9 am to 4:30 pm in winter. Admission is $3; $1.50 for four- to 12-year-olds and $1 for seniors.

The **Chase Home Museum of Utah Folk Art** (☎ 801-533-5760) is in the middle of the park, in Isaac Chase's adobe house, built in the 1850s. Enter the park at 600 E 1300 South. The museum displays such things as quilts, saddles, rugs, needlework and woodcarving. Hours are noon to 5 pm during weekends from mid-April to mid-October and daily from Memorial Day to Labor Day. Admission is free. Researchers can make an appointment to see the museum archives of books, photographs and recordings of Utah folk art.

Jordan River State Park

This state park (☎ 801-533-4496), 1084 N Redwood Rd, follows both banks of the Jordan River from 1700 South northward for about 8½ miles. To reach the ranger station, take N Temple to 900 West, go north on 900 West to 1000 North, then head west to 1084 N Redwood. Station hours are 8 am to 5 pm, Monday to Friday. Activities in the park include canoeing (put in at the south end and take out at the ranger station). At the ranger station, you can get maps showing boating and fishing areas, picnic sites, jogging, bicycling, equestrian and wheelchair exercise trails, a golf course and a model airplane field. Also ask about the best places to see shorebirds and waders during migrations and to watch birds and wildlife year-round. Beavers have been spotted here in summer. Most activities (golf and model-plane field excepted) are free. There is no overnight camping.

International Peace Gardens

Within Jordan River State Park, on the east bank of the river, lie the Peace Gardens (☎ 801-972-7800, 801-974-2411), 1000 S 900 West. Floral displays pay tribute to the culture of countries from all over the world. Hours are dawn to dusk from mid-May through September.

OUTSIDE THE CITY

Saltair & Great Salt Lake Marina

Saltair (☎ 801-531-8102), at I-80 exit 104 (Magna), 17 miles west of Salt Lake City, was a fashionable resort in the 1890s, restored in the early 1980s and destroyed by the 1987 floods (see Great Salt Lake sidebar). It has now been rebuilt on a smaller scale, has a small public exhibit about the lake, good lake views and is open year-round. It sometimes is the venue for concerts. Tourist concessions dispense information and sell snacks, souvenirs and gifts, including what they proudly proclaim to be 'Without a doubt the most delicious saltwater taffy that the world has ever known!'

Adjoining Saltair are beaches where people float in the saline waters just to see what it feels like to be unsinkable. The water is pretty cold except in summer. There are freshwater showers to wash off the briny water, which is very irritating to the eyes.

At the same exit is the marina (☎ 801-250-1898), formerly Great Salt Lake State Park, but now a private outfit with boating facilities but no camping. They plan to open a boat rental concession in the summer of 1998.

Lagoon Amusement Park & Pioneer Village

This is the second oldest amusement park (☎ 801-451-8000) in the country (opened in 1886) and it has several roller coasters and dozens of other rides. The Lagoon 'A' Beach water park offers plenty of water slides and pools. Live musical entertainment occurs daily in the summer. Pioneer Village has many historically accurate 19th-century buildings and visitors can ride stagecoaches or steam trains and watch gunslingers shooting it out. There is an old-time restaurant, modern food booths and picnic areas, pleasant gardens and a camping site (see Places to Stay).

The park is open during weekends from mid-April to late September and daily from Memorial Day to Labor Day. Hours are 11 am to midnight on busy days, earlier on

The Great Salt Lake

The huge lake that gave the city its name lies about 10 miles northwest of downtown. It is the largest lake in the USA west of the Great Lakes. So how big is the Great Salt Lake? That's hard to answer, because between 1873 and the present the lake has varied in size from 900 to 2500 sq miles. Maximum lake depths have varied from 24 to 45 feet – it is a large but shallow lake. Variations are caused by spring runoff raising lake levels and summer heat evaporating the water. A series of dry winters and hot summers will cause extremely low levels, and, conversely, wet winters and cooler summers will lead to high water levels. Evaporation rather than drainage is the main cause of water loss, so the lake has attained extremely high salinities of more than 20% (compared to 3.5% for seawater).

The prehistoric variation in lake levels was much greater. Sixteen thousand years ago the lake was part of Lake Bonneville, which was 900 feet higher and covered almost 20,000 sq miles. Then it suddenly dropped 350 feet when it burst through Red Rock Pass into the Snake River in Idaho. It receded to its present size about 8000 years ago. If you look at the nearby mountains, you can see terraces marking these ancient levels etched into the slopes about 900 and 550 feet above present lake levels.

In the 1980s the Great Salt Lake underwent devastating changes. In 1963, the record low depth of the lake left the surface only 4191 feet above sea level. During that time, several miles of I-80, the main interstate west of Salt Lake City, were built at 4207 feet above sea level. During the '60s and '70s the level rose slowly, but in the '80s, levels increased suddenly and dramatically. The winters of 1982-83 and 1983-84 both had record-breaking snowfalls. Skiers call it 'the greatest snow on earth,' but the ensuing snowmelts flooded the interstate. Crews worked feverishly to raise the freeway 7 feet, to 4214 feet above sea level. By the winter of 1986-87, lake levels had reached 4212 feet, breaking the 1873 record by several inches. Then, barely averting disaster, the lake began to recede.

For the time being, the interstate is safe again. But many other changes resulted from the sudden increase of water. The salinity dropped from 20% to 6% in some parts of the lake – still saltier than seawater but not much. The hard-working Utahans spent countless volunteer hours sandbagging creeks and rivers, building dikes and fighting the floods. Nevertheless, farmlands surrounding the lake were flooded and washed away. Evaporation ponds used for potash production were inundated. Many beaches, state parks, bird and wildlife refuges, and shoreline buildings were damaged or destroyed. If not for the timely actions of the locals, however, the toll would have been far greater.

The lake's wildlife was also hard hit. Before the flood, the lake had always been too saline for fish (except for a few areas near the mouths of rivers). Bacteria and small green algae grew in the salty water and became food for brine shrimp. Brine flies lived in great clouds on rotting vegetation in the marshes along the shoreline. The shrimp and the flies attracted great numbers of migrating birds, and these migrations were one of the natural spectacles of the lake. However, the flooding of coastal marshes caused a huge decline in the shrimp and fly populations, which in turn led to a massive decline in the number of migratory birds. Fortunately, in the last few years, the lake and its wildlife are recovering from the floods.

The Great Salt Lake has been declared a World Heritage bird sanctuary. Spring and summer migrants include many shorebirds, waders, gulls, terns and waterfowl. Some 80,000 California gulls, Utah's state bird, nest here. In good years, about a million Wilson's phalaropes feed here between mid-June and mid-August on their way south for the winter. Fall migrants are mainly ducks and geese, and during the winter, numerous ducks, gulls and occasionally bald eagles can be seen. White pelicans nest on islands in the lake. ■

quiet days. All-day park passes for ages four to 59 are $27 and include all attractions; cheaper partial passes for only the amusement park or water park are available. Pioneer Village and entertainment are included. Parking is $5.

To get there, take I-15 north to the Lagoon Drive exit, 17 miles north of downtown Salt Lake. The park is actually in the sizable town of **Farmington**, which is the seat of Davis County. Because of its proximity to Salt Lake City, Farmington doesn't have any hotels, though there are fast-food restaurants and gas stations.

Bingham Canyon Copper Mine

Billed as 'The Richest Hole on Earth,' this open-air mine (☎ 801-252-3234) is also the largest excavation that humans have ever dug. The gigantic 2½-mile-wide, half-mile-deep gash in the earth's surface has yielded millions of tons of copper and other metals. It is also an environmental disaster. The hazardous wastewater it has emitted over decades poses a threat to Salt Lake City's drinking water. The mine is operated by the Kennecott Corporation, which plans to clean up the area and has agreed to improve its mining practices. Government and other authorities, however, worry that the corporation will be unable to do a satisfactory cleanup.

The visitor center, which includes a museum, film presentation and overlook of the mine, is open 8 am till dusk daily from April to October. Admission is $3 per car, $2 per motorcycle.

The mine is 25 miles southwest of Salt Lake City. Take I-15 south to exit 301, then follow Hwy 48 west to the mine.

ACTIVITIES
Rentals

Utah Ski & Golf (☎ 801-355-9088), 134 W 600 South, is open daily from 8 am to 7 pm in summer, 7 am to 9 pm in winter, and rents skis, golf equipment, snowboards, ski clothing, mountain bikes and in-line skates. Ski-n-See (☎ 801-595-0407, 800-722-3685), 102 W 500 South, rents skis, snowboards and winter clothing. Canyon

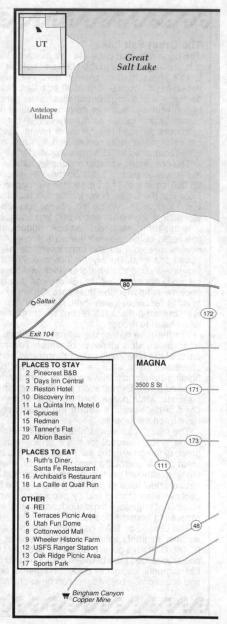

PLACES TO STAY
2 Pinecrest B&B
3 Days Inn Central
7 Reston Hotel
10 Discovery Inn
11 La Quinta Inn, Motel 6
14 Spruces
15 Redman
19 Tanner's Flat
20 Albion Basin

PLACES TO EAT
1 Ruth's Diner,
  Santa Fe Restaurant
16 Archibald's Restaurant
18 La Caille at Quail Run

OTHER
4 REI
5 Terraces Picnic Area
6 Utah Fun Dome
8 Cottonwood Mall
9 Wheeler Historic Farm
12 USFS Ranger Station
13 Oak Ridge Picnic Area
17 Sports Park

Bingham Canyon
Copper Mine

UTAH

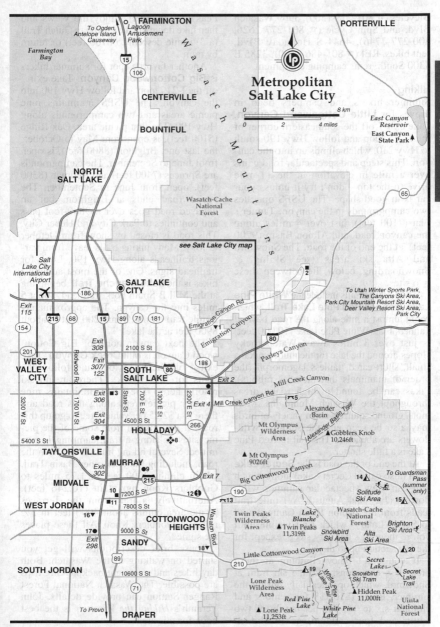

Metropolitan
Salt Lake City

Bicycles (☎ 801-278-1500), 3969 Wasatch Blvd, and Spin Cycle (☎ 801-277-2626, 800-277-7746), 4644 S Holladay Blvd, rent bikes. REI (☎ 801-486-2100), 3285 E 3300 South, rents camping equipment.

Hiking

Summer hikers and campers head in droves for **Little Cottonwood Canyon**. Take exit 7 off the southeastern corner of the I-215 loop and follow Hwy 190 south to Hwy 210, which climbs up into the canyon. This steep and spectacular road gains over a mile in elevation in the 11-mile drive to the top – don't try it unless your car is in good shape. The USFS operates two campgrounds in the canyon: Tanner's Flat (7100 feet), just over 4 miles along the canyon road, and Albion Basin (9700 feet), at the end of the road. The Snowbird and Alta ski areas (see Skiing & Snowboarding, below) lie between these two sites.

Good hiking trails include the **White Pine Lake Trail** and **Red Pine Lake Trail**, which begin almost a mile along the road beyond Tanners Flat. White Pine Lake (10,000 feet) is just over 3 miles away. Watch rocky slopes around the lake for the unique pika, a small, short-eared, tailless lagomorph (the order of mammals that includes rabbits). Pikas can be found in high rocky areas throughout the Wasatch Mountains. Marmots, ground squirrels and a variety of birds may also be seen and the summer wild-flowers are abundant. The trail to Red Pine Lake is a little shorter.

At the end of the road is the **Secret Lake Trail** (also called Cecret Lake) along which you can view spectacular summer wild-flowers (July and August). A 1-mile trail leads from the Albion Basin Campground to Secret Lake – which isn't visible until you're there. It's not very steep, except for the last section up to the lake.

If you don't fancy climbing at these breathless elevations, take the ski tram at Snowbird, which operates daily during the summer. Rides ($10; $8 for seniors and children six to 16; $29 per family of two adults and four children) go to Hidden

Peak (11,000 feet). Enjoy the views and then hike down via the Peruvian Gulch Trail (a 3½-mile descent to 8100 feet) or return by tram.

Another favorite spot for summer hikers is **Big Cottonwood Canyon**. Take exit 7 off the I-215 loop and follow Hwy 190 into the canyon. The USFS maintains nine picnic areas and two campgrounds along Hwy 190. The first picnic area, Oak Ridge (5100 feet), is open from May to October; the last one, Brighton (8800 feet), is open from June to September. The campgrounds are Spruces (7400 feet) and Redman (8300 feet), open from June to September. The paved road ends at Brighton, but an unpaved road goes over a 9800-foot pass and continues to Park City and Heber City. This road is closed by snow from October to May. Many hiking trails leave from various trailheads along Hwy 190. Look for trailhead signs. One of the most attractive hikes is the **Lake Blanche Trail**, beginning at the Mill B South Fork trailhead, about 5 miles into the canyon. The approximately 2-mile trail climbs from 6200 feet to about 8900 feet at the lake.

The next canyon north of Big Cotton-wood Canyon is **Mill Creek Canyon**. Take exit 4 off the I-215 loop and follow the signs for Mill Creek. (There are no ski resorts here.) The USFS maintains nine summer picnic areas along this road and there is a $2.25 per vehicle fee to go up this road. If you hike in from some of the picnic sites or along a trail, camping is permitted. Several hiking trails leave from the road, including the Alexander Basin Trail, which climbs 3000 feet in 1.75 miles to Gobblers Knob mountain (10,246 feet). Alternatively, a trail from the Terraces picnic area climbs about 4000 feet in 5½ miles to Gobblers Knob. All these places are signed.

These brief descriptions will get you started on walking in the Wasatch. Both day hikes and overnight backpacking trips are possible. The Wasatch National Forest Ranger Station can provide details. John Veranth's *Hiking the Wasatch* is the best book for this area.

Mountain Biking

Several books (see the Facts for the Visitor chapter) give detailed descriptions of rides in the area and information offices in Salt Lake have useful brochures. The ski tram at Snowbird (see Hiking above) will take your bike up for no extra charge and offers an all-day lift ticket for $15.

Bird Watching

With deserts and the Great Salt Lake to the west and mountains to the east, the Salt Lake area provides ample and varied birding opportunities. The Utah Wildlife Resources Division (☎ 801-596-8660) maintains a recorded message, updated weekly, of the most interesting avian visitors and reports on migrations.

Skiing & Snowboarding

An entire book could be written about Utah's skiing – this guide isn't it. Your best bet is to get a *Utah Winter Vacation Planner*. This free and recommended booklet is published each winter by Ski Utah (☎ 801-534-1779, fax 801-521-3722, ski.utah@worldnet.att.net, www.skiutah .com), 150 W 500 South, Salt Lake City, UT 84101. Available from the visitors bureau, it lists up-to-date prices and details of all nearby resorts and amenities, plus hotel packages in Salt Lake City. For current ski conditions, call 801-521-8102.

The Wasatch Range overlooking Salt Lake City provides great winter (and summer – see above) outdoor recreation. The skiing is world-class and the 2002 Winter Olympics will be held here and at nearby Park City. Four alpine ski resorts are within 30 miles of Salt Lake and several others are within an hour's drive, especially near Park City (see Park City, in the Wasatch Region chapter). Use Salt Lake as a base and ski in a different resort every day of the week! Skiers driving to the resorts should note that snow tires or chains are required from November to May. Some resorts are open for skiing more than 200 days a year!

A few ski lodges stay open in summer with much-reduced room rates (see Places

to Stay). In the winter, room rates increase dramatically. The ski season stretches from mid-November to early May. If you stay at a ski lodge during the peak season (around Christmas and during February to early March) expect to pay $40 to $100 per person for a dormitory room and several hundred dollars for a private room (single or double occupancy) or for an apartment sleeping up to eight people. Some places may include meals and/or lift passes in the rates. Remember, though, that much cheaper rooms can be had in Salt Lake City, and public transport (with ski racks) is available from downtown to the four closest ski resorts. The lodges that are not right at the ski resorts are also cheaper.

UTA Ski Buses (☎ 801-287-4636) collect passengers from several downtown hotels and stops at the four local ski areas. Service begins at 7 am and buses depart every hour or every half hour. One-way fare is $4.50. Lewis Bros Stages (☎ 801-359-8677, 800-826-5844, fax 801-359-5114, lbs@lewisbros.com) has roundtrip shuttles from downtown to the local ski areas and Park City for $18.

Snowbird This ski area (☎ 801-742-2222, 800-453-3000, fax 801-742-3300) is the closest to Salt Lake City, only 24 miles away in Little Cottonwood Canyon. It is also the highest in northern Utah at 11,000 feet, dropping to 7760 feet at the base. The 2500-acre ski area has 66 runs serviced by one quad and seven double chairs and a tram which carries up to 250 skiers to the top in about eight minutes. About 25% of the runs are beginner and 30% are intermediate. Snowbird not only allows snowboarding but encourages it – this is one of the best snowboarding areas in the country.

Adult all-day chair lift passes (9 am to 4:30 pm) are $47 including the tram and $39 for chairs only. Kids 12 and under ski free (two per adult) and seniors over 62 pay $34 or $27. Adult half-day passes are $39 or $32. Ski rentals, child care, children's programs and a ski school are available.

UTAH

Alta Alta, an 1870s mining town, became Utah's first ski resort in 1937. Only 2 miles beyond Snowbird, Alta (☎ 801-742-3333) has 2200 acres dropping from 10,550 to 8550 feet. Eight chair lifts and five tows service 40 runs, of which 25% are for beginners and 40% for intermediate skiers. All-day chair lift passes (9:15 am to 4:30 pm) are $28 for all chair lifts or $20 for beginner chair lifts. People over 80 ski free. Half-day passes are $21; $14 for beginners. Ski rental, child care and a ski school are available; there is no snowboarding.

Solitude This area (☎ 801-534-1400, 800-748-4754, fax 801-649-5276) is 28 miles from Salt Lake City in Big Cottonwood Canyon. There are 1200 skiable acres between 10,030 and 8000 feet. Seven chair lifts service 63 runs, of which 20% are for beginners and 50% for intermediate skiers. Snowboards are allowed. All-day lift passes (9 am to 4 pm) are $36; those over 70 and 10 and under (two kids per adult) ski free. Half-day passes are $30.

Just beyond the downhill area is the **Solitude Nordic Center** (☎ 801-536-5774, 800-748-4754) at 8700 feet. There are 13 miles of prepared cross-country ski trails, of which 30% are for beginners and 60% for intermediate skiers. All-day trail use is $10 for 11- to 69-year-olds.

Rentals and lessons in downhill, cross-country and snowboarding are all available. There is no child care (though ski lessons are available for ages four and up).

Brighton Just 2 miles beyond Solitude, Brighton (☎ 801-532-4731, 800-873-5512, fax 801-649-1787) has 850 acres between 10,500 and 8755 feet. Seven chair lifts service 64 runs, of which 21% are for beginners and 40% are for intermediate skiers. Snowboarding is allowed. All-day passes (9 am to 4 pm) are $29, and children under 10 ski free with an adult (two kids per adult). Seniors over 70 also ski free. Brighton offers night skiing from 4 to 9 pm for $20 or 12:30 to 9 pm for $29. Both skiing and snowboarding lessons and rentals are available.

Golf & Tennis
There are dozens of public and private golf courses in the Salt Lake City Area – the Salt Lake City Visitors Bureau or the yellow pages can give an exhaustive list. The following Salt Lake City municipal golf courses (☎ 801-484-3333 for tee times for all municipal courses) are easily accessible. Forest Dale (☎ 801-483-5420), 2375 S 900 East, has nine holes. Nibley Park (☎ 801-483-5418), 2780 S 700 East, has nine holes and a driving range. The remainder in this list have 18 holes and a driving range: Bonneville (☎ 801-583-9513), 840 S 2130 East; Glendale (☎ 801-974-2403), 1630 W 2100 South; Glenmoore (☎ 801-280-1742), 4800 W 9800 South; Mountain Dell (two courses, ☎ 801-582-3812), Parleys Canyon; Rose Park (☎ 801-596-5030), 1386 N Redwood Rd; and Wingpointe (☎ 801-575-2345), 3602 W 100 North.

The Salt Lake City Parks & Recreation Department (☎ 801-972-7800) has information about tennis and other activities in the city's many parks. Their biggest selection of tennis courts in one spot is by the Liberty Park pro shop (☎ 801-328-4711) – see the Liberty Park section, earlier in this chapter.

ORGANIZED TOURS
Various companies offer narrated city tours as well as tours to outlying sites like the Great Salt Lake or Bingham Copper Mine. Old Salty (☎ 801-359-8677) has 1½-hour city tours in open-air wagons pulled by locomotive-like contraptions. Their tours run late May to early October and cost $8/4 for adults/children. Gray Line (☎ 801-521-7060), in the Shiloh Inn at 206 S West Temple, has 3½-hour city tours that cost $17/9 for adults/children. Innsbruck Tours (☎ 801-534-1001) has three-hour city tours for $15. These last two will pick you up. AdvenTours (☎ 801-288-2118) has several tours starting at $22. Salt Island Adventures (☎ 801-583-4400, 888-725-8475) runs one-hour scenic cruises on the lake most days during the summer. Fares are $11 with discounts for children. Cruises can be combined with AdvenTours bus tours.

SPECIAL EVENTS

As in any big city, there are a variety of happenings each week. The Visitor Information Center has exhaustive events listings. The following is a selection of the most important annual events.

The **Utah Arts Festival** is held in the Triad Center, 350 W South Temple, in the last week of June. It is a juried event with hundreds of entries. Entertainment, ethnic food and children's art are featured. The **Highlands Festival** with Scottish dancing, bagpipes, crafts, food booths and highland games is held at Fort Douglas on the second Saturday of June. **Pioneer Day**, July 24, commemorates the arrival of Brigham Young's band of Mormon pioneers in 1847. For several days before the 24th, there are rodeo competitions and an arts festival. (Pioneer Day itself is celebrated with fireworks, picnics and a huge parade which organizers claim to be the third largest in the country. Pioneer Day is also celebrated in most Mormon towns.)

The **Utah State Fair** occurs in early to mid-September at the fairgrounds on N Temple near the Jordan River. For over a week there are rodeos, carnival rides, agricultural and livestock shows, arts and crafts displays and entertainment. During September weekends and ending the first weekend in October, **Oktoberfest** comes to the Snowbird resort with beer, live music and dancing.

Christmas Festivities begin in late November with the Christmas Lighting of Temple Square, during which about a quarter of a million light bulbs are switched on to illuminate the square. In December, various Christmas cultural events take place, such as performances of the *Nutcracker* ballet or Dickens' *A Christmas Carol*.

PLACES TO STAY

There are well over 100 places to stay in Salt Lake City and the immediate surroundings. The following represents a large selection – but there are more. Summer and winter are the high seasons and prices may be lower in late spring and fall. Winter rates in the middle and top-end price ranges may include access to UTA buses to the ski slopes and various ski packages. Because of heavy weekday business travel, many downtown hotels have lower weekend rates.

PLACES TO STAY – CAMPING

Two miles west of Temple Square, *Camp VIP* (☎ 801-328-0224, 800-226-7752, fax 801-363-5880), 1400 W North Temple, charges $20 for tents, $26 for RV hookups and has over 500 sites. (Despite this, it can fill in summer.) There are two pools, a spa, coin laundry, recreation room and showers. About 100 sites are found at the well-maintained *Mountain Shadows RV Park* (☎ 801-571-4024), 13275 S Minute Man Drive in Draper (east of 1-15 exit 294, 16 miles south of downtown), which charges a few dollars less and also has a pool and spa.

At the Lagoon Amusement Park (see Outside the City, earlier in this chapter) a campground (☎ 801-451-8100, fax 801-451-8015) is open from May to October. Sites are $15.50 for tents and $20 with full RV hookups. Showers and a coin laundry are available and guests get a discount on park passes. Reservations are recommended.

The USFS (☎ 801-524-5042) maintains four campgrounds in the Wasatch Mountains. In Little Cottonwood Canyon there is *Tanner's Flat* (7100 feet), with 59 sites and fishing nearby. Sites are $11 and open from late May to early October. *Albion Basin* (9700 feet) has 28 sites for $9, open from late June to early September. In Big Cottonwood Canyon, *The Spruces* (7400 feet) has 61 sites for $11, open from late May to early October. *Redman* (8300 feet) has 76 sites for $11, open from early June to late September. Both Spruces and Redman have fishing nearby. All four campgrounds have water; none have showers or RV hookups. RVs over 22 feet are not recommended. Open and closing dates depend on snow conditions.

PLACES TO STAY – BUDGET
Near Downtown

The *Avenues Youth Hostel* (☎ 801-359-3855, 800-881-4785, fax 801-532-0182, hisaltlakecity@sisna.com), 107 F St and

UTAH

2nd Ave, has dormitory beds for $14/17 for youth hostel members/nonmembers, and private rooms with funky furniture, some with private bath and phone, for $25 to $38.50 for singles and doubles. They total 61 beds in 21 rooms with 13 bathrooms, so various sleeping accommodations can be arranged. A kitchen, laundry, big-screen-TV lounge and message board are available and the guests are mainly young international travelers. Office hours are 7:30 am to 12:30 pm and 4 to 10:30 pm; there is no curfew. Credit card reservations are accepted.

At the south end of downtown is the smaller and homier *Ute Hostel* (☎ 801-595-1645, fax 801-539-0291, uteinth1@aol .com), 21 E Kelsey Ave, Salt Lake City, UT 84111, having 12 dorm beds in three rooms for $15 including tax, and two private rooms for $35, single or double occupancy. There are kitchen facilities and no curfew. They'll pick you up from the airport, bus or train station but won't take credit card reservations. You need to mail them a check or money order to secure a reservation.

There is a dearth of really cheap motels. *Allstar Motel* (☎ 801-531-7300), 754 W North Temple, has very basic rooms in the $30s. Other 'cheap' places are found along N Temple. The simple but decent *Marmalade Inn* (☎ 801-355-0293), 667 N 300 West, has 29 rooms, most with kitchenettes, starting at $40 a night or $210 a week. They are often full so make a reservation. The newly renovated downtown *Motel 6* (☎ 801-531-1252, fax 801-359-2859), 176 W 600 South, has a pool and charges $49/55 for singles/doubles, which is high for a Motel 6! It has more than 100 rooms, as do all the Motel 6s in the Salt Lake area.

A recommended budget choice is the older *Deseret Inn* (☎/fax 801-532-2900), 50 W 500 South, which has a spa, restaurant and lounge and 88 large, clean rooms with writing desks. Rooms with one bed are $41/47; rooms with two beds go up to $52; and king-suites are $55 to $65.

Beyond Downtown

The *Overniter Motor Inn* (☎ 801-533-8300, 800-914-8301), 1500 W North Temple, has adequate rooms in the $40s. The airport *Motel 6* (☎ 801-364-1053), 1990 W North Temple, has a pool and charges $43/49 for singles/doubles. Opposite is the *Chateau Motel* (☎ 801-596-7240), 1999 W North Temple, which has basic rooms starting in the $30s.

A decent mom-and-pop place is the *Colonial Village Motel* (☎ 801-486-8171, fax 801-486-8180), 1530 S main, with 34 cozy rooms from $36 to $46. North of town, the *Regal Inn* (☎ 801-364-6591), 1025 N 900 West, has rooms in the $30s and $40s. On the east side of downtown, the *Scenic Motel* (☎ 801-582-1527), 1345 Foothill Drive, charges $40/46. *Holiday Motel* (☎ 801-466-8733), 3035 S State, charges about the same. The Midvale *Motel 6* (☎ 801-561-0058, fax 801-561-5753), 496 N Catalpa Rd (near exit 301 off I-15 at 7200 South), is about $46/52 and the Woods Cross *Motel 6* (☎ 801-298-0289, 801-292-7423), 2433 S 800 West (at exit 318 off I-15) is $41/47. Both have a pool.

PLACES TO STAY – MIDDLE
Hotels
Near Downtown The *Royal Executive Inn* (☎ 801-521-3450, 800-541-7639, fax 801-521-3452), 121 N 300 West, has nice rooms for $59 to $65, including continental breakfast. Rates are occasionally lower. The inn has a courtesy van to the airport, a pool and a spa. The *Econo Lodge* (☎ 801-363-0062, 801-359-3926), 715 W North Temple, has a pool, laundry facilities and airport transportation; singles are $52 to $65 and doubles are $57 to $70.

The *Travelodge at Temple Square* (☎ 801-533-8200, fax 801-596-0332), 144 W North Temple, has clean rooms with coffee-makers for $50 to $70 – it's nothing special but the Temple Square location is excellent. Six blocks south is the similarly priced *Travelodge – City Center* (☎ 801-531-7100, fax 801-359-3814), 524 S West Temple, which has a pool and hot tub. Nearby is the *Super 8 Motel* (☎ 801-534-0808, 801-355-7735), 616 S 200 West, with rooms at $62.88/69.88 for singles/doubles in summer.

The attractive *Peery Hotel* (☎ 801-521-4300, 800-331-0073, fax 801-575-5014), 110 W 300 South, is an old hotel dating from 1910 and restored in 1985. The lobby is old-fashioned, the rooms, though not overly large, are comfortable and have touches of the past and one of the city's favorite bars is on the premises. Other amenities include a restaurant, exercise room, spa, sauna and airport van. Room rates, which include continental breakfast, are $60 to $100 (rates are lowest on weekends).

The *Quality Inn – City Center* (☎ 801-521-9230, 800-521-9997, fax 801-355-0733), 154 W 600 South, has an outdoor pool and spa, two restaurants, an exercise room, and comfortable, spacious rooms for $59 to $89 single and $69 to $99 double.

Beyond Downtown There are several hotels in the airport area. The *Super 8 Airport Motel* (☎ 801-533-8878, fax 801-533-8898), 223 N Jimmy Doolittle Rd, has a pool, spa and exercise room. Rates are $70/75 for singles/doubles including continental breakfast. Some rooms have microwaves, refrigerators and whirlpool baths. The *Days Inn* (☎/fax 801-539-8538), 1900 W North Temple, has nice rooms at $60 to $80 including continental breakfast and there are restaurants nearby. The *Comfort Inn – Airport* (☎ 801-537-7444, fax 801-532-4721), 200 N Admiral Byrd Rd, has a restaurant, lounge, room service, pool, spa and spacious rooms at $80 to $100, with some more-expensive suites. The *Holiday Inn Express* (☎ 801-355-0088, fax 801-355-0099), 2080 W North Temple, charges $70 to $95 for rooms, some of which have microwaves and refrigerators. Continental breakfast is included and there is a pool, spa and workout room.

Almost 2 miles south of the university on the east side of town, the *Skyline Inn* (☎/fax 801-582-5350), 2475 E 1700 South, is a small, clean, moderately priced motel with a pool and spa; rates are $60/65 including continental breakfast.

Other mid-range hotels lie well south of town. The *Days Inn – Central* (☎ 801-486-8780, fax 801-486-6611), 315 W 3300 South (just east of I-15 exit 306), has an indoor pool, spa, sauna and exercise room and rooms with queen-size beds for $60 to $80 including continental breakfast. The *Reston Hotel* (☎/fax 801-264-1054), 5335 College Drive (near exit 303 off I-15), has a pool, spa and restaurant. Good, comfortable rooms are $65 to $75.

The following hotels are near exit 301 off I-15, about 11 miles south of Temple Square. All have large, comfortable rooms with queen- or king-size beds and are good values if you don't mind the distance from downtown. *La Quinta Inn* (☎ 801-566-3291, fax 801-562-5943), 530 Catalpa Rd, has a pool and charges $50 to $70 including continental breakfast. A 24-hour restaurant is nearby. The *Discovery Inn* (☎ 801-561-2256, fax 801-561-4243), 380 W 7200 South, has an adjacent restaurant and rooms in the $70s, including continental breakfast. There is a pool and spa. Several other chain hotels can be found in this area.

B&Bs
The B&B tradition is catching on in Utah with new ones opening every year in Salt Lake City. These accommodations in private homes should be reserved in advance – though a phone call may sometimes yield same-day accommodations.

The closest B&B to downtown is the *Anton Boxrud B&B* (☎ 801-363-8035, 800-524-5511, fax 801-596-1316), 57 S 600 East, Salt Lake City, UT 84102. This historic 1901 home, elegantly furnished with antiques, has five lovely rooms with private baths and two with shared bath. There's an outdoor hot tub and smoking is not permitted. Rates, including full breakfast and complimentary evening refreshments, are $64 or $74 for a double with shared bath and $94 to $134 with private bath. The most expensive suites have whirlpool tubs. Just a little further east is the *Saltair B&B* (☎ 801-533-8184, 800-733-8184, fax 801-595-0332), 164 S 900 East, Salt Lake City, UT 84102. Built in 1903, this historic home was Salt Lake's first B&B. The five rooms have period furnishings; two have private baths. Adjoining the B&B are two cottages built around 1870 and now remodeled. Each has a modern kitchen, fireplace and sitting room and sleeps up to four people. There is a hot tub. Rooms start at $65 and go up to $130 and the cottages are $120 to $160, all including full breakfast and evening refreshments. Weekly discounts are offered.

The *Armstrong Mansion B&B* (☎ 801-531-1333, 800-708-1333, fax 801-531-0282), 667 E 100 South, Salt Lake City, UT 84102, is an 1893 home that was once the mayoral mansion. It has been remodeled into 14 comfortable rooms with modern amenities within a Victorian ambiance. All rooms have private baths and some have whirlpool baths or fireplaces. There is a honeymoon suite. Rates are $90 to $190 including gourmet breakfast and afternoon refreshments.

The most luxurious B&B is the *Brigham Street Inn* (☎ 801-364-4461, 800-417-4461, fax 801-521-3201), 1135 E South Temple, Salt Lake City, UT 84102. Just under 2 miles east of Temple Square, this elegant Victorian mansion has nine attractive rooms, each decorated by a different local interior designer to make it unique – every one is an artistic accomplishment. Most rooms have queen- or king-size beds and fireplaces for $125 to $140. One room with a twin bed is $85 and a suite with kitchen and double whirlpool bathroom is $185. All have private bath, phone and TV. A continental breakfast is served buffet-style and smoking is not allowed.

The *Pinecrest B&B* (☎ 801-583-6663, 800-359-6663), 6211 Emigration Canyon, Salt Lake City, UT 84108, is a 1915 country residence in the Wasatch foothills, about 12 miles east of downtown. The large and peaceful garden has a stream running through it. There are six rooms, all with private bath, two with spa/sauna and two with fireplace and kitchen. Two of the 'rooms' are cabins which can sleep a family and a huge suite can also accommodate a family. Rates are $75 to $180

double, depending on the room. Smoking is not allowed.

There are a dozen or more other B&Bs in the Salt Lake area – call the visitor center for a list.

PLACES TO STAY – TOP END
Near Downtown

The *Shilo Inn* (☎ 801-521-9500, fax 801-359-6527), 206 S West Temple, opposite the visitor center, is a fair value. This 12-story hotel has queen- or king-size beds in the spacious rooms, which have microwaves and refrigerators. Many have balconies. Facilities include free van to the airport (bus and train station too), a café and a restaurant with room service, 24-hour indoor pool, sauna, exercise room, coin laundry and gift shop. Rooms are $100 to $125 for one or two people and include a free continental breakfast.

The *Best Western Salt Lake Plaza* (☎ 801-521-0130, fax 801-322-5057), 122 W South Temple, is conveniently adjacent to Temple Square and a block away from the Family History Library. If you are spending several days in Salt Lake researching your family history, ask for a discount – you'll get it. Room rates range from $89 to $135 and suites are about $200. The better rooms, which include refrigerators and king-size beds, are in quieter parts of the hotel. Cheaper rooms have queen-size beds but all rooms are comfortable and spacious. Facilities include a restaurant, airport van, pool, spa, exercise room and coin laundry.

The *Best Western Olympus Hotel* (☎ 801-521-7373, fax 801-524-0354), 161 W 600 South, has almost 400 large rooms from $90 to $150 (depending on season) and some suites for $275. The thirteen-floor hotel is topped by a restaurant/lounge with great views. Meals and room service are available 24 hours. There is a heated year-round outdoor pool; a spa, exercise room and coin laundry; and free airport/ski area transportation.

The huge 17-story *Little America* (☎ 801-363-6781, 800-453-9450, fax 801-596-5911), 500 S Main, is a good full-service hotel with 850 large rooms and suites ranging from a very reasonable $80 to $140, depending on size, views and amenities. The hotel has both indoor and outdoor pools, spas, saunas and an exercise room. There's a coffee shop, a restaurant/lounge and room service.

The Inn at Temple Square (☎ 801-531-1000, 800-843-4668, fax 801-536-7272), 71 W South Temple, is in a 1930 Edwardian building refurbished for the 1990s. It offers the closest luxury lodging to Temple Square (which is across the street) and many rooms have good views of the square; some rooms have whirlpool bathtubs. The 90 rooms or suites are attractively furnished and elegantly old-fashioned. Mini-refrigerators with complimentary soft drinks are inside the rooms. Nearby pool and health club privileges are available. Smoking is not permitted throughout the hotel and no liquor is served. Rates include breakfast and range from $90 to $150 a room and $150 to $225 for a suite. Weekend discounts are available.

Another luxury hotel just a block away from Temple Square is the *Marriott* (☎ 801-531-0800, 800-345-4754, fax 801-532-4127), 75 S West Temple, a full-service hotel with more than 500 rooms and suites, and year-round swimming, sauna and exercise facilities. There are four restaurants and a lounge. Rates vary substantially depending on date, room and whether you use senior or AAA discounts. A weekend room in the low season can be snagged for as low as $80 but can be twice that midweek when they are busy.

There are several other large, good, full-service hotels within a few blocks of Temple Square.

Beyond Downtown

A fairly new and very comfortable full-service hotel, the *Holiday Inn – Downtown* (☎ 801-359-8600, 800-933-9678, fax 801-359-7186), 999 S Main, is set in beautifully landscaped grounds 1½ miles south of Temple Square. The hotel offers all the standard facilities plus a tennis court, putting green and playground. Spacious rooms with king-size beds range from $100 to $140.

The *Airport Hilton* (☎ 801-539-1515, 800-999-3736, fax 801-539-1113), 5151

Wiley Post Way, boasts a small lake with boats and a putting green nearby. There are two swimming pools, spa, exercise room and restaurant and lounge. Rooms are large and have coffeemakers. Rates start at $80 and more-expensive suites are available.

The *Radisson Hotel – Airport* (☎ 801-364-5800, 800-333-3333, fax 801-364-5823), 2177 W North Temple, offers the most luxurious lodgings close to the airport. Spacious and attractive rooms with coffeemakers and refrigerators, some with balconies and fireplaces, range from $80 to $140, including continental breakfast and a complimentary evening cocktail hour. There is a restaurant with room service and liquor license but no lounge bar. Amenities include pool, exercise room, spa and airport/train/bus station transportation.

The *University Park Hotel Suites* (☎ 801-581-1000, fax 801-584-3321), 480 Wakara Way, just east of the university, is a modern and luxurious full-service hotel with the usual amenities and good views of downtown or the mountains. Rooms are about $100 to $125, and suites are about $200, with weekend and other discounts available.

Ski Resorts

Both the Snowbird/Alta area in Little Cottonwood Canyon and the Solitude/Brighton area in Big Cottonwood Canyon have ski resorts, condos and lodges. Of the ski areas, Snowbird/Alta offers the greatest choice of accommodations. Some of these remain open in summer, when they offer cheaper accommodations than in winter. During the summer, they make good bases for hiking, mountain biking, rock climbing and other outdoor activities.

The ski-season rates vary during low, regular and holiday periods. The low periods are normally the first and last few weeks of the ski season, when snow conditions are the most erratic. The regular season runs from January through March. The holiday season, from about December 18 to New Year's Day, is the most expensive. There is often a post-holiday-season lull in January, when slopes are the least crowded of the regular season and low-season prices may be offered by many resorts, some of which may require a minimum stay of several days. Note that a sales tax of about 10% is added to the prices given and that lodges offering meals-inclusive packages add a further 15% service charge.

Ski resorts and airlines often join together to offer package deals that are cheaper than paying for flights and rooms separately. Ask your travel agent about these.

Budget travelers will not find any bargains at the ski resorts. To save money, stay in Salt Lake City and take a bus up to the resorts. The free and very useful annual *Utah Winter Vacation Planner*, available from the Utah Travel Council and many information centers (see Information), provides both skiing and accommodations information.

Snowbird The *Snowbird Resort* (☎ 800-385-2002, fax 801-742-3300), Snowbird, UT 84092-9000, operates the *Cliff Lodge*, with more than 500 rooms, as well as three condo complexes: the *Lodge at Snowbird*, the *Iron Blosam Lodge* and the *Inn at Snowbird*. These places house the majority of skiers as all are within walking/skiing distance of the chair lifts, ski rental and repair shops and skiing school. They require a four-night stay if the rental dates include a Thursday, Friday or Saturday night during the regular and holiday seasons. These lodges are generally newer and a little more upscale than most of the lodges in Alta.

The Cliff Lodge has a full-service spa with everything from herbal wraps to a giant whirlpool (adults only), child care, three restaurants, room service, bars and dancing. Other restaurants are nearby. The condo-complexes also have restaurants, child care, pools, saunas and spas. The lodge offers single-sex dormitories at $49/69 per person in low/regular season; and has a variety of studios, bedrooms, suites, efficiencies and one- or two-bedroom fully furnished condos with kitchens and fireplaces ranging from $125 to $575 in the low season and $209 to $959 in the regular season.

Alta There are more than a dozen places to stay in or near Alta, and many can be reserved through *Alta Reservation Service* (☎ 801-942-0404, fax 801-942-0965), 3332 East Little Cottonwood Rd, Sandy, UT 84092. This service also books Snowbird accommodations.

All the following are a short walk or ski from the chair lifts. *Alta Lodge* (☎ 801-742-3500, 800-707-2582, info@altalodge.com) offers 50 rooms ranging from dormitories at $95 per person to deluxe rooms, some with fireplaces, for $380 double (regular season). Prices include breakfast and dinner (add 10% tax and 15% service charge). They have a sauna and spa, as well as a children's program.

Alta Peruvian Lodge (☎ 801-742-3000, 800-453-8488, fax 801-742-3007) has a swimming pool but no child care; otherwise it is similar to the Alta Lodge at prices from $81 in dorms to $308 a double, plus taxes and including three meals. *Goldminer's Daughter Lodge* (☎ 801-742-2300, 800-453-4573) has a hot tub, sauna and exercise room. Dorm rooms cost $84 per person; bedrooms cost from $120 to $134 for singles and $188 to $200 for doubles; and suites from $228 a double to $370 for quadruple occupancy, plus taxes, including breakfast and dinner. Discounts of 10% to 20% are offered in the low season.

The most comfortable of the Alta lodges is the 56-room *Rustler Lodge* (☎ 801-742-2200, 888-532-2582, fax 801-742-3832, info@rustlerlodge.com). It has child care, a pool, sauna and spa. Regular-season rates are $100 per person in dorms and range from $230 to $550 a double in rooms and suites. Low-season rates drop to $90 in dorms and $200 to $490 in rooms and suites, plus taxes. Rates include breakfast and dinner. Next door, the 20-room *Snow Pine Lodge* (☎ 801-742-2000) offers dorms for $82 per person, and rooms, some with shared baths, range from $186 to $270 a double, plus taxes (regular season), including breakfast and dinner. It has a hot tub.

If you want more elegant accommodations and don't mind walking a few hundred yards to the chair lifts, *Canyon Services*

(☎ 801-943-1842, 800-562-2888, fax 801-943-4161, canyon@xmission.com), PO Box 920025, Snowbird, UT 84092-0025, has several dozen one-, two-, three- and four-bedroom condos and townhouses, some with lofts, sleeping four to 12 people. Most come with private hot tub, parking garage and full kitchen, and many have laundry facilities, balconies and fireplaces. Regular-season rates range from $280 for one bedroom to $550-$850 for three bedrooms and a loft. Holiday-season rates run about 10% higher and low-season rates around 30% lower.

There are several other small places (under 20 units) close to but not right by the lifts; Alta Reservation Service can help locate these.

Brighton/Solitude The Brighton/Solitude ski areas have far fewer places to stay. The *Brighton Lodge* (☎ 801-649-7908, 800-873-5512) is right by the lifts. It has 20 rooms, a hot tub and a pool. Double rooms are about $100 during regular season. A quarter mile from the slopes, *Brighton Chalets* (☎ 801-942-8824, 800-748-4824, fax 801-942-4480) features several cabins of various sizes complete with kitchen and fireplace and suitable for families. Regular-season rates go from about $100 to $300. There are several other small places near Brighton.

The *Village at Solitude* (☎ 801-536-5700, 800-748-4754, fax 801-649-5276) has 46 rooms and condos ranging from $180 for a standard room to $565 for a three-bedroom condo. There is a restaurant, lounge, pool, hot tub and exercise room, and childcare is available.

PLACES TO EAT

The main shopping malls have good food courts with a variety of fairly inexpensive dining – pizzas, burgers, sandwiches, Chinese, Mexican, Greek and so forth. These are handy for lunch downtown. The biggest selection is at the *Crossroads Plaza*, 50 S Main, right by Temple Square. Other malls with plenty of places to eat include *ZCMI*, 36 S State, and *Trolley Square*, 600 S 700

East. Besides the food court, Trolley Square stands out among the malls for its good restaurants (some of which are described below).

Many of the city's better hotels have good restaurants open to the public. The most upmarket include *JW's Steak House* (☎ 801-531-0800) in the Marriott at 75 S West Temple and the *Little America Dining Room* (☎ 801-596-5704), 500 S Main in the Little America Hotel, known for its hugely varied menu and especially for its Sunday brunch served from 9 am to 2 pm. Although I give dining hours for the establishments listed below, it's worth calling ahead if you are set on a particular place because hours do change.

Budget

Starving travelers with huge appetites and limited funds might try the following 'all-you-can-eat' restaurant. Salad, dessert and hot food are all featured at *Chuck-A-Rama* (☎ 801-531-1123), 744 E 400 South, and at several additional suburban locations. Buffet lunches are $6 (11 am to 4 pm, Monday to Saturday) and dinners are $8 (4 to 9 pm, Monday to Saturday, and 11 am to 8 pm on Sunday).

Other budget places include the *Old Spaghetti Factory* (see Italian), *Bill & Nada's Café* and various burger joints (see American) and most Mexican restaurants. Also check the Middle Eastern & Asian restaurants below; many of them have inexpensive lunch specials, sometimes all-you-can-eat.

Coffeehouses

The last few years have seen a dramatic increase in the number of coffeehouses in the city and most of them are great places to hang out. The coffee is good too! You can expect a variety of imported coffees served straight or as espresso or cappuccino in the following places. The oldest and best known is the *Salt Lake Roasting Company* (☎ 801-363-7572), 320 E 400 South, open 6:45 am to midnight, Monday to Saturday. They serve pastries and light lunches and dinners. Travelers should head upstairs to check out their extensive map collection both of local areas and the rest of the world. Also good is *Millcreek Coffee Roasters* (☎ 801-595-8646), 657 S Main, which serves light breakfasts and lunches. They're open from 6:30 am to 6 pm on weekdays and 8 am to 4 pm on Saturdays, with extended summer hours.

Another popular choice is the *Coffee Garden* (☎ 801-355-3425), 898 S 900 East, open from 7 am to 10 pm daily, till 11 pm on Friday and Saturday. *A Cup of Joe* (☎ 801-363-8322), 353 W 200 South, serves Italian ice cream and other desserts, a limited sandwich menu and carries international newspapers. Hours are 7 am to midnight, Monday to Saturday, and 9 am to 2 pm on Sunday. They sometimes have poetry evenings and such. Also try *Bad Ass Coffee Co* (☎ 801-537-7707), 45 E 200 South, and (☎ 801-265-1182), 3530 S State, which claims to be the world's largest roaster of Kona/Hawaiian coffee. They serve pastries and are open 6:30 am to 10 pm every day. There are plenty of other places.

Mexican

I like the food at the *Red Iguana* (☎ 801-322-1489), 736 W North Temple. Come here for the reasonable prices and well-prepared Mexican dishes – not for the ambiance, which is cheap and undistinguished. Hours are 11 am to 9 pm, Monday to Thursday, and to 10 pm on Friday and Saturday. Savvy locals know this place, so arrive early or be prepared to wait. The *Rio Grande Cafe* (☎ 801-364-3302), 270 S Rio Grande, is inexpensive and fun – it is housed in the historic Rio Grande Railway Depot. Hours are 11:30 am to 2:30 pm and 5 to 10 pm Monday to Saturday and 4 to 9 pm on Sunday. The pork carnitas are especially good and they serve a decent margarita as well. *La Frontera* is at 1236 W 400 South (☎ 801-532-3158) and at 1434 S 700 West (☎ 801-974-0172); both serve good-sized meals at reasonable prices. Hours are 10 am to 11 pm daily except Friday and Saturday, when they close at 11 pm.

The *Pierpont Cantina* (☎ 801-364-1222), downtown at 122 W Pierpont Ave, has a more extensive and expensive menu, though you are paying for the surroundings and wider selection rather than better Mexican food (not to say that the food isn't good). You can eat on the outdoor sidewalk or inside accompanied by festively loud Mexican music and surrounded by piñatas and other south-of-the-border touches. Plates are in the $9 to $18 range. The café is open 11:30 am to 10 pm from Monday to Thursday, till 11 pm on Friday, 4 to 11 pm on Saturday and 10 am to 10 pm on Sunday (with an all-you-can-eat buffet from 10 am to 2:30 pm).

Finally, I can't resist mentioning the delightfully named *Guadalahonky Mexican Restaurant* (☎ 801-571-3838), 136 E 12300 South. I can only wonder what the food is like.

Italian

For pizza, *Pie Pizzeria* (☎ 801-582-0193), 1320 E 200 South, is a popular university hangout and may have live entertainment on weekends. It's a little difficult to find this basement place but look hard – locals have voted this the best pizza in Utah. Hours are 11 am to 1 am, Monday to Thursday, till 3 am on Friday and Saturday, and noon till midnight on Sunday. The *Old Spaghetti Factory* (☎ 801-521-0424), Trolley Square (southwest of 500 South and 700 East) is very popular and inexpensive. A variety of spaghetti plates go for $4.50 to $9 including bread and salad and they're good. The plush bright red interior, complete with unusual antiques and a trolley from the days when Trolley Square was actually a transportation depot, make this a fun place to bring your kids. *Salt Lake Pizza & Pasta* (☎ 801-484-1804), 1063 E 2100 South, is a good choice as well for reasonably priced pizza and pasta and they have a great variety of microbrews to wash it down with.

There are several good, upscale Italian restaurants. *Fresco Italian Café* (☎ 801-486-1300), 1513 S 1500 East, offers yet a different Italian dining experience. The small but neat dining room is inside a house, and diners spill out onto a courtyard outside during warm weather. A no-smoking policy is enforced. Pasta and other Italian dishes are flavored with some unusual sauces – not necessarily to everyone's taste but local cognoscenti think highly of the unique offerings. Main courses are in the $11 to $22 range and their hours are 5 to 9:30 pm daily. Lunches may be served in summer.

Other top-quality Italian restaurants worth trying include the *Baci Trattoria* (☎ 801-328-1500), downtown at 134 W Pierpont Ave, which has a modern but beautiful décor; next door is the Club Baci – a popular private club. The same tasty food is served in both places. It's open from 11:30 am to 3 pm from Monday to Friday and 5 to 11 pm daily.

Finally, a new place that has received great reviews for its freshly made authentic meals (the owners are from Tuscany and most of the waitstaff are Italian) is *Michelangelo Ristorante* (☎ 801-466-0961), 2156 S Highland Drive, near 1100 East. Reservations are highly recommended for both lunch (11:30 am to 2:30 pm, weekdays) and dinner (6 to 10 pm, Monday to Saturday). A recent restaurant poll claims that Michelangelo's servers are the best-dressed in town, so you might want to wear something more than jeans and a T-shirt!

French

Despite its name, *Le Parisien* (☎ 801-364-5223), 417 S 300 East, serves both French and some Italian food at more modest prices than most French restaurants; dinner entrées are mostly in the teens and their lunches are bargain-priced. This elegant and popular restaurant has several private booths and an upstairs dining room with city views; a reservation is a good idea. Hours are 11 am to 10 pm from Monday to Thursday and to 11 pm on Friday and Saturday; 5 to 10 pm on Sunday. The less well-known *L'Hermitage* (☎ 801-583-5339), 1615 S Foothill Drive, has a fiercely loyal clientele who claim the fine French dinners served from Tuesday to Saturday are the best in town.

It's a fair drive to *La Caille at Quail Run* (☎ 801-942-1751), 9665 Wasatch Blvd (near the beginning of Little Cottonwood Canyon), but it's worth the drive to this beautiful restaurant. Set in 22 acres of landscaped gardens, the place bills itself as an 18th-century French chateau and does a nice job of fulfilling the promise. The food and service are very good at prices commensurate with the high quality and elegant surroundings. Reservations are required.

Historic Restaurants

There are several eateries with a sense of history, especially the *Lion House Restaurant* (☎ 801-363-5466), 63 E South Temple. This is on the ground floor of the Lion House, built in 1855 as quarters for some of Brigham Young's many wives. Hearty American food is served for weekday lunches (11 am to 2 pm). Meals are $4 to $10.

Lamb's Restaurant (☎ 801-364-7166), 169 S Main, founded in 1919, is Utah's oldest continually operating restaurant. It moved to its present location in 1939 and has maintained a 1930s atmosphere – it feels as if you are in a Bogart movie. The food is good and fairly inexpensive, too. Hours are 7 am to 9 pm daily, except Sunday.

The *Old Salt City Jail* (☎ 801-355-2422), 460 S 1000 East, housed in what used to be a jail house, has a 'singing sheriff' and other early Western touches. It's OK, though a bit touristy. The food is mostly meat, and main courses are in the $10 to $20 range. Seafood and a children's (Little Cowboy's) menu are available. Hours are 5 to 10 pm from Monday to Thursday, 4:30 to 11 pm on Friday and Saturday, and 4 to 9 pm on Sunday.

Archibald's (☎ 801-566-6940), 1100 W 7800 South, is well south of town in the historic mill built by Archibald Gardner in 1853. (There are many gift shops and a small museum.) American food is served and there is a patio for summer dining. Main courses are in the $6 to $15 range. Hours are 11 am to 9 pm Monday to Thursday, till 10 pm on Friday and Saturday, and 9 am to 4 pm on Sunday. ∎

Dinner is served from 6 to 10 pm daily (11 pm on Friday and Saturday). There is a Sunday brunch from 10 am to 1 pm.

Middle Eastern & Asian

Lebanese, Indian, Thai, Vietnamese, Afghan, Chinese, Tibetan or Japanese – you have a good choice of Asian restaurants in a city where the population is very predominantly Caucasian. Enjoy it here; you won't find many Asian restaurants in the rest of the state. Most of these restaurants have a good selection of vegetarian items on their menus.

The *Cedars of Lebanon* (☎ 801-364-4096), 154 E 200 South, has inexpensive lunches (including all-you-can-eat weekday lunch buffets for about $6) and pricier dinners with a good variety of Middle Eastern and vegetarian dishes. Middle Eastern carpets and music add to the ambiance and belly dancers entertain on Friday and Saturday nights. Dinner entrées range from $9 to $18. Hours are 11 am to 10 pm, Monday to Saturday. There is an adjoining deli with espresso and Middle Eastern groceries.

Across the street, the *Star of India* (☎ 801-363-7555), 177 E 200 South, also has an all-you-can-eat lunch buffet from 11:30 am to 2:30 pm, Monday to Saturday. For dinner, good medium-priced curries, tandoori specialties and other Indian dishes are served from 5:30 to 9:30 pm on Sunday, till 10 pm Monday to Thursday, and till 10:30 pm on Friday and Saturday. Another excellent choice for Indian meals is *Bombay House* (☎ 801-581-0222), 1615 S Foothill Drive, open for dinner from 5 to 10 pm, Monday to Saturday.

Bangkok Thai (☎ 801-582-8424), 1400 S Foothill Drive, in the Foothill Village shopping center, is generally considered one of the region's best Thai restaurants. It features a spice rating reminiscent of nearby ski slopes, ranging from a circle for Easy (Mild), through a double diamond for Expert (Authentically Hot) to a circle with a slash for Extreme, so everyone in your group can find the right level of spiciness or lack thereof. The restaurant is known for its 'Meatless Mondays' when

vegetarian entrées are $5/7 for lunch/dinner and it gets really crowded. It is open Monday to Friday for lunch and daily for dinner.

For genuine and well-prepared Afghan food, the place to go is *Baba Afghan* (☎ 801-596-0786), 55 E 400 South. They are open from 11:30 am to 2:30 pm for buffet lunches from Monday to Friday; dinner is served from 5 to 10 pm Tuesday to Saturday, till 9 pm on Sunday.

If you'd like to try authentic Tibetan cuisine, complete with tea served with butter and salt, head over to *House of Tibet* (☎ 801-364-1376), 145 E 1300 South, Space 409. They do buffet lunches from 11:30 am to 2:30 pm, Monday to Friday, à la carte lunches from noon to 2:30 pm on weekends and dinners from 5 to 9:30 pm every day. The recommended and inexpensive *Cafe Trang* (☎ 801-539-1638), 818 S Main, serves tasty and authentic Vietnamese cuisine 11:30 am to 9:30 pm daily, and till 10 pm on Friday and Saturday. They have Chinese food as well. There are several dozen other Chinese restaurants in Salt Lake City – the yellow pages are full of them – but I keep going back to the Trang. With 200 items on the menu, it's hard to run out of new things to try.

Japanese food has recently become popular in the city and there are several good places to choose from. The family-owned *Kyoto* (☎ 801-487-3525), 1080 E 1300 South, has authentic food at moderate prices and offers private dining rooms where guests sit on mats around a low table, Japanese style. Lunches are $5 to $10, dinners $10 to $17. Reservations for the private rooms are recommended and on weekends the place is always packed. Lunch is served 11:30 am to 2 pm from Monday to Friday; dinner is served daily 6 to 9:30 pm (till 9 pm on Sundays).

The well-recommended *Mikado* (☎ 801-328-0929), 67 W 100 South, which has been open since the 1950s, has authentic Japanese dining in a traditional ambiance – private *zashiki* dining rooms are available and there is a particularly good sushi bar.

Dinners are served 6 to 9:30 pm from Sunday to Thursday and to 10:30 pm on Friday and Saturday. Dinner prices range from $12 to $22, and a children's menu is available.

Shogun (☎ 801-364-7142), 321 S Main, has one of the better sushi bars in town, as well as a wide variety of other Japanese dishes. Its downtown location makes it popular with businesspeople. Lunch combos are in the $5 to $10 range; dinners go from $9 to $21, plus a special sushi combo for about $25. Hours are 11:30 am to 2 pm from Monday to Friday, 5:30 to 10 pm from Monday to Thursday, to 11 pm Friday and Saturday and to 9:30 pm on Sunday.

American

One of my favorite places is *Bill & Nada's Cafe* (☎ 801-359-6984), 479 S 600 East, the quintessential, unpretentious American diner. The service is friendly if occasionally offbeat, the food is satisfactory, the prices are low and the hours are perfect. This locally popular café provides good value 24 hours a day. Apart from the usual – full breakfasts (served anytime), sandwiches, grilled chicken, liver 'n onions etc – you'll find some offbeat dishes like scrambled eggs with brains (which I last ate in Peru!). In addition, the *City Weekly* rates their archaic jukebox as 'fantastic . . . , nostalgic' and the best in town.

Good value has not gone the way of the dinosaurs in the nicely named *Dodo Restaurant* (☎ 801-328-9348), 680 S 900 East, which serves excellent and moderately priced food. The varied selection is interesting and the ham and turkey used in the delicious sandwiches are smoked right on the premises. There is a pleasant outdoor patio. Their lunches are especially good (about $5 to $10), dinner entrées are in the $10 to $15 range and dessert-lovers will definitely not regret leaving room for that last course. Hours are 11 am to about 9 pm from Monday to Thursday and to 10:30 pm on Friday and Saturday. A Sunday brunch is served from 10 am to 2 pm.

You get Western food in an Old Wild West setting at *Diamond Lil's* (533-0547), 1528 W North Temple. The food is appropriate – prime rib, steak and barbecue are the big sellers, though seafood is available too. Meals range from $10 to $31 (the latter for a huge king crab/New York steak combo) with most dinners in the teens. It's open 11:30 am to 10 pm from Monday to Saturday. Top-quality steaks are also the specialty at *Ruby River* (☎ 801-359-3355), 435 S 700 East, where those with smaller appetites can get an 8-oz filet mignon for $15 and those with gargantuan appetites can get a 2-lb porterhouse steak for about $30. Chicken, fish and pasta are also offered, as are meaty sandwiches and salads for lunch. Hours are 11 am to 4 pm, Monday to Friday, and from 5 pm every night.

For more upmarket American food, head for the *Market Street Grill* (☎ 801-322-4668), 48 W Market (downtown at 350 South), which specializes in seafood. Specializes? Heck, it's probably the best seafood restaurant in the state as far as food quality goes, although it's popular and busy so don't go for a quiet intimate meal. It's open for breakfast and lunch from Monday to Saturday (6:30 am to 3 pm) and dinner daily from 4 pm. They also do Sunday brunch from 9 am to 3 pm. Excellent breakfasts are $4 to $8 (crab omelets, broiled halibut with eggs, trout with bacon and standard American breakfasts are among the many choices). Lunch salads, sandwiches, pasta and seafood plates are in the $6 to $14 range. Dinners include meat and seafood entrées ranging from Utah trout ($14) to filet mignon with Alaskan king crab legs ($45) with many fine seafood specialties in the teens. Come in before 7 pm to take advantage of the early bird special – prime rib or halibut for $13. It comes with chowder or salad, ice cream and beverage – a good deal. Next door is the *Market Street Oyster Bar* (☎ 801-531-6044), 48 W Market, a private club with similar food for lunch and dinner – temporary club membership is $5 for two weeks and you can usually get in for free by asking at the door for someone to sponsor you.

Next to the above pair is the *New Yorker* (☎ 801-363-0166), 60 Market. This, too, is an elegant and upmarket restaurant in a private club. Dinner entrées range from $20 to $30 or you can drop $50 for abalone. Daily fixed-price lunches are $8 and are popular with businesspeople in a hurry – the restaurant guarantees a 50-minute lunch. Lunch is served from 11:30 am to 2:30 pm from Monday to Friday and dinner from 6 pm daily except Sunday. Reservations are recommended.

Opposite, the *Barking Frog Grill* (☎ 801-322-3764), 39 W Market, specializes in well-prepared Southwestern cuisine. Dinner entrées range from fish tacos at $15 through Utah red trout ($18), high mesa lamb ($18.50), venison served with a chile crust, wild mushroom tamales ($22), a 16-oz porterhouse steak ($23) and a number of other choices. Service is friendly and helpful.

One of the best university-area restaurants is the *Market Street Broiler* (☎ 801-583-8808), 260 S 1300 East, which is a partner of the Market Street Grill (see above) and has similar food at slightly more moderate prices. Interestingly, the restaurant is housed in a renovated 1930s fire station and has a pleasant and popular outdoor patio. Hours are 11 am to 10 pm, Monday to Thursday and to 10:30 pm on Friday and Saturday. Sunday hours are 4 to 9:30 pm.

For dining out in the nearby countryside, head up to Emigration Canyon, northeast of the city. *Ruth's Diner* (☎ 801-582-5807), 2100 Emigration Canyon, is about 4 miles east of the university. In the 1930s, Ruth's was a diner and a pretty wild one at that, but is now a pleasant café with outdoor gardens and live musicians most evenings when the weather is warm. The place is popular and packed with locals who want to eat well-prepared and reasonably priced food out-of-doors – or inside in winter. The menu is varied but tends toward Mexican/American. Prices are in the $5 to $15 range for most items. Hours are 7 am to 10 pm daily. Breakfast is served from an ambitious 7 am to a relaxing 4 pm – with patio dining, friendly servers and tasty food, it's one of the best breakfasts in town.

Right next door to Ruth's is the *Santa Fe Restaurant* (☎ 801-582-5888). High ceilings, wooden beams, fireplaces, picture windows and Southwestern décor make this one of the more distinctive and popular restaurants in the Salt Lake area. It also has an outdoor patio. The menu is American with a Southwestern and Mexican flair. Lunches are in the $5 to $9 range; main dinner entrées from $10 to $18. Hours are 11:30 am to 2:30 pm from Monday to Friday, 5 to 10 pm from Monday to Saturday and from 10 am to 2:30 pm for Sunday brunch.

Vegetarian
While many of the restaurants above (especially the Middle Eastern & Asian section) have vegetarian entrées, the following don't make you pick through a varied menu to find a meatless dish. The award-winning *Park Ivy Garden Café* (☎ 801-328-1313), 878 S 900 East, is one of the city's favorites and is open 11 am to 9 pm, Monday to Saturday. They serve a variety of Mexican meals, salads, sandwiches and soups ranging from about $4 to $8. *Wild Oats Community Market* (☎ 801-355-7401), 812 E 200 South, and other locations, is a store specializing in vegetarian items; it also has a café. Hours are 8 am to 9 pm, Monday to Saturday and 10 am to 7 pm on Sunday (though the café closes about an hour before the store does). Another choice is the *Oasis Café & Restaurant* (☎ 801-322-0404), 151 S 500 East, which has some seafood items along with the vegetarian menu. The café is open 7 am to 10 pm, Monday to Friday, 8 am to 5:30 pm on weekends. The adjoining restaurant has similar hours but closes in the afternoons.

Brewpubs
If you feel like a burger and brew, a good place is the *Squatter's Pub Brewery* (☎ 801-363-2739), 147 W 300 South, whose microbrewery is right behind the bar. You can down a pint of draft pale ale, cream stout, best bitter or one of the brewmaster's seasonal ales along with your meal. The beer is among the best in Utah. The food is good

and plentiful too – not just burgers but a satisfying choice of soups, salads, sandwiches, pizza, chile and pub food like fish & chips or curry. Almost everything is under $10. The ambiance is pub-like and friendly – a good place to hang out. Fireplaces blaze in winter and there's a beer garden for summer. Hours are 11:30 am to midnight (1 am on Friday and Saturday) – but you have to be 21 to get in.

The *Salt Lake Brewing Company* (☎ 801-328-2329), 367 W 200 South, has similar brews to Squatter's but also has a pool room, and a restaurant that welcomes children. Other brewpubs include the *Red Rock Brewing Company* (☎ 801-521-7446), 254 S 200 West, which also allows children and brews its beer right there. They advertise more than 30 styles of beer and house food specialties are wood-fired pizza as well as other bar food served until midnight, or later on weekends. It's lines-outside-the-door popular at weekends. Also popular with the younger crowd is the *Desert Edge Brewery* (also called 'The Pub,' ☎ 801-521-8917), in Trolley Square, with an unusual interior reminiscent of a factory. They serve good sandwiches and bar food under $11 and there is a section seating children.

ENTERTAINMENT
Cinemas
There are dozens of movie theaters all over town – look in the entertainment sections of the city newspapers for cinema addresses, phone numbers and movie times. Note the discounted prices (as low as $1) if you go to afternoon matinee performances midweek.

If you want a change from popcorn and soda with your first-run movie, get a beer and a meal at *Brewvies* (☎ 801-355-5500), 677 S 200 West. You have to be 21 to enter.

For alternative movies, call the *Tower Theater* (☎ 801-297-4040), 876 E 900 South, or try the *Utah Film & Video Center* (☎ 801-534-1158) in the Salt Lake Art Center at 20 S West Temple, which could be showing just about anything. During the second half of January, the Tower Theater

shows some of the movies from the Sundance Film Festival, held in Park City.

Nightlife
The best listing of bars, concerts and nightclubs is in the free *City Weekly*, published on Thursday and available at hundreds of outlets, including many of the bars themselves. The free biweekly *Event*, published every other Thursday, is also a good information source. The Friday editions of the two city dailies have entertainment listings.

Many nightclubs are private clubs – you can buy a temporary two-week membership for $5 (which allows you to bring five guests) or you can hang out at the entrance and find a member to sponsor you for one night. You have to be 21 to get in to most places everywhere – and IDs are often checked. If you can't find a newspaper listing, call before showing up – nightclubs don't last forever!

There are dozens of popular nightspots, catering to a wide variety of tastes. Some popular ones include the following (all along S West Temple). The *Dead Goat Saloon* (☎ 801-328-4628), 165 S West Temple, is more or less underground, down a funky-looking iron stairwell and behind a formidable wooden door. This has been a popular drinking spot for both young locals and travelers since 1965. There is live blues or rock & roll with a $3 to $6 cover most nights. Pub lunches are served and there are pool tables. Hours are 11:30 am to 1 am during the week and 6 pm to 1 am on weekends. Also popular, featuring live and recorded rock & roll, blues and alternative music, is the hip private club *DV8* (☎ 801-539-8400), 115 S West Temple. The young crowd is cool and the cover can wander into the double digits. Decide for yourself whether it's worth it. Underage nightclubbers will find a no-alcohol zone on the ground floor. *Zephyr* (☎ 801-355-2582), 301 S West Temple, Salt Lake's oldest club, is a friendly private club sticking to fairly mainstream live music every night. It serves pizza and Italian food until late at night and the dance floor is usually packed (with dancers, not pizzas).

Other places include *Port-O-Call* (☎ 801-521-0589), 78 W 400 South, a private club with some live music and big-screen-TV sports – it is popular with singles and the college crowd. *Bricks Club* (☎ 801-328-0255), 579 W 200 South, is a huge place with different dance floors, a pool room and a stage where you are likely to see anything from a freak circus to an alternative band. The *Ashbury Pub* (☎ 801-596-8600), 22 E 100 South, floats between being a friendly neighborhood pub and a venue for a variety of live music. The *Holy Cow* (☎ 801-256-4901), 241 S 500 East, is a good bet for live music and dancing. *Ichabob's* (☎ 801-359-6660), 666 S State, is a bar with pool tables, live local bands and no membership fee. The *Sun Club* (☎ 801-531-0833), 200 S 700 West, is a friendly gay and lesbian bar/dance club. *The Library* (☎ 801-521-8300), 155 W 200 South, looks kind of like an enlarged version of Sherlock Holmes' study and books jazz bands. There are plenty of other places to prowl around.

For country & western bands and dancing, head on over to the *Westerner Club* (☎ 801-972-5447), 3360 S Redwood Rd, which claims the largest dance floor in Utah and offers free dance lessons on Monday, Tuesday and Wednesday nights. Pool tables and ranching paraphernalia contribute to the Western ambiance.

Don't forget to read the Brewpubs section above. Other good bars with no cover charge include *Junior's Tavern* (☎ 801-322-0318), 200 E 500 South, which is your basic beer bar with a jukebox and pool table. Small and cheap, it draws a mildly wild clientele of all ages and races. *Bar X* (☎ 801-532-9114), 155 E 200 South, is a good basic beer bar with a pool table.

Many of the better hotels have good clubs attracting people of all ages. These include the clubs at the Marriott, Embassy Suites, Red Lion, Holiday Inn Airport and Shilo Inn.

Performing Arts
See Nightlife (above) for entertainment information sources. The best new plays or musicals are presented year-round by the *Salt Lake Acting Company* (☎ 801-363-0525), 168 W 500 North. *Pioneer Theater Company* (☎ 801-581-6961), 300 S 1340 East at the university, has performances throughout the September-to-May school year. The *Promised Valley Playhouse* (☎ 801-240-5696), 132 S State, is a charming turn-of-the-19th-century theater presenting squeaky-clean productions.

Several professional and acclaimed companies share the elegant *Capitol Theater* (☎ 801-355-2787) venue at 50 W 200 South. These include the Utah Opera Company and Ballet West, each of which stages four classical productions during the season (fall to spring). Modern dance is presented by the Ririe-Woodbury Dance Company (☎ 801-328-1062).

The Utah Symphony Orchestra performs at frequent intervals around the year in *Abravanel Hall* (☎ 801-533-6683, 801-533-5626), which is next to the Salt Palace and lays claim to the best acoustics of any modern concert hall in the world.

The Salt Lake City Arts Council (☎ 801-596-5000) has information about various local cultural events.

SPECTATOR SPORTS
The Delta Center (☎ 801-325-7328), 301 W South Temple, hosts both National Basketball Association (NBA) and International Hockey League (IHL) games. The NBA Utah Jazz (☎ 801-355-3865) and the IHL Utah Grizzlies (☎ 801-530-7166, 801-325-7825) are the home teams and both have been doing well in recent years. Seats for the most important games are sold out well in advance but call anyway – you might get lucky. Otherwise, scalpers may be found near the center offering tickets for the best games at exorbitant prices.

Franklin Quest Field (☎ 801-485-3800), 77 W 1300 South, hosts the Salt Lake Buzz baseball team. The Buzz are the Minnesota Twins' AAA team (AAA being the highest level of professional minor league baseball play). Tickets are easier to come by for baseball games.

SHOPPING

Conventional shopping is available at a number of good malls. ZCMI (Zions Cooperative Mercantile Institution) (☎ 801-321-8745), 36 S State, is the oldest in Utah, though the approximately one hundred stores and restaurants within are all thoroughly modern. Opposite is the Crossroads Plaza (☎ 801-531-1799), 50 S Main, with about one hundred and fifty shops and restaurants. Free validated parking is available if you spend over $5 at one of the establishments in these two malls.

One place stands out for its typical handicrafts. Simply called Mormon Handicrafts (☎ 801-355-2141), in ZCMI, it sells beautiful handmade quilts, dolls and stuffed animals, clothes (especially baby clothes) and a host of other painstakingly made articles reminiscent of pioneer days. Quiltmaking supplies are available.

Trolley Square (☎ 801-521-9877), 600 S 700 East, is housed in what used to be the trolley-car depot, which went out of use after WWII. There are plenty of signs of the old days – a restaurant in a trolley car, stores in car barns, a photography exhibit etc. This attractive mall has a good selection of restaurants as well as shops. Free guided tours of some of the historical parts of Trolley Square are offered every 30 minutes from noon to 2 pm on Saturdays.

There are a number of good bookstores. Sam Weller Books (☎ 801-328-2586), 254 S Main, carries many books on the West and is the city's biggest independent bookstore. Deseret Book (☎ 801-328-8191), in ZCMI and several other locations, has the best selection of books for and about Mormons. Waking Owl Books (☎ 801-582-7323), 208 S 1300 East, is a readers' bookstore with a good choice of titles and an easy browsing atmosphere. A Woman's Place (☎ 801-583-6431), 1400 S Foothill Drive in the Foothill Village shopping center, has books by, for and about women.

REI (☎ 801-486-2100), 3285 E 3300 South, is a reliable source of high quality outdoor guidebooks and gear – everything from climbing ropes to sleeping bags. Rentals are available for your trip into the backcountry.

GETTING THERE & AWAY

Air

Salt Lake City International Airport, about 6 miles west of downtown, is by far the most important airport in Utah. Several major carriers including America West, American, Continental, Delta, Southwest, TWA, United and others fly out of state; Skywest/Delta Connection flies to the Utah cities of St George, Cedar City and Vernal. The local Alpine Air (☎ 801-575-2839) flies between Salt Lake City and Moab once or twice on most days.

The airport has two national terminals and a third terminal for international flights. Facilities include a tourist information office, money exchange, restaurants, lounge, car rentals, baggage lockers and shops.

Bus

Greyhound (☎ 801-355-9579), 160 W South Temple, provides long-distance bus service. There are several buses a day heading south on I-15 through Provo, St George and Cedar City to Las Vegas (Nevada) and Los Angeles. There are also several buses a day west to San Francisco, east to Denver (Colorado), and north to Portland (Oregon) and Seattle (Washington).

UTA (Utah Transit Authority) (☎ 801-287-4636) provides services to the nearby cities of Provo, Tooele, Ogden and the towns and suburbs in between. Fares are a very reasonable $2. Sunday services are limited to three buses each to Ogden and Provo but there are frequent departures during the rest of the week.

Train

Amtrak (☎ 801-531-0188) is in the Rio Grande Depot at 320 S Rio Grande near downtown. There is daily service between Chicago and Salt Lake via Denver, Thompson and Helper. The westbound train continues to San Francisco. Call Amtrak for information on other services available.

GETTING AROUND
To/From the Airport

A taxi downtown will cost about $10. The UTA Bus 50 goes downtown for $1 (exact change required) between about 6 am and 7 pm. There are 25 trips a day from Monday to Friday, 13 trips on Saturday and five on Sunday. UTA Bus 150 has five night buses from Monday to Saturday until about 11 pm. There is no holiday service. See below for local bus information.

Several shuttle services can take you to and from anywhere in the Salt Lake City/ Wasatch Front area. Call the airport transportation desk (☎ 801-575-2477) for information.

Bus

UTA (☎ 801-287-4636 between 6 am and 7 pm, Monday to Saturday) provides services throughout Salt Lake City and the surrounding areas. There are dozens of routes with scores of departures a day on the busier lines. Sunday services are limited to buses to the airport, Provo and Ogden. There is no holiday service.

Fares in the city are a flat $1 (exact change required) and free transfers are available on request. All-day passes are $2. There is a free fare zone from 400 South to North Temple (continuing along N Main to the State Capitol) and from West Temple to 200 East. If you enter and exit the bus between these streets, the ride is free. The most useful free fare bus is the No 23, which goes from 325 S West Temple to the State Capitol 60 times between 5:45 am and 7:20 pm from Monday to Friday and 11 times on Saturday. Many buses are wheelchair accessible or have bike racks. Seniors and disabled passengers get discounts.

Detailed bus maps and timetables are available from the visitors bureau, public libraries, shopping malls, and city and municipal buildings.

Taxi

The three main taxi companies, all with 24-hour service, are Yellow Cab (☎ 801-521-2100), Ute Cab (☎ 801-359-7788) and City Cab (☎ 801-363-5550).

Car Rental

All the major car rental companies have offices in Salt Lake City and at the airport.

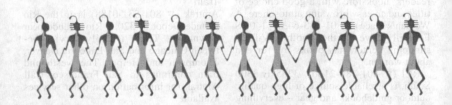

Wasatch Mountains Region

Salt Lake City is but one of several towns running north to south along the western front of the Wasatch Mountains. The towns combine into an urban chain stretching roughly from Ogden, 35 miles north of Salt Lake City, to Provo, 45 miles south – this area is home to well over half of Utah's residents. The steep-sided, forested mountains form a splendid backdrop to the urban areas and, perhaps more to the point, provide a reliable source of water for the area. Historically, nomadic Ute and Shoshone Indians roamed this well-watered area, and it became the first region to be settled by the Mormon pioneers.

Today, the Wasatch Mountains provide the winter visitor with 11 ski resorts within 55 miles of Salt Lake City. Four are best reached from Salt Lake City itself, and three others are most accessible from Park City to the east. Yet another three are found northeast of Ogden, and the last is north of Provo.

The summer visitor can enjoy the beautiful scenery by hiking, camping, fishing, visiting underground caves, sightseeing and relaxing. The towns themselves have interesting historical buildings, museums, festivals and plenty of good places to stay and eat. In fact, a visitor could spend months enjoying the area without venturing more than 60 miles from Salt Lake City.

This chapter first covers the Ogden area in the north, continues with Park City and Heber City to the east, and finishes with the Provo area south of Salt Lake City.

ANTELOPE ISLAND STATE PARK

This 15-mile-long island, the largest in the Great Salt Lake, is connected to the mainland by a 7-mile causeway, which was flooded in the 1980s and reopened in the mid-1990s. Now a state park, the island is most famous for being the home of one of the largest bison (often called buffalo) herds

---

Where the Buffalo Roam

Once, tens of millions of bison roamed much of the western part of the continent; now, the 550- to 700-strong herd on Antelope Island is one of the few remaining.

Bison calves are normally born in March, April and May, and this is when the population is at its highest. Because of the finite food resources on the island, the herd is rounded up every fall (usually in late October), allowed to rest for a few days, then passed through corrals for veterinary inspection and tagging. A few animals are removed to keep the population stable, and the rest of the bison are allowed to roam freely throughout most of the island for the remainder of the year. Some are always kept at the corrals so visitors can get a close look. The fall herding and corralling of these animals is one of the area's famous wildlife spectacles.

Another wildlife spectacle is the spring and fall bird migration, when hundreds of thousands of shorebirds, waterfowl and seabirds use the island and causeway shorelines as a protected feeding place on their way to distant lands. One of the main food sources is the tiny brine shrimp, which are dense along the shoreline. In August, as many as 250,000 Wilson's phalaropes have been recorded, along with large numbers of other species. In addition, the island itself is the home of burrowing owls, several species of raptors and many other birds.

The visitor may also see one of the several dozen pronghorn antelope, bighorn sheep and deer, which share the island with badgers, porcupines, and numerous coyotes, jackrabbits, cottontails and various rodents. ■

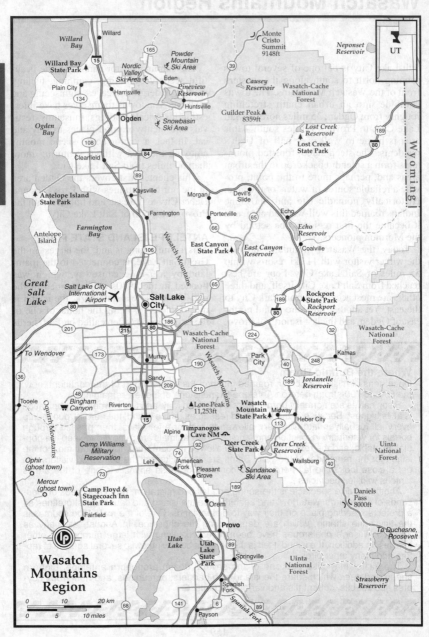

Wasatch Mountains Region

in the country. People also come for the spring and fall bird migration. (See the sidebar Where the Buffalo Roam.)

Another attraction is the Fielding Garr ranch, established in 1848 and inhabited until 1981, when it was taken over by the state park. This is the oldest continually inhabited Anglo home in the state. It is currently closed to the public, but there are plans to reopen it in 1999 or 2000 when a mountain bike trail is constructed to the ranch.

At this time, there are a few miles of paved roads, several miles of unpaved roads and 19 miles of hiking trails. More are in the works, but the planners are proceeding carefully to ensure minimum negative impact on the wildlife. Some trails are closed for parts of the year to allow the animals to breed and give birth without disturbance.

Day use of the state park is $3 per bicyclist and $7 per car. A campground (☎ 801-773-2941 for reservations and information) offers water and pit toilets (no showers) for $9 per site and is open year-round. There is a small marina that offers cruises from Salt Islands Adventures (☎ 801-583-4400) during the summer months. *Buffalo Point Restaurant* (☎ 801-776-6734), open daily in summer and with limited hours in other months, serves buffalo burgers and other snacks and sandwiches. There is a gift shop, basic grocery supplies, and horseback riding – all available seasonally.

The park is open year-round from dawn till dusk (about 7 am to 10 pm in summer, 8 am to 5:30 pm in winter). Get there by heading west from I-15 exit 335 (25 miles north of Salt Lake City; 10 miles south of Ogden) and following signs for about 7 miles to the park entrance, which is at the beginning of the 7-mile causeway (an interesting driving experience). This park is undergoing changes and developments in 1999; contact the state park headquarters (☎ 801-550-6165), 4528 W 1700 South, Syracuse, UT 84075.

OGDEN

The city is named after Peter Skene Ogden, a trapper who arrived in the Ogden river valley in 1826 and traded with the local Shoshone Indians. The pleasant area was the site of multiple rendezvous among the Indians, trappers and mountain men of the area during the 1820s and 1830s. There were no permanent structures until Miles Goodyear built a cabin in the 1840s (reputedly the oldest non-Native American building in Utah). In 1846, he built Fort Buenaventura. Goodyear was bought out by the Mormons soon after, and under Brigham Young's direction, founded the town in 1850.

After the completion of the first transcontinental railway in 1869, Ogden became an important railway town. The railway brought many non-Mormon settlers, and Ogden quickly developed a large non-Mormon population, whose frontier-town excesses often created tension with the sober Mormon inhabitants.

Since then, Ogden has seen the opening of Weber State University (in 1889) and Hill Air Force Base (in 1939). Today, Ogden is an important agricultural and manufacturing center. The military base is also an economic mainstay. The population of Ogden itself is about 70,000, but along with the surrounding communities, it is Utah's third most populous urban area. Ogden is the seat of Weber County. Its elevation of 4500 feet gives it a similar climate to Salt Lake City.

Orientation

Although laid out by Mormons in their typical wide-avenued grid pattern, the city's street names differ somewhat from most Mormon towns. The east-west streets begin at 1st in the north and continue to about 40th in the south; the north-south streets are named mainly after famous people, particularly American presidents. The most historic east-west street is 25th, and the most important north-south street is Washington Blvd, also called Hwy 89. I-15 skirts the city to the west.

Information

The visitors bureau (☎ 801-627-8288, 800-225-8824, staff@ogdencvb.org), 2501 Wall Ave (in Union Station), is open 8 am to

UTAH

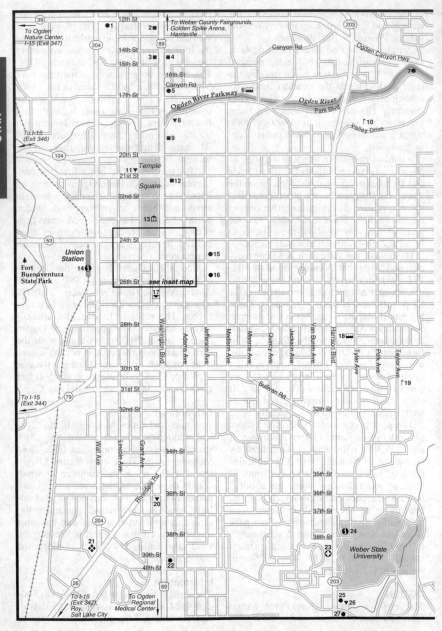

To Ogden
Nature Center,
I-15 (Exit 347)

To Weber County Fairgrounds,
Golden Spike Arena,
Harrisville

12th St
14th St
15th St
16th St
Canyon Rd
17th St

Canyon Rd

Ogden Canyon Hwy

Ogden River Parkway
Ogden River
Park Blvd

Valley Drive

To I-15
(Exit 346)

20th St

Temple

21st St

Square

22nd St

24th St

Union
Station

Fort
Buenaventura
State Park

26th St   see inset map

28th St

Washington Blvd
Adams Ave
Jefferson Ave
Madison Ave
Monroe Ave
Quincy Ave
Jackson Ave
Van Buren Ave
Harrison Blvd
Tyler Ave
Polk Ave
Taylor Ave

30th St

31st St

To I-15
(Exit 344)

32nd St

Sullivan Rd

32nd St

34th St

Wall Ave
Lincoln Ave
Grant Ave
Riverdale Rd

35th St

36th St

36th St

37th St

38th St

38th St

39th St

40th St

Weber State
University

To I-15
(Exit 342),
Roy,
Salt Lake City

To Ogden
Regional
Medical Center

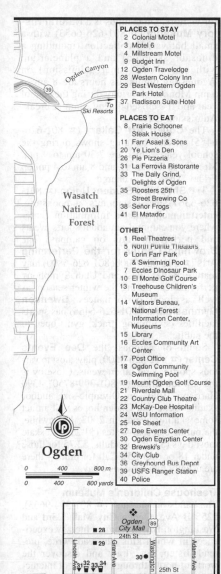

PLACES TO STAY
2 Colonial Motel
3 Motel 6
4 Millstream Motel
9 Budget Inn
12 Ogden Travelodge
28 Western Colony Inn
29 Best Western Ogden
    Park Hotel
37 Radisson Suite Hotel

PLACES TO EAT
8 Prairie Schooner
    Steak House
11 Farr Asael & Sons
20 Ye Lion's Den
26 Pie Pizzeria
31 La Ferrovia Ristorante
33 The Daily Grind,
    Delights of Ogden
35 Roosters 25th
    Street Brewing Co
38 Señor Frogs
41 El Matador

OTHER
1 Reel Theatres
5 North Pointe Theaters
6 Lorin Farr Park
    & Swimming Pool
7 Eccles Dinosaur Park
10 El Monte Golf Course
13 Treehouse Children's
    Museum
14 Visitors Bureau,
    National Forest
    Information Center,
    Museums
15 Library
16 Eccles Community Art
    Center
17 Post Office
18 Ogden Community
    Swimming Pool
19 Mount Ogden Golf Course
21 Riverdale Mall
22 Country Club Theatre
23 McKay-Dee Hospital
24 WSU Information
25 Ice Sheet
27 Dee Events Center
30 Ogden Egyptian Center
32 Brewski's
34 City Club
36 Greyhound Bus Depot
39 USFS Ranger Station
40 Police

Ogden

0   400   800 m
0   400   800 yards

Ogden City Mall
24th St
28
29
30
31 32 33 34
35 36
40
37 38
39
41
25th St
26th St
Lincoln Ave
Grant Ave
Washington Blvd
Adams Ave
Ogden Ave
0   150   300 m
0   150   300 yards

4:30 pm from Monday to Friday. Between Memorial Day and Labor Day, the bureau remains open later and may also open on weekends. The Wasatch National Forest Ogden Ranger Station (☎ 801-625-5112), 507 25th, and the National Forest Information Center (☎ 801-625-5306), inside the visitors bureau, have maps and national forest information from 8 am to 4:30 pm, Monday to Friday.

The library (☎ 801-627-6917) is at 2464 Jefferson Ave. The local newspaper is the *Standard-Examiner*. The downtown post office (☎ 801-627-4184) is at 2641 Washington Blvd. Recycle at Bloom Recyclers (☎ 801-393-5396), 2127 Wall Ave – it accepts glass, plastic, paper, aluminum and tin. There are two hospitals: McKay-Dee (☎ 801-627-2800), 3939 Harrison Blvd, and Columbia Ogden Regional Medical Center (☎ 801-479-2111), 5475 S 500 East. The police (☎ 801-629-8221) are at 2549 Washington Blvd.

Union Station
Built in the 1920s, the station (☎ 801-629-8444), 2501 Wall Ave, contains several museums in addition to the tourist information offices mentioned above. The structure itself is of interest to railway buffs. Inside is the **Browning-Kimball Car Museum**, with a classic collection of vintage American cars on display; the **Browning Firearms Museum**, which shows many guns developed by Ogden native, John M Browning (1855-1926); the **Railroad Museum**, which has an extensive model train system as well as historic locomotives; the **Natural History Museum**, which includes geological and fossil exhibits; and the **Myra Powell Art Gallery** with changing shows of local and national artists. There is also a gift shop and restaurant. Hours are 10 am to 5 pm, Monday to Saturday, plus 11 am to 3 pm on Sundays from June to September. One admission price of $3 for adults and $1 for children under 12 is valid for all exhibits.

Historic 25th Street
The blocks of 25th east of Union Station have numerous early Ogden buildings,

UTAH

some dating to the 1880s. The visitors bureau has a free *Historic Walking Tour* brochure detailing some of these. Mixed in with the historical buildings are private clubs, coffee shops, restaurants and dive bars – an interesting mix! Some of these places are described below in Places to Eat and Entertainment.

Eccles Community Art Center

Housed in a historic mansion, the center (☎ 801-392-6935), 2580 Jefferson Ave, features changing shows of local artists in various media. Hours are 9 am to 5 pm, Monday to Friday, and 10 am to 4 pm on Saturday; admission is free.

DUP Museum

This history museum (☎ 801-393-4460), 2148 Grant Ave, houses the usual artifacts found in DUP museums. Hours are 10 am to 5 pm, Monday to Saturday, May 15 to September 15. Admission is free. Outside is the **Miles Goodyear Cabin**, reputedly the oldest non-Native American house in Utah. The museum is within **Temple Square** – the tabernacle, 2133 Washington Blvd, can be visited, but the adjoining temple is for Mormons on church business only.

Fort Buenaventura State Park

On the grounds of this park (☎ 801-621-4808), 2450 A Ave, is an accurate, full-size replica of the original fort built in 1846. Guides in period dress will show you around and a 'mountain-man rendezvous' occurs over Labor Day weekend. Other programs are scheduled throughout the summer.

Outside the fort is a picnic site, a pond for fishing, canoeing or ice skating (depending on season), and a campsite for preregistered large groups. Daily hours are 8 am to 5 pm, March to November, and until dusk from April to September. Admission is $1 per person or $3 per carload.

Weber State University

This university, pronounced 'weeber,' (☎ 801-626-6975), 3750 Harrison Blvd, offers a variety of events and destinations for visitors. On campus is a **Natural History Museum** (☎ 801-626-6653) with a small but varied collection (including a dinosaur skeleton) and a planetarium with star shows (small admission) on Wednesday nights. Its hours are 8 am to 5 pm Monday to Friday during the school year and it's closed during summer break. Admission is free.

The **Collett Art Gallery** (☎ 801-626-6455) offers changing shows during the school year. Hours are 7:30 am to 9 pm, Monday to Thursday, and 8 am to 4 pm on Friday. There is no charge.

The **Shepherd Student Union** (☎ 801-626-6367) has restaurants, a bookstore, entertainment and an information center where you can find out about sports events and performing arts on campus. The **Browning Center for the Performing Arts** (☎ 801-626-7000, 801-626-6800) may feature Ballet West and Utah Symphony performances during the winter season, as well as local performances. **Swenson Gymnasium** (☎ 801-626-6466) has sports facilities (swimming, track, gym) open to the public.

South of campus, the **Dee Events Center** (☎ 801-626-8500) plays host to various sporting and other events. Close by is the new **Ice Sheet** (☎ 801-399-8750), 4390 Harrison Blvd, an Olympic-size indoor skating arena that Ogden hopes will attract some skating events in 2002. Meanwhile, the public can rent skates ($1.25) and skate most days ($3.25 for adults, $2.75 for those under 18 or over 55). Call for times – there are usually two sessions a day.

Treehouse Children's Museum

The hands-on museum (☎ 801-394-9663), 2255 B Ave, Ogden City Mall (23rd and Washington Blvd), features literacy experiences in which kids can read, write, pretend, listen, act, draw and discover the world of books through a variety of interactive programs. Hours are 10 am to 6 pm, Tuesday to Thursday; 10 am to 9 pm, Friday; noon to 7 pm, Saturday; noon to 5 pm, Sunday. Admission is $3 for kids 15 and under, $1.50 for adults.

Ogden Nature Center

This private reserve (☎ 801-621-7595), 966 W 12th, has trails through a variety of habitats. An exhibit room and naturalist guides are on the premises, and there is a picnic area. Raccoons, muskrats, porcupines, mule deer and various bird species may be seen, especially in spring and fall. In winter, the snow-covered trails are used by snowshoers and Nordic skiers. Hours are 10 am to 4 pm, Monday to Saturday. Admission is $1.

Ogden River Parkway

Following the banks of the Ogden River from near downtown to the mouth of Ogden Canyon, the parkway offers opportunities for picnicking, bicycling, playing tennis and golf, and running. Riverside trails begin at Washington Blvd and head east along the river as far as just beyond the Eccles Dinosaur Park (see below). Parking areas for the parkway are found off Washington Blvd on the north side of the river, Monroe Blvd on the south side of the river and at the Dinosaur Park.

Eccles Dinosaur Park

This park (☎ 801-393-3466), 1544 E Park Blvd (best reached along Ogden Canyon Hwy), is at the east end of Ogden River Parkway. It features life-size replicas of more than 100 dinosaurs in a wooded outdoor setting, with hidden loudspeakers emitting the grunts and roars that scientists think these animals may have made. The replicas are quite accurate and the place is sure to be a hit with younger kids. There is a café (☎ 801-627-3628), with DinoBurgers (of course), a gift shop and small playground. The park is open daily (weather permitting) April through October. Hours are 10 am to 6 pm (noon to 6 pm on Sunday) and admission is $3.50 for adults, $2.50 for seniors and $1.50 for three- to 17-year-olds.

Ogden Canyon & Monte Cristo Summit

The scenic, steep-walled canyon east of Ogden through the Wasatch Mountains continues on to Monte Cristo Summit (9148 feet), about 40 miles to the northeast; it is especially attractive in late September and early October for the fall colors. This is the route to Ogden's ski areas, and chains or snow-tires are required from November 1 to March 31. The Monte Cristo Summit is closed in winter due to heavy snow. The road is best reached by taking 12th Ave and driving east.

Hill Air Force Base Museum

For anyone interested in planes or the history of flight, this museum (☎ 801-777-6868) in Roy (drive 4 miles south on I-15 to exit 341 and follow signs) has dozens of historic aircraft on display outside and an indoor museum that shows a seven-minute video on request. There is a gift shop. Hours are 9 am to 4:30 pm, Monday to Friday, 9 am to 5:30 pm on weekends and closed January 1, Thanksgiving and Christmas. Admission is free.

Activities

There are three ski resorts east of Ogden; see the information in Ski Resorts, below. Easy **cross-country skiing** on groomed tracks is available at the Mount Ogden Golf Course in town (see below). The USFS can recommend more difficult terrain in the national forest. You can rent cross-country and downhill skis, snowboards and snowshoes at Alpine Sports (☎ 801-393-0066) between 30th and 31st, just off Harrison; Black Diamond (☎ 801-627-5733), 3701 Washington Blvd, which also has mountaineering and backpacking gear; and Miller's Ski & Cycle Haus (☎ 801-392-3911), 834 Washington Blvd, which also rents bikes.

You can **golf** a round at various nearby courses. The closest golf courses to central Ogden are the Mount Ogden Golf Course (☎ 801-629-8700), 3000 Taylor Ave (east end of 30th), which has 18 holes, and the nine-hole El Monte Golf Course (☎ 801-629-8333), 1300 Valley Drive, at the mouth of Ogden Canyon. There are about 10 more courses in the suburbs and surrounding communities – ask the visitors bureau or look in the yellow pages for more choices.

Ogden Parks Division (☎ 801-629-8284), 1875 Monroe Blvd, can inform you about city parks with public tennis courts. If you'd like to **swim**, the city also runs the Lorin Farr Park & Swimming Pool (☎ 801-629-8691), 1691 Gramercy Ave (where there is a water slide), and the Marshall White Center Pool (☎ 801-629-8346), 222 28th. Others are Ben Lomond Pool (☎ 801-625-1100), 1049 7th, and Ogden Community Pool (☎ 801-625-1101), 2875 Tyler Ave.

Summer hiking and winter cross-country skiing, snowshoeing and snowmobiling are popular activities in the nearby Wasatch National Forest. The ranger station is listed in Information, above. Also see the Ice Sheet (in Weber State University, above) for ice skating.

Special Events

There are several events every month in Ogden, especially in the summer – the visitors bureau has precise dates and a full list. The biggest annual event is **Pioneer Days** (☎ 801-629-8214), during the week leading up to July 24 (but not on Sunday), which includes a rodeo, fireworks, music, antique cars, a street festival, a parade and some other events. The **Weber County Fair** (☎ 801-399-8798), held in mid-August, takes place at the Weber County Fairgrounds and Golden Spike Arena (☎ 801-399-8544), 1000 N 1200 West, about 4 miles north of town.

Places to Stay – Camping

Century Camping Park (☎ 801-731-3800, fax 801-731-0010), 1399 W 2100 South, near I-15 exit 346, has tent/RV sites for $16 or RV sites for $21 with full hookups. There are hot showers, a coin laundry, store, playground and (in summer) a swimming pool.

There are many more camping areas about 10 to 20 miles east of town along scenic Ogden Canyon (Hwy 39) as it cuts through the Wasatch Mountains. Maps and details are available from the USFS (see Information, earlier in this section). These sites are open only in the summer, cost about $9 to $11, have water in most cases but no showers, and, though RVs are accepted, they

have no hookups. Many of these sites fill up with locals during summer weekends. Reservations can be made through Biospherics (☎ 800-280-2267); you will incur a $6 reservation fee in addition to site fees.

Distances given below are from the beginning of Ogden Canyon Rd at 12th and Harrison Blvd: *Anderson Cove*, 9 miles east of Ogden, has access to fishing and swimming in Pineview Reservoir, as does *Jefferson Hunt*, 10 miles east of Ogden. Between 17 and 19 miles east of Ogden are a slew of sites – *Magpie, Hobble, Botts, South Fork, Perception, Meadows* and *Willows*. All are along the Ogden River and offer fishing. Tiny Hobble lacks drinking water and is $5 (though often full). There is also *Maples*, 12 miles southwest of Anderson Cove, near the Snowbasin Ski Resort – this site is free but also lacks drinking water. *Monte Cristo Campground*, just below Monte Cristo Summit, 40 miles northeast of Ogden, has sites open from July to September.

See also Willard Bay State Park (later in this chapter), and Antelope Island State Park (earlier in this chapter) for other camping options.

Places to Stay – Budget

Rates are slightly higher in summer. Some hotels have larger rooms with kitchenettes, which cost a few dollars more. Many offer weekly discounts.

The cheapest motels are found along Washington Blvd and look fairly run-down. The *Colonial Motel* (☎ 801-399-5851), 1269 Washington Blvd, has basic rooms, which are often full, at $29/36 (single/double). The *Budget Inn* (☎ 801-393-8667), 1956 Washington Blvd, is similar. For a few dollars more, the nicer *Big Z Motel* (☎ 801-394-6632), 1123 W 21st (near I-15 exit 346), has some rooms with kitchenettes and a restaurant on the premises.

The (almost) downtown *Motel 6* (☎ 801-627-4560, fax 801-392-1878), 1455 Washington Blvd, charges $37/43 for singles/doubles and has a pool. The Riverdale *Motel 6* (☎ 801-627-2880, fax 801-392-1713), 1500 W Riverdale Rd (near I-15 exit

342), is one of the fancier members of the Motel 6 chain, offering a pool, restaurant, private club with dancing and a tennis court; rooms are $39/45 (a good value). Also at about this price, the *Western Colony Inn* (☎ 801-627-1332, fax 801-392-0600), 234 24th, has decent rooms. The *Millstream Motel* (☎ 801-394-9425), 1450 Washington Blvd, has a restaurant, antique car museum and a garden. Adequate rooms start around $38, though there are more expensive rooms with kitchenettes.

The *Super 8 Motel* (☎ 801-731-7100, fax 801-731-2627), 1508 W 21st (near I-15 exit 346), charges $39.88/44.88 for standard singles/doubles and has a café, convenience store and gas station adjoining it.

Places to Stay – Middle
The *Best Rest Inn* (☎ 801-393-8644, 800-343-8644, fax 801-399-0954), 1206 W 21st (near I-15 exit 346), is a good value. Nice rooms with microwaves and refrigerators are in the low $50s, including continental breakfast. The pleasant grounds have a pool, and the motel features a restaurant, café, private club (occasional entertainment) and exercise room. Geared to freeway travel, the hotel has 24-hour service in the restaurant and in the adjoining gas station and store. The *Ogden Travelodge* (☎ 801-394-4563, fax 801-394-4568), 2110 Washington Blvd, also with good rooms and a pool, is similarly priced and is convenient for downtown.

The *Best Western High Country Inn* (☎ 801-394-9474, fax 801-392-6589), 1335 W 12th (close to I-15 exit 347), charges in the $50s and $60s and has a pool, spa, coin laundry and restaurant. It offers ski packages in winter.

Places to Stay – Top End
The *Best Western Ogden Park Hotel* (☎ 801-627-1190, fax 801-394-6312), 247 24th, is a full-service downtown hotel with an indoor pool, spa, game and exercise rooms, beauty salon and concierge. There is a restaurant with 24-hour room service and a private club with occasional entertainment. Rooms are $80 to $110 with a full breakfast and sub-stantial weekend discounts. With almost 300 rooms, this is Ogden's biggest hotel. There are several more expensive suites with balconies and whirlpool baths.

The *Radisson Suite Hotel* (☎ 801-627-1900, fax 801-394-5342), 2510 Washington Blvd, is a centrally located, older hotel on the National Register of Historic Places. Most of the units are suites ranging from about $90 to $190 – they have refrigerators and wet bars. A few smaller, cheaper rooms are available. Rates include full breakfast. The hotel has a sauna, spa, exercise room, two restaurants and a private club with weekend entertainment.

Places to Eat
Ogden has well over 100 restaurants, so there's plenty to choose from – here's a selection.

If you like to start the day with a jolt of coffee, *The Daily Grind* (☎ 801-629-0909), 252 25th, features an espresso bar and specialty coffees, as well as pastries, sandwiches and light lunches. This building is one of the oldest in Ogden. Hours are 7 am to 6 pm Monday to Wednesday, 7 am to 11 pm on Thursday and Friday and 8 am to 11 pm on Saturday. The nearby *Delights of Ogden* (☎ 801-394-1111), 258 25th, open 11 am to 4 pm weekdays and 11 am to 3 pm on Saturdays, also features gourmet coffees as well as a 'delightful' lunch menu.

For 24-hour dining, head over to *The Cookery* (☎ 801-393-8691), 1254 W 21st, adjoining the Best Rest Inn. All the motels with restaurants mentioned under Places to Stay (above) are decent choices for breakfast, lunch and dinner. *Jeremiah's* (☎ 801-394-3273) at the Best Western High Country Inn is open from 6 am to 10 pm, Monday to Saturday, 7 am to 9 pm on Sunday, and has been well recommended for the heartiest breakfasts in Ogden.

Good American food (steak and seafood) is served at *Ye Lion's Den* (☎ 801-399-5804), 3607 Washington Blvd, which has been here for more than three decades. It's open 11:30 am to 2 pm from Monday to Friday, 5 to 9:30 or 10 pm from Monday to Saturday and noon to 7 pm on Sunday. Also

UTAH

recommended is the attractive, 50-year-old *Gray Cliff Lodge* (☎ 801-392-6775), 5 miles up Ogden Canyon Rd. The menu features local trout. It's open 5 to 10 pm from Tuesday to Friday, to 11 pm on Saturday, 10 am to 2 pm for Sunday brunch and 3 to 8 pm for Sunday dinner. Both these places are rather pricey but worth it.

Another slightly cheaper option for American food in a pioneering atmosphere is the *Prairie Schooner Steak House* (☎ 801-392-2712), 445 Park Blvd. Here you have the pleasure of dining in covered wagons – yee haaa! Hours are 11 am to 2 pm, Monday to Friday, 5 to 10 pm from Monday to Thursday, 5 to 11 pm on Friday and Saturday, and 4 to 9 pm on Sunday. Or try the *Timber Mine* (☎ 801-393-2155), 1701 Park Blvd (just east of the Dinosaur Park), with an old Western mine atmosphere. Hours are 5 am to 10 pm from Monday to Thursday, to 11 pm on Friday and Saturday, and to 9 pm on Sunday. Both places serve steak and seafood with entrées in the teens and $20s. Also east of the Dinosaur Park is *The Greenery* (☎ 801-392-1777), 1875 Valley Drive, a plant-filled modern restaurant serving lighter and less expensive American fare – sandwiches, salads and desserts. Hours are 11 am to 10 pm, Monday to Thursday, till 11 pm on Friday and Saturday and till 9 pm on Sunday.

Roosters 25th Street Brewing Co (☎ 801-627-6171), 253 25th, is a microbrewery with good beer in turn-of-the-19th-century surroundings. It serves up yuppified pub grub (prices in the teens), or you can just enjoy a beer.

There are several good Italian restaurants, including *La Ferrovia Ristorante* (☎ 801-394-8628), 210 25th, in a 1908 'Commercial Victorian' building restored in 1985. Hours are 11 am to 9 pm, Tuesday to Thursday, and to 10 pm on Friday and Saturday. *Berconi's Pasta House* (☎ 801-479-4414), 4850 Harrison Blvd, is also good; it's open 11:30 am to 2 pm, Monday to Friday, 4:30 to 10 pm, Monday to Saturday, to 9:30 pm on Sunday. A clone of Salt Lake's *Pie Pizzeria* (☎ 801-621-0484), near

the University at 42nd and Harrison Blvd, is open from 11 am to midnight, Monday to Thursday, till 1 am Friday and Saturday, and noon to 11 pm on Sunday.

El Matador (☎ 801-393-3151), 2564 Ogden Ave, is considered the best Mexican restaurant by local cognoscenti. It is open daily for lunch and dinner. Also try the nearby *Señor Frog's* (☎ 801-394-2323), 465 25th, which is comparably good.

There are dozens of Chinese restaurants – you'll find about six to choose from just south of 36th.

For ice cream, the traditional place to go is *Farr Asael & Sons* (☎ 801-393-8629), 274 21st. This old-fashioned ice-cream parlor was established in 1920.

Entertainment

Country Club Theater (☎ 801-393-5864), 3930 Washington Blvd, offers movies at very low prices. Both of the following have four screens: *Carmike Ogden City Plaza* (☎ 801-392-1122), 23rd and Grant Ave, and *Carmike Riverdale Center* (☎ 801-627-1061), 4109 Riverdale Rd. Other cinemas include *North Pointe Theaters* (☎ 801-782-9822), 1610 N Washington Blvd, and *Reel Theatres* (☎ 801-392-7474), 151 12th.

Ballet, theater, symphony recitals and other performing arts are featured at Weber State University (see above). Also call the Ogden Symphony Ballet Association (☎ 801-399-9214, 801-399-0453), 2580 Jefferson Ave, for its performance schedules and information. The *Ogden Egyptian Center* (☎ 801-627-2117, 800-337-2690), 2415 Washington Blvd, dates from the 1920s and has been newly renovated in sumptuous style after the original glittering Egyptian facade. It will be used for various cultural events.

The private clubs in the hotels above provide entertainment or are just a place for a quiet drink. Other choices are found along 25th. The *City Club* (☎ 801-392-4447), 264 25th, in a 'Commercial Victorian' 1898 brick building, has an extensive Beatles collection. *Brewski's* (☎ 801-394-1713), 244 25th, is a popular college hangout. The

Roosters brewpub (see Places to Eat, above) is across the street and there are several others in the area. Some places have live music on weekends.

Getting There & Away
Greyhound (☎ 801-394-5573), 2501 Grant Ave, has an early morning bus and an evening bus to Salt Lake City and on down I-15 to Las Vegas. It also has buses north, east and west out of the state.

UTA (☎ 801-621-4636 from 6 am to 7 pm, Monday to Saturday) has local services to Salt Lake City and intermediate points as well as services around Weber County. An important UTA bus stop is at 25th and Washington Blvd – there is an information booth here. Buses for Salt Lake City leave frequently (at least once an hour) from about 4:30 am to 11 pm, Monday to Saturday, and three times on Sunday. There is no service on major holidays. The fare is $2.

Salt Lake City has the nearest passenger train station.

OGDEN-AREA SKI RESORTS
There are three ski resorts in the mountains east of Ogden, all accessed via the steep-walled Ogden Canyon. Apart from Ogden, you can stay at the ski resorts or in the villages of Eden and Huntsville. (Eden and Huntsville are on the banks of Pineview Reservoir, a popular spot for boating, fishing, swimming and water-skiing in summer.) All the resorts have ski shops, instructors and places to eat.

Nordic Valley
This very tiny, 85-acre resort (☎ 801-745-3511) is the closest to Ogden (15 miles) and offers the cheapest skiing in the state. The nearest accommodations are in Eden (1 mile) or Huntsville (12 miles). The elevation goes from 5400 to 6400 feet, with two double lifts and 18 runs; 30% are designated for beginners and 50% for intermediate skiers. All-day (9:30 am to 4 pm) lift passes are $15 and $5 for those over 65. Lighted night skiing from 5:30 to 10 pm is $10. Snowboarding is permitted.

Powder Mountain
This resort (☎ 801-745-3771, 801-745-3772, fax 801-745-3619, powdermtn@aol.com) is 19 miles from Ogden, 6 from Eden and 3 from Huntsville. The elevation goes from 7600 to 8900 feet, and the 1600 acres of skiing include about 40 runs serviced by two double lifts and one triple, and three tows. In addition, 1200 acres of powder skiing are serviced by snowcat and there are another 1200 acres of backcountry powder, giving more than 30 more runs for expert powder hounds. Only 10% of the terrain is for beginners and 60% is for intermediate skiers. All-day (9:30 am to 4:30 pm) lift passes are $27/21/16 for adults/seniors over 65/children 12 and under. Lighted night skiing (4:30 to 10 pm) is $14.50/10 for adults/children. Combined day and night lift passes are $33/21 for adults/children. Multiple-day rates for three or more days are discounted. Snowcat powder skiing is $12 per ride or $40 for four rides. Snowboarding is allowed. Ski/snowboard rental and lessons are available.

The resort's small *Columbine Inn* provides slope-side rooms and suites for $75 to $220. Four lodges provide snacks and meals during the day and one remains open until 10 pm.

Adjoining *Powder Ridge Village* (☎ 800-272-8824, fax 801-531-9011) offers fully furnished condos with kitchens sleeping four for $125 to $185 (depending on the season), sleeping seven for $155 to $215 and sleeping nine for $185 to $245. There is a hot tub and heated swimming pool.

Snowbasin
This 1800-acre resort (☎ 801-399-1135, fax 801-399-1138) will be the host for Downhill and Super G skiing events in the 2002 Winter Olympics. Accommodations are available in Huntsville (6 miles), Eden (16 miles) and Ogden (17 miles). The elevation is 6400 to 8800 feet, a vertical drop of 2400 feet – Utah's third largest. In addition, a new run with a 2900-foot drop is being constructed for the Olympics. There are currently four triple lifts and one double servicing the 39 runs. Terrain is 20% for

beginners and 50% for intermediate skiers. All-day (9:30 am to 4 pm) lift passes are $27/20 for adults/kids and $19 for adults over 65. There are lessons and rentals, and snowboarding is allowed.

Places to Stay & Eat
Eden The *Snowberry Inn B&B* (☎ 801-745-2634), 1315 N Hwy 158, Box 795, Eden, UT 84310, 8 miles from the slopes, has an outdoor spa, billiards room, and five rustic rooms with private bath and spa. Rates with full breakfast are $85/65 for doubles/singles, with discounts for multiple nights. Ski packages are available.

Wolf Creek Village (☎ 801-745-0222, 801-745-0223, 800-933-9653, fax 801-745-3732), 3720 N Wolf Creek Drive, Eden, UT 84310, 4 miles from the slopes, has 16 one-, two- and three-bedroom condos sleeping four to 10 people for $90 to $130, with multiple-day discounts and ski packages available. Condos have full kitchens and hot tubs; sauna and exercise facilities are available. Similar lodgings are offered at the nearby *Condominiums in Ogden Valley* (☎/fax 801-745-2621, 800-345-8824), 3615 N Wolf Creek Rd. These places are north of Eden.

For camping near Pineview Reservoir, see Places to Stay – Camping in Ogden.

Huntsville *Jackson Fork Inn* (☎ 801-745-0051, 800-255-0672), 7345 E 900 South, Huntsville, UT 84317, has eight rooms, most with private spas. There is a restaurant for complimentary continental breakfast and for dinner at extra cost. Rates are from $50/90 without/with the spa for two people. The restaurant is open to the public for dinner and Sunday brunch. The inn rents snowmobiles for about $100 a day.

The *Heritage Inn B&B* (☎ 801-745-3226), 7355 E 200 South, Huntsville, UT 84317, is a modern inn with antique furnishings. Two rooms with private, jetted tubs and four-poster beds are $90 a double, including a full breakfast. Almost next door, the *Shooting Star Saloon* (☎ 801-745-2002), 7350 E 200 South, has been in operation since 1879, making it Utah's oldest continu-

ally running saloon. It serves beer and burgers, and has a pool table. The burgers are known far and wide, and the saloon, though a simple place and a little hard to find, is often crowded with people from all over the place – German tourists, Harley-Davidson bikers from New York and local cowboys were all there on my last visit.

For a light snack, try the homemade bread and honey sold by the Trappist monks at the *Abbey of Our Lady of the Holy Trinity* (☎ 801-745-3784), 4 miles east of Huntsville.

For camping in the Huntsville area, see Places to Stay – Camping, in the Ogden section, earlier in this chapter.

WILLARD BAY STATE PARK
Willard Bay State Park (☎ 801-734-9494), 650 N 900 West, PO Box A, Willard, UT 84340, lies on a small bay on the northwest shore of the Great Salt Lake. The park includes mud flats hosting thousands of migrating shorebirds in March to May and September to November. In summer, the birding is also good, and there is boating and fishing. Ice fishing is possible in winter.

The park has two sections. To reach the north unit, take exit 360 off I-15 (at Willard, 14 miles north of Ogden) and head a short way west; to reach the south unit, take exit 354 from I-15 and head 3 miles west – there are signs.

The north unit is larger and more popular for boating and fishing; it has boat rentals. The south unit is less developed but perhaps better for birding. Both have boat launch areas. There are more than 60 campsites in the north (showers available) and about 30 in the south. Rates are $10 for camping (tents or RVs – no hookups) and $4 for day use.

OGDEN TO PARK CITY
Thirty-nine-mile-long I-84 runs from I-15 just south of Ogden to I-80 going southeast. Another 23 miles south on I-80 brings you to the Park City exit. Along this drive there are two county seats and access to three state parks – none of major importance to travelers.

Morgan Area

The town of **Morgan**, 23 miles southeast of Ogden on I-84, is the seat of Morgan County. The county fair is held annually in August. There are no hotels, but there are a few places to eat.

Seven miles east of town on the north side of I-84 is the **Devil's Slide** geological formation. Just past this is the exit for **Lost Creek State Park** (☎ 801-829-6866), 15 miles northwest of the interstate. The park, which surrounds a small reservoir, offers boating, trout fishing (ice fishing in winter) and primitive camping.

East Canyon State Park (☎ 801-829-6866) is 10 miles south of Morgan along Hwy 66 (there are other access routes). This park also surrounds a reservoir and has a marina (boat rentals available in summer only), fishing, boating and camping (showers available but no hookups). Bald eagles overwinter near the reservoir. In winter, ice fishing is possible, though the road may get snowed in temporarily. There is an $11 camping fee, and sites may fill in the summer, so arrive early or call ahead. The campground is closed in winter.

Coalville

Coalville, the Summit County seat, is midway between Morgan and Park City. The coal fields discovered in the 1850s are no longer mined. The county fair here is also in August; call the City Hall (☎ 435-336-5981) for information.

The small motels on Main St charge about $30 to $50 for basic doubles (more during winter holidays) and can provide accommodations for Park City skiers. Call the *Blonquist Motel* (☎ 435-336-2451, 800-371-2451) or *Moore's Motel* (☎ 435-336-5991). For simple meals try *Denise's Home Plate* (☎ 435-336-2249). *Holiday Hills Campground* (☎ 435-336-4421), 500 W 100 South, is open year-round, with tent and RV sites for $11/18, showers, groceries and a seasonal swimming pool.

Rockport State Park

This is yet another state park around a reservoir with the usual fishing, boating and camping, but Rockport is popular for windsurfing as well. The campground ($11 per day) has showers but no RV hookups and is open all year. There is primitive camping as well ($7). Day use is $4. Rockport State Park (☎ 435-336-2241) is 5 miles east of I-80 exit 156.

PARK CITY

At the foot of Utah's largest ski resort and with two other resorts nearby and five more within an hour's drive, Park City is the Southwest's most important skiing town. The skiing is world-class – Park City is the headquarters of the United States Ski Team and many events will be staged here during the 2002 Olympics.

Park City was not always this way, of course. After silver was discovered here in 1868, the city became a booming mining town. Most of it burned down in 1898 but was quickly rebuilt. When the mining boom went bust in the early 20th century, the town faded in importance and Utah's governor suggested shutting down this 'ghost town' in the 1950s. But the locals persevered and began building the first ski areas in the 1960s. Today, the town has grown into a sprawl of condos and apartments catering to skiers, but fortunately the turn of the 19th-century downtown area has been well preserved and forms an attraction in itself.

At 6900 feet in elevation, the town has plenty of winter snow. Summer daytime temperatures average in the upper 70s°F, but nights can be chilly. Park City is 5 miles south of I-80 exit 145 and 32 miles west of Salt Lake City.

Information

The Visitor Information Center (☎ 435-649-1000, 800-453-1360, fax 435-649-4132) is at 528 Main (in the Park City museum). During the summer (Memorial Day to Labor Day) and ski season (mid-November to mid-April), it is open 10 am to 7 pm daily, except Sunday (noon to 6 pm). During off-season months, hours are noon to 5 pm daily. The library (☎ 435-645-5140) is at 1255 Park Ave. The local weekly newspaper is the *Park Record* – continuously published

UTAH

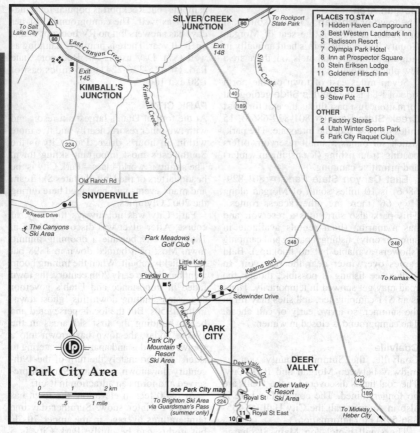

PLACES TO STAY
1 Hidden Haven Campground
3 Best Western Landmark Inn
5 Radisson Resort
7 Olympia Park Hotel
8 Inn at Prospector Square
10 Stein Eriksen Lodge
11 Goldener Hirsch Inn

PLACES TO EAT
9 Stew Pot

OTHER
2 Factory Stores
4 Utah Winter Sports Park
6 Park City Raquet Club

Park City Area

```
0        1        2 km
0    .5        1 mile
```

for over a century. The post office (☎ 435-649-9191) is at 450 Main. The Health & Emergency Center (☎ 435-649-7640) is at 1665 Bonanza Drive. The police (☎ 435-645-5050) are in the municipal offices at 445 Marsac Ave. The Recycling Center (☎ 435-649-9698), at 1825 Woodbine Rd (behind Anderson Lumber on Kearns Blvd), takes glass, cans and paper (no plastics) daily during daylight hours.

Park City Museum

This small museum (☎ 435-649-4135), 528 Main, which keeps the same hours as the

visitor center, has exhibits of mining and local history, and you can visit the old Territorial Jail in the basement. It's free.

Downtown Walking Tour

The visitor center has brochures describing the historic town center (Main St and Park Ave) for self-guided walks. Locals in period dress lead walking tours in the summer. There are over a dozen commercial galleries along Main St and Park Ave, some of which have changing exhibits in various media by regional artists, as well as pieces from other countries. Especially interesting is the Kimball Art Center (☎ 435-649-8882), 638 Park Ave.

Park City Silver Mine Adventure

This silver mine is 1500 feet below the ground and 1½ miles south of Park City on Hwy 224. Visitors wear miner hardhats and bright-yellow rain ponchos and descend into the depths using a mine shaft hoist. During the tour, you ride an underground mine train into century-old silver-mine shafts carved out of the rock; there is some wheelchair-accessible walking. Old mining equipment is on display, sometimes dynamite blasting is going on (okay, it's simulated) and guides who are ex-miners give lively talks. The tour is an interesting slice of mining history and fun for all. Participants should wear warm clothes (it's a moist 47° to 55°F underground) and sturdy footwear.

The Silver Mine Adventure (☎ 435-655-7444) is offered year-round and costs about $19 for adults, $14 for seniors and children four to 12 (no younger children allowed). At the surface is a mining museum with some hands-on exhibits (dig for gems), which is included in the tour price. Those not wishing to go underground can visit the museum alone for $8.50/7. Mine hours are 10 am to 7 pm, December through March and July through August; 10 am to 6 pm in other months. Underground tours last about two hours, are limited to 32 participants and leave on the hour.

Winter Sports

Downhill Skiing The free and recommended *Park City Winter Vacation Planner*, published each winter, is available from visitors bureaus and information centers. It gives up-to-date prices and details of the area's ski resorts and accommodations. Budget travelers should note that Park City offers the most expensive skiing and accommodations in the Southwest. Skiing starts in mid- to late November and ends in mid-April, depending on snow conditions.

The **Park City Mountain Resort**, Utah's largest ski area (☎ 435-649-8111, 800-222-7275, fax 435-647-5374), offers 2200 skiable acres and will be the site of the

Olympic giant slalom and snowboarding events in 2002. This resort offers 14 lifts (one of which begins from downtown Park City and three of which carry six passengers) and 93 runs. It can handle over 26,600 passengers an hour, so lift lines tend to be short! Elevations range from 6900 to 10,000 feet. 17% is beginner terrain, and 44% is for intermediate skiers. All-day lift passes (9 am to 4 pm) are $52 for adults, $23 for kids under 12, $25 for seniors 64 to 69, and free for those over 70. Half-day adult passes (1 to 4 pm) are $37. Night skiing (4 to 9 pm) is $18 for adults, $8 for kids. Rates drop after March 31 till the resort closes (usually around April 19, weather dependent). Multi-day discounts and lessons are available.

On the southeastern outskirts of Park City, **Deer Valley Resort** (☎ 435-649-1000, 800-424-3337) strives to be the most luxurious ski resort in the USA; it certainly is luxurious. Fourteen lifts service 67 carefully groomed runs covering 1100 acres between 7200 and 9400 feet, and expansions are planned. Deer Valley will be the site of Olympic slalom, freestyle and mogul events in 2002. 15% of the terrain is for beginners and 50% is for intermediate skiers. All-day adult passes (9 am to 4 pm) are $54 ($57 on holidays), children 12 and under are $29, and those over 65 are $38. Half-day (1 to 4 pm) adult passes are $38. There is a ski school, ski rentals and childcare facilities but no snowboarding.

Four miles north of Park City on Hwy 224 (there are buses), **The Canyons** (☎ 435-649-5400, 800-754-1636, fax 435-649-7374) provides good skiing at more reasonable prices, although its ticket prices are catching up with those of other resorts in Park City. (This area was called Park West until 1994 and Wolf Mountain until 1997; older maps and books may use these names.) Nine lifts service 74 runs on 2000 acres between 6800 and 9380 feet – 16% is for beginners and 38% for intermediate skiers. This new resort has expanded considerably in recent years and continues to grow. It recently opened groomed half-pipe runs designed for professional snowboarding; The Canyons is definitely the best place for snowboarding in Park City and one of the best in all the Southwest. Both skiing and snowboarding lessons are available.

Sundance also offers ski facilities not far from Park City (see the Sundance Resort section later in this chapter).

Cross-Country Skiing Try White Pine Touring (☎ 435-649-8701, 435-649-8710), 201 Heber Ave, for ski rentals, instruction and guides on its 13 miles of groomed trails in and around Park City. Trails are suitable for all levels. Day passes are $8 for 13- to 64-year-olds, free to others.

Sledding & Ski Jumping Near The Canyons is the new **Utah Winter Sports Park** (☎ 435-658-4200, fax 435-647-9650), site of the Olympic ski jumping, bobsledding and luge events in 2002. There are 5-, 10-, 18-, 38-, 65- and 90-meter ski jumping hills and a 120-meter hill under construction. Bobsled (ridden by teams of four) and luge (light toboggan for one person) runs can also be seen. Admission to look around the site is $5 per car or $10 per van (during competitions, entry fees are higher); you may see athletes practicing.

Alpine ski jumping lessons are offered every few days. These last two hours and cost $28 for adults, $19 for 13- to 17-year-olds and $15 for children 12 and under.

Helmets are provided, but you need your own skis. Students begin on small hills and may progress through the 5-, 10-, 18- and 38-meter hills depending on their ability. During the summer, ski jumping is still practiced – jumpers land in a lake rather than on snow.

Recreational rides on the bobsled runs are also available on a limited basis by advance reservation. Tickets go on sale October 1 and cost $125; the bobsled run lasts about a minute! Despite the cost, the thrill of a super-fast descent on an Olympic bobsled meant that all dates for the 1997-98 winter season were sold out by Thanksgiving 1997 and the Sports Park may re-evaluate its policies for future years.

In addition to bobsled runs, there are 'rocket rides' on individually controlled sleds. Runs on these also last about a minute and cost $27. Because this is an Olympic training facility, the Sports Park may be closed to recreational use on some days, so call as early as possible for hours and rates.

The Park City Mountain Resort (☎ 435-649-8111) keeps a lift open in summer. For $6, you can descend thousands of feet on a wheeled sled within cement tracks winding back down the mountain or ride the lift back down. Call them for details.

Hot-Air Ballooning
Hot-air balloon rides are offered throughout the year and cost about $150 per person per hour, though companies sometimes offer 'specials' starting at $50 for 30 minutes (look for flyers at the visitor center). There are about a dozen ballooning companies in the Park City area and all should be FAA certified, licensed and insured. Some companies include ABC Ballooning (☎ 435-649-2223, 800-820-2223), Park City Adventure Center/Balloon Affaire (☎ 435-649-1217, 435-649-3343), Great Balloon Escape (☎ 435-645-9400, 800-287-9401) and Sunrise Balloons (☎ 801-649-9009).

Fishing
Jans (☎ 435-649-4949, 800-745-1020, sports@jans.com), 1600 Park Ave, and also the Fly Shop (☎ 435-645-8382, 800-324-

6778), 2065 Sidewinder Drive, have fly-fishing equipment for sale or rent. Lessons and guides are available.

Golf

Play 18 holes of golf at the Municipal Golf Course (☎ 435-649-8701), 1541 Thaynes Canyon Drive, or the highly rated Park Meadows Golf Club (☎ 435-649-2460), 2000 Meadows Drive, designed by Jack Nicklaus. Both are near the city – other courses are a short drive away. During summer, the Park City Mountain Resort has miniature golf.

Mountain Biking

Jans (see Fishing), and White Pine Touring (see Cross-Country Skiing), offer bicycle and helmet rentals (about $27 a day, less for kids and more for high-performance bikes), local information, maps and tours. All three ski resorts have biking trails and may have ski lifts open to take bikes up. (Deer Valley Resort definitely keeps lifts open in summer.)

Other Activities

Park City Racquet Club (☎ 435-645-5100), 1200 Little Kate Rd, and Prospector Athletic Club (☎ 435-649-6670), in the Inn at Prospector Square, offer indoor/outdoor recreation year-round. Both have racquetball and tennis courts, a swimming pool, spa and gym. Park City Stables (☎ 435-645-7256), at the Park City Mountain Resort, rents horses for guided trail rides. High Country Rafting (☎ 435-645-7533) offers six-person rafts, with and without guides, for floats on the Provo River.

Special Events

The **Sundance Film Festival** (☎ 801-328-3456), lasting almost two weeks in the second half of January, is a major festival showcasing independent film-makers. Tickets are often sold out well in advance, so call as far ahead as possible. (Despite the festival's name, the majority of the films are actually screened in Park City, not at the Sundance Resort. As the festival has grown, some films are

now screened at Salt Lake City's Tower Theater.)

In late February **Winterfest** features a snow sculpture contest and other events. During the ski season, various **competitions** take place, ranging from skiing to bobsledding events. Symphony, chamber music, bluegrass, jazz and other music events take place during various **summer concert** series. The **Art Festival** (☎ 435-649-8882) in early August features more than 200 artists (the 30th annual event takes place in 1999). **Miners Day** with a parade and contests is held over Labor Day weekend. Contact the visitor center to find out about other events.

Places to Stay

The Park City area offers well over 100 condominium complexes, upscale hotels and B&Bs, with almost 4000 rooms and 13,000 beds (about twice the number of permanent residents). There are a few chain hotels/motels but no cheap ones. This is a booming ski town, and new places are opening every year in anticipation of the 2002 Olympics, so I can give only a selection below.

Room rates are high, especially during the peak season around Christmas and New Year's, when vacationers have to pay premium prices and commit to a minimum stay of several nights. The top rates given below are for this short period; at other times rates drop 20% or more.

The cheapest winter rates begin in mid- or late November when skiing begins, and run to shortly before Christmas, when the highest rates kick in. From early January to the end of March are the mid-rates, though there is often a brief low season during the slack period immediately after the Christmas/New Year's peak season. Thus, early to mid-January represents the best prices and snow conditions for the budget-conscious skier. Prices again drop in April until the skiing stops, which is usually mid- to late April.

However, keep in mind that during the Sundance Film Festival (see Special Events, above), some hotels are fully booked, so if

UTAH

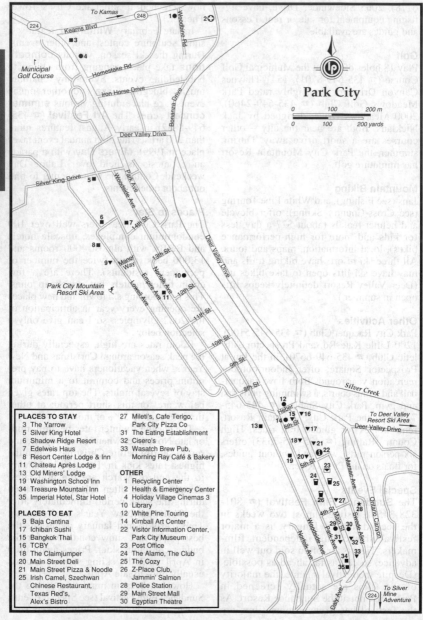

Park City

To Kamas

Kearns Blvd

Municipal
Golf Course

Homestake Rd

Iron Horse Drive

Deer Valley Drive

Silver King Drive

Park Ave

Woodside Ave

14th St

Manor Way

13th St

Norfolk Ave

12th St

Empire Ave

Lowell Ave

11th St

10th St

9th St

8th St

Park City Mountain
Resort Ski Area

Deer Valley Drive

Silver Creek

Heber

5th St

Main St

Park Ave

Swede Alley

Marsac Ave

Ontario Canyon

4th St

Woodside Ave

Norfolk Ave

Daly Ave

To Deer Valley
Resort Ski Area
Deer Valley Drive

To Silver
Mine
Adventure

0   100   200 m
0   100   200 yards

PLACES TO STAY
3 The Yarrow
5 Silver King Hotel
6 Shadow Ridge Resort
7 Edelweiss Haus
8 Resort Center Lodge & Inn
11 Chateau Après Lodge
13 Old Miners' Lodge
19 Washington School Inn
34 Treasure Mountain Inn
35 Imperial Hotel, Star Hotel

PLACES TO EAT
9 Baja Cantina
17 Ichiban Sushi
15 Bangkok Thai
16 TCBY
18 The Claimjumper
20 Main Street Deli
21 Main Street Pizza & Noodle
25 Irish Camel, Szechwan
   Chinese Restaurant,
   Texas Red's,
   Alex's Bistro

27 Mileti's, Cafe Terigo,
   Park City Pizza Co
31 The Eating Establishment
32 Cisero's
33 Wasatch Brew Pub,
   Morning Ray Café & Bakery

OTHER
1 Recycling Center
2 Health & Emergency Center
4 Holiday Village Cinemas 3
10 Library
12 White Pine Touring
14 Kimball Art Center
22 Visitor Information Center,
   Park City Museum
23 Post Office
24 The Alamo, The Club
25 The Cozy
26 Z-Place Club,
   Jammin' Salmon
28 Police Station
29 Main Street Mall
30 Egyptian Theatre

your trip coincides with the festival, plan to book a room early.

Many lodgings have a variety of accommodations ranging from 'economy' rooms to expensive multi-bedroom condos with a kitchen, fireplace and perhaps a spa. Make precise requests to get what you want. Because prices vary so much from month to month (even day to day!) and from unit to unit within one establishment, use the prices given below only as an approximate guide. Using a reservation service (see below) is a convenient option.

Several lodgings close altogether in summer and others offer rates as low as half the winter prices. The cheapest times to stay here are May and October, when not much is going on.

Vacation Packages Deciding where to stay among the many choices depends partly on what's available (many lodges run at full or almost full capacity in winter). Skiers may want to use a ski tour operator who can put together entire packages – accommodations, lift passes, ski rentals, flights, car rentals or transfers and other services.

Operators specializing in the Park City area include the following:

Avenir Adventures (☎ 435-649-2495, 800-367-3230, fax 435-649-1192, avenir@burgoyne .com)

Condo Destinations (☎ 801-466-1101, 800-444-9104, fax 801-466-6655)

Deer Valley Central Reservations (☎ 435-649-1000, 800-424-3337, fax 435-645-6538)

EB Ski Tours & Travel (☎ 801-531-9777, 800-313-2754, fax 801-531-7054)

Lynx Ski Travel (☎ 970-453-4131, 800-422-5969, fax 970-453-5529, lynx@colorado.net)

Park City Custom Vacations (☎ 435-645-7902, 800-646-7333, fax 435-645-7720)

Park City Mountain Resort Vacations (☎ 435-649-0493, 800-222-7275, fax 435-649-0532)

Park City Reservations (☎ 435-649-9598, 800-453-5789, fax 435-649-3353)

Park City Travel and Lodging (☎ 435-645-8200, 800-421-9741, fax 435-645-8252)

Ski Reservation Headquarters of Utah (☎ 435-649-2526, 800-522-7669, fax 435-645-8666)

Utah Ski Reservations (☎ 435-649-6493, 800-882-4754, fax 435-645-8419)

Reservation Services The following services specialize mainly in finding places to stay for visitors to the Park City area. They also arrange lift tickets on request. Rates given are per night and range from low winter rates in budget rooms to peak winter rates in the most comfortable luxury lodgings. The cheapest places go fast, so make reservations early. Don't forget to add the 10.25% lodging tax to all rates. Summer rates are substantially cheaper.

Because the services listed below have rooms all over the area, skiers should check carefully about the distance from the room to the nearest resort (you can ski or walk in from some places), bus line or parking area, and exactly what facilities are offered – kitchen, laundry, fireplace, spa, views, maid service, front desk, restaurant and so on. The following services are all in Park City; this is just a selection of some of those that have been around for a few years and have a wide selection of rooms. The *Park City Winter Vacation Planner* and *Ski Utah* list dozens more.

ABC Reservations (☎ 435-649-2223, 800-820-2223, fax 435 649 8619) combines a variety of lodging with all area activities ranging from ballooning to sleigh rides.

Blooming Enterprises (☎ 435-649-6583, 800-635-4719, fax 435-649-6598, blooming@xmission.com) has 50 units from $125 for low ski-season studios to $3000 for peak-season luxury homes. There are four- to seven-day minimums.

Budget Lodging (☎ 435-649-2526, 800-522-7669, fax 435-645-8666) has 50 units, including hotel rooms sleeping one to four ($70 to $140) to three-bedroom condos sleeping 10 ($120 to $400) and four-bedroom condos ($300 to $525). Yep, this is considered 'budget' for Park City.

Central Reservations of Park City (☎ 435-649-6606, 800-243-2932, fax 435-649-6654) represents hundreds of units ranging from $100 to $1400 a night.

Deer Valley Lodging (☎ 435-649-4040, 800-453-3833, fax 435-645-8419) offers 300 deluxe accommodations near luxurious Deer Valley Resort. One-bedroom ($235 to $700) to four-bedroom ($550 to $2500) condos and private homes may require a four- to seven-day minimum stay.

David Holland's Resort Lodging (☎ 435-655-3315, 800-754-2002, fax 435-645-9132) represents over 400 properties ranging from $120 to $800 a night.

Identity Properties (☎ 435-649-5100, 800-245-6417, fax 435-649-5107, ski@pclodge.com), has almost 200 units from studios ($135 to $250) to four-bedroom townhouses and condos ($390 to $870).

Park City Reservations (☎ 435-649-8800, 800-453-5789, fax 435-649-3353, pcres@xmission .com) has 350 condo properties ranging from dorms ($80 to $100 for one to four people), one-bedroom units ($110 to $250) to five-bedroom condos and houses ($325 to $580), plus properties at Deer Valley that are about twice these prices. Three- to seven-day minimums are required.

R&R Properties (☎ 435-649-6175, 800-348-6759, fax 435-649-6225, lodging@ditell.com) has 58 rooms, studios and luxury condos and homes ($115 to $1200).

Places to Stay – Camping
The nearest campsite is the *Hidden Haven Campground* (☎ 435-649-8935, fax 435-649-9256), 2200 Rasmussen Rd, 1 mile northwest of I-80 exit 145 along the north frontage road (6 miles north of Park City). Tent sites are $13, and RV sites are $17 to $20, depending on hookups used. There are showers, a playground, and fishing in the stream.

Also see the campgrounds and state parks under Coalville (above) and Heber (below).

Places to Stay – Budget
The *Dudler Dorms* downtown on Main St has rooms sleeping one to four people for $80 to $100 per night, which can be reserved through Park City Reservations (see above). *Chateau Aprés Lodge* (☎ 435-649-9372, 800-357-3556, fax 435-649-5963), 1299 Norfolk Ave, is a two-minute walk from the Park City lifts. There are men's and women's dormitories ($25 per person) and 32 rooms with bath for $72/82/92 for two/three/four people.

The *Star Hotel* (☎ 435-649-5746, 888-649-8333, fax 435-649-8333), 227 Main,

has 10 rooms sharing three bathrooms in an older family house (just like staying with grandma!). Rates are $85/150 (single/double), including home-cooked breakfast and dinner during the ski season. In summer and fall, rates are $65 for a single or double, without meals.

Budget travelers with cars can also stay at Heber City (19 miles south), Coalville (24 miles north) or Salt Lake City (about 30 miles).

Places to Stay – Middle
B&Bs All of the following are nonsmoking establishments. The *Imperial Hotel* (☎ 435-649-1904, 800-669-8824, fax 435-645-7421), 221 Main, PO Box 1628, Park City, UT 84060, in a restored building dating from 1904, has both antiques and modern amenities. Ten rooms are around $60 to $95 in summer and $140 to $195 in winter, including a full breakfast and afternoon refreshments. There is an indoor hot tub.

The *Old Miners' Lodge* (☎ 435-645-8068, 800-648-8068, fax 435-645-7420), 615 Woodside Ave, PO Box 2639, Park City, UT 84060, which dates from 1893, is decorated with period pieces. There are nine rooms and three suites. An outdoor hot tub is open year-round, and a fireplace and full breakfast are included. Rates run $60 to $115 in summer, $95 to $190 in winter.

The *Washington School Inn* (☎ 435-649-3800, 800-824-1672, fax 435-649-3802), 543 Park Ave, PO Box 536, Park City, UT 84060, is a B&B in a renovated stone school dating to 1889. You'll find both period furnishings and modern amenities, including an indoor spa and sauna. In winter, 12 rooms go for $145 to $235 and three suites with fireplaces are $225 to $350, including full breakfast and afternoon refreshments. Summer rates are $125 to $175.

Hotels & Condos *Edelweis Haus* (☎ 435-649-9342, 800-438-3855, fax 435-649-4049, edelhaus@aol.com), 1482 Empire Ave, is less than a quarter mile from Park City lifts and requires a six-night minimum in winter. This is a condo-hotel with about 50 rooms and maid service twice a week.

A pool, spa and sauna are available. Hotel-style rooms with microwaves, refrigerators and coffeemakers run about $60 in summer, $100 to $145 in winter. One- and two-bedroom condos with full kitchens are up to $130 in summer, $170 to $360 in winter.

The *Best Western Landmark Inn* (☎ 435-649-7300, fax 435-649-1760), 6560 N Landmark Drive (I-80 exit 145), is 5 miles north of Park City, but it has a shuttle to ski areas. There is an indoor pool, a spa, exercise room and an adjoining 24-hour restaurant. Room rates are $69 to $99 in summer, $119 to $164 in winter.

The *Radisson Inn Park City* (☎ 435-649-5000, 800-333-3333, fax 435-649-2122), 2121 Park Ave, has indoor and outdoor pools, a spa, sauna, exercise equipment, restaurant with room service and lounge with entertainment; 131 hotel rooms go for $160 to $200 in winter. Many rooms have fine views, but it's a couple of miles to the slopes. *Treasure Mountain Inn* (☎ 435-655-4500, 800-344-2460, fax 435-655-4504), 255 Main, is right downtown and has a pool, spa, fireplace and game area; studios ($90 to $170) to two-bedroom condos ($165 to $250) are available in winter.

The *Olympia Park Hotel* (☎ 435-649-2900, 800-234-9003, fax 435-649-4852), 1895 Sidewinder Drive, is a good full-service hotel. There's a concierge, pool, spa, sauna, exercise room, massage service, two restaurants, a bar, room service, a ski shop and rental, lift ticket sales, car rental and more. Rooms are about $120 in summer, $150 to $200 in winter, and there are some condos up to $350. Nearby is the *Inn at Prospector Square* (☎ 435-649-7100, 800-453-3812, fax 435-649-8377), 2200 Sidewinder Drive, which has a restaurant, bar and complete athletic club. Rooms are $70 to $100 in summer, $100 to $180 in winter. Studios and one-, two- and three-bedroom condos are $80 to $200 in summer and $110 to $480 in winter.

The *Resort Center Lodge & Inn* (☎ 435-649-0800, 800-824-5331, fax 435-645-9132), 1415 Lowell Ave, is right at the base of the Park City lifts. It offers a pool, spa, sauna, massage service, and a restaurant and bar. There is tennis and mini-golf in summer. Hotel rooms are $80 to $180, studios are $120 to $300 and one- to four-bedroom condos run from $220 to $1600; five-day minimums are preferred in winter, and lower rates are available in summer. *Shadow Ridge Hotel & Conference Center* (☎ 801-649-4300, 800-451-3031, fax 435-645-9132), 50 Shadow Ridge Rd, is a block from the ski area. Amenities include a pool, spa, sauna, exercise room and restaurant with room service. Hotel rooms and studios to three-bedroom condos go for $120 to $750.

The Yarrow (☎ 435-649-7000, 800-927-7694, fax 435-645-7007), 1800 Park Ave, a full-service resort hotel and conference center opposite a golf course, is located half a mile from the Park City ski area. It offers a pool, spa, sauna, restaurant, bar, room service, concierge, ski rental/repair shop, ticket sales and more. Its hotel rooms, efficiencies and one-bedroom condos cost $215 to $475 in winter, $115 to $275 in summer.

The *Goldener Hirsch Inn* (☎ 435-649-7770, 800-252-3373, fax 435-649-7901, ghi@mail.burgoyne.com), 7570 Royal East, is an Austrian-style hotel with 20 double rooms located at mid mountain in the Deer Valley ski area. There is a good restaurant and bar with aprés-ski entertainment. Bedrooms and suites range from $325 to $700 with continental breakfast. Many rooms have fireplaces and terraces.

The *Silver King Hotel* (☎ 435-649-5500, 800-331-8652, fax 435-649-6647), 1485 Empire Ave, is two (long) blocks from the Park City ski area. Amenities include indoor and outdoor pools, a spa, sauna, exercise area and concierge. Studios and one- or two-bedroom condos have kitchens, fireplaces, laundry areas and jetted tubs. Winter rates are $240 for a studio, $295 to $540 for one- to three-bedroom suites. Holiday rates are $260 to $630, shoulder ski season rates are $140 to $365 and summer rates are $99 to $325. The hotel also runs the nearby *Silver Cliff Village*, which has two-bedroom condos with the same features for $160 to $475, depending on season.

Places to Stay – Top End

The last few places described in the previous section would belong in the Top End category in other chapters of this book, especially their most expensive suites and condos. For the very best top-end places, either of the Deer Valley reservation services mentioned earlier will be able to help.

One lodge stands out above the rest, however. The *Stein Eriksen Lodge* (☎ 435-649-3700, 800-453-1302, fax 435-649-5825), 7700 Stein Way, is at 8200 feet, mid-mountain on the slopes of the Deer Valley ski area. Amenities include two restaurants, including the best in the area (the Glitretind), room and pool-side service, a bar with music, a pool, spa, sauna, exercise room, massage service, games, shops, a concierge and a huge fireplace in the lobby. Summer guests can use mountain bikes and enjoy the extensive grounds. Most rooms have superb views; suites may include a kitchen, fireplace, laundry area, private hot tub and balcony. It is the most luxurious and attentive ski lodge in Park City, but it comes at a high price. Winter rates are $450 to $650 for bedrooms, $925 to $1500 for suites and over $2000 for the Grand Suite! Summer rates start at $175, though they were recently offering mid-week, low-season specials for $129.

Places to Eat

Scores of places to eat do a thriving business in the ski season when reservations are recommended. Most cut back operations in the summer and the months immediately before and after skiing. Call ahead to check on hours. Prices are relatively high, but the food quality is also among the best in the state.

Hotel Restaurants Most of the better hotel restaurants are good if you are staying there, and worth visiting even if you're not a guest. The most famous is the elegant *Glitretind* (☎ 435-649-3700), serving fresh continental cuisine in the Stein Eriksen Lodge. You don't get a choice of french fries or mashed potatoes here – it's 'crisped bliss potatoes' or 'garlic potato puree.' The restaurant is open for breakfast, lunch and dinner, and Sunday brunch is $25 – which gives you an idea of the prices. During winter only, an adjacent dining room is famed for its game menu – venison, caribou, bison and other meats. Reservations are recommended.

The *Goldener Hirsch Inn* (☎ 435-649-7770) serves breakfast, lunch and dinner daily during winter and Wednesday to Sunday in summer – reservations recommended. The menu is continental with a strong Austrian/German influence, and most entrées are in the $20s. The *Grub Steak Restaurant* (☎ 435-649-8060) in the Inn at Prospector Square is named for its excellent steaks and has a huge salad bar. It offers chicken and seafood as well. This restaurant is open for lunch, dinner and Sunday brunch and has live music on weekends.

Main Street This street is the historic heart of Park City, along which restaurants abound. Browse the following selection (there are many others), arranged approximately from south to north. Many places have outdoor dining areas (in summer).

The *Wasatch Brew Pub* (☎ 435-649-0900), 250 Main, is a microbrewery producing at least five unpasteurized beers for all tastes – ask about brewery tours. Its slogan is 'We drink our share and sell the rest.' Open at 11 am, it serves soups, salads, sandwiches and specialties for lunch (all under $10) and a variety of dinners ($8 to $16). There's a sports bar, pool table and dart board.

The *Morning Ray Café & Bakery* (☎ 435-649-5686), 268 Main, opens at 7 am with good breakfasts and lunches featuring gourmet coffees and pastries (a great selection), soups and salads. *Cisero's* (☎ 435-649-5044), 306 Main, is a reasonably priced and popular Italian restaurant. *The Eating Establishment* (☎ 435-649-8284), 317 Main, was established in 1972 and is one of the area's most enduring and reasonably priced places to eat. Hearty breakfasts ($4 to $8) are served from 8 am to 4 pm and a good, similarly priced selection of sandwiches and specialties for lunch and slightly pricier dinners are served till 10 pm.

The 400 block of Main St is the heart of the restaurant district. Family-run *Mileti's* (☎ 435-649-8211), 412 Main, has been a favorite for over two decades (a long time in this ski town). It serves good pastas ($11 to $17) and Italian specialties ($14 to $22) for dinner only. The popular *Cafe Terigo* (☎ 435-645-9555), 424 Main, serves nouvelle American café cuisine for lunch and dinner ($15 to $20 entrees).

Park City Pizza Co (☎ 435-649-1591), 430 Main, is open 11 am to 11 pm, and it delivers – pizzas, what else? No surprises either at *Szechwan Chinese Restaurant* (☎ 435-649-0957), 438 Main, serving inexpensive lunch specials and pricier dinners ($9 to $17, or $28 for Peking duck). The oddly named *Irish Camel* (☎ 435-649-6645), 434 Main, is open daily for dinner and for lunch on weekends. It serves Mexican-influenced meals (entrées $6 to $16) and humped potatoes with blarney on the side. *Texas Red's* (☎ 435-649-7337), 440 Main, serves chili ($3.50 and up), barbecue ($8 to $17) and Texan-style catfish and chicken-fried steak for lunch and dinner in a Western setting. Don't like cowboy cookin'? Next door is *Alex's Bistro* (☎ 435-649-5252), 442 Main, a dinner restaurant with jazz and blues entertainment and nouvelle cuisine entrées in the $10 to $15 range.

Ichiban Sushi (☎ 435-649-2865), 586 Main, has a good sushi bar and a fine selection of traditional Japanese dinners in the $10 to $21 range. The *Main Street Deli* (☎ 435-649-1110), 525 Main, open from 7:30 am to 9 pm, has an excellent selection of inexpensive breakfasts, sandwiches and baked goods. Also a good value for the budget-conscious is *Main Street Pizza & Noodle* (☎ 435-645-8878), 530 Main, with lunches and dinners for $7 to $11. *The Claimjumper* (☎ 435-649-8051), 573 Main, is a popular restaurant in an older building, open for straightforward, well-prepared steak and seafood dinners (about $12 to $25). *Bangkok Thai* (☎ 435-649-8424), 605 Main, serves authentic Thai dinners every night with

entrées in the $11 to $19 range. *TCBY* (☎ 435-649-4000), 632 Main, a national chain, serves tasty frozen yogurt desserts.

Other Restaurants The *Baja Cantina* (☎ 435-649-2252), at the Park City Mountain Resort, serves reasonably priced Mexican lunches and dinners.

The *Stew Pot* (☎ 435-645-7839), 1375 Deer Valley Drive South (in Deer Valley Plaza), serves soups, salads, sandwiches and daily specials from 8 am to 9 pm in winter. Not only does it have good views from the deck, it's one of the cheaper places to eat in the Deer Valley area.

Entertainment
During the summer, concerts of all kinds take place in the various resorts and other venues around town; call the visitor center for details. Often, there are ongoing free performances downtown during the summer – recently there were free Wednesday evening concerts from 6 to 8 pm June through August in the city park bandstand and various live events on Main St from 1 to 4 pm on summer Saturdays. Park City Performances (☎ 435-649-9371) puts on plays or musicals during summer in the historic *Egyptian Theater*, 328 Main.

Holiday Village Cinemas 3 (☎ 435-649-6541), 1776 Park Ave, screens movies year-round. The Park City Film Series (☎ 435-649-9747) screens foreign and independent movies at the Santy Auditorium in the library at 8 pm on Fridays and Saturdays.

There are plenty of private clubs; to gain admission, you must either obtain a guest membership or be sponsored by a member, but both are easy to do. These are good places for live bands, especially in winter. The majority are on or near the 400 block of Main St. *Z-Place* (☎ 435-645-9722), 427 Main, the largest club in the area (with a capacity of about 1000), features live rock & roll, country & western and other music genres. Downstairs is the *Jammin' Salmon* (☎ 435-658-3474) with more live music on weekends. *The Club* (☎ 435-649-6693), 449 Main, is very popular for dancing to recorded music – go early. Next door, *The Alamo* (☎ 435-649-2380), 447 Main, is another good possibility and has pool tables, too. Across the street, *The Cozy* (☎ 435-649-6038), 438 Main, offers a variety of live bands (reggae one week, grunge the next), a large dance floor and a game/TV room. *Mileti's* (☎ 435-649-8211), 412 Main, has jazz on occasion. You can catch blues and rock at *Cisero's* (435-649-6800), 306 Main, after eating dinner inside the adjoining Italian restaurant. It has sports on a big-screen TV and dancing to DJs on nights without live bands. The Wasatch Brew Pub (see Places to Eat, above) is a good place for a beer and isn't a private club. There are plenty of other venues, including several in the better hotels.

Check out the Diversions section of the *Park Record* on Thursday, or pick up a copy of the free monthly *Park City's EAR* for entertainment, arts and recreation news.

Shopping
The Factory Stores at Park City (☎ 435-645-7078), near I-80 exit 145, has dozens of factory-outlet stores selling everything from boots to books. There are plenty of antique stores, art galleries, craft shops and boutiques on Main St.

Getting There & Away
Lewis Bros Stages (☎ 435-649-2256 in Park City, 801-359-8677 in Salt Lake City, 800-826-5844, lbs@lewisbros.com) provides vans between Salt Lake City Airport and Park City several times a day for $16 to $20 one way. They'll pick up and drop off at many Park City hotels; reservations are required. They also provide service to other ski resorts in the Salt Lake area.

Getting Around
Park City Transit (☎ 435-645-5122, 435-645-5130) runs free buses two or three times an hour throughout the day along Main St and Park Ave to most areas of town. Schedules and bus maps are available from the Visitor Information Center, or ask any bus driver.

HEBER CITY & MIDWAY AREA
An agricultural center founded in 1859, Heber City makes a good base from which to visit the surrounding valley and mountains. At an elevation of almost 5600 feet, Heber City is the Wasatch County seat and has a population of 5200.

Midway is a small town (population 1500) 3 miles west of Heber City and has natural hot springs.

Orientation & Information
Main St (Hwy 40) runs north-south and is Heber City's main commercial street. 100 S westbound takes you to Midway.

The chamber of commerce (☎ 435-654-3666), 475 N Main, is open 9 am to 5 pm, Monday to Friday plus weekends in the summer. The Uinta National Forest Heber Ranger Station (☎ 435-654-0470), 2460 S Hwy 40, is open 8 am to 5 pm Monday to Friday. The library (☎ 435-654-1511) is at 188 S Main. The local weekly newspaper is the *Wasatch Wave*. The post office (☎ 435-654-0881) is at 125 E 100 North. The County Hospital (☎ 435-654-2500) is at 55 S 500 E. The police (☎ 435-654-3040) are at 75 N Main.

Things to See & Do
The **Heber Valley Historic Railroad** (☎ 435-654-5601, 801-581-9980 in Salt Lake), 450 S 600 West, uses a steam locomotive built in 1904 and two old diesel engines for sightseeing trips. From late June to Labor Day, three trips a day are offered, ranging from 1 to 3½ hours roundtrip. From Memorial Day to late June and from Labor Day to mid-October, two trips a day are offered. For the rest of the year, trips are usually on weekends, though weekday trips are sometimes available. Trips are also offered in winter (2¼ hours). You should call ahead because some departures are sold out ahead of time by tour groups or charters. Also, if you insist on a steam train, call ahead as the diesels are used for about 75% of departures. Fares are $17 roundtrip for the 3½-hour ride, $15 for those over 65 and $10 for three- to 12-year-olds. Trips lasting 2¼ hours are $15/13/9 and 1-hour trips are $8/7/5.

Heber City

0   250   500 m
0   500   500 yards

PLACES TO STAY
5 Alpine Lodge
9 Swiss Alps Inn
11 Hylander Motel
13 Mac's Motel
15 National 9 High
   Country Inn & RV Park
16 Danish Viking Lodge

PLACES TO EAT
2 Wagon Wheel
12 Granny's Drive-In
14 Song's Chinese Restaurant
17 Claimjumper Steakhouse

OTHER
1 Chamber of Commerce
3 Post Office
4 Police
6 County Hospital
7 Reel Theaters
8 Library
10 Heber Valley Historic Railroad

The **State Fish Hatchery** (☎ 435-654-0282), on Hwy 113 a mile south of Midway, is one of the world's biggest trout hatcheries. Visiting hours are 8 am to 4:30 pm.

About 15 miles southwest of Heber City along Hwy 189 is the beginning of scenic and steep-walled **Provo Canyon**, which you drive through en route to Provo. A few miles after the canyon begins, the 600-foot-high double **Bridal Veil Falls** can be seen on the south side. An **aerial tramway** climbs 1753 feet to the top of the canyon with great views of the falls. Locals say this is the world's steepest tramway. It operates

Memorial Day to Labor Day (or slightly longer, weather permitting); fares are about $8/4 for adults/children. Bring binoculars or a spotting scope to watch the Rocky Mountain goats that are often seen in the area.

On the north side of Hwy 189 near the entrance to Provo Canyon is the **Alpine Loop Road** (Hwy 92), one of the most scenic, steep, narrow and twisting roads in the area – not recommended for long RVs or trailers. Parts of the loop are closed by snow in winter. In later September and early October, the route has spectacular fall colors. The road passes both Sundance Resort and

Timpanogos Cave National Monument, described below. About 4 miles from Hwy 189 and 2 miles beyond Sundance, a USFS tollbooth charges $3 per car unless you have a Golden Age, Eagle or Access Pass or are a resident. (Coming the other way, there is a tollbooth at the national forest boundary about 2 miles west of Timpanogos Cave.) It takes almost an hour to drive the 16 miles without stops. Along the way, you can take in impressive vistas of 11,750-foot **Mt Timpanogos**. The mountain can be climbed by trails leaving from either Mt Timpanogos or Timpooneke Campgrounds, both on Hwy 92 and described under Places to Stay, below. It's about 9 miles to the summit, but the trails are closed by snow from late October to early July – there is a permanent snowfield near the summit. To learn about the many other summer hiking possibilities in the area, contact the Uinta National Forest ranger stations in Heber City (☎ 435-654-0470), Provo (☎ 801-377-5780) or Pleasant Grove (☎ 801-785-3563) for maps, camping regulations and hiking information.

During winter, Heber City makes a good base for skiing in Park City or Sundance – both just under 20 miles away. Likewise, you can cross-country ski or snowshoe in the Uinta National Forest.

The Heber Airport (☎ 435-654-5831), a mile south of town, offers glider rides and instruction.

Other area excursions include driving to Wasatch Mountain and Deer Creek State Parks, both described below, and to Strawberry Reservoir, 26 miles southeast (described in the Northwestern Utah chapter).

Special Events

Early February sees dogsled and snowmobile racing. The Wasatch County Fair is held in Heber City in early or mid-August. Midway celebrates its European heritage during Swiss Days, held during the last weekend in August or first weekend in September.

Places to Stay – Camping

The RV park next to the *National 9 High Country Inn* (see below) has 36 sites with hookups for $20 during May to October. The *Mountain Spaa Resort* (see below) also has a few sites. Six miles north of town, near the Provo River at Jordanelle Reservoir, the *Heber Valley RV Park* (☎ 435-654-4049) has about 100 sites open year-round, mostly for RVs though tents are allowed. Rates are $11 to $18 depending on facilities used. There are showers and good trout fishing nearby.

The Uinta National Forest has more than 30 campgrounds open during the summer only. Several lie along or just off the Alpine Loop Drive (Hwy 92), and some can be reserved through Biospherics (☎ 800-280-2267). Alternatively, call the Provo Ranger Station (☎ 801-377-5780) or Pleasant Grove Ranger Station (☎ 801-785-3563) for information. From east to west along or near Hwy 92, camping areas are as follows: *Mt Timpanogos* (6800 feet elevation), *Altamont* (reserved groups only), *Timpooneke* (7400 feet), *Echo* (6000 feet, only four sites), *Little Mill* (6000 feet), *North Mill* (reserved groups only) and *House Rock* (5800 feet). These all have water, no RV hookups, and charge $11 per night. Other areas can be reached by forest roads off the main loop.

Also see Around Heber City, below.

Places to Stay – Budget to Middle

Hotel prices tend to be a little higher in summer and can get rather expensive during summer weekends. Weekly discounts and ski packages are often available. Addresses given below are in Heber City, unless otherwise indicated.

Mac's Motel (☎ 435-654-0612), 670 S Main, charges from the $30s for simple rooms. *Alpine Lodge* (☎ 435-654-0231, 800-371-0232), 90 N Main, also has rooms in the $30s and some more expensive suites with kitchenettes.

All the following have rooms in the $40 to $60 range. The *Hylander Motel* (☎ 435-654-2150, 800-932-0355, fax 435-654-2109), 425 S Main, is well run and a good value. Rooms all have microwaves and refrigerators and there is also a pool. The *National 9 High Country Inn* (☎ 435-654-0201, 800-345-9198), 1000 S Main, has a pool and spa, and a restaurant next door.

Rooms are pleasant, all with microwaves and refrigerators. There is RV camping and a small play area for children. A laundry room is available and continental breakfast is included. The *Danish Viking Lodge* (☎ 435-654-2202, 800-544-4066, fax 435-654-2770), 989 S Main, has a pool, spa, sauna, playground and coin laundry. Most rooms have refrigerators, and there are a few suites with kitchens and private spas for around $70. *Swiss Alps Inn* (☎ 435-654-0722), 167 S Main, has a pool, spa, sauna and playground. There is a restaurant opposite the motel.

In Midway, the *Mountain Spaa Resort* (☎ 435-654-0721, 435-654-0807), 800 N Mountain Spaa Lane (at 600 N 200 E), has rustic cabins starting around $50. There is a restaurant. They have two naturally heated mineral-water swimming pools and horse rentals, but are open only in summer.

Places to Stay – Top End
The 140-room *Homestead Resort* (☎ 435-654-1102, 800-327-7220, fax 435-654-5087, info@homestead-ut.com), 700 N Homestead Drive, Midway, UT 84049 is the area's premier year-round resort. Some buildings date to the 1880s (though most are modern), and the attractive grounds are extensive. There are (depending on the season) an 18-hole golf course or 12½ miles of cross-country ski tracks; golf or ski lessons; horse, mountain bike, cross-country ski or snowmobile rentals; horse-drawn buggy or sleigh rides; tennis courts, mineral-water bath, indoor and outdoor swimming pools, spa, sauna, lawn games, play area, gift shop, coffeeshop and the best restaurant in the area. (Some facilities are available to the public.)

Guests can also bathe in the natural hot springs adjoining the resort; recently, scuba diving was a new option, though you should call ahead about this. Rates are $89 to $139 for rooms, $159 to $314 for suites and $229 to $550 for condos and private houses for up to eight people. Some rooms and suites come with one or more of these amenities: fireplace, antique furnishings, and private hot tub, sun deck or patio. The

highest rates are mid-December to early January (three-night minimum required) and summer weekends. All-inclusive, one-week ski or golf vacation packages are available.

Places to Eat
The *Wagon Wheel* (☎ 435-654-0251), 220 N Main, is a family-style restaurant serving American food from 6 am to 10 pm. For a decent burger while avoiding the fast-food chains, there's *Granny's Drive-In* (☎ 435-654-3097), 511 S Main, which has 44 flavors of thick milkshakes; hours are 11 am to 9 pm, Monday to Thursday and to 10 pm Friday and Saturday. *Song's* (☎ 435-654-3338), 930 S Main, serves good Chinese and American lunches and dinners. For a reasonably priced steak, try the *Claimjumper* (☎ 435-654-4661), 1267 S Main.

The restaurants near or at the hotels above are all OK. The most upscale is *Simon's* at the Homestead Resort. Its Sunday brunch (10 am to 3 pm, $14) attracts people from as far as Salt Lake City, especially during fall when the drive over is very pretty. Dinners are served nightly, and reservations are advised, especially on weekends.

Entertainment
Reel Theaters (☎ 435-654-1181), 94 S Main, shows movies.

Getting There & Away
Greyhound passes through Heber City on its daily run along Hwy 40 between Salt Lake City and Denver, Colorado. Most people drive.

AROUND HEBER CITY
Wasatch Mountain State Park
This large state park (34 sq miles) offers fine mountain views, a good 27-hole golf course (which becomes a cross-country ski track in winter), hiking and horse trails (which turn into snowmobile trails in winter), a visitor center and developed camping with showers. These amenities make it one of the most popular state parks in the area. Reservations (☎ 800-322-3770) for summer weekend camping

are advised. Every year, snow closes the campgrounds from late October through April.

The park (☎ 435-654-1791), PO Box 10, Midway, UT 84049, is 2 miles northwest of Midway and can be reached in summer via scenic but partly unpaved Guardsman Pass (Hwy 224) south of Park City. There are about 140 campsites in different areas of the park that cost $8 (tents) or $14 to $16 (RV hookups); day use is $4. The golf course can be reached at ☎ 435-654-0532.

Deer Creek State Park

As usual for the area, this state park (elevation 5417 feet) surrounds a reservoir and offers fishing, boating and windsurfing in the summer, and ice fishing in winter. In addition, there are fine mountain views.

The park (☎ 435-654-0171), PO Box 257, Midway, UT 84049, is 9 miles southwest of Heber City via Hwy 189. Camping is available from April to October; there are showers, a grocery store and a boat launch. A marina rents boats in summer. Day use is $4; camping is $10. Weekend reservations (☎ 800-322-3770) are recommended during summer – there are only about 30 sites.

Sundance Resort

Owned and developed by actor/director Robert Redford, this year-round resort (☎ 801-225-4107, 800-892-1600, fax 801-226-1937), RR 3, Box A-1, Sundance, UT 84604, offers an elegant rustic getaway in a scenic wilderness setting. Tucked under Mt Timpanogos, the resort offers excellent skiing in winter and an arts program, hiking and mountain biking during summer. The resort is 2½ miles along Hwy 92 from the north end of Provo Canyon (Hwy 189).

Skiing goes from mid-December to April. Three lifts and a tow service 41 runs in 450 acres between 6100 and 8250 feet. 20% are for beginners and 40% for intermediate skiers. All-day lift passes (9 am to 4:30 pm) are $35 for adults, $22 for children under 12 and free for seniors over 65. Half-day passes are $27/16 for adults/children. The charge for using the resort's 9 miles of groomed cross-country ski tracks is $8 (all day) or $5 (after 2 pm); free for skiers under 12 and under and over 65. Ski rentals and lessons are available.

Mountain bikes can be rented in summer. The ski lifts run weekends and holidays (occasionally midweek) in summer and can lift mountain bikes, so you can either hike or bike back down. Horses are available for rent, and guided day rides are an option.

Outdoor theater programs for adults and children are scheduled from mid-June to August each year. Performances take place every evening except Sunday. Other events occur through the summer season. During the rest of the year, weekend theatrical performances and special film screenings are presented. There is an autumn arts program. During the summer there are activities for kids – theater, crafts, games, riding, hiking and so on – usually scheduled as three-day kids' camps for children 6 to 11.

Call the resort for information about all these activities.

Places to Stay & Eat *Sundance* has about 90 rustic wooden cottages/cabins and a few four- and five-bedroom mountain homes (call for rates). Winter rates range from about $200 for a standard room to $435 for a master suite with full kitchen, living room and fireplace. (Rates may be higher over the Christmas period.) Ski packages (stay three nights, ski free) are offered. Summer rates are $180 to $335 and theater packages are offered. In spring (April to about mid-May) and fall (Labor Day to about mid-December) rates are $150 to $280. Multi-night special packages can be arranged year-round.

There are two restaurants. The *Tree Room*, the most elegant and expensive, features Redford's private Native American art collection. Dinner reservations are recommended. The *Foundry Grill* serves breakfast, lunch and dinner in a more casual atmosphere. The adjoining *Owl Club* is a private club with food service and live music on high-season weekends. In addition, fast-food is served at *Creekside* and at *Bearclaw's Cabin* at the bottom and top of the ski area, respectively – great views. There is a small grocery store.

Timpanogos Cave National Monument

The three beautiful caves of this national monument, at an elevation of 6730 feet in the foothills of Mt Timpanogos, are a popular stop for those driving the Alpine Scenic Loop. Lovely geological formations and underground pools make the mildly strenuous access very worthwhile.

The caves are reached by a 1½-mile trail leaving the visitor center in American Fork Canyon. The climb to the caves is over 1000 feet, and there is no wheelchair or stroller access. All cave visitors must be accompanied by a park ranger, and guided tours are limited to 20 people. The trail is closed by snow for most of the year, and the caves are open only from mid-May to mid-October.

Tour tickets must be bought at the visitor center and cost $6; $5 for six- to 15-year-olds and $3 for those under six. Tours depart from the cave entrance every 10 minutes, and you will be assigned a specific time to be at the entrance. Visitor center hours (in summer) are 7 am to 5:30 pm, but afternoon tours are often filled by late morning, especially during midsummer weekends. Therefore, arrive early, preferably midweek, for the shortest waits. Allow an hour for the 1½-mile trail climb to the entrance. Each tour lasts just under an hour, and cave temperatures are 43°F year-round, so bring a sweater. In the visitor center, exhibits, a slide show and gift shop help pass the time, or ask rangers for suggestions about local trails.

Tickets can be purchased in advance for any day at the visitor center or by mail, prepaid, two weeks in advance. Call to check for price changes. Special tours are occasionally given. Information and tickets are available from Timpanogos Cave National Monument (☎ 801-756-5238), RR 3, Box 200, American Fork, UT 84003.

There is a snack bar and picnic area but no overnight camping.

PROVO

Provo, 44 miles south of Salt Lake City along I-15, is the Utah County seat and the second largest city in the state. Although Provo's population is only about 101,000, it combines with its neighbor **Orem** to the north (84,000 inhabitants) and over a dozen smaller nearby towns (see Around Provo, below) to make a sizable metropolitan area.

Provo is named after Canadian fur trapper Etienne Provost, who trapped here in 1824-1825. The earliest European visit, however, was the Spanish Domínguez-Escalante missionary expedition, which spent a few days in the area in 1776, preaching to the Ute inhabitants. Despite these brief incursions, the land remained under Ute control until Brigham Young sent 150 settlers to the valley in 1849. Short wars were fought between the Mormons and the Utes, but the settlers prevailed and several more towns were quickly founded nearby.

Provo rapidly grew into the leading Mormon town in the area. In 1875, the Brigham Young Academy (now Brigham Young University) opened, and it has grown into the world's largest church-established university. Most of the 30,000 students are strict Mormons, and the school and city have a squeaky-clean feel to them. More than other Utahan cities, Provo has held on to its early Mormon heritage; the population is largely white, conservative and middle class. The university and schools are the town's biggest employers, but the computer industry is a fast-growing second economic contributor as well. Provo consistently ranks near the top among various 'most-livable cities' polls.

The many late-19th- and early-20th-century buildings, the university, the several good museums, the proximity of skiing at Sundance (15 miles), beautiful mountain scenery along the Alpine Loop Drive (see Heber City & Midway Area, above) and the attractions of nearby Utah Lake (the state's largest freshwater lake) make Provo a tempting destination for travelers. In addition, the quality and reasonable prices of hotels make this a cheaper base than Salt Lake City and Park City.

UTAH

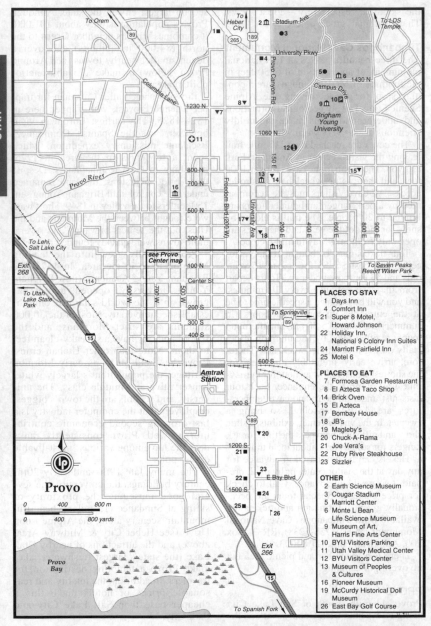

PLACES TO STAY
1   Days Inn
4   Comfort Inn
21 Super 8 Motel,
    Howard Johnson
22 Holiday Inn,
    National 9 Colony Inn Suites
24 Marriott Fairfield Inn
25 Motel 6

PLACES TO EAT
7   Formosa Garden Restaurant
8   El Azteca Taco Shop
14 Brick Oven
15 El Azteca
17 Bombay House
18 JB's
19 Magleby's
20 Chuck-A-Rama
21 Joe Vera's
22 Ruby River Steakhouse
23 Sizzler

OTHER
2   Earth Science Museum
3   Cougar Stadium
5   Marriott Center
6   Monte L Bean
    Life Science Museum
9   Museum of Art,
    Harris Fine Arts Center
10 BYU Visitors Parking
11 Utah Valley Medical Center
12 BYU Visitors Center
13 Museum of Peoples
    & Cultures
16 Pioneer Museum
19 McCurdy Historical Doll
    Museum
26 East Bay Golf Course

Orientation

University Ave (Hwy 189), running north from I-15 exit 266, is the main drag through town. Center St, running east from I-15 exit 268, crosses University Ave at Provo's meridian (or zero) point. (Don't confuse University Ave with University Parkway, which leaves I-15 at exit 272, crosses University Ave at about 1600 N and leads to the university.)

Information

The Utah Valley Visitors Bureau (☎ 801-370-8393, 800-222-8824, fax 801-370-8050), in the historic courthouse at 51 S University Ave, is open from 8 am to 5 pm, Monday to Friday, and from 9 am to 6 pm on weekends. The Uinta National Forest Ranger Station (☎ 801-377-5780), 88 W 100 North, is open 8 am to 5 pm, Monday to Friday. The city library (☎ 801-379-6650) is at 425 W Center. The local newspaper is the *Daily Herald*. The post office (☎ 801-374-2000) is at 95 W 100 South. The medical center (☎ 801-373-7850) is at 1034 N 500 West. The police (☎ 801-379-6210) are at 351 W Center.

Brigham Young University (BYU)

This campus (☎ 801-378-4636) is huge and has much of interest, not least of which is the sober appearance mandated by the student dress code – no cutoffs, long hair, bikinis or beards here! Visitor parking is off Campus Drive south of the Marriott Center, reached from University Parkway along 450 East. The visitor center (☎ 801-378-4678), open 8 am to 5 pm, Monday to Friday, has campus information and gives tours at 11 am and 2 pm, or by appointment.

The following museums are on campus and are all free and worthwhile. Most will give tours by appointment. The beautiful new **Museum of Art** (☎ 801-378-2787) is one of the biggest in the Southwest and covers many periods and styles. Hours are 10 am to 4 pm, Monday to Friday (until 9 pm on Thursday) and noon to 5 pm on Saturday. There is a charge for occasional special exhibits. The **Harris Fine Arts Center** (☎ 801-378-2881) has two art gal-

leries open from 9 am to 5 pm, Monday to Friday.

Head to the **Monte L Bean Life Science Museum** (☎ 801-378-5051) for dioramas of Utahan and other wildlife. Hours are 10 am to 9 pm on weekdays, 10 am to 5 pm on Saturdays. The **Museum of Peoples & Cultures** (☎ 801-378-6112), located at the very southwest corner of campus, concentrates on Native Americans (including South Americans) and people of the Near East. Hours are from 9 am to 5 pm, Monday to Friday. The **Earth Science Museum** (☎ 801-378-2232), at the northwest corner of campus, has an extensive dinosaur exhibit as well as others. Hours are 9 am to 9 pm on Monday, 9 am to 5 pm from Tuesday to Friday, and noon to 4 pm on Saturday. A $1 donation is suggested.

The university sponsors many artistic (☎ 801-378-4322) and athletic (☎ 801-378-2981) events, including concerts, theater, dance, football, basketball, baseball and other sports, which are often held at Cougar Stadium at the northwest end of campus.

McCurdy Historical Doll Museum

In addition to thousands of dolls in all kinds of costumes, this museum (☎ 801-377-9935), 246 N 100 East, has a doll shop and doll hospital. Hours are 1 to 5 pm, Tuesday to Saturday, and admission is $2; $1 for three- to 11-year-olds.

Pioneer Museum

This historical museum (☎ 801-377-7078), 500 W 600 North, has Western art and local Indian and pioneer artifacts. Hours are 1 to 4 pm, Monday to Friday from Memorial Day to Labor Day. Call for other hours. Admission is free.

Historic Buildings

The Utah County Travel Council has a free brochure/map describing over 20 buildings. Among these is the **Utah County Courthouse**, 51 S University Ave (within which the travel council office is located). Built in the 1920s, it's one of Utah's finest public buildings. There are several historic buildings along Center and in Provo Town Square

(Center at University Ave) – the storefronts here retain a realistic early-20th-century appearance. Construction on the Mormon **Tabernacle**, 100 S University Ave, began in 1883; the tabernacle is the site of organ recitals. Only Mormons on church business can enter the impressive, modern, sparkling-white Mormon Temple that dominates the city to the northeast at 2200 N Temple Drive.

Provo Bay
The bay is on the east side of Utah Lake, southwest of Provo. The marshes on the south side of the bay attract wetland birds such as white pelicans, white-faced ibis, ducks, geese and herons. They are also seen in the waterfowl management area on the north shore, just east of the municipal airport. The birds take up residence from March to November; April and November are the best months.

For the south side, drive west from I-15 exit 263 for about 4 miles on Hwy 77. At the Spanish Fork River bridge, a dirt road leads north to the marsh. There are trails. For the north side, go west on W Center, then south on 1600 W or 3110 W.

Seven Peaks Resort Water Park
This park (☎ 801-373-8777), 1330 E 300 North, has dozens of wave-makers, slides (including one of the world's highest), tubes, twists, and pools. There are picnic areas and sports facilities, including an 18-hole golf course and horseshoe pits. Hours are 10 am to 7 pm daily from Memorial Day to Labor Day. Admission is $15 for 10- to 62-year-olds, $12 for four- to nine-year-olds. Babies and seniors are free.

An ice-skating rink is open from December to March and costs $5; $3 for children.

Trafalga Family Fun Center
Arcade games, miniature golf, batting cages, a miniature racetrack and bumper boats are featured at this center (☎ 801-225-0195), 168 S 1200 West in Orem (take I-15 exit 274). It's open year-round; call for hours. Admission is free and you pay for individual activities.

Utah Lake State Park
The largest freshwater body in the state, Utah Lake offers fishing, boating and swimming in its 150 sq miles. The state park includes several hundred yards of shoreline and has boat launching areas; it also encompasses the mouth of the Provo River, where canoeing is popular. In winter, there is an ice-skating rink ($3; $2 for six- to 11-year-olds), ice fishing and cross-country skiing.

The state park (☎ 801-375-0733, 801-375-0731) is at 4400 W Center (the west end of Center). There is a visitor center and showers. Day use is $4; camping from April to October costs $10. Make reservations at ☎ 800-322-3770.

Golf
You can play a round at several public courses: Seven Peaks Resort (☎ 801-375-5155), see above; East Bay Golf Course (☎ 801-373-6262), 1860 S East Bay Blvd (27 holes); and Cascade Fairways (☎ 801-225-6677), 1313 E 800 North, Orem (nine holes).

Special Events
The year's main event is Freedom Days, which begins about the third week in June. Festivities include sports contests, a carnival, music and arts events and a parade, and culminate with a grand fireworks display on the Fourth of July.

Places to Stay – Camping
In addition to the campgrounds listed, also see the state parks in this chapter.

Provo KOA (☎ 801-375-2994), 320 N 2050 West, charges from $15.50 for tent sites to $21 for RV sites with full hookups and has two Kamping Kabins for $28 a double. Amenities include a pool, playground, showers and coin laundry. *Lakeside Campground* (☎ 801-373-5267), 4000 W Center (near Utah Lake State Park), charges $13 for tents and $18 for RV hookups. Fee includes use of a pool, showers, play areas, grocery store, coin laundry and canoe rental.

The Uinta National Forest Pleasant Grove Ranger Station (☎ 801-785-3563), at 390 N 100 East, Pleasant Grove, UT

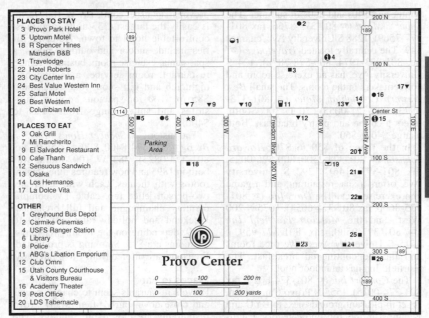

PLACES TO STAY
3 Provo Park Hotel
5 Uptown Motel
18 R Spencer Hines
   Mansion B&B
21 Travelodge
22 Hotel Roberts
23 City Center Inn
24 Best Value Western Inn
25 Safari Motel
26 Best Western
   Columbian Motel

PLACES TO EAT
3 Oak Grill
7 Mi Rancherito
9 El Salvador Restaurant
10 Cafe Thanh
12 Sensuous Sandwich
13 Osaka
14 Los Hermanos
17 La Dolce Vita

OTHER
1 Greyhound Bus Depot
2 Carmike Cinemas
4 USFS Ranger Station
6 Library
8 Police
11 ABG's Libation Emporium
12 Club Omni
15 Utah County Courthouse
   & Visitors Bureau
16 Academy Theater
19 Post Office
20 LDS Tabernacle

Provo Center

UTAH

84062, 10 miles north of Provo, administers most of the local USFS campgrounds northeast of Provo. The nearest is *Hope Campground*, 6 miles northwest on Hwy 189, then 4 miles south on USFS Rd 27. It's open late May to late September, has water but no showers or hookups and costs $8. Also see Spanish Fork, below.

Places to Stay – Budget
Hotel prices tend to be a little higher in summer.

Hotel Roberts (☎ 801-373-3400), 192 S University Ave, is a decent old hotel dating from the late 1800s. Basic rooms are about $20/25 for singles/doubles with bath, or $12/15 with shared bath down the creaky hall. Some renovated rooms are more expensive. The hotel won't take reservations for the cheapest rooms, which are often full.

All the following provide clean budget rooms and have seasonal pools. *Motel 6* (☎ 801-375-5064), 1600 S University Ave,

charges $33/39 for singles/doubles. The nice *Uptown Motel* (☎ 801-373-8248), 469 W Center, charges $30/40 for singles/doubles or slightly more with a kitchenette. Other hotels in the $30s or low $40s include the *City Center Inn* (☎ 801-373-8489, 801-374-9529), 150 W 300 South, the *Safari Motel* (☎ 801-373-9672, 800-723-2742), 250 S University Ave, and the *Best Value Western Inn* (☎ 801-373-0660, 800-500-5003, fax 801-373-5182), 40 W 300 South. All have some rooms with kitchenettes.

If you head north on 500 West, it becomes State St in Orem. Three small motels along State St charge about $30 a double.

Places to Stay – Middle
All these hotels (except the Super 8) have pools. The *National 9 Colony Inn Suites* (☎ 801-374-6800, 800-524-9999, fax 801-374-6803), 1380 S University Ave, has a spa, sauna, coin laundry and good-size rooms with kitchenettes in the $30s in

winter and $40s and $50s in summer. The *Super 8 Motel* (☎ 801-375-8766, fax 801-377-7569), 1288 S University Ave, charges $49. The centrally located *Travelodge* (☎/fax 801-373-1974, 800-578-7878), 124 S University Ave, has an exercise room and coffeemakers in the rooms. The small *Best Western Columbian Motel* (☎ 801-373-8973, 800-321-0055), 70 E 300 South, offers a coffee and pastry breakfast. Both charge $40 to $60.

In the range of $50 to $70, *Howard Johnson* (☎ 801-374-2500, 800-326-0025, fax 801-373-1146), 1292 S University Ave, offers a spa, restaurant, and a game and exercise area. The *Days Inn* (☎ 801-375-8600, fax 801-374-6654), 1675 N 200 West, and the *Marriott Fairfield Inn* (☎ 801-377-9500, fax 801-377-9591), 1515 S University Ave, have nice rooms and include continental breakfast. The Fairfield Inn has an indoor pool.

The *Comfort Inn* (☎ 801-374-6020, fax 801-374-0015), 1555 N Provo Canyon Rd, is set in pleasant grounds next to BYU and is almost in the Top End category. Facilities include an indoor pool, spa, gift shop and coin laundry, and the $60 to $85 room rates (which go up for special BYU events) include continental breakfast. There are a few honeymoon suites with private spa for $125. Restaurants are nearby, though none are on the premises.

Places to Stay – Top End
The *Best Western Cotton Tree Inn* (☎ 801-373-7044, fax 801-375-5240), 2230 N University Parkway (north of BYU), is set in attractively landscaped grounds along the Provo River. Some rooms have balconies and river views. There are indoor and outdoor pools, a spa, coin laundry and restaurant. Rooms are $70/75, and there are a few suites for up to $150.

The *Holiday Inn* (☎ 801-374-9750, fax 801-377-1615), 1460 S University Ave, has an exercise room, business center and a restaurant with room service. Rates are $70 to $90, including continental breakfast.

The *Provo Park Hotel* (☎ 801-377-4700, 800-777-7144, fax 801-377-4708, provopark@itsnet.com), 101 W 100 North, is easily the largest (333 units) and most comfortable hotel in town. Hotel facilities include indoor and outdoor pools, a spa, sauna, exercise room, business center, restaurant, room service, a lounge bar/nightclub and gift shop. Rates are about $85 to $100 for spacious rooms; mini-suites and suites range from $125 to $400.

The historic *R Spencer Hines Mansion B&B* (☎ 801-374-8400, 800-428-5636, fax 801-374-0823), 383 W 100 South, was built in 1895 and now features nine elegant rooms with themes, each with a private, two-person jetted tub, cable TV, complimentary champagne and full breakfast. Weekend and holiday rates are $99 to $199, depending on the room; weekdays, all rooms are $95. Smoking is prohibited. Free tours are offered from 1 to 4 pm daily.

Places to Eat
Provo's restaurants seem to change names and close down fairly often. Many Provo restaurants are closed on Sundays. The area around Provo Town Square (Center St at University Ave) has interesting early buildings with a variety of restaurants from which to choose.

Mexican There are several Mexican restaurants around Provo Town Square. Best known and priciest (though not expensive) is *Los Hermanos* (☎ 801-375-6714), 16 W Center, open from 11 am to 10 pm, Monday to Thursday and to 11 pm on Friday and Saturday. It has musicians occasionally. *Mi Rancherito* (☎ 801-373-1503), 368 W Center, open 11 am to 9:30 pm, Monday to Thursday, to 11 pm Friday and Saturday, advertises $4.50 lunch specials and is quite good. The *El Salvador Restaurant* (☎ 801-377-9411), 332 W Center, serves the typical and inexpensive El Salvadoran snack, pupusas, which are thick corn tortillas stuffed with cheese or beans or occasionally something else – I love them. Other El Salvadoran and Mexican food is also served from 11:30 am to 10 pm daily except Sunday.

Away from the center, a good choice is *El Azteca* (☎ 801-373-9312), 746 E 820 North, which has been serving authentic Mexican food for over 30 years. Hours are 5 to 10 pm daily except Sunday. They also run the *El Azteca Taco Shop* (☎ 801-375-9690), 46 W 1230 North, with both drive-through and dine-in service from 11 am to 10 pm, Monday to Thursday, till 11 pm on Friday and Saturday. *Joe Vera's* (☎ 801-377-3393), 1292 S University Ave, (in Howard Johnson's) is open from 6:30 am to 10 pm daily except Sunday, when it closes at 9 pm. They have a liquor license.

Asian *Cafe Thanh* (☎ 801-373-8373), 278 W Center, is a locally popular place serving both Vietnamese and Chinese meals. Lunch specials are around $4, with dinners in the $5 to $9 range. It's open from 11:30 am to 9:30 pm, Monday to Thursday, and to 10 pm on Friday and Saturday.

Close to BYU, *Formosa Garden Restaurant* (☎ 801-377-5654), 265 W 1230 North, specializes in Mandarin Chinese and Mongolian barbecue. Hours are 11 am to 9 pm, Monday to Thursday, to 10 pm on Friday and Saturday. There are a dozen other Chinese restaurants in town; several along State St in Orem are open on Sunday.

More upscale dining is available at *Osaka* (☎ 801-373-1060), 46 W Center, which serves traditional Japanese food and has 'shoji rooms' (private dining areas partitioned by sliding rice-paper screens). It has lunch specials from 11 am to 3 pm, dinners from 5 to 10 pm and is closed Sunday.

Bombay House (☎ 801-373-6677), 463 N University Ave, is the place to go for a curry or other Indian food, and the food and service are good. It's open from 11:30 am to 2:30 pm, and 5 to 10 pm daily except Sunday.

Italian *La Dolce Vita* (☎ 801-373-8482), 61 N 100 East, is one of the best values. It is open 11 am to 10 pm, Monday to Friday and 4 to 10 pm on Saturday. Most meals are about $10 or less. At the north end of town, the upscale but affordable *Olive Garden* (☎ 801-377-0062), 504 W 2230 North, is open from 11 am to 10 pm daily, to 11 pm Friday and Saturday.

The *Brick Oven* (☎ 801-374-8800), 111 E 800 North, is a good choice for pizza and has some pasta dishes. Its hours are 11 am to 11 pm, Monday to Thursday, and to 12:30 am on Fridays and Saturdays.

American There's always the unremarkable but affordable *JB's* (☎ 801-375-1133), 366 N University Ave, open 6 am to 11 pm daily (or midnight Friday and Saturday). Starving? Economizing? Fill up at *Chuck-A-Rama* (☎ 801-375-0600), 1081 S University Ave, which has a variety of all-you-can-eat salad and cooked buffets and claims to have been here since the mid-1960s. The *Sensuous Sandwich* (☎ 801-377-9244), 163 W Center, serves deli sandwiches from 10:30 am to 8 pm, Monday to Saturday.

For inexpensive steaks, head over to the *Sizzler* (☎ 801-374-1516), at 1385 S University Ave, which has a salad bar and serves lunch and dinner every day. Nearby is the more upscale *Ruby River Steakhouse* (☎ 801-371-0648), 1454 S University Ave (in the Holiday Inn), also open daily and serving seafood as well as steak, with most entrées in the $15 to $20 range.

Magleby's (☎ 801-374-6249), 1675 N 200 West, next to the Days Inn, is also upscale and handy for BYU. It specializes in fresh seafood, though it serves meat and pasta as well from 11 am to 10 pm, Monday to Thursday, to 11 pm on Friday, and 4 to 11 pm Saturday. This pleasant restaurant is completely nonsmoking. Another good all-around dinner choice is the *Oak Grill* (☎ 801-370-3547), 101 W 100 North (in the Provo Park Hotel), open from 6 to 10 pm daily and also nonsmoking.

For desserts, the *Carousel Ice Cream Parlor* (☎ 801-374-6667), 2250 N University Parkway, is open from 11 am to 11 pm, Monday to Thursday, and to midnight on Friday and Saturday.

Entertainment
For films check out *Academy Theater* (☎ 801-373-4470), 56 N University Ave;

Carmike Cinemas (☎ 801-374-6061), 175 W 200 North; or *Movies 8* (☎ 801-375-5667), 2424 N University Parkway.

See Brigham Young University, above, for telephone numbers to call for performing arts events on campus.

Because almost all BYU students are strict Mormons, bars aren't a big part of the entertainment scene. *ABG's Libation Emporium* (☎ 801-373-1200), 190 W Center, is a tavern/restaurant open Monday to Saturday and with live music on Friday and Saturday. There are a few other bars nearby. *Club Omni* (☎ 801-375-0011), 153 W Center, has three huge dance floors in an alcohol- and smoke-free environment for patrons aged 18 and over.

Getting There & Away

Bus Greyhound (☎ 801-373-4211), 124 N 300 West, has two to four buses a day north and south along I-15.

UTA (☎ 801-375-4636) has buses along University Ave going to Salt Lake City and other local towns at least every hour during the week, but only three times on Sundays, and never on holidays. Free schedules are available at the BYU Bookstore, Albertsons Supermarket, 560 W Center, and Smith's Supermarket, 350 N 200 West.

Train Amtrak (800-872-7245) has an early-morning train to Denver, Colorado and points east, and a late-evening train to Salt Lake City with connections to Los Angeles and San Francisco, California. The train station is at 600 S 300 West.

Getting Around

UTA (see above) provides local bus services.

You can rent bikes at Gourmet Bicycle (☎ 801-377-3969), 1155 N Canyon Rd, Provo, and at Guy's Bike Shop (☎ 801-798-9479), 410 N Main, Spanish Fork.

AROUND PROVO

There are over a dozen towns close to Provo, some of which have tourist facilities and sites of interest.

Lehi

This small town is at the north end of Utah Lake, off I-15 exit 282.

It's worth a stop at **Hutchings Museum of Natural History** (☎ 801-768-7180), 55 N Center. The varied exhibits offer a bit of everything – Native American and pioneer artifacts, art, fossils, minerals, bird and egg collections, and more. Hours are 9:30 am to 5 pm Monday to Saturday. Admission is $2.50, $1.50 for kids under 12.

Most visitors stay in Provo (14 miles to the south) or Salt Lake City (30 miles to the north), although there is a *Best Western Timpanogos Inn* (☎ 801-768-1400, fax 801-768-1444), 195 S 850 East, with an indoor pool, spa, free breakfast and 59 rooms for $60 to $85.

Springville

This town of 16,000 inhabitants is 7 miles south on Hwy 89 (S State St) and is the home of the **Springville Museum of Art** (☎ 801-489-2727), 126 E 400 South, completed in 1937 and considered to be one of Utah's best art museums. Some of the 13 galleries trace the history of art in the state and others have a variety of changing exhibits. The grounds hold many sculptures. Hours are 10 am to 5 pm, Tuesday to Saturday (till 9 pm on Wednesday) and from 3 to 6 pm on Sunday. Admission is free (except for special events). A 12-minute video on the museum is shown to interested visitors, and the museum sponsors a series of Sunday evening concerts from September to early May.

Spanish Fork

Spanish Fork is 8 miles south of Provo. The Escalante-Domínguez expedition passed through in 1776, praising the beauty of the area. Mormons settled here in 1850, and soon after, Mormons from Iceland formed the first Icelandic settlement in the USA. Monuments to these events are found in the city park at 51 S Main (Escalante-Domínguez) and at 895 E 300 South (Icelandic tower). The town has a population of about 12,000.

The Spanish Fork Ranger Station (☎ 801-798-3571), 44 W 400 North, Spanish Fork, UT 84660, has information about four USFS campgrounds along USFS Rd 058 and other roads in Hobble Creek Canyon east of Springville. They are open in summer only and have water. Fees are $7 to $11; distances are 7 to about 30 miles east of Springville. The ranger station also has information about the Nebo Loop, described under Payson in the Central Utah chapter. The chamber of commerce (☎ 801-798-8352), 40 S Main, also has visitor information. There are a couple of hotels.

Northern Utah

This chapter covers the area north of Ogden and the Great Salt Lake. Geographically, the area has two distinct regions – one dry and desolate, the other mountainous and forested.

North and northwest of the Great Salt Lake, the land is very arid, saline and extremely barren with very few inhabitants, human or otherwise. Even desert lovers are stunned by the sheer unlivability of this terrain. The remote area does attract visitors, however, who come to see where America's first transcontinental railroad was finally linked.

The countryside northeast of the Great Salt Lake, by contrast, is a scaled-down continuation of the Wasatch Mountains region described in the previous chapter. Today, two small Mormon towns dominated by

beautiful temples are overlooked by forest-clad mountains reaching over 9000 feet in elevation. Snow sports in winter, and camping, hiking and water sports in summer are the big attractions for northern Utahans. Visitors to the small towns of Brigham City and Logan will find them quintessential, old-fashioned American communities with strong Mormon ties.

Brigham City & the Northwest Corner

BRIGHAM CITY
Settled in 1851 by Mormons and originally named Box Elder, this town was soon

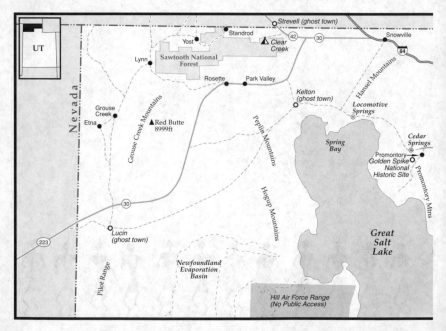

renamed to honor Brigham Young, who gave his last public speech here. Brigham City (population approximately 20,000) remains staunchly Mormon and today serves as an agricultural center, especially for the local orchards.

The pleasant town is dominated by mountains to the east. Despite being close to this green and mountainous region, it is, in fact, the seat of Box Elder County, which encompasses the desolate region to the west. This odd pairing occurred simply because there are no (Utahan) settlements of any size west of Brigham City.

Orientation & Information

Brigham City is 2 miles east of I-15, about 50 miles north of Salt Lake City. Main St runs north-south and is the main thoroughfare.

The chamber of commerce (☎ 435-723-3931), 6 N Main St, is open from 9 am to 12:30 pm and 1:30 to 5 pm, Monday to

Friday (hours may be curtailed off-season). The library (☎ 435-723-5850) is at 26 E Forest St. The post office (☎ 435-723-5234) is at 16 S 100 West. The hospital (☎ 435-734-9471) is at 950 S 500 West. The police station (☎ 435-723-3421) is at 20 N Main St.

Brigham City Museum Gallery

This museum (☎ 435-723-6769), 24 N 300 West, has changing art shows and permanent exhibits of local history. The photographs taken a century ago are particularly interesting; some buildings can still be identified. Hours are 11 am to 6 pm, Tuesday to Friday, and noon to 5 pm on Saturday. Admission is free.

Mormon Tabernacle

If you're passing Brigham City on I-15, take the short detour to see the city's tabernacle, built in 1896 to replace one destroyed by fire. With 16 spires and a steeple sweeping skyward, this church (☎ 435-723-5376),

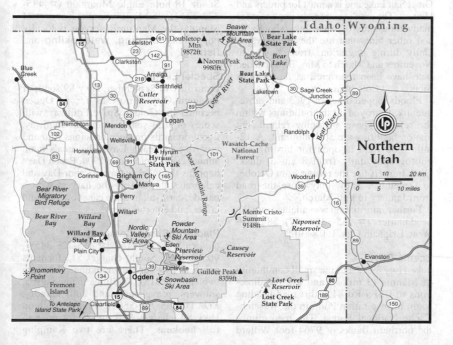

UTAH

251 S Main St, is considered one of Utah's finest. It's open daily from 9 am to 9 pm; free tours are given from May to October.

Other Buildings

The restored turn-of-the-19th-century **train station** (☎ 435-723-2989), 833 W Forest St, has a museum and is of interest to railroad buffs. The Box Elder **County Courthouse**, 1 S Main St, built between 1855 and 1857 and expanded in 1910, is a noteworthy building. Next door, the chamber of commerce occupies the brick-red **firehouse** built in 1910 and can tell you of other historical buildings.

Also drive 4 miles south to **Willard**, known for its many late-19th-century stone houses built in Welsh style.

Bear River Migratory Bird Refuge

Sixteen miles west of Brigham City, this refuge encompasses almost 74,000 acres of marshes on the northeastern shores of the Great Salt Lake and is a must for birders and hunters. The area is extremely important for many thousands of waterfowl, shorebirds and other birds that use the refuge, especially during migrations from August to November and March to May. Birds banded here have been recovered as far away as Siberia and Colombia.

Floods topped dikes in 1983 and subsequently destroyed all the buildings within the refuge. These are being rebuilt, but visitor facilities are still minimal. A 12-mile-loop road is open for birding and photography daily from 8 am to dusk. Duck hunters use the refuge from October to December. Snow may close the road from January to mid-March.

Further information is available from the headquarters (☎ 435-723-5887), 58 S 950 West, Brigham City, UT 84302.

Scenic Drive

Take Hwy 89 east to the small community of Mantua (3 miles), and ask for directions to USFS Rd 84, a dirt road heading south to Inspiration Point in the Wasatch-Cache National Forest. The road climbs the northern flanks of 9764-foot Willard

Peak, reaching Inspiration Point (9422 feet, 17 miles from Brigham City), which offers fine views over the Great Salt Lake and, weather permitting, into Nevada and Idaho. Four-wheel drive is recommended, though high-clearance vehicles make it in dry weather.

Crystal Springs

Built around natural hot springs, this facility includes a pool, water slide and a picnic area. The springs (☎ 435-279-8104, 435-547-0777), 10 miles north at 8215 N Hwy 69 in Honeyville, are open daily from late morning to evening; hours vary. Admission is $8, or less if you don't use the water slide. There is a campground open April to September with showers and a spa. Sites are $9 for tents or $18 for RV hookups.

Activities

Play **golf** at nine-hole Brigham City Golf Course (☎ 435-723-5301), 900 N Main St, or 18-hole Eagle Mountain (☎ 435-723-3212), 960 E 700 South. Just east of Mantua, the Mantua Reservoir is locally popular for **boating, water-skiing** and **fishing**.

Special Events

From July to September, Hwy 89 south of Brigham City almost as far as Ogden becomes the Golden Spike Fruitway, with scores of fruit stands lining the highway. Local orchards produce delicious fruit and give rise to Peach Days, the area's main annual event, held since 1904. Peach Days happens the weekend after Labor Day and celebrates the end of the harvest with a parade, carnival, antique car show, arts and crafts, and entertainment.

Places to Stay – Camping

Golden Spike RV Park (☎ 435-723-8858), 905 W 1075 South, charges $13 for tents or up to $19 for full hookups. There are two cabins ($15). Facilities include a spa, showers, playground and coin laundry. *KOA* (☎ 435-723-5503), 4 miles south on Hwy 89, charges $16 to $22 for none to full hookups. There are two Kamping

Kabins for $27. Facilities include showers, pool, playground, coin laundry and a store. The USFS runs *Box Elder Campground* (☎ 435-753-2772, 800-280-2267 for reservations), 2 miles south of Mantua. It's open mid-May through September. Sites are $9; there is water but no hookups or showers. Also see Crystal Springs, above.

Places to Stay – Budget
Rates go up during special events. The decent *Galaxie Motel* (☎ 435-723-3439, 800-577-4315), 740 S Main St, is next door to a family restaurant and charges in the $30s in summer, in the $20s in winter. The smaller *Bushnell Motel* (☎ 435-723-8575), 115 E 700 South, charges in the upper $20s and $30s. Both have some rooms with kitchenettes.

Places to Stay – Middle
The *Howard Johnson Inn* (☎ 435-723-8511, 800-446-4656, fax 435-723-8511), 1167 S Main St, has a pool, spa, refrigerators in many rooms and an adjoining restaurant. Rates include continental breakfast and are in the $50s. The modern new *Crystal Inn* (☎ 435-723-0440, 800-408-0440, fax 435-723-0446), 480 Westland Drive, has a pool, spa, exercise room and spacious rooms with microwave, refrigerator and laptop modem hookups. Some rooms also have spas. Rates are $65 to $100, including continental breakfast.

About 10 miles northeast on Hwy 89/91, halfway to Logan, is the *Best Western Sherwood Hills Resort* (☎ 435-245-5054, 435-245-4183). Amenities include three pools, spas, saunas, golf and tennis, and horse, bike, cross-country ski and snowmobile rentals. There is a good restaurant open daily for breakfast, lunch and dinner. During the summer, the resort presents outdoor theater and musical revues and hosts murder-mystery dinners. Rooms range from the $50s to the $80s; honeymoon and other suites are about $120.

Places to Eat
A fun stop for inexpensive meals is the family-run *Idle Isle* (☎ 435-734-2468), 24 S

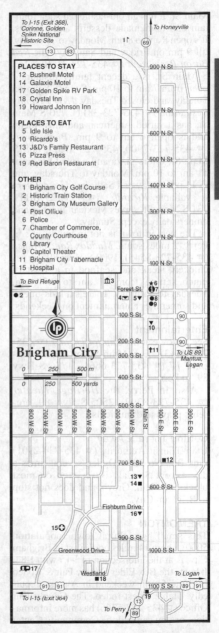

PLACES TO STAY
12 Bushnell Motel
14 Galaxie Motel
17 Golden Spike RV Park
18 Crystal Inn
19 Howard Johnson Inn

PLACES TO EAT
 5 Idle Isle
10 Ricardo's
13 J&D's Family Restaurant
16 Pizza Press
19 Red Baron Restaurant

OTHER
 1 Brigham City Golf Course
 2 Historic Train Station
 3 Brigham City Museum Gallery
 4 Post Office
 6 Police
 7 Chamber of Commerce,
    County Courthouse
 8 Library
 9 Capitol Theater
11 Brigham City Tabernacle
15 Hospital

Brigham City

Main St. It has an old-fashioned soda fountain and homemade desserts and candies. It's open 8 am to 8 pm, Monday to Thursday, till 9 pm on Friday and Saturday. The *Red Baron Restaurant* (☎ 435-723-3100), 1167 S Main St, is a decent family restaurant open from 7 am to 10 pm, 8 am to 8 pm on Sunday, and closed Tuesday. *J&D's Family Restaurant* (☎ 435-723-3811), 720 S Main St, has a varied American and kids' menu and is open 6 am to 9 pm. *Pizza Press* (☎ 435-723-7900, 435-723-5752), 868 S Main St, offers pizza and a salad bar from 11 am to 10 pm, Monday to Thursday, and to 11 pm Friday and Saturday; free delivery is available. *Ricardo's* (☎ 435-723-1811), 131 S Main St, serves Mexican lunches and dinners daily except Sunday.

The best in town is not in town – it's in Perry, 2 miles south. *Maddox Ranch House* (☎ 435-723-8545), 1900 S Hwy 89, serves chicken, steak and seafood in a Western ranch setting from 11 am to 9:30 pm, Tuesday to Saturday. There's a kids' menu and sometimes entertainment on weekends.

Entertainment
See a movie at the *Capitol Theater* (☎ 435-723-3113), 53 S Main St, or *Walker Cinemas IV* (☎ 435-723-6661), 1776 S Hwy 89, in Perry.

Also in Perry, the *Heritage Theater* (☎ 435-723-8392), 2505 S Hwy 89, presents plays and musicals.

Getting There & Away
Utah Transit Authority (☎ 435-734-2901) runs Bus No 30 to Ogden several times a day except Sunday. Buses stop on most blocks of Main. Greyhound does not stop in Brigham City.

TREMONTON
This small agricultural town (population 5000), about 14 miles northwest of Brigham City, is at the intersection of I-15 with I-84. It hosts the Box Elder County Fair & Rodeo held the fourth weekend in August, reputedly Utah's oldest rodeo. The County Fair Office (☎ 435-257-5366) has more information, or you can call the Community Center

(☎ 435-257-3371), 150 S Tremont St, for tourist information. The center houses a small museum, open on weekdays.

Belmont Hot Springs (☎ 435-458-3200), 10 miles north at Plymouth, has hot pools ($5) and a golf course open from late April to mid-October. There is an RV park here.

Places to Stay & Eat
The tiny *Marble Motel* (☎ 435-257-3524), 116 N Tremont St, has adequate rooms in the low $30s. The better *Sandman Motel* (☎ 435-257-7149), 585 W Main St, charges $35 to $45. The best is the *Western Inn* (☎ 435-257-3399, 800-528-7414, fax 435-257-3256), 2301 W Main St, which charges $45 to $50 and is convenient for I-15 exit 40 (the other motels are in town).

Next to the Western Inn, *Denny's* (☎ 435-257-1919), 2341 W Main St, serves breakfast, lunch and dinner. *Saigon Towers* (☎ 435-257-0443), 26 S Tremont St, serves Chinese food.

GOLDEN SPIKE NATIONAL HISTORIC SITE
Between the 1830s and early 1860s, more than 30,000 miles of railway tracks were laid in the USA, all east of the Missouri River. In 1863, work began on a transcontinental system. The Union Pacific Railroad was built westward from Omaha, Nebraska, and the Central Pacific Railroad pushed eastward from Sacramento, California. On May 10, 1869, the two railroads met at Promontory Summit and were linked by ceremonial golden spikes – now the nation could be crossed by train. The face of the American West was changed forever.

New tracks bypassed the site in 1903, and modern trains take a different route, but the historic site contains almost 2 miles of track laid on the original roadbed where the railroads were linked. Visitors can watch exact replicas of the original steam engines chugging along the tracks, and various talks and demonstrations of track-laying and life in the 1860s are given by folks in period costume. A 1½-mile, self-guided walk and a 9-mile, self-guided auto tour are good opportunities for taking a closer look at the area. The visitor center has booklets describing the tours, audio-visual programs and exhibits about the history of the transcontinental railroad. There is a gift and book shop.

Information

The visitor center (☎ 435-471-2209), PO Box 897, Brigham City, UT 84302, is open from 8 am to 6 pm from late May to early September and to 4:30 pm otherwise. It is closed on New Year's Day, Thanksgiving and Christmas.

Steam train demonstrations happen at 10:30 am, 1:30, 3:30 and 5 pm from late May to early September and at 9:30 am, 11:30 am, 1:30 and 4 pm from late April to late May and September to mid-October. There are also steam demonstrations during the last weekend of the year. The rest of the year the trains don't run – it may be possible to look at them in the engine house with a ranger.

Admission is $7 per car or $3.50 per person, from late April till mid-October, $4/2 at other times and free during special events. Golden Age, Access and Eagle Passes are honored.

There are no camping sites or restaurants; picnic sites are available. Food vendors attend the special events.

The site is 32 miles west of Brigham City along paved and signed roads.

Special Events

There is an annual reenactment of the Golden Spike Ceremony every May 10, which is very popular. The annual Railroader's Festival takes place on the second Saturday of August and features reenactments and a variety of events ranging from spike-driving contests to buffalo-chip-throwing contests. (No, a buffalo chip is not a large french fry – it's an authentic, sun-dried buffalo turd especially imported from the herd on Antelope Island. See the Wasatch Mountains Region chapter.) The last weekend of the year sees the annual Railroader's Film Festival and Winter Steam Demonstration, with classic Hollywood railroading films. The annual March

for Parks is the third Saturday in April, and the Park Service's birthday is August 25. Admission to the park is free for all of these events.

From mid-March to mid-April, especially just after dawn, you may see sage and sharp-tailed grouse performing courtship rituals in the sagebrush areas near the visitor center.

AROUND GOLDEN SPIKE NATIONAL HISTORIC SITE

About 5 miles east of Golden Spike, a turnoff to the south leads to **Promontory Point**. A 40-mile road, half paved and half gravel, follows the eastern coast of the Promontory Mountains Peninsula (the biggest land mass jutting into the Great Salt Lake). There are fine views of the lake and the Wasatch Mountains behind. The road has no facilities, and the southernmost point is private.

Adventurous drivers can follow the old **Central Pacific Railroad** bed for about 90 miles west through uninhabited desert. A dirt and gravel road heads west from the Golden Spike NHS and passes Locomotive Springs National Waterfowl Management Area, goes through the ghost town of Kelton, climbs over the steep Peplin Mountains, and emerges at the ghost town of Lucin near the Nevada border. Parts of the drive (particularly over the Peplin Mountains) require 4WD; some parts may be passable to cars in good weather. The section in the best condition is between Locomotive Springs and Kelton, both of which are reached by decent gravel roads from the north. The area is remote; it's rarely traveled (not marked on many maps), and drivers must carry emergency food and water, spare tires, fuel etc. Occasional 'Scenic Backway' signs point the way. The BLM (☎ 801-907-4300 in Salt Lake City) has more information.

The small community of **Corinne**, about 5 miles before Brigham City on the way back from Golden Spike NHS, used to be an important railroad town. Several 19th-century buildings can be seen, including the Methodist Church built in

UTAH

1870 and considered Utah's oldest non-Mormon church.

If, instead of returning to Brigham City, you take Hwy 83 north to I-84, you'll see **Thiokol**, a rocket manufacturing plant spread out over several square miles. Windowless buildings, countless 'No Trespassing' signs, occasional glimpses of rockets and miles of forbidding fencing give the area a somewhat menacing air.

THE NORTHWESTERN MOUNTAINS

From Snowville, Utah's northernmost town on I-84, paved Hwy 30 cuts across the northwestern corner of the state on its 90-mile run to the Nevada border, passing several mountain ranges. Rock hounds roam some slopes, looking for variquoise in the Hansel Mountains south of Snowville and variscite in the Grouse Creek Mountains north of Lucin.

In the Raft River Mountains, there's a free campground in the Sawtooth National Forest at Clear Creek, open from June to October. Water is available from springs. Reach the campground from Strevell on Hwy 42, a mile into Idaho; there is a signed gravel road for Yost and Clear Creek, about 10 miles south of Strevell. Hiking, exploration by 4WD vehicle and wildlife observation are all possible activities. Most of the Sawtooth National Forest is in Idaho; for more information, contact the USFS (☎ 208-678-0430), 2621 S Overland Ave, Burley, ID 83318.

Tiny **Snowville** (population 250) has the *Outsiders Inn* (☎ 435-872-8293, fax 435-872-8183), 50 S Stone Rd, with rooms in the $30s. Eat at *Mollie's Café* (☎ 435-872-8295), 15 E Main St.

The only settlement along Hwy 30 to Nevada is even tinier **Park Valley**, with the simple *Palmer's Motel* (☎ 435-871-4755) offering rooms in the $30s. A café is open from Monday to Saturday, and there's a gas station.

After Hwy 30 crosses into Nevada, it becomes Hwy 233 and continues 35 miles to I-80. From there, it's another 32 miles back to Utah at Wendover (see the Western Utah chapter).

Bridgerland

LOGAN

Logan, with a population of 38,000, is the Cache County seat and the largest town in northern Utah. The drive northeast of Logan through Logan Canyon is very scenic and especially popular in the fall for the beautiful colors. Legend has it that the local Shoshone Indians called it 'the house of the Great Spirit' long before the white man recognized the valley's beauty.

Founded by Mormons in 1859, the city quickly became an important agricultural center. In 1888, Utah State University was founded here, although it was originally known as the Agricultural College of Utah. During the late 1800s, many other important buildings were constructed and can still be seen by the curious visitor. Not the least of these buildings is the magnificent Mormon Temple, which dominates the city.

Agriculture continues to fuel the economy. Ranching and dairy farming are important, and Cache Valley cheeses can be bought in the supermarkets of many Western states. There is also a meat-packing plant and some light industry. The tourist industry is growing; visitors come for the beautiful scenery, historical setting and local cultural activities. The elevation of 4525 feet gives the town a pleasant, four-season climate, and snow activities are popular in winter.

Orientation & Information

Hwy 91 (Main St), is the major street, running north-south. Hwy 89 (400 N) eastbound leads into scenic Logan Canyon.

The chamber of commerce (☎ 435-752-2161, 800-882-4433), 160 N Main St, Logan UT 84321, is open 8 am to 5 pm from Monday to Friday and Saturday in summer. The Wasatch-Cache National Forest Logan Ranger Station (☎ 435-755-3620), 1500 E Hwy 89, is open 8 am to 4:30 pm from Monday to Friday. The library (☎ 435-750-9870) is at 225 N Main St. The local newspaper is *The Cache Citizen*. The post office

UTAH

PLACES TO STAY
9   Alta Motel
      & Alta Manor Suites
10 Comfort Inn
12 Best Western Weston Inn
22 Center Street B&B
26 Best Western Baugh Motel
29 Days Inn
31 Western Park
32 Super 8 Motel,
      Crystal Inn

PLACES TO EAT
3   El Toro Viejo
5   El Sol
6   Angie's
7   Frederico's Pizza
16 Cafe Ibis
18 Copper Mill
19 Glaucer's Restaurant
20 The Bluebird

25 Gia's Restaurant
27 Cottage Restaurant

OTHER
1   Cache Valley Mall
2   Hospital
4   Municipool
8   USFS Ranger Station
11 Library
13 Post Office
14 Police
15 Chamber of Commerce,
      DUP Museum
17 Logan Temple
21 Tabernacle Square
23 The White Owl
24 Capitol Theater
      (Ellen Eccles Theater)
28 Community Recreation
      Center
30 Willow Park Zoo

(☎ 435-752-7246) is at 151 N 100 West. The hospital (☎ 435-752-2050) is at 1400 N 500 East. The police station (☎ 435-750-9900) is at 45 W 200 North.

Historic Main Street
Many turn-of-the-19th-century buildings are on or just off the three blocks of Main between 200 N and 100 S. The building at 160 N Main St was originally the US Federal Building but now houses the chamber of commerce (which has self-guided-walk leaflets for 14 buildings on the street) and the **DUP Museum** (☎ 435-752-5139)

with local historical exhibits. It is open on summer afternoons, Tuesday to Friday, and other times by arrangement.

Opposite, at 179 N Main St, is the **County Courthouse**, built in 1883 and Utah's oldest county building still being used for its original purpose. Its cupola has been restored.

A block south, in a park-like setting, is the Mormon **Tabernacle** (☎ 435-755-5598), built between 1864 and 1891. The thrifty and dedicated Mormon community was using the building for meetings two decades before its completion. The building was restored (again) in 1997, and the public is welcome; tours are given in summer.

The old Capitol Theater, 43 S Main St, dates from 1923, and is once again being used for performances as the **Ellen Eccles Theatre**, after renovations completed in 1993. Similarly, the **Lyric Theatre**, 28 W Center St, dates from 1913 and boasts a ghost as well as repertory arts. A favorite building on the walk is the **Bluebird Restaurant**, 28 N Main St, which was built in 1914 and has been operating since 1923 (see Places to Eat, later in this chapter).

Mormon Temple

Built between 1877 and 1884, the temple is Utah's third oldest; reputedly 25,000 people worked on it. Although it is open only to Mormons on church business, the visitor cannot miss the massive, 170-foot tall, twin-towered building, which is perched on a green hilltop and visible from many parts of Logan. You are welcome to walk the grounds around the temple at 175 N 300 East.

Utah State University

About 20,000 students and more than 2000 staff enliven Logan's cultural scene. The campus is famous for **Old Main** (☎ 435-797-1000), the late-19th-century center of university life. The **Taggart Student Center** has an information desk (☎ 435-797-1710), restaurants serving the locally popular student-made Aggie Ice Cream and other meals, a movie theater and other services. The **Nora Eccles Harrison Museum of Art** (☎ 435-797-0163) has both permanent exhibits and changing shows in various media. Hours are 10:30 am till 5 pm, Tuesday to Friday (till 8 pm on Wednesday) and 2 to 5 pm on weekends. Admission is free.

The university has many concerts, festivals and sports events; call ☎ 435-797-3000 or ☎ 435-797-3040 for date and ticket information.

Alliance for the Varied Arts

This art space (☎ 435-753-2970), 43 S Main St in the Capitol Theater, has changing shows of regional and national artists. Receptions with refreshments, free to the public, are held every few weeks at the start of each new show. Otherwise, it opens from noon to 6 pm, Wednesday to Saturday. Work is for sale.

Willow Park Zoo

The small zoo and aviary (☎ 435-750-9893), 419 W 700 South, are open daily from 9 am to dusk. Admission is 25¢. Picnic and playground areas are available.

Activities

You can **golf** a round at the new 18-hole Logan River Golf Course (☎ 435-750-0123), 1 mile south on Hwy 89/91. The 18-hole Birch Creek Golf Course (☎ 435-563-6825) is 7 miles north in Smithfield. The Community **Recreation Center** (☎ 435-750-9877), 195 S 100 West, has tennis, racquetball, a gym and a sauna. **Swim** at the Municipool (☎ 435-750-9890) at 114 E 1000 North.

Winter sports are popular in the Logan area. Snow starts falling in late October, and the best months for snow sports in the nearby mountains are December through April. Over a dozen places in and around Logan rent snowmobiles, or cross-country and downhill skis and snowboards. Downhill skiing/snowboarding is practiced at Beaver Mountain (see Beaver Mountain Ski Area, later in this chapter) and snowmobiling and cross-country skiing are popular in Logan Canyon, Hardware Ranch and the Wasatch-Cache National Forest, where almost 200 miles of snowmobile trails are maintained. Both the chamber of commerce and the USFS Ranger Station have details of rental places and trails.

Special Events

Festival of the American West This major annual event lasts eight days, beginning the last Friday in July. Sponsored by Utah State University, the festival includes a historical pageant held every evening (except Sunday) with acting, dancing and singing. There is also a fair open daily (except Sunday) with Western entertainment, craft demonstrations, mountain men and Indians, and food stands. Advance tickets are sold at the university ticket office (☎ 435-797-1143, 800-225-3378, 800-249-2583).

Other Events Summerfest Art Fair brings arts and crafts booths to the tabernacle lawn every June. The Fourth of July is celebrated with many events on or close to the date, including a fireworks show in Logan and a rodeo in neighboring Hyrum (7 miles south). The Saturday closest to the Fourth features a vintage car and hot-rod rally and parade that attracts tens of thousands of attendees to Logan's Main Street. The Cache County Fair & Rodeo is held the second week of August; it has been held in Logan since 1892.

Places to Stay – Camping

Riverside RV Park (☎ 435-245-4469), 445 W 1700 South (east of Hwy 89/91), has showers and coin laundry and charges $16.50 with hookups or $10 for tents. *Western Park* (☎ 435-752-6424), 350 W 800 South (enter via 600 South), has showers and charges $15; there are no tent sites.

Hardware Ranch Rd, which leaves east from Hyrum as Hwy 101, enters Blacksmith Canyon after a few miles, and 9 miles from Hyrum it passes *Pioneer Campground*, run by the Wasatch-Cache National Forest. Open from May to October, the campground provides water and toilets for a $9 fee. Free dispersed camping is allowed in the forest. (See also Hyrum State Park and Logan Canyon Scenic Drive, later in this chapter.)

Places to Stay – Budget

The *Alta Motel* (☎ 435-752-6300), 51 E 500 North, has simple rooms (no phones) in the mid-$30s. The *Zanavoo Lodge* (☎ 435-752-0085), 2½ miles up Logan Canyon, has rustic, basic rooms (no TVs or telephones) for about $30.

Places to Stay – Middle

The *Days Inn* (☎ 435-753-5623, fax 435-753-3357), 364 S Main St, has pleasant rooms, many with microwaves, refrigerators and coffeemakers for about $36/44 for singles/doubles and mini-suits with spas and kitchenettes for around $60. The hotel has an indoor pool, spa, coin laundry and free continental breakfast. The *Super 8 Motel* (☎ 435-753-8883, fax 435-753-2577), 865 S Main St, has clean rooms from $38.88/42.88, including continental breakfast. The *Comfort Inn* (☎ 435-752-9141, fax 435-752-9723), 447 N Main St, has an indoor pool, spa, exercise area and coin laundry. Spacious rooms are $55/60; mini-suites with refrigerators and jetted tubs are $65, including continental breakfast.

The *Best Western Weston Inn* (☎ 435-752-5700, fax 435-752-9719), 250 N Main St, has an indoor pool, spa, sauna, exercise room and coin laundry. Good rooms are about $50/60, including full breakfast. The *Best Western Baugh Motel* (☎ 435-752-5220, fax 435-752-3251), 153 S Main St, is set in agreeable gardens with a pool, sun deck and picnic area. Its restaurant opens from 6 am to 10 pm daily, except on Sunday (8 am to 2 pm). Most rooms are about $45/50. A few suites with fireplaces, refrigerators or spas are about $80.

The new *Crystal Inn* (☎ 435-752-0707, 800-280-0707, fax 435-787-2207), 853 S Main St, offers spacious rooms with microwaves, refrigerators and VCRs for $50 to $80, including continental breakfast. Amenities include an indoor pool, spa, exercise room and coin laundry.

Alta Manor Suites (☎ 435-752-0808, fax 435-752-2445), 42 E 500 North, has eight nonsmoking one- and two-bedroom suites in an elegantly restored house. Each suite has a full kitchen with free coffee, sitting room, fireplace, whirlpool tub, cable TV and laptop dataports. Rates are $80 to $100, including continental breakfast.

Center Street B&B (☎ 435-752-3443), 169 E Center St, Logan UT 84321, has 16 nonsmoking suites and two rooms. Part of the property dates to the 1800s. Suites are individually theme decorated with period or modern furniture, ranging from Victorian to Space Odyssey. These are priced at $55 to $135 (to $180 on weekends) and have modern amenities and in-suite breakfasts; some have spas and giant-screen TVs. The two rooms with shared bath are of a simpler Victorian style for $25/30. This is Logan's oldest B&B.

See also *Best Western Sherwood Hills Resort*, under Brigham City.

Places to Eat

The favorite of many visitors is the 1920s-style *Bluebird Restaurant* (☎ 435-752-3155), at 19 N Main St, which almost transports you into an early Hollywood movie. The back room has a wraparound mural of Logan's history and various antiques on display. It's not all hype – the building dates from 1914 and has been a restaurant since the 1920s. Hours are 11 am to 9 pm, Monday to Thursday, and to 10 pm on Friday and Saturday. Lunches are $4 to $9; dinners are $7 to $14, and no alcohol is available. Predictably, this restaurant serves traditional American fare.

Many locals favor *Angie's* (☎ 435-752-9252), 690 N Main St. Its atmosphere is the converse of the Bluebird – it's large, modern, squeaky-clean and a little plastic-looking, but it offers a decent selection of very reasonably priced American food. Angie's is open 6 am to 11 pm daily. A more atmospheric place for very inexpensive American family dining is *Glauser's Restaurant* (☎ 435-752-1681), 25 W Center St, open 6 am to 9 pm, Monday to Saturday. Neither serves alcohol.

Cafe Ibis (☎ 435-753-4777), 52 Federal Ave, is a combination deli/juice bar/coffeehouse/health-food store popular with the university crowd. Snacks, desserts and inexpensive light meals are available from 7:30 am to 9 pm, Monday to Thursday, till 11 pm on Friday, from 8:30 am to 11 pm on Saturday and 10 am to 5 pm on Sunday.

The *Cottage Restaurant* (☎ 435-752-5260), 51 W 200 South, serves good American food, ranging from sandwiches to steak and seafood, in an old-fashioned, homey atmosphere. Prices range from $4 to $20; hours are 6 am to 10 pm daily except on Sunday (8 am to 2 pm). The *Copper Mill* (☎ 435-752-0647), 55 N Main St (top of the Emporium Building), specializes in prime beef and seafood (entrées between $13 and $20) and some cheaper choices. There's a decent salad bar (as well as alcohol). It's open 11 am to 9:30 pm from Monday to Thursday, and to 10:30 pm on Friday and Saturday.

The best choice for Italian food is *Gia's Restaurant* (☎ 435-752-8384), 119 S Main St, open daily from 11 am to 10 pm. Meals are $6 to $16 and alcohol is served. *Frederico's Pizza* (☎ 435-752-0130), 1349 E 700 North, is convenient to the university; it's open from 11 am to 10 pm daily, to 11 pm on Friday and Saturday.

For Mexican dining *El Toro Viejo* (☎ 435-753-4084), 1079 N Main St, is quite good. Hours are 11 am to 10 pm daily. *El Sol* (☎ 435-752-5743), 871 N Main St, is an older Mexican place with very cheap set lunches and dinners.

There are several Chinese restaurants along Main St, most of which offer inexpensive all-you-can-eat lunch buffets.

The *Zanavoo Lodge* (☎ 435-752-0085), 2½ miles out of town into Logan Canyon, serves satisfying American dinners in a casual, rustic setting. Hours are 5 to 10 pm daily except Sunday, and entrées range from $8 to $16. Prime rib is its weekend specialty.

Entertainment

The major arts event is the Utah Festival Opera Company performing at the historic *Ellen Eccles Theatre* (☎ 435-752-0026), 43 S Main St, (formerly the Capitol Theater). Three or four operas are offered from mid-July to mid-August. Also popular is the Old Lyric Repertory Company, with four plays during the season from late June to late August at the 1913 *Lyric Theatre* (☎ 435-752-1500, 435-797-0305), 28 W Center St. Both companies rotate their performances so theater-goers can enjoy them all in three or four days. Both theaters offer various other cultural events throughout the year.

Catch a movie at the *Cache Valley 3* (☎ 435-752-7762, 435-753-3112), 1300 N Main St, in the Cache Valley Mall; *Cinefour* (☎ 435-753-6444), 2297 N Main St; *Movies*

5 (☎ 435-787-9438), 2440 N Main St; *Reel Time* (☎ 435-752-5098), 795 N Main St; *Cinema Theater* (☎ 435-753-1900), 60 W 100 North; or *Utah Theatre* (☎ 435-752-3072), 18 W Center St.

Also see Utah State University, above.

For a beer, big-screen sports TV and a game of pool, head over to *The White Owl* (☎ 435-753-9165), 36 W Center St.

Getting There & Away
Logan Cache Airport (☎ 435-752-5955), 2500 N 900 West, can arrange charters or rentals; there are no commercial flights.

Greyhound (☎ 435-752-4921), at the airport, has a daily evening bus to Salt Lake City (1½ hours) and a couple of buses a day up to Idaho.

AROUND LOGAN
RV Jensen Living Historical Farm
This 'American Family Farm – 1917' (☎ 435-245-4064) lies 6 miles southwest of Logan on S Hwy 89/91 in Wellsville. Run by university students in period clothing, the farm operates as it would have in 1917. Visitors are welcome to tour the historic buildings, watch the daily use of antique farm implements and enjoy the animals.

There are scheduled special events such as sheepshearing by hand, horseshoeing and threshing grain with a steam engine. The farm is open 10 am to 4 pm, Tuesday to Saturday, June through August. Events are also scheduled for several Saturdays during the year – call for dates. Adult admission is $5; $4 for seniors and students, and $3 for kids under 13. Family tickets are $15.

Wellsville Mountains
This is reputedly the highest range in the world rising from such a narrow base, so there are no roads and only a few steep trails up the almost-vertical sides. The area is in the Wasatch-Cache National Forest (call the Logan Ranger Station for information and maps). Hikers must carry water and know what they are doing. There are no campsites, and wilderness camping is permitted but not recommended, due to scarcity of flat areas and water, and the high elevation.

Access is from the small town of **Mendon** (elevation 4435 feet), 10 miles west of Logan. From Mendon, drive 2 miles west on 300 North to park at the trailhead (5400 feet). The trail switchbacks 3 miles up to the ridge (8100 feet) with excellent views. From here a trail goes northwest for about a mile to a vista point (8585 feet) that is one of Utah's best hawk-watching spots during fall migration, which peaks in September. Golden eagles and many other raptors have been recorded.

Alternatively, follow the ridge southeast 2 miles to Stewart Pass (8400 feet); a trail drops eastward to the Coldwater Lake trailhead (6000 feet, about 2 miles) from where a dirt road returns to Mendon (3½ miles). Or, from Stewart Pass continue south along the ridge to the highest points, Wellsville Cone (9356 feet, about 1½ miles) and Box Elder Peak (9372 feet, another mile). Many fossils, especially coral, have been found at Wellsville Cone.

Hyrum State Park
Seven miles south of Logan, near the small town of **Hyrum** (with places to eat but no hotels) is this park on Hyrum Reservoir, locally popular for fishing, boating, water-skiing and camping in summer. In winter, ice fishing and snowmobiling are the things to do.

The Ranger Station (☎ 435-245-6866) is at 405 W 300 South, Hyrum, UT 84319. There are picnic areas, boat launch areas, and 41 campsites with hot showers. Day use is $4, camping is $10 from April to November. Reservations for busy summer weekends can be made by calling ☎ 800-322-3770.

Hardware Ranch Road
This road, which leaves east from Hyrum as Hwy 101, is a designated 'Scenic Backway.' After a few miles it enters Blacksmith Canyon, where there are spots to fish for trout along the Blacksmith Fork of the Bear River. There are many primitive roads, hiking trails and camping possibilities in the area. During fall, the brilliant foliage colors make Blacksmith Canyon a popular and attractive drive.

In winter, there are **snowmobile trails** in the canyon. The paved road is plowed for the 18 miles between Hyrum and Hardware Ranch, which is a game management area and the center of an extensive snowmobile trail network. With the arrival of snow, 800 head of elk (Utah's state animal) are fed at the ranch, and there are sleigh rides to view the animals from January to March. A visitor center (☎ 435-753-6168) has information, exhibits, a café and snowmobile rentals. In spring, the elk move off into the forest.

Forest-service roads north of Hardware Ranch lead to Bear Lake Summit on Hwy 89 (see Logan Canyon Scenic Drive, below), a distance of about 25 miles. Follow USFS Rd 054 and USFS Rd 055, but be aware that these dirt roads become impassable after wet weather or spring thaw. Fall colors are lovely along here, too. The roads become groomed snowmobile trails in winter.

LOGAN CANYON SCENIC DRIVE

Logan Canyon (Hwy 89) northeast of Logan is one of Utah's best-known scenic areas: Native Americans, mountain men, fur trappers and Mormon pioneers all noted its beauty. Today, Hwy 89 is used by countless drivers in the summer to visit Bear Lake and/or continue to Yellowstone and Grand Teton National Parks in Wyoming. Likewise, fall travelers admire foliage colors splashing the steep limestone walls of the canyon. In the winter, many take this road to ski, snowmobile or continue on to the famous ski resort of Jackson Hole, Wyoming. Many hiking trails, dirt roads, fishing spots, campgrounds and picnic areas line the 40-mile drive through Logan Canyon to Bear Lake.

The drive begins as Hwy 89 crosses the Logan River at the east end of town and enters the canyon. There are several geological and historic markers along the road – just pull over to read them. There are also plenty of fishing and picnicking spots. Good stopping places include the following:

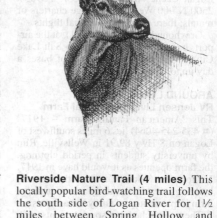

Riverside Nature Trail (4 miles) This locally popular bird-watching trail follows the south side of Logan River for 1½ miles between Spring Hollow and Guinavah campgrounds – moose have been seen here.

Wind Caves Trail (5 miles) Caves and arches eroded by wind and ice, 900 feet above the canyon floor, are reached by a 1-mile trail leaving from opposite the Malibu-Guinavah campgrounds.

Fucoidal Quartzite (8½ miles) A geological sign interprets the rock here; this place is one of several popular rock-climbing areas in the canyon.

Jardine Juniper Trail (10 miles) This is reputedly the world's oldest juniper tree – more than 3000 years old. A 5-mile trail leaves Wood Camp and climbs almost 2000 feet to the tree. There are good views and spring flowers in May and June, fall colors in September.

Logan Cave (12 miles) The cave is about a third of a mile long and can be explored with flashlights – there are no facilities. It is closed (with bars) from October to mid-May to protect a colony of Townsend's big-eared bats, which hibernate in the cave and are sensitive to human disturbance.

Naomi Peak Trail (19 miles) After 19 miles, drive west 7 miles to Tony Grove Lake (8100 feet) from where a 3-mile trail reaches Naomi Peak (9980 feet), the highest in the Bear River Range. The peak is surrounded by meadows awash with spring flowers in July and August – spring comes late at this elevation! Several other trails leave from Tony Grove Lake campground.

Beaver Mountain Ski Area (24 miles) Hwy 243 exits Logan Canyon to the ski area, described below.

Bear Lake Summit (29 miles) At 7800 feet, this is the highest point on the drive. Nearby is the relatively flat, half-mile long **Limber Pine Nature Trail**, with views of Bear Lake and many flowers in June and July. The Hardware Ranch Road drive exits near the trailhead.

Bear Lake Overlook (30 miles) The overlook is on the right of the road. Great views and interpretive signs make this an essential pullout. Beyond the lake you can see Bear River, which is the longest US river that does not empty into the sea. Instead, it rises in Utah's Uinta Mountains and passes through Wyoming and Idaho before discharging into the Great Salt Lake.

Places to Stay – Camping
The Wasatch-Cache National Forest operates several campgrounds in Logan Canyon. Most open in May and close in September/October; those over 6000 feet have shorter seasons. Actual dates vary, depending on weather conditions. All campgrounds have sites for $9 to $11, pit or flush toilets, and drinking water, except Wood Camp, which is $6 and lacks water. Sites fill up on summer weekends; arrive early or reserve by calling ☎ 800-280-2267. Day-use fees are the same as camping fees on Friday and Saturday, half price from Sunday to Thursday. Most campgrounds have only about 12 sites, except Malibu-Guinavah (40 sites), Tony Grove (36 sites) and Sunrise (27 sites).

The campgrounds are *Bridger* (5000 feet elevation, 3 miles into Logan Canyon); *Spring Hollow* (5100 feet, 4 miles); *Malibu-Guinavah* (5200 feet, 5 miles, which has an amphitheater with weekend-evening presentations); *Preston Valley* (5500 feet, 8 miles); *Lodge* (5600 feet, 9 miles plus 1½ miles to right); *Wood Camp* (5600 feet, 10 miles); *Lewis M Turner* (6000 feet, 19 miles); *Tony Grove Lake* (8100 feet, 19 miles plus 7 to left); *Red Banks* (6500 feet, 20 miles); and *Sunrise* (7800 feet, 30 miles, 6 miles before Garden City).

BEAVER MOUNTAIN SKI AREA
This small (464 acres) ski area (☎ 435-753-0921) is 25 miles up Logan Canyon and 1½ miles to the left (or 13 miles from Garden City). A day lodge has food, ski rentals and instruction. Three lifts service 16 runs between 7200 and 8840 feet elevation. Thirty-five percent of the runs are for beginners, 40% for intermediate skiers. A full-day (9 am to 4 pm) lift pass is $20, or $15 for a half day. Children and those over 65 pay $15 for all day; seniors over 70 ski free. Ski/snowboard rentals are available.

Half a mile beyond the ski-area turnoff is **Beaver Creek Lodge** (☎ 435-753-1076, 435-946-3400), which rents horses and mountain bikes (in summer), snowmobiles and rooms with kitchenettes from $65 midweek, $80 on weekends. Otherwise, Garden City has the closest overnight accommodations for skiers.

Both cross-country ski and snowmobile trail systems are found in the area.

GARDEN CITY & BEAR LAKE
Despite its name, Garden City is just a village of a few hundred inhabitants on the west shore of Bear Lake at 5890 feet above

UTAH

sea level. The village provides lake visitors with places to stay and eat and is very busy in summer. Bear Lake extends into Idaho, covers 112 sq miles and supports four endemic fish species, which are sought after by anglers. The lake's deep-blue color is caused by limestone particles suspended in the water.

Information

Bear Lake Visitors Bureau (☎ 208-945-2072, 800-448-2327) is a few miles north in Idaho. There is a tourist information center in Garden City at the intersection of Hwy 89 and Hwy 30 (open during the summer).

Bear Lake State Park

Three areas on the west, south and east sides of the lake are all administered by the park (☎ 435-946-3343, 800-322-2770 for camping reservations), PO Box 184, Garden City, UT 84028. In addition, there are a few more facilities on the Idaho end (☎ 208-945-2790).

During summer, boating, fishing and even scuba diving are popular activities. In the early 1990s, low water levels left the marina high and dry, but at this time the lake is at almost record-high levels, and the marina has been expanded to 350 boat slips. (I recommend you call the park about water levels.) The best fishing is in early spring and late fall for cut-throat trout. During the January spawning season, anglers dip nets through the ice to catch the endemic Bonneville cisco. Day use is $4 per vehicle, or $1.50 for cyclists and walk-ins; camping is $6 to $15, depending on the site.

The **Bear Lake Marina**, 1 mile north of Garden City, is the main park head-quarters and is open all year. There is a visitor center, picnic area, swimming, boat rental, launch ramps and a 13-site campground with showers for $11 per site – reservations are recommended in summer.

The **Rendezvous Beach** area is 8 miles south of Garden City on the south end of the lake. There are picnic areas, a sandy beach and small-watercraft activity. Three campgrounds (with showers) have a total of about 140 campsites for $11 to $15 (with hookups).

The **Eastside** area is 12 miles north of Rendezvous Beach and offers boat launches and picnic areas all year. The shore slopes steeply here, and scuba divers use the area. About 100 primitive campsites are $6 – drinking water is available but limited.

Summer Activities

Apart from the state park, several of the resorts under Places to Stay rent boats or jet skis. Beaver Creek Lodge, 12 miles away near Beaver Mountain Ski Area (see above) has horse and bike rental.

Winter Sports

Garden City is the center of a large network of **snowmobile trails**. Bear Lake Funtime (☎ 435-946-3200, 800-516-3200), 1217 S Bear Lake Rd, rents snowmobiles and gives tours, as does Beaver Creek Lodge.

Special Events

The popular Raspberry Days festival is held the first Thursday to Saturday in August with parades, entertainment and, of course, raspberries. Garden City is known throughout Utah for its raspber-ries, which (in summer) are served in sev-eral locations as delicious sundaes and almost-solid milkshakes.

In mid-September, the Mountain Man Rendezvous, with reenactments of the old fur-trapping days, is held at Rendezvous Beach (camp reservations suggested).

Places to Stay – Camping

Apart from Bear Lake State Park (above), there is the *KOA* (☎ 435-946-3454), three-quarters of a mile north of Garden City. Open May through October, it offers showers, adults' and kids' pools, a play-ground, store and coin laundry. Sites are $15.50 to $21.50 (with hookups) and $24 to $35 for a few Kamping Kabins, which sleep up to four. The campground may open in winter with limited facilities.

There is also camping at the Blue Water and Ideal Beach Resorts (see below).

Places to Stay – Budget

The eight-room *Cactus Café & Motel* (☎ 435-946-3233), 205 N Bear Lake Blvd, is the cheapest at $40/50 for simple rooms with one/two beds. They open only from April through October.

Places to Stay – Middle

Bear Lake Motor Lodge (☎ 435-946-3271), 50 S Bear Lake Blvd, has a restaurant and charges $45 to $70 for rooms; some have kitchenettes. The *Eagle Feather Inn* (☎ 435-946-2846), 135 S Bear Lake Blvd, PO Box 262, Garden City, UT 84028, is a three-roomed B&B with a hot tub for guests. Rooms are $60.

Harbor Village at Bear Lake (☎ 435-946-3448, 800-324-6840), 785 N Bear Lake Blvd, has a restaurant, bar, swimming pool, spa, exercise facilities and one- and two-bedroom units with kitchenettes. One-bedroom units are $109 a double, and two-bedroom units are $200 a double.

The *Blue Water Beach Resort* (☎ 435-946-3333, 800-756-6795), 2126 S Bear Lake Blvd, offers RV camping, cabins and condos at various prices (call them). They also have a full range of boat rentals ranging from canoes to jet skis.

Ideal Beach Resort (☎ 435-946-3364, 800-634-1018), 2176 S Bear Lake Blvd, rents fully furnished one-, two-, and three-bedroom condos with kitchens from $325 per half week, as well as motel rooms from $60 per night. There are two pools, a spa, a sauna, tennis courts and miniature golf on the premises. They also operate *Sweetwater RV Park & Marina* (☎ 435-753-1707) next door, with boat rentals of all kinds.

Places to Eat

Apart from the Places to Stay mentioned above, stop by *La Beau's* (☎ 435-946-8821), 69 N Bear Lake Blvd, or one of the other little drive-ins nearby for a raspberry milkshake (in summer).

Entertainment

Pickleville Playhouse (☎ 435-946-2918), 2049 S Bear Lake Blvd, showcases local theatrical talent during its late June to early September season. Show time is at 8 pm most days, and there is a steak barbecue at 6:30 pm, before the show.

SOUTH OF BEAR LAKE

Hwys 30 and 16 lead 65 miles southeast of Garden City to connect with I-80 at Evanston, Wyoming, by the Utah border. Tiny **Randolph**, seat of Rich County, is halfway (no hotels). From Evanston, Hwy 150 leads 90 miles south to Kamas; this scenic route (the Mirror Lake Hwy) accesses the Uinta Mountains and is described in the chapter Northeastern Utah.

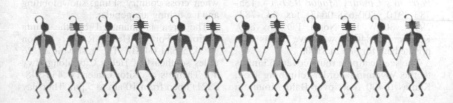

Northeastern Utah

High wilderness terrain dominates northeastern Utah. The few small towns are all a mile above sea level, and the highest mountains in the state, the rugged Uintas, rise a farther 8000 feet above the towns. These mountains are relatively undeveloped – self-sufficient camping, backpacking, fishing and hiking are prime activities. East of the Uintas, the Flaming Gorge National Recreation Area provides record-breaking fishing and the Green River is known for good river running.

Near the Colorado border lies Vernal, the region's largest town with a population of just 8000. A short drive leads to Dinosaur National Monument, one of the largest dinosaur fossil quarries in the West, where fascinating exhibits show fossilized dinosaurs still being worked on. Northeastern Utah capitalizes on its dinosaur attraction; local tourist brochures dub the region 'Utah's Dinosaurland.'

This chapter begins with the western edge of the Uinta Mountains and continues through the Uintas to the area around Vernal.

MIRROR LAKE HIGHWAY (HWY 150)

The highway begins in the small community of **Kamas**, 16 miles southeast of exit 156 on I-80. Kamas is the western gateway to the Uinta Mountains; information about camping and so on can be obtained from the Wasatch-Cache National Forest **Kamas Ranger Station** (☎ 435-783-4338), 50 E Center, open from 8 am to 4:30 pm daily from July to September, and Monday to Friday the rest of the year. You can stay in *Patricia's Country Manor B&B* (☎ 435-783-2910, 800-658-0643, fax 435-783-2910), 80 W 100 North, PO Box 849, Kamas, UT 84036, with five rooms with private bath for $85 to $100.

The scenic alpine route covers 65 miles to the Wyoming border, climbing from Kamas (6400 feet) over Bald Mountain

Pass (10,620 feet and 30 miles away) and continuing at elevations of over 8000 feet into Wyoming. Evanston, Wyoming, is 23 miles north of the border and has hotels; a further 65 miles north brings you to Garden City (see the Northern Utah chapter).

Snow closes this high mountain road for most of the year. Snowplows clear the first 15 miles from Kamas to give access to cross-country skiing and snowmobiling, but Bald Mountain Pass is open only from June to October, depending on weather conditions. The road provides beautiful vistas of the western Uintas and passes by scores of lakes for fishing and trailheads for both short hikes and extended backpacking trips.

Travelers should visit or call the Kamas Ranger Station to obtain detailed information about outdoor recreational opportunities. The USFS operates more than two dozen campgrounds along the approximately 40 miles of highway that lie within the national forest. Most campgrounds cost $9 to $11 and provide outhouses and water; none have RV hookups. Many campgrounds have hiking, nature trails or fishing. The few that don't provide drinking water are free. Campgrounds can fill up on summer weekends – either arrive early or make a reservation (☎ 800-280-2267).

STRAWBERRY RESERVOIR AREA

This large reservoir offers the usual water attractions – summer boating and year-round fishing. In addition, backcountry roads lure motor bikers and 4WDs. The 7600-foot elevation in high-plains country ensures cool summers and icy winters, when cross-country skiing, snowmobiling and ice fishing are popular.

The area is managed by the Uinta National Forest, Heber Ranger Station (☎ 435-654-0470). The reservoir is 26 miles southeast of Heber City along Hwy 40. There is a visitor center (☎ 435-548-2321) open from 10 am to 5 pm, Thursday

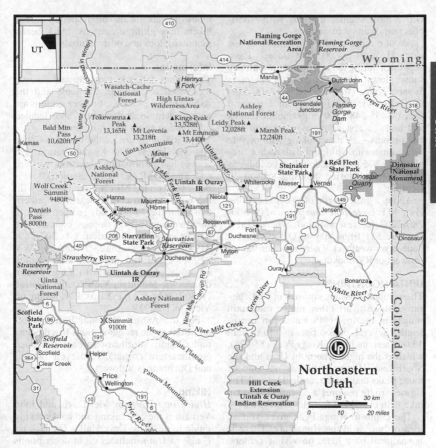

to Monday, May through October, at the northwest end of the reservoir. There are a couple of short nature trails by the center and you can visit a fish hatchery. The reservoir is stocked with salmon and various trout species.

Camping from May to October costs $11.50 or $20 with RV hookups; there is water but no showers. Camping reservations (☎ 800-280-2267) can be made for some sites, but most are first-come, first-served. *Strawberry Bay*, on the west side of the reservoir, has almost 300 sites of which about 30 have hookups. Other campgrounds

lack hookups, including *Renegade Point* on the southwest corner with about 70 sites, *Soldier Creek* on the east side with more than 150 sites and *Aspen Grove* on the southeast side with 60 sites. All four have boat launch areas. Day use and boat launching is $3.

The marinas at Strawberry Bay (☎ 435-548-2261) and Soldier Creek (☎ 435-548-2696) are in operation during the sailing season. Both offer boat rentals, a gas station, a dock rental, fishing supplies and a convenience store. There is a café at Strawberry Bay. Renegade Point and Aspen

UTAH

Grove have smaller marinas with small-boat rentals and a basic store.

About 6 miles northwest of the reservoir along Hwy 40 is 8000-foot Daniels Pass, kept open during the long winter months by snow plows. Here there is the *Daniels Summit Lodge* (☎ 435-654-0907, 800-519-9969, fax 435-654-1013) with a general store (☎ 435-548-2300), snowmobile rentals and tours, a restaurant, a gas station and eight rooms – all nonsmoking with private bath, some with whirlpool bath and/or fireplace, for $75 to $95 a double. The lodge is very popular during hunting season in October.

About a mile north of the pass along Hwy 40 is *Lodgepole Campground* (☎ 800-280-2267 for reservations), where USFS sites are $11 from May to October (dates depend on weather). There is water but no showers or RV hookups.

UINTA MOUNTAINS

These mountains are unusual in that they run east-west; all other major mountain ranges in the lower 48 states run north-south. Several peaks rise to more than 13,000 feet, including Kings Peak (13,528), which is the highest point in Utah and the Southwest. However, this is not one of those peaks that can be reached by car! The shortest route requires a 32-mile roundtrip hike with over 4000 feet elevation gain.

The climb to Kings Peak gives you an idea of how wild the Uintas are. There is no national park here, no visitor centers, scenic overlooks, snack bars or lodges. The central summits are within the High Uintas Wilderness Area, which covers almost 800 square miles in which no logging or development is allowed. There are no roads – and neither mountain biking nor off-road driving is permitted. You have to hike, ride a horse or cross-country ski.

There are hundreds of lakes in the high country. Over 600 of these are stocked with trout and whitefish each year (some are stocked by airplane), and the fishing is considered to be some of the best in the West. Alpine wildlife is plentiful: deer are the most commonly seen large mammals, but

moose and elk are also often spotted. Lucky hikers may glimpse martens, black bears, mountain lions and other animals.

Information

The Uintas fall into two national forests: the Wasatch-Cache in the west and the Ashley in the east. Forest ranger stations are an excellent source of maps and detailed information about the entire range.

The following are for the Wasatch-Cache National Forest: The Kamas station (see above) has information about the western end. The Bear River Ranger Station (☎ 435-642-6662) on the Mirror Lake Highway (in the northwestern corner near the northern exit from the forest land) is open only in summer; at other times, contact the Evanston Ranger Station (☎ 307-789-3194), PO Box 1880, Evanston, WY 82931. From the northern side (which offers the shortest access to Kings Peak), contact the Mountain View Ranger Station (☎ 307-782-6555), PO Box 129, Mountain View, WY 82939.

For the Ashley National Forest, refer questions to the ranger stations listed below under Manila (northeastern corner), Vernal (southeastern corner), Roosevelt (south) and Duchesne (southwest).

Hiking

High Uinta Trails by Mel Davis and John Vernath is the best hiking and backpacking guide to the area. Dave Hall's *The Hiker's Guide to Utah* includes eight descriptions of Uinta hikes.

The hiking season here is about June to October in the lower elevations, July to September in the upper elevations, and just July and August for the highest peaks. Even in midsummer, be prepared for cold, drenching rain; you need warm and waterproof gear. Definitely bring insect repellent. Many trails are remote and not recommended for beginners. Experienced backpackers should carry an emergency kit.

Trips can range from day hikes to extended backpacking trips of many days. About 20 trailheads give access to a huge variety of trails from all sides of the Uintas.

Generally speaking, the west is more crowded than the east.

Those wishing to climb **Kings Peak** will find the shortest access is from Henrys Fork trailhead on the north side (though you can reach the summit via other longer trails). From the Mirror Lake Highway, 2 miles north of the Bear River Ranger Station, head east on unpaved USFS Rd 058, which reaches Bridger Lake and Stateline Reservoir (about 40 miles). From here go north several miles on USFS Rd 072, then south on USFS Rd 017/077 about 12 miles to Henrys Fork. The most direct approach is a 32-mile drive south of Mountain View, Wyoming.

Henrys Fork offers a primitive campground, a parking area and a sign with a trail map, though none for sale. From the trailhead (9400 feet) the trail climbs 16 miles almost to the top. The last few hundred feet involve scrambling to the rocky summit, where you can sign your name in the logbook. Congratulations!

Fishing

Hundreds of lakes are stocked with fish, and the fishing is very good. Serious anglers should read *Lakes of the High Uintas*, a series of booklets listing all necessary access and permit information. The booklets are published by the Utah Wildlife Resources Division (☎ 801-538-4700), 1594 W North Temple, Salt Lake City, UT 84114, and also available in Vernal (☎ 435-789-3103), 152 E 100 North. Many backpackers supplement their rations with fresh fish.

Places to Stay

Backcountry camping is free and no permits are required. Ranger stations can suggest areas in which to camp. They also have lists of drive-in campgrounds on all sides of the range, most of which provide drinking water, toilets and fire pits. Most cost $6 to $8; a few are free, others are more expensive and price increases are possible in the near future. Due to snow, most drive-in campgrounds operate from about May to October.

DUCHESNE & AROUND

Pronounced 'doo-SHANE' (rhymes with 'blue train'), this small town of 1500 is the seat of Duchesne County (although Roosevelt, 28 miles east, is larger and has more facilities). Duchesne is a southern gateway to the Uintas.

Orientation & Information

Main St (Hwy 40) is the main thoroughfare.

The city hall (☎ 435-738-2464), 165 S Center, provides basic visitor information. The Ashley National Forest Duchesne Ranger Station (☎ 435-738-2482), 85 W Main, Duchesne, UT 84021, is open 8 am to 5 pm from Monday to Friday, plus 8 am to 4:30 pm on Saturday in summer and fall.

Starvation Lake State Park

This park (☎ 435-738-2326), PO Box 584, Duchesne, UT 84021, is 4 miles northwest of Duchesne. The Starvation Reservoir has a boat launch area and boat rentals in summer. Water-skiing, windsurfing, sailing and fishing are popular. Two campgrounds (with showers and a playground but no hookups) have about 60 sites for $10 in summer, less in winter when the water may be shut off. Day use is $3.

North of Duchesne

Twenty-two miles northeast of Duchesne, **Altamont** has the *Altamont Motel* (☎ 435-454-3341) and the small but comfortable *Falcon's Ledge Lodge* (☎ 435-454-3737, fax 435-454-3392), which has a restaurant and spa. Rooms start around $100; fly-fishing and bird-shooting enthusiasts stay here.

Further north, there are many campgrounds in the Ashley National Forest and trailheads leading into the high Uintas. You need a USFS map to find the roads.

Hwy 35, northwest of Duchesne, passes through **Tabiona**, 26 miles away, where there is the small *Sagebrush Inn* (☎ 435-848-5420/5637). Hwy 35 continues through Hanna to USFS Rd 144, which leads to *Defa's Dude Ranch* (☎ 435-848-5590), Hanna, UT 84031, about 50 miles from Duchesne. The ranch offers inexpensive cabins (bring bedding and utensils) and horseback trips; facilities include a restaurant and RV hookups. It is open May to October. Three USFS campgrounds are on this road, too.

Trails lead into the Uintas from the ends of all these roads, which are passable in ordinary vehicles in good weather.

Special Events
The Duchesne County Fair & Rodeo is held around the third week in August.

Places to Stay & Eat
The *Rio Damian Motel* (☎ 435-738-2217), 23 W Main, has standard rooms from $45 and manages two nearby motels with cheaper rooms. Some have kitchenettes. RV spaces are $14 with hookups.

Cowan's Cafe (☎ 435-738-5609), 57 E Main, serves daily breakfast, lunch and dinner. *Well's Club* (☎ 435-738-9693), 47 E Main, is a bar that serves reasonable food. There are also a few drive-in places.

Getting There & Away
The Greyhound bus stops at the Conoco Gas Station (☎ 435-738-5961), 432 W Main, on its twice-daily run between Salt Lake City and Denver, Colorado.

ROOSEVELT & AROUND
Roosevelt, with a population of 5000, was founded in 1905 and named after President Theodore Roosevelt who once camped nearby. It is the largest town in Duchesne County and the center of the region's cattle and oil industries. Driving north of Roosevelt and Duchesne, you'll see occasional oil pumps.

Information
The chamber of commerce (☎ 435-722-4598), 48 S 200 East, is open 8 am to 5 pm, Monday to Friday. The Ashley National Forest Roosevelt Ranger Station (☎ 435-722-5018), PO Box 338, Roosevelt, UT 84066, is at 244 W Hwy 40. The post office (☎ 435-722-3231) is at 81 S 300 East. The medical center (☎ 435-722-4691) is at 250 W 300 North. The police station (☎ 435-722-4558) is at 255 S State.

North of Roosevelt
With USFS maps, you can find several campgrounds and trailheads into the Uintas. Hwy 121 north through Neola runs into USFS Rd 118, which reaches two USFS campgrounds and the *U-Bar Ranch* (☎ 435-646-4118; in Park City ☎ 435-645-7256, 800-303-7256, fax 435-655-9908). This rustic ranch, located about 30 miles from Roosevelt, has six log cabins ($54/64 for one/two beds) and a cabin sleeping 10 for $109. Bathrooms are shared and meals are $25 per day ($19 for children under 12). Horseback rides are $20 an hour or $98 per day (children must be six or older). Fishing and overnight pack trips are available. Call the ranch about possible cross-country skiing or snowmobiling packages.

A few miles east, near Whiterocks, is *J-L Ranch Outfitter & Guides* (☎ 435-353-4049, fax 435-353-4181), a rustic ranch with rooms ($95 for doubles with bath and continental breakfast; $12 per extra person

Roosevelt

PLACES TO STAY
7   Frontier Motel
9   Regal Motel

PLACES TO EAT
4   Marion's Variety
    & Confectionery
7   Frontier Grill

OTHER
1   Medical Center
2   Greyhound Bus Depot
3   Uinta Theater
5   Roosevelt Twin Theater
6   Chamber of Commerce
8   Post Office
10 Police
11 Ranger Station

up to four people). It offers guided fishing and pack trips.

There are several other remote campgrounds in the Ashley National Forest north of Roosevelt as well as other guest ranches.

Nine Mile Canyon

A gravel and dirt road leaves Hwy 40, 11 miles southwest of Roosevelt (1.6 miles west of Myton), and heads about 80 miles southwest over the West Tavaputs Plateau to Hwy 191/6, about 8 miles southeast of Price. About halfway along this signed backcountry road is Nine Mile Canyon, known for many petroglyphs and pictographs dating from the Fremont Indian culture. (Rock walls with petroglyphs actually stretch for about 40 miles.) The road is graded and passable to cars in good weather; several side canyons have tracks for which 4WD is advised. Carry water and food, as no services are available. Further information and brochures are available from the Roosevelt, Vernal or Price tourist or BLM offices.

Ouray National Waterfowl Refuge

The refuge (☎ 435-545-2522) includes marshlands along the Green River that form an oasis for migrating ducks and geese flying over the desert. At least 15 species of waterfowl nest on the refuge in summer, but numbers peak in October and April during migrations.

Refuge headquarters (☎ 435-789-0351) are at 266 W 100 North in Vernal. To reach the refuge, take Hwy 40 (16 miles east of Roosevelt or 14 miles west of Vernal) and then drive 14 miles south on Hwy 88. There is a self-guided auto tour covering 9 miles within the refuge, which is open year-round.

Special Events

Uinta Basin in Celebration, the first Thursday to Saturday in August, includes rural events ranging from parades to pig chasing, food stands to fireworks. This is the area's biggest fair.

Also see the section Uintah & Ouray Indian Reservation, below.

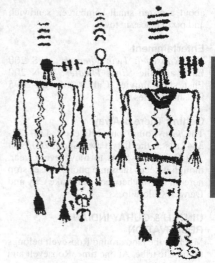

Places to Stay & Eat

Prices for accommodations go up for special events weekends. At other times, nine basic rooms with kitchenettes at the *Regal Motel* (☎ 435-722-4878), 160 S 200 East, are about $30. The *Western Hills Motel* (☎ 435-722-5115), 737 E 200 North, charges in the $30s and has a restaurant (☎ 435-722-4562) serving inexpensive breakfast, lunch and dinner daily.

The *Frontier Motel* (☎ 435-722-2201, 800-248-1014, fax 435-722-2212), 75 S 200 East, charges $35 to $50 for decent rooms. It has a seasonal pool and a spa. Attached is the *Frontier Grill* (☎ 435-722-3669), 65 S 200 East, a nice family restaurant and bar open from 6 am to 9:30 pm daily.

The *Best Western Inn* (☎ 435-722-4644, fax 435-722-0179), 1 mile east of town on Hwy 40, has a seasonal pool, year-round spa and exercise room. Pleasant rooms are $45 to $60 in summer, $40 to $50 the rest of the year. *JB's Restaurant* (☎ 435-722-0778) next door serves breakfast, lunch and dinner every day.

Marion's Variety & Confectionery (☎ 435-722-2143), 29 N 200 East, was established in 1933 and has an old-fashioned soda fountain and lunch counter. In addition, there are about a dozen small hamburger, sandwich and pizza places in town.

Entertainment
The *Roosevelt Twin Theater*, 21 S 200 East, and the *Uinta Theater*, 41 N 200 East, show movies. Call ☎ 435-722-2095 for show times.

Getting There & Away
The Greyhound bus office (☎ 435-722-3342) is at the Jiffy Pawn Shop, 200 N at 300 East, but seems to move every year, though it keeps the same phone. Buses stop here on the run between Salt Lake City and Denver, Colorado.

UINTAH & OURAY INDIAN RESERVATION
Much of the land around Roosevelt belongs to the Ute tribe. At one time, Roosevelt and many other areas were part of the reservation, but in the late 19th and early 20th centuries the reservation was cut in size, and homesteaders and oil prospectors moved in. There is talk of increasing the reservation area again. Today, about 3000 Utes live on or near the reservation.

Information
The Ute Tribal Offices (☎ 435-722-5141) are in Fort Duchesne, PO Box 190, UT 84026, about a mile south of Hwy 40 and 8 miles east of Roosevelt. The Ute Public Relations Department (☎ 435-722-3736), PO Box 400, also has information. Non-Utes can freely travel the reservation by road. Tribal permits (obtainable in Fort Duchesne or in sporting or fishing stores) are required for fishing, hunting, camping, boating or backcountry use.

A tribal museum (☎ 435-722-4992) is next to the Bottle Hollow Motel on Hwy 40. Ute history, customs and crafts are explained and displayed. Hours are from 9 am to 4 pm, Monday to Friday.

Special Events
The main public Indian event in northeastern Utah is the annual Northern Ute Powwow and Rodeo held for several days

around the Fourth of July; the 30th annual powwow was in 1998.

Other events, held throughout the year, are more tribal in nature, and no photography or other recording devices are allowed. Contact the tribal offices for information about the Bear Dance (in April or May) and the Sun Dance (in July or August).

Places to Stay & Eat
The tribe operates *Bottle Hollow Motel* (☎ 435-722-3941), on Hwy 40 in Fort Duchesne. Rooms are quite basic and the place closes in winter. In summer, there's a restaurant (closed Sunday) and a gift shop selling beadwork items typical of the Utes.

VERNAL
Northeastern Utah's mineral wealth (oil, natural gas, Gilsonite and other deposits) as well as stock grazing make Vernal an important industrial and agricultural center. Tourism has also become an important industry in recent years and the town has the best motel selection in the area.

There are two major tourist attractions in this far northeastern corner of Utah. To the north lies the geological and scenic splendor of Flaming Gorge and to the east lies the fascinating Dinosaur National Monument. In addition, river running on the Green River and its tributaries is increasingly popular.

Vernal was settled in 1878. In the late 1800s, outlaws used to hide out in the area because it was remote and inaccessible. Today, Vernal (population of 8000) is the Uintah County seat and the cultural and commercial center of 'Dinosaurland.'

Information
The Welcome Center (☎ 435-789-4002), in the state park at 235 E Main, is open daily 8 am to 9 pm in summer, 9 am to 5 pm the rest of the year. The center provides both local and regional information for travelers arriving from Colorado or Wyoming. Also call Dinosaurland Travel Board (☎ 435-789-6932, 800-477-5558) for area information.

UTAH

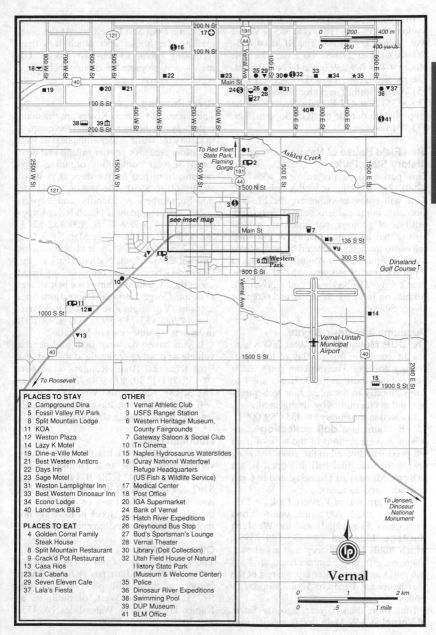

PLACES TO STAY
2   Campground Dina
5   Fossil Valley RV Park
8   Split Mountain Lodge
11 KOA
12 Weston Plaza
14 Lazy K Motel
19 Dine-a-Ville Motel
21 Best Western Antlers
22 Days Inn
23 Sage Motel
31 Weston Lamplighter Inn
33 Best Western Dinosaur Inn
34 Econo Lodge
40 Landmark B&B

PLACES TO EAT
4   Golden Corral Family
    Steak House
8   Split Mountain Restaurant
9   Crack'd Pot Restaurant
13 Casa Rios
23 La Cabaña
29 Seven Eleven Cafe
37 Lala's Fiesta

OTHER
1   Vernal Athletic Club
3   USFS Ranger Station
6   Western Heritage Museum,
    County Fairgrounds
7   Gateway Saloon & Social Club
10 Tri Cinema
15 Naples Hydrosaurus Waterslides
16 Ouray National Waterfowl
    Refuge Headquarters
    (US Fish & Wildlife Service)
17 Medical Center
18 Post Office
20 IGA Supermarket
24 Bank of Vernal
25 Hatch River Expeditions
26 Greyhound Bus Stop
27 Bud's Sportsman's Lounge
28 Vernal Theater
30 Library (Doll Collection)
32 Utah Field House of Natural
    History State Park
    (Museum & Welcome Center)
35 Police
36 Dinosaur River Expeditions
38 Swimming Pool
39 DUP Museum
41 BLM Office

Vernal

The Ashley National Forest Vernal Ranger Station (☎ 435-789-1181) is at 355 N Vernal Ave, Vernal, UT 84078. The BLM (☎ 435-781-4400) is at 170 S 500 East. The post office (☎ 435-789-2393) is at 67 N 800 West. The medical center (☎ 435-789-3342) is at 151 W 200 North. The police station (☎ 435-789-5835) is at 437 E Main. Recycle in the drop-off bins outside the IGA Supermarket, 575 W Main.

Utah Field House of Natural History State Park

This park and its museum (☎ 435-789-3799), 235 E Main, is well worth a visit. Kids will enjoy encountering the life-size dinosaurs in the gardens outside; inside are exhibits of geology, paleontology, natural history and local area history. A gift shop sells dino-treasures. Museum hours are from 8 am to 9 pm June to August, and 9 am to 5 pm the rest of the year (closed on New Year's Day, Thanksgiving and Christmas). Admission is $2 for those six and older, or $5 per family.

Museums & Historic Sights

The **DUP Museum**, 500 West 200 South, has an extensive, free display of local pioneering artifacts. The museum entry was a tithing house built in 1887. Hours are 1 to 7 pm Monday to Saturday, June to September, and at other times by arrangement.

Located in the library (☎ 435-789-0091), 155 E Main, is a **doll collection** comprising representations of the wife of each US president dressed in the gown she wore during the inaugural ball. It's open 10 am to 8 pm, Monday to Thursday, and to 6 pm on Friday and Saturday.

On the grounds of Western Park (☎ 435-789-7396), 302 E 200 South, you will find the County Fairgrounds and the **Western Heritage Museum** (☎ 435-789-7399), which holds local history and art shows. There is a gift shop. Summer hours are 9 am to 6 pm, Monday to Saturday; the rest of the year hours are 10 am to 5 pm, Monday to Friday.

Built more than 70 years ago, the **Bank of Vernal** at 3 W Main (today called Zions First National) was constructed with bricks that came from Salt Lake City. At the time, mailing the bricks cost much less than freighting them, so they arrived by US mail – and prompted a change in mailing regulations soon after!

River Running

The Green and Yampa Rivers are the main waterways in the area and both have rapids to satisfy the white-water enthusiast as well as calmer areas for gentler rafting and float trips. Several companies organize trips ranging from one to five days at costs of about $60 to $650. The season is May to mid-September. A friendly and experienced local company is Hatch River Expeditions (☎ 435-789-4316, 800-342-8243, fax 435-789-8513), 55 E Main, PO Box 1150, Vernal, UT 84078. It also does trips through Canyonlands National Park on the Colorado River. Other companies are listed under the Mountain Biking (see below) and Flaming Gorge National Recreation Area sections. You might also try Adrift Adventures (☎/fax 435-789-3600, 800-824-0150) in Jensen, 13 miles east of Vernal.

If you have your own boat and need a vehicle or passenger shuttle at the end of a float trip, call River Runners Transport (☎ 435-781-1180, 800-930-7238, fax 435-781-3048), 126 S 1500 West. This outfit will also rent rafts, kayaks and miscellaneous river-running equipment.

Mountain Biking

The Welcome Center has brochures listing various rides in the area. Dinosaur River Expeditions (☎ 435-781-0717, 800-247-6197, fax 435-649-8126), 540 E Main, has river tours and bike tours or combinations thereof. The bicycle stores in town do not rent bikes (though they have in the past).

Other Activities

The Dinaland Golf Course (☎ 435-781-1428), 675 S 2000 East, has 18 holes. **Swim** indoors at the public pool (☎ 435-789-5775), 170 S 600 West, or outdoors at Naples Hydrosaurus Waterslides (☎ 435-789-1010), 1701 E 1900 South. Spend all day at the water-slide pool for $6, or $3.50 for a half day, or $1.50 for swim only.

Vernal Athletic Club (☎ 435-789-5816), 1180 N Vernal Ave, rents all the equipment you need and has information about local **cross-country skiing** areas.

Special Events
From mid-June through early August, Vernal hosts events including a Western musical performed on many evenings, a rodeo and all sorts of other Western events ranging from cowboy poetry contests to Wild West shootouts. The Uintah County Fair is held in early August. Other events are held in nearby communities. Dates vary, so call the chamber of commerce.

Places to Stay – Camping
Fossil Valley RV Park (☎ 435-789-6450), 999 W Hwy 40, has showers and is open year-round. Most sites are $18 with hookups; a few tent spaces are $10. *Vernal KOA* (☎ 435-789-8935), 1800 W Sheraton Ave, has a pool, playground, showers, store, recreation area and coin laundry; it's open from May to September. Sites are $14 or $18 with hookups and Kamping Kabins go for $25. *Campground Dina* (☎ 435-789-2148, 800-245-2148), 930 N Vernal Ave, has similar facilities (plus mini-golf) for $6 per person in tents or $18 with TV hookups and is open year-round.

In Jensen, 13 miles east of Vernal, the *Dinosaur Village Campground* (☎ 435-789-5552) has showers and charges $10 to $14. It is open April through November. Other campgrounds are listed below in Around Vernal.

Places to Stay – Budget
Vernal is growing as a tourist center, and prices are rising accordingly; summer prices can be $10 or $20 higher than the rest of the year.

The clean and well-run *Sage Motel* (☎ 435-789-1442, 800-760-1442), 54 W Main, has 26 fairly large rooms for $35 to $46 during the summer. There is a family restaurant attached. Slightly cheaper are the small *Lazy K Motel* (☎ 435-789-3277),

1500 E 775 South, and the *Dine-a-Ville Motel* (☎ 435-789-9571), 801 W Hwy 40, which has a pool.

Places to Stay – Middle
B&Bs *Landmark B&B* (☎ 435-781-1800, 888-738-1800), 288 E 100 South, has eight rooms with private bath and three suites with fireplaces and double-sized spa tubs. Rates are $65 to $75 for the rooms and $135 to $175 for the suites. From Monday to Thursday, the suites are $100. There is no smoking and an extended continental breakfast is included.

Hotels The *Split Mountain Lodge* (☎ 435-789-9020), 1015 E Hwy 40, has 40 nice rooms (some with microwaves and refrigerators) for $40 to $60 in summer. There is a restaurant attached. The *Econo Lodge* (☎ 435-789-2000, fax 435-789-0947), 311 E Main, is conveniently located downtown; it has a restaurant next door and provides complimentary morning coffee. Clean rooms are mostly in the $40s and some in the $50s.

The *Days Inn* (☎ 435-789-1011, fax 435-789-0172), 260 W Main, has a pool and free continental breakfast included in its rates, which start at $40/46 for singles/doubles and go up to about $60 in the summer. The similarly priced *Weston Lamplighter Inn* (☎ 435-789-0312, fax 435-789-4874), 120 E Main, has a pool, restaurant and play area for kids. The *Weston Plaza* (☎ 435-789-9550, fax 435-789-4874), 1684 W Hwy 40, has an indoor pool, a spa, coin laundry, restaurant and bar (with occasional music and dancing). Rooms are good-sized and are mainly in the $50s.

The *Best Western Antlers* (☎ 435-789-1202, fax 435-789-4979), 423 W Main, has a restaurant, pool, spa, exercise room and play area for kids. Pleasant rooms are $60 to $95 in summer, $15 to $30 less off-season. The *Best Western Dinosaur Inn* (☎ 435-789-2660, fax 435-789-2467), 251 E Main, is convenient to downtown and has a pool, spa, playground, restaurant and bar. Attractive rooms are $65 to $100 in summer.

UTAH

Places to Eat

The locally popular *Crack'd Pot Restaurant* (☎ 435-781-0133), 1089 E Hwy 40, is open 5 am to 10 pm with a wide variety of American meals ranging from inexpensive daily specials to reasonably priced steak and seafood. There is a lounge bar adjoining the restaurant.

Try the inexpensive *Seven Eleven Cafe* (☎ 435-789-1170), 77 E Main, open from 6 am to 9:30 pm. Filling American dinner specials for $6 to $9 are a good value if you are hungry. For steaks, the *Golden Corral Family Steak House* (☎ 435-789-7268), 1046 W Hwy 40, is a good value; it serves chicken and fish as well. The hotel restaurants are all reasonable places for American food.

For Mexican food, try *Casa Rios* (☎ 435-789-0103), 2015 W Hwy 40, *La Cabaña* (☎ 435-789-3151), 56 W Main, and *Lala's Fiesta* (☎ 435-789-2966), 550 E Main.

Entertainment

Catch a movie (☎ 435-789-6139 for schedules) at *Tri Cinema*, 1400 W Hwy 40, or at the *Vernal Theater*, 40 E Main.

For a beer, the *Gateway Saloon & Social Club* (☎ 435-789-9842, 435-789-5075), 773 E Main, is a private club featuring live entertainment or karaoke on some nights. *Bud's Sportsman's Lounge* (☎ 435-789-9963), 65 S Vernal Ave, has a big-screen TV, pool tables and food.

Getting There & Away

Air The airport is at 830 E 500 South. Skywest Airlines (☎ 435-789-7263, 800-453-9417) has two or three flights a day to and from Salt Lake City.

Bus Greyhound (☎ 435-789-0404), in Frontier Travel at 15 S Vernal Ave, has one or two buses a day on the Denver-Salt Lake City run and on to other points.

AROUND VERNAL
State Parks

Six miles north of Vernal, **Steinaker State Park** (☎ 435-789-4432) is a popular fishing, boating and water-skiing area during the summer. There is a sandy beach, boat ramp, picnic area and campground with water, but no showers. Camping costs $8 ($5 after the water is shut off in winter); day use is $3.

Red Fleet State Park (same phone) has nearly the same attractions and facilities as Steinaker. In addition, a 1½-mile hike (roundtrip) passes fossilized dinosaur tracks. The park, located 12 miles northeast of Vernal, is not marked on all maps – head north on Hwy 191 for about 10 miles and you'll see a sign for the park on your right.

Driving Tours

The Welcome Center in Vernal has several brochures with details of driving tours. The two most popular are outlined below – ask at the Welcome Center for others.

Drive Through the Ages From 4 miles north of Vernal on Hwy 191 to the entrance of Flaming Gorge, about 30 miles farther, the road passes some 20 geological strata and formations representing about a billion years of geology (almost 25% of our planet's existence). About 20 signs and pull-offs along the way explain these geological phenomena as well as present natural history.

Petroglyphs & Red Cloud Loop Leave Vernal westbound on 500 North. After about 3 miles go through the community of Maeser and turn right on Dry Fork Canyon Rd. About seven more miles brings you to the McConkie Ranch, where there are hundreds of Indian petroglyphs spread over a mile along a canyon wall. There is a small admission fee – note that this is private property, so follow the owners' signed instructions.

After the petroglyphs, the road continues northwest into the Ashley National Forest as USFS Rd 018. Low-slung cars may want to turn back at this point. This is the scenic Red Cloud Loop, along which several dirt sections may require high clearance or 4WD – ask at the ranger station for details. The road is closed by snow in winter. USFS Rd 018 loops around for about 45 miles through beautiful high forests and alpine meadows with fine Uinta mountain views before emerging at Hwy 191, 19 miles north of Vernal. Many people do the loop starting at Hwy 191 and emerging at Dry Fork because the signs are easier to follow.

There are many possibilities for hiking, fishing, camping and picnicking along this route – the ranger station has maps and details.

FLAMING GORGE NATIONAL RECREATION AREA

Flaming Gorge was named by John Wesley Powell, who explored the area in 1869 during his historic first descent of the Green and Colorado Rivers. Between 1957 and 1964, the Bureau of Reclamation built the Flaming Gorge Dam across the Green River, which backed up for more than 90 miles to form the present reservoir. The reservoir straddles the Utah-Wyoming state line, but the visitor center and most of the best scenery, campsites and other facilities are on the Utah side.

As with many of the artificial lakes of the Southwest, fishing and boating are prime attractions. The lake is stocked with half a million fish annually and the fishing is some of the best in the Southwest. Various fishing records have been set here and the season is year-round.

Flaming Gorge, however, provides more than just fishing and boating. The scenery is quite spectacular and there are plenty of hiking, camping, picnicking and backpacking opportunities in the summer. In winter, cross-country skiing, snowshoeing and snow camping are all possible. Wildlife, including big game such as moose, elk, pronghorn antelope and mule deer, are quite common. Bighorn sheep, black bears and mountain lions are occasionally seen also. Hunting is allowed in season with appropriate permits.

The elevation of the lake is 6040 feet above sea level, which ensures pleasantly warm but not desperately hot summers – daytime highs average about 80°F. The main season is May to October. At other times, most services are shut down, though there are still places to stay and eat, and the main roads are kept open with snowplows in winter.

Orientation

A 35-mile drive due north from Vernal on Hwy 191 (see Drive Through the Ages, above) leads to Greendale Junction at the entrance of the recreation area. From the junction, Hwy 191 continues 6 miles to the northeast past the Flaming Gorge Dam and the Visitor Center, then a farther 3 miles through the small community of Dutch John (population 300) and on up the east side of the area into Wyoming. Heading west from Greendale Junction, Hwy 44 passes the Red Canyon Visitor Center (3 miles, plus 3 on a side road) and goes on to the small town of Manila (about 28 miles), continuing up the west side of the lake into Wyoming. All these roads are paved.

Information

The Flaming Gorge Dam and Reservoir are managed by the BLM and the surrounding area is part of the Ashley National Forest. Information is available from the USFS or BLM in Vernal or at the USFS Flaming Gorge Headquarters (☎ 435-784-3445), PO Box 278, Manila, UT 84046. The Manila office is open from 8 am to 4:30 pm, Monday to Friday, plus weekends in summer.

The Flaming Gorge Dam Visitor Center (☎ 435-885-3135) is open from 8 am to 8 pm, Thursday to Saturday, till 7 pm Sunday to Wednesday in the summer; 9 am to 5 pm the rest of the year. The Red Canyon Visitor Center (☎ 435-889-3713) is open from 9:30 am to 5 pm daily from mid-May to late September. Audio-visual displays, exhibits about the area and a bookstore are all here. The views from the center are impressive; even better views are possible from a short, paved interpretive trail to various overlooks. Both visitor centers have schedules of nature walks, fireside talks and similar events led by rangers.

Admission to Flaming Gorge National Recreation Area is free for the Drive Through the Ages tour and visiting the dam and nearby sites. The USFS requires a

UTAH

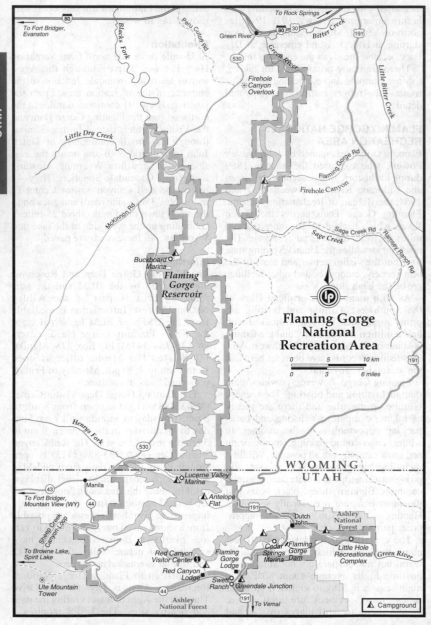

Flaming Gorge National Recreation Area

0   5   10 km
0   3   6 miles

▲ Campground

recreational pass ($2 per day, $5 for 16 days, $20 per year) for people wishing to hike, fish, hunt, ski, boat or do similar recreational activities.

Flaming Gorge Dam

Free guided tours leave from the visitor center between 9 am and 4:30 pm during the summer. An elevator within the dam will drop you 42 floors to the base of the structure, which rises 502 feet above bedrock. At other times, you can walk along the top of the dam. The visitor center has exhibits, audio-visual displays and a store selling maps and books.

Swett Ranch National Historic Site

Half a mile northeast from Greendale Junction on Hwy 191 brings you to a signed road to Swett Ranch, 1½ miles away. This ranch dates to the early 1900s and provides a glimpse of what life was like before roads opened up the area. Hours are 9 am to 5 pm Thursday to Monday, Memorial Day to Labor Day.

Sheep Creek Canyon

A 13-mile paved loop road leaves Hwy 44 about 15 miles west of Greendale Junction, returning to Hwy 44 about 7 miles further north. The loop road goes through Sheep Creek Canyon Geological Area; brochures from the visitor centers and roadside signs interpret the geology of the area. The scenery is dramatic and there are picnicking areas but no campgrounds. Snow closes the loop road in winter.

Spirit Lake Road

Two miles along the Sheep Creek Canyon loop road, unpaved USFS Rd 221 branches to the west and leads about 20 miles to Spirit Lake, where you can camp ($6) from June through September/October or stay at the *Spirit Lake Resort* (☎ 435-880-3089 in summer, 435-783-2339 other times), which has rustic cabins (from $32 a double to $60 for a big cabin with 16 bunks), a restaurant serving breakfast, lunch and dinner, horse rentals ($10 an hour) and paddle boats ($5 an hour). The resort is open Memorial Day

to the end of elk-hunting season in October. The road is passable to cars in good weather.

Near the beginning of USFS Rd 221, a sign for **Ute Mountain Tower** points the way up 2-mile-long USFS Rd 005, a steep dirt road leading to the only fire tower left standing in Utah. A hike will bring you to the top (8834 feet above sea level), where you can take in great views and read signs explaining what being a fire lookout here was like in the 1930s. A couple of miles after the Ute Tower turn, USFS Rd 096 leads about 2 miles to Browne Lake, where there is a free USFS campground (no water). These roads are all closed by snow in winter.

Hiking & Backpacking

In addition to the hike to the Ute Mountain Tower (above), there are a number of day hikes in the area. These range from short day hikes such as the popular 5-mile walk along the Canyon Rim Trail to a strenuous climb up Leidy Peak, the highest point near Flaming Gorge at 12,028 feet.

The **Canyon Rim Trail** begins at the Red Canyon Visitor Center and ends at the Greendale overlook a mile west of Greendale Junction off Hwy 44. The terrain is gently rolling and elk are sometimes seen. Several campgrounds are close to parts of the walk.

The **Leidy Peak Trail** leaves Browne Lake (see Spirit Lake Rd, above) from the southeast corner and climbs almost 4000 feet in 8 miles to Leidy Peak.

Rangers at the visitor centers or forest-ranger stations can suggest several more hikes as well as overnight backpacking trips. Recreational passes are required.

Fishing

You can fish at any time in Flaming Gorge Reservoir, which has produced record-breaking trout, salmon, bass and other fish (see sidebar). You need a recreational pass and a fishing permit, available from ranger stations, marinas or lodges in the area. Day permits are $5; season permits cost $40.

Fly-fishing for trout is excellent on the Green River (below the dam for obvious

Flaming Gorge Fishing Records
Fishing, especially for trout, is a big deal at Flaming Gorge. Some of Utah's state fishing records have been set in this artificial lake, including:

Mackinaw (or lake) trout – 51 lbs 8 oz
brown trout – 33 lbs 10 oz
rainbow trout – 26 lbs 2 oz
Kokanee salmon – 5 lbs 5 oz
smallmouth bass – 4 lbs 6 oz

reasons!) and some of its tributaries. These rivers are carefully managed with occasional closures and various catch-and-release and other regulations designed to maintain the high quality of fishing – ask about current conditions at the ranger stations or you risk being fined for breaking the rules.

The very best fishing is had by local experts. If you're not one, then local guides can be hired who'll show you the places to go and the lures to use. Guides aren't cheap – more than $100 per day per person in small groups – but they get you the best fishing. See the next section for marinas and the Places to Stay & Eat section, below, for lodges with guides.

Boating & River Running

In this case, 'boat' describes everything from fishing boats, pontoons and power/ski boats on the lake to rafts and canoes on the river. Fishing boats rent for $35 to $80 a day, depending on size, pontoon boats for about $160 and ski boats for about $200. Raft rentals range from $30 to $80, depending on size, and inflatable kayaks for one person are about $20. Half-day and hourly rates are available.

The Flaming Gorge Reservoir has two marinas on the Utah side and another in Wyoming. All three offer lake boat rentals, gas, camping, boat launch area, store and guided fishing trips. **Lucerne Valley Marina** (☎ 435-784-3483, 888-820-9225,

fax 435-784-3433), PO Box 10, Manila, UT 84046, is 7 miles east of Manila on the Lucerne Peninsula. It has the longest season, with limited boat rentals beginning sometime in March and ending in November (depending on weather). It also has a few house boats to rent for $600 to $1060 for three to seven days for a 36-foot boat, or $950 to $1650 for a 50-foot boat (from May 15 to September 15). Substantial discounts are offered in spring and fall.

Cedar Springs (☎ /fax 435-889-3795), PO Box 337, Dutch John, UT 84023, a little over a mile west of Flaming Gorge Dam, is open from about April to October. Apart from rentals, it also offers guided fishing and boat tours. Four hours of fishing is $200 for one/two people and $300 for three/four anglers. Boat tours last 90 minutes and are $75 to $125 for two to six passengers. There is also **Buckboard Marina** (☎ 307-875-6927), 23 miles northeast of Manila in Wyoming. In addition to the marinas, there are several other boat launch areas for privately owned boats.

River rafts and kayaks can be rented from **Flaming Gorge Flying Service** (☎ 435-885-3338, 435-885-3370), PO Box 368, Dutch John, UT 84023, at the Dutch John airport; and **Flaming Gorge Recreational Services** (☎ 435-885-3191, fax 435-885-3350), PO Box 367, Dutch John, UT 84023. This service provides fishing guides as well as shuttle vehicles to pick you up at the end of a raft trip. There are raft launch areas for privately owned boats on the Green River, a short way below the dam. Life jackets must be worn by all boaters and recreational passes are required.

The most popular rafting section is the first 7 miles below the dam, pulling out at Little Hole about three hours after entry. A shuttle bus (up to eight passengers) will meet you and bring you and your raft back for about $30, if arranged in advance. There are several minor (Class I and II) rapids; for more experienced rafters, bigger rapids are found below Little Hole. Summer weekends are very popular – reserve a raft rental in advance or come midweek.

Winter Activities

Solitude is what the locals say you'll find in winter. Cross-country skiers will find marked trails following the Canyon Rim Trail (see Hiking & Backpacking, above) and around Swett Ranch and several other areas. Plenty of unmarked possibilities exist for the adventurous skier.

Snowmobilers use the forest roads to the east; the Dowd Springs picnic area just south of the Sheep Creek Canyon loop road is the base for snowmobiling, but there are no facilities apart from a plowed parking area and restrooms.

If you get up to the highland lakes (for example, Browne and Spirit Lakes), you'll find a few anglers on the ice. You can join them. Brrr!

Places to Stay & Eat

Camping The Ashley National Forest operates about two dozen campgrounds in the Flaming Gorge area and just outside it. Campgrounds are open May to October in lower elevations and for a briefer period up higher. Reservations (☎ 800-283-2267) for some of the more popular campsites are suggested.

Free USFS campgrounds (bring your own water) are available at *Browne Lake* and *Deep Creek* (3 miles along unpaved USFS Rd 539, leaving Hwy 44 about 3 miles south of the Sheep Creek Canyon loop). In addition, there are several free USFS campsites on the lake that can be reached by boat only.

More than a dozen other campgrounds scattered around the south end of the area provide drinking water and toilets but no showers or hookups ($9 to $11). Lakeside campgrounds have boat launch ramps. A favorite campground is *Lucerne Valley*, near to the marina, where more than 150 sites are available at $10 a night; open April to October. Pronghorn antelopes roam the Lucerne Peninsula and visitors often see them. *Antelope Flat*, 10 miles west of Dutch John on the east side of Flaming Gorge Lake, is another popular campground with more than 100 sites. *Firefighters Memorial* campground has more than 90 sites conveniently located between Greendale Junction

and the dam, but not on the lake. Other campgrounds are smaller. Also see Spirit Lake Rd, above.

There is a private campground in Manila. The *Flaming Gorge KOA* (☎ 435-784-3184), a quarter mile east on Hwy 43 from Hwy 44, is open from April to October (dates depend on weather) and facilities include a pool, showers, play area, grocery store and coin laundry. Sites are $13 for tents or $19 with hookups.

Cabins & Motels – Flaming Gorge The *Red Canyon Lodge* (☎ 435-889-3759) is near the Red Canyon Visitor Center. It provides simple rustic cabins with shared bathrooms for $36 (one queen-size bed) or $46 (two queen-size beds in two rooms). Cabins with private bathrooms are $15 more. Each cabin has an outdoor picnic table and fire ring. Luxury cabins with two queen-size beds and a queen-size sofa, a kitchenette, private bath and covered porch rent for $110. All cabins have a wood-burning stove. The lodge has a full restaurant and a grocery and tackle store. It is next to small Green Lake, where there is private fishing and boat rental; fishing guides are available. Bicycles and horses can also be rented. The lodge is open daily from April to October and by arrangement on weekends in other months.

The *Flaming Gorge Lodge* (☎ 435-889-3773, fax 435-889-3788, greenriverherald@ union-tel.com) is just off Hwy 191 between Greendale Junction and the dam. Motel rooms for one to four people are $52 to $71 and condominiums run $92 to $110 – these come with a kitchen. November through February rates are lower. Facilities include a restaurant, café, store and river-raft rentals. Guided fishing trips and boat tours are available and cross-country skis are rented in winter.

There is a simple restaurant serving hamburgers and such in Dutch John. It is open in summer only.

Hotels & Motels – Manila With a population of about 300, Manila manages to be the Daggett County seat. It is just outside the west end of Flaming Gorge and has a few small hotels.

The *Flaming Gorge Bunkhouse* (locally called Grubbs' after the friendly owners) (☎ 435-784-3131, 435-784-3268) has simple but adequate rooms for about $40 in the summer (less in winter) and a café serving home-cooked meals. *Steinakers' Motel* (☎ 435-784-3104) has five cheap and basic rooms. *Niki's Inn* (☎ 435-784-3117) has 10 decent rooms around $50 and a restaurant nearby. The *Vacation Inn* (☎ 435-784-3259, 800-662-4327, fax 435-263-3404) is the biggest place, with two dozen rooms with kitchenettes going for about $50. It may close in winter.

DINOSAUR NATIONAL MONUMENT

Dinosaurs have inspired many people's imaginations perhaps more than any other animal group – it is hard to believe that they have been extinct for tens of millions of years. Although dinosaurs once roamed over much of the earth, in only a few places have the right geological and climatic conditions combined to preserve the beasts as fossils. One of the largest dinosaur fossil beds in North America was discovered here in 1909 and the site was protected by national monument status in 1915.

Today visitors can wander through a dinosaur quarry in which hundreds of bones have been exposed and left in plain sight. This productive quarry has been completely enclosed within a building to protect the fossils from weathering. Apart from dinosaur bones, the starkly eroded canyons of the national monument provide the visitor with scenic drives, hiking, camping, backpacking and river running.

Orientation

Dinosaur National Monument straddles the Utah-Colorado state line and is best reached from Hwy 40. The park headquarters and most of the land is within Colorado, but the dinosaur quarry (which is the only place that such fossils can be seen in the site where they were found) is in Utah. Reach the quarry by driving north from Jensen (13 miles east of Vernal) on a 7-mile paved

road. The headquarters are just off Hwy 40, 25 miles east of Jensen and about 4 miles into Colorado.

Information

Information is available from Dinosaur National Monument Headquarters (☎ 970-374-3000), 4545 Hwy 40, Dinosaur, CO 81610. The visitor center at the headquarters has an audio-visual program, exhibits, bookstore and information (but no fossils). It is open from 8 am to 4:30 pm, Monday to Friday, plus weekends in summer; closed New Year's Day, Thanksgiving and Christmas. Entrance to this visitor center is free; entrance to all other parts of the monument (including the dinosaur quarry) is $10 per (private) vehicle or $5 per cyclist/bus passenger. Golden Age, Access and Eagle Passes are accepted. Visitors can ask for free park literature including a map, the *Echoes* newspaper with general park information and other brochures covering specific topics.

Summer daytime temperatures average in the mid to upper 80°s F – carry drinking water if hiking. Snow during the winter may close some of the areas described below though the road to the quarry is usually open.

Dinosaur Quarry

This educational spot (☎ 435-789-2115) is open daily from 8 am to 7 pm from Memorial Day to Labor Day weekends, and 8 am to 4:30 pm the rest of the year (closed New Year's Day, Thanksgiving and Christmas). The Jurassic rock layer that holds the fossils is well worth seeing – it gives an idea of how hard paleontologists work to transform the solid rock into, on the one hand, the beautiful skeletons seen in museums and, on the other hand, the scientifically accurate interpretation of what life was like for the dinosaurs.

Rangers, brochures, audio-visual presentations and exhibits are here to help you understand what you see. Rangers also have information about the rest of the monument and there is a schedule of ranger-led events (walks, talks, tours). There is also a gift and bookstore.

During the busy summer, park your car in the lower lot and either walk about a half mile to the quarry or wait for the frequent and free shuttle bus. Disabled visitors can drive all the way to the small parking lot at the quarry, as can the general public during off-peak periods.

Scenic Drives & Hiking Trails

Several drives with scenic overlooks and interpretive signs lead to various trailheads for short nature trails or access to the backcountry.

The **Cub Creek Rd** goes east of the dinosaur quarry for 11 miles, ending at Josie Morris' cabin. Josie Morris was a tough woman who lived here for some 50 years – legend has it that Butch Cassidy was among her many suitors. Along the road (which is paved except for the last 2 miles) you can stop at three **nature trails** (1¼ to 2 miles long), see Indian petroglyphs, learn about geology, have a picnic or camp at one of the two campgrounds here.

The paved **Harpers Corner Rd** leaves Hwy 40 at the park headquarters and heads north for 31 miles into the heart of the backcountry, crossing over the Utah-Colorado state line a few times. This scenic and popular drive has several pull-outs with vistas and interpretive signs, picnic areas and trailheads but no campgrounds. Trails include the very short **Plug Hat Butte Nature Trail** (4 miles from the headquarters), the difficult 4-mile (one way) **Ruple Point Trail** (25 miles from headquarters) and the moderate 1-mile (one way) **Harpers Corner Trail** at the end of the road. Both the Ruple Point and Harpers Corner Trails lead to dramatic views of Green River canyons. The Harpers Corner Trail is especially recommended for good views and the sunsets are often memorable.

The unpaved **Echo Park Rd** leaves the Harpers Corner Rd 25 miles north of the headquarters. Vehicles with high clearance or 4WD are recommended for this 13-mile drive, which drops steeply down to Echo Park at the confluence of the Yampa and Green Rivers. The steep road can get very slick or impassable after rain – beware. There is a primitive campground in a splendid setting at Echo Park and hiking is encouraged though there are no maintained trails. The road is not passable to large motor homes or trailers, though ordinary cars can make it in dry weather – check at the visitor center first. People with trucks or 4WDs could also explore the rough **Yampa Bench Rd**, which leaves Echo Park Rd about 8 miles from Harpers Corner Rd. The 38-mile-long Yampa Bench Rd has views of the Yampa River and comes out on Hwy 40 at Elk Springs, Colorado, about 34 miles east of monument headquarters. Again, this road becomes impassable after heavy rains.

The paved but narrow **Jones Hole Rd** leaves from 4 miles south of the dinosaur quarry and goes 48 miles around the west and north sides of the monument to Jones Hole National Fish Hatchery (☎ 435-789-4481). The hatchery is open to the public daily from 7 am to 3:30 pm. The **Jones Hole Trail** from here descends 4 miles to the Green River. Along the way, the trail passes Indian petroglyphs and crosses Ely Creek, where backcountry camping (with a permit) is allowed.

The unpaved **Island Park Rd** leaves from about 15 miles along the Jones Hole Rd and descends 12 miles to Rainbow Park on the Green River; there are two primitive campsites. The warnings for the Echo Park Rd apply here as well.

Other paved roads lead to **Deerlodge Park** on the Yampa River at the east end of the monument and the scenic **Gates of Lodore** on the Green River at the northeast end of the monument. Both places have campgrounds and ranger stations; they are open in summer and are accessed by roads from Colorado.

All vehicles (including bicycles) must travel on designated roads; off-road vehicle travel is prohibited.

Backpacking

Most hikers take one of the trails described above. A few prefer to backpack into remote areas. There are designated backcountry campsites only on the Jones Hole Trail (see above). Otherwise, wilderness camping is allowed anywhere that is at least a quarter mile from an established road or trail. Backpackers must register with a ranger at one of the visitor centers or ranger stations, where they receive free permits and can review the best routes with a ranger.

River Running
The Yampa River is the only major tributary of the Colorado River that has not had its flow severely impounded by major dams. Both the Yampa and Green Rivers offer excellent river-running opportunities, with plenty of exciting rapids and white water amidst splendid scenery. Trips range from one to five days and normally go from mid-May to early September. Two excellent local companies are listed under Vernal and about 10 others are authorized by the National Park Service to do tours – call the monument for a current list.

Experienced rafters wishing to go alone need a permit obtainable from the River Ranger Office (☎ 970-374-2468) between 8 am and noon, Monday to Friday. Permits are limited and most are issued many months in advance (especially for multiday trips) so plan well ahead.

Fishing
Fishing is permitted only with the appropriate state permits, available from sports stores or tackle shops in Vernal, or Dinosaur, Colorado. Check with park rangers about limits and the best places.

Places to Stay
There are no lodges or restaurants in the monument so camping is your only option. The main campground is *Green River*, 5 miles east of the dinosaur quarry along Cub Creek Rd. There are 85 sites and modern bathrooms and drinking water but no showers or hookups. Camping is $10 from April to October and reservations are not taken. The campground may fill on summer weekends but rarely fills midweek. During the winter the water is turned off and camping is free. Nearby *Split Mountain* has four group campsites available by reservation only ($20 per night plus $10 reservation fee), bathrooms and drinking water (turned off in winter).

Free camping is permitted at *Rainbow Park* (two sites) and *Deerlodge Park* (eight sites), neither of which have drinking water. *Gates of Lodore* (17 sites) and *Echo Park* (nine sites) have drinking water and cost $5 in summer (free in winter; no water). You must carry out garbage as there is no trash collection at these sites. See the Scenic Drives & Hiking Trails section above for descriptions of how to get to these places, and call the visitor centers to check on dates and availability.

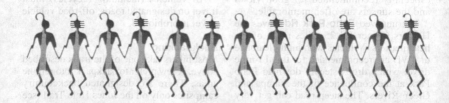

Western Utah

The grim names on local maps describe western Utah: Snake Valley, Black Rock Desert, Skull Valley, Little Sahara, Blood Mountain, Disappointment Hills, Skull Rock Pass, Confusion Range. This is harsh desert country. The map shows few settlements or paved roads southwest of the Great Salt Lake, but the many dirt roads crisscrossing the area indicate that, even in this difficult land, people have tried to eke out an existence through mining and ranching. A large portion of western Utah is inaccessible even to the hardiest desert rat – military testing, training and proving grounds allow no public access.

Western Utah was never home to many people. Small bands of nomadic Indians hunted through the area and there are two small Goshute Indian reservations, which offer little of interest to non-Indians.

The inhospitable terrain did not deter the famous Pony Express riders, who galloped across western Utah in the 1860s. The Pony Express Trail can still be followed, and it is one of the area's most interesting driving excursions (sturdy, reliable vehicles only). Other attractions are stark scenery, the Bonneville Salt Flats (famed as the site of many land speed records), the occasional museum in one of the small towns on the edges of the region and gambling on the Nevada/ Utah border.

This chapter begins in the north along I-80 and then moves south.

WENDOVER

Two hours (125 freeway miles) west of Salt Lake City, Wendover straddles the Nevada/ Utah border and provides northern Utahans with a taste of the glitter and gambling that Nevada is famous for. There are hotels on both sides of the state line, but only those on the Nevada side can legally operate a casino. Not all visitors come for gambling – the Bonneville Salt Flats are only a short drive away.

Orientation & Information

Wendover Blvd, parallel to and south of I-80, is the main thoroughfare. Utah addresses are E Wendover Blvd; Nevada addresses are W Wendover Blvd.

The Welcome Center (☎ 702-664-3414, 800-426-6862), 937 W Wendover Blvd, is open from 8:30 am to 5 pm daily. There is also a visitors bureau in the Bonneville Speedway Museum (see below). The Wendover Clinic (☎ 702-644-2220) handles medical emergencies. Wendover is on Utah time, but the rest of Nevada is one hour behind Utah.

Things to See & Do

The **Bonneville Speedway Museum** (☎ 435-665-7721), 950 E Wendover Blvd, on the east edge of town, is full of classic American cars, including some of the cars that set land speed records on the salt flats. There are also photographs, trophies and other racing mementos, as well as a souvenir shop. Hours are flexible, though the museum is open daily in summer. Admission is $2; $1 for six- to 12-year-olds.

For **gambling**, catch the shuttle bus that runs along Wendover Blvd linking hotels with casinos on the Nevada side. There is complete 24-hour gambling action and occasional entertainment, but the few casinos are subdued compared to those in most Nevada gambling towns. Five casinos are found along W Wendover Blvd.

There is a **golf course** (☎ 702-664-4300, 800-852-4330) south of Wendover Blvd at the west end of town.

Danger Cave was used by prehistoric Indians 10,000 years ago. It lies a couple of miles northeast of Wendover, but despite being marked on many maps, there are no facilities at all.

Places to Stay – Camping

State Line RV Park (☎ 702-664 2221, 800-848-7300) is just off Wendover Blvd at the

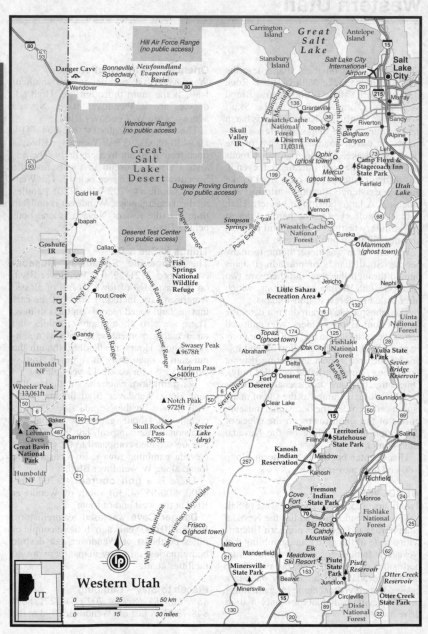

UTAH

Western Utah

Carrington Island

Great Salt Lake

Antelope Island

Hill Air Force Range
(no public access)

Stansbury Island

Salt Lake City International Airport

Salt Lake City

Murray

80
ALT 93

Danger Cave

Bonneville Speedway

Newfoundland Evaporation Basin

Wendover

80

201

215

138

Grantsville

Wasatch-Cache National Forest

36

Tooele

Bingham Canyon

Riverton

Sandy

Alpine

Wendover Range
(no public access)

Stansbury Mountains

▲ Deseret Peak 11,031ft

Oquirrh Mountains

73

Lehi

Camp Floyd & Stagecoach Inn State Park

Great Salt Lake Desert

Skull Valley IR

Ophir (ghost town)

Mercur (ghost town)

Fairfield

Utah Lake

199

Onaqui Mountains

ALT 93

Dugway Proving Grounds
(no public access)

Faust

Vernon

68

Gold Hill

Ibapah

Dugway Range

Simpson Springs

Pony Express Trail

Wasatch-Cache National Forest

36

Eureka

Deseret Test Center
(no public access)

Goshute IR

Callao

Mammoth (ghost town)

Goshute

Fish Springs National Wildlife Refuge

Jericho

Nephi

Nevada

Deep Creek Range

Trout Creek

Thomas Range

Little Sahara Recreation Area

6

132

Uinta National Forest

Confusion Range

Gandy

House Range

Topaz (ghost town)

174

125

Fishlake National Forest

28

Yuba State Park

Humboldt NF

Swasey Peak ▲ 9678ft

Abraham

Oak City

Sevier Bridge Reservoir

Wheeler Peak 13,061ft

Marjum Pass 6400ft

Delta

50

Pavant Range

Scipio

50
6

Sevier River

Fort Deseret

Deseret

Gunnison

Notch Peak ▲ 9725ft

50

Clear Lake

50

89

Baker

50 6

Skull Rock Pass 5675ft

Sevier Lake (dry)

Flowell

15

Salina

Lehman Caves

487

Garrison

Fillmore

Territorial Statehouse State Park

Great Basin National Park

San Francisco Mountains

257

Kanosh Indian Reservation

Meadow

Humboldt NF

21

Kanosh

Richfield

Frisco (ghost town)

Cove Fort

Fremont Indian State Park

Monroe

24

Milford

70

Big Rock Candy Mountain

Fishlake National Forest

25

Manderfield

Marysvale

62

Wah Wah Mountains

Minersville State Park

Elk Meadows Ski Resort

153

Piute State Park

Piute Reservoir

Western Utah

Minersville

Beaver

Junction

Otter Creek Reservoir

UT

0   25   50 km
0   15   30 miles

15

130

20

Circleville

Dixie National Forest

89

22

Otter Creek State Park

state line. It has RV sites with hookups for $19 on weekends, $16 midweek. There is a coin laundry and guests can use facilities at the nearby State Line Inn.

On the Nevada side, the Red Garter Casino has a free RV parking area (no facilities) for RV folks who want to park and play. Behind the casino is a *KOA* (☎ 702-664-3221) that has showers, a pool and a playground. Fees range from $15 (tents) to $22 (full hookups). Kamping Kabins are $27 on weekends, less midweek.

Places to Stay – Budget

Because gamblers descend on the town on weekends, many hotels raise their prices on Fridays, Saturdays, holidays and for special events. Summer rates may also be higher.

The *Motel 6* (☎ 435-665-2267, fax 435-665-2696), 561 E Wendover Blvd, charges $34/40 for singles/doubles midweek, $10 more on weekends. It has a pool. The *Western Ridge Motel* (☎ 435-665-2211, fax 435-665-2883), 895 E Wendover Blvd, also has a pool and rooms at varying sizes and rates from $30 to $70, midweek to weekends. Others to try in this price range are the *Bonneville Motel* (☎ 435-665-2500), 389 E Wendover Blvd, and the *Western Motel* (☎ 435-665-2215, fax 435-665-2223), 645 E Wendover Blvd, both of which have a pool, and the *Heritage Motel* (☎ 435-665-7744, 800-457-5927, fax 435-665-2975), 505 E Wendover Blvd.

Places to Stay – Middle

Hotels The *State Line Inn* (☎ 435-665-2226, 800-848-7300, fax 435-531-4090), 295 E Wendover Blvd, has a pool and spa and is near the Silver Smith Casino, outside which stands the giant figure of Wendover Will waving you in. Rooms are pleasant and reasonably sized; there are some larger rooms and a few suites. Doubles start from $40s midweek and from the $60s on weekends; suites are more expensive. A 24-hour restaurant is adjacent.

The *Best Western Salt Flat Inn* (☎ 435-665-7811, fax 435-665-2383), 999 E Wendover Blvd (near I-80 exit 2), features a pool, sauna, spa and exercise room. It includes a continental breakfast in the rates, but the nearest restaurant is half a mile away. Large rooms are in the $40s midweek from mid-September to mid-May, in the $60s midweek in summer and $65 to $75 on weekends.

The *Super 8 Motel* (☎/fax 702-664-2888) is on W Wendover Blvd in Nevada next to the Red Garter Casino, where there is a bar and 24-hour restaurant. Summer midweek rates are $52.88/60.88 for singles/doubles with one bed, $65.88 for doubles with two beds. Rates are lower from October to March, higher on weekends.

Casinos The *Nevada Crossing Hotel & Casino* (☎ 702-664-2900, 800-537-0207, fax 702-664-4024), 1035 W Wendover Blvd, has a pool, spa and casino next door (with restaurant, bar and occasional entertainment). Rooms are in the $40s midweek, in the $50s on weekends. This place is popular with truck drivers because of the service station next door. The *Silver Smith Resort & Casino* (☎ 702-664-2231, 800-848-7300) is the oldest of Wendover's casinos, but it's kept up very well and has rooms around $50. The *Peppermill Inn & Casino* (☎ 702-664-2255, 800-648-9660) has slightly cheaper rooms. Also try the *Red Garter Hotel & Casino* (☎ 702-664-2111, 800-982-2111).

Places to Eat

The casinos have the food scene wrapped up, with inexpensive all-you-can-eat buffets, 24-hour restaurants and coffee shops. There are several fast-food places as well.

Getting There & Away

The Greyhound bus (☎ 435-665-2595) stops at 215 E Wendover Blvd on its runs between Salt Lake City and San Francisco.

BONNEVILLE SALT FLATS

The salt flats are the remnants of ancient Lake Bonneville, which once covered all of northern Utah and beyond. Today, all that remains is the Great Salt Lake and the thousands of acres of salt flats that create a super-smooth surface for car racing (see the

Speed Limit: 763 MPH

Cars, tents and entire garages mushroom on the flats in the third week of August during the **Bonneville National Speed Trials**. Other speed trials occur from July to October, usually sponsored by the Southern California Timing Association (☎ 805-526-1805) or the Utah Salt Flats Racing Association (☎ 435-785-5364). (Also call the Wendover Welcome Center or BLM for details.) The speed trials are threatened by salt deterioration, particularly after higher than average rainfall, and some events have been canceled.

The first records made at Bonneville were in 1914, when Teddy Tezlaff unofficially reached 141.73 mph in a Blitzen Benz. English racing driver Sir Malcolm Campbell (one of my childhood heroes) was the first person to drive over 300 mph, in his *Bluebird Special* on September 3, 1935 on a perfectly groomed, 1-mile course laid on the salt flats. Since then, American Craig Breedlove, driving *Spirit of America*, broke the 400, 500 and 600 mph barriers at Bonneville – the last on November 15, 1965.

Jet-powered cars have recently been breaking records in the Black Rock Desert in neighboring Nevada. Here, in 1996, Breedlove unofficially reached 675 mph before crashing. He was watching on October 15, 1997 (50 years and a day after the first aircraft broke the sound barrier) when Englishman Andy Green caused a sonic boom by driving the jet-car *ThrustSSC* to 763.035 mph – the first-ever supersonic world land-speed record. ■

sidebar Speed Limit: 763 MPH). Unfortunately, problems of salt deterioration and shrinkage blamed partially on natural cycles and partially on local mining activities have resulted in the flats shrinking by approximately 1% every year since the 1960s. The area is managed by the BLM (☎ 801-977-4300), which, with the help of Reilly Industries and car-racing enthusiasts, will soon begin pumping salty waste water from a potash mining plant in an attempt to retard salt loss from the flats.

The salt flats are visible from I-80 a few miles northeast of Wendover. A paved side road leads to a parking area and you can drive on the hard-packed salt during late summer and fall. Obey all signs – parts of the flats are thin and can trap vehicles. Salt is very corrosive to vehicles; a BLM ranger told me that he wouldn't take his own vehicle out there! If you decide to take your car, wash it afterwards.

TOOELE
Tooele (pronounced 'too-will-uh') was settled by Mormon pioneers in 1849 and is the Tooele County seat. Agriculture has been overtaken by industry as the main economic base – mining, a military munitions depot and proving grounds, and landfills are important.

Tooele is the area's largest town. It's a pleasant place with 17,000 inhabitants and provides accommodations for people wishing to visit the local museums, nearby ghost towns and surrounding countryside. Salt Lake City is only 35 miles away.

Orientation & Information
Hwy 36 (Main) is the major street and runs north-south; Vine is the major east-west street.

The chamber of commerce (☎ 435-882-0690, 800-378-0690), 201 N Main (above the Key Bank), is open from 9 am to 4 pm Monday to Friday. The library (☎ 435-882-2182) is at 47 E Vine. The post office (☎ 435-882-1429) is at 65 N Main. The medical center (☎ 435-882-1697) is at 211 S 100 East. The police (☎ 435-882-8900) are at 323 N Main.

Things to See & Do
The **Tooele County Museum** (☎ 435-882-2836, 435-882-0110), 35 N Broadway (half a mile east of Main on Vine), is in the old

railway station, which dates to 1909. The exhibits emphasize local mining history and the railway. Outside, there are vintage carriages, a steam engine and a replica mine. A miniature railway operates on Saturdays. From Memorial Day to Labor Day, hours are 1 to 4 pm, Tuesday to Friday (sometimes earlier), and 11 am to 4 pm on Saturday, or by appointment the rest of the year. Admission is by donation.

Another historical museum, the **DUP Museum**, 39 E Vine, is housed in an 1867 stone courthouse and an older log cabin alongside. Inside are pioneer photographs and artifacts. Hours are from 11 am to 3 pm on Saturdays in July and August, or call the numbers posted in the window for an appointment.

Play nine holes of **golf** at Oquirrh Hills Course (☎ 435-882-4220), 700 East and Edgemont.

Special Events

Tooele County Arts Festival is held the last weekend in May or the first in June. Tooele County Fair & Rodeo is held in mid-August, and the Gem and Mineral Show is held the last weekend in September.

Places to Stay

The small *Villa Motel* (☎ 435-882-4551), 475 N Main, has simple rooms in the low $30s (a few dollars more with a kitchenette). The *Valley View Motel* (☎ 435-882-3235), 599 Canyon Rd at the south end of town, has 10 rooms with kitchenettes for about $38.

The *Comfort Inn* (☎ 435-882-6100, fax 435-882-6102), 491 S Main, offers a pool, spa, exercise room and coin laundry. Rooms have a refrigerator and microwave. Rates are $50 to $70 in summer, in the $40s at other times, including breakfast. Suites and larger rooms with kitchenettes go up to $95.

The *Best Western Inn* (☎ 435-882-5010, fax 435-882-5746), 365 N Main, has an indoor pool, spa and coin laundry. Pleasant rooms with refrigerators run about $60/65 for singles/doubles in summer, less at other times, including continental breakfast.

Places to Eat

The local favorite is the *Glowing Embers Restaurant* (☎ 435-882-0000), 494 S Main. It serves reasonably priced American meals from 6 am to 9 pm daily (to 10 pm on Friday and Saturday). A decent little Mexican restaurant is *Los Laureles* (☎ 435-882-2860), 23 N Main, open from 11 am to 10 pm except on Sunday. *Tooele Pizza & Restaurant* (☎ 435-882-8035), 21 E Vine, is open from 10 am to 10 pm, Monday to Saturday; it has eat-in or takeout pizzas and other fare.

Getting There & Away

UTA (☎ 435-882-9031) runs bus 38 to Salt Lake City and bus 51 to Grantsville – there is no Sunday service.

AROUND TOOELE
Benson Grist Mill

This grist (grain) mill was built around 1860 using wooden pegs and leather to hold the timbers together. It operated until about 1940 and has recently been restored. Inside, the original machinery remains on display; outside are several period buildings. The mill is usually open 10 am to 4 pm, Tuesday to Saturday, from June through August. You can call ☎ 435-882-7678 or 435-882-7137 to arrange tours at other times. The mill is 8 miles north of Tooele, just west of Hwy 36 on Hwy 138.

Grantsville

Settled in 1850 by Mormon pioneers, this small town, 11 miles northwest of Tooele, is a strange hodgepodge of elegant Victorian homes, modern tract housing and everything in between. The chamber of commerce (☎ 435-884-3411), in the city hall at 429 E Main, has area information.

The main attraction is the **Donner-Reed Memorial Museum** (☎ 435-884-3348 for the curator, or call the chamber of commerce), 90 N Cooley (a block north of 300 W Main) in an adobe house dating from the 1860s. Inside, exhibits describe the Donner-Reed Party's wagon train, which was caught by winter snows in the Sierra Nevada in 1847. Almost half the group died and the survivors resorted to cannibalism to survive – a famous story of the early Western frontier. The museum is opened on request. Outside is Grantsville's first **jail**, a small, portable, iron-grill box, which is open even if the museum is closed. Photograph your traveling companions languishing inside!

The little *Donner Motel* on the 100 block of E Main rents rooms, and the *Skyline Restaurant* (☎ 435-884-3272), 58 W Main, serves meals.

Stansbury Mountains

These mountains are just west of Grantsville and include 11,031-foot Deseret Peak. They are part of the Wasatch-Cache National Forest (☎ 801-524-5042 in Salt Lake City). Drive 5 miles south of Grantsville and then head west another 4 miles to South Willow; there are several free USFS campgrounds along this road, but they lack drinking water and are closed October to May.

At the end of the road past the campgrounds (12 miles from Grantsville) is a parking area and trailhead at 7400 feet. From here, a 4-mile trail reaches **Deseret Peak**, which offers superb views.

Bingham Canyon Copper Mine Overlook

This overlook provides good views of the world's largest open-pit mine (described in the Salt Lake City chapter). To reach the overlook, head east of Tooele on Vine and follow signs along Middle Canyon Rd. The first 7 miles are paved and another 4 miles are unpaved, though passable to cars in good weather.

Vehicles with high clearance or 4WD can continue past the overlook, down Butterfield Canyon and finally reach paved roads in the Salt Lake Valley. This route is closed by snow in winter and not recommended after heavy rains.

Ghost Towns

Head south from Tooele on Hwy 36 for 12 miles, then east on Hwy 73 for 5 miles to signs for **Ophir**, where you'll find deserted mining buildings and a few occupied

houses – please respect the residents' property. There's little to see here unless you are interested in old mining towns.

Four miles beyond the Ophir turnoff on Hwy 73 is a sign for **Mercur**. There is a small mining museum (☎ 801-268-4447) open from 10 am to 7 pm, Thursday to Monday (sometimes Tuesday and Wednesday) from Memorial to Labor Day.

PONY EXPRESS TRAIL

Over 130 miles of the original Pony Express Trail, passing markers indicating several stations, can be followed on a backcountry byway operated by the BLM (☎ 801-977-4300 in Salt Lake City). Use your imagination to think about riding through here in Pony Express days (see the sidebar Delivering Mail by Trusty Steed). Most of the road is maintained gravel or dirt and is passable to ordinary cars in good weather. In winter, snow may close the route or necessitate the use of 4WD; in summer, heavy rains may bog down vehicles. Spring and fall are the best traveling times. There are no services, and drivers should carry extra food and water, fill up with gas and check tires and spares before departing. Primitive camping is allowed along the trail, which is signed.

The trail begins at **Fairfield**, about 25 miles southwest of I-15 at Lehi along Hwy 73. Here you'll find the **Camp Floyd/ Stagecoach Inn State Park** (☎ 801-254-9036), where thousands of troops were housed in the 1850s and 1860s. The 12-room inn dates from 1858 and has been restored (no accommodations). The park and inn are open weekends and most weekdays from about Easter to September; there is a picnic area and small museum. Hours are 11 am to 5 pm; admission is $3 per car, or $1 for cyclists and bus passengers.

Beyond Fairfield on Hwy 73, a sign indicates the (newly paved) Pony Express Trail to **Faust Junction**, about 16 miles west, where the trail intersects Hwy 36, about 30 miles south of Tooele; this is another easy access point to the trail. There is an interpretive exhibit about 2 miles west of Hwy 36, one of several that can be read by the curious traveler. The road continues past the Onaqui Mountains, where wild horses are often seen, and climbs over 6100-foot-high Lookout Pass, the highest point on the trail.

Simpson Springs Station, 25 miles west of Faust Junction, is the best restored of the Pony Express stations along the route. Nearby is a small BLM campground with water (purification advised) and toilets ($3 a night).

West of Simpson Springs, the trail passes the Dugway Range to the north and the Thomas Range to the south, both good rockhounding areas. A small sign indicates a rough road into the Dugways, which are known for geode beds. Topaz Mountain in the Thomas Range is known for topaz. About 40 miles west of Simpson Springs is the **Fish Springs National Wildlife Refuge** (☎ 435-831-5353), an oasis in the desert where 220 species have been recorded. Ducks, geese, herons and other waterfowl flock to the refuge, especially during spring and fall migrations. Tundra swans overwinter here from late December to early March. No camping is permitted, but daylight visits are allowed along an 11-mile loop road giving views of

the marshes, springs and dikes of the refuge. Bird checklists and information are available at the entrance.

A sign interprets the few rocks that remain of **Boyd Station**, halfway between the refuge and **Callao**, 25 miles west. Callao is home to about 200 people who work in local agriculture.

A road south of Callao goes 15 miles to Trout Creek; there is a picnic area (no drinking water, free camping allowed) about 4 miles along this road. Side roads from the Trout Creek Rd head west into the 12,000-foot **Deep Creek Mountains** – a remote, high and rarely visited wilderness. The forested mountains are the

---

Delivering Mail by Trusty Steed

Those who complain that mail delivery is too slow would not have been happy in the mid-1800s, when a letter took two months to reach California from the East Coast of the USA. Delivery was by boat to Caribbean Panama, by mule to the Pacific Coast, and by boat again up to San Francisco, California.

The Pony Express was founded in 1860 to speed mail across the country. Expert horsemen who weighed under 120 lb were hired to ride the almost 1900 miles from St Joseph, Missouri, to Sacramento, California. This was done in relays, passing through home stations roughly 60 miles apart where riders changed, and through swing stations about 12 miles apart where horses were changed. Speeds averaged 190 miles per day, though 'Buffalo Bill' (William F Cody) rode a record 322 miles in less than 22 hours, using 21 different horses. The fastest run was the delivery of President Lincoln's inaugural address, which took just seven and a half days. The Pony Express service lasted only 19 months – its end came with the completion of a transcontinental telegraph system in 1861. ■

haunts of mountain lions, bobcats, elk, mule deer, bighorn sheep and other wildlife. Climbing and hiking is best from June to October – the peaks are snow-bound during the rest of the year. Access is best from the Trout Creek Rd side – access from the west requires permits from the **Goshute Indian Reservation** (☎ 435-234-1138/1139/1136, fax 435-234-1162), PO Box 6104, Ibapah, UT 84034. The west side is much drier. Trail descriptions are found in *Hiking the Great Basin* by John Hart. The dirt road continues south of Trout Creek for about 50 miles to intersect paved Hwy 6/50 just across the state line in Nevada, near Great Basin National Park.

The Pony Express Trail continues 13 miles northwest of Callao to the signed remnants of **Canyon Station** and on through Clifton Flats, from where a signed dirt road heads north to **Gold Hill**, a few miles from the trail. Gold Hill is one of the largest ghost towns in Utah – a few people still live here, but the town is largely deserted. The Pony Express Trail ends at **Ibapah**, 28 miles from Callao. Here there is a gas station, store and a paved road leading north into Nevada and emerging at Wendover, 60 miles away. South of Ibapah is the Goshute Indian Reservation, most of which requires a permit to visit.

EUREKA

This small mining town (population 700) is the gateway to Hwy 6/50, which slashes southwest across the deserts of western Utah, reaching Great Basin National Park just across the state line in Nevada. Once, thousands of people lived in Eureka – today the mining boom is over and the town has shrunk. It calls itself 'The Friendliest Town on America's Loneliest Highway.'

Information

The city hall (☎ 435-433-6915), built in 1899 at 241 W Main, has tourist information. The medical clinic (☎ 435-433-6905) is at 330 W Main.

Things to See

Upstairs in the city hall and next door in the old railway station, informative exhibits of the **Tintic Mining Museum** deal mainly with the mining history of the area. The museum is open weekends in summer and erratically or on request at other times; curators' phone numbers are posted in the railway station window, or call the Tintic Historical Society (☎ 435-433-6842), PO Box 218, Eureka, UT 84628. The society gives **walking tours** of the area.

Booklets available at the Tintic Mining Museum describe several **ghost towns** within a short drive of Eureka. Silver City and Mammoth are the best known.

Special Events

The annual Tintic Silver Festival takes place the third weekend in August. Mining tours by the Tintic Historical Society are the highlight.

Places to Stay

Little Valley, about 10 miles south of Vernon, has free camping in the Wasatch-Cache National Forest – almost 30 miles from Eureka. Bring drinking water. The campground is open May to October. There is also camping at Little Sahara Recreation Area (see below).

Carpenter Station (☎ 435-433-6311), 202 W Main, has four rooms for $32/35 (single/double) and a general store, coin laundry and gas station.

LITTLE SAHARA RECREATION AREA

The BLM manages almost 95 sq miles here, of which almost half are sand dunes. Little Sahara is a mecca for ORV (off-road vehicle) users who roar around the dunes. The BLM brochure states, 'Each year several people are seriously injured or killed in the dunes through negligence. Always check for steep drop-offs before powering over the crest of a dune.'

A herd of pronghorn antelope roams the area. A unique sub-species of giant four-wing saltbush found here and nowhere else grows twice as fast and has half the chromosomes of regular saltbush plants.

Information is available from the BLM (☎ 435-743-6811 in Fillmore or 435-896-8221 in Richfield). A visitors center (with exhibits) is open with varying hours from March to October.

There are four campgrounds, two of which have designated safe areas for kids to play in the sand. The campgrounds have picnic tables, charcoal grills, toilets and drinking water from March to October only. In winter, toilets and water are available at the visitors center.

Day-use fees are $5 per vehicle, which includes camping. Spring and fall are the most heavily used periods, especially weekends.

Little Sahara is 21 miles south of Eureka or 35 miles north of Delta.

DELTA
This town of 3500 people is an agricultural center for the farms irrigated by the Sevier River; alfalfa and grain crops are important. Industry is not absent, however. The Intermountain Power Plant, 18 miles north of town, is the largest coal-fired power plant in the known universe. Delta's main importance for travelers is as the 'Gateway to Great Basin National Park,' which lies almost 100 miles west. Delta has the best selection of hotels and services west of I-15 (in Utah).

Information
The chamber of commerce (☎ 435-864-4316), 76 N 200 West, is open from 10 am to 2 pm, Monday to Friday (summer hours may be longer). The library (☎ 435-864-4945) and police (☎ 435-864-2755) are at the same address. The post office (☎ 435-864-2811) is at 86 S 300 East. The medical center (☎ 435-864-5591) is at 126 S White Sage Ave.

Things to See & Do
The **Great Basin Museum**, a small regional museum (☎ 435-864-5013), 328 W 100 North, has pioneer, mining and historical exhibits. One exhibit has part of a barracks from the Topaz War Relocation Center (see Around Delta, below). Hours are 10 am to 4 pm, Tuesday to Saturday,

and 1 to 4 pm on Monday. Admission is free but donations are encouraged.

You can take a guided tour (by appointment) of the cheese-making plant at the **Delta Valley Farms Cheese Company** (☎ 435-864-2725), 1365 N 1250 East. There's a restaurant here.

Play nine holes of **golf** at Sunset View Course (☎ 435-864-2508), 3000 E 1500 North. **Swim** year-round at West Millard Outdoor Pool (☎ 435-864-3133), 201 E 300 North.

Places to Stay – Camping
The oddly named *Kitten Klean Trailer Park* (☎ 435-864-2614), 181 E Main, has showers and sites with hookups for $12, without hookups for $6. The *Antelope Valley RV Park* (☎ 435-864-1813), 776 W Main, has 96 sites from $10 for tents to $18 with RV hookups. There are showers and a playground.

The Fishlake National Forest (☎ 435-743-5721 in Fillmore) runs about 20 sites at *Oak Creek Campground*, 17 miles east of Delta or 4 miles northeast of Oak City on paved roads. Drinking water and toilets are available from mid-May to October. Camping is $5 and there is trout fishing in Oak Creek.

Places to Stay – Budget
Summer rates (given below) are a few dollars more than at other times. One of the cheapest is the *Rancher Motel & Cafe* (☎ 435-864-2741), 171 W Main, with basic but clean and larger-than-average rooms in the mid-$20s. The *Budget Motel* (☎/fax 435-864-4533), 75 S 350 East, is the largest of the cheap hotels, with 29 rooms. Rates are $30/35, or about $40 for seven larger rooms with kitchenettes.

Other places with rooms in the $20s and low $30s include the *Diamond D Motor Lodge* (☎ 435-864-2041), 234 W Main, and *Deltan Inn Motel* (☎ 435-864-5318), 347 E Main.

Places to Stay – Middle
The *Best Western Motor Inn* (☎ 435-864-3882, fax 435-864-4834), 527 E Topaz

Blvd (near the intersection of Hwy 6 and Hwy 50), is by far the best and largest (82 rooms) place in town. There are seasonal swimming and kids' pools, a coin laundry and the Jade Garden Restaurant next door. Rooms are about $45 to $70 in summer, depending on room size.

Places to Eat

The restaurant selection is limited and American food predominates, but meals are reasonably priced and quite good. *Top's City Cafe* (☎ 435-864-2148), 313 W Main, serves simple, inexpensive meals all day, as does the *Rancher Motel & Cafe* (☎ 435-864-2741), 171 W Main, which also has Mexican food. Upstairs at the Rancher, the more upscale *Gold Room* serves steak and seafood.

Chef's Palace (☎ 435-864-2421), 225 E Main, is locally recommended, serves steak and seafood dinners and has a salad bar (closed Sunday). *The Loft* (☎ 435-864-4223), 411 E Main, is also good for similar dinners from Wednesday to Saturday. The *Jade Garden Restaurant and Lounge* (☎ 435-864-2947), 540 E Topaz Blvd, is a good family restaurant open daily for breakfast, lunch and dinner. The *Pizza House* (☎ 435-864-2207), 69 S 300 East, serves soups, salads and sandwiches as well as pizza and pasta (closed Sunday).

Two miles north of town, the *Delta Valley Farms Restaurant* (☎ 435-864-3566), 1365 N 1250 East, is a local favorite family restaurant serving lunches from 10 am to 4 pm (closed Sunday). It is next to a cheese-making plant (see Things to See & Do, above).

Entertainment

The *T&T Twin Theaters* (☎ 435-864-4551), 420 E Topaz Blvd, are closed on Sunday.

AROUND DELTA

The Great Basin Museum and the city park near the chamber of commerce have memorials to the **Topaz War Relocation Center**, about 14 miles northwest of Delta. This is where thousands of US citizens of Japanese descent were 'relocated' during WWII. Not much apart from a memorial remains at the site itself.

Fort Deseret is about 10 miles southwest of Delta. Some maps describe it as a state park – it's no more than a picnic area near the crumbling remains of a fort built by Mormon pioneers in the 1860s. A few miles west is the **Great Stone Face** – a rock outcrop that locals claim resembles Joseph Smith, founder of the Mormon church. (Use faith, imagination or hallucinogens to see the prophet.)

Two state waterfowl management areas offer birding opportunities, especially during spring and fall migrations. These are **Topaz** (15 miles northwest) and **Clear Lake** (20 miles south).

The **Fishlake National Forest** (see Fillmore & Around in the Central Utah chapter) is about 15 miles east of Delta. There is camping, fishing and hiking in the small Canyon Mountains, which reach over 9000 feet.

About halfway between Delta and the Nevada state line are the **House Range** mountains, with several gravel or dirt roads leading to rockhounding sites. The **Notch Peak Rd**, 43 miles west of Delta along Hwy 6/50, is a good gravel road giving access to the area – a 50-mile loop brings you back to Hwy 6. Locals say that Notch Peak is the largest limestone mountain in Utah. Swasey Peak (9678 feet), north of Notch Peak, is known for trilobite fossils. Much of the area is managed by the BLM (☎ 435-743-6811), 15 E 500 North, Fillmore, UT 84631, which administers over 40% of Utah's lands. The BLM can provide further information about this remote area.

GREAT BASIN NATIONAL PARK (NEVADA)

This park, 100 miles west of Delta and just over the state line in Nevada, has two main attractions – Lehman Caves and Wheeler Peak. The visitor center can recommend several other hiking trails to see a natural arch, alpine lakes, bristlecone pines and other mountains within the park.

Information

Get information from the Superintendent (☎ 702-234-7331), Great Basin NP, Baker, NV 89311. Entrance is free. The visitor center is open daily except New Year's Day, Thanksgiving and Christmas. Hours are 8:30 am to 4:30 pm, extended to 6 pm in summer.

For descriptions of the backcountry, read Michael Kelsey's *Hiking and Climbing in Great Basin National Park*.

Lehman Caves

Most visitors come for these caves, which are thick with beautiful geological formations. Entrance to the caves is from near the visitor center and only allowed if you go on a ranger-led tour. Tours last 90 minutes and cover more than half a mile of the almost 2 miles that have been explored. Be prepared for a few stairways, narrow passages and a constant 50°F cave temperature – bring a sweater. Tours leave hourly from 8 am to 6 pm from Memorial Day to Labor Day, with more frequent departures on weekends. Four to six tours a day are offered the rest of the year. Tours cost $4, $3 for children ages six to 15 and $2 for seniors over 62. Buy tickets at the visitor center as soon as you arrive. In summer, more expensive specialized caving tours may be offered.

Wheeler Peak

At 13,061 feet, Wheeler Peak is Nevada's second-highest mountain and the only one that boasts a (small) year-round ice field. A scenic road climbs 12 miles to Wheeler Peak Campground at about 10,000 feet. From here a strenuous 5-mile (one-way) trail climbs to the summit. Apart from the ice field, see the bristlecone pines, which are about 4000 years old and said to be the world's oldest living species. There are various other trails. The entire road is open from about June to September or October, depending on snow conditions. Hiking is difficult because of snow in winter and spring, when cross-country skiing is a possibility.

Places to Stay & Eat

This is one of the more remote areas in the National Park System, with far fewer visitors than the famous parks of southern Utah or the Grand Canyon. The nearest sizable town is Ely, almost 70 miles west, with about 20 hotels. Delta (100 miles) and Beaver (124 miles) offer lodging choices on the Utah side, and Milford (94 miles) has just one hotel.

Within the park there are small campgrounds that may fill during the summer, especially on weekends. *Lower Lehman Creek Campground*, 2 miles beyond the visitor center along the Wheeler Peak Rd, is open all year. Three other campgrounds are open in summer only. Fees are $5, and there are toilets and water but no showers. Free backcountry camping is permitted in most of the park – ask at the visitor center for recommendations. A café at the visitor center is open from Easter to October.

The little town of Baker, Nevada, just outside the park, has the *Silver Jack Motel* (☎ 702-234-7323), the *Whispering Elms Motel and Campground* (☎ 702-234-7343) and a couple of places to eat. Also try the *Border Inn* (☎ 702-234-7300) on the state line along Hwy 6/50, with a restaurant serving meals all day. These places offer simple rooms around $40.

HWY 21

This is another lonely road crossing western Utah, running 112 miles from I-15 at Beaver to Garrison near the Utah-Nevada line, and another 12 miles to Great Basin National Park. It offers the fastest link between Great Basin and the national parks of southwestern Utah. Rock hounds claim this is one of the best areas in the state to prospect for semiprecious stones – a rockhounding brochure is available in Beaver (southwestern Utah).

Starting from the state line, you drive through Garrison, a blink-and-you'll-miss-it town with no tourist facilities. The road continues through almost uninhabited and sparsely vegetated desert and climbs over a 7000-foot pass in the eerily named **Wah Wah Mountains** about 50 miles into Utah. Near mile marker 54, a gravel road heads south for about 15 miles into the Wah Wahs, providing access to remote hiking and camping possibilities – bring plenty of water.

Another 15 miles brings you to the San Francisco Mountains, once important for silver. **Frisco** is a ghost town visible from Hwy 21 near mile marker 63; a historical marker tells the story near a turnoff that leads into the remains.

Frisco once had a population of several thousand and was served by a railway, but its mining heyday came to a dramatic end in 1885 when the main silver mine literally caved in.

Today, several buildings still stand. Be careful when exploring the area as buildings are nearing a state of collapse, and there are mine shafts nearby. Other ghost towns can be found close by.

Milford

This small town, 82 miles from the state line and 30 miles from Beaver, offers the last services before Nevada, but is otherwise of little interest. Information is available from the Milford City Office (☎ 435-387-2711), 302 S Main. Amtrak trains (☎ 800-872-7245) between Salt Lake City and Los Angeles stop here in the middle of the night.

The *Station Motel* (☎ 435-387-2481), 485 S 100 West, has about two dozen simple but clean rooms in the $30s. The attached *Station Restaurant* (☎ 435-387-2804) serves American and Chinese food from 9 am to 10 pm daily. Also try the *Hong Kong Cafe* (☎ 435-387-2251), 433 S Main, or the *Old Hickory Inn* (☎ 435-387-5042), 485 W Center.

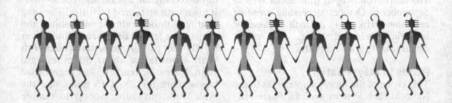

Central Utah

This chapter covers the rough triangle delineated by I-15, I-70 and Hwy 6 between Spanish Fork (see the Wasatch Mountains chapter) and Green River (see the Southeastern Utah chapter). I-15 runs along the west side of the San Pitch Mountains and Pavant Range, which are high, forested and scenic extensions of the Wasatch Mountains. A 7000-foot pass at the south end of the Pavant Range allows I-70 to take off eastward through Utah and on across the continent. I-70 soon intersects with Hwy 89, which follows the east side of the San Pitch and Pavant Mountains.

I-15 and Hwy 89 trace historically significant routes, and the towns found along them were among the first settled by the Mormon pioneers in the 1850s. There were

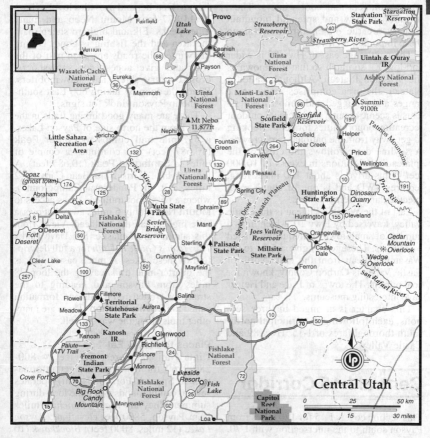

several minor 'wars' between the Mormon pioneers and the Ute Indians as well as between Mormons and 'Gentiles' (non-Mormon whites). These altercations are described in various museums in the area.

The towns along I-15 have been changed and modernized as freeway towns tend to be, but those along Hwy 89 have a definite early Mormon feel to them suggested by their turn-of-the-19th-century Main St architecture, magnificent temples and traditional, clean-living, friendly inhabitants. The whole area is mountainous and, with few exceptions, towns here lie between 5000 and 6000 feet above sea level with warm summers and cool winters. Thus, Mormon history and splendid mountain scenery are the major attractions along these important highways.

The next range east of Hwy 89 is wider and lower – so much so that it's known as the Wasatch Plateau. Although called a plateau, the area comprises many small ranges and is rugged and almost roadless. This is scenic country with remote outdoor recreation opportunities for people looking to get away from the national-park crowds. A skyline drive follows the crest of the 'plateau' at elevations in excess of 10,000 feet – this drive is about 100 miles long, requires 4WD and is one of Utah's most spectacular wilderness roads.

East of the Wasatch Plateau is the Castle Valley, traversed by Hwy 10, which links a number of small towns infrequently visited by tourists. These towns give access to the Wasatch Plateau from the east. North of Castle Valley is Carbon County, known for coal mining. The towns of Price and Helper have interesting museums.

This chapter is arranged in three sections, each following the principal north-south thoroughfares of I-15, Hwy 89 and Castle Valley.

Central I-15 Corridor

This section covers I-15 for 120 miles from Payson south to the intersection with I-70.

PAYSON

Mormon rancher James Pace and others settled here in the 1850s and gave the town its name. Payson, with 11,000 inhabitants, is 15 miles south of Provo and the gateway to the Nebo Loop Scenic Byway. The chamber of commerce (☎ 801-465-2634, 801-465-5200) is in the City Center Complex at 439 W Utah Ave.

Nebo Loop Scenic Byway

This beautiful road climbs from Payson at 4500 feet to more than 9000 feet before dropping to 5100 feet at Nephi, about 40 miles away. The paved road is open from June to October and provides lovely views of 11,877-foot Mount Nebo and many other peaks. Elk and bighorn sheep roam the area and the fishing is good. During the winter, the roads are open part of the way and give access for snowshoers, cross-country skiers and snowmobilers. Reach the loop by taking 600 East southbound in Payson (look for signs).

There are many good hiking trails in the area. From the north side of Payson Lakes, a 5½-mile trail climbs to **Loafer Peak** (10,687 feet) and continues a couple of miles to **Santaquin Peak** (10,685 feet). A tougher hike starts from Bear Canyon (2 miles east of Ponderosa Campground), where a 6500-foot trailhead gives access to **Mount Nebo**, only 5 miles away but over a mile higher than the trailhead. Views from this summit are fantastic. See Dave Hall's *The Hiker's Guide to Utah* for a full description of these hikes. A much easier walk is the quarter-mile trail leaving the loop 28 miles from Payson and heading to the strangely eroded red sandstone formation called the **Devil's Kitchen**. There are many other trails along the way as well.

Places to Stay & Eat

Uinta National Forest Service (☎ 800-280-2267 for reservations; get information in Spanish Fork or Nephi) operates several campgrounds along the loop during summer. They are *Maple Bench* (8 miles from Payson, 5800 feet elevation); *Payson Lakes* (12 miles, 8000 feet); *Blackhawk* (16 miles, 8000 feet); and *Ponderosa* (36 miles, 6200 feet). These have water and toilets and cost $7 to $11. There are picnic sites, and backcountry camping is also permitted.

In Payson, the *Comfort Inn* (☎/fax 801-465-4861), 830 N Main (just off I-15 exit 254), has more than 60 spacious rooms, a few with kitchenettes, for $55 to $90, including continental breakfast. Facilities include a pool, spa, sauna, exercise room and coin laundry. There's also the much cheaper *Cherry Lane Motel* (☎ 801-465-2582), 240 E 100 North, with 10 modest rooms in the low $30s.

Next to the Comfort Inn, the *Cobblestone Family Restaurant* (☎ 801-465-9283), 840 N Main, is open 24 hours. There's also *Mi Rancherito* (☎ 801-465-0460), 41 E 100 North, for good Mexican food.

NEPHI & AROUND
As the Mormon pioneers pushed further south, they settled area after area. Nephi, named after a Mormon prophet, was established in 1851. It is about 40 miles south of Provo, has about 3500 inhabitants and is the Juab County seat.

Hwy 132 east of Nephi passes the end of the Nebo Loop after 6 miles and continues through **Fountain Green** to **Moroni**, 21 miles away. Both are early Mormon towns founded in 1859, the latter named after an angel. Both have places to eat but no hotels. This is one of the most important sheep- and turkey-raising regions in the West. (Foreign visitors might remember that the US Thanksgiving holiday is traditionally celebrated with a turkey dinner.) Fountain Green celebrates Lamb Days in mid-July with a parade, games and entertainment. Eight miles south of Moroni, Hwy 132 intersects with Hwy 89 just north of Ephraim (see Central Hwy 89 Corridor, below).

Orientation & Information
Nephi is west of I-15 between exits 228 in the north and 222 in the south. Follow the signs from I-15 to Main, the primary thoroughfare.

There is limited tourist information at the Juab County Center (☎ 435-623-2411),

160 N Main, and at the chamber of commerce (☎ 435-623-5203), 4 S Main, in the DUP Museum (☎ 435-623-5202), which is open from 9 am to 5 pm, Monday to Friday. The Uinta National Forest Nephi Ranger Station (☎ 435-623-2735), 740 S Main, Nephi, UT 84648, has information about the Nebo Loop. The post office (☎ 435-623-1832) is at 10 N Main. The police station (☎ 435-623-1626) is at 21 E 100 North. The medical center (☎ 435-623-1242) is at 549 N 400 East.

Yuba State Park
Twenty-five miles southwest of Nephi along I-15, this park (☎ 435-758-2611), PO Box 159, Levan, UT 84639, contains the Sevier Bridge Reservoir, which has a boat launch area for fishing and boating. Park beaches were recently closed due to contamination. The campground is open all year, has showers and charges $11. Day use is $4.

Special Events
The annual Ute Stampede (☎ 435-623-4407), held during the second Thursday to Saturday in July at the county fairgrounds, has taken place for more than 60 years. It is a major event featuring a rodeo, parades, crafts, contests, cooking, carnivals, concerts and car shows.

Places to Stay – Camping
The *KOA Kampground* (☎ 435-623-0811) is 6 miles east of town along Hwy 132, near the exit for the Nebo Loop. Open from mid-May through September, it has a pool, game room, grocery store and coin laundry, and charges $14.50 for tents, $19 with hookups and $26 for Kamping Kabins. In Nephi itself, there is *High Country RV Park* (☎ 435-623-2624), 899 S Main. (See also the Nebo Loop Scenic Byway and Yuba State Park, above.)

Places to Stay – Budget
Prices rise during the Ute Stampede. From October to April, rates are often lower. The *Safari Motel* (☎ 435-623-1071), 413 S Main, which has a pool surrounded by a lawn and shade trees, is a good value with

rooms in the $30s in summer, $20s in winter. Cheaper rooms are available at the *Starlite Motel* (☎/fax 435-623-4000), 675 S Main, which has a pool and some rooms with kitchenettes. The *Super 8 Motel* (☎ 435-623-0888, fax 435-623-5025), 1901 S Main, charges $40.88/43.88 for singles/doubles or $46.88 for doubles with two beds.

Places to Stay – Middle
Roberta's Cove Motor Inn (☎ 435-623-2629, 800-456-6460), 2250 S Main (by I-15 exit 222) lacks a pool but has a picnic/barbecue area and very pleasant rooms with coffeemakers ranging from $35 to $55. The *Best Western Paradise Inn* (☎/fax 435-623-0624), 1025 S Main, has an indoor pool, spa and rooms from $45 to $60.

Places to Eat
JC Mickelson's (☎ 435-623-0152), 2100 S Main, open from 6 am to 10 pm daily, is the best in town. It serves American food at moderate prices.

Getting There & Away
Greyhound buses (☎ 435-623-0823) stop at 563 N Main on their two or more daily runs up and down I-15 (Salt Lake City to Las Vegas, Nevada).

FILLMORE & AROUND
Fillmore was almost the geographical center of the territory of Utah, which is why it became the territorial capital in 1851, even before the town was settled. A statehouse was built, but Fillmore's capital status lasted only till 1856.

Today, Fillmore is the seat of Millard County, both named after Millard Fillmore, 13th president of the USA, who was supportive of the Mormons. It has 2500 inhabitants and is the center of agriculture in the region. Fillmore is clearly a rural town. Although the statehouse is near the town center, I noted a horse in the backyard of a house just two blocks away. Another house had peacocks strutting around the garden. Walk around and enjoy this small town.

Orientation & Information
Fillmore is east of I-15 between exits 167 in the north and 163 in the south. Main is the main drag through town.

A tourist information booth in North Park, 500 N Main, operates from late spring to early fall. The Fishlake National Forest Fillmore Ranger Station (☎ 435-743-5721), 390 S Main, Fillmore, UT 84631, is open 8 am to 5 pm, Monday to Friday. The BLM (☎ 435-743-6811), 35 E 500 North, is open from 8 am to 4:30 pm, Monday to Friday; it provides information about BLM areas west of Fillmore. The library (☎ 435-743-5314) is in the city hall at 75 W Center. The post office (☎ 435-743-5748) is at 60 E Center. The medical center (☎ 435-743-5591) is at 674 S Hwy 99. The police (☎ 435-743-5302) are at 765 S Hwy 99.

Territorial Statehouse State Park
This park (☎ 435-743-5316), 50 W Capitol Ave (off 50 S Main), contains Utah's oldest government building. Only one wing was completed by 1855, after which the territorial legislature decided to move to Salt Lake City. Three floors with 14 rooms furnished with period pieces have exhibits of interesting old photos and pioneer memorabilia. Outside is a rose garden, an 1867 stone school, 1880s log cabins and a picnic/play area. Call ahead for guided tours. Summer hours are 8 am to 8 pm, Monday to Saturday and 9 am to 6 pm on Sunday. Winter hours are 9 am to 6 pm, Monday to Saturday. Admission is $2 per person or $5 per car load.

Fishlake National Forest
Head east on 200 South to reach the Fishlake National Forest along Chalk Creek Rd – the many fishing and picnic places here are popular with the locals in summer.

About 7 miles south of Fillmore, Hwy 133 intersects with I-15. Take Hwy 133 south through the pioneer Mormon villages of **Meadow** and **Kanosh**, settled in the 1850s and largely undisturbed by freeway traffic. Kanosh is named after Paiute Indian Chief Kanosh, who is buried in the village cemetery. From Kanosh, Corn Creek Rd heads east into the Pavant Range of the Fishlake National Forest, which offers many camping, hiking and fishing opportunities. The unpaved **Paiute ATV Trail** (All Terrain Vehicles) also takes off from here and follows a 200-mile loop into the wilderness, crossing three mountain ranges, mostly in USFS and BLM lands. The trail can also be accessed at Richfield and Marysvale (both of which have ATV rentals) and other places. Information and maps are available in Fillmore and Richfield.

Flowell Lava Beds

Drive west on Hwy 100 (400 North) to Flowell, 6 miles away. From there head south for 3 miles to the end of the paved road, and continue on dirt roads into lava beds caused by eruptions thousands of years ago. There are lava tubes, extinct volcanoes and many interesting geological formations within this natural devastation – the BLM and tourist booth in Fillmore and the chamber of commerce in Delta (see the Western Utah chapter) have maps and information.

Cove Fort

Thirty miles south of Fillmore is Cove Fort, built in 1867 on the spot indicated by Brigham Young. Restoration of the solid-looking structure was completed by the Mormon Church in 1994, and Mormon guides in period dress tell interesting stories of the fort's history. One of several forts built along the Mormon corridor between Salt Lake City and St George, Cove Fort is the only one that has been fully restored. The 12 rooms are furnished with antiques. The fort is open daily from 8 am till dusk (weather permitting), and guided visits are free. The site is reached from exit 135 on I-15 or exit 1 on I-70.

I-15 south of here is described in the Southwestern Utah chapter. I-70 east reaches Fremont Indian State Park (15 miles) and intersects with Hwy 89 (23 miles), both described in the next section.

Places to Stay – Camping

Wagons West RV Camp (☎ 435-743-6188), 545 N Main, has showers and a coin laundry

and charges $10 without hookups, $15 with hookups. The *KOA* (☎ 435-743-4420), 800 S 270 West, near I-15 exit 163, has showers, coin laundry and a store; fees are $14/19 without/with hookups and Kamping Kabins are $24 to $28. They are open from March to mid-December.

The Fishlake National Forest has campgrounds – the nearest is 14 miles southwest to Kanosh, then 6 miles southeast to *Adelaide Campground*. This campground is open from May to October, has drinking water and toilets, and costs $6 a night. The Paiute ATV Trail passes nearby.

Places to Stay – Budget

The *Spinning Wheel Motel* (☎ 435-743-6260), 65 S Main, has simple but clean rooms with one or two beds, some with kitchenettes, for $25 to $35. The pleasant *Fillmore Motel* (☎ 435-743-5454), 61 N Main, charges about $26 for a double or $36 for a double with two beds. Some rooms have microwaves and refrigerators.

Places to Stay – Middle

The *Best Western Paradise Inn* (☎ 435-743-6895, fax 435-743-6892), 1025 N Main (near exit 167), features an indoor pool, spa and restaurant next door. Good rooms with one bed are about $50; spacious rooms with two beds are around $60 a double in summer, less at other times. The slightly cheaper *Rodeway Inn* (☎ 435-743-4334, fax 435-743-4054), 1060 S Main (near exit 163), also has an indoor pool and spa and includes a continental breakfast. There's also the new *Suite Dreams B&B* (☎ 435-743-6622, 435-743-6862), 172 N Main, which has large, nonsmoking rooms with private spas.

Places to Eat

The *Garden of Eat'n* (☎ 435-743-5414), next to the Best Western, is the town's best restaurant, featuring American fare, a salad bar and a cocktail bar. Prices are reasonable with dinners at around $10. Hours are from 6 am to 10 pm (to 11 pm in summer).

Deano's Pizza (☎ 435-743-6385), 96 S Main, features soups, sandwiches, salads and pizzas to eat in or take out – and a miniature golf course, pool tables and video arcade! Hours are 11 am to 10 pm, Monday to Saturday. The *Cowboy Cafe* (☎ 435-743-4302), 31 N Main, features local home cooking from 6 am to 10 pm. *Caleb's Country Grill* (☎ 435-743-6876), 590 N Main, serves breakfast, lunch and dinner.

Entertainment
The *Avalon* (☎ 435-743-6918), 35 N Main, shows movies. For a beer, stop by the *Arrowhead Trail Tavern* (☎ 435-743-5144), 21 N Main, which has pool tables and live music and dancing on weekends.

Getting There & Away
The Greyhound bus (☎ 435-743-6876) stops by Caleb's Country Grill, 590 N Main, on its two daily runs between Salt Lake City and Las Vegas, Nevada.

Central Hwy 89 Corridor

This section follows Hwy 89 for 140 miles as it parallels I-15 east of the San Pitch Mountains and Pavant Range. The historic road passes through some of Utah's most traditional Mormon towns, several of which have early Western buildings lining their main streets. Hwy 89 avoids freeway traffic, which makes it a fine alternative to I-15 if you have extra time and want to experience some of Utah's early history.

SKYLINE DRIVE
This gravel and dirt road parallels Hwy 89 and traverses 90 miles of the Wasatch Plateau from Hwy 6 in the north to I-70 in the south. The scenic but difficult drive reaches 10,900 feet and is passable only in summer and fall, when many people come to look at wildflowers and fall colors. 4WD vehicles are needed to complete the drive, although easier sections passable to cars can be accessed from towns along Hwy 89 or Hwy 10. Most of

the drive is within the Manti-La Sal National Forest, and information is obtainable from ranger stations in Price, Ephraim and Ferron.

The drive begins near the Tucker Rest Area, 30 miles east of Spanish Fork along Hwy 6. It follows USFS Rd 150 for most of its length except the final few miles along USFS Rds 001 and 009 in the Fishlake National Forest. There are campgrounds at *Gooseberry* about a third of the way along the drive, and at *Ferron Reservoir* and *Twelvemile Flat*, two-thirds of the way. These have drinking water, toilets and fire pits and are open from June to September. Fees are about $7. The first is also reachable from Fairview or Huntington along Hwy 31, the second area from Ferron or Gunnison along forest roads. Free primitive camping is allowed and there are plenty of hiking trails. There's mountain wildlife, especially mule deer and elk, and more for observant naturalists. Other campgrounds and recreation opportunities are available in the lower reaches of the national forest. During the winter, many parts of the area attract cross-country skiers and snowmobilers.

FAIRVIEW
Settled by Mormons in 1859, Fairview is a minor agricultural center for the surrounding sheep and turkey farms. The town's Mormon roots are strong, as they are in most towns in the area. Barely 1000 people live here, yet the town attracts visitors with its excellent museum. Fairview is also an important gateway to the Skyline Drive. The city hall (☎ 435-427-3858), 85 S State, has visitor information.

Fairview Museum of History & Arts
This is one of my favorite small-town museums (☎ 435-427-9216), at 85 N 100 East. Originally housed in a school built in 1900, part of the collection was moved next door in 1995 into the splendid new Horizon Building, built specifically to house a life-size replica of the 15,000-year-old Columbian mammoth unearthed under Huntington Reservoir dam in 1988. The

new building also houses a fine collection of Norman Rockwell lithographs, many other paintings and sculptures by mainly regional artists, a collection of Indian and pioneer memorabilia, and a gift shop.

Next door, the old Heritage Building houses the work of Fairview's Lyndon Graham, a sculptor and wood carver who has produced wonderfully detailed miniatures of stagecoaches, trains and even Cinderella's carriage. Also here is the 'National Shrine to Love and Devotion' – a sculpture of a Fairview couple, Peter and Celestia Peterson, who were married for 82 years, setting a world record. Arts and crafts and pioneer rooms and furniture are also here. Outside, old farm implements are scattered about. There's something for everyone and it's free; donations are welcomed.

The Horizon Building is open year-round from 10 am to 5 pm, Monday to Saturday, and 2 to 5 pm on Sunday. In summer, it closes at 6 pm. The Heritage Building stays open the same hours in summer but is closed in winter except by appointment, although there are plans to stay open year-round.

Skyline Drive

Hwy 31 east of Fairview intersects with the Skyline Drive after 9 miles. The paved road is kept open in winter and provides access to cross-country skiers and snowmobilers. The Gooseberry campground is a short way north along the drive.

Special Events

Pioneer Days in the week leading up to July 24 (anniversary of Brigham Young's arrival in Salt Lake City) is celebrated with rodeos, a demolition derby, food, arts and crafts, and entertainment. Lace Day is held at the museum on a Tuesday in mid-July with demonstrations of how to make different kinds of lace.

Places to Stay & Eat

The small *Skyline Motel* (☎ 435-427-3312), 236 N State, has doubles in the $30s. The *Mariposa Cafe* (☎ 435-427-3294), 44 S State, has been the place to eat (under various names) since 1937 and serves Mexican and American food from 7:30 am to 9 pm, Monday to Saturday, and 9 am to 8 pm on Sunday. There's also the *Home Plate Cafe* (☎ 435-427-9300), 215 N State.

MT PLEASANT

Settled by Danes in 1859, the town retains much of its early character. Main St has many old buildings and is on the National Register of Historic Places. The small **Old Pioneer Museum**, 150 S State, is open from 9 am to 4 pm Monday to Friday. The **Wasatch Academy**, 120 S 100 West, is Utah's oldest continuously operating secondary school – it dates from 1875.

Mt Pleasant is 5 miles south of Fairview and has about 2000 inhabitants. Hwy 116 leads west to Moroni (see Nephi & Around, above). The city hall (☎ 435-462-2456), 115 W Main, has local information. The police (☎ 435-462-2724) are here, too. The area's hospital (☎ 435-462-2411) is at 1100 S Medical Drive.

Places to Stay & Eat

The *Mt Pleasant City Park* (☎ 435-462-2456) allows tents and RVs during the July celebrations here and in Manti.

Larsen House B&B (☎ 435-462-9337, 800-848-5263), 298 S State, Mt Pleasant, UT 84647, is a splendidly restored 1890s building with stained-glass windows and hand-painted designs on the ceiling. Six rooms with private baths rent for about $75 a double with full breakfast served in your room. Smoking is prohibited. There's also the *Fiddler's Green Inn B&B* (☎ 435-462-3276), 3564 W Hwy 116, Mt Pleasant, UT 84647, with three rooms.

The new *Horseshoe Mountain Resort* (☎ 435-462-9330, 800-462-9330), 850 S Hwy 89, has a pool, hot tub and restaurant (☎ 435-462-9533). Large rooms with microwave and refrigerator are $60 to $75, including continental breakfast.

There are several places to eat around Main and State – the town's major intersection. The *Backroads Restaurant* (☎ 435-462-3111), 70 State, serves American fare from 7:30 am to 10:30 pm daily.

SPRING CITY

Spring City is about 6 miles south of Mt Pleasant. Named after a spring that flows year-round, this village was settled in 1852 and has about 800 inhabitants. The whole town is on the National Register. The **city hall** (☎ 435-462-2244), 46 N Main, was built in 1893; you can get information and buy booklets describing the town's buildings there. On the Saturday before Memorial Day there is a tour of the old homes. There is also a small **DUP Museum** in the 1899 schoolhouse at 40 S 100 East.

The *Horseshoe Mountain Inn* (☎ 435-462-2871), 310 S Main, has three rooms for about $40, including breakfast, and allows camping. Nearby is the Horseshoe Mountain Pottery (☎ 435-462-2708), 278 S Main, where you can buy locally made ceramics and get local information.

EPHRAIM

Ephraim, with over 3000 inhabitants, is the biggest town in the area. It's also a major turkey-farming center. The town was settled in 1854 and has several historic buildings.

Information

The city offices (☎ 435-283-4631), 5 S Main, have local information. The Manti-La Sal National Forest Ephraim Ranger Station (☎ 435-283-4151), PO Box 692, Ephraim, UT 84627, is at 540 N Main. The library (☎ 435-283-5143) is at 30 S Main. The post office (☎ 435-283-4189) is at 45 E 100 North. The police (☎ 435-283-4602) are at 15 S Main.

Things to See & Do

The late-19th-century **Mercantile Co-op Store**, 100 North and Main, has been restored and is Ephraim's best known historic building. The two buildings south of it are also historic and house an art gallery and gift shop. Another noteworthy building is the Homestead B&B (see B&Bs, below). You can see other old buildings by just walking around.

Snow College, a junior college (☎ 435-283-4021) of more than 200 students at 150 E 100 North, dates to 1888 and provides much of the area's cultural life with concerts, plays and other performances – call for a schedule.

Special Events

The Scandinavian Festival held over Memorial Day weekend celebrates the Scandinavian heritage of Sanpete County. Now you know why so many of the locals are blond.

Places to Stay

Camping The USFS *Lake Hill Campground* is reached by heading east on 400 South and following Hwy 29 for 8 miles. The 12-site campground is at 8500 feet, has water and toilets but no showers, and is open June to October. Overnight use is $7. The road continues past an agricultural experimental station (with self-guiding trail) and on to the Skyline Drive about 5 miles away.

Motels Two small motels charge in the $30s: the *Iron Horse Motel* (☎ 435-283-4223), 670 N Main, and *Travel Inn Motel* (☎ 435-283-4071), 330 N Main. The new *Sleep Inn* (☎ 435-283-4566), 450 S Main, has a hot tub, VCR rentals and 58 rooms in the $50s, including continental breakfast. Prices increase dramatically during special events in the area.

B&Bs *Ephraim Homestead B&B* (☎ 435-283-6367), 135 W 100 North, Ephraim, UT 84627, features 'The Granary,' an 1860s two-story log cabin furnished with period pieces (spinning wheel, wood stove, fireplace, antique beds and claw-footed tub). It rents for $85 a couple, including breakfast delivered to your room. 'The Barn' was built in 1981, using old materials and furnished in 19th-century style. Two rooms sharing a bath rent for $45 and $55. Breakfast is served in the 1880s Victorian house where the owners live. Grounds include swings for kids and porches for adult relaxation. No smoking or liquor is allowed, but children are welcome and the owners are friendly. Units can sleep families.

There is also the *W Pherson House B&B* (☎ 435-238-4197), 224 S Main, with three rooms in the $60s and an antique store.

Places to Eat

The best of half a dozen simple places to eat along Main is the *Palate Pleaser* (☎ 435-283-5550), 89 S Main, open for lunch and dinner from Tuesday to Saturday.

MANTI

This is one of Utah's earliest towns, settled in 1849. It is overlooked and dominated by a magnificent temple dedicated by Brigham Young in 1877 and completed in 1888. Manti is the Sanpete County seat and has around 2000 inhabitants. There is a huge population increase during the annual Mormon pageant – a major highlight that attracts more than 100,000 visitors. Otherwise, there's little to do apart from looking at the particularly well-preserved old buildings.

Information

The History House Visitors Center (☎ 435-835-8411), 402 N Main, is two blocks from the temple and provides both local and church information during the summer. Sanpete County tourist information is available at ☎ 800-281-4346. The library (☎ 435-835-2201) is at 2 S Main. The post office (☎ 435-835-5081) is at 140 N Main. The small medical clinic (☎ 435-835-3344) is at 159 N Main. The police (☎ 435-835-2191) are at city hall, 50 S Main.

Palisade State Park

This park (☎ 435-835-7275, 800-322-3770 for reservations), PO Box 650070, Sterling, UT 84642-0249, offers opportunities for camping (see Places to Stay, below), swimming, fishing and nonmotorized boating. Canoes can be rented. There is an 18-hole golf course with pro shop (☎ 435-835-4653). Cross-country skiing, skating, tubing and ice fishing are winter activities. The park is 5 miles south of Manti (or 1 mile north of **Sterling**, which has a store and gas station) then 2 miles east on Palisade Lake Rd. Day use is $3.

Special Events

Mormon Miracle Pageant The pageant (☎ 435-835-3000) is a major Mormon Church event held annually since 1967. Several hundred performers tell the story of Mormon beginnings and migration to Utah, and the spectacle attracts over 100,000 visitors. Until 1996, it was held for over a week in mid-July; in 1997 it was held in late June. The pageant takes place on the grassy slopes of the hill below the Manti Temple (which is open only to Mormons on church business). The many visitors somewhat overwhelm the small town, and although the community copes valiantly, there has been talk of moving the pageant to a bigger location.

County Fair The Sanpete County Fair, featuring a rodeo, square dance, carnival, parade and other activities, is held around the third week of August.

Places to Stay

Camping *Yogi Bear's Jellystone Camp Park Resort* (☎ 435-835-2267), on Hwy 89 at the north end of Manti, has showers, a pool, playground, game room, coin laundry, store and various activities including Yogi Bear (in person to meet the kids) and horseback rides. The campground has 70 sites costing $17/21 without/with hookups.

The USFS *Manti Community Campground* (☎ 435-283-4151 in Ephraim), 7 miles east along 500 South and Manti Canyon, has seven sites ($7) from June to October. There are toilets and drinking water. The road continues 8 miles farther to the Skyline Drive and provides winter access to cross-country skiing and snowmobiling.

At Palisade State Park, there's a campground open from April to October that has hot showers. Fees are $11 for camping ($5 during winter without services). Campsites often fill on summer weekends.

Motels During the pageant, book in advance and expect substantially higher rates. Towns with more rooms are Ephraim (85 rooms, 8 miles), Salina (190 rooms, 33 miles), Richfield (nearly 500, 55 miles) and Nephi (nearly 200, 45 miles).

Manti Motel & Outpost (☎ 435-835-8533), 445 N Main, and *Temple View Lodge* (☎ 435-835-6663), 260 E 400 North (with great Temple views), have simple rooms around $40. The Manti Motel has kitchenettes in some rooms. *Manti Country Village* (☎ 435-835-9300, 800-452-0787, fax 435-835-6286), 145 N Main, is the biggest (23 rooms) and most comfortable motel, with large rooms, a spa and a restaurant. Rates are about $50.

On Hwy 89, 5 miles south of Manti, the *Palisade Lodge* (☎ 435-835-4513) has swimming pools, spas, a water slide, sauna, gym and racquetball. Over 50 rooms range from motel-style to family cottages to deluxe rooms, renting from about $40 to over $100. Camping areas are also available. There are barbecue and picnic areas but no restaurant.

B&Bs These are historic Mormon buildings with attractive period furniture, but they are renovated so all units have private bathrooms. None permit smoking.

The oldest is the *Brigham House Inn* (☎ 435-835-8381), 123 E Union, Manti, UT 84642, built in the 1860s and 1870s, with four rooms in the $60 to $80 range. The *Manti House Inn B&B* (☎/fax 435-835-0161), 401 N Main, has a restaurant open on weekends and sometimes at midweek – advance reservations are required. Its seven rooms and suites run $60 to $125. One suite has an in-room spa and balcony. The *Yardley B&B* (☎ 435-835-1861), 190 W 200 South, has five rooms for about $50 to $75 and a more expensive suite. Some rooms have four-poster beds or fireplaces. The *Old Grist Mill Inn B&B* (☎ 435-835-6455, fax 435-528-7798), 780 E 500 South, has nine rooms in a converted mill; rates are $55 and up. New B&Bs are opening; call the visitors center for details.

Just outside Palisade State Park, the *Cedar Crest Inn* (☎ 435-835-6352), 819 Palisade Lake Rd, has seven rooms. There is a hot tub and a restaurant (reservations essential); some rooms have refrigerators and microwaves. Rooms are $50 to $60; one two-bedroom unit is about $80.

Places to Eat

Choices (☎ 435-835-9550), 115 N Main, serves American meals all day. There are also a couple of fast-food places and a restaurant at the Manti Country Village.

During the pageant only, food concession stands appear near the temple.

GUNNISON

When settled in 1860, this town was given the delightful name of Hogs Wallow but was renamed in honor of Captain John Gunnison, who was killed near here by Indians. A park at the north end (intersection of Hwys 89 and 28) has a tourist information booth in summer as well as a pool and playground. Gunnison is 17 miles south of Manti.

Rooms, some having refrigerators and microwaves, are $40 to $50 at the 15-room *Gunnison Motel* (☎ 435-528-7840), 12 N Main. The tiny *Country Paradise Motel* (☎ 435-528-7521), 395 S Main, is cheaper. There are several simple restaurants.

SALINA

Hwy 89 intersects with I-70 exit 54 at Salina, 33 miles south of Manti, and the two highways continue together to the southwest for 30 miles. Settled in 1863, Salina (Spanish for 'salt mine') is known for its salt deposits. Locals find prime snowmobiling in Salina Canyon, along I-70 southeast of town. There are a few 19th-century buildings in Salina, but otherwise there's little of interest in this town of 2300 apart from several hotels serving travelers.

Orientation & Information

Salina is 1½ miles north of I-70, and there are hotels both in the center and by the freeway.

The city offices (☎ 435-529-7304), library (☎ 435-529-7753) and police (☎ 435-529-3311) are all at 90 W Main. You'll find the post office (☎ 435-529-7221) at 35 N

100 East. The medical clinic (☎ 435-529-7411) is at 310 W Main.

Places to Stay – Camping
Butch Cassidy Campground (☎/fax 435-529-7400), 1100 S State, has a pool, playground, showers and coin laundry. It is open year-round and charges $20 with full hookups in summer, less in other seasons. Tent sites are $6. *Salina Creek RV Camp* (☎ 435-529-3711), 1385 S State, has showers and coin laundry; only RV sites are available ($16).

The nearest USFS campground is *Maple Grove* (☎ 435-743-5721), 11 miles northwest on US 50, then 4 miles west. The campground is open mid-May to October and has toilets and water. Sites cost $6.

Places to Stay – Budget
Most hotels raise their prices from May to October. The *Lone Star Motel* (☎ 435-529-3642), 785 W Main, has simple, clean rooms in the $30s (summer rate). The *Wasatch Motel & Cafe* (☎ 435-529-7074), 395 W Main, also offers budget rooms.

Places to Stay – Middle
Henry's Hideaway (☎ 435-529-7467, fax 435-529-3671), 60 N State, has a pool, spa, laundry, restaurant and rooms with coffeemakers for $40 to $55, or $30 in winter.

Out near I-70, the *Budget Host Scenic Hills Motel* (☎ 435-529-7483, fax 435-529-3616), 75 E 1500 South, has reasonably sized, clean rooms, some with kitchenettes, for about $35 to $50. Nearby is the *Safari Motel & Restaurant* (☎/fax 435-529-7447), at 1425 S State, which has a pool and pleasant rooms for about $45 to $60. The *Best Western Shaheen Motel & Restaurant* (☎ 435-529-7455, fax 435-529-7257), 1225 S State, has a pool, restaurant and comfortable rooms for $55 to $70.

The *Victorian Inn B&B* (☎ 435-529-7342), 190 W Main, Salina, UT 84654, is a restored 1896 house. Four large rooms with king-size beds and antique bathtubs rent for $75 to $90, including full breakfast. Smoking is not permitted. It closes from September to May.

Places to Eat
Mom's Cafe (☎ 435-529-3921) is at 10 E Main, has been in Salina since 1929 and is locally popular. 'Mom' serves up home cooking at reasonable prices from 7 am to 10 pm.

The *Safari Restaurant* (☎ 435-529-7696) is a truck stop and service station – big meals for hungry drivers are served from 6 am to 10 pm (midnight in summer). *Shaheen's Restaurant* (☎ 435-529-7600, 435-529-7455), 1229 S State, is a coffee shop and steak house, open from 6 am to 10 pm. The restaurant at *Henry's Hideaway* is open from 7 am to 10 pm and has a lounge bar.

Getting There & Away
Greyhound buses (☎ 800-231-2222) stop at the Scenic Hills Motel, the only stop in Sevier County. No tickets are sold here.

RICHFIELD
Richfield was settled in 1864; now it's an important agricultural center as well as the largest town for 100 road miles in any direction. It has 6500 inhabitants and is the Sevier County seat.

Orientation & Information
Richfield lies east of I-70, between exits 37 in the south and 40 in the north.

There is an information booth (☎ 435-896-1789) in an 1880s building in the city park, 400 N Main, open daily (except Sunday) from 10 am to 7 pm in the summer. At other times call either the chamber of commerce (☎ 435-896-4241) in the basement of the county courthouse, 250 N Main, or the County Travel Council (☎ 435-896-8898, 800-662-8898). The Fishlake National Forest Richfield Ranger Station (☎ 435-896-9233), 115 E 900 North, Richfield, UT 84701, is open from 8 am to 5 pm, Monday to Friday. Also here is the BLM (☎ 435-896-8221).

The post office (☎ 435-896-6231) is at 93 N Main. The library (☎ 435-896-5169) is at 83 E Center. The hospital (☎ 435-896-8271) is at 1100 N Main. The police (☎ 435-896-8484) are at 75 E Center.

UTAH

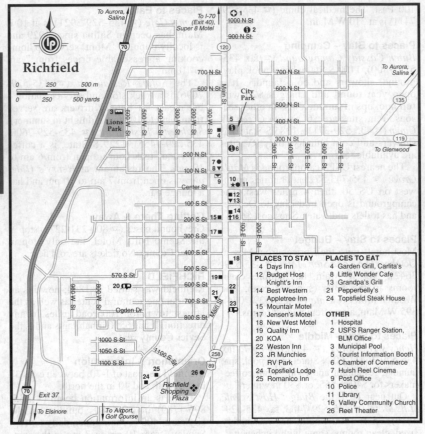

Richfield

PLACES TO STAY
4 Days Inn
12 Budget Host Knight's Inn
14 Best Western Appletree Inn
15 Mountair Motel
17 Jensen's Motel
18 New West Motel
19 Quality Inn
20 KOA
22 Weston Inn
23 JR Munchies RV Park
24 Topsfield Lodge
25 Romanico Inn

PLACES TO EAT
4 Garden Grill, Carlita's
8 Little Wonder Cafe
13 Grandpa's Grill
21 Pepperbelly's
24 Topsfield Steak House

OTHER
1 Hospital
2 USFS Ranger Station, BLM Office
3 Municipal Pool
5 Tourist Information Booth
6 Chamber of Commerce
7 Huish Reel Cinema
9 Post Office
10 Police
11 Library
16 Valley Community Church
26 Reel Theater

Things to See & Do

The information booth has a brochure detailing the town's historic buildings. Highlights include the **Ramsay Home**, 57 E 200 North, built in 1873 and now housing a small museum, open 11 am to 5 pm, Monday to Friday, in summer. Other buildings to see include the **post office**, built in 1917; the **library**, built by the Carnegie Foundation in 1913; behind it, a 19th-century **log house** called the Pioneer Relic Hall; and the **Valley Community Church**, 200 South and Main, built in 1880.

You can **golf** nine holes at the municipal course (☎ 435-896-9987), 1255 W

1700 South, or go **swimming** at the municipal pool (☎ 435-896-8572), 600 W 500 North, for $1.

Richfield is also an access point for the **Paiute ATV Trail** (see Fillmore & Around, above). Five Star Rental (☎ 435-896-7368), 25 E 900 North, rents ATVs.

Places to Stay – Camping

Richfield KOA (☎ 435-896-6674), 600 W 600 South, has showers, a pool (summer only), playground, game room, store and coin laundry. Sites are $16 or $20 with full hookups. *JR Munchies* (☎ 435-896-9340), 745 S Hwy 89, is an RV park (no tents) with hookups for about $15. It has showers and a coin laundry.

Places to Stay – Budget

Rates from June to September (given below) are several dollars higher than the rest of the year. *Jensen's Motel* (☎ 435-896-5447), 290 S Main, has basic rooms in the $20s or low $30s. The *New West Motel* (☎ 435-896-4076, fax 435-896-4520), 447 S Main, has nicer rooms in the $30s. *Topsfield Lodge & Steak House* (☎ 435-896-5437), 1200 S Main, has adequate rooms in the $30s. The similarly priced *Mountair Motel* (☎ 435-896-4415), 190 S Main, has a seasonal pool and a few more expensive rooms with kitchenettes.

Places to Stay – Middle

Motels in this section give $10 to $20 discounts off-season. The attractive and friendly *Romanico Inn* (☎ 435-896-8471, 800-948-0001), 1170 S Main, is a good deal with pleasant rooms for about $40, though it will often drop its price to match the bottom-end places. There is a spa and coin laundry, and some more expensive rooms have kitchenettes. Another decent choice is the *Budget Host Knight's Inn* (☎/fax 435-896-8228), 69 S Main, which has a pool and a restaurant next door and charges $44/54 single/double.

The *Super 8 Motel* (☎ 435-896-9204, fax 435-896-9614), 1575 N Main (by exit 40), has nice rooms for $49/53 for singles/doubles with one bed – more for two beds. Restaurants are close by. The *Weston Inn* (☎ 435-896-9271, fax 435-896-6864), 647 S Main, has similar prices and good rooms. Facilities include a restaurant, indoor pool and spa.

The remaining chain hotels all have more than 50 rooms. Both the *Days Inn* (☎ 435-896-6476), 333 N Main, and the *Quality Inn* (☎ 435-896-5465), 540 S Main, have a pool, spa and exercise room. The Days Inn has a restaurant and bar; its rooms have refrigerators and rent for about $60/70 for singles/doubles. The Quality Inn has some rooms with kitchenettes and a few suites with private spas. Their rates, which include continental breakfast, range from $45/55 for standard rooms or up to $90 for larger units.

The *Best Western Appletree Inn* (☎ 435-896-5481, fax 435-896-9465), 145 S Main, has a pool and rates include continental breakfast. Spacious rooms are about $50/60 for singles/doubles, more with two beds. A few two-room units are about $80 to $100.

Places to Eat

The *Little Wonder Cafe* (☎ 435-896-8960), 101 N Main, is a locally popular diner serving cheap breakfasts and lunches from 6 am to 5 pm. *Pepperbelly's* (☎ 435-896-2097), 680 S Main, serves decent Mexican food in unusual 1950s gas station surroundings. Hours are 11 am to 9:30 pm, Monday to Thursday, till 10:30 pm on Friday and Saturday.

Otherwise, hotel restaurants are your best bet. *Grandpa's Grill* (☎ 435-896-1742), 89 S Main, next to the Budget Host Knight's Inn, has inexpensive American meals and serves breakfast all day. The more upscale *Garden Grill* and *Carlita's* are both in the Days Inn (☎ 435-896-6476). The Garden Grill serves American food from 6 am to 10 pm daily. Carlita's serves Mexican dinners and has a liquor license. The *Topsfield Lodge Steak House* (☎ 435-896-5437), 1200 S Main, is open from 5:30 to 10 pm Monday to Saturday. The fireplace makes this a homey restaurant, with good steaks and seafood mainly in the $10 to $18 range.

Entertainment

The *Reel Theater*, 1150 S Hwy 89, and the *Huish Reel* (both ☎ 435-896-4400), 131 N Main, show movies.

Getting There & Away

The nearest Greyhound stop is in Salina (see Getting There & Away in the Salina section, above).

MONROE

This small town of 1800 inhabitants was first settled in 1864 and retains several early buildings. Monroe is located 10 miles south of Richfield on minor roads. Just east of town are the **Mystic Hot Springs**

(☎ 435-527-3286), with a natural soaking pool open all year, heated swimming pool open in summer, showers and tent/RV camping for $10/15. The springs are free for campers; $5 for others.

Peterson's B&B (☎ 435-527-4830), 95 N 300 West, Monroe, UT 84754, is open from April to October with two rooms for $65 double, including full breakfast. Smoking is prohibited.

FREMONT INDIAN STATE PARK

The Fremont Indians, who lived throughout much of Utah, were contemporaries with but distinct from the Ancestral Puebloans, who lived to the south during the roughly 1000 years leading up to the 15th century. The Fremont culture is poorly understood – this state park outlines some of our current knowledge of these people.

The visitor center (☎ 435-527-4631) has good exhibits, particularly of prehistoric rock art. Two very short trails (wheelchair accessible) pass petroglyphs on nearby cliffs, and there is a longer nature trail as well. Rangers lead interpretive walks and give talks in summer. The center is open 9 am to 5 pm daily (to 6 pm in summer) except New Year's Day, Thanksgiving and Christmas. Admission is $5 per car or $2 for walkers and bikers. Rangers know of good local mountain-biking routes.

The park is near I-70 exit 17. The *Castle Rock Campground*, 3 miles from the visitor center in the Fishlake National Forest (☎ 800-322-3770 for reservations) has toilets and drinking water and is open from April to October. Sites are $7 and include park admission.

From a short distance west of the park, USFS Rd 113 heads south to the remains of the old mining town **Kimberly** and continues east to Marysvale. Alternatively, after Kimberly, take USFS Rd 123 south, emerging at Beaver Canyon (Hwy 153 east of Beaver). Between 6000 and 11,000 feet above sea level, these Fishlake National Forest roads are packed dirt, but are often passable to cars in dry weather; all are closed by snow in winter and spring. Summer wildflowers, fall colors,

fine views of 12,000-foot peaks in the Tushar Range and glimpses of wildlife make this a good way to leave or access the Fremont Indian State Park.

MARYSVALE

This small town of 400 is an access point for the Paiute ATV Trail (see Fillmore & Around, above). Local businesses rent out ATVs and horses – guides are available. Marysvale hosts a rodeo in July. The town is on Hwy 89, 11 miles south of I-70. Hwy 89 continues south for 16 miles to Junction (see the Southwestern Utah chapter).

Places to Stay & Eat

The *4-U Motel* (☎ 435-326-4388) and the *Sportsman's Lodge & Cafe* (☎ 435-326-4258), both in the town center, each have basic rooms in the $20s and $30s. Nearby, *Moore's Old Pine Inn* (☎ 435-326-4565, 888-887-4565) claims to be Utah's oldest historic hotel and has nine rooms, suites and cabins from $40 to $90, including breakfast.

Five miles north on Hwy 89 is the *Big Rock Candy Mountain Resort* (☎ 435-326-2000, 888-560-7625). The mountain is a multicolored massif on the west side of the road, which bears a resemblance to a giant pile of candy and was made famous in a song by Burl Ives. The supposedly therapeutic mineral waters from the mountain are bottled and sold. The resort has nine large modern motel rooms (each named after a candy, with a complimentary bag in each room) for $59, and seven cabins for $39 to $89. All are nonsmoking and have TVs and telephones. There is a restaurant, hot tub, one-hour float trips on the Sevier River, ATV and mountain-bike rentals, horseback rides, a camping area, grocery and souvenir store.

East of the Wasatch Plateau

This section begins with the coal-mining towns of Carbon County and continues southeast along Hwy 10 through the towns of the Castle Valley. This colorful but dry region was settled relatively late in the 1870s and 1880s, after pioneers had settled the moister valleys west of the Wasatch Plateau. The many imposing buttes and austere eroded geological formations in the area led to it being locally called 'Castle Country.'

The discovery of coal and the arrival of the railway in 1883 attracted many immigrants from diverse backgrounds to Carbon County, and the Mormon heritage that predominates in the valleys west of here is diluted. The towns in this area, of which Price is the most important, are between 5000 and 6000 feet above sea level.

HELPER

Named after the 'helper' locomotives that once pulled coal-laden trains over the steep Soldier Summit nearby, Helper was a major railroad and coal-mining center. Today, many historic buildings along Main are boarded up or for sale. Nevertheless, almost 3000 people still live here, the train continues to stop every day, a good museum is worth visiting and art galleries and gift shops are attempting to revitalize downtown. Price, 10 miles to the southeast, has information and other visitor services.

Things to See & Do
The **Western Mining & Railroad Museum** (☎ 435-472-3009), 296 S Main, is a good introduction to the area. Models, photographs, artifacts, paintings and audio-visual displays describe anything from mining disasters to Butch Cassidy holdups. Outside is a collection of antique mining and railroad equipment. The museum is open 10 am to 6 pm Monday to Saturday, from May to September, and noon to 5 pm, Tuesday to Saturday, October to April. A donation is suggested.

The museum is in a 1914 hotel; other turn-of-the-century buildings along Main have put Helper on the National Register.

The **Bristlecone Ridge Hiking Trail** at *Price Canyon Campground* leads up into the mountains nearby, gaining almost 700 feet in 1 mile and reaching an area

Bristlecone pines are the oldest living things on earth.

where bristlecone pines can be seen – the oldest living things on earth. Deer are also often seen. The campground, 8 miles north of Helper, is run by the BLM (☎ 435-636-3600 in Price). It's open from June to October, has water but no showers and costs $6. There is a picnic area.

In December, Helper's Christmas lights display is especially colorful, which is why Helper is called **Utah's Christmas Town**. Lights are turned on in the last

Butch Cassidy
Local historians tell how Butch Cassidy, along with two others, pulled off a major payroll heist at the Castle Gate Mine office in 1897. (The town of Castle Gate was just north of Helper. The mine closed and the town is no longer.) One of Cassidy's accomplices was shot the next year by a posse who thought they had killed Cassidy. When the robber was buried, Cassidy himself is said to have shown up to watch the proceedings. ∎

week of November and an electric light parade takes place on the second weekend in December.

Getting There & Away

Bus The Greyhound bus has a flag stop (bus stops on demand only) as it passes Helper between Price and Provo.

Train Amtrak (☎ 800-872-7245) has daily trains through Denver, Colorado to Chicago, Illinois and to Provo with connections to Salt Lake City. The train station is near the Western Mining & Railroad museum.

SCOFIELD STATE PARK

At almost 7600 feet above sea level, Scofield Reservoir is one of the highest in the state. The park on its shores offers a short summer season of boating, fishing and water-skiing. During winter, ice fishing, cross-country skiing and snowmobiling are popular. Campgrounds on the north and east sides of the reservoir are open from May to September or October; they offer showers, boat-launch facilities and fish-cleaning areas. Day use is $4; camping is $11.

Information is available from PO Box 166, Price, UT 84501-0166. Call ☎ 435-448-9449 in summer or ☎ 435-637-8497 in winter. Trail maps showing snowmobile trails climbing up to Skyline Drive are available in winter. The park is about 14 miles northwest of Helper on Hwy 6, then 12 miles southwest on Hwy 96. It can also be reached from Fairview via Hwy 31 and Hwy 264 – a steep route that crosses the Skyline Drive and is closed in winter.

The tiny mining town of Scofield, just south of the reservoir, was the site of Utah's most disastrous mining accident (described at the museum in Helper). Tombstones of victims can still be seen in the town cemetery.

PRICE

Founded as an agricultural center in 1879 and named after William Price, an early Mormon bishop, Price quickly became a coal-mining and railroad center, attracting immigrants from many countries. This diverse heritage is celebrated during Price's annual events.

Coal mining continues to be important. Uranium and natural gas are also mined, and there is some farming in the area. The Carbon County seat and home of the College of Eastern Utah, Price has almost 10,000 inhabitants. The town, which has an excellent museum, is a good base for exploring the area.

Orientation

Hwy 6 is the major highway. It skirts Price to the west and south with three freeway-style exits enabling drivers to enter town. Street names such as 1st North and 100 North are both used in Price; in this chapter, I use the 100 North system.

Information

The Castle Country Travel Office (☎ 435-637-3009, 800-842-0789) and the chamber of commerce (☎ 435-637-2788) are both at 90 N 100 E and are open from 9 am to 5 pm, Monday to Friday. The Prehistoric Museum next door has some tourist information during museum hours. The Manti-La Sal National Forest Price Ranger Station (☎ 435-637-2817) is at 599 W Price River Drive. The BLM (☎ 435-636-3600), 125 S 600 West, is open from 7:45 am to 4:30 pm, Monday to Friday. The post office (☎ 435-637-1638) is at 95 S Carbon Ave. The library (☎ 435-636-3188) is at 159 E Main. The hospital (☎ 435-637-4800) is west of town at 300 N Hospital Drive. The police (☎ 435-636-3190) are at 81 N 200 East.

College of Eastern Utah Prehistoric Museum

The collection at this museum (☎ 435-637-5060), 155 E Main, is a fine surprise. Several well-displayed dinosaur skeletons, plenty of superb Indian artifacts, a kids' area, local art and a good gift shop combine to make this a recommended stop. It's free but deserves a donation ($2 per adult is suggested). Hours are 9 am to 6 pm Monday to Saturday, and noon to 5 pm on Sunday from April to September; 9 am to 5 pm Monday to Saturday the rest of the year.

UTAH

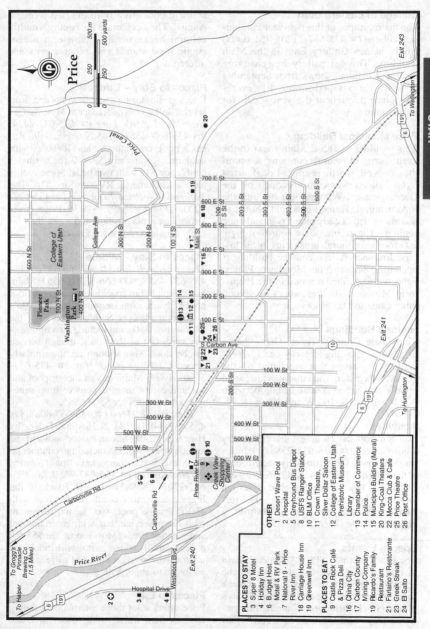

Price

500 m
500 yards
0   250   500
0   250   500

To Wellington

To Helper

To Grogg's Pinnacle Brewing Co (1.5 Miles)

Exit 243

Exit 241

Exit 240

College of Eastern Utah

Pioneer Park

Washington Park

Price River

Price River Dr

Carbonville Rd

Westwood Blvd

Hospital Drive

Creek View Shopping Center

Price Canal

College Ave

600 N St
500 N St
400 N St
300 N St
200 N St
100 N St
Main St
100 E St
200 E St
300 E St
400 E St
500 E St
600 E St
700 E St
100 S St
200 S St
300 S St
400 S St
500 S St
600 S St
S Carbon Ave
100 W St
200 W St
300 W St
400 W St
500 W St
600 W St

To Huntington

PLACES TO STAY
3 Super 8 Motel
4 Holiday Inn
6 Budget Host Motel & RV Park
7 National 9 - Price River Inn
18 Carriage House Inn
19 Greenwell Inn

PLACES TO EAT
9 Castle Rock Café & Pizza Deli
16 China City
17 Carbon County Mining Company
19 Farlaino's Restorante
21 Ricardo's Family Restaurant
23 Greek Streak
24 El Salto

OTHER
1 Desert Wave Pool
2 Hospital
5 Greyhound Bus Depot
8 USFS Ranger Station
10 BLM Office
11 Crown Theatre, Silver Dollar Saloon
12 College of Eastern Utah Prehistoric Museum, Library
13 Chamber of Commerce
14 Police
15 Municipal Building (Mural)
20 King-Coal Theaters
22 Mecca Club & Cafe
25 Price Theatre
26 Post Office

College of Eastern Utah

The main campus of this two-year community college (☎ 435-637-2120), 451 E 400 North, houses **Gallery East** in the Main Building. This art gallery has changing local and national shows from September to June. Various performing arts events take place throughout the year – call for information.

Price Municipal Building

This building at 185 E Main (next to the Prehistoric Museum) contains a mural that is well worth seeing. Local artist Lynn Faucett was commissioned by the Depression-era WPA project to paint the indoor mural. Faucett used old photos to accurately depict early pioneers in authentic settings. The result is a four-foot-high, 200-foot-long mural illustrating local history. Entrance is free and the building is open from 8 am to 5 pm Monday to Friday. Faucett also painted a mural in the Prehistoric Museum; she has works in several other cities and states as well.

Historic Buildings

The Castle Country Travel Office has a brochure detailing nearby early-20th-century buildings that are listed on the National Register. The buildings are found mainly on Carbon Ave and Main between 300 N and 100 S, 100 W and 200 E.

Activities

You can **golf** the 18-hole Carbon Country Club Course (☎ 435-637-2388), 4 miles north of town. Or **swim** daily, year-round, at the Desert Wave Pool (☎ 435-637-7946), 240 E 500 North. The complex offers lap swimming as well as wave action. The surrounding Washington Park has **tennis**, a playground and other facilities.

Special Events

The Black Diamond PRCA Rodeo is held in mid to late June. Greek Days on the second weekend in July offers Greek food, music, dancing and tours of Utah's oldest Greek Orthodox Church. International Days and the Carbon County Fair are held concurrently in the first week in August. They celebrate the county's multicultural background; a parade, a rodeo, ethnic-food stands and other events are offered.

Places to Stay – Budget

Prices go up during special events and drop several dollars from October to May. *Budget Host Motel & RV Park* (☎ 435-637-2424, fax 435-637-4551), 145 N Carbonville Rd, has a pool, coin laundry and RV sites with hookups. Rooms are $35/40 for a single/double, or $45 with two beds. Some rooms have a kitchenette. RV sites are $16. The *National 9 – Price River Inn* (☎ 435-637-7000, 435-637-8889), 641 W Price River Drive, has a playground and more than 90 fairly standard rooms for $38/46.

Places to Stay – Middle

The *Greenwell Inn* (☎ 435-637-3520, fax 435-637-4858, 800-666-3520), 655 E Main, has 125 plain but spacious rooms, an indoor pool and spa, exercise rooms and Ricardo's Restaurant adjacent. Summer rates are in the $40s or low $50s and include a complimentary breakfast at Ricardo's, though service can be slow. Almost opposite, the similarly priced *Carriage House Inn* (☎ 435-637-5660), 590 E Main, has an indoor pool and spa and a few more expensive mini-suites with kitchenettes for $50 to $65.

The *Super 8 Motel* (☎ 435-637-8088, fax 435-637-8483), 181 N Hospital Drive (by Hwy 6 exit 240), has an indoor pool and spa and charges $48/55, including continental breakfast. Some rooms have spas. Nearby, the *Holiday Inn* (☎ 435-637-8880, fax 435-637-7707), 838 Westwood Blvd, is the biggest and most comfortable hotel with 150 rooms, a pool, spa, sauna, restaurant with room service, bar with entertainment and meeting areas. Most rooms are $55/60; a few small suites with whirlpools or microwaves, refrigerators and coffeemakers go for up to about $90.

Places to Eat

Price offers a lot more international dining choices than most small towns in Utah.

The *Greek Streak* (☎ 435-637-1930), 84 S Carbon Ave, is a little hole-in-the-wall place serving some of the best Greek snacks and pastries in Utah. It is open from 7 am to 9 pm, Monday to Saturday. For Mexican food, try the inexpensive and good *El Salto* (☎ 435-637-6545), 19 S Carbon Ave, which is closed on Sunday. *China City* (☎ 435-637-8211), 350 E Main, serves steak, seafood and Chinese fare from 11 am to 10 pm daily. *Farlaino's Restorante* (☎ 435-637-9217), 87 W Main, serves Italian dinners from 5:30 to 9 pm, Wednesday to Saturday; *Farlaino's Cafe* on the same premises is open for breakfast and lunch from 7 am to 2 pm Monday to Saturday.

The *Carbon County Mining Company* (☎ 435-637-9959), 355 E Main, is locally popular for good steaks and 'Italian night' on Wednesdays. The *Castle Rock Café & Pizza Deli* (☎ 435-637-8480), 700 W Price River Drive (in the Creek View Shopping Center) is open 9:30 am to 9 pm daily and is a good bet for pizzas and sandwiches. *Grogg's Pinnacle Brewing Co* (☎ 435-637-2914), 1653 N Carbonville Rd (2 miles northwest of town), has microbrewed beers and serves pizzas, steaks and other food. Hours are 11 am to 10 pm, Monday to Thursday, to 11 pm on Friday and Saturday, and noon to 8 pm on Sunday.

Ricardo's (☎ 435-637-2020) in the Greenwell Inn offers midpriced American and Mexican meals from 6 am to 9 pm. The *Holiday Inn Restaurant* (☎ 435-637-8880) is a more upmarket American restaurant, open from 6 am to 10 pm.

Entertainment

Movies are shown at *King-Coal Theaters* (☎ 435-637-1233), 1171 E Main, *Crown Theatre* (☎ 435-637-1705), 30 W Main, and *Price Theatre* (☎ 435-637-2740), 30 E Main.

For a beer, try *Mecca Club & Cafe* (☎ 435-637-9958), 75 W Main, which is in the 1913 Mahleres-Siampenos Building and has been a bar (with many different names) since the building was constructed. (It serves meals, too.) Across the street, the *Silver Dollar* (☎ 435-637-9446), 36 W Main, has live music on weekends. There are several other bars within a block.

Getting There & Away

The Greyhound bus (☎ 435-637-7153) stops at the Phillips 66 Service Station, 277 N Carbonville Rd, with one or two daily buses to Green River and Denver, Colorado or to Salt Lake City.

See Helper for train information.

WELLINGTON

There's little reason to stop in this mining town of 1800 people, 5 miles southeast of Price, unless you want a meal or a place to stay. Pioneer Day (July 24) is celebrated with a rodeo and other events.

Two miles east of Wellington, off Hwy 6/191, is the signed turnoff to the north along Soldier Creek Rd to the **Nine Mile Canyon** backroad, described in the Northeastern Utah chapter.

Hwy 6/191 continues 54 miles southeast of Wellington to intersect with I-70. Green River, 4 miles east of this intersection, is described in the Southeastern Utah chapter.

Places to Stay & Eat

The *Mountain View RV Park* and the *National 9 Inn* (☎ 435-637-7980, fax 435-637-8929) are both at 50 S 700 East. The RV park charges $14 with hookups; there is a playground and RVers can use the hotel facilities. RV park facilities are limited from mid-November to mid-March – no water. The hotel has an indoor pool and decent rooms for about $35/45 for singles/doubles. Also at this address is the *Outlaw Café* (☎ 435-637-6884), open daily from 5 am to 10 pm (from 6 am in winter and from 7 am on Sundays). The food is inexpensive American cooking, and breakfast is served all day. Check out the photos of famous outlaws on the walls.

There's also the small and basic *Pillow Talk Motel* (☎ 435-637-7706), 430 E Main, with cheaper rooms.

Cowboy's Country Kitchen (☎ 435-637-4223), 31 E Main just off Hwy 6/191, is a locally popular country-style steak house and lounge bar with dancing on occasion.

HUNTINGTON & AROUND

This mining town, settled in 1878, has 2800 inhabitants. The massive Huntington Canyon Power Plant is 9 miles west of town and can be seen from several miles away. Huntington is 20 miles south of Price on Hwy 10.

Cleveland-Lloyd Dinosaur Quarry

This National Natural Landmark is operated by the BLM (☎ 435-636-3600 in Price). Over a dozen species of dinosaur were buried here 150 million years ago, and their fossilized bones are currently being excavated. A visitor center has information and a gift shop; behind this is a large hut built over the quarry itself. Within, you can see partially excavated dinosaurs and the tools used to uncover them. If the quarry building is closed, there's not much to see – certainly no dinosaur fossils lying around for the casual collector! A short nature walk and a driving tour through the stark high desert scenery are available.

The quarry and visitor center are open daily from 10 am to 5 pm, Memorial Day to Labor Day, and on weekends from Easter to Memorial Day, but phone the BLM to confirm. The site is remote (I saw a North American badger crossing a road near the quarry) and accessible only by dirt roads passable by car in dry weather but not in wet or snowy conditions. Hwy 155 to the quarry leaves Hwy 10 eight miles north of Huntington; it is 17 miles to the site.

Cedar Mountain Overlook

Six miles west of the quarry, a dirt road heads south for 20 miles, climbing 2000 feet through forest to the overlook. There are fine views, a short nature trail, interpretive geological markers, toilets and picnic areas. The road is closed by snow in winter and passable to cars only when dry. The BLM has maps and information.

Desert Lake State Waterfowl Reserve

This small lake is a few miles northwest of the dinosaur quarry (there are signs). Reserve headquarters (☎ 435-653-2900) are in the village of Elmo. This is an unusual marsh and lake area in the desert – waterfowl and shorebirds pass through in spring and summer. During the summer, access is limited when the birds are breeding, so call ahead.

Huntington State Park

This park (☎ 435-687-2491), PO Box 1343, Huntington, UT 84528, is 2 miles north of town. A lake offers fishing, boating, waterskiing and swimming. Ice skating, cross-country skiing and ice fishing are all possible winter activities. There are picnic areas and a campground with showers, which are turned off in winter. Day use is $4; camping is $11.

Huntington Canyon

Hwy 31 west of town leads up to the Skyline Drive and down to Fairview, 44 miles away (both described earlier in this chapter). The scenic road parallels Huntington Creek for part of its length and provides access to Manti-La Sal National Forest campgrounds and fishing areas and, in winter, to snowmobiling and cross-country skiing. Look for beaver dams across the creek.

Places to Stay & Eat

Campgrounds in Huntington Canyon, with water and toilets but no showers, are located at *Bear Creek* (8 miles), *Forks of Huntington* (18 miles) and *Old Folks Flat* (21 miles from Huntington). Sites are open from June to September and cost $6. Beyond are several highland lakes (for fishing and boating) as well as hiking trails. The ranger station in Price has complete details and maps of the area.

The *Village Inn Motel* (☎ 435-687-9888), 310 S Main, has decent rooms, some with kitchenettes, for $34 to $46. The *Canyon Rim Cafe* (☎ 435-687-9040), 505 N Main, serve meals from 6 am to 8 pm daily.

CASTLE DALE & AROUND

Nine miles south of Huntington, Castle Dale was settled in 1875. The town is the Emery County seat and has a population of about 2000. As with other towns in the area, mining has been the main industry and continues to be so, despite a disastrous fire that killed 27 miners in 1984. A block south of the museum outside the courthouse is the Wilberg Memorial, commemorating the miners.

The chamber of commerce (☎ 435-381-2547) is at 410 E Main.

Museum of the San Rafael

This modern new museum (☎ 435-381-5252), 96 N 100 East, was built to house dinosaurs excavated in Emery County. Other exhibits highlight the geology and natural history of the San Rafael, Indian artifacts (including the famous Sitterud Bundle) and occasional local art shows. Hours are 10 am to 4 pm, Monday to Saturday year-round, and noon to 4 pm on Sundays in summer. A donation of $2 per adult is suggested.

County Pioneer Museum

This museum (☎ 435-381-5154) in the city hall diagonally across from the Museum of the San Rafael, features historical displays and re-creations of pioneer homes and buildings. Hours are 10 am to 4 pm, Monday to Friday, and noon to 4 pm on Saturday. Admission is by donation.

Joes Valley Reservoir

Paved Hwy 29 goes westward from Hwy 10, 2 miles north of Castle Dale, through Orangeville and along Cottonwood Creek to Joes Valley Reservoir in the Manti-La Sal National Forest, 22 miles away. (Ranger stations in Price and Ferron have information.) There are three monuments along the route with parking and historical markers. Campgrounds are available (see below). A small marina rents boats in summer and a store and restaurant are open May to early November. Cross-country skiing is popular in winter when mule deer are often seen.

West of the reservoir, a dirt road (passable in dry weather only) climbs about 15 miles to the Skyline Drive.

San Rafael River & Swell

This geologically interesting area southeast of Castle Dale is remote and rarely visited – it used to be the hideout of outlaws. Much of it is BLM land; the office in Price has maps and information. You can explore by 4WD and camp almost anywhere, but be prepared in case you break down – you may not see other people.

The best road is a gravel one that leaves Hwy 10 two miles north of Castle Dale. After 13 miles, a signed turn to the south leads 6 miles to **Wedge Overlook**, which offers great views of the San Rafael River, 1200 feet below, and mountainous buttes in the distance. Returning from the overlook to the 'main' road, you can continue southeast on the Buckhorn Draw Rd for 30 miles or so to emerge at exit 129 on I-70, 30 miles west of Green River. The road crosses the San Rafael River on a suspension bridge – there is a campground near with toilets but no drinking water. The road is normally passable in ordinary cars except after heavy snow or rain.

The swell continues south of I-70 and into southeastern Utah – see San Rafael Desert and Goblin Valley State Park in the Southeastern Utah chapter.

Special Events

The historical Castle Valley Pageant in late July or early August is a reenactment of the pioneering history of the valley. Also in August is the Emery County Fair with horse races and a rodeo.

Places to Stay & Eat

At Joes Valley Reservoir is the USFS-run *Joes Valley Campground*, with water but no showers, open from late May to mid-October. Sites are $8 for one car, $15 for two. About 10 miles before the reservoir, an unpaved road follows Cottonwood Creek to the north, reaching *Indian Creek Campground* in another 10 miles. The campground is operated by the USFS from June to September, has water but no showers and costs $6.

The *Village Inn Motel* (☎ 435-381-2309, fax 435-381-5121), 375 E Main, has a couple dozen rooms, some with kitchenettes, in the $30s. Opposite is *Big Mama's Pizza & Deli* (☎ 435-381-5080), 340 E

Main, which may be closed on Sundays. There are also a couple of fast-food outlets.

FERRON

Settled in 1877, Ferron is surrounded by mountains covered with salt deposits. This town is 11 miles south of Castle Dale and has 1800 inhabitants. The city hall (☎ 435-384-2350), 15 S State, has information. The Manti-La Sal National Forest Ferron Ranger Station (☎ 435-384-2372, 435-384-2505), PO Box 310, Ferron, UT 84523, is at 98 S State.

Things to See & Do

The **Presbyterian Church** was built in 1907 and is on the National Register.

Millsite State Park (☎ 435-384-2552) is 4 miles west of town and has a nine-hole **golf course** (☎ 435-384-2887) and a lake with boat launch facilities (day use $4) and camping. Ice fishing is popular in winter and trout fishing is popular at other times.

Ferron Canyon is west of the state park and within the Manti-La Sal National Forest. A good dirt road passes several overlooks before reaching **Ferron Reservoir**, 28 miles away and the Skyline Drive,

2 miles beyond. The road is open from about June to September. There is camping, a boat launch area, and a lodge with cabins, a café and boat rentals. In winter, the canyon is a popular snowmobiling and cross-country skiing route.

Special Events

The Southern Utah Junior Livestock Show takes place in July. The city's main festival is Peach Days, which has been celebrated annually since mid-September 1906.

Places to Stay & Eat

The campground at *Millsite State Park* is open all year, has showers in summer and charges $11. The USFS *Ferron Reservoir Campground* has water but no showers and is open mid-June to mid-September for $7. Also by the reservoir, the *Sky Haven Lodge* (☎ 435-748-2224, 435-835-5342 in Manti) rents cabins in summer.

Castle Country Motel (☎ 435-384-2311), 45 S State, has a dozen run-down rooms for about $30. Next door, Tony's serves breakfast, lunch and dinner. *Gilly's Inn & Convenience Store* (☎ 435-384-3333), 15 N State, has nine nicer rooms for $37/43 (singles/doubles). The store closes at 10 pm.

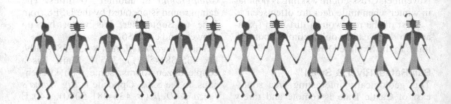

Southwestern Utah

Locals call this part of the state 'Color Country' and colorful it certainly is. Almost every imaginable hue of red, from subtle pinks to vivid vermilions, seems to be represented in the wonderfully odd geological formations – and not only red but shades of orange, gray, yellow, brown and even blue can be seen. The shifting position and intensity of the sun, coupled with seasonal changes, make every vista a unique one. The landscape is mind-blowing and has to be seen to be believed.

An older nickname for the area is 'Dixie,' because the warm climate reminded early settlers of states in the southern USA – the settlers even grew cotton here. Indeed, much of the area is now part of the Dixie National Forest.

Relatively little is known of the Indians who lived in this part of Utah. Ancestral Puebloans inhabited the area from about 1400 years ago and their pictographs can be seen, but little remains in the way of buildings as found in other parts of the Southwest. Small groups of Paiute Indians were living in southwestern Utah when the first Europeans arrived – in this case, the Spanish Domínguez-Escalante missionaries who quickly passed through in 1776. During the next 75 years, a few Anglos explored the area, but it was not until the Mormons arrived in 1851 that permanent white settlement occurred.

Mormon history tells of how the pioneers tried to befriend the Indians with gifts of food and clothing. Nevertheless, the Paiute did not take kindly to Mormons turning large tracts of land into towns, ranches, farms and mines. The Indians lost their best hunting grounds and water supplies, thus disrupting their traditional way of life. Instead, they were encouraged to live like white people – not an easy or alluring option. Few Indians wished to change and, inevitably, there were several wars in the 1850s and 1860s.

Settlement of this part of Utah continued the historical pattern set in central Utah; two main Mormon pioneering routes can be identified. Interstate 15 now follows the main route used by Mormons to extend their influence into the southern part of the state. They were attracted by both iron mining and lower elevations in the area. Accordingly, Brigham Young sent out large groups of Mormon families to settle the region, extract much-needed iron and establish St George at a warm 2880-foot elevation. This town, which later became Brigham Young's winter home, is now by far the largest city in the southern two-thirds of the state, though its population of only 45,000 attests to the low population density of the southern Utahan wilderness.

The second Mormon pioneering route was on the east side of the Markagunt Plateau, along what today is Hwy 89. Several early towns can be visited and this route gives excellent access to forests, mountains, and Zion and Bryce Canyon National Parks on either side. Hwy 9 joins I-15 and Hwy 89, passing through Zion National Park – a spectacular but very narrow, steep and switchbacking road that poses problems for RVs and other large vehicles.

This chapter follows these two corridors from north to south and ends with the lovely drive along Hwy 12 from Bryce Canyon to Capitol Reef National Park.

I-15 Corridor & Zion National Park

East of I-15, the mountains start high in the 12,000-foot Tushars east of Beaver, drop to 11,000 in the Markagunt Plateau east of Cedar City and drop farther to about 7000 feet in Zion National Park east of St George.

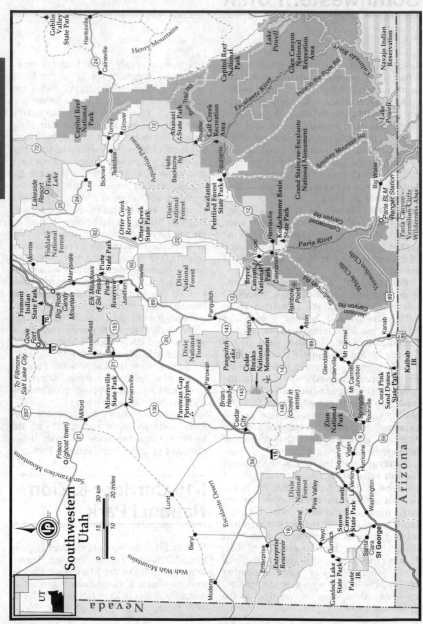

BEAVER

Settled by Mormons in 1856, Beaver was named after the beaver dams (no longer seen) on the nearby river. It became the gateway of a mining boom to the west soon after its founding. Beaver was a tense place to live in the early days, with differences between the rough, tough miners and the Mormon farmers escalating to occasional violence. The area was a fitting background for the birthplace of outlaw Butch Cassidy, who was born here in 1866 and grew up in nearby Junction.

Today the town is the Beaver County seat, has more than 2000 inhabitants and is both an agricultural center and a crossroads town with a good hotel selection. I-15 runs north-south. Hwy 153 leads eastward into the high Tushar Mountains, which offer winter skiing and cool summer recreation. Hwy 21 heads west into the deserts of western Utah.

Information

The Beaver County Travel Council (☎ 435-438-2975, 800-280-2975) has an office open in summer in the log cabin behind the library. The Fishlake National Forest Beaver Ranger Station (☎ 435-438-2436) is at 575 S Main, Beaver, UT 84713. The post office (☎ 435-438-2321) is at 20 S Main. The library (☎ 435-438-5274) is at 55 W Center. The hospital (☎ 435-438-2531) is at 85 N 400 East. The police (☎ 435-438-2862) are at 40 S 100 East.

Old Courthouse Museum

This three-story Victorian brick building, 90 E Center, was constructed between 1877 and 1882 and served as a courthouse for almost a century. Now it's a small museum with Indian and pioneer artifacts and geological exhibits. The old basement jail can be toured – call Donna Spencer (☎ 435-438-2898) for an appointment. The museum is open from 11 am to 5 pm, Tuesday to Saturday, from June to August. There is a small outlet for local handicrafts.

Historic Buildings

Scores of other late-19th- and early-20th-century buildings appear throughout the town center, many of them noted on the National Register of Historic Places. Several can be seen (from the outside) between Center and 200 North, and between 400 West and 300 East. Parts of **Fort Cameron**, built in 1872 by the US Army to keep peace between miners and Mormons, are seen at the east end of town along 200 North.

Minersville State Park

Locals favor this state park (☎ 435-438-5472), PO Box 1531, Beaver UT 84713, which circles a reservoir 12 miles west of Beaver along Hwy 21. In summer, visitors fish (mainly for trout) and boat; in winter, ice fishing is possible. There is a boat ramp, picnic area and campground with 29 RV hookups and showers. Rates are $3 for day use and $5/11 for tent/RV camping. Water is turned off in winter.

Activities

You can **golf** nine holes at the Canyon Breeze Course (☎ 435-438-2601), 2 miles east on Hwy 153, or **swim** at the municipal pool (☎ 435-438-5066), 465 E 300 North.

Places to Stay – Camping

Beaver Canyon Campground (☎ 435-438-5654), 1419 E 200 North, is open from May to October and has showers, coin laundry, a playground and (surprise!) a decent Mexican restaurant. Rates are $10/12 without/with hookups. *United Beaver Camperland* (☎ 435-436-2808), near exit 109, has a pool, showers, coin laundry and a store, and is open year-round. Rates are $9 (tents) and $12 to $15 (RVs). Both campgrounds are large and well run. *Beaver KOA* (☎ 435-438-2924), 1428 N Manderfield Rd, has a pool, playground, showers, coin laundry and a store, and is open from February to November. Rates are $14 to $17 without/with hookups. *Delano Trailer Park* (☎ 435-438-2418, 435-438-2419), 480 N Main, has showers and a few $8.50 RV sites with hookups located next to a small motel.

Also see East of Beaver (below) and Minersville State Park (above).

UTAH

PLACES TO STAY
1   Super 8 Motel
2   Best Western Paradise Inn
3   Beaver KOA
6   Days Inn
7   Delano Motel & Trailer Park
10 Paice Mansfield Motel
17 Granada Inn Motel
18 Best Western Paice Inn
19 Aspen Lodge

PLACES TO EAT
4   El Bambi Cafe
5   Arshel's
18 Cottage Inn

OTHER
4   Greyhound Bus Stop
8   Swimming Pool
9   The Show House
11 Renegade Bar
12 Hospital
13 Library & Beaver County
     Travel Council
14 Post Office
15 Old Courthouse Museum
16 Police
20 Cache Valley Cheese

Beaver

Places to Stay – Budget

From late October to April, rates are often significantly lower. The cheapest hotels have about a dozen rooms each. The following have simple rooms, some with kitchenettes, in the $20s or low $30s: *Aspen Lodge* (☎ 435-438-5160), 265 S Main; *Granada Inn Motel* (☎ 435-438-2292), 75 S Main; *Paice Mansfield Motel* (☎ 435-438-2410), 10 W Center.

Places to Stay – Middle

The 11-room *Delano Motel* (☎ 435-438-2418, 800-288-3171, fax 435-438-2115),

480 N Main, has satisfactory rooms for about $34/38 for singles/doubles. The attractive *Sleepy Lagoon Motel* (☎ 435-438-5681), 882 S Main, has a pool and good rooms in the low $40s. The *Super 8 Motel* (☎ 435-438-3888, fax 435-438-1780), at exit 112, has a whirlpool bath, free continental breakfast and decent rooms for $39.88/43.88.

The good-looking *Best Western Paice Inn* (☎ 435-438-2438, fax 435-438-1053), 161 S Main, has flower beds in front and a collection of carved wooden birds, duck decoys and wildlife art brightening the lobby. Pleasant doubles are in the $50s. There is a pool, sauna and spa, and a good restaurant next door. With only 24 rooms, the inn is often full. The larger *Best Western Paradise Inn* (☎ /fax 435-438-2455), 1451 N 300 West, is similarly priced, convenient to the freeway, and has a pool, spa and an adjacent restaurant.

The *Quality Inn* (☎ 435-438-5426, fax 435-438-2493), by exit 109, has a pool and spa, and a restaurant next door. Good-sized rooms, some with private spas, are $40 to $60. *Days Inn* (☎ 435-438-2409, 800-325-2525, fax 435-438-3248), 645 N Main, charges $50 to $70 including continental breakfast. There is an indoor jacuzzi and some larger jacuzzi-suites with kitchenettes from $70 to $80.

Places to Eat
Arshel's (☎ 435-438-2977), 711 N Main, is a locally popular small restaurant that has been here for half a century; it is a good budget choice. Open from 6 am to 9 pm (10 pm in summer), it serves home-style cooking. Main courses run about $7 to $10; big hamburgers and sandwiches are around $4; no beer is served. For inexpensive 24-hour dining, there's *El Bambi Cafe* (☎ 435-438-2983), 935 N Main – the Greyhound bus stops here.

The rustic *Maria's Cocina* (☎ 435-438-5654), 1419 E 200 North (in the Beaver Canyon Campground), serves as authentic a Mexican meal as you'll find in the area – good and reasonably priced. It is open for dinner only (5 to 9 pm).

The town's hotel restaurants are generally good. Foremost among them is the *Cottage Inn* (☎ 435-435-5855), 171 S Main (by the Paice Inn). The old-fashioned cottage interior is cozy, featuring antiques and a doll collection. Meals are generally American fare, with most entrées under $14. Hours are 7 am to 10 pm.

Entertainment
The Show House (☎ 435-438-0502), 55 N Main, screens movies. Plays are performed in summer at the Old Courthouse and the nearby old Opera House. The *Renegade*

Bar is a private club with beer, pool and country & western music.

Shopping
Cache Valley Cheese (☎ 435-438-2421), 330 W 250 South, gives tours of its cheese-making plant and sells factory-fresh cheeses and ice cream.

Getting There & Away
The Greyhound bus (☎ 435-438-2229) stops at the El Bambi Cafe, 935 N Main, several times a day southbound to St George and Las Vegas, Nevada; eastbound to Denver, Colorado, along I-70; or northbound to Salt Lake City.

EAST OF BEAVER
Hwy 153 heads east into the Tushar Mountains, emerging at Junction, 40 miles away. The first half is paved and the east side is graveled and passable to cars. The graveled road is closed by snow from about October to June.

Most of the land along Hwy 153 is part of the Fishlake National Forest (☎ 435-438-2436 in Beaver), which has small campgrounds at *Little Cottonwood* (6 miles east of town) and *Mahogany Cove* (12 miles). Both have water and no showers, cost $6 and are open May to October. Several other campgrounds are located along unpaved side roads. Several lakes and streams offer fishing – the Beaver ranger station has details. In October, fall colors make the drive especially pretty.

Elk Meadows Ski & Summer Resort
Eighteen miles east of Beaver at 9200 feet above sea level (the road is paved and open up to here all winter), this resort (☎ 435-438-5433, 800-248-7669, fax 435-438-2598), PO Box 511, Beaver, UT 84713, has 200 skiable acres. This is one of the smallest of Utah's alpine ski resorts, but it enjoys a reputation for good powder. The skiing season goes from Thanksgiving to early April, and five lifts service 30 runs between 9200 and 10,400 feet in elevation; 14% of the runs are for beginners and 62% for intermediate skiers. Adult lift tickets are

$25 (9 am to 4 pm) or $18 for half a day. Children ski for $15 all day and those over 65 ski free. There are ski rentals, a ski school (for skiers aged four to adult), snowboarding, a grocery/liquor/convenience store, places to eat and condos for rent.

During summer, the resort is a good base for fishing the nearby lakes, reservoirs and streams. Hiking, picnicking and mountain biking are also popular – a mountain-bike shop offers rentals and guided trips. Horses are also available for rent or overnight pack trips. Naturalists will find plenty of mule deer, elk, yellow-bellied marmots and other wildlife to observe.

A popular fishing area is **Puffer Lake**, 4 miles east of Elk Meadows. There are boat rentals starting at around $55 a day, a fishing and grocery store, and very rustic cabins starting around $35 a day – bring your own bedding and kitchen utensils.

Elk Meadow Condos are right at the base of the ski slopes. Most come with a full kitchen and fireplace or wood stove. Winter rates for a studio sleeping two range from $80 to $110 (higher prices on weekends and holidays); a two-bedroom/one-bathroom condo sleeping six rents for $95 to $140; a three-bedroom/two-bathroom condo sleeping 10 costs $150 to $195; and

homes sleeping 12 or more go for $275 to $375, plus tax. Stays of three midweek nights qualify for 10% to 20% discounts. Summer rates are $55 to $70 for a studio, $74 to $90 for a two-bed/one-bath, $105 to $120 for a three-bed/two-bath and $180 to $230 for a house.

PAROWAN
Founded by Mormons on January 13, 1851, this is the oldest settlement in southern Utah. Today, this small town (population 1900) is both the Iron County seat and the gateway to Brian Head Ski Resort and Cedar Breaks National Monument, south on Hwy 143. It offers cheaper lodging than the Brian Head Ski Resort.

Information
The city office (☎ 435-477-3331), 5 S Main, open from 9 am to 4 pm Monday to Friday, has information and brochures about the area's historic heritage. A visitor center (☎ 435-477-8190), 73 N Main, is open in summer. The police (☎ 435-477-3383) are at 22 E Center.

Things to See
Historic buildings in town range from log cabins to a **rock church** built at Center

---

Southern Utah – Being Loved to Death?
The southern third of Utah, south of I-70, is a spectacular area containing five of the most famous national parks in the country, as well as numerous national monuments and state parks. So magnificent are the multi-hued canyons, cliffs, bridges, buttes, spires and other formations that no trip to the Southwest is complete without a visit to the region.

Unfortunately, massive increases in tourism during the 1980s and 1990s have meant that the most publicized areas are swamped by visitors, especially during the summer. National park lodges are booked up months in advance, and the main roads to and through the parks sometimes see traffic more like a city rush hour than a leisurely drive through stunning scenery.

Park authorities and wilderness watchdog groups are well aware of the dilemma, and they are scrambling to come up with management plans that will both protect parks and allow adequate access for millions of visitors. By the late 1990s, it is likely that private cars will be banned from some areas and buses will transport travelers from parking areas outside the park boundaries to visitor centers inside. Meanwhile, throngs of people continue to pour into the area – and you are one of those people. If you want to avoid the worst of the crowds, yet still have a memorable visit, here are some suggestions.

and Main in the 1860s and now housing a small DUP museum, open 1 to 5 pm Monday to Saturday during the summer, or by appointment. Across the street to the south, the adobe **Jesse N Smith Home** was built in the 1850s and also can be toured – call the Parowan Hostess Committee (☎ 435-477-8728). Other historic buildings are found close by, as well as in **Paragonah**, 4 miles north.

The **Parowan Gap Petroglyphs**, an extensive array of chiseled symbols and pictures, line a gravel road 11 miles west of Parowan along 400 North. The area is on BLM land (information in Cedar City). Many hundreds of designs were made by Indians crossing the pass over a period of about 1000 years.

Special Events

Cowboy Days & Poetry Gathering, held over Memorial Day weekend, features everything from sheepshearing to mule races and cowboy poetry readings. The Iron County Fair, which runs for a week around Labor Day, features a rodeo, carnival, horse racing and many other events. Christmas in the Country is a candle-lit foot procession and Christmas lighting ceremony held Thanksgiving weekend.

There are also historic-home tours, a bazaar and entertainment.

Places to Stay

Camping *Sportmen's Country* (☎ 435-477-3714), 492 N Main, has showers and a fast-food restaurant. Rates are $11 with hookups, substantially less without. The Dixie National Forest (☎ 435-865-3700 in Cedar City) operates the small *Vermillion Castle* campground, 4 miles south along Hwy 143. The campground has water but no showers and is open from mid-May to mid-November. Sites cost $7.

Motels Prices are highest in the summer, around Christmas and during winter weekends, and lowest in the spring after skiing season. The *Crimson Hills Motel* (☎ 435-477-8662), 400 S Hwy 91, has 17 rooms in the mid $30s. *Days Inn* (☎ 435-477-3326, fax 435-477-3473), 625 W 200 South, has 44 standard rooms, some with microwave and refrigerator, from $35 to $65. There is a restaurant.

The nicest place is the alpine-style *Best Western Swiss Village Inn* (☎ 435-477-3391, fax 435-477-8642), 580 N Main. It has a pool, spa and restaurant. Pleasant rooms cost around $60.

UTAH

The period between Memorial Day and Labor Day is the peak season – so avoid those months if possible. Many tourists try to do the 'Big Six' (Zion, Bryce Canyon, Capitol Reef, Canyonlands and Arches National Parks in southern Utah, plus Grand Canyon National Park in northern Arizona) in an exhausting 10-day or two-week tour – consider visiting just one or two of these parks for a longer period of time.

Hike or better still backpack away from the crowds – even during the height of tourist season in midsummer, camping permits for the backcountry in most but not all national parks are available on a day's notice even when drive-in campsites and park lodges have been filled to capacity for weeks.

Use your common sense: don't litter; stay on established trails (cutting trails causes erosion); be considerate of other visitors (loud music may not enhance everyone's experience – natural tranquillity is a rare pleasure); never attempt to feed or touch wild animals; and drive carefully.

Consider visiting and spending time in some of the less-well-known state parks and national monuments, all of which have superb scenery. And remember the area's Indian and pioneering history by visiting museums, historic buildings and routes, and ghost towns – sometimes you'll be the only one there. ■

B&Bs *Grandma Bess' B&B* (☎ 435-477-8224), 291 W 200 South, has two rooms for $50. *Janet Lynn House* (☎ 435-477-1133, 800-891-1132), 390 E 200 South, has a spa and exercise/game areas. Three rooms with shared bath are $60 and one with private bath is $75. *Adam's Historic B&B* (☎ 435-477-8295), 94 N 100 East, has three rooms with private bath from $60 to $120 (all are nonsmoking).

Places to Eat
The Days Inn and Swiss Village Inn motels have the best restaurants, but they sometimes close in the middle of the day. The *Parowan Cafe* (☎ 435-477-3593), 33 N Main, is a small family restaurant open 7 am to 8:30 pm Monday to Saturday. *La Villa Mexican Restaurant* (☎ 435-477-1541), 13 S Main, serves lunch and dinner daily. *Pizza Barn* (☎ 435-477-8240) is at 595 W 200 South, and there are a few other fast-food places.

Getting There & Away
The Greyhound bus (☎ 800-231-2222) stops on Main at Center for Salt Lake City; Las Vegas, Nevada; and Denver, Colorado. Advance reservations are required.

BRIAN HEAD
At 9700 feet above sea level, Brian Head is Utah's highest town and has about 100 permanent residents and many more transient ones. Only 14 miles south of Parowan but almost 4000 feet higher, the town is reached on paved, but steep and winding, Hwy 143. Brian Head Ski Resort is southern Utah's largest.

This is an uncrowded place to visit in summer, and lift lines are not a problem in winter. The resort is steadily gaining popularity because of this, and new hotels and condos are being built. After skiing ends in spring, the town is almost deserted.

Information
The folks at the Brian Head town offices (☎ 435-677-2029), PO Box 190068, Brian Head, UT 84719, and the chamber of commerce (☎ 435-677-2810, fax 435-677-2154, www.brianheadutah.com), PO Box 325, Brian Head, UT 84719, have information. The medical clinic (☎ 435-677-2700) operates in winter only.

Altitude sickness can be a problem. Sleeping at Parowan (6000 feet) is one solution. If you feel altitude sick, a hasty descent will quickly provide relief (see Health in the Facts for the Visitor chapter).

Winter Activities
Brian Head Ski Resort (☎ 435-677-2035, 800-272-7426, fax 435-677-3883) offers great **downhill skiing** from Thanksgiving to early April. Six lifts service 53 runs between 9600 and 10,920 feet elevation. Of more than 500 skiable acres, 38% are for beginners and 43% for intermediate skiers. Adult day passes (9 am to 4:30 pm) are $35; half day (from 12:30 pm) are $27. Children under 12 and seniors over 60 pay $20/15 for full/half day. Youths 12 to 20 pay $32. Discounts are available for multi-day passes. Snowboards are allowed on most runs. Skis rent for $17 a day and snowboards for $25. There is night skiing on weekends, and child care and instruction daily.

Those who prefer **cross-country skiing** can rent equipment from Brian Head Cross Country & Mountain Bike (☎ 435-677-2012) or Georg's Ski & Mountain Bike Shop (☎ 435-677-2013). Brianhead Sports (☎ 435-677-2014) rents skis, snowboards and clothing. Several other places rent skis. **Snowmobile** rentals and tours are available from Crystal Mountain Recreation (☎ 435-677-2386). Groomed ski and snowmobile tracks lead to Cedar Breaks National Monument and other areas; wilderness skiing is also possible.

Summer Activities
The resort is quiet in summer – year-round action is a recent occurrence at Brian Head. The deliciously cool climate (daytime highs in the 70°s F) attracts lowlanders fed up with their summer basting. **Mountain biking** is good; rentals are available at Georg's (see above) and the resort's Brian Head Mountain Bike Park. Some ski lifts become bike lifts in

summer. The *Brian Head Mountain Bike Guide* is a recommended free annual magazine with details of many local trails from Brian Head down to Parowan, Panguitch, Duck Creek and Cedar City. The biking season is June to October.

From July to October, the road up to 11,307-foot Brian Head Summit is open – go south 2 miles from town, then head east 3 miles on an unpaved road passable to cars. Great views!

Places to Stay

There are no bottom-end lodgings. Reservations are unnecessary in summer (when discounts are offered) but suggested in winter. New lodgings are opening annually. Most are within walking distance of the skiing area.

The largest place is the *Brian Head Hotel* (☎ 435-677-3000, 800-272-7426, fax 435-677-2211) at the base of the skiing area. There are 180 rooms and one-, two- and three-bedroom suites ranging from $95 to more than $300 in winter, $65 to more than $200 in summer. Amenities include a restaurant and bar, spa and sauna, and an exercise room. *The Lodge at Brian Head* (☎ 435-677-3222, 800-386-5634, fax 435-677-3202) has 70 units with rooms starting in the $60s midweek in winter and larger apartments for up to $250. There is a sauna, spa, indoor pool and restaurant.

There are many condominiums for those wishing to have a kitchen and fireplace. Try the *Brian Head Reservation Center* (☎ 435-677-2042, 800-845-9718, fax 435-677-2827), PO Box 190055, Brian Head, UT 84719, representing 30 condos with one, two or three bedrooms sleeping up to eight, all with kitchens and one or two bathrooms. All are convenient to the skiing area. Winter rates range from $100 for a one-bedroom condo sleeping two to $205 for a three-bedroom condo sleeping eight. Holiday rates are about 50% higher and summer rates are about 30% lower. Another agency is *Brian Head Condo Reservations* (☎ 435-677-2045, 800-722-4742, fax 435-677-3881), PO Box 190217, Brian Head, UT 84719, with 100 condos from $80 to $400.

Chalet Village Condom... 677-2025, 800-942-8908 ... 2031) has 40 fairly b... kitchens, ranging from studios to ... bedroom condos at $65 to $140 in winter, with the normal holiday increase and summer savings. *Copper Chase Condominiums* (☎ 435-677-2890), PO Box 190145, Brian Head, UT 84719, has a pool, spa and exercise room, and 80 studios, one-, two- and three-bedroom condos for $129 to $269 in winter. *Evergreen Luxury Condominiums* (☎ 435-677-2050, 800-237-1410, fax 435-677-3660) has 20 various units ranging from about $50 to more than $300.

Places to Eat

The *Edge Restaurant* (☎ 435-677-3343) serves steaks and seafood and has been around longer than most of the eateries in Brian Head. It's one of the better and pricier places. To economize, look into the Brian Head Mall, where you'll find a few moderately priced choices. The two hotels listed above have good restaurants. Most places close in the spring after skiing ends and reopen in the summer.

CEDAR BREAKS NATIONAL MONUMENT

This area has spectacular geological formations but is unusual because of its altitude atop the Markagunt Plateau. Cars can reach it only in summer (late May to October); during winter, it is the province of snowmobilers and cross-country skiers.

From Brian Head south to Hwy 14 is about 10 miles – half of this road is within the national monument. West of the road, erosion has formed a massive natural amphitheater, 3 miles wide and over 2000 feet deep. Inside are fantastically eroded formations: ridge after ridge of spires and columns colored yellow, orange, red, purple and brown by iron and manganese. East of the road lies the plateau, carpeted with wildflowers from late June to mid-August, peaking in late July.

Most visitors simply drive through, stopping at the four scenic overlooks, each

...out 10,400 feet above sea level, for stunning views of the amphitheater. There are also two hiking trails, each 2 miles long. The **Alpine Pond Trail** leads through a conifer forest to a pond; the **Wasatch Ramparts Trail** follows the southern end of the amphitheater, passing ancient bristlecone pines and offering good views. Maps are available from the visitor center.

Information

The visitor center, near the south entrance of the monument, is open from 8 am to 6 pm from Memorial Day to Labor Day and 8 am to 5 pm to early October. Facilities include an exhibit, book and souvenir shop, and restrooms. Park rangers provide information and lead scheduled walks, talks and other programs. Admission to the monument is $4 per car if you are using the facilities in season; free out of season or if you simply drive through. Golden Age, Eagle and Access Passes are accepted.

Further information is available from Cedar Breaks National Monument (☎ 435-586-9451), PO Box 749, Cedar City, UT 84720.

Places to Stay

Almost a mile from the visitor center is a Park Service campground and picnic area. The campground has water, toilets and fire grills; it is open from June to September on a first-come, first-served basis. The 30 sites sometimes fill by mid-afternoon. Camping fees are $9. Prepare for near-freezing night temperatures at this elevation.

CEDAR CITY

Mormon settlers were sent south from Parowan in November 1851 to found Cedar City and extract the nearby iron ore. This venture largely proved a failure (it was cheaper to import iron by railroad from the East, so the people turned to ranching. After Zion National Park was established in 1919, tourism began to play an important role in the economy.

Today, Cedar City hosts a Shakespearean Festival, which draws theater-goers from within and beyond the state, and several other cultural events. Less than an hour's drive from Zion, Cedar Breaks and Brian Head, it is a natural stopping place for travelers. The town, southern Utah's second largest (20,000 inhabitants), is 5800 feet above sea level and has about 20 hotels from which to choose.

Information

The chamber of commerce (☎ 435-586-4484), 286 N Main, is open from 8 am to 5 pm Monday to Friday. In summer, hours are extended to 7 pm, and 9 am to 1 pm on Saturday.

The Dixie National Forest Cedar City Ranger Station (☎ 435-865-3200, 435-865-3799 for a recorded message), PO Box 627, Cedar City, UT 84720, is at 82 N 100 East. The BLM (☎ 435-586-2401) is at 176 E DL Sargent Drive, at the north end of town. These government offices are open 8 am to 4 pm Monday to Friday.

The library (☎ 435-586-6661) is at 136 W Center. The local newspaper is the *Daily Spectrum*. The post office (☎ 435-586-6701) is at 333 N Main. The medical center (☎ 435-586-6587) is at 595 S 75 East. The police (☎ 435-586-2956) are at 110 N Main. Raindance Laundromat (☎ 435-586-6964), 430 S Main, has about 40 coin-operated washers.

Southern Utah University (SUU)

Founded in 1897, this four-year college (☎ 435-586-7700), 351 W Center, has more than 5000 students. Visitors can see two early buildings, **Old Main**, built in 1898, and the old **Administration Building**, dating from 1904.

The **Braithwaite Fine Arts Gallery** (☎ 435-586-5432) is in the eastern part of the campus near Old Main. Both permanent and changing shows of local and national artists, past and present, are on display. Hours are 10 am to 10 pm Monday to Saturday (shorter hours in winter). Admission is free.

Near the gallery, the university **library** (☎ 435-586-7933) displays local Paiute Indian artifacts.

UTAH

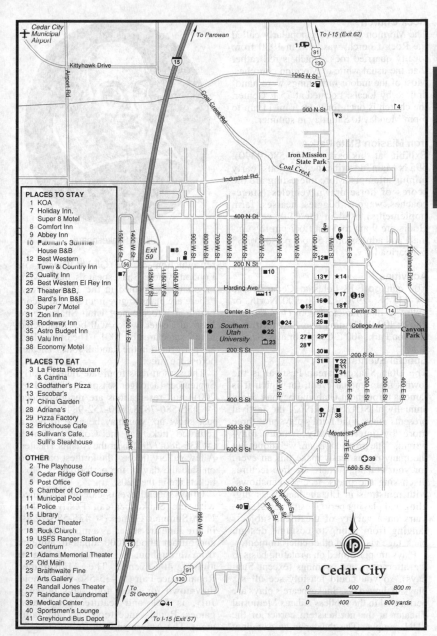

PLACES TO STAY
1 KOA
7 Holiday Inn,
  Super 8 Motel
8 Comfort Inn
9 Abbey Inn
10 Paxman's Summer
   House B&B
12 Best Western
   Town & Country Inn
25 Quality Inn
26 Best Western El Rey Inn
27 Theater B&B,
   Bard's Inn B&B
30 Super 7 Motel
31 Zion Inn
33 Rodeway Inn
35 Astro Budget Inn
36 Valu Inn
38 Economy Motel

PLACES TO EAT
3 La Fiesta Restaurant
  & Cantina
12 Godfather's Pizza
13 Escobar's
17 China Garden
28 Adriana's
29 Pizza Factory
32 Brickhouse Cafe
34 Sullivan's Cafe,
   Sulli's Steakhouse

OTHER
2 The Playhouse
4 Cedar Ridge Golf Course
5 Post Office
6 Chamber of Commerce
11 Municipal Pool
14 Police
15 Library
16 Cedar Theater
18 Rock Church
19 USFS Ranger Station
20 Centrum
21 Adams Memorial Theater
22 Old Main
23 Braithwaite Fine
   Arts Gallery
24 Randall Jones Theater
37 Raindance Laundromat
39 Medical Center
40 Sportsmen's Lounge
41 Greyhound Bus Depot

Cedar City

| 0 | 400 | 800 m |
| 0 | 400 | 800 yards |

Rock Church

The Mormon Tabernacle, popularly called the Rock Church, was built in 1930 from locally quarried rock, which is red rather than the usual white of Mormon churches. Most of the indoor furnishings were hand-crafted by locals. Located at 75 E Center, the church is open for tours from 11 am to 5 pm Monday to Saturday in summer.

Iron Mission State Park

Exhibits at this park (☎ 435-586-9290), 595 N Main, describe the Mormons' early mining attempts. More interesting are the scores of horse-drawn vehicles (stage-coaches, wagons, buggies, hearses, farm implements) used in the 19th century. Hours are 9 am to 5 pm (to 7 pm in summer) and admission is $1 per person or $3 per carload.

Activities

You can **golf** 18 holes at Cedar Ridge (☎ 435-586-2970), 200 E 900 North, or **swim** at the municipal pool (☎ 435-586-2869), 400 W Harding Ave. Play **tennis** at Canyon Park, 400 E Center, or at SUU.

Special Events

The Utah Shakespearean Festival is the town's main annual event, for which it is famous throughout Utah and beyond. Held annually at SUU since 1962, the festival presents three of the Bard's plays plus three more by internationally famous play-wrights. The productions are well done, but the many extras really make this an event for your calendar. There are free lectures discussing the plays, free 'Greenshows' with minstrels in Elizabethan dress jug-gling and playing period instruments, sem-inars on a variety of theatrical subjects ranging from acting to costume design, backstage visits and other entertainment.

Plays are performed on a rotating basis in the afternoons and evenings (except Sun-days), so you could feasibly see all six plays in three days. Shakespeare's plays are performed in the roofless Adams Memorial Theater at the northeastern corner of the SUU campus. The theater is an excellent

William Shakespeare

reproduction of the Globe Theater in London, where Shakespeare's plays were originally performed in the 16th century. (There are plans to give it a roof and incor-porate it into the new Utah Shakespeare Festival Center, which will be constructed in this same area by 2001.) The other plays are performed in the Randall Jones Theater across the street.

The season runs from late June to early September (a longer season is planned by 2001) and reservations are recommended (☎ 435-586-7878, 800-752-9849). If you just show up, you may be able to buy a returned ticket at the Courtesy Booth (☎ 435-586-7790), near the Adams Theater. A few gallery tickets (the farthest back) go on sale the day of the performance. Most tickets are in the $20s.

Other special events can be combined with the Shakespearean Festival. The Utah Summer Games (☎ 435-586-7228) in late June are styled as a mini-Olympics and attract about 7000 amateur athletes from throughout the state competing in almost 40 events. The Midsummer Renaissance Fair (☎ 435-586-5943), held downtown for about four days in early July, is free and features magicians, games, Renaissance food and entertain-ment. The American Folk Ballet (☎ 435-

586-7872) has performances in the Centrum (in the middle of the SUU campus) in late July.

Other special events include the Paiute Powwow in early June, a Winterfest in early December and the SUU Theater Season (☎ 435-586-7878), offering five or six plays performed for week-long runs between October and May.

Places to Stay – Camping

Cedar City KOA (☎ 435-586-9872), 1121 N Main, has showers, a pool, a playground, a grocery store and coin laundry. Sites range from $15 to $21 and there are a few Kamping Kabins for $26 a double. *Country Aire RV Park* (☎ 435-586-2550), 1700 N Main, has similar facilities for $13 to $18. Also see Hwy 14 East of Cedar City (below).

Places to Stay – Budget

During the Shakespearean Festival (especially weekends) rates can be 50% higher than other times and there are few truly cheap places. The cheapest is the *Economy Motel* (☎ 435-586-4461), 443 S Main, with shabby rooms from $20, but friendly owners. The *Valu Inn* (☎ 435-586-9114, fax 435-586-4614), 344 S Main, has double rooms in the $40s in summer and around $30 at other times.

The *Zion Inn* (☎ 435-586-9487), 222 S Main, has standard doubles in the $50s in summer and the $30s the rest of the year. The *Astro Budget Inn* (☎ 435-586-6557), 323 S Main, is similarly priced and has a pool. The *Super 7 Motel* (☎ 435-586-6566), 190 S Main, has nice double rooms for $45 to $65 in summer, $40 the rest of the year. The *Super 8 Motel* (☎ /fax 435-586-8880), 145 N 1550 West, has decent rooms for $50/55 for singles/doubles in summer, including coffee and a pastry breakfast.

Places to Stay – Middle

B&Bs Travelers preferring the B&B experience should book early, especially for the Shakespearean Festival. No smoking is allowed in these places.

Paxman's Summer House B&B (☎ 435-586-3755), 170 N 400 West, is a Victorian house with many period furnishings. Four rooms with a queen-size bed and private bath rent for $55 to $80. The *Willow Glen Inn* (☎ 435-586-3275) is 2 miles north of town at 3308 N Bulldog Rd. There are nine rooms from $45 (shared baths) to a two-bedroom suite with kitchenette for $100 a double, $10 per extra person.

The *Theater B&B* (☎ 435-586-0404), 118 S 100 West, has three rooms for $50 each during the theater season. The *Bard's Inn B&B* (☎ 435-586-6612), 150 S 100 West, has seven rooms from $65 to $80.

Hotels All the hotels in this section have a swimming pool and nicely kept, generally spacious rooms. The *Rodeway Inn* (☎ 435-586-9916), 281 S Main, features a sauna, a whirlpool and a restaurant. Doubles are $64 to $74 in summer, with some two-bedroom units for a few dollars more.

The *Abbey Inn* (☎ 435-586-9966, 800-325-5411, fax 435-586-6522), 940 W 200 North, looks nice and has a spa and coin laundry. Rooms come with a microwave and refrigerator. Doubles with two queen-size beds or one king-size bed are $65 to $80 in summer, and a couple of suites with spas go for about $140. Continental breakfast is included.

The *Comfort Inn* (☎ 435-586-2082, 800-627-0374, fax 435-586-3193), 250 N 1100 West, has a spa and coin laundry. Big double rooms are $65 to $80 in summer, $49 to $73 at other times; rates include continental breakfast. Even larger units, some with kitchenettes or spas, some with two bedrooms, cost about $20 more.

The *Quality Inn* (☎ 435-586-2433, fax 435-586-7257), 18 S Main, has 50 pleasant rooms with microwave and refrigerator, but all are up a flight of stairs – no elevator. Rates are $66 to $86 for a double in summer, including continental breakfast.

The *Best Western Town & Country Inn* (☎ 435-586-9900, fax 435-586-1664), 189 N Main, is by far the biggest place in town with 157 rooms – it's more like two hotels separated by 200 North. Despite the sprawl, it's well run. Facilities include two pools, two spas, a game room, coin laundry, National Car Rental, a steak house and a pizza parlor. There are half a dozen other restaurants within a block. Double rooms with continental breakfast are $71 to $91, depending on the season, and there are a few more expensive suites.

The *Best Western El Rey Inn* (☎ 435-586-6518, fax 435-586-7257), 80 S Main, has a spa, a sauna and an exercise room. Doubles vary from $49 to $65 for (a few) small rooms, $69 to $89 for larger rooms and up to $125 for a few suites, some with private spa.

The *Holiday Inn* (☎ 435-586-8888, 800-432-8828, fax 435-586-1010), 1575 W 200 North, has a pool, spa, sauna, a well-equipped exercise room and a coin laundry. There is a restaurant and bar with room service (7 am to 10 pm, 6 am to 11 pm in summer). Comfortable rooms run in the $80s in summer, in the $60s in winter.

Places to Eat

With 30 or 40 places in town, you certainly won't go hungry.

Downtown, the place to go for reasonably priced American-style meals is *Sullivan's Cafe* (☎ 435-586-6761), 301 S Main. In business since 1946, the café is popular – hours are 6 am to 10 pm, but they say they'll rustle up breakfast any time. The café has a large salad bar and also serves potatoes in a variety of ways. It adjoins *Sulli's Steakhouse*, which offers more upmarket dining, cocktails, a salad bar, an Italian menu and entrées in the $9 to $25 range. Hours here are 6 to 10 pm, from 5 pm for festival-goers.

Another fine steak choice (some seafood) is *Milt's Stage Stop* (☎ 435-586-9344), 5 miles east of town along Hwy 14 in Cedar Canyon in rustic Western surroundings. Hours are 6 to 10 pm and entrées run $15 to $30. This restaurant has been around for years and is popular – make a reservation before driving up there.

Adriana's (☎ 435-586-7673), 164 S 100 West, with an Olde Worlde ambiance, is famous among festival-goers. Good Amer-

ican food is served, including a selection of healthful items, at quite reasonable prices – under $10 for lunch and $10 to $20 for dinner.

Escobar's (☎ 435-865-0155), 155 N Main, serves good inexpensive Mexican food all day but does not serve beer. Also good, and with a beer license, is *La Villa* (☎ 435-586-8088), 2581 N Main, and *La Fiesta Restaurant & Cantina* (☎ 435-586-4646), 890 N Main, open from 11 am to 10 pm Monday to Saturday, with a full liquor license.

The long-established *China Garden* (☎ 435-586-6042), 170 N Main, is open from 11 am to 10 pm and has daily inexpensive lunch specials. For pizza, try *Godfather's Pizza* (☎ 435-586-1111), 241 N Main, or the *Pizza Factory* (☎ 435-586-3900), 124 S Main.

The *Brickhouse Café* (☎ 435-865-1770), 227 S Main, offers gourmet coffees, vegetarian selections, light meals and desserts from 7 am to 11 pm on weekdays and 8 am to 11 pm on Saturdays.

Entertainment

For 24-hour movie information, call ☎ 435-586-7469. Movies are shown downtown at the *Cedar Theater* (☎ 435-586-6539), 33 N Main, and on the outskirts at *Fiddler's Three Theaters* (☎ 435-586-5924), 170 E Fiddlers Canyon Rd.

The Playhouse (☎ 435-586-9010), 1027 N Main, doesn't show plays (see Special Events, above, for that) but does have pool tables and dancing some nights. Also try the *Sportsmen's Lounge* (☎ 435-586-6552), 900 S Main.

Getting There & Away

Air Skywest Airlines (☎ 435-586-3033, 800-453-9417) flies to and from Salt Lake City two times a day. The airport is 2 miles northwest of downtown Cedar City.

Bus Greyhound (☎ 435-586-9465), 1355 S Main (in a Texaco Station), runs two buses a day each way between Las Vegas, Nevada, and Salt Lake City. Another two go between Las Vegas and Denver, Colorado.

Getting Around

National Car Rental is at the airport (☎ 435-586-7059) and at the Best Western Town & Country Inn (☎ 435-586-9900). Speedy Rental (☎ 435-586-7368), 650 N Main, is another choice.

HWY 14 EAST OF CEDAR CITY

This paved scenic route leads 40 miles over the Markagunt Plateau ending in Long Valley Junction at Hwy 89. The road crests at 10,000 feet with splendid views of Zion National Park to the south. Much of the road is within the Dixie National Forest (Cedar City Ranger Station has maps and information), and there are campgrounds, hiking trails, fishing lakes and lodges. (Distances below are east of Cedar City.)

Cedar Canyon Campground (11½ miles) has about 20 sites at 8000 feet, open June to about October. Sites cost $5 and have water.

At 9200 feet **Navajo Lake** (25 miles) has a small marina with boat rentals, a lodge with cabins, a store, a small restaurant and *Spruce* and *Navajo Lake Campgrounds*, both on the lake with about 70 sites between them, and *Te-Ah Campground* with an additional 40 sites about 1½ miles away. These facilities are open Memorial Day to October – the campsites are $7 and have water.

A large area around Navajo Lake is a Dante-esque jumble of jagged black rocks, the result of a prehistoric lava flow. There are several places where you can pull off to take a closer look.

The **Duck Creek Area** (30 miles) has tiny Duck Lake and Aspen Mirror Lake, both good for trout fishing, as is Duck Creek. There is a small visitor center, open in summer, various hiking trails and *Duck Creek Campground* with 80 sites for $7. In **Duck Creek Village** (population 60, elevation 8000 feet), there are some small, rustic lodges that fill up on summer weekends with hikers and watersports enthusiasts, on fall weekends with color-watchers, and on winter holiday weekends with skiers and snowmobilers, during which times reservations are recommended. The area has been used for making various movies, of which *How the West Was Won* is perhaps the best known.

Falcon's Nest (☎ 435-682-2556, 800-240-4930, fax 435-682-2564), on Hwy 14, rents rooms for $55 double and cabins (sleeping six) for $65 to $70 double and $5 per extra person. A restaurant is open on weekends. Also on Hwy 14, the *Duck Creek Village Inn* (☎ 435-682-2565) has motel rooms at $49 to $64 for one to four people ($11 more on holiday weekends) and cabins sleeping up to eight for $70 to $80 double ($10 for additional people). Its restaurant is open daily except Wednesdays in summer. *Pinewoods Resort* (☎ 435-682-2512, 800-848-2525, fax 435-682-2543), just off Hwy 14 also has a restaurant as well as mountain bike and snowmobile rental. Six two-bedroom condos with kitchen, living room and bathroom are $85 to $95 double. Nearby, the *Inn at Cedar Mountain* (☎ 435-682-2378, 800-897-4995, fax 435-682-2379, inncedar@color-country.net) has eight large nonsmoking units sleeping four/six/eight people for $79/99/119. Each has a kitchen but no TV. There is a hot tub. *Meadeau View Lodge* (☎ 435-682-2495) offers rooms with breakfast for about $60 to $70 a double.

A couple of miles east of Duck Creek Village, a signed dirt road to the south leads about 10 miles to **Strawberry Point**, with superb vistas of the color country to the south. It is passable only late May to October.

ST GEORGE

Under an hour southwest of Cedar City along I-15, St George has a noticeably different climate with its elevation at 2880 feet (3000 feet below Cedar City). Summers are hot, with frequent highs over 100°F, and winters are mild.

Founded in 1861 as a cotton-farming center, St George was named after a Mormon leader, George A Smith (no dragon-slaying stories here). Within a decade, the cotton-growing mission failed for the same reason the iron mission to the north failed – cheaper cotton became available from the East when the railroad arrived.

Despite harsh conditions, the Mormons persevered, partly because of Brigham Young's insistence. In the 1870s, he spent the last few winters of his life here and ensured the building of the most impressive Mormon Temple and Tabernacle in southern Utah.

Today, the mild winter weather continues to promote prosperity in St George. It is southern Utah's largest city (45,000 inhabitants) and one of the region's fastest growing ones (only 7000 inhabitants in 1970). Despite the growth, it remains a fine Mormon town with wide streets, historic buildings and a spacious feel.

There are several golf courses and St George claims to have the best year-round golf in the state. With the golf and mild winter weather, and the proximity of cooler Zion National Park to the east and Pine Valley Mountains to the north for summer relief, St George relies on tourism as an economic mainstay.

There's little to do here unless you're an avid golfer or enjoy visiting pioneer buildings, but its excellent range of hotels makes St George a good base for visiting Zion and other nearby parks. The city is the Washington County seat.

Information

The chamber of commerce (☎ 435-628-1658, fax 435-673-1587, hotspot@infowest.com), 97 E St George Blvd, is open from 9 am to 5 pm, Monday to Friday, and from 9 am to 1 pm on Saturday. The Dixie National Forest Pine Valley Ranger Station (☎ 435-652-3100, 435-628-4491), open 8 am to 5 pm Monday to Friday, and the BLM (☎ 435-673-4654, 435-628-4491) are both at 345 E Riverside Drive. The library (☎ 435-634-5737) is at 50 S Main. The local newspaper is the *Daily Spectrum*. The post office (☎ 435-673-3312) is at 180 N Main. The medical center (☎ 435-634-4000) is at 544 S 400 East. The police (☎ 435-634-5001) are in the city offices, 175 E 200 North.

Historic Buildings

Brochures detailing some two dozen old buildings are available from the tourist information offices. The highlights are described below.

Utah's first **Mormon Temple** was built here between 1871 and 1877 – a magnificent building interesting both for its architecture and the difficult history of its construction. The Temple (like all Mormon temples) is open only to church members on official business, but a visitor center (☎ 435-673-5181), 250 E 400 South, open daily from 9 am to 9 pm (10 pm in summer), has audio-visual and other displays and hosts lectures about the temple's history and church beliefs in general.

The **Mormon Tabernacle**, on Tabernacle and Main, was built between 1863 and 1876. The red-brick and white-spired building is open daily and guided tours (☎ 435-628-4072) are offered from 11 am to 5 pm. The **Brigham Young Winter Home** (☎ 435-673-2517), 89 W 200 North, is where the Mormon leader spent his winters from 1873 until 1877. Many of the original furnishings remain. Hours are from 9 am to 5 pm (until sunset in summer), and there are free guided tours. Across the street, lining the west side of 100 West between St George Blvd and 300 North, are several other pioneer homes, two of which house the Seven Wives Inn (at 217 N 100 West).

The **Old County Courthouse**, was finished in the 1870s and now houses the chamber of commerce. Just north of it is a 1930s building housing the **DUP Museum** (☎ 435-628-7274), 135 N 100 East, which displays interesting pioneer artifacts; it is open during rather irregular hours (supposedly 10 am to 5 pm Monday to Saturday).

In the suburbs, the **Jacob Hamblin Home** (☎ 435-673-2161), Hamblin Drive in Santa Clara, is an early 1860s building – the area's earliest surviving house. It is open from 9 am to 5 pm (later in summer) and free guided tours are offered. The **Washington Cotton Mill** (☎ 435-673-0375), 375 W Telegraph in Washington, is a large three-story factory built in the 1860s. It is now used for local events and can be toured.

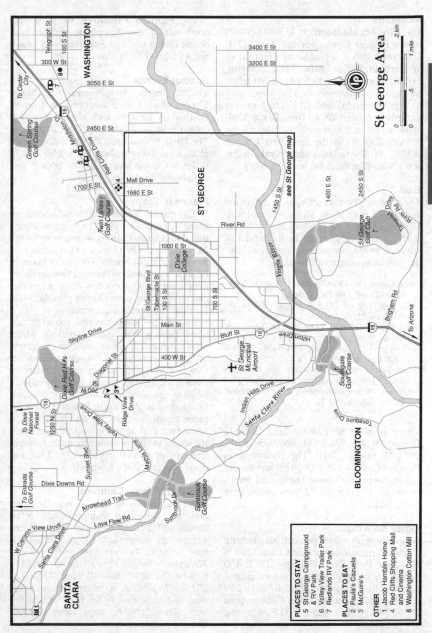

St George Area

To Cedar City

Telegraph St
100 S St
300 W St
WASHINGTON
3400 E St
3200 E St
3050 E St
2450 E St
Green Spring Golf Course
Middleton Dr
Red Cliffs Drive
Mall Drive
1680 E St
1700 E St
ST GEORGE
see St George map
1450 E St
1400 E St
2450 S St
River Rd
Twin Lakes Golf Course
St George Golf Club
Tanner Dr
River Rd
1000 E St
Dixie College
Virgin River
St George Blvd
Tabernacle St
100 S St
700 S St
Skyline Drive
Dixie Red Hills Golf Course
Main St
Bluff St
St George Municipal Airport
Diagonal St
700 W
18
Hilton Drive
Brigham Rd
To Arizona
15
Southgate Golf Course
400 W St
1250 N St
18
To Dixie National Forest
Valley View Drive
Ridge View Drive
Indian Hills Drive
Santa Clara River
Tonaquint Drive
BLOOMINGTON
To Entrada Golf Course
Dixie Downs Rd
Sunset Blvd
Mathis
Sunbrook Dr
Sunbrook Golf Course
W Canyon View Drive
Santa Clara Drive
Arrowhead Trail
Lava Flow Rd
SANTA CLARA

0   1   2 km
0   .5   1 mile

PLACES TO STAY
5 St George Campground & RV Park
6 Valley View Trailer Park
7 Redlands RV Park

PLACES TO EAT
2 Paula's Cazuela
3 McGuire's

OTHER
1 Jacob Hamblin Home
4 Red Cliffs Shopping Mall and Cinema
8 Washington Cotton Mill

Museums

The **City Art Museum** (☎ 435-634-5942) in the Pioneer Center for the Arts, 47 E 200 North, has a permanent collection of Western art, Indian artifacts and changing exhibits. Hours are 6 to 8 pm on Monday, noon to 5 pm Tuesday to Thursday, noon to 8 pm on Friday and 10 am to 5 pm on Saturday. Admission is free. **Dixie College**, a two-year community college, also has art displays in the Fine Arts Center, 200 S 700 East. The huge mural on the south wall illustrates the area's history.

Golf

The following courses are open to the public and charge from about $7 for nine holes to $28 for 18 holes. Green fees are higher in winter when tee times are best reserved in advance. In roughly ascending order of cost, the following courses are available.

Twin Lakes (☎ 435-673-4441), 660 N Twin Lakes Drive, nine holes/par 27
Dixie Red Hills (☎ 435-634-5852), 1000 N 700 West, nine holes/par 34
Southgate (☎ 435-628-0000), 1975 S Tonaquint Drive, 18 holes/par 70
St George Golf Club (☎ 435-634-5854), 2190 S 1400 East, 18 holes/par 73
Green Spring (☎ 435-673-7888), 588 N Green Spring Drive, Washington, 18 holes/par 71
Sunbrook (☎ 435-634-5866), 2240 Sunbrook Drive, 18 holes/par 72

There is also the new 18-hole Entrada Course (☎ 435-674-7500, 800-975-7550), 2511 W Entrada Trail. The Bloomington Country Club (☎ 435-673-2029) has a more expensive private course (reciprocal memberships), 18 holes/par 72. New courses are being built.

Other Activities

After your golf round, you can play **tennis** at the Vernon Worthen City Park, 200 S 400 East, or at Dixie College, 700 E 400 South. Or go **swimming** at the municipal pool and hydrotube (☎ 435-634-5867), 250 E 700 South, or at the Dixie College pool (☎ 435-673-8386), 425 S 700 East by the Dixie Center.

The **Pioneer Primitive Park** on the north side of town has picnic benches and desert hiking trails to Sugarloaf – a small hill with good city views.

Special Events

The St George Arts Festival fills Main Street during Easter weekend. A Cotton Festival is held in and around the old cotton mill in Washington in early May. The Dixie Round-up, a PRCA rodeo, takes place in mid-September. In October, there is the St George Marathon and later in the month, the World Senior Games.

Places to Stay

St George has about 2400 hotel rooms in about 40 hotels, which is the biggest selection of accommodations in southern Utah. Nevertheless, when I tried to get a room in St George, most hotels were fully booked because a convention brought thousands of people into town for a few days. Even the cheapest motels were charging in the $40s for their few remaining rooms.

Because St George has year-round attractions, there are no specific periods when rates are more expensive, with the exception of Easter weekend and the sports events in October. Although November to January is usually the quietest season, periodic lulls in tourism can produce lower rates at other times as well. Weekends, however, may be more expensive in some hotels. The following rates are approximate midweek rates for spring to fall, assuming there are no conventions or special events – but look for deep discounts if the town is quiet.

Places to Stay – Camping

Camping, mainly in RVs, is popular here, and the following campgrounds offer almost 900 sites among them. Winter reservations are suggested. All the following have toilets, showers and coin laundry. *McArthur's Temple View RV Resort* (☎ 435-673-6400, 800-776-6410, fax 435-673-6419), 975 S Main, is the largest with more than 260 sites (mainly for RVs) at $16 for tents, $21 with full hookups. There's a pool, spa and recreation area.

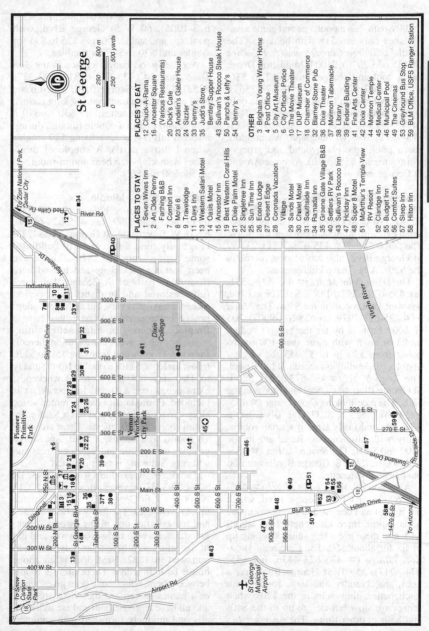

PLACES TO STAY
1 Seven Wives Inn
2 An Olde Penny
   Farthing B&B
7 Comfort Inn
8 Morel 6
9 Travelodge
11 Days Inn
13 Western Safari Motel
14 Oasis Motel
15 Ancestor Inn
19 Best Western Coral Hills
21 Dixie Palm Motel
22 Singletree Inn
25 Sun Time Inn
26 Econo Lodge
27 Desert Edge
28 Coronada Vacation
   Village
29 Sands Motel
30 Chalet Motel
31 Southside Inn
34 Ramada Inn
35 Greene Gate Village B&B
40 Settlers RV Park
43 Sullivan's Rococo Inn
47 Holiday Inn
48 Super 8 Motel
51 McArthur's Temple View
   RV Resort
52 Claridge Inn
55 Budget Inn
56 Comfort Suites
57 Sleep Inn
58 Hilton Inn

PLACES TO EAT
12 Chuck-A-Rama
16 Ancestor Square
   (Various Restaurants)
20 Dick's Cafe
23 Andelin's Gable House
24 Sizzler
33 Denny's
35 Judd's Store,
   Bentley Supper House
43 Sullivan's Rococo Steak House
50 Pancho & Lefty's
54 Denny's

OTHER
3 Brigham Young Winter Home
4 Post Office
5 City Art Museum
6 City Offices, Police
10 The Movie Theater
17 DUP Museum
18 Chamber of Commerce
32 Blarney Stone Pub
36 Dixie Theater
37 Mormon Tabernacle
38 Library
39 Federal Building
41 Fine Arts Center
42 Dixie Center
44 Mormon Temple
45 Medical Center
46 Municipal Pool
49 The Cinemas
53 Greyhound Bus Stop
59 BLM Office, USFS Ranger Station

Settlers RV Park (☎ 435-628-1624), 1333 E 100 South, has a pool, spa and game area; RV sites only are $18 with hookups. The small *St George Campground & RV Park* (☎ 435-673-2970), 2100 E Middleton Drive, has a pool and charges from $12 to $16. *Valley View Trailer Park* (☎ 435-673-3367), 2300 E Middleton Drive, has RV sites only at $14 with hookups. *Redlands RV Park* (☎ 435-673-9700, 800-553-8269, fax 435-673-9711), 650 W Telegraph, Washington, has a pool, spa, playground and grocery store; sites are $15 to $20. Also see Around St George, below.

Places to Stay – Budget

The *Western Safari Motel* (☎ 435-673-5238), 310 W St George Blvd, is one of the cheapest with simple rooms in the $20s. The *Oasis Motel* (☎ 435-673-3551), 231 W St George Blvd, also has modest rooms in the $20s. A few have kitchenettes.

The *Dixie Palm Motel* (☎ 435-673-3531, fax 435-673-5352), 185 E St George Blvd, has well-kept rooms in the $30s. The *Motel 6* (☎ 435-628-7979, fax 435-674-9907), 205 N 1000 East, is by far the biggest budget motel in town with more than 100 rooms going from $30/36 to $37/43 for singles/doubles, depending on season. It has a pool. The *Sands Motel* (☎ 435-673-3501), 581 E St George Blvd, has a pool and rooms in the $30s. The nice-looking *Desert Edge* (☎ 435-673-6137), 525 E St George Blvd, has a pool, spa and fairly large if spartan rooms, many with kitchenettes. Rates are in the $30s and $40s. The *Southside Inn* (☎ 435-628-9000), 750 E St George Blvd, is similar but has no kitchenettes.

Also good is the *Chalet Motel* (☎ 435-628-6272), 664 E St George Blvd, which has a pool and decent double rooms in the $30s. Some have kitchenettes for about $40, and there are a few suites sleeping up to six for about $60. The *Coronada Vacation Village* (☎ 435-628-4436, fax 435-674-4717), 559 E St George Blvd, has a pool, spa, laundry and large rooms with kitchenettes; they start in the $20s when things are slow but can go up to the $40s and $50s at other times. The *Ancestor Inn*

(☎ 435-673-4666, 800-864-6882, fax 435-673-1005), 60 W St George Blvd, with pool, spa and sauna, charges $25 to $35 for singles and $30 to $45 for doubles.

Another good budget choice is the *Sun Time Inn* (☎ 435-673-6181, 800-237-6253), 420 E St George Blvd, which has a pool and spa. Pleasant nonsmoking rooms, some with kitchenettes, are $30 to $40 a single, $40 to $45 a double (though during a recent lull it was advertising $19 singles when I drove past!). A couple of mini-suites with king-size beds and in-room spa go for $60 to $80.

Places to Stay – Middle

B&Bs *Greene Gate Village* (☎ 435-628-6999, 800-350-6999, fax 435-628-6989), 62-78 W Tabernacle, St George, UT 84770, is actually nine different early buildings, some dating from the 1870s. Most have been literally picked up and moved here from other parts of St George, then carefully restored and furnished with period pieces. The rooms vary, but all have modern private bathrooms, and some may have a fireplace, balcony or kitchenette, sitting room, hot tub or some combination thereof. Individual rooms and suites are $50 to $110 (most under $85) for a double from Sunday to Thursday and $10 more on weekends; extra people are $10 and full breakfast is included. Entire houses can be rented – one sleeps up to 22 people and has a $225 minimum charge for six guests. There are about 18 rooms and suites, a pool, spa, large grounds with picnic and barbecue areas and a library. Smoking is not permitted.

The *Seven Wives Inn* (☎ 435-628-3737, 800-600-3737, seven@infowest.com), 217 N 100 West, St George, UT 84770, is made up of two houses. The first was built in 1873 and named after one of the owners' great-grandfathers, who had seven wives and hid in the attic room here after polygamy was outlawed in 1882. Next door is an adobe house built in 1883. There are 13 rooms between them, which have been given women's names (seven are the wives' names), and all have a private bath and are individually and uniquely furnished with antiques;

some have fireplaces or balconies. Rates are $55 to $125, including full breakfast. There is a pool, and each house has a living room with fireplace, books and games. The friendly owners can tell you about area history. No smoking allowed.

The above two places have been around since the early 1980s, have good reputations and are often booked up – reservations are recommended. A newer place is *An Olde Penny Farthing Inn* (☎/fax 435-673-7755), 278 N 100 West, St George, UT 84770, a restored pioneer house with five nonsmoking rooms with private bath. Rates are $55 to $110.

Hotels The *Sleep Inn* (☎ 435-673-7900, fax 435-673-8325), 1481 S Sunland Drive, has a pool and spa and very clean rooms for $40 to $55. *Sullivan's Rococo Inn* (☎ 435-628-3671, fax 435-673-6370), 511 S Airport Rd, is near the airport on the bluff overlooking St George from the west, a location that provides good city views. There is a pool, spa and steak house (dinner only). Rooms are a little worn but quite large and feature refrigerators and either two queen-size beds or a king-size bed; they are reasonably priced in the $40s.

The *Claridge Inn* (☎ 435-673-7222, 800-367-3790, fax 435-634-0773), 1187 S Bluff, has a pool, spa and pleasant rooms, all nonsmoking, in the $40s for a double, including continental breakfast. The *Super 8 Motel* (☎ 435-628-4251, fax 435-628-6534), 915 S Bluff, has a seasonal pool and fairly good rooms for $39.88 to $48.88 for one to four people. The *Travelodge* (☎ 435-673-4621, fax 435-628-2635), 175 N 1000 East, has a pool and satisfactory rooms for about $40/50 for singles/doubles and a couple of suites for $70. Another reasonable choice at this price is the *Budget Inn* (☎ 435-673-6661, fax 435-674-7119), 1221 S Main, which has adults' and kids' pools, spa and free continental breakfast.

The *Days Inn* (☎ 435-673-6123, fax 435-673-7030), 150 N 1000 East, with garden-like grounds, outdoor pool, spa and sauna, has decent rooms mainly in the $50s, including continental breakfast. The simi-

larly priced *Comfort Inn* (☎ 435-628-4271, fax 435-628-5196), 999 E Skyline Drive, has a pool and nice spacious rooms and also offers continental breakfast. The friendly *Singletree Inn* (☎ 435-673-6161, 800-528-8890, fax 435-673-7453), 260 E St George Blvd, and the *Econo Lodge* (☎ 435-673-4861, fax 435-628-4878), 460 E St George Blvd, are close to the historic center, have a pool and spa, and include continental breakfast for rooms in the $50s.

Also close to downtown is the *Best Western Coral Hills* (☎ 435-673-4844, fax 435-673-5352), 125 E St George Blvd – the best hotel in the center. There are three pools (indoor, outdoor, kids'), spas, an exercise room, a game room, a putting green and restaurants nearby. Spacious, comfortable rooms, some with balconies, are $50 to $65 for a double. Suites with spas cost $20 or $30 more. There are two other Best Western properties in town.

The *Ramada Inn* (☎ 435-628-2828, fax 435-628-0505), 1440 E St George Blvd, has nice rooms in the upper $50s. There is a pool and spa, and continental breakfast is included.

Places to Stay – Top End
The better rooms in the B&Bs listed above fall into the Top End category.

Comfort Suites (☎ 435-673-7000, fax 435-628-4340), 1239 S Main, has 123 mini-suites, each with a sitting area and a microwave. There is a pool and spa. Rates are $50 to $90 for a double (highest rates at Easter, October and weekends), including a continental breakfast. The *Hilton Inn* (☎ 435-628-0463, fax 435-628-1501), 1450 S Hilton Drive, has 100 rooms, among them the largest and most comfortable in St George. There is a pool, spa, sauna and tennis court. A golf course and health club (for a fee) are within short walking distance. A restaurant and lounge are on the premises. Double rooms run $70 to $110.

The *Holiday Inn* (☎ 435-628-4235, fax 435-628-8157), 850 S Bluff, is the largest hotel in town with 164 comfortable rooms, some with refrigerators or balconies. Facilities include two pools as well as a spa, exercise room, playground, tennis court, putting green, game room, coin laundry and business services. A restaurant and bar are on the premises and there is room service. Double rooms are $70 to $100 and a few mini-suites go up to $140.

Places to Eat

For dining with some local atmosphere, the best-known place is *Dick's Cafe* (☎ 435-673-3841), 114 E St George Blvd. It has been here since 1935 under the motto 'Where the West Meets the Guest' – American dining amid Western trappings. It is open from 6 am to 9:30 pm daily in summer (shorter hours otherwise) with midpriced meals (around $5 for breakfast or lunch, $7 to $14 for dinner). There's both a coffee shop and a more old-fashioned diner area; no alcohol is served.

Andelin's Gable House (☎ 435-673-6796), 290 E St George Blvd, is known for its fine, five-course, fixed-price dinners, homemade rolls and desserts as well as its conventional American menu. The ambiance here is Olde Worlde, with antiques everywhere and 'wenchresses' wearing 18th-century outfits. The place is very popular, partly because it's within walking distance of several good hotels, though locals consider this to be one of the town's better restaurants, too. It is open from 11:30 am to 10 pm Monday to Saturday. Lunches (burgers, sandwiches, salads) are $5 to $8; dinners are $8 to $25. This is a no-smoking, no-alcohol restaurant.

McGuire's (☎ 435-628-4066), 531 N Bluff, is an upmarket restaurant, serving some Italian and continental dishes as well as American dinners from 5:30 to 10:30 pm Monday to Saturday. Most entrées cost between $10 and $23; it has a liquor license.

The northwest corner of Main and St George Blvd is called **Ancestor Square** and has several decent restaurants as well as interesting shops in quaint surroundings. *Basila's Greek & Italian Cafe* (☎ 435-673-7671) has good and authentic food and is locally popular for business lunches, etc.

It is open Monday to Saturday for lunch (11 am to 2:30 pm, about $5 to $9) and dinner (5 to 9:30 pm, entrées from $10 to $25). It serves alcohol. Also in Ancestor Square is the *Pizza Factory* (☎ 435-628-1234) and the *Pasta Factory* (☎ 435-674-3753) for both eat-in and takeout Italian food. *JJ Hunan Chinese Restaurant* (☎ 435-628-7219) serves a huge variety of Chinese dishes from 11:30 am to 9:30 pm daily (8:30 pm on Sunday). Good Mexican food is served at *Los Hermanos* (☎ 435-628-5989), on the west side of Ancestor Square, open from 11:30 am to 9:15 pm Monday to Saturday in summer, shorter hours otherwise.

Other good places for Mexican food are *Paula's Cazuela* (☎ 435-673-6568), 745 W Ridge View Drive, which is closed on Sundays, and *Pancho & Lefty's* (☎ 435-628-4772), 1050 S Bluff, open daily from 11:30 am to 10 pm. Both are inexpensive and serve alcohol. Also a good value if you're hungry is the *Chuck-A-Rama* (☎ 435-673-4464), 127 N Red Cliffs Drive, with a variety of all-you-can-eat buffets.

If you like steak or seafood, the best place in town is *Sullivan's Rococo Steak House* (☎ 435-673-3305) at the Rococo Inn. There are great city views from the dining room. Hours are 11 am to 4 pm on weekdays and 5 to 10 pm every day. Most dinners are in the $20s; lunches are inexpensive. For less expensive steaks, head over to the *Sizzler* (☎ 435-628-1313), 405 E St George Blvd, which serves breakfast, lunch and dinner.

For something different, make a reservation (required) at the *Bentley Supper House* (☎ 435-628-6999) in the Greene Gate Village B&B, where they serve old-fashioned, home-cooked country dinners in a pioneer setting on Thursday, Friday and Saturday nights. The old-fashioned *Judd's Store* (☎ 435-628-2596), 62 W Tabernacle (part of the Greene Gate Village), serves traditional shakes using ancient machines in a turn-of-the-19th-century setting.

Both *Denny's*, located at 155 N 1000 East (☎ 435-673-4908) and 1215 S Main (☎ 435-628-6607), are open 24 hours.

Entertainment

From October to May, Dixie College (☎ 435-673-4811) hosts a Celebrity Concert Series as well as plays and musicals at the *Fine Arts Center Theater* (☎ 435-628-3121), 225 S 700 East. Also call the Dixie Center (☎ 435-628-7003) for other cultural entertainment.

Tuacahn Amphitheater (☎ 435-652-3200, 800-746-9882), 10 miles northwest of town, has outdoor presentations of an epic musical, *Utah!*, in which a large cast sings, dances and acts its way through the tales of the first Mormon pioneers, including Jacob Hamblin whose house can be toured en route to the amphitheater. Special effects such as floods and fires are enhanced by the natural red-rock scenery. There are daily performances from mid-June through Labor Day; tickets range from $16 to $26 for adults, $10 to $17 for six- to 12-year-olds.

The Mormon influence remains strong, and there is little in the way of bars and nightclubs. For a beer and a game of pool, try the simple *Blarney Stone Pub* (☎ 435-673-9191), 800 E St George Blvd, which has occasional live music on weekends.

Movies (☎ 435-673-1994) are shown at six cinema complexes around town.

Getting There & Away

Air The airport is on a bluff overlooking downtown from the west – nice views. Skywest Airlines has six daily flights to and from Salt Lake City, two flights to Las Vegas, Nevada, and sometimes flights to other destinations.

Bus Greyhound (☎ 435-673-2933) leaves from the McDonald's at 1235 S Bluff, with two buses (one around midnight, the other late morning) to Salt Lake City, as well as buses to Denver, Colorado, and Las Vegas.

St George Shuttle (☎ 435-628-8320, 800-933-8320) has seven vans a day direct to Las Vegas Airport for $20.

Getting Around

For a car rental try Budget (☎ 435-673-6825), 116 W St George Blvd; Dollar (☎ 435-628-6549), 1175 S 150 East; National

(☎ 435-673-5098), at the airport; and Thrifty (☎ 435-674-2234), 280 N Bluff.

AROUND ST GEORGE

South of town, I-15 swings southwest; after 8 miles, it crosses the Arizona state line and 30 miles farther, the Nevada state line, on its way to Las Vegas about 120 miles southwest of St George. Joshua trees can be seen near the Utah/Arizona line – an unusual species for Utah. **Mesquite**, on the Nevada state line, has a casino with relatively inexpensive but comfortable accommodations for the nearest gambling to southwestern Utah.

Snow Canyon State Park

Snow? Ha! Not in this hot desert country. The park derived its name from early pioneers. The scenery is volcanic and well worth seeing: cinder cones and lava flows mixed in with the usual Southwestern sandstone cliffs and petroglyphs. The desert vegetation is interesting. There are hiking trails; a 1-mile hike leads to lava caves, and longer hikes go to arches and canyons. Summers are searingly hot, so come prepared with plenty of water and sun protection. Other seasons are more pleasant.

The *campground* has showers and 21 tent sites ($12) and 14 RV sites with hookups ($14); reservations (☎ 800-322-3770) are recommended during spring and fall weekends. Primitive camping (no facilities) is possible along the longer trails.

The park is 9 miles north of St George on Hwy 18 and then left; the road continues through the park to Ivins, Santa Clara and back to St George. This 24-mile loop is a popular drive or bike ride. Day use is $4 per vehicle. For further information, contact the park (☎ 435-628-2255).

Veyo Area

Veyo is a tiny village 19 miles north of St George on Hwy 18. **Veyo Pool** (☎ 435-574-2300) is a swimming pool filled by naturally warmed spring water. It has been in use since the 1920s, thus making it a historic spot by Utahan standards. Note the nearby (extinct) volcano on the west side of Hwy 18, which provides the warmed waters. There is picnicking and a café along with a rock-climbing area. It is open from May to Labor Day from 11 am to nightfall (or later). Swims are about $4. The pool is signed to the east of Hwy 18, 19 miles north of St George.

Ten miles southwest of Veyo, **Gunlock State Park** offers fishing and boating. There is no campground or development yet, so entrance is free – information is available from Snow Canyon State Park.

Five miles north of Veyo, there is free camping at the BLM-owned **Baker Dam Reservoir**, which has no water for drinking but does offer decent fishing and boating. A few miles farther north is the **Mountain Meadows Massacre Monument**, marking the site where Mormons killed about 120 non-Mormon pioneers in 1857 for reasons that are still unclear.

Enterprise Area
This agricultural town of 1100 inhabitants is 19 miles north of Veyo. The *Cottonwood Motel* (☎ 435-878-2603, 435-878-2433) at the east end next to a gas station, store and country café, has six rooms. Rooms are in the $30s midweek, more expensive on weekends.

Paved and then gravel roads lead 11 miles west to **Enterprise Reservoir** with fishing, boating and the USFS *Honey Comb Rocks Campground*, open from mid-May to November, with water but no showers. Sites cost $8. This campground is remote and uncrowded, especially midweek. The USFS also operates the free but waterless *Pine Park Campground*, about 10 miles west of the reservoir turnoff. This is a poor road, though cars can just make it in dry weather.

Pine Valley Area
To reach the village of **Pine Valley**, exit Hwy 18 at Central, between Veyo and Enterprise, and head a few miles east. The village is 32 miles from St George and its 6500-foot elevation gives some relief from the lowland heat. A fine, white-wood church, built in 1868, is the

oldest continually operating Mormon church in Utah. It is open for tours.

The small *Pine Valley Lodge* (☎ 435-574-2544) offers 10 rustic rooms and cabins ranging from about $25 to $50 – higher rates on weekends. The cabins sleep up to four and are the cheapest; bring your own bedding. There are public coin showers and laundry, a store and a café. The *Pine & Thistle B&B* (☎ 435-574-2746), 49 N 300 East, Pine Valley, UT 84722, has two rooms with a shared bath for $65 double and one with a private bath for $85 double, including breakfast. Lunch and dinner are available with advance notice. Nearby is the *Brandin' Iron Steak House* (☎ 435-574-2261), which serves dinners on Fridays and Saturdays year-round.

Half a mile to the east, you enter the Dixie National Forest and within 3 miles pass a cluster of five small campgrounds (with a total of about 70 sites) at 6800 feet. These are popular, especially during weekends in the May-to-October season. All campgrounds have water but no showers and cost $9. Arrive early or call ☎ 800-280-2267 for a reservation.

Several hikes and backpacking trips are possible from the campgrounds up into the Pine Valley Mountains – the ranger station in St George can provide maps and information about the trailheads as well as other campgrounds in the Dixie National Forest.

Leeds Area
Leeds, a small town of 500, has a couple of places to eat and an RV park. It is off I-15 exit 22, 13 miles northeast of St George.

Over a thousand people lived in **Silver Reef** in the late 19th century, drawn to it by silver mining. Today, most of the buildings have disappeared, although a few dilapidated ruins remain. The Wells Fargo building has been restored and now houses a small museum and art gallery (☎ 435-879-2254), open 9 am to 5 pm Monday to Saturday. Silver Reef is just over a mile northwest of Leeds by a signed, paved road.

South of Leeds is **Quail Creek State Park** (☎ 435-879-2378), 4 miles east of

STEPHEN TRIMBLE

CHUCK PLACE

LEE FOSTER

CHUCK PLACE

Top: Downtown Salt Lake City
Bottom Left: Mormon Temple in Salt Lake City, Utah

Middle Right: Mormon Tabernacle Choir, Salt Lake City, Utah
Bottom Right: Mormon Temple, Logan, Utah

RALPH LEE HOPKINS

STEPHEN TRIMBLE

ROB RACHOWIECKI

Top: Zion Canyon, Zion National Park, Utah
Bottom Left: Wasatch Mountains, Utah

Bottom Right: Bryce Canyon National Park, Utah

I-15 exit 16 toward Hurricane. The reservoir provides the usual fishing and boating, and there is a small campground with water but no showers for $8. Day use is $4.

Fort Pearce & Dinosaur Tracks
The ruins of Fort Pearce can be reached by heading east from River Rd on 1450 S and, after 2 miles, following signs along a dirt road for another 6 miles. From Fort Pearce, two more miles of dirt road lead to the dinosaur tracks, where there are interpretive signs. Cars can drive the road in good weather. There are also dinosaur tracks northeast of Washington, but you have to hike in the last few hundred yards – ask at the St George Chamber of Commerce for precise directions.

HURRICANE
With more than 7000 inhabitants (1998 estimate), this is a growing town whose population has doubled in the past decade (Hurricane attracts retirees), resulting in plenty of new construction that can create traffic bottlenecks. The area is famous for its peaches and is the main town between Zion National Park (25 miles east) and St George (20 miles west).

Information
The small chamber of commerce is at Main and 100 S next to the old Bradshaw Hotel and is open 10 am to 5 pm Monday to Saturday (it may move soon). Information is offered at the museum as well.

Things to See & Do
The **Pioneer and Indian Museum**, 35 W State near Main, showcases the area's history and is open from 9 am to 5 pm Monday to Saturday. The old **Bradshaw Motel**, Main at 100 S, built in 1906, was the first home in the area and can now be visited: see the old doctor's office, a doll collection and turn-of-the-century furniture.

A mile north of town, the **Pah Tempe Hot Springs** (☎ 435-863-2879, fax 435-635-2353), 825 N 800 East, Hurricane, UT 84737, fill a series of dip pools and a swimming pool. Fees are $10 for all day, $5 for

two- to 12-year-olds. Massage and yoga programs are offered and there are picnicking, camping and B&B facilities. This is a quiet, no-smoking, alcohol-free establishment and bathing suits are required.

The new **Sky Mountain Golf Course** (☎ 435-635-7888) offers 18 holes, par 72.

Hurricane hosts the **Washington County Fair** in August.

Places to Stay & Eat
New places open every year. Summer rates are given below; prices drop about $10 in winter. Very cheap motels are nowhere to be found, but there is a hostel. There are several restaurants and the usual fast-food places, but name changes and new owners in this fast-growing town seem to be the order of the day. Ask locally for recommendations.

Camping *Pah Tempe Hot Springs* (see above) has tent sites for $20 for one person and $10 for each additional person, including use of the hot springs. RV hookups are an extra $6. *Robert's Roost* (☎ 435-635-0126), 113 W 400 South, has 15 RV sites with showers and coin laundry. *Willowind RV Park* (☎ 435-635-4154), 1150 W 80 South (just off Hwy 9), charges $12 to $18 for tent and RV sites and has hookups, showers and a spa. *Brentwood RV Resort* (☎ 435-635-2320), 150 N 3700 West (4 miles west on Hwy 9), has about 200 sites for $16 with hookups and a few tent sites for $12. Facilities include showers, a restaurant, pool, spa and playground as well as minigolf, putting and tennis; there's a waterslide park nearby.

Other Accommodations The *Dixie Hostel* (☎ 435-635-8202, 435-635-9000), 73 S Main (junction of Hwys 9 and 59), charges $15 per person in dorms and has a few private doubles. Kitchen, laundry and linen are provided and reservations are suggested.

Park Villa Motel (☎ 435-635-4010, fax 435-635-4025), 650 W State, has a pool and spa and is a good place to stay. Most rooms have kitchenettes and rent for $45 to $60 in summer, less in winter. The *Best Western Weston Lamplighter* (☎ 435-635-4647, fax 435-635-0848), 280 W State, has a seasonal pool and spa. Rooms are in the $50s and $60s in summer, less in winter, and include continental breakfast.

Three new chain hotels have opened in the last couple of years. The *Super 8 Motel* (☎ 435-635-0808, fax 435-635-0909), 65 S 700 West, has a pool and spa open in summer; rooms are in the $50s, including continental breakfast. *Days Inn* (☎ 435-635-0500, 435-635-0272), 40 N 2600 West (about 2 miles west on Hwy 9), boasts an indoor pool and spa, with standard rooms for $40 to $60 and mini-suites with refrigerators and microwaves for about $80. Nearby, *Comfort Inn* (☎ 435-635-3500, fax 435-635-2425) has an outdoor pool and spa, and good-sized rooms, some with microwaves and refrigerators, for $40 to $75.

Pah Tempe Hot Springs B&B (see above) has rooms with shared bath for $45/55 single/double; rooms with two beds and private bath for $55 to $85 for one to four people; and similarly priced rooms with two beds, fireplace and shared bathroom. Rates include taxes, full breakfast and use of the hot springs. There are a total of six rooms and reservations are requested.

About 10 miles east of Hurricane on Hwy 9 in the tiny community of **Virgin** is *Snow Family Guest Ranch* (☎ /fax 435-635-2500), which offers nine Western-style B&B rooms for $75 to $150, depending on room and season. The guest ranch has horses for rent and offers guided trail rides.

GRAFTON GHOST TOWN & ROCKVILLE

Grafton has several buildings, including a church, a large two-story house and general store – all standing empty and mute save for the wind ghosting through them. The site has gained fame since it was the setting for the bicycle scene in *Butch Cassidy and the Sundance Kid*, starring Robert Redford (who owns the Sundance Ski Resort in Utah).

Grafton is reached from Rockville, a few miles southwest of Springdale. From Hwy 9, turn south on 200 East (also called Bridge Lane – it crosses the river). The road is signed as a 'Scenic Byway' and reaches Grafton in 4 miles (turn right at a fork about halfway). The last section is dirt, but it's passable to cars.

In Rockville, population 250, several small nonsmoking B&Bs offer full breakfast. The best-established include *Handcart House* (☎ 435-772-3867), 244 W Main, Rockville, UT 84763, which has four rooms with private baths and antique furniture. Rates are about $60 to $80 for two people. The *Blue House* (☎ 435-772-3912), 125 E Main, Rockville, UT 84763, has four rooms for about $10 less. Newer places include the *Hummingbird Inn* (☎ 435-772-3632, 800-964-2473), 37 W Main, Rockville, UT 84763, with four rooms with private bath. There is a game room and spa. The two-room *Serenity House* (☎ 435-772-3393, 800-266-3393), 149 E Main, Rockville, UT 84763, is cheaper.

SPRINGDALE

With a permanent population of 350, Springdale's main claims to fame are its position at the entrance to Zion National Park and its many hotels. Most of these are along Zion Park Blvd (lower address numbers are closest to the park entrance). There are nice mountain views from most parts of town.

Tourist information is available in summer; look for a sign. Year-round, you can contact the Zion Canyon Chamber of Commerce (☎ 435-722-3757), PO Box 331, Springdale, UT 84767-0331. Emergency medical care is available from May through October at Zion Medical Clinic (☎ 435-772-3226).

Things to See & Do

The **OC Tanner Amphitheater** (☎ 435-652-7994) has a variety of musical and theatrical events and a multimedia sound-and-light show about Zion – happenings occur nightly throughout the summer. The **Southern Utah Folklife Festival** is held here in September.

The **Zion Canyon Cinemax Theater** (☎ 435-772-2400) is just 200 feet from the entrance to Zion National Park in Springdale. The theater has a giant movie screen (82 feet wide and six stories high), and showings of *Zion Canyon – Treasures of the Gods* take place every odd hour from 9 am to 9 pm in summer. The film starts with the Ancestral Puebloan dwellers of the area and continues with the history and legends of Zion. Every even hour from 10 am to 8 pm has screenings of *The Great American West*, featuring the lives of Indians, explorers and pioneers in the West. Hours are 11 am to 7 pm in winter. Admission is $7 for adults and $4.50 for children.

Bicycles, kayaks and inner tubes (for tubing down the Virgin River) are available for rent – just look for signs.

Places to Stay – Camping

Zion Canyon Campground (☎ 435-772-3237), PO Box 99, Springdale, UT 84767, 479 Zion Park Blvd, has a restaurant, store, playground and coin laundry. You can take a dip in the Virgin River, which runs by. There are almost 200 sites for $15 (tents) to $19 with hookups, several camping cabins for about $40 and a few motel rooms for $65 to $75. Showers are available for walk-ins ($3). More camping sites are available in the national park.

Places to Stay – Middle

Motels Roughly April to October is the high season; Memorial Day to Labor Day is particularly busy and hotels charge much more. An idea of summer/winter differences are given for some hotels below, but you can expect winter discounts on all of them. Reservations are recommended during the busy period, especially on weekends, though you can usually find somewhere to stay on most days if you don't arrive late in the day. (St George is almost an hour away.)

Very cheap places do not exist in the high season, but the midpriced places are clean and a fair value. Among the least expensive are the camping cabins (see Place to Stay – Camping, above) and the *El Rio Lodge*

(☎ 435-772-3205, 888-772-3205), 995 Zion Park Blvd, with just 11 rooms for $47/52 with one/two beds in summer. It has great views from the sun deck. The rustic-looking and popular *Pioneer Lodge* (☎ 435-772-3233, 800-772-3233, fax 435-772-3165), 838 Zion Park Blvd, has about 40 standard double rooms in the upper $50s during summer, $35 to $45 in winter. It has a restaurant, pool and spa. The *Terrace Brook Lodge* (☎ 435-772-3932, 800-342-6779, fax 435-772-3596), 990 Zion Park Blvd, has a pool and two dozen rooms for about $52/60 for singles/doubles in summer, in the $40s in winter. Some rooms have good views.

The facilities at the *Zion Park Motel* (☎ 435-772-3251), 855 Zion Park Blvd, include a pool, playground, picnic area and coin laundry. About 20 rooms with two queen-size beds rent for $59 double, three rooms with a double bed are $45; two apartments (sleeping up to six) with kitchenettes rent for about $100. The pleasant *Bumbleberry Inn* (☎ 435-772-3224, 800-828-1534, fax 435-772-3947), 897 Zion Park Blvd, has a popular restaurant, a garden and pool, indoor racquetball court and spa, and a game room with air hockey and pool table. Forty-eight sizable clean rooms, most with mountain views, are $59 to $75.

The *Canyon Ranch Motel* (☎ 435-772-3357, fax 435-772-3057), 668 Zion Park Blvd, has a shaded lawn, pool and spa. Rooms are in homey cottages, most with good views. Doubles are $59 to $69; some have kitchenettes and may have a queen- or king-size bed, or two beds. Winter rates are $44 to $54. The *Best Western Driftwood Lodge* (☎ 435-772-3262, fax 435-772-3702), 1515 Zion Park Blvd, is quietly situated on the outskirts of town, 2 miles from the park entrance. The grounds are attractive and the views are good. Many rooms have balconies or porches and run $70 to $82 for a double, including continental breakfast. Two-bedroom family units are $100 to $108. There is a pool and spa.

Flanigan's Inn (☎ 435-772-3244, 800-765-7787, fax 435-772-3396), 428 Zion Park Blvd, just over a quarter of a mile from the park entrance, has a pool and picnic area on nice grounds – good views. A decent restaurant and lounge are on the premises. Most doubles are about $80; a few units have kitchenettes for $90; suites are about $150. Breakfast is included. The *Cliffrose Lodge* (☎ 435-772-3234, 800-243-8824, fax 435-772-3900), 281 Zion Park Blvd, is set in five acres of trees and gardens bordered by the Virgin River. There is a pool, playground and coin laundry. All rooms are large, have good views and rent for $119 to $145 from May through October. You are paying for the view and location: closest lodgings to the park entrance. Off-season discounts range from 25% to 60% lower.

The *Zion Park Inn* (☎ 435-772-3200, 800-934-7275, fax 435-772-2449), 1215 Zion Park Blvd, is a new resort and conference center with 120 rooms. Rates are in the $80s for doubles, $110 to $135 for units with kitchens, and $135 to $150 for suites. There is a restaurant, an outdoor pool open from April through October and a year-round outdoor spa.

B&Bs Built of local sandstone in the 1930s, quaint *O'Toole's B&B* (☎ 435-772-3457, fax 435-772-3324), 980 Zion Park Blvd, Springdale, UT 84767, has two small, antique-filled rooms with shared bath ($69) and a larger suite with private bath, kitchen and sitting room ($125). In the garden, a small cabin built in the 1920s has three bedrooms, each with private bath, for $65 or $79. There is a spa; smoking is prohibited; children are allowed by prior arrangement; full breakfast is included.

Half a mile from the park entrance, the *Harvest House* (☎ 435-772-3880), 29 Canyon View Drive, Springdale, UT 84767, is a modern house (built in 1989), with four spacious and light bedrooms, all with private bath. Two rooms have sun decks; there is a spa; smoking is not allowed. Rates range from $80 to $100 a double, including full breakfast.

The very friendly *Zion House* (☎/fax 435-772-3281), 801 Zion Park Blvd, Spring-

dale, UT 84767, has four large rooms, each with mountain views. Two share a bathroom and one has a kitchenette. Smoking is prohibited. Rates are $70 to $95 for two people.

Places to Eat

The most popular place in town is the *Bit & Spur Mexican Restaurant & Saloon* (☎ 435-772-3498), 1212 Zion Park Blvd, which serves dinner from 5 to 9:30 pm; the saloon stays open till midnight. The Mexican food is good and you can have equally tasty (and more pricey) Southwestern cuisine as well. The *Pioneer Family Restaurant* (☎ 435-772-3467), 828 Zion Park Blvd, next to the Pioneer Lodge, is locally popular and serves home-style breakfast, lunch and dinner. The *Panda Gardens* (☎ 435-772-3535), 805 Zion Park Blvd, serves excellent Chinese food from noon to 11 pm.

Zion Pizza & Noodle Company (☎ 435-772-3815), 868 Zion Park Blvd, has inexpensive Italian food as well as salads, microbrews and espressos. *Pizza to Go* (☎ 435-772-3462), 479 Zion Park Blvd, next to the Zion Canyon Campground, has pizza and other Italian food to eat in or take out – it's even open for breakfast in summer if you wake up craving a pepperoni pizza. *Oscar's Café & Deli* (☎ 435-772-3232), 61 Zion Park Blvd, near the park entrance, has the great motto 'We cook because we like to' and is locally recommended. The new *Loghouse Restaurant* (☎ 435-772-3000, fax 435-772-3100), 2400 Zion Park Blvd, at the far west end of town, is a huge, log-roofed establishment with great views and a wildlife museum. It's open daily for upscale but casual American lunches and dinners. They plan on opening a lodge.

Several motels offer good restaurants. The *Shonesburg Restaurant* (☎ 435-772-3522), in the Bumbleberry Inn, serves home-style American food from 7 am to 9:30 pm in summer, 8 am to 8 pm in winter, closed Sunday. Here you'll find yummy bumbleberry pies and pancakes. Never heard of bumbleberries? You have now. The more upmarket *Switchback Grille* at the Zion Park Inn is open from 7 am to 10 pm and features wood-fired pizza and grilled steaks and chicken. *Flanigan's Inn Restaurant*, open from 7 am to 10 pm in summer, is one of the fanciest places in this casual town – great dining views. It features contemporary Western cooking.

ZION NATIONAL PARK

The white, pink and red rocks of Zion are so huge, overpowering and magnificent that they are at once a photographer's dream and despair. Few photos can do justice to the magnificent scenery found in this, the first national park established in Utah.

The highlight is Zion Canyon, a half-mile-deep slash formed by the Virgin River cutting through the sandstone. Everyone wants to follow the narrow paved road at the bottom, straining their neck at colorful vistas of looming cliffs, domes and mountains with evocative names such as the Great White Throne or Mountain of the Sun. So popular is this route that it has become severely overcrowded with vehicles and the NPS will be implementing a

shuttle bus service in 1999 to mitigate this problem. (See the sidebar The Price of Popularity, below.) Other scenic drives are less crowded and just as magnificent. For those with the time and energy, day and overnight hikes can take you into spectacularly wild country.

Orientation

Three roads enter the park. Hiking trails depart from all three roads, leading you further into the splendor.

At the southern end, the paved Zion-Mt Carmel Hwy (Hwy 9 between Mt Carmel Junction and Springdale) is the most popular route and leads past the entrance of Zion Canyon. This road has fine views, but it is also exceptionally steep, twisting and narrow for much of its length. A tunnel on the east side of Zion Canyon is so narrow that escorts must accompany vehicles over 7 feet, 10 inches (2.4m) wide or 11 feet, 4 inches (3.46m) tall (call ☎ 435-772-3256 in advance to arrange an escort; a fee is charged). Bicycles are prohibited in the

---

The Price of Popularity

In the late 1970s, there were about a million annual visitors to Zion National Park – about the number for which the park facilities had been intended. The popularity of the park has grown tremendously since then, and now more than 2½ million visitors arrive annually, with more coming each year.

The pressure on the park is enormous, yet federal funding has not grown commensurably and the Park Service is struggling to cope with visitor problems. Problems? Hundreds of thousands of feet combine to erode the most popular trails, which must be paved. Exhaust fumes from many thousands of cars slowly pollute the area. Unthinking visitors feed wildlife, draw graffiti, dump litter, pick flowers, defecate on the trails, make unnecessary noise or ignore trail markers.

Zion has to be seen to be believed, but you can see it without making an unnecessarily heavy impact. Don't drop trash (carry a resealable plastic bag for diapers, toilet paper, sanitary pads, sardine cans and other odorous objects). Don't disturb the wildlife – never feed or try to touch animals. Respect the beauty of the area in the same way you would respect a museum, a home, a church, a school, a treasure . . . a national park is all of these and more.

Various solutions to the overcrowding problem have been discussed. The National Park Service is required to protect the parks for the enjoyment of the public, and this, the Park Service says, precludes the obvious solution of limiting the number of visitors. There are plans for creating large parking areas at the main park entrance and making all visitors walk or ride shuttle buses within the canyon. (This option has worked well in Yosemite National Park in California.) ■

tunnel unless they are transported on a vehicle. The Zion Canyon Rd itself is an offshoot from Hwy 9, dead-ending about 7 miles up the canyon. The main visitor center and campgrounds lie at the mouth of Zion Canyon, and lodging is nearby, either in the canyon or Springdale. The elevation in Zion Canyon is about 4000 feet, and at the east entrance, 5700 feet.

For the middle of the park, paved **Kolob Terrace Rd** leaves Hwy 9 at the village of Virgin (elevation 3550 feet), climbs north into the Kolob Plateau for about 9 miles and then becomes gravel for a few more miles to Lava Point (elevation 7890 feet), where there is a ranger station and primitive campground. This road is closed by snow from about November to May. The road continues out of the park past Kolob Reservoir, to Hwy 14 and Cedar City as a dirt road that becomes impassable after rain. There is also another dirt road that branches off to I-15. This is the least used of the three roads into the park.

At the north end, the paved **Kolob Canyons Rd** leaves I-15 at exit 40 and extends 5 miles into the park. There is a visitor center at the beginning of the road, but no camping. The road, which is more than 5000 feet above sea level, is open all year, and there are several scenic lookouts over the Finger Canyon formations.

There is so much to see in Zion that entire books have been written about it. The descriptions below are necessarily brief, but remember that free maps and information are available from the entrance stations and visitor centers. Likewise, you can read one of the hiking guidebooks.

Zion National Park is undergoing major changes. In addition to an increase in the number of shuttle buses into Zion Canyon during 1999 and 2000, the main visitor center will be moving from the mouth of Zion Canyon to near the expanded parking areas/shuttle bus stop at the entrance of the park. Check at the visitor center for the most up-to-date information. The NPS plans to extend the shuttle route through Springdale, enabling hotel guests to leave

their cars at the hotel and hitch a ride all the way into the canyon.

Information

The main visitor center (☎ 435-772-3256), on Hwy 9 near the mouth of Zion Canyon, less than a mile from the south entrance near Springdale, will be moving to the park entrance in 1999. The building now housing the visitor center will become a cultural museum with exhibits focusing on the geology, wildlife, archaeology and history of the area.

Park rangers answer questions about any aspect of the park and present a variety of programs, including Junior Ranger Programs for six- to 12-year-olds. These run from Memorial Day to Labor Day, last 2½ hours, and are offered twice a day from Tuesday to Saturday at a charge of just $2. Parents can get a couple of hours to themselves! Other free programs (discussions, talks, demonstrations, hikes etc) run from March to November during the day and in the evening. Visitor center hours are 9 am to 5 pm daily, 8 am to 8 pm in summer.

The smaller Kolob Canyons Visitor Center (☎ 435-586-9548), at the beginning of Kolob Canyons Rd, is open from 8 am to 4:30 pm and also has park exhibits, information, books and maps.

Entrance to the park is $5 per person (on foot, bicycle or motorbike) or $10 per private vehicle. Tickets are valid for seven days, and Golden Age, Eagle and Access Passes are accepted. The south and east entrance stations (at either end of the Zion-Mt Carmel Hwy) and the visitor centers provide park maps and informative brochures.

In an emergency, call the visitor centers or ☎ 435-772-3322 or ☎ 911 24 hours a day.

Further information is available from the Superintendent, Zion National Park, Springdale, UT 84767.

Climate & When to Go

From as early as March to as late as November, the campgrounds may fill, and during the Memorial Day to Labor Day high season they are often full by late

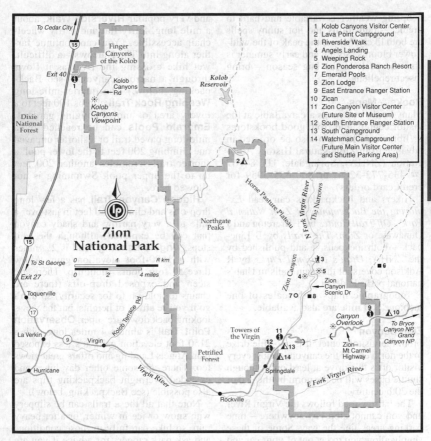

1 Kolob Canyons Visitor Center
2 Lava Point Campground
3 Riverside Walk
4 Angels Landing
5 Weeping Rock
6 Zion Ponderosa Ranch Resort
7 Emerald Pools
8 Zion Lodge
9 East Entrance Ranger Station
10 Zican
11 Zion Canyon Visitor Center
   (Future Site of Museum)
12 South Entrance Ranger Station
13 South Campground
14 Watchman Campground
   (Future Main Visitor Center
   and Shuttle Parking Area)

UTAH

Zion
National Park

To Cedar City
Exit 40
Finger
Canyons
of the Kolob
Kolob
Canyons
Rd
Kolob
Canyons
Viewpoint
Dixie
National
Forest
Kolob
Reservoir
Horse Pasture Plateau
Northgate
Peaks
The Narrows
N Fork Virgin River
Zion Canyon
To St George
Exit 27
Toquerville
La Verkin
Hurricane
Virgin
Rockville
Springdale
Kolob Terrace Rd
Towers of
the Virgin
Petrified
Forest
Virgin River
E Fork Virgin River
Zion Canyon Scenic Dr
Zion
Canyon
Canyon
Overlook
Zion–
Mt Carmel
Highway
To Bryce
Canyon NP,
Grand
Canyon NP

morning, so plan on an early arrival if camping. Almost half of the park's annual visitors arrive in the Memorial Day to Labor Day period. Conversely, only about 7% of the annual visitors come in the December to February period.

Summer weather is hot (well over 100°F is common), so be prepared with plenty of water and sun protection. Temperatures drop into the 60°s F at night, even in midsummer. The summers are generally dry with the exception of about six weeks from late July to early September, when the so-called 'monsoons' –

short but heavy rainstorms – occur, transforming dry canyon walls into waterfalls.

Fall is my favorite season, with beautiful foliage colors peaking in September on the Kolob Plateau and October in the Zion Canyon. By October, daytime weather is pleasantly hot and nights are in the 40°s and 50°s F.

There is snow in winter, but the main roads are plowed and though it may freeze at night, daytime temperatures usually rise to about 50°F. Hikers climbing up from the roads will find colder and more wintry (snow and ice) conditions.

Spring weather is variable and hard to predict – rainstorms and hot sunny spells are both likely. May is the peak of the wildflower blooms. Spring and early summer is also the peak of the bug season – bring insect repellent.

Books & Maps

Many books and maps are available at the visitor centers and from good bookstores or libraries. They can also be ordered in advance from Zion Natural History Association (ZNHA), Springdale, UT 84767 (☎ 435-772-3264, or 800-635-3959 for credit card orders).

Hikers and backpackers can read *Exploring the Backcountry of Zion National Park – Off Trail Routes* by T Brereton and J Dunaway, or *Zion: The Trails* by B Lineback – both inexpensive and published by the ZNHA. *Utah's National Parks* by R Adkison covers all the main trails in Utah's national parks in detail.

Topographic maps with scales of one inch:one half mile are also available.

Zion Canyon

From the visitor center, it is a 7-mile drive to the north end of the canyon; almost every visitor does this drive at least once, though shuttle buses will be the norm by the end of the 20th century.

The narrow road follows the Virgin River and you cannot stop just anywhere – nine parking areas line the way. Some of these simply allow you to get out of your car and take a photograph, but most are trailheads.

In order of increasing difficulty, the best trails accessible from the Zion Canyon road are outlined below. Which have the best views? All of them! There are signs at the trailheads. (All distances listed below are one-way.)

You can stroll or roll along the paved **Pairus Trail**, which stretches paralleling the road for almost 2 miles from the Watchman Campground to the main park junction. Bicycles, dogs and wheelchairs use this trail – the only trail bicycles and dogs are allowed on. Take an easy walk near the canyon's end along the paved

and very popular **Riverside Walk**, about a mile long, fairly flat and partly wheelchair accessible. (You can continue farther along into The Narrows – a difficult, wet hike crossing the river as it flows through a narrow canyon – see Backpacking, below.) The quarter-mile-long **Weeping Rock Trail** climbs 100 feet to a lovely area of moist hanging gardens. **Emerald Pools** can be reached by a mile-long paved trail or a shorter unpaved one climbing 200 feet to the lower pool; a shorter trail scrambles another 200 feet up to the upper pool. Swimming is not allowed here.

Hidden Canyon Trail has a few long drop-offs and climbs 750 feet in just over a mile to a very narrow and shady canyon that can be explored, although the trail stops. **Angels Landing Trail** is 2½ miles with a 1500-foot elevation gain. Allow three to four hours roundtrip. There are steep and exposed drop-offs (there are chains to hold on to for security) so don't go if you're afraid of heights, but the views looking back down are super. **Observation Point Trail** is almost 4 miles long with a 2150-foot elevation gain; it's less exposed than Angels Landing and offers great views too. There are some other day hikes and extended overnight backpacking trips are also possible (see Backpacking, below).

Note that all these trails can be slippery with snow or ice in winter, or after heavy rain, so hike carefully in those conditions and ask park rangers for advice if you are unsure.

Zion-Mt Carmel Hwy

The road east of Zion Canyon is somewhat of an engineering feat, with many switchbacks and a long tunnel giving access to vehicles (though check the Orientation section for vehicle restrictions). East of the tunnel, the geology changes into slickrock, with many carved and etched formations of which the mountainous Checkerboard Mesa is a memorable example. It's just over 10 miles from the Zion Canyon turnoff to the east exit of the park, and there are several parking areas along the road. Only one has a marked trail (though other short walks are possible) – the half-mile-long **Canyon Overlook Trail**, which climbs more than 100 feet and gives fine views into Zion Canyon, 1000 feet lower. The trailhead is just east of the mile-long tunnel (there is a second, much shorter, tunnel).

Kolob Canyons Rd

This 5-mile-long road penetrates the Finger Canyons area at the north end of the park. It is about a 40-mile drive from the main visitor center, out of the park along Hwys 9 and 17 to I-15, then north to exit 40. Perhaps visitors don't think it worth driving 40 miles just to see one more short scenic drive. Whatever the reason, this road is much less busy than the above two, and this is one of its attractions. The other is the scenery, which is just as stupendous as in the south part of the park.

There are several parking areas. One gives access to the 2.7-mile-long **Taylor Creek Trail**, with a 450-foot elevation gain and the possibility of wet feet – the trail crosses the creek many times. A little farther, the Lee Pass overlook gives access to the **La Verkin Creek Trail**, which drops 700 feet in 7.2 miles to the **Kolob Arch** – the biggest arch in the park and one of two vying for the title of 'biggest arch in the world' (the other is Landscape Arch in Arches National Park, in southeastern Utah). Fit hikers can do the roundtrip (14.4 miles) to the arch in a day. This trail continues even farther for extended backpacking trips. The last parking area has a picnic site at **Kolob Canyons Viewpoint**. From here, the half-mile **Timber Creek Overlook Trail** climbs about 100 feet to a small peak.

Kolob Terrace Rd

This 11-mile road reaches Lava Point (7890 feet), a cool relief from the Zion Canyon summer heat. Though not as crowded as the main park roads, it's still busy in the high season and is as scenically rewarding. Three trails leave the road. The **Hop Valley Trail** is an alternate way of reaching Kolob

Arch; it's about 7 miles and an 1100-foot elevation drop along the watered Hop Valley – green fields amidst red cliffs. The **Wildcat Canyon Trail** is 6 miles long and begins along Kolob Terrace Rd, emerging at Lava Point. Beginning at Lava Point makes it more of a descent – either get a car shuttle or walk back the way you came. Also from Lava Point, the **West Rim Trail** goes about 14 miles to Zion Canyon – this is mainly a backpackers' trail.

Backpacking

You can backpack and wilderness camp along the over 100 miles of trails in Zion. Starting from Lee Pass on the Kolob Canyons Rd in the north, you could backpack along a number of connected trails emerging at the east entrance of the park. This entire traverse of the park is about 50 miles. A variety of shorter backpacking options are suggested in Adkison's book and by park rangers.

The most famous backpacking trip is through **The Narrows** – a 16-mile journey through canyons along the North Fork of the Virgin River. In places the canyon walls are only 20 feet apart and tower hundreds of feet above you. The hike requires wading and sometimes swimming the river many times. It is usually done from Chamberlain's Ranch (outside the park) to the Riverside Walk Trail at the north end of Zion Canyon so hikers move with the river current. The trip takes about 12 hours and camping for a night is recommended. This hike is limited to June to October and may be closed from late July to early September because of flash flood danger. The few miles at the north end of Zion Canyon can get very crowded with hundreds of day hikers.

All backpackers for all routes need to obtain a permit from either visitor center. Permits cost $5 per person per night. Normally, permits are issued the day before or the morning of the trip – there is rarely any problem with selecting a route, with the exception of The Narrows, for which you may need to wait a day or two. Camping is allowed in the backcountry, but there are several restricted areas. Rangers will warn you about restrictions and also give you current information about the availability of water. Unlike many desert parks, Zion has a number of springs and rivers flowing year-round. None of these sources is clean and all water must be boiled or treated. Maximum group size is 12 people. Animals are not allowed.

Campfires are not allowed, so you need to carry a camping stove or food that doesn't need to be cooked. Sun protection is essential – sunblock, hat, dark glasses and long sleeves. Insect repellent is needed in spring and early summer. Backpacking supplies are limited in Springdale – stock up in St George.

Day hikes do not require a permit with the exception of people attempting The Narrows in one day.

Many backpacking trips require either retracing your footsteps or leaving a vehicle at either end of the trip. If you don't have two vehicles, ask at the main visitor center in Zion Canyon, which has a 'Ride Board' where you can connect with other backpackers. Also, Zion Lodge (☎ 435-772-3213) has a shuttle desk and will arrange a ride for you for a fee. Costs are reasonable for groups; for example, a shuttle to the top of The Narrows is $56 for the first passenger but only $1.25 for each additional person.

Horseback Riding & Biking
Three-hour guided rides from the Zion Lodge up the Sandbench Trail are offered daily from March to October by Bryce-Zion Trail Rides (☎ 435-772-3810, 435-679-8665, or call the lodge) for about $38 a person. Riders must be eight or older and weigh under 220 pounds. Sandbench Trail climbs almost 500 feet in 2 miles with great views. Easier, one-hour trail rides (minimum age five) are $15.

Bicycles are prohibited in the mile-long tunnel on the Zion-Mt Carmel Hwy (they can go through in a vehicle) and on all park trails except the Pairus Trail. Biking on park roads is allowed but not very easy because of the steep grades, narrow roads and heavy traffic.

Other Activities
Open-air **tram tours** run from Zion Lodge up and down the canyon several times a day in summer, offering narrated tours and photo stops. **Rock climbing** is permitted in most areas – contact the visitor center for information about routes and restrictions. Climbers should have their own gear, as guides and equipment are not available. **Fishing** is poor but permitted with a Utah fishing license.

Places to Stay & Eat
Between the south entrance and the main visitor center are two Park Service campgrounds, *Watchman* with 170 sites and *South* with 141 sites. Both offer water, barbecue grills, picnic tables and toilets but no showers; sites are $10. Watchman is open year-round, South from March to October, both on a first-come, first-served basis. Campgrounds usually fill up in the afternoon, so arrive early.

Lava Point has a free six-site campground – there's no water. The Zion Canyon Campground in Springdale lets anyone shower for $3. Just outside the east entrance, *Zican* (also called *Mukuntuweep*; ☎ 435-648-2154) has a store, restaurant, showers and several dozen tent sites ($15) and RV sites ($18 to $20).

Zion Lodge (☎ 435-772-3213, reservations at 303-297-2757, fax 435-772-2001) is beautifully set in the middle of Zion Canyon. It offers about 80 comfortable motel rooms and 40 cabins – most have excellent views and private porches. Reservations should be made well in advance; summer dates are sometimes filled months ahead. Motel rooms sleep five and rent from about $80 a double to $95 for five. A few suites are $110 to $120 for two to four people. The cabins are $75 to $95 for one to four people.

The *Zion Lodge Restaurant* is open from 6:30 to 9:30 am, 11:30 am to 2:30 pm and 5:30 to 9 pm – dinner reservations are requested. There is also a *Snack Bar* open all day in summer. Otherwise, stay and eat in Springdale.

Outside the east entrance and 5 miles north from Hwy 9 on North Fork County

Rd is the new *Zion Ponderosa Ranch Resort* (☎ 435-648-2700, 800-293-5444). The resort is signed from Hwy 9 and the last 2.2 miles are gravel. The resort features a pool, hot tub, hot showers, horseback riding, mountain biking, ATV tours, tennis, volleyball, basketball, horseshoes, archery, a playground, a climbing wall, a game room and a restaurant. All-inclusive packages include all the above activities (and fishing and boating at extra charge) plus all meals. Children's activities are offered. Tent sites are $45 to $49 per person; cowboy cabins, which have shared bath and sleep up to six, cost $89/69/65/59/55/49 per person for one to six people with a $10 weekend surcharge; and rustic-looking but modern log cabins with private bath and wet bar are $139/109/99/89/85/79. These are peak rates from late May through early September; there are fewer activities in spring and fall with cheaper rates. The resort is closed in January and February. Lodging-only is available outside the peak season.

Southern Hwy 89 Corridor

In southwestern Utah, Hwy 89 follows the Sevier River Valley at more than 6000 feet above sea level. It retraces the route of Mormon pioneers as they moved south down the east side of the Markagunt Plateau. South of the Sevier River, Hwy 89 has a junction with Hwy 9 (for Zion) and continues on to Kanab and into Arizona. This route is described north to south.

JUNCTION, CIRCLEVILLE & AROUND

Tiny Junction (population 151) is the Piute County seat. The turn-of-the-19th-century red-brick **County Courthouse** (on Hwy 89) is the town's most interesting building and has a tourist information office open in summer. The Piute County Fair is held in Junction every August.

Butch Cassidy

Circleville, 5½ miles southwest of Junction on Hwy 89, is where **Butch Cassidy** grew up. His (unrestored and dilapidated) childhood home is on the west side of Hwy 89, just over 2 miles south of Circleville.

Piute Lake State Park

This park, 7½ miles north of Junction, offers a boat launch area but no other development. It's popular for fishing and boating, and you can wilderness camp for free.

Otter Creek State Park

This park (☎ 435-624-3268), PO Box 43, Antimony, UT 84712, also offers a boat launch, and the trout fishing is reputedly good. The lake attracts many species of water birds, especially in spring and fall migrations, and raptors are often seen in winter – both golden and bald eagles have been recorded. A campground with hot showers is open all year, though it often snows in winter; fees are about $10. Day use is $4. Opposite the park entrance is *Otter Creek RV Park* (☎ 435-624-3292, 800-441-3292), open from mid-March through October. It rents boats, has a café and showers, and charges $15 for RV sites with hookups, less without. The park is 15 miles east of Junction along Hwy 62 (which continues to Hwy 24 and

Loa, 45 miles away; see the Central Utah chapter for more information).

Places to Stay & Eat
The *Last Go-Round Cafe & RV Park* (☎ 435-577-2024), 135 W Center, a block west of the Junction courthouse, has drinking water but no showers. Sites are $12 with hookups, $7 without, and home-cooked breakfast, lunch and dinner is served. *Double W Campground* (☎ 435-577-2527), 85 S Hwy 89 in Circleville, has showers and coin laundry and charges from $7 to $14 for sites. The Fishlake National Forest operates the free *City Creek Campground*, which has drinking water. It is 6 miles northwest of town off Hwy 153. All these places are open from about May to October.

The *Junction Motel* (☎ 435-577-2629), 300 S Main, under a sign that reads 'A Li'l Bit Country,' offers five rooms, some with kitchenettes, from $18 and up. It may close in winter. The *Country Motel* (☎ 435-577-2839), 30 W Main in Circleville, has four rooms in the $20s. Next door is *Kaye's Cafe*. *Butch Cassidy's Hideout* (☎ 435-577-2008, fax 435-577-2009), 339 S Hwy 89 in Circleville, has a café and a few inexpensive rooms.

PANGUITCH
Founded in 1864, this town of 1500 inhabitants is a center for the local ranching and lumbering communities and is the Garfield County seat. Many early buildings remain. Panguitch is in the midst of a scenic region – Hwy 89 to the south, Hwy 143 to the west and Hwy 12 to the east have all been designated 'Scenic Byways.' The northern gateway to Bryce Canyon National Park (24 miles east), Panguitch is a popular stopping place for travelers. Zion is about 70 miles southwest. The elevation of 6666 feet makes for pleasant summer weather.

Orientation & Information
Hwy 89 is the main drag through town and comes in along Main from the north, then turns east at Center. Main south of

Center becomes Hwy 143 leading to Panguitch Lake.

The Garfield County Travel Council (☎ 800-444-6689) has regional travel information year-round. There is also an information booth (☎ 435-676-8131), 800 N Main, open 9 am to 5 pm from May to October. The Dixie National Forest Powell Ranger Station (☎ 435-676-8815), PO Box 80, Panguitch, UT 84759, at 225 E Center, is open from 8 am to 4:30 pm Monday to Friday. The library (☎ 435-676-2431) is at 25 S 200 East. The post office (☎ 435-676-8853) is at 65 N 100 West. The hospital (☎ 435-676-8811) is at 224 N 400 East. The police (☎ 435-676-8807) are at 45 S Main.

Things to See & Do
The new **Paunsagaunt Wildlife Museum** (☎ 435-676-2500), 250 E Center, has a fine display of more than 300 professionally mounted animals in realistic backgrounds. Most are from the West, though there are also animals from Africa, Asia and Europe. Indian artifacts and fossils are also exhibited. Hours are 9 am to 10 pm daily from May through October. Admission is $4; $2.50 for six- to 12-year-olds.

The **DUP Museum**, 100 E Center, is open on summer afternoons and at other times by appointment (curators' telephone numbers are posted on the door). Some of the **red-brick houses** in town date from the 1870s – ask at the information centers about historic buildings.

Special Events
Pioneer Day (July 24) is celebrated with a rodeo. The Garfield County Fair takes place in August.

Places to Stay – Camping
The *Big Fish KOA* (☎ 435-676-2225), 555 S Main, has a pool, showers, playground, coin laundry and grocery store. It is open from April to October. Sites range from $16 to $21; five Kamping Kabins are $28 a double. *Hitch-n-Post* (☎ 435-676-2436), 420 N Main, has showers and coin laundry. A few tent sites are $10; RV sites with hookups are $13.50. *Sportsman's Paradise RV Park*

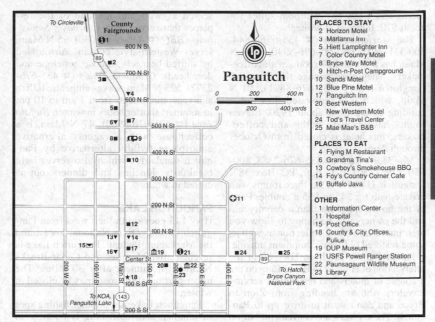

PLACES TO STAY
2 Horizon Motel
3 Marianna Inn
5 Hiett Lamplighter Inn
7 Color Country Motel
8 Bryce Way Motel
9 Hitch-n-Post Campground
10 Sands Motel
12 Blue Pine Motel
17 Panguitch Inn
20 Best Western
New Western Motel
24 Tod's Travel Center
25 Mae Mae's B&B

PLACES TO EAT
4 Flying M Restaurant
6 Grandma Tina's
13 Cowboy's Smokehouse BBQ
14 Foy's Country Corner Cafe
16 Buffalo Java

OTHER
1 Information Center
11 Hospital
15 Post Office
18 County & City Offices,
Police
19 DUP Museum
21 USFS Powell Ranger Station
22 Paunsaugunt Wildlife Museum
23 Library

Panguitch

To Circleville
County Fairgrounds
800 N St
700 N St
600 N St
500 N St
400 N St
300 N St
200 N St
100 N St
Center St
100 S St
200 S St

200 W St
100 W St
Main St
100 E St
200 E St
300 E St
400 E St

To Hatch,
Bryce Canyon
National Park

To KOA,
Panguitch Lake

UTAH

(☎ 435-676-8348), 2153 N Hwy 89 (2 miles north), has showers, coin laundry and a store. Sites cost from $9 to $13 and are closed in winter.

The private *Red Canyon* (☎ 435-676-2690, 435-676-2243) is about 10 miles east of town on Hwy 12. It has showers, a grocery store and an Indian souvenir store. Sites range from $9 to $14; it's open from March to October. Just to the east is the Dixie National Forest (☎ 435-676-8815) with its own *Red Canyon* campground; no showers here and sites are $8 each. Contact the USFS for other sites in the area.

Places to Stay – Budget to Middle
Prices are highest from May to October, when some over-pricing occurs because there's nowhere else to go. Try not to arrive late in the day if you want to snag a cheap-ish room. Many hotels charge $10 to $30 less in midwinter. Summer rates are given here.

The following places offer doubles in the $40s and $50s in summer. *Tod's Travel Center* (☎ 435-676-8863), 445 E Center, has 12 rooms in the low $40s and is one of the cheapest places. *Bryce Way Motel* (☎ 435-676-2400, 800-225-6534, fax 435-676-8445), 429 N Main, is one of the bigger hotels with 26 pleasant rooms, an indoor pool and a café. Slightly cheaper, decent rooms are available at *Blue Pine Motel* (☎ 435-676-8197, 800-299-6115, fax 435-676-2128), 130 N Main. The *Color Country Motel* (☎ 435-676-2386, 800-225-6518, fax 435-676-8484), 526 N Main, has a swimming pool, spa and clean rooms. The *Sands Motel* (☎ 435-676-8874, fax 435-676-8445), 390 N Main, has a swimming pool and standard rooms. The *Hiett Lamplighter Inn* (☎ 435-676-8362, 800-322-6966), 581 N Main, has very clean rooms with no smoking allowed. The well-run and friendly *Horizon Motel* (☎ 435-676-2651, 800-776-2651, fax 435-676-8420), 730 N Main, has pleasant rooms and a few two-bedroom suites for about $70. It closes in winter.

The *Marianna Inn* (☎ 435-676-8844, 800-331-7407, fax 435-676-8340), 699 N Main, has a spa and 24 rooms with coffee-makers. They also manage the 'historic' *Panguitch Inn* (☎ 435-676-8871), 50 N Main, which is a renovated downtown building dating from about 1920. Eleven rooms have private baths and coffee-makers; this hotel is closed from October through April.

Mae Mae's B&B (☎ 435-676-2388, 800-550-2388), 501 E Center, PO Box 387, Panguitch, UT 84759, has three rooms with private bath for $45 to $55 a double. Parts of the house are more than a century old and the owners will be happy to show you their interesting bottle collection as well as some restored old farm equipment outside.

About 7 miles south on Hwy 89 at the intersection of Hwy 12 to Bryce Canyon are a couple of motels and restaurants serving travelers who are heading from Zion to Bryce and don't want to drive up to Panguitch. These places are convenient, but no cheaper and less interesting than Panguitch.

Places to Stay – Middle to Top End
All the places above are small. By far the largest hotel is the *Best Western New Western Motel* (☎ /fax 435-676-8876), 180 E Center, with 55 rooms. This is the most comfortable place in town and offers an outdoor pool, indoor spa, exercise equipment and coin laundry. Standard double rooms with one or two queen-size beds are $55 to $75, and there are a few units with two bedrooms and refrigerators for $85 to $125. Winter rates drop into the $40s.

Places to Eat
Foy's Country Corner Cafe (☎ 435-676-8851), 80 N Main, is open from 6 am to 9:30 pm daily – it is a popular and reasonably priced, if rather bland, family restaurant that has been here since 1935. The *Flying M Restaurant* (☎ 435-676-8008), Main at 600 North, is a good choice for breakfast – it serves homemade pancakes, bread and rolls. Lunch and dinner are

served as well and it's one of the few places that serves beer. *Cowboy's Smokehouse BBQ* (☎ 435-676-8030), 95 N Main, serves Western-style cookin' surrounded by stuffed bear, elk, moose, antelope and deer heads. *Grandma Tina's* (☎ 435-676-2377), 523 N Main, serves authentic Italian and vegetarian meals from 7 am to 10 pm in summer; shorter hours in winter. *Buffalo Java* (☎ 435-676-8900), 47 N Main, is a coffeehouse with a vaguely alternative atmosphere (wildly alternative by Panguitch standards), which also serves light breakfasts, lunches and dinners but is closed in winter.

PANGUITCH LAKE
Hwy 143 goes south then west from Panguitch into the Dixie National Forest and the Markagunt Plateau. Panguitch Lake is reached after 15 miles and Cedar Breaks National Monument after 30 miles. The upper portion of the road may be closed in winter.

Panguitch Lake is a popular fishing spot in summer, and ice fishing is possible in winter. Anglers claim the trout fishing is particularly good. Snowmobiling, cross-country skiing and snowshoeing are all practiced, though there's not much in the way of rentals. However, with a snowmobile trail network of more than 200 miles passing the lake, this will probably change. It's about 10 miles around the lake, and the area has been discovered – there are many lots for sale and numerous private cabins have been built. The fall colors make this a beautiful drive in September and October.

Places to Stay
The Dixie National Forest (☎ 435-865-3200 in Cedar City) runs *White Bridge* campground, with sites for $9, on Hwy 143 14 miles southwest of Panguitch and 3 miles before reaching the lake. The USFS *Panguitch Lake North* and *Panguitch Lake South* campgrounds are on opposite sides of Hwy 143, almost 20 miles southwest of Panguitch. Sites at the south campground are $7; the north campground sites are $9

and up. All have water but no showers or RV hookups and are open from sometime in May to October, depending on weather. Day use at these campgrounds is $4.50. Near these campgrounds, *Panguitch Lake General Store & RV Park* (☎ 435-676-2464) has a convenience store open year-round with winter fishing and snowmobile supplies. From May through October it has RV sites for $17 with hookups, but no showers. Nearby, *Blue Springs Lodge* (☎ 435-676-2277, 800-987-5634) has six nonsmoking cabins with kitchenettes and lofts; they'll sleep six with no problem. Rates are $85 for up to six people in summer, $65 in winter.

The *Bear Paw Lakeview Resort* (☎/fax 435-676-2650, bearpaw@color-country.net) on Hwy 143 on the east shore is a friendly place with a store, boat and mountain bike rentals, a restaurant, RV sites with hookups for $16, and 10 cabins for $50 to $60. It is open from May through October.

The newly remodeled and attractive *Beaver Dam Lodge* (☎ 435-676-8339, fax 435-676-8068), on the north shore along North Shore Rd has a convenience store, boat rentals ($45 a day), mountain bikes ($25 a day), a restaurant and lounge, and rooms with two beds for $85, with four beds for $110. The *Deer Trail Lodge* (☎ 435-676-2211), on the northwest corner of the lake, has tent sites for $8, RV sites with hookups for $15, a restaurant, three cabins sleeping four for $50 to $85 and four small bedrooms sharing two showers for $25 double. Nearby, the *Rustic Lodge* (☎ 435-676-2627, 800-427-8345), has showers, a restaurant with liquor license, boat rentals, tent sites for $10, RV sites with hookups for $16, and 11 cabins of various sizes for $60 to $85. All these are open year-round and offer lodging discounts in winter.

HATCH

Hatch, with barely 100 year-round residents, is one of a handful of tiny Mormon towns along Hwy 89 (all described below) that provide services for people driving the 80 miles from Zion to Bryce Canyon National Parks. Hatch is at 7000 feet and has pleasant

summers. There is a Garfield County information booth on the south side of town, open from 9 am to 5 pm in summer only. Hatch is 24 miles from Bryce.

The **Mammoth Creek Fish Hatchery** (☎ 435-735-4200) is a mile south of town on Hwy 89, then 3 miles west. Trout are raised for release in local lakes; you can tour the facilities from about 8 am to 5 pm. The road, which continues west of the hatchery into the Dixie National Forest, is a popular snowmobiling route in winter.

No, Hatch was not named after the hatchery – it was named after the family who pioneered the area in the 1870s. For more about the area's history, drop by the small **DUP Museum**, a block from the center of town.

Places to Stay & Eat

Riverside Motel & Campground (☎ 435-735-4223, fax 435-735-4220), on Hwy 89 one mile north of town, has riverside tent sites for $14 and RV sites with hookups for $17. There are hot showers, coin laundry, a playground, pool and convenience store. The motel has 13 pleasant rooms in the $40s (one bed) or $50s (two beds), and there is a restaurant open from 7 am to 10 pm. Rates and restaurant hours are less in winter.

The *Mountain Ridge Motel & RV Park* (☎ 435-735-4258, 800-870-4258), 106 S Main, has showers and coin laundry. Tent sites are $10; RVs with hookups are $13. The motel has seven rooms in the $40s for doubles. It closes from November through April.

The *New Bryce Motel & Restaurant* (☎ 435-735-4265), 227 N Main, has 20 standard rooms in the $40s and $50s. The restaurant serves American food from 7 am to 10 pm. Cheaper rooms can be found at the *Galaxy Motel & Restaurant* (☎ 435-735-4327), 216 N Main, closed in winter. A new place is *Sunset Cliffs Motel* (☎ 435-735-4369, 800-662-5152, sunsetcl@color-country.net) with 18 rooms, a restaurant, a convenience store and a gas station.

There are a couple of restaurants in town; try *Escobar's*, 138 N Main, for Mexican food.

GLENDALE

Glendale (population 250) is 24 miles south of Hatch at an elevation of 5500 feet. It is the center of an apple-growing region.

The *Glendale KOA* (☎ 435-648-2490, fax 435-648-2037), 5 miles north on Hwy 89, has showers, game rooms, a pool, playground, store, horse rental and coin laundry. It is open from May to October and charges from $15 to $19. A few Kamping Kabins are $28 for two. In town is the cheaper and smaller *Bauer's Canyon Ranch* (☎ 435-648-2564), with a few tent sites and about 20 RV spaces for $9 to $14. There are showers.

The historic *Smith Hotel* (☎ /fax 435-648-2156), on Hwy 89 at the north end, was built in the 1920s and has been restored as a seven-room B&B. Rooms run about $40 to $65. The simple *Homeplace B&B* (☎ 435-648-2194), 200 S Main, Glendale, UT 84729, has three rooms in the $50s.

ORDERVILLE & MT CARMEL JUNCTION

In 1875, the Mormons founded Orderville, almost 5 miles south of Glendale, as a commune or kibbutz-like venture called 'The United Order,' which lasted about a decade (about 450 people live here now). A small **DUP Museum** on Hwy 89 at the northeast end of town explains the story and is open on request. Information is available at the city offices (☎ 435-648-2534). There is a small medical center (☎ 435-648-2108) at 425 E State. The Kane County Fair & Rodeo takes place here in late August. There are several gift stores selling local rocks, gems, minerals and jewelry.

Four miles south of Orderville, Mt Carmel Junction (population approximately 130) is where Hwy 89 meets eastbound Hwy 9 going to Zion.

Places to Stay & Eat

Orderville The *Starlite Motel* (☎ 435-648-2060) has more than 50 rooms, some with kitchenettes. Rooms start in the $30s but can go to twice that in the high season. The *Parkway Motel* (☎ 435-648-2380) has seven rooms and may be a little cheaper. The *Hummingbird B&B* (☎ 435-648-2415), PO Box 25, Orderville, UT 84758, has three rooms for $40 to $60.

Eat at *Marcella's Restaurant* (☎ 435-648-2063), next to the Starlite Motel. All the above places are along Hwy 89.

Mt Carmel Junction *East Zion Trailer Park* (☎ 435-648-2326), at the junction of Hwy 89 and Hwy 9, has no showers and charges $12 with hookups. *Mt Carmel Motel & Trailer Park* (☎ 435-648-2323) is on Hwy 89, 1½ miles north of the junction, near the separate community of Mt Carmel. It has showers, is open from March to November, and has cheap tent and $12 RV sites. It also offers six basic rooms in the $20s.

The *Best Western Thunderbird Motel* (☎ 435-648-2203, fax 435-648-2239), on the southwestern corner of the junction of Hwy 89 and Hwy 9, is the best hotel between Panguitch and Zion. Facilities include a pool, spa, nine hole/par 34 golf course, coin laundry and the *Thunderbird Restaurant* (☎ 435-648-2262), open from 7 am to 10 pm in summer, shorter hours in winter. Rooms are in the $60s in summer, $40s in winter. Nearby, the *Golden Hills Motel* (☎ 435-648-2268, 800-648-2268, fax 435-648-2558) has decent rooms in the $30s for singles and the $40s for doubles, less in winter. The *Golden Hills Restaurant* (☎ 435-648-2602) is on the premises, serving breakfast, lunch and dinner.

The *Sugar Knoll Manor B&B* (☎ 435-648-2335) is on Hwy 89, 2½ miles north of the junction.

CORAL PINK SAND DUNES STATE PARK

Over half of this 3700-acre park is covered with shifting pink sand dunes. Roaring up and down the loose sand in off-road vehicles (ORVs) seems to be the main attraction here, although there is an area for hiking, a short nature trail and a visitor center. Day use is $4. A campground with showers and picnic areas is $11 (no water in winter). The park is reached via a 12-mile paved road heading southwest from Hwy 89. The signed turnoff is 6 miles southeast of Mt Carmel Junction or 13 miles north of Kanab. Dirt roads provide alternate access routes. More information is available from ☎ 435-874-2408, PO Box 95, Kanab, UT 84741.

A mile north of the park, a road heads east for a couple of miles to the waterless *Ponderosa Campground*, managed by the BLM. Sites are $3.

KANAB

The remote town of Kanab was permanently settled by Mormons in 1874, although a fort had been built there a decade earlier. Local historians say that for more than half a century Kanab was farther from a railway than any incorporated town in the USA. The Grand Canyon and Colorado River to the southeast, the mountains to the north and the deserts to the west helped maintain Kanab's inaccessibility until the advent of roads.

Kanab was 'discovered' in the 1930s by the film industry and almost 100 movies have been filmed here – John Wayne, Clint Eastwood and dozens of other actors have made their appearance in Kanab.

The area is certainly spectacular, surrounded by the Vermilion Cliffs and a network of dirt roads on BLM land. Paved roads quickly lead to the area's famous national parks – Zion (40 miles), Bryce Canyon (80 miles), north rim of the Grand Canyon (80 miles) and Glen Canyon National Recreation Area (74 miles).

Because of its early isolation, the Kanab area was one of the most staunchly Mormon parts of Utah. Today, other churches have joined the LDS Church in Kanab, but some of the remote, small communities on the Utah/Arizona border are said to be defiantly traditional Mormon, with polygamy quietly being practiced despite the church ruling against it.

Kanab has 3500 inhabitants and is the Kane County seat. The elevation of 4925 feet means the summers get hot, but not unbearably so, with highs normally in the 90°s F. Winter snows are usually brief. Ranching has been the traditional industry, but tourism is now a major part of Kanab's economy.

PLACES TO STAY
3 Quail Park Lodge
4 Shilo Inn
7 Brandon Motel
8 Super 8 Motel
11 Treasure Trail Motel
12 Best Western Red Hills Motel
14 National 9 Aiken's Lodge
17 Parry Lodge
21 Canyonlands International Hostel
24 Hitch'n Post RV Park
25 Budget Host K Motel
26 Sun-n-Sand Motel
27 Kanab RV Corral

PLACES TO EAT
9 Wok Inn
10 Chef's Palace
17 Parry Lodge Restaurant
18 Houston's Trail's End Restaurant
23 Nedra's Too

OTHER
1 Hospital
2 BLM Office
5 Swimming Pool
6 Frontier Movie Town
13 Gazebo
15 Kanab Theater
16 Post Office
19 Travel Information Center
20 Heritage House
22 Police

Kanab

Orientation

Hwy 89 snakes through town and most motels lie along it. The highway enters from the east along 300 South, turns north on 100 East, west on Center, and north again to leave town along 300 West. Hwy 89 heads south along 100 East toward the Grand Canyon. The Arizona state line is 3 miles south.

Information

The county Travel Information Center (☎ 435-644-5033, 800-733-5263, kanetrav@ xpressweb.com), 78 S 100 East, is open from 8 am to 5 pm Monday to Friday in winter, and 8 am to 6 pm Monday to Saturday from Memorial Day to Labor Day. The BLM (☎ 435-644-2672), 318 N 100 East, is open from 8 am to 4:30 pm Monday to Friday. The library (☎ 435-644-2394) is at 533 E 300 South. The post office (☎ 435-644-2760) is at 39 S Main. The hospital (☎ 435-644-5811) is at 355 N Main. The police (☎ 435-644-5854) are at 140 E 100 South.

Historic Buildings

The best known historic building is the **Heritage House** (☎ 435-644-2542), 100 South at Main, built in the 1890s from local materials and open for free guided tours from 9 am to noon, 1 to 5 pm, Monday to Saturday in summer. Both the house and the information center have brochures detailing a walking tour of 16 historic houses.

Moqui Cave

Five miles north of town on Hwy 89, the cave (☎ 435-644-2987) houses a gift shop and collections of local Indian artifacts, fluorescent minerals and fossils. It's open 8:30 am to 7 pm in summer, 9 am to 6 pm in spring and fall, and closed on Sundays and in winter. Admission is $3.50, $3 for seniors, $2.50 for teenagers and $1.50 for six- to 12-year-olds.

Frontier Movie Town

This attraction (☎ 435-644-5337, 800-551-1714), 297 W Center, is a movie set where 'gunfights' are staged during the summer. It also has Wild West displays, a photo-shop where you can dress in 19th-century costumes, movie memorabilia, Indian artifacts, a gift shop and Western restaurant and saloon. Admission is free. Hours are 8 am to 11 pm, March through October, and 10 am to 5 pm in winter. On most evenings there are cowboy dinners with entertainment.

Backcountry Drives

There are many unpaved roads leading into the Vermilion Cliffs and White Cliffs areas. Some roads are passable to ordinary cars, others require 4WD and most are impassable after heavy rain. The BLM has good maps and information.

A popular drive is the **Johnson Canyon/ Alton Amphitheater Backway**, which leaves Hwy 89 nine miles east of Kanab and heads north for 30 or 40 miles, emerging at either Glendale or Alton. The first few miles are paved, and the remainder is gravel in fair condition. The road passes a Western movie set (on private land about 6 miles north of Hwy 89) and has good views of local geology. For a few miles, the road enters the newly formed Grand Staircase-Escalante National Monument (see that section later in the chapter).

Activities

For a popular hike to the Vermilion Cliffs, 400 feet above the city, follow 100 East north to the well-marked Squaw Trail. After 1 mile the trail leads to some great views.

You can **golf** at Coral Cliff (☎ 435-644-5005), 700 E Hwy 89, which has a nine hole/par 36 course, **swim** at the city pool (☎ 435-644-5870), 44 N 100 West, or play **tennis** at the city park, 500 N 100 East.

Special Events

The Fourth of July is the highlight of local events with fireworks, a parade, a concert, games and cookouts.

Places to Stay

The May-to-October season sees high prices and high occupancy. Call ahead to get the best choice of rooms.

Places to Stay – Camping

Hitch'n Post RV Park (☎ 435-644-2142, 800-458-3516), 196 E 300 South, offers showers and tent and RV sites for $10 to $18. *Crazy Horse Campark* (☎ 435-644-2782), 625 E 300 South, offers showers, a pool, a playground and coin laundry. Sites range from $10 to $17. *Kanab RV Corral* (☎ 435-644-5330, fax 435-644-5464), 483 S 100 East, is a 'Good Sam' park with mainly RV sites for $20; a few tent sites are cheaper. There's a pool, laundry and showers.

Places to Stay – Budget

Canyonlands International Hostel (☎ 435-644-5554), 143 E 100 South, is one of the few dorm-style hostels in the Southwest and attracts international budget travelers. It's a private hostel, so you don't need a card. Bunk beds are about $10, and there are lockers for your possessions. There's a kitchen (with free coffee and buffet breakfast included), reference library and travel information, coin laundry, TV lounge and yard.

Decent doubles in the $40s or low $50s are available at the small *Quail Park Lodge* (☎ 435-644-2651, fax 435-644-8115), 125 N 300 West; the *Budget Host K Motel* (☎ 435-644-2611, fax 435-644-2788), 330 S 100 East; the *National 9 Aiken's Lodge* (☎ 435-644-2625, 800-524-999), 79 W Center; and the *Brandon Motel* (☎ 435-644-2631), 223 W Center – all these are clean and have a pool, and some rooms have kitchenettes. Prices drop to the high $20s out of season and some places may close in winter.

Other places to try in this price range include the *Treasure Trail Motel* (☎ 435-644-2687, 800-603-2687), 150 W Center, and the *Sun-n-Sand Motel* (☎ 435-644-5050, 800-654-1868), 347 S 100 East, both with a pool.

Places to Stay – Middle

The *Parry Lodge* (☎ 435-644-2601, 800-748-4104, fax 435-644-2605), 89 E Center, has 89 rooms and has long been *the* place to stay in Kanab. Many of the actors who made films here stayed at Parry's and there is plenty of movie memorabilia, as well as a coin laundry, a pool, old-fashioned entertainment (in summer) and a restaurant and bar. The place has some character and the rooms, despite being older, are OK. High-season rates are in the $50s for a single or the $60s for a double, with some smaller, slightly cheaper rooms.

The *Super 8 Motel* (☎ 435-644-5500, fax 435-644-5576), 70 S 200 West, has a big pool and hot tub and charges about $70 in summer and $40 in winter.

The following modern motels all offer large, clean rooms, a pool, a spa, coin laundry and continental breakfast. *Holiday Inn Express* (☎ 435-644-8888, 800-574-4061, fax 435-644-8880), 815 E Hwy 89, has rooms in the $80s. *Best Western Red Hills Motel* (☎ 435-644-2675, fax 435-644-5919), 125 W Center, has some rooms with refrigerators and/or balconies for $85 to $95 in the summer. The *Shilo Inn* (☎ 435-644-2562, fax 435-644-5333), 296 W 100 North, is the biggest hotel in town with 119 rooms, some with kitchenettes or refrigerators. Summer rates are $70 to $100, with a few pricier mini-suites.

Places to Eat

Nedra's Too (☎ 435-644-2030), 310 S 100 East, is a cozy place open for inexpensive breakfast, lunch and dinner. (The original Nedra's Cafe is across the line in Fredonia, Arizona.) The menu has some interesting Western specialties – deep-fried ice cream, Navajo tacos (taco fillings on top of fry bread), chimichangas and other Mexican food and standard American fare. *Chef's Palace* (☎ 435-644-5052), 153 W Center, is a slightly more upmarket family restaurant specializing in steak – there's a salad bar and good burgers for the kids. It is open from 6 am to 11 pm daily in summer, to 10 pm in winter.

Houston's Trail's End Restaurant (☎ 435-644-2488), 32 E Center, is a rustic, fun, Western-style place serving reasonably priced American and Mexican chow from 6 am to 10 pm, March to December. For Chinese food, the *Wok Inn* (☎ 435-644-5400),

86 S 200 West, is locally recommended. It is open for lunch Monday to Friday and dinner daily. *Parry Lodge Restaurant* (in the hotel) is perhaps the closest to upscale that Kanab has, with good American breakfasts and dinner in a setting emphasizing the famous film stars who have dined here. It may close in winter.

Entertainment

Kanab Theater (☎ 435-644-2334), 29 W Center, shows movies. There are free concerts some evenings in the *gazebo* on Center. The *Old Barn Theater*, in the Parry Lodge, may have old-fashioned melodramas on summer evenings.

Bryce Canyon to Capitol Reef

Hwy 12 leaves Hwy 89 between Panguitch and Hatch and heads east past Bryce Canyon and three state parks, terminating at Torrey on Hwy 24, about 4 miles from Capitol Reef National Park. The 122-mile-long Hwy 12 is one of the most scenic roads in Utah; it is not conducive to fast driving.

BRYCE CANYON NATIONAL PARK

The Grand Staircase, a series of step-like uplifted rock layers stretching north from the Grand Canyon, culminates in the Pink Cliffs formation at Bryce Canyon National Park. These cliffs were deposited as a 2000-foot-deep sediment in a huge prehistoric lake some 50 to 60 million years ago, slowly lifted up to between 7000 and more than 9000 feet above sea level, and then eroded into wondrous ranks of pinnacles and points, steeples and spires, cliffs and crevices, and the strangely named formations called *hoodoos*. The 'canyon' is actually a series of amphitheaters eroded from the cliffs by the weather, rather than a real canyon formed by a river.

The similarity, yet variety, of the formations is strange at first sight. These odd hoodoos lined up one behind the other have

been likened to military platoons – superficially made up of identical soldiers yet each one unique upon closer inspection. The pink-red color of the rock is also incredibly variable – a shaft of sunlight can suddenly transform the view from merely magnificent to almost other-worldly.

Orientation

Scenic Hwy 12, the main paved road to the park, cuts across the northern portion. (There is no entrance fee for driving through this northern corner.) From Hwy 12 (14 miles east of Hwy 89), Hwy 63 heads south to the official park entrance about 3 miles away. From here, an 18-mile, dead-end drive continues along the rim of the canyon. Rim Rd climbs slowly past turnoffs to the visitor center (at almost 8000 feet), the lodge, campgrounds, scenic viewpoints and some trailheads, ending at Rainbow Point, 9115 feet above sea level. Trailers are allowed only as far as Sunset Campground, about 3 miles south of the entrance. Vehicles over 25 feet in length have access restrictions to Paria View in summer. Plans are in the works for a new shuttle bus system to cut down on parking/driving problems.

Information

The visitor center (☎ 435-834-5322, fax 435-834-4102) is the first main building along Hwy 63 after you officially enter the park. It is open from 8 am to 4:30 pm daily (except New Year's Day, Thanksgiving and Christmas), with extended hours from late spring to early fall. The center has exhibits about the park, audio-visual programs and a bookstore; rangers answer questions and (mainly during the summer) lead discussions, hikes etc. Free Junior Ranger Programs are offered for six- to 12-year-olds.

The entrance fee to the park is $5 per person (bicycle, motorbike, foot and non-commercial bus passengers) or $10 per private vehicle. Tickets are valid for seven days, and Golden Age, Eagle and Access Passes are accepted. The entrance station and the visitor center provide free park maps and informative brochures.

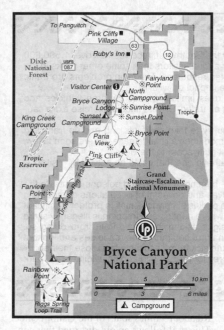

To Panguitch
Pink Cliffs ■
Village
63
Ruby's Inn ■
12
Dixie
National
Forest
USFS
087
Fairyland
※Point
Visitor Center ❶
North
Campground
Bryce Canyon
Lodge
※ Sunrise Point
Sunset ▲
Campground
※ Sunset Point
Tropic ●
King Creek
Campground ▲
Paria
View
※ Bryce Point
Tropic
Reservoir
Pink Cliffs
Under-the-Rim Trail
Grand
Staircase-Escalante
National Monument
Farview
Point ※

Bryce Canyon National Park

0   5   10 km
0   3   6 miles

Rainbow
Point ※

Riggs Spring
Loop Trail

▲ Campground

Further information is available from the Superintendent, Bryce Canyon National Park, UT 84717.

Climate & When to Go

The park is open year-round, with the five months of May to September seeing about 75% of the approximately 1.6 million annual visitors. Summer high temperatures at the 8000- to 9000-foot elevation of the rim may reach the 80°s F, but it's hotter below the rim, so carry water and sun protection when hiking. Summer nights can be chilly, with temperatures in the 40°s F. June is relatively dry, but in July and August the torrential late-summer storms descend – these are usually short-lived and transform the scenery in a matter of minutes.

Snows blanket the ground from about November to April, but most of the park's roads remain open. A few are unplowed and designated for cross-country skiing or snow-shoeing. The main Rim Rd is occasionally closed after heavy snow, but only until the

snowplows have done their job. January is the slowest month.

Flora & Fauna

Mule deer are frequently seen, especially early and late in the day. Drive carefully to avoid hitting them. Although other medium-to-large mammals are present, they are rarely seen. You will probably see plenty of chipmunks, ground squirrels and prairie dogs, however.

At least 164 bird species have been recorded in the park, especially in summer. My favorites are the ravens, which are often seen soaring close to the lookout areas – they are extremely agile and acrobatic for such large birds.

The visitor center has lists of animals and plants present in the park. Under *no* circumstances should you feed wildlife. (See the sidebar From Wildlife to Junk Food Junkies, below.)

Scenic Drives

Almost all visitors take all or part of the Rim Rd drive, normally in their own cars, although a shuttle bus system is being planned and may be implemented soon.

Near the visitor center, short side roads go to several popular viewpoints overlooking the Bryce Amphitheater. Further away from the visitor center, the Rim Rd passes half a dozen small parking areas and viewpoints on its way to Rainbow Point – all are worth a look.

Hiking

The views from the rim are superb, but you can gain a completely different perspective by getting away from the traffic and taking a hike, either along the rim, or better still, below the rim. Hikes below the rim descend for quite a ways and the uphill return at more than 8000 feet can be strenuous, so allow enough time and carry extra water. Also remember that most trails skirt steep drop-offs; if you suffer from fear of heights, these trails are not for you. During the July-August thunderstorm season, early morning departures are a good way to avoid the storms, which usually occur in the afternoon.

UTAH

From Wildlife to Junk Food Junkies

Bryce Canyon, the smallest national park in the Southwest, receives well over 1,500,000 visitors each year. Although this is far fewer annual visitors than some other parks in the region receive, it does strain the park's limited resources. The main problems are traffic congestion, trail damage, litter and negative impact on wildlife.

The congestion is eased somewhat by rules limiting access by large vehicles and trailers. In addition, a shuttle bus cuts down on traffic. Drivers should exercise extra caution when driving the busy park roads.

Trail problems are caused by visitors who try to take shortcuts and end up trampling vegetation and eroding the ground. One person does a little damage, others soon follow, and before long there is an ugly, washed-out gully scarring the view.

The litter problem is a sad and rather pathetic one that could be solved by visitors – please don't litter.

The impact on wildlife has been severe – hunting, trapping and poisoning outside the park have eliminated grizzly bears and wolves and devastated populations of mountain lion, black bear, elk and bighorn sheep – the park is simply too small to protect significant numbers of these species. Within the park (where hunting and trapping is illegal), visitors continue to feed smaller wildlife despite signs asking them to refrain from doing so. Feeding lures the animals away from their natural habitats to the roadsides and lookout areas, where they may be hit by cars, become sick from unsuitable food, lose their ability to find their own food in winter or become prey for predators. Feeding wildlife in the park is illegal – and subject to penalties. ∎

The easiest hike is along the **Rim Trail**, which is 5½ miles long (one way) and skirts the Bryce Amphitheater. It passes several viewpoints near the visitor center, so shorter sections can be done. The trail climbs about 550 feet from Fairyland Point to Bryce Point (or reverse it for more downhill). The 1-mile section between the North Campground and Sunset Point is the most level and parts are paved and accessible to wheelchairs and strollers.

There are many trails descending below the rim. One of the most popular is three-quarters of a mile from Sunrise Point at 8000 feet down to the **Queen's Garden**, 320 feet below. From here, you can either return the way you came or continue descending farther, connecting with the **Navajo Trail** for a more strenuous hike. These trails tend to be fairly heavily used in summer and are among the few that may remain open even in winter.

One trail suitable even for those with a fear of heights is the mile-long **Whiteman Connecting Trail**, which leaves the Rim Rd about 9 miles south of the visitor center. This trail follows an old dirt road that connects with the Under-the-Rim Trail; the descent is about 500 feet and you return the way you came.

One of the two most popular longer loop trails is the **Fairyland Trail**, which leaves from Fairyland Point north of the visitor center and includes 3 miles of the Rim Trail in the total 8 miles of the loop – there is a 900-foot elevation loss and gain. The other is the 7-mile-long **Peekaboo Trail**, which leaves from Bryce Point and involves an 800-foot elevation change. Both hikes go up and down more than the elevation change may suggest – allow half a day. The scenery is superb on both walks; the Peekaboo loop is also used by horses.

One of the most strenuous day hikes is the **Riggs Spring Loop Trail**, which leaves from Rainbow Point. It is almost 9 miles long and involves almost 1700 feet of descent/ascent. This can be done in a day if you're fit, but many prefer to make it an overnight trip.

Backpacking

Few visitors camp in the backcountry below the rim on any given night, though there are 10 designated campsites below the rim and most can accommodate up to six backpackers. So if you want to get away from the crowds, shoulder a pack and get down below the rim for a night or two. Permits are $5.

All backpackers must register at the visitor center. Park rangers will issue your permit, tell you the few places where you'll find water, discuss your route with you and show you where camping is permitted. Note that campgrounds are primitive – no facilities at all. All water below the rim must be purified. You must be self-sufficient – hiking gear is not available for rent. No fires are allowed; eat cold food or carry a stove. Carry out *all* your trash.

From November to April, backcountry camping may be difficult because many trails are snow-covered and hard to find. One or two campsites should be accessible even then – the rangers will know.

The **Under-the-Rim Trail** is the longest in the park, at 22 miles from Bryce Point to Rainbow Point. You could add the Riggs Spring Loop to make your trip more than 30 miles (one way), or you can use various connecting trails to make the trip as short as 2 miles roundtrip. All backcountry campsites are along the Under-the-Rim and Riggs Spring Trails.

Stargazing

Bryce Canyon is remote and doesn't suffer much from pollution. Visibility is usually more than 100 miles year-round, and it can exceed 150 miles in the crisp, clear winters. The s targazing is superb and astronomy evenings are presented by park rangers during the summer.

Winter Activities

The 1-mile road to Fairyland Point is not plowed in winter and access is by snowshoe or cross-country skis. The Rim Trail and other areas may be reached this way too. You can borrow snowshoes from the visitor center. Snowmobiles are prohibited.

Organized Tours

Canyon Trail Rides (☎ 435-679-8665), PO Box 128, Tropic, UT 84776, operates horse or mule tours into the backcountry. Two-hour rides to the canyon floor are $25 (no riders under five years old) and half-day loop tours are $35 (no riders under eight). There is a 220 pound weight limit. Bus tours along the park roads are available, starting around $10. The Bryce Canyon Lodge (see Places to Stay & Eat, below) also has information – the tours start there. Comparably priced trail rides are offered by lodges outside the park.

Places to Stay & Eat

Inside the Park The Park Service operates *North Campground* near the visitor center and *Sunset Campground* more than a mile south. There are toilets, drinking water, picnic tables and barbecue grills. Sites are $10 a night and a few remain open year-round. During the summer, all of the more than 200 sites are often full by noon or early afternoon. Between the two campgrounds is a *General Store* that offers basic food, camping supplies and coin-operated showers and laundry from April to May. (See Outside the Park, below, for places to shower in winter.)

The *Bryce Canyon Lodge* (☎ 435-834-5361, fax 435-834-5464), near the visitor center, is open from April through October. The attractive Western building dates from 1924 and has almost 120 units. There is a restaurant (open from 6:30 am to 9:30 pm; dinner reservations requested), coin laundry and occasional entertainment. Reservations (☎ 303-297-2757) are more or less essential, especially in summer when the lodge can be fully booked several months in advance.

Motel rooms with two queen-size beds, bath and private porch are about $80 to $95 (plus tax) for two to five people. Suites are $115 a double. Cabins with two double beds, bath, fireplace and porch are $90 to $100 for two to four people.

Outside the Park The places below are motels and campgrounds within a few miles of the park entrance. Also see the sections Tropic, Kodachrome Basin State Park, Panguitch and Hatch for places to stay within 25 miles of the park. Bryce Central Reservations (☎ 800-462-7923) can find places to stay in the whole area.

The *Best Western Ruby's Inn & Campground* (☎ 435-834-5341, fax 435-834-5265) is a huge, popular and unrelentingly 'Western' complex on Hwy 63, just over a mile north of the park entrance. It has a campground, hotel, restaurant and store (food, beer, camping stuff, fishing stuff, funny stuff, souvenir stuff, Indian crafts, sundries). Facilities include a pool, spa, post office and coin laundry. Horse, bike and ski rentals are available.

The campground has 200 sites ranging from $14 (tents) to $22 (hookups) open from April to October – its coin showers and laundry stay open all year. The well-run motel has almost 400 large and surprisingly pleasant rooms. Rates are $90 to $110 in summer (when reservations as far in advance as possible are advised) and about half that from January through March. A few family suites (two bedrooms) are about $130. Its restaurant/steak house is open from 6:30 am to 9:30 pm, and there is also a deli for making your own picnic. The motel offers 'chuck wagon' dinners (cowboy-style barbecue and entertainment) during the summer. Also during the summer there is Western entertainment, including a rodeo most evenings (not Sunday) for a few dollars. Yeeeeee haaaa!

Pink Cliffs Village (☎ 435-834-5351, 800-834-0043, fax 435-834-5256) is near the junction of Hwys 12 and 63, about 3 miles north of the park. It has an RV park, about 70 rooms, coin laundry, a pool and a restaurant/bar at prices a little lower than Ruby's Inn, but the facilities are much more modest, including dorm beds from $15. However, Ruby's is more likely to have rooms available on short notice.

Foster's Motel & Restaurant (☎ 435-834-5227, fax 435-834-5304) is on Hwy 12 a couple of miles west of the junction with Hwy 63. It offers 40 simple but clean rooms in the $60s in summer, less in

winter. The restaurant isn't bad – it's open from 7 am to 10 pm from May to October but has limited winter hours. There's a store and service station here.

Bryce Canyon Pines Motel & Campground (☎ 435-834-5441, fax 435-834-5330) is on Hwy 12 about 3 miles west of Hwy 63. It has a pool, store, restaurant, campground and coin laundry. Rooms are in the $60s and $70s in summer, less in winter. Rooms are nice enough – some have fireplaces or kitchenettes. The restaurant is open from 6:30 am to 9:30 pm. The campground is open from April to October and charges $10 to $18.

The Dixie National Forest borders much of Bryce Canyon National Park. Unpaved USFS Rd 087 heads south from Hwy 12 almost 3 miles west of Hwy 63. It reaches *King Creek Campground* after 7 miles. This campground is open from June to September, has water but no showers and costs $7. The similar *Pine Lake* National Forest campground is reached by taking USFS Rd 16 to the north off Hwy 12 from opposite Hwy 63, and then USFS Rd 132. It's almost 20 miles from the park entrance. The ranger stations in Panguitch and Escalante have maps and information.

TROPIC

This small town of about 400 inhabitants lies at 6300 feet on Hwy 12, about 7 miles east of the junction with Hwy 63. Tropic can be seen from some Bryce Canyon lookouts; a 6-mile trail leads from Sunset Point into the village.

Ebenezer Bryce, an early Bryce Canyon rancher for whom the park is named, lived in a wooden cabin that has been moved to the south end of town and now houses a small museum. A small information center is open at the east end of town during the summer.

Places to Stay & Eat

Summer prices are high; winter prices can drop as much as 50%. The fairly basic *Bryce Pioneer Village* (☎ 435-679-8546, 800-222-0381, fax 435-679-8607) has about 30 rooms and 20 cabins, some with kitchenettes, for about $40 to $70. There are also showers, 20 RV sites with hookups and a restaurant hosting Western-style cookouts and outdoor 'cowboy breakfasts' in the summer. It closes in winter. *Doug's Place Country Inn* (☎ 435-679-8600, 800-993-6847, fax 435-679-8605) has 28 standard motel rooms for about $65 a double in summer or from $35 in winter, a restaurant open 7 am to 10 pm in summer, a gas station and a grocery store. The *Bryce Valley Inn* (☎ 435-679-8811, 800-442-1890, fax 435-679-8846), with 65 clean, modern rooms for $60 to $85, is perhaps the best motel in town. There is a hot tub, coin laundry, store, deli and the *Hungry Coyote Restaurant*, which serves steaks and American and Mexican food from 6 to 10 am and 4 to 10 pm.

There are several small B&Bs, all with no-smoking policies. The *Bryce Point B&B* (☎/fax 435-679-8629), PO Box 96, Tropic, UT 84776, has six attractive and peaceful rooms with private showers in the $70s for a double. *Francisco's B&B* (☎ 435-679-8721, 800-642-4136), PO Box 3, Tropic, UT 84776, has three rooms with private baths in a log house on a small working farm. There is a spa. Summer rates are $60/70 for singles/doubles. *Fox's Bryce Trails B&B* (☎ 435-679-8700, fax 435-679-8727), PO Box 87, Tropic, UT 84776, has five modern rooms in the $70s. *Neimann's B&B* (☎ 435-679-8643), 320 Hwy 12, Tropic, UT 84776, has three rooms for $80, open in summer only.

The *Pizza Place* (☎ 435-679-8888) offers eat-in, takeout or delivered pizzas.

KODACHROME BASIN STATE PARK

Dozens of red, pink and white sandstone chimneys, and many other formations, make this one of the state's most colorful parks. There are several hiking and mountain-biking trails. Horses can be rented from mid-April to mid-October from Scenic Safaris (☎ 435-679-8536, 435-679-8787) at its Trailhead Station in the park. It also sells basic groceries and camping supplies and offers stagecoach rides.

Park information is available from (☎ 435-679-8562), PO Box 238, Cannon-ville, UT 84718. The park's campground has hot showers, offers 24 sites and is open all year. Day use is $4; camping is $12. The elevation here is 5800 feet. The park is 14 miles south of Tropic by paved road. A sign in Cannonville, on Hwy 12 five miles south of Tropic, points the way to the park, which is a further 9 miles by paved road. Many of the sights within the park are accessible only by trails or dirt roads that may be impassable after heavy rain. South of the park is the new Grand Staircase-Escalante National Monument (see below).

ESCALANTE & AROUND

The biggest settlement on Hwy 12, Escalante has 850 inhabitants and lies halfway between Bryce Canyon and Capitol Reef National Parks. Many people speed through en route to one of the parks, but the Escalante area itself is also one of great beauty (see Grand Staircase-Escalante National Monument, below). The elevation here is about 5600 feet.

Information

The Interagency Information Center (☎ 435-826-5499), PO Box 246, Escalante, UT 84726-0246, 755 W Main (Hwy 12 at the west edge of Escalante), is open 7:30 am to 5:30 pm daily, April to October, and 8 am to 5 pm Monday to Friday at other times. The BLM, Dixie National Forest and National Park Service all are represented at this information center. Information, permits, brochures, maps and guidebooks are available here. There is also a city information booth near Main and Center, which has brochures detailing local historic buildings. It is open in summer only. Escalante Outfitters (☎ 435-826-4266), 310 W Main, has information, arranges shuttles, and sells maps and outdoor gear. The post office (☎ 435-826-4314) is at 230 W Main.

Escalante Petrified Forest State Park

This park is about 2 miles northwest of town along Hwy 12 and a paved access road. There are 1¾ miles of trails leading through a small 'forest' of petrified wood;

a small lake with a boat ramp and opportunities for boating, windsurfing and fishing for trout and sunfish; and a 22-site campground with hot showers, open all year. Day use is $3; camping is $10. Information is available from PO Box 350, Escalante, UT 84726 (☎ 435-826-4466, 800-322-3770 for camping reservations).

North of Escalante

Most of the area north of the town is part of the Dixie National Forest – maps and information are available in Escalante. Various roads lead to campgrounds, fishing and hiking.

Posy Lake Rd goes north from Escalante. After 13 miles, a right fork, USFS Rd 153, becomes **Hell's Backbone Rd** and the left fork, USFS Rd 154, goes 2 miles to *Posy Lake Campground*, with 23 sites open in summer. There is water and a small lake (8700 feet) for fishing and boating; the fee is $6. Beyond Posy Lake, the road climbs up over the Aquarius Plateau at about 10,000 feet and emerges at Bicknell on Hwy 24, 25 miles away. Herds of pronghorn antelope roam the plateau and can often be seen in summer and fall – binoculars are suggested. The road is mainly dirt, but it is passable to cars in dry weather and closed by snow in winter.

The Hell's Backbone Rd passes *Blue Spruce Campground* at 7800 feet, about 5 miles after the fork. Six sites with water cost $6 in summer. The rough but highly scenic road continues east and south for about another 20 miles, emerging on Hwy 132 near Boulder – cars can make it through in dry weather if driven carefully. Snow closes the road in winter. The road skirts the **Box-Death Hollow Wilderness** – a real wilderness area with no campgrounds or roads and only rudimentary trails.

These two roads give access to other rougher roads, with trails and backpacking opportunities. Primitive camping is permitted.

Places to Stay & Eat

Triple S RV Park (☎ 435-826-4959), 495 W Main, has showers, coin laundry and 30 sites for $10 to $14; three camping cabins are about $22. (For more camping options, see also North of Escalante, above, and the state parks and national monument.)

Budget travelers head over to Escalante Outfitters (see Information, above), which has bunkhouses with both shared and private bath facilities for $15 to $30 a person. It also has the *Esca-latte* coffee shop.

Four modest motels offer simple rooms for $35 to $50 in the busy summer season (less out of season) and they may close in winter. Rates may go up on busy summer weekends. These are the *Quiet Falls Motel* (☎ 435-826-4250), 75 S 100 West, which has some kitchenettes; the *Padre Motel* (☎ 435-826-4276), 20 E Main; the *Moqui Motel* (☎ 435-826-4210), 480 W Main, which has some kitchenettes and a few RV sites with hookups and showers; and the *Circle D Motel* (☎ 435-826-4297, fax 435-826-4402), 475 W Main, which is the biggest of these with 29 clean rooms and a restaurant attached serving breakfast, lunch and dinner.

The new *Prospector Inn* (☎ 435-826-4653), 380 W Main, has more than 50 standard rooms in the $50s in summer, including continental breakfast. It has a restaurant and is the town's best motel. There's also the *Rainbow Country B&B* (☎ 435-826-4567, 800-252-8824, fax 435-826-4557), 586 E 300 South, with four rooms for $40 to $60, depending on season.

The best restaurant is the little *Cowboy Blues Diner* (☎ 435-826-4251), 530 W Main, with Southwestern cuisine but no alcohol. Waits can be long in summer. Meals are also served at the *Golden Loop Cafe* (☎ 435-826-4433), 39 W Main, and the hotels mentioned above.

GRAND STAIRCASE-ESCALANTE NATIONAL MONUMENT

Created in 1996 by President Bill Clinton, this 2656-square-mile monument is the newest and largest park in the Southwest. It links the area between Bryce Canyon and Capitol Reef National Parks (in the west and east, respectively) and Glen Canyon National Recreation Area in the southeast.

The name refers to the 'grand staircase' geological strata (see Bryce Canyon National Park, earlier in the chapter) and the Escalante River, one of the most important in the area.

Although the monument seems huge, earlier proposals were to make its western extent link up with Zion National Park, thus creating by far the largest protected area in the lower 48 states. The final area was a compromise between what ecologists wanted to conserve and the desires of some local inhabitants who were opposed to the creation of the monument. Utahan legislators had hoped to develop the area's mining potential, especially the coal-rich Kaiparowits Plateau. The creation of the federal monument came as a controversial surprise for many Utahans; however, some of the folks who live in the area are trying to harness the tourism potential as an alternative to mining. As one local councilwoman put it, 'You have to play the hand which you were dealt.'

Like other national monuments, Grand Staircase-Escalante is part of the federal park system, but it is not managed by the NPS. It is a BLM-managed area and thus many of the NPS restrictions do not apply here. Hunting and grazing are allowed with the proper permits, for example. Also unlike most NPS lands, the monument is not a solid area but rather a patchwork with areas of state lands (including Kodachrome Basin State Park) and private lands (including townships and ranches) that are surrounded by monument land. Finally, unlike NPS lands, development of a tourist infrastructure will be minimal, leaving a vast desert area suitable for adventurous exploration.

Travelers who have the time and necessary outdoor equipment will find the area has some of the least visited and most spectacular scenery in the country. Despite the remoteness, the few water sources are rarely clean and water must be chemically treated or boiled; it's best to bring water with you. Firewood is not always available and when it is, campfires are often illegal, so you need to carry a stove. Biting insects are a problem in spring and early summer – combine long sleeves and pants with repellent. Help may be hard to find in the event of an accident in remote areas. Talk to the appropriate agency for information about remote drives and hikes.

Orientation

Scenic Hwy 12 crosses some of the northern parts of the monument between the towns of Tropic, Escalante and Boulder. Hwy 89 crosses parts of the southern reaches of the monument east of Kanab. Three unpaved roads cross the monument roughly north to south between Hwys 12 and Hwy 89, and a fourth unpaved road crosses the monument from Hwy 12, dead-ending at the Glen Canyon National Recreation Area. These four roads, described below, provide the main access into the monument. (In addition, the Burr Trail from Boulder to Lake Powell crosses the northeastern corner of the monument – see Boulder, below.) They are passable to cars in good weather, though high clearance is advised. After heavy rain or snow, the roads may be impassable even with 4WD and should not be attempted if a storm is approaching. After light rains, parts of the roads have a clay surface, which becomes dangerously slippery. In dry weather, prepare for dusty or washboarded conditions. Always carry extra water and food in case of breakdown, foul weather or other emergency.

Information

Current information about this new area (regulations and/or facilities may change over the next few years) is available in advance from the BLM Escalante Resource Area Office (☎ 435-826-4291), PO Box 225, Escalante, UT 84726. If you are already in the region, the BLM at the Interagency Information Center in Escalante or the BLM office in Kanab both have maps and information.

To access many places in the Escalante area you'll need a good USGS or BLM map. Recommended reading is *Hiking the Escalante* by Rudi Lambrechtse, with background information and many hikes, originally published in 1985 and due for a revision in the near future.

Skutumpah/Johnson Canyon Roads

This is the most westerly route through the monument and the least-used of the cross-monument roads. The unpaved Skutumpah Rd heads southwest from a few miles west of Kodachrome State Park and goes through the Bull Valley Gorge and around the southern end of Bryce Canyon's pink cliffs (the 'Grand Staircase'). After about 34 miles, Skutumpah Rd intersects with the 16-mile, paved Johnson Canyon Rd, which goes past the White Cliffs and Vermilion Cliffs areas on the way to Hwy 89 and Kanab.

Cottonwood Canyon Road

This scenic backway goes 46 miles east and then south of Kodachrome State Park, emerging at Hwy 89 near Paria Canyon (see the sidebar Paria Canyon-Vermilion Cliffs Wilderness Area). This dirt road cuts about 50 miles off the drive between Bryce Canyon and Lake Powell and is therefore quite popular. About 10 miles east of Kodachrome State Park, a 1-mile road goes to Grosvenor Arch, an unusual double natural rock arch. There are picnic benches here.

The road then continues south along the west side of the Cockscomb, a distinctive long and narrow ridge caused by a flexure in the earth's crust. The Cockscomb divides the Grand Staircase from the Kaiparowits Plateau to the east. Further south, the road follows the Paria River valley, where there are numerous hiking possibilities.

A few miles west of where Cottonwood Canyon Rd meets paved Hwy 89 is the Paria BLM Ranger Station, which has information about both Grand Staircase-Escalante and Paria Canyon. A few miles west of the ranger station, a dirt road heads north from Hwy 89 for about 5 miles to the Paria Valley and an old Western movie set on monument land.

Paria Canyon-Vermilion Cliffs Wilderness Area

This remote area crosses the Utah-Arizona state line south of the Grand Staircase-Escalante National Monument. It is extremely rugged country with access only on foot. Experienced canyoneers enjoy the Paria Canyon because of the amazing Buckskin Gulch arm – miles of slot canyons so deep and narrow that the sun almost never shines directly into them. Hiking Buckskin Gulch-Paria Canyon to the exit point near Lees Ferry, Arizona, requires four to six days. Trailheads for the canyon are along dirt roads off Hwy 89 in Utah, near the Paria Ranger Station (no phone), about midway between Kanab and Page. The station is open from March to November and it posts weather information and flash flood warnings when closed. The area is managed by the BLM in Kanab, although much of the canyon is in Arizona.

The best time to do this adventurous hike is spring or fall. Winter is too cold and summer downpours create deadly flash floods. The hike must be done in the direction of river flow (north to south). The Arizona Strip Interpretive Association has published a waterproof *Paria Hikers Guide*, available from BLM offices for $8. Also read Annerino's *Adventuring in Arizona*. A hiking permit costs $5 per person per night. You can camp at the *White House Campground* near the Paria Ranger Station ($5 per site). After that, there are no maintained trails, campgrounds or signs through the Paria Canyon, so a map or hiker's guide is useful. Despite the remoteness of the area, it has been discovered and many people do the hike in season.

A car shuttle between the trailhead and the exit point can be arranged by the Marble Canyon Lodge or Cliff Dwellers Lodge. (See Marble Canyon & Lees Ferry Area in the Grand Canyon & Lake Powell chapter.) ■

Smoky Mountain Road

This dirt and gravel scenic backway crosses the rugged Kaiparowits Plateau between Escalante and Big Water (on Hwy 89 near the western end of Glen Canyon National Recreation Area). The 78-mile-long road leaves Hwy 12 from downtown Escalante but sees little traffic. The southern section has good views of Lake Powell. Most of the road is on monument land – the last few miles are in Glen Canyon.

Hole-in-the-Rock Road

Both the scenery and the history are wild along this scenic backway, which stretches about 60 miles southeast of Escalante.

Pioneering Mormons followed this route in 1879-1880 on their way to settle new lands in southeastern Utah. Little did they know that the precipitous walls of Glen Canyon of the Colorado River blocked their way. More than 200 pioneers literally blasted and hammered their way through the cliff, creating a route wide enough to lower their 80 wagons – a feat that is remembered and honored today by markers along the road. The final part of the descent cannot be seen – the Glen Canyon Dam flooded it along with countless other historical sites.

The dirt and gravel road leaves Hwy 12 about 5 miles east of Escalante and is passable to ordinary cars when dry. There are no camping or other facilities, although self-contained wilderness camping is possible. The BLM can tell you of side trails to arches and other scenic features. The main road stops short of the hole in the rock, but hikers can continue through down to Lake Powell, a scrambling descent that can be done in less than an hour. There are no taxis for the climb back up.

Hiking the Escalante Canyon

Escalante is near the headwaters of the Escalante River, which flows southeast to Lake Powell, nearly 90 miles away. You can hike the entire length, but you'll get wet – the 'trail' frequently crosses the river. Some canyoneers carry an inflatable air mattress to float gear across in the deepest sections. There are no campgrounds. The first third is

monument land, the rest is within Glen Canyon National Recreation Area.

Road access is from Hwy 12 at Escalante or from the Hwy 12 bridge midway between Escalante and Boulder, near Calf Creek Recreation Area. Trail access is from several trails heading east from Hole-in-the-Rock Rd, so you can do a day hike or a backpacking trip for as many nights as you want. (For details, read Lambrechtse's book.) The canyon scenery is quite marvelous, with sheer cliffs and soaring arches, waterfalls and pools, and many side canyons where the chances of seeing anyone are slim indeed. You may, however, encounter Indian artifacts – it is illegal and immoral to disturb these.

The best seasons are spring and fall – summer sees high temperatures and flash flood danger. Note that there are almost no signs and little development, so you need to be completely self-sufficient. Get local information about current conditions before beginning any hike. Obtain a free permit from the Interagency Information Center in Escalante.

Adventurous backpackers will find plenty of other opportunities to get away from it all in the monument, but there are almost no trails or signs – you really need to be experienced and prepared.

Calf Creek Recreation Area

This BLM-managed area is 15 miles east of Escalante on Hwy 12. It has a small campground and offers a scenic, popular and fairly easy hike to Calf Creek Falls, almost 3 miles away to the north. A pool below the falls is good for swimming, and other more difficult hikes are possible. Day use is $2. Call ☎ 435-826-5499 for information.

Places to Stay

The *Calf Creek Campground* (see the previous paragraph) has 13 sites and water but no showers. It is open from April to October and costs $7. The *Deer Creek Campground* is about 10 miles east of Boulder on Burr Rd and has five sites (no water or fee). Apart from these two simple campgrounds, there are no developed camping facilities within

. Wilderness camping at no …ed in most areas that are 300 …om a water source.

BOULDER

This tiny village (population 250) is about 25 miles northeast of Escalante on Hwy 12 and is a memorable drive. At one point the road follows the 'Hogsback,' a knife-edge ridge with great views all around for passengers, though drivers had better keep their eyes on the road. (I find that driving it east to west is the most scenic.) If you want even more excitement, there's the Hell's Backbone Rd (see North of Escalante, above).

On the north side of Boulder is **Anasazi State Park** (☎ 435-335-7308), an archaeological site that dates from 1050 to 1200 AD. A short trail leads through some of the excavated and restored ruins, and a museum has audio-visual programs and exhibits about the prehistory of the area. The site is small and provides intellectual rather than scenic stimulation – it's a worthwhile stop if you are interested in the pre-Columbian history of the Southwest. Hours are 8 am to 6 pm in summer, 9 am to 5 pm at other times. Admission is $2 per person over six, or $5 per carload. There is a picnic area but no camping.

Burr Trail is a scenic backway that heads east from Boulder and crosses the northeastern corner of the Grand Staircase-Escalante National Monument (one of the few paved roads in the monument) and then reaches the Waterpocket Fold area of Capitol Reef National Park. Burr Trail crosses the park as a scenic unpaved road and continues to Bullfrog Marina on Lake Powell, about 70 miles from Boulder. The spectacular dirt-road drive is passable in a car after good weather, though high clearance or 4WD are sometimes necessary. Heavy rains or snow can make the road impassable. Recently, Garfield County officials have claimed ownership of this road and want to pave or at least grade it, but the National Park Service wants to keep it as a primitive road to preserve the wildness of the area. The dispute is being settled in court.

Places to Stay & Eat

Pole's Place (☎ 435-335-7422, 800-730-7422), near the state park, has a café, groceries, gift shop and 12 motel rooms in the $40s. Nearby, the *Circle Cliff Motel* (☎ 435-355-7353) is a house painted shocking pink. It has just three rooms for under $30.

The *Boulder Mountain Lodge* (☎ 435-335-7460, 800-556-3446, fax 435-335-7461), at the junction of Hwy 12 and Burr Trail at the east end of Boulder, is the most upscale place, with a hot tub, 20 comfortable rooms and a decent restaurant. They can arrange local jeep or horse tours. The atmosphere is laid back to casually classy. This is a new place, and rates and services are evolving. Expect doubles in the $70 to $95 range.

There's a fast-food place too, and four RV sites are available at *Hall's Store* (☎ 435-335-7304). USFS camping is found along Hwy 12 (see Torrey & Area, below).

TORREY AREA

Hwy 12 terminates at Hwy 24 at the village of Torrey, about 40 very scenic miles northeast of Boulder. Located 11 miles west of the Capitol Reef National Park visitor center, Torrey provides the closest hotels to the park; other nearby towns, including Bicknell and Teasdale, provide more places to stay and eat. Although still a pleasantly sleepy rural village, Torrey has several good places to stay and eat.

Information

A booth in Torrey, on the north side of Hwy 24 at Hwy 12, has tourist information and brochures during the summer. Otherwise, try contacting the Wayne County Travel Council (☎ 800-858-7951, capreef@ xmission.com), PO Box 7, Teasdale, UT 84773. Also in Teasdale, 3 miles west of Torrey, is the Dixie National Forest Teasdale Ranger Station (☎ 435-425-3702), PO Box 99, UT 84773, 118 Main.

Outfitters

Hondoo Rivers & Trails (☎ 435-425-3519, 800-332-2696, fax 435-425-3548), 90 E Main, runs horse and jeep expeditions from half a day to several nights. Wild Hare Expeditions (☎/fax 435-425-3999, 888-304-4273, thehare@color-country.net), 116 W Main, arranges shuttles and guided driving and hiking tours from two hours to several days in length.

Bicycle tours and rentals are available from Pedal Pusher (☎ 435-425-3270, 435-425-3378), 151 W Main, or Buffalo Jacks (☎ 435-425-3711, 800-909-2000), at the Hwy 24/12 intersection. Pleasant Creek (☎ 435-425-3315, 800-892-4597) offers horseback rides from one hour to several days in length.

Places to Stay – Camping
Thousand Lakes RV Resort (☎ 435-425-3500, 800-355-8995), a mile west of Torrey on Hwy 24, has showers, coin laundry, a pool, picnic area and grocery store. It's open April through October and sites are $11 (tent) to $17 (hookups), or $26 for three camping cabins. Nearby, the *Sandcreek RV Park & Campground* (☎ 435-425-3577) has tent spaces for $9, RV hookups for $15 to $18, and showers for the public at $2.50. There is a store, coin laundry and espresso bar. It is open April through October.

The *Boulder Mountain Homestead RV Park* (☎ 435-425-3374, 800-769-4644), on Hwy 12 four miles south of Hwy 24, has 10 RV sites with hookups for $14 from March through October but no laundry or showers. Also see the Chuckwagon Lodge and Aquarius RV Park, below.

The Fishlake National Forest *Sunglow Campground* is almost 2 miles east of Bicknell (6 miles west of Torrey) amid red-rock cliffs. Water is available but no showers. Seven sites are open from mid-May to October; the fee is $8.

About 17 to 22 miles south of Torrey (20 to 25 miles north of Boulder) along Hwy 12 in the Dixie National Forest, the small *Oak Creek, Pleasant Creek* and *Singletree Campgrounds* all have water, no showers and $8 sites during summer.

Places to Stay – Budget
Reservations are a good idea during the busy summer season. In winter, prices plummet and some places close.

Torrey *Capitol Reef Inn & Cafe* (☎ 435-425-3271), 360 W Main, has 10 simple but good clean rooms, one with kitchenette, in the low $40s for a double. Its gift shop specializes in local maps, guidebooks and books about the Southwest as well as arts and crafts. The unpretentious but appealing café is open from 7 to 11 am and 5 to 9 pm and serves surprisingly commendable food at reasonable prices. The small menu tends toward health-conscious rather than blue-plate specials, and they do a good job with local trout served with fresh vegetables and brown rice. Espressos, beer and wine are available, and jazz or classical music plays in the background. The whole operation closes down from November to March.

Chuckwagon Lodge & General Store (☎ 435-425-3335, 800-863-3288, fax 435-425-3434), 12 W Main, has modern air-conditioned rooms with two queen-size beds for about $50/60 single/double in summer. Older, small rooms with fans and one bed are about $35/40. There is a pool and spa. The facility also runs a small campground with showers and coin laundry, open from April to October, for $9 to $16.

The *Boulder View Inn* (☎ 435-425-3800, 800-444-3980), 385 W Main, has 11 large rooms, some with microwaves, for $46/52 single/double, including continental breakfast. Winter rates are lower and the inn may close if there's not much business. Also try the nearby *Torrey Trading Post* (☎ 435-425-3716) with a few basic cabins for about $30.

Two miles west of town, the *Cactus Hill Guest Ranch* (☎ 435-425-3578, 800-507-2624), 830 S 1000 East, is a working farm with six rooms for $45 to $55.

Bicknell The clean *Sunglow Motel & Restaurant* (☎ 435-425-3821), 63 E Main, has 17 standard rooms for about $28/40 for singles/doubles, $46 with a king-size bed. The inexpensive café is open from 6:30 am to 10 pm daily. The *Aquarius Motel & Restaurant* (☎ 435-425-3835, 800-833-5379, fax 435-425-3771), 240 W Main, has 27 basic but adequate rooms for $35 to $50 in summer, from the $20s out of season.

Some rooms have kitchenettes. Its inexpensive restaurant is open 6 am to 10 pm daily. The motel also runs the nearby *Aquarius RV Park* (☎ 435-425-3771) with about a dozen cheap RV sites with hookups but no showers.

Places to Stay – Middle

Torrey The *Wonderland Inn & Restaurant* (☎ 435-425-3775, 800-458-0216, fax 435-425-3212), at the junction of Hwys 24 and 12, is on a little hill with pleasant views. The inn has a coin laundry, an indoor pool, a spa, a sauna and a restaurant open 7 am to 9 pm (shorter hours in winter). Fifty good rooms are about $60/70 for singles/doubles in summer.

The *Days Inn* (☎ 435-425-3111, fax 435-425-3112), at the junction of Hwys 24 and 12, has an indoor pool and a spa. Rates are $60 to $90 for a double in summer, and some mini-suites with a whirlpool tub go up to about $100; rates include continental breakfast.

The *Best Western Capitol Reef Resort* (☎ 435-425-3761, fax 435-425-3300), 2600 E Hwy 24 (about 2 miles west of the park boundary), has a pool, spa and tennis court, and arranges horseback riding. Many of the 50 units have good views; mini-suites have terraces, microwaves and refrigerators. The restaurant is open 7 am to 10 pm (9 pm in winter). Rates are in the $80s from June to September (over $100 for mini-suites), from the $50s November through March and in between at other times.

The comfortable *Skyridge B&B* (☎/fax 435-425-3222), 950 E Hwy 24, Torrey, UT 84775, has five rooms for $80 to $130 double. Rooms are attractively furnished and decorated; one has a private hot tub and others have private decks. There is a spa for all guests, and the huge grounds invite walkers and cyclists. Rates include a full Southwestern breakfast and evening drinks/snacks.

Teasdale The *Cockscomb Inn B&B* (☎/fax 435-425-3511), PO Box 8, Teasdale, UT 84773, at 97 S State, has four nonsmoking rooms with private bath, some with kitchen

facilities, for $55 to $70. A three-day minimum stay is required.

The *Lodge at Red River Ranch* (☎ 435-425-3322, 800-205-6343), PO Box 69, Teasdale, UT 84773, is a nice Western-style wooden lodge by the Fremont River. Amenities include a reading/game/exercise area, huge lounge with fireplace, and expansive grounds with walking trails and access to 5 miles of river fishing. Fifteen rooms and suites, all with fireplaces and balconies, rent for $90 to $160, including continental breakfast. The lodge closes in winter.

A few other B&Bs and cabins have opened in tiny Teasdale recently; check with the information booth in Torrey.

Places to Eat

Torrey is your best bet for meals. Apart from the hotel restaurants (the Capitol Reef Inn & Café is especially noteworthy), there's the friendly *Café Diablo* (☎ 435-425-3070), 599 W Main, with excellent Mexican and Southwestern cuisine at moderate prices. It opens for lunch and dinner daily in summer; call for winter hours.

Entertainment

Wayne Theater (☎ 435-425-3123), 11 E Main, Bicknell, shows movies on Thursday, Friday and Saturday nights. It occasionally has country & western music evenings. Ask at the information booth in Torrey about local Western plays, musicals or dinner theater during the summer tourist season.

LOA & FISH LAKE

The small town of Loa, 27 miles west of Capitol Reef, was settled in the 1870s. Mormon missionaries named it after Mauna Loa in Hawaii. It has barely 500 inhabitants but is the Wayne County seat. This is ranching and farming country – you'll begin to see a lot of sheep as you enter the better irrigated lands of central Utah. The Fishlake National Forest Loa Ranger Station (☎ 435-836-2800, 435-836-2811), 138 S Main, Loa, UT 84747, is open from 8:30 am to 4:30 pm Monday to Friday.

RALPH LEE HOPKINS

KIM HAMMAR

STEPHEN TRIMBLE

Top Left: Headwaters of Beaver Creek, Tushar
  Mountains, Utah
Bottom: Rock formations, Grand Staircase-Escalante
  National Monument, Utah

Top Right: Winter at Bryce Canyon National Park, Utah

RALPH LEE HOPKINS

BONNIE KAMIN

RALPH LEE HOPKINS

BONNIE KAMIN

Top: Sunrise Point, Bryce Canyon National Park, Utah
Bottom Left: Kayak on Lake Powell, Utah

Middle Right: La Sal Mountains near Canyonlands
  National Park, Utah
Bottom Right: Las Vegas, Nevada

About 20 miles northwest of Loa, **Fish Lake** is an attractive lake in the Fishlake National Forest. Unlike many of Utah's lakes, this is a natural one, not a reservoir. The elevation of 8800 feet makes it a cool summer destination. Prairie dog colonies are visible and if you are lucky you may catch sight of moose. The fall sees beautiful colors and excellent fishing (with a license). Trout fishing is especially good. In winter, the road up to the lake is usually open and provides access for cross-country skiing and snowmobiling.

Places to Stay & Eat

Loa The *Road Creek Inn B&B* (☎ 435-836-2485, 800-388-7688, fax 435-836-2489), PO Box 310, Loa, UT 84747, at 98 S Main in a restored 1912 general store, is the nicest hotel in town. The people are friendly, and dinners in their restaurant are home-cooked and good – especially the trout. (They'll tell you where to catch it yourself, too.) This B&B has a gym, spa, sauna and game room with billiards. Thirteen attractive rooms are $70 to $100, including breakfast.

There's also *Wayne Wonderland Motel* (☎ 435-836-9692), 42 N Main, with 12 simple rooms from the $30s. They have planned a renovation and summer rates will be higher.

Fish Lake The USFS operates several campgrounds in the area, all with water but no showers or hookups; the fee is $8. These are open from May to October and reservations can be made for some sites (☎ 800-280-2267), or call the USFS for information. *Bowery* and *Mackinaw* campgrounds both have boat ramps. Free dispersed camping is allowed on roads and trails away from the lake.

The *Bowery Haven Resort* (☎ 435-638-1040 in season, 435-943-7885 off season), Fish Lake, UT 84701, is open from mid-May to October. It has rustic cabins (outside bathrooms) in the $30s and modern motel rooms and cabins in the $60s, each with kitchenette (no utensils). Units sleep up to four.

Fish Lake Resorts (☎ 435-638-1000), Hwy 25, Fish Lake, UT 84701, operates both the *Fish Lake Lodge* and *Lakeside Resort*. Rustic cabins start at about $40 and go up to almost $100 for large modern family cabins. They are open year-round.

These places offer marinas with boat rentals, fishing guides, stores selling food and fishing supplies, RV hookups and showers (in summer, and restaurants as well as various accommodations.

CAPITOL REEF NATIONAL PARK

Just as Bryce Canyon isn't a canyon, Capitol Reef isn't a reef. The red-rock cliffs and ridges of the park were formidable barriers to early pioneers, who named them 'reefs.' Atop the red cliffs are whitish, domelike formations, reminiscent of the Capitol dome of the nation's capital – hence the name.

Interesting for its archaeology, history and desert wildlife, Capitol Reef is also a textbook example of geology at work. For hundreds of millions of years, layer after layer of rock was deposited here. Then, some 65 million years ago, the earth's surface buckled up and folded, then became partly eroded to form what is today the 100-mile-long Waterpocket Fold, most of which lies within the park and provides extremely scenic views. Other park attractions are

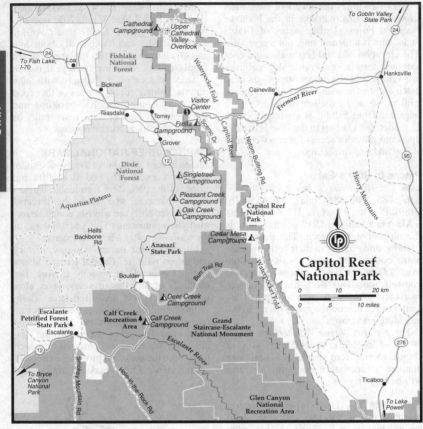

Indian petroglyphs, old Western pioneer buildings and fruit orchards, and great driving and hiking opportunities.

With more than 375 sq miles, this is the second largest park in the state and receives about 700,000 annual visitors – a much lower number than most of the other parks. Those venturing beyond the standard scenic drive will enjoy a relatively uncrowded visit.

Orientation

Hwy 24 cuts through the northern section of this long, thin park – the Waterpocket Fold can be seen stretching off to the north and south. Unpaved roads that are partly outside the park itself lead north and south of the highway to give good looks at the geological formations. This is an isolated area – Hwy 24 wasn't built until the 1960s.

Information

The visitor center (☎ 435-425-3791) is on Hwy 24 at the junction with the paved scenic drive. People driving through on Hwy 24 can cross the park without payment, but visitors taking the scenic drive pay $4 per vehicle or $2 per person; Golden

Age, Access and Eagle Passes are accepted. Entrance is valid for a week.

The visitor center is open 8 am to 7 pm from Memorial Day to Labor Day and from 8 am to 4:30 pm otherwise (closed Christmas). Various ranger-led programs and activities are scheduled during the summer. Visitors will find books and maps for sale, exhibits, audio-visual presentations and information available throughout the year. Brochures describing the places below in some detail are also provided at the center. If you drive away from the main roads, carry extra water in case of breakdown. Further information is available from the Superintendent, Capitol Reef National Park, UT 84775.

Climate & When to Go

The park is open year-round. Rainfall and humidity are low; annual rainfall averages just over seven inches, of which over half falls between June and October. Summer thunderstorms make for ever-changing skies but also introduce flash flood dangers. At the visitor center (5400 feet), summer temperature highs occasionally reach more than 100°F. Evenings usually cool into the 60°s F. Biting insects are the worst from mid-May to late June. Spring and fall are more pleasant months for hiking. The dry winter months see average highs in the 40°s F and lows around 20°F, although temperatures below 0°F are possible. Snowfall is light but may close some roads briefly.

Fruita

At the junction of the Fremont River and Sulphur Creek, Fruita was a settlement established by Mormon pioneers in 1880. Today, the park's visitor center is here and nearby are several picturesque, rustic, turn-of-the-19th-century buildings as well as a campground. A prominent formation, The Castle, rises just north of the visitor center.

Visitors like to stop by the well-tended Fruita orchards, which produce apricots, cherries, peaches, apples and pears. From early March to the end of April the orchards are a mass of flowers. The fruit is harvested from mid-June to mid-October and can be picked and eaten at no charge inside any unlocked orchard. During designated harvest days, fruit can be picked in quantity for a fee.

The Mormon pioneers weren't the first to arrive, of course. Fremont Indians lived here a thousand years ago; visitors can view the Indian petroglyphs on a cliff just over a mile east of the visitor center along Hwy 24. Park rangers can suggest other places where Indian artifacts can be seen.

Scenic Drive

Pick up brochures describing this drive and others at the visitor center. The scenic drive is part pavement and part gravel, passable to all vehicles. This 25-mile roundtrip drive south from the visitor center gives a look at the western side of the Waterpocket Fold. Several scenic viewpoints, dirt side roads and trailheads invite further exploration.

Notom-Bullfrog Road

This dirt and gravel road follows the east side of the Waterpocket Fold and is accessible to ordinary vehicles in dry weather but may be impassable after heavy rains. The road heads south from Hwy 24 just outside the eastern park boundary and remains outside the park for the first 20 miles, then enters the park for about 17 miles. About 34 miles south of Hwy 24, it intersects the Burr Trail Rd – head west on the only road that climbs over the Waterpocket Fold (steep sections, great views) or head east to leave the park and head toward Lake Powell, almost 40 miles away. The road gives access to many trailheads.

Cathedral Valley Roads

Two roads leave Hwy 24 a few miles east of the park boundary and head northwest to the Cathedral Valley area at the north end of the park – a scenic desert landscape of peaks and pinnacles. River Ford Rd is just over 3 miles east of the park and Caineville Rd is almost 11 miles east of the park. Both reach Cathedral Valley, so you can make a roundtrip without backtracking (80 miles total). Caineville Rd is longer, but River Ford Rd involves fording the Fremont River. Both roads require high-clearance vehicles – you can usually manage without a 4WD in good weather.

Hiking

The following is a varied selection of some of the most popular, easily reached and rewarding short hikes in the park. Getting away from the road gives rewarding and satisfying vistas. Some trails are very short and suitable for almost anyone. Just over 2 miles west of the visitor center on Hwy 24, a short unpaved but good road goes south to Panorama Point and the **Goosenecks Trail**. This 200-yard-long trail is almost flat and reaches an overlook with great views. From the same trailhead, the **Sunset Point Trail** goes a third of a mile to an equally scenic lookout – a favorite at sunset.

A few miles along the Scenic Drive, a good dirt road goes east to the Grand Wash parking area. The **Grand Wash Trail** continues east. It's a fairly flat and easy walk through the cliffs of the Waterpocket Fold, going through an impressive 'narrows' section before emerging at Hwy 24, 2¼ miles away. Either arrange a car shuttle or return the way you came. Much more strenuous hikes leave from the same trailhead. The 1.8-mile **Cassidy Arch Trail** climbs steeply to the west, switchbacking to the top of cliffs looking down upon the arch. (Butch Cassidy's outlaws supposedly had a hideout near here.) The **Frying Pan Trail** heads north from the arch trail and follows the high ridges back to Cohab Canyon and the Fruita Campground (about 5 miles).

At the end of the Scenic Drive, a good unpaved road dead-ends in the Capitol Gorge. From here, you have the choice of the **Capitol Gorge Trail** to the east or **Golden Throne Trail** to the west. The mile-long gorge trail is easy and leads enticingly into the Waterpocket Fold; petroglyphs are visible on the cliff walls. The 2-mile-long Golden Throne trail climbs steeply to the cliff tops and gives fine views of the Golden Throne landmark.

Backpacking

You can hike and camp almost at will in this desert wilderness as long as you have a permit, available for free from the visitor center. Rangers supply you with maps and information while they register you, so they'll know where you are in the event of an accident.

Backpacking trips usually involve taking poorly marked trails where little piles of stones (cairns) are the only markers and the path is hard to see. You can camp almost anywhere as long as it's more than 100 feet away from water and a half mile away from and out of sight of the main roads. Backpacking at Capitol Reef is a desert wilderness adventure – if you lack experience, get full advice from park rangers and start with an easy trip. Get maps or use a guidebook – Adkison's *Utah's National Parks* details several good backpacking trips.

This dry desert environment does not recover quickly from human impact – the normal rules of no fires, no garbage and no cutting of vegetation are even more important here. Leave campsites as you found them. Don't bury garbage, as it decomposes very slowly and desert critters try to dig it up.

Places to Stay

The *Fruita Campground* has 70 sites and is open all year on a first-come, first-served basis for $8. Some sites can be driven to, others require a short walk (50 yards) from the parking area. Walk-in sites are usually available if you arrive by early afternoon, even in summer. Water and grills are provided, but there are no showers.

Free primitive camping is possible at *Cathedral Campground* at the end of the River Ford Rd and at *Cedar Mesa Campground*, about 23 miles south along the Notom-Bullfrog Rd. Each has five sites, picnic tables, grills and pit toilets but no water. They are open year-round.

There are no lodges. Motels and other campgrounds are found in Torrey and Loa to the west and Caineville to the east.

CAINEVILLE

This small settlement is approximately 20 miles east of the Capitol Reef visitor center and halfway to Hanksville (see the Southeastern Utah chapter). It offers the *Sleepy Hollow Campground* (☎ 435-456-9130) with $10 tent sites, $14 RV sites with hookups and $3 public showers. The *Caineville Cove Inn* (☎ 435-456-9133, 435-456-9900, fax 435-456-9142), has a pool and 16 rooms for about $60 (double) in summer.

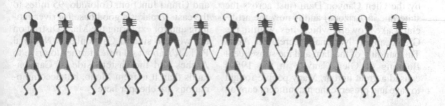

Southeastern Utah

'Canyonlands' is what Utahans call the southeastern corner of their state. And canyons there certainly are here – sheer-walled and majestic, arid and desolate. They were formed by the Colorado River and many of its tributaries, most notably the Green and San Juan Rivers. Utah's largest and wildest national park, appropriately enough named Canyonlands, is found here, along with the exquisite Arches National Park and numerous other protected areas.

This is one of the most inhospitable yet beautiful terrains in the world. Not a great deal is known about the prehistoric Indians who lived here – their art and buildings can be seen throughout the area, but the reasons for their departure remain unclear.

The canyons proved to be formidable barriers to any kind of exploration or travel. Even the hardy Mormon pioneers settled this corner of the state well after other parts of Utah. Towns were tiny and distances were great until the discovery of uranium and the consequent post-WWII mining boom. Suddenly, dirt roads appeared everywhere (evidence of the search for radioactive pay dirt) and populations swelled. As more people moved here in the 1950s, word began to get out about the spectacular but unforgiving nature of this corner of the world. Slowly, tourists started drifting in to see these fantastic canyonlands.

It is ironic that the greatest canyon of them all has been destroyed. The Glen Canyon of the Colorado River was flooded by the Glen Canyon Dam (just across the state line in Arizona) and is now the artificial Lake Powell, which lies within the Glen Canyon National Recreation Area. The building of the dam and the subsequent flooding of Glen Canyon in the 1960s caused a great uproar. Many people fought to save and preserve the magnificent canyon and the many Indian ruins within it. These are now lost. Today, Lake Powell is a mecca for boaters and anglers and receives millions of visitors every year – but there are still Southwestern desert rats who refuse to visit what they call 'Lake Foul.'

Author Edward Abbey was one of the strongest protestors against the flooding of Glen Canyon. He wrote not so much for the preservation of the desert Southwest itself, but rather for its incalculable quality of untouched remoteness. It is another irony that in so unerringly evoking the stark beauty of life in the canyonlands in his books, he inadvertently attracted to the Southwest hundreds of thousands of people seeking that very remoteness.

Today, southeastern Utah is experiencing a tourist boom, which has had a negative impact in many areas and a positive one in others. The canyonlands are one of the most splendid areas in the Americas, and that splendor needs to be cared for. Travel lightly, slowly, thoughtfully, respectfully. You are only one of millions, but your voice and actions count. (See the sidebar Southern Utah – Being Loved to Death? in the Southwestern Utah chapter.)

Green River & Around

Green River, with almost 1000 inhabitants, is the only town of any size along I-70 between Salina, 108 miles to the west, and Grand Junction, Colorado, 95 miles to the east. It makes a good base for river running and for exploring the Maze District on the western side of Canyonlands National Park. It's about 40 miles farther to drive to Arches and the eastern side of Canyonlands than it is from Moab, but accommodations are cheaper here.

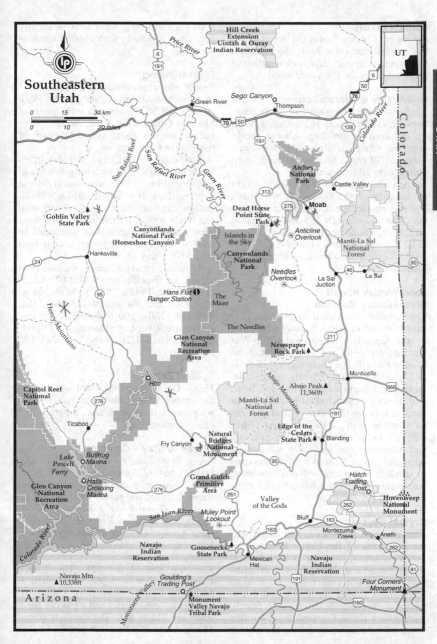

GREEN RIVER

Settled in 1878 on a ford of the Green River, the town today calls itself the 'world's watermelon capital,' and melon growing and tourism are the main industries.

Orientation & Information

The I-70 business loop north of the freeway between exits 158 and 162 becomes Main St, the town's main drag. Almost everything lies along this street. Westbound drivers on I-70 won't find any services until Salina, over 100 miles away.

The visitor center (☎ 435-564-3526) is in the museum at 885 E Main. It sells maps and guidebooks for hikers and river runners. The post office (☎ 435-564-3329) is at 20 E Main. The library (☎ 435-564-3349) is at 85 S Long. A small clinic (☎ 435-564-3434) is open during business hours at 110 Medical Center Drive.

John Wesley Powell
River History Museum

The Colorado and Green Rivers were first explored and mapped in 1869 and 1871 by the legendary one-armed Civil War veteran, geologist and ethnologist, John Wesley Powell. The museum (☎ 435-564-3427), 885 E Main, has all the details, including a replica of the wooden boat, with Powell's chair lashed to it, that was used in making the historic first descent by a white man of these rivers. Other exhibits focus on the Indians, geology and history of the area. The museum is open daily from 8 am to 8 pm from April to October and 9 am to 5 pm in winter. Admission is $2 for adults, $1 for children or $5 per family.

Crystal Geyser

This cold-water geyser erupts from near the east bank of the Green River about every six hours, shooting as high as 100 feet in the air and lasting for several minutes. The visitor center may be able to help with a timing prediction and directions for the 10-mile drive along poorly signed back roads. Located about 4 miles south of town along the river, the geyser marks a swimming spot that is locally popular – especially with kids on summer vacation.

River Running

People with experience and a boat can put in from the **Green River State Park** (☎ 435-564-3633), about a mile south of Main on Green River Blvd. Another river access point is about 10 miles north of town in the Gray Canyon.

A few local outfitters run day trips for about $40 to $50 including lunch and transportation. These are mainly float trips with a few small rapids. Small groups can sometimes book a trip with one day's notice. Larger groups or longer trips can be arranged, but you need to book in advance. Longer trips cost well over $100 a day.

Reputable local companies include Holiday River Expeditions (☎ 800-624-6323, fax 801-266-1448), 1055 E Main; Moki Mac River Expeditions (☎ 435-564-3361, 800-284-7280), 100 Silliman Lane; and Adventure River Expeditions (☎ 435-564-3454, 435-943-0320, 800-331-3324), 185 Broadway.

Special Events

Melon Days around the third weekend in September is the annual harvest festival with sports, dancing, music, a parade and other entertainment.

Places to Stay – Camping

Green River State Park (☎ 435-564-3633, fax 435-564-3223), on Green River Blvd, has 42 year-round sites for $10. You'll find water, showers and plenty of shade but no hookups. *Green River KOA* (☎ 435-564-3651), 550 S Green River Blvd, is open from April to October and charges $14 to $20. It has a pool, coin laundry, convenience store and recreation area. There are three Kamping Kabins for $26. The *United Campground* (☎ 435-564-8195), 910 E Main, has a pool (summer only), showers, play areas, coin laundry and a grocery store. Rates are $14 to $18. The similarly priced *Shady Acres RV Park* (☎ 435-564-8290,

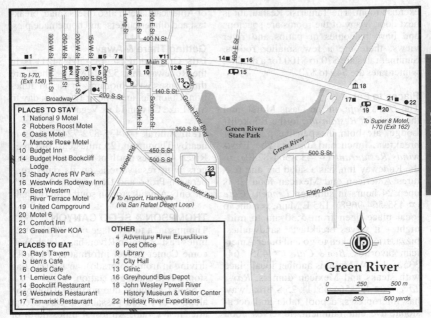

Green River

PLACES TO STAY
1 National 9 Motel
2 Robbers Roost Motel
3 Oasis Motel
7 Mancos Rose Motel
10 Budget Inn
14 Budget Host Bookcliff Lodge
15 Shady Acres RV Park
16 Westwinds Rodeway Inn
17 Best Western River Terrace Motel
19 United Campground
20 Motel 6
21 Comfort Inn
23 Green River KOA

PLACES TO EAT
3 Ray's Tavern
5 Ben's Cafe
6 Oasis Cafe
11 Lemieux Cafe
14 Bookcliff Restaurant
16 Westwinds Restaurant
17 Tamarisk Restaurant

OTHER
4 Adventure River Expeditions
8 Post Office
9 Library
12 City Hall
13 Clinic
16 Greyhound Bus Depot
18 John Wesley Powell River History Museum & Visitor Center
22 Holiday River Expeditions

UTAH

800-537-8674), 360 E Main, has showers, coin laundry and a store.

Places to Stay – Budget
Summer rates are substantially higher than the rest of the year. One of the cheapest places is *Mancos Rose Motel* (☎ 435-564-9660), 20 W Main, which has 17 simple rooms for $25 to $40 in summer. Also in this price range, the *Oasis Motel* (☎ 435-564-3471), 118 W Main, has 20 basic but OK rooms. The similarly priced *Budget Inn* (☎ 435-564-3441, fax 435-564-3442), 60 E Main, has about 30 modest rooms.

The *Motel 6* (☎ 435-564-3436, fax 435-564-8272), 946 E Main, is the largest hotel in town, with over 100 budget rooms and a pool. Summer rates run $42/48 for singles/doubles; winter rates are about $30/36. Others in this price range are the *National 9 Motel* (☎ 435-564-8237, 800-474-3304, fax 435-564-3625), 456 W Main, and the small *Robbers Roost Motel* (☎ 435-564-3452), 225 W Main, which has a pool and spa.

Places to Stay – Middle
The *Budget Host Bookcliff Lodge* (☎ 435-564-3406, 800-493-4699, fax 435-564-8359), 395 E Main, has about 80 rooms, a pool in summer, a restaurant open from 6 am to 10 pm (7 am to 9 pm in winter) and adequate rooms for about $45/55 for singles/doubles (one bed) or $60 to $80 (two beds) in summer, $30 and up in winter. The *Westwinds Rodeway Inn* (☎ 435-564-3421, 800-845-2389, fax 435-564-8162), 525 E Main, has a restaurant. Rooms are nice enough and cost in the $60s in summer. The *Super 8 Motel* (☎ 435-564-8888, fax 435-564-8890), 1248 E Main, has an indoor pool and spa. Pleasant rooms are about $60, including coffee and pastries for breakfast.

The *Comfort Inn* (☎ 435-564-3300, fax 435-564-3299), 1065 E Main, has an indoor pool, a spa and an exercise room, and includes a continental breakfast. Rooms run $60 to $80. The *Best Western River Terrace* (☎ 435-564-3401, fax 435-564-3403), 880 E Main, has an outdoor pool, a spa and an exercise room. The Tamarisk Restaurant is next door. Many of the rooms are spacious and have balconies or patios and river views; there are a few smaller rooms. Summer rates are $70 to $100 for a double; winter rates are $49 to $70.

Places to Eat

The *Oasis Cafe*, in the Oasis Motel, and the *Bookcliff Restaurant*, in the Bookcliff Lodge, are both inexpensive places for breakfast, lunch and dinner. The *Westwinds Restaurant* (☎ 435-564-8240), in the Rodeway Inn, has a salad bar and features American and Mexican food; it is open 24 hours in summer. *Lemieux Cafe* (☎ 435-564-9698), 135 E Main, is a cheap local place open from 5:30 am to midnight – it serves breakfasts, sandwiches, pizza, fried chicken to go and other American favorites. *Ben's Cafe* (☎ 435-564-3352), 115 W Main, is another local place with steaks and Mexican dinners. *Ray's Tavern* (☎ 435-564-3511), 25 S Broadway, has microbrews, a pool table and occasional live entertainment. It serves good burgers, steak, seafood and pizza in a Western setting.

The most upscale eatery in town is the *Tamarisk Restaurant* (☎ 435-564-8109), 870 E Main, open 6 am to 10 pm. It has river views and a reasonably priced menu

---

The Edible State Flower

Utah's state flower, the sego lily *(Calochortus nuttallii)*, grows from a bulb that can remain dormant in the soil during dry years, sprouting only when enough precipitation falls in the winter and spring. The lily, which blooms from May to July, has three delicate white petals, each with a purple mark on the inside at the base. The flower takes its name from the Ute Indians, who called it 'sago' and showed the early Mormons how to dig for the bulb, which is starchy and nutritious. ■

---

of American fare; it also offers salad, breakfast and dinner buffets, and homemade pies.

Getting There & Away

Bus Greyhound (☎ 435-564-3421) is in the Rodeway Inn, 525 E Main. There are three buses each morning to Grand Junction, Colorado, and one or two each day to Salt Lake City and Las Vegas.

Train Amtrak (☎ 435-872-7245) stops in nearby Thompson (25 miles east of Green River; 40 miles north of Moab) for passengers with reservations on its daily runs between Provo and Denver, Colorado. It's the only Amtrak stop in southeastern Utah.

THOMPSON & SEGO CANYON

Thompson, a tiny village on I-70 about 25 miles east of Green River, has a Utah Welcome Center (travel information for folks driving in from Colorado), an Amtrak flag stop, a café and a gas station.

Sego Canyon is due north of Thompson along a dirt road passable to cars except after heavy rain. Almost 4 miles north of Thompson, a variety of prehistoric rock art is visible on the cliffs to the left, near a creek ford. There is also a ghost town (Sego) in the canyon – you can wander among the ruins of the small mining town that was abandoned around 1950. The canyon is within the Book Cliffs – a 250-mile-long escarpment stretching from Price, Utah, to Grand Junction, Colorado.

SAN RAFAEL DESERT & REEF

The San Rafael Desert lies more than 2000 feet below the San Rafael Swell (see the Central Utah chapter). The two are separated by the San Rafael Reef, a natural barrier that stretches southwest of Green River. I-70 west of Green River goes through the north end of the San Rafael Desert before climbing up past the reef and into the swell – a very scenic freeway drive through remote and almost uninhabited territory.

A 100-mile loop road from Green River (over half of which is unpaved but passable to ordinary vehicles in dry weather) leaves town along Airport Rd. The visitor center has a brochure describing the route in detail and can advise you of road conditions. You can camp almost anywhere, but there are no facilities. Carry at least a gallon of water per person per day. The drive gives access to several side roads that require 4WD or foot travel and get you into canyons with Indian petroglyphs and scenic overlooks. This road eventually reaches Hwy 24 just south of the entrance road to Goblin Valley (see below). This road also provides the only access to the remote western **Horseshoe Canyon** and **Maze** sections of Canyonlands National Park. Further details of these areas are given in Canyonlands National Park, later in this chapter.

GOBLIN VALLEY STATE PARK

This park is about 46 miles southwest of Green River. Reach it along Hwy 24 and turn right on a signed 12-mile-long road, the last 7 miles of which are unpaved but passable to cars. The park is near the southern end of the **San Rafael Swell**, and various dirt roads continue beyond the park into the beautiful, rugged and relatively untraveled San Rafael area. The BLM in Price, the visitor center and state park in Green River, and the park itself have maps and information about these drives, for which high clearance is recommended and 4WD might be necessary. The BLM office in Hanksville also has maps and information, although these BLM lands are administered from Price.

The park itself is full of goblins: tortured and twisted rock formations that imaginative visitors have also described as ghosts, giant mushrooms and toadstools, chess pieces, spooks and assorted other weirdoes. A couple of 1- to 2-mile trails wind their way through the eroded rocks. This would be a great place to spend Halloween with your kids. A year-round campground provides 21 sites with barbecue grills, water and showers. Day use is $4; camping is $10.

The park headquarters are at Green River State Park. Make camping reservations at ☎ 800-322-3770.

HANKSVILLE

At the junction of Hwys 24 and lage of under 500 inhabitants is a convenient stopping place on the way between the area's various natural attractions.

The BLM (☎ 435-542-3461), 406 S 100 West, has maps and information about the lands surrounding Hanksville, especially the Henry Mountains (see below). Hours are 7:45 am to noon and 12:45 to 4:30 pm, Monday to Friday.

Places to Stay & Eat

Red Rock Campground & Restaurant (☎ 435-542-3235), 226 E 100 North, has 60 sites, showers and a coin laundry; it's open from late March to early November. Sites are $9 for a tent to $14 with hookups. The cheaper *Jurassic Park* (☎ 435-542-3433), 100 S Center, has about 40 sites, half for tents and half with hookups. There are showers and it's open all year.

Hotels in Hanksville are simple but adequate and charge $40 to $50 for a double in summer. *Whispering Sands Motel* (☎ 435-542-3238, fax 435-542-3429), 132 S Hwy 95 at the south edge of town, has two dozen rooms each with two queen-size beds and cable TV. It is close to *Blondie's Eatery* (☎ 435-542-3255), which offers basic breakfast, lunch and dinner. Nearby is *Stan's Burger Shak* (☎ 435-542-3441); his burgers are better than his spelling.

The slightly cheaper *Desert Inn* (☎ 435-542-3241, fax 435-542-3231), 197 E Hwy 24, is fronted by a whimsical metal dinosaur fence. There's also the *Poor Boy Motel* (☎ 435-542-3471), 322 E 100 North.

Friendly *Fern's Place* (☎ 435-542-3251), 99 E 100 North, has eight rooms, some with kitchenettes, and gets a thumbs up from readers. *Joy's B&B* (☎ 435-542-3252), PO Box 151, Hanksville, UT 84734, at 296 S Center, has three nonsmoking rooms.

HENRY MOUNTAINS

This 11,000-foot-high range was the last to be named and explored in the lower 48 states. It is remote and scenic and boasts a herd of bison that was introduced here in the 1940s. Now it's one of the country's last wild bison herds, with some 200 head freely roaming the range.

The bison usually graze high in the summer and drop down into the western flanks of the Henrys in winter. The BLM in Hanksville can tell you where the animals have been sighted recently. Pronghorn antelopes, mule deer and bighorn sheep are also seen in the Henrys. A good source book for the area is *Hiking & Exploring Utah's Henry Mountains and Robbers Roost* by MR Kelsey.

Access from Hanksville is south from the BLM station along 100 East.

The BLM operates three small (about 10 sites) campgrounds in the area. All have pit toilets and water but no showers or RV hookups. *Lonesome Beaver* is about 25 miles south of Hanksville along 100 East, which becomes Sawmill Basin Rd. The elevation here is 8000 feet, and the area is open from May to October. There is a $4 fee. The free *McMillan Springs* campground is a further 10 miles in; it usually is open from May to November. Both these campgrounds can also be reached from Hwy 95 via the Bull Mountain Scenic Backway, signed at about 20 miles south of Hanksville. At 6300 feet *Starr Springs* is open from April to November; the fee is $4. It is at the south end of the range, reached by a signed 4-mile dirt road from Hwy 276, about 17 miles beyond the junction with Hwy 95.

Note that some of these roads are unpaved – check with the BLM for current conditions.

The BLM also runs the free and waterless *Hog Spring* campground off Hwy 95 about 35 miles south of Hanksville.

Hwy 95 turns southeast and, about 45 miles from Hanksville, crosses Lake Powell near its north end at Hite (there's a bridge), then continues past magnificent scenery into Utah's far southeastern corner. About 25 miles south of Hanksville, Hwy 276 heads southwest and reaches Lake Powell at Bullfrog Basin, where the lake can be crossed by car ferry. Both these places are described in the Grand Canyon & Lake Powell chapter.

Arches National Park to Blanding

Approximately 20 miles east of Green River, Hwy 191 branches off of I-70 and heads southeast. This stretch of highway gives access to the town of Moab, and to Arches and Canyonlands National Parks, containing some of the most spectacular scenery in the Southwest. Be aware that Horseshoe Canyon and the Maze (both in Canyonlands NP) are not accessible from Hwy 191 – see their section for further information.

ARCHES NATIONAL PARK

The arches and bridges found in the Southwest are all formed by erosion of sandstone – the difference between the two is that arches are carved by erosion from the weather and from rockfall, while the bridges begin by erosion from rivers. Sometimes it is difficult to tell which is which after a river has dried up or shifted.

Arches National Park boasts the greatest concentration of arches in the world (a good place to see bridges is at Natural Bridges National Monument, described later in this chapter). To qualify as an arch, a formation must be at least 3 feet across; over 2000 have been found in the national park, including the spectacularly elongated Landscape Arch, which is over 100 feet high and 300 feet across. This is probably one of the largest arches in the world, but it is eroded to the point where it is likely to collapse in the near geological future. That means any minute in the next few thousand years, so it probably won't happen when you're under it. Roads and hiking trails make many of the most spectacular arches accessible to everyone.

The relatively small park covers about 115 sq miles. In 1997, the US House of Representatives passed a bill that would add almost 5 sq miles to the northeastern corner of the park. At the time of writing, this bill was going before the Senate.

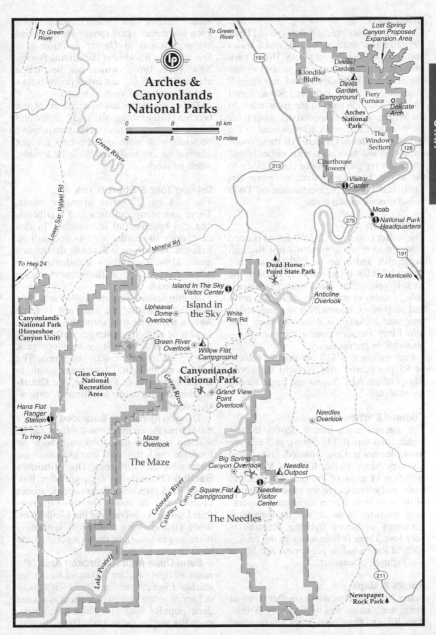

Orientation

The park is easily reached along paved Hwy 191, 20 miles southeast of I-70 and 5 miles northwest of Moab. From Hwy 191, a park road reaches the entrance station and visitor center almost immediately and continues 9 miles to a 'Y' near Balanced Rock. From the Y, a 2½-mile road to the right leads to the Windows Section, a good destination for those with little time. A 10-mile road to the left goes to Devils Garden. All these roads are paved and have numerous pullouts and trailheads for great views or scenic hikes to the arches. In addition, there are some dirt roads suitable for high-clearance or 4WD vehicles or mountain bikes.

Information

The visitor center (☎ 435-259-8161) is open 7:30 am to 6 pm from mid-April through September and 8 am to 4:30 pm at other times. It is closed December 25 (though the park is open). The usual things are available – audio-visual shows, exhibits, book and map sales, information and ranger-led programs including a daily two-hour hike into Fiery Furnace during the summer – reservations are necessary.

Park entrance is $10 per private vehicle or $5 per person; this is valid for seven days. Golden Age, Access and Eagle Passes are accepted.

Climate & When to Go

The summer is the busiest period, though highs often top 100°F. Spring and fall are more pleasant and less crowded. Snowfall is not very heavy at the 4000- to 5500-foot elevation of most of the park's roads and trails, and winter can be the most enchanting of times to visit. Winter nighttime temperatures are often in the 20°s F; daytime temperatures are above freezing. Rainfall is very low. There is little water in the park – carry at least a gallon per person per day as you sightsee in summer.

Books & Maps

In the 1950s, Arches was a smaller national monument, access was by the sandy Willow Flats Rd, and there were just a few hundred annual visitors. That's when Edward Abbey got a job here as a park ranger. He described his experiences in *Desert Solitaire – A Season in the Wilderness* (Ballantine Books, New York, 1968), which has become a classic. Other books are listed under Books in the Facts for the Visitor chapter.

The visitor center has free park maps and brochures describing all roads, trails and major features. It also sells inexpensive booklets with more details. Pets are not allowed on any trails and must be leashed when on roads.

Driving Tour & Short Hikes

The park has 22 miles of paved roads. There are many pullouts and trailheads that can become full in summer. In this case, drive to another area as you will be ticketed for parking outside of designated areas. Drive carefully – accidents occur when drivers stare at the scenery rather than the road.

Highlights include the following. Just over 2 miles from the entrance is **Park Ave**, a mile-long trail through impressive sandstone cliffs that emerges farther along the road. Arrange to have someone pick you up, or return the way you came. The trail drops over 300 feet from south to north. Just north of Park Ave, the **Courthouse Towers** on the left form an impressive skyline.

The gravity-defying **Balanced Rock** (9 miles from the entrance) on the right can be reached by a 0.3-mile-loop trail; both the roadside and the trail perspectives are impressive and different. The **Windows Section** (2½ miles to the right after Balanced Rock) has several very scenic arches visible from the road. The three-quarter-mile Double Arch Trail and the 1-mile Windows Trail are easy and highly rewarding hikes to get you right up to several of the most impressive arches.

Sand Dune Arch and **Broken Arch** (8½ miles straight on after Balanced Rock) are reached from the same trailhead – it's about 0.2 miles to the first (where there is a sand dune popular with kids) and a 1.3-mile, easy, flat loop to the second. There are very

The Desert's Delicate Skin

Travelers to deserts of the Southwest are often told to avoid stepping on the **cryptobiotic crust** – but what is this odd-sounding stuff? The crust is a unique combination of living organisms such as lichen, cyanobacteria, fungi and algae that forms a dark, powdery coating on the high deserts of the Colorado Plateau. It acts both as a protective covering and as a binding agent for tiny soil particles, retarding erosion, absorbing moisture and providing nutrients (especially nitrogen) for desert plants and the animals that rely on them. The cryptobiotic crust may not look like much, but it is the delicate and fragile basis of life in the desert.

In some ways, the crust is tough stuff – it survives the scorching summer sun, freezing winters, irregular downpours and windstorms. But it's not built to withstand a hiking boot: the force of a footprint crushes and kills the crust. Millions of visitors, billions of footprints – the crust can suffer irreversible damage. Worse damage is caused by bicycle or vehicle tires; the crust breaks down in a continuous strip that makes the desert especially vulnerable to erosion. That's why you are told to stay on established roads and trails, and to step on the rock or in the sandy washes when traveling off the trail. ■

UTAH

good views from these trails. A short way beyond is **Skyline Arch**, which is visible from I-70. This arch almost doubled in size with a 1940 rockfall – a quarter-mile trail will take you underneath to see the result.

Hiking

Many visitors' favorite is the **Delicate Arch Trail**. About 2½ miles beyond Balanced Rock, a good road leads almost 2 miles right to **Wolfe Ranch**. (Here a log cabin built in 1908 by an early pioneer is quite well preserved and enables you to imagine how tough life must have been then.) Just east of the ranch, a footbridge crosses Salt Wash, beyond which a short path leads to views of Ute Indian rock art. The footbridge marks the beginning of the moderately difficult arch trail that goes over slickrock (where it is marked by rock cairns), past pockets of vegetation and fine vistas, culminating in a wall-hugging narrow ledge to Delicate Arch itself – one of the most beautiful in the park and well worth the 3-mile roundtrip hike.

Expect some steep drop-offs on this trail, but no shade or water (carry at least a quart). Another (more distant) view of the arch is obtained by taking the road about a mile beyond the ranch and hiking 0.4 miles to an overlook – again, steep sections.

Nineteen miles from the visitor center, **Devils Garden** is at the end of the paved road. A variety of trails here allow you to hike from 2 to 7 miles, roundtrip. One trail, which passes about 10 arches (including **Landscape Arch** – the biggest, described above), is close to the park campground and therefore is very popular. The 2-mile roundtrip to Landscape Arch (passing Tunnel Arch and Pine Tree Arch) is quite easy and busy; beyond, the trail gets less crowded but is rougher and less obvious, though fairly straightforward for experienced hikers. It offers spectacular views of the La Sal Mountains.

Guided Hikes About 5 miles north of Balanced Rock is **Fiery Furnace**. This maze of canyons offers the opportunity to hike off-trail (don't step on that cryptobiotic crust) and get thoroughly lost. Forget your water and you're buzzard bait. Actually, because of the disorienting nature of the furnace and the damage done by so many people, the park requires you to go as part of a ranger-led group (limited to 25). Space fills up fast and there could be a two-day waiting period. Sign up at the visitor center up to two days in advance. The Fiery Furnace hike leaves at 10 am and 2 pm from April to October and costs $6 for those over 12 and $3 for seven- to 12-year-olds. If staffing permits, other ranger-led hikes are offered.

Driving & Hiking off the Main Road

There are three unpaved roads in the park. The **Salt Valley Rd** is suitable for cars most of the time (inclement weather may close the road). It leaves the main road just over a mile before the end and heads 9 miles west to the very scenic **Klondike Bluffs**. This gives you a chance to get away from the densest crowds – though a good number of cars do make it out here! From here, a trailhead gives access to a 2.4-mile roundtrip hike to **Tower Arch**, with great views of the arch and other formations, but some loose footing on sandy sections.

From Klondike Bluffs, an unnamed 10-mile dirt road leads back to the main park road at Balanced Rock. This requires 4WD and is best done from north to south (going the other way involves a steep and sandy climb that may be impassable). This road also goes near Tower Arch.

From Balanced Rock, the Willow Flats Rd goes west (soon meeting the road described above). This used to be the way into the park (back when Abbey worked here) and is in fair shape for most vehicles to the park boundary (4 miles). From there it requires high clearance or 4WD to reach Hwy 191, about another 4 miles. The distant views and solitude are the main attractions on this road – there are no important arches nearby. Before you go, ask rangers at the visitor center about road conditions.

Mountain Biking

Bicycles are welcomed on paved and unpaved roads maintained for vehicles, but there are no bike trails. Biking is not allowed on any foot trails.

Backpacking

Because most of the park is easily reached on day trips and because of the heat and scarcity of water, few visitors backpack, though this is allowed with permits obtained from the visitor center. Backpacking here is not recommended for beginners and you should talk to the rangers for the best suggestions. They'll help, not hinder you – unless you aren't prepared. Backpackers must carry a gallon of water per day (minimum), bring a stove (fires are prohibited), camp at least a mile away from roads and refrain from trampling the cryptobiotic

---

Park Etiquette

From a few hundred annual visitors in the days of Edward Abbey to 100,000 in the 1980s to almost a million in the 1990s, the popularity of Arches National Park has soared. The NPS surveyed park patrons to find out what measures would improve their visits – perhaps surprisingly, many people would like the park to limit the number of visitors at the major scenic points. Therefore, the parking lots at scenic areas are limited in size and when they are full you should move on to another one. Parking and other regulations are enforced to help protect the desert from the onslaught of visitors.

Hikers should stay on trails where they exist. When hiking in the backcountry, hike on the sandstone, slickrock or sandy washes. Avoid stepping on the desert vegetation, which is particularly vulnerable (see the sidebar The Desert's Delicate Skin). 4WD vehicles and mountain bikes can only be used on the paved and unpaved roads, not on hiking trails or off-road. ATVs and ORVs cannot be used anywhere in the park. ■

crust. There are no designated backcountry campsites.

Rock Climbing

Sites marked on USGS maps are off limits (ie, most of the famous arches), but rock climbing is permitted in much of the park. Climbers should ask at the visitor center for advice and a free permit.

Places to Stay

The scenic *Devils Garden* campground is at the road's end about 20 miles north of the entrance. It has 52 sites, picnic tables, grills, water and toilets, but no showers. All campers must register at the visitor center on a first-come, first-served basis. The fee is $10. It's usually full by early to mid-morning in the summer high season, so arrive at the visitor center early. Registration begins at 7:30 am. In winter, water is turned off but can be obtained at the visitor center.

There are also two group campsites near Devils Garden for tent campers only. One has space for up to 33 people and seven vehicles (no RVs) and the other for 55 people and 10 vehicles. Fees are $3 per person per night with 11 people minimum plus a $10 reservation fee per group. Make reservations through the NPS Reservations Office (☎ 435-259-4351, fax 435-259-4285), 2282 S West Resource Blvd, Moab, UT 84532.

There are many places to stay in nearby Moab.

DEAD HORSE POINT STATE PARK

This state park, although small, compares in dramatic scenery to the nearby Arches and Canyonlands National Parks and deserves the 22-mile side trip along paved Hwy 313 (which leaves Hwy 191 11 miles northwest of Moab). The lovely drive's most exciting section is near the end – the road crosses a narrow neck of land only 30 yards wide with 2000-foot cliffs all around.

The view from the end is simply fabulous – the Colorado River below has almost looped back on itself forming a splendid 'gooseneck' opposite the point. A rough

footpath follows the edge allowing views in all directions. Canyonlands National Park can be seen to the southwest, immediately behind the gooseneck.

There is a visitor center (☎ 435-259-2614) open from 8 am to 6 pm in summer and 9 am to 5 pm in winter. Slide shows, exhibits, information and a gift shop are here. Rangers lead walks and give talks in summer. A short nature trail is nearby.

The 21-site *Kayenta Campground* nearby has water but no showers. There are RV hookups in summer only. Reservations can be made (☎ 800-322-3770) or just show up early. Even in the busy summer, the campground usually has space until midday or early afternoon. Day use is $4; camping is $9.

CANYONLANDS NATIONAL PARK

Covering 527 sq miles, this is the largest and wildest national park in Utah – indeed, parts of it are as rugged as almost anywhere on the planet. Sheer-walled and spectacular canyons provide great scenic beauty but also prevent you from getting around very easily. Take the primitive campgrounds at the Doll House and the Horsehoof Arch, for example. They are only 5 miles apart as the crow flies – but separated by the Cataract Canyon of the Colorado River. With a 4WD vehicle you'll cover 230 miles of (often very rough) road to get from one campground to the other! Not only canyons awe the visitor; there are arches, bridges, needles, spires, craters, mesas and buttes – just about every Southwestern geological formation you can imagine.

There's plenty of water, too, but it's usually 2000 inaccessible feet below you in the rivers. Only one campground in the park has drinking water in summer. Most areas are completely waterless – even visitor centers (they'll sell you bottled water). If you plan on anything more than a casual day trip to the main overlooks, load up several large containers of water – a gallon per person per day is considered minimal in summer.

The difficult terrain and lack of water make this the least developed and least visited of all the major Southwestern national parks.

Orientation The canyons of the Colorado and Green Rivers divide the park into *three completely separate* and very different areas (called 'districts' by the NPS). Imagine the canyons in a 'Y' shape. The long northeast-southwest arm of the Y is the Colorado River and the northwest arm is the Green River. The most developed district of the park is 'Island in the Sky' – the area enclosed by the two rivers at the top of the Y. This is easily reached by paved Hwy 313, about a 30-mile drive from Moab. To the southeast of the Colorado is 'The Needles' – about a 75-mile drive from Moab via paved Hwys 191 and 211. To the west of the two rivers is the 'Maze' – about 130 miles from Moab and accessible by dirt roads. In addition, 'Horseshoe Canyon,' an unconnected unit northwest of the Maze, is also reached by dirt roads. There are no bridges over the canyons within the park, so each district is described separately later in this chapter.

Island in the Sky and The Needles have visitor centers, developed campgrounds and paved roads leading to scenic overlooks and picnic areas. They also have dirt roads and hiking trails. The Maze and Horseshoe Canyon have only dirt roads (most accessible only to 4WD), hiking trails and primitive campgrounds – these areas have fewer visitors.

Information Maps, guidebooks, and information for all park areas are available from the Moab Visitor Center (see Moab) or the NPS headquarters in Moab (☎ 435-259-7164), 2282 S West Resource Blvd, Moab, UT 84532, open 8 am to 4:30 pm, Monday to Friday. Also see the separate park districts below.

Entrance to the park is $10 per vehicle or $5 per person, valid for seven days and for all the different districts. Golden Age, Access and Eagle Passes are accepted. In winter and in the remote Maze district, fees aren't collected.

Pets are not allowed on hiking or backcountry 4WD trails, even inside a vehicle.

ATVs are not allowed anywhere. There are no lodges in the park.

Climate & When to Go If you've read the earlier national park descriptions, you'll find the pattern familiar. Summer has average temperatures in the 90°s F (often over 100°F) and short but heavy thunderstorms in July and August. Biting insects are worst in late May and June when you should carry repellent. Spring and fall are the most pleasant seasons. January, the coldest month, has average highs around 40°F and lows in the teens. Winter snows aren't very heavy but can close some roads. The best months overall are April and October – but don't tell anyone. Summer months are busy with driving visitors while spring and fall are busy with backcountry users.

Backcountry Permits & Reservations Permits are required for all backcountry camping, backpacking, mountain biking, 4WD trips and river trips. They are in addition to the park entrance fee. Backpackers pay $10 per group (maximum seven people in the Island and Needles districts; maximum five in the Maze). Mountain-bike or 4WD groups pay $25 for up to three vehicles (nine people maximum in the Maze, 10 in the Needles and 14 in the Island). River trips are $25 per group in Cataract Canyon and $10 per group in flatwater areas (16 people maximum). Permits are valid for up to 14 consecutive days. In addition, certain backcountry sections of the Needles are open for day use by horses, bikes and 4WD vehicles and cost $5 per day per vehicle or per group of up to seven bikes or horses.

Reservations can be made with the NPS Reservations Office (☎ 435-259-4351, fax 435-259-4285), 2282 S West Resource Blvd, Moab UT 84532. They answer questions from 8 am to 12:30 pm (until 4 pm if staff are available) Monday to Friday. For backpacking, mountain-biking and 4WD trips, reservations can be made no earlier than the second Monday in July for the following calendar year. They must be made at least two weeks in advance, and are especially recommended for spring and fall. For raft trips and day use, reservations are taken at the beginning of January for the same year.

If you don't have a reservation, permits can be obtained on a space-available basis the day before or the first day of your trip from the visitor center in which your trip begins. Call the visitor center to find out if permits are available, but be aware that reservations by phone are not accepted.

Books Apart from general Utah outdoor books, dedicated Canyonlands travelers will find the following useful: *Canyon Country Mountain Biking* by FA Barnes & T Kuehn; *Hiking, Biking and Exploring Canyonlands National Park and Vicinity* and *River Guide to Canyonlands National Park*, both by MR Kelsey; and *Mountain Biking Moab* by D Crowell. There are many others.

Exploring the Backcountry Hiking, biking and 4WD are used to explore the backcountry. These activities are described below under the three Canyonlands districts. Mountain bikers and all vehicles must use roads (both paved and unpaved) and cannot bike/drive on hiking trails or off roads. Everyone should use high-scale topographic maps as signs are few and trails not always clear. Outfitters in Moab and other places can arrange guided backcountry trips or you can do it yourself.

River Running Guided river trips are available from Green River for the river of that name and from Moab for the Colorado River. All outfitters in these towns take care of the logistics and obtain the necessary permits. A limited number of permits (see above) are available to members of the public who have the appropriate skills, experience and boating equipment. Write to the park headquarters as far in advance as possible for applications and information.

The trip from Green River down to the confluence with the Colorado is a scenic one with relatively easy rapids. The same is true of the Colorado above the confluence. Almost immediately below the confluence, however, the Colorado goes through the wild white water of Cataract Canyon – navigable by experienced or guided boaters only. Beyond this canyon, the river eases off as it approaches Lake Powell in the Glen Canyon National Recreation Area. A useful book is *River Guide to Canyonlands National Park* by MR Kelsey.

Rock Climbing Climbing is permitted in most parts of the park. However, there is no climbing in the Horseshoe Canyon unit, on any archaeological site or cultural resource, or on any arch or natural bridge marked on USGS maps, with the exception of Washerwoman Arch. All climbing must be free or clean-aid climbing. The soft rock in The Needles is unsuitable for climbing. Climbers are encouraged to check with a ranger prior to a climb.

Canyonlands – Island in the Sky

This is the most easily reached and popular district. The heart is a 6000-foot-high mesa (the 'Island in the Sky') surrounded by a sandstone bench called the White Rim, 1200 feet below. From this rim, cliffs tumble a further 1000 feet to the rivers.

Information The Island in the Sky Visitor Center (☎ 435-259-4712) is open 8 am to 4:30 pm daily, extended to 5 or 6 pm from spring to fall and closed Thanksgiving, December 25 and January 1. From spring to fall, especially on weekends, interpretive activities are offered.

Main Drive & Short Hikes The visitor center is on the mesa top about 2 miles after the park boundary (pay entrance fees here). Paved roads continue to the edge of the 'island' with superb vistas of the White Rim, the rivers below and the national park stretching off into the distance. Most visitors take this paved road. From the visitor center, the road goes 12 miles south to Grand View Point; at about the halfway point of the drive, another paved road forks to the northwest and leads to Upheaval

Dome, 5 miles away. Along these 17 miles of paved roads are several overlooks and trails – all well worth a stop. The best are described below. Note that some trails, though easy, cross slickrock and are marked by cairns, or come close to cliff edges, so keep your eyes open.

A brochure describes the vegetation around the **Mesa Arch Nature Trail**, 6 miles south of the visitor center. The easy, half-mile loop trail passes Mesa Arch, which is on the very edge of the rim and makes a dramatic frame for the desert country below. The best light for photography is at dawn or in the afternoon.

At the picnic area almost a mile before the end of the road to Grand View Point, the **White Rim Overlook Trail** is an almost 2-mile roundtrip, but it isn't difficult and gives some of the best views of the Colorado River over 2000 feet below. Another easy 2-mile walk is the **Grand View Trail** at the road's end – many people say it has the best views in the park. Even if you are not up to hiking these trails, a stop at **Grand View Point Overlook** is a must.

Turning northwest 6 miles south of the visitor center leads to a picnic area and the **Upheaval Dome Trail**. An interpretive pamphlet describes the geology of this area. The trail is an easy half mile one-way to the Upheaval Dome Overlook with fine views of a crater thought to have been the result of a meteor crashing into the planet. The trail continues a further half mile (but becomes a little more difficult) to Crater View Overlook.

The **Green River Overlook** has some of the best views of that river. The overlook is behind the Willow Flat Campground, reached by a short unpaved road at the beginning of the road to Upheaval Dome.

Longer Hikes & Backpacking There are plenty of possibilities for half-day, all-day or overnight trips. These are strenuous because they involve the steep and often slippery descent down to the White Rim, and then the climb back out. About seven foot trails descend from the paved road down to the White Rim Rd – these form the basis of the longer hikes and backpacking trips. The trails have little or no shade or water, so you should be well prepared to deal with these hazards. The lack of water limits most backpacking trips to what you can carry. Permits are required.

White Rim Loop Built partially by uranium prospectors after WWII, this 4WD track goes all the way around the Island in the Sky. It is about 100 miles long and is reached from the visitor center by the steeply descending Shafer Trail Rd. This circuit is a great favorite for 4WD trips, mountain-bike trips and, to some extent, backpacking trips. The Park Service is trying to maintain the wilderness quality by limiting the number of vehicles using the road.

Park rangers regularly patrol the route to assist people whose vehicles break down or who have other problems. They also check for permits.

Places to Stay Six or 7 miles by road beyond the visitor center, *Willow Flat Campground* has 12 sites open all year. There are pit toilets and fire grills but no water – you must haul it in from Moab. Camping is free on a first-come, first-served basis.

Near the Upheaval Dome Trail is the *Syncline Campsite* for backpackers only. Backpackers can also camp at large in many designated areas. There are no facilities or reliable water supplies and permits are required (see Backcountry Permits & Reservations, earlier in this chapter).

Along the White Rim Rd are 10 primitive campgrounds for backpackers and 4WD or mountain-bike users. Each has two campsites limited to three vehicles and 15 people. None have water. Permits are required.

There are occasional cancellations and no-shows – call the park about the chance of doing this very popular drive on short notice.

Canyonlands – The Needles

Paved roads make this spikily scenic area almost as popular as Island in the Sky. It is named after the mind-boggling landscape of striped white and orange spires, which really has to be seen to be believed. There are plenty of arches as well, many hidden in the backcountry and accessible only by hiking trails or 4WD roads. Also found in the backcountry are Ancestral Puebloan sites and petroglyphs, many of which are difficult to reach.

Note that Newspaper Rock State Park, described later in this chapter, is passed on Hwy 211 about 18 miles before The Needles – these two are usually combined into one visit.

Information The Needles Visitor Center (☎ 435-259-4711) is open 8 am to 4:30 pm daily, extended to 5 or 6 pm from spring to fall and closed Thanksgiving, December 25 and January 1. From spring to fall, especially on weekends, interpretive activities are offered. Water is available at the visitor center.

Main Drive & Short Hikes The visitor center is 2½ miles beyond the park boundary – pay your entrance fee (unless you already have a pass from another area) and obtain maps here.

From the visitor center, the paved road continues for almost 7 miles to **Big Spring Canyon Overlook**; various stopping places, trails and paved and unpaved side roads line the way. Some of the best include the following.

Almost a mile beyond the visitor center, a left turn leads past rangers' housing and continues, unpaved, to the **Cave Spring Trail**, 1½ miles from the main road. This easy, 0.6-mile loop trail is fun and diverse: it crosses sandy areas and slickrock, descends two ladders, and passes thick vegetation in wet areas, Fremont Indian artwork and the remains of an old cowboy camp. A pamphlet describes these various facets of the walk.

Almost 3 miles beyond the visitor center, a side road to the left goes to a pump house with water year-round. A little farther is Squaw Flat Campground, again to the left. About 5 miles from the visitor center is the 0.6-mile loop **Pothole Point Trail** – one of

the easiest in the park and with nice views from boulders on a short side trail. A pamphlet describes the geology and biology of the potholes along the trail. Just before the road ends, the **Slickrock Trail** offers a fairly easy 2.4-mile loop, with a 0.6-mile spur – fine views. At road's end, the **Big Spring Canyon Overlook** also has great views and is the beginning of a longer trail.

Day Hikes Good day hikes abound. Three of the best (scenic and only moderately difficult) are suggested here. They are not for the total novice, however. The trails often cross slickrock, where the trail is marked by rock cairns   keep your eyes peeled or you can get lost. Shoes or boots with good rubber soles for traction are recommended. There is little shade and rarely any water (which, if found, must always be purified). Carry a gallon of water per person per day in the hottest months. See Climate & When to Go, earlier in this chapter.

From Squaw Flat Campground, climb up a short way along the **Squaw Canyon Trail** for fine views of The Needles. Return via the **Big Spring Canyon Trail** (roundtrip of 7½ miles) or the less used and more difficult **Lost Canyon Trail** (roundtrip 9 miles). These trails provide a good cross-section of slickrock, canyons, seasonal streams and distant views, and are a little more demanding than the earlier ones.

A still longer hike is from the Big Spring Canyon Overlook along the **Confluence Overlook Trail**, which leads 5½ miles to a point overlooking where the Green and Colorado Rivers meet – you can see the gray-green waters of the one mixing slowly with the reddish main flow of the other. Head back the way you came. You must climb a ladder at one point on this trail.

4WD Roads & Hikes The Needles is the park's best backpacking area because a network of hiking trails allows you to reach some primitive campgrounds over long stretches on 4WD roads. 4WD vehicles will have a hard time negotiating the infamous **Elephant Hill**, a couple of miles west of Squaw Flat – this is for experienced 4WD

UTAH

drivers only. Other roads are less difficult. Mountain bikers may find the 4WD roads a little too rough for comfort – though not impassable. Wide vehicles or those with long wheelbases are likely to have difficulty on some of the tight, steep switchbacks. (The NPS says that some drives involve considerable risk of vehicle damage!) The roads lead to backcountry campsites and various hiking trails. Because the roads are short, you can hike there.

One of the most amazing trails is the **Joint Trail**, accessed by a 9-mile drive from Squaw Flat Campground (4WD only). You can hike in and camp with advance permits and reservations. The trail itself is only about a mile, one way, but goes through a very narrow slot canyon for several hundred yards (very large people or those carrying big backpacks may have problems). The same access road also leads to the 5-mile **Chesler Park Loop** with beautiful views.

As with all 4WD trails in the park, you need a permit and reservations well ahead of time.

Places to Stay *Squaw Flat Campground* is just over 3 miles beyond the visitor center. There are 26 sites available year-round on a first-come, first-served basis. The campground may be full by early afternoon, so arrive early to ensure a place. There is drinking water and an $8 fee.

There are three group campsites nearby that must be reserved as far in advance as possible and at least two weeks ahead. Reservations cost $10 plus $2 per person. The campsites are *Split Top* with space for three vehicles and 15 people, *Wooden Shoe* (five vehicles, 25 people) and *Squaw Flat* (10 vehicles, 50 people).

There are primitive waterless campgrounds in the backcountry – these are for backpackers, mountain bikers and those using 4WD. Five campgrounds can be reached by 4WD and are limited to 10 people with three vehicles. Numerous others are reached by hiking trails with only minimal sections on the roads and are limited to seven people. There are also some areas where you can camp anywhere (with some limitations). See Backcountry Permits & Reservations, earlier in this section, for permit and fee information.

About 2 miles east of the visitor center on Hwy 211, a short signed road leads out of the park to *Needles Outpost* (cell ☎ 801-979-4007). Open year-round, it has a campground for $10. Showers ($4, or $2 for campground users) are available. Gas, food, meals, maps, information, jeep tours and bike rentals are also available, and they have an 8-inch astronomical telescope that can be used by reservation.

Canyonlands – Horseshoe Canyon & The Maze

The only access to these two remote western sectors of Canyonlands National Park is via dirt roads. There is no drinking water anywhere (though seasonal water exists and must be purified), so this area is for experienced and prepared desert rats.

The Hans Flat Ranger Station (☎ 435-259-2652, 435-259-6513) is open from 8 am to 4:30 pm daily from spring through fall only, and has information about both sectors.

You can reach both Horseshoe Canyon and the Maze directly from Green River via a long (47 miles to Horseshoe Canyon, 40 additional miles to the Maze) dirt road. An easier way is via the dirt road that heads southeast from Hwy 24 just south of the turnoff to Goblin Valley State Park. Follow this road 30 miles to Horseshoe Canyon or turn off it after 25 miles onto the road for the Maze. This latter road is suitable for cars only as far as the Hans Flat Ranger Station; after that you need 4WD.

Horseshoe Canyon The most important area here is the Great Gallery, where you can see superb rock art left by prehistoric Indians over thousands of years. The life-size figures are magnificent. Please don't disturb them in any way – even touching them with fingers deposits body oils that damage the millennia-old art. (Damaging the art is also a criminal offense.)

The Great Gallery can be reached by a 7-mile roundtrip hike from the 'main' dirt road, though you can get closer with 4WD. Rangers may lead hikes here in the spring to fall season. The access is downhill to the site.

The Maze The only access to this remote jumble of colorful canyons is via 4WD tracks or hiking trails east of the Hans Flat Ranger Station. This is one of the wildest areas in the Southwest. The few roads are very poor and can be closed by rain or snow – call the ranger station for current conditions. Short-wheelbase, high-clearance 4WD is the best choice for vehicles. Hiking trails cut miles from the vehicle routes. I recommend contacting the ranger before beginning any trip.

Places to Stay Overnight camping, as elsewhere in the park, is by permit only. There are several designated camping areas in the Maze that must be used by those driving or mountain biking. There are also designated camping areas west of the Maze in an area administered by the Glen Canyon National Recreation Area with similar camping rules. None have any facilities and campers must provide their own washable, reusable toilet systems. Hikers have more camping flexibility, but trails are often technical and may require a rope to raise and lower backpacks. The usual permits are required.

No camping is allowed in Horseshoe Canyon, but you can camp on the rim on BLM land. Carry water.

MOAB

You could say that Moab stands for Mormons, ores, actors and bikers – which sums up the town's history. Mormons set up a mission here in 1855, but Indians drove them away. In the late 1870s, Mormon farmers returned and weathered repeated attempts by Indians to oust them. Moab became a ranching and farming center, and many of today's roads and tracks in the area follow the hoof prints of early cattle roundups.

Oil prospectors became interested in the area's mineral wealth in the 1920s. The big strike didn't come until the 1950s, however, when valuable uranium ores were discovered and the population tripled in three years. The uranium boom was successful for a few years, and a handful of people made their fortunes. Miners wove a network of 4WD roads, which now are used by tourists. They also left scars on the landscape including radioactive tailings ponds. (Tailings are the waste product of mineral extraction processes; normally only a fraction of 1% of ores is usable product.) Some mining, especially of salt and potash, still goes on.

The influx of prospectors put Moab on the map, and word began to spread of the grand scenery in southeastern Utah. Actors arrived and movies were filmed including some John Wayne Westerns and Indiana Jones footage, though the most memorable footage may be the TV commercials of cars that were helicoptered to the tops of nearby mesas. (I never did trust those TV commercials.)

The mineral boom is now bust, and although films are still shot here, tourism has been the economic mainstay of recent years. Vacationers swell the population greatly outside of winter. Mountain bikers and 4WD-vehicle drivers have discovered the miners' roads and have begun using them. Mountain bikers have found that slickrock surfaces provide challenging and very scenic rides in the area.

Moab, with over 6000 permanent residents, is the seat of Grand County and the largest town in southeastern Utah. It is a semirural yet trendy town with chic restaurants and art galleries, and about 50 companies offering biking, river-running, backpacking and 4WD tours and rentals. Some 60 hotels and B&Bs provide over 1500 rooms and there are a further 1100 campsites. Despite, or perhaps because of, the large numbers of services, tourists swamp the place from spring to fall, and reservations are advised.

Much of the populace is delighted to profit from the influx of tourists. Others decry what Western writer Page Stegner calls 'an infestation of mountain-bike

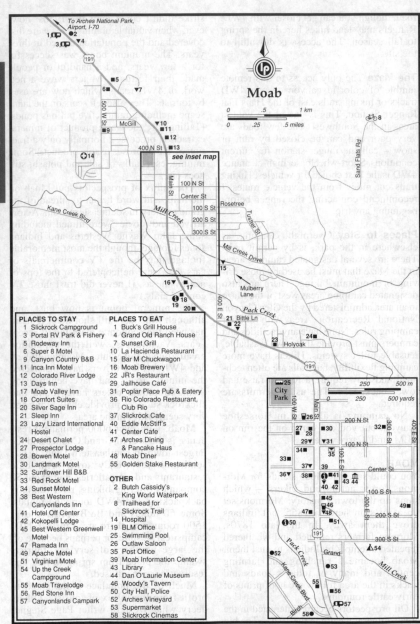

To Arches National Park,
Airport, I-70

Moab

0   .5   1 km

0   .25   .5 miles

see inset map

McGill

Kane Creek Blvd

Mill Creek

Main St

Mill St

100 N St

Center St

100 S St

200 S St

300 S St

Rosetree

Tusher St

Mill Creek Drive

Mulberry
Lane

Pack Creek

Bittle Ln

Holyoak

Sand Flats Rd

PLACES TO STAY
1 Slickrock Campground
3 Portal RV Park & Fishery
5 Rodeway Inn
6 Super 8 Motel
9 Canyon Country B&B
11 Inca Inn Motel
12 Colorado River Lodge
13 Days Inn
17 Moab Valley Inn
18 Comfort Suites
20 Silver Sage Inn
21 Sleep Inn
23 Lazy Lizard International
   Hostel
24 Desert Chalet
27 Prospector Lodge
28 Bowen Motel
30 Landmark Motel
32 Sunflower Hill B&B
33 Red Rock Motel
36 Sunset Motel
38 Best Western
   Canyonlands Inn
41 Hotel Off Center
42 Kokopelli Lodge
45 Best Western Greenwell
   Motel
47 Ramada Inn
49 Apache Motel
51 Virginian Motel
54 Up the Creek
   Campground
56 Moab Travelodge
56 Red Stone Inn
57 Canyonlands Campark

PLACES TO EAT
1 Buck's Grill House
4 Grand Old Ranch House
7 Sunset Grill
10 La Hacienda Restaurant
15 Bar M Chuckwagon
16 Moab Brewery
22 JR's Restaurant
29 Jailhouse Café
31 Poplar Place Pub & Eatery
36 Rio Colorado Restaurant,
   Club Rio
37 Slickrock Cafe
40 Eddie McStiff's
41 Center Cafe
47 Arches Dining
   & Pancake Haus
48 Moab Diner
55 Golden Stake Restaurant

OTHER
2 Butch Cassidy's
   King World Waterpark
8 Trailhead for
   Slickrock Trail
14 Hospital
19 BLM Office
25 Swimming Pool
26 Outlaw Saloon
35 Post Office
39 Moab Information Center
43 Library
44 Dan O'Laurie Museum
46 Woody's Tavern
50 City Hall, Police
52 Arches Vineyard
53 Supermarket
58 Slickrock Cinemas

City Park

0   250   500 m

0   250   500 yards

100 W St

Main St

100 W St

200 N St

100 N St

Center St

100 S St

200 S St

300 S St

100 E St

200 E St

300 E St

400 E St

Kane Creek Blvd

Pack Creek

Mill Creek

Bitlh

Grand

Holyoak

blight.' Like it or not, Moab is bursting at the seams – one Grand County councilmember writes 'tens of thousands of bikers, hikers, jeepers, spring-breakers, lycra-clad yuppies, foreign tourists and other refugees from the urban world are following the encouragement of the guidebook authors. . . . It ain't pretty.'

Orientation & Information

Hwy 191 becomes Main St, the main drag through town.

The multi-agency Moab Information Center, corner of Main and Center, is open for walk-in visitors from 8 am to 8 pm. The staff can answer almost any question you might have about the area's national parks, national forests, BLM areas, state parks, and county and city information. For information ahead of time, contact the Grand County Travel Council (☎ 435-259-8825, 800-635-6622, www.moab.net), PO Box 550, Moab, UT 84532.

Canyonlands National Park Headquarters (☎ 435-259-7164) is at 2290 SW Resource Blvd, and the Manti-La Sal National Forest Moab Ranger Station (☎ 435-259-7155) is next door; both open from 8 am to 4:30 pm, Monday to Friday. The BLM (☎ 435-259-6111) is at 82 E Dogwood.

The post office (☎ 435-259-7427) is at 50 E 100 North. The library (☎ 435-259-5421) is at 25 S 100 East. Recycle your carload of cans and bottles at the County Recycling Center (☎ 435-259-8640), 1000 E Sand Flats Rd. The hospital (☎ 435-259-7191) is at 719 W 400 North. The police (☎ 435-259-8938) are at 115 W 200 South.

Free newspapers to look out for in boxes and businesses around town include *Moab Happenings*, strongly geared to visitors, and *The Canyon Country Zephyr*, which has been 'Clinging Hopelessly to the Past Since 1989' and is recommended reading.

Dan O'Laurie Museum

The diverse collection shown at this museum (☎ 435-259-7985), 118 E Center, includes informative exhibits on everything from local archaeology to uranium to art. It is also the starting point of a self-guided walking tour of Moab's historic buildings – two dozen of them are within three blocks of the museum and are described in a free brochure. Hours are 1 to 8 pm, Monday to Saturday, from April to October; 3 to 7 pm from November to March. Admission is free.

Arches Vineyards

Oenophiles can visit the tasting room of Utah's only winery (☎ 435-259-5397, 800-723-8609), 420 Kane Creek Blvd. Local grapes are used. Hours are 11 am to 7 pm, Monday to Thursday, to 9 pm on Friday and Saturday.

Hole 'n the Rock

This 5000-sq-foot home (☎ 435-686-2250) carved out of solid sandstone, 15 miles south on Hwy 191, can be toured between 9 am and 5 pm; admission is $2.50; $1.50 for six- to 12-year-olds. There is a picnic area and gift shop.

Scenic Drives

Scenic drives ranging from easy paved roads to rugged and barely passable 4WD tracks are found all around Moab. The Information Center has free informative brochures. Most drives are on BLM or NPS land, and officials emphasize that there are many hundreds of miles of 4WD roads of all levels of difficulty and challenge. Please use them and don't drive off established roads – doing so damages the land and is usually illegal. Some of the best drives are outlined below.

The paved roads to the nearby parks and south to Monticello all have beautiful views. Other scenic paved roads include the **Colorado River Byway** (Hwy 128) northeast of Moab, following the Colorado River to Cisco, 44 miles away just off I-70. Highlights are views of the Fisher Towers and Castle Rock (seen in TV commercials and movies), the 1916 Dewey Bridge (one of the first to cross the Colorado – you can only walk over it now), and sights of rafts running the rapids of the Colorado River.

About 15 miles along Hwy 128, **La Sal Rd** heads south into the Manti-La Sal National Forest, climbing high by way of switchbacks (large RVs not recommended) into the forest and giving good views of canyon country below. The road emerges on Hwy 191, 8 miles south of Moab. This is a 60-mile loop from Moab, paved almost all the way but closed in during winter.

The **Potash Road** (Hwy 279) is named for the potash extraction plant near the end of it. Near the beginning of the road (which leaves Hwy 191 to the left about 3 miles north of Moab), a radioactive tailings pond is visible. Despite this, it's worth the drive because there are signed pullouts, side roads and short walks leading to Indian petroglyphs and dinosaur tracks. Also, the Corona Arch trailhead is about 10 miles along the road; a 1½-mile foot trail leads to this and another arch. Near the end of the drive, about 14 miles from Hwy 191, Jug Handle Arch is on the right. This unusual arch is only 3 feet wide, but 15 times as high. Shortly beyond, you reach the potash plant. The road continues as a 4WD track into the Island in the Sky district of Canyonlands National Park and Dead Horse Point State Park.

The BLM **Canyon Rims Recreation Area** lies to the east of Canyonlands National Park and is as scenic as the park. The area is reached by turning right off Hwy 191 32 miles south of Moab. The paved Needles Overlook Rd goes about 22 miles to a great view of the national park. About two-thirds of the way along this road, the gravel Anticline Overlook Rd stretches 17 miles north to a promontory with great views of the Colorado River. The road is passable to cars. The two roads combined make a good day trip, and there is camping in the area.

The Canyon Rims Recreation Area can also be reached via Kane Creek Blvd heading west from Moab. This soon becomes a gravel road following Kane Creek Canyon. About 10 miles out of Moab you must ford the creek, which may be impossible after heavy rains or spring snowmelt. The road continues in good enough shape for a ways, but past a certain point only 4WD vehicles can get through. Visitors to both the Anticline

Overlook and the Needles Overlook can see this jeep road winding along the canyon below. The road eventually ends at Hwy 211, a few miles east of the Needles area of Canyonlands National Park. The total drive is about 60 or 70 very scenic miles, and there are several side roads to explore – the BLM has maps and information.

Renting a 4WD vehicle costs about $90 (plus insurance) a day from Slickrock 4x4, Thrifty, Budget, Farabee Adventures and Canyonlands by Night. The last two companies as well as Adrift Adventures, Linn Ottinger Tours, Navtec, OARS and Tag-a-Long Expeditions offer half- and full-day guided 4WD tours for about $45 to $90 per person, depending on the difficulty and distance. See below for addresses and phone numbers, and be sure you understand the terms of the agency's insurance policy covering vehicle use off of paved roads.

River Running

This is the third of the triad of adventurous activities (along with biking and 4WD) that are big in Moab. The Colorado River northeast of Moab is easily accessible by Hwy 128, so this part of the river is a favorite for day trips, with some flat sections and some Class II to III rapids. Overnight trips offering greater excitement run through the Westwater Canyon of the Colorado (near the Colorado state line) and through the Cataract Canyon of the Colorado (in and beyond Canyonlands National Park). Trips on the Green River are available as well. You can paddle a canoe or raft, float on a raft or go by jet boat. Rafting season is April to September; jet-boat season goes longer. The highest water is usually in May and June.

You can either do it yourself or go on a tour. Most rafting tours cost $35 to $45 for a day; jet boats cost up to $70. Overnight tours of three to five days run about $400 to $800 per person. Children accompanying parents usually get discounts. Tours combining river trips with 4WD or mountain biking are available. Do-it-yourselfers can rent canoes, inflatable kayaks or rafts –

rates are around $20 to $40 a day for canoes and kayaks; around $60 to $100 a day for rafts (all come with life jackets and paddles). Permits are required well in advance for national park rivers, but you can run the rivers outside the parks with no problems.

One-day trips are often available at a day's notice, and half-day trips are an option. Overnight trips should be booked well in advance. Write to the companies for their brochures.

Rentals, shuttle or pick-up services, and half- or one-day trips are available from Adrift Adventures, Canyon Voyages, Red River Canoe Company, Tag-a-Long Expeditions, Tex's Riverways and Western River Expeditions.

One-day and multi-day river trips are available from the following companies: Sheri Griffith Expeditions is very experienced and has a variety of trips ranging from mainstream (pardon the pun) to tours for women only. Other experienced and recommended companies are World Wide River Expeditions, Adrift Adventures, Western River Expeditions, Tag-a-Long Expeditions, Navtec Expeditions, OARS and Moab Rafting Company. The latter also conducts overnight trips on the San Juan River (see also Bluff, later in this chapter).

Mountain Biking

There are dozens of mountain-bike routes in the area, the most famous of which is the **Slickrock Trail**, a 9.6-mile loop on BLM land beginning from the end of Sand Flats Rd about 3 miles east of town. This is a challenging trip that can take half a day; not recommended for novices. It has become so popular that there is now a $1 fee per biker and the trail can be very crowded.

The BLM and Travel Council have brochures describing other routes, and there are a host of books including *Canyon Country Mountain Biking* by FA Barnes & T Kuehne and *Mountain Biking in Canyon Rims Recreation Area* by P & B Utesch. Whichever route you select, please stay on the trails – the cryptobiotic crusts are being heavily impacted by riders leaving the trails.

The busiest biking seasons are spring and fall when thousands of riders visit the area. Summer is too hot and snow can cover trails in winter.

Mountain-bike rentals and tours are available from Kaibab Mountain Bike Tours & Cyclery, Nichols Expeditions, Rim Tours, Western Spirit Cycling and others.

Other Activities

Those interested in **horseback riding** can rent sturdy beasts for about $10 an hour or $60 a day including lunch. Breakfast and sunset rides with cookouts cost about $30. Overnight trips are also available. Call Cowboy Trails or the Pack Creek Ranch for information. **Golf** at the 18-hole/par 72 Moab Golf Course (☎ 435-259-6488), 2705 S East Bench Rd. **Butch Cassidy's King World Waterpark** (☎ 435-259-2837), 1500 N Hwy 191, has three pools, five slides, paddle boats, picnic areas, an amusement arcade and a pizza house. It's open May to September and charges $8.50 for all-day use for 13- to 65-year-olds, $6.50 for three- to 12-year-olds; half-day and multi-day discounts are given. There's also a **swimming pool** (☎ 435-259-8226) in the park at 181 W 400 North. Play **tennis** at Grand County Middle School Public Courts, 217 E Center.

Tour & Rental Companies

Rim Cyclery rents backpacking, climbing, skiing and camping gear. Others renting camping gear include Red River Canoe Company, Tag-a-Long Expeditions and Western River Expeditions. Canyonlands Field Institute is a nonprofit organization that organizes educational or cultural expeditions and seminars as well as hiking and river-running trips.

Scenic flights are available at the airport. Many local people and visitors and most NPS officials disapprove of them because the noise from the low-flying aircraft (and helicopters) ruins the quiet and scenic outdoor experience. In places like the Grand Canyon, aircraft noise is heard more often than not during busy summer periods. Although this is not yet the case in the

Moab area, scenic flights may begin to pose a serious problem.

The companies mentioned above (and listed below) seem to have decent reputations and have been around for a few years (or decades). New companies open every year. The Information Center lists 45 operators. Some of these offices may be closed in winter. To send mail to any of the companies listed here, add Moab, UT 84532 to the address.

Adrift Adventures
    378 N Main; PO Box 577 (☎ 435-259-8594, 800-874-4483, fax 435-259-7628)
Canyon Voyages
    690 S Main; PO Box 416 (☎ 800-733-6007, ☎ /fax 435-259-5659)
Canyonlands Field Institute
    1320 S Hwy 191; PO Box 68 (☎ 435-259-7750, 800-860-5262, fax 435-259-2335)
Cowboy Trails
    2231 S Hwy 191; PO Box 104 (☎ 435-259-8053, fax 435-259-2226)
Farabee Adventures
    83 S Main; PO Box 664 (☎ 435-259-7494, 800-806-5337, fax 435-259-2997)
Kaibab Mountain Bike Tours
    391 S Main; PO Box 339 (☎ 435-259-7423, 800-451-1133, fax 435-259-6135)
Lin Ottinger Tours
    600 N Main (☎ 435-259-7312)
Moab Rafting
    PO Box 801 (☎ 435-259-7238, 800-746-6622)
Navtec Expeditions
    321 N Main; PO Box 1267 (☎ 435-259-7983, 800-833-1278, fax 435-259-5823)
Nichols Expeditions
    497 N Main (☎ 435-259-3999, 800-648-8488, fax 435-259-2312)
OARS
    543 N Main (☎ 435-259-5865, 800-346-6277)
Pack Creek Ranch
    PO Box 1270 (☎ 435-259-5505, fax 435-259-8879)
Red River Canoe Company
    702 S Main (☎ 435-259-7722, 800-753-8216)
Rim Cyclery
    94 W 100 North (☎ 435-259-5333, fax 435-259-7217)
Rim Tours
    1233 S Hwy 191 (☎ 435-259-5223, 800-626-7335, fax 435-259-3349)

Sheri Griffith Expeditions
    2231 S Hwy 191; PO Box 1324 (☎ 435-259-8229, 800-332-2439, fax 435-259-2226)
Slickrock 4x4
    284 N Main (☎ 888-238-5337, ☎ /fax 435-259-5678)
Tag-a-Long Expeditions
    452 N Main (☎ 435-259-8946, 800-453-3292, fax 435-259-8990)
Tex's Riverways
    691 N 500 West; PO Box 67 (☎ 435-259-5101)
Thrifty
    711 S Main (☎ 435-259-7317, fax 435-259-4524)
Western River Expeditions
    1371 N Hwy 191 (☎ 435-259-7019, 800-453-7450, fax 435-259-6121)
Western Spirit Cycling
    478 Mill Creek Drive (☎ 435-259-8732, 800-845-2453, fax 435-259-2736, biking@westernspirit.com)
World Wide River Expeditions
    625 N Riversands (☎ 435-259-7515, 800-231-2769, fax 435-566-2722)

Special Events

Many of these celebrate the outdoor activities for which Moab is famous. Dates vary from year to year – call the Information Center. There is a half marathon in late March and a Jeep Safari around Easter weekend. During June there are one or two rodeos. Various horsy/agricultural/arty/outdoor events occur during the Grand County Fair in early August. October sees the Moab Gem & Mineral Show and the Fat Tire Bike Festival with tours, workshops, lessons, competitions and plenty of musical entertainment. This last is one of the biggest biking events in Utah and the town is packed full. For years it was held the week before Halloween but in 1997 was held mid-month.

Places to Stay

Whether camping or staying indoors, you have a wide variety of choices in and near Moab. Camping is possible at both public and private sites. Moab Central Reservations (☎ 435-259-5125, 800-505-5343, 800-748-4386, fax 435-259-6079, reservations@moab.net), 50 E Center, Moab, UT 84532, makes reservations for most of the places in town and will also make tour reservations. Other agencies include Moab Realty Property Management (☎ 435-259-6050, 888-879-6222, fax 435-259-5933) and Desert Highlights (☎ 435-259-4433, 800-747-1342, fax 435-259-4439).

The Moab high season is a long one – from mid-March to late October prices rise and reservations are recommended. If you don't have a reservation, arrive by early afternoon or your choices will be limited. High-season rates are given below, but rates during holiday weekends or special events may be higher. After the October Fat Tire Bike Festival is over, rates can drop 50% overnight. Moab's relative remoteness and independent spirit has produced few chain motels and many more privately owned ones.

Places to Stay – Camping

Up the Creek Campground (☎ 435-259-2213), 210 E 300 South, has 20 tent-only sites and showers within walking distance of downtown – the backpackers' choice. Rates are $7 from March through October. *Canyonlands Campark* (☎ 800-522-6848, ☎ /fax 435-259-6846), 555 S Main, has 150 sites, many with tree shade, and is open all year. It has a pool, playground, showers and coin laundry. Rates are $14 (tents) to $19 (full hookups).

Slickrock Campground (☎ 435-259-7660, 800-448-8873, fax 435-259-9402), 1301½ N Hwy 191, has almost 200 tree-shaded sites year-round. Facilities include a pool, spa, recreation area, playground, showers, coin laundry, groceries and a café open from March to October. Rates are $14.50 to $20. Camping cabins are $27 for two people, $33 for four. Nearby is *Portal RV Park & Fishery* (☎ 435-259-6108, 800-574-2028), 1261 N Hwy 191, with 36 RV sites with hookups ($17) and 10 tent sites ($12). It has a pool, showers, laundry and stocked private lakes (no license required) for trout fly-fishing. Rods are available, but you have to release the fish and pay an hourly fee of $10.

Moab Valley RV & Campark (☎ 435-259-4469), 1773 N Hwy 191 (the closest camp-ground to Arches), has over 100 sites as well as showers, coin laundry and a convenience store. Rates are $15 to $19. *Archview Campground* (☎ 435-259-7854, 800-813-6622), 12 miles north of Moab on Hwy 191 at Hwy 313, has 85 sites, half with hookups, for $15 to $19 in summer, $10 to $15 from October through March. A pool, laundry, showers, playground and store are on the premises.

Moab KOA (☎ 435-259-6682, fax 435-259-8703), 3225 S Hwy 191, has 150 sites, a pool, miniature golf, playground, showers, coin laundry and groceries. It is open from mid-March to October and charges $16 to $22. Kamping Kabins are $32. *Spanish Trail RV Park* (☎ 435-259-2411, 800-787-2751), 2980 S Hwy 191, has showers, laundry, and about 60 sites with hookups ($20) and 12 tent sites ($16).

There are Manti-La Sal National Forest campgrounds about 25 miles east of Moab in the La Sal Mountains, reached by gravel roads off La Sal Rd. Coming from Hwy 191, the free *Oowah Lake Campground* is first – it's open from June through September with six sites but no water. About 15 miles along La Sal Rd, a 5-mile gravel road goes to *Warner Lake Campground*, open from May through September; it has water and fishing but no showers and charges a $5 fee.

The BLM (☎ 435-259-6111) operates the *Big Bend, Hal Canyon* and *Oak Grove Campgrounds* along Hwy 128 next to the Colorado River. Big Bend is about 10 miles from Moab, has about 20 sites as well as pit toilets, picnic tables and grills, but no water; sites are $5. The others are much smaller with similar facilities. In the Canyon Rims Recreation Area, *Windwhistle Campground* is 5 miles west of Hwy 191 on the Needles Overlook Rd, and *Hatch Point Campground* is 25 miles west and north along the Anticline Overlook Rd. Both have water, pit toilets and charge $5 from April to October.

Showers Many places allow public use of their showers for $2 to $4. The Information Center has a list.

Places to Stay – Budget

The friendly *Lazy Lizard International Hostel* (☎ 435-259-6057), 1213 S Hwy 191, has five dorms that sleep six people each for $7 per person, and a few basic rooms at $20 a double. There are also a few teepees and log cabins for $25 or $32 double. Facilities include a hot tub, coin laundry, guest kitchen, a TV/video room and showers ($2 for nonguests).

Otherwise, the cheapest motels are in the $45 to $60 range for a double in the high season. These include the *Inca Inn Motel* (☎ 435-259-7261), 570 N Main, with small but tidy rooms that lack phones; this is one of the cheapest. Also try the old-fashioned *Hotel Off Center* (☎ 435-259-4244, 800-237-4685, fax 435-259-4220), 96 E Center. Rooms lack phones, and bathrooms may be down the hall. The *Silver Sage Inn* (☎ 435-259-4420), 840 S Main, has basic motel rooms with phones for $45 and is run by the Lutheran Church; profits go to charity. The *Colorado River Lodge* (☎ 435-259-6122), 512 N Main, has decent motel rooms with phones. The *Red Rock Motel* (☎ 435-259-5431), 51 N 100 West, has a spa, complimentary coffee and nice rooms with refrigerators – both of these are good deals by Moab standards.

Other basic economy places include the *Prospector Lodge* (☎ 435-259-5145, fax 435-259-8778), 186 N 100 West, and the *Sunset Motel* (☎ 435-259-5191, 800-421-5614, fax 435-259-5192), 41 W 100 North, which gives discounts for cash and has some more-expensive units with kitchens.

Places to Stay – Middle

Hotels For decent motels in the $60 to $80 range for a high-season double, try the following, arranged in roughly ascending order of cost. The *Virginian Motel* (☎ 435-259-5951, 800-261-2063, fax 435-259-5468), 70 E 200 South, has clean double rooms, more than half with kitchenettes. The friendly and helpful *Bowen Motel* (☎ 435-259-7132, 800-874-5439, bowen@ moab-utah.com), 169 N Main, has a pool and free morning coffee. The similar *Apache Motel* (☎ 435-259-5727, 800-228-6882,

fax 435-259-8989), 166 S 400 East, is quietly located four blocks from the main drag.

The *Kokopelli Lodge* (☎ 435-259-7615, 800-505-5343), 72 South 100 East, has eight rooms and a garden for barbecues. The price includes continental breakfast. The *Red Stone Inn* (☎ 435-259-3500, 800-772-1972, fax 435-259-2717), 535 S Main, has a coin laundry and 50 pleasant rooms (most with microwave and refrigerator, all with coffeemakers). The *Landmark Motel* (☎ 435-259-6147, 800-441-6147, fax 435-259-5556), 168 N Main, has a pool, kids' pool, spa and coin laundry. Its 36 large double rooms are in the $80s.

The *Super 8 Motel* (☎ 435-259-8868, fax 435-259-8968), 889 N Main, is by far Moab's largest motel, with 146 sizable, pleasant rooms, a pool, spa, coin laundry and an adjoining Denny's 24-hour restaurant. Rates are $79 for a single or double in midsummer; it's one of the better mid-priced chain motels. (Others include the Days Inn, Travelodge, Rodeway and Sleep Inn.)

Condos & Apartments The reservation services listed at the beginning of this section will find you condo and house rentals from $60 to $200 a night, or you can call the Information Center for a list. Most of these condo complexes have about six units or less and require advance reservations.

B&Bs There seem to be a couple of new B&Bs every year in Moab. Almost all of them have no-smoking policies.

The *Desert Chalet* (☎ 435-259-5793), 1275 E San Juan Drive, is a large log house with a hot tub and big storage area (for bikes and such). Guests have kitchen and laundry privileges as well as access to games, books and a slide projector. The five rooms with shared bathrooms cost about $55 to $75 for doubles. The *Canyon Country B&B* (☎ 435-259-5262, 800-435-0284), 590 N 500 West, Moab, UT 84532, is in a quiet residential area. It has a spa and a large backyard with a game area, and it rents bicycles. There are five rooms, two with shared bath, renting from $60 to $105 for a double. Both these places prefer no small children and rooms lack phones. Several other small B&Bs offer similar facilities; call the reservations agencies for further help.

Places to Stay – Top End
Hotel & Cabins *Comfort Suites* (☎ 435-259-5252, fax 435-259-7110), 800 S Main, is an all-suite hotel. Units have a kitchenette, pleasant living area and queen- or king-size beds. There is an indoor pool, a spa, exercise room and coin laundry. Suites are $85 to $110 for a double, $70 to $95 in winter, including continental breakfast. The *Ramada Inn* (☎ 435-259-7141, fax 435-259-6299), 182 S Main, has a pool, a spa and a good restaurant next door. Rooms are spacious and some have balconies. Rates are in the $90s, half that in winter. The *Moab Valley Inn* (☎ 435-259-4419, 800-831-6622, fax 435-259-4332), 711 S Main, has similar rates but smaller standard rooms, some with kitchenettes. With 127 units, it is Moab's second largest motel. It includes a continental breakfast and has a pool and spa.

The *Best Western Greenwell Motel* (☎ 435-259-6151, fax 435-259-4397), 105 S Main, has 72 nice rooms on spacious grounds that separate the rooms from highway noise. There is a pool. The restaurant is open from 7 am to 9 pm (later in high season). Rooms cost about $100, half that in winter. The *Best Western Canyonlands Inn* (☎ 435-259-2300, fax 435-259-2301), 16 S Main, is also in the heart of town, but it's reasonably quiet. It has a pool, spa, coin laundry and exercise room, and includes continental breakfast in the rates. Rooms have refrigerators and go for $80 to $125 from March to October – there are a few suites.

The new *Aarchway Inn* (☎ 435-259-2599, 800-341-9359, fax 435-259-2270), 1551 N Hwy 191, with 95 rooms about 3 miles north of town, has a pool and hot tub but lacks a restaurant for now. Rooms run $90, less in the off season.

The *Pack Creek Ranch* (☎ 435-259-5505, fax 435-259-8879), PO Box 1270, Moab, UT 84532, is about 15 miles south-

east of Moab; take La Sal Rd and, at the T junction shortly after leaving Hwy 191, go right and drive almost 6 miles. The 300-acre ranch is scenically located at over 6000 feet in the La Sal Mountains. There are about 10 rustic but comfortable cabins, some with two or three bedrooms, all with bathrooms and kitchens, some with fireplaces. Facilities include a pool, spa, sauna, playground, picnic areas, a reading room, coin laundry and restaurant. Summer rates are $125 per person including plentiful and tasty meals, less in winter when the restaurant may close. The restaurant is open to the public by reservation. There are hiking trails (cross-country skiing in winter). The owners know southeastern Utah extremely well and arrange horse-packing and river-running trips.

B&Bs One of the best is actually in Castle Valley, 20 miles northeast of Moab. The *Castle Valley Inn* (☎ 435-259-6012, fax 435-259-1501), 424 Amber Lane, CVSR Box 2602, Moab, UT 84532, has five rooms and three cottages, with excellent views of mountains such as sheer Castle Rock. All rooms have private baths, and the cottages have kitchenettes. The owners are well-traveled and friendly. Amenities include a hot tub, pleasant gardens and a living room with fireplace. Good lunches and dinners are available with advance notice. It may close in winter. Rates are $95 to $130 for double rooms, $155 for cottages.

Another good choice is the *Sunflower Hill B&B* (☎ 435-259-2974, 435-259-3065, innkeeper@sunflowerhill.com), 185 N 300 East. Parts of the house date from the 1800s, and there is a spa. There are 11 rooms ranging from a small single to luxury units with private balconies and patios or jetted tubs. Rates are $85 to $155, depending on the room.

Places to Eat
With so many tourists, it's hardly surprising that Moab has a good selection of restaurants. Most offer American fare.

For reasonably priced American breakfasts, *JR's Restaurant* (☎ 435-259-8352),

1075 S Hwy 191, seems to be popular with locals, perhaps because it's away from the central tourist traffic. It opens from 6 am to 2 pm. Serving breakfast only, the *Jailhouse Café* (☎ 435-259-3900), 101 N Main, is open from 7 am to noon (1 pm on weekends). The *Moab Diner* (☎ 435-259-4006), 189 S Main, serves full breakfasts, burger or sandwich lunches and full dinners, and has a wide selection of ice creams. Everything is reasonably priced, and it opens from 6 am to 10 pm in the high season. The *Golden Stake* (☎ 435-259-4848), 540 S Main, offers inexpensive family dining all day. *Cattleman's* (☎ 435-259-6585), 1991 S Hwy 191 in the truck plaza, is open 24 hours and serves breakfast any time. For more upscale day-long family dining, there's *Arches Dining & Pancake Haus* (☎ 435-259-7141), 196 S Main (next to the Ramada Inn), which has a mainly American menu.

For good and reasonably priced lunches and dinners, try the popular *Rio Colorado Restaurant & Bar* (☎ 435-259-6666), 2 S 100 West. It has an interesting Southwestern menu with items like Margarita chicken and Southwestern catfish as well as sandwiches and salads. Most items are under $10; steak or shrimp dishes are $11 to $15. Hours are 11:30 am to 10 pm, Monday to Saturday, and 10 am to 2 pm for Sunday brunch. *La Hacienda* (☎ 435-259-6319), 574 N Main, has Mexican food in the $5 to $13 range and has some 'gringo favorites' as well.

Buck's Grill House (☎ 435-259-5201), 1393 N Hwy 191, is a local favorite, open nightly at 5 pm. It serves good steaks in the $14 to $21 range and has a variety of other meat dishes (including venison, buffalo and rabbit) as well as vegetarian dishes and cheaper soups, sandwiches, burgers and a salad bar. The *Slickrock Cafe* (☎ 435-259-8004), 5 N Main, serves good Southwestern breakfasts, lunches and dinners in a relaxed and stylish Moab ambiance – it's popular with the biking and outdoor crowd.

Classier dining spots include the critically acclaimed *Center Cafe* (☎ 435-259-4295), 92 E Center, which opens at 5:30 pm. The gourmet food is fresh, well prepared, inventive and varied. There is a selection of

excellent coffees and a decent wine list. Entrées are in the $13 to $28 range. *Sunset Grill* (☎ 435-259-7146), 900 N Hwy 191, is in the hilltop house of the late billionaire Charlie Steen, who made a fortune mining uranium in his Mi Vida mine in the 1950s. The steep narrow road to the restaurant is not for novice drivers! Open from 5 to 10:30 pm, Sunset Grill specializes in Southwestern and continental cuisine, with most entrées in the $13 to $19 range. You can dine outside and enjoy the views, or indoors where most of the tables are next to windows. Built in 1896, *Grand Old Ranch House* (☎ 435-259-5753), 1266 N Hwy 191, is decorated with period photos and antiques. Open from 5 to 10:30 pm, it offers recommended American and German fare in the $12 to $20 range.

A popular bar is *Eddie McStiff's* (☎ 435-259-2337), 57 S Main, which runs a microbrewery (not on the premises) making a dozen varieties of beer, and offers a wide selection of moderately priced bar food as well as more expensive meals. Beer aficionados can try as many beers as they want for 65¢ for a 3-ounce glass or share a 54-ounce pitcher with friends for $8. There are pool, shuffleboard and foosball tables, as well as darts and big-screen sports TV, making the place boisterous and busy.

The *Poplar Place Pub & Eatery* (☎ 435-259-6018), 11 E 100 North, is in an 1886 building that has been completely renovated following a fire in 1989. It's a popular watering hole (microbrews and Guinness on tap) and serves decent pizza, Mexican food and salads. A newer and quieter place is the *Moab Brewery* (☎ 435-259-6333), 686 S Main, which brews its own on the premises and serves good snacks, lunches and dinners. It has pool tables and other games.

Finally, you can round off the day with a Western cookout at the *Bar M Chuckwagon* (☎ 435-259-2276), 541 S Mulberry Lane. It serves a meaty fixed-price cowboy dinner at 7:30 pm (but get there by 7 pm for the gunfights) followed by a Western music show – reservations are suggested; dinners cost about $15. It is open daily except Sunday from April to September.

Entertainment

The pubs mentioned above are popular gathering places. Other bars around town include the lively and popular *Woody's Tavern*, 165 S Main, which has pool tables and big-screen sports TV, and the *Outlaw Saloon* (☎ 435-259-2654), 44 W 200 North, with pool tables and weekend music and dancing. Private clubs include the *Club Rio* in the Rio Colorado Restaurant with weekend dancing to rock & roll and blues bands, and the *Sportsman's Lounge* (☎ 435-259-9972), next to the Cattleman's Restaurant, with country & western bands and dancing. They'll often help sponsor you.

Canyonlands by Night is a two-hour guided boat trip on the Colorado at sunset, with a sound and light show played on the cliff and canyon walls during the return. Call ☎ 435-259-5261 for reservations. Trips depart from 1861 N Hwy 191 (by the river bridge) at sunset nightly during the summer and cost $24; $12 for children under 18.

See movies at *Slickrock Cinemas* (☎ 435-259-4441), 580 Kane Creek Blvd.

Shopping

Good selections of books and maps are sold at Back of Beyond Books (☎ 435-259-5154), 83 N Main; B Osborne's Books & Magazines (☎ 435-259-2665), 50 S Main; TI Maps (☎ 435-259-5525), 29 E Center; and at the Visitor Information Center. To purchase a book in advance, get a mail-order catalog from Canyonlands Natural History Association (☎ 435-259-6003, 800-840-8978, fax 435-259-8263), 3031 S Hwy 191, Moab, UT 84532.

Lin Ottinger's Rock Shop (☎ 435-259-7312), 600 N Main, has everything for the rock hound – fossils, dinosaur bones, semi-precious stones, minerals, geodes, etc, as well as local jewelry. There are many other tourist-oriented gift shops and art galleries along Main – some are tacky, others are quite good and sell local artists' work.

Getting There & Away

For information on train and Greyhound bus service, see Green River, earlier in this chapter.

Air Alpine Air (☎ 435-259-2946, 801-575-2839 in Salt Lake City) flies between Salt Lake City and Moab once or twice on most days. The fare is about $165 roundtrip from Salt Lake City with advance purchase. The stand-by fare is $54 if you are flexible.

Taxi & Shuttle Bighorn Express (☎ 888-655-7433) has daily van shuttles between Moab and the Salt Lake City Airport for about $40. Taxis and shuttles are available from Coyote Shuttle (☎ 435-259-8656) and West Tracks Taxi (☎ 435-259-2294).

NEWSPAPER ROCK PARK

Formerly a state park and now administered by the BLM, this park showcases a large sandstone rock covered with over 300 petroglyphs chipped out by different Indian groups over a 3000-year period. Designs represent relatively recent mounted figures and much older pictures of animals and abstract art. The park is about 12 miles along Hwy 211, which begins at Hwy 191 14 miles north of the town of Monticello and ends at The Needles section of Canyonlands National Park.

There is a small, free campground with eight sites, pit toilets and grills, but no water. It is open year-round.

MONTICELLO

Pronounced 'Montisello,' this town at over 7000 feet in the Abajo Mountains foothills is greener and cooler than most towns in the region. Settled in 1888, it became a ranching area, and then oil and uranium were discovered. Ranching, mining and tourism are all important. Monticello has 2000 inhabitants and is the San Juan County seat (the highest in Utah).

Orientation & Information

Hwy 191 (Main St) is the main drag through town and runs north-south. Central St becomes Hwy 666, heading east into Colorado.

The multi-agency San Juan Visitor Center (☎ 435-587-3235, 800-574-4386, fax 435-587-2425), 117 S Main, (mailing address:

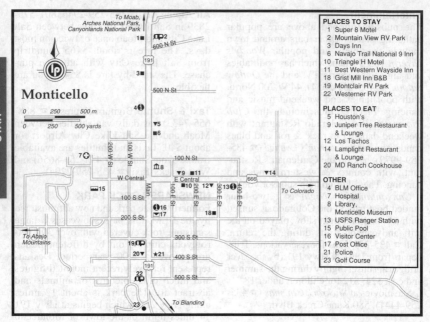

Monticello

0   250   500 m
0   250   500 yards

To Moab,
Arches National Park,
Canyonlands National Park

600 N St
500 N St
100 N St
W Central
E Central
100 S St
200 S St
300 S St
400 S St
500 S St

200 W St
100 W St
Main St

To Abajo
Mountains

To Colorado

To Blanding

PLACES TO STAY
1 Super 8 Motel
2 Mountain View RV Park
3 Days Inn
6 Navajo Trail National 9 Inn
10 Triangle H Motel
11 Best Western Wayside Inn
18 Grist Mill Inn B&B
19 Montclair RV Park
22 Westerner RV Park

PLACES TO EAT
5 Houston's
9 Juniper Tree Restaurant
    & Lounge
12 Los Tachos
14 Lamplight Restaurant
    & Lounge
20 MD Ranch Cookhouse

OTHER
4 BLM Office
7 Hospital
8 Library,
    Monticello Museum
13 USFS Ranger Station
15 Public Pool
16 Visitor Center
17 Post Office
21 Police
23 Golf Course

PO Box 490, Monticello), UT 84535, is open from 9 am to 5 pm, Monday to Friday in winter. From mid-April to October it is also open 10 am to 5 pm on weekends and may have longer weekday hours. The center has a bookstore and extensive information about Monticello and San Juan County and the national parks, national forests, BLM and state areas of southeastern Utah. The USFS Manti-La Sal Forest Ranger Station (☎ 435-587-2041) is at 496 E Central. The BLM (☎ 435-587-2141) is at 435 N Main.

The library (☎ 435-587-2281) is at 80 N Main. The post office (☎ 435-587-2294) is at 197 S Main. The hospital (☎ 435-587-2116) is at 364 W 100 North. The police (☎ 435-587-2273) are at 390 S Main.

Things to See & Do
The **Monticello Museum**, in the basement of the library, has Ancestral Puebloan and pioneer items of local interest.

The **Abajo Mountains** rise to 11,360 feet in the Manti-La Sal National Forest just

west of town. There are camping, hiking, backpacking, cross-country skiing and snow-mobiling opportunities. An unpaved road, closed by snow in winter, goes through the mountains to Newspaper Rock Park.

The nine-hole/par 35 **golf course** (☎ 435-587-2468) is at 549 S Main.

Special Events
Pioneer Days around July 24 is a locally popular event. The San Juan County Fair & Rodeo is held in mid-August.

Places to Stay
Camping *Mountain View RV Park* (☎ 435-587-2974), 632 N Main, has showers, coin laundry and 36 tent and RV sites from $8 to $14. Basic RV facilities are available at *Westerner RV Park* (☎ 435-587-2762), 516 S Main, with 28 sites. *Montclair RV Park* (☎ 435-587-2266), 348 S Main, has 20 RV hookups and eight tent sites.

The *Monticello KOA* (☎ 435-587-2884), 6 miles east on Hwy 666, is on a ranch with farm animals (including buffalo) and vintage farm implements. Open from May through September, it has a pool, spa, showers, a playground, coin laundry, game room and convenience store. They run jeep tours and present slide shows of the area. About 40 sites are $15 to $18.50 and two Kamping Kabins are $25.

Dalton Springs and *Buckboard* are two Manti-La Sal National Forest campgrounds accessible by paved roads about 6 miles west of town. Both are open from mid-May to October, have water and cost $6 a night.

See also Newspaper Rock Park and Moab, earlier in this chapter.

Hotels & B&Bs Summer rates (given below) are somewhat higher than winter rates. Higher rates will prevail during Pioneer Days, the county fair and other sporadic events.

The friendly *Navajo Trail National 9 Inn* (☎ 435-587-2251), 248 N Main, has singles/doubles in the $30s/40s in summer. The very clean and tidy *Triangle H Motel* (☎ 435-587-2274, fax 435-587-2175), 164 E Central, has double rooms from $42 to $62 (depending on size) in summer and in the $20s in winter.

The *Best Western Wayside Inn* (☎ 435-587-2261, fax 435-587-2920), 197 E Central, also has a pool and spa and charges in the high $60s for a double and in the $80s for a suite in summer. The *Super 8 Motel* (☎ 435-587-2489, fax 435-587-2070), 649 N Main, has an indoor pool and spa. Rooms are $51/59 for singles/doubles and $65 with two beds. Continental breakfast is included. The *Days Inn* (☎ 435-587-2458, fax 435-587-2191), 549 N Main, is Monticello's largest motel (43 rooms). It has an indoor pool and hot tub, and includes a continental breakfast in its rates – $66 to $80 for a double in summer.

The *Grist Mill Inn B&B* (☎ 435-587-2597, 800-645-3762, fax 435-587-2580), 164 S 300 East, has six large rooms with antique brass beds and a three-bedroom cottage. All rooms have private baths. Rates are $66 to $86, including complete breakfast, and dinners can be ordered. Amenities

include a spa, a reading room, sitting room with fireplace, TV room and outdoor deck.

Places to Eat
Houston's (☎ 435-587-2531), 296 N Main, is open from 6 am to 3 pm and serves inexpensive and tasty American and Southwestern food. The spicy pozole I had here was superb, and Houston's is a recommended choice for breakfast and lunch.

For Mexican/American lunch and dinner, try *Los Tachos* (☎ 435-587-2959), 280 E Central. For dinner, both the *Juniper Tree Restaurant & Lounge* (☎ 435-587-2870), 133 E Central, and the *Lamplight Restaurant and Lounge* (☎ 435-587-2170), 655 E Central, feature steaks and a salad bar. *MD Ranch Cookhouse* (☎ 435-587-3299), 380 S Main, is open for breakfast, lunch and dinner from mid-March to mid-November with good steaks, buffalo burgers and other ranch food in a Western setting.

There are also a few fast-food and pizza places.

BLANDING
Settled relatively late, in 1905, Blanding is now an agricultural center and the biggest town in San Juan County, with 3800 inhabitants. It has a state park with an excellent museum. The elevation is a pleasant 6000 feet.

Information
The Edge of the Cedars State Park museum has information. The library (☎ 435-678-2335) is at 25 W 300 South. The post office (☎ 435-678-2627) is at 90 N Main. The emergency clinic (☎ 435-678-3434) is at 400 W 930 North. The police (☎ 435-678-2334) are at 62 E 200 South.

Edge of the Cedars State Park
Well worth a stop, this park (☎ 435-678-2238), 660 W 400 North, has a short self-guided trail through Puebloan ceremonial and living quarters built between 700 and 1220 AD. These were excavated in the early 1970s, and an informative brochure about them is available at the **museum**, where there are good exhibits about this

UTAH

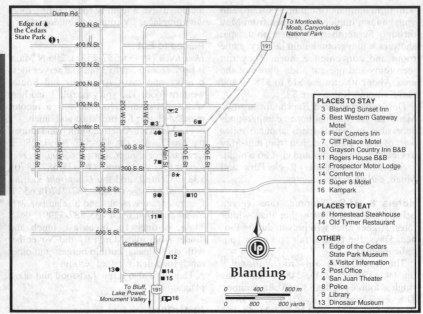

PLACES TO STAY
3 Blanding Sunset Inn
5 Best Western Gateway Motel
6 Four Corners Inn
7 Cliff Palace Motel
10 Grayson Country Inn B&B
11 Rogers House B&B
12 Prospector Motor Lodge
14 Comfort Inn
15 Super 8 Motel
16 Kampark

PLACES TO EAT
6 Homestead Steakhouse
14 Old Tymer Restaurant

OTHER
1 Edge of the Cedars State Park Museum & Visitor Information
2 Post Office
4 San Juan Theater
8 Police
9 Library
13 Dinosaur Museum

Blanding

prehistoric Indian culture. Audio-visual shows, talks and demonstrations are often given, and there is a small art gallery. Hours are 9 am to 5 pm (to 6 pm mid-May to mid-September); admission is $2.50 per person, $6 per carload. It is closed on New Year's Day, Martin Luther King Jr Day, Presidents' Day, Thanksgiving and Christmas.

Dinosaur Museum
This museum (☎ 435-678-3454), 754 S 200 West, has a small but well-displayed selection of dinosaur skeletons and life-size replicas. A movie hall features the history of dinosaurs in Hollywood. Fun! Hours are 9 am to 5 pm, Monday to Saturday, April 15 to October 15. Admission is $2; $1 for seniors and three- to 12-year-olds.

Nations of the Four Corners Cultural Center
This center (☎ 435-678-2072), 707 W 500 South, has a self-guided trail passing a Ute encampment, a Navajo hogan, a log cabin

and pioneer farm implements, representing the different cultures that have lived here. There are picnic tables and good views. Guided tours and special events take place in summer.

Recapture Reservoir
Four miles north of town, the reservoir has no developed facilities, but locals like to boat, swim, water-ski and fish for trout.

Special Events
The rodeo, ethnic folk fair and other activities leading up to the Fourth of July make this Blanding's most important annual holiday.

Places to Stay
Kampark (☎ 435-678-2770), 861 S Main, is open all year and has showers and a coin laundry. Rates are $10 to $14 for tents and RV hookups.

Devil's Canyon Campground, 9 miles north along Hwy 191, and *Nizhoni Camp-*

ground, 14 miles north along Mountain Rd (north on 100 East), are in the Manti-La Sal National Forest. Both have water, pit toilets and picnic facilities. Each costs $8 and is open May to October, though water may be turned off in October.

Winter (November to March) rates are well below the average summer rates given here. Rates around the Fourth of July and weekends are likely to be higher. *Blanding Sunset Inn* (☎ 435-678-3323), 88 W Center, has a spa and large rooms in the $30s. The *Cliff Palace Motel* (☎ 435-678-2264, 800-553-8093), 132 S Main, is similarly priced. The *Prospector Motor Lodge* (☎ 435-678-3231), 591 S Main, has better rooms in the $40s.

The turn-of-the-19th-century *Grayson Country Inn B&B* (☎ 435-678-2388, 800-365-0868), 118 E 300 South, has eight pleasantly old-fashioned rooms with private bath for $44/56 for singles/doubles. Smoking is not permitted. *Rogers House B&B* (☎ 435-678-3932, 800-355-3932, fax 435-678-3276), 412 S Main, is a 1915 house with four rooms including private jetted tubs for $50 to $70.

The *Four Corners Inn* (☎ 435-678-3257, 800-574-3150, fax 435-678-3186), 131 E Center, has nice large rooms in the $50s, including continental breakfast. The *Best Western Gateway Motel* (☎ 435-678-2278, fax 435-678-2240), 88 E Center, has a seasonal pool and rooms from $45 to $65, including continental breakfast. The cheapest rooms are small. The *Super 8 Motel* (☎ 435-678-3880, fax 435-678-3790), 755 S Main, charges $49/59 for large, new singles/doubles (or $65 with two beds). The *Comfort Inn* (☎ 435-678-3271, fax 435-678-3219), 711 S Main, has an indoor pool, a spa, exercise rooms, a game room and a coin laundry. Spacious and comfortable rooms, some with kitchenettes, are $55 to $90, including continental breakfast.

Places to Eat
Blanding is a dry town, so no alcohol is sold anywhere. The pleasant-looking *Old Tymer* (☎ 435-678-2122), 733 S Main, serves American breakfast, lunch and dinner daily, and is considered Blanding's best. The hamburger I ordered here was dried-out and overdone – and no beer to choke it down with. The new *Homestead Steakhouse* next to the Four Corners Inn may be better.

Entertainment
Melodramas are presented on some summer nights somewhere in town. Cheer the hero, boo the villain and have fun for about $5 (less for kids). Catch a movie at the *San Juan Theater* (☎ 435-678-2725), 20 S Main.

Around Four Corners

Extending from Blanding southeast to Four Corners (where Utah, Colorado, New Mexico and Arizona meet) and west to Lake Powell lies a sparsely populated and little visited triangle. While Lake Powell itself is a huge draw for those seeking watery fun in the sun, the rest of this region is largely deserted and a good place for those seeking solitude.

NATURAL BRIDGES NATIONAL MONUMENT
This compact area, 40 miles west of Blanding, became a national monument in 1908 – the first NPS land in Utah. Three natural bridges, all visible from a road and approachable by short hikes, are the highlight here. The three represent a natural aging process: there is a young, a middle-aged and an old bridge. My favorite is the oldest – the Owachomo Bridge – which spans 180 feet and rises over 100 feet above ground but is only 9 feet thick. This thin arch looks beautifully delicate. The Sipapu and Kachina natural bridges are the second and third largest known anywhere.

Orientation & Information
Hwy 275 branches off Hwy 95 and leads 6 miles to the visitor center, open 8 am to 6 pm in summer, to 5 pm in spring and fall,

to 4:30 pm in winter (closed Thanksgiving, Christmas and January 1). Audio-visuals and other exhibits, information, maps, books, toilets and water are available here at no charge. Ask about free ranger-led programs in summer.

Beyond the visitor center, the paved one-way Bridge View Drive provides a 9-mile loop with views of the bridges. Trailers are prohibited (leave them at the visitor center). There are no toilets or water on this drive, which is open daily from dawn till 30 minutes after sunset. Mountain biking is allowed only on this drive.

Entrance is $6 per car or $3 per hiker or biker; this is valid for seven days. Golden Age, Access and Eagle Passes are accepted.

Information is available from the Superintendent, Natural Bridges National Monument (☎ 435-692-1234), PO Box 1, Lake Powell, UT 84533.

Food, gas, and lodging are not available – Fry Canyon (25 miles from the visitor center), Blanding (37 miles) and Mexican Hat (45 miles) provide the closest services.

Bridge View Drive

This 9-mile loop has about 16 pullouts where you can park for photos – don't stop on the narrow road. From the three larger parking areas, trails lead to the bridges. One overlook gives views of the Horsecollar Ancestral Puebloan site.

Hiking

The following foot trails are described in the order in which they occur along Bridge View Drive. The **Sipapu Bridge Trail** is 0.6 miles long (one way) and involves stairs and ladders and a 500-foot descent. The **Horsecollar Trail** is an easy quarter-mile walk (one way). Don't hike on the fragile site itself; one misstep can destroy 1000 years of history. The **Kachina Bridge Trail** is three-quarters of a mile (one way) and has some steep stretches in the 400-foot descent. This bridge is the youngest. The **Owachomo Bridge Trail** is just a quarter-mile and fairly easy, with a 180-foot descent. All of the trails are very rewarding.

In addition, hikers can take loop trails that join any two or all three of the bridges. Seeing all three bridges this way involves a hike of over 8 miles, partly along steep and unmaintained trails, which puts it beyond the abilities of inexperienced walkers. Pick up a map at the visitor center. Don't hike off the trails.

The elevation here is 6500 feet and trails are open all year, but the steeper sections may be closed after heavy rains or snow. During the summer, carry at least a gallon of water per person per day and use sun protection. No water is available anywhere on the drive or trails. Carry a plastic bag for all litter. Use the toilets in the visitor center or campground.

Places to Stay

A small campground (13 sites) almost half a mile past the visitor center is open year-round. There are pit toilets, grills and picnic benches, but no water (obtainable at the visitor center). Camping is $6. The campground fills on summer afternoons, after which you are allowed to camp in the pullouts along Hwy 275 leading to the park – no facilities. No camping is allowed beyond the official campground, along Bridge View Drive or in the backcountry.

FRY CANYON

Founded as a uranium-mining center in 1955, Fry Canyon once had a post office and a school with 67 pupils. Today, all that remains is the *Fry Canyon Lodge* (☎ 435-259-5334) with a gas station, a store (they claim they used to sell more beer than anywhere else in Utah to thirsty prospectors!), a cozy '50s-style café and six rooms for $45 to $78 (more are planned). On Hwy 95 west of Natural Bridges National Monument, it is one of the remotest outposts in the Southwest.

HWY 261 – THE MOKI DUGWAY BACKWAY

Magnificently scenic Hwy 261 leaves Hwy 95 2 miles east of the Natural Bridges turnoff and heads south to Hwy 163, about 33 miles away.

Grand Gulch Primitive Area

Four miles south of Hwy 95 is the Kane Gulch Ranger Station, open from March to November; hours are irregular. This BLM station services the Grand Gulch Primitive Area to the west. Get maps and information in Monticello.

This area follows the wild Grand Gulch Canyon as it twists its way down to the San Juan River. It is wild and difficult country, with primitive trails and no developed camping. Despite this, the area is quite popular with adventurers seeking remote and beautiful wilderness. Spring and fall are the best times to visit; summer is too hot and snow may close the area in winter. Some areas may require a $5 permit for backpacking, which is the main activity.

There are hundreds of Ancestral Puebloan sites throughout the area – many have been vandalized by pot hunters. Prehistoric Indian sites (indeed, all Indian sites) are protected by law. Native Americans believe many of the sites to be of intrinsic religious significance, and archaeologists base their understanding of the peopling of the Americas on these early dwellings and ceremonial centers. Backcountry travelers should respect the spiritual and historical value of these places.

Unfortunately, people still try to remove artifacts or damage sites. This is illegal and, recently, the authorities have begun to crack down severely on offenders. Please report damage of archaeological sites to a ranger.

Moki Dugway

Less than 30 miles south of Hwy 95 the world falls away. This remains the most memorable driving experience of my first trip to the Southwest, over 20 years ago. The Moki Dugway is a (still unpaved) 3-mile section of road that hairpins down for over 1000 feet. From the top, the views of southern Utah and northern Arizona are among the best in the country. At the top of the Moki Dugway, an unpaved side road to the west leads about 5 miles to the **Muley Point Overlook**, which gives equally stunning – some say better – views.

Goosenecks State Park

Near the southern end of Hwy 261, a 4-mile paved road heads west to this state park. Here there are memorable views of the San Juan River, 1100 feet below, meandering in a series of massive curves over 6 miles as the river flows, but only 1½ miles as the crow flies. It's a worthwhile side trip.

There are pit toilets and a few picnic tables – you can camp for free although it is often windy. There is no water.

MEXICAN HAT & MONUMENT VALLEY

The tiny settlement of Mexican Hat (and adjoining Halchita) has about 150 inhabitants, most of whom work in the handful of hotels, restaurants and trading posts in town. The town was named after a distinctively sombrero-shaped rock that can be seen from Hwy 163 about 3 miles to the northeast. The whole area around here is scenically and geologically wonderful. The town lies on the north banks of the San Juan River. South of the river is the edge of the Navajo Indian Reservation – the largest in the country.

Monument Valley

Southwest of Mexican Hat, Hwy 163 enters the Navajo Indian Reservation and Monument Valley. This is one of the most scenic drives in the Southwest, with sand dunes rolling up to a clear blue sky punctuated by sheer red buttes and colossal mesas – you've probably seen the landscape in a TV commercial or a Hollywood Western. Half-and full-day tours of Monument Valley are available for about $30/60.

Goulding's Trading Post

Opened in 1924, Goulding's Trading Post is 2 miles west of Hwy 163 just before you cross from Utah into Arizona, about 25 miles southwest of Mexican Hat. The original trading post remains, now converted into an interesting museum of Indian artifacts and movie memorabilia. The $2 donation goes to local charities and it may close in winter. A theater presents a multimedia Earth Spirit Show featuring photography by Ric Ergenbright (whose Monument Valley photograph graced the front cover of the first edition of this book). There is also a modern gift shop selling high-quality Indian crafts, accommodations, food, and a convenience store and gas station.

Opposite the turnoff to Goulding's, a road heads southeast into Arizona and the Navajo-owned and -operated Monument Valley Navajo Tribal Park – tours, camping and scenic drives are all available. See the Northeastern Arizona chapter for more details.

Places to Stay & Eat

As usual in this part of the world, rates are much higher from about April to October, when reservations are recommended. Mexican Hat lodgings are rustic and simple.

Valle's Trading Post & RV Park (☎ 435-683-2226) has showers, coin laundry, and eight tent and 20 RV sites for $12. It provides shuttle service and arrangements for river runners.

Burches Indian Trading Company (☎ 435-683-2221) has showers, coin laundry and six RV sites with hookups for about $15. It also runs a motel with 40 modest double rooms for about $60. A reasonably priced restaurant and lounge are open all day and serve regional food. Burches can arrange local horseback rides.

The cheapest motel is *Canyonlands Motel* (☎ 435-683-2230) with 10 basic doubles in the $40s. The *Mexican Hat Lodge* (☎ 435-683-2222) has 35 doubles in the mid-$60s, with a restaurant on the premises.

The *San Juan Inn & Trading Post* (☎ 435-683-2220, 800-447-2022, fax 435-683-2210) has 36 rooms of various sizes going for $62 a double. It has a hot tub, exercise room and a popular restaurant/lounge open from 7 am to 10 pm, serving Navajo, American and Mexican food.

The comfortable *Goulding's Lodge* (☎ 435-727-3231, fax 435-727-3344), 25 miles away at Goulding's Trading Post (see above), has an indoor pool (closed in winter), coin laundry and a restaurant open from 7 am to 9:30 pm (shorter hours in winter). Because it is on the Navajo reservation, liquor is not served. Local tours are available. All of the 62 rooms have bal-

conies and outstanding views; rates are about $128 to $140 a double from June to mid-October, $62 to $74 from January to mid-March and intermediate rates at other times. A mile beyond the lodge is *Goulding's Campground* (☎ 435-727-3235) with showers, coin laundry and a convenience store. About 100 sites range from $14 for tents to $24 for full hookups. It is open from mid-March through January, with discounts in winter. The campground lies in a valley, which cuts down on the winds that often blow but also eliminates the views.

GLEN CANYON NATIONAL RECREATION AREA

The massive Glen Canyon Dam flooded Glen Canyon in the 1960s, forming Lake Powell, most of which lies in Utah. The lake is GCNRA's foremost attraction, with four marinas in Utah. However, Glen Canyon Dam itself, the main GCNRA Visitor Center, the largest and most developed marina (Wahweap), the biggest town on the lake (Page) and the main boating concession are all in Arizona, so the entire GCNRA is described in the Grand Canyon & Lake Powell chapter, including the **Lake Powell Car Ferry** between the Halls Crossing and Bullfrog marinas on Hwy 276 in Utah. (See the Lake Powell Ferry sidebar in that chapter.)

BLUFF

The 'Hole-in-the-Rock' pioneers (see Grand Staircase-Escalante National Monument, in the Southwestern Utah chapter) finished their arduous journey here, and established San Juan County's first non-Indian settlement in 1880. Some early pioneers' houses are still in use. About 300 people live here now.

The town is surrounded by red-rock scenery, of which the Navajo Twin sandstone pedestals are the most prominent. Driving west of town is spectacular. There are many **Ancestral Puebloan sites** hidden away in cliffs and canyons; tours are available or you can look for the sites yourself. The most famous are at Hovenweep (discussed later in this chapter). The best archaeological information is available at the museum at Edge of the Cedars State Park, 25 miles north in Blanding.

Bluff, on the north banks of the San Juan River, is near an ideal starting point for running that river. Across the river is the **Navajo Indian Reservation**.

Orientation

Arriving in town along Hwy 163/191 (Main St) from the southwest, you pass the following (in order): River House Inn, Calabre B&B, Cottonwood Steakhouse, Dairy Cafe, Turquoise Restaurant, Kokopelli Inn, Recapture Lodge, Pioneer House (left on 3rd East), Wild Rivers Expeditions, the post office and Cadillac Ranch RV Park. Then, from Main St, 6th East heads north to the Desert Rose Inn and Far Out Expeditions. This area north of Main is the historic part of Bluff. Main continues northeast and passes the Cow Canyon Trading Post & Restaurant, the Twin Rocks Café & Trading Post and the Bluff B&B.

Information

Blanding and Monticello have the nearest visitor centers. Informal visitor information is available from most Bluff businesses. There is a small public library behind the post office on the main road (Hwy 191/163). Brochures available at most of Bluff's businesses describe the earliest local buildings. Look for signs around town. There is no bank, but the Twin Rocks Café has an ATM.

River Running

Most trips begin at the Sand Island Recreation Area (see Places to Stay & Eat, below). Boaters must obtain permits from the BLM (☎ 435-587-2141), PO Box 7, Monticello, UT 84535, as far ahead as possible. A book of specific local interest is *San Juan Canyons: A River Runner's Guide* by D Baars & G Stevenson. The main season is March through October, though winter trips are sometimes possible.

Wild Rivers Expeditions (☎ 435-672-2244, 800-422-7654, fax 435-672-2365, wildriversexp@worldnet.att.net), PO Box 118, Bluff, UT 84512, has been guiding

river trips for four decades. Their motto is 'Educational Adventure with an Emphasis on Pleasure,' which sums them up well: trips are fun and you learn about geology, archaeology, Indian history and wildlife. White water is minimal to moderate. They run tours ranging from one-day adventures ($85) to seven-day Bluff to Lake Powell river trips with plenty of side explorations ($1075). A six-person minimum usually applies.

Organized Tours

Far Out Expeditions (☎ 435-672-2294), 7th East and Mulberry Ave, arranges off-the-beaten-track day trips to Monument Valley, including lunch with a Navajo family in a traditional hogan, a weaving demonstration and viewing of petroglyphs. Costs are $80 per person. Sunset tours to Monument Valley with a cookout are $95 per person. Custom day tours are from $75 per person (four people minimum for all these prices). Overnight tours can be arranged.

The Pioneer House Inn (see below) also arranges its own hiking, biking, jeep and river trips.

Places to Stay & Eat

Reservations for rooms and RV hookups are recommended in summer.

The BLM's *Sand Island Recreation Area*, 2½ miles west on the San Juan River, has pit toilets and six camping sites ($5) with grills and tables but no water. You can see petroglyphs half a mile away. Just follow the signs.

Turquoise Restaurant & RV Park (☎ 435-672-2219) has a few RV sites with hookups for $10 (no showers or tent sites). The restaurant (☎ 435-672-2279) serves a small menu of Navajo and American food from 7 am to 9 pm and 8 am to 8 pm on Sunday. The *Cadillac Ranch RV Park* (☎ 435-672-2262, 800-538-6195) has showers and 10 tent and 17 RV sites for $15. It opens from March through November.

The *Dairy Café* (☎ 435-672-2287) has some inexpensive motel rooms and a gas station, and caters to highway traffic with breakfast, lunch and dinner. The *River*

House Inn (☎ 435-672-2448) has seven basic rooms for about $38 a double. The clean *Kokopelli Inn* (☎ 435-672-2322, 800-541-8854, fax 435-672-2385) has 26 standard motel rooms for $48 for a single or double in summer. It also runs a grocery store next door and is planning on adding a pool and spa soon. The *Desert Rose Inn* (☎ 435-672-2239, 800-990-9472), 6th East and Black Locust Ave, has six rooms all with private baths in a century-old building. Rates are $69 to $79 double, including continental breakfast, and smoking and children under 12 are not permitted.

The *Recapture Lodge* (☎ /fax 435-672-2281), PO Box 309, Bluff, UT 84512, has a pool, spa, grounds with picnic and play areas, and a coin laundry, and arranges local tours and slide shows. There are 28 rooms in the $40s and $50s for a double (depending on room size and number of beds). The 1898 *Pioneer House Inn* (☎ 435-672-2446, 888-637-2582, fax 435-672-2365), 3rd East and Mulberry Ave, has nine rooms, some in the original pioneer house and some in new additions. Most rooms are $49 to $65 double, plus $10 for each additional person. A few rooms have kitchens. One huge group unit includes a kitchen and costs $140 for seven people and $10 for each additional person up to 13. All rooms have private bathrooms, and full breakfast is included.

The *Far Out Bunkhouse* run by Far Out Expeditions (see above) is a century-old bunkhouse with a kitchen and two rooms, each with six bunks and a private bath. Rates are $50 for one or two people, $55 for three or four people, $65 for five or six people and $130 for the entire bunkhouse.

The *Bluff B&B* (☎ 435-672-2220) and the cheaper *Calabre B&B* (☎ 435-672-2252, 800-317-9150, fax 435-672-2445) each have two rooms.

The *Twin Rocks Café* (☎ 435-672-2341) serves American food and Navajo tacos in a dining room with rock views. There is a trading post with high-quality local arts and crafts and a less expensive gift shop. The *Cottonwood Steakhouse* (☎ 435-672-2282) serves steak or barbecued chicken dinner both inside and outside (by a campfire under the old cottonwood tree) from March through November. The *Cow Canyon Trading Post & Restaurant* (☎ 435-672-2208) serves homemade dinners in summer from Thursday to Monday in the eccentric-looking building; the trading post is open daily and sells Indian arts and crafts.

HOVENWEEP NATIONAL MONUMENT

Hovenweep, meaning 'deserted valley' in the Ute language, is a remote place straddling the Utah/Colorado state line. Six sets of prehistoric Puebloan Indian sites are found here – this was once home to a large population before droughts forced them out in the late 1200s.

Established in 1923, Hovenweep soon built up a reputation for being in the middle of nowhere. Rangers told stories of visitors who arrived after spending many hours lost on the poorly signed and roughly surfaced dirt roads leading to the monument. Some visitors were so disheartened by their trip that their first question was not 'What is there to see here?' but 'Where am I and how the hell do I get back to civilization?!' These days, the scenery is certainly desolate – grayer and grimmer than the red-rock country to the west – but there are signs to the monument.

Information

The ranger station (☎ 970-749-0510) stays open from 8 am to 4:30 pm daily except Thanksgiving, Christmas and January 1. Rangers answer questions and sell maps and books. Occasionally, rangers may be gone on patrol. Vending machines sell drinks and snacks. Biting insects can be a problem in early summer (especially late May); bring repellent.

Further information is available from The Superintendent, McElmo Route, Cortez, CO 81321.

Hiking

Two loop hiking trails (one an easy half mile, the other 2 miles) leave from near the ranger station and pass a number of buildings in the Square Tower area. The trails give both distant and close-up views of the sites – please stay on the trails and don't climb on the buildings. They are ancient, fragile and easily damaged. It is illegal to move or disturb anything within the monument. Brochures describe each site in detail, as well as the plant life along the trails.

The Square Tower Ruin area is the best preserved and most impressive. The five other sites are isolated and more difficult to reach – several miles of rough hiking is usually involved. Ask the rangers for directions and advice.

Places to Stay

The campground, about a mile from the ranger station, is open year-round on a first-come, first-served basis. The 31 sites rarely fill except sometimes in summer. There are toilets, water and picnic facilities. There is a $10 fee.

The nearest hotels are over 40 miles away in Blanding and Bluff (or Cortez, Colorado). Limited food and supplies are available in Aneth, 20 miles south, or Hatch Trading Post, 16 miles west.

Getting There & Away

Most maps still show the roads to Hovenweep as unpaved. Access routes are now either paved or may have short gravel stretches suitable for all cars. The best route is east of Hwy 191 on Hwy 262 via Hatch Trading Post.

UTAH

Las Vegas

BONNIE KAMIN

Las Vegas, Nevada

'Fabulous' Las Vegas (population 425,000) has grown in 90 years from nothing to nearly half a million people – in 1997, it was the fastest growing city in the USA. If you've come for the gambling and glitter, you'll love it. At least for a few days, until your money disappears.

Even if you can't stand lounge singers, the incessant ding-ding-ding of slot machines, and the haggard countenance of down-and-out gamblers, Vegas does have inexpensive food and lodgings and is a great place to stop if you're driving to the Southwest. Las Vegas is also a major flight hub for travelers destined for Utah's national parks or the Grand Canyon.

History

The only natural feature to account for the location of Las Vegas is a small spring north of downtown, which was used by Paiute Indians and later by emigrants en route to California. The area became known to overland travelers as *las vegas*, 'the meadows.' Mormons established a small mission, but in 1902 most of the land was sold to a railroad company, and Las Vegas became a railroad town with ice works, hotels and saloons.

The Great Depression brought a collapse in mineral and crop prices, so in 1931 the state government legalized gambling and created agencies to tax it, turning an illegal activity into a revenue source and tourist attraction. Some gambling houses were established, but local Mormon conservatism did not encourage gaming. In the '40s and '50s, however, Las Vegas grew into a major city thanks to gangsters who bankrolled its growth, and thanks to the Hoover Dam, a New Deal project that provided the water and electricity. Bugsy Siegel's Fabulous Flamingo pioneered the new style of casinos – big and flashy, with lavish entertainment to draw in the gamblers. Today, tourism and gaming are the state's biggest industries, followed by mining and agriculture.

Orientation

Two main highways come into Las Vegas, I-15 and Hwy 95, but there are no exits marked 'Downtown' or 'the Strip.' For downtown, exit Hwy 95 at Las Vegas Blvd (exit 75) or I-15 at Charleston (exit 41). Interstate 15 parallels the Strip, so work out which cross street will bring you closest to your destination. If you want a Vegas overview, get off I-15 at Blue Diamond Rd (exit 33) and cruise the length of the Strip from south to north, all the way to downtown.

Downtown Las Vegas is the original town center; its main artery, Fremont St, is now a covered pedestrian mall lined with low-key casinos and hotels. Las Vegas Blvd goes through downtown and continues south for about 10 miles. The Strip, a 3-mile stretch of this boulevard, has most of the really big hotel/casinos, interspersed with vacant lots, garish shopping malls and fast-food outlets.

Most of the tourist areas are safe, but Las Vegas Blvd between downtown and the Strip can feel a bit threatening.

Information

The Nevada Commission on Tourism (NCT, ☎ 702-687-4322, 800-638-2328, www.travelnevada.com), Capital Complex, Carson City, NV 89710, sends free books, maps and information on accommodations, campgrounds and events.

The Las Vegas Visitor Center (☎ 702-892-7575, www.lasvegas24hours.com) is in the Convention Center at 3150 Paradise Rd. Another useful website is run by *The Insider* magazine (www.insidervlv.com). Note that quite a few businesses advertise as tourist offices, and they usually have maps, brochures and discount books, but they are basically agents selling tours and hotel packages. The Gay & Lesbian Community Center (☎ 702-733-9800), 912 E Sahara Ave, provides referrals for gay-friendly hotels, clubs and the like. (Like most of Nevada, Las Vegas is not particularly gay-friendly.)

University Medical Center (☎ 702-383-2000), 1800 W Charleston Blvd, has 24-hour emergency service.

Casinos

Most casinos entice gamblers with free booze, cheap food and glitzy entertainment. Inside, casinos are hideously gaudy, noisy and deliberately disorienting, with no clocks or windows. The Strip's new mega-casinos also feature gimmicky themes, attention-grabbing architecture and some non-gambling amusements.

Casinos listed below (from north to south) are worth visiting as attractions in themselves. At the time of writing, three new mega-casinos were under construction – the Bellagio, Paris and Venetian, all due to open in 1999.

Except for poker, all gambling pits the player against the house, and the house always has a statistical edge. Some casinos

Around Las Vegas

offer introductory lessons in blackjack, roulette and craps. To enter a gambling area, you must be 18 years old.

Stratosphere – Opened on the Strip in 1996, this casino/hotel has a landmark 1149-foot tower with a restaurant and two rides up top – a roller coaster ($5) and the free-fall Big Shot ($6). (☎ 800-998-6937)

Circus Circus – One of the original casino-cum-theme-parks, Circus Circus offers free circus acts in the tent-like interior. (☎ 800-634-3450)

Las Vegas Hilton – The casino (☎ 800-732-7117) has a flashy sci-fi theme, plus the popular 'Star Trek: The Experience' ride ($10). Grand Slam Canyon (☎ 702-794-3912) is a small amusement park behind the casino, with a roller coaster and water rides (day pass $16).

Treasure Island – The pirate ship and man-of-war in the lagoon out front stage a sea battle every 90 minutes from 4:30 pm to midnight. (☎ 800-944-7444)

Mirage – A fake volcano erupts out front every half hour. Inside is a re-created tropical rain forest, a dolphin tank and the white tigers used in the Siegfried & Roy stage show. (☎ 800-627-6667)

Caesar's Palace – You enter stylish Caesar's along a moving footpath, past classic columns and 'ancient' statues. Inside, the Forum is an imitation Roman street, with a painted sky that changes from dawn to dusk every three hours. (☎ 800-634-6001)

New York, New York – The hotel's façade re-creates the Manhattan skyline, with replicas of the Statue of Liberty, Brooklyn Bridge and more. The Manhattan Express roller coaster ($5) is a major rush. (☎ 800-693-6763)

MGM Grand – With over 5000 rooms, this is the world's largest hotel (☎ 800-929-1111). MGM Grand Adventure is a 33-acre theme park behind the main casino, with water rides, top-notch roller coasters and restaurants (day pass $12).

Tropicana – A tropical theme dominates at 'the Trop' (☎ 800-634-4000), and there's a giant water park out back.

Excalibur – It's decorated like a medieval castle with an overworked Arthurian theme. Dinner shows feature jousting knights. (☎ 800-937-7777)

Luxor – This casino is a remarkable glass-covered pyramid with a sphinx and an imitation of Cleopatra's needle out front (☎ 800-288-1000). Inside are Egyptian-theme rides ($5) and an IMAX movie theater ($8).

Other Attractions

There are many things to do apart from gamble, and discount coupons are available for most of them. The **Wet 'n Wild** water park (☎ 702-734-0088), 2601 Las Vegas Blvd S, looks mighty tempting on a hot day ($20).

The **Imperial Palace Auto Museum** (☎ 702-731-3311), at the Imperial Palace casino, has an excellent collection with lots of vehicles once owned by the rich and famous, from Hitler to Howard Hughes ($7). A Vegas favorite is the **Liberace Museum** (☎ 702-798-5595), at 1775 E Tropicana, with sequin capes, rhinestone jewelry, flashy cars and fabulous candelabra ($7). The **Guinness World of Records Museum**, 2780 Las Vegas Blvd S, is disappointing ($5). Those interested in local history should visit the **Nevada State Museum** (☎ 702-486-5205), in Lorenzi Park at 700 Twin Lakes Dr, with sepia photos and Indian artifacts ($2).

The **Old Las Vegas Mormon Fort State Historic Park** (☎ 702-486-3511), a mile north of downtown at 908 Las Vegas Blvd N, is unspectacular compared with modern Las Vegas, but it was here in the 1850s that an adobe quadrangle provided a refuge for travelers along the Mormon Trail.

Places to Stay

The best room deals are at the big casinos midweek, when doubles are as low as $35. On a busy Friday or Saturday, the same room might be $100 or more. Deals come and go by the hour, so call before you arrive. Budget-friendly casinos include *Circus Circus* (☎ 800-634-3450), the *Stardust* (☎ 800-824-6033) and the *Riviera* (☎ 800-634-6753). Also try free booking services such as the Las Vegas Tourist Bureau (☎ 800-522-9555) and City-Wide Reservations (☎ 800-733-6644).

Camping Some of the hotel/casinos on the Strip have RV parks for around $15 per night, including Circus Circus and the Stardust. These parking lots are not pleasant for tent campers, but they do

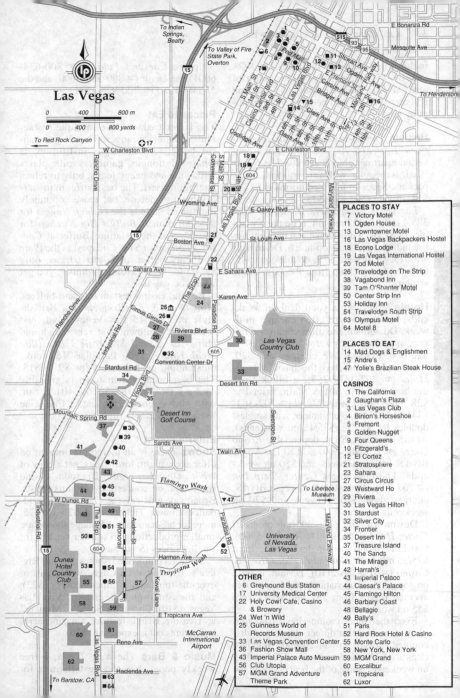

Las Vegas

To Indian Springs, Beatty

To Valley of Fire State Park, Overton

E Bonanza Rd

E Stewart Ave

Mesquite Ave

To Henderson

To Red Rock Canyon

W Charleston Blvd

E Charleston Blvd

Wyoming Ave

E Oakey Blvd

Boston Ave

St Louis Ave

W Sahara Ave

E Sahara Ave

Karen Ave

Riviera Blvd

Las Vegas Country Club

Convention Center Dr

Desert Inn Rd

Desert Inn Golf Course

Mountain Spring Rd

Sands Ave

To Liberace Museum

Flamingo Wash

Flamingo Rd

University of Nevada, Las Vegas

W Dunes Rd

Harmon Ave

Tropicana Wash

Dunes Hotel Country Club

E Tropicana Ave

McCarran International Airport

Reno Ave

Hacienda Ave

To Barstow, CA

To Red Rock Canyon

0   400   800 m
0   400   800 yards

PLACES TO STAY
7 Victory Motel
11 Ogden House
13 Downtowner Motel
16 Las Vegas Backpackers Hostel
18 Econo Lodge
19 Las Vegas International Hostel
20 Tod Motel
26 Travelodge on The Strip
38 Vagabond Inn
30 Tam O'Shanter Motel
50 Center Strip Inn
53 Holiday Inn
54 Travelodge South Strip
63 Olympus Motel
64 Motel 8

PLACES TO EAT
14 Mad Dogs & Englishmen
15 Andre's
47 Yolie's Brazilian Steak House

CASINOS
1 The California
2 Gaughan's Plaza
3 Las Vegas Club
4 Binion's Horseshoe
5 Fremont
8 Golden Nugget
9 Four Queens
10 Fitzgerald's
12 El Cortez
21 Stratosphere
23 Sahara
27 Circus Circus
28 Westward Ho
29 Riviera
30 Las Vegas Hilton
31 Stardust
32 Silver City
34 Frontier
35 Desert Inn
37 Treasure Island
40 The Sands
41 The Mirage
42 Harrah's
43 Imperial Palace
44 Caesar's Palace
45 Flamingo Hilton
46 Barbary Coast
48 Bellagio
49 Bally's
51 Paris
52 Hard Rock Hotel & Casino
55 Monte Carlo
58 New York, New York
59 MGM Grand
60 Excalibur
61 Tropicana
62 Luxor

OTHER
6 Greyhound Bus Station
17 University Medical Center
22 Holy Cow! Cafe, Casino & Browory
24 Wet 'n Wild
25 Guinness World of Records Museum
33 Las Vegas Convention Center
36 Fashion Show Mall
43 Imperial Palace Auto Museum
56 Club Utopia
57 MGM Grand Adventure Theme Park

include use of hotel facilities. A *KOA* (☎ 702-451-5527), a few miles south of town at 4315 Boulder Hwy, has tent and RV sites ($24 for two people) and a swimming pool.

Hostels The no-frills *Las Vegas International Hostel* (☎ 702-385-9955), in a converted apartment block at 1208 Las Vegas Blvd, is popular with international backpackers. Space in four-bed dorms is $12 to $14. Private rooms are $28.

Las Vegas Backpackers Hostel (☎ 702-385-1150), 1322 Fremont, is on the not-so-nice outskirts of downtown, but the facilities (including a pool) are top-notch. Dorm beds are $15; singles are $35; doubles are $45. Call for free pick-up from the Greyhound station.

Hotels Motels are a good deal on weekends, but casinos are often cheaper midweek. Downtown, the ultra-cheap and not very appealing *Ogden House* (☎ 702-385-5200), 651 Ogden Ave, charges only $20. Vegas' oldest hotel is the basic *Victory Motel* (☎ 702-387-9257), a block from the bus station at 301 S Main, priced at $28. The *Downtowner Motel* (☎ 702-384-1441), 129 N 8th, is a bit nicer, with singles/doubles for $25/35 ($35/45 on weekends). At the top of the Strip, dependable *Econo Lodge* (☎ 702-382-6001), 1150 Las Vegas Blvd S, is $35 midweek and $50 on weekends. The convenient *Center Strip Inn* (☎ 702-739-6066), 3688 Las Vegas Blvd S, charges about $40 midweek and $70 on weekends.

Downtown, the pleasant but older *El Cortez Hotel & Casino* (☎ 702-385-5200), 600 E Fremont, has singles/doubles from $25/35 midweek. *Gaughan's Plaza Hotel & Casino* (☎ 702-386-2110), 1 Main, is right on top of the bus station, and has above-average rooms from $35 midweek, from $55 on weekends.

Even the 'nice' casinos have packages (that is, rooms plus dinner shows and discounted meals), so call around. Standard rates are $70 to $95 midweek, $125 and up on weekends. Some of the best deals on the Strip are *Caesar's Palace* (☎ 800-634-6001), the *Luxor* (☎ 800-288-1000) and the *MGM Grand* (☎ 800-929-1111).

Places to Eat
The larger casinos have multiple restaurants in all price ranges. The all-you-can-eat buffet, a Las Vegas institution, is where gluttonous gamblers pile plates with wide and heavy loads, only to return later for dessert. The best buffet in town is a subject of debate, but those commonly mentioned include the *Golden Nugget* for a $9.50 dinner, *Bally's Big Kitchen* for $12.95, and the Palatium Buffet at *Caesar's Palace* for $14. Cheapest is the Plate of Plenty buffet at *Circus Circus*, only $3/4/5 for breakfast/lunch/dinner; you get what you pay for.

Beyond casino restaurants and buffets, *Mad Dogs & Englishmen* is a British-style pub at 515 Las Vegas Blvd, just south of downtown, that serves fish and chips for around $8. *Yolie's Brazilian Steak House*, 3900 Paradise Rd, cooks outstanding grilled meats for $9 to $15. The best restaurant in town is arguably *Andre's* (☎ 702-385-5016), 401 S 6th, with classic French cuisine, a fine wine list and predictably high prices.

Entertainment
Shows There is an incredible amount on offer every night; for listings, get a copy of *What's On in Las Vegas*. 'Big room' casino shows can be concerts by famous artists, Broadway musicals or flashy song-and-dance shows. Tickets cost $25 to $75, more for big-name acts. 'Lounge shows' are smaller productions, in smaller venues, for smaller prices ($8 to $20).

Some recommended shows are the Riviera's 'Evening at La Cage,' with a cast of over-the-top female impersonators ($22), and the Stratosphere's classic 'Viva Las Vegas' ($10). Cirque du Soleil's 'Mystère,' at Treasure Island, features amazing acrobatic stunts but is expensive ($70).

Music & Bars The *New Times*, a free weekly paper, has the best listings for

Marriage & Divorce
You can get hitched quickly in Nevada if you're over 18 years old and have proof of identity. If either party has been married before, the divorce must be final, and the date and location of the decree is required. Then get a marriage license from the nearest county courthouse ($27 cash), and find the Commissioner of Civil Marriages or a wedding chapel. Chapels come complete with a celebrant for as little as $30.

For a divorce, both parties must reside in Nevada for at least six weeks; then they can go to a lawyer or paralegal service and complete the papers. An uncontested divorce will take another one to four weeks, depending on how quickly the lawyer can obtain any necessary documents from other states. The cost can be as low as $250. ∎

nightlife outside the casinos. A popular dance spot among visitors and locals is *Club Utopia* (☎ 702-736-3105), 3765 Las Vegas Blvd S (across from the Monte Carlo), which plays techno-pop, hip-hop, alternative, and Top 40 music. The cover charge is usually $10 on weekend nights. Note that many dance clubs, including this one, have specific dress codes (for example, no jeans or sports attire).

On the corner of Sahara Ave and the Strip, the *Holy Cow! Cafe, Casino & Brewery* (☎ 702-732-2697) has some fine beers and a fun atmosphere. You'll notice it by the large plastic cow outside.

Getting There & Away
McCarran International Airport (☎ 702-261-5743) has direct flights from most US cities, and a few from Canada and Europe. Bell Trans (☎ 702-739-7990) and Gray Line (☎ 702-384-1234) provide airport shuttle service ($3.50 to $5 per person).

The Greyhound bus station (☎ 702-384-8009), downtown on Main, has regular buses to/from Los Angeles ($35) and San Diego, California ($42), plus connections to San Francisco via Reno.

Amtrak's Las Vegas route has been canceled, though a new LA-Vegas train may be running in 1999. Until then, Amtrak has express bus service from Los Angeles to the Las Vegas Greyhound depot ($34).

Getting Around
Local bus service is provided by Citizens Area Transport (CAT, ☎ 702-228-7433); bus No 301 runs up and down the Strip, 24 hours a day, all the way to downtown ($1.50).

The Strip Trolley (☎ 702-382-1404) does a loop from the Luxor to the Stratosphere and out to the Las Vegas Hilton every 25 minutes until 2 am ($1.30).

Dozens of agencies along the Strip offer rental cars for $25 to $45 per day. Try Budget (☎ 702-736-1212) or Thrifty (☎ 702-896-7600).

AROUND LAS VEGAS
Outside Las Vegas there are plenty of lower-key attractions, including the Lake Mead National Recreation Area and Hoover Dam, which straddle the Arizona/Nevada border (see the Western Arizona chapter).

Red Rock Canyon
This dramatic valley west of Vegas is noted for the steep Red Rock escarpment, rising 3000 feet on its western edge. It was created around 65 million years ago, when tectonic plates collided along the Keystone Thrust fault line, pushing a plate of gray limestone up and over another plate of younger red sandstone.

A 13-mile, one-way scenic loop starts at the BLM visitor center (☎ 702-363-1921) near Hwy 159. (From Vegas, go west on Charleston Blvd, which turns into Hwy 159.) The visitor center has maps and information about a number of short hikes in the area and is open daily from 8:30 am to 4:30 pm; the scenic loop is open from 8 am to dusk. (Sunset and sunrise are the best times for viewing.) The park day-use fee is $5. Camping at the Oak Creek site is available year-round on a first-come, first-served basis.

Toiyabe National Forest

The Spring Mountains form the western boundary of the Las Vegas valley, with higher rainfall, lower temperatures and fragrant pine forests. As an isolated mountain range surrounded by desert, Toiyabe has developed some distinct types of plant that are unique to the area.

Hwys 156 and 157 turn southwest off of Hwy 95 north of Las Vegas, climb into the forest, and are later connected by scenic 12-mile Hwy 158. Driving the loop is possible unless the roads are closed by snow. Sixteen miles north of Las Vegas, Hwy 157 follows Kyle Canyon up to the village of Mt Charleston. There, a USFS ranger station (☎ 702-872-5486) gives access to several hikes, including the demanding 9-mile trail up to Charleston Peak (11,918 feet). Campgrounds are open from mid-May to October and cost $10 per night.

Valley of Fire State Park

Near the north end of the Lake Mead National Recreation Area, 55 miles from Las Vegas, Valley of Fire is a masterpiece of desert scenery, with wonderful shapes in psychedelic sandstone. Hwy 169 runs through the park (entry $5), right past the visitor center (☎ 702-397-2088), which has hiking information and excellent exhibits. The winding side road to **White Domes** is especially scenic. The valley is at its most fiery at dawn and dusk, so consider staying in one of the park's two year-round campgrounds ($7).

Overton

Over 1000 years ago, a community of Ancestral Puebloans farmed here, but mysteriously abandoned their pueblo-like structures. Today, it's a little agricultural town with a couple of motels, bars, and other businesses along the dusty main street. Overton's **Lost City Museum** (☎ 702-397-2193), on Hwy 169, has a collection of artifacts going back 10,000 years and some adobe dwellings reconstructed on original foundations ($2). The museum is open daily from 8:30 am to 4:30 pm.

Arizona

RALPH LEE HOPKINS

Facts about Arizona

It's called the Grand Canyon State, and certainly the Grand Canyon is the one thing that schoolchildren from Nova Scotia to New Zealand will mention if quizzed about Arizona. But there's much more than canyons in this state, as visitors quickly discover. Deserts, mountains, forests and rivers provide a range of scenic attractions and outdoor activities. This variety is particularly enjoyed by Arizonans themselves, most of whom live in the hot desert cities of Phoenix and Tucson and in summer enjoy the cool mountains, forests and artificial lakes. Out-of-state visitors, on the other hand, are attracted more to the essentially Southwestern elements of the region, such as the spectacular canyons and mesas, the fascinating deserts and, of course, the Native American heritage.

Arizona has the third largest Indian population of the 50 states (after California and Oklahoma) and the two largest Indian reservations in the country (the Navajo and the Tohono O'odham). About 26% of the state is reservation land. Many tribes have retained much of their cultures, languages and traditions, all of which differ from tribe to tribe. Some of their ancient dances and ceremonies are open to the public, but many are not. However, all visitors can experience the Indian cultures in the villages, trading posts and crafts stores that dot the reservations, and in the Indian fairs, powwows and rodeos held regularly throughout the state.

Oraibi village, on the Hopi Reservation, was built in the 12th century and is one of only two places in the country that have been continuously occupied for more than 800 years. Visitors can learn about the ancestors of today's tribes through the fascinating ancient pueblos that have been preserved throughout the state, and in several excellent museums.

The southern reaches of the state have close ties to Mexico. Tucson has a wonderful selection of Mexican restaurants that are as good as those in Mexico itself! The Spanish heritage can be discovered in the centuries-old missions of southern Arizona established by Padre Kino and in the historic barrios of Tucson, where Spanish is as commonly heard as English.

Visitors interested in natural history can spot numerous species in Arizona found nowhere else in the USA. Southeastern Arizona is the undisputed hummingbird capital of the country, and many other rarities fly in from Mexico, including two species of tropical trogons. The tall, majestic saguaro and organ-pipe cacti are found only in parts of southern Arizona and in Mexico. These cacti provide nests and shelter for many desert birds and animals.

Arizona Trivia
Statehood: February 14, 1912 (48th state)
Area: 114,006 sq miles (sixth largest state)
Highest Point: Humphreys Peak (12,663 feet)
Lowest Point: Colorado River near Mexican border (70 feet)
Population (1996): 4,428,068 (21st most populous state)
Nickname: Grand Canyon State
State Capital: Phoenix
State Motto: *Didat Deus* (God enriches)
State Bird: Cactus wren
State Mammal: Ringtail
State Tree: Blue palo verde
State Flower: Blossom of saguaro cactus
State Reptile: Arizona ridge-nosed rattlesnake
State Fossil: Petrified wood
State Gem: Turquoise
State Neckwear: Bola tie

Arizona is one of three states where the wild pigs (javelinas) and the raccoonlike coatis are regularly glimpsed in the wild. The country's only poisonous lizard, the gila monster, lives here too.

Recent History

At the end of the Mexican War in 1848, the land north of the Gila River was claimed by the USA and incorporated into the New Mexico Territory, which then included Arizona. The USA soon realized that the best route from the Mississippi River to the burgeoning territory of California lay south of the Gila River, through the Mexican town of Tucson. US diplomat James Gadsden arranged for the USA to purchase the land between the present international border and the Gila River from Mexico. In 1854, the USA annexed the territory and Americans began to cross the area en route to California. Some travelers noted the potential mineral and agricultural wealth of the region and made the area their home, beginning the copper-mining and cattle-ranching industries that became mainstays of Arizona's economy.

Many of the settlers were from southern states and when the American Civil War broke out in 1861, Arizona declared itself a Confederate state. This resulted in the westernmost battle of the Civil War, when a small Confederate force was defeated by Union troops at Picacho Peak in 1862. The Confederate forces killed three Union soldiers before retreating to Tucson and dispersing, aware that they would soon be greatly outnumbered. When Arizona became a separate territory the following year, Tucson was the largest town, but Prescott was chosen as the territorial capital because Tucson was perceived as a bastion of Confederate loyalty. From 1867 to 1877, however, Tucson held the position of territorial capital, after which it was returned to Prescott and finally moved to the Anglo-founded town of Phoenix in 1889, where it has remained. Historians and Hispanics alike attribute this to the anti-Hispanic sentiment then prevalent in US politics.

Gila monster

Meanwhile, the US Army was fighting the Indian wars, protecting settlers and wresting the land from the Indians, who had little use for European concepts of land ownership. In 1864 the Navajos were forced to march from their land to the high plains of eastern New Mexico in the infamous 'Long Walk.' Over the next two decades a small number of Apache warriors under the leadership of Cochise and Geronimo fought far greater numbers of US settlers and soldiers using guerrilla tactics. Finally, the ever-growing numbers of Americans overwhelmed the dwindling Indian forces, and Geronimo surrendered in 1886, marking the end of the Indian wars.

The railroad had arrived a few years earlier and people from the East Coast started arriving in larger numbers. Mining towns grew up almost overnight and they were wild and dangerous places. As the memory of the Indian wars faded and the number of Anglos increased, the territory began to petition for statehood. The federal government in Washington, DC, didn't take these petitions very seriously; Arizona's reputation as a wild and lawless desert territory led politicians to suspect that statehood would prove a constant financial drain on the federal coffers. This opinion began to change after President Theodore Roosevelt visited Arizona in 1903 and supported the damming of the territory's rivers. The first dam, the Theodore Roosevelt Dam on the Salt River, was finished in 1911, providing year-round water for irrigation and drinking. This finally paved the way to statehood, and Arizona became the 48th state on February 14, 1912.

Over the next few decades, more dams were built and copper mining flourished.

ARIZONA

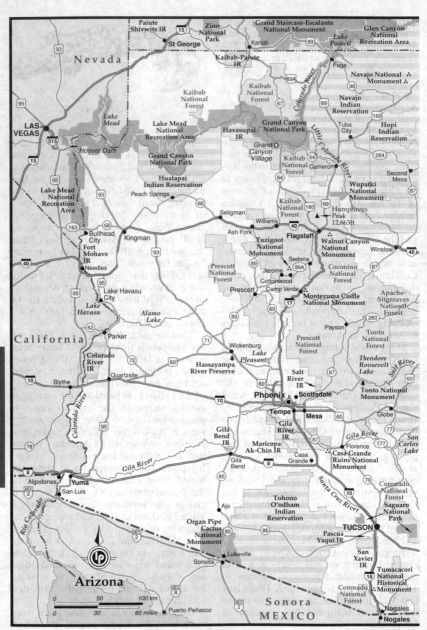

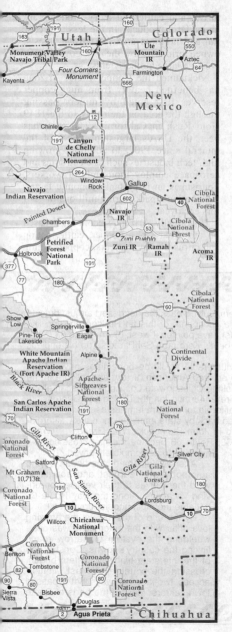

Some mines prospered, while others went bust and their accompanying towns dwindled to ghost towns. Irrigation increased crop yields, and cotton and cattle were important products. Tourists also started arriving, especially in the winter, and resorts and guest ranches for the wealthy began to appear in the Phoenix area in the '20s and '30s. Growth was steady but slow until WWII, when the population swelled with an influx of military personnel training for war in the deserts of Africa and other hot regions.

After the war, air conditioning became increasingly available and many veterans who had trained in Arizona decided to return and settle in what appeared to be a land of new opportunity. Growth was phenomenal and the small towns of Phoenix and Tucson quickly grew into the important cities they are today, with all the accompanying big-city problems of air pollution and urban crime. The warm climate has also attracted large numbers of retirees, some of whom spend winters in Arizona and summers in their northern home states. These 'snowbirds' are an important part of the socioeconomic fabric of the state.

Problems related to the scarce water resources remain among the foremost issues in Arizona. Dam after dam has been built, and every drop of water has a designated use, but there is not enough for the still-growing state. The simple solution, of course, would be to stop further building and development, but governmentally imposed limitations on growth are unlikely at best. And so growth continues, and the state desperately searches for water for its burgeoning desert cities.

The most recent water effort is the Central Arizona Project (CAP), which channels water hundreds of miles from the Colorado River to the Phoenix and Tucson areas. When CAP water arrived in Tucson households in 1994, residents shunned it, complaining that it looked bad and tasted worse and that the mineral content of the water was ruining their plumbing. In 1995, use of CAP water was temporarily put on hold, and legal steps commenced to reduce wasteful water use by residents. In 1997, another attempt to legalize CAP water for household use was electorally defeated, although the water is still used for irrigation. Paradoxically, the state has the world's highest water fountain and hundreds of golf courses sucking up moisture. The debate over water allocation and use will be among the most important issues the state faces as it moves into the 21st century.

Economy

Similarly to other Southwestern states, much of Arizona's economy has been directly linked to the scarcity of water and projects to divert water to agricultural areas and population centers. Where farmers and ranchers can tap water reserves, crops such as citrus fruits, hay, sorghum and cotton

thrive, and cattle and dairy products are major farm products. In the less arid central and northern areas, extensive forests, owned primarily by the US government, produce large lumber yields.

Nicknamed the Copper State, Arizona has benefited heavily from huge copper reserves first noted by miners passing through the area on their way to the 1849 Gold Rush in California. The state has been the USA's largest producer of the mineral since 1907. In addition, growing high-tech industries such as electronics and aerospace employ thousands of workers. Tourism is an important economic factor, with national parks luring millions of visitors each year.

Historically, Arizona's economy is based on the 'Four Cs' – copper, cattle, cotton and citrus. For many years, copper mining

Kickin' Down Route 66

Fenders! Huge, unwieldy, voluptuous fenders, pulling back the hot desert air just outside Tucumcari, New Mexico. It's 1949, and the occupants of this fat Hudson (looking like something out of a sci-fi serial from the '40s) have pointed it west, down Route 66 to the orange groves of Southern California. Maybe it's Kerouac's Sal Paradise on his endless ramble to find America.

That's the quintessential image that innumerable would-be bohemians have of the country's possibilities. Few highways have entered American history and folklore in the way that Route 66 has. In 1926 the road linking Chicago with Los Angeles became officially designated US Route 66 for its entire 2448-mile length. During the Depression, Route 66 was the main thoroughfare to California for migrant families escaping the dust bowl of the Midwest, some only to be turned back by state immigration at the California-Arizona border. This trip was immortalized in John Steinbeck's *The Grapes of Wrath*, which won the 1940 Pulitzer Prize. In 1938, Route 66 became the first cross-country highway to be completely paved.

After WWII, Americans began buying automobiles in earnest and sought to weld themselves to their vehicles on driving vacations. Along the way Route 66 became the most popular drive of all.

By the end of the 1950s, the growing love affair with the automobile was overwhelming the system of narrow roads linking the country's towns. Construction of the interstate highway system began, crossing the country with fast, limited-access, two-lane highways that bypassed town centers. Most of the parts of Route

was the most important industry. Copper was the main product of the $3.53 billion 1996 nonfuel mineral production in Arizona. The state leads the nation in copper production.

Citrus and cotton in the midst of the Southwestern desert is more of a surprise – irrigation from the Gila River has provided the necessary moisture. Cotton continues to be the most important crop, but citrus appears to have been replaced by several other 'C' crops – carrots, cauliflower, corn and celery – as well as other vegetables. The 1996 value of all farm marketings was $2.15 billion, of which about 60% was crops and 40% livestock and related products.

Today, all these have been surpassed by both manufacturing and tourism. Major products include aircraft and missiles

(Hughes Missile System Co employs many thousands in Tucson), electronics, metals, clothes and the printing and publishing industry. Tourism now brings in about $11 billion dollars annually. This growth has led to an expanded construction industry in the major metropolitan areas, and the value of construction in 1996 was $9.8 billion.

For Arizonans, more than 70% of jobs are in the service, trade and government sectors. Unemployment is 5.5%. Per capita income is about $21,000 per year.

Information
Telephone The Phoenix metropolitan area and surrounding Maricopa County use the 602 area code. The rest of Arizona uses the 520 area code, which was implemented in 1995.

66 that ran through northern Arizona and New Mexico were replaced by I-40. By 1984, the modern, efficient, soulless I-40 finally supplanted the last bit of Route 66, and the USA suddenly became a whole lot wider and the possibilities no longer so infinite. Williams was the last town on Route 66 to be bypassed by the freeway.

Many sections of old Route 66 fell into disuse and disrepair, but some sections, for example, Bill Williams Ave and Santa Fe Ave in Flagstaff, have been revived for nostalgic and historic reasons. The longest remaining sections of Route 66 are in western Arizona between Seligman and Kingman and between Kingman and Topock.

Today, Route 66 inspires a strange blend of patriotism, nostalgia and melancholy in most Americans. Emblematic of the enduring restless nature of the country, it has become America's Silk Road – exotic.

So exotic, in fact, that the road was the basis for the 1960s *Route 66* TV series and has appeared in many films, including *Bagdad Café*, released in 1988. (Bagdad is in California, near Siberia.) In 1946, a song by Bobby Troup reached the airwaves and by the 1990s more than 20 musicians had recorded '(Get Your Kicks on) Route 66,' including Perry Como, Bob Dylan, Buckwheat Zydeco, Asleep at the Wheel, Depeche Mode, the Rolling Stones, and – the most famous of all – Nat King Cole. ∎

ARIZONA

Driving Laws You must be at least 18 years old (16 with parental consent) to obtain a driver's license. Drivers and front-seat passengers are required to wear safety belts. Children under age five must use child restraints. You must be over 16 to obtain a motorcycle license. Motorcycle helmets are required for the rider and the passenger if under 18. The blood-alcohol concentration over which you are legally considered drunk while driving is 0.10%.

Drinking Laws You must be 21 to buy a drink in a store, bar or restaurant. Beer, wine and spirits are sold in grocery stores from 6 am to midnight except Sunday, when sales begin at 10 am. Restaurants must have licenses to serve alcohol; some licenses are limited to beer and wine. Bars close at 2 am and the sale of alcohol in them stops at 1 am. Alcohol is prohibited on most Indian reservations.

Time Arizona is on Mountain Standard Time (seven hours behind GMT). However, it is the only Western state that does not observe daylight-saving time. From late spring to early fall, therefore, Arizona is eight hours behind GMT. The exception is the Navajo Reservation, which, in keeping with those parts of the reservation in Utah and New Mexico, observes daylight-saving time.

Gambling The gambling laws in the state of Arizona are complicated. Casino gambling is illegal, but you can buy lottery tickets, bet on horse and dog races, and take part in bingo games organized by local church groups. Indian reservations have their own laws, and increasing numbers of tribes have been opening casinos in the past few years. Arizona state leaders are not happy with this and threaten to take the tribes to federal court if necessary. The Feds, however, seem to be leaning in favor of allowing the Indians to do what they want on the reservations, as long as they keep within federal laws. To avoid lawsuits, the tribes and the state recently agreed to permit casinos under a 10-year 'compact' in which gamblers could compete with machines or each other, but not against a dealer. Hence, games like blackjack (21) are not allowed, but poker, video keno, bingo and slot machines are. Profits are used to improve the reservations by investing in education and health programs and the like, though detractors say that associated problems such as alcoholism and prostitution make the picture less rosy than it might sound.

More than a dozen casinos operate on reservations throughout the state, attracting good-size crowds who don't have the time or money to make it to Las Vegas. Only the two Apache casinos serve alcohol.

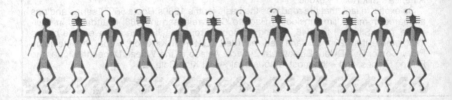

Phoenix

With more than a million inhabitants, Phoenix is the largest city in the Southwest and the seventh largest in the USA. It was surrounded by other towns before WWII, but rapid growth in the latter half of the 20th century has linked these into one huge, still-growing metropolitan area of more than 2.5 million people. Major towns adjoining Phoenix include Tempe (pronounced 'TEM-pee,' with 160,000 inhabitants), Scottsdale (population 180,000), Mesa (population 340,000), Sun City (population 45,000), Glendale (population 180,000), Chandler (population 145,000) and more than a dozen other communities. Together, they cover almost 2000 sq miles, an area that is locally called 'The Valley of the Sun' or just 'the valley.' Sunny it certainly is; with more than 300 days of sunshine a year, it's searingly hot in summer and pleasantly warm in winter.

The climate attracts winter visitors (locally called 'snowbirds') who leave their colder northern states to spend several months soaking up the rays. Fall, winter and spring are the main cultural and tourist seasons, when places charge the highest prices. Visitors arriving during summer vacation periods will find the lowest prices in the hotels and resorts, but also daytime high temperatures above 100°F for weeks on end, commonly reaching well over 110°F in midsummer. Clothing is appropriately casual – you can wear shorts almost anywhere in summer.

HISTORY

As early as 300 BC, the dry desert soil began yielding crops for the Hohokam people, who spent centuries developing a complex system of irrigation canals, only to mysteriously abandon them around 1450 AD. Remnants of the canals can be seen in the Pueblo Grande Museum.

Later, small groups of Pima and Maricopa Indians eked out an existence along the Gila and Salt Rivers, but there were no more permanent settlements until the mid-1860s when the US Army built Fort McDowell northeast of Phoenix. This prompted former soldier and prospector Jack Swilling to reopen Hohokam canals to produce crops for the garrison and led to the establishment of a town in 1870. Darrel Duppa, a British settler, suggested that the town had risen from the ashes of the Hohokam culture like the fabled phoenix, and the name stuck. Meanwhile, Charles Trumbull Hayden established a ferry crossing and trading post on the Salt River, southeast of Phoenix. Duppa, again putting his knowledge of the classics to work, commented that the location reminded him of the Vale of Tempe near Mt Olympus in Greece, and, once again, his suggestion stuck.

Phoenix began to establish itself as an agricultural and transportation center. The railway arrived from the Pacific in 1887 and by the time Phoenix became the territorial capital in 1889, it had about 3000 inhabitants. Settlers built many Victorian houses during the 1890s that today stand as Phoenix's oldest historical buildings. Tempe, too, was growing, and in 1886 the

More in Maricopa

Phoenix and adjoining towns in the valley are part of Maricopa County. The US Census Bureau released figures in March, 1998, estimating that Maricopa County's population increased by 82,789 in the single year from 1996 to 1997, making it the fifth most populous county in the nation, with a total of 2,696,198 residents. This was by far the largest population growth of any of the nation's 3142 counties during that year. ∎

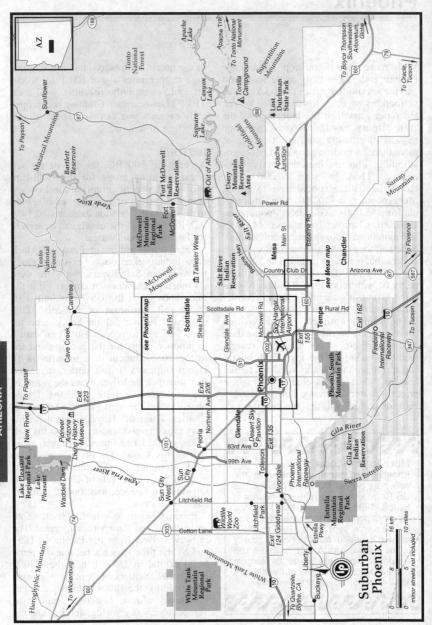

Suburban Phoenix

Arizona Normal School was established here, later to become Arizona State University (ASU). Other villages began to grow; Mesa was founded by Mormon settlers in 1878, and Scottsdale followed a decade later, named after army chaplain Winfield Scott, one of its first settlers.

The lack of water remained a major stumbling block to further growth until 1911, when construction workers finished building the Roosevelt Dam on the Salt River, the first of many large dams to be built in the state. The stage was set for growth and grow Phoenix did.

In 1926, Phoenix's railway link became transcontinental, enabling people from the East to pour into the state in increasing numbers. Many came for recreation – to stay in dude ranches and be cowboys for a few weeks, or to relax at the luxurious Arizona Biltmore resort, opened in 1929 and still one of the finest in the West. Others came for their health; the dry desert air was said to cure various respiratory ailments. Many of these visitors stayed, including Dwight and Maie Heard, who arrived in 1895 to cure Dwight's lung complaints. He became a leading businessman and editor, and with his wife, founded Phoenix's most interesting museum, the Heard.

The combination of recreation and culture has been the valley's main attraction ever since. Today's visitors come to golf, ride, swim and shop or simply relax. Many spend a day or two visiting the area's several fine museums, and during their stay, take in a world premiere at the theater or watch a professional basketball game, in the evening dining in one of the many casual restaurants that serve some of Arizona's most acclaimed meals. Relaxed sophistication is a hallmark of Phoenix, where a cowboy hat and jeans are rarely out of place and where ties are seldom required.

The early history of the area is not immediately evident to most visitors, who see a sprawling modern city. The two major causes of this pervasive modernity were the advent of air conditioning after WWII and the authorization of the Central

Phoenix rising

Arizona Project in 1968, which allowed the diversion of Colorado River water to Phoenix. Between WWII and today, the valley's population has grown almost six-fold; in the 1980s more than 100,000 new residents were arriving each year, making this the country's fastest growing area (see the sidebar More in Maricopa). Modern buildings have replaced most but not all of the old ones. The valley's economy continues to be, as always, driven by politics, the surrounding agriculture, transportation and tourism, but the recent growth has brought industry and manufacturing, especially of electrical and computer components, to the economic foreground.

ORIENTATION

At about 1100 feet above sea level, the valley is ringed by mountains that range from 2500 feet in elevation to more than 7000 feet. Because Phoenix grew to engulf many small towns, the city has several historical centers, of which Phoenix, Scottsdale, Tempe and Mesa are the most interesting. Most of this chapter is devoted to these towns.

Phoenix is the largest town and houses the state capitol, the oldest buildings and

ARIZONA

several important museums. Southeast of Phoenix lies Tempe, home of ASU and an active student population. East of Tempe, Mesa is the second largest town in the valley and is home to several museums and Arizona's main Mormon temple. Scottsdale, northeast of Phoenix and Tempe, is known for both its Western downtown area, now full of galleries, boutiques and crafts stores, and its many upscale resorts.

Other towns, including Chandler to the southeast and Glendale and Peoria to the northwest, are thriving residential and manufacturing communities off the travelers' normal circuit. Sun City and Sun City West, in the northwest of the valley, are among the largest retirement communities in the country, with little industry or tourism but numerous quiet streets and golf courses for the dynamic older residents. Paradise Valley, nestled between the arms of Phoenix and Scottsdale, is the valley's most exclusive residential neighborhood, and Apache Junction, at the far east end of metropolitan Phoenix, is the gateway to the wild Superstition Mountains and the Apache Trail leading into east-central Arizona.

Because the valley's roads run north-south or east-west, to get from one point to another you often have to take two sides of a triangle; this, combined with large distances and slow traffic, can make getting around a challenge. Grand Ave (Hwy 60), which heads diagonally northwest from Phoenix through Glendale and Peoria to Sun City, is an exception that is helpful to residents but of limited use to the traveler. Allow extra time for driving and be prepared to be patient if you use the bus.

Central Ave, running north-south in Phoenix, divides west addresses from east addresses; west of Central Ave, *avenues* are north-south bound, while east of Central Ave *streets* run north-south. Washington St, running west-east in Phoenix, divides north addresses from south addresses; thus 4100 N 16th St would be 16 blocks east of Central Ave and 41 blocks north of Washington (this is only an approximation – blocks don't always correspond exactly to 100-address increments).

This numbering system continues into Scottsdale and Glendale.

Tempe and Mesa each have their own numbering systems, which means you can drive from Phoenix's 4800 E Southern Ave to Tempe's 2800 W Southern Ave just by crossing the city limits. In Tempe, Mill Ave, running north-south, divides west addresses from east addresses, while the east-west flowing Salt River divides north from south addresses. In Mesa, north-south Center St divides west from east, and west-east Main St divides north from south. Other valley towns have similar systems.

To the east, Mesa's Main St becomes the Apache Trail in Apache Junction heading northeast along Hwy 88 into the Tonto National Forest and past the Roosevelt Dam. This unpaved and dramatic road is popular with Phoenix locals (see the East-Central Arizona chapter).

Major freeways leaving Phoenix include I-17 North (Black Canyon Hwy; this has many motels along it), I-10 West (the Papago Freeway), I-10 South (the Maricopa Freeway) and Hwy 60 East (the Superstition Freeway).

INFORMATION
Tourist Offices

The Valley of the Sun Convention and Visitors Bureau (☎ 602-254-6500, 602-252-5588, fax 602-253-4415), One Arizona Center, 400 E Van Buren, Suite 600, Phoenix, AZ 85004-2290, is open Monday to Friday from 8 am to 5 pm. This is the valley's most complete source of tourist information; ask for the free *Official Visitors Guide*. There is a CVB branch inside the Biltmore Fashion Plaza Shopping Mall at 24th St and Camelback Rd, opposite the Saks Fifth Avenue store. This branch is open during mall hours daily.

Individual towns each offer their own services. The Scottsdale Chamber of Commerce (☎ 602-945-8481, 800-877-1117, fax 602-947-4523), 7343 E Scottsdale Mall, is open Monday to Friday 8:30 am to 5 pm (6:30 pm in winter), Saturday 10 am to 5 pm and Sunday 11 am to 5 pm. The Tempe Convention and Visitors Bureau

(☎ 602-894-8158, 800-283-6734, tempe@goodnet.com), 51 W 3rd, Suite 105, and the Tempe Chamber of Commerce (☎ 602-967-7891), 909 E Apache Blvd, are open Monday to Friday from 8:30 am to 5 pm, and the Mesa Chamber of Commerce (☎ 602-969-1307) and the Mesa Convention and Visitors Bureau (☎ 602-827-4700, 800-283-6372, fax 602-827-0727), both at 120 N Center, are open Monday to Friday from 8 am to 5 pm. Other valley towns have chambers of commerce; call the main visitors bureau for details.

Statewide information is available at the Arizona Office of Tourism (☎ 602-230-7733), 2702 N 3rd St, Suite 4015, Phoenix, AZ 85004, and the Arizona State Parks Department (☎ 602-542-4174), at 1300 W Washington. The Arizona Game & Fish Department (☎ 602-942-3000) is at 2222 W Greenway Rd. The Tonto National Forest Headquarters (☎ 602-225-5200) are at 2324 E McDowell Rd, Phoenix, AZ 85006. The nearest ranger station (☎ 602-379-6446) is at 26 N MacDonald, Mesa.

The BLM offices are at 2015 W Deer Valley Rd (☎ 602-580-5500) and at 222 N Central Ave (☎ 602-417-9200); these are open Monday to Friday from about 8 am to 5 pm. The new Arizona Public Lands Information Center (☎ 602-417-9300, fax 602-417-9556, azplic@az.blm.gov), also at 222 N Central Ave, provides information about USFS, NPS, BLM and state lands and parks from 7:30 am to 4:30 pm Monday to Friday.

Money
Foreign exchange is available at the airport and many banks; call Bank of America (☎ 602-594-2891) or Bank One (☎ 602-221-2900) for addresses and hours of the nearest branch.

Post & Communications
The main post office (☎ 602-225-3158) is at 4949 E Van Buren, and the main downtown post office is at 522 N Central Ave. There are dozens of other branches in the valley. For postal information call ☎ 800-275-8777. The main Mesa post office (☎ 602-407-2019) is at 135 N Center and

the main Scottsdale post office (☎ 602-407-2042) is at 7242 E Osborn Rd.

Books & Periodicals
The huge new main library (☎ 602-262-4636) is at 1221 N Central Ave and there are many others throughout the city. The local daily is the *Arizona Republic*. The *New Times* is a free Thursday newspaper with the best entertainment listings of them all. Other free entertainment newspapers are *The Rep*, published by the Arizona Republic, also on Thursdays, and the new *Get Out*, also a Thursday weekly. Look for these in boxes around the city (there's one outside the visitors bureau building in the Arizona Center).

The bookstore scene is now dominated by the huge Barnes & Noble (four locations) and Borders Books (three locations). If you're after used books, Bookman's (☎ 602-835-0505), 1056 S Country Club Drive in Mesa, is the largest and there are many more. One of the best selections of periodicals and magazines is at The Book Store (☎ 602-279-3910), 4230 N 7th Avenue.

Medical & Emergency Services
The Samaritan Health Service (☎ 602-230-2273) operates several valley hospitals and provides 24-hour doctor referral; there are also many other hospitals and clinics. For 24-hour dentist referral, call the Arizona Dental Association (☎ 602-957-4864).

The Phoenix police (☎ 602-262-6151) are at 620 W Washington.

Recycling
The Office of Environmental Programs (☎ 602-256-5669, 602-262-7251) can tell you the location of the nearest drop-off recycling center.

Dangers & Annoyances
Phoenix is no more dangerous than any other large city in the USA or Europe. You are unlikely to run into gang or drug-related activities in the main tourist areas, but use the same precautions you would in any major city (see the Facts for the Visitor chapter).

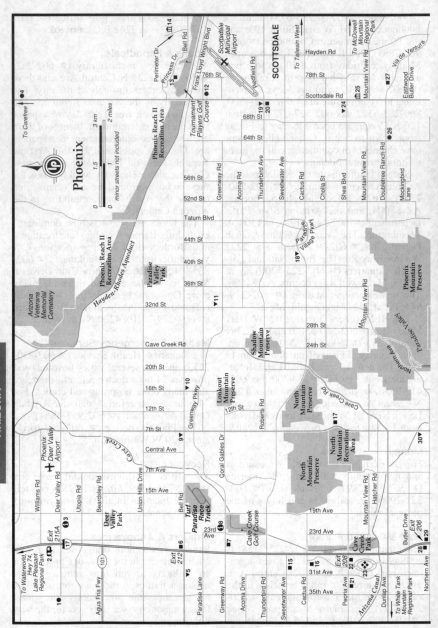

Phoenix

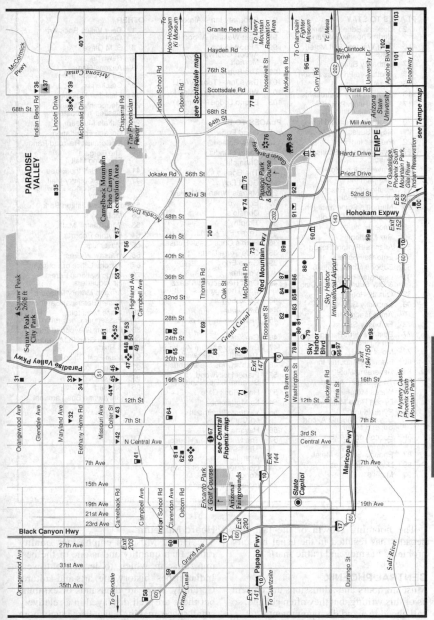

ARIZONA

PLACES TO STAY

2	Desert's Edge RV Park, North Phoenix RV Park
6	Best Western Bell Motel, Motel 6
7	Embassy Suites
13	Scottsdale Princess Resort
15	Motel 6
16	Ramada Inn – Metrocenter
17	Pointe Hilton Resort at Tapatio Cliffs
20	Scottsdale Fairfield Inn
21	Royal Suites
22	Premier Inn
27	Hyatt Regency Scottsdale Resort
28	Travelers Inn, Motel 6
29	Hampton Inn
31	Pointe Hilton Resort at Squaw Peak
35	Marriott's Camelback Inn
48	Courtyard by Marriott
49	Phoenix Inn
50	Ritz-Carlton
51	Arizona Biltmore Resort
59	Embassy Suites
60	Super 8 Motel, Motel 6
61	Lexington Hotel & City Square Sports Club
62	Quality Hotel
68	Embassy Suites
70	Ambassador Inn
73	Embassy Suites
77	Best Western Papago Inn & Resort
78	Motel 6
80	Flamingo Airporter Inn
81	Deserama Motel
82	Travelodge – Airport
83	Wards Motor Inn
84	Desert Rose Motor Hotel
85	Pyramid Inn, Days Inn, Phoenix Airport Super 8 Motel
86	Econo Lodge, Parkview Inn
87	Phoenix Sunrise Motel
89	Doubletree Suites
91	Motel 6
97	Rodeway Inn – Airport West
98	Best Western Airport Inn
99	Airport Hilton, Airport Courtyard by Marriott
100	The Buttes
101	Days Inn – Tempe/ASU
102	Whispering Wind Motel
103	Econo Lodge – Tempe

PLACES TO EAT

5	Good Egg
9	India Palace
10	Taste of India
11	Chompie's
18	The Eggery
19	Good Egg
24	Maria's When in Naples
30	El Bravo
32	Christo's
33	Timothy's
34	Texaz Bar & Grill
36	Ruth's Chris Steak House
38	Café Terra Cotta
39	Good Egg
40	Voltaire
42	Orbit Restaurant & Jazz Bar, The Eggery
43	Good Egg
44	5 & Diner
45	Fish Market, Top of the Market
46	Greekfest
47	Baby Kay's Cajun Kitchen, Tuchetti, Ed Debevic's
48	Ruth's Chris Steak House
52	Planet Hollywood, Steamers, RoxSand
53	Hard Rock Café
54	La Madeleine
55	Vincent Guerithault on Camelback
56	Havana Cafe
57	The News Coffee House, The Eggery
69	Avanti
71	Gourmet House of Hong Kong
74	India Delhi Palace

OTHER

1	Deer Valley Rock Art Center
3	BLM Office
4	Rawhide
8	Arizona Game & Fish Department
12	Crackerjax
14	Fleischer Museum
23	Metrocenter Mall, Castles 'n Coasters
25	Buffalo Museum
26	Cosanti Foundation
37	McCormick Railroad Park
38	The Borgata Shopping Mall
41	Char's Has the Blues
47	Town & Country Mall, Coyote Springs Brewing Company
52	Biltmore Fashion Park
58	Mr Lucky's
63	Park Central Mall
64	Rhythm Room
65	Mason Jar
66	Warsaw Wallies
67	Arizona Office of Tourism
72	Tonto National Forest Headquarters
75	Arizona Military Museum
76	Desert Botanical Garden
79	White Mountain Passenger Lines (bus)
88	Phoenix Greyhound Park
90	Pueblo Grande Museum & Ruins
91	Main Post Office
93	Phoenix Zoo
94	Hall of Flame
95	Big Surf
96	Greyhound Bus Terminal

ARIZONA

The booming growth of the last two decades has resulted in the usual big-city problems of smog and traffic snarls.

CENTRAL PHOENIX

Museum hours and admissions are current as of this writing, but they often change, so call ahead to avoid disappointment.

Heard Museum

The Heard Museum emphasizes quality rather than quantity and is one of the best museums in which to learn Southwest Indian tribes' history, life, arts and culture. Certainly, there are thousands of exhibits, but these are well displayed in a relatively small space, making a visit here much more relaxing than the torturous slog of many major museums. The kachina-doll room is outstanding, as are the audio-visual displays, occasional live demonstrations and the superb gift shop. If you are at all interested in Native American history and culture, this museum should be at the top of your list. Combined with a visit to the nearby Phoenix Art Museum, it makes a great cultural day.

The museum (☎ 602-252-8840), 22 E Monte Vista Rd, is open Monday to Saturday from 9:30 am to 5 pm (staying open to 9 pm on Wednesday) and Sunday from noon to 5 pm. Admission is $6 for adults; $4 for seniors; $3 for four- to 12-year-olds; free for Native Americans. You can take a free guided tour (noon, 1:30 and 3 pm, most days) or rent a 45-minute audio-tape tour for $3.

Phoenix Art Museum

This museum has recently undergone extensive renovation and expansion. Galleries show works from around the world produced between the 14th and 20th centuries; don't miss the collection of clothing from the last two centuries, and be sure to check out the many fine changing exhibitions. There is a restaurant.

The art museum (☎ 602-257-1880 or 602-257-1222 for a 24-hour recorded message), 1625 N Central Ave, is open 10 am to 5 pm daily (till 9 pm on Thursday and Friday) except Monday. Take a guided tour at 2 pm or sit in on the half-hour talks given daily at noon. Admission is $6 for adults; $4 for seniors and full-time students; $2 for six- to 18-year-olds. Admission is free to all on Thursday.

Heritage Square

Eight late 19th- and early-20th-century houses are preserved in Heritage Square (☎ 602-262-5029), the block southeast of 6th St and Monroe. This is about as historical as it gets in Phoenix. Try to ignore the surrounding skyscrapers and imagine thudding hooves and squeaking stagecoach wheels creating clouds of dust outside the buildings.

The square is open Tuesday to Saturday from 10 am to 4 pm and Sunday from noon to 4 pm, but it has shorter summer hours and is closed on holidays. Admission is free, but to tour the 1895 two-story restored **Rosson House**, the most splendid in the square, you'll have to pay a fee. Tours are offered every 30 minutes from 10 am to 3:30 pm Wednesday to Saturday and noon to 3:30 pm on Sunday; shorter hours are in effect in August. Admission is $3 for adults; $2 for people over 62 years old; $1 for six- to 12-year-olds. Also in the square, the **Arizona Doll & Toy Museum** (☎ 602-253-9337) is open during Heritage Square hours and charges $2; 50¢ for children. Other buildings are free and contain places to eat as well as arts and crafts shops.

Arizona Science Center

This new complex (☎ 602-716-2000), 600 E Washington, adjoining Heritage Square, contains a **museum** with 350 hands-on exhibits that encourage the visitor to explore and experiment with computers, bubbles, weather, physics, biology and more. There is also a five-story **giant-screen theater** with shows about the American West playing every hour from 11 am to 4 pm and occasional other shows (a NASA space show is currently featured daily). A **planetarium** has star shows every hour from 10:30 am to 3:30 pm. Also, there are **laser light** shows to the accompaniment of popular music at 9, 10:30 pm and midnight on Friday and Saturday nights and 7:30 and 9 pm on Sunday evenings. Pink Floyd and The Doors are the current offerings, plus a Beatles show at 7:30 pm on Sundays. Call for updates.

The museum is open daily from 10 am to 5 pm, except major holidays. Admission is $6.50 for adults; $4.50 for seniors and four- to 12-year-olds. Tickets for the theater, planetarium and laser shows are extra and sold on a first-come, first-served basis; seating is limited. Advance tickets can be purchased at the center only (no telephone sales). Planetarium shows are $9.50/7.50 and include museum admission; theater shows are $10/8, including the museum, and combined

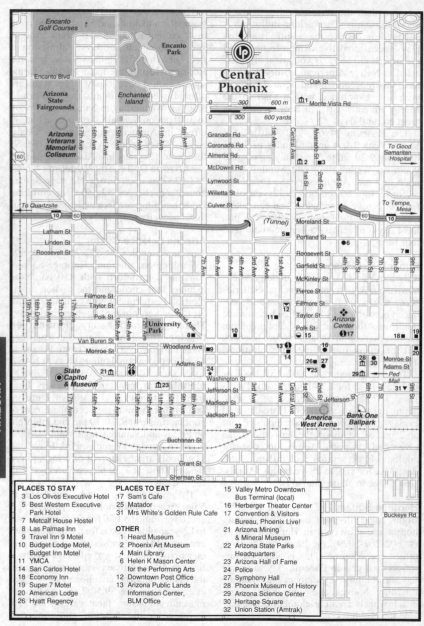

Central Phoenix

PLACES TO STAY
3 Los Olivos Executive Hotel
5 Best Western Executive
   Park Hotel
7 Metcalf House Hostel
8 Las Palmas Inn
9 Travel Inn 9 Motel
10 Budget Lodge Motel,
   Budget Inn Motel
11 YMCA
14 San Carlos Hotel
18 Economy Inn
20 American Lodge
26 Hyatt Regency

PLACES TO EAT
17 Sam's Cafe
25 Matador
31 Mrs White's Golden Rule Cafe

OTHER
1 Heard Museum
2 Phoenix Art Museum
4 Main Library
6 Helen K Mason Center
   for the Performing Arts
12 Downtown Post Office
13 Arizona Public Lands
   Information Center,
   BLM Office

15 Valley Metro Downtown
   Bus Terminal (local)
16 Herberger Theater Center
17 Convention & Visitors
   Bureau, Phoenix Live!
21 Arizona Mining
   & Mineral Museum
22 Arizona State Parks
   Headquarters
23 Arizona Hall of Fame
24 Police
27 Symphony Hall
28 Phoenix Museum of History
29 Arizona Science Center
30 Heritage Square
32 Union Station (Amtrak)

tickets for all three are $11/9. Laser shows are $7 for everyone and children under 12 must be accompanied by an adult.

Phoenix Museum of History
Displays here range from 2000-year-old archaeological artifacts to an exhibit about the sinking of the USS Arizona at Pearl Harbor in 1941. The museum (☎ 602-253-2734) is at 614 E Adams, adjoining Heritage Square. Hours are 10 am to 5 pm, Monday to Saturday, and noon to 5 pm on Sunday. Admission is $5 for adults; $3.50 for seniors; $2.50 for seven- to 12-year olds.

Arizona State Capitol Museum
The old state capitol building (☎ 602-542-4675), 1700 W Washington, built in 1900, is now a museum of Arizona history displaying documents and exhibits from late-territorial and early-state days. Hours are 8 am to 5 pm, Monday to Friday, and 10 am to 3 pm on Saturdays. Guided tours are offered at 10 am and 2 pm. Admission is free. (Arizona's state offices are in a new, nearby building.)

Arizona Mining & Mineral Museum
Apart from the rock and mining-history exhibits, the museum has a Rose Mofford room displaying memorabilia of the state's first woman governor. This free museum (☎ 602-255-3791), 1502 W Washington, is open Monday to Friday from 8 am to 5 pm and Saturday from 11 am to 4 pm.

Arizona Hall of Fame
This free museum (☎ 602-255-2110), housed in the 1908 Carnegie Library building at 1101 W Washington, presents changing exhibits on people who have contributed to Arizona's history in memorable and not-so-memorable ways. Hours are 8 am to 5 pm Monday to Friday.

OUTER PHOENIX
Desert Botanical Garden
This recommended, 145-acre garden in Papago Park exhibits thousands of species of arid-land plants from Arizona and around the world. The flowering season of March to May is the busiest and most colorful time to visit, but any month will provide you with insight into how plants survive in the desert. The garden (☎ 602-941-1225), 1201 N Galvin Parkway, has a gift shop and café, and offers occasional tours and events; it is open daily from 8 am to 8 pm (from 7 am, May through September) and is closed on Christmas. Admission is $7 adults; $6 for those over 60; $1 for five- to 12-year-olds.

The surrounding **Papago Park** has picnic areas, jogging, biking and equestrian trails, a city golf course and a children's fishing pond; it also houses the Phoenix Zoo.

Phoenix Zoo
The zoo (☎ 602-273-1341, 602-273-7771), 455 N Galvin Parkway, houses a wide variety of animals, including some rare ones, in several distinct and natural-looking environments. There is a children's petting zoo, walk-in aviary, camel rides and food facilities. The zoo is open May to Labor Day from 7 am to 4 pm and during the rest of the year from 9 am to 5 pm; it is closed on Christmas. Admission is $8.50 for adults; $7.50 for those over 60; $4.25 for four- to 12-year-olds. Narrated safari train tours cost $2 and last 30 minutes.

Arizona Military Museum
In the Arizona National Guard Military Preserve on the north side of Papago Park, you'll find this museum (☎ 602-267-2676), 5636 E McDowell Rd, which showcases the state's military history through photos, documents and weapons. Admission is free (donations accepted) and hours are 1 to 4 pm on weekends and 9 am to 2 pm on Tuesdays and Thursdays.

Hall of Flame
Opposite Papago Park at 6101 E Van Buren, the Hall of Flame (☎ 602-275-3473) exhibits more than 100 fire-fighting machines from 1725 onward and related paraphernalia. The hall is open 9 am to 5 pm, Monday to Saturday, and noon to 4 pm on Sunday; closed New Year's Day,

ARIZONA

Thanksgiving and Christmas. Admission is $5 for adults; $4 for those over 62; $3 for six-to 17-year-olds.

Pueblo Grande Museum

Pueblo Grande is a Hohokam village that has been partially excavated and then reburied for its protection. Parts of the excavation remain exposed for the visitor, and a nice little on-site museum (☎ 602-495-0900, 602-495-0901), 4619 E Washington, explains all that is known of the canal-building Hohokam culture. Admission is $2 for adults; $1.50 for seniors; $1 for five-to 18-year-olds; free on Sundays. Hours are 9 am to 4:45 pm, Monday to Saturday, and 1 to 4:45 pm on Sunday; the museum is closed on major holidays.

Mystery Castle

This 18-room fantasy was built between 1927 and 1945 by the reclusive Boyce Luther Gulley for his daughter, Mary Lou, who now gives tours of the oddly furnished property. Mystery Castle (☎ 602-268-1581), 800 E Mineral Rd (on the north border of Phoenix South Mountain Park),

is open October to June, Thursday to Sunday from 11 am to 4 pm; admission is $4 for adults; $3 for seniors; $1.50 for six- to 15-year-olds.

Deer Valley Rock Art Center

A small museum (☎ 602-582-8007), 3711 W Deer Valley Rd (just over a mile west of I-17 exit 215 A in northern Phoenix), interprets the significance and techniques involved in making the approximately 1500 prehistoric petroglyphs chipped into boulders along a quarter-mile trail outside. The rock art remains in the same place it was carved during thousands of years before the arrival of Europeans. Hours are 9 am to 5 pm, Tuesday to Saturday, and noon to 5 pm on Sunday; call about shorter summer hours. Admission is $3 adults; $2 for students and seniors; $1 for six- to 12-year-olds.

SCOTTSDALE
Old Town

Half a dozen blocks near the chamber of commerce constitute 'Old Town,' with some early-20th-century buildings and

The Desert as Muse

Frank Lloyd Wright (1867-1959), America's most iconoclastic well-known architect, lived, designed and taught in Scottsdale at **Taliesin West** (☎ 602-860-2700, 602-860-8810), 12621 Frank Lloyd Wright Blvd (Cactus Rd at 108th St). Set on 600 acres of desert, Taliesin West is an example of his organic architecture, which uses natural forms to shape most structures. Wright moved here in 1927 and set up a tent camp. He began building a decade later and wasn't finished until 20 years after that. Today, the natural rock, wood and canvas structures continue to be both living quarters and a teaching establishment.

Visits are limited to guided tours. One-hour tours are given daily on the hour, October to May from 10 am to 4 pm (call about summer hours), and cost $12 (discounted to $9 for students and seniors, and to $3 for three- to 12-year-olds). Ninety-minute tours are offered at 9 am, Monday to Saturday, and cost $16/12/4. Ninety-minute desert walks in the grounds are given at 11:15 am and 1:15 pm, Monday to Saturday; $14 for all. Three-hour 'behind the scenes' tours at 9 am Tuesdays and Thursdays are $30; call for reservations.

Paolo Soleri was a student of Frank Lloyd Wright who went on to develop his own form of organic architecture, which he termed 'arcology' (the combined form of architecture and ecology). Soleri's headquarters are at **Cosanti** (☎ 602-948-6145), 6433 Doubletree Ranch Rd, where you can see a scale model of his futuristic Arcosanti (see the Central Arizona chapter) and various other structures, and can pick up a souvenir at the gift shop. Hours are 9 am to 5 pm daily, and a $1 donation is suggested. ∎

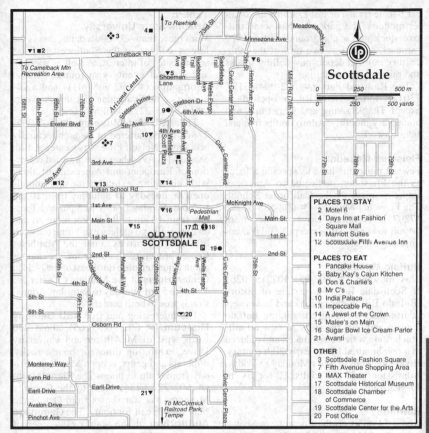

Scottsdale

To Rawhide

To Camelback Mtn
Recreation Area

Camelback Rd

Minnezona Ave

Meadowbrook Ave

Shoeman Lane

Stetson Drive

Arizona Canal

Stetson Dr

6th Ave

5th Ave

4th Ave

Winfield Scott Plaza

3rd Ave

Indian School Rd

1st Ave

Main St

1st St

2nd St

OLD TOWN
SCOTTSDALE

Pedestrian
Mall

McKnight Ave

Main St

1st St

2nd St

4th St

5th St

6th St

Osborn Rd

Monterey Way

Lynn Rd

Earll Drive

Avalon Drive

Pinchot Ave

To McCormick
Railroad Park,
Tempe

Camelback Rd

68th St

68th Place

69th St

70th St

Goldwater Blvd

Exeter Blvd

5th Ave

69th St

Goldwater Blvd

4th St

5th St

6th St

69th Place

70th Place

Marshall Way

Fishbein Lane

Scottsdale Rd

Brown Ave

Wells Fargo Ave

Buckboard Tr

Brown Ave

Brown Ave

Wells Fargo

Saddlebag Trail

Buckboard Ave

Civic Center Plaza

Hinton Ave (75th St)

Civic Center Blvd

75th St

75th St

73rd St

Miller Rd (76th St)

77th St

78th St

79th St

Civic Center Blvd

Civic Center Plaza

0   250   500 m
0   250   500 yards

PLACES TO STAY
2 Motel 6
4 Days Inn at Fashion Square Mall
11 Marriott Suites
12 Scottsdale Fifth Avenue Inn

PLACES TO EAT
1 Pancake House
5 Baby Kay's Cajun Kitchen
6 Don & Charlie's
9 Mr C's
10 India Palace
13 Impeccable Pig
14 A Jewel of the Crown
15 Malee's on Main
16 Sugar Bowl Ice Cream Parlor
21 Avanti

OTHER
3 Scottsdale Fashion Square
7 Fifth Avenue Shopping Area
8 IMAX Theater
17 Scottsdale Historical Museum
18 Scottsdale Chamber of Commerce
19 Scottsdale Center for the Arts
20 Post Office

some more recent buildings styled to look like those of the Old West. One of the oldest is the 'Little Red School House,' built in 1909 and now housing the **Scottsdale Historical Museum** (☎ 602-945-4499), 7333 Scottsdale Mall. Hours are 10 am to 5 pm, Wednesday to Saturday, and noon to 4 pm on Sunday; the museum is closed on holidays and throughout July and August. Admission is free.

Nearby, the **Scottsdale Center for the Arts** (☎ 602-994-2787), 7383 Scottsdale Mall, has art galleries and a sculpture garden, and hosts various performing arts. The

gallery is open Monday to Saturday from 10 am to 5 pm, and Sunday from noon to 5 pm; admission is free. West of the Scottsdale Mall, centered around Brown Ave and Main, old Western-style buildings house art galleries, restaurants and souvenir shops. The chamber of commerce offers brochures describing this popular area. There is free parking north of 2nd St, east of Brown Ave.

McCormick Railroad Park

If you're a train fan, don't miss the model steam trains at this park. You can ride the

5:12-scale trains, or just examine the smaller models. The park also has some full-size stock and a playground with a 1929 carousel, as well as two turn-of-the-19th-century railroad depots now selling snacks and railroad memorabilia.

The Railroad Park (☎ 602-994-2312), 7301 E Indian Bend Rd, is open daily except Thanksgiving and Christmas, and hours vary monthly. Admission is free and rides cost $1.

Fleischer Museum
Few art museums have as specific a focus as the Fleischer, dedicated to American Impressionism of the California School. The Fleischer Museum (☎ 602-585-3108), 17207 N Perimeter Drive, is open from 10 am to 4 pm daily except holidays; admission is free.

Buffalo Museum
This museum (☎ 602-951-1022), 10261 N Scottsdale Rd, is a mixture of history (Buffalo Bill memorabilia) and hokeyness (a life-size, mechanized, singing buffalo family) and tells the story of how 60 million buffalo were exterminated and reduced to a few hundred by the early 20th century. Hours are 9 am to 5 pm Monday to Friday. Admission is $3 for adults; $2 for six- to 17-year-olds.

Rawhide
About 14 miles north of downtown Scottsdale, Rawhide (☎ 602-502-5600), 23023 N Scottsdale Rd, is a re-created late-1800s Western town with saloons, showdowns, stagecoaches and all that stuff. Popular with tourists and fun for kids, it's open from 5 to 10 pm daily year-round; October to May hours are extended to 3 pm to 10 pm, Monday to Thursday, and 11 am to 10 pm on weekends. Admission is free, but attractions, such as the stagecoach, burro or train rides, the Indian village (with dance performances) and the children's petting zoo, charge an extra $2 to $4. A steak house is open from 5 pm daily, plus 11:30 am to 3 pm during winter weekends.

TEMPE
Arizona State University
With more than 43,000 students, this is the largest college in the Southwest and has several sites of interest, as well as sporting and cultural events year-round. General information (☎ 602-965-9011) and a 24-hour recorded calendar of campus events (☎ 602-965-2278) will help orient you.

The **ASU Art Museum** (☎ 602-965-2787), headquartered in the architecturally acclaimed Nelson Fine Arts Center at 10th St and Mill Ave, showcases a varied collection of European and American art along with changing exhibits; the museum is open Wednesday to Saturday from 10 am to 5 pm, Sunday from 1 to 5 pm and Tuesday from 10 am to 9 pm. For more art and an experimental gallery exhibiting the work of emerging artists, visit the Matthews Center branch of the museum, on campus about a quarter-mile northeast of the Nelson Center. Hours at the Matthews Center are 10 am to 5 pm Tuesday to Saturday. Admission is free to both centers.

The interesting and free **ASU Geology Museum** (☎ 602-965-7065), about 250 yards west of McAllister and University Drive, exhibiting dinosaur bones, rocks, minerals and gems, is open Monday to Friday from 9 am to noon. The **Planetarium** (☎ 602-727-6234), next to the Geology Museum, has star shows from October to May for $2; call for hours. The **Gammage Auditorium** at the southwest corner of campus at Mill Ave and Apache Blvd was Frank Lloyd Wright's last major building; tour the inside between October and May, Monday to Friday from 1 to 4 pm.

Tempe Historical Museum
Permanent and changing displays as well as interactive exhibits showcase Tempe's prehistory and modern history at this small museum. The museum (☎ 602-350-5100), 809 E Southern Ave, is open Monday to Thursday and Saturdays from 10 am to 5 pm, Sunday from 1 to 5 pm and is closed on Fridays and major holidays. Admission is $2.50 for adults; $2 for students and seniors; $1 for six- to 12-year-olds.

PLACES TO STAY
4 Tempe Mission Palms Hotel
11 Super 8 Motel of Tempe
13 Holiday Inn
14 Tempe-University Travelodge
15 Motel 6
16 Fiesta Inn
17 Motel 6

PLACES TO EAT
6 Coffee Plantation
8 India Palace

OTHER
1 Tempe Convention and
   Visitors Bureau
2 Gibsons,
   Balboa Jazz Café
   and other clubs
3 Valley Art Theater
5 Greyhound Bus Depot
7 ASU Geology Museum,
   Planetarium
9 ASU Art Museum
   (Nelson Fine Arts Center)
10 Gammage Auditorium
12 Tempe Chamber of Commerce

ARIZONA

Niels Petersen House

Architecture buffs may want to take a free
tour of this 1892 house that was remodeled in the 1930s and retains elements of
both periods. The house (☎ 602-350-5151),
1414 W Southern Ave, is open 10 am to
2 pm, Tuesday, Wednesday, Thursday and
Saturday.

MESA

There are quite a few museums in Mesa,
including the **Arizona Museum for Youth**
(see the Especially for Kids sidebar, later in
this chapter).

Mesa Southwest Museum

Animated dinosaurs, dioramas of ancient
Indians, an eight-cell territorial jail, gold
panning near the Dutchman's Mine and
changing art shows are just a few of the
many displays and interactive exhibits at
this museum with a Southwestern theme.

The Mesa Southwest museum (☎ 602-
644-2230), 53 N MacDonald, is open from
10 am to 5 pm, Tuesday to Saturday, 1 to
5 pm on Sunday, and is closed Mondays
and most holidays. Admission is $4 for
adults; $3.50 for seniors; $2 for three- to
12-year-olds.

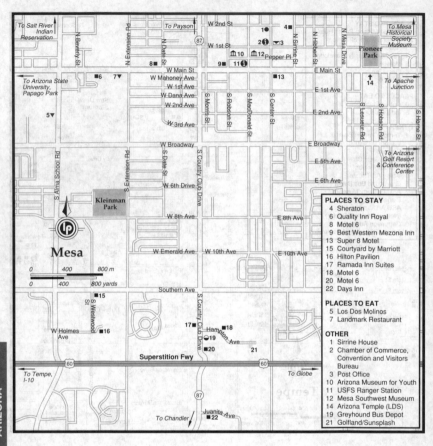

PLACES TO STAY
4 Sheraton
6 Quality Inn Royal
8 Motel 6
9 Best Western Mezona Inn
13 Super 8 Motel
15 Courtyard by Marriott
16 Hilton Pavilion
17 Ramada Inn Suites
18 Motel 6
20 Motel 6
22 Days Inn

PLACES TO EAT
5 Los Dos Molinos
7 Landmark Restaurant

OTHER
1 Sirrine House
2 Chamber of Commerce, Convention and Visitors Bureau
3 Post Office
10 Arizona Museum for Youth
11 USFS Ranger Station
12 Mesa Southwest Museum
14 Arizona Temple (LDS)
19 Greyhound Bus Depot
21 Golfland/Sunsplash

Two blocks away at 160 N Center, the museum also manages the **Sirrine House** (☎ 602-644-2760). Built in 1896, the now refurbished historic home is open October to May for guided tours during weekend museum hours and at other times on request; ask at the museum.

Mesa Historical Society Museum
Mesa's pioneer history is remembered through more than 4000 artifacts displayed at this museum (☎ 602-835-7358) at 2345 N Horne. The museum is open Tuesday to Saturday from 10 am to 4 pm

(though hours vary in summer) and admission is free.

Champlin Fighter Museum
The fighters here are of the airborne variety – this museum (☎ 602-830-4540), in Falcon Field Airport at 4800 E McKellips Rd, has one of the largest collections of fighter aircraft in the world. Thirty-three flyable airplanes from WWI to the Vietnam War are on display, and are explained in extensive supporting exhibits. The museum is open daily from 10 am to 5 pm and is closed Easter, Thanksgiving

and Christmas. Admission is $6.50 for adults; $3 for five- to 12-year-olds. Guided tours (call to reserve a spot) are given at 10:30 am, 1:30 and 3 pm.

Arizona Temple

This Mormon temple, 525 E Main, is Mesa's most noticeable building, but the inside is closed to the public. The adjoining visitor center (☎ 602-964-7164) and surrounding grounds are open, at no cost, from 9 am to 9 pm daily. Mormon guides give free tours of the grounds and visitor center, explaining the basic beliefs of the church.

SUBURBAN PHOENIX
Pioneer Arizona Living History Museum

About 25 authentic territorial buildings (carefully brought here from elsewhere) form a complete village inhabited by guides/interpreters in period dress at the Living History Museum. Daily performances in a turn-of-the-19th-century opera house and various other reenactments present a historically accurate depiction of pioneering life. The museum (☎ 602-465-1052) is almost 30 miles north of downtown Phoenix along I-17; take exit 225 to 3901 W Pioneer Rd (a good stop en route

---

Especially for Kids

Places like the zoo, the wildlife park, the Arizona Science Center, the Hall of Flame and Rawhide will interest the whole family, but the following are especially for kids.

Art exhibits and hands-on art workshops are aimed at elementary school children at the **Arizona Museum for Youth** (☎ 602-644-2467), 35 N Robson St, Mesa. Exhibitions and workshops change every few months, so call ahead for details. During the summer, the museum is open Tuesday to Friday from 9 am to 5 pm, Saturday from 10 am to 5 pm and Sunday from 1 to 5 pm. During the rest of the year, it's open Tuesday to Friday and also Sunday from 1 to 5 pm, and Saturday from 10 am to 5 pm. Admission is $2 for ages three and up. Preregistration for workshops is suggested.

Cool off in summer at **Waterworld** (☎ 602-581-1947), 4243 W Pinnacle Peak Rd (2 miles west of I-17 exit 217) with a six-story-high water slide; **Big Surf** (☎ 602-947 7873), 1500 N McClintock Drive, Tempe; and **Golfland/Sunsplash** (☎ 602-834-8318), 155 W Hampton Ave, Mesa. All offer acres of swimming pools, water slides and wave-making machines; Golfland also has tube floats, bumper boats, miniature golf and go-carts. They are open daily from Memorial Day to Labor Day, and admission is about $14 ($11.50 for four- to 11-year-olds).

Castles 'n Coasters (☎ 602-997-7575), 9445 E Metro Pkwy (by the Metrocenter Mall) is the area's largest amusement park with the 2000-foot-long Desert Storm roller coaster, complete with two 360° loops, providing fun for kids of all ages with strong stomachs. Smaller coasters are suitable for younger riders and there are a dozen other attractions, including four miniature golf courses, video arcades, go-carts and carousels. Desert Storm and major rides are $4; smaller rides are $1.50 and miniature golf is $6. All-day unlimited rides are $18; $23 with unlimited miniature golf. The park is open daily. Near downtown, **Enchanted Island** (☎ 602-254-2020), 1202 W Encanto Blvd, has 10 rides aimed at younger kids at 55¢ each; $8 for unlimited day use. It opens Wednesday to Sunday year-round, and some Mondays and Tuesdays.

Local 'Family Fun Parks' offering miniature golf, video games, batting cages, bumper boats, go-carts, volleyball and other activities year-round include the **Crackerjax** (☎ 602-998-2800), 16001 N Scottsdale Rd, and **Fiddlesticks** (☎ 602-961-0800), 1155 W Elliot Rd in Tempe (a mile east of I-10 exit 157), and (☎ 602-951-6060), 8800 E Indian Bend Rd, Scottsdale. They are open daily (hours vary seasonally) and you pay for the activities you want. Multiple-activity passes may be available. ■

ARIZONA

to Flagstaff). The museum is open Wednesday to Sunday from 9 am to 5 pm, and is closed June to September and on Christmas. Admission is $5.75 for adults; $4 for four- to 12-year-olds.

Wildlife World Zoo

This zoo specializes in rare and exotic species ranging from white tigers to black jaguars. The attractions include a walk-in aviary filled with tropical birds, a lory (parrot) feeding area, a petting zoo and an aquarium with seahorses, piranhas and electric eels. The zoo (☎ 602-935-9453), 16501 W Northern Ave (20 miles northwest of downtown Phoenix), is open 9 am to 5 pm every day of the year. Admission is $8 for adults; $5 for three- to 12-year-olds.

Out of Africa

See big cats from Africa and other continents, pet a lion cub or watch keepers swim with big cats at this wildlife park. The park presents a variety of continuous shows. Out of Africa (☎ 602-837-7779, 602-837-7677), 2 S Fort McDowell Rd (off Hwy 87 near the Fort McDowell Indian Reservation, almost 30 miles northeast of downtown Phoenix), is open 9:30 am to 5 pm year-round (closed Christmas, Thanksgiving and Mondays in winter). Admission is $12 for adults; $11 for seniors; $5 for four- to 12-year-olds.

Hoo-Hoogam Ki Museum

This small Pima-Maricopa Indian museum is on the Salt River Reservation at 10005 E Osborn Rd (at the intersection with Longmore, about 3 miles east of Old Town Scottsdale). The building is made of local materials, such as mesquite, saguaro ribs and adobe. See Pima baskets and Maricopa ceramics on display along with photographs that illustrate the history of the people, and visit the gift shop and café. The museum is open year-round Monday to Friday from 10 am to 4:30 pm, plus Saturdays from October to May from 10 am to 2 pm, and is closed major holidays. Admission is $1; 50¢ for children. Tribal offices (☎ 602-874-8000) are nearby.

SUBURBAN PARKS

Several large parks in the mountains ringing the valley provide residents with many hiking, cycling, horseback riding and picnicking areas. Some are very popular and of course get crowded; nevertheless, these parks are as wild as you can get near a major city. A useful book is *Day Hikes and Trail Rides In and Around Phoenix* by Roger and Ethel Freeman. ('Trail rides' in the title refers to horse trails.)

To begin getting away from city crowds, the Tonto National Forest is the best immediate bet. Outdoors, people must beware of dehydration and sunburn in summer; be sure to carry water and sun protection.

The following are some of the most important parks, going from south to north. Unless otherwise noted, expect the parks to close at night with no camping allowed. For more information on campgrounds, see Places to Stay, below.

Phoenix South Mountain Park

Covering 25 sq miles, this is the largest city park in the USA and is part of the Phoenix Mountain Preserve system (☎ 602-495-0222). The park provides more than 40 miles of trails used by hikers, mountain bikers and horseback riders from dawn until dusk. There are also good views and dozens of Indian petroglyph sites to admire. The park is on one of the lower ranges surrounding the valley, with South Mountain topping the landscape at 2690 feet. Reach the park by driving about 8 miles south of downtown Phoenix to 10919 S Central Ave. Rangers can help plan your visit (8 am to 5 pm), and maps are available outside during daylight hours. Rangers emphasize that you should not leave valuables in your car.

Estrella Mountain Regional Park

On the southwestern outskirts of the valley, this 31-sq-mile county park (☎ 602-932-3811) is at the north end of the extremely rugged Sierra Estrella, providing 34 miles of multi-use trails, a golf course, rodeo arena and picnicking areas, mainly in the northwest corner of the park.

If you walk out of the roadless and almost trailless southeast corner of the park into the main part of the Sierra Estrella, you'll find a mountain range so steep, slippery, waterless and wild that few people have walked it, despite its apparent proximity to the Southwest's largest city. (See Annerino's *Adventuring in Arizona*.)

The park is on the Gila River Indian Reservation; reach it by driving 5 miles south of I-10 along Estrella Parkway in Goodyear. The park is open 6 am to 10 pm; admission is free, but parking is $2.

Squaw Peak City Park

The 2608-foot summit of Squaw Peak affords one of Phoenix's most popular hikes (no bikes or horses are allowed), so much so that parking is very hard to find on weekends outside of summer; get there early in the morning. The park opens at 5:30 am and the parking areas may be full within two hours on winter weekends. The parking lots are along Squaw Peak Drive, northeast of Lincoln Drive between 22nd and 24th Sts. For information, call ☎ 602-262-7901.

McDowell Mountain Regional Park

Hiking, biking, horseback riding and camping are all permitted in this 33-sq-mile county park (☎ 602-471-0173). Access is along Fountain Hills Blvd from Shea Blvd east of Scottsdale. Of the miles of trails, none reaches 4034-foot Mt McDowell standing west of the park. The park is open from dawn till dusk and admission is $2 per vehicle. There is a camping area ($15 with water and electricity hookups).

White Tank Mountain Regional Park

This 41-sq-mile park (☎ 602-935-2505) is the largest in Maricopa County and offers good hiking, mountain biking, horseback riding and camping. Of the many trails, one leads to the 4018-foot summit of White Tank Mountain and another goes to a waterfall (which is sometimes dry). Park hours are dawn till dusk and admission is $2 per vehicle. To get to the park from Phoenix, drive 10 miles northwest on Grand

Ave (Hwy 60), then head 15 miles west on Olive Ave (the western extension of Dunlap Ave) to the park.

Lake Pleasant Regional Park

The Lake Pleasant Reservoir is formed by the new Waddell Dam on the Agua Fria River. The county park has an orientation center (☎ 602-780-9875) and offers boating, fishing, swimming, snacks, picnicking and camping (see Places to Stay). Admission is $4 per vehicle, $2 per boat or motorcycle and free for cyclists. If you only want to drive to the scenic overlook to view the lake and not use park facilities, admission is $1 per person.

From about March to November, Alaski Marina (☎ 602-697-8451) rents boats (sail and motor) and jet skis. Desert Princess Cruises (☎ 602-230-7600) provides a variety of cruises on the lake beginning at $25.95 for a sightseeing cruise; $39.95 to $75.95 for lunch, brunch and dinner cruises. Most cruises are two to 2½ hours. It also rents various boats and jet skis ($75 to $250 a day; hourly rates are available) and skis at its Pleasant Harbor Marina; make reservations at least a week in advance. Boat races and fishing tournaments are held regularly. To get to the park, drive about 27 miles north of downtown Phoenix on I-17 to Hwy 74, then continue about 12 miles west.

ACTIVITIES

In addition to the activities listed below, look in the yellow pages for skating rinks (both ice and roller), skydiving, gliding, bicycle rentals and other activities offered in the valley.

Golf, Tennis & Swimming

Serious golf players probably already know that the valley, despite its desert location, is a major golfing center with well over 100 greens that range from 'pitch and putt' to PGA championship courses. Information about these and other courses is available from the Arizona Golf Association (☎ 602-944-3035, 800-458-8484), 7226 N 16th, Phoenix, AZ 85020. Many of the resorts offer fine courses and package golfing or tennis vacations (see Places to Stay). Many of these courses charge $100 or more for a round.

Phoenix Parks and Recreation (☎ 602-262-6861 for general information) runs dozens of city parks with several golf courses, many tennis courts, swimming pools and other recreational programs. City courses generally offer the cheapest golfing, often at a quarter the price of the fancier places.

The city-run Encanto Park (☎ 602-262-6412), N 15th Ave and Encanto Blvd, a couple of miles north of downtown Phoenix, has a nine-hole (☎ 602-262-6870) and an 18-hole golf course (☎ 602-253-3963), a swimming pool, tennis, racquetball and basketball courts, lakes with ducks and rowboat rentals, and picnic areas to attract entire families. Try other 18-hole, city-run golf courses at Papago Park (☎ 602-275-8428); Maryvale (☎ 602-846-4022), 5902 W Indian School Rd; and Cave Creek (☎ 602-866-8076), 15202 N 19th Ave.

City-run tennis centers where courts can be reserved for about $2 to $6 an hour include City Center Courts (☎ 602-256-4120), 121 E Adams; Mountain View (☎ 602-788-6088), 1104 E Grovers Ave; Phoenix Tennis Center (☎ 602-249-3712), 6330 N 21st Ave; and Cave Creek Sports Complex (☎ 602-261-8011). Many of the parks have courts as well.

The city operates 27 swimming pools (call ☎ 602-258-7946 for general pool information). Also see the Especially for Kids sidebar.

Horseback Riding

As if to emphasize the valley's Western roots, almost 40 horse rental and riding outfits are listed in the Phoenix yellow pages. Short rides, often combined with a country breakfast or barbecue cookout, are popular activities, and overnight packing trips can be arranged. Rates are about $15 to $20 for an hour, reservations are suggested from late fall through spring, and it's too darn hot to do much riding in the summer, pardner.

Some better-known outfits include All Western Stables (☎ 602-276-5862), 10220 S Central Ave, and Ponderosa Stables (☎ 602-268-1261), 10215 S Central Ave, which lead rides into South Mountain Park. Papago Riding Stables (☎ 602-966-9793), 400 N Scottsdale Rd, Tempe, offers rides into Papago Park. For both short and overnight trips into the mountains east of Phoenix, contact Don Donnelly Stables (☎ 602-982-7822, 800-346-4403), 6010 S Kings Ranch Rd, Apache Junction, and Superstition Riding Stables (☎ 602-982-5488), N Meridian Drive in Apache Junction.

Tubing

Floating down the Salt River in an inner tube is a great way to relax and cool down in summer. To find a good starting spot, from 6800 E Main in Mesa, head north on Power Rd, which becomes Bush Hwy and intersects with the Salt River about 7 miles north of Main St. Follow Bush Hwy for a few miles east as it follows the river; the road reaches Saguaro Lake after about 10 miles.

Along the Bush Hwy, Salt River Recreation (☎ 602-984-3305, 602-984-1857, fax 602-984-0875) and Saguaro Lake Ranch Resort (☎ 602-380-1239) will give you information, rent tubes and provide van shuttles to several good starting places for short or all-day floats. Costs start at about $8.50 per person for shuttle and tube, but are less if you bring your own tube. (Rafts can also be rented.) Rent an extra tube for your cooler full of cold drinks (don't bring glass). Bring sunblock and shoes suitable to protect your feet from the bottom. Tubing season is mid-April through September, and weekends draw crowds of people bent on cooling off and partying on.

Hot-Air Ballooning

See the Outdoor Activities chapter for background information on this subject. Some experienced outfits include A Aerozona Adventures (☎ 602-991-4260) and Unicorn Balloon Company (☎ 602-991-3666, 800-468-2478), but many others are just as good.

Shooting & Archery

The Ben Avery Shooting Range (☎ 602-582-8313), northwest of I-17 on Hwy 74, provides practice facilities and competitions for a variety of firearms as well as archery, and has a campground for competition participants only. The Usery Mountain Recreation Area (☎ 602-984-0032), on Ellsworth Rd about 5 miles north of Hwy 60 in Mesa, offers extensive archery facilities and a 70-site campground (see Places to Stay – Camping, below).

ORGANIZED TOURS

Several companies offer tours in and around Phoenix. Gray Line (☎ 602-495-9100, 800-732-0327) runs three hour narrated city bus tours for $27 a person, and Vaughan's Southwest (☎ 602-971-1381) offers four-hour tours for a few dollars more. Both these and other companies do longer tours, such as a 14-hour tour to the Grand Canyon for about $80 (for people with really limited time!); children under 12 get discounts.

Arizona Carriage Company (☎ 602-423-1449, or 602-510-2243 mobile phone) gives horse-drawn carriage tours leaving from Main and Brown in Old Town Scottsdale. Carriages hold six people and tours start at $20 for a 15-minute ride.

Many companies offer 4WD tours into the surrounding desert that last anywhere from four hours to all day and stress various themes: ghost towns, cookouts, Indian petroglyphs and ruins, natural history, sunset tours and target shooting. Costs start around $50 a person. Some reputable companies include Arizona Desert Jeep Tours (☎ 602-947-7852), 835 E Brown in Scottsdale; Arrowhead Desert Tours (☎ 602-942-3361, fax 602-993-3304), 841 E Paradise Lane, Phoenix; and Wild West Jeep Tours (☎ 602-941-8355), 7127 E Becker Lane in Scottsdale.

Short rafting tours are offered by Desert Voyagers (☎ 602-998-7238, 800-222-7238). Short and long trips, some combined with jeep or horseback excursions, are offered by Cimarron River Co (☎ 602-994-1199).

SPECIAL EVENTS

Something is happening just about all the time from October to May in Phoenix, but few events occur during the searing summer. The chambers of commerce are knowledgeable about all the scheduled events and provide free calendars. Some of the most important include the following.

One of the biggest parades in the Southwest precedes the Fiesta Bowl college football game on New Year's Day at the ASU Sun Devil Stadium. Late January and early February sees Western events in Scottsdale, such as a horse-drawn parade, a rodeo, Pony Express reenactments and an All-Arabian Horse Show. Performers dress in Renaissance garb, joust and host many other medieval events on weekends from late February through early April during the Renaissance Festival, held on Hwy 60, 9 miles southeast of Apache Junction. Admission is $13 for adults; $6 for four- to 12-year-olds.

The Heard Museum hosts the Guild Indian Fair and Market during the first weekend in March, which has been held annually since 1958. View Indian dancers, eat Native American food, and browse and buy top-quality arts and crafts. Admission is $6 for adults; $3 for children.

In mid-March, watch the Phoenix Rodeo of Rodeos, held at the Veterans Memorial Coliseum, 1826 W McDowell Rd. The costumed Yaqui Indian Easter Ceremonies are held Friday afternoons during Lent and from Wednesday to Easter Sunday of Holy Week. The events occur in the main plaza of the village of Guadalupe at the south end of Tempe (call ☎ 602-883-2838 for information).

The Arizona State Fair takes place in the last two weeks of October. Simultaneously and continuing into mid-November, the Cowboy Artists of America exhibition is on display at the Phoenix Art Museum. The Thunderbird Hot-Air Balloon Classic lifts off in early November, and dance, song, and arts and crafts are featured at Pueblo Grande's Annual Indian Market during the second weekend in December.

ARIZONA

PLACES TO STAY

From very basic motels to ritzy resorts, the valley's hundreds of accommodations share one thing in common – prices plummet in summer. January-to-April rates can be two or even three times more expensive than summer rates in the top-end places, although at the cheapest ones, the seasonal price difference is not so vast. The price drop presents bargains for summer vacationers. Winter rates are overpriced because that is when hotels make enough money to offset the low rates in the stiflingly hot summers.

Reservation services for places in the mid-to-top price ranges (at no extra charge) include Phoenix/Scottsdale Hotel Reservations (☎ 619-627-9300, 800-728-3227); Experience Arizona Central Reservations (☎ 602-906-0017, 888-249-8470), 7000 N 16th St, Suite 120-237, Phoenix, AZ 85020; and Hospitality Network (☎ 602-200-9980, 800-331-5038, fax 602-200-9956), 100 W Clarendon Ave, Suite 1050, Phoenix AZ 85013. These outfits, like others listed in Sedona and Tucson, can also plan your entire Arizona vacation.

There are scores of B&Bs in the valley, most of which prefer advance reservations. The Arizona Association of B&B Inns (☎ 602-488-9636, 888-820-8299, fax 602-488-9636), PO Box 4948, Cave Creek, AZ 85327, can provide a statewide list of its members. Many B&Bs can be reserved through the Mi Casa Su Casa B&B reservation service (☎ 602-990-0682, 800-456-0682), PO Box 950, Tempe, AZ 85280, and some can be reserved through B&B Southwest (☎ 602-947-9704, 800-762-9704, fax 602-874-1316), 2916 N 70th St, Scottsdale, AZ 85251. Also call Arizona Trails B&B Reservations (☎ 602-837-4284, 888-799-4234), PO Box 18998, Fountain Hills, AZ 85269. Expect mid-range to top-end rates at most of these places.

The most elegant and expensive places to stay are the resorts, of which Phoenix has more than its share. These aren't just places to stay – they are places to spend an entire vacation. Sure, the staff will arrange a day trip to the Grand Canyon for you, but when you are spending hundreds of dollars a day for the resort facilities, it makes no sense just to sleep there.

The pricey resorts generally offer attractively landscaped grounds suitable for strolling or jogging, spacious rooms or suites (including presidential suites priced well over a $1000 a night) and extensive indoor and outdoor public areas. Expect a helpful staff, a variety of dining possibilities and room service, bars and entertainment, as well as several swimming pools, whirlpools, saunas, a fully equipped exercise/health center with instructors and trainers, and (at extra cost) massage, beauty treatments, tennis, racquetball and golf. Most can provide babysitting and some have children's clubs (again, at extra cost). Gift and sundries shops should be on the premises along with a hairdresser, and various other attractions may include anything from bicycle hire to basketball courts, video rental to volleyball and horseback riding to hot-air ballooning. Resorts also tend, inhospitably, to nickel-and-dime guests to death with very expensive local phone calls or $3 in-room coffee machines.

With most resorts having several hundred units running at full occupancy in winter, this is big business, and there are several dozen resorts and resort wanna-bes in the valley. This tradition started in Phoenix, but now Scottsdale is clearly the resort center of Arizona, if not the Southwest. Some of the major resorts and their main claims to fame are listed below, and you can expect them to have most of the features mentioned above. If you plan on vacationing in a valley resort, I suggest you contact the establishment for complete details or talk to a travel agent.

Places to Stay – Camping

Campers will usually find that summers are wretchedly hot for camping.

Boaters can camp at the free USFS *Bagley Flat Campground*, open year-round on Saguaro Lake (see Tubing, above), but there is no drinking water (treat the lake water) and access is by boat only. Call the Mesa Ranger Station (☎ 602-379-6446) for information. About 20 miles north of Scottsdale, via Carefree and the unpaved Seven Creeks Rd (USFS Forest Rd 24), the *Seven Creeks Campground* with 23 sites, and the *CCC Campground* with 10 sites, are open year-round and are free but lack drinking water; the elevation here is about 3500 feet. Call the Cave Creek Ranger Station (☎ 602-488-3441) for information. These sites are all in the Tonto National Forest.

The wildest camping is found east of the valley. The Tonto National Forest also runs *Tortilla Campground* 18 miles northeast of Apache Junction along Hwy 88, offering 77 sites October through April for $8, with water but no showers or hookups. *Lost Dutchman State Park* (☎ 602-982-4485), 6109 N Apache Trail, Apache Junction, AZ 85219, is 5 miles northeast of Apache Junction along Hwy 88. This campground offers nature trails and picnic sites ($3 day use per vehicle) nestled under the Superstition Mountains and 35 campsites for $8, with water but no showers or hookups.

You can camp at several of the suburban parks and recreation areas (see Suburban Parks, above, for more information about these): *Lake Pleasant Regional Park* offers dispersed primitive camping for $5, and two campgrounds with showers and about 100 tent sites ($8) and RV sites ($15 with hookups). *McDowell Mountain Regional Park* has about 70 campsites with water and electric hookups for $15, as well as showers. The campground closes from Memorial Day through September. The year-round campground at *White Tank Mountain Regional Park* offers 40 sites for $8, and provides showers but no hookups. *Usery Mountain Recreation Area* has a 70-site campground providing sites with hookups priced at $12; this campground is closed in summer.

For those 55 or older, the *Paradise RV Resort* (☎ 602-977-0344, 800-847-2280), 10950 W Union Hills Drive, in the retirement community of Sun City, features 950 RV sites with hookups for $35, as well as a pool, spa, sauna, exercise room, tennis courts and putting green. It's used mainly by long-stay visitors who get big weekly and monthly discounts.

Even larger adult-only RV parks (they should call them RV cities) are found in Mesa. All have extensive recreation facilities and are popular with long-stay visitors, so reservations are suggested. *Trailer Village* (☎ 602-832-1770), 3020 E Main, has almost 1700 sites priced at about $20. The *Mesa Regal RV Resort* (☎ 602-830-2821, 800-845-4752), 4700 E Main, has about 1800 sites priced at $30, as does the *Valle del Oro RV Resort* (☎ 602-984-1146, 800-626-6686), 1452 S Ellsworth. The *View Point RV and Golf Resort* (☎ 602-373-8700, 800-822-4404), 8700 E University Drive, offers more than 1300 sites priced at $30, as well as perhaps the most extensive recreational activities of any RV park in the valley.

Two north-Phoenix RV campgrounds with more than 200 sites each are near I-17 at exit 215: *Desert's Edge RV Park* (☎ 602-869-7021), 22623 N Black Canyon Hwy, with RV sites for adults only; and *North Phoenix RV Park* (☎ 602-581-6022), 2550 W Louise Drive, which allows families and limited tenting as well. Both charge $17 to $20 depending on services used, and both have showers, a pool, a spa, a recreation area and coin laundry.

Other family-oriented RV parks include the 360-acre *West World Equestrian Center of Scottsdale* (☎ 602-483-8800, 602-585-4392, 800-488-4887), 16601 N Pima Rd, offering 500 sites for $15, horseback riding and equestrian events, hiking, cookouts and outdoor recreation activities but no swimming pool. About a mile south of I-10 exit 124, 20 miles west of Phoenix, the *Phoenix West KOA* (☎ 602-853-0537), at 1440 N Citrus Rd in Goodyear, has almost 300 sites for $19 to $26 with hookups, as well as some tent sites, a pool, spa, playground and other activities.

About 100 more RV parks, many for adults only, are listed in the Phoenix yellow pages.

Places to Stay – Budget

Phoenix Central Phoenix has the region's best selection of cheap places to stay. Many young budget travelers head over to the friendly *Metcalf House Hostel* (☎ 602-254-9803), 1026 N 9th St. This hostel will not take telephone reservations but nearly always has space in the dorms, priced at $15 per person ($12 for HI/AYH members). Kitchen and laundry facilities are available.

The *YMCA* (☎ 602-253-6181), 350 N 1st Ave, rents single rooms with shared showers for $27 a night or $85 a week, and doubles for not much more. It is usually full and does not take reservations – show up around 9 am for the best chance at a room. The guests are primarily men, but women are welcome to stay in rooms on the women's floor and use the gym and other fitness facilities.

Most of the cheapest motels are along Van Buren. The downtown area is OK, but as you head east of 10th St, the neighborhood deteriorates into blocks of boarded-up buildings, used-car lots and streetwalkers' turf (police patrols periodically scout the area). The neighborhood from around 24th to about 36th Sts, north of the airport, is where many cheap hotels are located, some of which are acceptable though the area remains seedy. Many places will give weekly discounts.

For decent cheap lodging downtown, try the *Budget Lodge Motel* (☎ 602-254-7247), 402 W Van Buren, or the *Budget Inn Motel* (☎ 602-257-8331), 424 W Van Buren, offering double rooms around $36 in high season. Other adequate, inexpensive places nearby are the *Travel Inn 9 Motel* (☎ 602-254-6521), 201 N 7th Ave, with $40 doubles and the basic but adequate *Las Palmas Inn* (☎ 602-256-9161), 765 NW Grand Ave, which is just $30. Heading east, you could also try the basic *Economy Inn* (☎ 602-254-0181), 804 E Van Buren, and the *American Lodge* (☎ 602-252-6823), 965 E Van Buren, both charging about $30, or the *Super 7 Motel* (☎ 602-258-5540), 938 E Van Buren, which is $45 for a double.

You'll find adequate rooms within 2 to 4 miles of the airport in the following motels: The *Flamingo Airporter Inn* (☎ 602-275-6211), 2501 E Van Buren, charges about $35 for one or two people, as does the *Deserama Motel* (☎ 602-273-7477), 2853 E Van Buren. *Wards Motor Inn* (☎ 602-273-1601), 3037 E Van Buren, is in the high $30s for a double. The clean and often full *Desert Rose Motor Hotel* (☎ 602-275-4421, fax 602-273-6284), 3424 E Van Buren, charges in the $40s as does the *Pyramid Inn* (☎ 602-275-3691), 3307 E Van Buren. The *Parkview Inn* (☎ 602-273-7303), 3547 E Van Buren, and the *Phoenix Sunrise Motel* (☎ 602-275-7661), 3644 E Van Buren, are about $40 for a double in winter. Most of these have a pool.

Mixed in with these places along Van Buren are some more basic ones, some of which advertise 'Adult Movies,' as well as several decent chain motels that charge $55 to $100 in winter but drop prices to budget levels in summer. The cheapest chain is *Motel 6* with nine motels in Phoenix – call their toll-free number for a complete list. The cheapest is at 2323 E Van Buren (☎ 602-267-7511, fax 602-231-8701), with 245 rooms for $36/42 for singles/doubles. Most of the others have been renovated and charge in the $50s for a double in winter, in the $40s in summer. Many Motel 6s fill up in winter, especially during weekends, so make a reservation. There are also Motel 6s in Mesa, Tempe and Scottsdale.

Standard rooms start in the $50s during the high season at the *Super 8 Motel – Central* (☎ 602-248-8880, fax 602-241-0234), 4021 N 27th Ave, which has a pool and includes a continental breakfast. Two *Travelers Inn*s have good rooms at 8130 N Black Canyon Hwy (☎ 602-995-8451, fax 602-995-8496) and at 5102 W Latham (☎ 602-233-1988, fax 602-278-4598). Both places charge about $52/58 singles/doubles and also have a year-round pool and spa.

The *Ambassador Inn* (☎ 602-840-7500, 800-624-6759, fax 602-840-5078), 4717 E Thomas Rd, is a good value. Rooms have kitchenettes, and there is an adjacent restaurant as well as a spa, year-round pool and exercise area. Double rooms are $57, or $67 pool-side.

Tempe, Mesa & Scottsdale Phoenix has the cheapest budget rooms in the valley. Heading east into Tempe and Mesa, some basic motels with double rooms priced from $45 to $50 include *Whispering Wind Motel* (☎ 602-967-9935), 1814 E Apache Blvd, east of the intersection with McClintock Drive; several more places line the blocks between here and Price Drive. About half a mile farther, Apache Blvd becomes Main St in Mesa, where several cheap places line the half-mile around the *Del Rio Motel* (☎ 602-833-3273), 2200 W Main, and the *Roadrunner Motel* (☎ 602-834 8040), 2066 W Main. Almost all have pools.

The Motel 6 chain offers reasonably reliable budget accommodations and pools; the three in Mesa are at 336 W Hampton (☎ 602-844-8899, fax 602-969-6749), 630 W Main (☎ 602-969-8111, fax 602-655-0747) and 1511 S Country Club (☎ 602-834-0066, fax 602-969-6313). All charge about $48/54 for singles/doubles in winter. In the mile east of the Motel 6 on Main, there are several other basic, mom-and-pop motels. Tempe's three Motel 6s are similarly priced and are at 513 W Broadway (☎ 602-967-8696, fax 602-929-0814), 1612 N Scottsdale Rd/Rural Rd (☎ 602-945-9506, fax 602-970-4763) and 1720 S Priest Drive (☎ 602-968-4401, fax 602-929-0810).

Scottsdale, the resort capital of the valley, has very few budget places to stay, as you pay extra bucks for the swanky location. One of the least expensive places is the *Motel 6* at 6848 E Camelback Rd (☎ 602-946-2280, fax 602 949-7583) at $58/64 in winter.

Places to Stay – Middle
These hotels offer rooms in the $70 to $150 range during the high season. The places listed here are nice, but not luxurious; a $120 room in February can go for $60 in July, and is probably worth closer to the

lower end. Unfortunately, rates are difficult to pin down; most hotels will raise or lower rates depending on demand, which is high in winter. I give some sample summer rates, but expect big summer discounts everywhere. Most of these hotels give discounts to AAA or AARP members – ask for a discount for any reason you can think of. All the major chains have several properties in the valley and calling the chains will give you more possibilities. For middle to top-end accommodations, contacting the reservation agencies listed at the beginning of this section is a time- and labor-saving possibility if you have particular dates and desires in mind. All hotels below have pools and almost all have whirlpool/spas.

Phoenix The following are all close to the airport and provide a free shuttle; however, unless you want to stay near the airport, you can get a better value elsewhere. The *Best Western Airport Inn* (☎ 602-273-7251, fax 602-273-7180), 2425 S 24th, is about a mile from the terminal, has a sauna, restaurant and bar. High-season rates are $90 to $110, low season $65 to $75. The *Rodeway Inn – Airport West* (☎ 602-244-2211, fax 602-225-9170), 1202 S 24th, is a little cheaper and closer to the airport, providing standard rooms, a restaurant and bar. The *Days Inn – Airport* (☎ 602-244-8244, fax 602-244-8420), 3333 E Van Buren, about 3 miles from the terminal, also has a restaurant/bar. Standard rooms are in the $90s, around $60 off-season.

The *Phoenix Airport Super 8 Motel* (☎ 602-244-1627, fax 602-275-1126), 3401 E Van Buren, has a spa, exercise room and free coffee, but lacks a restaurant (there are some close by) and charges $84/89 a single/double. The *Travelodge – Airport* (☎ 602-275-7651, fax 602-275-7007), 2900 E Van Buren, includes a continental breakfast with rooms at around $70 and has a restaurant nearby. *Econo Lodge* (☎ 602-273-7121, fax 602-231-0973), 3541 E Van Buren, has a restaurant and rooms in the $60s in winter, making it the cheapest of the mid-range airport motels.

Right downtown, the *San Carlos Hotel* (☎ 602-253-4121, 800-528-5446, fax 602-253-6668), 202 N Central Ave, is the most fun. Built in 1927, it was downtown's swankiest hotel for decades, and although recently refurbished and comfortable, the hotel retains many of its early fixtures and atmosphere. The rooms ($89 to $109) are small, but there are more expensive suites (up to $159) if you need to spread out, and facilities include an exercise room, restaurant and bar. The *Los Olivos Executive Hotel* (☎ 602-528-9100, 800-776-5560, fax 602-258-7259), 202 E McDowell Rd, is smaller and more intimate than many business-oriented hotels; its 33 rooms, most with king-size beds and coffeemakers, cost about $80 (in the $40s off-season), and 15 mini-suites with kitchenettes cost $30 more. The hotel has tennis courts and a coffee shop open for breakfast and lunch on weekdays only.

On the north edge of downtown, the *Best Western Executive Park Hotel* (☎ 602-252-2100, fax 602-340-1989), 1100 N Central Ave, offers about 100 rooms that are as nice as some more expensive places downtown at $129 to $139 a double; 8th-floor suites with a view go for $180. The hotel has a restaurant, bar, room and pool-side service, sauna and exercise room. Phoenix has other good Best Western properties in this price range.

West of downtown Phoenix, the *Fairfield Inn* (☎/fax 602-269-1919), 1241 N 53rd Ave, near I-10 exit 139, is not conveniently located but is a good value in this price range, offering 126 nice rooms at $79 a double with complimentary continental breakfast.

North of downtown Phoenix, the *Lexington Hotel & City Square Sports Club* (☎ 602-279-9811, fax 602-631-9358), 100 W Clarendon Ave, charges $110 to $160 for standard hotel rooms. The relatively high rates include sports club amenities (available at no extra charge) that include large locker rooms, aerobics and well-equipped machine workout rooms with trainers, a dozen racquetball courts, a basketball court, spa, sauna and steam room.

There's also a restaurant open 6:30 am to 10 pm, a busy sports bar and nightclub, and free airport transportation. Prices drop on weekends – I've seen ads for $45 rooms during midsummer weekends. Nearby, the *Quality Hotel* (☎ 602-248-0222, fax 602-265-6331), 3600 N 2nd Ave, offers large rooms, several pools and a spa, playground, volleyball court, exercise area and putting green, a restaurant, bar and international coffee shop, and free airport transportation. Rates are $90 to $120.

Farther north there are the following: The *Best Western Bell Motel* (☎ 602-993-8300, fax 602-863-2163), 17211 N Black Canyon Hwy, has 100 rooms, with coffeemakers, refrigerators and hair-dryers. Continental breakfast is included. Winter rates are $80 to $110; summer rates can drop to the $40s. The *Hampton Inn* (☎ 602-864-6233, fax 602-995-7503), 8101 N Black Canyon Hwy, also provides a continental breakfast with its spotless, spacious rooms priced around $100. You'll find considerably cheaper, decent rooms at the 250-room *Premier Inn* (☎ 602-943-2371, fax 602-943-5847), 10402 N Black Canyon Hwy; it may require a two-night minimum stay.

The *Ramada Inn Metrocenter* (☎ 602-866-7000, fax 602-942-7512), 12027 N 28th Ave, has nice rooms for $100 to $130, with a restaurant and lounge. Nearby, the *Royal Suites* (☎ 602-942-1000, 800-647-5786, fax 602-993-2965), 10421 N 33rd Ave, offers 80 clean and modern mini-suites with kitchenettes. It charges $100 to $140, with discounts for longer stays. The *Phoenix Inn* (☎ 602-956-5221, 800-956-5221), 2310 E Highland Ave, has 120 new rooms, all with kitchenettes, for about $130 including continental breakfast.

At the south end of Phoenix, the *Quality Inn – South Mountain* (☎ 602-893-3900, fax 602-496-0815), 5121 E La Puente Ave, has good-sized, comfortable rooms and a restaurant open for breakfast and dinner. Winter rates are about $100.

Tempe Conveniently near ASU in Tempe, the *Tempe-University Travelodge* (☎ 602-

968-7871, fax 602-968-3991), 1005 E Apache Blvd, has winter doubles for $70, including in-room coffee and continental breakfast. Close to ASU, the *Super 8 Motel of Tempe* (☎ 602-967-8891, fax 602-968-7868), 1020 E Apache Blvd, has a spa, sauna and rooms in the $70s. *Days Inn-Tempe/ASU* (☎ 602-968-7793, fax 602-966-4450), 1221 E Apache Blvd, charges $60 to $90 for adequate rooms, including continental breakfast.

The *Econo Lodge – Tempe* (☎/fax 602-966-5832), 2101 E Apache Blvd, has 40 plain but clean rooms for $70 to $90. Decent doubles for about $70 are available at the 120-room *Travelers Inn* (☎ 602-413-1188, fax 602-413-1266), 1701 W Baseline Rd.

Rates at *Country Suites by Carlson* (☎ 602-345-8585, fax 602-345-7461), 1660 W Elliot Rd (near I-10 exit 157), range from $90 to $140 for rooms with limited to full kitchen facilities (some with sitting rooms) and include continental breakfast, the morning newspaper and airport transportation. The *InnSuites* (☎ 602-897-7900, 800-841-4242, fax 602-491-1008), 1651 W Baseline Rd (near I-10 exit 155), has pleasant rooms of various sizes priced from $110 to $120; all rooms include kitchenettes, and some have sitting rooms or full kitchens. Continental breakfast, evening cocktail hour and airport transportation are included. With two tennis courts and an exercise room, you can get a workout while the kids are on the playground, or you can relax in the spa.

Opposite ASU, *Holiday Inn* (☎ 602-968-3451, fax 602-968-6262), 915 E Apache Blvd, has spacious rooms with coffeemakers, some with balconies or wet bars, for about $140. Amenities include a restaurant (open from 6 am to 10 pm, with room service), lounge, spa and exercise room, and airport transportation.

Mesa There are three Mesa *Super 8 Motels* with winter doubles in the $70s. One is downtown at 3 E Main (☎/fax 602 834-6060). The *Days Inn-East Mesa* (☎ 602-981-8111, fax 602-396-8027), 5531 E Main,

has 60 decent rooms in the $80s, including continental breakfast. Similarly priced rooms are available at the *Days Inn* (☎ 602-844-8900, fax 602-844-0973), 333 W Juanita Ave, which also has some minisuites ($120 to $140).

The *Best Western Mesa Inn* (☎ 602-964-8000, fax 602-835-1272), 1625 E Main, charges $95 to $115 for standard rooms and has a complimentary evening cocktail hour, while the *Best Western Mezona Inn* (☎ 602-834-9233, fax 602-844 7920), 250 W Main, offers rooms for $10 less.

For good rooms priced around $120, including continental breakfast, try the *Hampton Inn* (☎ 602-926-3000, fax 602-926-4892), 1563 S Gilbert Rd. The *Quality Inn Royal* (☎/fax 602-833-1231, 800-333-5501), 951 W Main, offers comfortable rooms with balconies or patios from $100; a few units with kitchenettes go up to $150. Prices include continental breakfast, and the hotel has a spa, sauna, exercise room, and restaurant with a bar. *Ramada Inn Suites* (☎ 602-964-2897, fax 602-833-0536), 1410 S Country Club Drive, offers 120 units, ranging from studios to suites with two bedrooms and a sitting room, all with limited to full kitchen facilities. Rates range from $80 to $150, depending on the room, and include continental breakfast; there is an adjoining 24-hour coffee shop.

Scottsdale The *Scottsdale Fifth Avenue Inn* (☎ 602-994-9461, fax 602-947-1695), 6935 5th Ave, has comfortable rooms priced about $90 a double, and fashionable shopping is within walking distance. The *Days Inn at Fashion Square Mall* (☎ 602-947-5411, fax 602-946-1324), 4710 N Scottsdale Rd, offers standard rooms priced from $90 to $130 in winter, as well as a tennis court and putting lawn; continental breakfast is included. The *Scottsdale Fairfield Inn* (☎ 602-483-0042, fax 602-483-3715), 13440 N Scottsdale Rd, offers nice rooms for about $110, including continental breakfast.

The *Best Western Papago Inn & Resort* (☎ 602-947-7335, fax 602-994-0692), 7017 E McDowell Rd, has coffeemakers in

ARIZONA

its pleasant rooms, which are priced at $110 to $140. The 'resort' moniker refers to its sauna, exercise room and restaurant.

Places to Stay – Top End

As many top-end hotels cater to business travelers on an expense account, discounts can often be arranged for empty rooms on weekends. Many rooms are less than half price in summer. Refer to the Places to Stay and the Places to Stay – Middle introductions, above, for more details.

Phoenix The 24-story *Hyatt Regency* (☎ 602-252-1234, 800-233-1234, fax 602-254-9472), 122 N 2nd, is a huge downtown convention-center hotel with the expected amenities such as a health club, restaurants, room service, a concierge and shopping. More than 700 rooms, many with balconies, go for $160 to $260 a double; some suites go for more than $1000 on peak nights. This is the city's biggest hotel, and the revolving rooftop restaurant (the Compass) has great views and excellent Southwestern food.

There are several comfortable, full-service top-end hotels in the airport area. Among the most comfortable is the *Doubletree Suites* (☎ 602-225-0500, 800-800-3098, fax 602-225-0957), 320 N 44th, with 242 two-room suites, all with a kitchenette, as well as a restaurant, bar, sauna, fitness center, tennis court and free airport transportation. Winter rates are $170 to $270, depending on the room, and include a full breakfast.

Courtyard by Marriott (☎ 800-443-6000, 800-321-2211) has three Phoenix properties, including one by the airport, and three others in the valley. All have in-room coffee, a restaurant and bar, exercise equipment and comfortable rooms ranging from $140 to $200 in winter.

Embassy Suites (☎ 800-362-2779) has five locations, all of which offer two-room suites, most with microwaves or small kitchenettes. Each hotel has a spa, restaurant and bar, and includes a full breakfast and an evening drinks hour in its rates, which range from $140 to $280.

The ritziest hotel in Phoenix is, of course, the elegant *Ritz-Carlton* (☎ 602-468-0700, fax 602-468-0793), 2401 E Camelback Rd, offering attractive rooms in the $200 to $300 range and suites from about $400. Amenities include expensive but excellent restaurants, 24-hour room service, a bar with light entertainment, a fitness center with trainers and massage therapists, a spa, sauna, tennis court and golf privileges, including transportation to the courses. Traditionally elegant, The Grill is one of the best American grills in Arizona.

Much of the design for the city's first luxury resort, the *Arizona Biltmore* (☎ 602-955-6600, 800-950-0086, fax 602-954-2571), 24th St and E Missouri Ave, was influenced by Frank Lloyd Wright. This beautiful and historically interesting resort (opened in 1929) underwent various renovations in the early 1990s. Its modern facilities include two golf courses, several swimming pools and tennis courts, an athletic club and two very good restaurants. Standard rooms cost $350 to $395 in the high season ($145 to $175 in midsummer); premier rooms are $100 more; suites start at $620; and one- and two-bedroom villas with full kitchens are $1295 and $1745 per winter night.

The Hilton chain (☎ 800-944-4381, 800-445-8667) runs three Phoenix resorts. The *Pointe Hilton Resort at Squaw Peak* (☎ 602-997-2626, fax 602-997-2391), 7677 N 16th St, offers nine acres of pools, including water slides and a 'river' tubing area, as well as a popular kids' program, making this a good family choice. The *Pointe Hilton Resort at Tapatio Cliffs* (☎ 602-866-7500, fax 602-993-0276), 11111 N 7th St, and the *Pointe Hilton Resort on South Mountain* (☎ 602-438-9000, fax 602-431-6535), 7777 S Pointe Parkway (at the northeastern corner of Phoenix South Mountain Park), both have full resort facilities, including excellent (but expensive) golf courses. Rooms start around $250 in the high season. The South Mountain location has recently added a children's program as well. All three include a complimentary evening beverage service and have good restaurants, but the chain's best is the spectacularly located Etienne's Different Pointe of View, serving continental food atop Tapatio Cliffs.

Tempe The closest first-class hotel to ASU is the Southwestern-styled *Tempe Mission Palms* (☎ 602-894-1400, fax 602-968-7677, tempe@missionpalms.com), 60 E 5th St, with 300 rooms and suites, and in-room coffeemakers, tennis courts, golf privileges, a sauna and exercise room. Its restaurant has pool-side and room service, and there is a popular sports bar here. Rooms are around $200 in winter. Fairly similar facilities at slightly lower rates are offered at the 270-room *Fiesta Inn* (☎ 602-967-1441, fax 602-967-0224), 2100 S Priest Drive.

Tempe's best hotel, *The Buttes* (☎ 602-225-9000, 800-843-1986, fax 602-438-8622), 2000 Westcourt Way, is a cross between a comfortable business hotel and a resort. Attractively set on top of a small desert mountain, it offers a beautifully landscaped pool, water slide, spas, a sauna, exercise room, tennis courts and golf privileges, as well as the elegant Market Cafe (open from 6 am to 10 pm), the Top of the Rock restaurant (open from 5 to 10 pm), a bar, entertainment, 24-hour room service and airport transportation. The resort has rates in the $200s but offers some more expensive luxury rooms and suites.

Mesa The Sheraton and the Hilton chains present Mesa's best top-end hotels, both with almost 300 good-size rooms priced from $150 to $200. Both hotels have a spa, exercise room, tennis and golf privileges, a restaurant and bar, and some more expensive suites. The *Sheraton* (☎ 602-898-8300, fax 602-964-9279) is at 200 N Centennial Way (off Sirrine St), and the *Hilton Pavilion* (☎ 602-833-5555, fax 602-649-1886) is at 1011 W Holmes Ave.

The *Arizona Golf Resort & Conference Center* (☎ 602-832-3202, 800-528-8282, fax 602-981-0151), 425 S Power Rd, has almost 200 rooms, most with kitchenettes, and three restaurants, an exercise room,

golf and tennis. A bar has weekend entertainment. Room rates are $180 to $200, and two-room suites go up to $400.

Scottsdale Conveniently near Old Town and the shopping area, *Marriott Suites* (☎ 602-945-1550, fax 602-945-2005), 7325 E 3rd Ave, offers spacious two-room suites (many with balconies) with wet bars and coffeemakers for $230. Facilities include a fitness room, spa, sauna, restaurant and bar. However, many people looking for top-end accommodations in Scottsdale are looking for a destination resort. The following are among the best.

Marriott's Camelback Inn (☎ 602-948-1700, 800-242-2635, fax 602-951-8469), 5402 E Lincoln Drive, opened in 1936 and, with many dedicated customers, is considered a world-class resort. Highlights are 36 holes of excellent golf, a full-service spa and health club, several pools and tennis courts, and the highly rated Chaparral restaurant, serving pricey continental food. Everything else you might expect is here as well. Rates start around $350 for rooms with microwaves, refrigerators and coffeemakers; there are substantially pricier suites. Summer visitors can get a room for about $150 or occasionally even less – this is true of all the resorts.

Yet another world-class resort is the *Scottsdale Princess* (☎ 602-585-4848, fax 602-585-0086), 7575 E Princess Drive, the home of the annual PGA Phoenix Open. With 450 beautifully landscaped acres, this is one of the valley's largest full-scale resorts. The resort's La Hacienda restaurant serves the valley's most sophisticated and pricey Mexican food, and the Marquesa is simply the best Spanish (Catalan) restaurant in Arizona. Rooms start at $350, and casitas and suites are around $500. Also at these prices, an even larger property, the *Hyatt Regency Scottsdale* (☎ 602-991-3388, fax 602-483-5550), 7500 E Doubletree Ranch Rd, is popular with families. Enjoy the dozens of fountains and waterfalls, 11 pools, artificial beach, water slide, or playground on the 640-acre Gainey Ranch property while the kids take part in a program just for them. The resort's well-reviewed Golden Swan restaurant serves varied American fare.

Probably the most expensive is the almost overpoweringly opulent and modern *Phoenician* (☎ 602-941-8200, 800-888-8234, fax 602-947-4311), at 6000 E Camelback Rd, a world-class, super-deluxe resort with the usual amenities as well as some less usual activities such as archery, badminton and croquet. The resort's top-rated Mary Elaine's restaurant serves contemporary French cuisine and is one of the Southwest's most expensive and formal restaurants; there are several more casual eating choices as well.

PLACES TO EAT

Phoenix has the biggest selection of restaurants in the Southwest. From fast food to ultra fancy, it's all here. Serious foodies (I don't pretend to be one) will find several world-class kitchens that will lighten their wallets, if nothing else. A useful little book is *100 Best Restaurants in Arizona* by the serendipitously named Harry and Trudy Plate. This book is updated every year or two and, despite its name, squeezes about 150 restaurants into its covers; the reviews are fun. About two-thirds of these places are in the valley, and some of the very best are in the resorts listed above (you don't have to stay at the resorts to eat at the restaurants). Many of these resorts serve classy Sunday brunches that require reservations. In fact, reservations are recommended at all the fancier eateries.

Several free publications available from the chambers of commerce, visitors bureau and newsstands around the valley have extensive restaurant listings, though they lean toward the top end. The *New Times* weekly newspaper also has extensive listings at all price ranges. I give a varied selection of some of the best, including good lower-priced places. All addresses are in Phoenix, unless otherwise indicated.

Breakfast
While the diners and coffeehouses are often good choices, die-hard egg fans can have their breakfast omeleted, creped, Benedicted, scrambled, spiced or otherwise smashed at one of three *The Eggery*s at 5109 N 44th St (☎ 602-840-5734); 4326 E Cactus Rd (☎ 602-953-2342); and 50 E Camelback Rd (☎ 602-263-8554), or at the five related *The Good Egg*s at 2957 W Bell Rd (☎ 602-993-2797); 906 E Camelback Rd (☎ 602-274-5393); 3110 N Central Ave in the Park Central Mall (☎ 602-248-3897); 13802 N Scottsdale Rd (☎ 602-483-1090) in Scottsdale; 6149 N Scottsdale Rd (☎ 602-991- 5416), also in Scottsdale. All are open daily from 6:30 am to 2:30 pm and serve other brunch items in a bright and cheerful environment. Most breakfasts are $4 to $7.

Some folks prefer pancakes for breakfast; the best choice is the *Pancake House* (☎ 602-946-4902), 6840 E Camelback Rd. These come with a European twist – German, Dutch and apple pancakes are worth trying. Hours are 7 am to 2 pm.

Open wide at *Chompie's* (☎ 602-971-8010), 3202 E Greenway Rd, and 9301 E Shea Blvd in Scottsdale (☎ 602-860-0475), serving giant blintzes, bagels and huge puffy omelets for breakfast and the kind of sandwiches you can't get your mouth around for lunch. This is a genuine New York kosher deli with a wide variety of fresh bagels, bialys, knishes, sweet pastries and mouth-watering treats, all made on the premises. Hours are about 6 am to 9 pm. There's always a line for takeout and it's always noisily busy.

On a Sunday, you can defer breakfast into a leisurely brunch, which most of the valley's resorts serve from late morning through early afternoon. Prices are mainly in the $20s (though the Phoenician really goes to town with a $45 brunch) and though these are all-you-can-eat food-fests, the many varied choices are carefully prepared and delicious, and champagne and incredible desserts are included. Call any of the resorts for details.

Coffeehouses
Dozens of coffeehouses dot the valley, many providing entertainment in the eve-

nings. The *Coffee Plantation* (☎ 602-829-7878), 680 S Mill Ave in Tempe, is an espresso and cappuccino place popular with ASU students. It also serves light meals and a selection of tasty pastries, and may have entertainment in the evening. This location used to be open 24 hours, though recently it's been closing around midnight. Other Coffee Plantations have since opened in several of the valley's shopping malls.

For a good selection of coffees, light meals and imported beers and wines, try the *Orbit Restaurant and Jazz Bar* (☎ 602-265-2354), in the Uptown Plaza at Camelback Rd and Central Ave. It provides nightly entertainment (predominantly jazz) in a smoke-free environment. It opens from about 7 am to 11 pm, later on weekends.

Downtown, *The News* (☎ 602-852-0982), 5053 N 44th, features a newsstand with arty publications you can read along with your java.

Diners
The *5 & Diner* (☎ 602-264-5220), 5220 N 16th, is a lot of fun, with inexpensive, 24-hour food and friendly service in a '50s setting. The menu is the predictable pre-nouvelle American cuisine – burgers, fries, tuna melts, shakes etc. The diner's success has led to the opening of several others in the valley (check the phone book for more addresses) and in Tucson, but the new ones aren't open 24 hours – yet. If you like this kind of atmosphere, you'll enjoy the ever-popular *Ed Debevic's* (☎ 602-956-2760), 2102 E Highland Ave, which calls itself 'Short Orders Deluxe'; it makes great burgers and shakes, and also has a salad bar. Bring change for Elvis on the jukebox. The diner is open from 11 am to 9 pm daily, till 10 pm on weekends.

Steak Houses
Ruth's Chris Steak House, 2201 E Camelback Rd (☎ 602-957-9600) and 7001 N Scottsdale Rd (☎ 602-991-5988), both part of a nationwide chain known for superb steak, serve up huge steaks priced around $25 and slathered with melted butter but

nothing else; if you want vegetables or potatoes, you'll have to pay $4 or $5 more. (Perhaps they could make another buck by renting you a steak knife.) Seafood and the other meat dishes are also very good. Hours are 5 to 10 pm daily.

If you'd like a 'free' potato with your steak, try the *T-Bone Steakhouse* (☎ 602-276-0945), 10037 S 19th Ave, way south of town on the north side of Phoenix South Mountain Park, with some good city views. This hospitably Western steak house has a rustic setting and is locally popular for its mesquite-grilled steaks, which run in the teens and lower $20s. It opens for dinner only.

Phoenix is a major baseball spring-training center, drawing the sports fans who crowd into *Don & Charlie's* (☎ 602-990-0900), 7501 E Camelback Rd in Scottsdale. Here, baseball memorabilia and photos of sports personalities cover the walls and the food is meaty, with barbecue priced in the teens and steaks heading in the $20s. Hours are 5 to 10 pm daily.

Texaz Bar & Grill (☎ 602-248-7827), 6003 N 16th St, is not exactly a steak house but has huge, meaty meals – they don't skimp on potatoes and gravy. You can get a bowl of chili for $2 or an 18oz T-bone steak for $15; burgers and chicken-fried steaks are also popular. This fun, down-home place has every available space filled with Texan 'stuff' and is popular with locals and visitors. It's open for lunch and dinner daily, except Sunday when hours are 4 to 10 pm.

Seafood
The Californian *Fish Market* (☎ 602-277-3474), 1720 E Camelback Rd, offers a rustic, net-hung ground floor and a more elegant and pricier *Top of the Market* upstairs. The menu selection is almost as wide as the sea, and prices are equally varied, ranging from about $8 for your basic fish and chips downstairs to $36 for lobster upstairs. Hours are 11 am to 9:30 pm downstairs and 5 to 9:30 pm at the top.

The selection is also wide at *Steamers* (☎ 602-956-3631), 2576 E Camelback Rd

(Biltmore Fashion Park), open from 11 am to 10 pm daily (until 11 pm on Friday and Saturday). It also offers a few selections beyond the fish fare and most entrées are in the $18 to $25 range; there is also an oyster bar.

For relatively inexpensive but well-prepared fresh seafood in a simple setting, head over to *Seafood Central* (☎ 602-922-3474), 6990 E Shea Blvd, Scottsdale, which is open from 11:30 am to 10 pm (9 pm on Sunday). Most plates are in the $9 to $14 range. This restaurant also offers 'raw' seafood and daily specials.

Definitely check C-Fu Gourmet, listed under Chinese (below) for recommended seafood.

Soul Food & Southern

Mrs White's Golden Rule Cafe (☎ 602-262-9256), 808 E Jefferson, is a hole in the wall with hanging, hand-lettered menus, but greasy spoon it ain't. The food is cheap, well prepared and tasty, though you won't find any low-calorie plates here . The Golden Rule is to remember what you ate when you pay at the register at the end of your meal. It's open for lunch but not dinner, Monday to Friday.

For the valley's best Cajun catfish and crawfish, try *Baby Kay's Cajun Kitchen* in the Town & Country Mall at 2119 E Camelback Rd (☎ 602-955-0011) and 7216 E Shoeman Lane in Scottsdale (☎ 602-990-9080). Both are small, unpretentious places locally famed for delicious 'dirty rice,' a mixture of rice with sausage, onions, peppers and seasonings, and a whole bunch of other Southern specials. The Phoenix location serves lunch daily from 11 am to 3 pm; dinner is served from 5 to 10 pm (till 11 pm on Friday and Saturday) and from 4 to 9 pm on Sunday. Scottsdale has the same hours except lunches are Monday to Friday only. Dinner entrées are in the $8 to $15 range.

Southwestern

After enjoying great success as a Tucson favorite, the owners of *Café Terra Cotta* opened a second location in Scottsdale (☎ 602-948-8100), 6166 N Scottsdale Rd

at the Borgata Mall. The café is open from 11 am to 10 pm daily, and it stays open to 11 pm on Friday and Saturday. The menu has steadily become pricier, with most entrées now in the teens, but it remains innovative, even wild-sounding at times, with a few fairly straightforward choices for the less adventurous. Be sure to leave room for one of the heavenly desserts.

The classiest Southwestern restaurant is *Vincent Guerithault on Camelback* (☎ 602-224-0225), 3930 E Camelback Rd, serving food with the famous chef's French touch. With dinner entrées priced around $20, the restaurant is not outrageously expensive, considering the haute cuisine. The restaurant is open Monday to Friday from 11:30 am to 2:30 pm, and Monday to Saturday from 6 to 10:30 pm. It may open for Sunday dinner in the high season.

For somewhat cheaper Southwestern fare, visit *Sam's Cafe* (☎ 602-252-3545), downtown in the Arizona Center (Van Buren and 3rd St). Sam's is open daily from 11 am to 10 pm, staying open to midnight on Friday and Saturday. There are other Sam's at the Biltmore Fashion Park (☎ 602-954-7100) and at 10100 N Scottsdale Rd (☎ 602-368-2800).

Other American Cuisine

One of Mesa's best restaurants, the *Landmark* (☎ 602-962-4652), 809 W Main St in Mesa, has been serving good American food for more than two decades. Built as a Mormon church in the early 1900s, the restaurant is decorated with antiques and photos, and has a huge salad bar. The home-style, traditional American dinner entrées priced in the range of $10 to $18 (including salad bar) draw crowds of knowing locals. It is open daily for lunch and dinner.

You can't help but feel intrigued by a name like that of the *Impeccable Pig* (☎ 602-941-1141), 7042 E Indian School Rd in Scottsdale. Just as interesting as its name, the restaurant is in an antique shop and features a chalkboard menu listing a changing selection of American and continental repasts. Dinner entrées are priced in the upper teens, and you can do some shopping as well. Hours are 11 am to 3 pm Monday to Saturday, and 5 to 10 pm Tuesday to Sunday.

Scottsdale shoppers like to stop at the pink and white *Sugar Bowl Ice Cream Parlor* (☎ 602-946-0051), 4005 N Scottsdale Rd, which serves light meals but specializes in the cold stuff; it is open from 11 am to 11 pm daily.

If you're a jazz fan, *Timothy's* (☎ 602-277-7634), 6335 N 16th St, has American/international food with good live jazz for no additional cover. Dinners include steaks, seafood and international vegetarian plates, mostly in the \$20s but including homemade soup and green salad.

Planet Hollywood (☎ 602-954-7827), 2402 E Camelback (Biltmore Fashion Park), is a fun place for movie buffs. The restaurant looks like a cross between several movie sets and a cinema museum. A standard selection of burgers, pastas, sandwiches, salads and entrées are served from 11 am to midnight daily. If you're into theme dining, there's also the nearby *Hard Rock Café* (☎ 602-956-3669), 2621 E Camelback Rd.

French

If innovation isn't high on your list when eating French food, you'll find *Voltaire* (☎ 602-948-1005), 8340 E McDonald Drive in Scottsdale, perfect for traditional French dishes at more reasonable prices. The atmosphere is elegant, the service is attentive, and most entrées are priced around \$20; it is open for dinner Monday to Saturday but may close more days in summer.

Also good and reasonably priced (by French restaurant standards) is the *Citrus Café* (☎ 602-899-0502), 2330 N Alma School Rd (in Chandler, southeast of Tempe). It's out of the way but has earned high praises from local reviewers. This restaurant is open for dinner from Tuesday to Saturday.

The closest thing to French fast food is *La Madeleine*, serving French pastries, baguette sandwiches and light meals for breakfast, lunch and dinner every day.

Dinner entrées are mostly under \$10. La Madeleine has three locations: 3102 E Camelback Rd (☎ 602-952-0349); 10625 N Tatum Blvd (☎ 602-483-0730); and 7014 E Camelback Rd in Scottsdale Fashion Square (☎ 602-945-1663).

Italian

The valley probably has more noteworthy Italian restaurants than any other 'non-American' cuisine. The following is just a short selection.

For top-notch food in a sophisticated setting, dine at *Avanti*, 2728 E Thomas Rd (☎ 602-956-0900) and 3102 N Scottsdale Rd in Scottsdale (☎ 602-949-8333). Most entrées are in the \$20s, though simple pasta dishes are around \$15. Hours are 5:30 to 11 pm daily and, in Phoenix only, from 11:30 am to 3 pm Monday to Friday.

Christo's (☎ 602-264-1784), 6327 N 7th St, is a contemporary place serving excellent Italian meals in the teens – a good value considering the food quality. Hours are from 11:30 am to 2:30 pm, Monday to Friday, and from 5:30 to 10 pm Monday to Saturday.

Homemade pasta (you can watch it being made in the open kitchen) is the highlight at *Maria's When in Naples* (☎ 602-991-6887), 7000 E Shea Blvd in Scottsdale. Maria's serves pasta dishes in the teens as well as other more expensive entrées. Hours are 11:30 am to 2:30 pm, Monday to Friday, and 5 to 10 pm daily.

Families with small children enjoy the kids' menu and the wide selection of pizza and pasta dishes (many around \$10) at *Tuchetti* (☎ 602-957-0222), 2135 E Camelback Rd close to the Town & Country Mall. The decor is Italy à la Disney, and hours are from 11 am to 10 pm Monday to Thursday, from 11 am to 11 pm on Friday, noon to 11 pm on Saturday and 4:30 to 9 pm on Sunday.

Mexican

El Bravo (☎ 602-943-9753), 8338 N 7th, serves good combination plates for just \$5 and offers a choice of inexpensive à la carte Sonoran dishes as well as Navajo tacos.

ARIZONA

(The piñatas that decorate the dining area are for sale too.) This simple and genuine family restaurant has received great reviews but remains uncrowded because of its noncentral location. It is open Monday to Thursday from 10 am to 8 pm (until 9 pm Friday and Saturday).

A downtown favorite, the large, modern *Matador* (☎ 602-254-7563), 125 E Adams, is open from 7 am to 11 pm, so you can get a Mexican breakfast and a hangover-curing menudo as well as lunch and dinner mainly in the $6 to $9 range. Choices include a few non-Mexican items as well, and lines are often out the door with office workers grabbing breakfast or lunch, but these usually move quickly.

If you want great south-of-the-border food, try *Los Dos Molinos* at 8646 S Central Ave (☎ 602-243-9113) or at 260 S Alma School Rd in Mesa (☎ 602-835-5356). The food is New Mexican influenced, so it's hotter than Sonoran cuisine and delicious if you like chiles. These friendly, family-run restaurants have family members working the stove and tables; ask them to hold the hot sauce if you're not a hot-chile fan. The restaurants are open Tuesday to Saturday from 11 am to 9 pm. The Mesa location doesn't take credit cards, though with most dinners around $7 or $8, you hardly need them.

Mexican dining is normally inexpensive, though an exception is the very fine *La Hacienda* (☎ 602-585-4848) in the upscale Scottsdale Princess Resort. You'll find beautiful surroundings, strolling mariachis and superb food and service – though I have a hard time shelling out $25 for a Mexican entrée, even if it does get a Four Star Mobil rating. La Hacienda opens for dinner daily.

Indian

Most Indian restaurants offer all-you-can-eat lunch buffets for about $5. À-la-carte dinners, while somewhat pricier ($7 to $20), are freshly prepared and are also a good value.

Some locally popular places are *Taste of India* (☎ 602-788-3190), 1609 E Bell Rd;

India Delhi Palace (☎ 602-244-8181), 5050 E McDowell Rd; and three locations of *India Palace*, at 16842 N 7th St (☎ 602-942-4224), 933 E University Drive in Tempe (☎ 602-921-2200), and 4228 N Scottsdale Rd in Scottsdale (☎ 602-970-3300). Also popular in Scottsdale is *A Jewel of the Crown* (☎ 602-840-2412), 4141 N Scottsdale Rd.

Asian

Chinese There are scores of Chinese restaurants. A local favorite is the bustling *Gourmet House of Hong Kong* (☎ 602-253-4859), 1438 E McDowell Rd. The menu is very long and the prices low, the food is very good and the surroundings not particularly noteworthy. It is open daily from 11 am to 10 pm, staying open to 11 pm on Friday and Saturday. If you want more opulent surroundings with your Peking duck, *Mr C's* (☎ 602-941-4460), 4302 N Scottsdale Rd in Scottsdale, will take care of you. The food is classic and slightly pricey Cantonese; many say it's the best in town. Mr C's is open daily from 11 am to 2:30 pm and 5 to 10 pm, staying open to 11 pm on Friday and Saturday.

Out in Chandler is *C-Fu Gourmet* (☎ 602-899-3888), 2051 W Warner Rd. C-Fu? That's Sea Food and it is super fresh – you can see it swimming before it's cooked. A meal here is about $15 to $20 and selections vary from day to day depending on what's floating around; fish, crab, shrimp and other shellfish are available. This restaurant also has a good dim sum selection for lunch.

Thai *Malee's on Main* (☎ 602-947-6042), 7131 E Main in Scottsdale, open from 11:30 am to 2:30 pm and 5 to 9:30 pm daily, is perhaps the best of the many Thai restaurants in the valley. Most entrées are around $12.

Other Restaurants

Bavarian Point (☎ 602-830-0999), 4815 E Main in Mesa's Main St Plaza, is arguably the best and most authentic German restaurant in Arizona. Huge, tasty dinners run from $10 to $20; don't skip the delicious desserts. Hours are 11 am to 10 pm daily.

For Greek food, another 'best in Arizona' is *Greekfest* (☎ 602-265-2990), 1940 E Camelback Rd (it's set back from the road and has a small sign). Both food and ambiance are delightful, and the prices, in the teens for most dinner entrées, are reasonable. It is open for lunch Monday to Saturday from 11 am to 2:30 pm; dinner is from 5 to 10 pm, Monday to Thursday, until 11 pm on Friday and Saturday and until 9 pm on Sunday.

If you like Cuban food as much as I do, visit the *Havana Cafe* (☎ 602-952-1991), 4225 E Camelback Rd. The food is excellent and dinner entrées are priced in the teens. The cafe is open from 11:30 am to 9 pm, till 10 pm on Friday and Saturday and 4 to 9 pm on Sunday, though it may close on summer Sundays.

Eclectic, adventurous, risky, creative, international and transcontinental have all been used to describe fashionable *RoxSand* (☎ 602-381-0444), 2594 E Camelback Rd, in the Biltmore Fashion Park. The changing menu has roamed from Jamaican jerked rabbit to African pheasant to Japanese scallops (these entrées are in the $20s) as well as some cheaper and less adventurous options (such as a $10 pizza). This is a good place to eat a complete meal or just drop in for a super dessert. They are open daily for lunch and dinner.

ENTERTAINMENT

For what's going on, read the free alternative weekly *New Times*, published every Thursday and available at numerous boxes and other outlets around the city. On the same day, the Arizona Republic's *The Rep* and *Get Out* also have exhaustive entertainment listings, with an emphasis on popular music and nightlife.

Cinemas

There are dozens of cinema multiplexes throughout the valley showing the year's best and worst movies, including the huge new *AMC 24* (☎ 602-956-4262) in the Arizona Center with arm rests that fold up so you can cuddle with your date and steep seating so you don't have to peer through people's heads at the screen. There are some alternatives, including the *Valley Art Theater* (☎ 602-829-6666 or 6668), 509 S Mill Ave in Tempe, with regular Saturday midnight showings of *The Rocky Horror Picture Show* and a variety of foreign and alternatives flicks throughout the week. There is also the *IMAX Theater* (☎ 602-945-4629) in Scottsdale, one block east of Scottsdale Rd on Civic Center Blvd, showing documentary-type movies designed for the eight-times-larger-than-normal screen.

Nightlife

Many of the following spots are very busy on Friday and Saturday nights, but usually provide entertainment five to seven nights a week at varying cover charges. For more ideas, see Coffeehouses under Places to Eat, above.

The entertainment scene in Tempe, home of ASU, is aimed at students. Mill Ave between 3rd and 7th Sts is the off-campus nightlife center with several bars and clubs. There are plenty of cops hanging around at closing time, and their attitude is generally friendly. Places come and go, but some established places include *Gibsons* (☎ 602-829-7047, 602-967-1234), 410 S Mill Ave, a popular joint where decent live rock bands play, and the *Balboa Jazz Cafe* (☎ 602-966-1300), 404 S Mill Ave, with good live jazz as well as rock bands.

In downtown Phoenix, the Arizona Center provides a number of options aimed at the younger post-work crowd. If you can't make up your mind, *Phoenix Live!* (☎ 602-252-2502) allows you to circulate between various options. *Little Ditty's* has two pianos going full tilt and everyone singing along to old favorites. Can't remember the words? No worries. People hold up song boards with the 'lyrics' in huge letters, so everyone has fun. Next door, *Players Sports Bar & Grill* has sports TV and dozens of coin-operated machines ranging from basketball to foosball. Beyond that is *Decades*, a DJ-driven nightclub

ARIZONA

playing mainly techno and alternative rock for dancing. To make a night of it, there are several places to eat nearby.

Go west for the best in country & western. *Mr Lucky's* (☎ 602-246-0686), 3660 NW Grand Ave, has live country & western and dancing, and a corral outside with bull-riding competitions on weekends (with real bulls, not the mechanical kind; there's a $5 cover). Almost every patron is dressed in Western wear (I think I was the only man there without a cowboy hat). It's a short ride to *Toolies Country* (☎ 602-272-3100), 4231 W Thomas Rd, booking some of the best country & western bands in the valley. More upscale country & western places are found in some of the resorts, including *Rustlers Rooste* (☎ 602-431-6474) at the Pointe Hilton on South Mountain and the *Red River Music Hall* (☎ 602-829-6779) at Mill Ave and Washington in Tempe, hosting various country performances, musical reviews and big-name acts in a theater setting.

Jazz lovers can listen to KJZZ FM (91.5) on the radio or call the jazz hotline (☎ 602-254-4545) for a schedule of top performances. Also see Timothy's and The Orbit Restaurant and Jazz Bar under Places to Eat, above.

For good blues, stop by the popular and crowded *Char's Has the Blues* (☎ 602-230-0205), 4631 N 7th Ave, with some excellent acts most nights. *Warsaw Wallies* (☎ 602-955-0881), 2547 E Indian School Rd, is a small place but often has exceptional blues bands with low or no cover. Watch for the local band *The Rocket 88s* with an outstanding harpist. Good blues is also the staple of the *Rhythm Room* (☎ 602-265-4842), 1019 E Indian School Rd. *Coyote Springs Brewing Company & Cafe* (☎ 602-468-0403), 4883 N 20th St (at the Town & Country Mall), is a microbrewery serving good handcrafted beers and hosting fine local R&B bands on weekends. For a variety of alternative rock, the *Mason Jar* (☎ 602-956-6271), 2303 E Indian School Rd, is a good choice, with three to five bands attracting a young crowd of people dressed in black nightly.

Performing Arts

The following are the most highly acclaimed places to hear and see performing arts, but not much goes on here during the summer. For sold-out events, the ticket companies listed under Spectator Sports (below) can often help.

The *Herberger Theater Center* (☎ 602-252-8497), 222 E Monroe, has two stages that host productions put together by the Arizona Theater Company (☎ 602-256-6995), Ballet Arizona (☎ 602-381-0184), the Actors Theater of Phoenix (☎ 602-253-6701) and occasionally others.

The *Helen K Mason Center for the Performing Arts* (☎ 602-258-8128), 333 E Portland, is the home of the Black Theater Troupe and also hosts other African-American performers.

Symphony Hall (☎ 602-262-7272), 225 E Adams, is the home of the Arizona Opera (☎ 602-266-7464) and the Phoenix Symphony Orchestra (☎ 602-495-1999, 800-776-9080).

The *Gammage Auditorium* (☎ 602-965-3434), on the ASU Campus at Mill Ave and Apache Blvd, is the university's main center for performing arts.

The *Blockbuster Desert Sky Pavilion* (☎ 602-254-7200), north of I-10 exit 135 at 83rd Ave, is a huge outdoor amphitheater hosting big-name rock bands.

SPECTATOR SPORTS

Phoenix has some of the nation's top professional teams, but getting tickets for the best games is not always easy, as they sell out early. Call as far in advance as possible or, if nothing is available, look in the yellow pages under Ticket Sales or in newspaper classifieds for tickets (they're often overpriced). Also try the Ticket Company (☎ 602-279-4444, 800-279-4444, fax 602-266-2727), Ticket Connection (☎ 602-263-1111, fax 602-277-8282, tickets@4ticket.com) or Western States Ticket Service (☎ 602-254-3300, fax 602-254-3387, info@wstickets.com).

The NBA's Phoenix Suns (☎ 602-379-7867) play national championship-level basketball at the new America West Arena

(☎ 602-379-7800), 201 E Jefferson, from December to April. The new (women's) WNBA's Phoenix Mercury also play here. From May through August, the arena is home of the Arizona Rattlers (☎ 602-514-8383) arena football team, who were the 1994 world champions. The NHL's Phoenix Coyotes (☎ 602-379-2800) play ice hockey here from December to March. The West Coast Hockey League's Phoenix Mustangs (☎ 602-340-0001) play ice hockey at the Arizona Veterans Memorial Coliseum, in the State Fairgrounds at 1826 W McDowell Rd.

The NFL's Arizona Cardinals (☎ 602-379-0102) play professional football (fall to spring) at ASU Sun Devil Stadium in Tempe, the site of the 1996 Super Bowl, the nation's most prestigious football game. ASU student teams (such as the Sun Devils, ☎ 602-965-2381) also use the stadium.

The new Arizona Diamondbacks major-league baseball team played their first season in 1998 in the newly constructed Bank One Ballpark (☎ 602-462-6500), southwest of E Jefferson and S 7th Sts.

Professional players of golf compete for a seven-figure purse at the PGA Phoenix Open, held every January at the Tournament Players Club (☎ 602-585-3600, 602-585-4334, ext 237 for tee times), 17020 N Hayden Rd in Scottsdale.

You can watch horseracing at Turf Paradise (☎ 602-942-1101), 19th Ave and Bell, from October to May, and see greyhounds race year-round at Phoenix Greyhound Park (☎ 602-273-7181), 3801 E Washington. NASCAR car racing takes place at Phoenix International Raceway (☎ 602-252-2227 for tickets), 7602 S 115th Ave at Baseline Rd, Avondale. Drag racing is presented at Firebird International Raceway (☎ 602-268-0200), I-10 exit 162, Chandler.

SHOPPING

The question is not so much what to buy (you can buy just about anything) but where to go: The valley has several notable shopping malls. Scottsdale is the art gallery capital of Arizona. The Heard Museum has the best bookshop about Native Americans and the most reliable, excellent and expensive selection of Native American arts and crafts.

You may not be a fan of shopping malls, but the air conditioning does give them a certain allure when the mercury climbs in the summer. Shopping malls include the Metrocenter at I-17 exit 208 and Peoria Ave, the largest enclosed mall in Arizona, which has four department stores, standard shopping and many attractions for kids. The Park Central Mall, at Central Ave and Osborn Rd, is the city's oldest (but still reasonably fashionable) shopping center.

For more upscale shopping, visit the Scottsdale Fashion Square at Camelback and Scottsdale Rds in Scottsdale, or the more exclusive Biltmore Fashion Park at Camelback Rd and 24th St in Phoenix. Both provide a good selection of cheap to expensive restaurants, and the Biltmore is home to some of the valley's best eateries. Near the Biltmore, the Town & Country shopping center also has several decent restaurants.

Perhaps the fanciest selection of boutiques and galleries is at the Borgata, 6166 N Scottsdale Rd in Scottsdale, a mall designed to look like a medieval town. Also very trendy are the Fifth Avenue Shops east of Scottsdale Rd, where you'll find many galleries, boutiques and tourist-oriented shops. The block of Main west of Scottsdale Rd has about 20 galleries of all kinds and of a generally high quality. Look for the life-size metal horseman outside the Legacy Gallery at the corner – it's like a museum of bronze masterpieces with many items priced in the five figures. Many galleries are open from 7 to 9 pm on Thursday evening 'Art Walks.'

The outdoor Arizona Center is revitalizing downtown at 3rd St and Van Buren, with several popular bars, restaurants and a small selection of interesting shops.

If you need camping or outdoor gear, REI (☎ 602-967-5494), 1405 W Southern Ave in Tempe, has one of the largest selections in the Southwest and does mail order as well.

GETTING THERE & AWAY
Bus
Greyhound has a main terminal (☎ 602-389-4200) at 2115 E Buckeye and suburban bus stations in Tempe (☎ 602-967-4030), 502 S College Ave; in Mesa (☎ 602-834-3360), 1423 S Country Club Drive; and at Glendale, Chandler, Tolleson, Youngtown and Apache Junction. Phoenix is at the center of a fairly extensive bus network throughout and beyond the state. White Mountain Passenger Lines (☎ 602-275-4245), 319 S 24th St, has a 1 pm bus to Payson and Show Low, and the Arizona Shuttle Service (☎ 800-888-2749) has many vans a day linking Phoenix Airport with Tucson. Other local bus companies linking Phoenix Airport with Arizona towns beyond the valley are listed under Getting There & Away in those towns.

Train
Amtrak trains stop at the Union Station (☎ 602-253-0121), 401 W Harrison, on the south side of downtown Phoenix. Three night trains a week go to Yuma and Los Angeles, California, and three morning trains a week go to Tucson, east through New Mexico and on to Miami, Florida. Amtrak provides a daily bus connection to Flagstaff.

GETTING AROUND
To/From the Airport
Phoenix's Sky Harbor International Airport (☎ 602-273-3300 for the main switchboard; 602-392-0126 or 602-392-0310 for airport information) is 3 miles southeast of downtown. By far the largest airport in the Southwest, its three terminals (illogically called Terminal 2, 3 and 4) contain all the standard features of any major airport. There are economy long-term parking lots ($4 a day) within a short walk of the terminals and pricier short-term lots next to the terminals.

Valley Metro has two bus lines serving the airport. The Red Line operates every 15 to 30 minutes Monday to Friday from 4 am to 9:45 pm, driving to Tempe and Mesa along Apache Blvd and Main, or west into

downtown and then into north Phoenix. During weekends, buses run every 45 minutes from about 5 am to 9:20 pm. Bus No 13 operates every 30 to 60 minutes from 5:15 am to 8:30 pm from Monday to Friday and until 7:45 pm on Saturday, taking a westerly route along Buckeye Rd. Fares are $1 and transfers are available.

Several companies have vans providing airport-to-your-door service at any time. Fares are somewhat lower than taxis, which add a $1 airport surcharge in addition to their metered rates. Call ☎ 602-273-3307 for ground transportation at the airport.

Bus
Valley Metro (☎ 602-253-5000, 5 am to 8 pm Monday to Friday, 6 am to 7 pm on weekends) operates buses all over the valley from Monday to Friday and on a limited basis on Saturday. Some routes are limited-stop Express Services and most routes stop operating in the early evening. Fares are $1.25 (including one transfer) or $3.60 for an all-day pass. The latter can be bought at only a few locations such as the Main Downtown Bus Terminal at Central Ave and Van Buren; call Valley Metro for locations near you. A few Express Services cost $1.75. People over 65 or between six and 18 years old with a picture ID ride for half fare. Exact fare is required. As of May 1995, Valley Metro was the first city in the country to allow riders to pay with a credit card (Visa or MasterCard only).

Valley Metro also runs DASH buses from downtown out to the State Capitol, leaving every six to 12 minutes from 6:30 am to 6 pm, Monday to Friday. The flat fare for this route only is 30¢, and frequent downtown riders and groups can buy 250 DASH tokens for just $30 (☎ 602-495-5795). Valley Metro's FLASH buses offer free rides every 10 or 15 minutes around the ASU area and from there to the zoo and botanical gardens.

Car
All the main care-rental companies (Avis, Hertz, Enterprise etc) have airport offices

and many have offices in other parts of the valley or will deliver your car. Reserve a car in advance for the best rates.

Taxi

There are several 24-hour cab services, but with a $2 drop fee and fares of well over $1 per mile, you can rack up a pricey ride fairly rapidly in the large valley area. Renting a car is better for most longer rides. Some of the main cab companies are Ace Taxi (☎ 602-254-1999), AAA Cab (☎ 602-437-4000), Checker Cab (☎ 602-257-1818) and Yellow Cab (☎ 602-252-5252).

Bicycle

The following are a few of several bike rental shops: the Adventure Bicycle Co (☎ 602-649-3374), 1110 W Southern Ave in Mesa; Airpark Bicycle Center (☎ 602-596-6633), 15001 N Hayden Rd, and Wheels 'n Gear (☎ 602-945-2881), 7607 E McDowell Rd, both in Scottsdale; and Tempe Bicycles (☎ 602-966-6896), 330 W University Drive in Tempe.

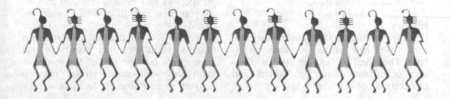

Grand Canyon & Lake Powell

The slogan on the Arizona license plate says it all: 'Grand Canyon State.' The Grand Canyon of the Colorado River is Arizona's most famous sight – indeed, it is arguably the best known natural attraction in the entire country. This grandest of all canyons has been declared a UN World Heritage Site to be protected for all people.

At 277 miles long, roughly 10 miles wide and a mile deep, the canyon sounds big. But its sheer size is not all that makes the sight so tremendous. The incredible spectacle of differently colored rock strata, the many buttes and peaks within the canyon itself, and the meandering rims give access to fantastic views that amaze the visitor. Staring from the many rim overlooks gives you a great impression of the grandeur, but walking down into the canyon on a short hike or a multi-day backpacking trip gives you a better sense of the variety in the landscape, wildlife and climate.

Although the rims are only 10 miles apart, as the crow flies, it is a 215-mile, five-hour drive on narrow roads from the visitor center on the South Rim to the visitor center on the North Rim. Thus the Grand Canyon National Park is essentially two separate areas that are treated separately in this chapter. I begin by describing the South Rim and continue with the areas south of the park. Then comes the remote and less-visited area to the north of the park, known as the Arizona Strip, which contains the North Rim of Grand Canyon National Park. Finally comes Page and the Glen Canyon Dam area, which is on the Colorado River just outside the northeastern corner of the park.

History

Scattered throughout the Grand Canyon are signs of ancient Native American inhabitants. The oldest artifacts are little twig figures of animals made by hunters and gatherers about 4000 years ago – a few of these can be seen in the Tusayan Museum, east of the Grand Canyon Village. More common are the hundreds of stone buildings left by Native Americans before their unexplained departure during the 12th century.

Cerbat people began living at the western end of the canyon around 1300 AD and were the ancestors of the present-day Hualapai and Havasupai tribes. Despite various attempts by Europeans to dislodge them, these two tribes continue to live in (what are now) reservations on the southwestern rim of the canyon. These reservations (described further in this chapter) abut the Grand Canyon National Park but can't be entered from the park.

The canyon's earliest European visitors were Spaniards who gazed into the depths in 1540. The canyon was difficult to reach and involved crossing large areas with little water. Because there didn't appear to be any mineral wealth and the area was generally considered magnificent but valueless, European visits were infrequent for over three centuries.

The first serious exploration was in 1869, when John Wesley Powell, a one-armed veteran of the Civil War, led an expedition along the Colorado River. Using simple wooden boats, they ran the entire length of the Grand and other canyons – a remarkable achievement. Powell led a similar expedition in 1871-72, which resulted in detailed scientific observations and his book, *The Exploration of the Colorado River of the West and Its Tributaries.*

During the late 1800s, Mormons began settling the remote Arizona Strip, and prospectors and miners ventured into the canyon in search of mineral wealth but found little. One miner, John Hance, arrived in 1883 and decided that catering to tourists would be more profitable than mining. He became one of the most colorful and well-known guides into the canyon, famous for his tall tales. Some

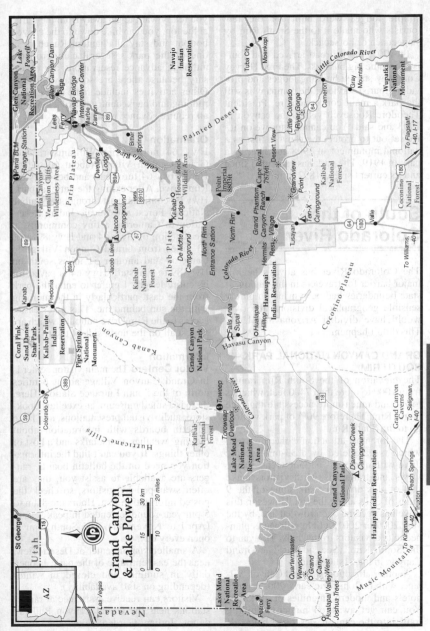

Grand Canyon
& Lake Powell

simple lodges were built for the few tourists who made it to the South Rim by stagecoach or horseback.

In 1901, the railroad arrived and tourism became big business. The Fred Harvey Company started building lodges and providing tourist services; the company is still the park's main concessionaire. President Theodore Roosevelt visited the canyon in 1903 and said 'You cannot improve on it.' He set out to protect the canyon, first as a national monument in 1908 and later as a park in 1919. The park has expanded since and its current size is 1892 sq miles.

South of the Colorado River

The Colorado River has always been a major barrier for travelers in this region. If state boundaries had been made on purely sensible geographical divisions, the river would have divided Arizona and Utah. This didn't happen.

GRAND CANYON NATIONAL PARK – SOUTH RIM

The elevation of the South Rim ranges from 7000 to more than 7400 feet, which is lower and much more accessible than the North Rim. Therefore 90% of park visitors go to the South Rim.

The foremost attraction is the rim itself, which is paralleled by a 33-mile scenic drive with numerous parking areas, scenic views and trailheads. Most visitors make part of this drive or walk some of the 9 miles of trails along the rim. However, this drive has become overcrowded and, by the year 2000 or 2001, a light railroad is planned to take visitors from nearby Tusayan to the South Rim. (See sidebar The Grand Canyon in the 21st Century.)

Another attraction is Grand Canyon Village, with both historic early-20th-century hotels and modern amenities of all kinds. You can get away on numerous hiking trails into the canyon, described below. If you really want to get away from the traffic at the top, you can hike down to the canyon bottom and stay at Phantom Ranch or at one of the park's several campgrounds, although advance reservations are necessary because there are so many visitors. Other activities include mule rides, river running and backcountry backpacking, but all require advance planning.

Orientation

Hwy 64 north from Williams reaches Grand Canyon Village (about 60 miles). Here, Hwy 64 turns east and becomes the Rim Drive. After exiting the national park, Hwy 64 continues east through the Kaibab National Forest and Navajo Indian Reservation to Cameron, a tiny community at the junction of Hwy 64 and Hwy 89. It is 53 miles from Grand Canyon Village to Cameron and another 51 miles south on Hwy 89 to Flagstaff. Hwy 64 is paved for its entire length. I prefer to enter the park from the east, particularly in the morning with the sun behind me. This gives easier access to the Rim Drive pullouts, which are almost all on the north side of the road.

Information

Visitor Centers The main visitor center is in Grand Canyon Village about 6 miles north of the South Entrance Station. Here, there is a small museum, an excellent bookstore, audio-visual presentations, and large bulletin boards with information about lodging, weather, tours, talks and a host of other things. If you can't find the information you need on the bulletin boards, rangers are available to assist you; they are often swamped by visitors, so check the posted information first. Hours are 8 am to 5 pm year-round, extended in peak season (April to November). The South Rim is open every day.

A smaller visitor center at Desert View, near the east entrance of the park, is open daily in summer and closed in winter (depending on staff availability).

Visitors can receive assistance at ranger stations near the Grand Canyon Railway depot, Indian Garden below the South

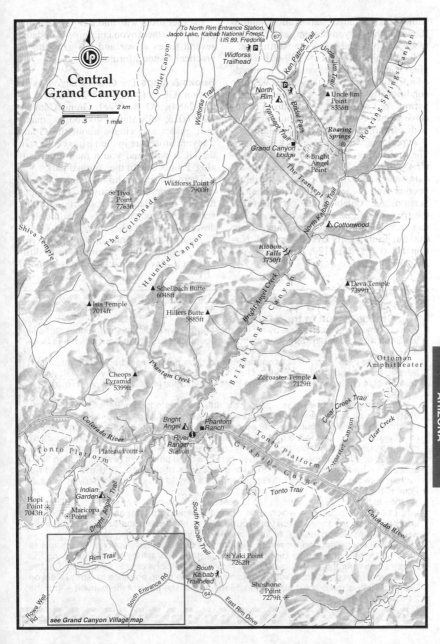

Central Grand Canyon

0   1   2 km

0   .5   1 mile

see Grand Canyon Village map

ARIZONA

Rim, the River ranger station and Phantom Ranch at the canyon bottom, and Cottonwood Campground below the North Rim.

Telephoning the park (☎ 520-638-7888) gives you an automated system with recorded information on everything from weather conditions to applying for a river-running permit. You can leave your address to receive written information or you can speak with a live ranger during business hours.

A park map and a seasonal newspaper, *The Guide*, are available at no charge to all visitors. *The Guide* is the best up-to-date source of park information available upon arrival. French, German and Spanish versions are available. Also very useful is the free *Grand Canyon Trip Planner*. You can receive information in advance from the Superintendent, Grand Canyon National Park, PO Box 129, Grand Canyon, AZ 86023.

Internet users will find the park's home page, www.thecanyon.com/nps, is updated several times a year and has a wealth of practical visitor information.

Books & Maps The Grand Canyon Association (GCA) (☎ 520-638-2481, fax 520-638-2484), PO Box 399, Grand Canyon, AZ 86023, sells almost 400 books, maps, trail guides and videos about the Grand Canyon. Stores are in the visitor centers, or the GCA will send you a mail-order catalog. Profits benefit the national park.

There are several hiking guides specifically for the Grand Canyon. The guides usually give plenty of background about geology and other matters in addition to describing the trails. *Hiking the Grand Canyon* by John Annerino gives descriptions ranging from easy rim hikes to difficult multi-day backpacking trails. *Official*

The Grand Canyon in the 21st Century

Grand Canyon National Park is by far the most heavily visited of all the national parks in the Southwest. For years, annual visitation has been close to five million, which has influenced and strained many aspects of the park.

During the busy summer season, hotels and campgrounds are booked up months in advance and parking lots are often filled to capacity. Drivers may have to wait just to park. People come for terrific views and instead get traffic jams. Clearly, overcrowding is a major concern.

Various solutions have been proposed and considered. The Park Service wants everyone to be able to enjoy the canyon (this is why the national park was created), so limiting the number of visitors is not an option. Instead, a plan is being implemented to limit the number of cars in the park. In November 1997, the government approved a $67 million program that will change the way most people visit the Grand Canyon. By the year 2000 or 2001, visitors will leave their cars in a huge parking lot (with more than 3000 spaces) in Tusayan, just outside the south entrance of the park, and use a light-rail system capable of carrying 47,000 passengers a day to the rim of the canyon. Mather Point is the proposed rail terminal point.

Once at the rim, visitors will be able to continue by foot, bicycle or shuttle bus. The current free shuttle-bus route, which runs along the West Rim from about March through October, will be expanded to run year-round and perhaps along some of the East Rim as well. If you are visiting in 2000 or later, check locally for what's going on.

Cars will not be banned, however. Visitors with overnight reservations will be able to drive up to their motel room or campground. Drivers will still be able to enter via the longer route from the east, though there may be restrictions on this eventually. But the busiest route, the short drive from Tusayan through the south entrance to Grand Canyon Village, will become a short railway trip all the way to the edge of the canyon – and the 21st century. ■

Guide to Hiking the Grand Canyon by Scott Thybony covers the major routes and gives information about permits and regulations. If you are less interested in the easy rim trails, try *A Guide to Hiking the Inner Canyon* by Scott Thybony. For hiking in the remotest areas of the north part of the park, there are *Grand Canyon Loop Hikes I & II* by George Steck. *Grand Canyon Geology Along Bright Angel Trail* by Dave Thayer will guide you through the geological features of that part of the canyon.

Fees & Permits Entrance to the park is $20 per private vehicle or $10 for bicyclists and pedestrians. The entrance ticket is valid for seven days and can be used at any entrance point, including the North Rim. Golden Access, Age and Eagle Passes are honored. Bus and train passengers either pay a lesser fee or may have the fee included in the tour. Note that this fee schedule may change when the train shuttle to the rim is implemented.

For backcountry camping, permits are required from the Backcountry Office (see Hiking & Backpacking, below).

Pets Pets are allowed (when leashed) on developed sections of the rim but nowhere below the rim (except guide/service dogs). Kennels are available, but leaving pets at home is encouraged.

Visitor Services Grand Canyon Village has most visitor services. However, prices here are substantially higher and lines longer than in Flagstaff, so think ahead.

Services available include hotels, restaurants, campgrounds, coin-operated laundry and showers, gift shops, pet kennels, churches and transportation services. Car towing and mechanics (☎ 520-638-2631) are available from 8 am to 5 pm and for 24-hour emergency service. A gas station is open daily; hours vary from 6 am to 9:30 pm in summer and 8 am to 6 pm in midwinter. A medical clinic (☎ 520-638-2551, 520-638-2469) is open 8 am to 5:30 pm, Monday to Friday, and 9 am to

noon on Saturday. The clinic's pharmacy (☎ 520-638-2460) is open 8:30 am to 5:30 pm, Monday to Friday, and till noon on Saturday.

Mather Shopping Center contains the following. A bank (☎ 520-638-2437) with foreign exchange is open 10 am to 3 pm, Monday to Friday, and 4 to 6 pm on Friday. A 24-hour ATM accepts American Express, Bank One, Plus, Star, Master Teller and Arizona Interchange Network cards. A post office (☎ 520-638-2512) is open 9 am to 4:30 pm, Monday to Friday, and 11 am to 1 pm on Saturday. Stamp machines in the lobby are accessible from 5 am to 10 pm daily.

Babbitt's General Store (☎ 520-638-2262) sells food, clothing and camping supplies (rentals are possible) from 8 am to 7 pm daily (closed New Year's Day, Thanksgiving and Christmas).

Recycling bins are found where there are trash containers. Visitors are urged to place recyclables in the designated bins.

Near the east entrance, the Desert View Service Center has a visitor center, general store, gas station (closed in winter), campground (closed in winter), cafeteria and the Watchtower, which is the highest point on the South Rim.

Water Woes

It's easy to forget that much of the Grand Canyon is essentially a desert. Visitors require water for drinking, cooking and washing, but the only available water must be piped in from a spring on the north wall of the canyon. A quick look over the rim will convince you that this was not the easiest pipe-laying project! Try to conserve water by taking short showers and not letting water run unnecessarily. When a storm broke the pipe in 1995, all water had to be trucked in. It's always a good idea to carry a few gallons of water in your car – you never know when you might need it in the Southwest. ■

ARIZONA

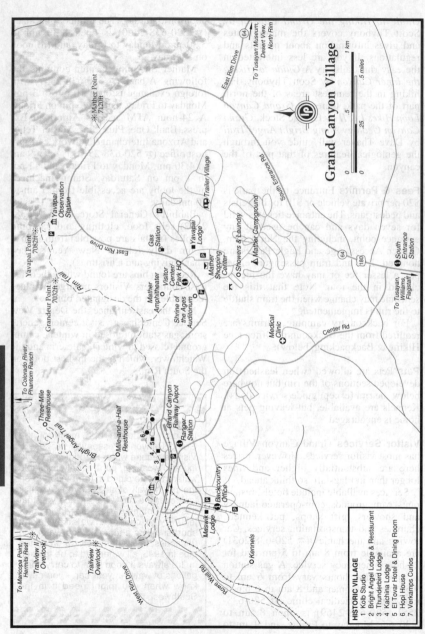

Grand Canyon Village

HISTORIC VILLAGE
1 Kolb Studio
2 Bright Angel Lodge & Restaurant
3 Thunderbird Lodge
4 Kachina Lodge
5 El Tovar Hotel & Dining Room
6 Hopi House
7 Verkamps Curios

Storm Watch

Weather-related problems can occur anytime in the Southwest, so seek local updates when traveling anywhere in the area. For example, severe storms in 1995 washed away parts of hiking trails and broke the main water supply to the Grand Canyon National Park, resulting in the closure of the park's most popular rim-to-rim trail (Bright Angel and North Kaibab) and cancellation of backpacking permits for five weeks. Toilet and washing facilities in park hotels, campgrounds and restaurants were severely disrupted, resulting in some temporary closures. ■

Climate & When to Go On average, temperatures are 20°F cooler on the South Rim than the bottom of the Grand Canyon. This means you could wake up on the rim to frost on the ground in April and be basking in the 80°s F by afternoon if you hike down into the inner gorge. The peak season ranges from about April to November, and the park is busiest from Memorial Day to Labor Day.

At the South Rim in summer, expect highs in the 80°s F and lows around 50°F. June is the driest month, but summer thunderstorms make July and August the wettest months. Weather is cooler and changeable in the fall, and snow and freezing overnight temperatures are likely by November. January has average overnight lows in the teens and daytime highs around 40°F. Winter weather can be beautifully clear, but be prepared for occasional storms that can cause havoc. (See the Storm Watch sidebar.)

The inner canyon is much drier with about eight inches of rain annually, about half that of the South Rim. Summer temperatures inside the canyon go above 100°F almost every day and often exceed 110°F in midsummer, which can be potentially lethal for unprepared hikers. Strong hot winds often blow in summer. Even in midwinter, freezing overnight temperatures

are rare, with average lows in the upper 30°s F and highs in the upper 50°s F.

Although the South Rim is open all year, the majority of visitors come in the peak season described above. Avoid that time if possible – it is very crowded indeed.

Dangers & Annoyances Each year, a few people fall to their deaths in the Grand Canyon. When visiting the rim of the canyon, stay inside guardrails and on trails. When hiking below the rim, use hiking shoes or boots rather than tennis shoes or sandals. Only a few trails below the rim are maintained; use extra caution when hiking on unmaintained trails.

Some 250 hikers a year on the most popular below-the-rim trails require ranger assistance to get out safely. The main problems are too much sun and too little water. Wear a hat and sunblock, and carry at least a gallon of water per person per day in summer. Hikers can (and do) run out of water and die. Even if it turns out you don't need it, carrying extra water may save someone else's life. Before attempting long hikes, speak with backcountry rangers about where you can replenish your water bottles. (See Hiking & Backpacking, below, and the Water Woes sidebar, above.)

Feeding wildlife is detrimental to the animals and illegal. It is also dangerous – observe them from a distance. Every year visitors are bitten, gored or otherwise injured by wild animals. Animals that are fed by visitors become used to human food and seek it out. Frequently, rangers have the sad task of shooting deer to spare them the pain of starving to death: their stomachs are so clogged with several pounds of indigestible food wrappers and plastic bags, they cannot feed anymore.

Other annoyances come from outside the park. Air pollution has seriously reduced visibility in the canyon in recent years. Smog from as far west as Los Angeles and sulfur emissions from the Navajo Generating Station near Glen Canyon Dam in the east are blown in. Sometimes, the far rim of the canyon is just a distant blur. Visitors find that winter usually offers the clearest visibility.

ARIZONA

The flow and characteristics of the Colorado River have changed and continue to change because of the Glen Canyon Dam. Half the species of fish in the river before the dam was built are now extinct. Anglers and river runners have had to adapt to these problems.

Hikers descending into the canyon to get away from the crowded rims have to listen to aircraft noise from the many tourist flights over the national park.

These annoyances are being recognized and corrected to some extent, but the political ramifications are very complex. The park periodically publishes a broadsheet, *The Canyon Constituent*, which provides some information about these problems and what is being done to solve them. Free copies are available from the visitor center or by writing to the park. This publication gives details of public meetings and addresses of agencies to whom concerned visitors can send their comments.

With so many visitors, crime is also a growing problem. Lock cars and hotel rooms. Do not leave valuable objects such as cameras in view inside your car.

Museums & Historical Buildings

In addition to the exhibits at the visitor centers, check out the following.

Yavapai Observation Station At Yavapai Point, at the northeast end of Grand Canyon Village, this station has a geology museum and spectacular views all the way down to Phantom Ranch at the canyon bottom. There is a bookstore and ranger-led activities. Winter hours are 8 am to 5 pm, extended to 6, 7 or 8 pm in other seasons.

Kolb Studio In Grand Canyon Village, this was a photography studio opened in 1904 and run by Emery Kolb until his death in 1976. Throughout the year, a variety of changing exhibits display photographs or other items related to the canyon. Hours are the same as the Yavapai museum's, and there is a bookstore. Several other nearby historic buildings date from the same period, including the El

Tovar Hotel and the gift shops of Hopi House and Verkamps Curios.

Tusayan Museum Located off of East Rim Drive, 23 miles east of Grand Canyon Village, this museum has exhibits and talks about Ancestral Puebloan life. This is where ancient twig figures of animals can be seen. You can visit the small Tusayan Ruin nearby; guided walks are offered several times a day in summer and less frequently in the off-peak season. Hours are 9 am to 5 pm in summer, with shorter winter hours. Admission is free.

Watchtower At Desert View near the east entrance, you can climb the stairs of the Watchtower (☎ 520-638-2736), built in 1932 and the highest point on the South Rim. Inside, the walls are decorated with reproductions of ancient petroglyphs as well as contemporary Native American artwork. There is a 25¢ admission to the tower and coin-operated telescopes are available. Hours are 8 am to 7:30 pm in summer, 9 am to 4:30 pm in winter.

Ranger-Led Activities

Call the park's information service (☎ 520-638-7888) or ask at a visitor center about free ranger-led activities. These occur year-round, though with much greater frequency in summer. Programs include various talks (including slide shows) and walks (some wheelchair accessible) throughout the day and into the evening. Guided walks range from a few hundred flat yards (40 minutes) to 3 miles below the rim (three to four hours). During the summer there are Junior Ranger activities for four- to 12-year-olds. This gives you an idea – there is plenty going on.

Volunteers can join the **Habitat Restoration Team**. Projects include planting native plants or removing exotic ones (sounds like weeding to me!), helping restore historic miners' cabins, collecting litter or doing maintenance work. A regular two-hour plant removal and restoration effort occurs at 8:30 am several mornings a week (depending on season) and families are encouraged to help and learn (minimum age is five). Information about this project and longer volunteer projects is available at the main visitor center.

The **Grand Canyon Field Institute** (☎ 520-638-2485, fax 520-638-2484), PO Box 399, Grand Canyon, AZ 86023, is the educational arm of the GCA (see Books & Maps, above). It offers in-depth classes of one to eight days from mid-March to mid-November. Some topics include geology, biology, ecology, Native Americans and photography. Classes are held both in classrooms and in the field, including hiking and multi-night backpacking trips. Contact the Field Institute for a course catalog.

Rim Trail

The paved Rim Trail is accessible to wheelchairs and extends for over 3 miles along the rim from **Yavapai Point** to **Maricopa Point**. It extends unpaved almost 7 miles farther west past several viewpoints to Hermits Rest (see the next section). The Rim Trail is the park's most popular walk and visitors can hike as far as they are comfortable. The rewards are beautiful views with many interpretive signs. Only foot and wheelchair traffic are allowed – no bicycles. During winter, snow or ice may temporarily cover the trail.

West Rim Drive

I don't single out any of the many stopping points on the Rim Drives because they are all spectacular and worth a stop.

The West Rim is accessible by road for 8 miles west of Grand Canyon Village (and by the Rim Trail described above). At the end of the drive and trail is **Hermits Rest** where there is a snack bar and the Hermit Trailhead down into the canyon; if you don't descend, you have to return the way you came.

Year-round you can hike the western Rim Trail or cycle along the road. From about mid-March to mid-October, cars are not allowed along the drive to Hermits Rest, but free shuttle buses operate every 15 minutes (see Getting Around, later in the chapter). In winter months you can

make this drive in your own car, although new shuttle-bus services planned for the 21st century may change this. Narrated bus tours are also available (see Organized Tours, below).

East Rim Drive

The East Rim is longer and a little less crowded than the West Rim but offers equally spectacular views. At this time, there are no free shuttle buses or walking trails, but you can drive, bike or take a narrated bus tour. The planned shuttle-bus service may provide access to the East Rim as well as the West Rim.

Tusayan, the most accessible of the park's approximately 2000 Ancestral Puebloan ruins, is along this road. The East Rim Drive ends at **Desert View**, about 25 miles east of Grand Canyon Village and the highest point on the South Rim. The road then leaves the national park through the Navajo Indian Reservation to Cameron. There are a couple of viewpoints into the smaller Little Colorado River canyon along the way. The Grand Canyon itself turns north at Desert View.

Hiking & Backpacking

For backpacking, the Backcountry Office (☎ 520-638-7875 from 1 to 5 pm Monday to Friday), PO Box 129, Grand Canyon, AZ 86023, has all relevant information. The office in the Maswik Transportation Center is open from 8 am to noon and 1 to 5 pm daily. Also see Books & Maps (above) for suggested reading.

The easiest walks are along the Rim Trail, described above. Hikes below the rim into the canyon are strenuous and some visitors prefer to use mules (see Organized Tours, below). Hikers meeting a mule train should stand quietly on the upper side of the trail until the animals have passed. Mule riders have the right of way.

Two important things to bear in mind when attempting any hike into the canyon: First, it's easy to stride down the trail for a few hours, but the steep uphill return during the heat of the day when you are tired is much more demanding. Allow two

ARIZONA

hours to return uphill for every hour of hiking downhill. Second, the temperatures inside the gorge are much hotter than at the rim and water is scarcely available. Carry plenty of water and protection from the sun. In summer, temperatures can exceed 110°F in the inner gorge.

The two most popular below-the-rim trails are the Bright Angel Trail and the South Kaibab Trail. These are the best-maintained trails and are both used by mule riders. Both are suitable for either day hikes or, with a permit and advance reservation, overnight backpacking trips. No permit is necessary for a day trip. Both trails are steep and strenuous. Nevertheless, they are considered the easiest rim-to-river trails in the canyon and even a short descent along part of these trails will completely alter your perspective – I recommend either or both. Day hikers should not expect to reach the river and return in one day.

Bright Angel Trail The trail leaves from the Rim Trail a few yards west of Bright Angel Lodge in Grand Canyon Village. From the trailhead at about 6900 feet, the trail drops to Indian Garden 4.6 miles away at about 3800 feet. Here, there is a ranger station, campground, restrooms and water. From Indian Garden, an almost flat trail goes 1½ miles to Plateau Point, with exceptional views into the inner gorge. The 12.2 miles roundtrip from the rim to Plateau Point is a strenuous all-day hike. Shorter hikes are of course possible – just walk down from the rim as far as you want. There are resthouses after 1½ miles (1130-foot elevation drop) and 3 miles (2110-foot elevation drop). The 1½-mile resthouse has restrooms; both have water in summer only.

From Indian Garden, the Bright Angel Trail continues down to the Colorado River (2450 feet elevation), which is crossed by a suspension bridge – the only bridge within

Geology of the Grand Canyon

Approximately two billion years of geologic history are exposed in the Grand Canyon – a huge amount of time considering the earth is just 4.6 billion years old. The oldest rock in the canyon, exposed just above the Colorado River, is the **Vishnu Schist**. Deposited in the Precambrian Era as sands, silts and muds interlayered with volcanic ash, these sediments were metamorphosed (hardened by heat and pressure) about 1.7 billion years ago by a collision of tectonic plates that baked and squeezed the entire region and uplifted the Mazatzal Mountains (which have since eroded). This metamorphism continued when **Zoroaster Granite** intruded into the Vishnu as molten magma. Between 1.2 billion and 800 million years ago, the area was covered by an ocean that rose and fell more than 18 times, depositing a thick series of marine sediments and volcanic flows; these were later metamorphosed into a rock unit named the **Grand Canyon Supergroup**.

The layers making up most of the canyon walls were laid during the Paleozoic (ancient life) and Mesozoic (middle life) Eras between 570 and 65 million years ago, which is why there are so many fossils in the Grand Canyon today. During much of this time, the entire Grand Canyon region was submerged under a tropical ocean, which rose and fell repeatedly. When sea levels were high, fine-grained clays and deep-sea oozes settled to the ocean floor – sediments that would later become thinly layered shales and limestones. When sea levels fell, the area became sandy beachfront property, complete with dunes, deltas and swamps, eventually forming siltstones and sandstones. Well-known examples include the **Redwall** and **Kaibab** limestones, the **Hermit** and **Bright Angel** shales, and the **Coconino** and **Tapeats** sandstones. Around 65 million years ago, tectonic forces once again uplifted the region and the sea retreated permanently. The final rocks to be deposited in the Grand Canyon were volcanic flows that erupted into the canyon about one million years ago.

the park. The Bright Angel Campground is a short way north of the bridge and 9½ miles from the South Rim. A few hundred yards beyond is Phantom Ranch. Water, food, accommodations and a ranger station are all here.

South Kaibab Trail This trail leaves the South Rim from near Yaki Point, about 4½ miles east of Grand Canyon Village. From the trailhead at 7262 feet it's more than 4800 feet down to the river and Bright Angel Campground, but the distance is only 6.7 miles. Clearly, South Kaibab is a much steeper trail than Bright Angel. It follows a ridge with glorious views. The first 1½ miles drop 1300 feet to Cedar Ridge and this makes a good short half-day hike.

From the Bright Angel Campground on the north side of the river, the **North Kaibab Trail** climbs to the North Rim at 8200 feet in 14 miles (see the North Rim section later in this chapter). You can cross the canyon rim to rim. Although extremely fit hikers can descend from the South Rim to the river and return or make a rim-to-rim crossing in one long day (the record for running rim to rim is now under four hours), the NPS strongly discourages such endeavors. Certainly, during the summer the extreme temperatures make such attempts very dangerous for inexperienced hikers.

Other Trails Although other trails receive little or no maintenance, several are not beyond the limits of any hiker with some experience. The least difficult are the **Hermit Trail**, which leaves from Hermits Rest at the end of the West Rim Drive, and the **Grandview Trail**, which leaves from Grandview Point of the East Rim Drive, 12 miles east of Grand Canyon Village. Both of these are steep and strenuous but offer

---

The tremendous depth and the unusually steep sides of the Grand Canyon are closely tied to the evolution of the Colorado River. The Grand Canyon lies within the **Colorado Plateau** geologic province, an area composed largely of flat-lying sedimentary and volcanic rocks. Both the Colorado Plateau and the Colorado River's source area in the Rocky Mountains has been rapidly uplifted several times since the end of the Mesozoic, with total uplift estimated as high as 10,000 feet. As its elevation increased, two separate stream systems – one flowing north and one flowing south – developed on opposite sides of the Colorado Plateau. Approximately six million years ago, a shift in the San Andreas Fault began opening the Gulf of California. Rivers that flowed south off the Colorado Plateau merged into what is now the lower Colorado River and emptied into this new sea. The headwaters of the river eroded northward through the Grand Wash Cliffs (near the present Arizona-Nevada border), connecting the river with the upper (north-flowing) Colorado River system. The upper Colorado River then changed its course from northward into Utah to southward into the Gulf of California, forming the modern Colorado River. This powerful new river cut through the hard Kaibab limestone, quickly incising the softer rocks below and forming the Grand Canyon as we see it today.

The hardness of different rocks determined many of the shapes and features of the Grand Canyon. In the upper canyon, erosion-resistant rocks formed stair-stepped cliffs and terraces such as the **Tonto Platform**, a wide, flat terrace that juts out into the canyon like a tabletop. Less resistant rocks formed slopes that are often covered in debris. The lower section of the canyon, called the Inner Gorge, is narrow and V-shaped. Composed largely of metamorphic rocks of similar hardness, each layer is eroded at about the same rate as its neighbors so none stand out farther than the others.

– Rhawn Denniston
Geologist

popular day hikes as well as backcountry camping possibilities.

Details of the many unmaintained trails and backcountry campgrounds in the canyon are beyond the scope of this book – read a backpacking guide book (see Books & Maps, above) and contact the Backcountry Office for further information.

Backpacking Itineraries Most overnight backpacking trips go from the South Rim to the river and return because rim-to-rim trips involve a five-hour car shuttle. Typically, three days and two nights are spent below the rim, with a choice of spending two nights at either Bright Angel or Indian Garden Campground, or one night at each (normally Bright Angel on the first night). If you arrange a shuttle, you could add a night at Cottonwood Campground on the way up to the North Rim. If your time is limited, a two day/one night trip is also rewarding. Because the Kaibab Trail is steep, this is the usual descent route, with the longer but less steep Bright Angel Trail used for climbing out. These two trails are called the 'corridor trails' and are recommended for first-time visitors.

If you want to hike but prefer a bed over a sleeping bag, you can stay at the canyon-bottom Phantom Ranch Lodge (see Places to Stay, below).

Backcountry Permits Permits are necessary for any overnight camping trip. Written applications are the only way to obtain a permit (phone reservations are not available). Applications can either be turned into the Backcountry Office in person; mailed to the Backcountry Office, PO Box 129, Grand Canyon, AZ 86023; or faxed (☎ 520-638-2125). If you stay at the Phantom Lodge, you don't need a permit but you do need advance reservations.

The number of permits issued is limited by the space available. Indian Garden (space for 46 campers), Bright Angel (104 campers) and Cottonwood (33 campers) are among the most popular campgrounds in the park and are often booked months in advance. Summer is extremely hot but

remains the most busy season, closely followed by the milder spring and fall. Numerous other smaller, less-developed campsites are available on unmaintained trails below the rim. Call or write the Backcountry Office for a complete listing and backcountry trip planner.

One permit is needed for each group. Most campsites are limited to a maximum of six people, so groups of one to six people have the best chance of getting the itinerary they request. A small number of sites are available for large groups of seven to 11 campers. For any itinerary, no more than two nights can be spent in one campground, except during the low season (November 15 to February 28) when you can spend up to four nights in one campground.

To obtain a permit, the following written information must be submitted.

- Group leader's name/address/phone
- Number of people in group
- License plate numbers of vehicles (one or two) to be left at trailhead
- Dates and names of campgrounds for proposed itinerary
- Alternative itineraries if the first itinerary is unavailable
- Credit card (Visa or MasterCard) number, expiration date, cardholder's name and signature, application date and amount authorized

The cost of each permit will vary depending on group size and itinerary. Fees are currently a nonrefundable $20 per permit, plus $4 per person per night. If you plan on numerous trips, you can obtain a $50 frequent-hiker permit that is valid for 12 months and waives the $20 fee, though the $4 per person per night fee still applies. Permits do not include the normal park entrance fees.

Applications are accepted for the current month and the next four (for example, applications postmarked January 1 can be made for trips beginning as late as May 31; trips beginning in June cannot be applied for until February 1). Mail or fax your application as far ahead as possible to allow for processing, which takes about three weeks. All applications will receive a reply by mail. If the application is approved, the permit will be enclosed. If you are forced to cancel your trip, there is no refund. If your proposed itinerary and all alternatives are full, your permit will be denied and no fee will be charged. If you do not receive a permit or denial before your trip, call the Backcountry Office to find out the status of your permit – occasionally you can pick up permits the day before your trip. Apply as far ahead as possible and give as many alternative itineraries as possible for the best chance of success. In 1996, the park received 25,000 permit applications and was able to issue 16,000 permits, so your chances are pretty good if you apply early and are flexible.

If you arrive at the Grand Canyon without a backcountry permit, don't give up. Head over to the Backcountry Office immediately and get on the waiting list for cancellations. Show up every morning at 8 am and you'll probably get a permit within a few days or even the same day if you are lucky. You have a better chance of getting a permit on short notice if you are prepared to hike unmaintained trails to less developed campgrounds (ask the ranger for advice) or if you avoid the peak season.

Although it may be tempting to try backpacking without a permit, remember that backcountry rangers patrol the trails and check permits on a regular and frequent basis, so you are quite likely to get caught and fined. Backpacking without a permit is considered a serious offense by the NPS.

River Running

You can run the Colorado River with a tour or arrange your own private trip. But before you throw a rubber raft into the back of a pickup and head up to the Colorado River, make sure you have serious river-running experience and a permit.

Obtaining a permit is straightforward but time consuming. Call or write the national park for an application, mail it and wait about 10 years. Then throw your raft into your pickup . . .

Most readers will go with a commercial tour and those who manage to get a private permit don't need information from me. (Sorry, no refunds if you bought this book expecting to learn how to get a private Grand Canyon river-running permit in 10 days instead of 10 years.)

Currently, well over 20,000 visitors a year run the river, almost all with commercial trips. These can be most simply divided into motorized and nonmotorized. The motorized trips are usually in huge inflatable boats that go twice as fast as the oar boats, but you have to put up with the roar of the engine. Nonmotorized trips are slow, but the only roar you'll hear is the roar of the rapids, mingled with gurgled screams. Whichever way you go, expect to get very wet during the day and spend nights camping on riverside beaches. This is not as primitive as it sounds – professional river guides are legendary for their combination of white-water abilities, gastronomy and information. David Lavender's *River Runners of the Grand Canyon* won't tell you how to run the river but will provide an entertaining history of the canyon's river runners.

Most trips run the river from Lees Ferry to Diamond Creek (in the Hualapai Indian Reservation), dropping more than 2000 feet in almost 300 miles and running scores of rapids. Passengers have the option of getting on or off at Phantom Ranch on the main rim-to-rim trail (the South and North Kaibab Trails) almost halfway into the entire river trip. Combining these options, you can take anything from a three- or four-day motorized trip of part of the canyon to a three-week nonmotorized trip of the entire canyon.

Nonmotorized trips are varied. Many are oar trips, where the captain controls the boat with large oars and the passengers hang on. Some are paddle trips, where the passengers paddle in response to the captain's commands. All these are generally in inflatable rafts, but a couple of companies do paddle trips in wooden dories, reminiscent of those used by John Wesley Powell in 1869. In addition, experienced kayakers

ARIZONA

can join commercial trips – the gear goes in the rafts.

Commercial trips aren't cheap – expect to pay up to $200 per person per day. Family discounts can be arranged, but small children are not allowed – minimum age requirements vary from trip to trip. The following companies are authorized to run the Colorado River through the national park. Their trips fill up several months (even a year) in advance, so contact them early for information.

Aramark-Wilderness River Adventures
Motor and oar trips. PO Box 717, Page, AZ 86040 (☎ 520-645-3296, 800-992-8022)
Arizona Raft Adventures, Inc
Motor, oar, paddle and kayak trips. 4050-F East Huntington Drive, Flagstaff, AZ 86004 (☎ 520-526-8200, 800-786-7238)
Arizona River Runners, Inc
Mainly motorized, some oar trips. PO Box 47788, Phoenix, AZ 85068-7788 (☎ 602-867-4866, 800-477-7238)
Canyon Explorations, Inc
Oar, paddle and kayak trips. PO Box 310, Flagstaff, AZ 86002 (☎ 520-774-4559, 800-654-0723, fax 520-774-4655)
Canyoneers, Inc
Motor, oar and kayak trips. PO Box 2997, Flagstaff, AZ 86003 (☎ 520-526-0924, 800-525-0924)
Colorado River & Trail Expeditions, Inc
Motor, oar, paddle and kayak trips. PO Box 57575, Salt Lake City, UT 84157-0575 (☎ 801-261-1789, 800-253-7328)
Diamond River Adventures, Inc
Motor and oar trips. PO Box 1316, Page, AZ 86040 (☎ 520-645-8866, 800-343-3121)
Expeditions, Inc
Oar, paddle and kayak trips. 625 N Beaver, Flagstaff, AZ 86001 (☎ 520-779-3769)
Grand Canyon Expeditions Co
Motor, oar, dory and kayak trips. PO Box O, Kanab, UT 84741 (☎ 801-644-2691, 800-544-2691)
Hatch River Expeditions, Inc
Motor and kayak trips. PO Box 1200, Vernal, UT 84078 (☎ 801-789-3813, 800-433-8966)
High Desert Adventures, Inc
Motor, oar and kayak trips. PO Box 40, St George, UT 84771-0040 (☎ 801-673-1200)
Moki Mac River Expeditions, Inc
Motor, oar and kayak trips. PO Box 21242, Salt Lake City, UT 84121 (☎ 801-268-6667, 800-284-7280)

OARS/Grand Canyon Dories
Oar, dory and kayak trips. PO Box 216, Altaville, CA 95221 (☎ 209-736-0805, 800-346-6277)
Outdoors Unlimited
Oar, paddle and kayak trips. 6900 Townsend Winona Rd, Flagstaff, AZ 86004 (☎ 520-526-4546, 800-637-7238)
Tour West, Inc
Motor and oar trips. PO Box 333, Orem, UT 84059 (☎ 801-225-0755, 800-453-9107)
Western River Expeditions, Inc
Motor and oar trips. 7258 Racquet Club Drive, Salt Lake City, UT 84121 (☎ 801-942-6669, 800-453-7450)

In addition, see Hualapai River Runners in the Hualapai Indian Reservation, below. Also see Organized Tours, below, for one-day, smooth-water raft trips.

Biking

Bicycles are allowed only on paved roads. Mountain biking on unpaved roads or on trails is not permitted – you need to go outside the park in the Kaibab National Forest for that. In fact, no wheeled vehicles of any kind are permitted on the trails (except for wheelchairs and baby strollers on the paved Rim Trail).

The story is told of a river runner who pushed a dolly loaded with 10 cases of beer down the Bright Angel Trail to his rafting group. He received a ticket for using a wheeled vehicle on the trail and also had to push the loaded dolly all the way back to the South Rim. Bummer!

Fishing

There is good trout fishing in the Colorado River and several of its tributaries. Licenses and tackle can be purchased at the general store in Grand Canyon Village.

Licenses are not available for purchase on the national park's North Rim – the nearest area to get a permit is Marble Canyon, where there are also guides.

Cross-Country Skiing

The higher North Rim area offers more snow for better cross-country skiing than the South Rim area (see also the Jacob

Lake section, later in the chapter). However, you can ski in the South Rim area in the Kaibab National Forest at the Grandview Ski Area when snow conditions permit. There are 18 miles of easy- to medium-difficulty, groomed and signed skiing trails near the east entrance of the park. The plowed parking area and access to the trails is on East Rim Drive, 10.1 miles north of the junction of Hwys 64 and 180, 2 miles east of Grandview Point.

About a half mile into the access trail is an information kiosk that describes routes and distances; the longest trail is 7½ miles. One trail has a canyon-view overlook, but all trails stay in the national forest and do not go to the South Rim of the national park.

Skiers are free to tour the national forest regardless of trails and there are no restrictions on camping unless you enter the park.

Organized Tours

Within the park, most tours are run by the Fred Harvey Company called Amfac (☎ 303-297-2757, fax 303-297-3175), 14001 East Iliff, Suite 600, Aurora, CO 80014. Inside the park, Amfac has a transportation desk (☎ 520-638-2631) at the Bright Angel Lodge and information desks at the visitor center and Maswik and Yavapai Lodges.

See Williams, in the Central Arizona chapter, for information about train tours to the Grand Canyon.

Bus Narrated bus tours leave from lodges in the Grand Canyon Village. These include a 2-hour West Rim tour, a 3¾ hour East Rim tour or a combination of both. Both leave twice daily year-round and cost about $12 and $19, with discounts for six- to 15-year-olds and for combining both tours. Sunset tours ($8) are offered in summer.

All-day tours (10 to 13 hours, departing daily with a four-adult minimum) visit the Sinagua Ruins around Flagstaff or visit the Navajo Reservation and Monument Valley with Navajo guides. These cost about $80 including lunch; children under 12 pay $50.

Some buses are wheelchair accessible by prior arrangement. Reservations are ad-

vised in summer but even then there are usually enough buses that you can get on a tour the next day by reserving at the transportation desk. Tax (6%) and guide tips are not included in these prices.

Mule A one-day trip to Plateau Point inside the canyon is offered daily. It takes about seven hours roundtrip, of which six hours are spent in the saddle. The cost is $100 plus tax and tips, including lunch.

Overnight trips to Phantom Ranch at the canyon bottom are offered daily. These take 5½ hours down and 4½ hours back up and cost about $255, including meals and dormitory accommodations. During winter only, three-day/two-night trips to Phantom Ranch cost $355. Rates don't include tax and tips, but there are discounts (about 20% to 25%) for second and additional persons in your group.

Reservations are suggested, although you can get on a waiting list if you don't have one. During winter, trips can often be arranged with a day's notice; during the summer the waiting list is much longer and a wait of several days or even weeks may be necessary.

These trips are strenuous – they are supposedly easier than walking, but I find them harder work than hiking! Riders must be in good physical shape and be able to mount and dismount without assistance, weigh under 200 pounds (including clothing and camera), be at least four feet, seven inches in height, be fluent in English (so they can understand instructions) and cannot be pregnant.

Horse and mule rides are also available from the town of Tusayan (see below).

You can ride your own horse into the park, but a permit is required from the Backcountry Office (see Hiking & Backpacking, above). Permit procedures and costs are the same as for backpackers, with an additional fee of $4 per horse per night; there is a limit of 12 horses per group of up to six people, or five pack animals for a single mounted rider. Horse trips are allowed only on the corridor routes and only Bright Angel and Cottonwood Campgrounds have overnight horse facilities. Feed must be carried.

Raft An all-day bus and boat tour includes an East Rim tour and drive to Glen Canyon Dam, a smooth-water float trip to Lees Ferry and a return trip by bus. About four hours are spent on the river and no white water is involved. The trip runs daily from May through October, and sometimes in late March, April and early November. Costs are $86, or $50 for children under 12, including picnic lunch. A minimum of four adults are required.

Wilderness River Adventures (see Page, below) does the same rafting trip but includes bus transportation to and from Page.

Special Events
The Grand Canyon Chamber Music Festival (☎ 520-638-9215), PO Box 1332, Grand Canyon, AZ 86023, has been presented at the Shrine of the Ages at Grand Canyon Village in September for more than a decade. Typically, about eight concerts are performed during a two-week period in mid-September. Tickets are $15; $5 for children and students.

Places to Stay
Reservations for all the places listed below are essential in summer and a good idea in winter. Cancellations provide a lucky few with last-minute rooms. Call to check. If you can't find accommodations in the national park, see Tusayan (6 miles south of Grand Canyon Village outside the South Entrance Station), Valle (31 miles south) and Cameron (53 miles east). Also see Williams (about 60 miles) and Flagstaff (about 80 miles) in the Central Arizona chapter.

Camping Campers should be prepared for freezing winter nights. Backcountry camping is available by reservation and permit only (see Hiking & Backpacking, above).

In Grand Canyon Village, *Mather Campground* has 320 sites (no hookups) for $15 (June to August) or $12 at other times. Make reservations (☎ 301-722-1257, 800-365-2267) up to five months in advance. Otherwise it's first-come, first-served. Even in summer, a few sites may be available in the mornings. Coin showers (6 am to 10 pm) and laundry (7 am to 9 pm) are available near the campground entrance. Nearby, the Fred Harvey *Trailer Village* has 80 RV sites with hookups for $19 year-round.

The *Desert View Campground* near the east entrance has 75 campsites on a first-come, first-served basis from April to October. They are often full by early morning so arrive early. There is water but no showers or RV hookups and fees are $10.

Lodges About 1000 rooms are available on the South Rim in a variety of lodges all run by Amfac Grand Canyon National Park Lodges (☎ 520-638-2631 for same-day information, 303-297-2757, fax 303-297-3175 for advance reservations), 14001 East Iliff, Suite 600, Aurora, CO 80014. In Grand Canyon Village, there are four lodges on the canyon rim – canyon-view rooms command higher prices. Two lodges, Maswik and Yavapai, are away from the rim, while Phantom Ranch is at the bottom of the canyon near the Colorado River. Approximate prices given below are the same for single or double occupancy; add tax (about 6%) and $7 to $14 per extra person. Prices vary by room, not by season.

On the rim, the most famous and expensive is the 1905 *El Tovar Hotel*, a rustic lodge with high standards of comfort and the best dining in the area. It was renovated in 1998 but still retains the historic flavor of the place. There are 78 small to midsized rooms from about $120 to $180. About 12 mini-suites are $190 to $280 and several have private balconies with canyon views.

Budget travelers use the rustic 1935 *Bright Angel Lodge & Cabins* with more than 30 simple lodge rooms, many with shared bath, from about $40 to $60. There are 42 cabins, all with bath, mostly for $65 to $115 and very popular. A few containing fireplaces and with canyon views are more than $200 – these are often booked up a year or more in advance. This is the park's cheapest lodge and one reader complained that his reservation was mishandled – I suggest calling to reconfirm.

Between these two places are the modern *Kachina Lodge* with 49 rooms and *Thunderbird Lodge* with 55 rooms, all comfortable motel-style units with private bath, some with canyon views. Rates are about $105 to $115.

A short walk away from the rim, the *Maswik Lodge* has almost 300 rooms with private baths. Most are motel-style units, some with balconies, for $75 to $110; there are a few slightly cheaper rustic cabins with baths. Near the visitor center, the *Yavapai Lodge* has about 360 reasonably sized motel rooms, all with private baths and some with forest views. Rates are $85 to $100. The Yavapai Lodge and the Maswik cabins may close in winter.

Phantom Ranch has basic cabins sleeping four to 10 people and segregated dorms sleeping 10 people in bunk beds. Most cabins are reserved for the overnight mule tours, but hikers may make reservations (from about $60 double) if space is available. There are separate shower facilities. Dorm rates are $21 per person, and bedding, soap and towels are provided. Meals are available in the dining hall by advance reservation only. Breakfast is $11.75; box lunch is $5.50; and dinner varies from $16.75 (stew) to $26.75 (steak). Meals are not fancy but are enough to feed hungry hikers. If you lack a reservation, try showing up at the Bright Angel Lodge transportation desk at 6 am to snag a canceled bunk (some folks show up earlier and wait). Snacks, limited supplies, beer and wine are also sold. Postcards bought and mailed here are stamped 'Mailed by Mule from the bottom of the Canyon.'

Places to Eat

By far the best place for quality food in an elegant setting is the historic *El Tovar Dining Room* where dinner reservations are recommended, especially in summer when they are often booked weeks ahead. Hours are 6:30 am to 2 pm and 5 to 10 pm. Continental (um, which continent?) dinner entrées are in the $15 to $25 range and smoking is not permitted.

More moderate prices and an American menu are available at the *Bright Angel Restaurant*, which is open from 6:30 am to 10 pm. Next door to the Bright Angel Lodge, the *Arizona Steakhouse* serves steaks and seafood from 5 to 10 pm from March through December. Canyonside snacks and sandwiches are sold from 8 am to 4 pm at the *Bright Angel Fountain* near the Bright Angel trailhead from March to October. Self-service dining is available at the *Maswik Cafeteria* from 6 am to 10 pm and at the *Yavapai Cafeteria and Grill* from 6 am to midnight from March through

ARIZONA

December. *Babbitt's Deli*, in the shopping center opposite the visitor center, has a dining area and carry-out food from 8 am to 6 pm.

Hermits Rest Snack Bar, at the end of the West Rim Drive, and *Desert View Fountain* near the east entrance, are both open daily for snacks and fast food; hours vary by season.

Entertainment
The El Tovar has a piano bar, and there's a lounge bar with live entertainment from Wednesday to Sunday at the Bright Angel Lodge. The Maswik Lodge has a sports bar.

Getting There & Away
The majority of people drive or arrive on bus tours. (See the Grand Canyon in the 21st Century sidebar, earlier in this chapter, for future plans.) The nearest airport is in Tusayan (see below).

See Flagstaff, in the Central Arizona chapter, for the Nava-Hopi Bus Company, which is the only regularly scheduled bus service into the park.

See Williams, in the Central Arizona chapter, for train service offered by the Grand Canyon Railway.

Canyon Airport Shuttle (☎ 520-638-0821, 520-638-0871, fax 520-638-0824) leaves the airport in Tusayan about every hour from 8 am to 5 pm, with several stops in Tusayan en route to the Maswick Transportation Center in Grand Canyon Village. One-way fare is $5; day passes (which you can use for a roundtrip) are $7; month passes are $45. This service also goes from Tusayan to Valle four times a day ($5 one way, $10 for a day pass). Park entrance fees are not included.

Grand Canyon Services (☎ 520-638-2023, 800-378-2023), has shuttle services to Williams, Flagstaff, Phoenix and Las Vegas, which require a five-passenger minimum. You can charter a van for your own tour.

Getting Around
Free Shuttle Buses Free shuttles operate along three routes from mid-March to Mid-

October (dates may be extended in the future). One goes around Grand Canyon Village, stopping at lodges, campgrounds, the visitor center, Yavapai Observation Station and other points. Bus stops are clearly marked. Buses leave every 15 minutes from 6:30 am to 9:45 pm and take 50 minutes for the entire loop.

The village loop bus connects with the West Rim shuttle at the Bright Angel trailhead (called the West Rim Interchange Stop). The West Rim shuttle operates every 15 minutes from 7:30 am to sunset, stops at eight scenic points along its route and takes 90 minutes roundtrip. When the shuttle is running, private cars are not allowed along the West Rim Drive. The shuttle buses are not wheelchair accessible, but visitors with wheelchairs can obtain a permit from the visitor center to drive along the West Rim.

A new service began in 1997 carrying passengers from the Backcountry Office, stopping at Yavapai Lodge and finishing at the South Kaibab trailhead and Yaki Point. Shuttles run every 30 minutes from one hour before sunrise to one hour after sunset and are especially useful to hikers on the South Kaibab trail.

Other Shuttles Ask at any of the transportation desks or call ☎ 520-638-2631 for other shuttle services. Shuttles to or from the South Kaibab trailhead (when the free shuttle is not running) cost $8 for one passenger and $3 for each additional passenger. There is a telephone at the trailhead.

Shuttles from rim to rim are available from May to October (when the North Rim is open), leave at 1:30 pm, take five hours and cost $60 one way or $100 roundtrip. Call Trans-Canyon Shuttle (☎ 520-638-2820). Other services are available on request.

TUSAYAN
Seven miles south of Grand Canyon Village and a couple of miles south of the south entrance, the sprawling community of Tusayan offers several motels, restaurants, souvenir shops and the Grand Canyon Airport, all strung along Hwy 64.

Information

The chamber of commerce (☎ 520-638-2901) has a visitors information booth in the IMAX Theater lobby. The Kaibab National Forest Tusayan Ranger Station (☎ 520-638-2443), PO Box 3088, Tusayan, AZ 86023, is at the north end of town and is open from 8 am to 5 pm Monday to Friday. The post office is opposite the IMAX Theater and an ATM is inside the theater. South Rim Travel (☎ 800-682-4393, fax 520-638-0238, sorimtravel@aol.com), PO Box 3651, Grand Canyon, AZ 86023, makes reservations for hotel rooms, transportation and complete packages in the South Rim area.

IMAX Theater

Using a film format three times larger than normal 70mm movie frames, a screen up to eight times the size of conventional cinema screens and a 14-speaker stereo surround system, the IMAX Theater presents *Grand Canyon – The Hidden Secrets*. This 34-minute movie plunges you into the history and geology of the canyon through the eyes of ancient Indians, John Wesley Powell and a soaring eagle. The effects are quite splendid and are a cheaper, safer and quieter way of getting an aerial perspective than taking a flight. The IMAX Theater (☎ 520-638-2468, fax 520-638-2807) is on Hwy 64, a few miles south of the park entrance. Shows are at 30 minutes past the hour from 8:30 am to 8:30 pm March through October and from 10:30 am to 6:30 pm the rest of the year. Admission is $7.75; $5.50 for three- to 11-year-olds. Credit cards are not accepted.

Horseback Riding

Apache Stables (☎ 520-638-2891, 520-638-2424) at the Moqui Lodge, a half mile south of the park entrance, has a variety of horseback rides available in both the national forest and national park from about March to November. Rides are $25 to $65 for one to four hours. Children as young as six can ride on the shorter trips.

Other Activities

The Kaibab National Forest provides many opportunities for outdoor fun. **Mountain biking** on dirt roads and trails (not allowed in the Grand Canyon) is permitted throughout the national forest. About 13 miles of groomed **cross-country skiing** trails are found on forest lands south of the national park; these trails are accessed from a national park parking area near Grandview Point. You can enjoy **hiking**, **backpacking** and **camping** without the crowds and without a backcountry permit from the NPS Backcountry Office. Of course, you don't get the canyon views either.

Places to Stay

Camping In the Kaibab National Forest, free dispersed camping is allowed as long as you are at least a quarter of a mile from paved highways. USFS roads provide access, but many are closed in winter. USFS Rd 686 heading west from Hwy 64, almost a mile south of the Ten-X turnoff, is often open year-round.

The USFS operates the *Ten-X Campground*, about 3 miles south of Tusayan. It is open from May through September and has 70 sites for $10 on a first-come, first-served basis. There is water but no showers or RV hookups. A large group site (25 to 100 people for $25 to $55) is available by reservation only (☎ 520-638-2443).

Grand Canyon Camper Village (☎ 520-638-2887) is at the north end of Tusayan, 1½ miles south of the park entrance. About 300 sites are available year-round, ranging from $15 for tents to $23 for full hookups. There are showers, a playground and minigolf. This place often has a tent site when everywhere else is full.

Hotels As with the Grand Canyon, reservations are recommended, especially in summer. Summer rates are pricey for what are basically motel rooms, but if you can't get a room on the South Rim and want to stay close to the canyon, this is what you're stuck with. Winter rates (November to March) are $30 to $50 lower. All motels are along Hwy 64.

The cheapest motel is *Seven Mile Lodge* (☎ 520-638-2291) with 20 rooms for about $80. *Moqui Lodge*, which is the closest to the park entrance and operated by Amfac (see Lodges in the Grand Canyon National Park – South Rim section, above), has 140 rooms at $95/100 for singles/doubles, including breakfast. Rooms vary somewhat in quality though not in price. It is closed from about November to March (subject to change). There is a desk for the Apache Stables (see Horseback Riding, above) and a decent restaurant and bar with Mexican and American food open from 6:30 to 10 am and 6 to 10 pm. On weekends, there is live country & western music.

The *Red Feather Lodge* (☎ 520-638-2414, 800-538-2345, fax 520-638-9216) has about 100 older rooms plus 130 added recently. Consequently, prices vary from about $90 to $140 in summer, $50 to $75 in winter. There is a seasonal pool as well as a spa, exercise room, game room and restaurant.

The *Holiday Inn Express* (☎ 520-638-3000, fax 520-638-0123) has 170 rooms for about $130, including continental breakfast. Rooms are new, modern and comfortable, but the hotel lacks a restaurant and swimming pool.

The *Quality Inn* (☎ 520-638-2673, fax 520-638-9537), has more than 200 pleasant rooms and mini-suites for $135 to about $200. The mini-suites, of which there are about 50, each have a microwave, refrigerator and separate sitting area. Most have balconies. There is a pool, spa, restaurant (open 6 am to 10 pm) and bar.

The *Best Western Grand Canyon Squire Inn* (☎ 520-638-2681, fax 520-638-2782) has 250 spacious rooms at $100 to $150 and a few suites for $200. There is a seasonal pool as well as a spa, sauna, tennis court, exercise room, coin laundry, gift shop and (at extra charge) a fun center with bowling, billiards and other games. A good restaurant, an inexpensive coffee shop (open 6:30 am to 10 pm) and a bar are on the premises.

Grand Canyon Suites (☎ 520-638-3100, 888-538-5353, fax 520-638-2747) has about 35 new nonsmoking one- and two-bedroom suites, each with its own Southwestern theme and all with microwaves, refrigerators and coffeemakers. Rates are in the $150 to $200 range, and include a

Grand Canyon Overflights

The idea of flying over the Grand Canyon at low altitude appeals to some people. However, passengers may want to consider that there have been many complaints about aircraft noise in the park and concerns about flight safety.

It is very difficult to get away from aircraft noise anywhere in the park for more than a few minutes. The NPS recently estimated that visitors have to tolerate aircraft noise during 75% of daylight hours. The natural quiet of the Grand Canyon is part of its magnificence and the current levels of aircraft noise are not acceptable in a national park.

While recent efforts to limit air pollution have met with some success, eliminating noise pollution has been a losing battle. Regulations to keep aircraft above 14,500 feet in 44% of the park and above the rim in the remaining area were a step toward limiting future increases in noise, but these regulations have not been adhered to and the number of flights has increased. In 1997, a new National Parks Overflights Act was proposed to limit aircraft noise in all national parks. It's a further step toward a noise-free canyon, but visitors will still find it almost impossible to get away from annoying aircraft noise.

Safety is another concern. Almost every year one or more tour aircraft crash in or near the canyon. Since the growth of air-tourism in the 1980s, more national park visitors have died in these accidents than in river-running, backpacking, hiking, mule-riding, train and car accidents combined. ■

continental breakfast, but there is no restaurant, pool or spa.

Places to Eat
Steakhouse at the Grand Canyon (☎ 520-638-2780), opposite the IMAX Theater, is open for dinner only. Otherwise, the hotel restaurants offer the best food, and there is a pizza place, Denny's and fast food.

Getting There & Away
Air The Grand Canyon Airport is at the south end of Tusayan. Flights to and from Las Vegas, Nevada operate several times a day with Grand Canyon Airlines (☎ 520-638-2407, 800-528-2413), Eagle Canyon Airlines (☎ 800-446-4584), Scenic Airlines (☎ 702-739-1900, 520-638-2436, 800-634-6801), Air Nevada (☎ 520-638-2441), Air Vegas (☎ 800-255-7474) and Las Vegas Airlines (☎ 702-647-3056, 800-634-6851).

Many of these flights include an overflight of the Grand Canyon. In addition, tours in airplanes and helicopters starting from and returning to the Grand Canyon Airport are available from about $50 for the shortest flights. Everybody will try and sell you one. (See the Grand Canyon Overflights sidebar.)

There are shuttles from the airport to Grand Canyon Village (see Getting There & Away in the South Rim section, above).

Car Rental Budget (☎ 520-638-9360) has cars available at the airport. Rates are cheaper at Flagstaff and Phoenix.

VALLE
Located about 25 miles south of the Grand Canyon National Park south entrance, Valle is the intersection of Hwy 64 to Williams and Hwy 180 to Flagstaff. There is no town here, just a couple of places to stay and eat, a gas station and an airport near the intersection. The recently opened **Planes of Fame** (☎ 520-635-1000) is an aircraft museum with several classic military and civilian aircraft in flying condition, as well as models and memorabilia. It opens daily except Thanksgiving and

Christmas; admission is $5; $2 for five- to 12-year-olds. The museum is in the airport, which is beginning to offer some flight services to the Grand Canyon.

Flintstones Bedrock City (☎ 520-635-2600) has 60 sites ($12 for tents and $16 for hookups). There are coin showers and laundry, a snack bar (Bronto Burgers and Dino Dogs) and a Flintstones recreation area complete with concretosaurs. The campground is open from mid-March through October.

The *Days Inn* (☎ 520-635-9203, fax 520-635-2345) has several sections with standard motel rooms around $100 in summer, half that in winter. There is a restaurant, gift shop, spa and seasonal pool. The gas station and grocery store are next door.

HUALAPAI INDIAN RESERVATION
This reservation borders many miles of the south side of the Colorado River northeast of Kingman. It contains the only road to the river within the Grand Canyon area. Back in the 1800s, when the area was being invaded by miners, the Hualapai fought hard to retain control of their lands. Today, most of the tribe works in ranching, logging or tourism. The reservation offers visitors a good opportunity to see some of the Grand Canyon area (outside the national park) accompanied by guides from a tribe that originally inhabited the region.

Orientation & Information
The tribal headquarters (☎ 520-769-2216), PO Box 168, Peach Springs, AZ 86434, and Hualapai Enterprises Tourism Office (☎ 520-769-2419) are at Peach Springs, a small community about 50 miles northeast of Kingman (see the Western Arizona chapter) or almost 40 miles northwest of Seligman (see the Central Arizona chapter) on Route 66. Hualapai Central Reservations (☎ 888-255-9550) has information about the tribally operated lodge, campground, river-running trips and bus tours.

Entrance into the reservation for sightseeing, picnicking and hiking is $7 per day per person (free for children under seven). No firearms are allowed on the reservation.

ARIZONA

Camping is available for $7 per night. Fishing costs $8 per day with a catch limit of eight fish. Permits can be bought in Peach Springs at the river-running office or lodge, both easy to find as you drive through on Route 66. (There is no charge for driving through on Route 66.)

Apart from 66, there are three roads of interest through the reservation. One is the paved road to the Havasupai Reservation (see the next section). The other two are unpaved.

From Peach Springs, 22-mile, unpaved **Diamond Creek Rd** heads north to the Colorado River. With the appropriate permit, you can drive to the Colorado River – 2WD cars with good clearance can usually make it except after heavy rains when you'll need a high-clearance 4WD. This is the only place within the canyon that the river can be reached by road.

Three miles west of Peach Springs on Route 66 is unpaved Buck and Doe Rd, which leads about 50 miles to Grand Canyon West (see Things to See & Do, below). This road is entirely within the reservation. Grand Canyon West can also be reached from Kingman by heading northwest on Hwy 93 for about 26 miles, then northeast along the paved Pearce Ferry Rd (heading toward Lake Mead) for about 30 miles, and then 21 miles east along the dirt Diamond Bar Rd. (This route is 20 miles shorter than driving from Kingman to Peach Springs.)

Things to See & Do
Peach Springs There's not much in Peach Springs apart from the tribal powwow held in late August. There's a small cultural center at the lodge.

Grand Canyon West This area has an airstrip and tribal office where permits, bathroom facilities and soft drinks are available. A tribally operated guided bus tour goes out to the canyon rim for $27.50 ($22 for three- to 11-year-olds) and includes a barbecue lunch on the rim and plenty of local lore and information as presented by the Hualapai guide – an interesting trip. The tour goes year-round.

A $7 permit (small children are free) allows you to drive 3 miles to the **Quartermaster Viewpoint**, which has a parking area and good views of the lower Grand Canyon but no facilities. A five-minute hike on a rough trail brings you to a small bluff with better views. You won't see many people – it's a far cry from the masses thronging the (admittedly more spectacular) South Rim of the national park.

River Running Hualapai River Running (☎ 520-769-2210, 520-769-2219, 800-622-4409, fax 520-769-2637), PO Box 246, Peach Springs, AZ 86434, offers one- and two-day river trips along the lower reaches of the Colorado River from May through October. Day trips run Monday to Friday; two-day trips run on weekends and include riverside camping. This company uses motorized rafts holding up to 10 passengers and the guides are Hualapai Indians. Both white-water and floating is involved. Rates are $221/321 per person for one/two days from Peach Springs; ask about discounts for groups of 10. Packages are also offered with rooms at the Hualapai Lodge before and after your trip. Children must be at least eight years old to participate.

Places to Stay & Eat
In Peach Springs is the tribe-operated *Hualapai Lodge* (☎ 888-216-0076), which opened in 1997 with 60 modern motel rooms for $75 single or double, and a restaurant open from 6 am to 9 pm. It provides shuttles to the Grand Canyon West. Otherwise there are no hotels on the Hualapai Reservation. The nearest off-reservation motels are in Truxton, about 10 miles west, or at Grand Canyon Caverns, 9 miles east of Peach Springs (see the Western Arizona chapter).

The Hualapai tribe operates a basic campground near the end of Diamond Creek Rd by the Colorado River. The elevation here is 1900 feet, which makes it extremely hot in summer. There are restrooms and picnic tables but no drinking water; bring everything you'll need.

HAVASUPAI INDIAN RESERVATION

This reservation is centered on Havasu Canyon, carved by Havasu Creek, a southern tributary of the Colorado River. It is the traditional home of the peaceful and energetic Havasupai Indians, who now offer Grand Canyon visitors a unique look at the canyon and river. Tribal headquarters are in Supai, which has been there for centuries – the only village within the Grand Canyon. The first European visitor was the Spanish priest, Francisco Garcés, in 1776. Just as in the old days, Supai can be accessed only by a steep 8-mile-long trail from the canyon rim. Below Supai, the trail leads past some of the prettiest waterfalls within the Grand Canyon.

Word has gotten out about this beautiful area. Although no roads directly connect Grand Canyon National Park's South Rim with the reservation, there are hundreds of daily visitors during the peak summer months. Nevertheless, it is much more tranquil than the South Rim.

Information

Information is available from the Havasupai Tourist Enterprise (☎ 520-448-2141), Supai, AZ 86435. All visitors pay an entry fee of $15; $12 in winter (November to March). The fee is valid for the length of your visit. The Supai Post Office distributes its mail by pack animals – postcards mailed from there have a special postmark to prove it. Until recently, all fees had to be paid with cash only, though the tourist enterprise tells me it now accepts Visa and MasterCard for reservations. Checks aren't accepted. The tribe levies a 5% tax on all goods and services. There is a small emergency clinic. Alcohol, firearms and pets aren't allowed.

Some visitors have expressed surprise that the village looks shabby, littered and unattractive. This is partly because the village is periodically flooded and partly because tribal members have a different concept of what is and isn't attractive. Come for the scenic and natural beauty and leave your urban planning ideas at home.

Things to See & Do

The 8-mile hike down to Supai is attractive, as it follows Havasu Creek and is lined with trees, but the most memorable sections are along the 4 or 5 miles of trail below the village. Here, there are four major **waterfalls** and many minor ones.

Just over a mile beyond Supai is Navajo Falls, the first of the four big falls. Next comes the 100-foot-high Havasu Falls, with a sparkling blue pool that is popular for swimming. Beyond this is the campground, and the trail then passes 200-foot-high Mooney Falls, the largest in the canyon. The falls were named after a miner who died in a terrifying climbing accident in 1880: although Mooney was roped, he was unable to extricate himself and hung there for many hours until the rope finally broke and he was killed. A very steep trail (chains provide welcome handholds) leads to the pool at the bottom, another popular swimming spot. Finally, 2½ miles farther is Beaver Falls. From there, it is a farther 4½ miles down to the Colorado River (about 8 miles below the campground).

Special Events

There are tribal dances held around Memorial Day and a Peach Festival in August. Call Havasupai Tourist Enterprise for exact dates.

Places to Stay & Eat

In Supai is the *Havasupai Lodge* (☎ 520-448-2111) with 24 modern rooms, all with canyon views, two double beds, air conditioning and private showers. There are no TVs or telephones – a plus for travelers wishing to get away from that stuff! Reservations are essential and should be made well in advance in the summer. Rates range from $75 to $96 for one to four people ($30 less in winter). Nearby is a small cultural center with tribal exhibits. Meals and snacks are served from 7 am to 6 pm daily at the *Village Cafe* (☎ 520-448-2981) near the lodge, and a general store sells food and camping fuel. Prices are high (though not prohibitive) because everything comes in by horse or helicopter. There are picnic tables.

ARIZONA

Two miles below Supai is the *Havasupai Campground* with 400 tent sites stretching along the river between Havasu and Mooney Falls. The campground suffered disastrous flooding in 1997 and tourists were evacuated. It has reopened since but may still be rather messy. There are pit toilets but no showers. You can swim in the river or pools, and there is a spring for drinking water, though it should be purified. Fires are not permitted, so bring a camp stove to cook. Camping fees are $10 per person ($9 in winter) and reservations (with Havasupai Tourist Enterprise) should be made because after hiking more than 10 miles in, you don't want to be turned back! The campground fills on holiday weekends and most days in summer. Don't leave gear unattended at the campground or anywhere else – thefts have occurred. There is no camping allowed elsewhere.

Note that the entrance fees are in addition to the lodge or campground fees. During summer, campers outnumber villagers so don't expect much in the way of cultural interaction. To enjoy the scenery and beautiful waterfalls, I suggest a three day/two night trip.

Shopping
The Havasupai are noted for basketmaking and beadwork. Their crafts are sold in the lodge's souvenir shop.

Getting There & Away
Seven miles east of Peach Springs on Route 66 is a signed turnoff to Hualapai Hilltop on the Havasu Canyon rim in the Havasupai Reservation. The 62-mile road is paved but has no gas stations or other services.

At Hualapai Hilltop is an unguarded parking area – try to arrive with as little stuff as possible and lock what you aren't taking to Supai in the trunk. Don't leave valuables. From the hilltop, a trail drops steeply and then flattens out, reaching Supai after about 8 miles and a 2000-foot elevation drop. The trail continues over a half mile through the village, then a farther 2 miles to the campground.

Havasupai Tourist Enterprise can arrange horses or mules by advance reservation (call two months ahead). Roundtrip fees per animal are $80 from hilltop to Supai, $110 from hilltop to campground, $40 from Supai to campground. If you want to hike down and hire a mule for the climb out, you can often arrange it when you get to Supai if you are flexible with your departure time ($50 one way). You can bring your own horse for a $15 trail fee – you supply feed. Mountain bikes are not allowed. Most visitors walk.

A helicopter service flies from the hilltop to Supai – this is mainly for tribal use.

CAMERON & AROUND
Cameron is a tiny community 52 miles east of Grand Canyon Village and 31 miles east of the national park's eastern entrance, a mile north of the intersection of Hwy 64 with Hwy 89. Although Cameron is on the western end of the Navajo Indian Reservation (see the Northeastern Arizona chapter), it is included here because it is on the main route from the South Rim to the North Rim of the Grand Canyon.

There are two excellent reasons to stop in Cameron. First, there is the historic **Cameron Trading Post**, opened in 1916 and still operating. It sells museum-quality Navajo rugs and other crafts, some of which date from the turn of the 19th century and sell for many thousands of dollars. Even if you're not in the market for the finest-quality rugs, it's worth stopping in just to see the attractive building and the beautifully displayed pieces, including some pre-European pots and items from several other tribes. The trading post sits scenically on the south side of the Little Colorado River. Next door is a motel, restaurant, RV park, grocery store, post office and a gift shop selling a huge variety of crafts and souvenirs at affordable prices.

The second reason to stop here is you're likely to be driving a long way to wherever you're going and Cameron surprisingly has the cheapest gas between Flagstaff and Page – gas up here!

About 10 miles west of Cameron on the way to the Grand Canyon is the **Little Colorado River Gorge Navajo Tribal Park** with a scenic overlook – it's worth a stop. Along the road are numerous stalls set up by Navajo families selling arts and crafts.

Right at the corner of Hwys 64 and 89 is the **Cameron Visitor Center**, open daily in summer and open erratically out of season. It has information about Navajo land as well as the Grand Canyon.

Places to Stay & Eat

The *Cameron Trading Post & Motel* (☎ 520-679-2231, 800-338-7385, fax 520-679-2350) has more than 60 pleasant Southwestern-style rooms, many with balconies, for $74 or $84 with one or two beds and a handful of suites with separate living quarters for $145 to $175. In summer it's difficult to get a room without a reservation and they don't take credit cards, so book ahead and mail them a check. Ask about discounts in winter. There are also RV sites with hookups for $15, but no tent sites or public showers. A restaurant and café serves decent meals and snacks but no alcohol (reservation land, remember?).

Eight miles south along Hwy 89 is the even smaller community of **Gray Mountain** where you'll find a gas station, small store and the *Anasazi Inn* (☎ 520-679-2214) with a restaurant and several dozen motel rooms around $70 in summer.

The Arizona Strip

Traditionally and geographically, this area north of the Grand Canyon has closer ties with Mormon Utah than Arizona. The Arizona Strip is wild, large, poorly roaded, a long way from Salt Lake City and remains the last holdout of the 19th-century practice of polygamy (see the sidebar The More the Merrier). The places described below, however, are on the few routes available to travelers from the South Rim of the Grand Canyon to the North Rim and beyond into

Utah. Don't expect to meet polygamists at every turn.

MARBLE CANYON & LEES FERRY AREA

Hwy 89 splits a few miles before crossing the Colorado River, with Hwy 89 heading northeast to Page and then swinging west to Kanab, Utah, and Hwy 89A taking a shorter route to Kanab through the Arizona Strip. Hwy 89A crosses the Navajo Bridge over the Colorado at Marble Canyon. This is the only road bridge into the Arizona Strip from the south and the only one on the Colorado River between Glen Canyon Dam and Hoover Dam in Nevada. Motorists use a new bridge; the original bridge was opened in 1929 and is now closed to vehicles, though you can park your car and walk across the old

---

The More the Merrier

Polygamy has not been condoned by the Mormon Church for more than a century, but the Arizona Strip is remote enough that old ideas die hard, particularly around Colorado City and Hildale (combined population 4500) on the Arizona/Utah border. Here, two independent Mormon churches, which split from the main church in 1929, determined 'to live marriage as much as we can,' according to a local church leader.

Until the 1950s, polygamists were jailed for their views, but in recent decades numerous families have openly practiced polygamy with few legal repercussions, although it remains technically illegal. Alma Aldebert Timpson, who was jailed in the 1940s for his beliefs in plural marriage, died in 1998 at the age of 92 and was buried in Colorado City. Records indicate that he had 66 children and as many as 347 grandchildren.

Colorado City is a tight-knit community and lacks visitor services. Although it's just a mile off Hwy 89A, inquisitive sightseers won't find any Welcome signs here. ■

ARIZONA

bridge, staring down onto the river almost 500 feet below. The bridge marks the southwestern end of the Glen Canyon National Recreation Area (GCNRA), described later in this chapter. At the west end is the Navajo Bridge Interpretive Center, run by the GCNRA and open from 9 am to 5 pm April through October. Almost immediately after the bridge, a side road to the right leads 6 miles to Lees Ferry, historically the only crossing point of the river for many miles and today the major put-in spot for river runners making the exciting descent through the Grand Canyon.

Lees Ferry is named after John D Lee, who established the Lonely Dell Ranch and primitive raft ferry here in 1872. Later, Lee was executed for his part in the Mountain Meadows Massacre (see Veyo Area in the Southwestern Utah chapter). The ferry operated until the Navajo Bridge was opened in 1929. Some of the historic ranch buildings near Lees Ferry can still be seen. The GCNRA has a ranger station (☎ 520-355-2234) here, and a booklet/map describing the ranch, ferry and area's history is available. Less than a mile southwest of Lees Ferry is the mouth of the spectacular Paria River Canyon (see the sidebar Paria Canyon-Vermilion Cliffs Wilderness Area in the Southwestern Utah chapter).

Places to Stay & Eat
The GCNRA runs the *Lees Ferry Campground* at Lees Ferry, with 54 sites for $10. There is drinking water, toilets and a nearby boat ramp but no showers or RV hookups. There are public coin showers ($2.50) at the Marble Canyon Lodge.

Summer rates are given below; they drop in winter. *Marble Canyon Lodge* (☎ 520-355-2225, 800-726-1789, fax 520-355-2227), on Hwy 89A half a mile west of Navajo Bridge, has about 60 rooms for $50/60 single/double (one bed) or $64 (two beds). There are a few cottages for $80 and apartments sleeping eight for $125. A restaurant is open from 6 am to 9 pm, and there is a coin laundry, store and bar.

Lees Ferry Lodge (☎ 520-355-2231, 520-355-2230), on Hwy 89A three miles west of Navajo Bridge, has 10 rooms at $50 a double. There is a restaurant and bar, and a fishing tackle shop and guide service next door.

Cliff Dwellers Lodge (☎ 520-355-2228, 800-433-2543) is under the Vermilion Cliffs, 8½ miles west of the Navajo Bridge. Twenty motel rooms (no TV or phone) rent for about $70 to $80 a double in summer. There is a restaurant, bar, store and gas.

JACOB LAKE AREA
Orientation & Information
Hwy 89A intersects with Hwy 67 at the small community of Jacob Lake, 41 miles west of Marble Canyon. Hwy 67 heads south to the North Rim of Grand Canyon National Park, 44 miles away, but is closed from December 1 to May 15. If a major snowstorm comes early, the road closes in November or even late October. Jacob Lake's high elevation (7921 feet) explains the long snow season. Hwy 89A remains open year-round, but winter travelers should carry chains or have 4WD.

A USFS visitor center (☎ 520-643-7298) in Jacob Lake, on Alt Hwy 89 near the intersection, has information, displays and interpretive programs on the Kaibab National Forest. The district headquarters are in Fredonia.

House Rock Wildlife Area
About 17 miles east of Jacob Lake along Hwy 89A is a signed turn-off to the south for unpaved USFS Rd 8910, which goes another 17 miles to this wildlife area on Kaibab National Forest land. House Rock

Condors at Vermilion Cliffs

The spectacular Vermilion Cliffs, which stretch along the north side of Hwy 89A for most of the way from Marble Canyon to Jacob Lake, were recently chosen as a release site for California condors, members of the vulture family. These endangered birds are magnificent – with a wingspan of 10 feet and weighing as much as 24 pounds, they are the largest land birds in North America. Before the arrival of Europeans, condors ranged throughout much of North America, but by the early 19th century they were found only west of the Rockies. The last confirmed sighting in Arizona was in 1924. By the 1980s, condors were extinct in the wild, but a small breeding population in the Los Angeles Zoo gave ornithologists hope that the birds could be reintroduced into the wild.

The first reintroduction was in Southern California, but this was not very successful because the release sites, though remote, were still too close to major metropolises. Condors require areas that are hundreds of miles from large cities and that provide mountain ridges or cliffs from which they can launch themselves for soaring flights. (The birds can fly as much as 50 miles in an hour under the right conditions.) The birds' preferred nesting areas are caves in inaccessible cliffs or mountains. The Vermilion Cliffs seem to meet these requirements, and six condors were initially released here in December 1996, with more releases in 1997 swelling the number to about 20. Inevitably, some condors have not survived; one was reportedly killed by a golden eagle and another died in a clash with power lines. Others, however, appear to be thriving and there have been recent sightings from both the Grand Canyon and Lake Powell. Keep your eyes open! ■

ARIZONA

Wildlife Area is known for a wild herd of buffalo, which you may be able to see with any luck (I did). Remember, however, the wildlife area covers more than 100 sq miles so your sightings are likely to be distant (mine were). Continuing past the ranch about another 10 miles will bring you to a couple of remote viewpoints overlooking the Marble Canyon area of the Grand Canyon National Park. Condors have been sighted here. (See the sidebar Condors at Vermilion Cliffs.) This road is closed by snow during the long winter.

Places to Stay & Eat

Free dispersed camping in the Kaibab National Forest is permitted as long as you are more than a quarter of a mile from the paved highway – several unpaved forest roads give access.

Jacob Lake Campground (☎ 520-643-7395) is near the USFS visitor center on Hwy 89A. More than 50 sites are $10 on a first-come, first-served basis. Two group sites (minimum $50 for 50 people) can be reserved. There is water but no showers or hookups. *De Motte Campground* is about 25 miles south on Hwy 67 and has 22 similar $10 sites. Both are USFS campgrounds open from mid-May through October, and Jacob Lake is open from April with no water or fee.

Kaibab Lodge Camper Village (☎ 520-643-7804), off Hwy 67 a mile south of Hwy 89A, has more than 100 sites from $10 (tents) to $22 (hookups) open from mid-May through October. There is water but no showers.

Jacob Lake Inn (☎ 520-643-7232) has simple motel rooms and cabins for about

$70 to $85 double ($100 for family units sleeping six) in summer. There is a restaurant and store. The *Kaibab Lodge* (☎ 520-638-2389 in season, 520-526-0924, 800-525-0924 year-round), on Hwy 67, 25 miles south of Jacob Lake, is open when the road is open. Rooms with private bath in duplex cabins rent from $70 for a double to $100 for rooms that sleep five. A restaurant serves breakfast and dinner.

GRAND CANYON NATIONAL PARK – NORTH RIM

The differences between the North and South Rims of the Grand Canyon are elevation and accessibility. The North Rim is more than 8000 feet above sea level with some points going over 8800 feet. Winters are colder, the climate is wetter and the spruce-fir forest above the rim is much thicker than the forests of the South Rim. Winter snows close the roads to car traffic until mid-May. The road closes by December 1 or earlier if there is heavy snow. There is only one road in, so visitors must backtrack more than 60 miles after their visit.

Because it's such a long drive from any major city or airport, only 10% of Grand Canyon visitors come to the North Rim. But the views here are spectacular. North Rim visitors are drawn by the lack of huge crowds and the desire for a more peaceful, if more spartan, experience of the canyon's majesty.

Orientation & Information

Forty-four miles from Jacob Lake is **Bright Angel Point**, which has the main visitors' services at the North Rim. Almost 30 miles of paved roads lead to various other overlooks. The park headquarters are at the South Rim. See the South Rim section for general information, entrance fees and backcountry permits. The park's automated telephone system (☎ 520-638-7888) has both South and North Rim information.

The North Rim Visitor Center (☎ 520-638-7864) is in the Grand Canyon Lodge (the North Rim's only hotel) and is open from 8 am to 8 pm from May 15 through

October 15. The usual NPS activities and information are available. The Backcountry Office (for backpackers) is in the ranger station near the campground, 1½ miles north of the visitor center/lodge. Other services available at the North Rim (in season) are a restaurant, gas station, post office, bookstore, general store, coin laundry and showers, medical clinic and tours. After October 15, all services are closed except the campground, which remains open weather permitting. After December 1, everything is closed.

Climate & When to Go

North Rim overnight temperatures drop below freezing as late as May and as early as October. The hottest month, July, sees average highs in the upper 70°s F and lows in the mid 40°s F. The North Rim is wetter than the South Rim although the rain pattern is similar. Winter snowfall is heaviest from late December to early March, when overnight temperatures normally fall into the teens and sometimes below 10°F, though very few people visit then.

During winter, you can ski in and, with a backcountry camping permit, camp. It takes about three days to ski in from where the road is closed, so this journey is for adventurous and highly experienced winter campers/skiers. In the past, snowcat shuttles were commercially available but were discontinued in 1997. Call the Backcountry Office for details and updates.

North Rim Drives

The drive on Hwy 67 through the Kaibab Plateau to Bright Angel Point takes you through thick forest. There are excellent canyon views from the point, but to reach other overlooks you need to drive north for almost 3 miles and take the signed turn east to **Point Imperial** and **Cape Royal**. It is 9 miles to Point Imperial, which is, at a lofty 8803 feet, the highest overlook in the entire park and has stunning views.

Backtrack about 4 miles from Point Imperial and then drive 15 miles south to Cape Royal where there are more great views and some short hiking trails.

TONY WHEELER

KIM HAMMAR

MARIA MASSOLO

MARIA MASSOLO

Top: Mule team on the South Kaibab Trail at the South Rim of Grand Canyon National Park, Arizona
Bottom Left: Mooney Falls, Havasupai Indian Reservation, Arizona

Middle Right: Grand Canyon, Arizona
Bottom Right: Kayaking rapids on the Colorado River, Grand Canyon, Arizona

Top: White House, Canyon de Chelly National Monument, Arizona

Bottom Left: Wa:k Powwow, San Xavier del Bac Mission, near Tucson, Arizona

Bottom Right: Petroglyphs and cacti, Saguaro National Park, Arizona

With 4WD and high clearance, you can take unpaved roads to several other outlooks along the North Rim. These roads may be closed by bad weather or other factors – information is available from any ranger or the park information line. Many of these roads require leaving the park, driving through USFS or BLM lands, then reentering the park.

One of the most spectacular of these remote overlooks is the **Toroweap Overlook** at **Tuweep**, far to the west of the main park facilities. An unpaved road, usually passable to cars, leaves Hwy 389 from 9 miles west of Fredonia and heads 55 miles to the Tuweep Ranger Station, which is staffed year-round. An alternative route is a 90-mile dirt road from St George, Utah. It is five more miles from Tuweep to the Toroweap Overlook, where there is primitive camping but no water or other facilities – you must be totally self-sufficient.

Hiking & Backpacking

The most popular quick hike is the paved half-mile trail from the Grand Canyon Lodge south to the extreme tip of **Bright Angel Point**, which offers great views at sunset. The 1½-mile **Transept Trail** goes north from the lodge through forest to the North Rim Campground, where there are also rim views.

Two trailheads, including the North Kaibab trailhead, are at a parking lot 2 miles north of the lodge. The **Ken Patrick Trail** travels through rolling forested country northeast to Point Imperial, about 10 miles away. This trail may be overgrown and require route-finding skills. About a mile along this trail, a fork to the right (east) becomes the Uncle Jim Trail, a fairly rugged 5-mile loop offering fine views from the rim.

Another rim possibility is the uncrowded **Widforss Trail**, which leaves from a side road north of the main visitors' area. This 5-mile trail (one way) offers both forest and canyon views.

A rugged, rarely used (and therefore crowd-free) inner-canyon hike follows the Old Bright Angel Trail, from the Ken Patrick Trail, through the Roaring Springs Canyon, to hook up with the North Kaibab Trail. Before embarking on this hike, consult with a North Rim ranger.

The **North Kaibab Trail** plunges down to Phantom Ranch at the Colorado River, 5,750 feet below and 14 miles away. This is the only maintained rim-to-river trail from the North Rim and it connects with trails to the South Rim. The first 4.7 miles are the steepest, dropping well over 3000 feet to **Roaring Springs** – a popular all-day hike and mule-ride destination. Drinking water is available at Roaring Springs from May to September only. If you prefer a shorter day hike below the rim, you can walk just three-quarters of a mile down to **Coconino Overlook** or 1 mile to the **Supai Tunnel**, 1400 feet below the rim, to get a flavor of steep inner-canyon hiking.

Hikers wishing to continue to the river will normally camp. **Cottonwood Campground** is 7 miles and 4200 feet below the rim and is the only campground between the North Rim and the river. Here, there are 14 backcountry campsites (available by permit only), drinking water from May through September and a ranger station. About 1½ miles below the campground a short side trail leads to pretty **Ribbon Falls**, a popular bathing spot but with no camping. Phantom Lodge and the Bright Angel Campground are 7 and 7½ miles below Cottonwood (see the South Rim section).

Because it is about twice as far from the North Rim to the river as from the South Rim, rangers suggest three nights as a minimum to enjoy a rim-to-river and return hike, staying at Cottonwood on the first and third nights and Bright Angel on the second. Fit and experienced hikers could enjoy a two-night trip, staying at Cottonwood both nights and hiking down to the river and back to Cottonwood on the second day. Faster trips, while technically feasible, would be an endurance slog and not much fun.

Hiking from North to South Rim requires a shuttle to get you back (see the South Rim for details).

ARIZONA

Backcountry Permits In the winter, the trails of the North Rim are regarded as backcountry-use areas, and snow can accumulate to five feet at the rim. Though the North Rim Campground (see Places to Stay, below) is closed, it is available for backcountry use. However, there are only two ways to get to the campground in winter – either hike from the South Rim up to the North Rim via the North Kaibab Trail or cross-country ski 52 miles from Jacob Lake, a route that takes three days.

Permits for Cottonwood Campground and any other backcountry campgrounds must be applied for as far in advance as possible from the Backcountry Office on the South Rim (see the South Rim section for full details). If you don't have an advance permit, get on the waiting list at the Backcountry Office (open 8 am to noon and 1 to 5 pm daily in season) in the North Rim ranger station near the campground as soon as you arrive. Your chances of getting a Cottonwood or Bright Angel Campground permit for the next day are slim; however, if you can wait two to four days, you'll probably get one. The ranger station can advise you of other, much more remote, backcountry campgrounds, most of which require a long drive on dirt roads followed by a hike.

A hikers' shuttle from the lodge to the Bright Angel trailhead is $5 for the first hiker and $2 for each additional hiker in your group. Ask at the lodge for tickets. Shuttles are available from 6 am to 8 pm.

Cycling
Mountain bikes are allowed on all paved roads and some unpaved roads on the North Rim. No wheeled vehicles are allowed on hiking trails.

Organized Tours
Van In season, daily three-hour narrated tours to Point Imperial and Cape Royal leave from the lodge and cost $20 ($10 for four- to 12-year-olds). A schedule is posted in the lobby.

Mule Trail Rides (☎ 520-638-9875 in season, 801-679-8665 otherwise), offers rides for $15 for an hour (minimum age is six), $35 for a half day (minimum age is eight) and $85 for an all-day tour into the Grand Canyon, including lunch (minimum age is 12). Advance reservations are recommended, or stop by their desk (open 7 am to 7 pm) in the Grand Lodge to see what is available. Mule rides are not available to the Colorado River except from the South Rim (see the South Rim section, above, for more information).

Places to Stay & Eat
Backcountry camping requires a permit (see Hiking & Backpacking, above).

The only other place to camp is *North Rim Campground*, 1½ miles north of the Grand Canyon Lodge, with 82 sites for $12 each. There is water, a store, snack bar and coin-operated showers and laundry, but no hookups. Make reservations (☎ 301-722-1257, 800-365-2267) up to five months in advance. Without a reservation, show up before 10 am and hope for the best.

The historic *Grand Canyon Lodge* (☎ 520-638-2611 in season, 303-297-2757, fax 303-297-3175 year-round for reservations) is usually full and reservations should be made as far in advance as possible. There are about 200 units: both motel rooms and a variety of rustic and modern cabins sleeping up to five people. All have private bath; only a few cabins have canyon views. Rates vary from $55 to $95 for a double and $70 to $110 for five people.

The lodge has a snack bar open from 6:30 am to 9 pm, a restaurant (☎ 520-638-2612) open 6:30 to 10 am, 11:30 am to 2:30 pm and 5 to 9:30 pm, and a bar open from 11 am to 10 pm. Dinner reservations are required and breakfast reservations are advised in the attractive restaurant.

A general store by the campground sells food and camping supplies from 8 am to 8 pm.

Getting There & Away
There is no public transport. A North to South Rim shuttle (☎ 520-638-2820) leaves daily at 7 am for $60 one way or $100 roundtrip and takes five hours.

FREDONIA

From Jacob Lake (7921 feet), Hwy 89A drops 3250 feet in 30 miles to Fredonia, which is much warmer. Founded by Mormons in 1885, Fredonia now has more than 1200 inhabitants and is the main town in the Arizona Strip. The larger Kanab, 7 miles north in Utah, has much better developed tourist facilities, but Fredonia has information about the Kaibab National Forest.

Information

The town offices and chamber of commerce (☎ 520-643-7241) are at 130 N Main. The Kaibab National Forest District Headquarters (☎ 520-643-7395), 430 S Main, is open from 7:30 am to 5 pm, Monday to Friday, and in summer from 8 am to 4:30 pm on Saturdays. The post office (☎ 520-643-7122) is at 85 N Main. The police (☎ 520-643-7108) are at 116 N Main.

Places to Stay & Eat

A few small places provide basic rooms in the $30s and may close in winter. *Blue Sage Motel & RV* (☎ 520-643-7125), 330 S Main, has a few RV hookups. Opposite is the *Ship Rock Motel* (☎ 520-643-7355), 337 S Main, which looks like the cheapest.

The *Grand Canyon Motel* (☎ 520-643-7646), 175 S Main, has stone cabins with kitchenettes in some units. The *Crazy Jug Motel* (☎ 520-643-7752), 465 S Main, charges in the $40s and is adding more rooms. Also try the *Jackson House* (☎ 520-643-7702), 90 N Main, with some rooms sleeping six or eight people.

Nedra's Cafe (☎ 520-643-7591), 165 N Main, serves Mexican and American food, Navajo tacos and breakfast any time between 6 am and 10 pm Monday to Saturday in summer.

Two miles north of town, just before the state line, *Travelers Inn Restaurant & Lounge* (☎ 520-643-7402), 2631 N Hwy 89A, serves American fare for lunch and dinner but is closed on Sunday. In winter, both places have reduced hours and may close.

AROUND FREDONIA

Pipe Spring National Monument

Ancient Indians and Mormon pioneers knew about this permanent spring in the arid Arizona Strip. Ranching began here in 1863 and a fort named **Winsor Castle** was built in 1870 to protect the ranchers from Indian attacks. In 1923, the 40-acre ranch was bought by the NPS as a historical monument documenting cowboy life on the Western frontier.

Today, visitors can relive late-19th-century cowboy life by touring the well-preserved ranch buildings and fort, examining historic exhibits and watching historically accurate reenactments by rangers in period costume. Tours of Winsor Castle are offered every half hour (last tour at 4 pm) and a short video is shown on request at the visitor center. At various times of year, cattle are rounded up and branded.

A visitor center (☎ 520-643-7105) is open from 8 am to 5 pm daily except New Year's Day, Thanksgiving and Christmas. There is a bookstore and snack bar. Admission is $2 for adults, and Golden Access, Age and Eagle Passes are honored. The monument is 14 miles west of Fredonia on Hwy 389. Further information is available from the Superintendent, HC65, Box 5, Fredonia, AZ 86022.

Kaibab-Paiute Indian Reservation

Fewer than 200 Paiutes live in this reservation, which completely surrounds the Pipe Spring National Monument. The tribally operated *Campground* (☎ 801-559-6537) is a half mile east of Pipe Spring. There used to be a casino here but it has closed. The desolate and abandoned-looking campground offers RV hookups for $5 and tent sites for $3.

Kanab Canyon

Marked on most maps as Kanab Creek, this is actually the largest canyon leading to the Colorado River's north side. In places, Kanab Canyon is 3500 feet deep and it effectively splits the relatively developed eastern part of the Arizona Strip from the

remote western part. From Fredonia, Kanab
Canyon goes south for 60 miles to the Grand
Canyon. Adventurous canyoneers enjoy
hiking this route, which is described in
Annerino's *Adventuring in Arizona*. Permits
are required in some stretches. Drivers of
high-clearance vehicles can drive through
the Kaibab National Forest to Hack Canyon
and Jumpup Canyon, two popular entry
points into the lower part of Kanab Canyon.

The Northwest Corner

This is the most remote part of the state.
Much of it is BLM land managed by
offices in Kanab and St George, Utah.
There are a few ranches and mines as well
as wilderness areas with absolutely no
development. They are reachable by a network of dirt roads. To explore this area,
you need a reliable high-clearance vehicle
and plenty of water and food. If you break
down, you might not see another car for
days. Consult with the BLM before you go.

The 'best' unpaved roads are the ones
heading to Tuweep Ranger Station and
Toroweap Overlook Campground (see
North Rim Drives, above).

Lake Powell Area

The next major canyon system on the Colorado River northeast of the Grand Canyon
is (was) Glen Canyon. Called 'The Canyon
That No One Knew,' in the 1950s it was the
heart of the largest roadless area in the continental USA. A few old-time river runners
and canyoneers tell of a canyon that rivaled
the Grand Canyon for scenic grandeur and
was full of ancestral Indian sites, but most
people hadn't even heard of this remote
wilderness area when work began on the
Glen Canyon Dam in 1956.

Conservationists fought hard against the
construction of the dam, realizing that not
only would the beautiful canyon be destroyed, but the character of the Southwest
would also change dramatically. Seven
years later, the dam was finished, and Glen
Canyon slowly began filling up to become

the second largest artificial reservoir in the
country, helping fuel the uncurbed population growth of the desert. The reservoir is
Lake Powell.

PAGE

Dam construction in the late 1950s gave
birth to this new town in the high desert. At
the height of construction 7500 people
lived here, but the population dropped considerably after work was finished. Since
the 1980s, the popularity of newly formed
Lake Powell as a boaters' resort has returned Page's population to peak levels.

Page is now the largest Arizonan town in
the huge area north of I-40 and is a regional
center for southeastern Utah as well. Tourists value Page not only as a convenient
stopping place between the two states
but also for the recreation opportunities
afforded by Lake Powell (7 miles from the
town center). The tourism industry is experiencing a boom and hotel rooms are overpriced and booked up in summer.

Information

The chamber of commerce (☎ 520-645-
2741, 888-261-7243, fax 520-645-3181,
chamber@page-lakepowell.com), 644 N
Navajo Drive, PO Box 727, Page, AZ
86040, is open from 8:30 am to 5 pm Monday to Friday in winter, with extended
hours and weekend openings in spring,
summer and fall. The Powell Museum (see
below) has visitor information and will
make motel and tour reservations. Numerous kiosks around town are stocked with
useful brochures. Locals wearing 'Community Host' badges wander around downtown ready to answer visitors' questions.

The library (☎ 520-645-2231) is at 697
Vista Ave. The post office (☎ 520-645-
2571) is at 44 6th Ave. The hospital (☎ 520-
645-2424) is at Vista Ave and N Navajo
Drive. The police (☎ 520-645-2463) are at
547 Vista Ave.

Things to See & Do

The small **Powell Museum** (☎ 520-
645-9496, fax 520-645-3412, museum@
page-lakepowell.com), 6 N Lake Powell

45

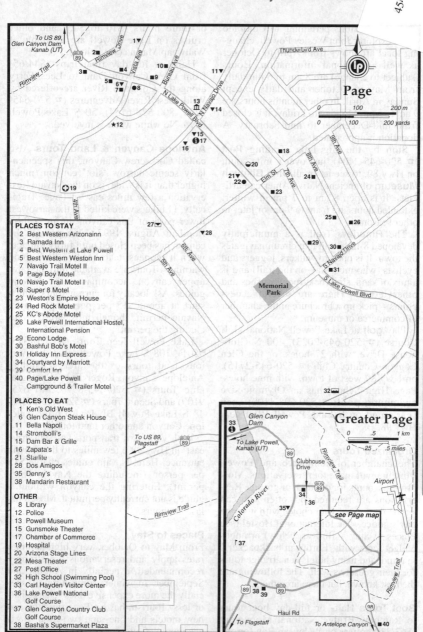

PLACES TO STAY
2 Best Western Arizonainn
3 Ramada Inn
4 Best Western at Lake Powell
5 Best Western Weston Inn
7 Navajo Trail Motel II
9 Page Boy Motel
10 Navajo Trail Motel I
18 Super 8 Motel
23 Weston's Empire House
24 Red Rock Motel
25 KC's Abode Motel
26 Lake Powell International Hostel,
     International Pension
29 Econo Lodge
30 Bashful Bob's Motel
31 Holiday Inn Express
34 Courtyard by Marriott
39 Comfort Inn
40 Page/Lake Powell
     Campground & Trailer Motel

PLACES TO EAT
1 Ken's Old West
6 Glen Canyon Steak House
11 Bella Napoli
14 Strombolli's
15 Dam Bar & Grille
16 Zapata's
21 Starlite
28 Dos Amigos
35 Denny's
38 Mandarin Restaurant

OTHER
8 Library
12 Police
13 Powell Museum
15 Gunsmoke Theater
17 Chamber of Commerce
19 Hospital
20 Arizona Stage Lines
22 Mesa Theater
27 Post Office
32 High School (Swimming Pool)
33 Carl Hayden Visitor Center
36 Lake Powell National
     Golf Course
37 Glen Canyon Country Club
     Golf Course
38 Basha's Supermarket Plaza

ARIZONA

Blvd, has exhibits pertaining to Colorado River explorer John Wesley Powell, changing local art shows from April to October as well as regional information. Hours (subject to change) are 8 am to 6 pm daily from May to October and daily except Sunday in April. In other months hours are 9 am to 5 pm Monday to Friday; it is closed from mid-December to mid-February. A donation is appreciated.

Stop by the Big Lake Trading Post (☎ 520-645-2404), just over a mile south on Hwy 89, to see its small **Diné Bikeyah Museum** of ancient Native American artifacts. It is open 8 am to 7 pm in winter; extended hours are 6 am to 9 pm or later in other seasons.

The **Rimview Trail** is a municipally developed 8-mile trail that circumnavigates the town. It is open to walkers, joggers and cyclists (who must stay on the trail) and is a mix of sand, slickrock, rocky washes and other terrain. There are several access points – pick up a brochure at the chamber of commerce or museum.

Play **golf** at Lake Powell National Golf Course (☎ 520-645-2023), 400 N Clubhouse Drive, with 27 holes, or the Glen Canyon Country Club (☎ 520-645-2715), on Hwy 89 west of town, with nine holes. Page High School has an Olympic-size **swimming pool** (☎ 520-608-4100) open year-round on S Lake Powell Blvd near Hwy 98.

Organized Tours

The chamber of commerce and Powell Museum will make tour reservations. Most offer discounts for children or groups. Reservations are required, but often you can get on the tour of your choice with just one day's notice. The International Hostel (see Places to Stay – Budget, below) arranges budget tours with 'European backpackers' in mind, and many hotels can arrange tours for their guests as well. The following are the best known, but there are others.

Boat Tours Half- or full-day boat tours to Rainbow Bridge National Monument ($63/83), cruises on Wahweap Bay for one or more hours ($10 to $45) and other cruises on Lake Powell are available at Wahweap Marina (see below).

Half- or full-day float trips ($44/65) from Glen Canyon Dam to Lees Ferry along the Colorado River are offered by Wilderness River Adventures (☎ 520-645-3279, 800-528-6154), 50 S Lake Powell Blvd. No white water is involved.

Antelope Canyon & Land Tours Also called Corkscrew Canyon, this spectacularly scenic narrow 'slot' canyon (much higher than it is wide) is on the Navajo Reservation a few miles east of Page. Tragically, 11 hikers were killed in the narrowest lower parts of this canyon during a flash flood in August 1997. This part of the canyon has been closed until further notice; when it reopens, take heed of flash flood warnings. Tours are available into the safer upper canyon, accompanied by Navajo guides. Ask locally for current tours, which start at about $15 per person plus a $5 Navajo permit, though most are $27 including the permit.

Lake Powell Jeep Tours (☎ 520-645-5501), 108 S Lake Powell Blvd, has various land tours of the area, including Antelope Canyon. Roger Ekis' Photographic Tours (☎ 520-645-8579, 801-675-9109) and Scenic Tours (☎ 520-645-5594), 48 S Lake Powell Blvd, also offer Antelope Canyon and other land tours.

With your own transport, you can drive east on Hwy 98 a few miles to the canyon entrance. Here, Navajo guides charge $15 per person (including the Navajo entry permit). Entering the canyon without a guide is not currently permitted. Most tours last 1½ hours.

Places to Stay

From May to October, very high summer rates apply and reservations are strongly recommended, especially in August and September. In winter, some hotels (especially the more expensive ones) charge half or less. Tourism has hit Page quickly, and new motels and one- and two-room B&B accommodations are scrambling to catch up. However, summer demand still exceeds available rooms, so you should arrive by early afternoon if you don't have a reservation. Rooms are generally clean and modern – no Route 66 motels or creaky Victorian hotels in Page. Note that there are campgrounds and a motel at Wahweap Marina, 5 miles away (see Glen Canyon National Recreation Area, below).

In the past few years, dozens of people have opened one or two rooms in their homes to provide simple B&B accommodations. Places open and close every year. The chamber of commerce and museum can help with B&B and last-minute accommodations.

Places to Stay – Camping

Page/Lake Powell Campground & Trailer Motel (☎ 520-645-3374), 949 S Hwy 98, has more than 70 sites, mainly for RVs with hookups ($19) and a few for tents ($15). There are showers, a pool, spa and coin laundry. Trailer motel rooms are about $60 a double.

Places to Stay – Budget

The very friendly *Lake Powell International Hostel* (☎ 520-645-3898, 800-545-5405), 141 8th Ave, PO Box 1077, Page, AZ 86040, charges $12 to $15 per person in dorms (up to six people) or about $35 to $40 for private double rooms in its *International Pension*. All have bathrooms. There are laundry facilities, kitchen privileges, outdoor barbecues and volleyball court, free coffee and free shuttles to the airport and Lake Powell. You don't have to have an HI/AYH card to stay here. The hostel is clean, well run and deservedly popular so call a week ahead to reserve a bed in summer.

The cheapest motels, which have simple but clean doubles in the $40s or low $50s in summer, include *Bashful Bob's Motel* (☎ 520-645-3919), 750 S Navajo Drive; the *Page Boy Motel* (☎ 520-645-2416), 150 N Lake Powell Blvd, which has a small pool; *Navajo Trail Motel I* (☎ 520-645-9508), 800 Bureau; *Navajo Trail Motel II*, 640 Vista Ave; *KC's Abode* (☎ 520-645-2947),

126 8th Ave; and *Red Rock Motel* (☎ 520-645-0062), 114 8th Ave. Call ahead for all of these!

Places to Stay – Middle

Weston's Empire House (☎ 520-645-2406, 800-551-9005, fax 520-645-2647), 107 S Lake Powell Blvd, has 70 nice motel rooms for about $70 as well as a pool, restaurant (6 am to 9 pm) and bar. The *Lake Powell Motel* (☎ 520-645-2477, 800-528-6154, fax 520-645-1031), about 4 miles north of the Glen Canyon Dam at the junction of Hwy 89 and Wahweap Marina Rd, has 24 reasonable rooms from $70 to $80. The motel sits on a hill with nice views and is away from road noise. It is closed from November through March.

The *Super 8 Motel* (☎ 520-645-2858, fax 520-645-2890), 75 S 7th Ave, has 40 standard rooms in the $80s (half price in winter). The *Econo Lodge* (☎ 520-645-2488), 121 S Lake Powell Blvd, has more than 60 units, including some large, family-size rooms with three queen-size beds and mini-suites with refrigerators for $70 to $95. It has a swimming pool.

Places to Stay – Top End

None of these hotels are luxurious, but their summer prices are in the Top End category.

The *Best Western Arizonainn* (☎ 520-645-2466, fax 520-645-2053), 716 Rimview Drive, has more than 100 rooms, some with balconies and distant lake views, for $100 to $110; a few 'suites' are pricier. There is a pool, spa, exercise room, restaurant (6 am to 10 pm in a separate building) and bar. A block away, the *Best Western at Lake Powell* (☎ 520-645-5988, fax 520-645-2578), 208 N Lake Powell Blvd, has 132 spacious rooms for $80 to $110 and some mini-suites for up to $140. There is a pool, spa and breakfast bar (extra charge). Opposite, the older *Best Western Weston Inn* (☎ 520-645-2451, 800-637-9183, fax 520-645-9552), 207 N Lake Powell Blvd, has 100 ordinary rooms, some with balconies, for around $90 to $100 for a double. There is a seasonal pool.

The *Holiday Inn Express* (☎ 520-645-9000, fax 520-645-1605), 751 S Navajo Drive, has 70 modern rooms for about $100, including a breakfast buffet. There is a pool and spa. The *Ramada Inn* (☎ 520-645-8851, fax 520-645-2523), 287 N Lake Powell Blvd, has 130 rooms, many have balconies with a view, for $110 in summer. The hotel features a nice pool area, coin laundry, restaurant (6 am to 10 pm), bar and room service. The new *Comfort Inn* (☎ 520-645-5858, fax 520-645-3255), 649 S Lake Powell Blvd, has 100 rooms, a few with kitchenettes, for $80 to $130 including continental breakfast. There is a pool and spa. The *Courtyard by Marriott* (☎ 520-645-5000, fax 520-645-5004), 600 Clubhouse Drive, offers 150 large and attractive rooms for about $150. There is a pool, spa, exercise area, restaurant (6 am to 10 pm) and bar. The hotel overlooks the national golf course.

Places to Eat
For an early breakfast, your best bet is one of the hotel restaurants (see above), which serve mainly American food.

Strombolli's (☎ 520-645-2605), 711 N Navajo Drive, serves pizza and other Italian specialties and is popular because of its large outdoor deck and cheap dinners, which are advertised as 'under $10.' More upscale Italian dining in a more intimate atmosphere is found at *Bella Napoli* (☎ 520-645-2706), 810 N Navajo Drive. This is considered by many to be the best restaurant in Page and is open from 5 to 9 pm daily in summer, till 10 pm on Fridays and Saturdays, closed on Sundays in fall and spring and closed entirely in winter. Dinners are in the $8 to $17 range, and there is a patio.

Glen Canyon Steak House (☎ 520-645-3363), 201 N Lake Powell Blvd, serves American food from 6 am to 10 pm. Page's 'Wild West' steak house is *Ken's Old West* (☎ 520-645-5160), 718 Vista Ave, open from 4 to 10 pm (11 pm on Friday and Saturday) with meaty meals priced from $10 to $20. The *Dam Bar & Grille* (☎ 520-645-2161), 644 N Navajo Drive, also serves good steaks but in modern surroundings that remind you why Page is here. It features a 'cook your own' grill if you feel like doing it yourself, though I don't know why you'd go to a restaurant to cook! It serves seafood and pasta as well (you don't have to boil the noodles) and it has sports TV and live music on weekends.

If you don't want American food, Mexican lunch and dinner is served at *Zapata's* (☎ 520-645-9006), 615 N Navajo Drive, and *Dos Amigos* (☎ 520-645-3036), 608 Elm. Eat Chinese at *Starlite* (☎ 520-645-3620), 46 S Lake Powell Blvd, or *Mandarin* (☎ 520-645-5516), 683 S Lake Powell Blvd.

Denny's (☎ 520-645-3999), on Hwy 89, is open 24 hours.

Entertainment
Movies are shown at the *Mesa Theater* (☎ 520-645-9565), 42 S Lake Powell Blvd.

Ken's Old West features live and recorded country & western music and dancing nightly except Sunday in the summer and a few times a week during other seasons. *Gunsmoke Theater* (☎ 520-645-1888), next door to the Dam Bar & Grille, has tourist-oriented Western musical entertainment and dinner nightly at 7 pm during the summer for $30. The show is $17.50 without dinner.

Getting There & Away
Airlines serving Page Airport change often. Currently, Great Lakes Airlines (☎ 520-645-3665, 800-274-0662) flies to Phoenix.

Bus services come and go. The International Hostel usually knows what's going on. Arizona Stage Lines (☎ 520-645-9356, 888-253-7420), 55 S Lake Powell Blvd (in the Mobil service station/Page Food Mart) recently instituted daily van service to Flagstaff.

Getting Around
Budget (☎ 520-645-3977) rents cars at the Page Airport. Rates are expensive and you can save money by renting in Flagstaff or Phoenix.

GLEN CANYON NATIONAL RECREATION AREA

When the Glen Canyon Dam was finished in 1963, the Colorado River and its tributaries (especially the San Juan River) began backing up for 186 miles. It took until 1980 to fill the artificial Lake Powell, flooding the canyon to a depth of 560 feet at the dam and creating almost 2000 miles of shoreline. The 1933-sq-mile Glen Canyon National Recreation Area (GCNRA) was established in 1972, primarily emphasizing activities on the lake, which accounts for 13% of the total area. The remainder is many square miles of remote backcountry, which can be explored on foot or by a few roads north of the confluence of the Colorado and San Juan Rivers.

Information

The Carl Hayden Visitor Center (☎ 520-608-6404) is at the dam, 2 miles north of Page (the only town close to the GCNRA). Hours are 7 am to 7 pm from Memorial Day to Labor Day and 8 am to 5 pm at other times. Most of the GCNRA is in Utah, but it is treated as a whole here. Entrance to the area costs $5 per vehicle or $3 per individual and is valid for up to seven days. Boats are $10 for up to seven days or $25 a year. Golden Age, Access and Eagle Passes are accepted. Up-to-date information is available in the free newspaper *Reflections*, available on arrival.

Five miles north of the visitor center is Wahweap Marina, the largest marina on Lake Powell. It offers complete visitors' services. Four more marinas are scattered along the shores of Lake Powell in Utah. All marinas have an NPS ranger station and there's a smaller visitor center at Bullfrog Marina. Details of services available in each marina are described under individual marina headings below. Aramark (☎ 602-278-8888, 800-528-6154, fax 601-331-5258), PO Box 56909, Phoenix, AZ 85079, is the concessionaire for houseboats and lodges at the lake.

The GCNRA also operates a ranger station at Lees Ferry and an interpretive center at Navajo Bridge on Hwy 89A

(see Marble Canyon & Lees Ferry Area, earlier in this chapter).

Further information is available from the Superintendent (☎ 520-608-6200), GCNRA, PO Box 1507, Page, AZ 86040.

Books & Maps The *Boater's Guide to Lake Powell* by Michael R Kelsey is for boaters interested in taking side hikes from the shore, including information about shore camping for people using small boats. *Lake Powell and its 96 Canyons: Boating and Exploring Map* by Stan Jones is an annotated map with plenty of other useful information.

Camping Regulations Rising and falling water levels have caused buried human waste to contaminate the lake and make some areas unsafe for swimming. These areas are closed and marked with yellow buoys and signs. In 1997, a new regulation was established that anyone camping within a quarter mile of the lake must use a portable toilet. Rangers can tell you which beaches have toilets. If you camp on a beach without a toilet, you can rent portable ones from the marinas. Human waste must be disposed of in designated dump stations.

Climate & When to Go The area is open year-round. The water-level elevation of 3700 feet makes the GCNRA cooler than Lake Mead and other downstream recreation areas, but summer temperatures can still rise to more than 100°F on some days. Average summer maximum temperatures are in the 90°s F, with water temperatures ranging from 70°F to 80°F from June to September. Overnight temperatures drop into the 70°s F, making sleeping comfortable. The humidity is low year-round and there is little rainfall. Summer is the most popular season with the highest rates for boat rentals and motel rooms.

Spring can be very windy, and cold water temperatures preclude swimming or water-skiing without a wet suit – in May the water averages a brisk 64°F. Fall water temperatures average 69°F in October; the lowest average is 46°F in February.

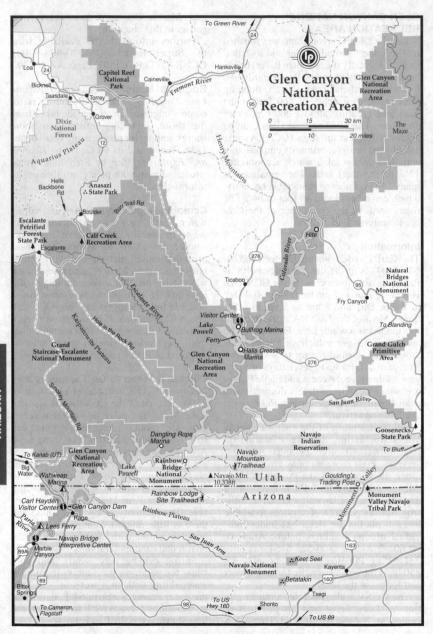

ARIZONA

Hikers and backpackers will find April to June and September to October the most pleasant months. In winter, overnight temperatures often fall into the 20°s F but rise into the 40°s F during the day in December and January, the coldest months.

Water levels fluctuate depending on season and water use. The highest levels are in late spring and early summer, when you can boat just a little farther into some of the side canyons.

Dangers & Annoyances Several people drown every year in boating, swimming or diving accidents, many of which are alcohol related. Lake Powell has no lifeguards, but the lake is patrolled by park rangers. Children under 12 are required by law to wear life jackets when on a boat, while everyone in a boat, regardless of age, is required to have a preserver immediately accessible (not stowed). Use common sense.

Glen Canyon Dam

Right next to the Carl Hayden Visitor Center, the dam can be visited on self-guided tours year-round. From April through October, free guided tours lasting 60 to 90 minutes leave hourly on the half hour until 90 minutes before the center closes. Tours take you along the top and then deep inside the dam in elevators that drop to near the bottom. The dam is 710 feet high and required over 5 million cubic yards of concrete to build.

Wahweap Marina

Only 7 miles from Page, Wahweap Marina & Lodge (☎ 520-645-2433, fax 520-645-1031) offers complete services – boat tours and rentals (see Water Sports and Houseboating, below), boat and car service and fuel, laundry, showers and a supply store. Call the marina directly for information and reservations less than seven days in advance. Otherwise, call Aramark (see Information, above) for reservations, which are strongly recommended in summer.

Wahweap Campground has about 180 sites without hookups on a first-come, first-served basis open from April through October. Sites are $12. Next door *Wahweap RV Park* has 123 year-round sites with hookups for $24, or $17 from November through March (when tenting is permitted). There are showers and a playground.

Wahweap Lodge has 350 comfortable rooms with coffeemakers, refrigerators, balconies or patios, for $150 to $160 from mid-June through September, about $120 in spring and fall and $100 in winter. Suites are $200 in summer. About half the rooms have lake views, and there are two pools and a spa. The lodge has room service, a moderately priced coffee shop and a good restaurant. Hours are 6 am to 10 pm (7 am to 9 pm in winter). A bar has live entertainment ranging from Native American dancing to piano music.

Aramark offers seven tours ranging from a one-hour ride on a steam-powered paddlewheel riverboat ($10) to a seven-hour tour to Rainbow Bridge ($83). There are discounts for three- to 11-year-olds. All tours leave from Wahweap Marina. Rainbow Bridge tours also leave from Bullfrog and Halls Crossing Marinas.

Bullfrog Marina

Bullfrog Resort & Marina (☎ 435-684-3000) is 96 miles upstream from the dam and is the lake's second largest marina. It is located on Lake Powell's north shore and the nearest town is tiny Hanksville, Utah, 72 miles north.

There is a GCNRA visitor center (open 8 am to 5 pm daily April to October, weekends in March and November, and closed in winter), a medical clinic (summer only), post office, ranger station, laundry, showers, boat rentals (see Water Sports and Houseboating, below), fuel and services, auto fuel and services, and an expensive supply store. Reservations (which should be made well in advance) for houseboats, the campground and Defiance House Lodge are provided by Aramark (see Information, above).

Bullfrog RV Park and Campground is open year-round with about 100 tent sites ($10) and 24 RV sites ($22). Ask at the ranger station about free primitive camping (no water) at several places along the shore. Note the new camping regulations (see Information, above).

Defiance House Lodge has about 60 comfortable rooms with TV, refrigerator and coffeemaker for $100 to $120 in summer, less in winter. A few housekeeping trailers, with two or three bedrooms, two bathrooms, fully equipped kitchen and electricity range from $120 a double to $160 for six people in summer, less in winter. The lodge has a restaurant open for breakfast, lunch and dinner year-round and a fast-food place open during the summer. There is also a bar.

A ferry connects Bullfrog Marina with Halls Crossing Marina. (See the Lake Powell Ferry sidebar.)

Halls Crossing Marina

Halls Crossing Marina (☎ 435-684-7000) is on the south shore of the lake, opposite Bullfrog. The nearest town is Blanding, Utah, 75 miles to the east. Services include a ranger station, boat rentals, fuel and service, auto fuel and service, laundry, showers, a supply store and an air strip. Services are provided by Aramark.

Halls Crossing RV Park and Campground has about 60 tent sites ($10) and 20 RV sites ($22). The ranger can suggest free campsites along the shore. *City Center Lodge* has 20 housekeeping trailers with kitchens; they sleep up to six for about $150 in summer, $100 from November through March. There is no restaurant.

Hite Marina

Hite Marina (☎ 435-684-2278) is 139 miles upriver from the dam and is the most northerly marina. Hanksville, Utah, is 45 miles northwest and is the nearest small town. Services at Hite include a ranger station, boat rentals, fuel and service, auto fuel and service, and a supply shop. Aramark provides reservations.

The marina has a free primitive campground (no water) and housekeeping trailers (see Halls Crossing Marina for details). Water is available from the boat ramp.

Dangling Rope Marina

This marina is about 40 miles upriver from the dam and can be reached only by boat. This is the closest marina to Rainbow Bridge National Monument (see below). Services include a ranger station, boat fuel and services, and a supply store.

Fishing

You can fish year-round. Spring and fall are considered the best times, although summer isn't bad. Bass, crappie and walleye are the main catches on the lake. Licenses are required and are available from any marina; you'll need Arizona and/or Utah licenses depending on where you fish.

Water Sports

The public can launch boats from NPS launch ramps at the marinas. Boats ranging from 16-foot runabouts to 59-foot houseboats sleeping 12 are available for rental from Aramark. Water skis and jet skis can also be rented, but the marinas aren't geared to renting kayaks or dinghies.

Water-skiing, scuba diving, sailing and swimming are summer activities. Average water temperatures of 62°F in November and 64°F in May are too chilly except for the most dedicated enthusiasts with wet or dry suits.

Aramark rents boats: A 16-foot skiff seating six with a 25-hp motor is $66 a day or $303 a week in summer. Skiffs are suitable for exploring and fishing. Larger boats with larger engines for towing water-skiers cost three or four times as much.

Water 'toys' include jet skis for about $220 a day or $1320 a week in summer and water skis and other equipment packages for $20 a day or $100 a week. See Houseboating, below, for winter discounts.

All marinas except Dangling Rope rent boats and skis. Jet skis are not available at Hite.

Houseboating

Houseboating is popular – hundreds of houseboats are available for rent and there are more every year. Despite the number of boats, the large size of the lake still allows

Lake Powell Ferry

The 150-foot-long *John Atlantic Burr* provides a link between Bullfrog and Halls Crossing Marinas year-round and holds 150 passengers, 14 cars and 2 buses. The 3.1-mile crossing takes 25 minutes and can save as many as 145 miles of driving, depending on your route. The ferry is usually out of service in February for maintenance, and boats may be delayed by bad weather. Phone Halls Crossing (☎ 435-684-8000) for information.

Fares

Foot Passengers

12 to 64 years	$2
5 to 11 years	$1
Other ages	free

Vehicles
(including driver and passengers)

Bicycle	$2
Motorcycle	$3
Vehicles under 20 feet	$9
Vehicles 20 to 70 feet	$12 to $38
Vehicles over 70 feet	$50

Schedule

Departs Halls Crossing	Departs Bullfrog
8 am	9 am
10 am	11 am
Noon	1 pm
2 pm	3 pm*

Additional Service
Mid-April through October

4 pm	5 pm

Additional Service
Mid-May through September

6 pm	7 pm

*The 3 pm boat may be delayed until 3:30 pm when school is in session.

Houseboats on Lake Powell are provided by Aramark (see Information, above), which also provides small boats, tours and lodging in marinas – these can be combined into a variety of packages. Houseboats can be rented from any marina except Dangling Rope and advance reservations are required.

Summer rates range from about $860 to $1620 for three days or $1500 to $2950 for a week in boats ranging from 36 to 52 feet in length and sleeping eight. Rates are about $2200 to $4300 for three days to a week for 59-foot boats sleeping 12. Four-, five- and six-day rentals are available and two-day rentals are available outside of summer. From about October to April (dates vary with boats and marinas), discounts of about 40% are offered.

All houseboats have tiny to midsize refrigerators, simple cooking facilities, a toilet and shower, a gas barbecue grill and 150-quart ice chests.

Larger boats may have some of the following: electric generator (allowing air conditioning, microwave, toaster, coffeemaker, TV, VCR and radio), canopies, swim slides and ladders. Luxury boats have all these features upgraded and with extra space. Boats are booked up well in advance in summer.

RAINBOW BRIDGE NATIONAL MONUMENT

On the south shore of Lake Powell, Rainbow Bridge is the largest natural bridge in the world and a site of religious importance to the Navajo. No camping or climbing on the bridge is permitted, but visitors can come by boat, horse or on foot. Primitive camping is allowed outside the monument, less than a mile from the bridge. Most people visit the bridge by boat tour (see Page, above) and then hike a short trail. Rainbow Trails & Tours in Shonto, on the Navajo Reservation, offers horseback trips to the monument. (See Shonto in the Northeastern Arizona chapter for details.)

Very few people arrive on foot. However, hikers leave from the Rainbow Lodge trailhead in Arizona (the lodge is abandoned)

ARIZONA

houseboaters to get away from others. Houseboats can sleep from eight to 12 people, but accommodations are tight so make sure you are good friends with your fellow shipmates.

or Navajo Mountain trailhead in Utah and walk about 14 miles to the monument. The trailheads are reached by dirt roads and the trails themselves are not maintained. This hike is for experienced backpackers only; you should carry water and be self-sufficient.

Both trailheads are on the Navajo Reservation and a tribal permit should be obtained from the Navajo Nation Recreational Resources Department (see the Northeastern Arizona chapter). The monument is administered by the GCNRA.

ARIZONA

Western Arizona

Western Arizona is not only the hottest part of the state, it is often the hottest area in the nation. The low-lying towns along the Colorado River (Bullhead City, Lake Havasu City and Yuma) boast average maximum daily temperatures of more than 100°F from June to September, and temperatures exceeding 110°F are not unusual. Balmy weather during the rest of the year attracts thousands of winter visitors, many of whom end up staying – western Arizonan cities have some of the fastest growing populations in the USA.

After the Colorado River leaves the Grand Canyon, it turns south and forms the western boundary of Arizona, referred to as Arizona's 'west coast.' Several dams form huge artificial lakes that attract those holiday-makers escaping the intense summer heat – water-skiing and jet-skiing, sailing and boating, fishing, scuba diving and plain old swimming are popular activities. In addition, travelers enjoy the wild scenery, visit dams, explore wildlife refuges and ghost towns, gamble in casinos and see perhaps the most incongruous of sights in the desert Southwest, London Bridge.

In the northwestern corner of the state, the massive Hoover Dam forms Lake Mead and the smaller Davis Dam forms Lake Mohave, both of which are major attractions within the Lake Mead National Recreation Area. The far shores of the Colorado River and the two lakes lie in the state of Nevada, which provides plenty of gambling opportunities for Arizonans and other visitors. The Nevada town of Laughlin, joined by a bridge across the Colorado to Bullhead City in Arizona, provides the closest full-service casinos to Phoenix and Tucson.

In the center of Arizona's western border is Lake Havasu, formed by the Parker Dam. Lake Havasu City, with the popular tourist destination of London

Bridge, is on the lake's eastern shore. The western shores lie in California. Yuma, Arizona's third-largest metropolitan area, is in the southwestern corner of the state adjoining a historically important crossing point of the Colorado River.

Northwestern Arizona

This section covers the area bounded by the Colorado River and Lake Mead to the north and west and does not include the Arizona Strip north of the Colorado. Most of the area falls into Mohave County, named after the Mohave Indians who originally lived in the area and now have reservations along the lower Colorado River. Other important Indian tribes in the region include the Hualapai and Havasupai, both of which have reservations bordering the southwestern reaches of Grand Canyon National Park and provide tourist services to the canyon (see the Grand Canyon & Lake Powell chapter).

The area features low to mid-elevation desert interspersed with several north-south mountain ranges that created a barrier to east-west exploration. The highest are the Hualapai Mountains. Pine-clad Hualapai Peak reaches 8417 feet. The more modest Cerbat Mountains and Black Mountains are rich in minerals. Below these, the Colorado River drops from 1221 feet at Lake Mead to only 482 feet at Lake Havasu City.

Northwestern Arizona was virtually unknown to Europeans until the mid-19th century. In 1857, Edward Beale, using camel caravans, surveyed a wagon route across northern Arizona near what is now Kingman. Twelve years later, John Wesley Powell made the first boat descent of the

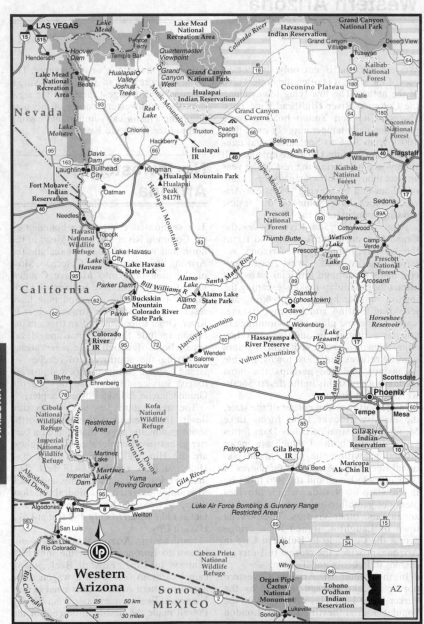

Western Arizona

0   25   50 km
0   15   30 miles

AZ

Grand Canyon, emerging at what is now Lake Mead. Lewis Kingman surveyed a railway route through northern Arizona in 1880; the railroad was completed in 1883. The area became an important mining region, with gold, copper, silver and turquoise all being important products. In the mid-1900s, mining declined and dams and irrigation projects led to some development of agriculture. Since then, centrally located Kingman has become the major trade and transportation center, and tourism has become important.

This section begins with Kingman and the surrounding area, and then follows the course of the Colorado, first east and then south.

KINGMAN

Although attracting fewer visitors than the nearby resorts of Bullhead City and Lake Havasu City, Kingman (population 35,000) provides an excellent base for exploring the northwestern corner of the state. Slightly cooler than the other towns due to its higher elevation, Kingman is also conveniently located at the intersection of I-40 with both historic Route 66 and Hwy 93, the main Phoenix-Las Vegas route.

Kingman is the major town along I-40 between California and Flagstaff and offers plenty of inexpensive and mid-priced accommodations. Founded by Lewis Kingman in 1880 as a railway stop on the soon-to-be-built Atchison, Topeka and Santa Fe Railroad, it is also the most historic of the area's larger towns. In 1887, Kingman became the seat of Mohave County. Several turn-of-the-19th-century buildings survive.

Orientation

I-40 cuts through the northern and western suburbs of Kingman. Drivers leave the freeway at exits 48 and 53 to enter town along Kingman's main street, Andy Devine Ave, named after a Hollywood actor who was raised here. Andy Devine Ave also forms part of historic Route 66 and most accommodations and services are found

along it. Streets and avenues east of 1st St are prefixed E (as in E Andy Devine Ave); west of 1st are prefixed W.

Information

The chamber of commerce (☎ 520-753-6106, fax 520-753-1049), 333 W Andy Devine Ave, is open from 8 am to 7 pm weekdays and from 9 am to 5 pm on weekends between Memorial Day and Labor Day. During the rest of the year it closes two hours earlier. The BLM (☎ 520-757-3161) is at 2475 Beverly Ave. The library (☎ 520-692-2665) is at 3269 N Burbank. The local newspaper is the *Kingman Daily Miner*. The post office (☎ 520-753-2480) is at 1901 Johnson Ave. The Kingman Regional Medical Center (☎ 520-757-2101) is at 3269 Stockton Hill Rd. The police (☎ 520-753-2191) are at 2730 E Andy Devine Ave.

Historic Walking Tour

The chamber of commerce has a map detailing this walk, which leaves from the Mohave Museum and goes down Beale to the area bounded by 3rd and 6th and Spring to Andy Devine Ave. Some of the oldest buildings include the old red-brick school, built in 1896 at 4th and Oak; Kingman's oldest adobe dwelling, built in 1887 diagonally across from the Bonelli House; and the Hotel Beale at 325 E Andy Devine Ave, built in 1899 and under restoration.

Mohave Museum of History & Arts

This attractive museum (☎ 520-753-3195), 400 W Beale, next door to the chamber of commerce, highlights local history and is open from 9 am to 5 pm on weekdays and from 1 to 5 pm on weekends, but is closed on major holidays. Admission is $2 for adults; 50¢ for children under 13.

Bonelli House

The Bonelli family came from Switzerland in 1858 and were early pioneers in Utah and Arizona. They built a house in Kingman in 1894 and rebuilt it in 1915 after it was destroyed by fire. Located at N 5th and Spring (☎ 520-753-1413), the house is now municipally owned; it is on the National

ARIZONA

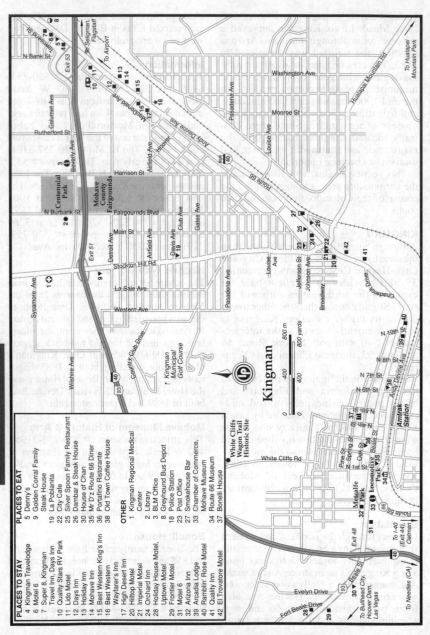

PLACES TO STAY
4   Kingman Travelodge
6   Motel 6
7   Super 8, Kingman
     Travel Inn, Days Inn
10 Quality Stars RV Park
11 Lido Motel
12 Days Inn
13 Holiday Inn
14 Mohave Inn
15 Best Western King's Inn
16 Best Western
     Wayfarer's Inn
17 High Desert Inn
20 Hilltop Motel
24 Imperial Motel
24 Orchard Inn
28 Holiday House Motel
29 Frontier Motel
31 Motel 6
32 Arizona Inn
39 Arcadia Lodge
40 Ramblin' Rose Motel
41 Quality Inn
42 El Trovatore Motel

PLACES TO EAT
5   Denny's
9   Golden Corral Family
     Steak House
19 La Poblanita
22 City Cafe
25 Silver Spoon Family Restaurant
26 Dambar & Steak House
30 House of Chan
35 Mr D'z Route 66 Diner
36 Portafino Ristorante
38 Old Town Coffee House

OTHER
1   Kingman Regional Medical
     Center
2   Library
3   BLM Office
8   Greyhound Bus Depot
18 Police Station
23 Post Office
27 Smokehouse Bar
33 Chamber of Commerce,
     Mohave Museum
34 Route 66 Museum
37 Bonelli House

Kingman

Register of Historic Places and is open to the public as an example of early Anglo architecture in Arizona. Hours are 1 to 4 pm Thursday to Monday, except major holidays. Admission is by donation.

Route 66 Museum
This new museum is due to open east of the chamber of commerce in 1999.

Hualapai Mountain Park
This park (☎ 520-757-3859) surrounds 8417-foot Hualapai Peak and offers a popular summer getaway for local residents. Fourteen miles southeast of Kingman (take Hualapai Mountain Rd from Andy Devine Ave), it features picnicking, camping, cabins, wildlife observation, 6 miles of maintained trails and 10 miles of undeveloped trails.

Near the park is Hualapai Mountain Lodge Resort (see Places to Stay, below).

Activities
You can **golf** nine holes at the Kingman Municipal Golf Course (☎ 520-753-6593), 1001 E Gates Ave. Valle Vista Golf Course (☎ 520-757-8744), 16 miles northeast of town on Route 66, has 18 holes.

At Centennial Park, north of I-40 between Burbank and Harrison, play **miniature golf** (☎ 520-757-5566, 520-757-5561), **swim** at the pool (☎ 520-757-7910), play **tennis**, or enjoy the other athletic facilities.

Special Events
As part of the Route 66 Fun Run, a car rally along Route 66 between Seligman and Topock held during the last weekend in April, there is a car show in Kingman, followed by dancing in the evening. There are also events in the small towns along the route; call the Route 66 Association of Arizona (☎ 520-753-5001) for details. Also see the Route 66 section, below.

The Arts Festival during Mother's Day weekend in May includes metal workers and woodcarvers as well as the more usual types of artists. The Mohave County Fair is held in mid-September and Andy Devine Days, which includes a parade, rodeo, gem show and other events, takes place during late September or early October.

Places to Stay – Camping
At *Hualapai Mountain Park*, more than 70 campsites are available for $6, most with picnic tables and grills. Eleven RV sites with hookups are $12. Water and toilets are available.

There are also 16 rustic cabins with beds, kitchens, and hot showers. Most cabins have a fireplace or wood-burning stove. Visitors supply their own bedding, cooking utensils and towels. Most cabins sleep two to four people and rent for $25 (propane heater), $30 (wood-burning stove), or $40 (fireplace). One cabin sleeps six and has a stove ($45) and another sleeps 10 and has a fireplace ($55). Stay five nights and get two free.

Campsites are on a first-come, first-served basis. Reserve cabins at the Mohave County Parks Department in Kingman (☎ 520-757-0915), 3675 E Andy Devine Ave, PO Box 7000, Kingman, AZ 86402, open from 8 am to 5 pm Monday to Friday. Credit cards are accepted. Cabins are very popular in summer, so book ahead. Cabins and campsites are open in winter, though snow may necessitate 4WD or chains.

The BLM runs *Wild Cow Campground*, 6 miles by steep dirt road south of Hualapai Mountain Park. Vehicles must be under 20 feet. This campground is open from May to October, has no water and is $4.

The *KOA* (☎ 520-757-4397, 800-562-3991), 3820 N Roosevelt (northeast of town), has mainly RV sites and a small tenting area. Rates are $16 to $20 for two people, with an extra $1 for sewage hookup and $3 for electric hookup. A swimming pool, game room, coin laundry, convenience store and miniature golf are available.

The *Quality Stars RV Park* (☎ 520-753-2277), 3131 McDonald Ave, offers sites from $12 to $18 depending on whether you use the hookups. There is a coin laundry and small pool.

Places to Stay – Budget
Cheap hotels are found along Andy Devine Ave (old Route 66). Prices may rise during

holidays or special-event weekends; make reservations for those dates and for most summer weekends. Winter rates are lower than the summer rates given below.

The cheapest places have basic double rooms in the $20s, including the *Arcadia Lodge* (☎ 520-753-1925), 909 E Andy Devine Ave; *Frontier Motel* (☎ 520-753-6171), 1250 W Beale; the *Lido Motel* (☎ 520-753-4515), 3133 E Andy Devine Ave; the *Mohave Inn* (☎ 520-753-9555), 3016 E Andy Devine Ave; the *Uptown Motel* (☎ 520-753-2773), 1239 W Beale; the *Holiday House Motel* (☎ 520-753-2153), 1225 W Beale; and the *Orchard Inn* (☎ 520-753-5511), 1967 E Andy Devine Ave.

For doubles in the $30s, the *High Desert Inn* (☎ 520-753-2935), 2803 E Andy Devine Ave; the *Ramblin' Rose Motel* (☎ 520-753-5541), 1001 E Andy Devine Ave; and the *Hilltop Motel* (☎ 520-753-2198), 1901 E Andy Devine Ave, are all good small motels. The latter two have pools. Also try the *El Trovatore Motel* (☎ 520-753-6918), 1440 E Andy Devine Ave, and the *Imperial Motel* (☎ 520-753-2176), 1911 E Andy Devine Ave, both of which have pools.

There are two *Motel 6*s, both with a pool. The one at 3351 E Andy Devine Ave (☎ 520-757-7151, fax 520-757-2438) is about $34 for one or two people, and the one at 424 W Beale (☎ 520-753-9222, fax 520-753-4791) charges $40/46 for singles/doubles in summer, $32/38 in winter and has a restaurant next door.

Places to Stay – Middle

The *Super 8 Motel* (☎/fax 520-757-4808), 3401 E Andy Devine Ave, lacks a pool but has nice enough rooms for $40.88/45.88. The following all have a pool. The *Arizona Inn* (☎ 520-753-5521), 411 W Beale, has an adjoining coffee shop, is convenient for the town center and charges about $32/41. The *Kingman Travelodge* (☎ 520-757-1188, 800-367-2250, fax 520-757-1010), 3275 E Andy Devine Ave, has nicer rooms for $45/50. The *Kingman Travel Inn* (☎ 520-757-7878, fax 520-692-8366), at 3421 E Andy Devine Ave, has decent rooms in the

$40s. There are two *Days Inn*s, both with a spa and some rooms with microwave and refrigerator, at 3023 E Andy Devine Ave (☎ 520-753-7500, fax 520-753-4686), which charges around $40/50 (up to $15 more during summer weekends), and at 3381 E Andy Devine Ave (☎ 520-757-7337), which is about $5 cheaper. The *Holiday Inn* (☎ 520-753-6262, fax 520-753-7137), 3100 E Andy Devine Ave, has large rooms from $49/54, dropping during winter.

The *Quality Inn* (☎/fax 520-753-4747), 1400 E Andy Devine Ave, has a sauna, a spa and exercise area, and a decent adjoining restaurant. Route 66 aficionados can examine the memorabilia in the lobby. Rooms cost about $60/70, including continental breakfast. The similarly priced *Best Western King's Inn* (☎ 520-753-6101, 800-750-6101, fax 520-753-6192), 2930 E Andy Devine Ave, has a spa, sauna and free in-room coffee. The *Best Western Wayfarer's Inn* (☎ 520-753-6271), 2815 E Andy Devine Ave, has a spa and spacious rooms with microwaves and refrigerators. This is considered Kingman's best motel. Rates are $66/71 with king-size beds or a little less with double beds. A few two-room units are $88.

Near Hualapai Mountain Park is the *Hualapai Mountain Lodge Resort* (☎ 520-757-3545), with rooms from $50 to $90 and a restaurant.

Places to Eat

The popular *Silver Spoon Family Restaurant* (☎ 520-753-4030), 2011 E Andy Devine Ave, is open from 5 am to 10 pm. Breakfasts cost between $3 and $5, and dinners are a good value in the $5 to $8 range.

The well-recommended *House of Chan* (☎ 520-753-3232), 960 W Beale, is open from 11 am to 10 pm and is closed on Sundays. The service is good and prime rib, steak and seafood are featured in addition to Chinese food. Dinners are in the $7 to $20 range.

Other possibilities include the inexpensive *City Cafe* (☎ 520-753-3550), 1929 E Andy Devine Ave, a locally popular greasy spoon. The *Dambar & Steak House* (☎ 520-753-3523), 1960 E Andy Devine Ave, specializes in large steaks ($10 to $20) in a sawdust-on-the-floor atmosphere. It is open from 4 to 10 pm. Cheaper steaks are served at the *Golden Corral Family Steak House* (☎ 520-753-1505), 3157 Stockton Hill Rd, open from 11 am to 10 pm. Grab a burger or blue plate special at the '50s style *Mr D'z Route 66 Diner* (☎ 520-718-0066), 105 E Andy Devine Ave. Light snacks and international coffees are served at the *Old Town Coffee House* (☎ 520-753-2244), 616 E Beale.

La Poblanita (☎ 520-753-5087), 1921 Club Ave, is one of the better Mexican restaurants with meals in the $5 to $9 range. Hours are 11 am to 10 pm Tuesday to Sunday. For Italian dining, the best is *Portafino Ristorante* (☎ 520-753-7504), in an atmospheric house at 318 Oak, open from 11 am to 2 pm, Tuesday to Friday, and 5 to 9 pm Tuesday to Sunday. Main entrées are $12 to $15, but pastas and pizzas are $6 to $10.

For 24-hour service, there's *Denny's* (☎ 520-757-2028), 3255 E Andy Devine Ave, or the *Flying J Truck Plaza* (☎ 520-757-7300), 3300 E Andy Devine Ave.

Entertainment
The *Smokehouse Bar* (☎ 520-753-9965), 2032 E Andy Devine Ave, has country & western music and dancing on weekends and sometimes midweek in summer. *The Movies* (☎ 520-757-7985), 4055 Stockton Hill Rd, is the local cinema.

Getting There & Away
Air Kingman Airport (☎ 520-757-2134) is 6 miles northeast of town off Route 66. America West (☎ 800-235-9292) flies between Kingman and Phoenix, stopping at Prescott, three or four times a day on weekdays.

Bus The Greyhound Bus Terminal (☎ 520-757-8400), 3264 E Andy Devine Ave, is behind the McDonald's Restaurant. Four daily buses go to Phoenix (four hours, $40), Tucson and El Paso, Texas. Four daily buses

go to Las Vegas, Nevada (two hours) and Salt Lake City, Utah. Two daily buses go to Flagstaff (three hours) and Albuquerque, New Mexico (11 hours). Two daily buses go to Los Angeles, California (eight hours).

Train Amtrak (☎ 800-872-7245) has a daily train west to Los Angeles and east to Flagstaff, Albuquerque and Kansas City, Missouri. Trains leave late at night or very early in the morning, and the station is on Andy Devine Ave between 4th and 5th.

ROUTE 66
Historic Route 66, once the main highway from Chicago to Los Angeles, has been largely forgotten in favor of the interstate freeway system (see the Route 66 sidebar in Facts about Arizona). The longest remaining stretch of what was once called 'The Main Street of America' stretches 160 miles from Seligman (see the Central Arizona chapter) to Topock on the Arizona-California border. Apart from Kingman, Route 66 winds through some empty and lesser-traveled northwestern Arizonan countryside. Every year, this desolate stretch is transformed into its bustling former self with the annual Route 66 Fun Run around the last weekend in April, when all manner of beautifully restored antique cars mix with old beaters along the highway. Traveling west from Seligman, you pass the following points.

Grand Canyon Caverns
These caverns, 23 miles west of Seligman on Route 66, are 210 feet underground. Tourists visiting them in the 1920s were lowered on a rope and the caverns became a popular roadside attraction during the Route 66 heyday. Today, an elevator takes people below ground, where a three-quarter-mile trail winds by the geological formations.

The *Grand Canyon Caverns and Motel* (☎ 520-422-3223, 520-422-3224), PO Box 180, Peach Springs, AZ 86434, is open year-round. Entrance, including a 45-minute guided tour, costs $8.50 for adults and $5.75 for four- to 12-year-olds. Hours are 8 am to 6 pm in summer and 10 am to 5 pm in winter. The motel charges about $40 to $63 for one to five people in summer and substantially less in winter. There is a restaurant open when the caverns are open. The caverns are a mile behind the motel.

Peach Springs

This village, 12 miles west of the Grand Canyon Caverns, contains the Hualapai Indian Reservation tribal offices and tourist lodge (see the Grand Canyon & Lake Powell chapter). During the Route 66 Fun Run, the tribe prepares a barbecue for passing motorists.

Truxton

This blink-and-you'll-miss-it town, 9 miles west of Peach Springs, has the basic and inexpensive (though prices rise dramatically during the Route 66 Fun Run) *Frontier Motel & Café* (☎ 520-769-2238) and an RV park. There is entertainment here during the Fun Run.

Valentine & Hackberry

Both Valentine, 10 miles west of Truxton, and Hackberry, 5 miles farther west and 25 miles from Kingman, are even smaller than Truxton. Valentine has an old dance hall with entertainment during the Fun Run. Hackberry features the eccentric **Old Route 66 Visitor Center** (☎ 520-769-2605), built in 1934 as the Hackberry General Store and now run by a Route 66 memorialist, Robert Waldmire, who says the center is 'open by chance or appointment' every day. Admission is free.

Oatman

This gold-mining town in the rugged Black Mountains about 25 miles southwest of Kingman was founded in 1906. Two million ounces of gold were extracted before the last mine closed in 1942, and the population of thousands plummeted to hundreds. Today, 500,000 visitors annually come through this self-styled 'ghost town' to see the old buildings, browse the gift shops, enjoy the weekend shenanigans (gunfights at high noon and Western dancing at night) and feed the wild burros.

Route 66 is the only important street through town. In early days, the torturously steep road through the Black Mountains was a major obstacle for drivers and it remains winding and narrow, slowing traffic through Oatman to a crawl: a natural tourist trap. Vehicles more than 40 feet long are prohibited. The chamber of commerce (☎ 520-768-6222) has information. The *Oatman Hotel* (☎ 520-768-4408) was rebuilt in 1920 after the first one burned down. The two-story adobe structure is on the National Register of Historic Places and the simple rooms are almost unchanged since Hollywood legends Clark Gable and Carole Lombard honeymooned here in the 1930s. Rooms start at $35 and the shared bathroom is down the hall. Nonguests can go upstairs to see the Gable-Lombard room, or grab a bite alongside the grizzled miners in the *Saloon & Restaurant* downstairs (the bar is wallpapered with $1 bills). The *Z-Inn* (☎ 520-768-4603) is another simple motel. There are several eateries, including *Cactus Joe's Cantina* (☎ 520-768-3242), which serves Indian fry bread, chile, burgers and rattlesnake!

Topock

This stretch of Route 66 ends in little Topock, where travelers continue on I-40. *Golden Shores Trailer Park* (☎ 520-768-1193) has spaces for RVs.

CHLORIDE

Founded in 1862 by silver miners, Chloride is the oldest mining town in Arizona and home to the oldest continuously operating post office in the state (since 1871).

In the late 1800s, some 5000 people lived here, working many mines. The most famous was the Tennessee Schuylkill Mine, which was closed in 1948 after six decades of operation. Locals claim it produced more than $100 million in gold, silver, lead and zinc.

Today, about 400 people live here and tourism is the economic mainstay. The town is quieter and more low-key than crowded Oatman (see above) and Jerome (see the Central Arizona chapter) mining towns. There are antique and art stores, old buildings and occasional melodramas, usually held on the first and third Saturdays of summer months. A signed dirt road goes 1.3 miles southeast of town to a rocky hillside with huge murals painted by artist Roy Purcell.

The chamber of commerce (☎ 520-565-2204), PO Box 268, Chloride, AZ 86431, has information. The visitor center is open daily on Tennessee Ave, the main street through town, which continues on to the murals. Visit the old jail, two blocks from the visitor center, with two tiny, grimly barred cells flanking the woodstove-heated guard's room.

Locals dress in turn-of-the-19th-century garb on Old Miners Day, the last Saturday in June. A parade and old-time music and dancing are featured. Watch out for gunfights and showdowns!

There is a small *RV park* (☎ 520-565-4492). The locally famous *Sheps General Store* (☎ 520-565-3643) rents four rooms for $25 to $45 (some include breakfast and/or a private bath). There are three homey cafés and a couple of Western saloons.

The easiest way to Chloride is to head 19 miles northwest from Kingman on Hwy 93 to mile marker 53; turn right for 3½ miles into town on Tennessee Ave.

LAKE MEAD NATIONAL RECREATION AREA (NRA)

The extreme heat and aridity of the far northwestern corner of Arizona made this one of the least hospitable areas of the USA, attracting prospectors and miners but few others. Then, between 1931 and 1936, the Hoover Dam (at that time the world's largest) was built. It backed up the Colorado River, flooding canyons, archaeological sites, wilderness areas and communities and producing Lake Mead, one of the world's largest artificial lakes. In 1953, the smaller Davis Dam was completed, forming Lake Mohave. The dams were built for flood control, irrigation, hydroelectricity and as a water supply to the burgeoning population of the Southwest and southern California.

When the dams were built, people decried the flooding as a destructive waste of archaeological, historical, natural and scenic resources. Today, the two lakes, surrounded by wild desert scenery, attract millions of annual visitors, ranging from curious day-trippers looking at the dams to vacationing families spending a week boating on the lakes. Barely an hour's drive from Las Vegas, the recreation area certainly doesn't suffer from a shortage of visitors.

Orientation

Hwy 93 (between Kingman and Las Vegas) crosses the Hoover Dam and passes the main visitor center and park headquarters. Hwy 68 (between Kingman and Bullhead City) goes near the Davis Dam. Both dams straddle the Arizona/Nevada state line, as does most of the recreation area. Minor paved and dirt roads provide access to a number of lodges, marinas, camping areas, boating areas and wilderness areas around the lakes.

The 2337-sq-mile recreation area encompasses both 110-mile-long Lake Mead and 67-mile-long Lake Mohave, about 700 miles of shoreline, and many square miles of desert around the lakes, in both Arizona and Nevada. In addition, the remote Shivwits Plateau area in Utah, reachable only by long dirt roads from the Arizona Strip north of the Grand Canyon, offers a largely unwatered, high-desert wilderness area administered by Lake Mead NRA.

Motels, developed campgrounds, restaurants, marinas, grocery stores and gas stations are available in three lakeside areas in Arizona and six in Nevada. There are also several undeveloped backcountry campgrounds and boat-launch areas.

Information

The Alan Bible Visitor Center (☎ 888-293-8990) in Nevada, 5 miles west of Hoover Dam, is open from 8:30 am to 4:30 pm (Pacific time) daily except Thanksgiving, Christmas and New Year's Day. The center has maps, books, information, exhibits, films and a small desert botanical garden.

ARIZONA

The smaller Katherine Landing Visitor Center (☎ 520-754-3272) in Arizona, 3 miles north of Davis Dam, is open 8 am to 4 pm. There are eight ranger stations. Get advance information from the Superintendent, Lake Mead NRA, 601 Nevada Hwy, Boulder City, NV 89005 (☎ 702-293-8906/8907).

Every year, people die in boating, swimming or diving accidents, many of which are alcohol related. Take care. In an emergency, contact a ranger or call the 24-hour emergency number (☎ 702-293-8932).

The area is open year-round and summer temperatures rise over 100°F most days (best for water activities), but winter highs are in the 50°s and 60°s (best for hiking and backpacking). Long hikes are not recommended in summer, when heat prostration is a real problem. Get the National Weather Service forecast by calling ☎ 702-736-3854.

Admission is free, although there is talk of implementing a fee in the future.

Hoover Dam

At 726 feet high, Hoover Dam remains one of the tallest in the world and is an impressive feat of engineering and architecture. There is an exhibit center, and guided tours (☎ 702-293-8387, 520-293-8321) leave from here at frequent intervals throughout the day between 8:30 am and 5:45 pm.

The standard tours leave every 10 minutes and take up to 80 people. These tours descend into the dam by elevator, last 40 minutes, and are followed by a 25-minute video presentation. The cost is $6 ($5 for those over 62; $2 for six- to 16-year-olds). One-hour 'behind the scenes' hardhat tours are limited to 15 people paying $25 each. These tours leave on demand.

Parking on the Arizona side is limited to several lots along Hwy 93; free shuttle buses take visitors to the dam. On the Nevada side, there is a parking area ($2) just past the exhibit center.

Hwy 93 crosses the Colorado River as a two-lane road over the dam. The narrow, steep and winding road down to the dam gets backed up for miles on busy days, so prepare for delays.

Davis Dam

You can visit the 200-foot-high Davis Dam, at the south end of Lake Mohave near Bullhead City, on a free self-guided tour from 7:30 am to 3:30 pm daily.

Fishing

The lakes are said to have some of the best sport fishing in the country. Striped bass (some are in excess of 50lb) are one attraction; rainbow trout, largemouth bass, channel catfish, black crappie and bluegill are also likely catches. November to February is the best time for trout and crappie; March to May is OK for trout, catfish, crappie and bass; June to August is best for catfish, bass and bluegill; September to mid-October continues to be OK for bass and, as the water cools, for crappie. Check with a visitor center or ranger station for current fishing tips.

You can fish year-round with a license, available at the boating marinas (which also have fishing supplies and charters). Those with a state fishing license (Arizona or Nevada) can fish from the appropriate shore. Boat anglers need a state license with a special-use stamp from the other state.

Boating

Free public boat-launch areas are available at the resort marinas mentioned below and elsewhere in the recreation area. Parking near the boat launches is available but limited to seven days.

Because of the large number of powerboats and the huge area of the lakes, small vessels such as canoes and rafts are not encouraged, except through the Black Canyon of the Colorado River, just below the Hoover Dam. Here, the water flows at a controlled three to five miles per hour and the 11-mile trip to Willow Beach Marina or the farther 13 miles to Eldorado Canyon are popular trips (backcountry camping is possible). Canoe launching is free but by permit only. Call ☎ 702-293-8204 from 8 am to 5 pm, Monday to Thursday, for permit applications, maps and information. Call at least two weeks in advance for weekend launching dates; only 30 canoe launches are allowed per day.

Boat Tours Lake Mead Cruises (☎ 702-293-6180) has four to six narrated cruises a day from Lake Mead Resort Marina to Hoover Dam (1¾ hours roundtrip). You also have the option to disembark at the dam, take a dam tour and return on a later trip. The boat is an air-conditioned, three-decked, Mississippi-style paddle wheeler. Fares are $16/6 for adults/children two to 12. Also available are two-hour weekend breakfast buffet cruises ($21/10), dinner cruises from Sunday to Thursday ($29/15) and dinner/dance cruises on Friday and Saturday ($43, adults only). Departure times vary with season, and reservations for meal cruises are recommended.

The more adventurous can do a raft tour from below the Hoover Dam, down the Black Canyon of the Colorado River to Willow Beach Resort. The motorized rafts will hold up to 45 passengers and the tour is $65 for adults, $35 for children under 12, and free for children under five. Lunch is included and a bus returns you to your starting point at Black Canyon Raft Tours (☎ 702-293-3776), Expedition Depot, 1297 Nevada Highway, Boulder City, NV 89005. Tours are from February to November and the roundtrip takes 5½ hours. During the summer months, you may see desert bighorn sheep, especially in the early hours of the day.

Boat Rentals Fishing, ski, patio and houseboats are available as well as jet skis. Seven Crown Resorts (☎ 800-752-9669), PO Box 16247, Irvine, CA 92623, operates the Lake Mohave Resort near Katherine Landing on Lake Mohave; the Temple Bar Resort on the southeast arm of Lake Mead; the Lake Mead Resort, near Boulder Beach by the Hoover Dam, Nevada; and the Echo Bay Resort on the north arm of Lake Mead, Nevada. All have small-boat rentals ranging from $60 per day for fishing boats to $225 a day for ski boats or jet skis (half-day and weekly rates are also available).

The Lake Mohave and Echo Bay Resorts have houseboats that sleep up to 6, 10 or 14 people and include kitchen, shower, refrigerator and air conditioner. Rates for the high season (June 15 to September 15 and Memorial Day weekend) range from $950 to $1950 for three days and two nights or $1550 to $2550 for seven days/six nights. During the rest of the year rates are $400 less. Add taxes of 5% in Arizona or 7% in Nevada. Houseboats travel about 8 miles and use about 5 gallons of gas per hour.

Forever Resorts (☎/fax 602-968-5449, 800-255-5561) also has houseboat rentals at Callville Bay Marina on the north side of Lake Mead, Nevada; and Cottonwood Cove Marina on the west side of Lake Mohave, Nevada. The boats sleep 10 and high-season rates are $1900 for three or four nights and $2995 for seven nights. Rates for the low season (November to April) are $795 and $1100 and the rest of the year rates are intermediate. Taxes and fuel are extra.

All the above places are authorized concessionaires of the National Park Service. In addition to boat rentals, they provide motel rooms and restaurants, grocery stores, gas stations, and fishing bait, tackle and license facilities.

Two things to consider when renting a boat: bring binoculars (they help to read buoy numbers) and make sure you are good friends with your shipmates – a boat sleeping 10 will be very cramped for 10 adults.

Places to Stay & Eat
Kingman and Bullhead City in Arizona, and Las Vegas, Boulder City and Laughlin in Nevada, all have accommodations.

RV campers can stay at the *Temple Bar, Echo Bay* and *Lake Mohave Resorts* for $18 daily or $350 monthly (including hookups). *Cottonwood Cove* charges $20 a night with hookups. The *National Park Service* (☎ 520-767-3401 at Temple Bar; 520-754-3272 at Katherine Landing) operates campgrounds for tents and RVs for $10. There are also campgrounds on the Nevada side.

Seven Crown Resorts and Forever Resorts (see Boat Rentals, above, for telephone

ARIZONA

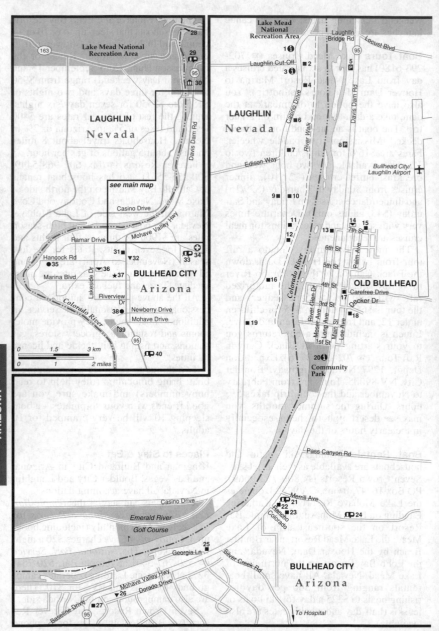

PLACES TO STAY
2   Don Laughlin's Riverside Resort
    Hotel & Casino
4   Flamingo Hilton Laughlin
6   Regency Casino
7   Edgewater Hotel & Casino
9   Ramada Express Hotel & Casino
10 Colorado Belle Hotel & Casino
11 Pioneer Hotel & Gambling Hall
12 Golden Nugget
13 River Queen Resort Motel
15 Palms Motel
16 Gold River Resort & Casino
17 Best Western Bullhead City Inn
18 Nevada Club Inn
19 Harrah's Laughlin Casino & Hotel
21 Bullhead RV Park
22 Motel 6
23 Days Inn
24 River City RV Park
25 Riverfront Motel, Econo Lodge
27 La Plaza Inn
29 Davis Camp
31 Hilltop House Motel
33 Silver Creek RV Park
40 Fiesta RV Resort

PLACES TO EAT
13 El Encanto Restaurant
26 El Palacio, China Szechuan
32 China Panda

OTHER
1   Laughlin Visitors Center
2   Riverside Cinemas
3   Laughlin Chamber of Commerce
5   Parking for Colorado River Ferries
8   Parking for Colorado River Ferries
14 Post Office (Branch)
20 Bullhead Area Chamber
    of Commerce
28 Davis Dam
30 Colorado River Museum
34 Hospital
35 Movie House
36 Post Office (Main)
37 Bullhead City Complex,
    Police Station
38 Back Bay Canoes
39 Chapparal Country Club

Bullhead City & Laughlin

```
0        400        800 m
0        400        800 yards
```

numbers) operate motels and restaurants at several of their resorts. The *Temple Bar Resort* (☎ 520-767-3211) is 47 miles by paved road east of the Hoover Dam. Rates range from $43 to $89 for fishing cabins, double rooms and kitchen suites sleeping four. The *Lake Mohave Resort* (☎ 520-754-3245) at Katherine Landing charges $60 to $83 for doubles, some with kitchens, or $175 for three-room houses with kitchens. Seven Crown Resorts also has similarly priced motels at *Lake Mead Resort* and *Echo Bay Resort*. Forever Resorts' *Cottonwood Cove Motel* (☎ 702-297-1464) on the Nevada shores charges $80 to $90 for doubles from mid-March to October and holidays, and $55 to $60 the rest of the year.

BULLHEAD CITY & LAUGHLIN
Bullhead City (population 29,000), or 'Bull' as some locals call it, is 34 miles west of Kingman at the south end of Lake Mohave. The town was established in the 1940s for the builders of Davis Dam and is now a popular vacation destination for tourists wishing to visit Lake Mohave or cross the bridge over the Colorado River to Laughlin, Nevada, which has the closest casinos to the major Arizona cities.

Orientation
Hwy 95 is the main thoroughfare and runs north-south, parallel to the Colorado River. Many places to stay and eat are found along or just off this strip. At the north end of town, a short bridge across the Colorado joins Bullhead City to Laughlin, Nevada.

Information
The Bullhead Area Chamber of Commerce (☎ 520-754-4121), 1251 Hwy 95, is open Monday to Friday from 8 am to 4 pm between April and October and 9 am to 5 pm the rest of the year. Saturday hours are 9 am to 3 pm. The main post office (☎ 520-758-5711) is at 1882 Lakeside Drive and a branch (☎ 520-754-3717) is at 990 Hwy 95. Bullhead Community Hospital (☎ 520-763-2273) is at 2735 Silver Creek Rd. The police (☎ 520-763-1999) are in the Bullhead City Complex, 1255 Marina Blvd.

The Laughlin Chamber of Commerce (☎ 702-298-2214), 1725 Casino Drive, is almost opposite the enormous Hilton Flamingo Casino. The Laughlin Visitors Center (☎ 702-298-3321) is at 1555 S Casino Drive. Both are open 8 am to 4:30 pm, Monday to Friday, and the visitors center is open till 7 pm on Friday.

Nevada time is one hour behind Arizona in the winter but is the same in summer (no daylight-saving time in Arizona).

Things to See & Do

The **Colorado River Museum** (☎ 520-754-3399), 355 Hwy 95, Bullhead City (located half a mile north of the Laughlin bridge) features local area history. Hours are 9:30 am to 2:30 pm daily, November to March, from Tuesday through Saturday in April, May, June, September and October, and closed in July and August. Admission is free.

You can visit the nearby Davis Dam and Lake Mohave Resort & Marina at Katherine Landing (see Lake Mead NRA, above).

In Laughlin, **gambling** is the main attraction. All the usual casino games are played. Also in Laughlin, Blue River Safaris (☎ 702-298-0910, 800-345-8990) by the Colorado Belle Casino; Laughlin River Tours (☎ 702-298-1047, 800-228-9825) by the Edgewater Casino; and Del Rio Cruises (☎ 702-298-6828, 800-742-3224) have various **river cruises**, depending on water levels. Blue River Safaris also has bus tours to local areas of interest. In Bullhead City, Back Bay Canoes (☎ 520-758-6242), 1450 Newberry Dr, has canoe and kayak rentals as well as guided trips.

Chaparral Country Club (☎ 520-758-6330), 1260 E Mohave Drive, off Hwy 95 at the south end of town, has a nine-hole **golf** course. Nearby, the Chaparral Health Club (☎ 520-763-2582), 1290 E Mohave Drive, features **racquetball** and a gym. A few miles farther south is the Desert Lakes Golf Course (☎ 520-768-1000), 5835 Desert Lakes Drive, with 18 holes. Over in Laughlin, the Emerald River Golf Course (☎ 702-298-0061), 1155 S Casino Drive, also has 18 holes.

A paved **river walk** follows the Nevada bank of the Colorado from the Laughlin bridge past all the casinos. It makes a pleasant 2½ mile stroll.

Places to Stay – Camping

RVs can park overnight in the casino parking lots. There are no hookups, but restaurants and gambling are right on your doorstep. There are several RV parks in Bullhead City; most prefer long-term visitors, require reservations and don't allow tents. Try the *Bullhead RV Park* (☎ 520-763-8353), 1610 Hwy 95, $15 per night; the *Fiesta RV Resort* (☎ 520-758-7671), 3190 Hwy 95, $21 per night; the *River City RV Park* (☎ 520-754-2121), 2225 Merrill Ave, $14 per night; or the *Silver Creek RV Park* (☎ 520-763-2444), 1515 Gold Rush Drive, $16.58 per night. More RV parks are near Hwy 95 south of Bullhead City.

Tent and RV sites are available at *Davis Camp*, run by Mohave County Parks (☎ 520-586-3977), on Hwy 95 almost a mile north of the Laughlin Bridge. Rates are $8 for tents, $15 for RVs with hookups. RV and tent camping is also available at Katherine Landing (see Lake Mead NRA, above).

Places to Stay – Budget

If arriving midweek, check the Laughlin casinos for the best values in town (see Places to Stay – Middle, below). Probably the cheapest place in Bullhead City is the *Palms Motel* (☎ 520-754-2644), 115 Palm Ave, with basic doubles starting as low as $18 midweek. Rooms at the *La Plaza Inn* (☎ 520-763-8080), 1978 Hwy 95, are quite nice and start at $22 midweek, $30 weekends. Both motels give weekly discounts. The *Motel 6* (☎ 520-763-1002), 1616 Hwy 95, has a pool and charges $24 for singles or doubles midweek, and $34 on weekends.

The *Riverfront Motel* (☎ 520-763-3869), 1715 Hwy 95, has kitchenettes in some rooms and charges in the low $30s midweek for a double. Also in the $30s midweek, the *Hilltop House Motel* (☎ 520-753-2198), 2037 Hwy 95, and the *Econo Lodge* (☎ 520-758-8080), 1717 Hwy 95, have nice rooms. The Econo Lodge also has more-expensive rooms (up to $60) with balconies and river views as well as suites (up to $90). Continental breakfast is included and some rooms have microwaves and refrigerators. There is a pool and coin laundry.

Places to Stay – Middle

Casinos The room rates at the Laughlin casinos vary greatly, but most casinos offer a good deal for accommodations and expect to make their money on gambling. The weekend travel sections of major newspapers in Arizona and California sometimes advertise special midweek rates. (In 1997, I stayed in a very comfortable double room at the Gold River for $13 using one of these special rates, and even lower prices are sometimes offered here and elsewhere!) You can expect to get nice double rooms in the teens or low $20s if you go midweek. These are the best lodging bargains in the Southwest, if you limit your gambling to what you can afford. The Laughlin Visitors Center has a free phone that connects directly to all the casinos so you can call to see which has the best deal. Or drive down Casino Drive and watch for the flashing neon '$15.95 FOR TWO' signs. Weekend and holiday rates jump drastically to $50 or more.

The casinos are along Casino Drive, except for the Avi, which is 12 miles south of Laughlin and run by the Fort Mojave Tribe:

Avi Hotel & Casino
  ☎ 702-535-5555, 800-284-2946
Colorado Belle Hotel & Casino
  ☎ 702-298-4000, 800-477-4837
Don Laughlin's Riverside Resort Hotel & Casino
  ☎ 702-298-2535, 800-227-3849
Edgewater Hotel & Casino
  ☎ 702-298-2453, 800-647-4837
Flamingo Hilton Laughlin
  ☎ 702-298-5111, 800-352-6464
Gold River Resort & Casino
  ☎ 702-298-2242, 800-835-7903
Golden Nugget ☎ 702-298-7111, 800-237-1739
Harrah's Laughlin Casino & Hotel
  ☎ 702-298-4600, 800-447-8700,
  800-427-7247
Pioneer Hotel & Gambling Hall
  ☎ 702-298-2442, 800-634-3469

Ramada Express Hotel & Casino
  ☎ 702-298-4200, 800-243-6846
Regency Casino ☎ 702-298-2439

Hotels The following are in Bullhead City. Most offer special lower rates whenever they aren't full. The *Nevada Club Inn* (☎ 520-754-3128), 336 Lee Ave, has a pool, a spa and a tennis court. Double rooms cost in the $50s or less midweek. The *Days Inn* (☎ 520-758-1711, fax 520-758-7937), 2200 Rancho Colorado Blvd, charges about $50 a double midweek, more on weekends, and has a few pricier suites. It has a pool, spa and coin laundry. The *River Queen Resort Motel* (☎ 520-754-3214), 125 Long Ave, also has rooms in this price range, some with kitchenettes, as well as a pool and the El Encanto restaurant. The *Best Western Bullhead City Inn* (☎ 520-754-3000), at 1124 Hwy 95, has a pool, spa and attractive rooms for $36 to $65.

Places to Eat

The casino restaurants in Laughlin have 24-hour service and very cheap buffet meals, but lines can be long.

In Bullhead City, *El Encanto* (☎ 520-754-5100), in the River Queen Resort Motel, is good for Mexican and American food from 11 am to 10 pm. Dinner entrées are in the $6 to $10 range. Another decent Mexican restaurant is *El Palacio* (☎ 520-763-2494), at 1884 Hwy 95. Next door, *China Szechuan* (☎ 520-763-2610), 1890 Hwy 95, is good for Chinese food, as is the *China Panda* (☎ 520-763-8899), 2164 Hwy 95.

Entertainment

The Laughlin casinos often have nightclub shows. Young people like the dance club action at *Tarzan's* in the Golden Nugget and the *Loser's Lounge* in Laughlin's Riverside Resort. Catch films at the *Movie House* (☎ 520-758-6360), 590 Hancock Rd, Bullhead City, or at the five-screen *Riverside Cinemas* (☎ 702-298-2535) next to Don Laughlin's Riverside Casino.

ARIZONA

Getting There & Away

Air The airport (☎ 520-754-2134) is at 600 Hwy 95. Services and carriers change frequently. America West (☎ 800-235-9292) operates several flights a day to and from Phoenix, some via Lake Havasu City.

Bus Try KT Services & Greyhound Bus (☎ 702-298-1934), with an office in the Riverside Casino, offering four buses a day to Kingman and on to Flagstaff, Phoenix or Albuquerque. There are also buses to Las Vegas and Los Angeles.

Tri-State Super Shuttle (☎ 520-704-9000, 800-801-8687) has two buses a day between Bullhead City and Las Vegas airport. They pick up at major hotels.

HAVASU NATIONAL WILDLIFE REFUGE

This is one of a string of wildlife refuges and other protected areas along the lower Colorado River. Habitats include marshes, sand dunes, desert and the river itself. Popular activities for this area include birding and, in the northern reaches, boating through the 16-mile-long Topock Gorge. Overwintering birds – geese, ducks and cranes – are all found here in profusion. After the migrants' departure, herons and egrets nest in large numbers. Many other species are seen, especially shore and marsh birds. Bald eagles and ospreys are often sighted in winter. Desert bighorn sheep are sometimes seen and the elusive

Bald eagle

bobcat is present (though rarely glimpsed), along with common desert mammals such as coyotes, rabbits and pack rats.

Orientation & Information

The section of the reserve north of I-40 is the Topock Marsh. South of I-40, the Colorado flows through Topock Gorge. The southern boundary of the reserve abuts the northern boundary of Lake Havasu State Park, about 3 miles north of London Bridge.

The refuge headquarters (☎ 619-326-3853), 1406 Bailey Ave, Suite B, PO Box 3009, Needles, CA 92363, is open 8 am to 4 pm Monday to Friday. (Limited funds/staff may cause the office to be closed at times.) It has maps, bird lists and information.

Boating

A day of canoeing or just floating through Topock Gorge usually begins at either *Golden Shores Marina* (☎ 520-768-2325) in Arizona or *Park Moabi Campground* (☎ 619-326-4777) in Needles, California. Both places are just north of where I-40 crosses the Colorado River and Park Moabi has boat rentals. Allow about seven hours for the float through the gorge. You can also paddle north into the marsh area. Power boaters should beware of submerged sandbars and other obstacles.

The Jerkwater Canoe Company (☎ 520-768-7753), PO Box 800, Topock, AZ 86436, offers canoe rentals and guided day trips through the gorge as well as a variety of overnight excursions along the river. Jetboat tours from Lake Havasu City are operated by Bluewater Charters (see Lake Havasu City, below).

LAKE HAVASU CITY

Parker Dam, finished in 1938, created 46-mile-long Lake Havasu. Until 1963, there was no town along the lake. Developer Robert McCulloch planned Lake Havasu City as a center for water sports and light industry/business. The city received a huge infusion of publicity when McCulloch bought London Bridge for $2,460,000, disassembled it into 10,276 granite slabs,

ARIZONA

and reassembled it at Lake Havasu City. The bridge, opened in London, England in 1831, was rededicated in 1971 and has become the focus of the city's English Village – a complex of restaurants, hotels and shops built in pseudo-English style. The village is the city's most immediately obvious tourist attraction.

The bridge move was a huge success, and today Lake Havasu City is host to millions of visitors coming not just to see the strange sight of London Bridge in the desert, but also to enjoy water sports, boat tours, shopping, golf and tennis. I've read a local claim that Lake Havasu City attracts more tourists than anywhere in Arizona except the Grand Canyon! The population has doubled in the last decade and is now about 43,000, making this city one of the fastest-growing communities in the Southwest. Although once known as a retirement community, the city now attracts young families. (The population's average age is 35.)

Orientation

Hwy 95, the main drag through town, runs north-south. McCulloch Blvd is the main east-west street and goes over London Bridge. You can't turn from Hwy 95 onto McCulloch Blvd; you have to turn a block before or after and reach McCulloch via Lake Havasu Ave.

Information

The chamber of commerce (☎ 520-453-3444, 800-242-8278, fax 520-680-0010), 314 London Bridge Rd, is open 9 am to 5 pm Monday to Friday. A visitor information center at the English Village is open daily from 9 am to 5 pm (4 pm in summer). The parking lot at the English Village costs $3 per day, but you can get a free 30-minute parking pass for the visitor center.

The library (☎ 520-453-0718) is at 1787 McCulloch Blvd. The post office (☎ 520-855-2361) is at 1750 McCulloch Blvd. The Havasu Samaritan Regional Hospital (☎ 520-855-8185) is at 101 Civic Center Blvd. The police (☎ 520-885-1171) are at 2360 McCulloch Blvd.

Activities

Boating Departing from the English Village, one-hour, narrated, day and sunset boat tours cost about $12 ($5 for children and free for kids under eight) – call Dixie Belle (☎ 520-855-0888, 520-453-6776) or Miss Havasupai (☎ 520-855-7979), across the bridge at the Island Fashion Mall. Also here is Adler Marine (☎ 520-855-1555), which offers sailboat tours and rentals. Bluewater Charters (☎ 520-855-7171, 888-855-7171) in the English Village has jet-boat tours at 9 am daily (subject to seasonal change); the tours cover 60 miles in three hours. Fares are $25, $12 for children, free for kids under 12.

Fishing, rowing, water-skiing and sightseeing boats can be rented from Lake Havasu Marina (☎ 520-855-2159), 1100 McCulloch Blvd, Resort Boat Rentals (☎ 520-453-9613) in the English Village; or the Havasu Landing Resort (☎ 619 858-4593), across the lake in California. Boat rentals vary from about $40 a day for a four-person fishing boat to as much as $300 a day for a decked ski boat. Jet skis and parasailing are available from the Water Sports Center at the Nautical Inn (☎ 520-855-2141, ext 429, or 520-453-6212).

Canoes and kayaks are rented (from $15 a day) and sold at WACKO, Western Arizona Canoe & Kayak Outfitter (☎ 520-855-6414, 520-680-9719). It also offers guided canoeing trips from $39 per person. (Also see Jerkwater Canoe Company in the Hasusu National Wildlife Refuge section, above.) Several other companies rent a variety of watercraft.

Fishing Fishing is possible year-round. The best months (usually) for the favored species are April to July and October and November for largemouth bass, May to July for striped bass, June to September for catfish, March to May for crappie and May to September for bluegill. Licenses, gear and information are available from the boat rental places and Bob Lee's Tackle Shop in the True Value Hardware Store (☎ 520-855-6744), 40 Capri Blvd. Lee & Regnier

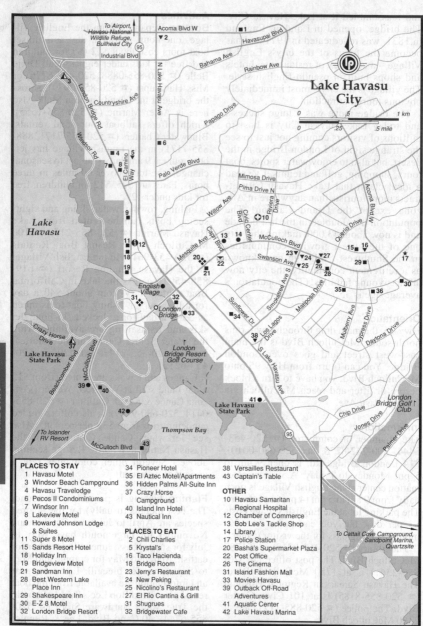

Lake Havasu City

PLACES TO STAY
1 Havasu Motel
3 Windsor Beach Campground
4 Havasu Travelodge
6 Pecos II Condominiums
7 Windsor Inn
8 Lakeview Motel
9 Howard Johnson Lodge & Suites
11 Super 8 Motel
15 Sands Resort Hotel
18 Holiday Inn
19 Bridgeview Motel
21 Sandman Inn
28 Best Western Lake Place Inn
29 Shakespeare Inn
30 E-Z 8 Motel
32 London Bridge Resort

34 Pioneer Hotel
35 El Aztec Motel/Apartments
36 Hidden Palms All-Suite Inn
37 Crazy Horse Campground
40 Island Inn Hotel
43 Nautical Inn

PLACES TO EAT
2 Chili Charlies
5 Krystal's
16 Taco Hacienda
18 Bridge Room
23 Jerry's Restaurant
24 New Peking
25 Nicolino's Restaurant
27 El Rio Cantina & Grill
31 Shugrues
32 Bridgewater Cafe

38 Versailles Restaurant
43 Captain's Table

OTHER
10 Havasu Samaritan Regional Hospital
12 Chamber of Commerce
13 Bob Lee's Tackle Shop
14 Library
17 Police Station
22 Post Office
26 The Cinema
31 Island Fashion Mall
33 Movies Havasu
39 Outback Off-Road Adventures
41 Aquatic Center
42 Lake Havasu Marina

CHUCK PLACE

ROB RACHOWIECKI

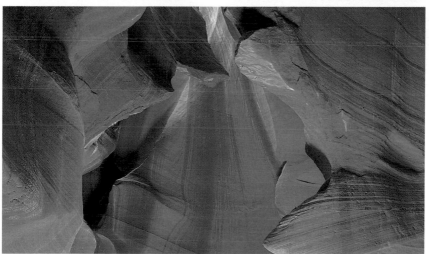

RALPH LEE HOPKINS

Top Left: Bell tower, San Xavier del Bac Mission, near Tucson, Arizona
Bottom: Antelope Canyon, Navajo Indian Reservation, Arizona

Top Right: Tsegi Overlook on South Rim Drive of Canyon de Chelly National Monument, Arizona

RALPH LEE HOPKINS

RICK GERHARTER

STEPHEN TRIMBLE

ROB RACHOWIECKI

Top Left: Red-tailed hawk on saguaro cactus
Bottom: Monument Valley, Arizona

Top Right: Presidio Historic District, Tucson, Arizona
Middle Right: Zuni Pueblo women in O'odham Tash celebration

(☎ 520-505-4665), 362 London Bridge Rd, Suite 2, are fishing guides.

Golf The London Bridge Golf Club (☎ 520-855-2719), 2400 Club House Drive off the south end of Acoma Ave, has two championship 18-hole courses. The Nautical Inn (see Places to Stay, below) has an 18-hole course (☎ 520-855-5585), tennis courts and other amenities. The London Bridge Resort Golf Course (☎ 520-855-4777), 1477 Queens Bay, has nine holes. All courses recommend calling for a tee time.

Other Activities You can take a quick trip on the ferry from English Village to the Havasu Landing Resort on the Chemehuevi Reservation across the lake in California. They'll take you to their small **casino** for those 18 years and older.

Outback Off-Road Adventures (☎ 520-680-6151), 1350 McCulloch Blvd, offers **4WD desert tours** for $65 a half day, $130 a full day with lunch. Groups of four or more and children get discounts.

London Bridge Racquet & Fitness Center (☎ 520-855-6274), 1401 McCulloch Blvd, in the Island Fashion Mall, has **tennis** and **racquetball** courts, a **pool**, gym and other amenities.

The Aquatic Center (☎ 520-453-2687), 100 Park Ave off Hwy 95, has a wave pool and water slide.

Special Events
The chamber of commerce has information on dozens of annual events, most of which occur from September to June. The most important are listed here.

Students flock to town during spring break in March, when hotels get busy and live bands entertain. The dedication of London Bridge on October 10, 1971 is celebrated annually during London Bridge Days, held during a week in October (dates vary) when concerts and dancing, sporting events and contests, art shows and a parade are featured. The World Jet Ski Finals are held at the Nautical Inn in October. Aficionados flock to the Annual Dixieland Jazz Festival held in mid-January; nonstop

jazz is played at the London Bridge Resort at the English Village. An all-concert ticket is about $40.

Places to Stay – Camping
Lake Havasu State Park (☎ 520-855-7851) has two campgrounds. The *Windsor Beach Campground* (☎ 520-855-2784), 2 miles north on London Bridge Rd, and *Cattail Cove* (☎ 520-855-1223), 15 miles south on Hwy 95, both offer showers, boat launch and tent/RV camping (no hookups) for $10 per day. Cattail Cove also has 40 RV sites with hookups for $15. Day use is $3. In addition, the park maintains more than 200 primitive shoreline campsites accessible only by boat.

The *Crazy Horse Campground* (☎ 520-855-4033), 1534 Beachcomber Blvd, has several hundred RV sites with full or partial hookups for $22 and 200 tenting sites for $10. Showers, a laundry room and a grocery store are available. The *Islander RV Resort* (☎ 520-680-2000), 751 Beachcomber Blvd, offers more than 500 sites with full hookups for $24. There are two pools, showers, a spa, boat launch, grocery store, laundromat and a clubhouse in the resort. The *Sandpoint Marina* (☎ 520-855 0459), 15 miles south on Hwy 95 near Cattail Cove, has 175 RV sites with hookups for $22. There are showers, a laundromat, grocery store, play area and boat rentals available.

There are more camping areas near Parker Dam and Parker (described later in the chapter) and on the California side of Lake Havasu.

Places to Stay – Houseboats
Houseboats sleeping up to eight people are available from H2O Houseboat Vacations (☎ 800-242-2628, fax 602-680-1005), PO Box 2100, Havasu Lake, CA 92363, on the California side of the lake opposite Lake Havasu City. Boats are available by the half week (Friday to Sunday or Monday to Thursday) or by the full week. Cheap winter rates are $595/895 for half/full week from November to February. High season (July and August)

rates are $1350/1995. Holiday rates can reach $2995 for Memorial Day weekend.

Places to Stay – Budget

Hotel rates vary tremendously from season to season; those given here are approximate. The winter season sees the lowest prices. Hotel costs rise in summer, which in Lake Havasu City stretches from March to November! Reservations are a good idea for summer weekends, holidays and some special events, when prices rise still further. Very cheap accommodations are hard to come by.

The cheapest places, offering doubles for around $30 in winter but about $40 or more during summer (weekly discounts are often available) include the following: the *E-Z 8 Motel* (☎ 520-855-4023, 800-326-6835), 41 Acoma Blvd, with a pool, spa and coin laundry; the *Havasu Motel* (☎ 520-855-2311), 2035 Acoma Blvd; the *Lakeview Motel* (☎ 520-855-3605), 440 London Bridge Rd; the *Shakespeare Inn* (☎ 520-855-4157, 800-982-3622), 2190 McCulloch Blvd, with a pool; and the *Windsor Inn* (☎ 520-855-4135, 800-245-4135), 451 London Bridge Rd, with a pool and spa. All the above advertise some rooms with kitchenettes.

Places to Stay – Middle

The *Super 8 Motel* (☎ 520-855-8844, fax 520-855-7132), 305 London Bridge Rd, has a pool and spa and summer weekday rates in the low $40s for doubles, more on weekends and less in winter. Other places charging in the $40s and $50s for a summer double include the *Bridgeview Motel* (☎ 520-855-5559), 101 London Bridge Rd, which has a pool; the *El Aztec Motel/Apartments* (☎ 520-453-7172, fax 520-855-1685, aztec@lakehavasucity.com), 2078 Swanson Ave, which has a pool and rooms with kitchenettes and BBQ areas; and the *Sandman Inn* (☎ 520-855-7841, 800-835-2410), 1700 McCulloch Blvd, with a pool, laundry room, and some (more expensive) suites and better rooms with kitchenettes. The *Havasu Travelodge* (☎ 520-680-9202, fax 520-680-1511), 480 London Bridge Rd,

offers morning coffee and pastries, has an indoor spa and charges in the $60s for a double.

These following three hotels are a decent value in their price range. The *Holiday Inn* (☎ 520-855-4071, fax 520-855-2379), 245 London Bridge Rd, has comfortable rooms from $50 to $90, many with refrigerators and balconies. There are some suites for $140. The hotel offers a pool and spa, coin laundry, restaurant, bar and entertainment (music with dancing) on most nights. The similarly priced *Howard Johnson Lodge & Suites* (☎ 520-453-4656, fax 520-680-4561), 335 London Bridge Rd, offers an indoor pool and spa, coin laundry and good standard rooms as well as larger units with kitchens. Some rooms have balconies and lake views. The *Island Inn Hotel* (☎ 520-680-0606, fax 520-680-4218), 1300 McCulloch Blvd, is one of the newer hotels and has a pool, spa, restaurant, bar and many rooms with balconies and lake views for $65 to $95. It also has pricier suites.

Other places with doubles in the $50 to $90 range (depending on season) include the *Best Western Lake Place Inn* (☎ 520-855-2146, fax 520-855-3148), 31 Wings Loop, offering a pool and fairly spacious rooms, and the *Pioneer Hotel* (☎ 520-855-1111, 800-528-5169), 271 Lake Havasu Ave, one of the largest places in town with almost 200 rooms, a heated pool, spa and laundry room.

For rooms with kitchens, try the *Hidden Palms All-Suite Inn* (☎ 520-855-7144), 2100 Swanson Ave, or the *Sands Resort Hotel* (☎ 520-855-1388, 800-521-0360, fax 520-453-1802), 2040 Mesquite Ave. One-bedroom units begin around $60 in winter, more in summer, and long-term discounts are available. The Sands Resort has more expensive two-bedroom suites as well. There is also the *Pecos II Condominiums* (☎ 520-855-7444), 465 N Lake Havasu Ave, which charges $395 per week for two-bedroom, two-bathroom condos. All these places have swimming pools.

The *Nautical Inn* (☎ 520-855-2141, 800-892-2141), 1000 McCulloch Blvd, was the first of Lake Havasu's resort hotels (some rooms show their age) and has a reputation for water sports: fishing, boating, water-skiing, jet-skiing and parasailing arc available. The inn also has a pool, spa, restaurant and bar, coin laundry and tennis and golf privileges. Large rooms sleep up to four people and rent for $100 to $150 in the high season. Reservations are recommended. Midpriced hotels offer comparable rooms if you don't need the water sports.

The *London Bridge Resort* (☎ 520-855-0888, 800-624-7939, fax 520-855-9209), 1477 Queens Bay Rd, has three pools, a spa, an exercise room, golf, tennis, three restaurants, shops and views of London Bridge. Rooms are big enough, but their olde worlde windowes are small. The hotel is next to London Bridge and rates reflect the location – anywhere from $60 to $160, depending on demand. There are a few pricier suites.

Places to Eat

A variety of restaurants are on or near the half mile of McCulloch Blvd between Smoketree Ave and Acoma Blvd.

Shugrues (☎ 520-453-1400), 1425 McCulloch Blvd, advertises American cuisine, which translates into several dozen entrées featuring fresh seafood, steak, chicken and pastas. Dinner entrées include soup or salad and range from about $10 to over $30, most in the mid-teens. Lunches are cheaper, and many tables have some sort of bridge view. Shugrues is open from 11 am to 3 pm and 5 to 10 pm. Another choice for midpriced, good American dinners is *Krystal's* (☎ 520-453-2999), 460 El Camino Way, open 4:30 to 10 pm daily.

Other good restaurants are found in the better hotels: the *Captain's Table* (☎ 520-855-2141) at the Nautical Inn, the *Bridge Room* (☎ 520-855-4071) at the Holiday Inn and the *Bridgewater Café* (☎ 520-855-0888) at the London Bridge Resort all serve breakfast, lunch and dinner at somewhat more economical prices than at Shugrues. The new Bridgewater Café, with its bridge views, is especially popular with younger adults. There's a slightly older crowd in the nearby *City of London*

Arms Pub & Restaurant (☎ 520-855-8782) at the English Village; decent pub food and imported British brews are featured.

The most upscale place is *Versailles* (☎ 520-855-4800), 357 S Lake Havasu Ave, with French and Italian cuisine, both good. The French menu is more expensive (most entrées in the mid-teens), but the budget-conscious will find a pleasing selection of pasta dishes around $10. The restaurant is open for dinner only (5 to 10 pm) and is closed on Mondays year-round, plus Tuesdays in summer.

For Mexican food, there's *El Rio Cantina & Grill* (☎ 520-680-0088), 2131 McCulloch Blvd, with nightly karaoke and a sports bar, and *Chili Charlies* (☎ 520-453-5055), 790 N Lake Havasu Ave, with pool tables and video games. If you prefer a chimichanga without the bar scene, head over to *Taco Hacienda* (☎ 520-855-8932), 2200 Mesquite Ave. This locally popular place has been here for two decades (eons by Lake Havasu City standards!). It's open from 11 am to 9 pm.

Italian-food lovers can try *Nicolino's Restaurant* (☎ 520-855-3484), 86 S Smoketree Ave, with a variety of entrées; it's closed on Sundays. Good Chinese food is served at *New Peking* (☎ 520-855-4441), 2010 McCulloch Blvd. Nearby is the reasonably priced *Jerry's Restaurant* (☎ 520-855-2013), 1990 McCulloch Blvd, which serves breakfast 24 hours a day.

Entertainment

Some hotels and restaurants mentioned above have nightlife, especially during spring break when students descend on the town. Favored places change often, so ask locally about where to dance or hear a band.

Catch a movie at *The Cinema* (☎ 520-855-3111), 2130 McCulloch Blvd, or the six-screen *Movies Havasu* (☎ 520-453-7900), 180 Swanson Ave. Dinner plays are performed by the *Drury Lane Repertory Players* (☎ 520-453-5605, 520-855-0888) at the London Bridge Resort. The chamber of commerce has other performing arts information.

ARIZONA

Getting There & Away
Air Lake Havasu City Airport (☎ 520-764-3330), 5600 N Hwy 95, is 7 miles north of town. America West (☎ 800-235-9292) has several daily flights to and from Phoenix and others to Bullhead City (though driving is quicker!). Flight schedules change frequently.

Bus KT/Greyhound buses leave from the Busy 'B' Shell Service Station (☎ 520-764-2440), 3201 N Hwy 95, 4 miles north of town. There are daily departures for Phoenix (about $30 one way) at 4:20 pm and to Las Vegas at noon.

PARKER
After almost 40 years of being a post office for the surrounding Colorado River Indian Reservation, Parker was founded in 1908 as a railroad town (there are no passenger trains today). The town became the base for the building of the Parker Dam and since then it has thrived, albeit on a smaller scale than Lake Havasu City and Bullhead City, on agriculture and tourism. Visitors come for water sports in the summer and for fishing and desert exploration in the mild winter. The area between Parker and the Parker Dam, known as the Parker Strip, has dozens of campgrounds, boat-launch areas and marinas.

Parker (population 3000) is the county seat for sparsely populated La Paz County (population 17,000).

Information
The chamber of commerce (☎ 520-669-2174, fax 520-669-6304), 1217 California Ave, is open from 9 am to 5 pm Monday through Friday. The library (☎ 520-669-2622) is at 1001 Navajo Ave. The post office (☎ 520-669-8179) is at Joshua Ave and 14th. Parker Hospital (☎ 520-669-9201) is at 1200 Mohave Rd. The police (☎ 520-669-2264) are at 1314 11th.

Colorado River Indian Tribes Museum
Members of four tribes live on the Colorado River Indian Reservation: Mohave, Cheme-huevi, Navajo and Hopi. Their culture, past and present, is preserved in the museum (☎ 520-669-9211, ext 335) at Mohave Rd and 2nd Ave, southwest of town. Reservation inhabitants are very active in agriculture and some of them make crafts and jewelry that are sold at the museum. Hours are 8 am to noon and 1 to 5 pm Monday to Friday. They sometimes close early, so call ahead.

Adjacent to the museum is the Reservation Administrative Center, where you can get tribal fishing and hunting permits and information about camping and hiking.

Parker Dam
This dam (☎ 619-663-3712) is 15 miles north of Parker and 19 miles south of Lake Havasu City. Completed in 1938, its closure formed 45-mile-long Lake Havasu. The dam looks small, but about 70% of its structural height is buried beneath the original riverbed, therefore making it the world's deepest dam. The dam can be visited on a self-guided tour from 8 am to 5 pm, Monday to Friday, except holidays. There is an orientation area with information and exhibits.

La Paz County Park
Eight miles north of Parker, this park (☎ 520-667-2069) has a tennis court, horseshoe pits, a playground, beach, boat ramp, swimming, and tent and RV camping. Camping rates are $10 to $14 for two people and day use is $2 per person. Weekly discounts are available. Opposite is the 18-hole Emerald Canyon Golf Course (☎ 520-667-3366).

Buckskin Mountain Colorado River State Park
This park (☎ 520-667-3231), 11 miles north of Parker, offers tent and RV camping, a boat ramp, beach, swimming, picnicking, a playground, recreation room, laundry, grocery store and ranger-led activities on weekends. A mile north is the Buckskin Mountain River Island Unit (☎ 520-667-3386), with more camping spaces in a scenic desert setting. Rates are $4 for day use and $12 to $20 for camping.

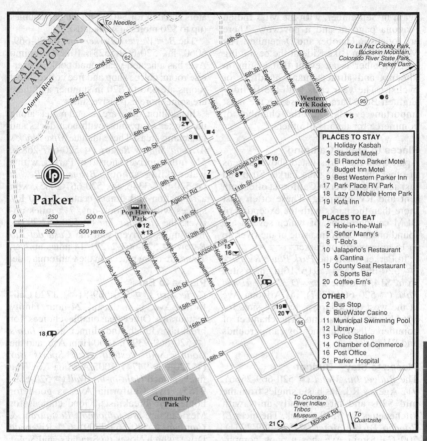

Parker

PLACES TO STAY
1 Holiday Kasbah
3 Stardust Motel
4 El Rancho Parker Motel
7 Budget Inn Motel
9 Best Western Parker Inn
17 Park Place RV Park
18 Lazy D Mobile Home Park
19 Kofa Inn

PLACES TO EAT
2 Hole-in-the-Wall
5 Señor Manny's
8 T-Bob's
10 Jalapeño's Restaurant
   & Cantina
15 County Seat Restaurant
   & Sports Bar
20 Coffee Ern's

OTHER
2 Bus Stop
6 BlueWater Casino
11 Municipal Swimming Pool
12 Library
13 Police Station
14 Chamber of Commerce
16 Post Office
21 Parker Hospital

ARIZONA

Activities

Many people bring boats, and launching areas are located along the Parker Strip. Launching is free or subject to nominal fees. **Fishing**, **water-skiing**, **jet-skiing**, **inner-tubing** and plain old messing around with boats are all extremely popular. Some rental services are available at the many places along the strip.

Parker's Olympic-size, public municipal **swimming pool** (☎ 520-669-5678), 1317 9th, is used for an annual Special Olympics competition.

The BlueWater Casino (☎ 520-669-7777, 800-747-8777), at 119 W Riverside Drive in the Moovalaya Safeway Shopping Plaza, operated by the Indian Reservation, is open 24 hours a day, and offers **bingo**, **slots** and **poker**.

Special Events

The year begins with SCORE 400 in late January. This is an off-road, 4WD jeep and pickup truck race that covers more than 300 miles and attracts 100,000 visitors. There are water-skiing races in February. March features a Balloonfest, the La Paz County Fair and the Enduro Power Boat Races. As the weather heats up, activities calm down. Things pick up again in September, with the Miss Indian Arizona pageant and a powwow. There are rodeos in October and December. The MS Best Dam Bike Ride at the beginning of November is an event that begins in Phoenix and attracts many hundreds of cyclists. The year ends with the Holiday Lighted Boat Parade. These are the most important events; call the chamber of commerce for details of others.

Places to Stay – Camping
Apart from the parks listed above, dozens of other places along the Parker Strip and just across the river in California offer both tent and RV camping. These often cost more than the parks with the exception of BLM campgrounds, of which several are found on the California side of the river up to 15 miles north of Parker.

In Parker itself, the *Park Place RV Park* (☎ 520-669-2675), 916 16th, has sites from $14, and the *Lazy D Mobile Home Park* (☎ 520-669-8797), off Arizona Ave at the west end of town, has RV sites for $16. Neither allow tents. The chamber of commerce lists other nearby campgrounds and RV parks.

Places to Stay – Budget
The *Budget Inn Motel* (☎ 520-669-2566), 912 Agency Rd, has basic singles from the mid $20s and larger family units with kitchenettes for $210 a week. The nicer *El Rancho Parker Motel* (☎ 520-669-2231), 709 California Ave, has a pool, complimentary coffee, and rates beginning in the low $30s.

Places to Stay – Middle
The pleasant *Kofa Inn* (☎ 520-669-2101), 1700 California Ave, has a pool and an adjacent 24-hour coffee shop. Rates start in the upper $30s. The *Stardust Motel* (☎ 520-669-2278, 800-786-7827), 700 California Ave, has a pool and rooms for similar rates as well as slightly more expensive rooms with kitchenettes. The *Holiday Kasbah* (☎ 520-669-2133, fax 520-669-2133), 604 California Ave, has a pool and complimentary continental breakfast. Rooms have refriger-

ators and rent for $40/45 for singles/doubles (up to $20 more on weekends).

The *Best Western Parker Inn* (☎ 520-669-6060, fax 520-669-5523), 1012 Geronimo Ave, has a heated year-round pool, an exercise room, coffee shop and free coffee. Most rooms are $50 to $70 in summer and there are some more expensive suites.

In addition, there are several motels along the Parker Strip, most with boat docks and launching areas. These include *Mike Mack's Arizona Shores Resort* (☎ 520-667-2685), 5½ miles upriver (north) of Parker, with a water-skiing school; *Branson's Resort* (☎ 520-667-3346, fax 520-667-2085), with a recreation and fitness center and 60 RV spaces with full hook-ups, 7½ miles upriver; the *Harbour Inn* (☎ 520-667-2931), 13½ miles upriver; and the *Casa del Rio Resort* (☎ 520-667-2727), 14 miles upriver. There are more places on the California side.

Places to Eat
Coffee Ern's (☎ 520-669-8145), 1720 California Ave, is a decent 24-hour family restaurant. Other reasonable choices for breakfast, lunch and dinner are *T-Bob's* (☎ 520-669-9396), 1000 Hopi Ave, and the *County Seat Restaurant & Sports Bar* (☎ 520-669-9474), 1005 Arizona Ave. The finely named *Hole-in-the-Wall* (☎ 520-669-9755), 612 California Ave, is good for home-style breakfasts. Good choices for Mexican fare are *Jalapeño's Restaurant & Cantina* (☎ 520-669-2309), 621 Riverside Drive, which closes on Sundays, and *Señor Manny's* (☎ 520-669-9237), 213 Riverside Drive, open daily from 11 am to 9 pm, and till 11 pm Thursday to Saturday. There are plenty of fast-food and other places in Parker and along the strip.

Getting There & Away
Greyhound/KT buses stop at the Hole-in-the-Wall restaurant at 4:15 pm for Phoenix and 10:15 am for Las Vegas.

QUARTZSITE
Quartzsite has about 2000 permanent residents, but during the winter the number swells to hundreds of thousands of people.

The attraction is gems and minerals. Several thousand dealers are on hand during the early January to mid-February gem and mineral shows that attract more than a million visitors who buy, sell, trade and admire.

These folks can't quite squeeze into the town's three tiny motels and so, as the chamber of commerce puts it, the desert around Quartzsite turns into a sea of aluminum. Thousands upon thousands of RVs stretch out as far as the eye can see – a strange sight, indeed.

The chamber of commerce (☎ 520-927-5600) is on the north side of I-10 exit 17. Hours are 9 am to 4 pm daily in January and February, cutting back to 9 am to 1 pm on Tuesday, Wednesday and Thursday from April to October. March and November hours vary. Call the chamber for a recorded message when it's closed.

Obviously, the January/February gem and mineral shows (there are as many as eight separate events) are the main thing to do. During this time there are also rodeos, balloon rides, stagecoach rides, cookouts, dances and other Western events. During the winter (November to March) there are less important, but still popular, shows and flea markets. During the prostrating heat of summer the population dwindles to a tiny fraction of the January crowds.

Near the center of town is a curious monument: a small stone pyramid topped by a metal camel. The memorial is to Haiji Ali, a Syrian camel driver who arrived in 1856 to help with US army experiments in using camels in the Southwestern deserts. These trials failed and Ali, who had become known as Hi Jolly, became a prospector and died here around 1902.

The Hi Jolly monument is Quartzsite's most loved landmark. Hi Jolly 'Daze,' with a parade and other festivities, occurs the weekend before Thanksgiving to welcome back winter visitors. Quartzsite is a friendly place and the gem shows have thrived annually since the first one in 1967.

There are petroglyphs, ghost towns, ruins, wildlife and desert scenery around Quartzsite – much of it along dirt roads or trails reachable by 4WD, horseback or on foot. If you have time, ask the chamber of commerce for exploration ideas. It sells a local map with 21 points of interest. Also read below for nearby places that can be visited by car.

The three tiny motels have about 30 rooms between them, so almost everyone stays in the many RV camps surrounding town. Most camps have hookups for RVs and charge up to $20 a night. The farther you park from the center, the less you pay.

The BLM (☎ 520-317-3200 in Yuma) runs the *La Posa Long Term Visitor Area* at the south end of town on Hwy 95. Here, for $50, you can camp (tent or RV) for as long as you want between September 15 and April 15. Permits for seven days cost $10. (A fee increase is planned for the 1998/99 season.) The permit allows you to use other BLM sites in the Yuma area. The rest of the year you can camp free, but you can stay in the same place for only 14 days. Facilities include toilets, water (no showers), and dump stations. South of La Posa at mile marker 99, and north of town at mile marker 112, are areas where you can camp for free anytime, but there are no services. A municipal RV dump station is a mile north of Quartzsite, where a $4 fee is charged.

Most people rustle up their own vittles on camp stoves or RV kitchens, but you'll find plenty of fast-food places and small restaurants on the I-10 business loop between exits 17 and 19.

The nearest place for a better selection of motels and restaurants is Blythe, California, 21 miles west along I-10, with more than a dozen motels of varying prices. (Drivers note that gas prices are about 10¢ per gallon more expensive in California.) Parker, 35 miles north, and Salome, 35 miles east, have more modest selections of motels.

SALOME

Salome is one of many little mining towns founded in the area around the turn of the 19th century. Some of these became ghost towns, others continue a precarious existence. Salome gained a mild notoriety in the 1920s through the antics of Dick Wick Hall, who published the *Salome Sun* broadsheet and ran the 'Laughing Gas Station' on the rutted road joining Wickenburg with Los Angeles. His broadsheet (no longer published) ran 'extravagant tales of the desert adaptations of species,' such as the story of his 'seven-year-old frog that never learned to swim because he didn't want to.' There is not much to do in Salome, but it's a place to stop if you don't feel like going the next 55 miles to Wickenburg.

The McMullen Valley Chamber of Commerce (☎ 520-859-3846), PO Box 477, Salome, AZ 85348 has information.

RV parks include the *Desert Gem* (☎ 520-859-3373) at $10.50 per night ($6 for tents) and the similarly priced *Mountain Pass* (☎ 520-859-3757), both with showers and located 2 miles west of town on Hwy 60. Others are near the tiny communities of Brenda and Hope, between Salome and Quartzsite.

There are four motels, of which the best are *Sheffler's Motel* (☎ 520-859-3001) and the *International Inn* (☎ 520-859-3452). Both have restaurants and Sheffler's has a pool. Rates are from $25 to $45 depending on the room and season. Cheaper (and very basic) places include the *Westward Motel* (☎ 520-859-3316) and *Circle N Motel* (☎ 520-859-3396).

ALAMO LAKE STATE PARK

Alamo Lake was formed in 1968 by a flood-control dam on the Bill Williams River. The lake has good fishing, which attracts an estimated 50,000 annual visitors, most of whom come in the spring and fall. Bass, bluegill and some crappies are the main catch. Winter brings many migrating waterfowl to the lake. Summer is hot enough to discourage heavy visitation.

Information is available from Alamo Lake State Park (☎ 520-669-2088), PO Box 38, Wenden, AZ 85357. A small store sells supplies and rents boats (12- to 16-footers; sample rates are $30 to $450 for six hours). There are picnic and boat launch facilities, showers, and 250 campsites at $8 for tents, $13 for RVs with hookups. Day use is $3.

From Wenden (5 miles east of Salome or 50 miles west of Wickenburg) a paved road runs 34 miles north to the lake.

The Lower Colorado

This section follows the lower Colorado River south of I-10 to where the river enters Mexico, a corner of the state that contains some of the West's wildest areas where, for whatever reason, very large things come in twos. Two huge military testing grounds with restricted entry cover most of the region. These are proving grounds and bombing ranges – the borders are clearly marked so you won't blunder into a firefight by accident. There are also two extremely rugged and remote national wildlife refuges protecting desert flora and fauna. (One of these, the Cabeza Prieta NWR, was established more than half a century ago, but has been threatened by, among other things, military training flights that disturb the wildlife.) Two other national wildlife refuges protect riparian habitats stretching along the Colorado River.

The parched land is crossed by two east-west interstate highways barreling through as straight as they can. Along the northern boundary runs I-10, linking Florida with Los Angeles, California. Toward the south, I-8 links Arizona to San Diego, California. In this bombed and beautiful southern region is Yuma, Arizona's rapidly growing, third-largest city.

KOFA NATIONAL WILDLIFE REFUGE

This is one of the wildest of the wildlife refuges. Three rugged mountain ranges, the Kofa, the Castle Dome and the Tank Mountains, meet together in a splendid tangle. The refuge covers just over 1000 sq miles, of which more than two-thirds is designated wilderness with vehicular access limited to a few dirt roads. Apart from these roads, visitor facilities are nonexistent. Bighorn sheep roam the area, but are hard to spot.

Most visitors drive in from the west on Hwy 95 to the entrance to Palm Canyon, about 29 miles south of Quartzsite, or 51 miles northeast of Yuma. A 7.2-mile dirt road (usually passable to cars) leads to a parking area from where a steep, rocky, half-mile trail climbs to views of Palm Canyon: a sheer-walled crack to the north within which a stand of California palms *(Washingtonia filifera)* can be seen. Botanists claim this is the only place in Arizona where these palms grow naturally. Best views are around midday; at other times the palms are in shadow. There are several other access points and poor dirt roads through the refuge. Off-road driving is prohibited.

Obtain information from Kofa NWR (☎ 520-783-7861), 356 W 1st St, PO Box 6290, Yuma, AZ 85366-6290. Hunting is allowed in season with appropriate licenses. Camping is allowed anytime, anywhere (except within a quarter mile of water holes), with a 14-day limit.

CIBOLA NATIONAL WILDLIFE REFUGE

Another of the string of refuges along the Colorado River, Cibola NWR is an important overwintering site for Canada geese (as many as 25,000 in midwinter), about 1000 greater sandhill cranes and many other waterfowl – a good place to watch for migrants from mid-November to late February. Some 237 species have been recorded, including the endangered Yuma clapper rail.

Information is available from Cibola NWR (☎ 520-857-3253), PO Box AP, Blythe, CA 92226. Hunting and fishing, with licenses and in the appropriate seasons, is permitted. Camping is not.

Refuge headquarters are most easily reached from I-10 at the Neighbors Blvd exit (about 8 miles into California). Head south for 13 miles to a sign for the Cibola NWR, cross over the Colorado River (back to Arizona) on the Cibola Farmers Bridge, and proceed 4 miles to the refuge headquarters. Hours are from 8 am to 4:30 pm Monday to Friday. From the headquarters,

the Canada Geese Drive auto tour road is open daily during daylight hours.

IMPERIAL NATIONAL WILDLIFE REFUGE

Named after the small Imperial Dam on the Colorado River, this is the southernmost of the string of protected areas on the lower Colorado. Overwintering waterfowl number many thousands from mid-December through February, which is the best time to visit for birding. The small **Martinez Lake** at the south end has some water-skiing and boating activity in summer.

Refuge headquarters (☎ 520-783-3371), PO Box 72217, Martinez Lake, AZ 85365, are on the north side of Martinez Lake. Hours are 7 am to 4 pm, Monday to Friday and possibly Saturdays in the winter, with shorter summer hours. An observation tower nearby gives views of the refuge, and a dirt road takes visitors to several observation points and a 1-mile interpretive trail. There is no camping. Hunting is permitted with licenses in season.

Two resorts are just outside the refuge: *Martinez Lake Resort* (☎ 520-783-0253, 520-783-9589, 800-876-7004, fax 520-782-3360), which is the main resort, and *Fisher's Landing* (☎ 520-783-6513, 520-783-5357). Both offer boating, RV camping, a grocery store and lounge. In addition, Martinez Lake has a boat rental, motel and restaurant. Fisher's Landing has tent camping. Basic motel rooms (some are trailers) in summer are $50 to $80 and sleep four to six; RV sites are about $20 at Martinez Lake and less at Fisher's Landing. These places are reserved weeks in advance for national holidays in summer.

Get there by driving east and north from Yuma on Hwy 95 for 22 miles, then take Martinez Lake Rd to the left. After 10 miles, you reach the resorts and a dirt road to the right goes 4 miles to the refuge headquarters.

YUMA

This town of 62,000 inhabitants is Arizona's third-largest metropolitan area, and one of the sunniest and driest. Weather records

ARIZONA

indicate that 93% of daylight hours during the year are sunny and rainfall averages about three inches annually. The low elevation (138 feet above sea level at the lowest point) ensures hot weather. In winter, temperatures in the 70°s F attract tens of thousands of winter visitors, many of whom spend the entire winter in trailer parks in and around the city. Triple-digit temperatures are expected almost daily from June to September, but the low humidity makes it bearable and there are plenty of swimming pools, air-conditioned sites of interest and water sports on the Colorado River for visitors to enjoy. The proximity of towns in Mexico is an added attraction. During the summer, however, Yuma serves mainly as a resting place on the drive between San Diego and Tucson or Phoenix.

Yuma was built where the Colorado River narrows, making it the easiest place to cross the river for hundreds of miles. This was known to the local Quechan, Cocopah and Mohave Indians, collectively known as the Yumas. Early Spanish explorers and later American adventurers soon discovered Yuma Crossing, as it became known. Some 30,000 people were estimated to have crossed the Colorado here after the California gold rush of 1849. Steamships made it up to here from the Gulf of Mexico along the Colorado, making Yuma Crossing an important river port.

The town was founded in 1854, after the area was purchased from Mexico by the USA, and was first known as Colorado City, then Arizona City. These terms were somewhat misleading when you consider that the 'city' population was only 85 in 1860, though it grew to more than 1100 by 1870. In 1873, Arizona City was renamed Yuma. Three years later, Arizona's Territorial Prison was opened here – a notorious hellhole that operated for 33 years until a new prison was built in Florence. The old jail can be visited and is a major local historical attraction.

Various 20th-century dam projects have changed the flow of the river, and today's Yuma Crossing site is very different from what it was in the 1800s. Nevertheless,

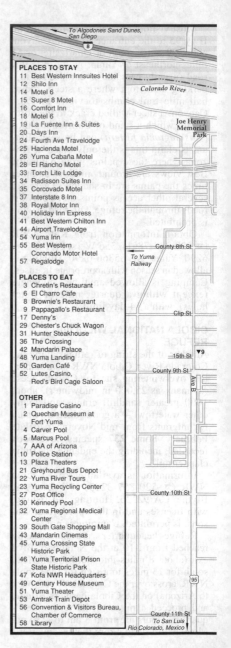

PLACES TO STAY
11 Best Western Innsuites Hotel
12 Shilo Inn
14 Motel 6
15 Super 8 Motel
16 Comfort Inn
18 Motel 6
19 La Fuente Inn & Suites
20 Days Inn
24 Fourth Ave Travelodge
25 Hacienda Motel
26 Yuma Cabaña Motel
28 El Rancho Motel
33 Torch Lite Lodge
34 Radisson Suites Inn
35 Corcovado Motel
37 Interstate 8 Inn
38 Royal Motor Inn
40 Holiday Inn Express
41 Best Western Chilton Inn
44 Airport Travelodge
54 Yuma Inn
55 Best Western
   Coronado Motor Hotel
57 Regalodge

PLACES TO EAT
3 Chretin's Restaurant
6 El Charro Cafe
8 Brownie's Restaurant
9 Pappagallo's Restaurant
17 Denny's
29 Chester's Chuck Wagon
31 Hunter Steakhouse
36 The Crossing
42 Mandarin Palace
48 Yuma Landing
50 Garden Café
52 Lutes Casino,
   Red's Bird Cage Saloon

OTHER
1 Paradise Casino
2 Quechan Museum at
   Fort Yuma
4 Carver Pool
5 Marcus Pool
7 AAA of Arizona
10 Police Station
13 Plaza Theaters
21 Greyhound Bus Depot
22 Yuma River Tours
23 Yuma Recycling Center
27 Post Office
30 Kennedy Pool
32 Yuma Regional Medical
   Center
39 South Gate Shopping Mall
43 Mandarin Cinemas
45 Yuma Crossing State
   Historic Park
46 Yuma Territorial Prison
   State Historic Park
47 Kofa NWR Headquarters
49 Century House Museum
51 Yuma Theater
53 Amtrak Train Depot
56 Convention & Visitors Bureau,
   Chamber of Commerce
58 Library

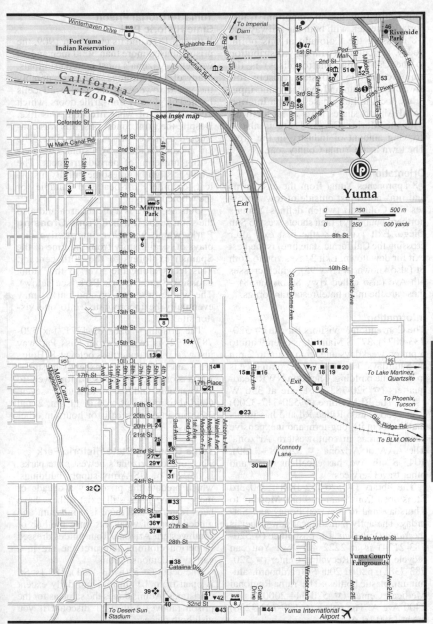

Yuma

Inset map labels:
45
46 Riverside Park
47
1st St
48
2nd St
49
50
51
52
53
54
55
56
57
58
3rd St
4th St
Orange Ave
Main St
Maiden Lane
Madison Ave
Giss Pkwy
Gila St
Ped Mall

Main map labels:
Winterhaven Drive
BUS 8
Fort Yuma Indian Reservation
Picacho Rd
S Quechan Rd
Pg Park Rd
To Imperial Dam
1
2
California
Arizona
Water St
Colorado St
W Main Canal Rd
see inset map
1st St
2nd St
3rd St
4th St
5th St
6th St
7th St
8th St
9th St
10th St
11th St
12th St
13th St
14th St
15th St
4th Ave
15th Ave
13th Ave
3
4
5 Marcus Park
6
7
8
Exit 1
Yuma
0   250   500 m
0   250   500 yards
8th St
10th St
Pacific Ave
Castle Dome Ave
11
12
13
10
14
15
16
Riley Ave
17
18
19
20
Exit 2
8
95
Main Canal
Magnolia Ave
95
10th Pl
11th Ave
10th Ave
9th Ave
7th Ave
6th Ave
5th Ave
4th Ave
17th St
17th Place
21
18th St
19th St
20th St
20th Pl
21st St
22nd St
3rd Ave
2nd Ave
1st Ave
Walnut Ave
Maple Ave
Madison Ave
Arizona Ave
22
23
24
25
26
27
28
29
30
31
Kennedy Lane
32
24th St
25th St
26th St
27th St
33
34
35
36
37
28th St
E Palo Verde St
Yuma County Fairgrounds
38
Catalina Drive
39
40
41
42
43
44
32nd St
BUS 8
Crest Drive
Windsor Ave
Ave 2E
Ave 2½E
To Desert Sun Stadium
Yuma International Airport
To Lake Martinez, Quartzsite
To Phoenix, Tucson
Gila Ridge Rd
To BLM Office

Yuma still remains an important transportation center, with both the railway and I-8 crossing the Colorado at this point. Today, agriculture (with easy distribution to the Californian metropolises) is the major economic mainstay, closely followed by tourism and the economic input of the local military bases. Yuma International Airport shares parts of its facilities with the Marine Corps. There is also a growing amount of industry in the area. The town is the Yuma County seat.

Orientation

I-8 approaches Yuma from the east, turns and runs north just outside of town, crosses the Colorado (which defines Yuma's northern boundary), then shoots west to San Diego. Exit 1 off I-8 (the first exit after crossing the California state line) is the best exit for downtown. Exit 2 takes you to 16th St (also known as Hwy 95), which crosses 4th Ave (also called Hwy 80 or Bus 8) – these are the main hotel/restaurant drags.

Information

The Convention & Visitors Bureau (☎ 520-783-0071), 377 S Main St, is open 9 am to 5 pm on weekdays and from 9 am to 2 pm on Saturdays. The chamber of commerce is in the same building. The Kofa NWR headquarters (☎ 520-783-7861) are at 356 W 1st St. The BLM office (☎ 520-317-3200) is at 2555 E Gila Ridge Rd and has information about its long-term and inexpensive camping areas in southwestern Arizona. The AAA of Arizona (☎ 520-783-3339), 1045 S 4th Ave, has excellent maps and other travel services.

The library (☎ 520-782-1871), 350 3rd St, is open from 9 am to 9 pm, Monday to Thursday, and to 5 pm on Friday and Saturday. The aptly named local newspaper is the *Yuma Daily Sun*. The post office (☎ 520-783-2124) is at 2222 4th Ave. You can recycle at Yuma Recycling Center (☎ 520-783-7381), 620 E 20th St (cardboard, aluminum, plastic bottles). The Yuma Regional Medical Center (☎ 520-344-2000) is at 2400 Ave A. The police (☎ 520-782-3236) are at 1500 1st Ave.

Yuma Territorial Prison State Historic Park

Between 1876 and its closure in 1909, the prison housed more than 3000 men and 29 women – Arizona's most feared criminals. Many of the buildings still exist, notably the guard tower and the rock-wall cells fronted by gloomy iron-grille doors, which give an idea of what life here was like. Despite the grim conditions, this was considered a model prison at the time. The jail is complemented by a small but interesting museum of period artifacts. The whole is slightly gruesome, mildly historical, definitely off-beat and suitable for the whole family!

Outside, there is a picnic area and also the soon-to-be finished **Yuma Crossing Park**, which will have interpretive displays of local history from the time of the Spanish explorers to the 20th century. This leads along the river to the Yuma Crossing State Historic Park (see below). The whole area (prison and parks) may eventually be incorporated into one visitor site.

The prison (☎ 520-783-4771, fax 520-783-4772) is reached from Giss Parkway just west of the underpass below I-8. Hours are 8 am to 5 pm daily except Christmas. Admission is $3 for adults, $2 for seven- to 13-year-olds, and free for kids under seven. Guided tours are offered at 11 am, 2 and 3:30 pm in winter; call for hours in other seasons.

Yuma Crossing State Historic Park

This, one of Arizona's newest state parks, is the site of US Army supply buildings, which predate the prison by a decade or more. Some parts still exist, others have been restored, and there is a museum and guided tours of what was once the hub of southwestern Arizona. Tour guides dressed in period clothing interpret the era in a variety of demonstrations.

The depot (☎ 520-783-4771), 180 1st St, is open from 10 am to 5 pm daily except Christmas. Admission is the same as for the prison (above) with a $1 discount if you visit both places.

Century House Museum

Sponsored by the Arizona Historical Society, this museum (☎ 520-782-1841), 240 S Madison Ave, is in one of the oldest houses in the southwestern corner of the state (built in 1891). There are exhibits of local historical interest and a garden full of exotic plants and birds. A good café and gift shop adjoin the house. Hours are 10 am to 4 pm Tuesday to Saturday. Admission is free (donations encouraged).

Quechan Museum at Fort Yuma

Across the river in California on Indian Hill Rd (off Picacho Rd), Fort Yuma was built in the 1850s. The building now houses a small museum (☎ 760-572-0661) operated by the Quechan tribe. A variety of photographs and historical artifacts can be viewed. The tribal offices are nearby. Museum hours are from 8 am to noon and 1 to 5 pm, Monday to Friday. Admission is $1 for those over 12. Get there by taking the first California exit on I-8 and head north.

Saihati Camel Farm

See and learn about camels, Asian water buffalo, desert foxes, Arabian horses, Watusi cattle and desert antelopes at this farm (☎ 520-627-2553), 15672 S Ave 1E, which offers guided tours ($3) of its breeding facilities by appointment only. Take Ave B (Hwy 95) south to County 16th St and turn left.

Peanut Patch

This peanut farm with gift shop (☎ 520-726-6292, 800-872-7688), 4322 E County 13th St (a few miles southeast of the airport), sells all kinds of peanut products. During the October-to-December harvest season, tours of the fields and shelling plant are available for free and last about a half hour. Hours are 9 am to 6 pm daily from October to April. If agriculture interests you, ask the chamber of commerce for suggestions about visiting local citrus and date farms.

McElhaney Cattle Company Museum

This free museum (☎ 520-785-3384), 36 miles east of Yuma, displays 19th-century

wagons and early antique cars. Take I-8 exit 30, head north to Welton Elementary School, turn right on Los Angeles Ave (old Hwy 80) and look for museum signs. Hours are 8 am to 4 pm Monday to Friday.

Algodones Sand Dunes

These rolling and completely barren dunes have been featured in several movies. You can admire them from the rest stop off I-8, 17 miles west of Yuma in California. You can't get to the dunes from the stop, however. Instead, leave I-8 at the Grey's Well exit and take the frontage road. This goes near remains of the old plank road by which cars and carriages crossed the sand dunes from 1915 to 1926.

Activities

Play **golf** or **tennis** at the Mesa del Sol Golf & Tennis Club (☎ 520-342-1283), 10583 Camino del Sol, off I-8 exit 12. It has seven tennis courts and the Arnold Palmer 18-hole championship golf course, for which advance reservations are recommended. Other options are the 18-hole courses at Desert Hills (☎ 520-344-4653, 520-341-0644), 1245 W Desert Hills Drive, and Arroyo Dunes (☎ 520-726-8350), 32nd St and Ave A, both next to the Yuma Convention Center (☎ 520-344-3800) and the

Visiting Mexico

The small town of Algodones is reached by driving 8 miles west from Yuma on I-8, then turning south on a road signed for Algodones and following it 2 miles to the border. The town has dozens of dentists and several drug stores, and visitors come for dental work and prescriptions at cheaper-than-US prices. There are also several restaurants and crafts stores.

The city of San Luis is 23 miles south of Yuma on Hwy 95. With 150,000 inhabitants, it is the largest city on the Arizona-Sonora border. It offers hotels, restaurants and plenty of shopping opportunities. ■

ARIZONA

closest to downtown. Desert Hills offers the greater challenge. There are nine tennis courts here, too. The chamber of commerce can suggest others.

You can **swim** in one of the three municipal swimming pools (☎ 520-343-8686 for hours and charges). Carver pool is at 5th St and 13th Ave; Kennedy pool is at 24th St and Kennedy Lane; Marcus pool is at 5th St and 5th Ave.

The Greyhound Park (☎ 520-726-4655), 4000 4th Ave, has **greyhound racing** from Wednesday to Sunday in the evenings and also afternoons on Saturdays and Sundays. They also have **horseracing**. The racing season runs from November to April. Admission is free; the air-conditioned club house charges $2.

Dove hunting season opens over Labor Day weekend (preceding the first Monday in September) and Yuma is extremely popular with hunters at that time.

Organized Tours

Yuma River Tours (☎ 520-783-4400), at 1920 Arizona Ave, has jet-boat tours to Imperial NWR, Imperial Dam and historic sites (petroglyphs, mining camps etc). Tour guides provide a chatty explanation of local history and Indian lore. Tours are $29/49/69 for 3/5/7 hours and include lunch. Sunset cruises and custom charters are also available. Children ages three to 12 go for half price. All tours leave from Fisher's Landing (see Imperial NWR, above). Tours run almost daily in winter, less frequently in the hot months.

The Yuma Railway (☎ 520-783-3456) leaves from the west end of 8th St about 6 miles west of downtown (the last section is unpaved). This vintage train (a 1941 Whitcombe diesel engine pulling a 1922 Pullman coach) makes two-hour runs along the Arizona-Sonora border. Departures are at 1 pm on Saturdays and Sundays from November to March, and 10 am on Saturdays in October, April and May. Fares are $10 for adults, $9 for those over 55 and $5 for those four to 16. A family picnic run is offered at 1 pm on the first Saturday of November to April, which costs just $16 for two adults and up to five children. Steak dinner runs are offered at 4 pm on the second and fourth Saturdays of November to May for $18/9 for adults/children (reservations are required 48 hours in advance). All these hours change often, so call ahead.

The *Colorado King 1* is a small, two-deck paddle boat offering narrated, three-hour Colorado River cruises from Fisher's Landing on Martinez Lake (see Imperial NWR, above). Departure times vary seasonally; call ☎ 520-782-2412 for information. Tickets are available from Fantastic Sam's Hair Care, 1640 S 4th Ave in Yuma. Costs are $25 or $15 for children 12 and under.

The visitors bureau has information about (and sometimes organizes and escorts) local tours during the winter.

Special Events

The cooler winter months see the most noteworthy events. The annual Silver Spur Rodeo during the first weekend in February has been held for more than half a century and features Yuma's biggest parade, arts and crafts shows and various other events along with the rodeo. Yuma Crossing Days, during the last weekend in February, celebrates the town's history. The Yuma County Fair is held at the beginning of April. During much of the year there are monthly Main Street Block Parties with free street entertainment for the whole family. Call the visitors bureau for information about other events.

Places to Stay

Winter rates (usually January to April) can be up to $30 higher than summer rates, especially on weekends. In addition, hotels are booked well in advance and charge the highest prices of the year during the opening days of dove-hunting season (Labor Day weekend). Rates vary substantially according to demand and those given below are only approximate.

Places to Stay – Camping

There are scores, if not hundreds, of campgrounds, but most are geared to RVs on a long-term basis during the winter. Most have age restrictions (ie, no children, sometimes only for people over 50) and prohibit tents. People planning on a long RV stay are advised to call the chamber of commerce for lists.

The BLM operates a number of sites on the California side of the Imperial Dam, including the Imperial Dam Long Term Visitors Area ($50 for unlimited use from September 15 to April 15; $10 for one week; drinking water is available) and the Squaw Lake Campground ($5 per night with showers and a boat launch). These areas are reached by taking 1st St east and north out of Yuma and across the river into California, then driving north for 24 miles on County Rd S24. Alternatively, take Hwy 95 east and north of Yuma for 18 miles, then turn left on the Imperial Valley Dam Rd to the dam, where the river can be crossed to California.

Places to Stay – Budget

All Yuma motels listed have swimming pools. Many budget hotels charge midrange prices in winter and dove-hunting season. They include the popular *El Rancho Motel* (☎ 520-783-4481), 2201 4th Ave, with doubles for $24 in summer and $30 in winter. Also reasonable at about this price is the *Interstate 8 Inn* (☎ 520-726-6110), 2730 4th Ave. The *Regalodge* (☎ 520-782-4571), 344 S 4th Ave, is one of the better budget motels near downtown and has rooms with refrigerators and some kitchenettes. Its summer rates start in the $20s, going up to the $30s in winter and more in dove season. Also try the *Yuma Inn* (☎ 520-782-4592), 260 4th Ave, the *Corcovado Motel* (☎ 520-344-2988), 2607 4th Ave, the *Hacienda Motel* (☎ 520-782-4316), 2150 4th Ave, and the pleasant *Torch Lite Lodge* (☎ 520-344-1600), 2501 4th Ave.

The *Motel 6* (☎ 520-782-9521, fax 520-343-4941), 1445 16th St, charges $25/31 for singles/doubles in the summer, $38/44 in winter. The other *Motel 6* (☎ 520-782-6561, fax 520-343-4923), 1640 Arizona Ave, is marginally cheaper.

Places to Stay – Middle

The *Yuma Cabaña Motel* (☎ 520-783-8311, 800-874-0811), at 2151 4th Ave, charges $30/35 in summer but $45/50 in winter and more in dove season. It also has some units with kitchenettes for about $10 more. The *Royal Motor Inn* (☎ 520-344-0550), 2941 4th Ave, is a bit cheaper.

The *Super 8 Motel* (☎ 520-782-2000, fax 520-782-6657), 1688 S Riley Ave, is one of the better members of that chain and offers rooms for $47/50 in summer and $55/58 in winter (one bed) or $5 more with two beds. The *Days Inn* (☎ 520-329-7790, fax 520-329-7790 ext 300), 1671 E 16th St, has rooms with refrigerators for $40 to $60 in summer and $20 more in winter. Rooms with spas are $10 more and continental breakfast is included. Both hotels have coin laundries.

The *Fourth Ave Travelodge* (☎ 520-782-3831, 520-783-4616), 2050 4th Ave, charges $32 to $52 in summer and $42 to $62 in winter (depending on the date and size of the room), including continental breakfast. Rooms come with coffeemakers, and there is a laundromat and an outdoor picnic and barbecue area. The *Airport Travelodge* (☎ 520-726-4721, fax 520-344-0452), 711 E 32nd St, is the closest to the airport, has a free airport shuttle, exercise equipment, restaurant and bar, and good rooms (all with coffeemakers and some with kitchenettes) in the $40s in summer, from $55 to $75 in winter. Also in this price range is the new *Comfort Inn* (☎ 520-782-1200), 1691 S Riley Ave, which opened in 1997. The *Holiday Inn Express* (☎ 520-344-1420, fax 520-341-0158), 3181 4th Ave, has a spa and complimentary breakfast and an evening cocktail hour. Most rooms have a refrigerator. Rates are $55 and up in summer, between $70 and $85 in winter.

Places to Stay – Top End

The line between middle and top-end hotels is hazy. The Best Western chain seems to have the town wrapped up at this level, but there are a few other choices. Here's my selection.

The *Best Western Coronado Motor Hotel* (☎ 520-783-4453, fax 520-782-7847), 233 4th Ave, is the most attractive hotel close to downtown. It features a spa, gift shop and

ARIZONA

complimentary continental breakfast. There is a decent midpriced adjoining restaurant. Rooms have a refrigerator; some have a microwave and/or spa. Some units have two bedrooms, and there are several suites. Summer rates start at $46/51; winter rates start at $56/61, with larger units going for $70 to $90 for a double, up to $150 (usually less) for a suite sleeping six.

The *Best Western Chilton Inn* (☎ 520-344-1050, fax 520-344-4877), 300 E 32nd St, is close to the airport and provides an airport shuttle. There is a restaurant and room service, a spa, adults' and children's pools, and a fitness center. Continental breakfast with the morning newspaper is included in the rates of $50 to $85 (up to $100 during Labor Day weekend). The cheapest rates are offered Friday to Sunday.

The *Best Western Innsuites Hotel Yuma* (☎ 520-783-8341, fax 520-783-1349), 1450 Castle Dome Ave, has a spa, two tennis courts, an exercise room, playground and snack bar. Rates include full breakfast, morning newspaper and evening cocktails. The large and attractive rooms have microwaves and refrigerators; the larger suites have spas. Rates run from $60 to $80 in summer, $70 to $100 in winter for one-room suites, $10 to $30 more for two-room suites. A few suites with spas are $100 to $160, depending on season.

The *La Fuente Inn & Suites* (☎ 520-329-1814, 800-841-1814, fax 520-343-2671), 1513 E 16th St, is a modern, Spanish-colonial-style building surrounding a landscaped garden and pool. There is a spa and exercise room. Rooms are mainly one- or two-room suites, many including microwaves and refrigerators. Rates, which include continental breakfast and evening cocktail hour, run from $50 to $70 in the summer and $70 to $100 in winter.

Radisson Suites Inn (☎ 520-726-4830, fax 520-341-1152), 2600 4th Ave, has a spa and offers free airport-shuttle service. All units are two-room suites with refrigerators, coffeemakers and microwaves. Rates, including continental breakfast and evening cocktails, are about $70 in summer and $100 in winter for doubles,

although rates often increase for special events.

The *Shilo Inn* (☎ 520-782-9511, 800-222-2244, fax 520-783-1538), 1550 Castle Dome Ave, is the fanciest place in town. Amenities include an exercise room, spa, sauna and steam bath, and the pool is said to be the town's largest. There is a good restaurant and lounge, room service and an airport shuttle. Some rooms have kitchenettes; others feature a balcony or open onto the courtyard. All have refrigerators. Rates range from $85 to $140; the kitchenette suites can go to $225.

Places to Eat

Restaurants can be fairly dead midweek in summer but bustling during the busy winter season. *Lutes Casino* (☎ 520-782-2192), 221 Main St, is a locally popular hamburger joint. Eclectically decorated and with a bar, pool tables, dominoes and arcade games, it claims to be Arizona's oldest pool hall. Read about its history on the souvenir menu. Kids are welcome. Daily hours are 10 am to 7 pm (6 pm on Sunday), with extended hours to 9 pm or 10 pm in winter.

Chester's Chuck Wagon (☎ 520-782-4152), 2256 4th Ave, is a simple place offering inexpensive American food from 6 am to 10 pm. *Denny's* (☎ 520-782-2202), 1435 E 16th St, has 24-hour family dining. *Brownie's Restaurant* (☎ 520-783-7911), 1145 4th Ave, is a local diner for cheap breakfast and other meals.

For more elegant breakfasts and lunches, *The Garden Café* (☎ 520-783-1491), 250 Madison Ave, is locally popular. It serves good coffees, pancakes, sandwiches, salads and desserts in a pleasant outdoor patio; there's also an indoor dining room. Tuesday to Friday hours are 9 am to 2:30 pm; weekend hours are 8 am to 2:30 pm. For lunches and dinners, *The Crossing* (☎ 520-726-5551), 2690 4th Ave, specializes in prime rib, catfish and ribs and also has Italian dishes. Hours are 11 am to 9:30 pm daily, except Sunday when it closes at 8:30 pm. Dinner entrées are in the $7 to $15 range.

Yuma Landing (☎ 520-782-7847), 195 4th Ave, is convenient for downtown, offers reasonably priced American food from 6 am to 2 am and advertises jazz nights on weekends in winter. One of Yuma's best places for steak and fresh seafood is the *Hunter Steakhouse* (☎ 520-782-3637), 2355 4th Ave, open Monday to Friday from 11:30 am to 2:30 pm and daily from 5 to 10 pm. Most dinner entrées range from $10 to $20.

Yuma has no lack of Mexican restaurants. I like *Chretin's* (☎ 520-782-1291), 485 15th Ave, a locally popular place tucked away inconspicuously on a residential street. The Chretin family operated a dance hall here in the 1930s and opened their restaurant in 1946 – history by Yuma standards. Hours are 11 am to 11 pm Monday to Saturday. *Pappagallo's* (☎ 520-343-9451), 1401 Ave B, is also out of the way and features weekday lunch specials for under $5. Hours are 11 am to 9 pm. Another good choice is *El Charro Cafe* (☎ 520-783-9790), 601 W 8th St, open from 11 am to 9 pm Tuesday to Sunday.

For Chinese food, the *Mandarin Palace* (☎ 520-344-2805), 350 E 32nd St, is both elegant and excellent. Hours are 11 am to 10 pm Monday to Saturday and 3 to 10 pm on Sundays. Most dinner entrées are $8 to $15.

Entertainment

Professional baseball teams do their spring training in sunny Yuma at the 7000-seat Desert Sun Stadium, south of town off Avenue A. Call ☎ 520-317-3394 for a schedule (most games are in February).

Yuma Theater (☎ 520-783-4566, 800-386-5477, fax 520-783-3858), 254 Main, presents musical reviews most evenings except Mondays from fall to spring. The 1997 review *Main Street Tonight* was a local success and is planned to repeat in future years. The visitors bureau provides dates of occasional performances by the local chamber orchestra, community theater and both classical and Mexican folkloric ballet companies.

Choose movies from the five screens of *Plaza Theaters* (☎ 520-782-9292), 1560 4th

Ave, or the four-screen *Mandarin Cinemas* (☎ 520-782-7409), 3142 S Arizona Ave.

For pool, dominoes and other games during the day, see Lutes Casino under Places to Eat, above. Next door is *Red's Bird Cage Saloon* (☎ 520-783-1050), 231 Main St, for pool, darts and drinking after Lutes closes. It sometimes has live entertainment. *Yuma Landing* restaurant offers live jazz on Friday and Saturday evenings in the cool months. For a wilder time, roar over to *Ron's Place* (☎ 520-726-9946), 2852 E Hwy 95 (16th St east of I-8), with pool, darts, bikers, dancing and DJs playing LOUD rock.

Across the river, the Quechan Tribe operates the *Paradise Casino* (☎ 619-572-0213, 619-572-7777, 888 777-4946), 450 Quechan Dr (north on 4th Ave and follow the signs).

For other entertainment ideas, check the Thursday and Friday editions of the *Yuma Daily Sun*.

Getting There & Away

Air The airport (south of 32nd St) is served by Skywest Airlines (☎ 800-453-9417), America West Express (☎ 800-235-9292) and United Express (☎ 800-241-6522). Many daily flights serve Phoenix, and several go to Los Angeles. Avis, Budget, Hertz and Enterprise rent cars at the airport.

Bus The Greyhound Bus Terminal (☎ 520-783-4403), 170 E 17 Place, has three buses a day to Phoenix; Tucson; Lordsburg, New Mexico; and El Paso, Texas. Departures are in the late morning, late evening and the middle of the night. Travel times are four hours to Phoenix, six to Tucson and 14 to El Paso. Four daily buses run to San Diego, California.

Yuma Transit Inc (☎ 520-627-1130), at the Greyhound terminal, has four daily departures to San Luis on the Mexican border. Fares are $3 each way.

American Shuttle Express (☎ 520-726-0906, 888-749-9862) has vans from Yuma to the Phoenix Airport.

Train The Amtrak station, 291 Gila St, doesn't sell tickets, but trains will stop for

ARIZONA

passengers with reservations (☎ 800-872-7245). Trains pass through Yuma on Monday, Wednesday and Friday in the dark, early hours of the morning, heading for Los Angeles, California, or El Paso, Texas, and beyond.

CABEZA PRIETA NATIONAL WILDLIFE REFUGE

This, the driest, wildest and most remote desert area in the Southwest, is 45 miles southeast of Yuma. The NWR headquarters (☎ 520-387-6483), 1611 N 2nd Ave, Ajo, AZ 85321, are on the eastern side of the refuge. You must have a permit to visit the area.

The Cabeza Prieta NWR was set aside in 1939 as desert bighorn sheep habitat and you may be lucky enough to catch sight of some. This is 135 sq miles of wilderness, with no facilities and only rudimentary dirt roads. The main track is called El Camino del Diablo (the Devil's Highway) and has been used for centuries. It emerges at Wellton, on I-8 about 30 miles east of Yuma and 110 miles from Ajo, and takes two days to drive. Many people have died of thirst and heat prostration along this route. It's a real desert experience.

You'll need a 4WD vehicle (preferably two, because it might be days between vehicles if yours breaks down). The north

and west boundaries of the refuge are bounded by bombing and gunnery ranges and entrance is occasionally prohibited when the military is carrying out war games.

With your permit you'll receive safety tips and other information. See Annerino's *Adventuring in Arizona* for a detailed description of El Camino del Diablo.

GILA BEND

About 40 miles north of Ajo and 60 miles west of Casa Grande, Gila Bend is a minor agricultural center, dependent on what's left of the Gila River after upstream damming. Cotton is an important crop here.

Information

The visitor center (☎ 520-683-2002), 644 W Pima, near the west exit of the town (exit 115), has a nice little museum. Hours are 8 am to 4 pm daily, but it may close on summer weekends.

Petroglyphs

In the early part of this millennium, Hohokam people carved hundreds of petroglyphs into boulders northwest of Gila Bend. See the petroglyphs by taking I-8 west of Gila Bend 13 miles to exit 102 (Painted Rocks Rd) and then driving 12 miles north. There's a free campground with toilets but no water.

Places to Stay & Eat

The *Wheel Inn RV Park* (☎ 520-683-2951, 800-684-2951), 606 W William near the center, has showers and RV hookups for $13. Tent camping is permitted.

Several cheap and basic motels have pools and offer rooms from the low $20s. These include the *Yucca Motel* (☎ 520-683-2211), 836 E Pima, and the *El Coronado Motel* (☎ 520-683-2281), 212 W Pima.

The *Super 8 Motel* (☎ 520-683-6311, fax 520-683-2120) at exit 119 has some nicer rooms for $45.88/49.88 for singles/doubles. A restaurant is next door. The *Best Western Space Age Lodge* (☎/fax 520-683-2273), 1046 E Pima, has good rooms with coffeemakers in the $60s and

$70s in winter, a little less in summer. It has a spa and a 24-hour restaurant next door serving inexpensive American and Mexican food.

Getting There & Away

Greyhound stops at the Circle K Store (☎ 520-683-2751), 500 W Pima, three times a day eastbound and westbound on I-8.

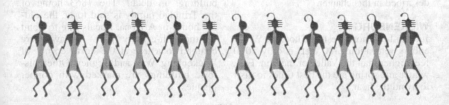

Central Arizona

North of greater Phoenix's Valley of the Sun there is nowhere to go but up. During the summer, droves of southern Arizonans head north to camp, fish, sightsee, shop and find cool relief. During the winter, many of the same folks make the trip in search of snow and skiing. This is not to say the area is just the province of canny locals. On the contrary, central Arizona, with the important town of Flagstaff, is the gateway to the Southwest's most famous destination, the Grand Canyon.

Apart from the outdoor activities in central Arizona's national forests, visitors will find many sights of historical and cultural interest. Several national monuments are sprinkled throughout the area, established to protect uninhabited but impressive Indian sites. Old mining towns either lie forgotten or flourish with a new lease on life as artists' communities. Prescott, the first territorial capital, preserves many buildings from its Wild West days. Sedona, a modern town amid splendid red-rock scenery, draws tourists seeking comfort and relaxation as well as New Agers looking for spiritual and psychic insights at the area's many vortexes. And Flagstaff, home of Northern Arizona University, provides museums, cultural events, nightlife and a laid-back atmosphere fueled by students, skiers and visitors from all over the world.

From Phoenix, you can drive north to Flagstaff in under three hours along I-17, or you can spend a few days wandering through the intriguing small towns that dot the countryside along and around Hwy 89 southwest of Flagstaff. This latter route is described in this chapter.

WICKENBURG

Just an hour northwest of Phoenix, Wickenburg (elevation 2100 feet) is only 1000 feet higher than the Valley of the Sun. Fall, winter and spring are the best times to visit to avoid the heat.

In the 1860s, prospector Henry Wickenburg found gold in the area and by 1866 Wickenburg had become a thriving community surrounded by gold mines. Today, much of the Old West heritage can still be seen in the small town's historic center and in the ghost towns in the area. In addition, Wickenburg has become a dude-ranch center, with several ranches offering cowboy-style vacations. Even if you're just passing through, this town merits a stop to see the Western buildings and the museum.

Orientation & Information

Wickenburg Way (Hwy 60), the main drag through town, runs east-west, intersecting in the middle of town with northbound Tegner (Hwy 93).

The chamber of commerce (☎ 520-684-5479, 800-942-5242, fax 520-684-5470, wburgcoc@primenet.com), 216 N Frontier, is open from 9 am to 5 pm, Monday to Friday, and has varying weekend hours. The library (☎ 520-684-2665) is at 160 N Valentine. The post office (☎ 520-684-2138) is at 2030 W Wickenburg Way. The hospital (☎ 520-684-5421) is at 520 Rose Lane. The police (☎ 520-684-5411) are at 155 N Tegner.

Historic Buildings

The downtown blocks between the railway line and the Hassayampa River contain about 20 buildings constructed between the 1860s and the 1920s – many are on the National Register. The chamber of commerce has a free brochure describing the buildings in detail. The 1863 home of the Trinidad family is said to be the oldest house in Arizona. Locals like to point out the 19th-century 'jail' – outlaws were chained to a tree at the north corner of Wickenburg Way and Tegner. Other historic buildings are marked with copper plaques.

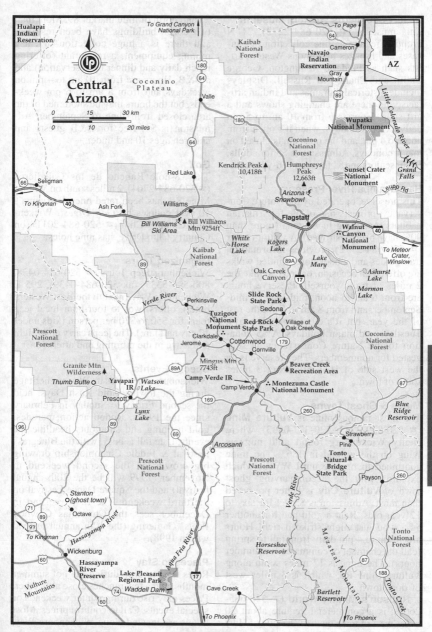

Central Arizona

Hualapai Indian Reservation

To Grand Canyon National Park

To Page

Cameron

Kaibab National Forest

Navajo Indian Reservation

Gray Mountain

AZ

Coconino Plateau

Valle

Little Colorado River

Wupatki National Monument

Coconino National Forest

Seligman

To Kingman

Ash Fork

Red Lake

Williams

Kendrick Peak 10,418ft

Humphreys Peak 12,663ft

Sunset Crater National Monument

Grand Falls

Arizona Snowbowl

Leupp Rd

Flagstaff

Bill Williams Ski Area

Bill Williams Mtn 9254ft

White Horse Lake

Rogers Lake

Walnut Canyon National Monument

To Meteor Crater, Winslow

Kaibab National Forest

Oak Creek Canyon

Lake Mary

Ashurst Lake

Mormon Lake

Verde River

Perkinsville

Slide Rock State Park

Sedona

Red Rock State Park

Village of Oak Creek

Tuzigoot National Monument

Clarkdale

Jerome

Cottonwood

Cornville

Coconino National Forest

Prescott National Forest

Granite Mtn Wilderness

Thumb Butte

Mingus Mtn 7743ft

Beaver Creek Recreation Area

Montezuma Castle National Monument

Yavapai IR

Watson Lake

Camp Verde IR

Camp Verde

Blue Ridge Reservoir

Prescott

Lynx Lake

Strawberry

Pine

Tonto Natural Bridge State Park

Payson

Arcosanti

Prescott National Forest

Prescott National Forest

Verde River

To Kingman

Stanton (ghost town)

Octave

Hassayampa River

Tonto National Forest

Wickenburg

Hassayampa River Preserve

Horseshoe Reservoir

Mazatzal Mountains

Vulture Mountains

Lake Pleasant Regional Park

Waddell Dam

Cave Creek

Bartlett Reservoir

Tonto Creek

Agua Fria River

To Phoenix

To Phoenix

0   15   30 km
0   10   20 miles

ARIZONA

Desert Caballeros Western Museum

This museum (☎ 520-684-2272), 21 N Frontier, features a fine collection of canvases and bronzes by famous Western artists such as Frederic Remington, George Catlin and Charles M Russell. Displays include historical dioramas and Indian artifacts, and there are changing shows and a gift shop. Hours are from 10 am to 5 pm daily except Sundays, when it's open from noon to 4 pm, and the museum is closed on major holidays. Admission is $5 for adults, $4 for seniors and $1 for six- to 16-year-olds.

Hassayampa River Preserve

This preserve, operated by the Nature Conservancy, protects one of the few riparian habitats remaining in Arizona (more than 90% have been destroyed). A visitor center (☎ 520-684-2772) provides information, trail guides and a bookstore. Guided walks are offered on occasion, or you can hike the 2 miles of trails yourself. Preserve hours are from 6 am to noon, mid-May to mid-September, and from 8 am to 5 pm the rest of the year, but it's closed on Mondays, Tuesdays and major holidays. A $5 donation to the Nature Conservancy is suggested for nonmembers. The preserve is on the west side of Hwy 60, about 3 miles south of town.

Mines & Ghost Towns

The most famous mine is **Vulture Mine** (☎ 520-859-2743, 520-377-0803), where Henry Wickenburg found gold nuggets lying on the ground in 1863. The mine continued to operate until WWII, which explains why the accompanying ghost town of **Vulture City** is better preserved than most. Admission is $5; $4 for six- to 12-year-olds. Rent a gold pan for another $4 – you just might strike it rich! Hours are 8 am to 4 pm daily from fall to spring (call the chamber of commerce for summer hours). The mine is 12 miles south along Vulture Mine Rd, which is 3 miles west of downtown.

Robson's Mining World (☎ 520-685-2609), is a commercial venture about 30 miles west of town on the west side of Hwy 71 and north of mile marker 89. More than two dozen buildings have been restored, and there is a huge collection of early mining equipment, a restaurant (offering lunch daily and dinner by reservation) and a B&B. Hours are from 10 am to 4 pm on weekdays and from 8 am to 6 pm weekends, but the hours may be shortened or the area closed from June to September. Admission is $4; free for B&B guests and children ages 10 and under.

Golf

The 18-hole Rancho de los Caballeros (☎ 520-684-2704), 2 miles south on Vulture Mine Rd, has been rated one of Arizona's 10 best courses by *Golf Digest*. Wickenburg Country Club (☎ 520-684-2011), on Country Club Drive, has nine holes.

Organized Tours

Wickenburg Jeep Tours (☎ 520-684-0438, 800-596-5337, fax 520-684-0439), 295 E Wickenburg Way (next to the Best Western hotel), offers two- to four-hour local jeep tours for $50 to $70 per person (kids under 12 pay half fare). The jeeps carry up to eight and leave in the morning and afternoon.

Special Events

Wickenburg celebrates its Western heritage during the town's Gold Rush Days, held the second Friday to Sunday in February since the 1940s. Rodeo action, parades, gold panning and shootouts headline the events. Late fall is busy, with the Bluegrass Festival & Fiddle Championship drawing big crowds on the second weekend in November (1999 will be the 20th annual festival) and the Square Dance Festival on the third weekend. The first weekend in December sees the Christmas Cowboy Poets' Gathering (the 10th annual festival was in 1998).

Places to Stay

Rates tend to drop during the hot summer months, and a few ranches close altogether. Prices may rise during winter weekends or special events. Call to confirm prices. Most hotels are located along Wickenburg Way.

Places to Stay – Camping

Horspitality RV Park (☎ 520-684-2519), 2 miles southeast of downtown on Hwy 60, has hookups, showers and horse stables. Rates are $15 per vehicle, and you should call for a reservation in winter. Similar facilities, plus a pool and recreation areas, are found at the adult-only *Desert Cypress Trailer Ranch* (☎ 520-684-2153), 610 Jack Burden Rd. Both places allow tents.

Self-contained campers can stay opposite the rodeo grounds for $2 per night, but water is not available.

Places to Stay – Budget

The *La Siesta Motel* (☎ 520-684-2826), 486 E Wickenburg Way, has a pool and café attached and has basic but adequate rooms in the $30s (perhaps the best budget choice). Other basic cheapies include the *Log Wagon Inn* (☎ 520-684-2531), 573 W Wickenburg Way; the *Capri Motel* (☎ 520-684-7232), 521-A W Wickenburg Way; and the *Westerner Motel* (☎ 520-684-2493), 680 W Wickenburg Way. The *Circle JR Motel* (☎ 520-684-2661), 741 W Wickenburg Way, has simple rooms in the $40s.

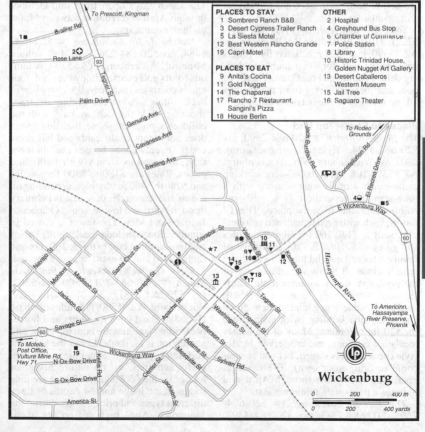

PLACES TO STAY	OTHER
1 Sombrero Ranch B&B	2 Hospital
3 Desert Cypress Trailer Ranch	4 Greyhound Bus Stop
5 La Siesta Motel	6 Chamber of Commerce
12 Best Western Rancho Grande	7 Police Station
19 Capri Motel	8 Library
	10 Historic Trinidad House,
PLACES TO EAT	Golden Nugget Art Gallery
9 Anita's Cocina	13 Desert Caballeros
11 Gold Nugget	Western Museum
14 The Chaparral	15 Jail Tree
17 Rancho 7 Restaurant,	16 Saguaro Theater
Sangini's Pizza	
18 House Berlin	

Wickenburg

ARIZONA

Places to Stay – Middle

The well-run *Americinn* (☎/fax 520-684-5461, 800-634-3444), 850 E Wickenburg Way, has a pool, spa and restaurant that is open from 7 am to 1:30 pm daily and from 5 to 8:30 pm Monday to Saturday. Some of the motel's 30 rooms have balconies. Rates range from $50 to $80.

The pleasantly Western-style *Best Western Rancho Grande* (☎ 520-684-5445, 800-854-7235, fax 520-684-7380), 293 E Wickenburg Way, is the best motel with a pool, spa and tennis court. All of the 80 rooms include a free morning newspaper, coffeemaker and refrigerator, and some mini-suites have kitchenettes. Most rooms are $60 to $80, up to $100 for the largest units available.

Sombrero Ranch B&B (☎/fax 520-684-0222), 31910 W Bralliar Rd, Wickenburg, AZ 85390, in a 1937 ranch, has five rooms with private baths for $75 a double, including deluxe continental breakfast. There is a pool and pleasant views from the ranch's hilltop location on the outskirts of town.

Places to Stay – Top End

The *Flying E Ranch* (☎ 520-684-2690, fax 520-684-5304, flyinge@primenet.com), 2801 W Wickenburg Way, Wickenburg, AZ 85390-1087, is a 20,000-acre working cattle ranch 4 miles west of town with a long-standing reputation as a well-run, comfortable and friendly place. The 17 rooms, each with private bath and refrigerator, start at $130/160 for singles/doubles and go up to $210/275. Take advantage of family rates and eat and play till you drop; costs include all meals served and use of the pool, spa, sauna, exercise room, shuffleboard, horseshoes, tennis, volleyball, basketball, table tennis and garden chess. Or try horseback riding (with instruction) for $20 for two hours. Many of the hearty meals are cookouts and are served family style (no alcohol is served, but you're welcome to bring your own). The ranch is open from November through April and requires a three-night minimum stay.

The *Kay El Bar Ranch* (☎ 520-684-7593, 800-684-7583, fax 520-684-4497, kelbar@juno.com), PO Box 2480, Wickenburg, AZ 85358, has eight rooms with private baths in a historic adobe ranch house (listed on the National Register of Historic Places) 2 miles north of town on Hwy 93. There is also a separate two-bedroom, two-bath adobe house with a living room and fireplace and a two-bedroom, two-bath casita with a fireplace. Ride horses, enjoy the excellent food, lounge by the pool, or play board games and read in the casual atmosphere of the large common area. Room rates are $140/255 for singles/doubles and include meals and horseback riding, but 21% taxes/tips are added; the separate adobe houses cost a little more. The ranch stays open from mid-October through April and requires a two- to four-night minimum stay.

Rancho de los Caballeros (☎ 520-684-5484, fax 520-684-2267), 1551 S Vulture Mine Rd, Wickenburg, AZ 85390, is famous for its golf course. Enjoy the pool, four tennis courts and nature walks, or try horseback riding, mountain biking or trapshooting while the kids are busy with the children's program. Note that this resort does not accept credit cards and has dress codes. Twenty adobe houses contain more than 70 spacious rooms with baths and patios. Rates are $180 to $300 for singles and $280 to $400 for doubles, depending on rooms and season. High season is February through April and low season is October to January and May. The resort is closed in summer. Rates include meals; golf, horses and trapshooting cost extra. A 20% tax and tip is added and no extra tips are expected.

Merv Griffin's Wickenburg Inn Dude Ranch (☎ 520-684-7811, 800-942-5362, fax 520-684-2981), 34801 N Hwy 89, Wickenburg, AZ 85390, is 8 miles north on Hwy 89. The 11 tennis courts and horseback riding facilities are both top class, and instruction is available. Enroll the kids in a children's program and enjoy arts and crafts activities, go on nature hikes, or lounge by the pool and spa. There are nine rooms in the lodge and 54 casitas of three different types and prices. Rates during the January to April high season are about

$300 to $400 a double (plus taxes), including all meals, tennis and two daily horseback rides. Family rates are available and prices drop substantially out of season.

Places to Eat

Wickenburg has many restaurants. For a start, try the following: the *Gold Nugget* (☎ 520-684-2858), 222 E Wickenburg Way, is open from 6 am to 10 pm daily and has a 'Gay '90s' Western atmosphere – 1890s, that is. American meals here are moderately priced and good. *Rancho 7 Restaurant* (☎ 520-684-2492), 111 E Wickenburg Way, has been locally popular for 60 years, featuring home-style American and Mexican cooking from 11 am to 9 pm daily. You can play darts, pool and shuffleboard in the adjoining bar. *Charley's Steak House* (☎ 520-684-2413), 1181 W Wickenburg Way, the town's best steak house, is open from 5 to 9 pm Tuesday to Saturday. The *House Berlin* (☎ 520-684-5004), 169 E Wickenburg Way, offers a haute-German cuisine for lunch and dinner daily except Monday. Dinner entrées are $9 to $14.

Sangini's Pizza (☎ 520-684-7828), 107 E Wickenburg Way, is open for lunch and dinner daily. They deliver. Try *Anita's Cocina* (☎ 520-684-5777), 57 N Valentine, for Mexican food served daily from 11 am to 9 pm. Eat Chinese at the *Sizzling Wok* (☎ 520-684-3977), 621 W Wickenburg Way, open from 11 am to 2:30 pm and from 4:30 to 9:30 pm daily. *The Chaparral* (☎ 520-684-3252), 45 N Tegner, serves homemade ice cream, pastries and snacks from 6 am to 6 pm daily.

Entertainment

The *Saguaro Theater* (☎ 520-684-7189), 176 E Wickenburg Way, screens movies. The *Rancher Bar* (☎ 520-684-5957), W Wickenburg Way by Los Altos Drive, has live country & western music and dancing on weekends. The *Rancho 7 Restaurant* has a popular bar.

Shopping

Art and antiques are big sellers in Wickenburg, and the chamber of commerce has a list of the several art galleries and antique shops downtown. The Gold Nugget Art Gallery (☎ 520-684-5849), behind the Gold Nugget Restaurant in the historic Trinidad House, and the Wickenburg Gallery (☎ 520-684-7047), 10 W Apache, are among the best. For a real whiff of the Old West, mosey into Ben's Saddlery (☎ 520-684-2683), 184 N Tegner; even if you aren't in the market for a saddle, the leathery smell makes it the most memorable shop in town.

Getting There & Away

Bus Greyhound (☎ 520-684-2601), 412 E Wickenburg Way (at the Subway Restaurant), has three night buses to Phoenix, a morning and an evening bus to Kingman and Las Vegas, and a morning bus to Los Angeles. Van shuttles to Phoenix Airport come and go; call the chamber of commerce for information.

Car From Phoenix, Hwy 60 is the most direct route, but going north on I-17 and then west on Hwy 74 is only marginally longer and much more scenic. Northwest of town, Hwy 93 to Kingman is called the Joshua Tree Parkway for the many stands of those plants lining the highway.

PRESCOTT

Founded in 1864 by gold prospectors, Prescott soon became Arizona's first territorial capital. This political decision was handed down by President Abraham Lincoln as the US Civil War was drawing to a close. He preferred the progressive small mining town to the more established, conservative Tucson, considered to have Confederate leanings. At this time, the various Indian ruins in the area were thought to be Aztec, and Prescott was named after William Prescott who had written a history of Mexico.

Although the gold has long since played out, vestiges of early territorial life remain in Prescott's many early buildings, including the first governor's mansion. Prescott's historic character and the cool elevation of 5346 feet attract many of Phoenix's two million residents seeking to escape the heat of summer, as it's only a two-hour drive.

ARIZONA

The town, almost surrounded by the Prescott National Forest, offers many outdoor recreation opportunities, and the tiny neighboring Yavapai Indian Reservation provides legal gambling. Two colleges, a small artists' community and galleries add to the town's bohemian air. Today, many of Prescott's 30,000 residents are involved to some degree in the tourist industry or in government, and the old territorial capital is now the Yavapai County seat.

Orientation
Hwy 89 runs generally southwest to northeast through town, becoming the north-south Montezuma, and then bending east sharply on the east-west Gurley. The main center of town is around the square formed by the intersection of Montezuma, Gurley, Sheldon and Pleasant.

Information
The chamber of commerce (☎ 520-445-2000, 800-266-7534, fax 520-445-0068, chamber@prescott.org), 117 W Goodwin, is open from 9 am to 5 pm, Monday to Friday, 9 am to 3 pm on Saturday, and 10 am to 2 pm on Sunday. The Prescott National Forest Bradshaw Ranger Station (☎ 520-445-7253), 2230 E Hwy 69, Prescott, AZ 86301, is open from 8 am to 4:30 pm Monday to Friday, and Saturday from April to September. The Forest Supervisor's Office (☎ 520-771-4700) is at 344 S Cortez, Prescott, AZ 86303.

The library (☎ 520-445-8110) is at 215 E Goodwin. The local newspaper is the *Daily Courier*. The main post office (☎ 520-778-1890) is at 442 Miller Valley Rd; the downtown branch is in the Federal Building at Goodwin and Cortez. Neighborhood Recycling Center (☎ 520-445-9108) is at 1327 N Hwy 89 or call the city recycling center (☎ 520-771-5849). The regional medical center (☎ 520-445-2700) is at 1003 Willow Creek Rd. The police (☎ 520-778-1444) are at 222 S Marina.

Historic Buildings
Montezuma St west of the Courthouse Plaza was once the infamous 'Whiskey

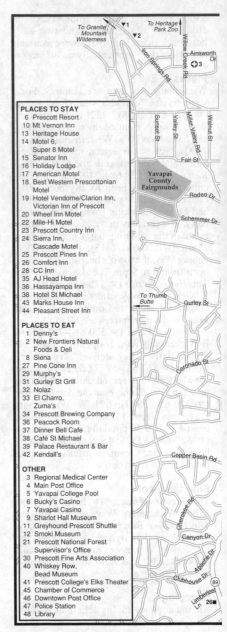

PLACES TO STAY
6   Prescott Resort
10 Mt Vernon Inn
13 Heritage House
14 Motel 6,
    Super 8 Motel
15 Senator Inn
16 Holiday Lodge
17 American Motel
18 Best Western Prescottonian
    Motel
19 Hotel Vendome/Clarion Inn,
    Victorian Inn of Prescott
20 Wheel Inn Motel
22 Mile-Hi Motel
23 Prescott Country Inn
24 Sierra Inn,
    Cascade Motel
25 Prescott Pines Inn
26 Comfort Inn
28 CC Inn
35 AJ Head Hotel
36 Hassayampa Inn
38 Hotel St Michael
43 Marks House Inn
44 Pleasant Street Inn

PLACES TO EAT
1   Denny's
2   New Frontiers Natural
    Foods & Deli
8   Siena
27 Pine Cone Inn
29 Murphy's
31 Gurley St Grill
32 Nolaz
33 El Charro,
    Zuma's
34 Prescott Brewing Company
36 Peacock Room
37 Dinner Bell Cafe
38 Café St Michael
39 Palace Restaurant & Bar
42 Kendall's

OTHER
3   Regional Medical Center
4   Main Post Office
5   Yavapai College Pool
6   Bucky's Casino
7   Yavapai Casino
9   Sharlot Hall Museum
11 Greyhound Prescott Shuttle
12 Smoki Museum
21 Prescott National Forest
    Supervisor's Office
30 Prescott Fine Arts Association
40 Whiskey Row,
    Bead Museum
41 Prescott College's Elks Theater
45 Chamber of Commerce
46 Downtown Post Office
47 Police Station
48 Library

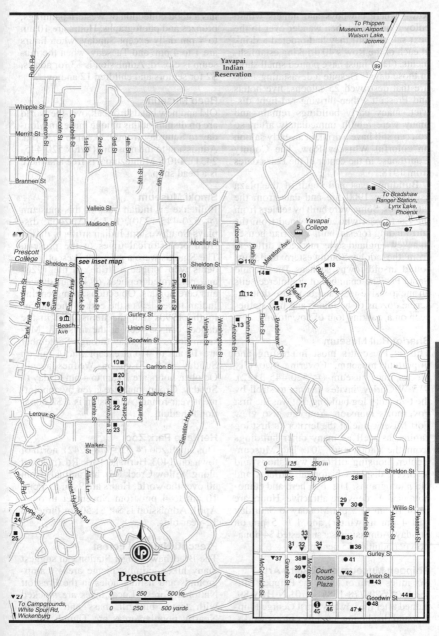

Row,' where cowboys and miners would enjoy a drink and then wander over to the next saloon until they had ordered a drink at each of the Row's 40 drinking establishments. (They must have poured small shots in those days!) Despite a devastating 1900 fire that destroyed 25 saloons, five hotels and Prescott's then-thriving red-light district, many early buildings remain and many were rebuilt immediately after, so you can still have a drink in an early saloon on colorful Whiskey Row. The County Courthouse in the center of the Plaza dates from 1918.

Buildings east and south of the plaza escaped the 1900 fire and date from the late 1800s. Some were built by settlers from the East Coast who, using wood from the surrounding forests, built Victorian houses in a New England style, markedly different from the adobe Southwestern buildings found in old towns such as Tucson and Santa Fe. The chamber of commerce sells an inexpensive map and brochure that describe dozens of buildings and five statues seen on a walking tour of downtown.

Sharlot Hall Museum
This is Prescott's most interesting and important museum. Covering two city blocks, the museum (☎ 520-445-3122), 415 W Gurley, invites visitors to stroll by the two-story log building that was the first governor's mansion. You can also view Fort Misery, one of the territory's first log cabins, as well as many other buildings from the 1860s and '70s. The Museum Center, housing offices, workshops and archives, displays historical artifacts and old photographs. The rose, herb and ethnobotanical gardens are attractive. Hours are from 10 am to 5 pm Monday to Saturday (till 4 pm in winter) and 1 to 5 pm on Sunday. Admission is a suggested $4 donation per adult or $5 per family.

Phippen Museum of Western Art
Six miles north of town, the Phippen Museum (☎ 520-778-1385), 4701 N Hwy 89, named after the cowboy artist George Phippen and displaying a number of his works, has a good collection of Western paintings, bronzes and photographs. Hours are 10 am to 4 pm daily except Sunday, when hours are 1 to 4 pm, and Tuesday, when the museum is closed. Admission is $3 for adults, $2 for seniors and children 12 and over.

Bead Museum
Old and new beads from all over the world are on display at this unique museum Monday to Saturday from 9:30 am to 4:30 pm. Admission to the museum (☎/fax 520-445-2431), 140 S Montezuma, is free and there is a bead shop.

Smoki Museum
Built like an Indian pueblo, this museum (☎ 520-445-1230), 147 N Arizona, displays Southwestern Indian artifacts dating from prehistorical times to the present. The Smokis were a group of Prescott residents who formed a 'tribe' in the 1920s and performed replicas of Indian dances and ceremonials. Objections from genuine Indian tribes led to the end of the dances in the 1990s, but the items used in the dances can be seen at the museum. Museum hours from May through September are 10 am to 4 pm, except 1 to 4 pm on Sunday and closed on Wednesday. In October, hours are 10 am to 4 pm Friday to Sunday. Group tours are given by appointment year-round. Admission is a $2 donation for adults.

Heritage Park Zoo
This small zoo (☎ 520-778-4242), north of town on 1403 Heritage Park Rd (reached along Willow Creek Rd), has animals from all over the world. Hours are 9 am to 5 pm, 10 am to 4 pm from November through April. Admission is $4; $1.50 for three- to 12-year-olds.

Prescott National Forest
The Bradshaw Ranger Station can suggest many hikes, climbs, picnic areas, campgrounds and fishing holes in the Prescott National Forest. Local lakes are stocked with trout, bluegill, bass and catfish. Nearby popular areas are Thumb Butte,

Lynx Lake and the Granite Mountain Wilderness.

Looming over the west side of town, **Thumb Butte** can be reached by driving 3 miles along Gurley and Thumb Butte Rd. Have lunch at the picnic area before hiking the 1.2-mile trail that makes it almost all the way to the summit, a thousand feet above town. The last 200 feet are the province of rock climbers.

To get to **Lynx Lake**, drive 4 miles east on Hwy 69, then 3 miles south on Walker Rd. Here you'll find fishing, hiking, camping, a store, a small-boat rental (summer only), a small Indian ruin and good bird watching (look for eagles and waterfowl in winter and migrants in spring).

The **Granite Mountain Wilderness** has a fishing lake, campgrounds, and hiking trails and is popular with rock climbers. To reach the area, head north on Grove Ave from downtown, which becomes Miller Valley Rd, then bear left on Iron Springs Rd, and just after reaching the national forest boundary about 4 miles from Prescott, turn right on unpaved USFS Rd 347 and continue for another 4 miles.

Try picnicking, fishing and camping at **Watson Lake**, about 4 miles north on Hwy 89. Just beyond are the **Granite Dells**, a landscape of 100-foot-high, rounded redrock outcrops that you can hike through or rock climb on.

Activities

Play **golf** at one of the two 18-hole courses offered at Antelope Hills (☎ 520-776-7888, 800-972-6818), 8 miles north of Prescott

---

Sharlot Hall

Twelve-year-old Sharlot Mabrith Hall arrived in Prescott in February 1882 after an arduous horseback trip from Kansas with her family. During the journey, she was thrown by her horse, receiving a back injury that plagued her for the rest of her life.

While helping run her family's ranch, she became fascinated with life on the frontier. Largely self-schooled, she began describing the gold miners, Indians and ranchers around her in a series of stories and poems that soon gained local admiration. In 1909 she was appointed Territorial Historian, the first woman to hold a political office in Arizona.

In 1924 she traveled to Washington, DC, to represent Arizona in the Electoral College. She caused a stir in the capital with her outfit that included a copper mesh coat provided by a local mine. There was no mistaking that Arizona was 'The Copper State.' During her visit to the east, she toured several museums; these inspired her to found a museum of Arizona history.

On her return to Prescott, Hall leased the first territorial capitol building and restored the governor's mansion. In 1928, she moved her extensive personal collection of historical artifacts into the mansion and opened it as a museum. She lived on the property, expanding and adding to the collection until her death in 1943. The museum bearing her name has continued to flourish since then. In 1981, Sharlot Hall was elected to the Arizona Women's Hall of Fame. ■

on Hwy 89. The old north course is one of Arizona's better public courses. There are also 18 holes at Prescott Country Club (☎ 520-772-8984), 14 miles east of town on Hwy 69. Children will enjoy miniature golf, bumper boats, a race track and arcade games at Castle Golf (☎ 520-772-0702), 6 miles east on Hwy 69.

On a hot day, go **swimming** at Yavapai College Pool (☎ 520-776-2231), 1100 E Sheldon. For information about **mountain biking**, visit the Bikesmith (☎ 520-445-0280), 723-A N Montezuma. Buy or rent **camping** and **climbing** equipment at Basecamp (☎ 520-445-8310), 142 N Cortez, or Granite Mountain Outfitters (☎ 520-776-4949), 320 W Gurley.

If you're interested in **gambling**, the Yavapai Indian tribe runs a casino on its tiny reservation. The casino, on Hwy 69 a mile northeast of town, is open 24 hours and offers mainly slots, bingo and video keno. Nearby is Bucky's Casino, in the Prescott Resort.

For **horseback riding,** try Trail Horse Adventures (☎ 520-771-8303, 800-723-3538) or the Prescott Ranch (☎ 520-636-9737, 800-684-7433), on Hwy 89 about 20 miles north of town.

Special Events

The chamber of commerce has a calendar listing many events and there is something going on every week from May through September. Popular events include the Phippen Western Art and Off-Street Arts & Crafts festivals, both held over Memorial Day weekend. Territorial Days, on the second weekend in June, features free 19th-century entertainment, tours of the Victorian houses and general old-fashioned fun. A Bluegrass Festival on the third weekend in June is held in an outdoor auditorium backed by the Granite Dells. Frontier Days, during the week leading up to the Fourth of July, has the world's oldest rodeo and other celebrations. The Faire on the Square provides arts, crafts and entertainment during Labor Day weekend. The Yavapai County Fair is held in late September.

Places to Stay

Approximate midweek summer rates are given below; winter rates (from November to March) are substantially lower. Summer weekends may be as much as $20 higher, and weekend reservations are always a good idea, especially for Frontier Days when prices go up the most.

Note that Prescott Valley, about 8 miles east along Hwy 69, has several other motels (mainly chains) that aren't any cheaper than Prescott's.

Places to Stay – Camping

Point of Rocks RV Park (☎ 520-445-9018), 3025 N Hwy 89 (4 miles north of town in the Granite Dells), has 100 RV-only sites for $17 with hookups. *Willow Lake RV Park* (☎ 520-445-6311) has about 170 RV sites with hookups for $19.50 and 30 tent sites for $14 (less in winter) as well as a pool, showers, a playground and a coin laundry. To get there, drive 4 miles north on Hwy 89, then head west on Willow Lake Rd and follow signs for about 4 miles.

The USFS (☎ 520-445-7253) operates many simple campgrounds. *White Spar*, 2½ miles south of town on Hwy 89, has 62 sites with picnic tables, grills, toilets, water but no showers, and is open all year for $7 a night. Similar facilities are available for $9 at *Lynx Lake* (see the Prescott National Forest, above) from April to early November, and *Hilltop*, near Lynx Lake, from mid-May through September. Reservations (☎ 800-280-2267) are possible for some sites.

USFS campsites with pit toilets but no water are available at *Granite Basin* in the Granite Mountain Wilderness (see above) year-round. Try the similar facilities at *Indian Creek*, 6 miles south on Hwy 89 and 1 mile left on USFS Rd 97, open from mid-May through September, and at *Lower Wolf Creek*, 7 miles south on Senator Hwy and 1¼ miles right on USFS Rd 97, open from mid-May to mid-November. These campgrounds were free when I checked, but a fee may be charged in the future.

Places to Stay – Budget

It's difficult to find a motel room under $40 in the summer. The *Motel 6* (☎ 520-776-0160, fax 520-445-4188), 1111 E Sheldon, has a pool, coin laundry and 79 rooms for $40/46 single/double midweek in summer, and $46/52 on weekends. The *Super 8 Motel* (☎ 520-776-1282, fax 520-778-6736), 1105 E Sheldon, has a small pool, a microwave for guest use and a coin laundry. Seventy decent rooms are $47/54 with one bed, $58 with two beds, and include a coffee-and-pastry breakfast.

The popular *Hotel St Michael* (☎ 520-776-1999, 800-678-3757, fax 520-776-7318), 205 W Gurley, is an old Whiskey Row hotel rebuilt in 1900. It has 72 older but clean rooms with baths for $42 to $54 ($10 more on weekends); a few family units and 'suites' are in the $60s and $70s. There's a restaurant, and rates include continental breakfast. The old and funky *AJ Head Hotel* (☎ 520-778-1776), 129 N Cortez, offers basic rooms with shared bathrooms in the $30s and rooms with private bathrooms for up to $60; ask about long-stay discounts. The restaurant and bar has entertainment some evenings.

Several independent motels offer rooms in the budget price range. The cheapest motel is the basic *CC Inn* (☎ 520-445-7007), 115 E Sheldon. Better places include the *American Motel* (☎ 520-778-4322); the *Holiday Lodge* (☎ 520-445-0420); the *Senator Inn* (☎ 520-445-1440), with a pool; and the *Heritage House* (☎ 520-445-9091), all on E Gurley. (Some of these motels charge opportunistically high rates in summer.) The small *Mile-Hi Motel* (☎ 520-445-2050), 409 S Montezuma, and the *Wheel Inn Motel* (☎ 520-778-7346, 800-717-0902), 333 S Montezuma, are also in this price range; the Wheel Inn includes continental breakfast.

Places to Stay – Middle

Hotels South of town on a quiet wooded road, the *Comfort Inn* (☎ 520-778-5770, 800-889-9774, fax 520-776-8404), 1290 White Spar Rd, has a spa, outdoor pool, and 61 rooms starting in the $60s midweek and the $70s on weekends, and some pricier mini-suites with kitchenettes. Continental breakfast is included. Several restaurants are nearby. Other hotels in this area that may be marginally cheaper are the *Sierra Inn* (☎ 520-445-1250, 800-513-2014), 809 White Spar Rd, which has 49 rooms (some with fireplaces), a pool and complimentary in-room coffee, and the small *Cascade Motel* (☎ 520-445-1232), 805 White Spar Rd, which offers kitchenettes.

The *Best Western Prescottonian Motel* (☎ 520-445-3096, fax 520-778-2976), at 1317 E Gurley, has a small pool, a spa, and a restaurant and bar open from 6 am to 11 pm. More than 120 large rooms with coffeemakers are $60 to $90 ($120 over July 4), including continental breakfast; suites are also available.

The historic *Hotel Vendome/Clarion Inn* (☎ 520-776-0900, fax 520-771-0395), 230 S Cortez, has charm dating to 1917. There are 17 rooms for $80 to $100 double, all with modern private bath, and four suites for $100 and up, depending on season. Rates include continental breakfast. The lobby with a cozy wooden bar is an attractive place for a drink.

B&Bs Several old houses have been attractively restored as B&Bs, and it's hard to choose the nicest. The following selection includes both middle and top-end places; there are others. None allow smoking indoors and many offer multi-day discounts.

The *Marks House Inn* (☎ 520-778-4632, 800-370-6275), 203 E Union, Prescott, AZ 86303, is an 1894, two-story, turreted and colonnaded Queen Anne house. The four double rooms range from $90 to $135 (the $135 is for the Queen Anne suite, with a sitting room in the turret), and prices include full breakfast and afternoon tea. The *Pleasant Street Inn* (☎ 520-445-4774), 142 S Pleasant, Prescott, AZ 86303, in a 1906 Victorian restored in 1991, offers two rooms and two suites, one with a fireplace, for $85 to $125 double.

The *Victorian Inn of Prescott* (☎ 520-778-2642), 246 S Cortez, Prescott, AZ 86303, is an 1893 Victorian house with three rooms priced in the $90s and a suite for $145 double, each with private bath. *Mt Vernon Inn* (☎ 520-778-0886, mtvrnon@ primenet.com), 204 N Mt Vernon Ave, is a turreted 1900 Victorian house set in a tree-filled garden. Four rooms, each with private bath and queen-size bed, go for $95 double; the price includes breakfast and afternoon refreshments. In addition, three cottages with equipped kitchens are $105 to $125 double (without breakfast).

At the south end of town, the *Prescott Country Inn* (☎ 520-445-7991), 503 S Montezuma, Prescott, AZ 86303, has 12 cottages, each different but all with baths and kitchenettes. Rates are $90 to $150, depending on the cottage, and prices include continental breakfast.

Out of the town center, the very popular *Prescott Pines Inn* (☎ 520-445-7270, 800-541-5374, fax 520-778-3665), 901 White Spar Rd, Prescott, AZ 86303, is centered on a 1902 country Victorian house surrounded by four guesthouses that contain a total of 13 rooms, two of which combine into a chalet sleeping up to eight, three of which have gas fireplaces, and eight of which have kitchens or kitchenettes. Most rooms are priced at $65 to $109 a double, $10 more on weekends. The full breakfast is optional and costs an extra $5, but coffee and cookies are free. Reservations are recommended – some rooms are booked months in advance.

Five miles east of town, the *Lynx Creek Farm B&B* (☎ 520-778-9573, 888-778-9573, lcf@bslnet.com), PO Box 4301, Prescott, AZ 86302, is set in orchards and surrounded by a small farm. Six large rooms, some with outdoor hot tubs and decks, others with wood-burning stoves, and all with king-size beds and private bathrooms, are $85 to $115 double. Four rooms convert into suites with kitchenettes at $105 or $135 double, including breakfast, and multi-night discounts are available.

Places to Stay – Top End

The historic *Hassayampa Inn* (☎ 520-778-9434, 800-322-1927, fax 520-445-8590), 122 E Gurley, was one of Arizona's most elegant hotels when it opened in 1927. Carefully restored in 1985, the hotel has a vintage hand-operated elevator, many of its original furnishings and hand-painted wall decorations. The 68 rooms vary (standard, choice, suite, suite with spa) and run $100 to $130 for a double and $150 to $175 for a suite; prices include full breakfast and an evening cocktail. The lovely dining room is open from 7 am (6:30 on weekdays) to 2 pm and from 5 to 9 pm.

The *Prescott Resort* (☎ 520-776-1666, 800-967-4637, fax 520-776-8544), 1500 Hwy 69, sits high on a hill overlooking Prescott from the east. The resort features Bucky's Casino (with machines and bingo), an indoor pool, a whirlpool, two tennis courts, racquetball, full exercise facilities, a massage service, a restaurant and room service, a bar with entertainment and dancing and a barber/beauty shop. Large rooms with balconies, coffeemakers and refrigerators are $140 double, and one-bedroom suites are $170; prices are discounted 20% during the winter.

Places to Eat

On the plaza, *Café St Michael*, underneath the Hotel St Michael, serves reasonably priced breakfasts, espressos and light meals throughout the day. The *Dinner Bell Cafe* (☎ 520-445-9888), 321 W Gurley, is an inexpensive, down-home diner open from 6 am to 1:50 pm daily except Sunday, when it's open 7 to 11:45 am, and Wednesday, when it's closed. This diner might be cheap and plain, but the food is good.

If you are staying out along the White Spar Rd, a good choice is the *Pine Cone Inn* (☎ 520-445-2970), 1245 White Spar Rd, which opens at 7 am for breakfast and serves good American lunches and dinners (steak and seafood); Prescottians drive out from town for a change of pace and to enjoy the frequent live music and dancing. Dinner entrées are in the $8 to $18 range.

Back in town, the following are all good for lunch or dinner. *Kendall's* (Famous Burgers & Ice Cream) (☎ 520-778-3658), 113 S Cortez, is a 1950s-style place that does not believe in small portions. It's open from 11 am to 8 pm daily (6 pm on Sunday). The popular *Gurley St Grill* (☎ 520-445-3388), 230 W Gurley, in a historic building, has burgers, sandwiches, pastas, pizzas and grilled chicken lunches and dinners at moderate prices. It also has a decent beer selection. Good microbrews and English-style pub food are featured at the *Prescott Brewing Company* (☎ 520-771-2795), 130 Gurley St, a large but usually crowded place. Bring the whole family. The newly renovated but old-fashioned-looking *Palace Restaurant & Bar* (☎ 520-541-1996), 120 S Montezuma, now has sandwiches for lunch and steaks and seafood for dinner served by waitstaff in late-19th-century clothing. Luckily, its old wooden bar, saved from the 1900 fire, still serves to prop up elbows.

For Mexican food, try *El Charro* (☎ 520-445-7130), 120 N Montezuma, open daily from 11 am to 8 pm, to 8:30 pm on Friday and Saturday. Next door is the new *Zuma's* (☎ 520-541-1400), 124 N Montezuma, with wood-fired pizzas, decent Italian food (all entrées under $8), an above-average selection of libations and a slightly alternative atmosphere. More upscale Italian and continental lunches and dinners (most entrées at $14 to $21) are served at the favorably reviewed *Siena* (☎ 520-771-1285), 111 Grove, which is closed on Monday.

Try Cajun and Creole cooking at *Nolaz* (☎ 520-445-3765), 216 W Gurley, open lunch and dinner from Monday to Saturday (the name is an acronym for New Orleans, Louisiana and Arizona). Sample the good beer selection and listen to live jazz or blues in the lounge on weekends when the place can be packed; it tends to be quieter on nights without music. Most dinner entrées are priced in the teens. *Murphy's* (☎ 520-445-4044), 201 N Cortez, definitely one of Prescott's best, was a general store in the 1890s. Much of the old charm remains, and the American food is good and fairly priced in the $12 to $24 range for dinner, much less at lunch. Hours here are 11 am to 3 pm and 4:30 to 10 pm. The *Peacock Room* (☎ 520-778-9434), in the Hassayampa Inn, serving a wide range of

breakfasts, lunches and dinners, is another highly recommended dining spot. It's open from 7 am (6:30 on weekdays) to 2 pm and 5 to 9 pm daily.

Finally, you can buy food to go or eat a sandwich or salad at *New Frontiers Natural Foods & Deli* (☎ 520-445-7370), 1112 Iron Springs Rd, open every day for health food. Nearby, *Denny's* (☎ 520-778-1230), 1316 Iron Springs Rd, is open 24 hours.

Entertainment

See movies at the *Plaza West Cinemas* (☎ 520-778-0207), 1509 W Gurley, or *Frontier Village 10* (☎ 520-445-9500), in the shopping plaza at 1771 E Hwy 69. Wander down Whiskey Row for a selection of bars and saloons, some of which have live music and dancing; there's a couple more to check out on Cortez north of Gurley. Nolaz (see Places to Eat, above) also offers live jazz.

The *Prescott Fine Arts Association* (☎ 520-445-3286), 208 N Marina, presents music and drama. Also check Prescott College's *Elks Theater* (☎ 520-445-3557), 113 E Gurley, and the *Yavapai College Performance Hall* (☎ 520-776-2015), 1100 E Sheldon, for a schedule of performances.

See Activities (above) for gambling casinos.

Shopping

Several antique stores line Cortez north of Gurley. The Prescott Fine Arts Association Gallery (☎ 520-778-7888), 208 N Marina, has a selection of works for sale by regional artists as well as changing art shows. Hours are 11 am to 4 pm, Wednesday to Saturday, and noon to 4 pm on Sunday. The chamber of commerce has brochures about other antique stores and art galleries.

Getting There & Away

Air Prescott Municipal Airport is 9 miles north on Hwy 89. America West Express has three or four flights a day to and from Phoenix.

Bus Greyhound (☎ 520-445-5470), 820 E Sheldon, has a 10 am bus to Camp Verde for $10; there you can connect with north-bound or southbound Greyhound services along I-17. Shuttle U (☎ 520-772-6114, 800-304-6114) runs several vans a day between Prescott and Phoenix Airport for $29 one way and $50 roundtrip. Also try Mountain High Shuttle (☎ 520-772-9700, 888-817-1358), which offers fewer trips but cheaper rates.

Getting Around
Car Rental Hertz (☎ 520-776-1399) has an office at the airport. Enterprise (☎ 520-778-6506), 202 S Montezuma, will deliver your car to the airport or anywhere in Prescott. Budget (☎ 520-778-3806) also has cars.

Taxi Ace City Cab (☎ 520-445-1616, 520-445-5510), at the Greyhound office, operates from 4:30 am to 2:30 am daily.

JEROME
Named after New Yorker Eugene Jerome, who invested $200,000 in the local United Verde Mine in 1882 (a chunk of money in those days), Jerome is the most celebrated of Arizona's old mining towns. Rich in copper, gold and silver, the area was mined by Indians before the arrival of Europeans. Jerome grew to 15,000 inhabitants by the 1920s, but the stock market crash and resulting economic depression shut down many of the mines. The last closed in 1953 and with only a few dozen residents, Jerome looked as if it would become another ghost town.

In the late 1960s, Jerome's spectacular location and empty houses were discovered by hippies, artists and retirees, and slowly Jerome became what it is today, a collection of late-19th- and early-20th-century buildings housing art galleries, souvenir shops, restaurants, saloons and a few B&Bs, all precariously perched on a steep hillside. The setting is quite extraordinary – the entire town looks about to slide off the mountainside. Indeed, many buildings did just that; the famous 'sliding jail' can be seen today 225 feet below its original location.

Most of the buildings lining Main St and the streets just to the north and south date from between 1895 and the 1920s, and all

of Jerome is part of a National Historic District. The chamber of commerce has a map showing each historic building's location, and you can view Jerome's historic homes on tours given the third weekend of May for $6.

The town, elevated a pleasant mile above sea level, has about 400 permanent residents and on a busy summer day has many more tourists than locals.

Orientation & Information
Hwy 89A loops and winds its way over the steep hills leading to and from Jerome, between Prescott and Cottonwood (long trailers are not recommended). The town slopes steeply down from the southwest to the northeast.

The chamber of commerce (☎ 520-634-2900), Drawer K, Jerome, AZ 86331, located in a hut on Hull Ave, is open from 10 am to 4 pm in summer and as staffing permits in winter. The library (☎ 520-639-0574) is at 111 Jerome Ave. The post office (☎ 520-634-8241) is at 120 Main. The police (☎ 520-634-7943) are in the town hall on Main St.

Things to See
The **Mine Museum** (☎ 520-634-5477), 200 Main, is run by the Jerome Historical Society (☎ 520-634-7349) and displays old photos, documents, tools and other memorabilia to explain Jerome's history. Hours are 9 am to 4:30 pm and admission is $1 for people 13 and over. The museum is housed in the 1898 Fashion Saloon.

A mile beyond the north (upper) end of Main St is the **Gold King Mine Museum** (☎ 520-634-0053), a miniature ghost town with frequent demonstrations of antique mining equipment, a walk-in mine, a gift shop and (don't ask me why) a children's petting zoo. Hours are 9 am to 5 pm daily except Christmas; admission is $3, $2.50 for seniors and $2 for six- to 12-year-olds.

The **Jerome State Historic Park** (☎ 520-634-5381), 2 miles beyond Jerome off Hwy 89A en route to Cottonwood, is in and around the 1916 mansion of colorful mining mogul 'Rawhide' Jimmy Douglas

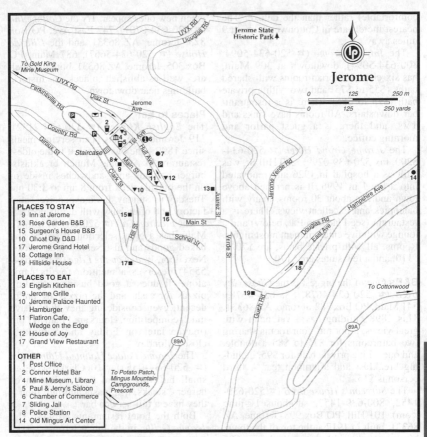

Jerome

0   125   250 m
0   125   250 yards

PLACES TO STAY
9 Inn at Jerome
13 Rose Garden B&B
15 Surgeon's House B&B
16 Ghost City D&D
17 Jerome Grand Hotel
18 Cottage Inn
19 Hillside House

PLACES TO EAT
3 English Kitchen
9 Jerome Grille
10 Jerome Palace Haunted Hamburger
11 Flatiron Cafe, Wedge on the Edge
12 House of Joy
17 Grand View Restaurant

OTHER
1 Post Office
2 Connor Hotel Bar
4 Mine Museum, Library
5 Paul & Jerry's Saloon
6 Chamber of Commerce
7 Sliding Jail
8 Police Station
14 Old Mingus Art Center

To Gold King Mine Museum

Jerome State Historic Park

To Cottonwood

To Potato Patch, Mingus Mountain Campgrounds, Prescott

(after whom the Arizonan town of Douglas is named). Of Jerome's museums, this gives the most thorough understanding of the town's mining history. View models, exhibits, a video presentation inside the mansion and old mining equipment outside. There is a picnic area with great views. Admission is $2.50; $1 for 7- to 14-year-olds. Hours are 8 am to 5 pm daily except Christmas.

Places to Stay

Camping The Prescott National Forest surrounds Jerome, and ranger stations in Prescott and Camp Verde have information. The *Potato Patch* campground, 6½ miles along Hwy 89A toward Prescott, has 14 sites open from April through November. Nearby, turn left along USFS Rd 104 and drive for 3 miles to *Mingus Mountain*, a campground with 27 sites open from May through November. Both of the campgrounds are free (this may change) and have pit toilets and picnic tables but no drinking water.

Hotels Don't expect luxury, as accommodations tend toward the historic (though comfortable) rather than the deluxe. The nearest motels are in Cottonwood, about 9 miles away.

The *Inn at Jerome* (☎ 520-634-5094, 800-634-5094), downtown at 309 Main, has six clean Victorian rooms with shared baths ($55 to $75) and two with a private bath ($75 to $85). There is a restaurant/bar downstairs. All rooms have sinks and TVs, and there is a guest parlor and morning coffee.

The *Jerome Grand Hotel* (☎ 520-634-8200, fax 520-639-0299), 200 Hill St, was built as a hospital in 1926 and renovated into a hotel in 1996. It is perched above town and has about 30 rooms, many with balconies and excellent views. There is a restaurant (see Places to Eat, below) and a lounge with live entertainment most nights. Rooms, all with private baths, are $70 to $110, and a few suites are $170.

B&Bs One of the biggest is the *Ghost City B&B* (☎ 520-634-4678, 888-634-4678), 541 Main, PO Box 382, Jerome, AZ 86331. This 1898 building has a verandah with great views, a hot tub, four rooms sharing two bathrooms for $75 to $85 a double, and one with a private bath for $95, including breakfast and afternoon tea. A third person is $15.

The *Surgeon's House B&B* (☎ 520-639-1452, 800-639-1452, surghouse1@juno .com), 101 Hill, PO Box 998, Jerome, AZ 86331, built in 1917 at the top of the town, has two rooms with private baths for $95 and $110. A suite with private bath and balcony, and a guesthouse with private bath and patio, are each $125 double. To relax, enjoy the views, soak in the hot tub or make an appointment for a massage. Full breakfast and assorted snacks are provided.

The *Rose Garden B&B* (☎ 520-634-3270), 120 Juarez, PO Box 313, Jerome, AZ 86331, offers one large private bedroom with bath and sitting room with fireplace for $89 double. You'll be the only guests. A long stairway leads up to Main St if you don't want to drive.

Several other small B&Bs are available, and the chamber of commerce knows when new ones appear. Try the *Cottage Inn* (☎ 520-634-0701), 747 East Ave, PO Box 823, Jerome, AZ 86331, and the *Hillside House* (☎ 520-634-5667), 687 Main, PO Box 305, Jerome, AZ 86331, both of which are well-established places in historic buildings near downtown.

Places to Eat

The *English Kitchen* (☎ 520-634-2132), 119 Jerome Ave, has been serving meals since 1899 – the owners say it is the oldest restaurant in Arizona. Munch breakfasts, burgers, salads and sandwiches inside or on the outside deck from 8 am to 3:30 pm Tuesday to Sunday. It's inexpensive, satisfactory and often busy with day-trippers.

The *Flatiron Cafe* (☎ 520-634-2733), 416 Main, has a great selection of coffee and baked goods and also serves light snacks. Next door, *Wedge on the Edge* (☎ 520-634-5554) deserves a mention for its name alone. It does a good business 'trading pizzas for cash' and the pizzas are pretty decent, even considering they don't have much competition. Hours are 11 am to 7 pm (maybe later on Friday and Saturday), closed Monday.

The *Jerome Palace Haunted Hamburger* (☎ 520-634-0554), 410 Clark, serves a small but varied and tasty selection of burgers, steaks, fish, pasta and pub food – they have a full-service bar.

Both the hotel restaurants are OK. The *Jerome Grille*, in the Inn at Jerome, serves reasonably priced American and Southwestern breakfast, lunch and dinner daily. The more upscale *Grand View Restaurant*, in the Jerome Grand Hotel, has varied but still mainly American cuisine.

The best and most expensive restaurant in the Jerome-Cottonwood area is the small (seven tables) but colorful *House of Joy* (☎ 520-634-5339), 416 Hull Ave, which is housed in a former bordello and retains a raffish decor. This restaurant is open Saturday and Sunday for dinner only, so reservations are essential and must be made several weeks in advance. The restaurant has a small continental menu offering good desserts. Most dinners are in the $20s, including the chef's soup and salad. Credit cards are not accepted here.

Entertainment
A good place to get drinks is *Paul & Jerry's Saloon* (☎ 520-634-2603), 206 Main, originally called the Senate Saloon when it first opened in 1899. Also have a look into the old *Connor Hotel*, a block away, which may or may not reopen as a hotel again though the funky old bar is still in business – everyone has different priorities. The bars may feature live music on weekends.

Shopping
A stroll along Main St will take you past plenty of art galleries, antique shops and souvenir stands. Serious gallery shoppers shouldn't miss the Old Mingus Art Center, about a mile from 'downtown' along Hwy 89A to Cottonwood. Here, there are a number of high-quality artists' studios and galleries, the best known of which is the 20,000-sq-foot Anderson-Mandette Art Studio (☎ 520-634-3438). The Raku Gallery (☎ 520-639-0239), 250 Hull Ave, showcases the best local ceramics among other art, and the Aurum (☎ 520-634-3330), 369 Main, has one of the best jewelry selections. Use these as a top-end gauge for the dozens of other galleries in town.

Getting There & Away
There is no public transport. If you're driving Hwy 89A from Prescott to Cottonwood, it's impossible to avoid Jerome as the road winds steeply through town. With so many tourists stopping, the town is a real bottleneck but has thus far avoided being cast purely as a tourist trap; allow the better part of an hour just to drive the last 14 miles from Prescott to Jerome and the next 4 miles out of Jerome toward Cottonwood. The map shows the one-way system through town. Vehicles pulling trailers over 20 feet are not recommended.

COTTONWOOD
Nine miles east of Jerome, Cottonwood is a good base for exploring various interesting sites in the area and offers modern motels.

Named after the trees growing alongside the Verde River, which flows north of town, Cottonwood was first settled in the 1870s. Despite its age, it is essentially a modern town; with almost 7000 inhabitants, it is the main trade center for the area. The elevation is a warm 3300 feet.

Orientation & Information
Hwy 89A is the main thoroughfare, though N Main St, about a mile north of Hwy 89A, is the heart of 'Old Town.' On the northwest border of Cottonwood is the smaller town of Clarkdale, and a couple of miles east is the neighboring village of Cornville.

The chamber of commerce (☎ 520-634-7593), 1010 S Main, is open from 9 am to 5 pm. The library (☎ 520-634-7559) is at 100 S 6th. The post office (☎ 520-634-9526) is at 700 E Mingus Ave. The hospital (☎ 520-634-2251) is at 202 S Willard. The police (☎ 520-634-4246) are at 816 N Main. Recycle at the bins in Verde Valley Plaza.

Clemenceau Heritage Museum
The Clemenceau (☎ 520-634-2868), 1 N Willard, in a wing of a 1924 school building, illustrates local history and has a model railroad exhibit. It's open from 9 am to noon on Wednesday and from 11 am to 3 pm Friday to Sunday; admission is by donation.

Tuzigoot National Monument
This monument (☎ 520-634-5564) contains a Sinaguan pueblo dating from 1125 to 1425 AD. The pueblo's two stories and more than 100 rooms once housed about 200 people; now the remnants can be visited on a short, steep trail (no wheelchairs) and are memorable for their location on a small ridge affording fine views of the Verde River Valley. Don't miss the visitor center's exhibit of Sinaguan artifacts. Hours are 8 am to 7 pm from Memorial Day to Labor Day and 8 am to 5 pm the rest of the year. Admission is $2 for adults; Golden Access, Age and Eagle Passes are honored. The site is 2 miles north of Cottonwood – follow signs from Hwy 89A.

Dead Horse Ranch State Park
This small area at the northern edge of town offers picnicking, fishing, nature trails, a playground and camping. The day-use fee is $4.

Verde Canyon Railroad
Restored locomotives provide four-hour guided roundtrips into the countryside north of Cottonwood Pass, traveling through roadless areas containing ancestral Indian sites and wildlife. Departing from 300 N Broadway in Clarkdale (the northern continuation of Cottonwood's N Main), the railroad (☎ 520-639-0010, 800-293-7245) has year-round departures Wednesday to Sunday. Times vary but are always in the morning with an occasional afternoon run on busy Saturdays. Moonlight rides are available near the full moon in summer. First-class tickets cost $55 and coach-class tickets are $36. Seniors over 65 pay $33 and kids under 12 pay $21. Reservations are required. Carriages are climate controlled and all passengers have access to open-air viewing cars. Food is available on the train and there is a café for a meal before you depart.

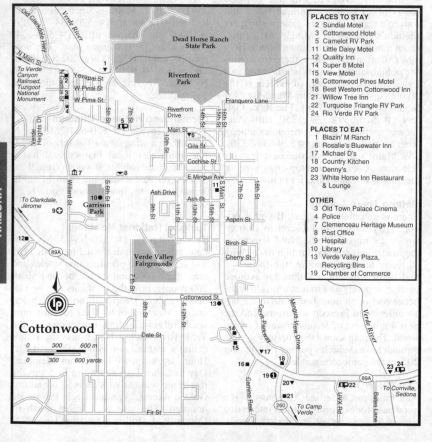

PLACES TO STAY
2   Sundial Motel
3   Cottonwood Hotel
5   Camelot RV Park
11 Little Daisy Motel
12 Quality Inn
14 Super 8 Motel
15 View Motel
16 Cottonwood Pines Motel
18 Best Western Cottonwood Inn
21 Willow Tree Inn
22 Turquoise Triangle RV Park
24 Rio Verde RV Park

PLACES TO EAT
1   Blazin' M Ranch
6   Rosalie's Bluewater Inn
17 Michael D's
18 Country Kitchen
20 Denny's
23 White Horse Inn Restaurant & Lounge

OTHER
3   Old Town Palace Cinema
4   Police
7   Clemenceau Heritage Museum
8   Post Office
9   Hospital
10 Library
13 Verde Valley Plaza, Recycling Bins
19 Chamber of Commerce

Cottonwood

ARIZONA

Places to Stay

Rates drop slightly outside of the summer high season, and motels are full for the Verde Valley Fair and Rodeo during the third or fourth weekend in April.

Places to Stay – Camping

The *Dead Horse Ranch State Park* (☎ 520-634-5283) at the north end of town has showers and 45 basic sites for $10, as well as some with hookups for $15. *Rio Verde RV Park* (☎ 520-634-5990), 3420 Hwy 89A, has showers, a coin laundry and more than 60 sites ($10 for tents or $20 with hookups). The *Turquoise Triangle RV Park* (☎ 520-634-5294), 2501 E Hwy 89A, has 60 RV sites with hookups for $22. *Camelot RV Park* (☎ 520-634-3011), 651 N Main, offers 50 RV-only sites for $17 with hookups. All of these campgrounds are open year-round.

Places to Stay – Budget

The least expensive in the area, with rooms starting in the mid-$30s, is the simple *Sundial Motel* (☎ 520-634-8031), 1034 N Main, but the 24 rooms are often filled with guests staying the week. Nearby, the recently renovated old *Cottonwood Hotel* (☎ 520-634-9455), 930 N Main, has rooms from $33 and with kitchenettes from $45.

In the newer part of town, there is the *Little Daisy Motel* (☎ 520-634-7865, fax 520-639-3447), 34 S Main, with 21 rooms, and the *View Motel* (☎ 520-634-7581), 818 S Main, which has 34 rooms, a pool, spa and hilltop location. Both are clean and offer some pricier rooms with kitchenettes; rates are from the upper $30s and lower $40s. Also in this price range is the 14-room *Cottonwood Pines Motel* (☎ 520-634-9975), 920 S Camino Real.

Places to Stay – Middle

The good *Super 8 Motel* (☎ 520-639-1888, fax 520-639-2285), 800 S Main, has a pool, spa and 52 pleasant rooms in the $50s for a double, including continental breakfast. The *Willow Tree Inn* (☎ 520-634-3678, fax 520-639-0407), 1089 S Hwy 260, has 30 standard rooms around $48 to $60, two with kitchens in the $70s. The *Quality Inn* (☎ 520-634-4207, fax 520-634-5764), 301 W Hwy 89A, has a pool, spa and restaurant open for lunch and dinner. Prices for 51 good-sized rooms, all with coffee-makers and some with refrigerators or microwaves, are in the $60s and $70s in summer, dropping to the $50s in winter.

The nicest motel is the *Best Western Cottonwood Inn* (☎ 520-634-5575, 800-350-0025, fax 520-634-5576, cottonwoodinn@verdenet.com), 993 S Main, providing a pool, spa and coin laundry as well as a restaurant and bar (with room service) that is open from 6 am to 10 pm in summer, 7 am to 9 pm the rest of the year. More than 70 standard rooms and 13 larger casitas, some with spa, are in the $70 to $120 range in summer.

The *Flying Eagle Country B&B* (☎ 520-634-0211), 2700 Windmill Lane, Clarkdale, AZ 86324, offers one room for $79 double and a guesthouse with kitchenette for $89 double. It has a spa.

Places to Eat

Michael D's (☎ 520-634-0043), 891 S Main, specializes in breakfasts and is open from 5:30 am to 2 pm Monday to Friday and from 7 am to 2 pm on Sunday. *Rosalie's Bluewater Inn* (☎ 520-634-8702), 517 N 12th, features good and inexpensive home-style cooking and is open from 7 am to 8 pm Tuesday to Sunday. The *Country Kitchen* (☎ 520-634-3696) by the Cottonwood Inn has reasonably priced family dining between 6 am and 10 pm daily.

The *White Horse Inn Restaurant & Lounge* (☎ 520-634-2271), on Hwy 89A by the Verde River, serves decent steak and seafood for lunch and dinner; hours are from 11 am to 2 pm and 5 pm to midnight daily except Sunday, when hours are noon to 9 pm. It features a sports bar and a deck overlooking the Verde River.

Blazin' M Ranch (☎ 520-634-0334, 800-937-8643, oldwest@blazinm.com), next to the entrance of Dead Horse Ranch State Park, has filling chuckwagon suppers with rootin' tootin' cowboy entertainment for

$16 ($8 for kids eight and under). The doors open at 5:30 with seating at 7 pm for dinner. Reservations are suggested. Come early if you want to visit the petting zoo. *Denny's* (☎ 520-639-3805), 2211 E Hwy 89A, is open 24 hours.

Out in Cornville, the *Manzanita Inn* (☎ 520-634-8851), 11425 E Cornville Rd, serves very good continental dinners in the $10 to $20 range (half that for lunches). Hours are 11 am to 2 pm and 4:30 to 8 pm Wednesday to Saturday, till 7 pm on Sunday.

Entertainment
The *Old Town Palace* (☎ 520-634-7167), 914 N Main, screens movies. The Verde Valley Concert Association (☎ 520-634-0636) arranges popular performances that often sell out throughout the year; call for details. Also see the Blazin' M Ranch in Places to Eat, above.

Getting There & Away
The Sedona-Phoenix Shuttle (☎ 520-282-2066) sends six buses a day between Phoenix Airport and Sedona, stopping at the Best Western Cottonwood Inn on runs in both directions.

CAMP VERDE & AROUND
On I-17 and 85 miles north of Phoenix, Camp Verde (elevation 3133 feet) is on the way to Jerome, Sedona and Flagstaff for travelers taking the quicker freeway rather than the long trip through Wickenburg and Prescott. Several places along the interstate north and south of Camp Verde are worth a look.

The Verde River was settled by Europeans in the 1860s and a fort was established at Camp Verde in 1865 to protect the pioneers from the local Yavapai and Tonto Apache Indians. In 1873 the Indians surrendered to General George Crook and were placed on a reservation near the fort, only to be moved to the San Carlos Apache Reservation in 1875. In the early 1900s the Yavapai started drifting back, and they now have a few very small reservations in the Camp Verde and Prescott areas.

Meanwhile, Camp Verde prospered and is now a town of about 6000 that provides services to the ranching and agricultural communities of the Verde River basin.

Orientation & Information
The center of town is about 2 miles east of I-17 exit 287. All places mentioned in this section are best reached from this exit unless I indicate otherwise.

The chamber of commerce (☎ 520-567-9294) is at 435 Main. The Prescott National Forest Verde Ranger Station (☎ 520-567-4121), PO Box 670, Prescott, AZ 86322-0670, is on Hwy 260 southeast of town, just past the Verde River. The post office (☎ 520-567-3175) is on Hwy 260 just west of town. The closest hospital is in Cottonwood. The police are reached at ☎ 520-567-6621.

Fort Verde State Historic Park
Only four buildings remain of the original 18 composing Fort Verde when it was decommissioned in 1891. These have been restored, and together with the original parade grounds and some foundations, serve to give the visitor an idea of what life was like here over a century ago. Visit the museum (☎ 520-567-3275) and pick up self-guided tour brochures describing the area. Volunteers in period costumes give interpretive demonstrations on weekends from fall through spring – call for hours. Fort Verde Day, on the second Saturday of October, has a full schedule of historical reenactments and other events.

Fort Verde is open from 8 am to 4:30 pm daily except Christmas. Admission is $2 for adults; $1 for seven- to 14-year-olds.

Montezuma Castle National Monument
Like nearby Tuzigoot, Montezuma Castle is an Ancestral Puebloan site built and occupied between the 12th and 14th centuries. The name refers to the splendid castle-like location high on a cliff; early explorers thought the five-story-high pueblo was Aztec and hence dubbed it Montezuma. A museum (☎ 520-567-3322) has

exhibits explaining the archaeology of this well-preserved site, which can be seen from a self-guiding, wheelchair-accessible trail. Entrance into the 'castle' itself is prohibited. Access the monument from I-17 exit 289, then follow signs for 2 miles.

Montezuma's Well is a separate site 10 miles northeast of the castle but is also administered as part of the monument. The well is a natural limestone sinkhole, 470 feet across and surrounded by the remnants of Sinaguan and Hohokam dwellings. Water from the sinkhole was used for irrigation by the Indians as it is today. Access is by a paved road from exit 293 or an unpaved road from exit 298; both have signs.

Both areas have picnic sites and are open from 8 am to 5 pm, to 7 pm from Memorial Day to Labor Day. Admission to the castle is $2 for adults, and the well is free; Golden Age, Access and Eagle Passes are honored. Despite its small size, Montezuma Castle receives nearly a million visitors annually due to its convenient location close to the freeway.

Coconino National Forest
East of Camp Verde, the Coconino National Forest provides wild and rugged country for backpacking, fishing, hunting and camping adventures. Several wilderness areas are completely undeveloped and provide real backcountry challenges, including canyoneering (see the Outdoor Activities chapter).

Further information is available from the Beaver Creek Ranger Station (☎ 520-567-4501), HC 64, Box 240, Rimrock, AZ 86335, or the Forest Supervisor in Flagstaff. The ranger station is near Beaver Creek Campground (see Places to Stay, below).

Arcosanti
Twenty-five miles south of Camp Verde and 2 miles east of I-17 exit 262, an unpaved road leads to this architectural experiment in urban living. Designed by architect Paolo Soleri, Arcosanti will be home to 5000 people who want to live in a futuristic, aesthetic, relaxing and environmentally sound development.

The space-age project is still under construction, but it's worth a look if you're in the area. Tours leave hourly from 9 am to 4 pm and cost $5. There is a café (noon till 3 pm), bakery (9 am to 4 pm) and gift shop selling the famous ceramic and cast bronze Soleri windbells. Simple accommodations range from $20/25 single/double for a basic room with shared bath, to $75 for a suite. Week-long and month-long seminars on various aspects of the project and various other events are also offered. For information contact Arcosanti (☎ 520-632-7135), HC 74, PO Box 4136, Mayer, AZ 86333.

River Running
The Verde River can be canoed, kayaked or rafted. The section from Clarkdale to Camp Verde is fairly flat, but the river becomes much wilder south of Camp Verde and to run this section you should be experienced. High water from January to April is the best time to try the descent from Camp Verde to the Horseshoe Reservoir, 60 miles south. The Verde Ranger Station has maps and information. Verde River Boat Rides (☎ 520-567-4087), 537 S Yaqui Circle, rents canoes ($35 per day) and other boats. River Otter Canoe Co (☎ 520-567-4116), 458 S 1st, also rents canoes and provides shuttles to anywhere in the Verde Valley for $30 and up.

Other Activities
Horseback Adventures (☎ 520-567-5502), in the Cowboys & Outlaws complex at I-17 exit 289, offers **horseback riding** year-round. East of the same exit, there is 24-hour **gambling** in the Cliff Castle Casino (☎ 520-567-6956), run by the Yavapai-Apache nation in the Best Western Lodge. There are about 500 machines and a card room.

Places to Stay
Camping The Coconino National Forest maintains both the *Clear Creek* campground, 6 miles southeast of Camp Verde on USFS Rd 9, open from April through October, and the *Beaver Creek* campground, 3 miles southeast of I-17 exit 298

along USFS Rd 618, open from April through September. Both campgrounds are small, have water but no showers and charge $5 per night.

Krazy K RV Park (☎ 520-567-0565), near exit 289, has RV sites for $15 and *Zane Grey RV Park* (☎ 520-567-4320, 800-235-0608), 4500 E Hwy 260, 6 miles southeast of town, is $20.

Motels Rates drop in winter. Basic rooms at the *Fort Verde Motel* (☎ 520-567-3486), 628 S Main, are all in the $30s and $40s and have two double beds. Near exit 287, the *Super 8 Motel* (☎/fax 520-567-2622), 1550 Hwy 260, has an indoor pool and spa and 46 decent rooms in the $50s. Close by, the new *Microtel Inn & Suites* (☎ 520-567-3000, microtel@verdevalley.com), 504 Industrial Drive, has about 60 bright rooms with coffeemakers, including 25 larger units with microwaves and refrigerators, for $40 to $65. Both places include a light continental breakfast. The *Best Western Cliff Castle Lodge* (☎ 520-567-6611, fax 520-567-9455), half a mile east of I-17 exit 289, has a pool and spa as well as a 24-hour restaurant in the adjacent casino. There are over 80 rooms and mini-suites priced from $50 to $100 (usually in the $70s for a double).

Places to Eat

You won't find anything approaching haute cuisine in Camp Verde, but you won't find haute prices either. A down-home, locally popular little place is the *Verde Cafe* (☎ 520-567-6521) at 368 Main, serving daily breakfast, lunch and dinner Monday to Thursday from 6 am to 3 pm, and Friday to Sunday from 6 am to 8 pm. Slightly more upscale family restaurants include *Bo's Valley View Restaurant* (☎ 520-567-3592), 102 Arnold at Main, open from 6 am to 9 pm daily, and the *Branding Iron Restaurant* (☎ 520-567-3136), open 5 am to 3 pm, in the Fort Verde Shopping Plaza. All three serve inexpensive American food. For Chinese, *Ming House* (☎ 520-567-9488), 288 S Main, is open daily from 11 am to 9 pm and has a $3.95 lunch buffet.

Getting There & Away

Greyhound (☎ 520-567-6663) stops several times a day heading to Phoenix or Flagstaff. There are connections to and from Prescott.

The Sedona-Phoenix Shuttle (☎ 520-282-2066) has a stop at the Camp Verde Chevron Gas Station (☎ 520-567-4300) near exit 287, with several buses each way between Sedona and Phoenix Airport.

SEDONA

Sedona, seated among splendid crimson sandstone formations at the south end of lovely Oak Creek Canyon, is one of the prettiest locations in Arizona. The year-round waters of Oak Creek attracted ancient Indian farmers as well as late-19th-century European settlers. Among the early settlers were the Schneblys, who established a rough road to Flagstaff through Oak Creek Canyon in 1901. When a post office was established in 1902, the village was named after Sedona Schnebly, one of the few women so honored by a Western town.

For decades, Sedona was a quiet farming community sending produce up from its balmy elevation of 4400 feet to Flagstaff, 2500 feet higher and 28 miles away over a twisting scenic road. In the 1940s and '50s, Hollywood began using Sedona as a major motion-picture location, but it wasn't until the 1960s and '70s that the beauty of Sedona's surroundings started attracting retirees, artists and tourists in large numbers and the town experienced much growth. Around 1980, New Agers (seekers of metaphysical and psychic enlightenment) began finding vortexes, or points where the earth's energy is focused, and these have attracted thousands more visitors. (See the sidebar In Search of the New Age.)

Sedona has about 16,000 residents (three times the 1980 population) but was not incorporated as a town until 1988, and rapid, poorly controlled growth took the area somewhat by surprise. The malls and strips look out of place among the red-rock scenery, although now the town is making some effort to blend in with its surroundings. (The McDonald's of Sedona does not boast the famous golden arches; instead, pastel green arcs are painted on a pink stuccoed wall.) Despite the random development, there are relatively few fast-food joints and the tourist development has tended toward the high-end curiously blended with the psychic. The town is home to several fine resorts, some of Arizona's best restaurants, fine art galleries and boutiques, and numerous New Age businesses, but very cheap motels do not exist here.

Sedona receives five to six million visitors a year. Despite the bustle, it is possible to get away from the crowds and enjoy the beautiful scenery on a 4WD tour, bike ride or hike. There's not much to do in town apart from eat, sleep, shop or try to experience a personal transformation. It's the environs that make Sedona an attractive, if pricey, destination.

Orientation

Hwy 89A is the main drag through town and runs roughly west-east, turning north at the east end where it heads to Flagstaff. Hwy 89A intersects with Hwy 179 from the south in the middle of town; this point is known as 'the Y.' Hwy 89A northeast of the Y is 'uptown,' where many of the tourist-oriented places are, and it continues north into Oak Creek Canyon. West Sedona, which is experiencing the most growth, is along Hwy 89A west of the Y. South of the Y, Hwy 179 leads in 7 miles to the Village of Oak Creek, a Sedona 'suburb' with several places to stay, and continues 8 miles more to I-17.

Information

The chamber of commerce (☎ 520-282-7722, 800-288-7336), Forest Rd and Hwy 89A, is open from 9 am to 5 pm daily except Sunday, when it closes at 3 pm. The Coconino National Forest Ranger Station (☎ 520-282-4119) is at 250 Brewer Rd, Sedona, AZ 86339. The library (☎ 520-282-7714) is at 3250 White Bear Rd. The post office (☎ 520-282-3511) is on Hwy 89A at Hwy 179. The medical center (☎ 520-204-3000) is at 3700 W Hwy 89A. The police (☎ 520-282-3100) are at 431 Forest Rd.

Chapel of the Holy Cross

Spectacularly located between red-rock towers 3 miles south of town, this chapel (☎ 520-282-4069) is open daily for non-denominational meditation or prayer from 9 am to 5 pm. To get there, go south on Hwy 179 and turn left on Chapel Rd.

Art Galleries

Many of the galleries have museum-quality shows. The **Sedona Arts Center** (☎ 520-282-3809), at the corner of Hwy 89A and Art Barn Rd, is in a former fruit barn and an adjacent modern building, and has changing exhibits, a gift shop, classes in performing and visual arts, and a variety of cultural events during the September to May season. Hours are Monday to Saturday from 10 am to 4:30 pm and on Sunday from 11 am to 4:30 pm.

There are scores of more commercial art galleries in Sedona. A good place to start is **Tlaquepaque** (☎ 520-282-4838), an attractive area of Mexican-style courtyards and fountains, with dozens of fine-art galleries and restaurants. This is a place to stroll and browse and enjoy the architecture as much as it is a place to shop. Tlaquepaque is on the west side of Hwy 179, a short walk south of the Y.

Red Rock State Park

This park has an environmental education center, visitor center (☎ 520-282-6907), picnic areas and six hiking trails ranging from less than a half mile to 1.9 miles in length. The 286-acre park protects riparian habitat and provides good birding and pleasant walking amid gorgeous scenery; you can fish in Oak Creek, but swimming and wading are not allowed. Ranger-led activities include nature walks, bird walks and full-moon hikes during the warmer months. The park is open from 8 am to 5 pm, to 6 pm in summer, and the visitor center is open from 9 am to 5 pm. Admission is $5 per private vehicle or $1 for pedestrians/cyclists. The park is 5½ miles west of the Y along Hwy 89A, then 3 miles left on Lower Red Rock Loop Rd.

Oak Creek Canyon

Although Oak Creek flows through Sedona and continues southwest of town, it is the section northeast of Sedona along Hwy 89A to Flagstaff that attracts the most attention. This is where the canyon is at its narrowest, and the red, orange and white cliffs are the most dramatic. Forests of pine and juniper clothe the canyon, providing a scenic backdrop for trout fishing in the creek.

Fish year-round at Rainbow Trout Farm (☎ 520-282-3379), about 3 miles north of Sedona on N Hwy 89A. This stocked trout farm rents a simple fishing pole for $1 and

then charges by the fish, from $3 for small ones to a bit more for those over 14 inches. You don't need a license and the staff will clean the fish for you, making this a good place for beginners and kids. Experienced anglers with licenses can ask at the Coconino Ranger Station for other fishing holes.

The USFS maintains six campgrounds in the canyon (see Places to Stay – Camping, below) as well as picnic areas. It also maintains the **Oak Creek Scenic Viewpoint**, 16 miles north of Sedona at the top of a particularly steep and winding section of N Hwy 89A.

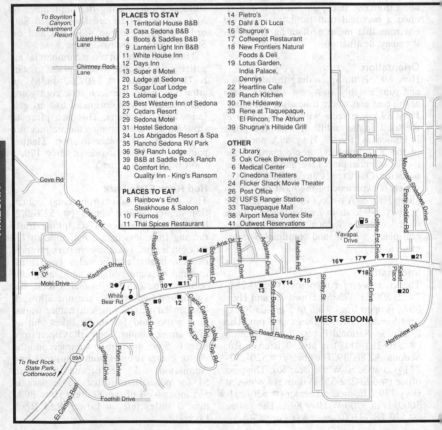

PLACES TO STAY
1 Territorial House B&B
3 Casa Sedona B&B
4 Boots & Saddles B&B
9 Lantern Light Inn B&B
11 White House Inn
12 Days Inn
13 Super 8 Motel
20 Lodge at Sedona
21 Sugar Loaf Lodge
23 Lolomai Lodge
25 Best Western Inn of Sedona
27 Cedars Resort
29 Sedona Motel
31 Hostel Sedona
34 Los Abrigados Resort & Spa
35 Rancho Sedona RV Park
36 Sky Ranch Lodge
39 B&B at Saddle Rock Ranch
40 Comfort Inn,
   Quality Inn - King's Ransom

PLACES TO EAT
8 Rainbow's End
   Steakhouse & Saloon
10 Fournos
11 Thai Spices Restaurant

14 Pietro's
15 Dahl & Di Luca
16 Shugrue's
17 Coffeepot Restaurant
18 New Frontiers Natural
   Foods & Deli
19 Lotus Garden,
   India Palace,
   Dennys
22 Heartline Cafe
28 Ranch Kitchen
30 The Hideaway
33 Rene at Tlaquepaque,
   El Rincon, The Atrium
39 Shugrue's Hillside Grill

OTHER
2 Library
5 Oak Creek Brewing Company
6 Medical Center
7 Cinedona Theaters
24 Flicker Shack Movie Theater
26 Post Office
32 USFS Ranger Station
33 Tlaquepaque Mall
38 Airport Mesa Vortex Site
41 Outwest Reservations

ARIZONA

Seven miles northeast of Sedona along N Hwy 89A, **Slide Rock State Park** (☎ 520-282-3034) is a very popular spot for swimming, picnicking and bird watching. Oak Creek sweeps swimmers (especially kids) through the natural rock chute from which the park derives its name. Hours here are 8 am to 6 pm (5 pm in winter) and admission is $5 per car or $1 for pedestrians/cyclists. Another popular swimming hole is **Grasshopper Point**, just over 2 miles north of town on the right side of N Hwy 89A.

Southwest of Sedona is **Red Rock Crossing**, best reached via Upper Red

Rock Loop Rd, off Hwy 89A. The area is managed by the USFS, which provides picnicking areas and parking on either side of this section of Oak Creek. The creek can be waded (usually with little difficulty), but there is no bridge. The highlights here, however, are the splendid views of Cathedral Rock above a pretty stretch of Oak Creek. Day use is $3 per vehicle; no camping.

Hiking & Mountain Biking

There are easy scenic trails in Red Rock State Park and more difficult ones in the

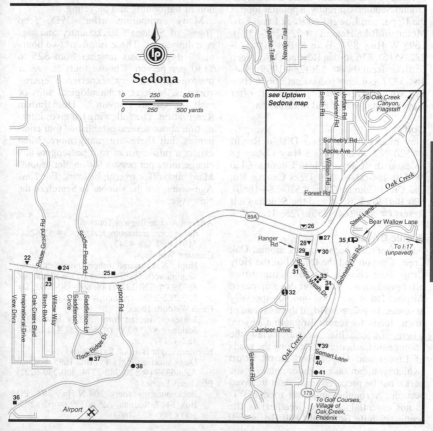

Coconino National Forest (surrounding Sedona on all sides). These provide a variety of hikes and rides for all abilities.

Hiking here is possible year-round, and although some higher trails may be closed in winter, they may be ideal in the heat of summer. Carry plenty of water on summer hikes to avoid dehydration; four quarts per person per day is suggested. The USFS ranger station sells good hiking maps and has up-to-date information. *Sedona Hikes* by R and S Mangum is a useful hiking guide available at local bookstores.

Ask about the ongoing development of Sedona Red Rock Pathways, which will eventually link up many of the biking trails around Sedona. Currently, a popular loop is the Upper and Lower Red Rock Loop Rds. Mountain Bike Heaven (☎ 520-282-1312), 1695 W Hwy 89A; Bike & Bean (☎ 520-282-3515), 376 Jordan Rd; and Desert Jeep & Bike Rentals (☎ 520-284-1099, 888-464-5337, gojeep@sedona.net), 6626 Hwy 179 (in the Desert Quail Inn), all offer bicycle rental, repair and information.

Golf
Play nine holes at Poco Diablo Resort (☎ 520-282-7333), 1752 S Hwy 179, or 18 holes at the Canyon Mesa Country Club (☎ 520-284-0036), 500 Jacks Canyon Rd; Oak Creek Country Club (☎ 520-284-1660), 690 Bell Rock Blvd; and the Sedona Golf Resort (☎ 520-284-9355), 7256 Hwy 179.

Scenic Drives
Aside from the scenic drives around Oak Creek Canyon and the Chapel of the Holy Cross (see above), the following drives offer good views. The short drive up paved **Airport Rd** is one good option, especially at sunset. **Dry Creek Rd**, at the west end of town, leads to scenic Boynton Canyon, where you can hike as well. View the photogenic Cathedral Rock along the roads of Lower and Upper **Red Rock Loop** (which you can take without entering the park), but be prepared for a short unpaved section. A rougher unpaved road (4WD is not essential in good weather) is the scenic 12-mile **Schnebly Hill Rd**, which

turns off Hwy 179 near Oak Creek and ends up at I-17 exit 320. This road is closed in winter.

Organized Tours & Activities
Sedona Trolley City Tours (☎ 520-282-5400, 520-282-6826) depart on the hour from their bus stop near the chamber of commerce. Narrated tours that last 55 minutes and cover Tlaquepaque and the Chapel of the Holy Cross leave at 10 am, noon, 2 and 4 pm; tours to West Sedona and Boynton Canyon leave at 11 am and 1, 3 and 5 pm. Tours are $7 each, or pay $11 for both; kids 12 and under pay $2. Other tour possibilities include horseback riding, hot-air ballooning and bicycling.

Many companies offer 4WD 'Jeep Tours' of Sedona's backcountry and surrounding areas. These run from two hours to all day at costs ranging from $25 to $130 per person. Choose tours to see or photograph scenery, experience energy vortexes, look at archaeological sites or visit the Grand Canyon or Hopi Indian Reservation. The following list gives information about several established tour companies, but there are many more. Most expect a minimum of four passengers and charge more per person for smaller groups. Many also offer overnight tours. For New Age tours, see the sidebar In Search of the New Age.

Arizona Archaeological Tours
    Some local archaeological sites. (☎ 520-284-5191, 800-488-4243)
Crossing Worlds
    Hopi, Navajo and other Indian cultures, Sedona vortexes. PO Box 623, Sedona, AZ 86339 (☎ 520-282-7148, 800-350-2693, fax 520-282-2401, crossing@sedona.net)
Earth Wisdom Tours
    Vortexes, Indian lore. 293 N Hwy 89A, Sedona, AZ 86336 (☎ 520-282-4714, 800-482-4714)
Northern Light Balloon Expeditions
    Daily sunrise flights. PO Box 1695, Sedona, AZ 86339 (☎ 520-282-2274, 800-230-6222)
Pink Jeep Tours
    Backcountry scenery. 204 N Hwy 89A, PO Box 1447, Sedona, AZ 86339 (☎ 520-282-5000, 800-873-3662)

Pink Jeep Tours Ancient Expeditions
Indian sites. 276 N Hwy 89A, PO Box 1447, Sedona, AZ 86339 (☎ 520-282-2137, 800-999-2137)

Red Rock Balloon Adventures
Daily morning flights. PO Box 2759, Sedona, AZ 86336 (☎ 520-284-0040, 800-258-3754)

Sedona Adventures
Jeep tours, vortexes, petroglyphs and scenery. 273 N Hwy 89A, PO Box 1476, Sedona, AZ 86339 (☎ 520-282-3500, 800-888-9494)

Sedona Art Tours
Local galleries and studios. 30 Kashmir Rd, Sedona, AZ 86339 (☎ 520-282-0788)

Sedona Red Rock Jeep Tours
Backcountry scenery, vortexes. 270 N Hwy 89A, PO Box 10305, Sedona, AZ 86339 (☎ 520-282-6826, 800-848-7728, fax 520-282-3281)

Trail Horse Adventures
One-hour to six-day horseback rides; must be at least six years old. Lower Red Rock Loop Rd (☎ 520-282-7252, 800-723-3538)

Special Events

The chamber of commerce has information about the many events throughout the year; most are oriented toward the arts. The annual all-day Jazz on the Rocks (☎ 520-282-1985), PO Box 889, Sedona, AZ 86339, celebrating its 18th year in 1999, features big-name musicians on the last Saturday in September. The concert usually sells out, so buy tickets ahead of time. Other noteworthy events are the Hopi Tribal Arts and Crafts Festival on the second weekend in May, Western Americana arts and crafts and car shows on the fourth weekend in May, the Sedona Arts Festival during the third weekend in October, and the lighting of the luminarias at Tlaquepaque during the second weekend in December. Both Tlaquepaque and the neighboring Los Abrigados Resort are fantastically lit up over the Christmas period.

Places to Stay

Sedona is a popular weekend getaway and many places raise their rates on Friday and Saturday; reservations are a good idea (especially during the Jazz Festival the last weekend in September). Because of the romantic views, some places don't have TVs in the rooms, so you'll have to enjoy the scenery, not the soap operas.

Sedona has a growing number of B&Bs, several of which are popular for their comfortable and attractive rooms and first-class service; however, prices are on the high side. Most places don't permit smoking and will give small discounts if you stay several nights.

There is a short low season from December (excluding the last week) through February when prices drop by 20% or more. Things sometimes get a little slow in midsummer, when it gets rather hot. Peak-season rates are given below.

Sedona is known for its deluxe accommodations and, apart from one hostel, offers no real budget places compared to most other towns in Arizona. This section is arranged by area and lodging type, rather than by price.

Reservation Centers Several agencies will make lodging reservations and arrange any kind of tour package you want around Sedona and much of central Arizona. They include *Go-Sedona* (☎ 520-282-2986, 800-467-3366); *Outwest Reservations* (☎ 520-282-5112, 800-688-9378, fax 520-282-0522, outwest@sedona.net), 841 Hwy 179, Sedona, AZ 86336; *Red Rock Reservations* (☎ 520-284-3627, 800-890-0521), 58 Bell Rock Plaza, Sedona, AZ 86351; and *Sedona Central Reservations* (☎ 520-282-1518, 800-445-4128).

Places to Stay – Camping

The USFS (☎ 520-282-4119) runs the following campgrounds in Oak Creek Canyon along N Hwy 89A. *Manzanita*, 6 miles from town, offers 19 sites; *Banjo Bill*, 8 miles from town, has eight sites; *Bootlegger*, 8½ miles from town, provides 10 sites; *Cave Springs*, 11½ miles down the road, has 78 sites; and *Pine Flat*, 12½ miles from town, offers 58 sites. Sites cost $10 and none of the campgrounds have hookups or showers. RVs and trailers are allowed only at Cave Springs and Pine

Flat. The official season is May through September, but some campgrounds may open for a couple of months longer. Most sites are on a first-come, first-served basis, and campgrounds are often full on Friday morning for the weekend. Reservations (☎ 800-280-2267) can be made at a few sites in Cave Springs only.

In Search of the New Age

Sedona is the foremost New Age center in the Southwest and one of the most important anywhere. The term 'New Age' loosely refers to a trend toward seeking alternative explanations or interpretations of what constitutes health, religion, the psyche and enlightenment. Drawing upon new and old factual and mystical traditions from around the world, 'New Agers' often seek to transform themselves psychologically and spiritually in the hope that such personal efforts will eventually transform the world at large.

You can't miss the New Age stores in town – many of them have the word 'crystal' in their names. They sell books, crystals and various New Age paraphernalia, distribute free maps showing vortex sites, provide information, and may arrange various spiritual or healing events. The Center for the New Age (☎ 520-282-2085), 341 Hwy 179, is open daily and is a good place to start. A recent glance through Sedona offerings include mainstream services such as massages, nutrition counseling and yoga classes, all the way through increasingly esoteric practices such as meditation, acupressure, herbology, tai chi, psychic channeling, aura photography, astrology, palmistry, tarot card and runes reading, aromatherapy, past-life regressions, crystal healing, shamanism, drumming workshops, reflexology, hypnotherapy and more . . .

The four best-known vortexes in the Sedona area are found on some of the local red-rock mountains. These include Bell Rock near the Village of Oak Creek east of Hwy 179, Cathedral Rock near Red Rock Crossing, Airport Mesa along the Airport Rd, and Boynton Canyon. Local maps show these four main sites, though some individuals claim that others exist.

Several people lead guided tours of vortexes and other important New Age sites. These tours differ from many of the standard vortex tours in that the guides believe in what they tell you, as opposed to simply showing you the place. Try the following (there are others):

Sedona Nature Excursions/Mystic Tours by Rahelio
1405 W Hwy 89A, PO Box 1171, Sedona, AZ 86339
(☎ 520-282-6735)

Spirit Steps Tours
PO Box 3151, West Sedona, AZ 86340
(☎ 520-282-4562, 800-728-4562, fax 520-204-1252)

Vortex Tours/Medicine Wheel Journeys
PO Box 535, Sedona, AZ 86339
(☎ 520-282-2733, 800-943-3266)

'New Agers' (for want of a better description) are generally gentle folk, but some have been criticized for performing rituals, such as chantings or offerings, in scenic areas. Chanting in a public scenic area can be as irritating as a loud radio, revving motorcycle or droning aircraft, and leaving offerings of crystals or food is tantamount to littering. If you want to participate in such public rituals, please keep your vocal interactions with the planet to a peacefully personal level, pick up your offerings when you're through, and leave nothing but your love, energy and blessings. ■

If you're camping with a large group, try one of the three USFS group sites at *Chavez Crossing*, just over 2 miles south of town on Hwy 179. These sites, open year-round and lacking showers and hookups, must be reserved and require a 10-person minimum and a $30 minimum fee.

RV resorts in/near Sedona are often full, so call ahead. *Sedona RV Resort* (☎ 520-282-6640, 800-547-8727), 6701 W Hwy 89A, 6½ miles west of the Y, has 196 RV sites with partial or full hookups and a few tent sites priced from $18 to $26, as well as four camping cabins for $38.50 a night. Facilities include a restaurant, pool, spa, playground, mini-golf and other games, coin laundry and showers. *Rancho Sedona RV Park* (☎ 520-282-7255), 135 Bear Wallow Lane, has a laundry, showers and 30 RV sites, most with full hookups, for $20 to $30. The similarly priced *Hawkeye Red Rock RV Park* (☎ 520-282-2222), 40 Art Barn Rd, offers coin showers that are available to the public. All three RV parks are open year-round, though reservations are suggested from spring through fall.

Places to Stay – Sedona
Hostel The *Hostel Sedona* (☎ 520-282-2772), 5 Soldiers Wash Drive, offers basic accommodations in two small, single-gender dormitories, each with eight bunks and a bathroom. Rates are $15 to $18 per person. There's also a room for a couple ($40) and an RV, which provides couple or family accommodation. Free tea and coffee is provided and there are simple kitchen facilities. Although basic, Hostel Sedona offers the only budget lodging in town and is often full, so call ahead for space.

Hotels The following are $50 to $80 for a double, which is considered budget during Sedona's lengthy high season. Most have rooms sleeping up to four or five. They are arranged in approximately increasing price.

The *Sugar Loaf Lodge* (☎ 520-282-9451), 1870 W Hwy 89A, offers 16 standard rooms with refrigerators and has a spa. The *White House Inn* (☎ 520-282-

6680), 2986 W Hwy 89A, has 22 motel rooms, some with kitchenettes. The *Lolomai Lodge* (☎ 520-282-2835, fax 520-282-0535), 50 Willow Way, has a spa and 12 quiet rooms with kitchenettes. *La Vista* (☎ 520-282-7301), 500 N Hwy 89A, and *Star Motel* (☎ 520-282-3641), 295 Jordan Rd, have 24 jointly managed units (☎ 800-896-7301) with standard rooms and much more expensive units with kitchenettes and suites. *Cedars Resort* (☎ 520-282-7010), Hwy 89A at Hwy 179, has 39 nonsmoking motel rooms, some with balconies, and a pool and spa. The *Super 8 Motel* (☎ 520-282-1533, 800-858-7245, fax 520-282-2033, super8@sedona.net), 2545 W Hwy 89A, has a pool, restaurant and 66 rooms for $70 to $80. It offers a choice of a king-size bed or two double beds, as well as packages with the Verde Valley Railroad (see Cottonwood, earlier in this chapter).

The following hotels are a bit pricier. Gaze at beautiful views from the *Sedona Motel* (☎ 520-282-7187), on Hwy 179 near 89A, which has 16 pleasant rooms with refrigerators and is often full. Summer rates are $70 to $90. The *Days Inn* (☎ 520-282-9166, fax 520-282-6208), 2991 W Hwy 89A, with a pool and spa, has 66 rooms, all with refrigerators and many with balconies or patios. Ten rooms have microwaves as well. Rates are $75 to $100, including continental breakfast. The *Sky Ranch Lodge* (☎ 520-282-6400, fax 520-282-7682) on Airport Rd is a good value by Sedona standards; its 94 rooms, pool and spa are in a nicely landscaped setting above town. Standard rooms are in the $75 to $100 range, and larger units with kitchenettes, fireplaces and good views go for up to $150.

The 23 rooms at the *Matterhorn Motor Lodge* (☎ 520-282-7176, fax 520-282-0727, mhl@sedona.net), 230 Apple Ave, all have balconies or patios overlooking uptown Sedona and Oak Creek. Amenities include in-room coffeemakers and refrigerators, and there is a pool and a spa. Rates are $75 to $95. The *Canyon Portal Motel* (☎ 520-282-7125, 800-542-8484), 280 N Hwy 89A, has a pool and more than

30 motel rooms, some with fireplaces, others with balconies or patios and many with views, priced in the $70 to $110 range. On a quiet street with a garden, the *Rose Tree Inn* (☎ 520-282-2065, 888-282-2065, fax 520-282-0083), 376 Cedar, has just five pleasant rooms, four with kitchenettes, as well as a spa; high-season rates are $85 to $125.

A few of the better motel chains are scattered on Hwys 89A and 179. The *Quality Inn – King's Ransom* (☎ 520-282-7151, fax 520-282-5208), 771 Hwy 179, has a pool, spa, restaurant and lounge, and offers 101 rooms, some with balconies or patios, priced in the $85 to $125 range. Next door, the *Comfort Inn* (☎ 520-282-3132), 725 Hwy 179, has a pool and spa and 53 rooms in the $85 to $105 range; prices include a continental breakfast.

Most of the 61 rooms at the *Best Western Arroyo Roble Hotel* (☎/fax 520-282-4001, 800-773-3662), 400 N Hwy 89A, have balconies or patios with good views for $100 to $140, and king-size or two queen-size beds. All have in-room coffeemakers. Enjoy the two pools, three spas, sauna, tennis court, game room and exercise room. Several villas with two bedrooms, two bathrooms, a fireplace and kitchen are in the $200 to $300 price range. The *Best Western Inn of Sedona* (☎ 520-282-3072, 800-292-6344, fax 520-282-7218), 1200 W Hwy 89A, has 110 modern rooms opening out onto view decks. Rooms have coffeemakers and refrigerators; some have fireplaces. There is a pool, spa and exercise room. Rates are $90 to $160, including continental breakfast.

L'Auberge de Sedona (☎ 520-282-1661, 800-272-6777, fax 520-282-2885), 301 L'Auberge Lane, Sedona, AZ 86339, is a 'Country French Inn' next to Oak Creek in uptown Sedona. Although there is a pool and spa, the emphasis is on relaxation and eating fancy French food (and I mean fancy French – this is one of the few places in Arizona where a jacket is required for men). The highlight is the 34 romantic one- and two-bedroom cottages scattered in the gardens and along the creek. With fire-

places and no TVs, the cabins run about $300 to more than $400 in the high season, while spacious rooms in the attractive lodge overlooking the cottages are $200 to $270. *The Orchards of L'Auberge*, under the same management but up the hill on Hwy 89A, overlooks the L'Auberge complex and affords the best views. The two are linked by a short aerial tram. Rooms here are more American style and run $170 to $200; most have private balconies and some have fireplaces.

B&Bs *A Touch of Sedona B&B* (☎ 520-282-6462, 800-600-6462), 595 Jordan Rd, Sedona, AZ 86336, in a residential area just north of uptown, offers five modern, individually decorated rooms with private baths (one with a kitchen) for $120 to $160.

In West Sedona, *Casa Sedona* (☎ 520-282-2938, 800-525-3756, fax 520-282-2259, casa@sedona.net), 55 Hozoni Drive, Sedona, AZ 86336, is a large Southwestern-style inn with 16 attractive, unique rooms featuring private whirlpool tubs, fireplaces, refrigerators and access to terraces with great red-rock views. There's a TV room, and guests can use VCRs in their bedrooms. Full breakfast and refreshments during the day are included in the rates, which go from $120 to $210.

The *Lodge at Sedona* (☎ 520-204-1942, 800-619-4467, fax 520-204-2128, lodge@sedona.net), 125 Kallof Place, Sedona, AZ 86336, has 13 rooms (three are suites) in a sprawling house set in 2.5 acres with lawn games and picnic areas. Rooms vary in size but all have private bathrooms and some have fireplaces, whirlpool baths, balconies or patios. There is a TV room. Rates range from $120 to $230 a double. The owners have a reputation for helpfulness and gourmet breakfasts.

Relax on the patio, splash in the pool, or soak in the hot tub at the hilltop *B&B at Saddle Rock Ranch* (☎ 520-282-7640, 520-282-6829), 255 Rock Ridge Drive, PO Box 10095, Sedona, AZ 86336. The 1926 ranch has been the setting for several Western movies and has a fantastic view. Three spacious and romantic guest rooms, each with

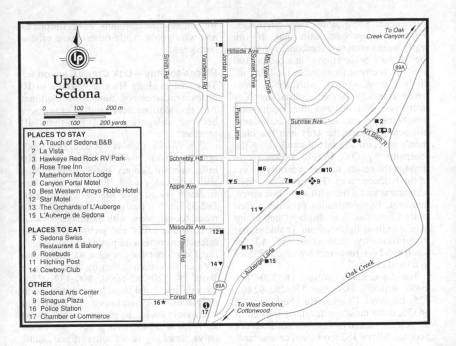

Uptown
Sedona

0   100   200 m
0   100   200 yards

PLACES TO STAY
1 A Touch of Sedona B&B
2 La Vista
3 Hawkeye Red Rock RV Park
6 Rose Tree Inn
7 Matterhorn Motor Lodge
8 Canyon Portal Motel
10 Best Western Arroyo Roble Hotel
12 Star Motel
13 The Orchards of L'Auberge
15 L'Auberge de Sedona

PLACES TO EAT
5 Sedona Swiss
   Restaurant & Bakery
9 Rosebuds
11 Hitching Post
14 Cowboy Club

OTHER
4 Sedona Arts Center
8 Sinagua Plaza
16 Police Station
17 Chamber of Commerce

To Oak
Creek Canyon

Hillside Ave
Smith Rd
Vanderen Rd
Jordan Rd
Sunset Drive
Mtn View Drive
89A
Sunrise Ave
Peach Lane
Art Barn Rd
Schnebly Rd
Apple Ave
Mesquite Ave
Wilson Rd
L'Auberge Lane
Oak Creek
Forest Rd
89A
To West Sedona,
Cottonwood

ARIZONA

private bath and fireplace, range from $125 to $150 a double and are often booked months ahead; a two-night minimum stay is requested and adult guests are preferred.

The rural *Territorial House B&B* (☎ 520-204-2737, 800-801-2737, fax 520-204-2230, oldwest@sedona.net), 65 Piki Drive, Sedona, AZ 86336, offers three rooms and a suite decorated in old Arizona 'Territorial' style for $100 to $180. All have private baths, and there is a spa. They work with *Boots & Saddles B&B* (☎ 520-282-1944, 800-201-1944, fax 520-204-2230, oldwest@sedona.net), 2900 Hopi Drive, Sedona, AZ 86336, which has four rooms with private baths and TV for $69 to $129 and arranges packages including golf, horseback riding and jeep tours.

Some small and slightly cheaper options include the following. *Moestly Wood B&B* (☎ 520-204-1461, fax 520-204-9005), 2085 Upper Red Rock Loop Rd, Sedona, AZ 86336, has two rooms with adjoining baths at $85 to $95, sells handcrafted wood products and has great views of Cathedral Rock, as does the nearby *Cathedral Rock Lodge* (☎ 520-282-7608, fax 520-282-4505), 61 Los Amigos Lane, Sedona, AZ 86336, with two rooms, a kitchen suite and a cottage priced from $75 to $125. *Lantern Light Inn* (☎ 520-282-3419), 3085 W Hwy 89A, Sedona, AZ 86336, has three rooms with baths at $90 to $120.

Resorts Sedona is known for several very upscale resorts. The *Los Abrigados Resort & Spa* (☎ 520-282-1777, 800-521-3131, fax 520-282-2614), 160 Portal Lane, Sedona, AZ 86336, is built in a Mexican style in keeping with its neighbor, Tlaquepaque. This is the place to stay if you want to be in the heart of Sedona and like to shop, exercise and enjoy spacious, comfortable suites. Prices for the 175 units range from $210 for a standard suite to $395 for a two-bedroom, two-bathroom suite with a kitchenette. Some suites have fireplaces, balconies or private patio spas. If you really want to impress someone, spring for the 'Historic Stone House,' at a cool $1500 a night. The resort's exercise facilities include a pool, saunas, whirlpools, three tennis courts, volleyball courts, aerobics instruction, Nautilus and other equipment, weight rooms, massage service and fitness instructors. Check the kids into the children's program and take a stroll along the footpaths by Oak Creek, which flows through the resort, or have a family picnic in the barbecue area. The resort has three restaurants and a bar with nighttime entertainment. Los Abrigados presents a fantastic Christmas light display (they claim over a million lights!) from Thanksgiving to mid-January. Admission ($5, $3 for seniors, $2 for four- to 12-year-olds) goes to a local charity.

The *Enchantment Resort* (☎ 520-282-2900, 800-826-4180, fax 520-282-9249), 525 Boynton Canyon Rd, Sedona, AZ 86336, is the most spectacularly located of the resorts, tucked in a canyon northwest of Sedona. All the 162 rooms and casitas have private balconies and great views; trails take you high above or far into the canyon. You'll get plenty of exercise with four pools, a dozen tennis courts (lessons are available), a croquet field and a fitness center, and can recover with a relaxing massage, sauna or soak in the spa. A children's program provides activities for the kids, and there is a fine innovative restaurant and bar. High-season rates are from about $270 for a large room to almost $700 for a two-bedroom, three-bathroom casita with kitchen, living room, deck with grill, and several balconies.

Poco Diablo Resort (☎ 520-282-7333, 800-528-4275, fax 520-282-2090), PO Box 1709, Sedona, AZ 86336, located 2 miles south of town on Hwy 179, has a nine-hole par 3 golf course, as well as two pools, four tennis courts, spas, and a restaurant and bar. About 140 large rooms and suites provide scenic views and include refrigerators, wet bars and coffee for $135 to $235 in the high season, or $250 to $360

for suites. Some rooms have fireplaces and whirlpools, while others have private balconies.

Places to Stay – Oak Creek Canyon

This area is along Hwy 89A, three to 10 miles northwest of downtown Sedona. Accommodations here tend to cross over between categories, so I list them all together.

Don Hoel's Cabins (☎ 520-282-3560, 800-292-4635), 9440 N Hwy 89A (10 miles north of Sedona) has 20 rustic cabins with kitchens priced at $60 to $90. The similarly priced *Slide Rock Lodge* (☎ 520-282-3531), 6 miles north of town, has 20 motel rooms, some with fireplaces, as well as barbecue grills and picnic tables, and offers free coffee and pastries in the morning. Couch potatoes beware – there are no TVs in the rooms. Nearby, the *Canyon Wren* (☎ 520-282-6900, 800-437-9736) has one small and three larger cabins with fireplaces, fully equipped kitchens and whirlpool tubs but no phones or TV, priced at $125 or $145 (two people per cabin only). Smoking is not allowed and continental breakfast is provided. *Oak Creek Terrace Resort* (☎ 520-282-3562, 800-224-2229), 4½ miles north of town, has 17 rooms and cabins, some with kitchenettes and fireplaces, ranging from $80 to $160.

The *Briar Patch Inn* (☎ 520-282-2342, fax 520-282-2399), 3190 N Hwy 89A, Sedona, AZ 86336, 3 miles north of town, has 16 rustic cabins, some with kitchenettes and/or fireplaces, attractively located on eight wooded acres right next to Oak Creek, making it convenient for swimming and fishing. Most cabins are for two; a few hold four people. Rates are $155 to $295 for a double. There are no TVs, but classical music performances may accompany breakfast, and occasional workshops and seminars keeps guests entertained. A two-night minimum stay is requested.

The *Junipine Resort* (☎ 520-282-3375, 800-742-7463, fax 520-282-7402), 8351 N Hwy 89A, Sedona, AZ 86336, 8 miles north of central Sedona, provides easy access to hiking, swimming and fishing in

Oak Creek. The 50 one- and two-bedroom townhouses (they are referred to as 'creek houses'), all with kitchens, living/dining rooms, fireplaces and decks and some with lofts, range from $180 to $250. Try the excellent restaurant if you're not in the mood to cook. There is a spa.

Places to Stay – Village of Oak Creek

This 'village' is about 7 miles south of Sedona on Hwy 179. The factory outlet mall on the 6600 block attracts shoppers and more places to stay are being added.

Hotels The *Desert Quail Inn* (☎ 520-284-1433, 800-385-0927, fax 520-284-0487, quail@sedona.net), 6626 Hwy 179, has 41 above-average rooms with refrigerators and in-room coffee, some with fireplaces and whirlpool tubs, for $90 to $150 in the high season. The activity-oriented inn has a spa and pool, is a rental center for jeeps and mountain bikes, and arranges golf and tennis.

Two pools, two spas, tennis courts, golf privileges at nearby courses and complimentary champagne make the *Bell Rock Inn* (☎ 520-282-4161, 800-881-7625, fax 520-284-0192), 6246 Hwy 179, one of the nicest motels in the area. Half of the nearly 100 rooms are mini-suites with fireplaces, and the red-rock views and pleasant pastel decor lend a Southwestern flavor. A restaurant and lounge provides weekend entertainment. Room rates are in the $80 to $140 range.

The *Holiday Inn Express* (☎ 520-284-0711, 800-822-3267, fax 520-284-3760), 6175 Hwy 179, has more than 100 rooms for $100 to $130, including continental breakfast and coffee available 24 hours a day. There is a pool and spa.

B&Bs Canyon Circle Drive is just off Bell Rock Blvd, which intersects with Hwy 179 on the west, about 7 miles south of Sedona. The road fronts the Coconino National Forest, providing easy access to the forest from nearby B&Bs. Two of Arizona's most luxurious B&Bs are found in this area.

The *Graham B&B Inn* (☎ 520-284-1425, 800-228-1425, fax 520-284-0767, graham@scdona.net), 150 Canyon Circle Drive, Sedona, AZ 86351, has six very comfortable and attractive rooms and four luxury casitas in the adjoining 'Adobe Village.' The owners claim that the Sedona Suite, priced at $229 a double, is the largest and most luxurious B&B suite in Arizona. It features a large Jacuzzi bathtub as well as twin showers, a living room with fireplace, a private patio with a fine view and, of course, a king-size bed. The other rooms, ranging in price from $139 to $189, all have private balconies and some have whirlpool bathtubs and/or fireplaces. The four casitas, each individually decorated and with a kitchenette, private deck, fireplace and Jacuzzi tub, rent for $269 to $369 depending on the unit and the season. Sip complimentary beverages in the library or by the swimming pool/spa. A two-night minimum stay is suggested.

Almost next door is the equally splendid *Canyon Villa B&B* (☎ 520-284-1226, 800-453-1166, fax 520-284-2114), 125 Canyon Circle Drive, Sedona, AZ 86351. This Mediterranean-style villa has 11 uniquely decorated rooms, some with Southwestern decor, with prices ranging from $135 to $215. Most rooms have balconies or patios, and many have whirlpool bathtubs and fireplaces. Enjoy the superb views from the pool while partaking of afternoon and evening refreshments.

The modern *Cozy Cactus B&B* (☎ 520-284-0082, 800-788-2082), at 80 Canyon Circle Drive, Sedona, AZ 86351, has five rooms with private baths and scenic views for $95 to $115 a double; two kitchens are available for guest use, and full breakfast and afternoon drinks are provided.

Places to Eat

Sedona has plenty of upscale restaurants but also a good selection of budget places serving decent food. Even the pricier places are often a reasonable value, providing high-quality, innovative dishes and agreeable surroundings. In fact, some visitors consider the cuisine to be as much of

ARIZONA

an attraction as the scenery. Reputable chefs are drawn to the town, rewarded both by the lovely setting and by an appreciative and (sometimes) discerning audience of food-loving travelers. Reservations are a good idea.

If you prefer to fix your own healthy meal, stop by *New Frontiers Natural Foods & Deli* (☎ 520-282-6311), 2055 W Hwy 89A. It is open from 8 am to 8 pm, Monday to Saturday, and 10 am to 8 pm on Sunday. You can eat your deli sandwich or other natural meal on a small outdoor patio (with parking lot views) – or take it out for a picnic.

For breakfast, the *Coffeepot Restaurant* (☎ 520-282-6626), 2050 W Hwy 89A, has been the place to go for decades. It's always busy and service can be slow, but meals are inexpensive and the selection is huge – it offers more types of omelets than most restaurants have menu items (it claims 101, but I didn't count). Opening at 6 am, the Coffeepot serves breakfast all day, and burgers, sandwiches, salads and Mexican food round out the lunch and dinner menus. Enjoy your food on the outdoor patio, or stare at the five-foot screen in the sports lounge if you can't bear to stay in Sedona without seeing how the Suns are doing. If 6 am isn't early enough for you, *Denny's* (☎ 520-282-5481), 1950 W Hwy 89A, is open 24 hours.

A couple of popular and inexpensive American family restaurants are conveniently located uptown. The *Hitching Post* (☎ 520-282-7761), 269 N Hwy 89A, is open from 7 am to 8:30 pm, and the *Ranch Kitchen* (☎ 520-282-0057), at the Y, is open from 6 am to 8 pm. For Southwestern food uptown, the *Cowboy Club* (☎ 520-282-4200), 241 Hwy 89A, looks like a saloon from the outside but has a large and determinedly Southwestern dining area with a good and interesting selection of snacks and meals at moderate prices. If you're feeling adventurous, you can order rattlesnake ribs with cactus condiments (vegetarians can stick to the cactus); standard food is available as well and desserts are good. Hours are 11 am to 10 pm daily.

Locals say the best American restaurant is the more expensive *Shugrue's* (☎ 520-282-2943), 2250 W Hwy 89A, offering dinner entrées in the teens and low $20s or lighter fare for less. Hours here are 11:30 am to 3 pm (with Sunday brunch beginning at 10 am) and 5 to 9 pm (till 10 pm on Friday and Saturday). *Shugrue's Hillside Grill* (☎ 520-282-5300), 671 Hwy 179, affords memorably panoramic red-rock views and both indoor and outdoor dining, as well as jazz entertainment on weekends. The seafood and meat menu is somewhat more adventurous and pricier than its simpler counterpart, so it draws a crowd. Hours are 11:30 am to 3 pm and 5 to 9:30 pm and reservations are recommended.

Shoppers at Tlaquepaque have several restaurants from which to choose. *El Rincon* (☎ 520-282-4648) serves very good Sonoran Mexican food from 11 am to 9 pm, Tuesday to Saturday, and noon to 5 pm on Sunday. It closes in February and has shorter hours from November to January. Prices are somewhat higher than most Mexican places but are still moderate. *The Atrium* (☎ 520-282-5060) is a plant-filled restaurant offering innovative bistro cuisine with dinner entrées in the $9 to $18 range and breakfasts and lunches from $3 to $8. *Rene at Tlaquepaque* (☎ 520-282-9225), long considered one of Sedona's best, is a nonsmoking restaurant with upscale continental cuisine (lamb is a specialty) and some unusual meats (pronghorn antelope, ostrich) and plenty of art on the walls. Though food, service and surroundings are top notch, diners dress neatly but casually. Lunch is served from 11:30 am to 4:30 pm. Dinner is served from 5:30 to 8:30 pm, with entrées in the high teens and $20s. Reservations are recommended.

The *Heartline Cafe* (☎ 520-282-0785), 1610 W Hwy 89A, serves imaginative and tasty continental cuisine with a Southwestern twist. The restaurant's name refers to a Zuni Indian symbol for good health and long life rather than low-cal cooking. It's a pretty place filled with flowers and has a patio for summer dining. Dinners, priced in the teens and low $20s, are a fair value, and lunches, most under $10, are also very good. Hours are 11 am to 3 pm, Monday to Saturday, and 5 to 9 or 10 pm daily.

For Italian dining, the *Hideaway* (☎ 520-282-4204), 251 Hwy 179 (in the Country Square Plaza), serves $8 to $15 dinners on a patio overlooking Oak Creek from 11 am to 9 pm daily. The more expensive *Pietro's* (☎ 520-282-2525), 2445 W Hwy 89A, considered by many to have northern Arizona's best Italian food, is open from 5 to 9 pm daily. Reservations are suggested. A recent and noteworthy competitor is *Dahl & Di Luca* (☎ 520-282-5219), 2321 W Hwy 89A, also open daily from 5 pm. Italian-food lovers can enjoy discovering which they like the best.

For Greek food, a good choice is the small and casual *Fournos* (☎ 520-282-3331), 3000 W Hwy 89A. Open for dinner from Thursday to Sunday, it specializes in seafood but also serves Sunday brunch; reservations are definitely recommended. Most dinner entrées are in the teens.

If you're dying for Swiss chocolates and other yummy chocolate things, get your fix at the *Sedona Swiss Restaurant & Bakery* (☎ 520-282-7959), 350 Jordan Rd. Before sampling the delectable desserts, pastries and gourmet coffees, go for a first-class Swiss-French meal in the pretty dining room next to the bakery. The inexpensive buffet lunch draws crowds, but it quiets down for dinner when entrées are in the teens or low $20s. Hours are 7 am to 9:30 pm Monday to Saturday.

Thai Spices (☎ 520-282-0599), 2986 W Hwy 89A, serves good, spicy and inexpensive authentic Thai food, including a wonderful coconut soup and some macrobiotic dishes. The restaurant is open from 12 to 3 pm, Monday to Friday, and 5 to 9 pm daily. Among the best Chinese restaurants are the *Lotus Garden* (☎ 520-282-3118, 520-282-3256), 164H Coffee Pot Drive (in Basha's Center), and *Ho's Mandarin House* (☎ 520-284-9088), 6486 Hwy 179 (at Castle Rock Plaza in the Village of Oak Creek). Both places are open from 11 am to 9 pm daily and to 10 pm on Friday and Saturday. For Indian food, the *India Pal-*ace (☎ 520-204-2300), 1910 W Hwy 89A (in Basha's), is open from 11:30 am and 5 to 10 pm.

Back in the Village of Oak Creek, try *Irene's* (☎ 520-284-2240), in the Castle Rock Plaza, serving home-style breakfast, lunch and dinner at moderate prices. Close by, the *Wild Toucan Restaurant and Cantina* (☎ 520-284-1604), 6376 Hwy 179, serves large portions of Mexican and American food inside or out on the patio and has a kids' menu. Entrées start at around $9. The restaurant at the *Bell Rock Inn* is open from 7 am to 9 pm and is quite good.

Of course, you're here to drop your jaw for the views as well as the vittles. So which restaurant has the most spectacular views in Sedona? Tough question. Certainly, *Rosebuds* (☎ 520-282-3022), 320 N Hwy 89A (in the Sinagua Plaza), was designed to be a contender – huge windows provide a memorable panorama. Serving mainly standard steak and seafood dinners in the $12 to $22 range, Rosebuds is open 11 am to 9:30 pm daily and to 10 pm on Friday and Saturday.

For even better views, dine watching a magnificent sunset out of town at the Enchantment Resort, where the *Yavapai Dining Room* (☎ 520-282-2900) serves superb food in a superb setting (make a reservation). The Southwestern cuisine has all sorts of interesting twists and the menu changes regularly. Seafood, meat and pasta dinner entrées range from $15 to $25, a fair value for the food and a bargain considering the location. The restaurant also puts together a good champagne Sunday brunch ($24) – again, make reservations. Hours are from 11:30 am to 2 pm and 6 to 9:30 pm daily.

All Sedona's resorts have good restaurants. The most famous is *L'Auberge de Sedona* (☎ 520-282-1667) in the resort of the same name. It's beautiful, elegant, romantic and very French. The high prices, small portions and formal dining are irresistible to many visitors; reservations and dinner jackets are required. The best value is the prix-fixe dinner menu that is changed daily and runs at about $60 for six courses. Otherwise, dinner entrées are around $30 and include French delicacies such as frog legs, pheasant, veal and snails.

Finally, if you are fed up with all this fancy stuff and just want a huge steak and country & western music, head over to *Rainbow's End Steakhouse & Saloon* (☎ 520-282-1593), 3235 W Hwy 89A, where you can stomp to live bands on weekends.

Entertainment

Read the monthly *Red Rock Review* for local events. Apart from the saloon at *Rainbow's End* (see Places to Eat, above), nightlife is fairly quiet, with mainly lounge entertainment at the resorts. The *Oak Creek Brewing Company* (☎ 520-204-1300), 2050 Yavapai Drive, serves hand-crafted beers on tap and has an outdoor patio and live music on most evenings – no cover charge when I was there. Hours here are 4 to 10 pm Monday to Thursday, 1 pm to midnight Friday and Saturday, and 1 to 10 pm on Sunday.

Check the *Sedona Arts Center* (see Art Galleries, earlier in this chapter) for cultural events, and *The Book Loft* (☎ 520-282-5173), 175 Hwy 179, for poetry readings.

The old-fashioned *Flicker Shack* (☎ 520-282-3777), 1½ miles west of the Y on Hwy 89A; the modern *Harkins 6 Theatres* (☎ 520-282-0222), 2081 W Hwy 89A; and *Cinedona Theaters* (☎ 520-282-0707), 3190 W Hwy 89A, show movies.

Shopping

Despite its size, Sedona is a prime shopping destination. The uptown area along Hwy 89A is the place to get souvenirs. Good bookstores here include Native & Nature (☎ 520-282-7870), 248 N Hwy 89A, stocking a selection of books about the Southwest, and the Happy Wanderer (☎ 520-282-4690), 320 N Hwy 89A, in the Sinagua Plaza, with an excellent selection of travel books. Sedona Kid Company (☎ 520-282-3571), 333 N Hwy 89A, is the place to go for the kids on your list. The Book Loft (☎ 520-282-5173), 175 Hwy 179, has new and used books.

Tlaquepaque (☎ 520-282-4838) has high-quality art galleries that are also high priced, but they are a good place to start for comparison shopping. Almost opposite is the Crystal Castle (☎ 520-282-5910), one of several stores selling New Age books and gifts. Continuing south along Hwy 179, Garlands's Navajo Rugs (☎ 520-282-4070), in the complex at the junction of Hwy 179 and Schnebly Hill Rd, has thousands of rugs to choose from as well as other Indian crafts. In the same complex is Sedona Pottery (☎ 520-282-1192), selling interesting ceramics. The Village of Oak Creek has Oak Creek Factory Outlets (☎ 520-284-2150), 6657 Hwy 179, with about 30 outlets providing many name brands at discounted prices.

Getting There & Away

Air Scenic Airlines (☎ 520-282-7935, 800-634-6801) arranges charters to and from Phoenix. The airport sits spectacularly atop a mesa.

Bus The Sedona-Phoenix Shuttle (☎ 520-282-2066, 800-448-7988, fax 520-204-5841) leaves Phoenix Airport every two hours between 10 am and 8 pm and returns from Sedona every two hours from 6 am to 4 pm. The fare is $35 one way or $60 roundtrip.

Getting Around

Car Rental Budget Rent A Car (☎ 520-282-4602) and AAAA Sedona Car/Jeep Rentals (☎ 520-282-2227, 800-879-5337) are at the airport. You can also try Enterprise (☎ 520-282-2052), 2550 W Hwy 89A; Sedona Rent A Car (☎ 520-282-2897), 3195 W Hwy 89A; and the jeep rentals in the Desert Quail Inn.

Taxi Call Bob's Sedona Taxi and Tours (☎ 520-282-1234) to get around the area.

FLAGSTAFF

Flagstaff was first settled by a flock of sheep, which arrived in the spring of 1876 accompanied by Thomas Forsyth McMillan, who settled down and built a cabin. On the Fourth of July of that year, a pine tree was stripped of its branches and a US flag hung from it to celebrate the country's centennial, hence the town's name. The arrival of the railroad in 1882 really put Flagstaff on the map. Cattle and sheep ranching became economic mainstays, and the surrounding forests formed the basis of a small logging industry.

By the end of the 19th century, Flagstaff was becoming an important town. The famous Lowell Observatory was founded in 1894, the still-functioning Hotel Weatherford was built in 1897, and the school that later became Northern Arizona University (NAU) was established in 1899. In the early 1900s, the Riordan Mansion and several other historic buildings were erected. Although Flagstaff didn't have the mineral resources of other parts of the state, the pleasant climate attracted settlers.

Today, ranching, forestry and the railroad have been supplanted by tourism, Flagstaff's major industry. During the summer, the city's 6900-foot elevation attracts lowland Arizonans escaping the heat as well as travelers from all over the world. From Flagstaff, it is less than a two-hour drive to the Grand Canyon and other attractions are even closer, such as impressive Sinagua Indian sites, the splendid (though inactive) volcano at Sunset Crater National Monument, beautiful Oak Creek Canyon and the 12,663-foot Humphreys Peak, Arizona's highest mountain. The Navajo and Hopi Indian Reservations are longer day trips. In winter, the nearby Arizona Snowbowl Ski Area provides convenient skiing.

Although 'Flag,' as locals call it, is a great base for trips into the surrounding area, it is also a destination in its own right, with museums, a historical downtown, cultural attractions and, thanks to NAU students and tourists looking for evening excitement, northern Arizona's best nightlife. Attracting international budget travelers, Flag is the Katmandu or Cuzco of Arizona.

With about 57,000 inhabitants, Flagstaff is Arizona's fourth largest urban area, and the largest between Phoenix and Salt Lake City. It is the seat of Coconino County, which, at 18,608 sq miles, is the second largest county in the USA (after California's San Bernardino County).

Orientation

Flagstaff is a major crossroads at the intersection of I-17 and I-40. Its main drag, Route 66 (also called Santa Fe Ave and marked both ways on maps), runs north of and roughly parallel to I-40, passing through the old town and by the visitor center, becoming the main motel strip away from downtown.

Information

The visitor center (☎ 520-774-9541, 800-842-7293, fax 520-556-1308), 1 E Route 66, is in the historic Amtrak railway station. The center is staffed from 7 am to 6 pm, Monday to Saturday, and from 8 am to 5 pm on Sunday, but the station is open from 6:15 am to 11:25 pm daily, and stands with free maps, events listings and accommodations brochures are available during those hours.

The Coconino National Forest Peaks Ranger Station (☎ 520-526-0866), 5075 N Hwy 89, Flagstaff, AZ 86004, has information about the forests north of Flagstaff and is open from 7:30 am to 4:30 pm Monday to Friday as well as summer Saturdays. The Mormon Lake Ranger Station (☎ 520-774-1147), 4373 S Lake Mary Rd, Mormon Lake, AZ 86001, provides information about the Coconino National Forest south of Flagstaff. Its office is open from 7:30 am to 4:30 pm Monday to Friday. Arizona Game & Fish (☎ 520-774-5045), 3500 S Lake Mary Rd, has hunting and fishing licenses, regulations and information. Hours are 8 am to 5 pm Monday to Friday.

The library (☎ 520-774-4000, 520-779-7670) is at 300 W Aspen Ave. The local newspaper is the *Arizona Daily Sun*. The main post office (☎ 520-527-2440) is at 2400 Postal Blvd and the downtown branch (☎ 520-527-2440) is at 104 N Agassiz. The medical center (☎ 520-779-3366) is at 1200 N Beaver. The police (☎ 520-556-2316, 520-774-1414) are at 120 N Beaver.

Winter snowstorms can close roads in northern Arizona. Call ☎ 520-779-2711 for road conditions.

ARIZONA

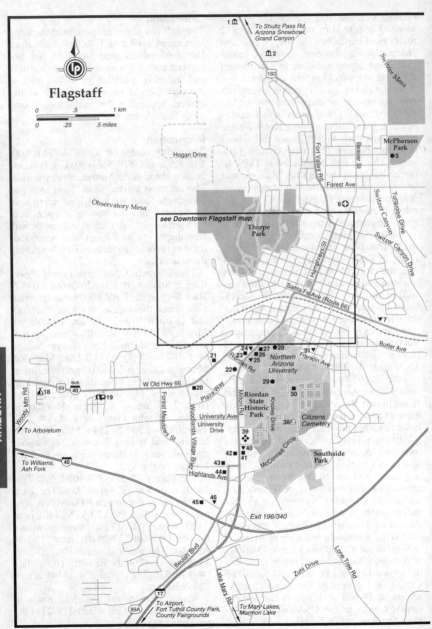

Flagstaff

0   .5   1 km

0   .25   .5 miles

To Shultz Pass Rd,
Arizona Snowbowl,
Grand Canyon

180

McPherson
Park
● 5

Hogan Drive

Observatory Mesa

Forest Ave

Switzer Mesa

Fort Valley Rd

Beaver St

Switzer Canyon Drive

Turquoise Drive

6 ⊕

see Downtown Flagstaff map

Thorpe
Park

Humphreys St

Santa Fe Ave (Route 66)

Butler Ave

▼ 7

24 ▼   ▼ 27   ● 28
23 ■   26 ■   31 ▼
21 ■   25 ▼   Franklin Ave
         Riordan Rd   Northern
22 ●   Arizona
            29 ●   University
W Old Hwy 66
20 ■   Plaza Way   Riordan   30
18 ▲   19   Forest Meadows St   Woodlands Village Blvd   Milton Rd   State   ●
         Historic   Knoles Drive
         Park   38 🏛   Citizens
To Arboretum   University Ave   Cemetery
         University   39 ◆
         Drive   ◆◆
To Williams,   42 ▼   ▼ 40
Ash Fork   43 ■   44 ■   41   McConnell Circle   Southside
40   Highlands Ave   Park
         45 ■   46 ▼
            Exit 196/340

Beulah Blvd

89   BUS   40

Woody Mtn Rd

89

ARIZONA

Lake Mary Rd

Lone Tree Rd

Zuni Drive

17

89A

To Airport,
Fort Tuthill County Park,
County Fairgrounds

To Mary Lakes,
Mormon Lake

1 🏛
🏛 2

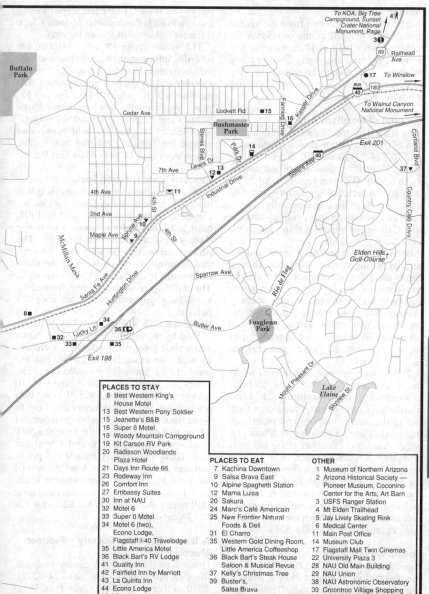

To KOA, Big Tree
Campground, Sunset
Crater National
Monument, Page

Railhead
Ave

To Winslow

To Walnut Canyon
National Monument

Buffalo
Park

Cedar Ave

Lockett Rd

Bushmaster
Park

Steves Blvd

Fanning Drive

Kaspar Drive

Park Dr

Lewis Dr

7th Ave

4th Ave

2nd Ave

Maple Ave

Spruce Ave

4th St

McMillan Mesa

Santa Fe Ave

Huntington Drive

Industrial Drive

Soliere Ave

Exit 201

Cortland Blvd

Country Club Drive

Elden Hills
Golf Course

Sparrow Ave

Rio de Flag

Butler Ave

Foxglenn
Park

Mount Pleasant Dr

Lake
Elaine

Skyview St

Exit 198

Lucky Ln

ARIZONA

PLACES TO STAY
8 Best Western King's
   House Motel
13 Best Western Pony Soldier
15 Jeanette's B&B
16 Super 8 Motel
19 Woody Mountain Campground
19 Kit Carson RV Park
20 Radisson Woodlands
   Plaza Hotel
21 Days Inn Route 66
23 Rodeway Inn
26 Comfort Inn
27 Embassy Suites
30 Inn at NAU
32 Motel 6
33 Super 8 Motel
40 Motel 6 (two),
   Econo Lodge,
   Flagstaff I-40 Travelodge
35 Little America Motel
36 Black Bart's RV Lodge
41 Quality Inn
42 Fairfield Inn by Marriott
43 La Quinta Inn
44 Econo Lodge
45 Motel 6,
   Days Inn I-40

PLACES TO EAT
7 Kachina Downtown
9 Salsa Brava East
10 Alpine Spaghetti Station
12 Mama Luisa
20 Sakura
24 Marc's Café Americain
25 New Frontier Natural
   Foods & Deli
31 El Charro
35 Western Gold Dining Room,
   Little America Coffeeshop
36 Black Bart's Steak House
   Saloon & Musical Revue
37 Kelly's Christmas Tree
39 Buster's,
   Salsa Brava
40 Perkins Family Restaurant
46 Delhi Palace

OTHER
1 Museum of Northern Arizona
2 Arizona Historical Society —
   Pioneer Museum, Coconino
   Center for the Arts, Art Barn
3 USFS Ranger Station
4 Mt Elden Trailhead
5 Jay Lively Skating Rink
6 Medical Center
11 Main Post Office
14 Museum Club
17 Flagstaff Mall Twin Cinemas
22 University Plaza 3
28 NAU Old Main Building
29 NAU Union
38 NAU Astronomic Observatory
39 Greentrice Village Shopping
   Plaza (Greentree 3 Cinemas,
   Mountain Sports)

Historic Downtown

Two blocks north and east from the visitor center, itself housed in the old Santa Fe Railway Depot built in 1926, you can see many late-19th- and early-20th-century buildings. The visitor center and the Pioneer Museum have a brochure describing almost 40 buildings.

Museum of Northern Arizona

In an attractive stone building set in a pine grove, this small but thorough museum (☎ 520-774-5211), at 3001 N Fort Valley Rd, is Flagstaff's most important and is worth a visit. Galleries feature exhibits on local Indian archaeology, history and customs (the Hopi kiva is especially worthwhile) as well as geology, biology and the arts. Call for information about its excellent changing exhibits.

Browse the gift and book store, and especially during summer, visit the exhibits, events and sales of Navajo, Hopi and Zuni art. To stretch your legs, try the short nature trail (which may be closed in the winter). Museum hours are 9 am to 5 pm daily except New Year's Day, Thanksgiving and Christmas. Admission is $5, seniors pay $4, students with ID pay $3 and children ages 7 to 17 pay $2.

The museum sponsors a variety of workshops and tours, ranging from half-day to multi-day trips exploring the surrounding country. The trips are led by local biologists, anthropologists and other professionals. Here's a sample tour: Photographing Ancestral Puebloan sites, led by a professional photographer, and visiting several Four Corners-area sites costs $370 for three days/two nights; the price includes instruction, transportation, lodging and some meals. For a full program of events and tours call the museum's education department (☎ 520-774-5213).

Lowell Observatory

Named after its founder, Percival Lowell, the observatory continues to be a working astronomical research center. Of the many important observations made here, the discovery of the planet Pluto in 1930 is one of the most famous. Eight telescopes are in use, including the historic 24-inch Clark refractor (which visitors can try out).

The visitor center (☎ 520-774-2096 for recorded information) has exhibits and various activities. Hours are 9 am to 5 pm in summer and 10 am to 5 pm in winter. Admission is $3 for adults; $1 for five- to 17-year-olds. Frequent night programs include lectures and stargazing through the magnificent telescopes, and are held year-round except for January; call for hours. The observatory is at 1400 W Mars Hill Rd.

Riordan State Historic Park

Brothers Michael and Timothy Riordan made a fortune from their Arizona Lumber Company in the late 1800s, and in 1904, built a 13,000-sq-foot mansion to house themselves and their two families. The park preserves this building with its original furnishings, which were of the then-fashionable and luxurious Craftsman style. The building is made of stone fronted by log slabs, giving it the false appearance of a palatial log cabin. The park is at 1300 Riordan Ranch St, surrounded by NAU.

Stop by the visitor center to see exhibits and a slide program. Visitors are welcome to walk the grounds and picnic, but entrance to the house is by guided tour only. Tours are worthwhile but limited to 20 people and reservations (☎ 520-779-4395) are recommended. Park hours are 8 am to 5 pm from mid-May to mid-September and 11 am to 5 pm the rest of the year; the park is closed Christmas Eve and Christmas Day. Tours leave hourly from 9 to 4 pm in summer and from noon to 4 pm the rest of the year. For a spooky tour, reserve space well in advance for an evening preceding Halloween. Admission is $4; $2.50 for 12- to 17-year-olds.

Arizona Historical Society – Pioneer Museum

Housed in the old 1908 county hospital, the Pioneer Museum (☎ 520-774-6272), 2340 N Fort Valley Rd, preserves Flagstaff's early history in photographs and memorabilia that ranges from vintage farm

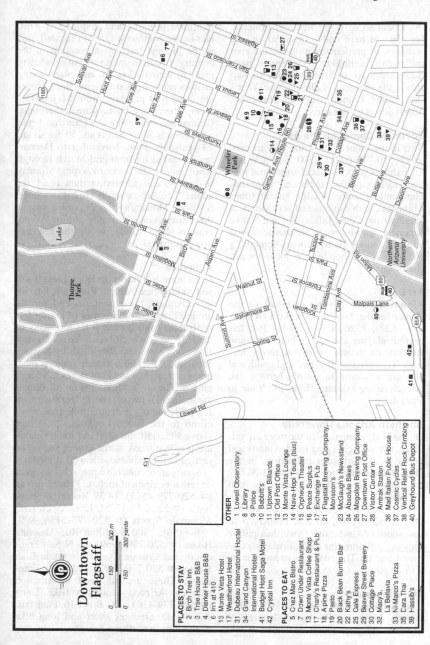

Downtown Flagstaff

0   150   300 m
0   150   300 yards

PLACES TO STAY

2 Birch Tree Inn
3 Tree House B&B
4 Dierker House B&B
6 Inn at 410
13 Monte Vista Hotel
17 Weatherford Hotel
31 Dubeau International Hostel
34 Grand Canyon
     International Hostel
41 Budget Host Saga Motel
42 Crystal Inn

PLACES TO EAT

5 Chez Marc Bistro
7 Down Under Restaurant
14 Nava-Hopi Tours (bus)
17 Monte Vista Coffee Shop
17 Charly's Restaurant & Pub
18 A pine Pizza
19 Pasto
20 Back Bean Burrito Bar
22 Kathy's
25 Cafe Express
29 Beaver Street Brewery
30 Cottage Place
32 Macy's,
     La Bellavia
33 Ni-Marco's Pizza
35 Cara Thai
39 Hassib's

OTHER

1 Lowell Observatory
8 Library
9 Police
10 Babbit's
11 Uptown Billiards
12 Old Post Office
13 Monte Vista Lounge
14 Nava-Hopi Tours (bus)
15 Orpheum Theater
16 Peace Surplus
21 Flagstaff Brewing Company,
     Monsoon's
23 McGaugh's Newsstand
24 Absolute Bikes
26 Mogollon Brewing Company
27 Downtown Post Office
28 Visitor Center in
     Amtrak Station
36 Mad Italian Public House
37 Cosmic Cyclas
38 Vertical Relief Rock Climbing
40 Greyhound Bus Depot

ARIZONA

equipment to early medical instruments. See the old barn and root cellar on the premises, or participate in one of the special events highlighting the area's past. Hours are 9 am to 5 pm Monday to Saturday; the museum is closed New Year's Day, Easter, Thanksgiving and Christmas. Admission is by donation.

Coconino Center for the Arts
Next to the Pioneer Museum, this art center (☎ 520-779-6921), 2300 N Fort Valley Rd, exhibits works by local artists and presents various performances and programs. The center's scope is wide and at times whimsical, with exhibits and performances ranging from Celtic folk music and Native American storytellers to an artistic miniature golf course. There's always something going on. A gift shop features local fine art. Hours vary.

Art Barn
Almost next to but not attached to the Center for the Arts, the Art Barn (☎ 520-774-0822), 2320 N Fort Valley Rd, has been displaying and selling both local and Reservation artists' work for three decades. The selection is varied and good, and you are welcome to simply browse the ever-changing exhibits. Hours are 9 am to 5 pm daily.

Northern Arizona University
On the NAU campus, visit the three art galleries, two with changing local exhibits and one with a permanent collection, in the **Old Main Building** (☎ 520-523-3471), 10 Knowles Drive. Admission is free; call for hours.

The **NAU Astronomic Observatory** (☎ 520-523-7170), on San Francisco St just south of University Drive, has public viewing sessions on clear Fridays year-round and on Thursdays in summer from 7 to 10 pm.

The Arboretum
The Arboretum (☎ 520-774-1441) at S Woody Mountain Rd has 200 acres of grounds and greenhouses dedicated to horticultural research and display. At 7150 feet on the southwest side of Flagstaff, this is the highest research arboretum in the country. Locals come to discover what to grow in their backyards, and plant-loving visitors can learn about alpine flora. Hours are 9 am to 4 pm daily from May to October, when plant displays are at their best. Guided tours are given at 11 am and 1 pm; admission is $3 for adults and $1 for six- to 18-year-olds. From November to December 23 and again from mid-March through April, hours are 9 am to 4 pm, Monday to Friday, and admission then is $1 for adults. The Arboretum is closed in winter. S Woody Mountain Rd is 2½ miles west of the visitor center on Route 66; the Arboretum is about 4 miles south (the last section is unpaved).

Activities
In addition to **hiking** on Humphreys Peak and **skiing** (see Around Flagstaff, later in this chapter), the mountains and forests around Flagstaff offer scores of hiking and **mountain biking** trails – far too many to describe here. A useful resource is *Flagstaff Hikes and Mountain Bike Rides* by R and S Mangum. The USFS ranger stations have maps and advice, and bookstores have trail guides. The closest hiking is on Mt Elden; the trailhead is just past the ranger station on Hwy 89, and it's a steep 3-mile (one way) climb to the Elden Lookout, 2300 feet above Flagstaff. Shorter and longer loops are possible – ask at the ranger station or just go to the trailhead; it's well signed.

Sports stores that have maps, books, gear or rental equipment include Peace Surplus (☎ 520-779-4521), 14 W Route 66; Babbitt's (☎ 520-774-4775), 12 E Aspen Ave; Mountain Sports (☎ 520-779-5156, 800-286-5156), 1800 S Milton Rd; Absolute Bikes (☎ 520-779-5969), 18 N San Francisco; and Cosmic Cycles Mountain Bike Rental (☎ 520-779-1092), 113 S San Francisco. These are all good information sources. Arizona Mountain Bike Tours (☎ 520-779-4161), PO Box 816, Flagstaff, AZ 86002, arranges short and long bike excursions in northern Arizona.

Flagstaff Mountain Guides (☎ 520-635-0145), PO Box 2383, Flagstaff, AZ 86003, offers guided nature hikes, and beginning to advanced **rock climbing**, winter climbing and backcountry skiing trips. Vertical Relief Rock Gym (☎ 520-556-9909), 205 S San Francisco, has 6000 sq ft of artificial indoor walls to practice rock climbing. Routes range from beginner level to the most difficult grades. Hours are noon to 8 pm daily, till 11 pm on weekdays. Rates are $12 a day plus $7 for equipment rental.

Hitchin' Post Stables (☎ 520-774-1719, 520-774-7131), 448 S Lake Mary Rd, has day-long **horseback riding** trips to Walnut Canyon and other destinations on request; Flying Hart Barn (☎ 520-526-2788), 8400 N Hwy 89, offers guided rides in the San Francisco Mountains. Both places offer horse-drawn sleigh rides in winter.

Jay Lively Rink (☎ 520-774-1051), 1850 N Turquoise Drive, has **ice skating** in winter and **roller skating** in summer. Rentals and lessons are available. You can **golf** 18 holes at Elden Hills (☎ 520-527-7997, 520-526-5125), 2380 N Oakmont Drive.

Organized Tours

The Gray Line subsidiary, Nava-Hopi Tours (☎ 520-774-5003, 800-892-8687, fax 520-774-7715), 114 W Route 66, has narrated bus tours of most nearby sites of interest, including the Grand Canyon and Indian reservations. Tours last seven to 11½ hours and cost about $35 to $75, depending on time and distance. Five- to 15-year-olds travel at half price, and motel pickup is included; national park admission and meals are extra. During the busy summer months, the company also runs city trolley tours. Tours can be booked through travel agents. Seven Wonders Scenic Tours (☎ 520-526-2501) arranges customized guided van tours to almost anywhere in northern Arizona.

Special Events

Flagstaff is busy throughout the summer with many ongoing events, often held simultaneously. The visitor center has details. Events include the Flagstaff Festival of the Arts, held from early July to mid-August and hosting plays, operas, concerts, films and other performances, many on the NAU campus. From late June to mid-August, in the Coconino Center for the Arts, there is a Festival of Native American Arts with performances and art exhibits. The Museum of Northern Arizona hosts Indian arts exhibits throughout the summer with some weekends highlighting the work of specific tribes, including the Zuni, the Hopi and Navajo. A rodeo and an Indian powwow are held in June, and the Coconino County Fair is held over Labor Day. Things quiet down during the rest of the year, although there's always something going on. The Flagstaff Winter Festival throughout February is also a big highlight, with sled dog races, skiing excursions and races, slide shows and musical evenings among the events.

Places to Stay

Flagstaff provides the best cheap and moderate lodging in this region, offering many motels and hotels as well as some youth hostels. There are no expensive destination resorts as in Sedona. Obviously, summer is the high season and hotel prices rise accordingly. In addition, weekends attract many of the two million sweltering inhabitants of the Valley of the Sun (2½ hours away by freeway) pushing room prices to a premium – a room that costs $20 in April can be $50 or more on an August weekend. Avoid summer weekends if possible; if you're up for dealing with the crowds, be sure to make reservations or arrive by early afternoon to have a reasonable hotel selection. At other times of year, you can easily find very cheap rooms. If you want to stay at a B&B, be aware that all the ones listed here are nonsmoking.

Flagstaff Central Reservations (☎ 520-527-8333 in Flagstaff, 800-527-8388, fax 520-527-4272, flagres@infomagic.com) makes reservations for the better motels and B&Bs in Flagstaff as well as northern Arizona.

Places to Stay – Camping

Campgrounds can fill up in summer, so be sure to make reservations where possible. *Fort Tuthill County Park* (☎ 520-774-3464, 520-774-5139), half a mile west of I-17 exit 337 and 3 miles south of Flag, has 100 sites for $9 and 14 sites with hookups for $13. There are showers, but facilities are basic. The campground is open from May to September; reservations cost an additional $5.

Woody Mountain Campground (☎ 520-774-7727), 2727 W Route 66, offers 146 sites, some with full hookups, for $16 to $21, as well as a pool, playground and coin laundry. It is open from April (sometimes earlier) to November 1. Nearby, the *Kit Carson RV Park* (☎ 520-774-6993), 2101 W Route 66, has 265 RV sites amid ponderosa pines available year-round, with full hookups for $20. *Black Bart's RV Lodge* (☎ 520-774-1912), 2760 Butler Ave (next door to the restaurant), provides hot showers and 110 sites with full hookups for $20; a few tent spaces are $10.

Flagstaff KOA (☎ 520-526-9926), 5803 N Hwy 89, has 200 year-round sites, many with full RV hookups, ranging in price from $18 to $24 depending on the season and facilities needed. Two Kamping Kabins are available for $29, and there is a playground, coin laundry and showers. The *Big Tree Campground* (☎ 520-526-2583), 6500 N Hwy 89, has 50 RV sites with hookups for $17 in the high season and tents for about $15, depending on the number of people at your site. A swap meet is held here Friday to Sunday during the summer. *J & H RV Park* (☎ 520-526-1829, 800-243-5264), 7901 N Hwy 89, has 55 RV sites with full hookups for $22 and does not allow tents; it's open April through October.

USFS campgrounds are listed under Lakes Southeast of Flagstaff, later in this chapter.

Places to Stay – Budget

There are plenty of cheap and basic motels along Route 66, especially along the 3-mile stretch east of downtown and near NAU southwest of downtown. Route 66 parallels the railway and the cheap places don't have soundproof rooms. Almost anytime from September to May you can cruise along here and find 15 or 20 motels advertising rooms for about $20, and some as cheap as $15 a double. (I don't list all the most basic cheapies here.) In summer, though, these same cheap places double and triple their rates, especially during a busy weekend when it's a sellers' market. At these times you need to make reservations or arrive in town by early afternoon to snag a cheapish basic room. Check the room before you pay, though – some are worse than others. They are perfectly satisfactory if you are paying $20 off-season but a poor value if you are paying $50 in summer. Budget travelers should avoid summer weekends.

Flagstaff is something of an international budget travelers' center – many of these travelers stay downtown in the interesting older hotels, some of which double as independent youth hostels (membership is not needed and linens are provided). These are good places to meet travelers and get up-to-date travel information.

The independently run *Grand Canyon International Hostel* (☎ 520-774-9421, 888-442-2696, fax 520-774-6047, info@grandcanyonhostel.com), 19 S San Francisco, was formerly called the 'Downtowner' and that huge neon sign is still visible. It charges $12 to $16 per person in dorm rooms and has some private doubles (shared bathroom) for $25 to $35. Breakfast is included and guests have use of a kitchen, BBQ area, laundry and TV/video room. The hostel offers pickup from the Greyhound station and arranges reasonably priced tours to the Grand Canyon and other local attractions.

Dubeau International Hostel (☎ 520-774-6731, 800-398-7112, fax 520-774-4060, dubeau@infomagic.com), 19 W Phoenix Ave, is in a motel dating from 1929. Rates are $13 per person in dormitories, each of which has a bathroom, and private rooms are about $27 a double. Rates include kitchen privileges with free tea/coffee (and you don't even have to wash the dishes!), use of the adjacent laundry, and pickup from the Greyhound station or airport. This hostel can hook you up with local tours, too.

Scenes of the movie *Casablanca* were filmed at the 1927 *Monte Vista Hotel* (☎ 520-779-6971, 800-545-3068, fax 520-779-2904), 100 N San Francisco, a popular place with many of the almost 50 rooms named after the film stars who slept in them. Rooms are comfortable and old-fashioned but far from luxurious (Humphrey Bogart handled it just fine). The cheapest, with shared bathrooms, are priced in the $30s for a double in summer. Rooms with a bathroom are around $50, and you'll pay a little more for one of the several suites. The shared-bathroom rooms save you $20 and are a better deal unless you really want the privacy. A few rooms with four beds are also available, which are used as dorms at $10 to $16 per person, depending on season. Check out the popular blues bar downstairs – I overdid it there one night but only had to drive the elevator to get to my room.

The *Weatherford Hotel* (☎ 520-779-1919, fax 520-773-8951, weathtel@infomagic .com), 23 N Leroux, dates back to 1897 and was then northern Arizona's finest hotel and is now Flagstaff's most historic. Until recently, it was a youth hostel but now has eight private rooms with a turn-of-the-19th-century feel (no TV or telephone) for $35 to $60 a double, depending on season. The popular Charly's (restaurant and pub) is downstairs and the recently renovated Zane Grey ballroom is an attractively old-fashioned place for a drink (open Thursday to Saturday evenings).

There are four *Motel 6*s, all with pools and more than 100 rooms each; summer doubles are in the upper $40s or $50s and often reserved weeks in advance (they're about $10 less at other times). They are, in increasing order of cost, at 2440 E Lucky Lane (☎ 520-774-8756, fax 520-774-2067); 2500 E Lucky Lane (☎ 520-779-6184, fax 520-774-2249); 2010 E Butler Ave (☎ 520-774-1801, fax 520-774-1987);

and 2745 S Woodlands Village Blvd (☎ 520-779-3757, fax 520-774-2137).

The clean *Budget Host Saga Motel* (☎ 520-779-3631), 820 W Route 66, has a pool and charges $50 to $60 in summer.

Places to Stay – Middle

Hotels Many of the standard chain motels are priced in the middle range. A *Super 8 Motel* (☎ 520-526-0818, fax 520-526-8786), 3725 Kasper Drive, lacks a pool but has 90 reasonable rooms in the $70s for a double, including a coffee/pastry breakfast. Another *Super 8 Motel* (☎ 520-774-1821, fax 520-774-7662), 2285 E Butler Ave, is slightly cheaper and has 100 spacious though slightly worn rooms and a pool, a sauna and a spa. Acceptable doubles for about $70 are offered at the *Flagstaff I-40 Travelodge* (☎ 520-779-5121, fax 520-774-5608), 2520 E Lucky Lane, with 140 rooms, an outdoor pool, indoor spa and some units with refrigerators, coffeemakers and microwaves.

Average chain motels with standard rooms in the $60 to $90 price range during summer include the *Best Western King's House Motel* (☎ 520-774-7186, fax 520-774-7188), 1560 E Route 66, with a pool and free continental breakfast; *Days Inn Route 66* (☎ 520-774-5221, fax 520-774-4977), 1000 W Route 66, with a pool and coffee shop; *Days Inn I-40* (☎ 520-779-1575, fax 520-779-0044), 2735 S Woodlands Village Blvd, with a spa, exercise room and continental breakfast; and the *Rodeway Inn* (☎ 520-774-5038), 913 S Milton Rd, with a pool and spa. There are two *Econo Lodges* at 2480 E Lucky Lane (☎ 520-774-7701, fax 520-774-7855), and 2355 S Beulah Blvd (☎ 520-774-2225), both with a pool (indoor at the first location), a spa and continental breakfast. *Crystal Inn* (☎/fax 520-774-4581, ☎ 800-654-4667), 602 W Route 66, has spacious rooms, a pool, spa and exercise room. Summer rates vary from $50 to $95; in winter you can find a room in the $30s.

Of the many hotels with summertime rates in the $70 to $100 range, one of the nicer places is the *Best Western Pony*

Soldier (☎ 520-526-2388, 800-356-4143, fax 520-527-8329, bwponyso@flagstaff .az.us), 3030 E Route 66, with 90 attractive rooms, an indoor pool and spa, restaurant and lounge, and complimentary continental breakfast. Unfortunately, it is close to the railway, which may bother light sleepers, though the desk clerk told me the rooms are reasonably soundproof. Away from the railway is the *Comfort Inn* (☎ 520-774-7326, fax 520-774-7328), 914 S Milton Rd, which also has pleasant rooms, free continental breakfast and a pool open in summer. Similar facilities are offered at the *Fairfield Inn by Marriott* (☎/fax 520-773-1300), 2005 S Milton Rd, with 135 rooms, and the 130-room *La Quinta Inn* (☎ 520-556-8666, fax 520-214-9140), 2015 S Beulah Blvd, both of which have above average rooms.

The *Inn at NAU* (☎ 520-523-1616, fax 520-523-1625), Building 33 on the east side of the NAU campus, is used as a training facility for NAU's School of Hotel & Restaurant Management. The inn's 19 nonsmoking rooms are spacious and well-maintained, and the student staff is eager to please. Rates range from $59 in winter to $84 in summer, including continental breakfast, and are a fair value. A restaurant and lounge serves lunch and dinner on some days.

B&Bs Cheaper options near downtown include the *Dierker House B&B* (☎ 520-774-3249), 423 W Cherry Ave, Flagstaff, AZ 86001, a 1914 antique-filled Craftsman house with three European-style rooms sharing a bath. You can grab something refreshing in the kitchen during the day. Rates are $45 to $65 a double. The *Birch Tree Inn* (☎ 520-774-1042, 888-774-1042, fax 520-774-8462, birch@flagstaff.az.us), 824 W Birch Ave, Flagstaff, AZ 86001, is a 1917 house with a wraparound verandah, a game room with billiards and an outdoor hot tub. Two rooms with shared bath are $69 and three more with private bath are $89 to $109, including a big breakfast and afternoon tea and snacks. A new place is the *Tree House B&B* (☎ 520-774-7598,

888-251-9390, rco@azaccess.com), 615 W Cherry Ave, Flagstaff, AZ 86001, with two suites, each with private entrance, bathroom, and sitting room with TV, both on the second floor of a 1915 home. Rates are $95 double, including breakfast served in your room and baked goods in the afternoon.

Away from downtown, *Jeanette's B&B* (☎ 520-527-1912, 800-752-1912, fax 520-527-1713), 3380 E Lockett Rd, Flagstaff, AZ 86004-4043, is a suburban home featuring ''30s style and grace.' Four rooms with private baths and eclectic art deco accouterments rent for $85 double. Jeanette is proud of her fine breakfasts.

The Christian *Arizona Mountain Inn* (☎ 520-774-8959), 685 Lake Mary Rd, AZ 86001 (a mile southeast of I-17), offers three B&B rooms with private baths. The 13 acres surrounding the inn have 16 cottages with baths, kitchens and fireplaces or stoves, ranging from one-bedroom A-frames to five-bedroom cabins. Rates are from $85 to $125. There are various outdoor activities available.

Places to Stay – Top End
Hotels Of several hotels charging more than $100 for a double in summer, the *Little America Motel* (☎ 520-779-7900, 800-352-4386, fax 520-779-7983), 2515 E Butler Ave, is one of the better ones, set amid acres of lawns and pine trees. The 250 spacious rooms have balconies, refrigerators and large TVs with Nintendo, and there is a pool, spa, and exercise room as well as a 24-hour coffee shop, a good restaurant and a lounge providing occasional entertainment. Rates are a good value at about $110 to $120; a few suites with fireplaces or saunas go up to about $200.

The *Radisson Woodlands Plaza Hotel* (☎ 520-773-8888, fax 520-773-0597), 1175 W Route 66, is the best hotel near downtown. The ambiance is trans-Pacific, with a Japanese restaurant and Southwestern coffee shop, severely square chandeliers and tightly clipped plants in the lobby, and contemporary desert colors in the guest rooms. Facilities include a pool, spa, sauna, steamroom and exercise equipment. Almost 200 large and attractive rooms are priced at $130 to $160 in summer; there are a few pricier suites. Room service is available and the restaurants are both very good.

The *Quality Inn* (☎ 520-774-8771, fax 520-773-9382), 2000 S Milton Rd, is a comfortable choice, offering most of the large, modern, Southwestern-style rooms with coffeemakers for $90 to $120 in summer. The hotel has a pool, and a 24-hour restaurant is next door.

Embassy Suites (☎ 520-774-4333, 520-774-0216, embassyflagstaff@thecanyon.com), 706 S Milton Rd, has 120 units with two rooms (bedroom and living room) and a kitchenette with a small microwave, refrigerator, coffeemaker and wetbar from $120 to $200 a double; prices include full breakfast and an evening cocktail hour. Most rooms are under $150. A spa and a pool are open in the summer, and there is an exercise room.

Comfi Cottages (☎ 520-774-0731, 888-774-0731) reservations at 1612 N Aztec, Flagstaff, AZ 86001, offers five quaint cottages, each with a kitchen stocked with your choice of breakfast items – cook your own whenever you feel like it. All cottages are about half a mile from downtown, with four around Beaver and Columbus Sts and one at 710 W Birch Ave. Most have gas fireplaces, washers and dryers, and all have yards or gardens with barbecue grills and bicycles available for use. Rents are $100 to $120 for the smaller cottages (with one bathroom and one or two bedrooms), $200 for the large one (with three bedrooms, two bathrooms, and sleeping up to six).

B&Bs The most upscale B&B is the *Inn at 410* (☎ 520-774-0088, 800-774-2008), 410 N Leroux, Flagstaff, AZ 86001, an elegant and fully renovated 1907 house with nine spacious bedrooms and two-room suites, each with private bath, coffeemaker and refrigerator, and most with a fireplace or whirlpool bath. This popular place charges $110 to $160 a double, including full gourmet breakfast and afternoon snacks.

Places to Eat
Summer tourists, winter skiers and year-round NAU students all influence the eating and entertainment scenes in Flag. Restaurants change their hours frequently and should be checked by phone out of season. Note that local laws prohibit smoking in all city restaurants.

Breakfast For breakfast (not to mention great coffees and light meals throughout the day), there are plenty of good choices in or near downtown. *Macy's* (☎ 520-774-2243), 14 S Beaver, a long-time favorite coffee shop, also serves good pastries and light meals. Students, outdoorsy types and coffee lovers crowd this place, which is open from 6 am to 8 pm daily and to 10 pm from Thursday to Saturday. Expect lines in the mornings – it's just a couple of blocks north of NAU. Neighboring *La Bellavia* (☎ 520-774-8301), 18 S Beaver, is equally casual, has just as much caffeine in its espressos and cappuccinos (though there are often breakfast lines here as well), and also serves quiches, pancakes, sandwiches etc. It is open from 6:30 am to 2:30 pm daily.

In the heart of downtown, *Cafe Express* (☎ 520-774-0541), 16 N San Francisco, has something for almost everyone except dedicated carnivores, including various coffees, vegetarian and natural-food meals and salads, juices, beer, wine, and pastries, which you can consume on the outdoor deck. It is open from 7 am to 10 pm and closes at 11 pm on Friday and Saturday. Opposite, *Kathy's* (☎ 520-774-1951), 7 N San Francisco, is a small, friendly place with good solid breakfasts, open from 6:30 am to 3 pm. The *Monte Vista Coffee Shop* (☎ 520-774-8211), in the historic hotel at 104 N San Francisco, is another good choice, open from 6:30 am to 6 pm.

American *Buster's* (☎ 520-774-5155), 1800 S Milton Rd (in the Greentree Village Shopping Plaza), has one of Flag's best fresh seafood selections, including an oyster bar, as well as steaks and prime rib. While most dinner entrées are in the teens, you can eat cheaper 'sunset dinners' between 6:30 and 7:30 pm (call to check hours). Inexpensive lunches include good salads, sandwiches and burgers. Its bar selection is excellent and Buster's is very popular (and often noisy) with locals and tourists. Hours are 11:30 am to 10 pm daily, and to 11 pm on Friday and Saturday.

The *Western Gold Dining Room* (☎ 520-779-2741), in the Little America Hotel at 2515 E Butler Ave, has a buffet at lunchtime and one of the best American dinner menus in town. Hours are 11 am to 2 pm, Monday to Friday, 5 to 10 pm daily, and 9 am to 2 pm for Sunday brunch.

Kelly's Christmas Tree (☎ 520-526-0776), 5200 E Cortland Blvd (in the Continental Shopping Plaza), has Christmas trees outside and an elegant turn-of-the-19th-century holiday air inside – don't ask me why. Chicken 'n dumplings and homemade pastries are house specialties and the rest of the menu is nicely varied. Most dinner entrées cost $10 to $20; hours are 11:30 am to 3 pm, Monday to Saturday, and 5 to 10 pm daily.

For big, old-fashioned steaks and beans ($15 to $24) in rustic 'singing cowboy' surroundings, head over to *Black Bart's Steak House Saloon & Musical Revue* (☎ 520-779-3142), 2760 E Butler Ave, open 5 to 10 pm daily and to 11 pm on Friday and Saturday (the cowboy music is no extra charge). For equally good steaks in a Western atmosphere without the singing hoopla, *Horseman Lodge Restaurant* (☎ 520-526-2655), 8500 N Hwy 89 (3 miles north of town), is a fine choice and is locally popular. It also has a wide selection of other American food.

New Frontiers Natural Foods & Deli (☎ 520-774-5747), 1000 S Milton Rd, has natural-food sandwiches, salads, soups, juices etc to go, or you can eat in the inexpensive deli. Hours are 9 am to 7 pm, Monday to Saturday, and 10 am to 6 pm on Sunday.

Several restaurants are open 24 hours. The *Little America Coffeeshop* (☎ 520-779-2741), 2515 E Butler Ave (in the top-end hotel), is perhaps the most upscale bet for food at 4 am. Other places to try for midnight munchies include *Perkins Family Restaurant* (☎ 520-779-1960), 1900 S Milton Rd, and the three *Denny's* at 2122 S Milton Rd (☎ 520-779-1371), 1996 E Route 66 (☎ 520-774-6795) and 2306 Lucky Lane (☎ 520-774-3413).

Mexican Of the dozen or so Mexican restaurants, *Salsa Brava* (☎ 520-774-1083), 1800 S Milton Rd, with Guadalajaran rather than Sonoran food, is a good, locally popular choice. Hours are 11:30 am to 9 pm, Monday to Thursday, to 11 pm on Friday, 8 am to 10 pm on Saturday, and 8 am to 9 pm on Sunday. It recently opened a second location at 2220 E Route 66 (☎ 520-779-5293) with a similar menu. Another good choice that is closer to Sonoran cuisine is *Kachina Downtown* (☎ 520-779-1944), 522 E Route 66, open from 11 am to 9 pm.

For cheaper Mexican food, *El Charro* (☎ 520-779-0552), 409 S San Francisco, is open 11 am to 9 pm, Monday to Saturday, and may have mariachis playing on weekends. The *Black Bean Burrito Bar* (☎ 520-779-9905), 12 E Route 66 (in a little alley/plaza), is a simple diner with big burritos and a few other items. Burrito fillings run from tofu to steak and are regular or large – the latter make a meal for anyone. You can eat in (no comfort here, but there's a good people-watching window) or take out. Most everything is $3 to $6. Hours are 11 am to 9 pm daily, to 2 am(!) on Friday and Saturday.

Italian *Mama Luisa* (☎ 520-526-6809), in the Kachina Square Shopping Center at 2710 E N Steves Blvd, is traditionally Flag's best Italian restaurant. Open for dinner only from 5 to 10 pm, Mama Luisa serves a wide range of Italian food for $9 to $18 in an appropriate cozy, red-checked-tablecloth setting. *Pasto* (☎ 520-779-1937), 19 E Aspen, has a courtyard and is vying with Mama Luisa for 'best Italian' honors. This popular little place is open from 5 to 10 pm Monday through Saturday, and 5 to 9 pm on Sunday.

Alpine Pizza (☎ 520-779-4109), 7 N Leroux, serves more than just pizza, has a pool table and is popular with young people. Hours are 11 am to 11 pm, to midnight on Friday and Saturday. *Ni-Marco's Pizza* (☎ 520-779-2691), 101 S Beaver, is open 11 am to 9 pm and is also popular with the student crowd. *Alpine Spaghetti Station* (☎ 520-779-4138), 2400 E Route 66, is a more family-oriented version of the downtown Alpine Pizza. It's open from 11:30 am to 9:30 pm, Monday to Saturday, and 4:30 to 10 pm on Sunday; they also deliver.

Asian The recommended Japanese *Sakura* (☎ 520-773-9118), in the Woodlands Plaza Hotel at 1175 W Route 66, has fresh seafood served either as sushi or grilled right in front of you. Steak and other food is also available sliced, diced and flamed tableside. Most entrées are in the teens. Hours are from 11:30 am to 2 pm and 5 to 10 pm daily except Sunday, when brunch starts at 10 am. At the other end of both the price range and the Asian continent is *Hassib's* (☎ 520-774-1037), 211 S San Francisco, which serves inexpensive Lebanese and Middle Eastern food from 11 am to 7 pm, Monday to Friday, and Saturday for lunch.

For Indian food, try the *Delhi Palace* (☎ 520-556-0019), 2700 S Woodlands Village Blvd, offering all-you-can-eat lunch buffets ($5.95) as well as à la carte items at dinnertime. Hours are 11:30 am to 2:30 pm and 5 to 10 pm.

New Zealand I've heard that New Zealand has six sheep for every person, which would explain why imported lamb ranks high on the menu of the *Down Under Restaurant* (☎ 520-774-6677), 413 N San Francisco (in the Carriage House Antique Mall). New Zealand wines, beers, venison, sea bass and mussels are among some of the imported foods available at this popular restaurant. Lunches ($3 to $9) include sausage rolls, meat pies and vegetarian frittata (a crustless quiche) served from 11 am to 3 pm. Dinners with entrées ranging from $10 to $24 are available from 5:30 to 9 pm.

Continental No roundup of Flag's restaurants is complete without the Cottage Place and Chez Marc, universally considered Flagstaff's two finest restaurants.

The *Cottage Place* (☎ 520-774-8431), 126 W Cottage Ave, has several intimate and pretty rooms in an early-20th-century house. The varied continental menu has entrées (including several vegetarian plates) ranging in price from the low teens to low $20s. The inviting and delicious appetizers pose a minor dilemma in that the entrées already include both soup and salad; it's best to come hungry. Hours are 5 to 9:30 pm and the restaurant is closed on Monday. Beer and wine are the only alcoholic beverages served.

The *Chez Marc Bistro* (☎ 520-774-1343), 503 N Humphreys, is classic French, complete with a French-born chef and a romantic, country-French atmosphere in a lace-curtained 1911 house. Dinner entrées are mainly in the high teens and low $20s and range from vegetarian to excellent seafood and meats. The extensive bar list includes French wines and single-malt scotches. It's a small, intimate place with fireplaces blazing inside in winter and an outdoor patio open in summer. Hours are 11:30 am to 3 pm and 5:30 to 9 pm. The owner recently opened *Marc's Café Americain* (☎ 520-556-0093), 801 S Milton, a modern American brasserie and wine bar, open from 11 am to 10 pm daily. The café serves a variety of innovative continental dishes, with prices around $7.50 for lunch and in the teens for dinner entrées.

Pub Grub Several bars near NAU serve decent food at reasonable prices, are popular with students (and professors) and often have entertainment later on, when food service can deteriorate. *Beaver Street Brewery* (☎ 520-779-0079), 11 S Beaver, is very popular for its microbrewery (five handmade ales are usually on tap) and well-prepared gourmet pizzas as well as other food. It opens at 11:30 am and has a beer garden in the summer. *Charly's* (☎ 520-779-1919), 23 N Leroux, on the ground floor of the historic Weatherford

Hotel, offers soups, salads and sandwiches for $4 to $8 as well as a small selection of steak, chicken and pasta dinners in the $11 to $16 range; it's perhaps overpriced but very convenient for the live music in two adjoining bars. Hours are 11 am to 10 pm.

Entertainment

For a relatively small town, Flagstaff has plenty going on. During the summer there are many cultural performances (see Special Events, earlier in this chapter) and skiers, students and passers-through seem to fuel a lively nightlife year-round. Read the Sundial (the Friday entertainment supplement to Flag's *Arizona Daily Sun*) and the free *Flagstaff Live* (published on the first and third Thursday of the month) to find out what's happening.

Half a dozen cinemas and multiplexes scattered around town show movies.

Flagstaff has plenty of bars, especially downtown, where you can relax to live music (usually for a $3 to $5 cover on weekends but often free during the week). Wander around a few blocks and make your choice. *Charly's* (see Places to Eat, above) and the *Exchange Pub* in the same building, have varied live music, ranging from bluegrass to blues, folk to fusion, jazz to jive. The *Monte Vista Lounge* (☎ 520-774-2403), in the Monte Vista Hotel at 100 N San Francisco, has good blues and alternative music. Next door to the hotel, the *Old Post Office* (☎ 520-214-9717), 106 N San Francisco, features live bands and DJs playing hip hop, techno and progressive sounds. The *Flagstaff Brewing Co* (☎ 520-773-1442), 16 E Route 66, and next door, *Monsoon's* (☎ 520-774-7929), 22 E Hwy 89, both have handcrafted beers and a variety of live rock & roll performances.

More sedate live music can be heard on weekends at the *Little America Lounge* (☎ 520-779-2741), 2515 E Butler Ave. For a livelier time, try the far-from-sedate country & western music, both live and recorded, at the *Museum Club* (☎ 520-526-9434), 3404 E Route 66. This popular barn-like place dates from the 1920s and '30s, and used to house a taxidermy

museum, which may account for its local nickname, 'The Zoo.' In the 1960s and '70s, big-name acts played here, but now mainly local country & western bands perform, usually at a $4 to $6 cover. For pure spectacle, The Zoo, with its open and friendly cowboy spirit and spacious dance floor (which the locals unsuccessfully try to hide with their huge Stetsons) is not to be missed. Check out the entrance, which is made from a single, forked trunk of a large ponderosa pine. The Zoo provides free roundtrip taxi service (☎ 520-774-2934) if you're planning on making a hard-drinkin' night of it.

Uptown Billiards (☎ 520-773-0551), 114 N Leroux, has plenty of pool tables and a good beer selection in a nonsmoking environment. The *Mad Italian Public House* (☎ 520-779-1820), 101 S San Francisco, is a decent pub with pool tables. Also shoot pool at the *Mogollon Brewing Company* (☎ 520-773-8950), 15 N Agassiz.

Shopping

For books about the Southwest and newspapers and magazines from all over, stop by McGaugh's Newsstand, 24 N San Francisco, open from 7:30 am to 9 pm, Monday to Saturday, and 8 am to 6 pm on Sundays. See Activities, earlier in this chapter, for stores that sell and rent outdoor equipment.

There are several galleries and crafts stores in the downtown area. Serious shoppers should stop by the Art Barn, Coconino Center for the Arts and the Museum of Northern Arizona to examine their selection of reliable arts and crafts, and then go comparison-shopping downtown.

Getting There & Away

Air America West Express has several flights a day to and from Phoenix. Flagstaff Pulliam Airport (☎ 520-556-1234) is 3 miles south of town on I-17.

Bus Greyhound (☎ 520-774-4573), 399 S Malpais Lane, sends buses between Flagstaff and Albuquerque (stopping in towns along I-40) four times a day; to Las Vegas (via Kingman and Bullhead City) every evening; to Los Angeles (via Kingman) twice a day; and to Phoenix five times a day.

Nava-Hopi Tours (☎ 520-774-5003, 800-892-8687), 114 W Route 66, has buses one to three times a day (depending on season) to the Grand Canyon for $12.50 one way, plus the national park entrance fee. Nava-Hopi also has buses to Phoenix stopping at Phoenix Airport ($22) and to Williams ($7).

There are no buses north to Page and Utah; however, the Grand Canyon International Hostel often runs a shuttle to the hostel in Page for $15 per person in season.

Train Amtrak (☎ 520-774-8679), 1 E Hwy 66, operates daily with its *Southwest Chief* service between Chicago, Illinois, and Los Angeles. Trains depart in the evening for Los Angeles (via Kingman) and in the morning for Chicago (via Winslow, Gallup and Albuquerque).

Getting Around

Bus Pine Country Transit (☎ 520-779-6624 between 8 am and 5 pm Monday to Friday) has three local routes running Monday to Friday between about 6 am and 6 pm. There is limited service on Saturday and no service on Sundays and major holidays. The visitor center has schedules.

Car Rental Flagstaff has offices of the following car-rental agencies: AAA Discount (☎ 520-774-7394); Avis (☎ 520-774-8421); Budget (☎ 520 779 0306); Enterprise (☎ 520-779-0494); Hertz (☎ 520-774-4452); National (☎ 520-779-1975); and Sears (☎ 520-774-1879).

Taxi In town, taxi service is provided by A Friendly Cab (☎ 520-774-4444), Sun Taxi (☎ 520-774-7400, 800-483-4488) and Arizona Taxi & Tours (☎ 520-779-1111). All of them provide long-distance service as well.

AROUND FLAGSTAFF

The places described here are within an hour's drive of Flagstaff. Also see Sedona

Grand Falls of the Little Colorado

The Grand Falls give an insight into Southwestern hydrography. The Little Colorado River is a minor tributary of the Colorado, and like many Arizonan rivers, it is nearly dry for much of the year. During spring runoff, however, the river swells and the Grand Falls come into being. The 185-foot drop is impressive, with muddy brown spray giving the falls their local nickname of 'Chocolate Falls.' The best time for viewing is March and April, although earlier in the year can be good if there has been enough winter precipitation. Occasional summer storms will also fill the falls.

The falls are on the Navajo Reservation. Drive 14 miles east of Flagstaff along I-40 to the Winona exit, then backtrack northwest about 2 miles to Leupp Rd. Head northeast on Leupp Rd for 13 miles to the signed turn for Grand Falls. An unpaved road, passable by car, leads 10 miles to the river and a quarter-mile trail goes to a falls overlook. At this time the Navajo tribe allows free access to the falls, where there are basic picnic facilities. ■

(earlier in this chapter) for Oak Creek Canyon, and the chapters on the Grand Canyon and Northeastern Arizona for longer day trips if your time is limited.

Sunset Crater National Monument

Sunset Crater (elevation 8029 feet) was formed in 1064-65 AD by volcanic eruptions that covered large areas with lava and much larger areas with ash. The devastation must have terrified the local people, who moved away after the main eruptions, returning a few decades later. Minor eruptions continued for more than 200 years, but no activity is predicted for the near future. Today, the Loop Rd (see below) goes through the Bonito Lava Flow and skirts the Kana-a Lava Flow. Overlooks and a mile-long interpretive trail enable visitors to get a good look at volcanic features, although walking on the unstable cinders of the crater itself is prohibited.

Combine your trip to Sunset Crater with a side trip to neighboring Wupatki National Monument for an excellent day-long excursion from Flagstaff, covering about 80 miles roundtrip.

Orientation Sunset Crater is reached by taking Hwy 89 north about 12 miles and then heading east on paved Hwy 545 (also known as the Sunset Crater/Wupatki Loop Rd). This leads through the monument and continues to and through Wupatki National Monument, rejoining Hwy 89 after 35 miles.

Information The visitor center (☎ 520-526-0502), about 2 miles from Hwy 89, houses a seismograph and other exhibits pertaining to volcanology and the region. Rangers give interpretive programs in summer. Hours are 8 am to 5 pm daily except Christmas. Admission is $3 for those over 16 and includes the Sunset Crater National Monument and the Wupatki National Monument (see below). A mile beyond the center is the Lava Flow Nature Trail, with a 1-mile interpretive trail (one-third mile via a short cut) across a lava field. The first 100 yards of the trail are wheelchair accessible.

No food or accommodations are available in the monument, but just west of the monument, the *Coconino National Forest Bonito Campground* has 44 sites for RVs and tents. The $10 sites have drinking water but no showers or hookups, and are available from April through September or October. Sites fill up on summer weekends, so come early.

Further information is available from the superintendent (☎ 520-556-7134), 2717 N Steves Blvd, Suite 3, Flagstaff, AZ 86004. (This office also supervises the Wupatki and Walnut Canyon National Monuments.)

Wupatki National Monument

This monument is off Hwy 89 about 30 miles north of Flagstaff, or can be reached by continuing along the Loop Rd from Sunset Crater. Wupatki has many Ancestral Puebloan sites that are different from those in most other national monuments in that they are freestanding rather than built into a cliff or cave. The pueblos have a distinct southern influence, indicating strong trading links with people from what is now southern Arizona and Mexico.

The pueblos seen today date mainly from the 1100s and early 1200s, although the area was inhabited from the 7th century. By about 1225, in common with many other Southwestern settlements, the people migrated from the area for reasons incompletely understood. Some of today's Hopi Indians are descended from the ancient inhabitants of Wupatki; the Hopi call their ancestors the Hisatsinom.

Information The narrow Loop Rd passes the visitor center and continues on past pullouts or short side roads that lead to the pueblos. Other pullouts along Loop Rd offer scenic views.

At the visitor center (☎ 520-679-2365), about 15 miles beyond Sunset Crater, there is a museum with exhibits interpreting the lives of the area's ancestral inhabitants as well as other exhibits of local interest, including a history of Navajo settlement in the area. The center's shop sells books and gifts but no food. In the summer, rangers may give talks or lead walks. Hours are 8 am to 5 pm (to 6 pm in summer) daily except Christmas.

There are no overnight facilities in the monument and the fee ($3 per person over 16) paid at Sunset Crater National Monument permits you to visit Wupatki as well. Golden Age, Access and Eagle Passes are honored.

Pueblos Of the hundreds of sites in the park, five pueblos are easily visited, and a sixth requires an overnight backpacking trip. The names of the pueblos are in the Hopi language, which doesn't always translate neatly into English. I give the approximate English equivalents where possible.

The largest of the pueblos, **Wupatki** ('tall house') is reached by a very short trail from the visitor center. Interpretive trail brochures are available for self-guided tours. The ball court found here is an example of the influence of more southerly cultures. From the Loop Rd just before reaching the visitor center, a 2½-mile side road leads to **Wukoki** ('wide house').

About 9 miles beyond the visitor center (5 miles from Hwy 89) there is a pullout with a short trail to **Citadel Pueblo**, which stands on top of a small hill, and the smaller nearby **Nalahiku** ('house outside the village'). Shortly after this pullout is a short road to the appropriately named **Lomaki** ('pretty house'). This is a well-preserved building reached by a quarter-mile trail that passes other smaller sites as it winds through Box Canyon. There are views of the San Francisco Mountains in the background.

Crack-in-the-Rock Pueblo can be visited only on a ranger-led, 16-mile round-trip, weekend backpacking tour; the trails pass petroglyphs and other sites en route. Trips are offered during weekends in April and October and cost $25. You must supply all equipment, food and water. Each trip is limited to 25 participants and these are chosen by a lottery system – you need to apply two months in advance to be included in the lottery. For further information about this trip, call the visitor center or write to Wupatki National Monument, Attention CIR Reservations, HC33, Box 444A, Flagstaff, AZ 86004.

Schultz Pass Road
This unpaved USFS road skirts the south flanks of the San Francisco Mountains and provides a longer but more scenic alternative to Hwy 89 during the summer. The road leaves Flagstaff from N Fort Valley Rd shortly past the Museum of Northern Arizona. Take Elden Lookout Rd to your right and in less than a mile you'll see Schultz Pass Rd (also called USFS Rd 420). Although unpaved, the road is passable to cars in the summer.

A drive down Schultz Pass Rd gives views of the San Francisco Mountains and access to the Kachina Peaks Wilderness Area, so named because of the religious significance of the mountains to the Hopi people. The road emerges at Hwy 89 about a mile south of the turn for the Sunset Crater/Wupatki Loop Rd.

Humphreys Peak
Arizona's highest mountain, the 12,663-foot Humphreys Peak in the San Francisco Mountains, is a reasonably straightforward though strenuous hike in summer and a snowy ascent for experienced outdoorspeople in winter. To get there in summer, drive up to the Arizona Snowbowl (see Downhill Skiing, below) and continue to the last parking lot near the Agassiz chair lift at 9500 feet. From the lift, a sign points the way. Note that this trail may be closed by the USFS. An alternative start is from a signed trail that leaves from the lower parking lot. The trails join in less than a mile.

The trail starts through forest, and eventually comes out above timberline where it is windy and cold, so hike prepared. The last mile of the trail is over crumbly and loose volcanic rock, so you'll need decent boots. The alpine tundra is very delicate, so it is essential that you stay on the trails; no camping or fires are allowed here. The elevation, steepness and loose footing make for a breathless ascent, but the views make the work worthwhile. The total distance is 4½ miles one way; allow six to eight hours roundtrip if you are in average shape.

Walnut Canyon National Monument
The Sinagua buildings at Walnut Canyon are not as immediately impressive as those at other nearby sites, but their spectacular setting makes this a worthwhile visit. The buildings are set in shallow caves in the near-vertical walls of a small limestone butte set like an island in the middle of the heavily pine-forested canyon.

The 1-mile-long **Island Trail** steeply descends 185 feet (with more than 200 stairs) and then encircles the 'island,' passing 25 cliff-dwelling rooms; many more can be seen in the distance. Before setting out on the Island Trail, consider that the 7000-foot elevation and the 185-foot steep climb out at the end could prove taxing for those with health problems.

A shorter, wheelchair-accessible **Rim Trail** affords several views of the rooms from a distance.

A visitor center (☎ 520-526-3367) is near the beginning of both trails and has a museum, bookstore and overlook. Rangers may give talks during the summer; the museum is open from 8 am to 5 pm (until 6 pm in summer) daily except Christmas. The Island Trail closes one hour before the visitor center. Admission is $3 per person over 16; Golden Age, Access and Eagle Passes are honored. You can eat at the picnic area, but no food or overnight facilities are available.

To get to the monument, drive 7 miles east of Flagstaff on I-40, take exit 204, then continue south for 3 miles. The monument is administered by the Sunset Crater/Wupatki superintendent.

Meteor Crater

This crater was once thought to be the remains of an ancient volcano, but scientists now agree that it was caused by a huge meteor crashing into our planet almost 50,000 years ago. The resulting crater, 570 feet deep and almost a mile across, was formed in the seconds after impact – it must have been one heck of a crash!

The cratered site was used as a training ground for some of the Apollo astronauts. Visit the on-site museum to see exhibits about meteors and space missions and to browse in the gift shop. Although you can't descend into the crater, you can walk the 3½-mile Rim Trail. However, apart from a big hole in the ground, there's not much to see and several readers suggest that it is an overpriced attraction.

The whole area (☎ 520-289-2362, 800-289-5898) is privately owned and operated. Hours are 6 am to 6 pm mid-May to mid-September and from 8 am to 5 pm the rest of the year. Admission is $8, $7 for seniors,

and $2 for six- to 17-year-olds. The crater is 40 miles east of Flagstaff; 5 miles south of exit 233 on I-40.

A coffee shop and picnic area are on the premises, and the *Meteor Crater RV Park* (☎ 520-289-4002) has 80 RV sites with hookups for $16 to $19 and a few tent sites for $12 to $14. Showers, coin laundry, a playground and groceries are available.

Lakes Southeast of Flagstaff

The Mormon Lake Ranger Station (see Information under Flagstaff) is the place to stop for information about the lakes and forests southeast of Flagstaff. Lakes are stretched out along paved S Lake Mary Rd (also called USFS Rd 3), beginning with **Upper Lake Mary**, 8 miles southeast of Flagstaff, and continuing with **Lower Lake Mary** and **Mormon Lake** about 25 miles away. Paved USFS Rd 82E leaves USFS Rd 3 between Lower Lake Mary and Mormon Lake and heads east 4 miles to **Ashurst Lake**. Other lakes can be reached by dirt roads.

The lakes vary greatly in size depending on local rainfall and water use (the Mary Lakes are formed by a dam on Walnut Creek). Upper Lake Mary usually has the most water and water-skiing is possible here. Fishing and boating are seasonal activities on the other lakes; call the ranger for current conditions.

Paved USFS Rd 3 continues south past Mormon Lake to the tiny community of Happy Jack (about 15 miles away), where the Long Valley Ranger Station (☎ 520-354-2216), HC 31, PO Box 68, Happy Jack, AZ 86024, provides information about the southern part of the Coconino National Forest. About 20 miles farther, USFS Rd 3 reaches Hwy 87, which goes to Payson.

Camping The Coconino National Forest operates the following campgrounds. Unless otherwise noted, all have drinking water but no showers or hookups, allow both tents and RVs, charge about $7 to $9 and are open May to September. They may fill on summer weekends, so arrive early.

Lake View, about 16 miles along USFS Rd 3 by Lower Lake Mary offers 30 sites and has a boat ramp. *Pine Grove*, with 46 sites, is a few miles farther and south of Lower Lake Mary. Nearby Ashurst Lake has boat ramps at *Ashurst* (23 sites) and *Forked Pine* (33 sites). *Dairy Springs* with 27 sites and *Double Springs* with 16 sites are both on the west side of Mormon Lake near the Mormon Lake Lodge (see Cross-Country Skiing, below) and are near a laundry. There are more campgrounds deeper into the Coconino National Forest, and free dispersed camping is allowed off dirt forest roads.

Skiing
Downhill Skiing at the Arizona Snowbowl (☎ 520-779-1951, snow report: 520-779-4577) is not world class, but it's pretty good, has been here more than 60 years and is popular with Arizonans. The elevation goes from 9200 to 11,500 feet, but only one chair lift makes this ascent and the highest runs are for experienced skiers only. Three shorter lifts and one tow offer intermediate and beginner skiing, and there are more than 30 runs. There are two day lodges: Hart Prairie, which offers lessons, ski rental and food, and the Agassiz Lodge, a quarter mile beyond, catering to experienced skiers only; no lessons or rentals are available, but there is food. The season begins sometime in December and ends sometime in April, depending on snow conditions.

All-day (9 am to 4 pm) lift passes cost $34, $19 for eight- to 12-year-olds, $14 for people over 65 and free if you are 70. Half-day (noon to 4 pm) passes are $21 on weekdays, $28 on weekends and $14 for kids and seniors. The ski school also has options ranging from beginners' two-hour group lessons, ski rental and an all-day pass for $50 to full-day private lessons costing $180 for one person and $80 for each additional person in your group. Snowboard rental with a two-hour lesson and an all-day pass is $60. Children's lessons are also offered.

During the summer, the longest lift (climbing to 11,500 feet) runs for sight-seeing from 10 am to 4 pm. The trip takes almost half an hour, provides fine views and costs $10 for adults, with discounts for seniors and kids ages six to 12.

To get to the Arizona Snowbowl, drive about 7 miles northwest of Flagstaff along N Fort Valley Rd (Hwy 180), then another 7 miles north on Snowbowl Rd. Sometimes the road from Hwy 180 to the Snowbowl requires chains or 4WD; ski buses for a few dollars are available. *Ski Lift Lodge & Stables* (☎ 520-774-0729, 800 472-3599) offers simple accommodations at this turn off.

Cross-Country The Flagstaff Nordic Center (☎ 520-779-1951), about 15 miles northwest of Flagstaff on Hwy 180 and affiliated with Arizona Snowbowl, offers nearly 30 miles of groomed trails, skiing lessons, rentals and food. Trail passes cost $10 for eight- to 69-year-olds (free for others) and snowshoers pay $5. If you continue past the Nordic Center, you'll find plenty of USFS cross-country skiing pullouts along Hwy 180, where you can park and ski for free (no facilities or rentals are provided). The season varies depending on snowfall but is generally not very long. Call the USFS to check conditions before you go.

Mormon Lake Ski Center (☎ 520-354-2240) is about 20 miles southeast of Flagstaff along S Lake Mary Rd and then 8 miles along USFS Rd 90. A day pass (10 am to 5 pm) for more than 20 miles of groomed trails costs $5 ($3 from 2 pm; group and family discounts are available) and the center offers ski rentals and lessons as well as snowshoe rentals. Call about moonlight tours on full-moon weekends.

The small *Mormon Lake Lodge* (☎ 520-774-0462, 520-354-2227) has a restaurant and rustic cabins for $40 to $95, depending on season and services. Snowmobiles are rented in winter, and during the summer there are cookouts, cowboy dinner theater and horseback rides.

WILLIAMS
Both the town and the mountain overlooking it were named after mountain man

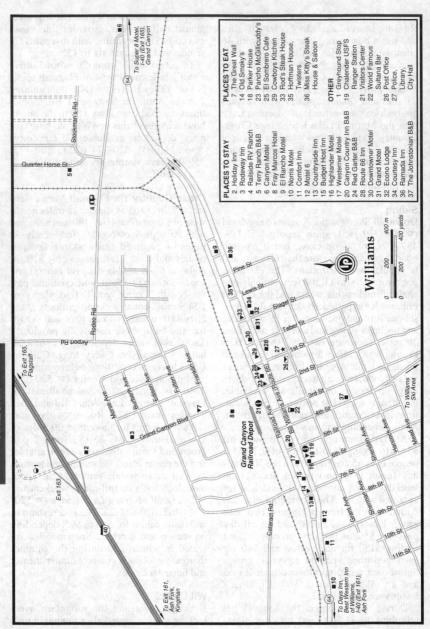

PLACES TO STAY

3   Holiday Inn
3   Rodeway Inn
4   Railside RV Ranch
5   Terry Ranch B&B
6   Canyon Motel
9   Fray Marcos Hotel
10 El Rancho Motel
11 Norris Motel
12 Motel 6
13 Countryside Inn
15 Budget Host Inn
16 Highlander Motel
17 Westerner Motel
20 Canyon Country Inn B&B
24 Red Garter B&B
28 Route 66 Inn
30 Downtowner Motel
31 Grand Motel
32 Econo Lodge
34 Courtesy Inn
36 Ramada Inn
37 The Johnstonian B&B

PLACES TO EAT

7   The Great Wall
14 Old Smoky's
18 Parker House
23 Pancho McGillicuddy's
25 El Sombrero Cafe
29 Cowboys Kitchen
33 Rod's Steak House
35 Hofman House;
    Twisters
36 Miss Kitty's Steak
    House & Saloon

OTHER

1   Greyhound Stop
19 Chalender USFS
    Ranger Station
21 Visitors Center
22 World Famous
    Sultana Bar
26 Post Office
27 Police;
    Library;
    City Hall

Williams

To Super 8 Motel,
I-40 (Exit 165),
Grand Canyon

To Exit 165,
Flagstaff

To Exit 163

To Exit 161,
Ash Fork,
Kingman

To Days Inn,
Best Western Inn
of Williams,
I-40 (Exit 161),
Ash Fork

To Williams
Ski Area

Grand Canyon
Railroad Depot

Stockman's Rd

Quarter Horse St

Rodeo Rd

Airport Rd

Pine St

Lewis St

Slagel St

Taber St

1st St

2nd St

3rd St

4th St

5th St

6th St

7th St

8th St

9th St

10th St

11th St

Morse Ave

Burbank Ave

Edison Ave

Fulton Ave

Franklin Ave

Railroad Ave

Bill Williams Ave (Route 66)

Sheridan Ave

Hancock Ave

Mead Ave

Grant Ave

Sherman Ave

Cataract Rd

Grand Canyon Blvd

0   200   400 m
0   200   400 yards

ARIZONA

Bill Williams, who passed through the area several times before his death in 1849. The first white settlers arrived in 1874, and Williams was soon ravaged several times by disastrous fires and developed a reputation as a lawless town. In 1901, when a railway to the Grand Canyon opened, Williams proclaimed itself 'The Gateway to the Grand Canyon' and began developing tourism, which is now the mainstay of the town's economy.

Eventually, roads became a cheaper way to visit the park, and the railway closed in 1969, only to return in 1989 as a popular historic steam train. Williams, 30 miles west of Flagstaff and 60 miles south of the Grand Canyon by good road, is the nearest town to the canyon with moderately priced lodging. The elevation is a cool 6770 feet.

Orientation & Information
The Business Loop of I-40 between exits 165 and 161 goes through downtown on Railroad Ave (westbound) and the parallel Bill Williams Ave (eastbound), the old Route 66. This becomes Hwy 64 en route to the Grand Canyon.

The visitor center (☎ 520-635-4061, 520-635-4207, fax 520-635-1417), 200 W Railroad Ave, is open from 8 am to 5 pm daily and is operated by both the chamber of commerce and the USFS. Pick up a walking tour brochure here if the turn-of-the-19th-century buildings downtown spark your interest. The Kaibab National Forest also has two ranger stations – Chalender (☎ 520-635-2676), 501 W Bill Williams Ave, and Williams (☎ 520-635-2633), behind the Best Western hotel west of town. The supervisor's office (☎ 520-635-8200) is at 800 S 6th.

The library (☎ 520-635-2263) is at 113 S 1st. The post office (☎ 520-635-4572) is at 114 S 1st. The police (☎ 520-635-4461) are at 113 S 1st.

Grand Canyon Deer Farm
This deer farm (☎ 520-635-4073, 800-926-3337), near I-40 exit 171, 8 miles east of town, is a petting and feeding zoo with several deer species, llamas, peacocks and

other animals. Fawning season (May to July) is a nice time to go with kids. Hours are 8 am to dusk June through August; 9 am to dusk March through May and September and October; and (weather permitting) 10 am to 5 pm November through February. It is closed on Thanksgiving and Christmas. Admission is $5 for adults, $3.75 for seniors and $2.75 for three- to 13-year-olds.

Grand Canyon Railway
The railroad uses turn-of-the-19th-century steam locomotives from late May through September and 1950s diesels the rest of the year. The trip is 2¼ hours to the Grand Canyon, with characters in period costume offering historical and regional narration, or strolling around playing a banjo and answering questions. Often, the train is held up by train robbers, but the sheriff usually takes care of them.

Roundtrips allow about 3½ hours at the canyon. Trains leave at 9:30 am daily except Christmas Eve and Christmas Day. A small museum, gift shop, breakfast area and cowboy performances at the Williams Train Depot (just north of the visitor center) make it worth getting there early. The train returns to Williams at 5:30 pm.

The fare was $3.95 when the railway opened in 1901. Today, most passengers travel coach class ($49.50 roundtrip, $19.50 for two- to 16-year-olds) in a 1923 car with free Coca Cola in a vintage bottle. Club Class (more room, free coffee, juice and pastries in the morning and a bar) is $64/34. First Class (reclining seats, continental breakfast, and afternoon champagne and snacks) is $114/84, and Deluxe Class (all the above plus seating in an upper-level, glass-dome car or in a luxury parlor car with access to an open-air rear platform) is $114; children are not allowed. Tax is an extra 8.8% and national park admission is $6 extra for adults. It's a short walk from the Grand Canyon train depot to the rim, but narrated bus tours of various lengths are also offered, as are various overnight packages with accommodations at either Williams or the Grand Canyon (hotel reservations essential). Contact the railway (☎ 520-773-1976, 800-843-8724, fax 520-773-1610) for more information or reservations.

Skiing

Williams Ski Area (☎ 520-635-9330), 4 miles south of town along 4th, has a poma lift that climbs from 7500 to 8150 feet and serves runs for beginner, intermediate and advanced skiers, as well as a few side trails. A short rope tow pulls beginners up the easiest slope. The lodge serves food and has a ski school as well as a downhill and cross-country ski and snowboard rental shop. The area is open from about mid-December until early April from 9:30 am to 4:30 pm from Thursday through Monday; during the schools' Christmas vacation it's open daily except Christmas Day. Full-day lift tickets are $21 on weekends and $16 midweek. Those over 60 and those 12 and under pay $16 on weekends and $13 midweek. For beginners using the rope tow only, prices are 25% less.

Try cross-country skiing in the Kaibab National Forest. Maintained trails are found at Spring Valley, 6 miles north of the Parks exit 178 on I-40 via USFS Rd 141. Stop by the forest ranger stations for information about undeveloped cross-country skiing areas, as well as snowshoeing, inner-tubing and sledding.

Other Activities

Play **golf** at the Elephant Rocks Golf Course (☎ 520-635-4936), a mile west of town near I-40 exit 161, with nine holes. Ask at the forest ranger station or visitor center about **hiking**, and see the following descriptions of camping areas under Places to Stay for **fishing** and **horseback riding** possibilities.

Special Events

Bill Williams Rendezvous Days over Memorial Day weekend features 'mountain man' events, such as shooting demonstrations using powder muskets as well as stage entertainment, a carnival, arts and crafts stalls, balloon rides, a parade and more. Apart from the usual fireworks display, the Fourth of July is celebrated with a carnival and barbecue. During the first weekend in August the town celebrates the Cowpuncher's Reunion & Old-Time Rodeo; another rodeo is scheduled over Labor Day weekend.

Places to Stay

Rates from mid-May to mid-September (given below) can be more than twice those charged in winter, and during special events, rates can climb even further. Reservations are advised in summer unless you arrive by early afternoon. See Tusayan in the Grand Canyon chapter for a reservation service that covers Williams and northern Arizona. There are more than 40 hotels and B&Bs; the following is a selection.

Places to Stay – Camping

Railside RV Ranch (☎ 520-635-4077), 877 Rodeo Rd, is the closest campground to the center, with 100 RV sites for about $20 with hookups; a handful of sites allow tents if the sites aren't taken by RVs. There's a $2 discount for tents and during the winter, and the campground offers showers, a game room and nightly Western entertainment in summer.

Near Cataract Lake, north of I-40 exit 161, *Cataract Lake County Park* (☎ 520-774-5139) offers 35 sites for $5 (May 1 to October 1) and boating/fishing access to the lake. *Red Lake Campground & Hostel* (☎ 520-635-9122, 800-581-4753, fax 520-635-5321, redlake@azaccess.com), on Hwy 64 eight miles north of I-40 exit 165, has 14 RV and eight year-round sites. Tenting costs $10, RVs with hookups cost $16 ($2 less from October to April), and there are coin showers, laundry and a grocery store. Summer reservations are recommended.

The *Circle Pines KOA* (☎ 520-635-4545, 800-732-0537, fax 520-635-2627), 1000 Circle Pines Rd (half a mile north of I-40 exit 167), has about 150 year-round sites ranging in price from $19 for tents to $25 for RVs with full hookups, and six Kamping Kabins available for $30. There are hot showers, a coin laundry, an indoor pool and spa, and a playground. Stable in the Pines (☎ 520-635-2626), at this campground, offers guided horseback rides from 30 minutes to all day, and can arrange overnight trips with advance notice. *Grand Canyon KOA* (☎ 520-635-2307, fax 520-635-9562), on Hwy 64 five miles north of I-40 exit 165, has 100 sites open from March through October at about the same price and with similar facilities (no stables).

The Kaibab National Forest operates the following campgrounds. All are open on a first-come, first-served basis from about May to October, with drinking water but no showers or RV hookups, and all offer fishing and boating (for those using paddles or small engines – call for limits) but no swimming. *Cataract Lake* is about a mile north of I-40 exit 161 (follow signs) and has 18 sites for $7. *Kaibab Lake*, almost 2 miles north on Hwy 64 from I-40 exit 165, has 70 sites for $11. Forest rangers give talks in summer, when the campground often fills early. To get to *Dogtown*, with 60 sites at $9, drive 4 miles south on 4th (becoming USFS Rd 173), then nearly 3 miles east on USFS Rd 140 and another mile on USFS Rd 132. To get to *White Horse Lake*, with 85 sites for $10, drive 9 miles south on 4th, then left about 8 miles southeast on USFS Rd 110, and left 3 miles more on USFS Rd 109.

Places to Stay – Budget
Red Lake Campground & Hostel (see above) has 32 hostel beds in rooms sleeping up to four people. Rates are $11 per person (more for private rooms) with winter discounts. The *Canyon Motel* (☎ 520-635-9371), on Rodeo Rd just off old Route 66 at the east end of town, has a Santa Fe Railroad carriage converted into a youth hostel, where 20 sleeper berths are available from April to October for $18 per person with showers, kitchen facilities and a pool. Simple motel rooms are about $50 in summer, $25 in winter. Early reservations are recommended at both hostels.

In Williams itself, you'll see a number of motels offering rooms for about $20 in winter, but in summer the same places charge $40 to $55 and fill up early. The most reliable of these include the 12-room *Highlander Motel* (☎ 520-635-2541, 800-800-8288), 533 W Bill Williams Ave; the *Budget Host Inn* (☎ 520-635-4415, 800-745-4415, fax 520-635-4781, budgethost@thegrandcanyon.com), 620 W Bill Williams Ave, with 26 rooms; and the 24-room *Courtesy Inn* (☎ 520-635-2619, 800-235-7029, fax 520-635-2610), 344 E Bill Williams Ave, which serves coffee and doughnuts for breakfast.

Other simple motels in the budget price range, all along Bill Williams Ave, include the *Downtowner Motel* (☎ 520-635-4041, 800-798-0071, downtowncr@thegrandcanyon.com), the *Grand Motel* (☎ 520-635-4601), the *Route 66 Inn* (☎ 520-635-4791, 888-786-6956, fax 520-635-4993, rt66inn@primenet.com), and the 24-room *Westerner Motel* (☎ 520-635-4312, 800-385-8608, fax 520-635-9313).

Places to Stay – Middle
The following have decent rooms for $50 to $70 in summer and reduced to $30 or less in winter. The pleasant *El Rancho Motel* (☎ 520-635-2552, 800-228-2370, fax 520-635-4173, elrancho@primenet.com), 617 E Bill Williams Ave, has 25 rooms with coffeemakers (some with microwaves and refrigerators) and a pool in summer. The *Norris Motel* (☎ 520-635-2202, 800-341-8000, fax 520-635-9202, ukgolf@primenet.com), 1001 W Bill Williams Ave, has a pool and spa, and all of its 33 rooms have refrigerators. Both of these hotels are a reasonable value for Williams and have free coffee, and both advertise 'British hospitality' (though they don't serve kippers and warm beer at odd hours of the day!).

Standard rooms at this price are also available at the 20-room *Rodeway Inn* (☎ 520-635-9127, 800-704-8083, fax 520-635-9801), 750 N Grand Canyon Blvd, the 42-room *Econo Lodge* (☎ 520-635-4085, fax 520-635-1326), 302 E Bill Williams Ave, and the *Motel 6* (☎ 520-635-9000, fax 520-635-2300), 831 W Bill Williams

Ave, the latter with an indoor pool and 50 better-than-average Motel 6 rooms. The independent *Countryside Inn* (☎ 520-635-4464, fax 520-635-1058), 710 W Bill Williams Ave, lacks a pool, but prices include a continental breakfast. It has some extra-large family rooms with refrigerators at a higher cost.

During summer, standard double rooms in the $70s and $80s are available at the *Comfort Inn* (☎ 520-635-4045, fax 520-635-9060, comfort@primenet.com), 911 W Bill Williams Ave, and the *Days Inn* (☎ 520-635-4051, fax 520-635-4411), 2488 W Bill Williams Ave, both of which have an indoor pool, a hot tub and more than 70 rooms. The *Super 8 Motel* (☎ 520-635-4700), 2001 E Bill Williams Ave, charges $70 to $80 for 40 doubles and has a pool.

Places to Stay – Top End
Hotels The *Ramada Inn* (☎ 520-635-4431, 800-462-9381, fax 520-635-2292), 642 E Bill Williams Ave, is very popular and its 96 attractive rooms are often full. The big draw here is the steak house (see Places to Eat, below), which offers entertainment. There is also a regular restaurant without music, and an outdoor pool and spa. Rooms cost around $90 to $120 in summer. The similarly priced *Best Western Inn of Williams* (☎ 520-635-4400, 800-635-4445, fax 520-635-4488), 2600 W Bill Williams Ave, sits pleasantly among pine trees a mile west of town. Its 79 rooms are large and attractive and have coffeemakers, and some pricier mini-suites are available. There is a seasonal pool and spa, and rates include a buffet breakfast; Denny's restaurant is next door. Also at this price, the *Holiday Inn* (☎ 520-635-4114, fax 520-635-26700), 950 N Grand Canyon Blvd, has well over 100 modern, large rooms as well as a pool, spa, sauna and restaurant/lounge.

The *Fray Marcos Hotel* (☎ 520-635-4010, fax 520-635-2180), 235 N Grand Canyon Blvd, is next to the Williams Grand Canyon Railway depot and is managed by the railway, which uses the hotel for a number of its overnight packages.

Although new, the hotel was built in the style of the original railroad hotel, part of which now forms a museum. About 90 large, attractive rooms rent for $119 a double in summer, $69 a double in winter and $99 a double in fall and spring. However, rooms are discounted if you buy a railway package.

Six miles east of Williams near I-40 exit 171, the *Quality Inn Mountain Ranch & Resort* (☎ 520-635-2693, fax 520-635-4188) features two tennis courts, an outdoor pool and spa (all seasonal), an outdoor game area and a restaurant and coffee shop; horseback rides are offered at extra cost. Most rooms have views of the forest or mountains and have TVs and in-room coffee. Rates are $90 for a single or double in summer, $60 in spring and fall; it closes in winter.

B&Bs The *Canyon Country Inn B&B* (☎ 520-635-2349, 800-578-1020, fax 520-635-9898), 442 W Bill Williams Ave, Williams, AZ 86046, has 13 rooms, pleasantly decorated with local arts and crafts. Summer rates are in the $75 to $95 range for a double with private bath. The *Johnstonian B&B* (☎ 520-635-2178), 321 W Sheridan Ave, Williams, AZ 86046, was built in 1900 and has four rooms priced from $65 to $110 in summer; three rooms share baths. Neither place allows smoking.

The smoke- and alcohol-free *Terry Ranch B&B* (☎ 520-635-4171, 800-210-5908, fax 520-635-2488, tranch@primenet.com), 701 Quarter Horse, Williams, AZ 86046-9520, has four rooms with turn-of-the-19th-century furnishings and private baths for $90 to $120 a double in summer. Downtown, the *Red Garter B&B* (☎ 520-635-1484, 800-328-1484), 137 W Railroad Ave, Williams, AZ 86046, also has four rooms with private baths in a restored 1890s bordello. Rates of $70 to $100 include a continental breakfast in the downstairs bakery. (The other B&Bs provide full breakfast.)

Places to Eat
Restaurant hours given below may be shortened in winter. For home-style break-

fasts, try *Old Smoky's* (☎ 520-635-2091), 624 W Bill Williams Ave, which is open from 6:30 am to noon, Monday to Saturday, and advertises 14 kinds of homemade breads as well as pancakes and cinnamon rolls. *Twisters* (☎ 520-635-0266), 417 E Bill Williams Ave, is a '50s-style 'Route 66' soda fountain with ice cream treats, hot dogs, burgers etc, served from 7 am to 10 pm in summer, 8 am to 8 pm in winter.

Simple family restaurants serving reasonably priced standard American food all day include the *Hoffman House* (☎ 520-635-9955), 425 E Bill Williams Ave, *Cowboys Kitchen* (☎ 520-635-2708), 117 E Bill Williams Ave, and *Parker House* (☎ 520-635-4590), 525 W Bill Williams Ave, all open 6 am to 9 or 10 pm, and *Denny's* (☎ 520-635-2052), 2550 W Bill Williams, open 24 hours a day.

Pancho McGillicuddy's (☎ 520-635-4150), 141 W Railroad Ave, is a 'Mexican cantina' popular with tourists; it also serves gringo food and has a patio outside. The restaurant is housed in one of the town's oldest buildings – constructed of stone in 1895, the building survived several fires that burned down other buildings in this block. This was once known as 'Saloon Row' with many bars, brothels and opium dens along here. If only walls could talk . . . Summer hours are noon to 10 pm and the cantina often has live entertainment. For Mexican and New Mexican food without the frills, try *El Sombrero Cafe* (☎ 520-635-9284), 126 E Railroad Ave, open for lunch and dinner daily except Tuesday. For Chinese food, there's *The Great Wall* (☎ 520-635-2045), 412 N Grand Canyon Blvd, open from 11:30 am to 8 pm, Monday to Friday, and 4 to 8 pm on Saturday.

At the Ramada Inn, *Miss Kitty's Steak House & Saloon* (☎ 520-635-9161) features live western or country & western bands most nights in the summer and on weekends in winter, and strives to make the atmosphere as Western as possible. Hours are 6 am to 2 pm (sorry, no singing cowboys at breakfast) and 5 to 10 pm. For a steak without all the hoopla, *Rod's Steak House* (☎ 520-635-2671), 301 E Bill

Williams Ave, has been here half a century and is the best place in town. Apart from good steaks priced in the teens, there are cheaper chicken and fish dinners and a kids' menu. Hours are 11:30 am to 9:30 pm (10 pm in summer).

Entertainment
Apart from those restaurants mentioned above, some of the 'old town' bars may have live music on weekends. Check out the *World Famous Sultana Bar* (☎ 520-635-2021), 301 W Bill Williams Ave, in a 1912 building with a checkered history, for '50s Route 66 theme nights.

Getting There & Away
Bus Greyhound (☎ 520-635-0870) has a morning eastbound bus and an afternoon westbound bus traveling on I-40, stopping at Williams Chevron gas station at 1050 N Grand Canyon Blvd. Nava-Hopi Tours (see Organized Tours in the Flagstaff section) stop at the Grand Canyon Railway depot on the way to and from the Grand Canyon (tickets are $9) and Flagstaff (tickets are $7).

Train Amtrak does not stop here; the only service is the Grand Canyon Railway.

Car Apart from the main highways, drivers enjoy the scenic Perkinsville Rd. This leaves town south along 4th and heads through forests and river valleys to Jerome, almost 50 miles away. Only the first half is paved, but ordinary cars can negotiate the unpaved section except after heavy rain or snow. See Annerino's *Adventuring in Arizona* for a detailed description.

ASH FORK
The countryside becomes flatter and grassier west of Williams. The small town of Ash Fork, 20 miles west along I-40, is home to about 1000 people and is a cattle ranching center. If you pull off the freeway and drive through town, you'll see big piles of stone slabs. These are Kaibab slate, a resource that leads Ash Fork to dub itself 'The Flagstone Capital of America.' Take

Hwy 89 south from Ash Fork to reach Prescott in 52 miles.

Orientation & Information

Ash Fork is north of I-40 between exits 144 and 146. The main streets are Lewis Ave (old Route 66, one way westbound) and Park Ave (one way eastbound). A tourism office (☎/fax 520-637-2442) on Park Ave is open intermittently.

Places to Stay & Eat

KOA (☎ 520-637-2521, fax 520-637-9869), three-quarters of a mile east of exit 144, has 75 tent and RV sites from $15.50 to $19.50 and a couple of Kamping Kabins ($26) year-round. Facilities include a pool, showers, playground and recreation area, but not all are open in winter. *Hillside RV Park* (☎ 520-637-2300), by the Exxon gas station near exit 144, is cheaper, especially for tenters.

The cheap and basic motels aren't much. *Ashfork Inn* (☎ 520-637-2514) on Lewis near exit 144, with more than 30 rooms in the $20s and $30s, looks like the best. Also try the *Copperstate Motel* (☎ 520-637-2335), 101 E Lewis; *Hi Line Motel* (☎ 520-637-2766), 124 E Lewis Ave; and the *Stagecoach Motel* (☎ 520-637-2551), 823 Park Ave.

The *Bull Pen Restaurant* (☎ 520-637-2330), on Park near exit 146, draws inter-state traffic 24 hours a day.

SELIGMAN

This small town (about 850 inhabitants) dates from 1886 when it became a railway town. Today, Seligman is of interest as one end of the longest remaining stretch of historic Route 66, the approximately 90 miles between Kingman and Seligman (compared to 70 miles along I-40). On the last weekend in April, a Route 66 Fun Run leaves Seligman westbound along Route 66 to Kingman (see the Western Arizona chapter). Everything seems to be along the main street, Chino Ave, including a Route 66 memorabilia store and a visitor center near the Deluxe Inn.

Places to Stay & Eat

KOA (☎/fax 520-422-3358) at the east end of town has 70 tent and RV sites for $15 to $20 and two Kamping Kabins for $28. There is a pool.

There are half a dozen inexpensive and basic motels along Chino Ave dating from the heyday of Route 66. These places include, in alphabetical order, the *Bil Mar Den Motel* (☎ 520-422-3470), the *Comfort Lodge* (☎ 520-422-3255), the *Deluxe Inn* (☎ 520-422-3244), the *Romney Motel* (☎ 520-422-3700), the *Historic Route 66 Motel* (☎ 520- 422-3204, fax 520-422-3581), and the *Supai Motel* (☎ 520-422-3663). Of these, the Route 66 Motel is considered to be the best with 15 rooms in the $50s – you are paying for the historic name.

The *Copper Cart Restaurant* (☎ 520-422-3241), 'downtown' on Chino Ave, serves American breakfasts, lunches and dinners and is the best. *Delgadillo's Snow Cap* (☎ 520-422-3291) is the traditional place for a '50s-style malt or milkshake.

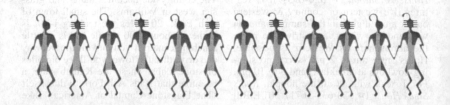

Northeastern Arizona

Some of Arizona's most beautiful and photogenic landscapes lie in the northeastern corner of the state. Between the fabulous buttes of Monument Valley on the Utah state border and the fossilized logs of the Petrified Forest National Park at the southern edge of the area lie lands that are locked into ancient history. Here is the Navajo National Monument, with ancient and deserted pueblos, and Canyon de Chelly, with equally ancient pueblos adjacent to contemporary farms. Here are mesas topped by some of the oldest continuously inhabited villages on the continent. Traditional and modernized Navajo hogans dot the landscape and Hopi kivas nestle into it. (Hogans are octagonal, usually earth-covered homes made of wood and earth, with the door facing east.) Native Americans have inhabited this land

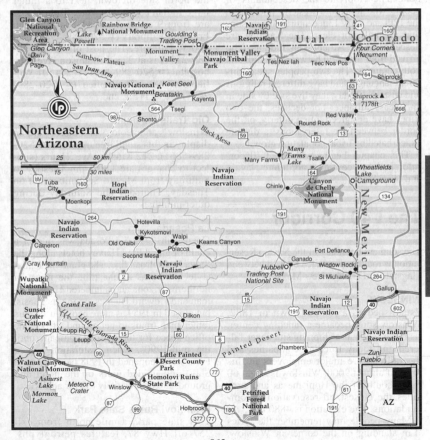

for many centuries; it is known today as the Navajo and Hopi Indian Reservations.

Tribal laws take precedence over state laws, although both tribes accept federal laws and are fiercely proud and patriotic citizens. The Navajo Indian Reservation is the biggest in the USA and spills over into the neighboring states of Utah, Colorado and New Mexico. It completely surrounds the Hopi Indian Reservation. It's the biggest reservation partly because its harsh landscape didn't seem to offer much when reservations were doled out.

The Navajo and Hopi are recent neighbors. The Hopi are the descendants of people who left more westerly pueblos in the 12th and early 13th centuries for reasons that are still not clear. The Navajos are descendants of Athapaskan Indians who arrived from the north between the 14th and 16th centuries. The two peoples speak different languages and have different religions and customs. Today, they live side by side in an uneasy alliance. For decades, the two tribes have disagreed, often bitterly, on the border between the reservations, a dispute exacerbated by tribal population growth.

This chapter begins with the I-40 corridor, and then continues north into Navajo and Hopi lands.

The I-40 Corridor

The southern boundary of the Navajo Reservation is roughly paralleled by I-40 between Flagstaff and Gallup, New Mexico.

WINSLOW
Established as a railroad town in 1882, Winslow soon became a ranching center. Its importance as a shipping site never faltered and today trucking companies and the railroad are major employers in this town of almost 9000. Winslow is about 60 miles south of the Hopi mesas and provides the closest off-reservation accommodations. The elevation is 4880 feet.

Many people may remember the lyrics 'I'm standing on the corner in Winslow,

Arizona, such a fine sight to see' from the '70s song *Take It Easy*, by the Eagles. The famous corner is downtown on old Route 66 at Kinsley Ave and 2nd and is in the heart of the oldest part of Winslow.

Orientation & Information
Old Route 66 (2nd and 3rd Sts) is the main drag through town and runs east-west parallel to and south of I-40 between exits 252 and 255. Second is one-way eastbound and 3rd is one-way westbound.

The chamber of commerce (☎ 520-289-2434, fax 520-289-2435) is by exit 253 on the north side of town, next to a rather large Indian carving by Peter Toth. Hours are from 9 am to 5 pm Monday through Friday. The library (☎ 520-289-4982) is at 420 W Gilmore. The post office (☎ 520-289-2131) is at 223 Williamson Ave. The hospital (☎ 520-289-4691) is at 1501 Williamson Ave. The police (☎ 520-289-2431) are at 115 E 2nd.

Old Trails Museum
Winslow's archaeology and history are on display in this small free museum (☎ 520-289-5861), 212 Kinsley Ave. Hours (subject to change) are 1 to 5 pm Tuesday to Saturday from May to September and on Tuesday, Thursday and Saturday during other months.

La Posada
Opened in 1930, La Posada was one of a chain of grand Fred Harvey hotels along the Santa Fe Railroad line. The grand hacienda-style hotel was at one time the finest in northern Arizona and numbered Harry Truman and Howard Hughes among its guests, but closed in 1959 as more people used cars rather than trains to get around. It became office space for the railroad company until the mid-1990s, when restoration began. Parts were reopened in 1998 (see Places to Stay) and guided tours of the hotel and grounds are offered daily ($5 for adults).

Homolovi Ruins State Park
This state park, a mile north from exit 257 off Hwy 87, features petroglyphs,

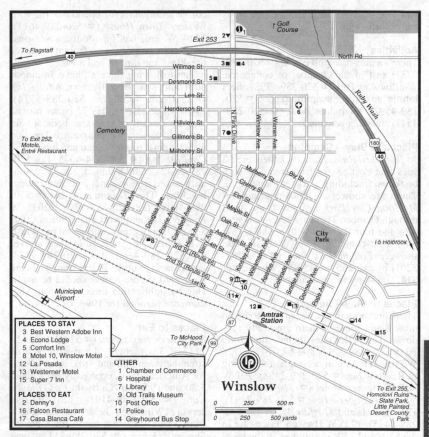

PLACES TO STAY
3 Best Western Adobe Inn
4 Econo Lodge
5 Comfort Inn
8 Motel 10, Winslow Motel
12 La Posada
13 Westerner Motel
15 Super 7 Inn

PLACES TO EAT
2 Denny's
16 Falcon Restaurant
17 Casa Blanca Café

OTHER
1 Chamber of Commerce
6 Hospital
7 Library
9 Old Trails Museum
10 Post Office
11 Police
14 Greyhound Bus Stop

Winslow

0   250   500 m
0   250   500 yards

ARIZONA

hundreds of small dwellings and four larger Pueblo sites attributed to the ancestors of the Hopi. Currently the eroded sites are under investigation, and federal laws prohibit the removal or disturbance of any artifacts found here. You will find unpaved roads and signed trails to many of the sites.

There is a visitor center open daily from 8 am to 5 pm. Day use is $3 per vehicle; see Places to Stay (below) for details about camping.

You can obtain more information from Homolovi Ruins State Park (☎ 520-289-4106), HC-63, Box 5, Winslow, AZ 86047.

McHood City Park

The Clear Creek Reservoir offers fishing, boating, swimming, picnicking and camping (see Places to Stay). Day use is $3 per vehicle.

Head south on Williamson Ave for about 1 mile (it becomes Hwy 87), turn left on Hwy 99 and continue for 4 miles to reach the park. For more information call the city parks office (☎ 520-289-4792) or recreation manager (☎ 520-289-3204).

Little Painted Desert County Park

This park (☎ 520-524-4251 in Holbrook) is 13 miles north from exit 257 on Hwy 87, and offers picnic facilities, walking trails and colorful views.

Activities
There's a nine-hole **golf** course (☎ 520-289-6737) east of the chamber of commerce. Winslow City Park (☎ 520-289-4792) offers **tennis**, an outdoor **swimming** pool (☎ 520-289-4592), an indoor pool (☎ 520-289-4543) and other activities.

Places to Stay – Camping
At *Homolovi Ruins State Park* there are 52 sites that cost $8 for tents and $13 with hookups (including park entrance fee). There are showers. The campground at *McHood City Park* is open from April through October. There are seven tent sites ($6) and four RV sites with hookups ($7) on a first-come, first-served basis, and showers. *Freddie's RV Park* (☎ 520-289-3201) by exit 255 has 45 RV-only sites for $14, and showers are available.

Places to Stay – Budget
There are more than a dozen old Route 66 motels and some of them are pretty run-down. The better ones include the *Motel 10* (☎ 520-289-3211, 800-675-7478), 725 W 3rd, with a family restaurant adjoining it; *Winslow Inn* (☎ 520-289-2458), 701 W 3rd; *Westerner Motel* (☎ 520-289-2825), 500 E 3rd; *Super 7 Inn* (☎ 520-289-2491), 1216 E 3rd; and *Mayfair Motel* (☎ 520-289-5445), 1925 W Hwy 66. Prices are in the $20s and $30s in summer, in the teens and $20s in winter.

Places to Stay – Middle
Several chain motels provide the best lodging, with summer prices substantially lower than in Flagstaff, 60 miles away. Expect off-season discounts of $10 to $15. Posted summer prices for the following hotels are about $50 to $70 a double.

The *Econo Lodge* (☎ 520-289-4687, fax 520-289-9377), 1706 N Park Drive, has 73 standard rooms. There is a seasonal pool, coin laundry and free coffee. The *Super 8 Motel* (☎/fax 520-289-4606), 1916 W 3rd, has 46 rooms and provides coffee and donuts for breakfast. The *Best Western Town House* (☎ 520-289-4611), 1914 W 3rd, has 68 rooms, a seasonal pool, coin laundry, a restaurant open for breakfast and dinner, and a bar.

The following three all have an indoor pool and spa. *Best Western Adobe Inn* (☎ 520-289-4638, fax 520-289-5514), 1701 N Park Drive, has 72 better rooms, all with queen- or king-size beds; a coin laundry; restaurant (open 6 am to 2 pm and 4 to 10 pm); room service and a bar. The *Comfort Inn* (☎ 520-634-4045, fax 520-289-5642), 520 Desmond, has 55 reasonably sized rooms and free continental breakfast. The 62-room *Days Inn* (☎ 520-289-1010, fax 520-289-5778), 2035 W Hwy 66, is the newest chain in town, has a guest laundry and continental breakfast.

The historic *La Posada* (see above) (☎ 520-289-4366, fax 520-289-3873, laposada@igc.org), 303 E 2nd, is being renovated. Some rooms should be available by publication time for $65 to $85; more are planned for 1999.

Places to Eat
The *Falcon Restaurant* (☎ 520-289-2342), 1113 E 3rd (actually located on a little street between 2nd and 3rd), is my choice for American food, open daily from about 5:30 am to 9:30 pm. Or try the *Casa Blanca Cafe* (☎ 520-289-4191), 1201 E 2nd, serving Winslow's best Mexican meals from 11 am to 9 pm (noon till 8 pm on Sunday). *Entré* (☎ 520-289-2141), near I-40 exit 252, serves good Chinese and American food from 11 am to 9:30 pm daily. *Denny's* (☎ 520-289-5117), at I-40 exit 253, is open 24 hours.

The hotel restaurants are adequate and there are several other inexpensive places around.

Getting There & Away
Greyhound (☎ 520-289-2171) stops at the Easy 8 Motel, 1000 E 3rd, a few times a day on its east- and westbound trips along I-40.

Amtrak (☎ 800-872-7245) has a morning eastbound train and an evening westbound train. There is no ticket office; call Amtrak for information.

HOLBROOK

Named after a railroad engineer, Holbrook was established in 1881 when the railroad reached this point. It soon became an important ranching center and the Navajo County seat. The proximity of the Petrified Forest National Park has added tourism to the town's economic profile. The elevation is 5080 feet and about 6000 people live here.

Information

The chamber of commerce (☎ 520-524-6558, 800-524-2459) is in the county courthouse at 100 E Arizona. The library (☎ 520-524-3732) is at 451 1st Ave. The post office (☎ 520-524-3311) is at 216 E Hopi Drive. The small medical center (☎ 520-524-3913) is at 500 E Iowa. The police (☎ 520-524-3991) are at 100 E Buffalo. The Greyhound bus (☎ 520-524-3832) stops at the Circle K Store at 101 Mission Lane several times a day heading east and west along I-40.

Things to See & Do

The **Navajo County Museum** is operated by the chamber of commerce in the 1898 county courthouse, 100 E Arizona. You can see the old city jail and learn about the area's history, which was pretty wild in the 19th century and rivals Tombstone's for sheer bloodiness. Visitors can obtain an invitation to a public hanging or stop by the nearby Bucket of Blood Saloon. The museum is free and worth a look. Hours are 8 am to 5 pm Monday to Friday. In summer, hours are extended to 8 pm and the museum is open from 8 am to 5 pm on Saturday. **Native American dancers** perform for free (tips appreciated) outside the museum at 7 pm from early June through mid-August. Photography is permitted. The chamber has a brochure describing the courthouse and other historic buildings nearby.

Play **golf** at the Hidden Cove Golf Course (☎ 520-524-3097), 2 miles north of I-40 exit 283. There is a **swimming pool** (☎ 520-524-3331) in the park at 507 7th.

Seventeen miles from town, **Rock Art Canyon Ranch** (☎ 520-288-3260), is a working ranch that offers tours of Chevelin Canyon, which contains many ancient petroglyphs. Horseback riding, wagon rides, a pioneer museum and other activities are offered at very reasonable prices, depending on the size of the group. Call for directions.

Special Events

The annual city festival is Old West Days in early June. The Navajo County Fair and Rodeo takes place in mid-September.

Places to Stay

With about 1200 rooms and 300 campsites, Holbrook offers plenty of accommodations, usually at attractive prices. Even in summer, you can find cheap lodging here. Light sleepers should note that Hopi Drive parallels the railway tracks.

Places to Stay – Camping

The *Holbrook KOA* (☎ 520-524-6689), 102 Hermosa Drive, is northwest of I-40 between exits 286 and 289. They have more than 100 tent and RV sites, showers, a pool, recreation room, playground and coin laundry. Rates are $18 to $22, with a small discount from mid-September to mid-May when the pool is closed. Kamping Kabins are $27. Summer reservations are suggested. The *OK RV Park* (☎ 520-524-3226), 1576 Roadrunner Rd, has showers and more than 100 tent and RV sites for $18.

Cholla Lake County Park (☎ 520-524-4251, 520-288-3717), 10 miles west of Holbrook (take I-40 exit 277 and follow signs to the south and east) has 12 $8 tent sites and eight $12 RV sites with partial hookups, with big discounts for stays of four days or longer. Day use costs $3. There are showers, a playground, a boat launch and fishing.

Places to Stay – Budget

Several hotels have basic rooms in the $20s, or even in the teens, year-round except during the County Fair.

ARIZONA

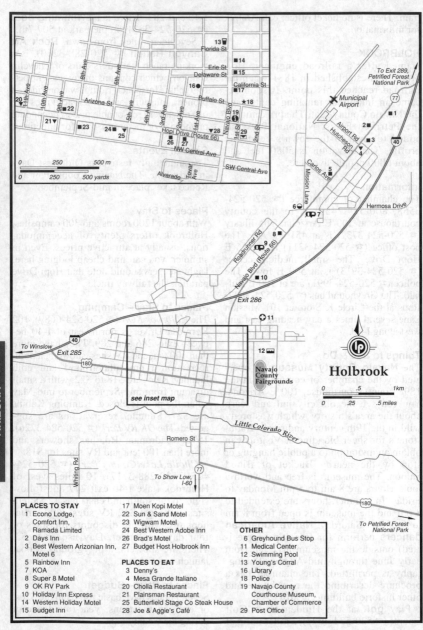

Holbrook

PLACES TO STAY
1 Econo Lodge,
   Comfort Inn,
   Ramada Limited
2 Days Inn
3 Best Western Arizonian Inn,
   Motel 6
5 Rainbow Inn
7 KOA
8 Super 8 Motel
9 OK RV Park
10 Holiday Inn Express
14 Western Holiday Motel
15 Budget Inn

17 Moen Kopi Motel
22 Sun & Sand Motel
23 Wigwam Motel
24 Best Western Adobe Inn
26 Brad's Motel
27 Budget Host Holbrook Inn

PLACES TO EAT
4 Mesa Grande Italiano
20 Cholla Restaurant
21 Plainsman Restaurant
25 Butterfield Stage Co Steak House
28 Joe & Aggie's Café

1 Denny's

OTHER
6 Greyhound Bus Stop
11 Medical Center
12 Swimming Pool
13 Young's Corral
16 Library
18 Police
19 Navajo County
   Courthouse Museum,
   Chamber of Commerce
29 Post Office

A selection of the cheapest places includes *Brad's Motel* (☎ 520-524-6929), 301 W Hopi Drive; the *Budget Host Holbrook Inn* (☎ 520-524-3809), 235 W Hopi Drive; the *Moen Kopi Motel* (☎ 520-524-6848), 464 Navajo Blvd; and the *Western Holiday Motel* (☎ 520-524-6216, fax 520-524-1521), 720 Navajo Blvd. The *Sun & Sand Motel* (☎ 520-524-2186, fax 520-524-2360), 902 W Hopi Drive, has a seasonal pool, as does the *Budget Inn* (☎ 520-524-6263), 602 Navajo Blvd. There are others.

Devotees of historic Route 66 schlockabilia won't want to miss the *Wigwam Motel* (☎ 520-524-3048), 811 W Hopi Drive. This motor court has a village of concrete wigwams doubling as rooms, each with restored 1950s-era furniture. Quite a sight! Rates start around $30 and the place may close in winter.

There's a *Motel 6* (☎ 520-524-6101, fax 520-524-1806) at 2514 Navajo Blvd that has a pool and 126 rooms for $27/31 for singles/doubles. This is Holbrook's biggest motel.

Places to Stay – Middle

The *Rainbow Inn* (☎ 520-524-2654, 800-551-1923), 2211 Navajo Blvd, is a standard clean motel and the only one in category that isn't part of a chain. Double rooms are about $40 for one queen-size bed or a little more for two beds. All rooms have refrigerators.

The remaining chain hotels all have pools. Although I give posted summer rates, many of the hotels in this section will drop their rates into the $30s and $40s if things are slow, even in summer. The *Super 8 Motel* (☎ 520-524-2871, fax 520-524-3514), 1989 Navajo Blvd, has a spa, coin laundry and $48 doubles. In-room coffee and breakfast pastries are included. The *Econo Lodge* (☎ 520-524-1448), 2596 Navajo Blvd, has a restaurant and standard rooms in the $40s including coffee and pastries. The *Best Western Adobe Inn* (☎ 520-524-3948, fax 520-524-3612), 615 W Hopi Drive, has rooms in the $50s with continental breakfast. The *Ramada Limited* (☎ 520-524-2566, fax 520-524-6427), 2608 Navajo Blvd, has an indoor pool/spa and rooms in the $50s including continental breakfast.

The *Days Inn* (☎ 520-524-6949, fax 520-524-6665), 2601 Navajo Blvd, has an indoor pool/spa and comfortable modern rooms in the $50s, including continental breakfast. Mini-suites with refrigerator and

ARIZONA

the $60s and $70s. The
zonian Inn (☎ 520-524-
-2253), 2508 Navajo Blvd,
ms for $50 to $65 and
adjoins the 24-hour Denny's restaurant. The
Comfort Inn (☎ 520-524-6131, fax 520-524-
2281), 2602 Navajo Blvd, also has a 24-
hour restaurant and includes free continental
breakfast. Rooms, some of which have microwaves and refrigerators, are in the $50s
and $60s. The *Holiday Inn Express* (☎ 520-
524-1466, fax 520-524-1788), 1308 Navajo
Blvd, has an indoor pool/spa and rooms for
about $60 including continental breakfast.

Places to Eat

There are many cheap and unremarkable
places to eat, mostly serving American food.
The *Plainsman* (☎ 520-524-3345), 1001 W
Hopi Drive, serves inexpensive breakfast,
lunch and dinner. The basic-looking and
cheaper *Cholla Restaurant* (☎ 520-524-
3529), 1102 W Hopi Drive, seems locally
popular and serves Mexican and American
food from 5 am to 9 pm. *Joe & Aggie's Cafe*
(☎ 520-524-6540), 120 W Hopi Drive, is an
inexpensive Mexican restaurant. The restaurants next to the Best Western Arizonian Inn
and the Comfort Inn are open 24 hours.

The best places in town include the *Butterfield Stage Co Steak House* (☎ 520-524-
3447), 609 W Hopi Drive, which is open
from 4 to 10 pm daily, and from 11 am in
summer. The steaks are in the teens and
there is a salad bar and seafood. Also good
is the *Mesa Grande Italiano* (☎ 520-524-
6696), 2318 Navajo Blvd, with the best
Italian food for miles around. Its hours are
11 am to 9 pm and meals are $5 to $13.

Entertainment

Young's Corral (☎ 520-524-1875), 865
Navajo Blvd, is a bar that sometimes has
live music and dancing on weekends.

PETRIFIED FOREST NATIONAL PARK

On my first visit many years ago, I had the
naive impression that some of the trees here
would still be standing in little glades,
eerily frozen in time. Parents traveling with
small kids might avoid major disappoint-

ment by explaining that the 'forest' is actually a bunch of horizontal fossilized logs,
some broken up, scattered around over a
large area. Nevertheless, they are impressive: some are greater than 6 feet in diameter and at least one spans a ravine, forming
a fossilized bridge.

The trees are conifers that date from the
Triassic (225 million years ago) and were
contemporary with ancient reptiles (some
fossils of which are seen in the visitor centers) and predate the dinosaurs. Washed by
floods into this area, logs were buried by
mud and then volcanic ash, and later became fossilized by the action of mineral-
laden water that left colorful deposits around
the wood cells. Slowly, these deposits turned
into stone. Much more recently, the area was
uplifted, which caused many of the logs to
break. Erosion then exposed the logs.

Before 1906, when parts of the forest
were designated a national monument, thousands of tons of petrified wood were taken
by souvenir seekers, builders and entrepreneurs. Since then, the area has been protected and now encompasses 146 sq miles.
All collecting is prohibited (punishable by
fines and imprisonment), but souvenirs of
similar wood collected outside the park are
sold in many stores in the area, particularly
in Holbrook and at the south park entrance.

Apart from the petrified logs, visitors can
see a few small ancient Indian sites (including one building made entirely from
blocks of fossilized wood), many petroglyphs and the picturesque scenery of the
Painted Desert – some 67 sq miles of picturesque lands that change colors as the sun
plays tricks with the minerals in the earth.
The original 1906 monument was the
southern part of the present park, and the
greatest concentration of petrified wood is
found here. The northern section gives outstanding views of the Painted Desert. Remnants of past Indian habitations are found in
the central and southern sections.

Orientation

The park straddles I-40 at exit 311, 25
miles east of Holbrook. From this exit, a
28-mile paved park road goes briefly north

ARIZONA

and then heads south, over the freeway, to emerge at Hwy 180, 18 miles southeast of Holbrook. Unless you want to make the complete loop from Holbrook, it is more convenient to begin at the north end if you are driving west and the south end if you are driving east. There is no other advantage to either direction.

Information
The Painted Desert Visitor Center near the north entrance, and the Rainbow Forest Museum near the south entrance, both have bookstores, exhibits about the park, and rangers who can provide information. At Painted Desert, there is a 20-minute film describing how the logs were fossilized, and at Rainbow Forest there are giant reptile skeletons. Between these two places, the park road passes more than 20 pullouts with interpretive signs and some short trails.

The park is open from 8 am to 5 pm in winter; hours may be extended in late spring and fall. From Memorial Day to Labor Day, hours are 7 am to 7 pm if staff is available. The park is closed on New Year's Day and Christmas. Entrance is $10 per vehicle; $5 per bus passenger or bike rider. Golden Age, Access and Eagle Passes are accepted. Visitors receive a (free) park map showing pullouts and parking spots along the road. Further information is available from the Superintendent (☎ 520-524-6228), Petrified Forest National Park, AZ 86028.

Hiking & Backpacking
Apart from some short trails at some of the pullouts, there are no trails into the park. Hikers can walk cross-country, but should speak with a ranger first to discuss their plans as there are no maintained or signed trails. Backpackers can hike into the backcountry and camp after obtaining a free permit from a ranger. There are no camping facilities or water away from the road, so hikers and backpackers need to carry all water. Campsites must be at least a mile from paved roads and no fires, firearms, pets or collecting are allowed. Backcountry

hiking and camping are permitted only in a designated wilderness area in the northern parts of the park. Almost half the park is off-limits to backcountry travel.

Places to Stay & Eat
Apart from backcountry camping, there are no overnight accommodations in the park. Snacks are available by the Rainbow Forest Museum and meals by the Painted Desert Visitor Center. There are a couple of picnic areas. In the town of **Chambers**, 22 miles east of the park, the *Best Western Chieftain Inn* (☎/fax 520-688-2754) has 52 standard rooms, a pool open from June through September and a restaurant open from 6 am to 9:30 pm. Rates are in the $60s for a double. Otherwise, stay in Holbrook.

Navajo Indian Reservation

The Navajo Indian Reservation, or the Navajo Nation as the Navajos themselves prefer to call it, covers about 27,000 sq miles. It's the largest reservation in the USA, and the Navajo tribe is the largest – about one in seven Native Americans in the USA is a Navajo. The reservation is mainly in northeastern Arizona, but also includes parts of neighboring Utah and New Mexico. About 75% is high desert and the remainder is high forest. The scenery is, in places, some of the most spectacular in North America, particularly in Monument Valley. Equally impressive are the beautiful (but uninhabited) ancient pueblos amid splendid settings in the Canyon de Chelly and Navajo National Monuments. After some background on the Navajo, this section will describe the highlights of the reservation, beginning with the tribal capital of Window Rock in the east and then moving west and north.

History
Anthropological research indicates that in the 14th and 15th centuries, many bands of

Athabaskan-speaking people migrated from the plains of Canada into the Southwest. The reasons for this migration aren't known, but by 1500 these people had established themselves in the Southwest. They were the ancestors of both the Navajo and the Apache Indians. In those days, they were a wandering people, hunting and gathering for food and occasionally raiding neighboring tribes. Influenced by the more sedentary and agricultural Pueblo tribes, the Navajos eventually began farming and making arts and crafts, but they never built any large stone villages such as the Pueblo Indians did.

The Navajo call themselves the *Diné* (the People) and explain their arrival in the Southwest quite differently. According to their legends, handed down orally through the generations, the Diné passed through three different worlds in various human, animal, spiritual and natural forms before finally emerging into the fourth world, called the Glittering World. Today's Diné maintain close links with their past worlds, and believe that their lives should be in harmony with all the elements of the present and the earlier worlds. Dozens of ceremonies and rituals, learned with painstaking care from tribal elders and medicine men, are done for various reasons to enable the people to live in harmony with the rest of the universe.

Contact with the Spaniards in the 16th, 17th and 18th centuries was surprisingly limited, considering the Spaniards' involvement with the Pueblo and Hopi peoples. The best-documented Navajo-Spanish interaction was the massacre of more than 100 Indians at Canyon de Chelly in 1805 in response to years of Navajo raids.

When the Anglos arrived in the 19th century, they tended to follow the better-known routes in New Mexico and southern Arizona. By the middle of the 1800s, the US Army was defeating tribes, including the Navajo, along the Western frontier and 'buying' the land from the Indians in exchange for peace. (This may have made sense to the Anglos, but it didn't to the Indians, who didn't value the European concept of land ownership.) Once their land had been purchased, the surviving tribes were often relocated onto distant reservations.

Canyon de Chelly, site of the massacre by the Spanish in 1805, also became the place where the US Army defeated the Navajo. During the winter of 1863-64, US Cavalry troops led by Colonel Kit Carson destroyed fields and property, killed anyone they found and drove the Indians up into the canyon until starvation forced their surrender. Thousands of Indians were rounded up and forced to march to Fort Sumner in the plains of eastern New Mexico (see Fort

ARIZONA

The Navajo Language

Navajo belongs to the Athapaskan language family, a group of languages that also includes Apache. Other tribes speaking Athapaskan languages live in Alaska, northwestern Canada, and coastal Oregon and California. The distribution of these tribes is considered evidence of migration patterns across the continent.

Some Navajo, especially the elders, speak only the Navajo language, but most speak both Navajo and English. All members of the tribe have a deep respect for the Navajo language whether they are fluent or not.

Navajo and English have very different sentence structures and Navajo is not an easy language for outsiders to learn. During WWII, the Navajo Code Talkers spoke a code based on Navajo for US military radio transmissions. The code was never broken. The Code Talkers are now famous for their wartime contribution and the remaining members of this unit are frequently honored at tribal functions. ■

Sumner in the Southeastern New Mexico section) in an episode that has gone down in tribal history as 'The Long Walk.'

Hundreds of Navajos died on the march or on the inhospitable new reservation. Despite this, the Navajo were one of the luckier tribes. A treaty in 1868 gave them a reservation of about 5500 sq miles in the heart of the lands on which they had lived for about half a millennium. The 8000 or so inhabitants of Fort Sumner along with about another 8000 scattered Navajos were allowed to settle on this new reservation. This grew over the years to its present size, and today more than half of the approximately 170,000 members of the Navajo Nation live on the reservation.

Information

The best information about the reservation is found at Window Rock (see that section later in this chapter). Other good information sources are the *Navajo Times* newspaper and KTNN radio station. This broadcasts out of Window Rock at 660 AM and has mainly Navajo language programming in the morning and English in the afternoon and evening. The music varies between country & western and traditional and recent Navajo music, much of which involves drums and song or flutes.

Money Banking facilities on the reservation are available at Norwest Banks in Window Rock, Tuba City, Chinle and Kayenta.

Time The Navajo Reservation, unlike Arizona, does observe Mountain daylight-saving time. Thus during the summer, the reservation is *one hour ahead* of Arizona; on the same time as Utah and New Mexico.

Photography Photography is permitted almost anywhere there's tourism. Taking photographs of people, however, is not appropriate unless you ask for and receive permission from the individual involved. A tip is expected.

Restrictions Alcohol and drugs are strictly prohibited throughout the reservation. The few hotels and restaurants in Navajoland provide clean (if pricey) accommodations and tasty food, but no alcohol. It is a violation of federal, state and Navajo tribal laws to disturb, destroy, injure, deface or remove any natural feature or prehistoric object.

Dangers & Annoyances Beware of farm animals on the roads as you drive through reservation land. Because most of the land is not fenced, animals will roam onto the highways. Hitting one can do as much damage to you as to the animal.

Be careful, as well, of the occasional drunk driver. Despite the ban on alcohol on the reservation, there are problems of drunk driving.

The phone system on the reservation occasionally goes dead for short or sometimes long periods. This is more likely to occur in remote locations and during severe weather.

Special Events

Summer and fall is the big tribal fair season in Navajoland. The following are the major events to which the general public is welcome. The world's biggest Indian event is the Annual Navajo Nation Fair, held over Labor Day weekend (Thursday through Sunday) in Window Rock. The fair has been taking place since 1946. Most visitors stay in Gallup, New Mexico, and travel to Window Rock for the intertribal powwow, Indian rodeo, traditional song and dance displays and competitions, a barbecue with Navajo food and many other events. Also, there is a Fourth of July powwow and rodeo held in Window Rock.

See Shiprock in the Northwestern New Mexico chapter for information on the oldest and most traditional fair, held in late September or early October. Similar events on a smaller scale are held during the Western Navajo Fair in Tuba City in mid-October, the Central Navajo Fair in Chinle, the Southwestern Navajo Fair in Dilkon (on Hwy 15, 6 miles east of Hwy 87) as well as the Eastern Navajo Fair in Crownpoint, New Mexico. These usually take place between July and October. The Navajoland

Tourism Department has the exact dates of these and other smaller rodeos and pow-wows that are held in many of the smaller towns on the reservation.

Private dances and sings (gatherings where singing is the main activity) are organized by individual families for particular religious or ceremonial occasions or for medicinal purposes. These could happen at any time of the year but are not advertised as they aren't tourist attractions.

Places to Stay
The few motels on the reservation are found at Window Rock, Chinle (by the Canyon de Chelly National Monument), Kayenta, Tuba City, Cameron (see the Grand Canyon chapter), Goulding's Trading Post (see Southeastern Utah), and Teec Nos Pos (near the Four Corners Monument). These are often full in summer; making reservations is a good idea. Most are expensive ($70 to $130 for fairly standard rooms); Tuba City and Teec Nos Pos are the only places on the reservation with relatively cheap and quite basic accommodations. Further details are given under each of these places.

Off-reservation towns offering conveniently close accommodations are Gallup and Farmington in New Mexico; Holbrook, Winslow, Flagstaff and Page in Arizona; and Goulding's Trading Post, Mexican Hat, Bluff and Blanding in Utah.

Some tribally operated campgrounds are found at or near Monument Valley, the Navajo National Monument, Chinle, Tsaile and Window Rock. RV facilities are very limited.

Coyote Pass Hospitality (☎ 520-724-3383, 520-674-9655), PO Box 91, Tsaile, AZ 86558, is run by Willie Tsosie, Jr. He can arrange stays with local families or in a traditional hogan in the Tsaile or Canyon de Chelly area. Accommodations are rustic (a sleeping bag is a good idea) and bathroom facilities are primitive (most hogans lack plumbing). Rates are about $80 to $90 including a Navajo breakfast; add $10 per extra person. Additional meals for longer stays can be arranged.

Shopping
The large Anglo towns on the perimeter of the reservation (Farmington, Gallup and Flagstaff) have galleries and pawn shops where Navajo rugs, silverwork, jewelry and other arts can be purchased. On the reservation itself, you can buy from trading posts, gift shops or museums, and it's likely that you will encounter Navajos offering their wares at tourist stops, roadside stands and in parking lots.

Buying items at 'official' stores is no guarantee of their quality; high- and low-quality wares appear on the trading-post shelves just as they do at roadside stalls. When you buy direct, you may find that you pay less and have more luck negotiating the price down; the sellers may still make more from the transaction than if they had sold their wares to a trading post. In addition, you may be able to talk directly to the artisan.

Getting There & Away
The Navajo Transit System (☎ 520-729-5449, 520-729-5457), Drawer 1330, Window Rock, AZ 86515, provides the only public transportation on the reservation using modern buses.

From Gallup, New Mexico (which can be reached by Greyhound Bus or Amtrak), Navajo Transit System has buses to Window Rock and Fort Defiance four times a day on weekdays and three times on Saturdays. The ride takes an hour. There is no Sunday service.

From Farmington, New Mexico (also reached by Greyhound), there is a daily 7 am bus Monday to Friday, returning from Window Rock at 2:25 pm. The fare is about $11 for the three-hour ride.

In Window Rock you can connect with a 3 pm bus (weekdays only) to Tuba City (four hours, $13) along Hwy 264 (with stops at Ganado, Keams Canyon (on the Hopi Reservation), the Hopi Cultural Center and several other small towns and villages. The bus returns from Tuba City at 6 am, Monday to Friday, leaving from the hospital and stopping at the Truck Stop Cafe.

Navajo Weaving

The Navajo are the best-known rug-weavers of the Native American tribes. A Navajo rug requires many months of labor and can involve several family members. Children tend the sheep, and various people participate in shearing, washing, carding, spinning and dyeing the wool before it even touches the loom. All is done by hand. The loom is a simple upright wooden frame, and the designs and colors are passed down from generation to generation, usually to the women. Legend has it that Spider Woman taught the women how to weave. You can watch weavers at work at some museums and trading posts; the Hubbell Trading Post near Ganado is a good place for this.

Navajo weavings were originally heavy blankets used in winter. When Anglos became interested in the work as a folk craft, they found that the origin of the rug could be recognized by the various designs and colors used in the rug. For instance, a Ganado Red was a rug with a red background coming from the settlement of Ganado. Rugs with geometrical designs in earth colors bordered by black were from the Two Grey Hills region from the eastern part of Navajo lands. And the Shiprock area was known for Yei rugs, depicting supernatural beings revered by the Navajo. Several other regional styles can easily be detected with a little experience.

Today, weavers from any part of the reservation can produce designs that were once specific to a particular area. While traditionally the designs have been geometric, some weavers currently use figurative designs. Such rugs are technically as valuable as the traditional ones.

Tips on Buying a Rug Whether used as a floor covering or displayed on a wall, a good quality rug can last a lifetime. Given the cost of purchasing a good quality rug, buying one is not for the average souvenir-seeker. It can take months of research, or can be bought on a whim if you see one you really love. If you're a more cautious shopper, visit museums, trading posts and crafts stores in Indian country. Talk to weavers, exhibitors and traders to learn about the various designs. Don't just look at the rugs – feel them. A good rug will be very tightly woven and even in width. Prices of rugs vary from the low hundreds to thousands of dollars. This reflects the size of the rug, the weeks of work involved, the skill of the weaver and whether the yarn is store-bought or hand-spun.

Be aware that cheap imitation rugs are available. These may look nice, but they aren't handmade by Navajos. Some are mass-produced in Mexico using Navajo designs. The staff at a reputable store can show you the difference. ∎

Another bus leaves from Fort Defiance (a few miles north of Window Rock) at 3:30 pm weekdays for Kayenta via Wheatfields, Tsaile, Chinle and other small villages. The bus returns at 5:55 am from Kayenta and costs about $12 for the 3½-hour trip.

Several daily buses connect Window Rock and Fort Defiance on weekdays; three do so on Saturdays.

WINDOW ROCK

The tribal capital is at Window Rock, a small town of about 3500 people almost on the New Mexico border, at the inter-section of Hwys 264 and 12. The town is named after a natural arch at the north end of town more than a mile north of the intersection.

Below the arch are the Navajo Nation Council Chambers (☎ 520-871-6417), which contain colorful murals and can be toured. During tribal council sessions, you can hear the 88 elected council delegates representing the 110 Navajo chapters (communities) discussing issues in the Navajo language. Full council sessions are held at least four times a year, usually on the third Monday of January, April, July and October.

Orientation & Information

Information about the whole reservation is available from Navajoland Tourism Department (☎ 520-871-6436, 520-871-7371, fax 520-871-7381), PO Box 663, Window Rock, AZ 86515. Their office is in a trailer 2 miles west of town on the south side of Hwy 264, by the Economic Development Building.

The main area of tourist interest is at the east end of town on Hwy 264 just east of Hwy 12. Here you'll find the huge FedMart shopping plaza (where the Navajo Transit System bus leaves from and where there is a cinema), bank, arts and crafts stores, the Navajo Nation Inn, the museum, botanical garden, zoo, post office and parks office all within a few hundred yards of one another.

Backpacking and other backcountry use anywhere on the reservation requires a permit from the Navajo Parks & Recreation Department (☎ 520-871-6636, 520-871-6647, fax 520-871-6637, 520-871-7040), PO Box 9000, Window Rock, AZ 86515. The office is next to the Zoo and Botanical Park on the east side of Window Rock. (Note that campgrounds mentioned in this chapter are not considered 'backcountry' and don't require a tribal permit beyond the camping fee.) Hunting (very limited), fishing and boating require tribal (not state) licenses obtainable from Navajo Fish & Wildlife (☎ 520-871-6451, 520-871-6452, fax 520-871-7040), PO Box 1480, Window Rock, AZ 86515.

Navajo Nation Museum & Library

This new museum (☎ 520-871-6673) was dedicated in the fall of 1997 and replaces the Navajo Tribal Museum, which used to be in an arts and crafts store. The first of many changing shows was a traveling exhibit of Navajo weavings from the Smithsonian Institution. Indian history and arts and crafts will also be highlighted (exhibits were being transferred from the old space at time of writing). A gift shop has an excellent selection of books about the Navajo and other tribes as well as other items.

In keeping with the traditional Navajo hogan, the museum's door faces east and is not immediately obvious from the highway. It is next to the Zoo & Botanical Park.

Navajo Nation Zoo & Botanical Park

At the east end of town on Hwy 264, this park (☎ 520-871-6573) shows native wildlife and Navajo architecture. Its hours are from 8 am to 5 pm daily except New Year's Day and Christmas. Admission is free.

St Michael's Mission Museum

Housed in an 1898 Franciscan mission, 3 miles west of Window Rock just off Hwy 264, this museum (☎ 520-871-4171) describes the missionary work of the Franciscans in Navajoland. Hours are 8 am to 5 pm Monday to Friday, and from 9 am to 5 pm on weekends from Memorial Day to Labor Day. Call for an appointment at other times.

Window Rock Tribal Park & Navajo Veterans Memorial

Below the sandstone arch that gives the town its name, there is a park with picnic areas and a memorial to all Navajo veterans. Camping is not allowed. The arch is important in Navajo ceremonies and may sometimes be off-limits during a particular ceremony.

Places to Stay & Eat

There are no developed campgrounds here. However, you can park your RV at *Tse Bonito Tribal Park* next to the Zoological & Botanical Park or at the unofficial *Summit Campground*, 9 miles west of Window Rock on Hwy 264. There are picnic tables but no water. A $2 per person fee is charged but might not be collected in the low season.

The *Navajo Nation Inn* (☎ 520-871-4108, 800-662-6189, fax 520-871-5466), is on Hwy 264 east of Hwy 12. There are 56 pleasant rooms decorated in modern Southwestern style. Rates range from $65 to $75 for a single and $5 for each extra person. A reasonably priced restaurant is open from 6:30 am to 9 pm daily (from 6 am in summer) that serves Navajo and American food. There are several fast-food restaurants.

Half a mile west of St Michael's Mission on Hwy 264, a new *Days Inn* was under construction in early 1998.

Shopping

Window Rock is the headquarters of the Navajo Arts and Crafts Enterprise (NACE), which runs a jewelry and crafts store (☎ 520-871-4090) next to the Navajo Nation Inn. The NACE was established in 1941 and is wholly Navajo operated. It guarantees the authenticity and quality of its products.

HUBBELL TRADING POST NATIONAL HISTORIC SITE

John Lorenzo Hubbell established this trading post at **Ganado** (30 miles west of Window Rock) in 1878 and worked here until his death in 1930. He was widely respected by Indians and non-Indians alike for his honesty and passion for excellence. Today, his trading post is operated by the NPS and looks much as it would have at the turn of the century. Indian artists still trade here.

Next to the trading post is a visitor center where respected Navajo women often give weaving demonstrations and men may demonstrate silversmithing. Helpful interpretive signs explain what is being woven, and rangers can help with questions. You can take photographs for a tip.

Tours of Hubbell's house (with a superb collection of early Navajo rugs and period furniture) are given several times a day. The trading post continues to sell local crafts, specializing in top-quality Navajo weavings worth thousands of dollars. If you can't quite scrape the money together, you can buy a postcard or a candy bar instead!

The site is open 8 am to 6 pm from June through September, 8 am to 5 pm otherwise, and closed New Year's Day, Thanksgiving and Christmas. Admission is free.

There's a picnic area but nowhere to stay. The visitor center has directions to and hours of a few small restaurants in Ganado village (some close on Sundays). Further information is available from the Superintendent (☎ 520-755-3475), PO Box 150, Ganado, AZ 86505.

CANYON DE CHELLY NATIONAL MONUMENT

Pronounced 'd-SHAY,' this many-fingered canyon contains several beautiful Ancestral Puebloan sites and is also important in the history of the Navajo. Ancient Basketmaker people inhabited the canyon almost 2000 years ago and left some pit dwellings dated to about 350 AD. These inhabitants evolved into the Pueblo people who built large cliff dwellings in the canyon walls between 1100 and 1300 AD. Droughts and other unknown conditions forced them to leave the canyon after 1300 AD and it is supposed that they were the ancestors of some of today's Pueblo or Hopi Indians.

The Navajo began farming the canyon bottom around 1700 and used the canyon as a stronghold and retreat for their raids on other nearby Indian groups and Spanish settlers. In 1805, the Spaniards retaliated and killed more than 100 Navajos in what is now called Massacre Cave in the Canyon del Muerto. The Spaniards claimed that the dead were almost all warriors but the Navajo say that it was mostly women and children. In 1864, the US Army drove thousands of Navajos into the canyon and starved them until they surrendered over the winter, then relocated them in eastern New Mexico after 'The Long Walk.' Four years later, the Navajos were allowed to return. Today, many families have hogans and farms on the canyon bottom. Most of the families live on the canyon rims in winter, and move to the canyon bottom in the spring and summer. The whole canyon is private Navajo property administered by the NPS. Please don't enter hogans unless with a guide and don't photograph people without their permission. A tip is expected if permission is given.

The mouth of the canyon opens at its west end near the village of **Chinle**. Here, the canyon walls are only a few feet high but soon become higher until they top out at about 1000 feet in the depths of the canyon. Two main arms divide early on in the canyon and several side canyons connect with them. A paved road follows the southernmost and northernmost rims of the

ARIZONA

canyon complex, affording excellent views into the splendid scenery of the canyon and distant views of uninhabited pueblos in the canyon walls. Most of the bottom of the canyon is off-limits to visitors unless they enter with a guide. The exception is a trail to the White House.

Information

The visitor center is near the mouth of the canyon just east of Chinle. There are exhibits about the canyon, a bookstore, information about guides and tours and a free newspaper guide. Inexpensive booklets with descriptions of the sights on South and North Rim Drives are available. Outside is a traditional Navajo hogan that you can enter (it's empty). Hours are 8 am to 5 pm daily, extended to 6 pm from May through September. Admission to the monument is free as long as you stick to the visitor center, paved rim roads and White House Trail. Further information is available from the Superintendent (☎ 520-674-5500), PO Box 588, Chinle, AZ 86503.

White House Trail

The trailhead is about 6 miles east of the visitor center on South Rim Drive, and the steep trail is about 1¼ miles one-way. Don't forget to carry water. The pueblo dates back to about 1040 to 1284 AD and is one of the largest in the monument.

Rim Drives

Both drives afford several scenic overlooks into the canyon. Lock your car and don't leave valuables in sight when taking the short walks at each scenic point.

South Rim Drive is about 19 miles long and passes six viewpoints before ending at the spectacular Spider Rock Overlook, with views down onto the 800-foot-high sheer-walled tower atop of which lives Spider Woman. The Navajos say that she carries off children who don't listen to their parents! This is a dead-end drive so you'll have to return the way you came.

North Rim Drive has four overlooks and ends at the Massacre Cave overlook, 15 miles from the visitor center. However, you can continue on the paved road to Tsaile, about 13 miles further east, from which Hwy 12 will take you to Window Rock or into the northern reaches of the reservation.

Monument staff suggest that the lighting for photography on the north rim is best in the morning and on the south rim in the afternoon.

Organized Tours

Ask at the visitor center information desk about all tours. Guides belong to the Tsegi Guide Association, PO Box 588, Chinle, AZ 86503. These are usually local Navajos who know the area well and can liven up your tour with witty commentary. (*Tsegi* is Navajo for 'canyon.') When writing to any of the addresses below, add Chinle, AZ 86503 after the PO Box.

Foot The Tsegi Guide Association offers guided four-hour hikes into the canyon at 9 am and 1 pm. The hike covers 4½ miles and costs $10 per person with a maximum of 15 and minimum of five (fewer people can split the $50 minimum fee). Five- to eight-year-olds pay $5. Two-hour guided night walks leave at dusk and cost $12. Register for all these at the visitor center.

For more difficult hikes or to visit more remote areas, you can hire a guide for $10 an hour (three hours minimum, 15 people per guide maximum). This can be arranged at the visitor center or in advance by calling the association.

Make sure to take along insect repellent if you go during spring or summer; the wash attracts hordes of mosquitoes in some places. Overnight hikes with camping in the canyon can be arranged, though this is infrequently done.

During the summer, free hikes may be led by park rangers. Inquire about this and register in advance at the visitor center.

Horse Justin Tso's Horseback Tours (☎ 520-674-5678), PO Box 881, is near the visitor center and has horses available year-round for $8 per person per hour plus $8 an hour for the guide. Tohtsonii Ranch (☎ 520-755-6209), PO Box 434, at the end of South Rim Drive, charges similar prices. The ranch offers four hour round-trip rides to Spider Rock. Twin Trails Horseback Tours (☎ 520-674-8425), PO Box 3068, is on the north rim, about 7 miles from the visitor center. They have horses available from mid-May to mid-October and offer various guided trips from two hours along the rim for $35 per person to all-day excursions to visit pueblos in the canyon for $70 per person. Overnight trips can be arranged.

4WD There are no roads into the canyon, only rough tracks, so you need 4WD. If you have your own vehicle you can hire a guide to go with you for $10 an hour (one guide can accompany up to five vehicles; three-hour minimum). Heavy rain may make the roads impassable.

Otherwise, you can take a Thunderbird Tour (☎ 520-674-5841), PO Box 548, from the Thunderbird Lodge near the visitor center. They don't bother with little 4WD vehicles. Instead, they use heavy-duty, army-style 6WD vehicles that can cross through streams that would stop a 4WD. Some Navajos refer to these as the 'shake-n-bake' tours. Half-day trips leave at 9 am and 2 pm and cost $36 ($27 for children under 13). They leave year-round. Full-day tours are $57 for everyone and include a picnic lunch. These may not leave in the low winter season.

You can rent a 4WD vehicle for $100 for three hours plus $30 for each additional hour from De Chelly Tours (☎ 520-674-3772, 520-674-5433), PO Box 2539.

Places to Stay

The *Cottonwood Campground* is near the visitor center. It has 96 sites on a first-come, first-served basis and a group site that can be reserved through the visitor center. There is some water but no hookups or showers. Camping is free and popular, so in summer get there early. During the summer, rangers may give talks. From November to March, water may be shut off. *Spider Rock Campground* (☎ 520-674-8261) is 10 miles east of the visitor center along South Rim

Drive. The remote campground, managed by the Navajo, is surrounded by piñon and juniper trees and is a pleasant getaway from the activity of the visitor center. Sites cost $10. There is no water or electricity, but the owner has bottled water and lanterns available. The Navajo Chapter House in Chinle has showers available for a fee.

Try the attractive *Thunderbird Lodge* (☎ 520-674-5841, fax 520-674-5844), half a mile from the visitor center. Comfortable rooms vary in size; some are in the old lodge (which dates from the late 1800s) but all have private baths and air-conditioning. Rates are in the $80s for a double; there are discounts from November to February. A few suites are $150. An inexpensive cafeteria offers tasty American and Navajo food from 6:30 am to 9 pm, with shorter winter hours.

A half mile west of the visitor center is the *Holiday Inn* (☎ 520-674-5000, fax 520-674-8264). They have a pool and the area's most upscale restaurant (though still not very fancy), open from 6:30 am to 10 pm. Although parts of the public areas incorporate an old trading post, the more than 100 rooms are modern. Rates range from $90 to $120 in summer.

In Chinle, just east of Hwy 191 and 3 miles west of the visitor center, is the *Best Western Canyon de Chelly Inn* (☎ 520-674-5875, fax 520-674-3715), with 100 pleasant motel rooms for $115 from May to October dropping into the $60s in winter. They have an indoor pool and an inexpensive dining room open from 6:30 am to 9 pm (10 pm in summer).

Places to Eat

Apart from the hotel restaurants, there are some fast-food restaurants and *Basha's*, the only supermarket for at least 50 miles.

Shopping

The Navajo Arts & Crafts Enterprise (see Window Rock, earlier in this chapter) has a store in Chinle (☎ 520-674-5338) at the intersection of Hwy 191 and Hwy 7. The Thunderbird Lodge gift shop also sells a good range of crafts and T-shirts. The walls of the Thunderbird cafeteria are often covered in high-quality Navajo rugs and paintings, which are for sale.

TSAILE

A small town at the northeast end of Canyon de Chelly, Tsaile (pronounced 'say-LEE') is the home of the Navajo Community College (☎ 520-724-6600). On campus, the modern six-story glass building housing the **Ned A Hatathlie Museum** (☎ 520-724-6650) has its entrance facing east, just like in a traditional hogan. The museum has exhibits about Indian history, culture and arts and crafts, a variety of which are offered for sale in the gift shop. Hours are from 8:30 am to 4:30 pm Monday to Friday; admission is by donation. The college bookstore has a superb selection of books about the Navajo.

South of the college and 2 miles off of Hwy 12 is the small (two sites) *Tsaile Lake Campground*, accessible by dirt road. RVs aren't recommended and there is no drinking water or facilities. Ten miles south of Tsaile on Hwy 12 is the larger and more attractive *Wheatfields Lake Campground* with nice lake views. There are pit toilets but no water. RV and tent sites are available for $2 per person. A nearby store sells food and fishing permits. Both Tsaile and Wheatfields Lakes are stocked with rainbow and cutthroat trout and offer some of Navajoland's best fishing.

FOUR CORNERS MONUMENT NAVAJO TRIBAL PARK

Make a fool of yourself as you put a foot into Arizona, another into New Mexico, a hand into Utah and another into Colorado. Wiggle your butt for the camera. Everyone does! The site is marked with a slab and state flags, and is surrounded by booths selling Indian souvenirs. This is the only place in the USA where four states come together at one point. Hours are 7 am to 8 pm, May to August, and 8 am to 5 pm at other times. Admission is a steep $2.50 per person (though might not be collected in winter). Seniors pay $1 and children under eight are free. There are basic toilets, and crafts and food stalls.

TES NEZ IAH

About halfway between Four Corners and Kayenta, this village has the small *Navajo Trails Motel* (☎ 520-674-3618) with basic double rooms in the $40s in summer – the cheapest motel in Navajoland.

KAYENTA

Established in 1908 by Richard Wetherill as a trading post, this town of about 5000 people (including the surrounding area) has in recent decades developed strong (if controversial) uranium- and coal-mining industries.

Kayenta has convenient (though pricey) tourist services for visitors to nearby Monument Valley and Navajo National Monument. Several vehicle tours to Monument Valley are provided by Crawley's Tour (☎ 520-697-3463, 520-697-3724), PO Box 187, Kayenta, AZ 86033; Golden Sands (☎ 520-697-3684), PO Box 458, Kayenta, AZ 86033 and Roland's Navajoland Tours (☎ 520-697-3524, fax 520-697-2382), PO Box 1542, Kayenta, AZ 86033. The visitor center (☎ 520-697-3572, 520-697-8198) can help with questions about the town and Navajoland, and has local crafts and books for sale.

Special Events

The Fourth of July Indian Rodeo attracts a lot of people over the nearest weekend. Besides the rodeo, there are horse races, food stalls, Navajo dances and sings and powwows. On weekends, Kayenta hosts a big flea market.

Places to Stay & Eat

The Navajo-operated *Best Western Wetherill Inn* (☎ 520-697-3231/3232, fax 520-697-3233) is 1½ miles north of Hwy 160 on Hwy 163. About 50 standard motel rooms with coffeemakers are almost $100 from April to October, about $50 to $70 in winter.

The *Holiday Inn* (☎ 520-697-3221, fax 520-697-3349), at the junction of Hwy 160 and Hwy 163, is the reservation's largest hotel, with 160 rooms and a few suites. Rates are about $130 for a double from July to October, dropping to about $80 in midwinter. There is a pool, a kid's pool, and a decent restaurant open from 6 am to 10 pm. They serve basic American food and Navajo tacos.

You could also try B&B accommodation with Sandy (☎ 520-697-8695) or Marcia (☎ 520-697-3389), both of whom advertise nonsmoking rooms.

The *Golden Sands Cafe* (☎ 520-697-3684) serves American and Navajo food near the Wetherill Inn, and the *Amigo Cafe* (☎ 520-697-8448), on Hwy 163 a short way north of the intersection with Hwy 160, which serves the best Mexican food on the reservation. Both are open for breakfast, lunch and dinner. The *Burger King* has an interesting exhibit on the

---

The High Cost of Coal

In satellite photos taken from 567 miles above the Navajo and Hopi Indian Reservations, the Peabody Coal Company's mine to the west of Kayenta looks like a blackhead. The fact that it appears at all is testimony to its size and to the size of the controversies surrounding the mine at Black Mesa. One of the main issues that arises is the use of groundwater. Coal mines use exorbitant amounts of water to transport the coal to smelters, depleting a vast supply of rainwater that has accumulated over the centuries.

Take into account that this land is desert and water is a precious resource for the Navajo and Hopi. Without the water, their ability to raise livestock and grow crops – the basis of their lifestyle – is threatened. Historically, treaties about tribal land have only defined the land, not the water under the surface. Bureaucracy takes over and the Indians find themselves fighting not only the federal bureaucracy, but also each other over disputed borders and use of land and resources. The issue is further complicated by the fact that Peabody is one of the primary employers on the reservation. ■

Navajo Code Talkers, whic Southwest's most unique place. There's also a *Busha* where you can pick up som long drive ahead.

About 10 miles west on Hwy 160 at the village of **Tsegi** is the *Anasazi Inn* (☎ 520-697-3793), with 60 simple motel rooms (many with good views) for about $90 in summer, less in winter. They have a dining room.

MONUMENT VALLEY NAVAJO TRIBAL PARK

The first time I saw the magnificent mesas and buttes of Monument Valley, shivers ran up and down my spine. The views are simply stupendous and I still get a thrill every time I drive up or down Hwy 163 and see the buttes perched on the horizon. Some people may have a feeling of déjà vu here: this is the landscape seen in famous Westerns like the classic 1939 production of *Stagecoach*, directed by John Ford, or *How the West Was Won* (1962).

Great views of Monument Valley are had from Hwy 163 but to really get up close you need to visit the Monument Valley Navajo Tribal Park (☎ 801-727-3353, fax 801-727-3287). Although most of the park is in Arizona, the area code is for Utah. The park is 24 miles north of Kayenta near the state line. A 4-mile paved road leads to a small visitor center with information, a few exhibits and crafts sales.

From the visitor center, a rough unpaved loop road covers 17 miles of stunning valley views. You can drive it in your own vehicle (ordinary cars can just get by) or take a tour. Self-driven visitors pay $2.50 ($1 for seniors, free for kids under eight). Several tour companies have booths next to the visitor center and offer two- to three-hour trips for about $20 a person. Horseback rides are around $30. Tours leave frequently in summer but may be infrequent or nonexistent in midwinter. Outfitters in nearby Kayenta and at Goulding's in Utah also offer tours. The road is open from 7 am to 7 pm, May through September, and 8 am to 5 pm the rest of the year; it's closed

ARIZONA

Christmas and open 8 am to noon on Thanksgiving. Call for hours for New Year's Day. Bad weather may also close the road.

Places to Stay

The tribally operated *Mitten View Campground* has coin-operated hot showers but no RV hookups. There are about 100 sites for $10 each and these may fill up in summer. They are available on a first-come, first-served basis and reservations are accepted only for groups in summer. The showers are closed in winter, when the sites cost $5 and can be very cold and windy (it snowed when I was there).

There are camping and motel facilities just across the state line at Goulding's Trading Post in Utah (see the Southeastern Utah chapter).

NAVAJO NATIONAL MONUMENT

This monument protects three Ancestral Puebloan sites. The small and fragile Inscription House has been closed since the 1960s, but the larger Betatakin and Keet Seel pueblos are open to public visitation and are both exceptionally well preserved, extensive and impressive. They are well worth a visit but are not very easy to get to. Thus part of their charm comes from your sense of achievement when they are reached. They can be visited only in summer.

Information

The visitor center (☎ 520-672-2366) is 9 miles north of Hwy 160 along paved Hwy 564. There are audio-visual shows and a small museum. There is a small but excellent gift shop, and information, ranger-led programs, camping and picnicking are available.

Hours are 8 am to 5 pm (Mountain Standard Time) except New Year's Day, Thanksgiving and Christmas. Admission is free.

Information is also available from the Superintendent, HC-71, Box 3, Tonalea, AZ 86044.

Betatakin

This pueblo is visible from the Sandal Trail, an easy 1-mile loop from the visitor center.

The view is a distant one and binoculars are definitely recommended. Trail signs point out local plants along the way. This trail is open year-round.

During the summer, you can make the 5-mile (roundtrip) hike to Betatakin, but only when guided by a ranger (unguided hikes are not permitted). These tours depart at 9 am from approximately mid-May through September.

You must obtain *your own* ticket for the hike at the visitor center. The tours are free (at time of writing) and limited to 25 people. Occasionally, there are 25 people waiting in line before the visitor center opens! The elevation (7300 feet at the visitor center, 6600 at Betatakin) means that the hike can be strenuous, especially on hot summer days, when you should carry plenty of water and sun protection, including a hat. Allow five to six hours for the roundtrip.

Keet Seel

This is one of the largest and best-preserved ancient pueblos in the Southwest and can be reached by foot or horseback only. Keet Seel is 8½ miles (one-way) from the visitor center, but the destination is worth the challenging trip if you are up to it. The hike involves a steep 1000-foot descent into a canyon and then a 400-foot gentle climb. The trail is often loose and sandy and may involve wading through a shallow streambed.

Although the 17-mile roundtrip can be done in a day, most visitors prefer to backpack in and stay at the primitive campsite below Keet Seel. There is no drinking water, so you must carry your own, and camping is limited to one night. At the site, visitors must register at a small ranger station. The pueblo may be visited only with the ranger and visitation is limited to 20 people a day and five people at a time, so you may need to wait. The last visit is at 3:30 pm. Entrance requires using a very long ladder, so it's not for people afraid of heights.

Keet Seel is open daily from Memorial Day weekend to Labor Day. The twenty daily permits are often taken early, and you should call up to two months in advance to reserve a permit. This must be picked up at the visitor center by 9 am on the day you begin your hike. A map and precise directions are available at the visitor center. The permit is free and allows you to cross Navajo land en route to the ruin, but hiking away from the main trail is not allowed. No fires are allowed so bring a stove or cold food.

Local Navajos provide horses for about $60 for experienced riders. Inquire at the visitor center.

Places to Stay

The campground at the visitor center is open from May through September and has 30 sites with water, but no showers or RV hookups. Camping is free on a first-come, first-served basis. A couple of large group sites are available by reservation. During other months, the campground remains open but the water is turned off. If the campground is full, there is a small overflow campground with no water.

SHONTO

This small Navajo village west of the monument has a store and offers horseback trips to Rainbow Bridge National Monument. (See the end of the Grand Canyon & Lake Powell chapter.) Contact Rainbow Trails & Tours (☎ 520-672-2397), PO Box 7218, Shonto, AZ 86054.

TUBA CITY

This town of more than 7000 inhabitants is a mile north of the intersection of Hwy 160 and Hwy 264. It was originally settled by Mormons in 1875 and is now the major town in the western half of the reservation. It was named after a Hopi chief. There is a small hospital (☎ 520-283-5201).

The **Tuba Trading Post** (☎ 520-283-4545) dates back to the 1880s and sells authentic Indian arts and crafts as well as food. A motel and restaurant are next door. The trading post has information about upcoming public dances and events on the Hopi and Navajo Reservations. **Dinosaur tracks** are seen 5 miles west along Hwy 160 on the north side of the road. Look for

a small sign and a few Navajo crafts stalls at the turnoff.

See the Navajo Reservation section earlier in this chapter for details on getting to and from Tuba City by bus.

Places to Stay & Eat

The *Grey Hills Inn* (☎ 520-283-6271, ext 141, fax 520-283-6604), PO Box 160, Tuba City, AZ 86045, is in the Grey Hills High School, a half mile east along Hwy 160 from the intersection with Hwy 264. Students operate a simple motel/youth hostel and reservations are accepted. Rooms with shared baths are $42 to $58 for one to four people from May to October, less in winter. Dorm beds are $15 per person and there are kitchen facilities.

The 80-room *Quality Inn* (☎ 520-283-4545, 800-644-8383, fax 520-283-4144) is part of the Tuba Trading Post complex. Rooms are in the $90s for a double from May to October, less at other times. Two mini-suites are $135. The *Hogan Restaurant* (☎ 520-283-5260) is on the premises, open daily from 6 am to 9 pm.

At the intersection of Hwy 160 and Hwy 264, truckers stop at the *Truck Stop Cafe* (☎ 520-283-4975).

Hopi Indian Reservation

The Hopi are the oldest, most traditional and most religious tribe in Arizona, if not the entire continent. Their earliest villages were contemporary with the ancestral cliff dwellings seen in several of the national parks in the area. Unlike the residents of those dwellings, however, who abandoned them about 1300 AD, the Hopi have continuously inhabited three mesas in the high deserts of northeastern Arizona for centuries. Old Oraibi, for example, has been continuously inhabited since the early 1100s AD and vies with Acoma Pueblo in New Mexico for the title of oldest continuously inhabited town in North America. It is thought that the ancestors of some of today's Hopi were also the people who migrated from other cliff dwellings 700 years ago.

The Hopi are a deeply religious and agricultural people. They are also private people and would just as soon be left alone to celebrate their cycle of life on the mesa tops. Because of their isolated location, they have received less outside influence than most other tribes and they have limited facilities for tourism.

When the Spaniards arrived, they stuck mainly to the Rio Grande valley and rarely struck out into the high deserts were the Hopi lived. Spanish explorers Pedro de Tovar and García López de Cárdenas, members of Coronado's expedition, were the first Europeans to visit the Hopi mesas in 1540, and Hopi guides led Cárdenas to see the Grand Canyon. In 1592, a Spanish mission was established at Awatovi and the zealous friars attempted to close down kivas and stop the religious dance cycle that is an integral part of the Hopi way of life. Because of this, the Hopi joined the Pueblo Revolt of 1680, drove out Spanish missionaries and destroyed the church. When the Spaniards returned to New Mexico in 1692, their attempts at reviving this mission failed and the entire area is now uninhabited and in ruins. Although unsuccessful in establishing their religion among the Hopi, the Europeans were, unfortunately, successful importers of disease: Smallpox wiped out 70% of the tribe in the 1800s.

Meanwhile, the Hopi were forced to deal with raids by Navajo and other groups. When the Navajo were rounded up for 'The Long Walk,' the Hopi, perceived as peaceful and less of a threat to US expansion, were left on their mesa tops. After the Navajo were allowed to return from their forced exile, they came back to the lands surrounding the Hopi mesas. Historically, the Hopi have distrusted the Navajo, and it is ironic, therefore, that the Hopi Reservation is completely surrounded by the Navajo Reservation.

Today, about 11,000 Hopi live on the 2410-sq-mile reservation, of which more than 1400 square miles are partitioned lands used by the Navajo. A complicated century-old legal conflict between the two tribes about the boundaries of the reservations was officially resolved by a US Senate bill in 1996, but there are still disagreements between the two tribes.

Orientation

The reservation is crossed by Hwy 264, which goes past the three mesas that form the heart of the reservation. These are pragmatically named, from east to west, First Mesa, Second Mesa and Third Mesa, and villages on the reservation will likewise be described from east to west. In addition, paved Hwys 6, 87 and 2 enter the reservation from the south, giving access from the I-40 corridor. Travel on paved highways is freely allowed but you can't drive or hike off the main highways without a permit.

Information

A tribal government coordinates activities among the 12 main Hopi villages and between the tribe and the outside world. Information is available from the tribe's Office of Public Relations (☎ 520-734-2441), PO Box 123, Kykotsmovi, AZ 86039. Tribal offices are open from 8 am to 5 pm Monday to Friday. Each village has its own leader, who often plays an important role in the religious practices of the village. Rules about visiting villages vary from place to place and you should contact each village (telephone numbers given below) to learn about their particular rules. These rules can change at any time. The village with the best tourism infrastructure is Walpi on First Mesa.

Outside each village and in prominent places on the highways are signs informing visitors about the villages' individual policies. All villages strictly prohibit any form of recording, be it camera, video- or audiotape, or sketching. Students of anthropology and related disciplines require tribal permits as well, and these are not issued without very careful scrutiny. As a general rule, the Hopi are not interested in having their culture dissected by outsiders. Alcohol and drug use are prohibited throughout the reservation. Visitors are allowed to attend some ceremonial dances but most are closed to the public.

As with the rest of Arizona (and different from the surrounding Navajo Indian Reservation) the Hopi Reservation does not observe daylight-saving time in summer.

There are no banks on the reservation, although an ATM is planned in the Circle M Store in Polacca. Cash is preferred for most transactions. There is a hospital (☎ 520-738-2211) at Keams Canyon and a new one will be built in Polacca. In emergencies, call the Hopi Police (☎ 520-738-2233).

Keams Canyon and Second Mesa have the only two motels on the reservation.

Special Events

There are scores of ceremonial dances throughout the year but most were closed in 1992 to the non-Indian public. There are two reasons for this. The first is that the religious nature of the Hopi dances was being threatened by visitors, and the second is that their remote mesa-top locations did not have the infrastructure (bathrooms, water, food, emergency services and space) to deal with scores of visitors.

The attendance of non-Indian visitors at dances is determined by each individual village. The Kachina Dances, which are held frequently from January to July, are mostly closed to the non-Indian public, as are the famous Snake or Flute Dances held in August. Social Dances and Butterfly Dances, held from late August through November, are often open to public viewing. All dances are very important to the Hopi people, who attend them in large numbers.

The dances are part of the Hopi ceremonial cycle and are performed in order to create harmony with nature. A particularly important aspect of this is ensuring rainfall for the benefit of all living things. The dances are expressions of prayer that require a traditional and responsible performance. The precise dates of performances are not known until a few weeks in advance. Village officials can tell you about dance dates close to when they happen and advise you whether they will be open to the public.

The best bet for tourists is to try and see a Social Dance or Butterfly Dance in the fall. These normally occur on weekends and go intermittently from dawn to dusk. See the 'Visitors' Etiquette' sidebar in the Facts for the Visitor chapter for information on visiting pueblos.

Shopping

Apart from kachinas, the Hopi are traditionally known for fine pottery, basketware and, more recently, jewelry and paintings. These crafts can be purchased from individuals or from stores on the reservation at prices below what you'd pay elsewhere. Hopi religious paraphernalia, however, is not offered for sale. Some reputable stores are mentioned under individual villages, but there are others.

KEAMS CANYON

This easternmost village houses federal government offices and officials, a small hospital, a crafts store and several churches. It is not a traditional Hopi village.

Keams Canyon Motel (☎ 520-738-2297) has basic rooms in the $40s. Nearby is a free campground with no water or facilities. There is a simple restaurant here serving American and Hopi food from 7 am daily.

FIRST MESA

This mesa is about 15 miles west of Keams Canyon. **Polacca** is a nontraditional village at the bottom of the mesa. A steep road climbs to the mesa top but large RVs and

Kachinas

Kachinas are several hundred sacred spirits that live in the San Francisco Mountains north of Flagstaff. At prescribed intervals during the year they come to the Hopi Reservation and dance in a precise and ritualized fashion. These dances maintain harmony among all living things and are especially important for rainfall and fertility.

The Hopi men who carefully and respectfully perform these dances prepare for the events over many days. They are important figures in the religion of the tribe, and it can be said that the dancers are the kachinas that they represent. This is why the dances have such a sacred significance to the Hopi and why the tribe is reluctant to trivialize their importance by turning a religious ceremonial into a tourist spectacle. The masks and costumes used by each kachina are often spectacular.

One of the biggest Kachina Dances is the Powamuya, or 'Bean Dance,' held in February. During this time, young Hopi girls are presented with kachina dolls that incorporate the girls into the religious cycle of the tribe. The dolls are traditionally carved from the eroded root of a cottonwood tree, a tree that is an indicator of moisture. Over time, these dolls have become popular collectors' items and Hopi craftsmen are producing them for the general public as an art form. Not all kachinas are carved for the tourist trade: some are considered too sacred. Other tribes, notably the Navajo, have copied kachina dolls from the Hopi.

In March 1992, Marvel Comics, the well-known comic-book publisher, issued an *NHL Superpro* comic book in which there was a story about kachinas trying to violently capture a Hopi ice-skating champion who was not living a traditional lifestyle. The Hopi people considered this an inaccurate and blasphemous portrayal of the sacred nature of the kachina's role in Hopi life. It was also the last straw in many years of inappropriate actions regarding Hopi religious practices, and most Kachina Dances are now closed to tourists. ∎

trailers will not make it; leave them in Polacca. The first village on the mesa is **Hano**, inhabited by Tewa-speaking Pueblo Indians who arrived in 1696 after fleeing from the Spaniards. They have been integrated into the Hopi tribe. Hano runs into the Hopi village of **Sichomovi** (you can't tell the difference), which is an 'overflow' of Walpi. Note that the mesa is occasionally closed to visitors during Kachina Dances.

At the very end of First Mesa is the tiny village of **Walpi**. This was built around 1200 AD in a spectacular setting on a finger-mesa jutting out into space. It is the most dramatic of the Hopi villages. The mesa is so narrow at this point that you can't drive in; cars must be left in a parking area near the entrance to the village. There is no water or electricity, so the handful of

year-round residents have to walk into Sichomovi to get water.

At the parking area is a tourist office (☎ 520-737-2262, 520-737-2670). Between about 9:30 am and 4 pm you can hire a Hopi guide here for a 45-minute Walpi walking tour. Fees are $5; $4 for 11- to 17-year-olds; $3 for five- to 10-year-olds and those over 65. The guides speak excellent English and the tour is a highlight of a visit to Hopiland.

There are many artisans living on First Mesa who sell pots, kachina dolls and other crafts. There are always several in front of the tourist office and they'll give you detailed verbal explanations of the work they sell. I always end up buying a kachina here – the work is good and priced fairly.

Cameras and recorders are not allowed on the tours. Leave them locked in your car.

SECOND MESA

This is 10 miles west of First Mesa and is called 'the center of the universe' by the tribe. The **Hopi Cultural Center** (☎ 520-734-6650) is here, with a small but informative museum – no photography or note-taking allowed. Admission is $3 ($1 for children 12 and under) and hours are 8 am to 5 pm Monday to Friday; shorter hours on summer weekends. It may close on major holidays.

Next door is the *Hopi Cultural Center Restaurant & Inn* (☎ 520-734-2401, fax 520-734-6651), PO Box 67, Second Mesa, AZ 86043, with 33 modern nonsmoking rooms for $80/85 in summer, $60/65 in winter. They are often fully booked in summer so call as far ahead as possible. The restaurant is open 6 am to 9 pm in summer, 7 am to 8 pm in winter and serves American food and some Hopi dishes like lamb stew. Nearby is a free RV area with no facilities.

Crafts are sold in the Cultural Center complex; in the nearby Hopi Arts and Crafts Guild (☎ 520-734-2463), which has good silverwork, and at Takurshovi, 1½ miles east of the Cultural Center, which has both high-quality arts (including baskets) and cheap 'Don't Worry, Be Hopi' souvenirs.

Also on Second Mesa are three Hopi villages that often have dances, a few of which may be open to public viewing. Call the villages between 8 am and 5 pm from Monday to Friday for information or ask at the Hopi Cultural Center. **Shungopavi** (☎ 520-734-2262) is the oldest village on the mesa and is famous for its Snake Dances, where dancers carry live rattlesnakes in their mouths. These are religious events, not circus acts,

and tourists have been banned since 1984. Kachina Dances held here are generally off-limits too, but Social and Butterfly Dances may be open to public viewing. The other villages are **Mishongnovi** (☎ 520-737-2520) and **Sipaulovi** (☎ 520-734-2570), both of which may have some dances open to the public.

THIRD MESA

Ten miles west of Second Mesa, this area includes both villages on the mesa and others to the west of it. The first is **Kykotsmovi** (☎ 520-734-2474), founded in the late 1800s and now the tribal capital.

On top of the mesa is **Old Oraibi**, which Hopis say has been continuously inhabited since the early 12th century. Oraibi is a couple of miles west of Kykotsmovi. The roads are unpaved and dusty so residents ask you to park next to crafts shops near the village entrance and visit on foot, to avoid unnecessarily stirring up clouds of dust.

Many of the residents left in 1906, after a disagreement led to a 'pushing contest.' The disagreement was over educational philosophies and school funding. One faction wanted US-funded schools for their children while the other preferred a more traditional approach. The traditionalists lost and left to establish the new town of **Hotevilla** (☎ 520-734-2420) and, soon after, **Bacavi** (☎ 520-734-2404). Despite the relative newness of these, their inhabitants remain very much traditionals.

On the Highway leading to Oraibi is the Monongya Gallery (☎ 520-734-2344) and in Oraibi itself is Old Oraibi Crafts, both with good crafts selections.

There are picnic areas off Hwy 264 just east of Oraibi and just east of Kykotsmovi on Oraibi Wash.

ARIZONA

East-Central Arizona

East of Phoenix, between the high desert of northeastern Arizona and the low Sonoran Desert of southeastern Arizona, lies not desert but primarily mountainous and forested land. Two geographic features stand out in this area: the Mogollon Rim, between 1000 and 2000 feet high, which separates the Colorado Plateau from the lower deserts of Arizona; and the forested lands near the rim, composed of national forests and the Fort Apache, San Carlos and Tonto Apache Indian Reservations.

Whether national forests or Apache lands, east-central Arizona is a highland area that offers cool respite for the citizens of Phoenix and Tucson. These cities' inhabitants dominate tourism in the area. Travelers from outside of the Southwest,

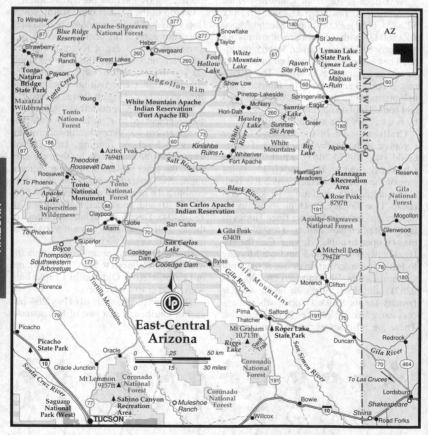

most of whom have forests at home, tend to focus more on the unique desert areas surrounding this part of Arizona.

PAYSON & AROUND

Only 90 miles northeast of Phoenix, Payson's pleasant altitude of 5000 feet and the surrounding Tonto National Forest lure Valley of the Sun residents seeking escape from the summer heat. The main thing to do is enjoy the countryside and the mild climate; hiking, fishing and hunting in the forests surrounding Payson are all popular pastimes. The town is the gateway to 'Rim Country,' and north of Payson is the world's largest stand of ponderosa pine.

Founded by gold miners in 1882, the town soon became a ranching and logging center. As Phoenix grew, so did tourism in Payson. Retirement communities, tourism and the government sector contribute the most to the local economy, although ranching remains important in surrounding areas.

Orientation & Information

Hwy 87, known as the Beeline Hwy, is the main drag through town and runs north-south.

The chamber of commerce (☎ 520-474-4515, 800-672-9766, fax 520-474-8812), 100 W Main, is open Monday to Friday from 8 am to 5 pm, and weekends from 10 am to 2 pm. The Tonto National Forest Payson Ranger Station (☎ 520-474-7900), 1009 E Hwy 260, Payson, AZ 85541, is open daily May to October, from 7:45 am to 4:30 pm, but is open weekdays only during the rest of the year.

The library (☎ 520-474-2585) is at 510 W Main. The post office (☎ 520-474-2972) is at 100 W Frontier. The hospital (☎ 520-474-3222) is at 807 S Ponderosa. The police (☎ 520-474-5177) are at 303 N Beeline Hwy.

Museums

The famous Western novelist Zane Grey lived in a cabin about 20 miles from Payson. The cabin burned down in 1990, but a few mementos were rescued and can be seen at the little **Zane Grey Museum** (☎ 520-474-6243), 503 W Main, open Monday through Saturday from 10 am to 4 pm, 11 am to 2 pm on Sunday. The **Rim Country Museum** (☎ 520-474-3483), 700 Green Valley Parkway, explores the history of Native Americans, mining, cattle and lumber in the area; it is wheelchair accessible and open Wednesday to Sunday from noon to 4 pm; admission is $1.

Payson Zoo

There are more than 50 animals, many of which have 'starred' in movies, at the small Payson Zoo (☎ 520-474-5435), 7 miles east of town along Hwy 260. Hours are 10 am to 3:30 pm (weather permitting); admission is $4 ($1 for kids under 13) and includes a guided tour.

Tonto Natural Bridge State Park

Spanning a 150-foot-wide canyon and measuring over 400 feet wide itself, the Tonto Natural Bridge was formed from calcium carbonate deposited over the years by mineral-laden spring waters. This is the largest travertine bridge in the world. You can go under it, walk over it or see it from several viewpoints along the short but steep trail. A guest lodge was built here in the early 1900s (everything had to be lowered into the canyon). It's been renovated and tours are available on weekends, but the lodge is currently not in operation.

To get to the park (☎ 520-476-2261, 520-476-4202), PO Box 1245, Payson, AZ 85547, drive 11 miles north from Payson on Hwy 87, then 3 miles west on a 14%-grade paved road (perhaps the steepest paved road in Arizona). The park is open April through October from 8 am to 6 pm, and the other months from 9 am to 5 pm, but is closed on Christmas. Admission is $5 per vehicle (up to four passengers; additional passengers are $1).

Historic Schoolhouse

Arizona's oldest-surviving schoolhouse, a one-room log cabin built in 1885 and used until 1916, is in the village of **Strawberry**, 19 miles north of Payson on Hwy 87 (and

ARIZONA

1000 feet higher) and 2 miles west on Fossil Creek Rd (turn at the Strawberry Lodge). Its restored interior is open during summer weekends and other times by appointment; telephone numbers are displayed at the entrance.

Activities

The USFS ranger stations can advise you about outdoor activities in the Payson area.

There are many rivers and lakes suitable for **fishing**, but only Woods Canyon Lake east of Christopher Creek has boat rentals and a bait shop. If you're really into fish, learn about the life of a trout at the Tonto Fish Hatchery (☎ 520-478-4200), about 5 miles north of Kohl's Ranch (see Places to Stay, below); it's open from 8 am to 4 pm daily.

Although there are many trails in the forest surrounding Payson for **hiking** and **mountain biking**, the best known is the 51-mile-long Highline Trail following the base of the Mogollon Rim from Pine to Christopher Creek. This and other trails are also suitable for **horseback riding**; you can rent horses and get trail information at the OK Corral (☎ 520-476-4303) in Pine and at Kohl's Ranch (☎ 520-478-4211).

Forest roads give access to hunters and anglers but are usually closed in winter, when they are used for **cross-country skiing**. The best-known road is the General Crook Trail (USFS Rd 300), which follows the top of the Mogollon Rim from Pine, past Woods Canyon Lake and on to the Show Low area.

You can also hike, ride or ski into the several undeveloped roadless wilderness areas to the east and west of town.

If you're looking for less outdoorsy recreation, you can play **golf** at Payson's 18-hole course (☎ 520-474-2273) at 1504 W Country Club Drive, or **swim** and play **tennis** at Rumsey Park (☎ 520-474-2774, 520-474-5242).

The Tonto Apache Tribe operates the **Mazatzal Casino** (☎ 800-777-7529) on Hwy 87 half a mile south of Payson. There are slots, keno, bingo, poker and a restaurant and lounge.

Special Events

Payson has more than 50 annual events ranging from dog shows to doll sales, the most famous of which is the Annual Oldest Continuous Rodeo, held every August since 1884. The Gila County Fair is held the second weekend in September, and the state's Old Time Fiddlers Contest is in late September.

Places to Stay

Although Payson is a popular year-round getaway, summer weekends see the most action. Accommodations are often booked weeks ahead and prices rise, especially during the major festivals. There are no bottom-end accommodations as far as prices are concerned; however, in keeping with its forested surroundings, Payson's accommodations tend towards the rustic, though there are modern chain motels.

Camping Free dispersed camping is allowed almost anywhere in the national forest, as long as you are a quarter-mile from a paved road.

Several developed USFS campsites sit along Hwy 260 east of Payson. *Ponderosa* is 15 miles east, *Tonto Creek* is 17 miles east on Hwy 260 and then a short drive north on USFS Rd 289, and *Christopher Creek* is 21 miles east and a short way south on USFS Rd 159. These three are open from May to September, have water but no showers or RV hookups, and charge about $9 a night on a first-come, first-served basis. Tonto Creek remains open in winter with no water or fee. Other primitive campgrounds are scattered along dirt roads in the forest, especially along USFS Rd 199 northeast of Payson; call the ranger station for details.

The *Houston Mesa Campground* (☎ 520-472-7658), a mile north of town along Hwy 87, has about 100 campsites roughly divided into thirds for tenting, RVing and horse-camping. Sites are $12 and up. There are showers. *Oxbow Estates RV Park* (☎ 520-474-2042), about 4 miles south of Payson off Hwy 87, offers tent and RV sites with hookups year-round and has

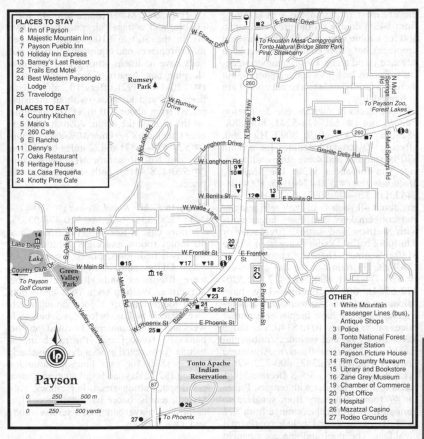

PLACES TO STAY
2 Inn of Payson
6 Majestic Mountain Inn
7 Payson Pueblo Inn
10 Holiday Inn Express
13 Barney's Last Resort
22 Trails End Motel
24 Best Western Paysonglo Lodge
25 Travelodge

PLACES TO EAT
4 Country Kitchen
5 Mario's
7 260 Cafe
9 El Rancho
11 Denny's
17 Oaks Restaurant
18 Heritage House
23 La Casa Pequeña
24 Knotty Pine Cafe

OTHER
1 White Mountain Passenger Lines (bus), Antique Shops
3 Police
8 Tonto National Forest Ranger Station
12 Payson Picture House
14 Rim Country Museum
15 Library and Bookstore
16 Zane Grey Museum
19 Chamber of Commerce
20 Post Office
21 Hospital
26 Mazatzal Casino
27 Rodeo Grounds

Payson

ARIZONA

showers, a coin laundry and a recreation room. Sites are $18.75 and summer reservations are recommended. A cluster of RV and mobile-home parks (tents aren't allowed) sits 4 miles east of Payson along Hwy 260.

Motels & Hotels Rates vary greatly depending on demand; double rooms start in the $60s during most summer weekends, in the $80s during holiday weekends. However, midweek in winter, the same room could be $40.

Some of the cheaper places include the *Trails End Motel* (☎ 520-474-2283, 800-

474-2283), 811 S Beeline Hwy; the *Travelodge* (☎ 520-474-4526, fax 520-474-0263), 101 W Phoenix; *Star Valley Motel & RV Park* (☎ 520-474-5182), 4 miles east of town on Hwy 260; *Ye Olde Country Inn* (☎ 520-478-4426), 13 miles east of town on Hwy 260; and, 19 miles north of Payson on Hwy 87 in Strawberry, the *Windmill Corner Inn* (☎ 520-476-3064, 800-476-3064) and *Strawberry Lodge* (☎ 520-476-3333). The Windmill Corner Inn has eight pleasant rooms with TVs and coffeemakers for about $60/70 for one/two beds; weekend reservations are needed. The friendly Strawberry Lodge offers some of the cheapest rooms in the area (ranging from $48 a double on the ground floor to $60 for a room upstairs with a balcony and fireplace), but you need to reserve weeks in advance (send a check) for summer weekends. Rooms lack TVs and telephones, but there is a family-style restaurant open 7 am to 8 pm daily.

Nicer places in town include the *Payson Pueblo Inn* (☎ 520-474-5241, 800-888-9828, fax 520-472-6919), 809 E Hwy 260, offering 40 standard doubles for around $70 in summer and some suites with private spa for about $130. The *Majestic Mountain Inn* (☎ 520-474-0185, 800-408-2442, fax 520-472-6097), 602 E Hwy 260, has about 40 rooms, all with refrigerators and coffeemakers, and many larger units with wetbars and patios, fireplaces or whirlpool baths. Doubles vary from $85 to $140 in summer. There is no pool.

All the 99 rooms at the *Inn of Payson* (☎ 520-474-3241, 800-247-9477, fax 520-472-6564), 801 N Beeline Hwy, have balconies or patios, coffeemakers and refrigerators; three have fireplaces; summer prices range from $110 to $140. The lodge has a pool, spa and includes continental breakfast. The *Best Western Paysonglo Lodge* (☎ 520-474-2382, 800-772-9766, fax 520-474-1937), 1005 S Beeline Hwy, caters to and is popular with seniors. Prices for 47 rooms that vary from standard to mini-suites with fireplaces range from $72 to $130 in summer and include continental breakfast. The pool and spa are open in summer only, and a family restaurant is next door. Also in this price range is the *Holiday Inn Express* (☎ 520-472-7484, fax 520-472-6283), 206 S Beeline Hwy.

B&Bs *Barney's Last Resort* (☎ 520-472-7911, 602-837-0378), 208 E Bonita, Payson, AZ 85541, has four rooms with private bath and TV for $69 to $79, with a $10 weekend surcharge. Full breakfast is included.

Cabins You can fish from your front porch at the rustic *Christopher Creek Lodge* (☎ 520-478-4300), 22 miles east of Payson

on Hwy 260. Motel rooms are $45 for a double, and cottages sleeping two to five are in the $60 to $100 range. Cottages have fireplaces and equipped kitchens, but beds have no linens – bring your own or a sleeping bag. Nearby *Grey Hackle Lodge* (☎ 520-478-4392) offers 10 cabins with fireplaces and kitchens (without utensils) priced from about $50 to $110 depending on the size of the cabin. Also at Christopher Creek are *Creekside Mountain Cabins* (☎ 520-478-4557) and, 2 miles beyond on Colcord Rd, *Mountain Meadow Cabins* (☎ 520-478-4415), both with comparable prices.

Resorts *Kohl's Ranch Resort* (☎ 520-478-4211, 800-331-5645, fax 520-478-0353), 17 miles east of town on Hwy 260, offers 40 motel rooms and eight cabins, some with two bedrooms, priced from $95 to $205. All the cabins and some of the rooms have fireplaces and kitchenettes. The attractive, Western-style rock-and-wood main lodge features a good dining room (see Places to Eat, below) and bar with weekend entertainment. Located on the banks of Tonto Creek, the ranch offers fishing (pole rental at $5 a day), horseback riding ($35 for two hours), mountain biking ($20 a day) and cookouts, and has a pool, spa, putting green, horseshoes, volleyball, tennis, bocce ball, shuffleboard, a children's playground, an exercise room and a game room.

Places to Eat

The unpretentious *260 Cafe* (☎ 520-474-1933), 803 E Hwy 260, is a good place for early risers, serving home cooking from 5 am to 9 pm. Other decent inexpensive places with American family dining include the *Knotty Pine Cafe* (☎ 520-474-4602), 1001 S Beeline Hwy, and the *Country Kitchen* (☎ 520-474-1332), 210 E Hwy 260. *Denny's* (☎ 520-474-4717), 317 S Beeline Hwy, is open 24 hours.

The town's best Italian food is served at *Mario's* (☎ 520-474-5429), 600 E Hwy 260, open from 10:30 am to 9 pm daily, and till 10 pm on Friday and Saturday.

There's an adjoining sports lounge. For Mexican food, dine at *El Rancho* (☎ 520-474-3111), 200 S Beeline Hwy, or the slightly more upscale *La Casa Pequeña* (☎ 520-474-6329), 911 S Beeline Hwy, which has a lounge and live music on weekends.

The *Heritage House* (☎ 520-474-5501), 202 W Main, is a tea room serving fancy sandwiches, soups and salads on a pleasant patio. The *Oaks Restaurant* (☎ 520-474-1929), 302 W Main, serves excellent prime rib, steaks and seafood in a pleasant country-home atmosphere, and is open Wednesday to Sunday from 11 am to 2 pm and 5 to 8 pm, till 9 pm on Friday and Saturday. This is Payson's most upscale restaurant, and dinner entrées are around $15.

Out at Christopher Creek, the *Kohl's Ranch Dining Room* (☎ 520-478-4211) is open to the public with a Western-style menu. Hours are 7 am to 9 pm, till 10 pm on Friday and Saturday, closed 2 to 5 pm from Monday to Thursday. Also, there's *Creekside Steakhouse* (☎ 520-478-4557), about 5 miles east of Kohl's Ranch, serving breakfast, lunch and dinner daily.

Entertainment
See a movie at the *Payson Picture House* (☎ 520-474-3918) in the Payson Plaza at Bonita and Mariposa.

Various bars and lounges provide drinks and live entertainment on weekends.

Shopping
Payson has a sprinkling of antique shops, especially around the 800 block of N Beeline Hwy. The bookstore next to the public library has a good selection.

Getting There & Away
White Mountain Passenger Lines (☎ 520-474-6749), 814 N Beeline Hwy, has buses to Phoenix ($22) at 10:15 am and to Show Low ($20) at 3:20 pm. There is no service on Sundays and major holidays.

SCENIC HWY 260
Hwy 260 continues about 70 miles beyond Christopher Creek to Show Low. The tiny

towns along the highway are the bases for camping, hiking and fishing in the wild and scenic Tonto and Apache-Sitgreaves National Forests.

Young
About 10 miles beyond Christopher Creek, dirt Hwy 288 heads south from Hwy 260 through the Tonto National Forest and past the historic village of Young as it winds its way to Lake Roosevelt. This is cattle country, and the small and remote ranching area can only be reached by unpaved roads.

In the late 19th century, this was the site of a bloody feud between farmers and sheep and cattle ranchers that left anywhere between 19 and 30 people dead (historians are not in agreement). Historical markers in the area document some of the details.

There's no real town as such, but do stop at the unique *Antler Cafe* (☎ 520-462-3265) on Hwy 288 for a beer or burger. Eclectic historical artifacts hang from every wall and ceiling beam. The cafe will rent one of three rooms for about $35 or suggest other accommodations in the area, including the inexpensive *Valley View Cabins* (☎ 520-464-3422) and the new *Pleasant Valley Inn* (☎ 520-462-3593) with spacious rooms with coffeemakers for about $65. The Antler Cafe hosts country dances on weekends.

Just off the highway (look for a sign), the Tonto National Forest Pleasant Valley Ranger Station (☎ 520-462-3311), PO Box 450, Young, AZ 85554, can provide information about camping, hiking and fishing in the surrounding forest and wilderness areas. The ranger station is open Monday to Friday from 7:45 am to 4:30 pm, and on Saturday and Sunday from Memorial Day to Labor Day from 7:45 am to 2:30 pm. During the rest of the year it closes on weekends and for lunch.

Forest Lakes
Back on Hwy 260, the tiny community of Forest Lakes sits about 4 miles east of the turnoff to Young. The General Crook Trail intersects with Hwy 260 near here,

the only place along its length where you can get onto a paved road. The 7700-foot elevation provides a cool climate for fishing and hiking in the surrounding Apache-Sitgreaves National Forest (for information stop by the ranger station in Heber).

During the winter, you can try the groomed cross-country ski trails at *Forest Lakes Touring Center* (☎ 520-535-4047), which also rents canoes in summer and has motel-style rooms with microwave and mini-fridge for $58, and one- and two-bedroom cabins with kitchenettes for $62 and $72. Cooking utensils are not supplied and there is a two-day minimum on weekends; discounts are available midweek. It has RV hookups for $18.

Otherwise, stay at the *Forest Lake Lodge* (☎ 520-535-4727), which offers 20 motel rooms with microwaves and refrigerators for about $70 a double on summer weekends; prices include a continental breakfast. Almost a mile east of the lodge, the *Rustic Rim Hideaway* (☎ 520-535-9030) has A-frame cabins that sleep up to eight people, each with two bedrooms, a fully equipped kitchen, bathroom, patio and barbecue grill. Rates are about $110 for four people and $5 for each additional person, but rates go up during holidays, when minimum-stay requirements may also apply.

Heber-Overgaard
This town's main draw is the Apache-Sitgreaves Heber Ranger Station (☎ 520-535-4481), PO Box 968, Overgaard, AZ 85933, at the east end of this small twin community about 15 miles east of Forest Lakes. The station is open from 8 am to 4:30 pm, Monday to Friday, plus 9 am to 1 pm on Saturdays, and provides details of the many remote campgrounds in the area as well as information about good fishing spots near Forest Lakes. The most accessible campground is *Canyon Point*, just off Hwy 260 about 2 miles west of Forest Lakes; the campground offers showers and more than 100 sites for $12 (about half of which have partial hookups available for $15) and is open from early May through

September. Other more primitive campgrounds are along the General Crook Trail and along several other dirt roads. They too are open in summer only.

You can stay at the *Best Western Sawmill Inn* (☎ 520-535-5053, 800-372-9564, fax 520-535-4164), 1877 Hwy 260, with a spa, exercise room and 43 rooms for $65 a double including continental breakfast. Some rooms have microwaves and refrigerators. There is also the cheaper *Canyon View Motel* (☎ 520-535-4598), 1842 Hwy 260.

From Heber you can take Hwy 277 to the small village of Snowflake (en route to Holbrook and northeastern Arizona) or continue east on Hwy 260 to Show Low.

Snowflake & Taylor
Technically beyond Hwy 260, these towns are included because they offer a couple of places to stay just outside the Apache-Sitgreaves National Forest. The small **Stinson Pioneer Museum** (☎ 520-536-4331), 102 N 1st East, Snowflake, is open 10 am to 3 pm, Monday to Saturday.

The *Best Western Silver Creek Inn* (☎ 520-536-2600, fax 520-536-3250), on Hwy 77 halfway between Snowflake and Taylor, provides a spa, exercise room and continental breakfast; some rooms have microwaves and refrigerators and run $50 to $69 a double. Cheaper rooms are available at the *Cedar Motel* (☎ 520-536-4606), 39 S Main in Snowflake.

SHOW LOW
Named after the 1876 card game in which the winner won a ranch by showing the lowest card (it was the deuce of clubs, the name of the main street), Show Low sits at 6400 feet on the Mogollon Rim at the intersection of five highways. This compact town is the gateway to the White Mountains, a region of forests and mountains popular with Arizonans. Along with neighboring Pinetop-Lakeside, it's a center for Mogollon Rim activities such as hunting, fishing, camping and horseback riding in spring, summer and fall, and skiing and snowmobiling in winter.

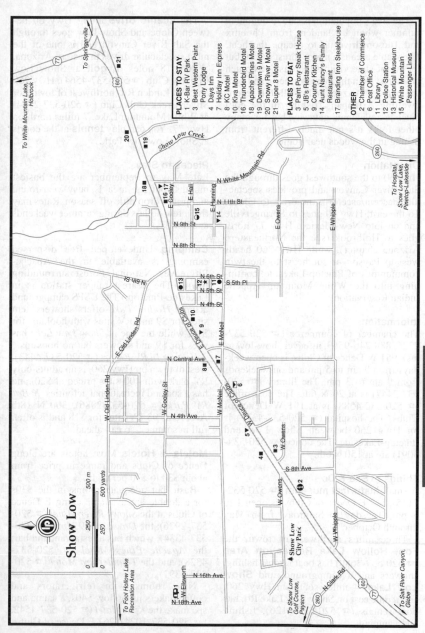

Show Low

PLACES TO STAY
1 K-Bar RV Park
3 Best Western Paint
   Pony Lodge
4 Days Inn
7 Holiday Inn Express
8 KC Motel
10 Kiva Motel
16 Thunderbird Motel
18 Apache Pines Motel
19 Downtown 9 Motel
20 Snowy River Motel
21 Super 8 Motel

PLACES TO EAT
3 Paint Pony Steak House
5 JB's Restaurant
9 Country Kitchen
14 Aunt Nancy's Family
   Restaurant
17 Branding Iron Steakhouse

OTHER
2 Chamber of Commerce
6 Post Office
11 Library
12 Police Station
13 Historical Museum
15 White Mountain
   Passenger Lines

To Springerville
To White Mountain Lake, Holbrook
To Hospital, Show Low Lake, Pinetop-Lakeside
Show Low Creek
N White Mountain Rd
E Hall
E Gooley
E Hunning
E Hill St
E Owens
E Whipple
N 9th St
N 8th St
N 6th St
S 5th Pl
N 5th St
N 4th St
E McNeil
S Clark Rd
N 9th St
E Old Linden Rd
N Central Ave
W Cooley St
W Old Linden Rd
W McNeil
W Owens
S 8th Ave
W Whipple
N Clark Rd
N 16th Ave
N 18th Ave
W Ellsworth
Show Low City Park
To Fool Hollow Lake Recreation Area
To Show Low Golf Course, Payson
To Salt River Canyon, Globe

0   250   500 m
0   250   500 yards

ARIZONA

The area's population is said to double in summer when lowlanders from Phoenix and Tucson drive up to escape the heat. The whole area is a major forest resort, but for out-of-state visitors there isn't as much of interest as in the more northerly and central parts of Arizona. After all, for desert-dwelling Arizonans, fishing in the cool pines is a welcome getaway, but for many other folks it's not much different from fishing in the woods near home.

Orientation

Hwy 60 to the southwest goes through the Salt River Canyon and provides spectacular descent/ascent in the drive to Globe. To the east, Hwy 60 goes to Springerville and on into New Mexico. Hwy 77 north goes to Holbrook (see the Northeastern Arizona chapter), while Hwy 260 heads west to Payson or southeast to the twin communities of Pinetop-Lakeside, continuing into the White Mountain Apache Indian Reservation.

Information

The chamber of commerce (☎ 520-537-2326, 888-746-9569, info@ci.show-low.az.us), 951 W Deuce of Clubs, is open weekdays from 9 am to 5 pm and on weekends from 9 am to 3 pm. The library (☎ 520-537-2447) is at 20 N 6th. The post office (☎ 520-537-4588) is at 191 W Deuce of Clubs. The hospital (☎ 520-537-4375) is on Hwy 260 between Show Low and Pinetop-Lakeside. The police (☎ 520-537-5091) are at 150 N 6th.

Things to See & Do

A small **historical museum** (☎ 520-532-7115), 542 E Deuce of Clubs, is open 1 to 5 pm, Tuesday to Saturday, from May through October.

Three miles northwest of town, the **Fool Hollow Lake Recreation Area** (☎ 520-537-3680) has boat ramps, fishing, showers and a campground, and **Show Low Lake**, 4 miles south on Hwy 260, and a mile east on Show Low Lake Rd, has boat rentals (☎ 520-537-4126), fishing and camping.

The **scenic drive** along Hwy 60 between Globe and Show Low goes through the Salt River Canyon and is one of the most spectacular drives in eastern Arizona.

Play 18 holes of **golf** at Show Low Country Club (☎ 520-537-4564), Hwy 260 and Old Linden Rd (northwest of town), or Silver Creek Golf Club (☎ 520-537-2744) at White Mountain Lake, 7 miles north on Hwy 77. You can play **tennis** at the courts at Show Low City Park.

Places to Stay

Late May to September are the busiest months, but the area is busy year-round and prices drop little off-season. Rates may rise a few dollars during summer weekends and holidays.

Camping Undeveloped free dispersed camping is available in the Apache-Sitgreaves National Forest surrounding town. (The nearest ranger station is in Lakeside-Pinetop.) The USFS campground at *Fool Hollow Lake* offers showers, tent sites for $9 and RV sites with hookups for $15, while the one at *Show Low Lake* has sites for $9 and showers but no hookups.

Venture In RV Resort (☎ 520-537-4443), west of town on Hwy 260, is an adults-only RV park with 400 sites priced at $20, and has a spa and recreational activities. *K-Bar RV Park* (☎ 520-537-2886), 300 N 18th Ave, rents 93 RV sites for $18 and is often full in summer, so call ahead.

Motels & Hotels Most hotels are along Deuce of Clubs and range in price from about $30 to $70 per night.

Basic but adequate rooms in the $30s for a double are available along E Deuce of Clubs at the *Snowy River Motel* (☎ 520-537-2926); the *Downtown 9 Motel* (☎ 520-537-4334), which has a restaurant and bar; the *Apache Pines Motel* (☎ 520-537-4328); and the *Thunderbird Motel* (☎ 520-537-4391).

Nice rooms with refrigerators and coffeemakers in the low $40s, a sauna and spa make the *Kiva Motel* (☎ 520-537-4542, fax 520-537-1024), 261 E Deuce of Clubs, a good choice, but call ahead as there are only 20 rooms. The *KC Motel* (☎ 520-537-4433, 800-531-7152), 60 W Deuce of Clubs, has a spa and 33 nice rooms in the $50s.

The *Super 8 Motel* (☎ 520-537-7694, fax 520-537-1373), 1941 E Deuce of Clubs, offers standard rooms priced in the $40s and low $50s. The *Days Inn* (☎ 520-537-4356, fax 520-537-8692), 480 W Deuce of Clubs, has what they say is the largest year-round Jacuzzi-style pool in Arizona, and more than 120 standard rooms with coffeemakers, microwaves and refrigerators for about $70. JB's Restaurant is conveniently in the same complex and provides room service. The similarly priced *Holiday Inn Express* (☎ 520-537-5115, fax 520-537-2929), 151 W Deuce of Clubs, has a spa, pool, 40 rooms (some with microwaves and refrigerators) and includes a continental breakfast in its rates. The *Best Western Paint Pony Lodge* (☎ 520-537-5773, fax 520-537-5766), 581 W Deuce of Clubs, has 50 nice rooms priced in the $70s.

Places to Eat
Food in Show Low definitely leans toward standard American. For family breakfasts, lunches and dinners, try *JB's Restaurant* (☎ 520-537-1156), 480 W Deuce of Clubs, or the *Country Kitchen* (☎ 520-537-4774), 201 E Deuce of Clubs. The homier *Aunt Nancy's Family Restaurant* (☎ 520-537-4839), in a large house at 21 N 9th, serves food Monday to Saturday from 7 am to 7:30 pm, and Sunday to 2 pm.

For steak and Western food, dine at the *Paint Pony Steak House* (☎ 520-537-5773), 581 W Deuce of Clubs, open from 11 am to 2 pm and 5 to 10 pm, or the *Branding Iron Steakhouse* (☎ 520-537-5151), 1261 E Deuce of Clubs, open similar hours.

There are also a couple of Mexican, Chinese, pizza and fast-food places, but none are outstanding.

Getting There & Away
White Mountain Passenger Lines (☎ 520-537-4539) has an 8 am bus to Phoenix via Snowflake, Heber-Overgaard, Forest Lakes, Christopher Creek, Payson, Mesa, Tempe and Sky Harbor Airport. Buses don't run on Sundays or major holidays, and the fare is $40 one way. The bus leaves from Phoenix at 1 pm, arriving in Show Low at 5:30 pm.

PINETOP-LAKESIDE
Southeast of Show Low along Hwy 260, Pinetop and Lakeside (averaging an elevation of 7000 feet) were originally separate towns, but now have combined services and extend for several miles along the highway with many motels, cabins and stores. This is the biggest resort in the White Mountains, indeed in eastern Arizona.

Orientation & Information
Hwy 260, running northwest-southeast, and known as White Mountain Blvd in town, winds its way between three public lakes as it heads east to Springerville. Show Low has the nearest bus terminal.

The Pinetop-Lakeside Chamber of Commerce (☎ 520-367-4290, fax 520-367-1247, plcofc@whiteriver.com), 674 E White Mountain Blvd, is open from 9 am to 5 pm (till 4 pm in winter), Monday to Friday, plus 9 am to 3 pm on summer weekends. The USFS Apache-Sitgreaves Lakeside Ranger Station (☎ 520-368-5111), 2022 W White Mountain Blvd, is open Monday to Friday from 8 am to 4:30 pm, and summer Saturdays from 8 am to noon.

The Arizona Department of Game & Fish (☎ 520-367-4281, 520-367-4342), 2878 E White Mountain Blvd, provides fishing and hunting information and permits (as do several outfitters along White Mountain Blvd).

The library (☎ 520-368-6688) is at 1595 W Johnson Lane. The Pinetop Post Office (☎ 520-367-4756) is at 712 E White Mountain Blvd, and the Lakeside Post Office (☎ 520-368-6686) is at 1815 W Jackson Lane. The nearest hospital is near Show Low on Hwy 260. The police (☎ 520-368-8802) are at 1360 Niels Hansen Lane.

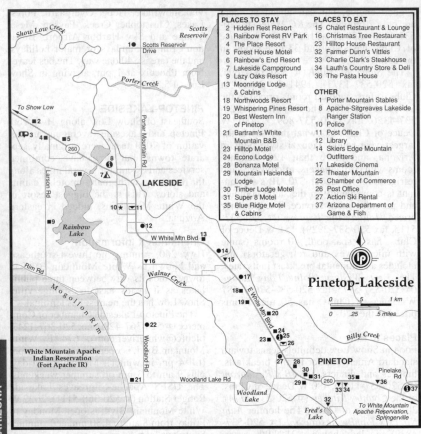

PLACES TO STAY
2   Hidden Rest Resort
3   Rainbow Forest RV Park
4   The Place Resort
5   Forest House Motel
6   Rainbow's End Resort
7   Lakeside Campground
9   Lazy Oaks Resort
13 Moonridge Lodge
    & Cabins
18 Northwoods Resort
19 Whispering Pines Resort
20 Best Western Inn
    of Pinetop
21 Bartram's White
    Mountain B&B
23 Hilltop Motel
24 Econo Lodge
28 Bonanza Motel
29 Mountain Hacienda
    Lodge
30 Timber Lodge Motel
31 Super 8 Motel
35 Blue Ridge Motel
    & Cabins

PLACES TO EAT
15 Chalet Restaurant & Lounge
16 Christmas Tree Restaurant
23 Hilltop House Restaurant
32 Farmer Dunn's Vittles
33 Charlie Clark's Steakhouse
34 Lauth's Country Store & Deli
36 The Pasta House

OTHER
1   Porter Mountain Stables
8   Apache-Sitgreaves Lakeside
    Ranger Station
10 Police
11 Post Office
12 Library
14 Skiers Edge Mountain
    Outfitters
17 Lakeside Cinema
22 Theater Mountain
25 Chamber of Commerce
26 Post Office
27 Action Ski Rental
37 Arizona Department of
    Game & Fish

Pinetop-Lakeside

Fishing & Boating

The chamber of commerce has brochures describing more than 60 White Mountain lakes and streams suitable for fishing, and the USFS ranger station and Department of Game & Fish (see above) are also excellent sources of information. Right in town, Rainbow Lake, Woodland Lake and Scotts Reservoir all offer fishing and boating, and Rainbow Lake has boat rentals. Also in town, the private Fred's Lake offers license-free fishing; you pay for your catch by the pound. Fred's provides fishing tackle and will even cook your fish for you.

Other Activities

Pinetop-Lakeside is a base for **cross-country skiing** and **hiking** as well as other activities in the White Mountains. Thirty miles east of town on Hwy 260, the Sunrise Ski Area (see White Mountain Apache Indian Reservation later in this chapter) has **downhill skiing**; pick up any last-minute gear in Pinetop-Lakeside. Skiers Edge Mountain Outfitters (☎ 520-367-6200), 560 W White Mountain Blvd, rents and sells skiing, fishing and camping gear, and rents mountain bikes for $15 a day, with multi-day discounts. Action Ski Rental (☎ 520-367-3373), 713 E White

Mountain Blvd, rents skis in winter and mountain bikes in summer. There are numerous **mountain-biking** trails.

For **horseback riding**, try Porter Mountain Stables (☎ 520-368-5306), Pinetop Lakes Stables (☎ 520-369-1000) and Thunderhorse Ranch (☎ 520-368- 5593).

The White Mountain Trail System is a new series of loop trails totaling about 200 miles and designed for hiking, biking and horseback riding. Planning began in 1997; the USFS ranger station has details.

Play **golf** and **tennis** at the Pinetop Lakes Golf & Country Club (☎ 520-369-4531), a mile east of Hwy 260 at the south end of Pinetop-Lakeside.

Also see the White Mountain Reservation for casino **gambling**.

Special Events
The White Mountain Native American Art Festival & Indian Market in mid-July brings together many of the region's best Native American artists for shows, sales and demonstrations. The Bluegrass Music Festival in mid-August is a popular event for bluegrass music fans. The year's biggest event is the Fall Festival held in late September with many fun events for the whole family.

Places to Stay
Slightly higher in elevation and more rural than Show Low, Pinetop-Lakeside has a wide variety of motel rooms, cabins, condos and rustic accommodations set in the forest. The location brings higher prices, as prices rise to what the market will bear, double what they are off-season. Two- or three-day minimum stays may apply at many places during summer. Also see White Mountain Apache Indian Reservation, later in this chapter.

Places to Stay – Camping
Pick up a USFS map to find several roads heading northeast into the forest where free dispersed camping is allowed.

Opposite the ranger station, the USFS *Lakeside Campground* offers more than 80 sites for $10 each, and provides drinking water but no showers or hookups. A boat ramp and boat rental are available, and the campground is open May through September.

The *Rainbow Forest RV Park* (☎ 520-368-5286), 3720 Rainbow Lake Drive, offers a few tent sites for $10 and 44 RV sites with hookups for $15, and is open from mid-April to mid-October.

Places to Stay – Budget
Basic motel rooms are priced in the $40s and $50s in summer and include the following along White Mountain Blvd in approximately increasing order of price. These are small mom-and-pop operations – don't expect luxury! The *Hilltop Motel* (☎ 520-367-4451), 577 E White Mountain Blvd, has an adjacent restaurant. The *Blue Ridge Motel & Cabins* (☎ 520-367-0758), 2012 E White Mountain Blvd, has rooms with refrigerators and offers more expensive cabins as well. The *Moonridge Lodge & Cabins* (☎ 520-367-1906, mnridge@whitemtns.com), 596 W White Mountain Blvd, has a few motel rooms along with more expensive cabins.

The *Forest House Motel* (☎ 800-440-2220, ☎/fax 520-368-6628), 2990 W White Mountain Blvd, has 17 clean rooms, all with microwaves, refrigerators and coffeemakers, sleeping two to six at $40 to $65 (weekends) and $32 to $55 (midweek). For another $10 you can have a private kitchen. The *Bonanza Motel* (☎ 520-367-4440), 850 E White Mountain Blvd, has simple rooms and a few more-expensive units with kitchenettes. The *Mountain Hacienda Lodge* (☎ 520-367-4146, fax 520-367-0291), 1023 E White Mountain Blvd, has 22 standard motel rooms in the $50s. The nearby *Timber Lodge Motel* (☎ 520-367-4463, 800-522-4463), 1078 E White Mountain Blvd, has 31 rooms in the $60s.

Places to Stay – Middle
Motels & Hotels Standard modern motel rooms at the *Econo Lodge* (☎ 520-367-3636, fax 520-367-1543), 458 E White Mountain Blvd, and at the *Best Western*

Inn of Pinetop (☎ 520-367-6667, fax 520-367-6672), 404 E White Mountain Blvd, are both priced in the $90s during summer weekends and have indoor spas. The *Super 8 Motel* (☎ 520-367-3161, fax 520-367-2445), 1202 E White Mountain Blvd, has a pool and slightly cheaper rooms. Unless you prefer modern chain-motel rooms, you'll save money by staying in a more rustic setting.

Cabins The small *Lazy Oaks Resort* (☎ 520-368-6203), 1075 Larson Rd, sits on a quiet street along Rainbow Lake; the resort offers boat rentals as well as cabins with kitchens, fireplaces and one or two bedrooms that sleep from two to 10 people for $60 to $120. With 35 cabins, a sauna and a spa, the *Whispering Pines Resort* (☎ 520-367-4386, 800-840-3867), 237 E White Mountain Blvd, is the biggest cabin resort. The one- and two-bedroom cabins each have a kitchen and a fireplace, and will sleep from two to eight people for $60 to $120. The cabins at the *Hidden Rest Resort* (☎ 520-368-6336, 800-260-7378), 3448 Hwy 260, have fireplaces, kitchens and porches, and some have private spas; prices range from $60 to $100 for a double.

The 24 comfortable cottages at *The Place* (☎ 520-368-6777), 3179 Hwy 260, range from small studios to two-bedroom units, each with kitchen and fireplace; prices range from $75 to $90 for two, and $85 to $110 for four people. For a group, try either the three-bed, two-bath or a four-bed, three-bath cottage – rates for these are $180 and $250 for six and eight people.

The *Northwoods Resort* (☎ 520-367-2966, 800-813-2966, fax 520-367-2969), 165 E White Mountain Blvd, has 15 pleasant one- to three-bedroom cabins, each with fireplace and kitchen, starting at $90 a double. *Rainbow's End Resort* (☎ 520-368-9004), 267 Trout Rd, has seven cabins on the lake for $65 to $95 double, all with kitchenettes and some with fireplaces. Boats can be rented. There are comparably priced cabins at the Blue Ridge Motel & Cabins and Moonridge Lodge & Cabins (see above).

B&Bs *Bartram's White Mountain B&B* (☎ 520-367-1408, 800-257-0211), 1916 W Woodland Lake Rd, Route 1, Box 1014, Lakeside, AZ 85929, offers five attractive nonsmoking rooms with private bath for $85 a double, and includes a seven-course breakfast.

The *Coldstream B&B* (☎ 520-369-0115), PO Box 2988, Pinetop, AZ 85935, at the southeast end of Pinetop (call for directions) rents five rooms with private bath for $95 to $145 a double, and provides a hot tub, pool table, bicycles and afternoon tea as well as full breakfast.

Places to Stay – Top End
Frank Smith & Associates (☎ 520-369-4000) assists with expensive condo rentals.

Places to Eat
For breakfasts and meals throughout the day, try the *Hilltop House Restaurant* (☎ 520-367-4617), 579 E White Mountain Blvd. *Farmer Dunn's Vittles* (☎ 520-367-3866), next to Fred's Lake, serves home-style breakfasts, lunches and dinners, and will cook the trout you just caught in the lake. Get picnic items or sit down for breakfast or lunch at *Lauth's Country Store & Deli* (☎ 520-367-2161), 1753 E White Mountain Blvd. They open at 7 am. Decent and inexpensive Italian dinners are served at *The Pasta House* (☎ 520-367-2782), 2188 E White Mountain Blvd.

As in Show Low, the best places serve American food. The following four are all open for dinner and serve meals in the $10 to $20 range. *Charlie Clark's* (☎ 520-367-4900), 1701 E White Mountain Blvd, has been a favorite steak house for decades. Hours are 5 to 10 pm. The *Christmas Tree Restaurant* (☎ 520-367-3107), 455 Woodland Rd, serves great American food amid a rustic Christmas décor; the varied menu is not limited to steak and seafood, offering chicken 'n dumplings as the house specialty. It closes on Tuesdays (and Mondays in winter) and you can dine outside in summer. The *Chalet Restaurant & Lounge* (☎ 520-367-1514), 348 E White Mountain Blvd, offers steaks and seafood and has the biggest salad bar in town; open for dinner daily in summer, it's closed on Sunday and Monday the rest of the year.

Entertainment
The *Lakeside Cinema* (☎ 520-367-8866, 520-367-8867), 20 E White Mountain Blvd, shows movies year-round. *Theater Mountain* (☎ 520-368-8888), 537 S Woodland Rd, puts on plays and musicals in summer – boo the villain.

WHITE MOUNTAIN APACHE INDIAN RESERVATION
Lying between the Mogollon Rim and the Salt and Black Rivers, this reservation is a separate entity from the San Carlos Apache Indian Reservation, which is south of the Salt River and described later in this chapter.

Like the Navajo, with whom they share linguistic similarities, the Apache were relatively late arrivals in the Southwest, arriving in the 14th century from the plains of Canada. They were a hunting people. Living in temporary shelters and moving often, they frequently raided other Indian tribes and, later, Europeans. Of the many different Apache groups living in the Southwest, the White Mountain Apache were willing to accommodate US expansion more than most, and many of the US Army's famous Apache scouts were secured from this group.

The White Mountain Apache were fairly isolated until the 1950s, when tribal leaders decided to take advantage of modern lifestyles and began long-term development planning. Building roads and dams, they created some of the Southwest's best fishing lakes. A ski resort and, most recently, a casino, attract the tourists.

For those seeking outdoor recreation, the more than 2500 sq miles of forest offer some of the greatest outdoor recreation in the state, including hiking, cross-country and downhill skiing, fishing, camping and boating. Because it's under tribal jurisdiction, you don't need state licenses for fishing, boating or hunting, but you do need relatively inexpensive tribal permits for these activities, as well as for camping, hiking, cross-country skiing and snowmobiling.

Hon-Dah Casino & Resort
The casino is 2 miles south of Pinetop-Lakeside at the junction of Hwy 260 and Hwy 73. Hon-Dah, which means 'welcome' in the Apache language, provides gamblers with card games and slot machines 24 hours a day. The complex includes the *Hon-Dah Resort* (☎ 520-369-0299, 800-929-8744), which opened in 1998 with 128 comfortable rooms and a restaurant and lounge with entertainment. (This is one of the few Indian reservations where responsible alcohol use is permitted.) Weekend rates are $99 for standard rooms, $109 for parlor-suites and $180 for full suites; rates drop $20 midweek. There is also a gas station (cheapest gas in the area), store and the *Hon-Dah RV Park* (☎ 520-369-7400), with 120 sites at $17.

Whiteriver
About 20 miles south of Pinetop-Lakeside tucked in a river valley, Whiteriver (population 3800) is the tribal capital and main information source; inquire at the Tribal Office (☎ 520-338-4346, fax 520-338-4778), PO Box 700, Whiteriver, AZ 85941, in the middle of town on the main road, Hwy 73.

Obtain permits and information from various outfitters and lakes in the area or from the Tribal Game & Fish Department (☎ 520-338-4385), PO Box 220, Whiteriver, AZ 85941, open Monday to Friday from 8 am to 5 pm and summer Saturdays from 8 am to 3 pm. The office is next to the White Mountain Apache Shopping Center, at the south end of town on Hwy 73. Here, you'll find a supermarket, bank, post office, restaurant and motel. The simple *White Mountain Apache Motel* (☎ 520-338-4927) offers 20 standard rooms ($55 a double) and a restaurant open 7 am to 8 pm.

Fort Apache
Built as a US Army post in 1870, the fort remains in much better condition than most

ARIZONA

structures from that period. The two dozen or so remaining buildings at the fort give the visitor a sense of army life on the Western frontier a century ago. The fort was closed in 1922 and became an Indian boarding school, which contributed to its preservation. Stop by the **Apache Cultural Center** (☎ 520-338-4625), open Monday to Friday from 8 am to 5 pm (with extended summer hours) to learn about the history of the fort and the soldiers and scouts stationed there. The center also has informative exhibits about the tribe's cultural heritage and an excellent display of basketry. Admission is $3 for five- to 62-year-olds, $2 for seniors.

To get to the fort, drive 3 miles south of Whiteriver on Hwy 73, then follow the sign leading a mile east.

Kinishba

Of various ancient buildings on the reservation, those at Kinishba are the only ones open to the public. Built by Native Americans in the 13th and 14th centuries, the extensive pueblo buildings are not in very good condition and you can view them only from the outside. To visit the ruins, drive about 5 miles south of Whiteriver on Hwy 73, then head west a couple of miles along a signed dirt road.

McNary

The small town of McNary, on the north side of the reservation, was founded in 1916 as a logging center. You can pick up a fishing permit and supplies at the grocery store (☎ 520-334-2217).

Hawley Lake

This lake is one of the two most developed fishing areas on the reservation (see Sunrise Park Resort, below, for the other). You can rent boats from the marina (☎ 520-335-7511) from mid-May to mid-October, and can pick up fishing permits at the store. Other facilities include a gas station and a campground that offers tent sites for $7 and RV sites with hookups for $17, as well as showers and laundry. *Hawley Lake Resort* (☎ 520-335-7511, 800-537-0990) has 10

motel rooms and eight cabins, all with kitchenettes, for $60 to $100. During the winter, you can go ice fishing if the weather is OK; the road is plowed and usually open, although the store and cabins are closed. This is a good place to start asking around about the many more isolated and less developed fishing holes in the area.

Sunrise Park Resort

This area offers excellent fishing, well-developed skiing in winter, and a comfortable hotel. The entire enterprise is run by the White River Apache Indian Tribe.

Winter Activities Spreading across three peaks, the highest stretching to 11,000 feet, the **Sunrise Ski Area** (☎ 520-735-7669, 520-735-7600) has runs that drop 1800 feet to the lower of two base areas. The approximately 60 runs are serviced by seven chair and four tow lifts, and are evenly divided among beginner, intermediate and advanced levels. Snowboarders are welcome. Adult all-day (9:30 am to 4 pm) lift tickets cost $32; kids under 13 pay $18, seniors (65 to 69) pay $13, and those over 70 ski free. Adult half-day passes cost $26; kids pay $14. Try night skiing on Friday and Saturday until 9 pm ($15 for adults or $10 for kids). Services include ski and snowboard rental, child care, children's programs and a ski school (☎ 520-735-7518). Call ☎ 800-772-7669 for a snow report.

Two miles from the alpine ski area, the **Sunrise Sports Center** (☎ 520-735-7335) offers $6 passes for 6 miles of groomed cross-country trails and $6 snowshoeing passes as well as snowmobile tours, ice fishing, cross-country-skiing lessons and ski, snowshoe and sled-tube rentals. The Sports Center is open from 7 am to 5 pm every day except Tuesday.

Summer Activities At 9100 feet, **Sunrise Lake** has some of the best trout fishing in the area. Other lakes are close by. The Sunrise Sports Center has boat rentals and fishing gear as well as bike rentals, and can make arrangements for horseback riding.

Sunrise began as a fishing and skiing area, but mountain biking, horseback riding, sailing and other activities are becoming more popular.

Places to Stay Next to the Sunrise Sports Center is a year-round RV park offering sites with electrical hookups for $7 and tent camping in summer. Sites are booked through the Sports Center.

The *Sunrise Park Hotel* (☎ 520-735-7669, 800-554-6835, fax 520-735-7315) is near the lake and a couple of miles from the ski area. Free shuttle buses run frequently in winter, and the restaurant, swimming pool, spa, sauna and bar – with winter weekend entertainment – keep guests relaxed and happy. Rates start around $60 for a standard double, $75 to $85 for a deluxe room (some with spas); or $195 for a suite with a kitchenette and spa and lift ticket included. During the high season (winter weekends, holidays and mid-December through the first week in January) room prices jump to between $95

and $125, and suites to $300. The hotel offers a variety of special packages to tie in with resort activities; call for details.

GREER

Halfway between Sunrise and Springerville on Hwy 260, Hwy 373 turns south into the town of Greer. Founded in 1879, Greer (elevation 8500 feet) has a permanent population of 94 residents, most of whom are involved in tourism.

In summer Greer provides a cool getaway with convenient fishing and shady hikes. In winter the town is an excellent base for skiing, with the Sunrise Park Resort just 15 miles away and cross-country skiing, if conditions permit, outside your door. (It doesn't always snow, even at this elevation.) Lee Valley Outfitters (☎ 520-735-7454) leads horseback-riding trips in summer, and the Greer Lodge arranges romantic horse-drawn sleigh rides when winter conditions permit. Snowmobiles can be rented (☎ 520-735-7617). The small Circle B Market (☎ 520-735-7540) has

food, fishing information, maps and cross-country ski rentals.

Places to Stay & Eat

Camping The USFS has two camp-grounds on Hwy 373. *Benny Creek* offers 30 sites for $6 with no drinking water. *Rolfe C Hoyer* offers 100 sites for $12 and has drinking water, lake access and a boat ramp, but no showers or RV hookups. Both are open mid-May to mid-September.

Motels & Hotels Most of the places are pretty rustic, and two-night minimum stays are usually required. For basic motel rooms in the $40s, try the *Tripp Inn* (☎ 520-735-7540) at the Circle B Market. The *Molly Butler Lodge* (☎ 520-735-7226) opened in 1910 and claims to be the oldest lodge in Arizona; it offers rooms for $30 to $45 a double and has a good restaurant.

Surrounded by forest and with a deck overlooking the town of Greer, the *Peaks at Greer* (☎ 520-735-7777, fax 520-735-7204), PO Box 132, Greer, AZ 85927, is the fanciest place in town. Rooms with two queen-size beds cost about $100 double (you pay $15 more for each additional person), the honeymoon suite costs $150, and larger suites sleeping four to six people cost $150, or $160 with a loft. The resort does not allow smoking, and the recommended restaurant is open for breakfast, lunch and dinner.

Cabins *Big 10 Cabins* (☎ 520-735-7578, fax 520-735-7390, bigten@cybertrails .com) offers nine quaint, rustic cabins with fireplaces and kitchenettes from $75 a double. There is also a carry-out pizza house (☎ 520-735-7608) open for lunch and dinner; they serve roasted chicken as well. The *Greer Mountain Resort* (☎ 520-735-7560), at the north end of Greer, has a restaurant open from 7 am to 3 pm, and eight housekeeping cottages priced from $50 to $85 a double.

Rivers Edge Resort (☎ 520-735-7477) has fishing outside your door and one- and two-bedroom cabins with kitchenettes for $55 and $65 a double. *Greer Point*

Trails End Cabins (☎ 520-735-7513) has one-, two-, and three-bedroom cabins with kitchens for $60 to $100 for two people. Some of the B&Bs below also have cabins.

B&Bs At the far south end of Greer, the attractive *Red Setter Inn B&B* (☎ 520-735-7441, fax 520-735-7425), PO Box 133, Greer, AZ 85927, is one of the newest and most modern (though rustic-looking) places in town. Nine attractive rooms with private baths and some with a fireplace, spa, deck or patio are $120 to $160 a double, including full breakfast. Smoking and children under 16 are not allowed.

The *Greer Lodge* (☎ 520-735-7216, 520-737-7217), PO Box 244, Greer, AZ 85927, offers nine B&B rooms for $120 a double and eight cabins for $75 to $95 a double.

The *Snowy Mountain Inn* (☎ 520-735-7576), PO Box 337, Greer, AZ 85927, off Hwy 373 amid the trees, offers four rooms with private baths for $70 a double as well as seven log cabins with fireplaces and lofts that sleep four for $110. The restaurant serves gourmet continental cuisine in a high-ceiling dining room decorated with artifacts from around the world.

The *White Mountain Lodge B&B* (☎ 520-735-7568, 888-493-7568, fax 520-735-7498), PO Box 143, Greer, AZ 85927, is in an 1892 farmhouse; rooms with private baths cost from $65 to $85 a double including full breakfast, cabins with kitchens and fireplaces range from $80 to $100, not including breakfast.

This list isn't exhaustive so check around for others.

SPRINGERVILLE & EAGAR

Founded as a small trading post in 1879, Springerville, with a population of 2000, has become an important ranching center as has the adjacent town, Eagar (population 4500). Surrounded by volcanic hills, the two towns along the Little Colorado River sit at a comfortable 7000 feet, drawing tourists to the cool climate. The area has the added attraction of being close to two archaeological sites currently under excavation.

Information

Springerville, although smaller, offers more information than neighboring Eagar. Add 'AZ 85938' when writing to any of the Springerville addresses listed here. The Round Valley Chamber of Commerce (☎ 520-333-2123), 318 E Main, Springerville, is open daily from 9 am to 4 pm. The Apache-Sitgreaves National Forest Supervisors Office (☎ 520-333-4301), 309 S Mountain Rd (Alt Hwy 180), PO Box 640, Springerville, is open Monday to Friday from 7:30 am to 4:30 pm. A short way north on Hwy 180, the Springerville USFS Ranger Station (☎ 520-333-4372), PO Box 640, is open the same hours.

The library (☎ 520-333-4694) is at 367 N Main in Eagar. The Springerville Post Office (☎ 520-333-4962) is at 5 Main. The Eagar Post Office (☎ 520-333-4764) is at 113 W Central Ave. The hospital (☎ 520-333-4368) is at 118 S Mountain Rd. The police (☎ 520-333-4240, 520-333-4000) are at 418 E Main in Springerville.

Casa Malpais

At the Casa Malpais site, a great kiva, underground burial chambers, a plaza, numerous buildings, two stairways and many rock art panels were created by the Mogollon people in the mid-13th century and abandoned in the late 14th century. The site lies 2 miles northeast of Springerville and can be visited only on guided tours led by researchers; tours leave daily from the **Casa Malpais Archaeology Center**.

The center (☎ 520-333-5375), 318 Main, PO Box 807, Springerville, AZ 85938 (in the chamber of commerce building), has a very small museum, a short video about the site, and an excellent bookstore for material on archaeology and Southwest Indians. Hours are 9 am to 4 pm daily. In summer, tours are offered at 9 and 11 am and 2:30 pm, with fewer departures in winter. Tours are weather dependent, last about 90 minutes, and involve a half-mile walk with some climbing. Fees are $4; $3 for those over 55 or between 12 and 18 years old. Groups can make reservations for tours at other times. Call about the center's participatory archaeological research program.

Raven Site

Built and occupied between 1100 and 1450 AD, this Mogollon pueblo shows the influence of other Ancestral Puebloan cultures. More than 600 rooms have been identified at this site, located 1 mile down an unpaved road west of Hwy 191, about 12 miles north of Springerville or 16 miles south of St Johns.

The adjacent **White Mountain Archaeological Center** (☎ 520-333-5857), HC 30, St Johns, AZ 85936, has a museum and gift shop. Guided tours of the site leave several times a day. Tours cost $4; $3 for those between the ages of 12 and 17 and over 60. Self-guided tours are available at the same price. The center is open daily from May through mid-October from 10 am to 5 pm, and is closed in the other months.

During summer, guided hikes lasting half a day (three hours) cover 2 miles and cost $18; $15 for nine- to 17-year-olds. Full-day guided hikes, lunch included, are $48; $40 for nine- to 17-year-olds.

If you're a real archaeology fan, try one of the summer archaeological programs that last all day (8:30 am to 5 pm, including orientation lecture, lunch, lab and field work). Rates are about $65 for a day; $45 for nine- to 17-year-olds. Multi-day programs (reservations required) can be arranged, with kitchen and camping facilities available. Tent sites are $5 and RV hookups are $7 per person. Bunkhouse accommodations may sometimes be available on request.

Cushman Art Museum

Housed in the Springerville Church, the Cushman Museum is the place to see a small but high-quality collection of European art, from the Renaissance to the early 20th century, without being surrounded by hordes of other museum-goers. The private Renee Cushman collection was willed to the Mormon Church, which displays it at

ARIZONA

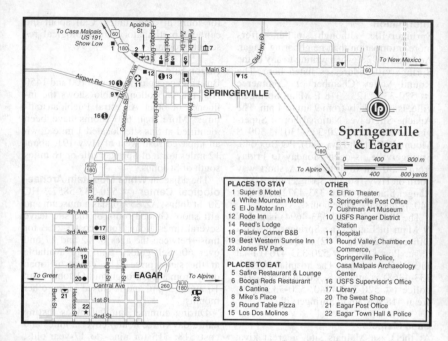

PLACES TO STAY
1 Super 8 Motel
4 White Mountain Motel
5 El Jo Motor Inn
12 Rode Inn
14 Reed's Lodge
18 Paisley Corner B&B
19 Best Western Sunrise Inn
23 Jones RV Park

PLACES TO EAT
5 Safire Restaurant & Lounge
6 Booga Reds Restaurant
   & Cantina
8 Mike's Place
9 Round Table Pizza
15 Los Dos Molinos

OTHER
2 El Rio Theater
3 Springerville Post Office
7 Cushman Art Museum
10 USFS Ranger District
   Station
11 Hospital
13 Round Valley Chamber of
   Commerce,
   Springerville Police,
   Casa Malpais Archaeology
   Center
16 USFS Supervisor's Office
17 Library
20 The Sweat Shop
21 Eagar Post Office
22 Eagar Town Hall & Police

the Springerville Church on request. The church is two blocks north of Main on Aldrice Burk Rd; look for the sign. At the church, a poster on the door gives the phone number of the current curator – call for an appointment. The chamber of commerce usually has the curator's telephone number as well.

Springerville Volcanic Field
The mountains west of town have the gently sloping appearance of volcanoes, which is exactly what they are. More than 400 volcanic vents have been mapped in this volcanic field, which covers almost 1200 sq miles and is the third largest of its kind in North America. The chamber of commerce has a brochure describing the area, with a suggested self-guided auto tour.

Fishing & Boating
The closest lake is **Nelson Reservoir**, about 6 miles southeast of the Hwy 260/180 intersection. This USFS-owned reservoir

has a boat ramp (electric motors only), restrooms and trout-fishing year-round (ice fishing in winter).

Three miles west of Eagar on Hwy 260 and then about 20 miles south on mainly paved Hwy 261, **Big Lake** offers excellent trout-fishing at about 9100 feet in the Apache-Sitgreaves National Forest; the marina has a boat ramp and rentals. There are several other lakes accessible from this road. Near Big Lake, Rainbow, Brookchar, Cuthroat and Grayling are USFS campgrounds open during summer, with drinking water but no showers or RV hookups. Rates are about $10 to $12. The season is usually May through September, though the marina and some campgrounds may remain open till November without water. Some lakes are suitable for ice fishing in winter. Call or visit the ranger station in Springerville for more details.

Fishing permits and supplies are available at Sport Shack (☎ 520-333-2222), 329 E Main, Springerville, or Western

Drug (☎ 520-333-4321), 105 E Main, Springerville.

See also Lyman Lake State Park, below.

Other Activities

The Springerville-Eagar area makes a good base for **hiking**, **horseback riding** and **mountain biking** in summer, **hunting** in the fall, and **skiing** during the winter and spring in the surrounding mountains and forests. Ask at the ranger station for details. You can rent alpine and cross-country skis, snowboards and mountain bikes at the Sweat Shop (☎ 520-333-2950), 74 N Main, Eagar. The fishing supplies stores (see above) have hunting and camping supplies. The Sunrise Ski Area in the White Mountain Apache Reservation is 23 miles away.

Special Events

The Fourth of July is celebrated, Western style, with a rodeo, fireworks, dancing and other events.

Places to Stay – Camping

The USFS offices can tell you about campgrounds in the Apache-Sitgreaves National Forest (some of the closest are at Greer and Big Lake, see above). *Casa Malpais Campground & RV Park* (☎ 520-333-4632), 1½ miles northwest of Springerville on Hwy 60, offers RV sites with hookups for $16 and a few tent sites for $10, as well as showers and a recreation area. *Jones RV Park* (☎ 520-333-4650), 425 E Central in Eagar, offers basic tent camping and RV hookups for $5/10, but lacks showers.

Places to Stay – Springerville

The *White Mountain Motel* (☎ 520-333-5482), 333 E Main, has basic rooms in the $20s, or in the $30s for bigger rooms, some with kitchenettes. Friendly *Reed's Lodge* (☎ 520-333-4323, 800-814-6451, fax 520-333-5191), 514 E Main, has an outdoor spa, a game room, gift shop, morning coffee, and a few bicycles to loan. It's a pleasant old Western inn, and John Wayne (who owned a ranch nearby) used to hang out here. Clean and comfortable older rooms are $28/34 single/double, or $38 with two beds, and newer 'deluxe' roc are $10 more. Also good, and similarly priced, is the *El Jo Motor Inn* (☎ 520-333-4314), 425 E Main.

The *Rode Inn* (☎ 520-333-4365), 242 E Main, has a restaurant and lounge and rooms in the $30s and $40s. The *Super 8 Motel* (☎ 520-333-2655, fax 520-333-5450), 123 W Main, has standard rooms for $40/46 for singles/doubles.

Places to Stay – Eagar

The *Best Western Sunrise Inn* (☎ 520-333-2540, fax 520-333-4700), 128 N Main, offers a spa, exercise room, and rooms from $50 to $90 during summer weekends; prices include continental breakfast. Four

---

Archaeology in Action

The Mogollon people left fewer sites than did some other cultures living in the early part of the second millennium, but two that did survive are currently being excavated in the Springerville area. Ever wondered what archaeologists do for a living? You can watch them work at Casa Malpais or Raven Site.

If you really want to get involved, ask about the participatory research programs, but be aware that research procedures are deliberate and painstaking. The archaeologist uses brushes and hand trowels to slowly and gingerly loosen centuries of debris from the sites. Each object found, be it an entire pot or just a tiny shard or scrap of wood, must be carefully labeled and recorded. Archaeologists must know exactly where one piece was found in relation to the next in order to build up an accurate record of the history of the site. A helper who removes an artifact and says 'Look what I found!' is no help at all; archaeologists must know exactly where the item was found and what was underneath, over and next to it. The work requires care and attention but can be very rewarding. ∎

...1910 *Paisley Corner B&B* (...565), 287 N Main, Eagar ...s is PO Box 458, Springer-...8), are furnished with antiques, have private baths, and are priced around $75.

Places to Stay – Ranches

The following guest ranches offer rustic getaways with horseback riding and other rural activities (call or write for details): *South Fork Guest Ranch* (☎ 520-333-4455), PO Box 627, Springerville, AZ 85938; *Sprucedale Guest Ranch* (☎ 520-333-4984), PO Box 880, Eagar, AZ 85925 in winter, or HC 61, Box 10, Alpine, AZ 85920 in summer; *Aspen Meadow Guest Ranch* (☎ 520-333-5206), PO Box 879, Springerville, AZ 85938.

Places to Eat

Booga Reds Restaurant & Cantina (☎ 520-333-5036), 521 E Main, serves inexpensive Mexican and American food from 5:30 am to 9 pm daily. *Los Dos Molinos* (☎ 520-333-4846), 900 E Main, prides itself on its hot homemade salsa, which is certainly good, as is their inexpensive Mexican food. They are open from 5 to 9 pm, Tuesday to Sunday, and serve lunch on Saturdays only.

The *Safire Restaurant & Lounge* (☎ 520-333-4512), 411 E Main, opens at 6 am daily and serves a good variety of reasonably priced American food, with some Italian and Mexican plates and nightly dinner specials. About a mile east of Springerville on Hwy 60 at D St, *Mike's Place Steak House & Saloon* (☎ 520-333-4022) offers daily dinners in a Western setting – good steaks!

Round Table Pizza (☎ 520-333-4565), 211 S Mountain Ave in the Round Valley Plaza, has dine-in, take-out and delivered pizza for lunch and dinner daily.

Entertainment

The *El Rio Theater* (☎ 520-333-4590), Main St at S Mountain Ave, screens movies. *Little River Lounge* (☎ 520-333-5790), 262 W Main, Springerville, has Western entertainment and dancing on weekends.

Shopping

The K5 Western Gallery in the lobby of Reed's Lodge is open from 6 am to 10 pm daily, and has a fine selection of local art.

LYMAN LAKE STATE PARK

Lyman Lake was formed when settlers dammed the Little Colorado River in 1915, bringing fine fishing, boating and water sports to an area where, even at 6000 feet, summer temperatures are often over 90°F. You can rent a boat at the small marina, or bring your own and use the boat ramp. Rangers offer special programs in summer, including tours of nearby petroglyphs and sites. A small herd of buffalo lives in the park. Day use costs $3.

The park (☎ 520-337-4441), off Hwy 191 about 12 miles south of St Johns, offers tent camping for $8, partial RV hookups for $13, and provides showers.

ST JOHNS

This town of 3400 inhabitants is 29 miles north of Springerville and is the Apache County seat. Local history is the focus of the Apache County Museum (☎ 520-337-4737), just west of downtown at 180 W Cleveland. It's open free of charge Monday to Friday from 9 am to 5 pm. The chamber of commerce (☎ 520-337-2000) is at the same address. The Apache County Fair is usually held the third weekend in September.

Places to Stay & Eat

The *Super 8 Motel* (☎ 520-337-2990, fax 520-337-4478), 75 E Commercial, charges $38/42 for singles/doubles. The *Days Inn* (☎ 520-337-4422, fax 520-337-4422), 125 E Commercial, has a restaurant and lounge. Rooms are in the $40s, including continental breakfast. There are several other restaurants in town.

CORONADO TRAIL SCENIC ROAD

In 1540 Francisco Vásquez de Coronado arrived in what is now Arizona (see Coronado National Memorial in the Southeastern Arizona chapter) and headed northeast in search of riches and the legendary Seven Cities of Cibola. During his travels he found many Native American pueblos but no gold. His route took him northeast toward present-day Clifton and then north through Alpine towards Springerville and beyond. The portion of Hwys 180 and 191 between Springerville and Clifton roughly parallels the historic route and has been named after Coronado.

Although the road from Springerville to Clifton is only 120 (paved) miles long, the route takes about four hours to drive. The slowest section is the last third. Parts of the steep and winding road climb to 9000 feet before dropping to 3500 feet at Clifton, and many hairpin bends slow you down to 10 mph. There are scenic views and lookout points where you can occasionally pull over, but trailers over 20 feet long are not recommended. The fall colors, peaking in September and October, are among the most spectacular in the state, especially those on aspen-covered Escudilla Mountain near Alpine. Many unpaved side roads can get you into pristine forest for hiking, camping, fishing, hunting and cross-country skiing, but winter snows can sometimes close the road south of Alpine for several days. There are several USFS campgrounds along the main road, and others on unpaved side roads. The Apache-Sitgreaves Ranger Stations in Clifton, Alpine and Springerville have detailed local information.

Note that there are no gas stations along the 90 miles between Alpine and Morenci.

ALPINE

At 8050 feet, Alpine is one of the highest towns in Arizona. Early settlers proudly named the town after the Swiss Alps, but although the forested surroundings and rolling mountains are beautiful, the resemblance requires a stretch of the imagination. About 600 people live here, although you can hardly tell as there's not much of a town center. Alpine is an excellent base for outdoor activities in the surrounding Apache-Sitgreaves National Forest.

Orientation & Information

The town is loosely scattered around the junction of Hwy 180 and Hwy 191. The

chamber of commerce (☎ 520-339-4330), PO Box 410, Alpine, AZ 85920, can send you local information. The Apache-Sitgreaves Alpine Ranger Station (☎ 520-339-4384), PO Box 469, Alpine, AZ 85920, is at the junction, and is open Monday to Friday from 8 am to 4:30 pm. The library (☎ 520-339-4925) and post office (☎ 520-339-4697) are both on Hwy 180.

Escudilla Mountain Wilderness

A well-maintained, 3-mile hiking trail climbs to a fire lookout at 10,877 feet on Escudilla Mountain, affording the best and highest views in the area. To get to the trailhead, take Hwy 180 6 miles north of Alpine, then turn right on USFS Rd 56 for 5 miles, passing Terry Flat. The unpaved road is passable to cars in good weather.

Hannagan Recreation Area

At over 9000 feet and about 20 miles south of Alpine along Hwy 191, the Hannagan Recreation Area is the highest part of the Coronado Trail, and offers plenty of summertime mountain biking and hiking, as well as some of the best cross-country skiing and snowmobiling in the state. You can fish in a small nearby lake, and camp in one of the many campgrounds near the area. Stop at the ranger station to pick up more information. The Hannagan Meadow Lodge is open year-round.

Activities

If you're into **mountain biking**, pick up a trails map at the USFS ranger station. Hannagan Meadow Lodge has horse, ski and snowmobile rentals. These services may be available in Alpine. In summer, play 18 holes of **golf** at the Alpine Country Club (☎ 520-339-4944), 3 miles east and then south on County Rd 2122. A couple of miles north of town, Williams Valley Rd is popular with mountain bikers in summer and becomes a groomed **cross-country skiing** area in winter.

Places to Stay

Camping *Alpine Village RV Park* (☎ 520-339-841), on Hwy 180 near the junction, has coin showers and tent and RV sites with hookups for about $5/15. *Meadow View RV Park* (☎ 520-339-1850), on Hwy 191 south of the junction, only has RV sites for about $15.

Free dispersed camping is allowed throughout much of the forest, and there are many USFS campgrounds. The closest developed USFS campsites are at *Alpine Divide*, 4 miles north of town on Hwy 180, offering 12 sites for $6 from mid-May to mid-September. The water is shut off in winter when you can camp for free. *Luna Lake*, 6 miles east on Hwy 180, offers 50 similar sites for $8. Fishing and boat rental are nearby, and the campground is closed in winter. There are free USFS campgrounds (no water) at *Hannagan Meadows*, 21 miles south of Alpine, at *KP Cienega*, 5 miles farther south, then 2 miles by dirt road, and at *Stray Horse*, about 6 miles farther south. There are more USFS campgrounds farther afield.

Hotels, Cabins & B&Bs Standard rooms in the $30s and rooms with kitchenettes in the $40s or $50s are available at the *Mountain Hi Motel* (☎ 520-339-4311), the *Sportsman's Lodge* (☎ 520-339-4576), *Alpine Cabins* (☎ 520-339-4440) and *Coronado Trail Cabins* (☎ 520-339-4772), all near the Hwy 191/180 junction.

The *Tal-Wi-Wi Lodge* (☎ 520-339-4319), PO Box 169, Alpine, AZ 85920, 4 miles north of town on Hwy 180, offers 20 rooms ranging from standard motel rooms to rooms with hot tubs and fireplaces for $55 to $95. Their restaurant and lounge are open erratically. *Hannagan Meadow Lodge* (☎ 520-339-4370, 800-547-1416), about 20 miles south of town along Hwy 191, provides 16 attractively rustic rooms and cabins from $70 to $100. Their restaurant is open in summer and winter, during the seasonal recreation periods. Facilities are limited in spring and fall.

Places to Eat
The *Blue Spruce Restaurant* (☎ 520-339-4378) and the *Bear Wallow Café* (☎ 520-

339-4310) are among your best bets for American meals.

CLIFTON & MORENCI
Gold prospectors arrived in the 1860s, but discovered that the area's copper deposits were a better source of mineral wealth. By 1873, miners founded the town of Clifton, which soon became a major mining center and the Greenlee County seat.

A huge underground copper mine operated in neighboring Morenci from the 1870s until the 1930s. Later, as an open-pit mine, it slowly engulfed the town. In the 1960s, Phelps Dodge Morenci Inc buried the old town and built a modern, company-owned town at the present site. Six miles above Morenci, an overlook from Hwy 191 gives dizzying views of the biggest producer of copper in the country. As you look down on this open-pit mine 2 miles in length, 200-ton trucks with tires 9 feet in diameter crawl like insects at the bottom. Free mine tours are offered Monday to Friday at 9 am and 1 pm; call Phelps Dodge (☎ 520-865-4521 ext 435) for tour times and an appointment. The tours last three to four hours and children under nine are not permitted.

Today, most of the miners live either in Morenci (population 2000), 4 miles from Clifton, or in Safford, an hour's drive away. Although Clifton (population 3000) remains the county seat, most of the once-splendid buildings lining historic Chase Street (off Hwy 191 in the center) are boarded up; it's still worth a stroll. For a history lesson, stop by the **Greenlee Historical Museum** (☎ 520-865-3115) at 317 Chase between 2 and 4:30 pm on Tuesday, Thursday or Saturday, or call to make an appointment.

Rockhounds search the surrounding hills for treasures; the chambers of commerce in Clifton and Safford can suggest where to look.

Information
The chamber of commerce (☎ 520-865-3313) is in the old railway depot on Hwy 191 at the south end of town. Hours are

9 am to 5 pm, Monday to Friday. The USFS ranger station (☎ 520-68-1301) is 10 miles southeast of Clifton at the junction of Hwy 191 and Hwy 75.

Places to Stay & Eat

Standard motel rooms are available in the $40s at the *Rode Inn* (☎ 520-865-4536), 186 S Coronado Blvd (Hwy 191 at the south end of Clifton), and in the $50s at the *Morenci Motel* (☎ 520-865-4111) on the main street in Morenci. The Morenci Motel has a restaurant and lounge.

At 265 Chase, the *Chase Creek Boarding House* (☎ 520-865-3891) offers beds in dorm rooms for $23 and private doubles for $38 in a restored building. Almost next door is the *Java Garden* with specialty coffees and snacks. Several restaurants are along Hwy 191.

SAFFORD

Founded in 1874 near the confluence of the Gila and San Simon Rivers, Safford (elevation 2900 feet) soon grew into an important agricultural center for farmers along the Gila River Valley. Many of the early settlers were Mormons; they also founded the neighboring town of Pima and settled in the small towns throughout the valley. More than 60% of Graham County's irrigated 55 sq miles grow cotton (one of Arizona's 'Four Cs,' along with copper, cattle and citrus), and local tourism, such as it is, is second to agriculture in the local economy.

Safford is the Graham County seat. There's not much to see in town itself (population 8000), though several motels make this the most convenient gateway for the Coronado Trail to the northeast, the San Carlos Apache Indian Reservation to the northwest and the Swift Trail up lofty Mt Graham to the southwest.

Orientation & Information

Safford is mostly spread out along east-west Hwy 70, also called Thatcher Blvd and 5th St in the town center.

The chamber of commerce (☎ 520-428-2511), 1111 W Thatcher Blvd, is open Monday to Friday from 8 am to 5 pm, and 10 am to 3 pm on weekends. It has a display on local industries (cotton, copper and the controversial new astronomy observatory on Mt Graham) as well as tourist information. The Coronado National Forest Ranger Station (☎ 520-428-4150) is on the 3rd floor of the post office building. The BLM (☎ 520-428-4040) is at 711 14th Ave, Safford, AZ 85546.

The library (☎ 520-428-1531) is at 808 7th Ave. The post office (☎ 520-428-0220) is at 504 5th Ave and Thatcher Blvd. The hospital (☎ 520-348-4000) is at 1600 20th Ave. The police (☎ 520-428-6884) are at 525 10th Ave.

Museums

The new **Discovery Park** (☎ 520-428-6260), 1651 Discovery Park Blvd (2 miles south along 20th Ave), is slowly developing its historic, scientific, ecological, agricultural and mining exhibits. The main focus is the **Gov Aker Observatory**, with a 20-inch reflecting astronomical telescope, a space-flight simulator and astronomy exhibits. This observatory will arrange tours of the observatory at Mt Graham (see sidebar). You can wander around the park daily, year-round. The Gov Aker Observatory is open from 3 to 9 pm on Friday and Saturday (call to confirm hours). Observatory admission includes a look through the telescope and costs $4; $3 for six- to 11-year-olds. Rides on the flight simulator are $6.

At Eastern Arizona College, located 3 miles west in Thatcher, the **Museum of Anthropology** (☎ 520-428-8310) displays artifacts of Native American culture, archaeology and anthropology; the collection is available weekdays to students and researchers during the school year (September to May). Six miles farther west in the village of Pima, the **Eastern Arizona Museum** (☎ 520-485-9400) has exhibits describing the influences of various peoples on the Gila Valley; hours are 2 to 4 pm, Wednesday to Friday. Displays at the **Graham County Historical Society Museum** (☎ 520-348-3212), 808 8th Ave,

ARIZONA

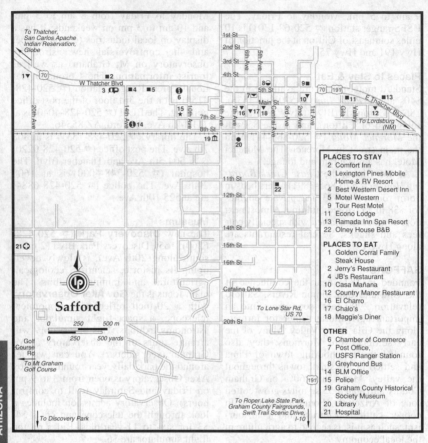

Safford

PLACES TO STAY
2 Comfort Inn
3 Lexington Pines Mobile Home & RV Resort
4 Best Western Desert Inn
5 Motel Western
9 Tour Rest Motel
11 Econo Lodge
13 Ramada Inn Spa Resort
22 Olney House B&B

PLACES TO EAT
1 Golden Corral Family Steak House
2 Jerry's Restaurant
4 JB's Restaurant
10 Casa Mañana
12 Country Manor Restaurant
16 El Charro
17 Chalo's
18 Maggie's Diner

OTHER
6 Chamber of Commerce
7 Post Office, USFS Ranger Station
8 Greyhound Bus
14 BLM Office
15 Police
19 Graham County Historical Society Museum
20 Library
21 Hospital

show life in pioneer days. The museum is open Monday and Tuesday from 1 to 4 pm or by appointment. All three museums are free.

Roper Lake State Park

This park (☎ 520-428-6760), 101 E Roper Lake Rd, Safford, AZ 85546, on the east side of Hwy 191 about 6 miles south of Safford, offers camping, boating, fishing, swimming and a hot springs. Day use costs $4 per vehicle. About 2½ miles farther south on Hwy 191, the Dankworth Ponds Unit also has fishing and a mineral hot spring, for day use only.

Hot Springs

Several natural mineral hot springs, with temperatures ranging from 98° to 108°F, are about 6 miles south of Safford. There are hot tubs at Roper Lake. Two commercial spas charge $5 to use their hot tubs and offer massage and reflexology treatments for $25 and up. Call Essence of Tranquility (☎ 520-428-9312) or Kachina Mineral Springs (☎ 520-428-7212) for rates and directions.

There are other springs in the Safford area, but few have been developed. Ask at the BLM office in town for directions to the lesser-known ones.

Swift Trail Scenic Drive

Hwy 366, popularly known as the Swift Trail, is a paved road up the Pinaleno Mountains almost to the top of 10,713-foot **Mt Graham**. The highest peak south of the White Mountains, Mt Graham also has the highest base-to-top elevation change of any peak in the state. The road begins from Hwy 191 almost 8 miles south of Safford and climbs 34 miles to the summit. This is part of the Coronado National Forest; stop by the Safford ranger station for detailed information.

The road passes through a succession of ecological zones, beginning with desert (the transition between the Sonora and Chihuahua Deserts) and climbing into dense, mainly coniferous, forests of the Canadian and Hudsonian zones. These are the haunts of squirrels, wild turkeys, deer, bears, mountain lions and many other species.

Development on Mt Graham

Mt Graham is one of the 'sky islands' of southeastern Arizona, separated from other summits in the area by lowlands. Because plants and animals living near the top of the mountain have been isolated from similar species living on other nearby ranges, some have evolved into different species or sub-species; this makes these high peaks a living natural laboratory for the study of evolution.

However, because Mt Graham is the highest mountain in the area and a long way from city lights and other sky pollutants, it has been chosen as the site of a major telescope observatory. Currently under construction, the project threatens the habitat of the Mt Graham red squirrel, among other 'sky island' species, and is therefore embroiled in controversy. Mt Graham is also a sacred site for some Apache Indians, an additional conflict. A small exhibit in the Safford Chamber of Commerce describes the astronomy project in glowing terms as a source of more employment and tourism for the area. ∎

There are several USFS campgrounds and picnic areas along the way as well as access to good hiking, fishing and hunting. The winding road is not recommended for extra-long RVs or trailers, and the top gravel section is closed by snow in winter.

The Columbine Visitor Station, more than 20 miles along the Swift Trail, offers maps and information and is open daily from 9 am to 6 pm from Memorial Day to Labor Day.

Activities

Play **golf** at the 18-hole Mt Graham Golf Course (☎ 520-348-3140), 4 miles southwest of town. Graham County Park and Fairgrounds, 2 miles out along Hwy 191, offers **tennis**, **racquetball**, **skating**, **horseracing** in March and April, and **stock-car racing** from March to November, along with other activities. The **swimming** pool (☎ 520-348-3222, open summer only) is in Firth Park behind the chamber of commerce.

Special Events

The Eastern Arizona Old Time Fiddlers perform in February. The Graham County Fair is in October. The Cowboy Arts & Crafts Fair is in November. The chamber has details of other events throughout the year.

Places to Stay – Camping

Several USFS campgrounds (☎ 520-428-4150 for information) along the Swift Trail (see above) all cost $6 to $9 and have water but no showers or hookups. *Arcadia*, at 6700 feet about 11 miles from Safford along Hwy 366, has 17 sites open from March to November, depending on the weather. The four others, open from about mid-May to late October, are at around 9000 feet and are between 20 and 30 miles up Hwy 366. *Riggs Flat* is the biggest campground with 26 sites but is also the farthest away from town; drive 28 miles along Hwy 366, which becomes unpaved USFS Rd 803, and continue on the gravel road for 5 miles. This campground offers fishing at Riggs Flat Lake. Along the way are *Shannon*, *Hospital Flat* and *Soldier Creek* campgrounds, each with about 10 or 12 sites.

The three camping areas at Roper Lake State Park have a total of 75 sites that range from $8 for tents to $14 for RVs with hookups; the campgrounds have showers. *Lexington Pines Mobile Home & RV Resort* (☎ 520-428-7570), 1535 Thatcher Blvd, provides $14 RV sites for adults only. *Red Lamp Mobile Home Park* (☎ 520-428-3382), 3 miles west in Thatcher at 3341 W Main, has showers, a pool, and tent and RV sites with prices starting at $10. Three miles east of Safford along Hwy 70, *Ivanho Mobile Home Park* (☎ 520-428-3828), 3201 E Hwy 70, offers RV sites only for about $12. Each of these has about 35 sites and may be filled with long-term visitors in winter.

Places to Stay – Budget
The *Tour Rest Motel* (☎ 520-428-3881), 110 W Thatcher Blvd, looks worn but is clean and has comfortable beds and some rooms with refrigerators; rates are in the $20s. For double rooms priced around $30, try the *Motel Western* (☎ 520-428-7850), 1215 W Thatcher Blvd, which has a small pool. Another cheap place is the *Pioneer Lodge & Cafe* (☎ 520-428-0733), 2919 W Hwy 70 in Thatcher. Rooms start around $40 at the *Econo Lodge* (☎ 520-348-0011), 225 E Thatcher Blvd, which has a pool and free coffee in the lobby. Some of the 40 rooms have microwaves and refrigerators.

Places to Stay – Middle
Room rates are about $50 to $70 a double and include a continental breakfast at the 45-room *Comfort Inn* (☎ 520-428-5851, fax 520-428-4968), 1578 W Thatcher Blvd. The *Best Western Desert Inn* (☎ 520-428-0521, fax 520-428-7653), 1391 W Thatcher Blvd, has 70 double rooms with coffeemakers in the $65 to $75 range. Both hotels have a seasonal pool and are next door to a restaurant. The *Ramada Inn Spa Resort* (☎ 520-428-3200, 800-555-3664, fax 520-428-3288), 420 E Thatcher Blvd, has an indoor pool, a spa, sauna, two

restaurants and a bar. More than 100 rooms from $100 to $135 have coffeemakers and refrigerators, and seven have whirlpool baths. Continental breakfast and evening cocktails are included.

Olney House B&B (☎ 520-428-5118, 800-814-5118, olney@zekes.com), 1104 Central Ave, Safford, AZ 85546, has a spa and charges $80 per couple in three rooms with shared bath or in two cottages with kitchenettes.

Places to Eat
Standard American fare is offered at the *Country Manor Restaurant* (☎ 520-428-3200), opposite but part of the Ramada Inn and open 24 hours; *Jerry's Restaurant* (☎ 520-428-5613), next door to the Comfort Inn; and *JB's* (☎ 520-348-9083), next to the Best Western Desert Inn. For cheap steaks, stop by the *Golden Corral Family Steak House* (☎ 520-428-4744), at the corner of W Hwy 70 and 20th Ave. *Maggie's Diner* (☎ 520-428-5009), 417 Main, offers homemade breakfast and lunch amid 1950s memorabilia.

Casa Mañana (☎ 520-428-3170), 502 1st Ave, open Monday to Thursday from 11 am to 9 pm and Friday and Saturday till 10 pm, has been here for 45 years and has tasty Mexican food. There are also a couple of good Mexican restaurants open for lunch and dinner in the historic part of downtown: *El Charro* (☎ 520-428-4134), 601 Main, closed on Sunday, and *Chalo's* (☎ 520-348-9889), 616 6th Ave, closed on Monday.

Getting There & Away
The Greyhound bus (☎ 520-428-2150) stops at 404 5th. Buses leave three times a day for Phoenix or Lordsburg, New Mexico, and beyond.

SAN CARLOS APACHE INDIAN RESERVATION
About 2900 sq miles of lakes, rivers, forests and desert belong to the San Carlos Apache Tribe. More than 8000 people live on the reservation, and of those, 3000 live in the tribal capital of San Carlos on

Hwy 70. Cattle ranching is the primary business, but some logging, mining and tourism also bring in revenue. Most tourists come for outdoor recreation, although there is also a casino on the reservation. There are no motels except for the tribal casino hotel, but you can camp at various campgrounds, including those at San Carlos Lake and Seneca.

A maze of unpaved roads penetrates the reservation, leading to scores of little lakes and river fishing areas as well as primitive camping areas. You'll need a high-clearance pickup or 4WD vehicle for many of them; contact the San Carlos Recreation and Wildlife Department for a detailed map and information.

Trout fishing on the Black River is especially good, and big-game hunting is permitted in season. The reservation claims that the world's-record largest antlers were taken from an elk here. Local guides can help you find rich hunting grounds for a high fee.

Information

To camp, hike, fish, hunt and drive off the main highways, you'll need a permit from the San Carlos Recreation and Wildlife Department (☎ 520-475-2343), PO Box 97, San Carlos, AZ 85550. The office occupies a big building on Hwy 70 in San Carlos – you can't miss it.

For other information, contact the San Carlos Tribal Offices (☎ 520-475-2361, fax 520-475-2567).

San Carlos Apache Cultural Center

A small but informative museum tells of the history and culture of the tribe and offers educational programs. The Center (☎ 520-475-2894) is in the community of Peridot, near mileage marker 260 on Hwy 70, about 20 miles east of Globe. Hours are 9 am to 5 pm, Tuesday to Saturday; admission is $3, $1.50 for seniors, $1 for students and free for those under 12.

San Carlos Lake

Formed by the Coolidge Dam on the Gila River, this is the largest lake wholly in Arizona; when full, it covers 30 sq miles and has 158 miles of shoreline, although it will shrink after prolonged dry spells. The lake has excellent fishing, and recently yielded the state's record-winning catfish (65 lb), largemouth bass (16 lb 1 oz) and crappie (4 lb 10 oz). Near Coolidge Dam (10 miles south of San Carlos) there is a marina and a convenience store as well as a campground with RV hookups, water and tent spaces, but no showers. Fees are $5 a person.

Seneca

There is a small lake and campground (no drinking water or RV hookups) here, just off Hwy 60 about 33 miles northeast of Globe. Camping is $5 a person.

Apache Gold Casino

The casino (☎ 520-425-8000) is on the north side of Hwy 70 at the western edge of the reservation, five minutes east of Globe. It offers 24-hour gambling and a restaurant serving alcohol. There are RV hookups, and the *Best Western Apache Gold Resort* (☎ 520-402-5600, 800-272-2438, fax 520-402-5601) has a pool, spa and 74 rooms in the $55 to $75 range.

Special Events

Sunrise Ceremonies, held in the summer, feature traditional dances in honor of young girls' coming of age. Some of these dances may be open to the public; call the tribal office for dates and details.

The Apaches love rodeo. The tribal rodeo and fair, held in San Carlos over Veterans Day weekend (closest weekend to November 11) also features traditional dancing. A spring roundup rodeo is held in April, and other rodeos and dances may be held throughout the year.

GLOBE

The discovery of a globe-shaped boulder formed of almost pure silver sparked a short-lived silver boom here in the 1870s, followed by the development of a long-lasting copper mining industry. Globe (population 6000, elevation 3500 feet)

ARIZONA

became the Gila County seat, a distinction it retains even though most of the copper mining has moved to the nearby towns of Miami and Superior. Globe offers the best accommodations in the area, and its various attractions provide a pleasant rural alternative to Phoenix (80 miles west).

Orientation & Information
Hwy 60, the main thoroughfare, is called Ash St, then Willow St, and finally Broad St as it snakes through town from east to west.

The Globe-Miami Chamber of Commerce (☎ 520-425-4495, 800-804-5623), 1360 N Broad, is open Monday to Friday from 8 am to 5 pm. The Tonto National Forest Ranger Station (☎ 520-402-6200) is on Six Shooter Canyon Rd at the south end of town. The library (☎ 520-425-6111) is at 339 S Broad. The post office (☎ 520-425-2381) is at 101 S Hill. The hospital (☎ 520-425-3261) is between Globe and Miami south of the Hwy 60/88 intersection. The police (☎ 520-425-5752) are at 175 N Pine.

Historic Downtown
Many turn-of-the-19th-century buildings still line Broad St south of Hackney Ave, making the downtown area a pleasant place to walk, less touristy than other old-town centers. The chamber of commerce has a walking-tour brochure describing more than 20 buildings.

Gila County Historical Museum
Find out about the area's history in this museum (☎ 520-425-7385) behind the chamber of commerce. The building used to be the home of a mine-rescue training station, so the museum has plenty of mining artifacts. Hours are 10 am to 4 pm, Monday to Friday, plus weekends by appointment.

Cobre Valley Center for the Arts
The turn-of-the-19th-century Gila County Courthouse houses this arts center (☎ 520-425-0884), 101 N Broad. A variety of local artists' works are on display Monday to Saturday from 9 am to 5 pm, and Sunday

from noon to 5 pm. An upstairs theater hosts local performances.

Besh-Ba-Gowah Archaeological Park
A small pueblo built by the Salado people in the 1200s and abandoned by the early 1400s is the principal site here. There are also some signs of earlier Hohokam occupation. Visit the museum's fine collection of Salado pottery and its ethnobotanical garden between 9 am and 5 pm daily; admission is $2 for those over 12 years old. Contact the park office (☎ 520-425-0320), 150 N Pine, about guided tours or walk around by yourself (follow the signs south of town).

Activities
Cobre Valley Country Club (☎ 520-473-2542), off Hwy 88 just north of Hwy 60, offers a nine-hole **golf** course and **tennis** and **racquetball** courts.

Far Flung Adventures (☎ 520-425-7272, 800-359-2627), PO Box 2804, Globe, AZ 85501, offers one- to five-day Salt River **rafting** trips. High water is February to June.

Special Events
Of the yearly events, most interesting are the Historic Homes Tour held over a weekend in mid-February, the Gila County Fair in mid-September and Apache Days, with tribal arts and traditional dancing, on the fourth Saturday in October.

Places to Stay – Camping
For free dispersed camping and some small developed campgrounds, drive south of Globe along Six Shooter Canyon Rd, past the USFS ranger station (which can provide a map); the road becomes USFS RD 122. The small *Gila County RV Park* (☎ 520-425-4653, 800-436-8083), 300 S Pine, offers sites with full hookups for $15 and tent sites for $7.

Places to Stay – Budget
Basic double rooms with one bed in the upper $20s and lower $30s are available at the *Willow Motel* (☎ 520-425-9491), 792 N

Willow; the *Belle Aire Motel* (☎ 520-425-4406), 1600 N Broad; the *El Rancho Motel* (☎ 520-425-5757, fax 520-425-8402), 1300 E Ash; and the *El Rey Motel* (☎ 520-425-4427), 1201 E Ash. Rooms with two beds cost a bit more. The *Copper Manor Motel* (☎ 520-425-7124, fax 520-425-5266), 637 E Ash, has standard rooms in the $40s; there is a pool and a 24-hour restaurant next door.

Places to Stay – Middle

Motels The *Cloud Nine Motel* (☎/fax 520-425-5741, 800-256-8399), 1699 E Ash, rents 80 comfortable rooms, some with spas and refrigerators, priced from $55 to $80 a double. It has a pool. The *Best Western Copper Hills Inn* (☎ 520-425-7151, fax 520-425-2504), on Hwy 60 a short way east of the intersection with Hwy 88 (in Miami), has a pool, restaurant and bar, and 68 rooms with refrigerators in the $55 to $75 range. The *Days Inn* (☎ 520-425-5500, fax 520-425-4146), 1630 Ash, has a pool, spa and 42 rooms, many with microwaves and refrigerators, for $50 to $65, including continental breakfast. If you don't need a pool, the

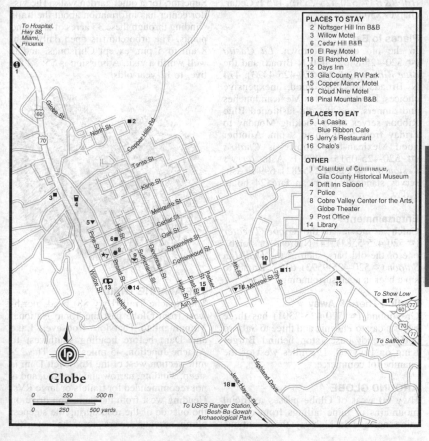

PLACES TO STAY
2 Noftsger Hill Inn B&B
3 Willow Motel
6 Cedar Hill B&B
10 El Rey Motel
11 El Rancho Motel
12 Days Inn
13 Gila County RV Park
15 Copper Manor Motel
17 Cloud Nine Motel
18 Pinal Mountain B&B

PLACES TO EAT
5 La Casita,
  Blue Ribbon Cafe
15 Jerry's Restaurant
16 Chalo's

OTHER
1 Chamber of Commerce,
  Gila County Historical Museum
4 Drift Inn Saloon
7 Police
8 Cobre Valley Center for the Arts,
  Globe Theater
9 Post Office
14 Library

To Hospital,
Hwy 88,
Miami,
Phoenix

To Show Low

To Safford

To USFS Ranger Station,
Besh Ba Gowah
Archaeological Park

Globe

0   250   500 m
0   250   500 yards

Holiday Inn Express (☎ 520-425-7008, fax 520-425-6410), on Hwy 60 at Hwy 88, has 45 comfortable rooms in the $50s, including continental breakfast.

B&Bs The *Pinal Mountain B&B* (☎ 520-425-2562), 360 Jess Hayes Rd, PO Box 1593, Globe, AZ 85502, offers two non-smoking rooms with private bath for $75. Housed in a renovated school dating from 1907, the *Noftsger Hill Inn* (☎ 520-425-2260), 425 North, has smaller rooms with shared bath as well as more expensive rooms with private bath and king-size beds; prices range from $45 to $65. *Cedar Hill B&B* (☎ 520-425-7530), 175 E Cedar, charges $50.

Places to Eat
In the old center of town, *La Casita* (☎ 520-425-8462), 470 N Broad, and the *Blue Ribbon Cafe* (☎ 520-425-4423), 474 N Broad, are both good, inexpensive choices. La Casita serves Mexican lunches and dinners, and the old-fashioned Blue Ribbon serves home cooking Monday to Friday from 6:30 am to 9 pm. Another good Mexican-food choice is *Chalo's* (☎ 520-425-0515), 902 E Ash. *Jerry's Restaurant* (☎ 520-425-5282), 699 E Ash, serves standard American fare 24 hours a day.

Entertainment
Catch a movie at the *Globe Theater* (☎ 520-425-5581), 141 N Broad, or stop by one of the old bars, such as the *Drift Inn Saloon* (☎ 520-425-9573), 636 N Broad, to sip a beer in aged surroundings.

Getting There & Away
Greyhound (☎ 520-425-2301) has three buses a day to Phoenix and three to Safford and beyond; buses stop behind Burger King on Hwy 60, 1½ miles west of the chamber of commerce.

AROUND GLOBE
Hwy 60 west of Globe passes artificial mountains of mine tailings from copper mines north of the highway; these continue

for several miles through the small towns of Claypool and Miami. From here, the road winds through the Devil's Canyon section of the Pinal Mountains, affording vistas of jagged ridges. Twenty-five miles west of Globe, the mining town of **Superior** has a couple of cheap motels, the *El Portal* (☎ 520-689-2886) and *Apache Tear Village RV Park & Motel* (☎ 520-689-5800). Visit the chamber of commerce (☎ 520-689-2441), 151 Main, for information about the area.

You can stop by the outstanding **Boyce Thompson Southwestern Arboretum** (☎ 520-689-2811), about 3 miles west of Superior, for a quiet garden walk. The visitor center has information about the trails winding through these 35 acres of arid-land plants. The arboretum is open daily from 8 am to 5 pm, except Christmas, and is well worth a visit. Admission is $5; $2 for five- to 12-year-olds.

THE APACHE TRAIL
The Apache Trail (Hwy 88) heads northwest from Globe past the Tonto National Monument to Theodore Roosevelt Lake and Dam before heading southwest to Apache Junction, 45 miles away. The 22-mile section west of the Roosevelt Dam is steep, winding, narrow and unpaved, and is not recommended for trailers or large RVs. Heading west from the dam, you drive on the outside of the road during the steepest climb; nervous drivers prefer the 'security'

of traveling west to east in order to hug the cliff wall rather than the drop-off. This is one of the most spectacular drives in the area. Once you're back on paved highway, the trail will take you past the small community of Tortilla Flat and the ghost town of Goldfield before reaching Apache Junction and the greater Phoenix area.

Tonto National Monument

About 28 miles northwest of Globe along the well-paved section of the Apache Trail, the Tonto National Monument protects a highlight of the area: a two-story Salado pueblo built in a cave. Like most other pueblos, it was mysteriously abandoned in the early 1400s.

From the visitor center (☎ 520-467-2241), a paved half-mile footpath climbs gently to the site, with good views of the saguaro-cactus-studded hillsides in the foreground and Theodore Roosevelt Lake in the distance. The visitor center has a museum and water but no food or camping facilities.

If you call or write ahead, you can arrange to join a free ranger-led, three-hour hike to an upper site along an unpaved footpath. Further information is available from the Superintendent, Tonto National Monument, HC 02, Box 4602, Roosevelt, AZ 85545. The monument is open from 8 am to 5 pm daily, but the trail closes an hour earlier. Admission is $4 per private vehicle; $2 per bicyclist or bus passenger. Golden Eagle, Age and Access Passes are honored.

Theodore Roosevelt Lake & Dam

Built of brick on the Salt River in 1911, this was the first large dam to flood the Southwest and, at 280 feet, is the world's highest masonry dam. At a hot 2100-foot elevation, the lake attracts water-sport enthusiasts year-round; swimming, water-skiing and boating are popular activities from spring to fall. The fishing is great throughout the year, and bass and crappie are two favored catches.

A marina and the Tonto Basin Ranger Station (☎ 520-467-3200), PO Box 649, Roosevelt, AZ 85545, are about 1½ miles east of the dam, just off Hwy 88, and are open Monday to Friday from 7:45 am to 4:30 pm. The Roosevelt Lake Marina (☎ 520-467-2245) has groceries, fishing and camping supplies, a snack bar and a boat ramp; boat rentals range from fishing boats for $45 a day to ski boats for $250 a day. You can also rent jet skis and water-skiing gear.

Places to Stay There are several USFS campgrounds in the area. *Windy Hill Campground*, with 348 campsites, is the largest in the USFS system, and has showers, drinking water and boat ramps but no RV hookups. Rates are $8 to $18 depending on the site. To get to the campground, drive about 6 miles east of the dam on Hwy 88, then head north on USFS Rd 82 for 2 miles to the lake. Ask at the ranger station about smaller campgrounds in the area.

Apache Lake

This long, narrow lake is west of Roosevelt Lake and is reached via the steep, unpaved portion of the Apache Trail. About 12 miles west of Roosevelt Dam, the Apache Lake Marina (☎ 520-467-2511) offers a boat ramp and rentals, tent and RV camping with hookups, and a small lodge with standard motel rooms priced in the upper $50s and rooms with kitchenettes priced in the $70s. These are often booked months ahead for summer holiday weekends.

Tortilla Flat

The Wild West look makes this little village a popular stop for drivers on the Apache Trail. You can pick up food and souvenirs, or spend the night in the campground, which offers sites without drinking water for $8. Tortilla Flat is 27 miles west of the dam and 17 miles east of Apache Junction.

Goldfield Ghost Town

Three or 4 miles before you get to Apache Junction, you'll come across Goldfield Ghost Town. This ghost town has been renovated; try your hand at gold panning, eat at the Western steak house, or examine the old artifacts in the mining museum. Hours are 10 am to 6 pm and admission is $4; $2 for six-to 12-year-olds.

Superstition Wilderness

Supposedly home to the fabled Lost Dutchman Mine, this rugged area is filled with hiking trails and mining stories. It is a

designated wilderness, so no development or vehicles are allowed. You can hike in on foot and camp anywhere, but be prepared – there's some remote and difficult terrain in here.

The Superstition Wilderness lies east of Apache Junction and south of the Apache Trail and is part of the Tonto National Forest. Ranger stations in Roosevelt and Mesa have maps and information.

Tucson & Southern Arizona

When isolated groups of Spanish explorers straggled through in the 1530s, this region of desert, mountain ranges and grasslands was inhabited by the Tohono O'odham (called the Papago until 1986) and the closely related Pima Indians, who were perhaps the descendants of the Hohokam people, whose culture disappeared around 1400 AD. The Apache Indians, who arrived later on, lived in the far southeast of present-day Arizona.

The first big Spanish expedition was in 1540, led by Francisco Vásquez de Coronado, who entered the area near present-day Sierra Vista on his way north in search of the 'Seven Cities of Cibola.' His descriptions are the earliest we have of the region, which had been largely ignored by the Spanish for well over a century until the Jesuit priest Padre Eusebio Francisco Kino arrived in the late 1600s and spent two

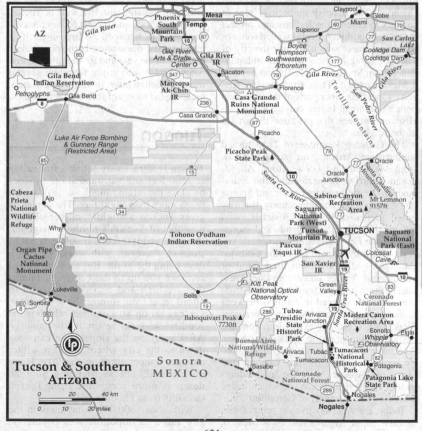

ARIZONA

decades establishing missions primarily among the Pima people. One of the churches he founded, Mission San Xavier del Bac, south of Tucson, is still used today. It is the finest example of Spanish colonial architecture in Arizona, rivaling the missions of New Mexico for architectural beauty and historical interest. Kino was also responsible for introducing cattle into the area.

With the missions came immigrants: Spanish settlers from the Mexican colonies. They lived in an uneasy truce with the Indians until 1751, when the Pimas rebelled against the unwanted new arrivals and killed or forced out many settlers and missionaries. The Spanish authorities sent in soldiers to control the Indians and protect the settlers, building several walled forts, or *presidios*, one of which became the city of Tucson. After Mexico won its independence from Spain in 1821, Tucson became a Mexican town. Thus southeastern Arizona, more than other parts of the state, had both a traditional Indian culture and a rich Hispanic heritage that predated the arrival of the Anglos.

The Gadsden Purchase of 1853 turned southeastern Arizona, on paper at least, from Mexican into US territory. Anglos began to arrive, homesteading the grasslands in the southeastern corner and finding that it made good ranching country. But they failed to realize that the Apaches, who inhabited the desert grasslands and mountains of the far southeastern corner of Arizona, didn't much care about the Gadsden Purchase – after all, from their point of view, it was Apache country and not Mexican in the first place. Tensions arising from this difference erupted in conflicts between Indians and Americans. Although such conflicts marked the US expansion from the east through most of the 1800s, the ones in Apache territory were especially fierce. Led by legendary warrior-chiefs Cochise and Geronimo, Apaches were the last holdouts in the so-called Indian Wars, which lasted until the 1886 surrender of Geronimo.

Today, the Apaches live on reservations in east-central Arizona and New Mexico, and what used to be their territory is now cattle ranching and mining country, where rolling vistas of ranchlands are studded with small but steep mountain ranges, the 'sky islands' of southeastern Arizona. The most dramatic are the Chiricahuas, protected in a national monument of the same name. The early ranchers and miners begot some of the classic tales of the Wild West, and now tourists flock to small towns like Tombstone and Bisbee, which retain much of their Old Western look.

West of these ranchlands lies the Sonoran desert, home of the majestic saguaro cacti, which are a symbol of this region. The Sonoran desert is also home to the Tohono O'odham Indians, who live west of Tucson on Arizona's second largest Indian reservation. And in between is Tucson itself, a major tourist destination both for travelers throughout the year and for the often-retired 'snow birds' who enjoy spending several months each winter in the Tucson area, escaping the snows of their northern homes.

Tucson

Tucson is attractively set in a flat valley at 2500 feet and surrounded on all sides by close mountain ranges, some of which reach more than 9000 feet. The elevation gives Tucson a slightly milder climate than that of Tucson's northern neighbor, Phoenix (at 1100 feet). It still gets hot in summer, however, with weeks of 100°F days being the norm. But an hour's drive can take you up to the cooler mountains that are high and accessible enough to afford relief from summer heat. In winter, you can ski on Mt Lemmon, which is the southernmost ski resort in the country. After a day on the slopes, you can drop down to the city where pleasant winter daytime temperatures in the 70°s F are not unusual. The surrounding Sonoran desert is more accessible from Tucson than it is from Phoenix.

With about 500,000 inhabitants in the city and a metropolitan area population exceeding 750,000, Tucson is Arizona's second largest city. More than 20% of Tucson's inhabitants are Hispanic, and this is reflected both in the language and the food. Spanish is frequently spoken and Mexican restaurants abound. Indeed, a few years ago the mayor declared Tucson to be the Mexican food capital of the world.

Tucson is the home of the University of Arizona (U of A), which has about 35,000 students and plays an important role in Tucson's economy. Also important to the city's economy are tourism and high-tech industries such as Hughes Missile Systems

Company and IBM Corporation, which employ thousands of Tucsonans. The Davis-Monthan Air Force Base also adds to the economy. It is one of the largest aircraft storage bases in the country and if you drive along Kolb Rd on the east side of town, you'll witness the eerie sight of almost 5000 mothballed aircraft lined up as far as the eye can see.

HISTORY

Visitors to downtown Tucson see 'A Mountain' looming over the city to the south-west. Its proper name is Sentinel Peak, but

Metropolitan Tucson

0   6   12 km
0   4   8 miles

PLACES TO STAY
3 Sheraton El Conquistador Resort
5 Spencer Canyon Campground
6 Rose Canyon Campground
7 White Stallion Ranch
8 Lazy K Bar Guest Ranch
9 Red Roof Inn
10 Motel 6
13 Westward Look Resort
15 Loew's Ventana Canyon Resort
16 Molino Basin Campground
17 Westin La Paloma Resort & Country Club
18 Hacienda del Sol Guest Ranch Resort
20 Casa Tierra B&B
22 Gilbert Ray Campground
23 Justin's Water World & RV Park
26 Suncatcher B&B
33 Voyager RV Resort
35 Cactus Country RV Resort

PLACES TO EAT
19 Hidden Valley Inn

OTHER
1 Biosphere 2
2 Breakers
4 Mt Lemmon Ski Area
11 Foothills Mall, Thunder Canyon Brewery
12 Tohono Chul Park & Tea Room
14 Finger Rock Canyon Trailhead
21 Arizona-Sonora Desert Museum
24 Old Tucson Studios
25 International Wildlife Museum
27 BLM Office
28 Davis-Monthan Air Force Base
29 Pima Air & Space Museum
30 Casino of the Sun
31 Mission San Xavier del Bac
32 Desert Diamond Casino
34 Pima County Fairgrounds, Tucson Raceway
36 RW Webb Winery & Brewery
37 Colossal Cave

ARIZONA

its nickname comes from the giant 'A' whitewashed onto the mountain by students from the U of A in 1915 and now repainted by freshmen as an annual tradition. But the peak's history goes back much farther than 1915. When the Spaniards arrived, the village below A Mountain was known as 'Stjukshon,' meaning 'at the foot of the dark mountain' in the Indian language. The Spaniards pronounced it 'Took Son' and later the Anglos dropped the 'k' sound, giving the city's name its current pronunciation of 'TOO-sahn.'

The first permanent Spanish settlement in Tucson was in 1775, when a large walled presidio was built here to house a garrison that protected settlers from the Indians. The Presidio District is now the most historic in Tucson, though almost nothing remains of the original buildings. Most of the oldest buildings date back to the mid-1800s, when arriving Anglos nicknamed the Hispanic fort 'the Old Pueblo.' The name has stuck and is often heard today as a nickname for Tucson. 'The Old Pueblo is expecting another 110° day' announce weather forecasters cheerily on the radio.

Anglos began to arrive in greater numbers after the Butterfield Stage Company started passing through Tucson in 1857. War with the Apaches prompted the construction of Fort Lowell in Tucson in 1866. Between 1867 and 1877, Tucson was the territorial capital. The town was a wild place in those days, and soldiers on drinking sprees added to the general mayhem. In 1873, in an attempt to minimize carousing by the army, Fort Lowell was moved to its present location 7 miles northeast of town. It was abandoned in 1891 and there is a museum and a small historic district on the site today. Meanwhile, in 1880 the railroad had arrived and Tucson, already Arizona's largest city, continued growing. The university opened in 1891, and an air of sophistication and coming-of-age descended on the wild city. Despite being the largest city in the territory, it was first denied the position of political capital in favor of Prescott and then in 1889 by Phoenix, which was less than half Tucson's size. There were various reasons for

this, not least the fact that Phoenix was a predominantly Anglo city while Tucson thrived on its Hispanic roots.

It was not until the 1920s that Phoenix finally eclipsed Tucson in size, and Tucson grew a little more slowly until WWII brought an influx of young men to train at the Davis-Monthan Air Force Base. After WWII, many of these trainees came back to Tucson and this, along with the widespread development of air conditioning, ensured Tucson's rapid growth in the latter half of the 20th century.

ORIENTATION

Tucson lies mainly to the north and east of I-10 at its intersection with I-19, which goes to the Mexican border at Nogales. Downtown Tucson and the main historic districts are east of I-10 exit 258 at Congress St/Broadway Blvd.

Congress/Broadway Blvd is a major west-east thoroughfare. Most west-east thoroughfares are called streets, while most north-south thoroughfares are called avenues (although there are a sprinkling of Rds and Blvds, etc). Stone Ave, at its intersection with Congress, forms the zero point for Tucson addresses. Streets are designated west and east and avenues north and south from this point.

Downtown Tucson is quite compact and is best visited on foot, although you have to battle the heat from May to September. Away from downtown, major thoroughfares are at 1-mile intervals, with minor streets and avenues (mainly residential) filling in the spaces in a checker-board arrangement.

About a mile northeast of downtown is the U of A campus, with some worthwhile museums, and just over a mile south of downtown is the square mile of South Tucson. This is a separate town inhabited mainly by a traditional Hispanic population with few tourist sites, but it does have some cheap and funky restaurants with tasty Mexican food. The rest of the city is mainly an urban sprawl of shopping malls and residential areas interspersed with golf courses and parks. The main section of the city, between Campbell Ave and Kolb Rd, is known as midtown.

The south end of town is the industrial area where you'll find Tucson International Airport, the Davis-Monthan Air Force Base and industrial parks. You'll go past this to visit San Xavier del Bac, Arizona's most impressive Spanish colonial site.

The north end of town is the Catalina Foothills, bounded by the steep and rugged Santa Catalina Mountains and home to the pricier residential districts, resorts and country clubs. Northwest of town, the city oozes around the western edge of the Catalinas into the I-10 corridor to Phoenix. This is where most of the current development is taking place.

East and west of town are wilderness areas, parts of which are protected by the east and west units of Saguaro National Park. These areas and many outlying areas are described at the end of the Tucson section.

INFORMATION
Visitor Centers

The Convention and Visitors Bureau (☎ 520-624-1817, 800-638-8350, fax 520-884-7804, mtcvb@azstarnet.com), 130 S Scott Ave, is open 8 am to 5 pm, Monday to Friday, and 9 am to 4 pm on weekends. It is closed on major holidays and may also close on summer weekends. Ask for its free *Official Visitors Guide*.

The Coronado National Forest Supervisor's Office (☎ 520-670-4552), inside the Federal Building at 300 W Congress, Tucson, AZ 85701, is open from 8 am to 4:30 pm, Monday to Friday. Also, the Santa Catalina Ranger Station (☎ 520-749-8700), 5700 N Sabino Canyon Rd, AZ 85715, in the visitor center at the entrance to Sabino Canyon, is open similar hours and is also open from 8:30 am to 4:30 pm on weekends.

The BLM Tucson Office (☎ 520-722-4289) is at 12661 E Broadway Blvd, and the Arizona Game & Fish Department (☎ 520-628-5376) is at 555 N Greasewood Rd (south of Speedway Blvd over 2 miles west of I-10).

Foreign Embassies

The Mexican Consulate (☎ 520-882-5595) is at 553 S Stone Ave.

Money

Foreign exchange is available at most banks; a $5 fee is charged if you don't have an account. The Tucson airport does not offer currency exchange.

Post

The main post office (☎ 800-275-8777) is at 1501 S Cherrybell Strav. (Strav is short for Stravenue, one of Tucson's few diagonal street/avenues!) The downtown branch is at 141 S 6th Ave and there are numerous other branches.

Books & Periodicals

The main library (☎ 520-791-4393) is open daily at 101 N Stone Ave. There are many other branch libraries. The U of A libraries (☎ 520-621-6441) have both extensive and excellent collections, including a superb map room open to the general public.

The local newspapers are the morning *Arizona Daily Star*, the afternoon *Tucson Citizen* and the free *Tucson Weekly*, published on Thursdays. The *Citizen* leans to the right and the *Star* is less conservative. The best source of entertainment, arts and current events news is the *Weekly*. Two glossy but quite informative local magazines are the monthly *Tucson Lifestyle* and the quarterly *Tucson Guide*.

Radio

Tucson's community radio station, KXCI, 91.3, is funded by listeners and has an eclectic and excellent range of programs. Most are from all over the musical spectrum (with the notable exceptions of classical music and top 40 stuff, and the inclusion of local talk shows from 6 to 7 pm). This is my favorite station in the Southwest.

Medical & Emergency Services

Pima County Medical Society (☎ 520-795-7985) gives doctor referrals during business hours. Ask A Nurse (☎ 520-544-2000)

ARIZONA

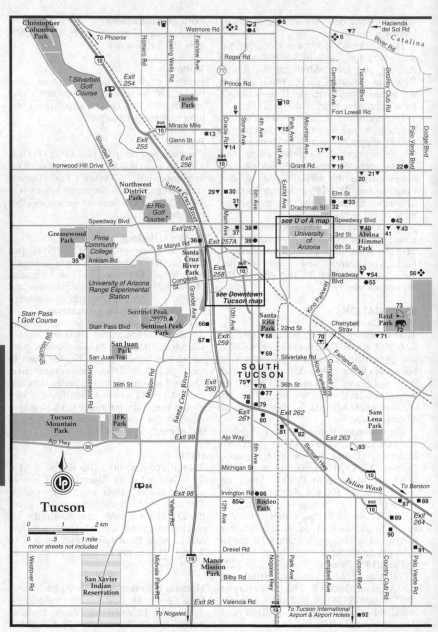

ARIZONA

Tucson

0   1   2 km
0   .5   1 mile
minor streets not included

ARIZONA

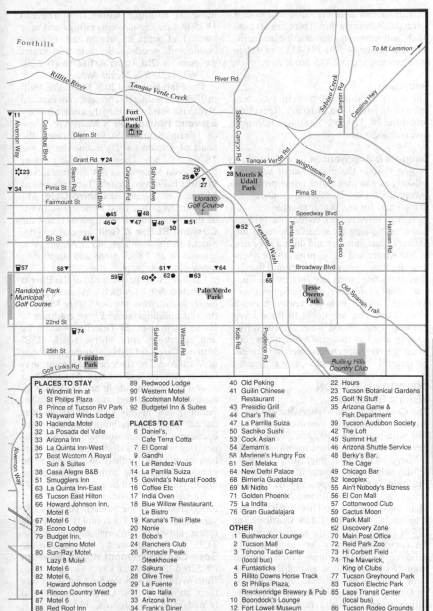

PLACES TO STAY
- 6 Windmill Inn at St Philips Plaza
- 8 Prince of Tucson RV Park
- 13 Wayward Winds Lodge
- 30 Hacienda Motel
- 32 La Posada del Valle
- 33 Arizona Inn
- 36 La Quinta Inn-West
- 37 Best Western A Royal Sun & Suites
- 38 Casa Alegre B&B
- 51 Smugglers Inn
- 63 La Quinta Inn-East
- 65 Tucson East Hilton
- 66 Howard Johnson Inn, Motel 6
- 67 Econo Lodge
- 78 Budget Inn, El Camino Motel
- 79 Sun-Ray Motel, Lazy 8 Motel
- 80 Sun-Ray Motel, Lazy 8 Motel
- 81 Motel 6
- 82 Motel 6, Howard Johnson Lodge
- 84 Rincon Country West
- 87 Motel 6
- 88 Red Roof Inn
- 89 Redwood Lodge
- 90 Western Motel
- 91 Scotsman Motel
- 92 Budgetel Inn & Suites

PLACES TO EAT
- 6 Daniel's, Cafe Terra Cotta
- 7 El Corral
- 9 Gandhi
- 11 Le Rendez-Vous
- 14 La Parrilla Suiza
- 15 Govinda's Natural Foods
- 16 Coffee Etc
- 17 India Oven
- 18 Blue Willow Restaurant, Le Bistro
- 19 Karuna's Thai Plate
- 20 Nonie
- 21 Bobo's
- 24 Ranchers Club
- 26 Pinnacle Peak Steakhouse
- 27 Sakura
- 28 Olive Tree
- 29 La Fuente
- 31 Ciao Italia
- 33 Arizona Inn
- 34 Frank's Diner
- 40 Old Peking
- 41 Guilin Chinese Restaurant
- 43 Presidio Grill
- 44 Char's Thai
- 47 La Parrilla Suiza
- 53 Sachiko Sushi
- 53 Cock Asian
- 54 Zemam's
- 58 Marlene's Hungry Fox
- 61 Seri Melaka
- 68 New Delhi Palace
- 68 Birriería Guadalajara
- 69 Mi Nidito
- 71 Golden Phoenix
- 75 La Indita
- 76 Gran Guadalajara

OTHER
- 1 Bushwacker Lounge
- 2 Tucson Mall
- 3 Tohono Tadai Center (local buc)
- 4 Funtasticks
- 5 Rillito Downs Horse Track
- 6 St Philips Plaza, Breckenridge Brewery & Pub
- 10 Boondock's Lounge
- 12 Fort Lowell Museum
- 22 Hours
- 23 Tucson Botanical Gardens
- 25 Golf 'N Stuff
- 35 Arizona Game & Fish Department
- 39 Tucson Audubon Society
- 42 The Loft
- 45 Summit Hut
- 46 Arizona Shuttle Service
- 48 Berky's Bar, The Cage
- 52 Chicago Bar
- 52 Iceoplex
- 55 Ain't Nobody's Bizness
- 56 El Con Mall
- 57 Cottonwood Club
- 60 Cactus Moon
- 60 Park Mall
- 62 Discovery Zone
- 70 Main Post Office
- 72 Reid Park Zoo
- 73 Hi Corbett Field
- 74 The Maverick, King of Clubs
- 77 Tucson Greyhound Park
- 83 Tucson Electric Park
- 85 Laos Transit Center (local bus)
- 86 Tucson Rodeo Grounds

provides medical information and doctor referrals 24 hours a day. There are 10 hospitals and many smaller health care facilities. The police (☎ 520-791-4452, or 911 in emergencies) are at 270 S Stone Ave.

Recycling

There are 10 drop-off recycling centers open daily from 7 am to 10 pm. Recycling Info-Line (☎ 520-791-5000) has information and addresses.

Dangers & Annoyances

People visiting the major tourist sites are unlikely to run into major crime problems except theft. (See Dangers & Annoyances in the Facts for the Visitor chapter.)

Visitors often remark on the river bridges that cross nothing but sand. In the monsoon season of late summer and during the rains of late winter and early spring, these rivers flow in earnest, sometimes in raging floods. Because heavy rains are infrequent, Tucson's road drainage system becomes overwhelmed for a few hours several times a year. Roads that are liable to flood have warning signs. Flood waters occur infrequently and last for only a few hours, but when they do happen unsuspecting drivers get trapped or swept away. Obey all signs.

DOWNTOWN TUCSON
Historic Buildings

The Convention and Visitors Bureau has a brochure detailing a downtown walking tour with more than 40 sites. Some of the more noteworthy ones are mentioned here.

Many of the most interesting and colorful historic buildings are in the **Presidio Historic District**, especially in the few blocks between Franklin and Alameda and Main and Court Aves. This district merits a leisurely stroll. **La Casa Cordova**, at 175 N Meyer Ave, at the northern end of the Tucson Museum of Art (see below) is believed to be the oldest house, dating from 1848, and can be visited during the same hours as the museum. Just north of La Casa Cordova is the **Romero House**, dating from 1868 and now part of the Tucson Museum of Art School. Behind the

museum, buildings dating from 1862 to 1875 feature saguaro-rib ceilings and now house La Cocina Restaurant and six interconnected, good-quality arts and crafts galleries of **Old Town Artisans** (☎ 520-623-6024), 186 N Meyer Ave.

The **Fish House**, 120 N Main Ave, built in 1868 for political representative Edward Nye Fish, and the roughly contemporary **Stevens House**, 150 N Main Ave, home of Hiram Sanford Stevens, formed the heart of Tucson's social scene during the 1870s and '80s. They now house parts of the Tucson Museum of Art. Restaurants in historic buildings include Tucson's oldest Mexican restaurant, **El Charro Cafe**, 311 N Court Ave, in a 1900 stone house (most of the earlier houses were adobe), and the **Cushing St Bar & Grill**, several lengthy blocks to the south at 343 S Meyer Ave, housed in an 1880s store and displaying many old photographs.

Cushing St is the north end of the **Barrio Historico** district, which was an important business district in the late 1800s. Many of the old buildings around here continue to house businesses. **El Tiradito** is a quirky and crumbling little shrine south of El Minuto Cafe on Cushing on the west side of Main Ave. The story behind the shrine is one of passion and murder. Apparently a young herder was caught making love with his mother-in-law and was shot dead by his father-in-law at this spot, where he was buried. Pious locals burned candles here because it was unconsecrated ground. The practice continues today, with candle-burners praying for their own wishes to be granted. If a candle burns throughout the night, your wish will be granted!

Between the Presidio and Barrio Historico districts is the modern Tucson Convention Center (TCC) complex. Only one house survived the construction of the TCC. At the northwest end is hidden the **Sosa-Carrillo-Frémont House Museum** (☎ 520-622-0956), at 151 S Granada Ave. Built in the 1850s by the Sosa family, it was then bought by the Carrillo family and rented briefly by John C Frémont, Arizona's fifth governor. The restored house is

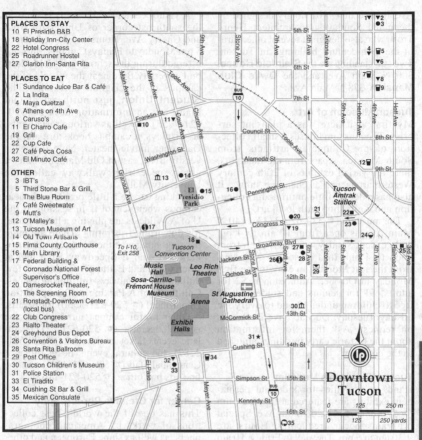

PLACES TO STAY
10 El Presidio B&B
18 Holiday Inn-City Center
22 Hotel Congress
25 Roadrunner Hostel
27 Clarion Inn-Santa Rita

PLACES TO EAT
1 Sundance Juice Bar & Café
2 La Indita
4 Maya Quetzal
6 Athens on 4th Ave
8 Caruso's
11 El Charro Cafe
19 Grill
22 Cup Cafe
27 Café Poca Cosa
32 El Minuto Café

OTHER
3 IBT's
5 Third Stone Bar & Grill,
     The Blue Room
7 Café Sweetwater
9 Mutt's
12 O'Malley's
13 Tucson Museum of Art
14 Old Town Artisans
15 Pima County Courthouse
16 Main Library
17 Federal Building &
     Coronado National Forest
     Supervisor's Office
20 Damesrocket Theater,
     The Screening Room
21 Ronstadt-Downtown Center
     (local bus)
22 Club Congress
23 Rialto Theater
24 Greyhound Bus Depot
26 Convention & Visitors Bureau
28 Santa Rita Ballroom
29 Post Office
30 Tucson Children's Museum
31 Police Station
33 El Tiradito
34 Cushing St Bar & Grill
35 Mexican Consulate

Downtown Tucson

now an 1880s period museum open 10 am
to 4 pm Wednesday to Saturday; admission
is free. It is operated by the Arizona Historical Society, which offers guided walking
tours (☎ 520-622-0956 to register) of historic Tucson at 10 am on Saturdays from
October through March for $4.50.

In addition to the oldest buildings, the
downtown area has several notable newer
buildings from the early 20th century. The
Pima County Courthouse, at 115 N
Church Ave, is a colorful blend of Spanish
and Southwestern architecture with an
impressive mosaic-tile dome. **El Presidio**

Park, on the west side of the courthouse,
covers what was the southern half of the
original presidio and also houses a Vietnam
Veterans Memorial. A few blocks south is
the elegant, whitewashed St Augustine
Cathedral, 192 S Stone Ave, begun in 1896.
Stained-glass windows and a Mexican-style
sandstone façade were added in the 1920s.
Two blocks to the southeast is the **Temple
of Music & Art**, 330 S Scott Ave, built in
1927 and recently gloriously restored as the
home of the Arizona Theater Company. A
block northeast of it is the **Tucson Children's Museum** (see below), 200 S 6th

Ave, housed in a 1901 library designed by the noted Southwestern architect Henry Trost, who also designed several other turn-of-the-19th-century buildings in Tucson. Two still standing are the **Steinfeld House**, 300 N Main Ave, and the **Owl's Club Mansion**, 378 N Main Ave.

Tucson Museum of Art

My first visit here was a pleasant surprise. The museum houses a small collection of pre-Columbian artifacts from South America. Apart from the Inca pots, there are varied exhibits of 20th-century Western art as well as changing shows. It also has a decent little multimedia collection and a gift shop with local art.

The museum (☎ 520-624-2333), 140 N Main Ave, is open from 10 am to 4 pm daily except Sunday, when it's open from noon to 4 pm. It is closed on Mondays from the last Monday in May to the first Monday in October. Admission is $2 for adults, $1 for seniors and students, and free to children under 12 and to everyone all day Tuesday. Docents give free tours on request. Ask them for information about the historic early buildings attached to the complex.

Tucson Children's Museum

Hands-on activities for kids and permanent exhibits are featured at this museum (☎ 520-884-7511), 200 S 6th Ave. Special programs occur frequently. Hours are 9:30 am to 5 pm, Tuesday to Friday, 10 am to 5 pm on Saturday and noon to 5 pm on Sunday. Admission is $5 for adults, $4 for seniors and $3 for two- to 16-year-olds. On Sundays, a $12 family pass will admit four family members, and the museum is free on the third Sunday of each month.

UNIVERSITY OF ARIZONA

This fine campus houses some excellent museums and several notable outdoor sculptures. This is not just a place for students; it's a worthwhile stop for everyone. Note that hours can change when school is not in session and during school holidays; call ahead.

A visitor center (☎ 520-621-5130) is at the southeast corner of University Blvd and Cherry Ave. Hours are from 8 am to 5 pm Monday to Friday. Campus tours are offered during the school year. **Old Main** on University Blvd near the middle of the campus is the original university. The **Student Union**, just northeast of Old Main, has an information desk (☎ 520-621-7755) as well as various restaurants, art displays, a campus bookstore and the Gallagher movie theater. Note that University Blvd, east of Old Main, becomes a grassy pedestrian walkway called the University Mall.

Parking can be a little problematic near campus when school is in session; if the U of A Wildcats are playing a home game, it's downright frustrating. There are large parking garages at the northeast corner of Park Ave and E Speedway Blvd and at Cherry Ave and E 4th. These charge a few dollars but are always full during games. Call the U of A Parking & Transportation Department (☎ 520-621-3550) for details.

Other useful campus numbers are the general operator (☎ 520-621-2211), athletic events ticket information (☎ 520-621-2287), the cultural events ticket office at Centennial Hall (☎ 520-621-3341) and the fine arts box office (☎ 520-621-1162).

Center for Creative Photography

This has one of the world's best collections of works by American photographers, as well as some European and other artists. The small public gallery displays some images by various famous photographers and changing exhibits throughout the year. Most of Ansel Adams's and Edward Weston's work, as well as images by many other photographers, are stored in the archives. Serious photography buffs can call for an appointment to view the works of one or two particular photographers; this is a remarkable opportunity rarely offered elsewhere. The center (☎ 520-621-7968), 1030 N Olive Ave, is open from 11 am to 5 pm, Monday to Friday, and from noon to 5 pm on Sunday. Admission is free.

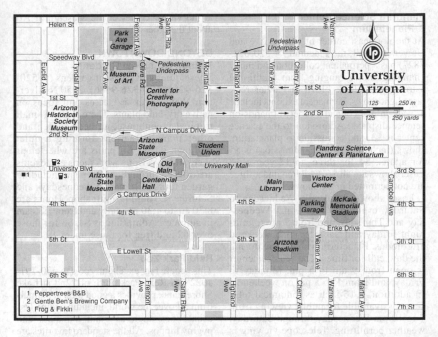

University
of Arizona

1 Peppertrees B&B
2 Gentle Ben's Brewing Company
3 Frog & Firkin

University of Arizona Museum of Art

This museum (☎ 520-621-7567), across the street from the photography center, displays changing shows of mainly student works. These exhibits range widely in quality but are always intriguing. There are also fine permanent collections of European art and a variety of sculptures. Hours are 9 am to 5 pm, Monday to Friday, and noon to 4 pm on Sunday during the school year; summer weekday hours are 10 am to 3:30 pm. Admission is free.

Arizona State Museum

This museum focuses on the Indian inhabitants of the region, with archaeological and cultural artifacts. One of the permanent exhibits entitled 'Paths of Life: American Indians of the Southwest' is a state-of-the-art representation of the past and present lives of several tribes; this exhibit is especially worth seeing. The state museum (☎ 520-621-6302) is in two buildings on the north and south sides of University Blvd, east of

the campus entrance at Park Ave. 'Paths of Life' is in the north hall; admission is free. Hours are 10 am to 5 pm, Monday to Saturday, and noon to 5 pm on Sunday.

Arizona Historical Society Museum

This is the society's flagship museum; it also manages the Sosa-Carrillo-Frémont House Museum (see Historic Buildings, above) and the Fort Lowell Museum (see Beyond Downtown, below). The museum (☎ 520-628-5774) is right outside the campus boundary at 949 E 2nd. The society has a research library here. The collection is a comprehensive trip through Tucson's history as a Spanish colonial, Mexican, territorial and state city. Anything from colonial silverware to vintage automobiles can be seen in this wide-ranging selection of historical artifacts. Changing exhibits keep bringing locals back. Hours are 10 am to 4 pm daily except Sunday (noon to 4 pm) and closed some major holidays. It's free, but donations are appreciated.

Flandrau Science Center & Planetarium

At the northeast corner of Cherry Ave and University Mall, the Flandrau (☎ 520-621-7827) has a permanent collection and many changing shows ranging from traditional astronomy to Pink Floyd and other rock laser-light shows. Permanent exhibits include a 'walk-in' meteor and a variety of hands-on science displays. Admission to the science center is $3, and admission to planetarium shows (including exhibits admission) is $5 for adults; $4 for three- to 12-year-olds. Laser shows are all $6. Children under three are not permitted in the shows.

Laser shows are usually Wednesday to Saturday evenings (7 to 9 pm Wednesday and Thursday, and from 7 pm to midnight Friday and Saturday) and weekend afternoons. Planetarium shows are during the day; call for times. The science center is open from 9 am to 5 pm, Monday to Friday, and from 1 to 5 pm on weekends. In addition, a 16-inch astronomical telescope is available for public viewing from 7 to 10 pm Wednesday through Saturday, weather permitting. Telescope viewing is free. Various other scientific events are scheduled throughout the year.

Mineral Museum

This free museum (☎ 520-621-4227) in the basement of the Flandrau is open 9 am to 5 pm on weekdays and 1 to 5 pm on weekends. Minerals, meteorites and gemstones from all over the world are exhibited, with an emphasis on local stones.

Campus Sculptures

Beginning with *The Flute Player*, commissioned in 1979 and now standing in front of the main library, the U of A has steadily acquired an eclectic collection of about a dozen sculptures scattered throughout the campus. The most controversial? The huge *Curving Arcades (Homage to Bernini)* at the main eastern entrance at University Mall and N Campbell Ave. My favorite? The whimsical *25 Scientists* in front of the new chemistry and biology building on University Mall, just west of the main library. Ask at the visitor center or the Museum of Art about the others.

BEYOND DOWNTOWN
Tucson Botanical Gardens

These quiet and pleasant gardens (☎ 520-326-9255, 520-326-9686), 2150 N Alvernon Way, cover 5½ acres and focus on native dry-land plants. There is also a small tropical greenhouse, an herb garden and other plant attractions forming a quiet midtown oasis. All paths are wheelchair accessible. Various workshops and events are offered throughout the year, including garden tours at 10 am on Wednesdays and Saturdays. There is a gift shop. Hours are 8:30 am to 4:30 pm daily and from 7:30 am in summer. Admission is $4, $3 for those over 62 and free for those under 12.

Reid Park Zoo

This small but excellent zoo (☎ 520-791-4022), in Reid Park north of 22nd at Lake Shore Lane, provides a good look at animals from all over the world, including some less usual ones such as giant anteaters and pygmy hippos. All the standard favorites are here, and the compact size of the zoo makes it a great excursion for children because they don't get overwhelmed and tired out. The small size means fewer animals, but the cages are still of a reasonable size and there are some well-themed exhibits, especially the South American area. There is a gift shop and a fast-food restaurant. Hours are 9 am to 4 pm daily except Christmas; hours may be extended during some months. Admission is $3.50, $2.50 for those over 62 and 75¢ for five- to 14-year-olds accompanied by an adult.

Outside the zoo, the surrounding Reid Park provides picnic areas, playgrounds and a duck pond with paddle boat rentals in summer – definitely a kids' fun day out.

Fort Lowell Museum

The army set up camp here in 1873 after moving from downtown Tucson. After Geronimo surrendered, Fort Lowell's important role in the Indian Wars faded, and the army shut it down in 1891. Only weath-

Apache leader Geronimo

ered ruins remain today, but the museum is housed in reconstructed officers' quarters with furnishings and exhibits of the fort's heyday. The museum (☎ 520-885-3832) is in Fort Lowell Park off the 2900 block of N Craycroft Rd. Museum hours are 10 am to 4 pm, Wednesday to Saturday, and admission is free. The surrounding park has a playground, duck pond and picnic areas. Across Craycroft Rd, a short way north of the fort, Fort Lowell Rd heads west past several early houses in the small Fort Lowell historical district.

Pima Air & Space Museum
With 200 plus aircraft representing a history of aviation, this museum (☎ 520-574-9658, 520-574-0462), 6000 E Valencia Rd, sits on the south side of the Davis-Monthan Air Force Base. It's a must-see for aircraft buffs. The museum also operates the Titan Missile Museum (see Green Valley in the South of Tucson section, later in this chapter). The Pima Museum is open 9 am to 5 pm every day except Thanksgiving and Christmas. Admission is $7.50 for adults, $6.50 for those over 62 or with military ID and $4 for 10- to 17-year-olds. Admission is free after 4 pm. From 10 am to 3 pm, wheelchair-accessible tram tours cost another $2.

Across the street, note the approximately 5000 mothballed aircraft at Davis-Monthan. The best way to see them is to drive north on Kolb Rd and then west on Escalante Rd. Free tours of the base are given at 9 am on Monday and Wednesday only and they require reservations well in advance (☎ 520-228-4570).

Tohono Chul Park
This small desert oasis, surrounded by encroaching development, is a good place to see desert flora and fauna in a natural setting. There are demonstrations and ethnobotanical gardens, an exhibit room with changing shows, gift shops, plant sales and a tea room. A variety of docent-led tours are offered. The park (☎ 520-575-8468), 7366 N Paseo del Norte near Ina Rd, is open from 7 am to dusk daily; the other attractions have shorter hours. Admission is free, but a $2 donation is suggested.

ACTIVITIES
The Convention and Visitors Bureau can provide lists of golf courses, tennis courts and other local attractions.

Hiking & Backpacking
Tucson is ringed by mountains. The Rincons to the east and the Tucson Mountains to the west are easily explored from Saguaro National Park (see Around Tucson, later in this chapter). The Santa Ritas, topped by 9453-foot Mt Wrightson, are visible in the distance, to the south (see Green Valley & Around, later in this chapter).

The Santa Catalina Mountains, topped by 9157-foot Mt Lemmon, form Tucson's northern boundary and prevent the city from expanding farther north. The Santa Catalinas, which lie within the Coronado National Forest, are the best loved and most visited of Tucson's mountain ranges. There are several trailheads on the north side of town, including the Finger Rock Canyon (Mt Kimball) trailhead at the far north end of Alvernon Way, which leads steeply up past Finger Rock – an obvious point on the northern skyline from many parts of Tucson. (Note that Alvernon Way in midtown Tucson stops at Fort Lowell Rd. You have to take Campbell Ave north to Skyline Drive and then head east to pick up Alvernon Way again to reach this trailhead.) Other trailheads are found in Sabino Canyon and Catalina State Park (see below).

Take extra precautions when hiking around Tucson in summer, when dehydration can be a potentially lethal problem. You should carry water with you at all times and drink a gallon of water per day. Sunburn can be debilitating, so protect yourself. Also, watch out for those spiny plants. It's worth carrying tweezers and a comb – they help remove cactus spines from your skin.

Backpackers should contact a USFS ranger station about suitable places to camp and where to leave their cars.

Books Useful books about hiking in the Tucson area are *Tucson Hiking Guide* by Betty Leavengood, *Trail Guide to the Santa Catalina Mountains* by Pete Cowgill and Eber Glendening, and *Hiking Guide to the Santa Rita Mountains of Arizona* by Bob and Dotty Martin. The Summit Hut (☎ 520-325-1554), 5045 E Speedway Blvd, is an excellent source of hiking books, maps and equipment.

Sabino Canyon This is the most popular and accessible part of the Santa Catalinas. There is a visitor center that includes a USFS ranger station (☎ 520-749-8700), open weekdays from 8 am to 4:30 pm and on weekends from 8:30 am to 4:30 pm. Maps, hiking guides and information are available here, and there is a short nature trail nearby. The visitor center is at the entrance of the canyon at 5900 N Sabino Canyon Rd, where there is also a large parking lot.

Roads continue beyond the visitor center into the canyon, but only shuttle buses (☎ 520-749-2861 for recorded information) are allowed to drive on these. The Sabino Canyon Rd goes a scenic 3.8 miles up the canyon, crossing the river several times. Narrated shuttle bus tours spend 45 minutes doing the roundtrip and stop at nine points along the way. Tours leave every half hour from 9 am to 4:30 pm, and ticket holders can get on and off at any point whenever they feel like it. There are several riverside spots and picnic places on the way. At the top is a trailhead for hikers wanting to go high into the Santa Catalinas. Fares are $6; $2.50 for three- to 12-year-olds. In addition, full-moon shuttle tours are given by

---

Kids' Stuff

Your first choice for children in the heat of summer will certainly be the amusement places listed under Water Sports. The Tucson Children's Museum, open year-round, appeals to younger kids. The Flandrau Science Center shows are aimed at older kids and teenagers. The Reid Park Zoo and the Arizona-Sonora Desert Museum are good for the entire family, as is the Pima Air & Space Museum, especially if your kids are plane nuts.

Also fun for younger kids is the Discovery Zone (☎ 520-748-9190), 6238 E Broadway Blvd, where kids (and adults) can crawl, climb, swing and slide on the giant indoor jungle gym. The Zone is open from 10 am to 8 pm daily and till 9 pm on Friday and Saturday. Admission is $6 for three- to 12-year-olds and $4 for toddlers. Two places that offer miniature golf, go-carts, bumper boats, batting cages and other fun stuff are Funtasticks (☎ 520-888-4653), 221 E Wetmore, and Golf 'N Stuff (☎ 520-885-3569), 6503 E Tanque Verde Rd. ■

reservation on the nights around a full moon. Call ☎ 520-749-2327 for dates and reservation information.

Another road goes 2½ miles to the Bear Canyon trailhead. A shuttle bus (no narration or stops) takes hikers there every hour from 9 am to 4 pm. The fare is $3; $1.25 for three- to 12-year-olds. From the trailhead a 2.3-mile (one-way) hike leads to Seven Falls, a scenic and popular spot for picnics and swimming, but there aren't any facilities (allow 3½ hours roundtrip). From the falls, the trail continues up as high as you want to go.

Bicycles are allowed on the roads only before 9 am and after 5 pm and not at all on Wednesday and Sunday. Hikers can walk along the roads at any time from dawn to dusk. You don't have to take a shuttle to get to a trailhead; starting from the visitor center, there are plenty of hiking possibilities. The Phoneline Trail, skirting Sabino Canyon high on its southeastern side, is a popular alternative to taking the road.

Several picnic areas with grills, tables and bathrooms are in the area. Camping is not allowed within those areas. Backpackers can hike into the Santa Catalinas and wilderness camp almost anywhere that is more than a quarter mile away from a road or trailhead.

Catalina State Park This park is in the western foothills of the Santa Catalinas and is popular for hiking, picnicking, bird watching and camping. You'll find both short nature trails and trailheads for long-distance hiking and backpacking. Horseback riding is permitted and one trail is specifically developed for horses. The Equestrian Center has boarding for horses. Natural swimming holes occur along some of the trails and make good day-hike destinations. Ask the ranger for directions. (See Places to Stay – Camping, later in this chapter.) For information on the campground.) For more information call Catalina State Park (☎ 520-628-5798), PO Box 36986, AZ 85740. The park is about 15 miles north of downtown along Oracle Rd (Hwy 77). Day use is $4 per vehicle.

Mt Lemmon You can spend a couple of days hiking up to Mt Lemmon's summit along the many trails in the Santa Catalinas, or you can head east on Tanque Verde Rd, pick up the Catalina Hwy and drive to the top in an hour. This is a favorite getaway for Tucsonans wishing to escape the summer heat. Along the way are four USFS campgrounds and several pullouts with great views. The road is narrow and winding, however, and requires some concentration, as well as a $5 per vehicle toll. Several hiking trails intersect with the highway. Near the top of the drive is the Palisades Ranger Station (no phone) with information about the area, or call the Sabino Canyon Ranger Station (☎ 520-749-8700).

At the top is the small village of **Summerhaven** where there are cabins to rent, some restaurants, a picnic area and a ski area (see Skiing, below). During the summer you can take scenic rides on the chair lift from 10:30 am to 5 pm for $6 ($2 for three- to 12-year-olds). Families pay $12 for two adults and up to four children. Gas up in Tucson; there's no gas on Mt Lemmon.

Rock Climbing
Mt Lemmon (see above) has good rock climbing – route books are available from the Summit Hut (see Books, above). Rocks and Ropes (☎ 520-882-5294), 330 S Tooele Ave (hard to find, so call for directions), is an indoor rock-climbing facility with equipment rental.

Bird Watching
Southeastern Arizona is a mecca for bird watchers, who come from all over the USA to see birds found nowhere else in the country. Many of these are from Mexico. The most notable are the 16 species of hummingbirds, eight of which are uncommon or rare. While the months between April to September see the most species, there's always a few around. By comparison, most eastern states have only one hummingbird species and most western states have half a dozen or so.

Sightings of two trogon species are highly prized. Both species are colorful, with green heads and wings, red bellies and white tails. The eared trogon is very rare and is sure to excite any birder; the elegant trogon is less rare but still uncommon. The latter has a yellow bill and a white band on its chest. Ramsey Canyon near Sierra Vista (see the Southeastern Arizona chapter) is one of the most celebrated spots for hummers and trogons. In addition, the various species of common desert birds such as roadrunners, gila woodpeckers, elf owls and cactus wrens attract out-of-state birders wanting to add to their life lists.

The best resource for bird watchers is the Tucson Audubon Society, 300 E University Blvd, Tucson, AZ 85705. It has an excellent nature shop (☎ 520-629-0510) with a fine selection of bird guides and related materials. Hours are 10 am to 4 pm, Monday to Saturday, and to 6 pm on Thursday. A research library is also available. The nature shop has information about monthly meetings and slide shows held from September to May, as well as a variety of field trips, many of them free. The society has published an essential handbook for birders: *Finding Birds in Southeastern Arizona* by William A Davis and Stephen M Russell. A bird-sightings and information hotline (☎ 520-798-1005) is updated weekly.

Skiing

Mt Lemmon Ski Area (☎ 520-576-1400, 520-576-1321) is the most southerly ski area in the USA. One chair services 16 runs between 9150 and 8200 feet. These are mainly for intermediate and experienced skiers. There is also a rope tow for beginners. Rentals, lessons and food are available. Depending on the weather, the slopes are open from mid-December to early April. Weekend lift tickets are $28; $12 for children under 13. Weekday tickets are $25/8.

Skating

Iceoplex (☎ 520-290-8800), 7333 E Rosewood (near Speedway and Kolb), has ice skating year-round – a cool getaway from Tucson's heat. Sessions are $6.50 and skate rentals are $2.50. Call for session times.

If you prefer roller or in-line skating, try Skate Country at 2700 N Stone Ave (☎ 520-622-6650) or 7980 E 22nd (☎ 520-298-4409). Both rent skates for about $2 and charge $2 to $4, depending on times. The latter has longer hours.

Skateboarders can check out the new (free) facility at Randolph Skatepark, 200 S Alvernon, open from noon till dusk. It has various pipes, ramps and rails.

Hot-Air Ballooning

Several companies offer hot-air-balloon flights over the desert and foothills. Flights usually take place in the calm morning air, last about an hour and then finish with a traditional champagne breakfast. Costs are about $125 per person. Flights may be canceled in windy weather and in summer because of the extreme heat. Most companies can arrange flights on a day's notice. Experienced companies include Balloon America (☎ 520-299-7744) and A Southern Arizona Balloon Excursion (☎ 520-624-3599, 800-524-3599).

Horseback Riding

Several stables offer excursions by the hour, half day or longer. Summer trips tend to be short breakfast or sunset rides because of the heat. Desert cookouts can be arranged. One of the most reputable companies is Pusch Ridge Stables (☎ 520-825-1664), 13700 N Oracle Rd, which also offers overnight pack trips. Nearby, Walking Winds Stables (☎ 520-742-4422), 10811 N Oracle, specializes in Catalina State Park rides. At the other end of town is Pantano Stables (☎ 520-751-1951), 4450 S Houghton Rd. Several others advertise locally. Rates start around $20 for the first hour, but are much less for subsequent hours.

Golf

There are so many courses in Tucson and so many people who come to golf them that an entire book could be written about it. The following is only a sampling of the facilities available. Tucson Parks & Recreation (☎ 520-791-4336 for golf information and tee reservations) maintains five municipal 18-hole golf courses; these are good-quality courses that charge anywhere from about $10 to more than $40 for 18 holes, depending on the course and the season (winter is the most expensive).

There are many more expensive golf courses at various resorts and clubs in Tucson. Some courses that come recommended are Starr Pass Golf Club (☎ 520-670-0400), 3645 W Starr Pass Blvd, 18 holes, par 71; Omni Tucson National Golf & Conference Resort (☎ 520-575-7540), 2727 W Club Drive, 27 holes, par 73; and Westin La Paloma Resort & Country Club (☎ 520-299-1500) 3800 E Sunrise Drive, 27 holes, par 72. Rates at these courses are well over $100 in winter.

Tee Time Arrangers (☎ 520-296-4800, 800-742-9939) can arrange tee times and entire golf vacations. The Convention and Visitors Bureau can send you off a booklet with detailed golf course information.

Tennis
Most high schools and the U of A have tennis courts open to the public after school hours. Municipal public tennis centers can be found at Fort Lowell Park (☎ 520-791-2584), 2900 N Craycroft Rd; Himmel Park (☎ 520-791-3276), 1000 N Tucson Blvd; and Randolph Park (☎ 520-791-4896), 100 S Alvernon Way.

Water Sports
Tucson Parks & Recreation (☎ 520-791-4873) manages about two dozen swimming pools throughout the city. Many hotels have their own pools.

During the summer, water parks offer something a little more exciting than swimming laps. Breakers (☎ 520-682-2530), 8555 W Tangerine Rd (1½ miles east of I-10 exit 242, 16 miles north of downtown), has a huge wave pool for surfing, as well as water slides and nonwave pools. Hours are 9 am to dusk; admission is $11.95 for adults, $7.95 for kids under 48 inches tall and free for children under three. Children under 13 must be accompanied by an adult. Justin's Water World & RV Park (☎ 520-883-8340), 3551 S San Joaquin Rd (8 miles west of I-19 exit 99 along Ajo Way, then 2 miles north), has many swimming pools, toddlers' paddling pools, water slides galore, a tubing area and an 'Atlantis – The Lost Continent' attraction. Hours are 10 am to 5 pm Friday to Sunday and holidays. Admission is $9 for six- to 60-year-olds.

ORGANIZED TOURS
Gray Line (☎ 520-622-8811) offers standard coach and van tours of the city and its surroundings as well as excursions all over the state. Tours of Tucson and southeastern Arizona are offered by Tucson Tour Company (☎ 520-297-2911) and Off the Beaten Path Tours (☎ 520-529-6090). Trail Dust Jeep Tours (☎ 520-747-0323) takes you into the desert in open jeeps. The Center for Desert Archaeology (☎ 520-885-6283) has tours led by archaeologists to sites in downtown Tucson and the surrounding desert. Old Pueblo Tours (☎ 520-795-7448) specializes in historical tours of Tucson. Note that some tours don't operate in the summer heat.

SPECIAL EVENTS
Hundreds of events happen year-round, of course. The following is a selection of some of the most notable and important. The Convention and Visitors Bureau has a complete listing of events and exact dates.

The Southern Arizona Square and Round Dance & Clogging Festival attracts thousands of dancers, who gather at the Tucson Convention Center in late January.

In the first half of February, the Tucson Gem and Mineral Show attracts exhibitors and visitors for what is said to be the largest show of its kind in the world. The Fiesta de los Vaqueros, held from the last Thursday to Sunday of February, features the world's largest nonmotorized parade followed by a rodeo and other cowboy events – even the city's schools are closed for the last two days of what is locally called 'Rodeo Week.'

The Tohono O'odham tribe hosts many Southwestern Indian tribes for several days of food, dances, singing and other entertainment during the Wa:k Pow Wow,

held at the San Xavier del Bac Mission in early March.

See Deer Dances on the tiny Pascua Yaqui Indian Reservation on the Saturday before Palm Sunday (one week before Easter) and the Saturday before Easter Sunday. The reservation is almost 5 miles west of I-19 exit 95 along Valencia Rd, then a mile south along Camino de Oeste.

In April, the Tucson International Mariachi Conference and the Waila Festival (Tohono O'odham music) celebrate ethnic music. The International Film Festival lasts for almost two weeks in the middle of the month. The Pima County Fair, with carnival rides galore and many other events, takes place in April at the county fairgrounds. Also in April and repeated in December is the 4th Avenue Street Fair, celebrated with hundreds of arts and crafts booths and free street entertainment.

Tucson's Hispanic heritage is celebrated during Cinco de Mayo at JF Kennedy Park on or close to May 5 with parades, dances, music, arts and crafts booths, and Mexican food. Also in early May is the Tucson Folk Music Festival. Things slow down somewhat during the hot summer months, although a June blues festival at Mt Lemmon brings out music lovers enjoying the cool pines and tunes. Mexican Independence Day is celebrated at JF Kennedy Park in mid-September.

In mid- to late October the Fiesta de los Chiles celebrates this most Southwestern of all agricultural products at Tucson Botanical Gardens. There's also the Tucson Blues Festival held at Reid Park. Another 4th Avenue Street Fair kicks off the December holiday season and many of the Christmas celebrations have a strong Hispanic flavor.

PLACES TO STAY

As with Phoenix, December through April is the high season in Tucson, when rooms are at a premium. During major events like the Gem and Mineral Show and the Fiesta de los Vaqueros, prices rise above their already high winter rates. Prices drop substantially in the low season, from May to September, when some places, especially the pricier resorts, charge less than half of their high-season rates. Because of this seasonal variation, the prices given for the following can only be used as a rough guide.

Places to Stay – Camping

The USFS (☎ 520-749-8700) operates four simple campgrounds on the Catalina Hwy going up to Mt Lemmon. None take reservations and all can fill over weekends, so arrive early in the day. About 12 miles from the Tanque Verde Rd turnoff is *Molino Basin*. Open from mid-October to mid-April, the campground is at an elevation of 4500 feet and has more than 40 sites at $5 but no water. A few miles farther is *General Hitchcock* at 6000 feet, open year-round with 12 sites at $5 but no water. About 8 miles farther is *Rose Canyon* at 7000 feet with a trout-fishing lake and drinking water, but no showers or RV hookups. The 74 sites are open from mid-April till mid-October and cost $9. *Spencer Canyon*, open about the same dates and also with drinking water, is 4 miles farther at 8000 feet, with 70 sites for $8. Nearby Summerhaven has stores and restaurants.

Campgrounds in the Tucson valley often fill up in winter, so arrive early or make reservations if possible. The campground at *Catalina State Park* has 48 campsites that fill up on a first-come, first-served basis. Fees are $10 or $15 with electrical hookups, and water and showers are available. A group campground (minimum of 20 people) can be reserved. For more information call Catalina State Park (☎ 520-628-5798), PO Box 36986, AZ 85740. The park is about 15 miles north of downtown along Oracle Rd (Hwy 77).

Gilbert Ray Campground (☎ 520-883-4200), on Kinney Rd a couple of miles east of the Arizona-Sonora Desert Museum, has 152 sites open year-round, some with electrical hookups. There's water but no showers. Site rates are $6 or $9.50 with hookups.

Justin's RV Park (☎ 520-883-8340) is next to Justin's Water World (see Water Sports, above) and has 225 sites with hookups for $15. This is an adult-only park except during months when Water World is open.

Some RV resorts with more than 1000 sites provide entertainment and recreational facilities for adults only. These are often full with long-term RVers in winter, when reservations are essential and weekly and monthly discounts are often given. *Voyager RV Resort* (☎ 520-574-5000, 800-424-9191, fax 520-574-5037, vrv@primenet.com), 8701 S Kolb Rd near I-10 exit 270, charges $25 to $32 and was recently voted the nation's best adult RV resort. *Rincon Country West* (☎ 520-294-5608), 4555 S Mission Rd, a short way west of I-19 exit 99, is similarly priced and is for seniors only.

If you have kids, there's the 260-site *Cactus Country RV Resort* (☎ 520-574-3000, 800-777-8799, fax 520-574-9004), 10195 S Houghton Rd, a half mile north of I-10 exit 275. There are various recreational facilities and sites for $25 with hookups. There are also five tent sites for $15. Another family choice is *Prince of Tucson* (☎ 520-887-3501, 800-955-3501),

3501 N Freeway near I-10 exit 254. It has recreational facilities and more than 200 sites for $25.

There are many more smaller RV resorts (the Convention and Visitors Bureau can send a listing), but the above should get you started.

Places to Stay – Budget

The *Roadrunner Hostel* (☎ 520-628-4709, roadrunn@azstarnet.com), 346 E 12th St, Tucson, AZ 85701, is an independent hostel opened in summer of 1998 and aimed at international travelers. Currently, it has two six-room dorms for men and women at $13 a night or $70 a week, but there are plans to expand. It offers free pick-up from the Greyhound as well as bedding, a kitchen, laundry and 24-hour access. Guests can rent bicycles, or use the Internet, for an extra $5.

Young budget travelers like to stay at *Hotel Congress* (☎ 520-622-8848, 800-722-8848, fax 520-792-6366, hotel@hotcong.com), 311 E Congress, right downtown. The best alternative music club, as well as a bar, café and cybar (with Internet access), is downstairs – music can be loud until 1 am. The hotel dates back to the 1920s and has some charm. There are 40 old-fashioned rooms; most are small and have a double bed, and a few midsized ones have two. Five rooms provide two to four dorm beds for $15 per person – these aren't exactly a youth hostel but are for hostelers. Only travelers with HI/AYH or international student cards can stay in these budget rooms and reservations are not accepted. You can reserve one of the private rooms with private showers. Rates are from $29 single in summer to about $55 from December to April. Doubles are about $35 to $70. Youth-hostel-card holders get a 20% discount on the private rooms, and seniors and students get a 10% discount. Weekly discounts are available.

Outside of downtown, cheap, basic, independent mom-and-pop type motel rooms start around $30 in the winter (more during the Gem and Mineral Show in early February). However, they can be hard to find; they are often booked up by long-term clients who pay by the week. In the summer, rooms can be found in the $20s.

There are two main areas for cheap and basic motels, with a few pricier chain-owned places thrown in. The cheapest area is on the south side of South Tucson around the intersection of 6th Ave with I-10 exit 261, and southeast from there along Benson Hwy as far as Alvernon Way. The other area is north of downtown along Stone Ave or Oracle Rd, north of Speedway Blvd, and west of Oracle Rd on Miracle Mile. These are not the most salubrious of neighborhoods but are OK if you are driving rather than walking.

At I-10 exit 261 the hotels are the very cheapest: *Budget Inn* (☎ 520-884-1470), 3033 S 6th Ave; *El Camino Motel* (☎ 520-624-3619), 297 E Benson Hwy; and the *Sun-Ray Motel* (☎ 520-622-9737), 220 E Benson Hwy. For a few dollars more, the decent *Lazy 8 Motel* (☎ 520-622-3336), 314 E Benson Hwy, has a pool and restaurant and includes breakfast – summer rates in the low $30s and winter rates in the $35 to $45 range make this a good budget choice. Also near exit 261, the *Econo Lodge* (☎/fax 520-623-5881), 3020 S 6th Ave, has a pool and spa. In summer it charges a reasonable $35/40 for singles/doubles and only a few dollars more in winter but can get overpriced during the February Gem and Mineral Show when its official rates go up into the $70s (as do many other cheap motels). Budget travelers should avoid Tucson at this time unless they're attending that show.

Farther southeast along Benson Hwy are about a dozen basic motels. Some cheap but adequate ones are the *Western Motel* (☎ 520-746-9892), 3218 E Benson Hwy (one of the cheapest); the *Redwood Lodge* (☎ 520-294-3802), 3315 E Benson Hwy, with a pool; and the *Scotsman Motel* (☎ 520-294-7002), 3526 E Benson Hwy.

North of downtown, the cheapest motels are likely to charge about $40 or even $50 for a double in winter, but they are more convenient to the center of town. One of the cheapest OK places here is the *Hacienda Motel* (☎ 520-623-2513), 1742 N Oracle Rd, with a pool and some rooms with kitchenettes. Other nearby cheapies are found on the same block and along Miracle Mile, mixed in with a couple of mid-range places.

The Motel 6 chain is well represented in Tucson. All locations have pools and more than 100 rooms. Winter rates for singles are between $43 and $50, and $49 to $55 for doubles; summer rates drop into the $30s or low $40s for doubles. Here's a listing of your choices in increasing order of cost: *Motel 6 Benson N* (☎ 520-622-4614, fax 520-624-1584), 755 E Benson Hwy; *Motel 6 Benson S* (☎ 520-628-1264, fax 520-624-1731), 1031 E Benson Hwy (both near I-10 exit 262); *Motel 6 Congress* (☎ 520-628-1339, fax 520-624-1848), 960 S Freeway; *Motel 6 22nd* (☎ 520-624-2516, fax 520-624-1697), 1222 S Freeway; *Motel 6 East* (☎ 520-746-0030, fax 520-741-7403), 4950 S Outlet Center Drive; and *Motel 6 North* (☎ 520-744-9300, fax 520-744-2439), 4630 W Ina Rd.

Places to Stay – Middle

Hotels Remember that a $99 room in late February can be $49 in July and $139 during the Gem and Mineral Show. Always ask about discounts.

Hotels offering satisfactory lodging in the $60 to $85 range for a double in winter (except for the Gem and Mineral Show) include the following. The two *Red Roof Inns*, one at 3700 E Irvington Rd (☎ 520-571-1400, fax 520-519-0051) and another at 4940 W Ina Rd at I-10 exit 248 (☎ 520-744-8199, fax 520-519-0051) are among the cheapest in this range. Both have a pool and more than 100 rooms; the first location has a 24-hour coffee shop. The *Wayward Winds Lodge* (☎ 520-791-7526, 800-791-9503, fax 520-791-9502), 707 W Miracle Mile, has 40 good-sized rooms, some with kitchenettes, and a swimming pool on pleasant grounds. Continental breakfast is included and it's a good value. The cheapest good hotel very close to the airport is *Budgetel Inn & Suites* (☎ 520-889-6600, fax 520-889-4100), 2548 E Medina Rd, with more than 100 rooms. It has a pool, spa, and exercise room and offers continental breakfast.

ARIZONA

Howard Johnson Lodge (☎ 520-623-7792, fax 520-620-1556), 1025 E Benson Hwy, has 136 rooms, many with balconies or patios. It also has a pleasant pool, a spa, sauna and coffee shop on the premises. A free airport shuttle is available. There's also the *Howard Johnson Inn* (☎ 520-622-5871, fax 520-620-0097), 1010 S Freeway, with 107 rooms and similar services plus a continental breakfast. A little over half a mile west of downtown by the freeway is the *La Quinta Inn – West* (☎ 520-622-6491, fax 520-798-3669), 664 N Freeway, which has 133 rooms and a pool; there's a coffee shop nearby. Continental breakfast is included.

Three *Super 8*, two *Days Inn* and five *Best Western* chain motels are in the $70 to $125 range – rates vary according to demand. Among the best of these is *Best Western Inn at the Airport* (☎ 520-746-0271, 800-772-3847, fax 520-889-7391, iaatucson@aol.com), 7060 S Tucson Blvd, right outside the airport, with 150 rooms, a pool, spa, restaurant and tennis court; continental breakfast is included. Also good is the *Best Western A Royal Sun Inn & Suites* (☎ 520-622-8871, 800-545-8858, fax 520-623-2267), 1015 N Stone Ave, with 79 large rooms (including several hot-tub suites), all with refrigerators and VCRs, some with balconies. There is a pool, spa, sauna, exercise equipment, restaurant and lounge with room service and occasional entertainment. The hotel is situated in a nondescript commercial area but is only about a mile from downtown.

The following are some good hotels with rooms in the $90 to $125 range for doubles in winter. *La Quinta Inn – East* (☎ 520-747-1414, fax 520-745-6903), 6404 E Broadway Blvd, has a pool, spa and many rooms with balconies or patios, all with coffeemakers. *La Quinta Inn – Airport* (☎ 520-573-333, fax 520-573-7710), 7001 S Tucson Blvd, has large new rooms by the airport entrance. Both provide continental breakfast.

The *Holiday Inn – City Center* (☎ 520-624-8711, fax 520-623-8121), 181 W Broadway Blvd, is right downtown next to the Tucson Convention Center and is popular during conventions. It has a pool, restaurant and bar, and more than 300 rooms. Also good downtown is the *Clarion Inn – Santa Rita* (☎ 520-622-4000, fax 520-620-0376), 88 E Broadway Blvd. This older hotel has been fully renovated and has about 150 rooms and 40 pricier suites, all with microwaves and coffeemakers. It has a pool, spa, exercise room and the Café Poca Cosa (see Places to Eat, below) and includes continental breakfast.

Try the *Smugglers Inn* (☎ 520-296-3292, 800-525-8852, fax 520-722-3713, smuggler@rtd.com), 6350 E Speedway Blvd, with attractive gardens and spacious rooms with balconies or patios. Facilities include a pool, spa, tennis court, putting green, restaurant and bar. Room service, weekend entertainment and pickup from the airport are available.

The *Tucson East Hilton* (☎ 520-721-5600, fax 520-721-5696, tehilton@primenet.com), 7600 E Broadway Blvd, has a pool, spa, restaurant, bar, room service and a more expensive 7th-floor 'Summit Level' with extra services such as complimentary breakfast, a cocktail hour and newspapers.

The *Windmill Inn at St Philips Plaza* (☎ 520-577-0007, 800-547-4747, fax 520-577-0045), 4250 N Campbell Ave, is in one of the more upscale shopping plazas. The 122 attractive suites are decorated in Southwestern style and have microwaves, wet bars and refrigerators. Winter rates are $130 to $140, with newspapers, coffee and pastries delivered to your room every morning. There is a pool, a spa and a lending library of paperback bestsellers as well as bicycles for guest use.

B&Bs There are about 40 B&Bs in Tucson, and I give a selection of some of the best-established, though there are others that are just as good. The most practical way to obtain a description of facilities and prices of B&Bs (both in Tucson and southern Arizona) is to make reservations through Old Pueblo Homestays (☎/fax 520-790-2399, 800-333-9776, jaws1926@aol.com), PO Box 13603, Tucson, AZ 85732, or with Casa Alegre (see below), which represents several B&Bs. Also refer to the agencies listed in the Phoenix chapter that also represent Tucson B&Bs, or get a listing from the visitors bureau.

Casa Alegre (☎ 520-628-1800, 800-628-5654, fax 520-792-1880, alegre123@aol .com), 316 E Speedway Blvd, Tucson, AZ 85705, is a peaceful 1915 house that is convenient to U of A and downtown and is decorated with historical memorabilia. Five rooms with baths range from $80 to $105, and there is a pool and spa. *El Presidio* (☎ 520-623-6151, 800-349-6151, fax 520-623-3860), 297 N Main Ave, Tucson, AZ 85701, has three suites (two with kitchenettes) within an adobe home. Bathrobes and fruit are some of the features offered at this garden oasis in the heart of the city. Rooms cost from $85 to $125.

Peppertrees B&B (☎/fax 520-622-7167, 800-348-5763), 724 E University Blvd, Tucson, AZ 85719, is a quick walk away from U of A. Four large guest rooms in the 1905 house cost $110, and two guesthouses, equipped with TVs, phones, laundry facilities, full kitchen and two bedrooms, are $170 – about 30% less in summer. Gourmet breakfasts and an afternoon tea are included in the price. *La Posada del Valle* (☎/fax 520-795-3840), 1640 N Campbell Rd, Tucson, AZ 85719, is also close to U of A and has a beautiful courtyard. It features five rooms with private entrances and bathrooms. Three rooms cost $90; the more luxurious costs $115 and a cottage goes for $145. Rates include breakfast and an afternoon tea.

Take Broadway all the way east to the Saguaro National Park and look for signs before the fork in the road to get to the luxurious and remote *Suncatcher B&B* (☎/fax 520-885-0883, 800-835-8012), 105 N Avenida Javelina, Tucson, AZ 85748. This B&B has four rooms all individually decorated to resemble some of the world's most exclusive hotels. It also has a pool and spa. Rates are $140 to $170 in winter, $80 to $100 in summer.

Casa Tierra (☎ 520-578-3058, fax 520-578-8445, casatier@azstarnet.com), 11155 W Calle Pima, Tucson, AZ 85743, is just west of the western section of Saguaro National Park. Take Kinney Rd to Mile Wide Rd then turn left at the second set of mailboxes. Sounds remote? It is – a modern-day adobe surrounded by desert. The three rooms, each with private bathrooms, patios, microwaves and refrigerators are between $75 and $95, including breakfast. A three-bedroom, three-bathroom house sleeping eight rents for $1400 a week (no breakfast). There are two hot tubs, one for the B&B and one for the house. This B&B closes from June through September.

Places to Stay – Top End
Hotels The grand dame of Tucson hotels is the sedate and beautiful *Arizona Inn* (☎ 520-325-1541, 800-933-1093, fax 520-881-5830), 2200 E Elm, built in 1929. The 14-acre grounds are attractively landscaped and the public areas are elegant and traditional. A pool, tennis and croquet are available. The rooms, decorated in Southwestern style, are spacious though the bathrooms are not very large (people spent less time in them in 1929, perhaps). There are 70 rooms and 16 suites with patios or fireplaces. The restaurant is good enough to attract the local citizenry, and you can order room service. The service is friendly and unpretentious, yet professional. Expect to pay $180 to $230 in the winter.

Ranches & Resorts Although Phoenix and Scottsdale are undeniably the resort capitals of the Southwest, Tucson does have a growing number of fine resorts that rival the Valley of the Sun for beauty, comfort and diversity of facilities. Note that 7.5% tax and 15% gratuities may be added to ranch rates that include meals and riding. They normally require a minimum stay of two to four days and give weekly discounts. These are often destinations in themselves rather than a place to stay for a couple of days while touring the Southwest.

Lazy K Bar Guest Ranch (☎ 520-744-3050, 800-321-7018, fax 520-744-7623, lazyk@theriver.com), 8401 N Scenic Drive, Tucson, AZ 85743, offers horseback riding twice a day on desert and mountain trails. Tennis, mountain biking and hayrides are

ARIZONA

some of the other activities. The style is very much family-oriented with plenty of activities for children and large sit-down dinners with all the guests. The ranch has 23 rooms in adobe buildings, all with air conditioning and private baths. Rates are about $200 to $300 a double, depending on season, with discounts for children.

White Stallion Ranch (☎ 520-297-0252, 888-977-2624, fax 520-744-2786), 9251 W Twin Peaks Rd, Tucson, AZ 85743, is a quiet, peaceful, family-style ranch where you can groom your own horse before a ride, let the children roam free in a petting zoo, relax on a patio and listen to the birds or take a challenging hike throughout the desert mountain wilderness. This 3000-acre ranch is open from October to May and has 32 rooms at about $300 double.

Fifteen miles east of Tucson, *Tanque Verde Guest Ranch* (☎ 520-296-6275, 800-234-3833, fax 520-721-9426), 14301 E Speedway Blvd, Tucson, AZ 85748, sits in the Rincon Mountains, offering plenty of opportunities for hiking, riding and nature walks (it has an extensive birding list). For more 'resort-style' activities, there are two pools, five tennis courts, a spa, exercise room and basketball courts. But 100 head of horses remind you what Tucson ranches are about. This is one of the more famous and comfortable ranches in the area, with 70 well-decorated 'casitas,' attentive service, great food and beautiful surroundings. Depending on season, rates are about $200 to $400 double.

Loew's Ventana Canyon Resort (☎ 520-299-2020, 800-234-5117, fax 520-299-6832), 7000 N Resort Drive, Tucson, AZ 85715, is in a spectacular setting surrounded by the golf course. The resort also features a shopping arcade, impeccable and comfortable rooms, a beauty salon, elegant dining, two 18-hole golf courses, several tennis courts, extensive fitness activities and entertainment. Room rates are from $300 to $400, with more expensive suites as well. Similarly priced places with top-notch golfing and resort facilities include *Sheraton El Conquistador Resort & Country Club* (☎ 520-544-5000, 800-325-7832, fax 520-

544-1222), 10000 N Oracle Rd, Tucson, AZ 85737; *Omni Tucson National Golf Course & Spa* (☎ 520-297-2271, 800-528-4856, fax 520-742-2452), 2727 W Club Drive, Tucson, AZ 85742; and *Westin La Paloma* (☎ 520-742-6000, 800-937-8461, fax 520-577-5886), 3800 E Sunrise Drive, Tucson, AZ 85718. Each of these are big resorts with about 200 to 500 rooms; call for complete details.

If you're not looking for on-site golf but do want extensive resort facilities at a more moderate price, a good bet is *Westward Look Resort* (☎ 520-297-1151, 800-722-2500, fax 520-742-1573, wlrres434@aol.com), 245 E Ina Rd, Tucson, AZ 85704. It was originally a dude ranch and retains much of its original intimate style. There is a top-notch restaurant, and the rooms have views of either the mountains or the city. Swimming pools, tennis courts, a fitness center, spas and bicycles keep guests occupied. Winter rates here are $180 to $300.

Another good choice is *Hacienda del Sol Guest Ranch Resort* (☎ 520-299-1501, 800-728-6514, fax 520-299-5554), 5601 N Hacienda del Sol Rd, Tucson, AZ 85718. This is more for people who just want to relax in an authentic Southwest setting with lovely views without all the golf and tennis hoopla. The resort dates from 1929 and they say that Clark Gable, Spencer Tracy and other stars used to stay here. It does offer tennis, croquet, horseshoes, a whirlpool and a small swimming pool, but with only 33 units, everything is much lower key than other resorts. Horseback riding and golf can easily be arranged if you want. There is a gourmet restaurant on the premises. Most of the rooms are about $160 double, with five suites at $200 and three casitas at about $280, all including continental breakfast.

Note that these resorts give summer visitors huge discounts – 60% less is not uncommon.

PLACES TO EAT

Tucson has a well-deserved reputation for Mexican food and if you like it, you'll never be at a loss for a place to eat. If you don't like Mexican food, you'll still find an extensive and varied selection of excellent American and international restaurants, as well as Southwestern cuisine.

Cafés & Diners

The popular and busy *Coffee Etc* (☎ 520-881-8070), 2830 N Campbell Ave, serves breakfast 24 hours a day, as well as burgers, sandwiches, soups, salads, light meals and, of course, a variety of coffees. There is another branch (☎ 520-544-8588) at 6091 N Oracle.

For home-style breakfast, the friendly *Marlene's Hungry Fox* (☎ 520-326-2835), 4637 E Broadway Blvd, is a good choice favored by locals, some of whom have been eating breakfast here for years. It features 'double yolk eggs' and is open from 6 am to 2 pm on weekdays and 6:30 am to 2 pm on weekends. Another friendly and funky local place that has good breakfasts and lunches at low prices is *Bobo's* (☎ 520-326-6163), 2938 E Grant Rd, near what Tucsonans call 'the airplane corner' (an airplane was parked on the corner for many years before being hauled off in 1998). Pancakes are stuffed with fruit or, if you're feeling adventurous, get the UFO, which is a pancake made with spinach and melted cheese. It is open from 5:30 am to 2:30 pm. Another local favorite greasy spoon (there are many more for you to discover) is *Frank's* (☎ 520-881-2710), 3843 E Pima, open at 6 am weekdays, 7 am Saturday, 8 am Sunday, and closing daily at 2 pm.

Good downtown spots for breakfast include *Cup Cafe* (☎ 520-798-1618), 311 E Congress, in the same building as the Hotel Congress and Club Congress, recommended for people searching for something more eclectic and artistic. The breakfasts are good, as are the light meals. Hours are from 8 am to 1 am daily. Also good and locally popular is *Grill* (☎ 520-623-7621), 100 E Congress, open 24 hours.

For breakfast in the desert, head to the *Tohono Chul Tea Room* (☎ 520-797-1222), 7366 N Paseo del Norte, where you can dine on a pleasant patio or indoors from 8 am to 5 pm daily. The varied menu features both Mexican and American food,

and they serve an English-style high tea from 2:30 to 5 pm.

If you want your eggs Benedict served in the most elegant of surroundings, try the dining room at the *Arizona Inn* (☎ 520-325-1541), 2200 E Elm (see Places to Stay, above). It is open to the public; breakfast hours are 7 to 10 am.

Vegetarian

The *Blue Willow Restaurant* (☎ 520-795-8736), 2616 N Campbell Ave, serves both vegetarian and meat dishes, but the emphasis is vegetarian. The breakfasts are some of the best in town, and its soups, salads and sandwiches are both good and an excellent value. The place is popular, with a slightly alternative clientele of all ages, and there's sometimes a wait during which you can browse its interesting card and poster shop. It has an attractive patio with a shade roof and mist-makers to keep you cool. Hours are 7 or 8 am (depending on season) to 10 pm; it's open until 11 pm on Friday and Saturday and 9 pm Sunday. Beer and wine are served.

For alcohol-free, all-vegetarian meals, try *Govinda's Natural Foods* (☎ 520-792-0630), 711 E Blacklidge Drive. As the name suggests, food is Indian-influenced and is served buffet-style by Hare Krishna types. The atmosphere is meditative and vegan food is also available. Hours are from 11:30 am to 2:20 pm, Wednesday to Saturday, and 5 to 9 pm Tuesday to Saturday. Another alcohol-free, all-vegetarian place is *Sundance Juice Bar & Café* (☎ 520-620-1699), 621 N 4th Ave. This one has a Middle Eastern and Mediterranean influence and is open 11 am to 9 pm Monday to Saturday. *Guilin Chinese Restaurant* (☎ 520-320-7768), 3250 E Speedway Blvd, is a new authentic Chinese restaurant with mainly vegetarian and some vegan offerings. It has been well-reviewed locally and is open from 11 am to 9 pm on weekdays, to 10 pm on weekends.

Mexican

There must be more than 100 Mexican restaurants in Tucson. A worthwhile culinary adventure would be to spend a few months eating at every one!

With so many Mexican places from which to choose, it's hard to narrow them down to a manageable list, but here are some of my favorites. The least expensive restaurants are generally in or near South Tucson. For Mexican fast food, check out *Birriería Guadalajara* (☎ 520-624-8020), 304 E 22nd – very tasty and beats the heck out of any American fast food. The menu here is in Spanish, but the servers will translate for you. Hours are from 7 am to 10 pm daily, till about midnight on Friday and Saturday. For sit-down dining, there are half a dozen good places along S 4th Ave between 22nd and I-10, any one of which provides satisfactory food. *Mi Nidito* (☎ 520-622-5081), 1813 S 4th Ave, frequently gets the best reviews and there's often a wait; they don't take reservations. Hours are 11 am to 10 pm Wednesday, Thursday and Sunday, and to 2 am on Friday and Saturday.

There are several good choices downtown. One of the cheapest and most interesting is *La Indita* (☎ 520-792-0523), 622 N 4th Ave. Apart from the excellent Mexican food, this is one of the few places where you can also try Michoacan Tarascan Indian dishes. Hours are from 11 am to 9 pm, Monday to Friday, 6 to 9 pm on Saturday, and 9 am to 9 pm on Sunday. There is another *La Indita* (☎ 520-623-2766) at 2332 N 6th Ave, with similar food but no alcohol, open from 11 am to 9 pm Monday to Friday.

Mexican food in more upscale environments costs a few dollars more but has some innovative twists and is still an excellent value. Recommended downtown places include the excellent *Café Poca Cosa* (☎ 520-622-6400), 88 E Broadway Blvd (in the Clarion Inn – Santa Rita), with beautifully presented, freshly prepared, innovative meals and a full bar. The menu changes often and reservations are requested. Hours are 11 am to 9 pm, Monday to Thursday, to 10 pm on Friday and Saturday. Around the corner is *Little Café Poca Cosa* (no phone), 20 S Scott, open from 7:30 am to 2:30 pm, Monday to Friday; alcohol is not served.

El Minuto Cafe (☎ 520-882-4145), just south of downtown at 354 S Main Ave, has been in business for six decades and is famous for its chiles rellenos, among other dishes. Hours are 11 am to 10 pm, Monday to Thursday, and to 11 pm on Friday and Saturday. It recently opened a branch at 8 N Kolb Rd (☎ 520-290-9591). The oldest place in town is *El Charro Cafe* (☎ 520-622-1922), 311 N Court Ave, which they say has been in the same family since 1922 and is very popular with tourists and locals alike. Its carne seca used to be dried on the roof in the old days. Hours change seasonally and it opens for breakfast sometimes. There are also branches at 6310 E Broadway (☎ 520-745-1922) and at the airport, for your last (or first) Mexican meal.

La Parrilla Suiza (☎ 520-747-4838), 5602 E Speedway Blvd, and (☎ 520-624-4300), 2720 N Oracle Rd, serves grilled Mexico City-style food and is part of a chain with 18 restaurants in Mexico. Hours are 11 am to 10 pm, Sunday to Thursday, to 11 pm Friday and Saturday. *El Saguarito* (☎ 520-297-1264), 7216 N Oracle Rd, is open from 7 am to 9 pm Monday to Saturday, and serves both health- and heart-conscious food using canola oil rather than the traditional lard. *La Fuente* (☎ 520-623-8659), 1749 N Oracle Rd, often has strolling mariachis in the evening to give you that extra Mexican ambiance. It is open from 11:30 am to 10 pm daily and till 11 pm on Friday and Saturday.

Guatemalan

Maya Quetzal (☎ 520-622-8207), 429 N 4th Ave, is a small, friendly place that has been very well received locally and serves delicious dishes at pequeño prices. It has a little outdoor patio and is open from 11 am to 2 pm and 5 to 8:30 pm, till 9 pm Friday and Saturday and is closed on Sunday.

Asian

Cock Asian (☎ 520-320-5502), at 2547 E Broadway Blvd, has great Vietnamese/Chinese food, which many locals claim is the best in town, and is a good value. Hours are from 11 am to 9 pm, Monday to Saturday. *Old Peking* (☎ 520-795-9811), 2522 E Speedway Blvd, is a good choice for standard Chinese cuisine. It is open from 11:30 am to 9:30 pm daily. Also try the *Golden Phoenix* (☎ 520-327-8008) at 2854 E 22nd. Hours are 11 am to 9:30 pm. *Seri Melaka* (☎ 520-747-7811), 6133 E Broadway Blvd, serves reasonably priced Malaysian food and some Chinese dishes. Hours are 11 am to 9:30 pm.

Sakura (☎ 520-298-7777), 6534 E Tanque Verde Rd, serves a varied Japanese menu including sushi and teppan (fun, table-side chopping and pyrotechnics) with prices as varied as the menu. Hours are from 11 am to 2 pm Monday to Friday, 5 to 10 pm Sunday to Thursday, and until 11 pm on Friday and Saturday. Dedicated sushi fans should try *Sachiko Sushi* (☎ 520-886-7000), 1101 N Wilmot Rd. It lacks any kind of ambiance, but the sushi is possibly the best in town and other Japanese/Korean food is served. It's open for lunch from Monday to Saturday and dinner daily; hours vary. Kimono-clad waitresses will provide a touch of tradition at *Shogun* (☎ 520-888-6763), 3971 N Oracle Rd, where authentic Japanese meals and an extensive sushi bar are available 11:30 am to 2:30 pm, Monday to Saturday, and from 5 to 10 pm nightly (till 11 pm on Friday and Saturday).

A couple of places stand out for Thai cooking. *Karuna's Thai Plate* (☎ 520-325-4129), 1917 E Grant Rd, has inexpensive lunch buffets (including vegetarian selections) and is very popular, though alcohol isn't served. Hours are 11:30 am to 3 pm and 5 to 9 pm (till 10 pm on Friday and Saturday) and 5 to 10 pm on Sunday. *Char's Thai* (☎ 520-795-1715), 5039 E 5th St, has super-spicy plates (though mild dishes are also available) and is open weekdays for lunch and daily for dinner.

India Oven (☎ 520-326-8635), 2727 N Campbell, serves great Punjab food and has an inexpensive lunch buffet. It's very popular; service can be slow. Hours are 11 am to 3 pm and 5 to 10 pm daily. Other recommended Indian places are *Gandhi* (☎ 520-292-1738), 150 W Fort Lowell Rd, and *New Delhi Palace* (☎ 520-296-8585),

at 6751 E Broadway Blvd, both of which are open from 11:30 am to 2:30 pm and 5 to 10 pm.

African

Well, Ethiopian, to be precise. At *Zemam's* (☎ 520-323-9928), 2731 E Broadway Blvd, you eat your food with injera bread instead of cutlery. It's definitely a different dining experience, but a delicious and very inexpensive one that has proved quite popular in Tucson. If you don't know where to start with Ethiopian cuisine, order a combination plate with three entrées. Alcohol isn't served, but you can bring your own. Hours are 11:30 am to 2:30 pm and 5:30 to 9 pm daily except Monday.

Italian

If expense is not a concern, try elegant *Daniel's* (☎ 520-742-3200), 4340 N Campbell Ave in St Philips Plaza, one of the best places in town. It specializes in Tuscan-style meals, and most dinner entrées are in the $20s, except for several less-expensive pasta selections. Hours are 5 to 9 pm daily. Recommended, less-expensive choices include *Ciao Italia* (☎ 520-884-0000), 1535 N Stone Ave, open only from 5 to 10 pm, Tuesday to Saturday, and *Caruso's* (☎ 520-624-5765), 434 N 4th Ave, with a great patio and open 4:30 to 10 pm, Tuesday to Thursday and Sunday, till 11 pm on Friday and Saturday.

French

Le Rendez-Vous (☎ 520-323-7373), 3844 E Fort Lowell Rd, looks like a little Southwestern house in a parking lot and has a refreshingly unpompous atmosphere. The food is recommended and a bit cheaper than most French restaurants of this caliber. Its hours are from 11:30 am to 2 pm, Tuesday to Friday, and 6 to 10 pm Tuesday to Sunday.

Le Bistro (☎ 520-327-3086), 2574 N Campbell Ave, is a local favorite – excellent authentic French food with entrées mainly in the teens. Hours are 11 am to 2:30 pm on weekdays and 5 to 9:30 pm daily (till 10:30 pm on Friday and Saturday).

Greek

Athens on 4th Ave (☎ 520-624-6886), 500 N 4th Ave, has delicious Greek food and though prices have crept up since the last edition, it's inexpensive. The restaurant is small; reservations are a good idea. Hours are 5 to 10 pm, Monday to Thursday, and to 11 pm on Friday and Saturday. A little more upscale and very good is the *Olive Tree* (☎ 520-298-1845), 7000 E Tanque Verde Rd. Restaurant hours are from 11:30 am to 9 pm, Monday to Thursday, to 10 pm on Friday and Saturday, and 5 to 9 pm on Sunday.

Southwestern

Cafe Terra Cotta (☎ 520-577-8100), 4310 N Campbell Ave, in St Philips Plaza, is the best Southwestern restaurant in Tucson. The food is as good as any of the other places at prices that are definitely more moderate. The menu is innovative, even wild-sounding at times, but there are also a few fairly straightforward choices. The appetizers sound so appetizing that many people order two of them and forgo an entrée, supposedly to leave room for one of the divine desserts. There is a pleasant patio and appropriate Southwestern décor. Hours are from 11 am to 9:30 pm, till 10 pm on Fridays and Saturdays. Note that they plan to move to a new, larger location near 3500 E Sunrise on December 31, 1999.

Another moderately priced restaurant with a delicious and eclectic Southwestern menu but a decidedly un-Southwestern ambiance is the *Presidio Grill* (☎ 520-327-4667), 3352 E Speedway Blvd. It is open 11 am to 10 pm, till midnight on Friday and Saturday. Sunday brunch begins at 10 am.

The renowned *Janos* (☎ 520-884-9426), considered by many to be the most upscale Southwestern restaurant in town, lost its lease on the 1855 Stevens House downtown and recently moved to 3770 E Sunrise Dr, in the Westin La Paloma resort.

Cajun

New in town is *Nonie* (☎ 520-319-1965), 2526 E Grant Rd, a New Orleans bistro serving authentic French Creole and Cajun cuisine. If crawfish, jambalaya, alligator and fried pickles are your idea of good food, the cooks know how to prepare them here. Wash 'em down with a Voodoo beer. (Okay, there are plenty of less offbeat Cajun options as well.) Prices are reasonable; hours are from 11 am to 3 pm, Tuesday to Friday, and 5 pm to 1 am Tuesday to Sunday.

Steak

There are plenty of steak houses that serve what Southwestern food used to be until the good chefs like Janos Wilder (of Janos, listed above) came along and reinvented the concept. For those on a budget, *El Corral* (☎ 520-299-6092), 2201 E River Rd, is a good choice. Service is a little amateurish but aims to please. Prime rib is the specialty of the house and a great deal at under $10. Kids' cheeseburgers are $2. Hours are 5 to 10 pm daily; reservations aren't taken and there's always a line outside.

The same owners run the *Pinnacle Peak Steakhouse* (☎ 520-296-0911), 6541E Tanque Verde Rd, where the atmosphere is Wild Western and fun, if slightly touristy. Wooden sidewalks pass dance halls and saloons as you swagger into the dining room. The sign outside warns 'Stop! No Ties Allowed'; if you've got one on, you can donate it to the rafter decorations. The food is inexpensive and good. Hours are 5 to 10 pm daily.

The *Hidden Valley Inn* (☎ 520-299-4941), 4825 N Sabino Canyon Rd, has that Old Wild West look to bring in the crowds as well as reasonably priced steaks. It's a great family place with hundreds of animated models of the Old West around the walls – kids can wander around and look at them while waiting for a meal. Hours are 11 am to 3 pm and 4:30 to 10 pm daily.

The most upscale steak house is the *Ranchers Club* (☎ 520-321-7621), in the Sheraton Hotel at 5150 E Grant Rd. No, it doesn't feel like a hotel restaurant. You can pay well over $30 for a steak grilled to perfection, weighing a pound and a half and feeding two. Hours are 11:30 am to 2 pm and 5 to 10 pm, Monday to Friday, and 5 to 10 pm on Saturday.

ARIZONA

Brewpubs

Not quite restaurants and not quite bars, brewpubs have surged in popularity in Tucson recently. The classic student hangout is *Gentle Ben's Brewing Company* (☎ 520-624-4177), 865 E University Blvd, which serves many classes of students with decent pub grub from 11 am to 10 pm, Monday to Saturday, and noon to 9 pm on Sunday, washed down with a choice of half a dozen excellent brews. Opposite, the newer *Frog & Firkin* (☎ 520-623-7507), 874 E University Blvd, styles itself after a British pub, though the pub fare tends towards Italian – both beer and food are good. It opens at 11 am and closes at 1 am. Both places have live music some nights – Frog & Firkin is famous for its Wednesday Sinatra nights, when pasta is served and the band plays Sinatra's hits.

Breckenridge Brewery & Pub (☎ 520-577-0800), 1980 E River Rd, is a stylish place with decent brews (see the vats up on the second level) and good food at reasonable prices. It's in the posh St Philips Plaza, which gives you an idea of what to expect. Foothills Mall, 7401 N La Cholla Blvd, also has a good place to unwind after some hard shopping (or just relax while someone else does the shopping): the *Thunder Canyon Brewery* (☎ 520-797-2652) with lots of different beers to choose from between 11 am and midnight, and standard American pub food (plus fish 'n chips, mate).

The *Pusch Ridge Brewery & Restaurant* (☎ 520-888-7547), 5861 N Oracle Rd, makes an attempt to elevate the menu beyond ordinary pub grub – it's reasonably successful and the beer selection should please everyone.

ENTERTAINMENT

Read the free alternative *Tucson Weekly*, which is published every Thursday and available in red boxes throughout the city, for updates on local happenings. The daily papers also have entertainment information every day, especially in the Friday 'Starlight' section of the *Arizona Daily Star* and the Thursday 'Calendar' section of the *Tucson Citizen*.

Cinema

There are a dozen or more cinema multiplexes showing the year's best and worst movies. A few of them have decent movies screening every day for as low as $1.50. Check the dailies for details. Some theaters frequently screening more artistic, alternative and foreign movies include *The Loft* (☎ 520-795-7777), 3233 E Speedway Blvd; *The Screening Room* (☎ 520-622-2262), 127 E Congress; and *The Gallagher* (☎ 520-621-3102), at the student union on the U of A campus.

Nightlife

Tucson's Hispanic and Western heritages and the U of A have all influenced the city's nightlife. Every week you can get a good variety of mariachi, tejano, country & western, cowboy, blues, rock, jazz and alternative music. In addition, the local Indian tribes occasionally provide days or evenings of dancing and music. Be prepared to pay a cover (usually $2 to $6) at most of these places.

For mariachi and other Mexican music, restaurants like *La Fuente* (☎ 520-623-8659), 1749 N Oracle Rd, or *Gran Guadalajara* (☎ 520-620-1321), 2527 S 4th Ave, are good places to start. This is dinner music, admittedly, but if you like what you hear, your server or the locals can direct you to lesser-known places.

There are several fun boot-scooting country & western bars. *The Maverick, King of Clubs* (☎ 520-748-0456), 4702 E 22nd, is a friendly place with live country music most nights. The *Cactus Moon* (☎ 520-748-0049), 5470 E Broadway Blvd, is loud, brash and the place to see and be seen if you're into two-stepping to recorded music. Come dressed in the latest Western wear. *Bushwacker Lounge* (☎ 520-887-9027), 4635 N Flowing Wells Rd, is a bit lower key and has live bands on weekends. Call these places if you are interested in dance lessons.

Club Congress (☎ 520-622-8848), 311 E Congress, stands out as the best alternative music place, with plenty of dancing room, though a few live acts are more of the listening variety. DJs take over early in the week. Check out the listings in the *Tucson Weekly* to find out what's going on from Thursday to Sunday.

There are several other places to bar-hop downtown, such as *Cushing St Bar & Grill* (☎ 520-622-7984), 343 S Meyer Ave (on the corner of Cushing), with mainly jazz and blues attracting college students. A whole bunch of places along 4th Ave include *The Blue Room* (☎ 520-770-1377), 536 N 4th Ave, with mainly blues; *Third Stone Bar & Grill* (☎ 520-628-8844), 500 N 4th Ave, with both rock and alternative bands; *Mutt's* (☎ 520-628-8664), 424 N 4th Ave, with a hard-drinking crowd; and *O'Malley's* (☎ 520-623-8600), 247 N 4th Ave, with rock bands on weekends and pool during the week. *Café Sweetwater* (☎ 520-622-6464), 340 E 6th St, has a small but lively bar attached to its restaurant and features modern and Latin jazz, with occasional blues bands. *Cottonwood Club* (☎ 520-326-6000), 60 N Alvernon Way, is another jazz club.

The *Chicago Bar* (☎ 520-748-8169), 5954 E Speedway Blvd, presents blues, rock and reggae bands and is popular with students. *Berky's Bar* (☎ 520-296-1981), 5769 E Speedway Blvd, attracts an older crowd and often has decent live bands (mainly blues) and dancing, sometimes with no cover charge. *Boondocks Lounge* (☎ 520-690-0991), 3360 N 1st Ave, is a pretty good blues venue.

Catch bluesman Sam Taylor for a taste of Tucson's local talent. Taylor also hosts a blues and R&B hour at 5 pm on Saturdays on KXCI, 91.3 FM, Tucson's community radio station. The Tucson Blues Society hotline (☎ 520-617-4617) has information about events, and the Tucson Jazz Society operates a jazz events hotline (☎ 520-743-3399).

There are many dance clubs, some of which are favored by the gay and lesbian community. Women like *Ain't Nobody's Biz-ness* (☎ 520-318-4838), 2900 E Broadway Blvd, while gay men hang out at *IBT's* (☎ 520-882-3053), 616 N 4th Ave, and both lesbians and gay men dance up a storm at

Hours (☎ 520-327-3390), 3455 E Grant Rd. Dance clubs with a straight though alternative clientele include *The Cage* (☎ 520-885-3030), 5851 E Speedway Blvd, where drinks are cheap and the crowd is young.

Some older theaters now function as performance venues for musicians playing anything from a cappella through punk to zydeco, and where dancing is sometimes allowed. These include the *Rialto Theater* (☎ 520-740-0126), 318 E Congress, and the *Santa Rita Ballroom* at 6th Ave and Broadway Blvd.

Performing Arts

There are several places to hear and see performing arts. The following are the most highly acclaimed. During the summer, not much happens at these places.

The renovated 1920s *Temple of Music & Art* (☎ 520-884-4875), 330 S Scott Ave, is the home of the Arizona Theater Company (☎ 520-884-8210, or 520-622-2823 for the box office), which produces shows from October to May. The *Tucson Convention Center* (☎ 520-791-4101, or 520-791-4266 for the box office), 260 S Church, has a Music Hall, the Leo Rich Theater and a huge convention area that plays host to many events, including performances by the Arizona Opera Company (☎ 520-293-4336), from October to March; the Tucson Symphony Orchestra (☎ 520-882-8585), November to March; and sporting and theatrical events. The U of A *Centennial Hall* (☎ 520-621-3364, or 520-621-3341 for the box office), 1020 E University Blvd, hosts a variety of excellent international acts throughout the academic year and presents Ballet Arizona (☎ 602-381-1096, 888-322-5538) from December to May.

Tucson has a lively theater scene, with several local companies, some offering year-round performances of alternative and avant-garde productions. One of the best is the *Damesrocket Theater* (☎ 520-623-7852), 125 E Congress. See the newspapers listed under Entertainment, above, for other current offerings.

Although cultural performances dwindle in summer, you can catch plenty of fun and

ARIZONA

free events at *Downtown Saturday Night*, held along Congress and Broadway Blvd between Stone and 4th Aves the first and third Saturday of every month from about 7 am to 10 pm. Galleries stay open late and there are plenty of free street performances. Downtown Saturday Night is sponsored by the Tucson Arts District (☎ 520-624-9977). A variety of free music performances take place in the spring and the summer in some of the city parks. Call the city parks' outdoor entertainment department (☎ 520-791-4079) for details.

SPECTATOR SPORTS

Phoenix has most of the top professional sports teams in Arizona, although the minor league Tucson Sidewinders (☎ 520-325-2621) play baseball at Tucson Electric Park (☎ 520-740-2680), 2500 E Ajo Way, from April to September. Every March, major league teams have their spring training here or at Hi Corbett Field (☎ 520-791-4873) in Reid Park at E 22nd and Randolph Way. The Gila Monsters (☎ 520-903-9000) play professional ice hockey at the TCC (☎ 520-791-4266) from October through March. Inexpensive tickets for these sports are easy enough to obtain.

It's exactly the opposite for some college sports – the U of A Wildcats have top-ranked teams. Tickets for the U of A men's basketball team (winners of the 1997 NCAA championship) are in great demand when the November to February season gets underway. Most games are sold out. Football tickets are also in demand, depending on who is playing. The women's softball team has won the Women's College World Series championships most years of the 1990s, though seats to see them play from February to May are usually available. Tickets for other college sporting events are easy to get and very inexpensive from the campus box office (☎ 520-621-2287).

The Tucson Chrysler PGA Golf Tournament (☎ 520-571-0400) is held at the Tucson Omni National Golf Course in mid-February. In March the Welch's/Circle K LPGA Golf Tournament is held at the Randolph municipal golf course. Both attract top pro golfers.

Greyhounds race year-round at Tucson Greyhound Park (☎ 520-884-7576), 2601 S 3rd Ave. Stock-car races take place at Tucson Raceway (☎ 520-762-9200), 12500 S Houghton Rd (go southwest of town on I-10 to the Houghton Rd exit) on Saturday evenings from spring to fall. Horse racing happens at Rillito Downs (☎ 520-293-5011), 4502 N 1st Ave, during winter Saturday afternoons.

SHOPPING

Southwestern arts and crafts are of the most interest to travelers. Small but exquisite pieces of jewelry can easily be carried and bulky items can be shipped.

Some of the best arts and crafts stores are in the Presidio Historic District (see Downtown Tucson, earlier in this chapter). Another good place for quality arts and crafts is St Philips Plaza at the southeast corner of River Rd and Campbell Ave. Prices are high, but so is the quality. Particularly good stores here are the Obsidian Gallery (☎ 520-577-3598) for art and jewelry, Bahti Indian Arts (☎ 520-577-0290) for varied Native Americana and the Turquoise Door (☎ 520-299-7787) for stunning jewelry.

Farther north is De Grazia's Gallery in the Sun (☎ 520-299-9191), 6300 N Swan Rd, which is the former home, present resting place and gallery of famous local artist Ted De Grazia, whose simple depictions of Southwestern people and life can be found on calendars, postcards and prints. You can view some of his originals in the adjoining museum (admission is free) and purchase reproductions. Morning Star Traders (☎ 520-881-2112), 2002 E Speedway Blvd, specializes in high-quality and antique Southwestern Indian crafts.

For fun shopping and browsing, you can't beat 4th Ave between University Blvd and Congress. Here you'll find books and beads, antiques and African art, jewelry and junk, clothes and collectibles, and all sorts of treasures. Then head west along Congress for the Arts District.

Several large, enclosed shopping malls are in Tucson. Four of the most noteworthy are Tucson's oldest major mall, El Con Mall (☎ 520-795-9958), 3601 E Broadway Blvd; the Tucson Mall (☎ 520-293-7330), 4500 N Oracle, which is the city's largest; the renascent Foothills Mall (☎ 520-742-7191), at Ina Rd and La Cholla Blvd; and Park Mall (☎ 520-748-1222), 5870 E Broadway Blvd. Call the malls for information about their free shuttle services to and from the major hotels and resorts.

For bookstores, the following stand out. The Book Mark (☎ 520-881-6350), 5001 E Speedway Blvd, has the biggest selection of new books in town while the two Bookman's at 1930 E Grant Rd (☎ 520-325-5767) and 3733 W Ina Rd (☎ 520-579-0303) have the largest selection of used books, tapes and CDs in Arizona. Tucson Maps and Flags (☎ 520-887-4234), 3239 N 1st Ave, has travel titles and maps. Antigone Books (☎ 520-792-3715), 600 N 4th Ave, has books by and about women and nonsexist books for kids. There are also several of the new, large chain bookstores around town.

GETTING THERE & AWAY
Air
Tucson International Airport (☎ 520-573-8000) is approximately 9 miles south of downtown. It has a few direct flights into a limited number of cities in Mexico. Flights to other countries involve connections at larger airports. Therefore, international airport facilities in Tucson are a bit limited; there are immigration and customs facilities but no international currency desks. Many of the major carriers have direct flights to and from Tucson and many large US cities.

The terminal has a pricey parking lot, or you can try the Park 'n Save lot at Tucson Blvd and Corona, near the main entrance. A frequent, free shuttle connects Park 'n Save with the terminal.

Sun Tran (☎ 520-792-9222) has buses during the day to the Laos Transit Center at Irvington and Liberty Ave, about halfway between the airport and downtown. This is bus No 25. From here you have to connect to another bus. The fare is 85¢ and a transfer is free. Bus No 11 leaves from the airport and goes north through town along Alvernon Way. You can connect with many east-west routes from this line. Timetables and bus maps are available at the airport.

A more convenient option is using Arizona Stagecoach (☎ 520-889-1000, 520-881-4111), which has door-to-door, 24-hour van service to anywhere in the metropolitan Tucson area. The fare varies from $9 to more than $20, depending on the location. The fare usually works out to be roughly half of what a taxi would cost.

Bus
The Greyhound terminal (☎ 520-792-3475) is at 2 S 4th Ave. Several buses a day run east along I-10 to New Mexico, and northwest along I-10 to Phoenix, connecting to the rest of Arizona and California. Greyhound also connects with (and sells tickets for) Citizen Auto Stage vans to Nogales every hour from 7 am to 7 pm for $6.50, with stops at towns along I-19. Greyhound also connects with Los Rapidos buses for Douglas ($20), via Sierra Vista and Bisbee, leaving five times a day.

Arizona Shuttle Service (☎ 520-795-6771), 5350 E Speedway Blvd, has hourly vans to Phoenix Airport from 4 am to 11 pm. The fare is $22 with discounts for roundtrips, children and groups.

Train
Amtrak's Tucson Station (☎ 520-623-4442), 400 E Toole Ave, near downtown, has three night trains each week to Phoenix, Yuma and Los Angeles, and three morning trains east through New Mexico and on to Florida.

GETTING AROUND
Bus
Sun Tran (☎ 520-792-9222 from 6 am to 7 pm on weekdays and 8 am to 5 pm on weekends and holidays) has buses all over the metro Tucson area from early morning into the evening every day, but there are no night buses. Fares are 85¢ with a free transfer. There are discounts for monthly passes and also for students, seniors and

disabled people. Passes and timetables are available at dozens of outlets around town; call Sun Tran for the nearest one. There are many park-and-ride lots around town and some buses have bike racks. Major transit centers are the Laos Transit Center near Irvington and Liberty Ave to the south; the Ronstadt-Downtown Center at Congress and 6th Ave; and the Tohono Tadai Center at Stone Ave and Wetmore Rd to the north.

Sun Tran Trolley is an old-fashioned-looking trolley (fit with air conditioning) linking U of A (it leaves from Old Main) with the 4th Ave shopping area, Congress and the Arts District, historical downtown, and the Ronstadt-Downtown Center. Trolleys run two or three times an hour from about 10 am to 6:30 pm, Monday to Friday, and less frequently on Saturday (no Sunday service). Trolleys run until 11 pm on the nights of Downtown Saturday Night and when the U of A has a home game. Trolley fare is 25¢.

Car
All the main companies have offices in the airport and many have offices in other parts of the valley or will deliver your car.

Taxi
You'll find a plethora of cabs operating 24 hours. A fare from the airport to downtown is around $15. Cab rates can vary somewhat, so call several companies to ask for the best deal. Companies include Yellow Cab (☎ 520-624-6611), Allstate Cab (☎ 520-798-1111) and Checker Cab (☎ 520-623-1133). Apart from the cab rank at the airport, you need to phone to get a cab – they don't cruise the streets.

Bicycle
Tucson takes pride in being bike-friendly, with bike lanes on many major roads. Public libraries have free maps of the bike-lane system. Tucson's bike shops can provide you with information, rentals (about $20 a day) and details of mountain biking off the main roads. Check out Bargain Basement Bikes (☎ 520-624-9673), 428 N Fremont Ave; the Bike Shack

(☎ 520-624-3663), 940 E University Blvd; or Full Cycle (☎ 520-327-3232), at 3232 E Speedway Blvd. Helmets are required for cyclists under 18.

AROUND TUCSON
Mission San Xavier del Bac
Founded by the Jesuit Padre Kino in 1700, this is Arizona's oldest European building still in use. Most of the mission was destroyed in the Pima Indian uprising of 1751, but it was rebuilt by Franciscans in the late 1700s and today looks very much like it did 200 years ago. Much of the building has been restored, and work continues on the frescoes inside. A visit to San Xavier is a highlight of many people's trip to Tucson.

Catholic masses are held daily. The church itself (☎ 520-294-2624) is open daily from 8 am to 6 pm, and the church museum and gift shop is open from 9 am to 5 pm. Admission is free and donations are accepted. Photography is permitted when religious ceremonies are not taking place.

Nicknamed 'the white dove of the desert,' its dazzling white walls are a splendid site as you drive south on I-19 (take exit 92 to get there). The mission is on the San Xavier Indian Reservation (part of the Tohono O'odham tribe), and the plaza on the south side of the mission parking lot has several stores selling Indian jewelry, arts and crafts, and snacks.

Especially colorful religious ceremonies are held on the Friday after Easter, the Fiesta of San Xavier in early December, and Christmas. Call the mission for details.

Arizona-Sonora Desert Museum
The ASDM is a living museum representing the flora and fauna of the Arizona-Sonora Desert and, as such, is more like a zoo than a museum. It is one of the best of its kind in the country. Just about any local desert animal you could think of is displayed, often in quite natural-looking settings. The grounds are thick with desert plants too, many of which are labeled. You'll see scorpions and saguaros, coatis and coyotes, bighorn sheep and rattlesnakes, golden

Golden eagle

eagles and tiny hummingbirds, javelinas and agaves. It's all here.

Docents are on hand to answer questions about the live animals and to show other exhibits throughout the day – you might get a chance to pet a snake! There are two walk-through aviaries, one dedicated solely to hummingbirds; a geological exhibit featuring an underground cave (kids love that one); an underground exhibit with windows into ponds containing beavers, otters and ducks (indeed, these are found along the riparian corridors of the desert); and much more. It's one of the best things to see in the Tucson area and a great way to learn about the natural history of the desert.

Allow a minimum of two hours (a half day is better) and come prepared for outdoor walking. Strollers and wheelchairs are available. There is a gift shop, art gallery, restaurant and café.

The drive out to the ASDM, 2021 N Kinney Rd, is about 14 miles west along Speedway Blvd, which crosses over the very scenic Gates Pass. The narrow and winding Gates Pass Rd is impassable for trailers and RVs, which must take the longer route west along Ajo Way – follow the signs. A visit to the ASDM can be combined with a visit to the Old Tucson Studios, the International Wildlife Museum or Saguaro National Park (West) to make a full-day outing.

The ASDM (☎ 520-883-2702) is open 8:30 am to 5 pm daily, and from 7:30 am to 6 pm in summer. (On summer Saturdays, it's open until 10 pm.) Admission is $8.95 for those over 12, and $1.75 for six- to 12-year-olds.

Old Tucson Studios

This film set was used in hundreds of Western movie productions from 1939 onward. Unfortunately, 65% of it burned down one night in 1995 (no one was hurt), but it has now been rebuilt, expanded and reopened as a Western theme park, though movies can still be shot here. Visitors are treated to shootouts, stagecoach rides, saloons, sheriffs and Wild West events galore; it is fast regaining its status as Tucson's most popular tourist spot. Old Tucson (☎ 520-883-0100) is on Kinney Rd a few miles southeast of the ADSM (see Arizona-Sonora Desert Museum, above, for directions). Hours are 10 am to 6 pm daily, and admission is $14.95 ($9.95 for four- to 11-year-olds) plus tax. All Pima County Residents, AAA and AARO members get discounts.

International Wildlife Museum

Housed in an odd castle-like building at 4800 W Gates Pass Rd (between Speedway Blvd and Gates Pass), this museum (☎ 520-617-1439) is a taxidermist's delight. Hundreds of animals from all over the world have been killed and expertly mounted. There are various hands-on exhibits and hourly movies about wildlife but no live animals. Hours are 9 am to 5 pm daily; admission is $6 for adults, $4.75 for students and those over 62 and $2 for six- to 12-year-olds.

Biosphere 2

This place is unique. It is a 3-acre glassed dome built to be completely sealed off from Biosphere 1, that is, the biosphere on which you are living. Inside the dome are seven different micro-habitats, ranging from tropical forest to ocean environment, designed to be completely self-sustaining. In 1991, eight bionauts entered Biosphere 2 for a two-year tour of duty during which they would be physically cut off from the outside world. Although this experiment could be used as a prototype for future space stations, it was a privately funded endeavor.

The bionauts emerged two years later, all thinner but otherwise in pretty fair shape. The experiment was much criticized, however, because the dome leaked gases and it was opened a few times to allow a bionaut to emerge for medical treatment and to bring in supplies. Carbon dioxide rose to unhealthy levels inside. There were also the accompanying petty wranglings that happen when entrepreneurs, scientists, businesspeople and glory-seekers come together.

Since then, bionauts have entered on shorter missions, but there are none planned at this time. The facility is now operated by Columbia University and the public can tour the site and enter parts of the biosphere. There is a restaurant, gift shop and the *Biosphere 2 Hotel* (☎ 520-896-6222, fax 520-896-6471) with 27 rooms, all with coffeemakers, mini-fridge bars and balconies, for $80 ($50 in summer). It has a pool, tennis courts and an exercise room.

Biosphere 2 (☎ 520-896-6200) is 5 miles northeast of the junction of Hwy 77 and Hwy 79, about 30 miles north of Tucson. It is open daily from 8:30 am to 5 pm and guided tours are offered all day. Admission is $12.95 for adults, $10.95 for those over 62 and $6 for 12- to 17-year-olds. If you are staying at the hotel, tickets are $10. Other discounts are often given – ask about discount coupons at the Convention and Visitors Bureau.

Colossal Cave

This dry limestone cave is six stories under the ground and was a legendary outlaw hideout. It's a 'dry' cave because there is no dripping water and geological formations are no longer growing. A half-mile trail takes you through several different chambers with many geological formations. Parts of the cave are still unexplored. Entrance includes a guided tour that lasts about 45 minutes. The temperature inside is a pleasant 72°F year-round.

Colossal Cave (☎ 520-647-7275) is open every day for tours from 9 am to 5 pm from mid-September to mid-March and from 8 am to 6 pm the rest of the year. It stays open one hour later on Sundays and holidays. Tours last about 50 minutes and leave at least every half hour (every 10 minutes when it's busy). Admission is $7.50; $4 for six- to 12-year-olds. The cave is 8 miles north of I-10 exit 279, about 25 miles southeast of Tucson. Alternatively, head southeast on Old Spanish Trail and follow the signs.

RW Webb Winery & Microbrewery

Enjoy a local wine-tasting or sample the microbrews, then pick up a bottle of whatever tickles your tastebuds. Hours are 10 am to 5 pm, Monday to Saturday, and noon to 5 pm on Sunday. The winery (☎ 520-762-5777) is near I-10 exit 279 (about 20 miles southeast of downtown).

Gambling

The Casino of the Sun (☎ 520-883-1700, 800-344-9435) is inside the Pascua Yaqui Indian Reservation at 7406 S Camino de Oeste. Take I-19 exit 95 and go west on Valencia Rd for almost 5 miles and then south on S Camino de Oeste, following the signs. The Desert Diamond Casino (☎ 520-294-7777, 520-889-7354) is inside the San Xavier Indian Reservation at 7350 S Nogales Hwy. From I-19 exit 95, go east on Valencia Rd for 1½ miles, then south on Nogales Hwy for 1½ miles. The casinos are open 24 hours a day and offer slots, keno, bingo and poker games. They have cheap food buffets, but no alcohol is served.

SAGUARO NATIONAL PARK

The park has two sections, Saguaro East and Saguaro West, which are about 30 miles apart and separated by Tucson. Not too many cities in the USA can claim they have a national park on their doorstep!

Neither section has any drive-in campgrounds or lodges and only Saguaro East allows overnight backpacking, so for the most part Saguaro National Park is explored as a day trip from Tucson. As the park's name implies, its main purpose is to preserve large stands of the giant saguaro cactus and associated habitat.

Flora & Fauna

Young saguaro seedlings are vulnerable to intense sun and frost, so they often grow in the shade of palo verde or mesquite trees, which act as 'nurse trees.' Saguaros begin growing slowly, taking about 15 years to grow to a foot in height and about 50 years to reach 7 feet. They are almost a hundred years old before they begin to take on their typical many-armed appearance.

Most of the saguaros in the park are old ones. This is because the area is the north-eastern corner of the saguaros' range and more prone to killer frosts. In addition, ranching was allowed in some parts of the park as late as 1979 and the cattle trampled the saguaro seedlings and compacted the ground, causing the nurse trees to die. Now ranching has stopped, but occasional frosts and even vandalism and theft continue to be problems for the young plants. Nevertheless, there are some signs of recovery and stands of young saguaro are being monitored by park authorities.

Saguaros are only part of the landscape. Various birds make nests in holes in these giant cacti. Gila woodpeckers and flickers (a kind of woodpecker) excavate holes in the plants. The holes form hard scar tissue on the inside of the plant, which protects the nest and the cactus. In subsequent years, owls, cactus wrens, kestrels and other birds may use these nests, which are often 20°F cooler than the outside. On the ground are many other kinds of cacti and a variety of vegetation that is home to javelinas, desert tortoises, gila monsters, jackrabbits, coyotes, kangaroo rats, rattlesnakes, roadrunners, tarantulas and many other animals.

Late April is a good time to visit the park, when the saguaros begin blossoming with lovely white flowers – Arizona's state flower. By June and July, the flowers give way to ripe red fruit that has been traditionally picked by desert Indians; they use them both for food (as fruit and jam) and to make saguaro wine.

Saguaro East

Also called the Rincon Mountain District, this is the larger and older section of the park and encompasses both the desert and mountain country of the Rincon Mountains and their western slopes. The saguaro grows only up to about 4000 feet and then the scenery gives way first to oak woodland, then pine and finally, at elevations of more than 7000 feet, to mixed conifer forest.

Information The park is open daily from sunrise to sunset. The visitor center (☎ 520-733-5153) at the park entrance is open from 8:30 am to 5 pm daily except Christmas and is the only place with drinking water. It has a bookstore, information, an audio-visual display and exhibits. Ranger-led programs are offered, especially in the cooler months. The park is 15 miles east of downtown along Old Spanish Trail. Admission is $4 per private vehicle or $2 for walkers, cyclists or bus passengers. All Golden Age, Access and Eagle Passes are honored. Further information is available from the Superintendent, Saguaro National Park, 3693 S Old Spanish Trail, AZ 85730-5601.

Cactus Forest Drive This paved, one-way, 8-mile loop road gives access to a couple of picnic areas (no water), some nature trails of varying lengths and views of the saguaro forest. The road is accessible to all vehicles, including bicycles. In addition, a 2½-mile trail off the drive is suitable for mountain bikes only.

Hiking & Backpacking There are almost 130 miles of trails in Saguaro East. The easiest is the quarter-mile, wheelchair-accessible Desert Ecology Nature Trail, which leaves from the north end of Cactus Forest Drive. Progressively longer trails strike off into the park, including the Tanque Verde Ridge Trail, which climbs fairly steeply from the south end of Cactus Forest Drive up into the Rincon Mountains, where the highest elevation is Mica Mountain at 8666 feet. There are six designated backcountry camping areas, most

ARIZONA

of which lack water. Campers must have permits, which are available at the visitor center at no charge up to two months ahead of your chosen date. Permits must be picked up by noon on the day you start your hike to allow enough time to reach the first camping area. Horses are also permitted on trails.

Saguaro West

Also called the Tucson Mountain District, this is just north of the Arizona-Sonora Desert Museum, and a drive through the area can be combined with a visit to the ASDM. Saguaro West is much lower than Saguaro East, with the highest point being 4687-foot Wasson Peak.

Information The visitor center (☎ 520-733-5158) on Kinney Rd, 2 miles northwest of the ASDM, is open from 8:30 am to 5 pm daily except Christmas, with similar facilities to Saguaro East. The two paved roads through the park (Kinney Rd and Picture Rocks Rd) are open 24 hours a day. Unpaved loop roads and hiking trailheads close at sunset, however. Admission to this part of the park is free. The visitor center has a free map of the park.

Bajada Loop Drive The unpaved, 6-mile Bajada Loop Drive begins 1½ miles west of the visitor center and can normally be negotiated by ordinary vehicles. Apart from the fine views of cactus forests, there are several picnic areas as well as trailheads.

Hiking Short, paved nature trails are found near the visitor center. Longer trails climb several miles into the Tucson Mountains and give access to Indian petroglyphs as well as fine views. The King Canyon trailhead is just outside the park boundary almost opposite the ASDM. This trailhead is open until 10 pm. Although night hiking is permitted, camping is not. The nearest campground is the Gilbert Ray Campground about 4 miles southeast of the park (see Places to Stay – Camping, earlier in the chapter).

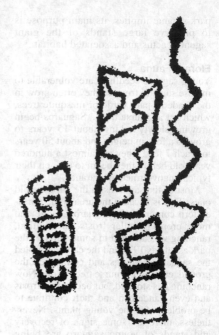

Between Tucson & Phoenix

Most people barrel through from city to city along I-10 in a couple of hours. It is not a particularly attractive ride except for the view of Picacho Peak at almost the halfway point. There are several worthwhile side trips, however, for travelers with a little time.

PICACHO PEAK STATE PARK

Picacho Peak (3374 feet) is an obvious landmark on the west side of I-10 exit 219, 40 miles north of Tucson. The westernmost 'battle' of the American Civil War was fought here, with the Confederate forces killing two or three Union soldiers. The Confederates then retreated to Tucson and dispersed, knowing their forces would soon be greatly outnumbered.

The state park (☎ 520-466-3183) provides camping, picnicking and two steep hiking trails to the summit of the peak. Fixed ropes and ladders are used to aid hikers, but no technical climbing is involved. It's about 2 miles and 1500 feet up to the top. Day use is $4 per vehicle (up to four passengers).

The *campground* has about 100 sites open year-round. Rates are $10 for tents, $15 for hookups. There is drinking water and showers. Sites are available on a first-come, first-served basis. The 1800-foot elevation makes this a hot stop in summer.

A short way outside the state park, in the community of Picacho, is the *Picacho Peak KOA* (☎ 520-466-7401). It offers a pool, recreation area and about 100 sites, most with full hookups ($21). There are a few tent sites.

CASA GRANDE AREA
Casa Grande
The small town of Casa Grande is a few miles northwest of the I-10 interchange with I-8, on Hwy 238. Though it was founded in 1878, little remains of that era and it is essentially a modern town. The ruins of Casa Grande (described below) are about 30 miles away and have nothing to do with the town apart from the name.

From I-10 exit 194, Florence Blvd goes west into Casa Grande, passing a visitor center on the left and reaching the small **Heritage Hall Historical Museum** (☎ 520-836-2223), at 110 W Florence Blvd, 4 miles west of the freeway. The museum is open from 1 to 5 pm daily, except Mondays and holidays, from September 15 to June 1 (closed in summer).

Today, Casa Grande is known for its two huge factory outlet shopping malls that sell brand-name products at discounted prices. At I-10 exit 194 is the Casa Grande Mercado & Factory Stores and at exit 198 is the Tanger Outlet Center.

There are annual Indian dances and a powwow during **O'odham Tash**, held in mid-February. Get information from the O'odham Tash office (☎ 520-836-4723, fax 520-426-1731).

Places to Stay & Eat The *Sunland Motel* (☎ 520-836-5000) near exit 198 has basic rooms in the $20s and low $30s. There are a couple of other cheap places on Florence Blvd west of the museum. The *Motel 6* (☎ 520-836-3323, fax 520-421-3094) is at exit 200 and charges $39/45 for singles/doubles in winter, $10 less in summer. The *Best Western Casa Grande Suites* (☎ 520-836-1600, fax 520-836-7242) is just over a mile west of exit 194 along Florence Blvd. Rooms are roughly in the $90s in winter, in the $60s in summer, and there is a pool. The *Holiday Inn* (☎ 520-426-3500, fax 520-836-4728), 777 N Pinal Ave, charges about the same, has a pool, and has a restaurant open from 6 am to 10 pm. There are plenty of chain restaurants along Florence Blvd and at the interstate exits.

Casa Grande Ruins National Monument
Once a major Hohokam Indian village covering about 1 sq mile, this site was abandoned around 1350 AD and little remains today except for one building, the Casa Grande (big house).

The Casa Grande is quite imposing. About 30 or 40 feet high, it is built of mud walls several feet thick. The mud was made from caliche, the rock-hard soil of the area that is the bane of the modern gardener. A huge amount of work went into constructing the building, which is the most unusual Hohokam structure standing today. Rain and human intrusion have caused some damage, but the general structure of the building remains clear. To prevent further erosion, Casa Grande has been capped by a large metal awning built in the 1930s, an effective, if incongruous, preservation tool. You cannot enter the building itself. From the outside it is still impressive though, and you should also check the girders of the modern roof protecting the ruin. I found a pair of owls nesting there.

The site, about 20 miles north of I-10 exit 212 or 14 miles east of I-10 exit 185, has a visitor center (☎ 520-723-3172) with a good small museum explaining the general history of the Hohokam and this ruin

ARIZONA

in particular. There are picnic tables, drinking water and a bookstore, but no overnight facilities. The monument is open daily except Christmas, from 8 am to 5 pm. Admission is $4 per vehicle, or $2 per bike or bus passenger. Golden Age, Access and Eagle Passes are honored.

Florence

Founded in 1866, this is one of Arizona's earliest Anglo towns. Arizona's second governor, Richard C McCormick, named it after his sister. Today, this small town is the Pinal County seat and the home of the Arizona State Prison, which replaced Yuma's notorious prison in 1909. Now about 8000 people live here (including the prisoners) and the elevation is a toasty 1493 feet.

Few travelers stay overnight because of the proximity to Phoenix, but there is a motel and Florence makes a good base for seeing Casa Grande, just 10 miles west. There are several historic buildings; the most interesting is the 1878 adobe brick courthouse (with assorted later additions) in **McFarland Historical State Park** (☎ 520-868-5216), Main at Ruggles Ave, which offers various exhibits about Florence's past. This is open from 8 am to 5 pm, Thursday to Monday; admission is $2; $1 for teenagers and younger folk. Also visit the **Pinal County Historical Museum** (☎ 520-868-4382), 715 S Main, which has a surprisingly varied collection of a little bit of everything to do with the area. The museum is open noon till 4 pm from Wednesday to Sunday; admission is $1 for adults.

The visitor center (☎ 520-868-4331), 912 N Pinal, Florence, AZ 85232, is open from 9 am to noon and from 1 to 4 pm, Monday to Friday, with shorter hours in summer. It has a brochure describing some of the historic buildings.

The *Blue Mist Motel* (☎ 520-868-5875, fax 520-868-0660), at the junction of Hwys 287 and 79, has about 20 simple rooms in the $30s and $40s. Some rooms have kitchenettes for a few dollars more, and there is a pool. There are several little restaurants along Hwy 287 as you head west toward the Casa Grande Ruins.

Gila River Arts & Crafts Center

The name doesn't sound particularly interesting, but this is an above-average stop on the freeway. The name comes not from the river, but from the Gila River Indian Reservation, Arizona's earliest reservation, established in 1859 for the Pima and Maricopa Indian tribes. It was relatively good acreage until the early 20th century, when dams caused the river to run almost dry, ruining the Indians' agricultural livelihood.

After years of poverty and government neglect, the Indians have finally begun to benefit from Phoenix's growth by building this center. Although only a half mile from I-10 exit 175, it's different from the average freeway stop. The center has a museum (☎ 520-315-3411) about the Pima and Maricopa tribes and a gift shop selling arts and crafts from most Southwestern tribes. Part of the museum is outside, with a park containing a variety of Southwest Indian dwellings. A restaurant serves up mainly American food along with a few Indian items. There is a grocery store and a basic RV park next door, which has showers and charges $13 for hookups, less without. The tribal office (☎ 520-562-3311) is in Sacaton several miles to the east, but the museum can provide information.

West of Tucson

Hwy 86 heads west of Tucson toward some of the driest parts of the Sonora Desert. Much of the land is part of the Tohono O'odham Indian Reservation, the second largest in the country, but there is little here for the curious traveler. Highlights of a trip out west are the Kitt Peak Observatory and the Organ Pipe Cactus National Monument.

Much of the area is particularly well described in Bowden's *Blue Desert*.

BUENOS AIRES NATIONAL WILDLIFE REFUGE LOOP

From Robles Junction, on Hwy 86 about 20 miles west of Tucson, Hwy 286 goes south to the 175-sq-mile Buenos Aires National

Wildlife Refuge. This was formerly ranchland and became a refuge operated by the US Fish & Wildlife Service in 1985. There are about 200 miles of dirt roads in the area, a good one for grassland birding. There is an ongoing project to reintroduce the masked bobwhite, a small, quail-like bird that became extinct in Arizona around the turn of the 19th century. The refuge is open daily during the daylight hours, and guided tours are occasionally offered. Backpacking and overnight camping are permitted at about 100 sites, none of which have facilities. Information is available from Buenos Aires NWR (☎ 520-823-4251), PO Box 109, Sasabe, AZ 85633. Their office is open from 7 am to 3:30 pm Monday to Friday.

At the south end of the NWR is the border village of **Sasabe**, with the *Rancho de la Osa Guest Ranch* (☎ 520-823-4257, 800-872-6240, fax 520-823-4238, osagal@aol .com), PO Box 1, Sasabe, AZ 85633. The ranch is in a 100-year-old Spanish hacienda, and horseback riding, bird- and wildlife-watching and walking are the main activities. Advance reservations and a two-night minimum are usually required. Rates are approximately $160 per person (more for a few suites) with excellent Southwestern meals and riding included. They have a liquor license and espresso bar. Summers are hot (elevation 3500 feet) and rates are lower then. The 17 guest rooms are rustic but comfortable and attractively decorated with Mexican antiques. Each has a private bathroom and a fireplace or wood-burning stove. There is a pool and spa. This ranch makes a nice desert getaway.

A few miles east of the refuge is the little village of **Arivaca** with several buildings dating from the 1880s. There is a café but no motel. From Arivaca, you can return to Tucson via the paved road to Arivaca Junction and then I-19, the quickest way, or take the unpaved **Ruby Road** to Nogales. This is a scenic route with plenty of border history. The road is passable to ordinary cars in dry weather but should be avoided in rain; it passes through the Coronado National Forest (see Nogales) where you can camp almost anywhere. There are some small lakes along the way that attract wildlife.

The Buenos Aires NWR and Ruby Road make an interesting trip, which few people make, so you'll get away from the crowds. Birders will want to have Davis and Russell's *Finding Birds in Southeastern Arizona* and drivers/historians will find useful information in Annerino's *Adventuring in Arizona*.

TOHONO O'ODHAM INDIAN RESERVATION

This large desert and mountain reservation of almost 4500 sq miles is home to the Tohono O'odham, who are traditionally an agricultural people. They still practice farming and, since the Spaniards introduced cattle, ranching as well. Maize, beans and cotton are important crops and naturally growing saguaro fruit is harvested for jams and a kind of wine. Mesquite beans are also an important part of the diet and various other naturally occurring plants are harvested. Small branches of the reservation are around the Mission San Xavier del Bac (see Around Tucson, earlier in this chapter) and just north of Gila Bend, but the majority of the land is in the deserts beginning about 25 miles west of Tucson.

As you drive west out of Tucson, you'll see a humpbacked mountain that stands out above all the others. This is Baboquivari Peak, at 7730 feet the highest in this area and sacred to the tribe. To the north of it is Kitt Peak (6875 feet), home of the observatory described below. The tribal capital is Sells, almost 60 miles west of Tucson on Hwy 86.

The Tohono O'odham have little interest in tourism. Their only tourist facility is the Desert Diamond Casino on the San Xavier section of the reservation (see Gambling, earlier in this chapter). The Indians are known for their fine basket work, which can be purchased from a couple of shops in Sells, the gift shop at Kitt Peak and the Gu-Achi Trading Post at Quijotoa, on Hwy 86, 23 miles west of Sells.

The main event is the annual Tohono O'odham All-Indian Tribal Fair & Rodeo, which attracts Indians from many tribes and is open to the general public. The rodeo is the main attraction, but there are also some dances and the chance to eat Indian food and buy basket work. This is usually held in February. For information, call either the Tucson Visitor Center or the Tribal Office (☎ 520-383-2221, fax 520-383-2417), Sells, AZ 85634. Other events are held at the San Xavier Mission and the O'odham Tash Indian Celebration in Casa Grande in February.

Sells has a couple of places to eat and some stores but no accommodations. Dirt roads leading off the main highway are often in poor shape and a permit may be required to travel on them. Contact the tribe for details.

KITT PEAK NATIONAL OPTICAL OBSERVATORY

Both Baboquivari and Kitt Peaks are visible from Tucson and if you look very carefully, you can just make out the white telescope domes on top of Kitt Peak, even though it is a 55-mile drive (or about 40 miles as the crow flies). This attests both to the clarity of the desert air and the size of the telescopes.

This is the largest observatory in the world and includes 22 telescopes, one of which is a solar telescope used for studying the sun via a series of mirrors. The largest telescope has a diameter of 4 meters and is housed in a 19-story-high dome.

There is a visitor center (☎ 520-318-8726, 520-318-8200) with a museum, gift shop and information, but no food, though there are picnicking areas if you bring your own. Guided tours, lasting about an hour and visiting two or three telescopes, leave daily at 10 am, 11:30 am and 1:30 pm. (You don't get to look through the telescopes.) Self-guided tours are also possible. The observatory is open from 9 am to 3:45 pm daily except New Year's Day, Thanksgiving, and Christmas Eve and Christmas Day. A $2 donation is suggested. The nearly 6900-foot elevation often means snow in winter, and the steep road up the mountain may occasionally be closed to automobiles.

A few times a year, the observatory offers a night visit with public viewing. This is very popular and should be booked well in advance. Call for details.

ORGAN PIPE CACTUS NATIONAL MONUMENT

The organ pipe is a species of giant columnar cactus. It differs from the saguaro in that it branches from its base – both species are present in the monument, so you can compare them. Organ-pipe cacti are common in Mexico, but this national monument is one of the few places in the USA where they are commonly seen. The third species of columnar cactus found here (and nowhere else in the USA) is the senita, which, like the organ pipe branches from the bottom but has fewer pleats in its branches, which are topped by the hairy white tufts that give the senita its nickname of 'old man's beard.'

This is prime and mainly undisturbed Sonoran Desert habitat. Not only do three types of large columnar cacti grow here, but an excellent variety of other desert flora and fauna also thrive. In spring, in years that have the right combination of winter rains and temperatures, the monument can be carpeted with wildflowers – mid-February to April is the best time for this. Cacti flower at different times, particularly from late April to early July, although some species can flower in March or as late as October.

There are many animals present, but the heat and aridity of the desert force them to use survival strategies that make them hard to see. The best survival strategy is to hide out in a hole or burrow during the day, which means that early morning and evening are the best times to look for wildlife. Walking around the desert by full moon or flashlight is also a good way to catch things on the prowl, but wear boots and watch where you step, because rattlesnakes will be out and about, particularly in late spring and summer.

The monument offers six hiking trails ranging from a 200-yard paved nature trail to strenuous climbs of over 4 miles. Cross-country hiking is also possible, but have a topographical map and a compass and know how to use them – a mistake out here is deadly if you get lost and run out of water. There are also two scenic loop drives of 21 and 53 miles. These start near the visitor center and are steep, winding and unpaved. They are passable to cars except after heavy rain, but motor homes and trailers are not recommended. Other roads are passable only to 4WD vehicles. Carry extra water in your car in case of a breakdown. There are several picnic sites along the way, but no water.

Information

A visitor center (☎ 520-387-6849), Route 1, Box 100, Ajo, AZ 85321, is on Hwy 85, 22 miles south of Why. It is open from 8 am to 5 pm daily and has information, drinking water, a bookstore, a small museum and a slide show. Ranger-led programs take place from about October to April. Admission to the monument is $4 per vehicle, or $2 per bike or bus passenger. Golden Eagle, Age and Access Passes are honored. There is no charge to drive through the monument on the main road, Hwy 85 from Why to Lukeville.

Winter is the most pleasant season to visit. Summer temperatures soar above 100°F most days from June to August, although nights are pleasant, with lows typically 30°F lower than daytime highs. The summer monsoons make July to September the wettest months, although the rains tend to be of the brief, torrential variety and rarely stop anyone for more than an hour or two. Winter temperatures are pleasant, with January, the coolest month, experiencing average highs of 67°F and lows of 38°F.

Places to Stay

More than 200 sites are available at the campground by the visitor center. There is drinking water but no showers or RV hookups. Sites cost $8 on a first-come, first-served basis. From mid-January through March they are often full by

noon. Free backcountry camping (no water) is only allowed with a permit; you can obtain one at the visitor center.

Lukeville (see below) has the nearest accommodations outside of the monument. There are basic RV sites at Why, 22 miles north, and a variety of accommodations at Ajo, 32 miles north (see below).

LUKEVILLE & SONOITA (SONORA)

Lukeville is a small border town that is 5 miles south of the Organ Pipe Visitor Center. You can stay at the small *Gringo Pass Motel & RV Park* (☎ 602-254-9284) with rooms from about $55 to $75, RV sites with hookups for $15 and tent sites for $11. There are showers, a pool and a recreation room. A coffee shop is nearby.

A couple of miles south, across the border in Mexico, Sonoita offers several decent restaurants, gift shops and a few motels. Another 60 miles southwest brings you to the small Mexican seaside resort of Puerto Peñasco (Rocky Point) on the Sea of Cortez, offering hotels, restaurants, swimming and scuba diving. It is a four-hour drive from Tucson and is the nearest beach to that city. (See the Crossing the Border sidebar.)

Tourist cards and Mexican car insurance are available at the border, which is open from 6 am to midnight.

AJO

Prospectors roamed the area in the late 1800s, and in 1911 industrial copper mining began. Ajo (pronounced 'AH-ho') became a major mining town, and a mile-wide open-pit mine can be seen just south of town. Falling copper prices finally closed the mine in 1985 and Ajo became hard hit by unemployment. Some of the miners left and housing costs dropped, attracting retirees and reviving the town. The town plaza, built in Spanish-colonial style and flanked by two architecturally similar white churches, is very attractive and has several pleasant restaurants and shops.

Information

The chamber of commerce (☎ 520-387-7742), on the main highway near the plaza, is open from 9 am to 4 pm from Monday to Friday, with reduced hours in summer.

Things to See & Do

The **Ajo Historical Society Museum** (☎ 520-387-7105), in an attractive church close to the copper mine, south of town, is usually open in the afternoon except in summer. The **Ajo Country Club** (☎ 520-387-5011), 7 miles northeast of town, has a nine-hole golf course.

Try the **Windowpane Observatory** (☎ 800-727-4367), PO Box 842, Ajo, AZ 85321, with a 17½-inch telescope and other equipment available for public astronomical viewing by reservation. Viewing starts at $25 an hour and astronomers are on hand to give instruction and explain what you see.

A few miles west of Ajo is one of the most rugged regions in the country, the **Cabeza Prieta National Wildlife Refuge**, a stretch of barren desert traversed only by dirt roads. See the Western Arizona chapter for details.

Places to Stay

The *Shadow Ridge RV Resort* (☎ 520-387-5055), 431 N 2nd Ave (Hwy 85), *Belly Acres RV Park* (☎ 520-387-6907), 2050 N Hwy 85, and *La Siesta RV Resort & Motel* (☎ 520-387-6569), 2561 N Hwy 85, are all just off the main highway north of town and offer sites with hookups in the $15 to $21 range. The La Siesta Motel has 11 simple rooms in the $30s and $40s.

The little *Marine Resort Motel & RV Park* (☎ 520-387-7626), 1966 N Hwy 85, has 20 large, clean motel rooms with refrigerators and coffeemakers for about $45 to $65 in winter, less in summer. RV hookups are available.

The 1925 *Guest House Inn B&B* (☎ 520-387-6133), 700 Guest House Rd, Ajo, AZ 85321, has four comfortable rooms decorated in a Southwestern motif and with private baths for about $80 a double. The *Mine Manager's House Inn B&B* (☎ 520-387-6505, 800-266-7829, fax 520-387-6508), 601 Greenway Drive, Ajo, AZ 85321, is in one of Ajo's earliest houses (it was built in 1919), situated on a hill with fine views.

Five rooms and suites, all with private bath, range from $75 to $110 double. There is a hot tub.

South of Tucson

I-19 due south of Tucson heads to Nogales, on the Mexican border 62 miles away. The freeway exits and speed limits are all in kilometers along here, as a courtesy to Mexican drivers and to prepare US drivers for the metric change in Mexico. While most people barrel along I-10 bent on reaching either Mexico or Tucson in an hour, there is a lot to see along this route, which follows the Santa Cruz River Valley and has been a historical trading route since pre-Hispanic times. The most interesting site is San Xavier del Bac, just south of Tucson (described earlier under Around Tucson). If you continue on farther south, you'll find the following sites.

GREEN VALLEY & AROUND

Green Valley is a retirement community of more than 20,000 people at I-19 exits 69, 65 and 63. (These are exits at kilometer intervals, so they come up pretty quickly.) The chamber of commerce (☎ 520-625-7575, 800-858-5872), just west of exit 63, is open year-round from 9 am to 5 pm Monday to Friday (as well as 9 am to noon on Saturdays from September to May). A huge open-pit copper mine can be seen west of the freeway near here.

Titan Missile Museum

During the Cold War, the USA had dozens of Intercontinental Ballistic Missiles armed with nuclear warheads and ready to fly within a few seconds of receiving a launch order. Fortunately, that order never came. With the SALT II treaty, all the missiles and their underground launch sites were destroyed except for this one, which has been kept as a national historic landmark. The nuclear warhead was removed, but the rest remains as it was during the tense 1960s and '70s, when the push of a button could have started a cataclysmic nuclear war.

The public can tour the entire complex. The museum (☎ 520-574-9658, 520-574-0462) is west of I-19 exit 69. Guided tours (reservations recommended, ☎ 520-625-7736 during business hours) leave hourly from 9 am to 4 pm daily except Thanksgiving and Christmas, November to April. From May to October the museum is closed on Mondays and Tuesdays. Tours involve stair climbing, but wheelchair-accessible tours can be arranged. Admission is $7.50 for adults, $6.50 for those over 62 or with military ID and $4 for 10- to 17-year-olds.

Asarco Mineral Discovery Center

Asarco, one of the nation's largest producers of non-ferrous metals, operates four copper mines in Arizona, including the Mission Complex open-pit mine between Tucson and Green Valley. The discovery center (☎ 520-625-7513) is a mining museum opened in 1998. Hours (subject to change) are 10 am to 5 pm Tuesday to Sunday; admission is free. Open-pit mine tours lasting one hour cost $6 for adults, $5 for seniors and $4 for five- to 12-year-olds. The last tour leaves at 3:40 pm. The center is just west of I-19 exit 80, and the mine is 4 miles farther west.

Madera Canyon Recreation Area

This canyon gives access to hiking trails into the Santa Ritas, including two trails up the biggest peak, Mt Wrightson (9453 feet), in the Coronado National Forest (the ranger station is in Nogales, ☎ 520-281-2296). These trails are 5.4 and 8.1 miles respectively, and there are numerous others. The riparian habitat in the canyon attracts an unusually large variety and number of birds, and this is one of the most popular places for birding in southeastern Arizona. Parking may be difficult to find, especially on weekends, when an early arrival is essential. Madera Canyon is about 12 miles east of I-19 exit 63 and there are signs. Day use is $5 per vehicle. The elevation is a pleasant pine-shaded 5200 feet.

The USFS runs the 13 campsites at *Bog Springs Campground* on a first-come, first-served basis. There is water but no showers or hookups. The fee is $5. There is also a USFS-run picnic area.

Santa Rita Lodge (☎ 520-625-8746), HC 70, Box 5444, Sahuarita, AZ 85629, has about eight rooms and four larger cabins, all with kitchenettes, which are popular with birders and usually booked in advance from March to May. Rates are $78 for rooms and $93 for cabins. The lodge has hiking information.

Whipple Observatory

A new paved road leads up to the observatory from I-19 exit 56. The multi-mirror telescope atop Mt Hopkins at 8550 feet is one of the largest in the world. It can be visited only by a bus tour ($7; $2.50 for six- to 12-year-olds) beginning at the visitor center at 9 am on Monday, Wednesday and Friday from mid-March all through November. Tours last six hours and are limited to 26 participants by reservation only (☎ 520-670-5707).

Ten miles below the observatory, a visitor center shows a film and has exhibits about the telescope (admission is free). The visitor center is open from 8:30 am to 4:30 pm Monday to Friday; it may close in winter.

Places to Stay

The *Green Valley RV Resort* (☎ 520-222-2969), 19001 S Richfield Ave, west of I-19 exit 69, has 300 RV sites with full hookups for $28 and is often full with wintering snowbirds, so reservations are recommended. There is a pool and recreation area.

The *Best Western Green Valley* (☎ 520-625-2250, fax 520-625-0215), at 111 S La Canada, west and south of I-19 exit 65, has a restaurant, a bar, a pool and a spa, and 108 pleasant rooms with coffeemakers, microwaves and refrigerators from $95 to $135 from January through March (much less in summer). The closely priced *Holiday Inn Express* (☎ 520-625-0900, fax 520-393-0522), at I-19 exit 69, has 60 rooms with similar amenities, an indoor pool and spa, and includes continental breakfast.

Also refer to Madera Canyon Recreation Area, above.

TUBAC & AROUND

Tubac is one of the biggest arts and crafts villages in the Southwest and is also among the most historic. If history and/or crafts shopping interest you, Tubac is definitely a worthwhile stop.

There was a Pima Indian village here before Spanish missionaries arrived in the late 17th century, followed by settlers in the 18th century. A Pima revolt in 1751, which the Indians lost, led to the building of Tubac Presidio in 1752, which fell into disuse when the garrison moved to Tucson in 1776. A Spanish/Pima garrison was established a few years later. Tubac became part of Mexico after 1821, but, in 1848, Apache Indians forced the settlers out again. After the Gadsden Purchase of 1853, Americans revived mining operations and Tubac briefly became Arizona's largest town in 1860. Activities ceased during the Civil War, and then afterwards Tubac became a sleepy farming community. After an art school opened in 1948, Tubac began its transformation into a major artists' community.

Information

Tubac is east of I-19 exit 34. It's a small village and is easily visited on foot. The chamber of commerce (☎ 520-398-2704), on Burruel St at Calle Iglesia, answers questions during the week. The Tubac Center for the Arts (☎ 520-398-2371) is near the entrance of town at Plaza Rd and Calle Baca, and has local art exhibits, performances and information. It is open from 10 am to 4:30 pm, Tuesday to Saturday (plus Mondays in winter), and from 1 to 4:30 pm on Sunday. It may close in summer. Most of the approximately 80 galleries, art studios and crafts stores in town have a map showing the location of the shopping district and shops, most of which are open from 10 am to 5 pm daily, year-round.

Tubac Presidio State Historic Park & Museum

The presidio (see above) now lies in ruins, but you can see the 1885 schoolhouse and other historic buildings nearby. The exhibits in the museum (☎ 520-398-2252) tell about the history of Tubac. Hours are 8 am to 5 pm daily except Christmas, and admission is $2; $1 for seven- to 14-year-olds. The park is at the east end of Tubac and has picnicking facilities.

The 4½-mile-long **Juan Bautista de Anza National Historic Trail** winds along the Santa Cruz River from the park to Tumacacori (see below) but is unpleasantly hot in summer and may require wading the river – check with either the Tubac Chamber of Commerce or the Tumacacori Visitor Center for recommendations. The trail commemorates de Anza's route from Mexico to found San Francisco in 1775/76.

Tumacacori National Historical Park

Three miles south of Tubac at I-19 exit 29 are the well-preserved ruins of the Tumacacori (pronounced 'too-ma-CA-co-ree') Franciscan Church, built in 1800 but never completed. Although abandoned in the late 1800s, the church was protected as a national monument in 1908. It gives the visitor an idea of the Spanish history of the area. There is a visitor center (☎ 520-398-2341) with a museum, gift shop and picnic area. Mexican and Indian artists demonstrate their techniques on weekends. Hours are from 8 am to 5 pm daily except Thanksgiving and Christmas. Admission is $2 per person over 16, and Golden Age, Access and Eagle Passes are honored. Ask here about visiting two other missions that are part of the park but not always open.

Special Events

The Tubac Arts & Crafts festival is held every February and lasts several days. Anza Days on the third weekend in October features historical reenactments and cultural events.

A mass is said in the Tumacacori Church on Christmas Eve, and a couple of times a year besides. Call the Tumacacori Visitor

Center for information. An Indian arts and crafts fair is held in Tumacacori in early December.

Places to Stay & Eat

Tubac Trailer Tether (☎ 520-398-2111), in the center of town, has overnight RV parking with hookups for $15. *Mountain View RV Park* (☎ 520-398-9401), at 1½ miles south of I-19 exit 48, has a pool, playground, nearby pizza joint and about 80 sites with hookups for about $20 (less for tents). Reservations are recommended in winter, when snowbirds take spaces for weeks at a time.

Tubac Country Inn B&B (☎ 520-398-3178), at Plaza Rd and Burruel in downtown Tubac, PO Box 1540, Tubac, AZ 85646, has four large rooms with private baths (two with kitchenettes) opening onto a porch and garden. On the Tubac outskirts, *Secret Garden Inn B&B* (☎ 520-398-9371), PO Box 1561, Tubac, AZ 85646, has two rooms surrounded by gardens. *Valle Verde Ranch B&B* (☎/fax 520-398-2246), PO Box 157, Tubac, AZ 85640, on the frontage road just south of Tubac, has a spa, three rooms and two casitas with kitchenettes.

The *Amado Territory Inn* (☎ 520-398-8684, fax 520-398-8186), near I-19 exit 48, has nine rooms decorated in territorial (19th-century ranch) style, all with private baths and with patios or decks. There is an adjoining restaurant. These B&B rooms are nonsmoking and run $80 to $140 in winter but may close in summer.

Tubac Golf Resort (☎ 520-398-2211, 800-848-7893, fax 520-398-9261) is a mile north of Tubac. Apart from the 18-hole golf course, there is a tennis court, pool, spa, and a good restaurant and bar. Rooms are all spacious and some have fireplaces, living rooms or kitchenettes attached. Winter rates are $135 to $185, depending on the size of the room. Summer rates are $70 to $120.

The restaurants adjoining the Amado Territory Inn and the Tubac Golf Resort are both good. There are several quaint eateries in town. A popular one is *Tosh's* (☎ 520-398-3008), Camino Otero at Burruel St, with Mexican food and a bar.

It opens daily from 11 am to 8 pm (with shorter summer hours).

NOGALES & AROUND

Nogales (pronounced 'noh-GAH-lez'), Arizona, and Nogales, Sonora, are towns separated only by the USA/Mexico border. You can easily walk from one into the other. The twin towns are locally called *Ambos Nogales* or 'Both Nogales.'

Nogales, Arizona, is the Santa Cruz County seat and has about 20,000 inhabitants. The elevation here is 3865 feet. Many visitors come to shop for Mexican goods just across the border. Nogales is Arizona's most important gateway into Mexico and is also the major port of entry for the agricultural produce Mexico sells to the USA and Canada.

Information

Steep hills, a dividing railroad, one-way streets, a confusing street system and poor local maps make getting around Nogales difficult for visitors. It's not a big town, though, so relax and you'll eventually find where you want to go.

The chamber of commerce (☎ 520-287-3685, fax 520-287-3688), in Kino Park off Grand Ave, is open 8 am to 5 pm Monday to Friday. The Mexican Consulate (☎ 520-287-2521), 480 Grand Ave, is open from 8:30 am to 3 pm, Monday to Friday, and 9 am to 2 pm on Saturday. Call ☎ 520-287-3609 for US Immigration.

The Coronado National Forest Ranger Station (☎ 520-281-2296) is near I-19 exit 12. The library (☎ 520-287-3343) is at 518 Grand Ave. The post office (☎ 520-287-9246) is at 300 N Morley Ave. The hospital (☎ 520-287-2771) is at 1171 W Target Range Rd.

Pimeria Alta Historical Society Museum

This historical museum (☎ 520-287-4621) is in the old town hall (built in 1914) at 136 Grand Ave and gives a good introduction to the area. Hours are 10 am to noon and 1:30 to 5 pm, Tuesday to Friday, and 10 am to 4 pm on Saturday; admission is free.

Visiting Mexico

Most visitors go to shop for a few hours and perhaps have a meal in Nogales, Sonora (Mexico). Park on the US side (many lots around Crawford and Terrace Ave charge $4 a day) and walk over into the Nogales, Sonora, shopping district. US dollars and credit cards are accepted and prices are good (though not much cheaper than nearby Arizona), but the quality varies so shop around. Bargaining is certainly possible. All kinds of Mexican goods are available, such as pottery, stoneware, silver, tin, glass, weavings, leather, basketry and wood carvings.

From Nogales, buses and trains continue farther into Mexico. The bus terminal is about 3 miles south of the border (take a taxi) and there are frequent departures. There is also a daily train south to Guadalajara and Mexico City. Information is available near the border. Drivers can obtain car insurance from Sanborn's (☎ 520-281-1873), 2921 Grand Ave.

For border crossing information, see the Crossing the Border sidebar earlier in this chapter.

Winery

Arizona Vineyards (☎ 520-287-7972), 1830 Hwy 82, has tours and tastings of its colorfully named 'Arizona Dust' and 'Coyote Red' wines.

Places to Stay

Camping *Mi Casa RV Park* (☎ 520-281-1150), 2901 Grand Ave, is about 3 miles north of town on Hwy 89. RV sites are $16 with hookups, and there are showers and a few cheap tent sites. The USFS-operated *Upper/Lower White Rock* campgrounds are on Peña Blanca Lake, 9 miles west of I-19 exit 12, north of Nogales. There are 15 sites with water but no showers or hookups available year-round on a first-come, first-served basis. Sites are $5 and there is fishing and boating. (Also see Patagonia Lake State Park, below.)

Hotels & Motels Winter rates (given below) are about 20% higher than summer rates.

The cheapest place is the independent *Arroyo Motel* (☎ 520-287-4637), 20 Doe St, with basic rooms around $30. There's a similarly priced place (it has gone through recent name changes) on Grand Ave south of the Days Inn.

All the following motels have pools. The *Motel 6* (☎ 520-281-2951, fax 520-281-9592), 141 W Mariposa Rd, east of I-19 exit 4, offers 79 singles/doubles for $38/44 in the winter. There are two Best Westerns, each with a spa and about 45 small but clean rooms in the $40s and $50s, including continental breakfast. The *Best Western Time Motel* (☎ 520-287-4627, fax 520-287-6949), 921 Grand Ave, is usually a few dollars cheaper than the *Best Western Siesta Motel* (☎ 520-287-4671, fax 520-287-9616), 673 Grand Ave, which has some rooms with microwaves and refrigerators.

The *Super 8 Motel* (☎ 520-281-2242, fax 520-281-2242 x 400), 547 W Mariposa Rd, on the east side of I-19 exit 4, has a spa, a restaurant open 6 am to 9 pm and a bar. More than 100 rooms are in the $40s (one bed) and $50s (two beds) for a double. The *Days Inn* (☎ 520-287-4611, fax 520-287-0101), 844 Grand Ave, has 98 rooms, a spa, restaurant and lounge, and includes a continental breakfast. The *Americana Motor Hotel* (☎ 520-287-7211, 800-874-8079, fax 520-287-5188), 639 Grand Ave, has a restaurant open from 6:30 am to 10 pm, room service, a bar with poolside service and 90 good-sized older double rooms from $40 to $65.

North of Nogales at I-19 exit 17 is the *Rio Rico Resort* (☎ 520-281-1901, 800-288-4746, fax 520-281-8017), with almost 200 rooms situated on a hilltop with a view. It features a pool, spa, sauna, an 18-hole championship golf course, four lighted tennis courts, an exercise room and horseback riding. A restaurant, lounge, outdoor barbecues and weekend entertainment are also provided. Most rooms have a private patio or balcony, a coffeemaker, and are about $150 a double in winter. More expensive suites are available. This golf resort is a good alternative

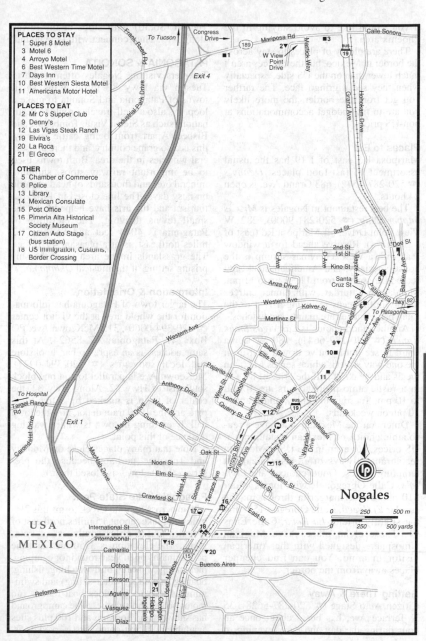

PLACES TO STAY
1 Super 8 Motel
3 Motel 6
4 Arroyo Motel
6 Best Western Time Motel
7 Days Inn
10 Best Western Siesta Motel
11 Americana Motor Hotel

PLACES TO EAT
2 Mr C's Supper Club
9 Denny's
12 Las Vigas Steak Ranch
19 Elvira's
20 La Roca
21 El Greco

OTHER
5 Chamber of Commerce
8 Police
13 Library
14 Mexican Consulate
15 Post Office
16 Pimeria Alta Historical
    Society Museum
17 Citizen Auto Stage
    (bus station)
18 US Immigration, Customs,
    Border Crossing

To Tucson

Congress Drive

Frank Reed Rd

Mariposa Rd

Calle Sonora

189

W View Point Drive

Maslick Way

Hohokam Drive

BUS 19

Exit 4

Industrial Park Drive

Grand Ave

3rd St

2nd St
1st St

Don St

Bankerd Ave

C Ave

D Ave

Kino St

Bayre Ave

Santa Cruz St

Patagonia Hwy

82

Anza Drive

Western Ave

Kolver St

Belleia St

To Patagonia

Martinez St

Perkins Ave

Morley Ave

Western Ave

Sage St

Ellis St

Pajarito St

Sonoita Ave

West Loma St

Chenoweth Ave

Anthony Drive

Quarry St

Potrero Ave

89

To Hospital
Target Range Rd

Walnut St

MacNab Drive

Curtis St

Adams St

Castellana St

Exit 1

Carondelet Drive

MacNab Drive

Oak St

Arroyo Blvd

Grand Ave

Morley Ave

Western Drive

Noon St

Elm St

Beck St

Hudgins St

Sonoita Ave

Terrace Ave

West Ave

Crawford St

Court St

East St

Nogales

0   250   500 m
0   250   500 yards

19

International St

USA

MEXICO

Internacional

Camarillo

Ochoa

Pierson

Aguirre

Vásquez

Díaz

Reforma

Lopez Mateos

Hidalgo

Obregon

Ingeniero

Elias

Buenos Aires

MEX 15

ARIZONA

if you would like to avoid staying in the Phoenix area.

There are plenty of places to stay across the border in Mexico, but their prices aren't much lower than on the US side, especially when they see a gringo face. The farther you get from the border, the more likely you are to find budget accommodations at non-US prices.

Places to Eat

Mariposa Rd east of I-19 has the usual assortment of fast-food places. *Denny's* (☎ 520-287-4572), 683 Grand Ave, is open 24 hours.

The best restaurant in Nogales is *Mr C's Supper Club* (☎ 520-281-9000), 282 W View Point Drive, off Mariposa Rd (east of I-19 exit 4). Reserve ahead for a window seat with a view. Guaymas shrimp is the house specialty, and American steak and seafood are served from 11:30 am to 11 pm, Monday to Saturday, with dinner entrées mainly in the teens including a visit to the salad bar. Lunches are mainly sandwiches.

Another good choice is *Las Vigas Steak Ranch* (☎ 520-287-6641), 180 W Loma (hard to see until you've driven past it on the one-way street), which serves Mexican meals and steaks at half the price of Mr C's in a rustic atmosphere. Hours are 10 am to 10 pm, Tuesday to Friday, and 8 am to 10 pm on weekends.

Diners on the Mexican side have a reasonable choice of Mexican restaurants at US prices, but even in the USA, Mexican restaurants always offer tasty meals at tempting prices. Good choices are *Elvira's*, Calle Obregón 1, with meals under $10 and a free margarita thrown in; the similar *El Greco*, Calle Obregón 152; and the slightly pricier *La Roca*, Calle Elías 91. These clean places have Mexican atmosphere designed with the American visitor in mind. You can find cheaper places away from the border.

Getting There & Away

Citizen Auto Stage (☎ 520-287-5628), 35 N Terrace Ave, has buses about once an hour during the day and early evening to Tucson ($6.50) with stops at the towns along I-19. They connect with Greyhound.

PATAGONIA & SONOITA

Travelers visiting Nogales often return to Tucson via Hwy 82 through the small towns of Patagonia and Sonoita to make a loop. It's also a well-traveled route to destinations such as Sierra Vista, Tombstone and Bisbee. Apart from being cattle country, this is also grape country, and there are several wineries in the area. Both towns used to be important railway stops, shipping mineral ores and thousands of head of cattle on busy days. The line closed in 1962, but tourism and the arts have helped keep the small towns thriving. The elevation of Patagonia is 4044 feet and Sonoita, 12 miles northeast, is at a pleasant 4970 feet. The grasslands in the area were the surprising setting of the musical *Oklahoma*.

Information & Orientation

The larger town of Patagonia has information for the whole area at the visitor center (☎ 520-394-0060), 315 McKeown Ave, PO Box 241, Patagonia, AZ 85624. At this same address is an espresso bar, bookstore and local souvenirs (☎ 520-394-0077). McKeown Ave is parallel to and one block southeast of Hwy 82. Along Hwy 82, the center of town is marked by a tree-filled park and the 1900 train depot, now the town hall. Everything in town is within walking distance of this point.

Note that many places close on Monday and Tuesday (perhaps because the preserve – see below – is closed then.)

Patagonia Lake State Park

A dam across Sonoita Creek forms this 2½-mile-long lake, about 15 miles northeast of Nogales and 7 miles southwest of Patagonia. The elevation is 3750 feet, and the park remains open year-round for camping, picnicking, walking, bird-watching, fishing, boating (including water-skiing) and swimming. A marina provides boat rentals (no motor boats) and supplies. The campground has showers and hookups and 100 plus sites available on a first-come, first-served basis.

Crossing the Border

You can freely walk across the border into Mexico for shopping or a meal at any of the border towns. Returning from Mexico into the USA, however, is another matter. You need to carry a passport on your return to show the US immigration authorities. US citizens on a day trip don't need passports if they carry their birth certificates (if they were born in the USA) or a naturalization certificate. Although a US driver's license will sometimes suffice, don't count on it. US resident aliens need to carry their resident alien card when returning to the USA.

If you want to enter Mexico for more than a border day trip, you need a passport and a Mexican tourist card, which will be checked a few miles inside the country. The tourist card is available for free at the border upon producing a passport. US citizens can obtain a tourist card with a birth certificate, but a passport is a more convenient and quickly recognized document and enables you to change money and perform other tasks. Mexican tourist cards are valid for up to 180 days, but normally much less time is given. Ask for as many days as you will need. A few nationalities require a Mexican visa; recently, these included Australians, New Zealanders and some European, African and Asian nationals, but the situation changes. If in doubt, check with the Mexican consul in your home country or in Tucson and Nogales. Be warned that even the Mexican consul might not be aware of the latest changes. If you are heading just to Puerto Peñasco, four hours drive from Tucson, you don't need a tourist card.

Travelers into Mexico cannot bring in guns or ammunition without a special permit. Recently, an Arizona man crossing into Mexico was found to have some ammunition (left over from a hunting trip) in his vehicle. He was arrested and now, almost a month later, remains jailed in Mexico, even though he didn't have a gun.

You can bring almost anything bought in Mexico back into the USA duty-free as long as it's worth a total of less than $400 and doesn't include more than a quart of booze or 200 cigarettes. Many handicrafts are exempt from the $400 limit. Fresh food is prohibited, as are fireworks, which are illegal for personal use in Arizona. Importing weapons and drugs is also illegal, except for prescribed drugs, which are cheaper in Mexico – some visitors without health insurance fill their prescriptions in Mexico.

Traveling by Mexican public transport is a little more adventurous than the equivalent in the USA. However, it's also much more far-reaching and you can get almost anywhere on a bus at reasonable cost. If you prefer to bring your own car, you should get Mexican car insurance; US car insurance is not normally valid in Mexico. Car insurance can easily be bought at one of many places at the border (Sanborn's in Nogales and Tucson are reputable) or through the American Automobile Association. Rates are $10 to $15 a day for comprehensive coverage, but if you buy insurance by the week or month, rates drop substantially. Remember: Mexico's legal system is Napoleonic, that is, you are guilty until proven innocent, and you are likely to be arrested and held after a car accident unless you can show Mexican car insurance covering the accident.

Nogales is the main Arizona/Mexico border crossing and is also the safest. Along the southeastern Arizona border, drug smuggling and international car theft are frequent occurrences, and west of Nogales, illegal immigration is a concern. Immigration and customs officials are working to control these problems. Not all officials are honest, however. Both Mexican and US officers have broken the law in recent years. This is a recognized problem that the USA is working to solve, but travelers should be aware that a small percentage of officials on both sides of the border is corrupt. The best defense is to make sure that your documents are perfectly in order, to travel by day and to not allow officials to intimidate you for any reason. It is most unlikely that you will have any problems. ■

These can fill up in summer. Rates are $5 for day use, $10 for camping and $15 with hookups. Information is available from Patagonia Lake State Park (☎ 520-287-6965), PO Box 274, Patagonia, AZ 85624. The main gate is closed from 10 pm to 5 am.

Patagonia-Sonoita Creek Preserve

This has been managed by The Nature Conservancy since 1966, the Conservancy's first project in Arizona. Sonoita Creek is the home of four endangered species of native fish, and the splendid riparian habitat along the creek attracts more than 260 species of birds, including rarities from Mexico, and this in turn attracts some 30,000 visitors a year, especially birders.

Birding is good year-round, although March to September is considered to be the best time, with peaks of migrants in late April and May, and then again in late August and September. Beware of insects in spring and summers (chiggers are bad in July and August!) and wear long pants and insect repellent.

The preserve is reached by going northwest on N 3rd or 4th Ave in Patagonia, then south on Pennsylvania Ave. The preserve is across a small creek, which you may have to drive through or wade across. Entrance is free for Nature Conservancy members; nonmembers are asked to make a $5 donation. There is a visitor center and trails but no camping or picnicking facilities. Hours are 7:30 am to 4 pm, Wednesday to Sunday, and short guided tours are given at 9 am on Saturday mornings, by reservation. Further information is available from the preserve (☎ 520-394-2400), PO Box 815, Patagonia, AZ 85624.

Wineries

There are six wineries in the area, and most offer tastings and perhaps tours. Stop by the visitor center for information about Patagonia's Santa Cruz Winery (☎ 520-394-2888). Near tiny Elgin, a few miles east of Sonoita, the Village of Elgin Winery (☎ 520-455-9309) and Sonoita Vineyards

(☎ 520-455-5893) advertise tours and tastings from 10 am to 4 pm daily.

Special Events

The Sonoita Quarter Horse Show is the oldest in the country and runs in early June. Sonoita is home of the Santa Cruz County Fair & Rodeo Grounds (☎ 520-455-5553) with a rodeo over Labor Day weekend. The county fair is held the fourth weekend in September.

Places to Stay & Eat

Patagonia has a hotel, guest ranch and an increasing number of B&Bs. Sonoita has the best restaurants.

The *Stage Stop Inn* (☎ 520-394-2211, 800-923-2211, fax 520-394-2212), 303 W McKeown in Patagonia, is a modern motel with a Western facade. More than 40 rooms are $70 a double or $80 with a kitchenette, and there is a small pool, restaurant and saloon bar.

The *Circle Z Ranch* (☎ 520-394-2525, 888-854-2525), PO Box 194, Patagonia, AZ 85624, is a working cattle ranch a few miles southwest of Patagonia on Sonoita Creek. From November to mid-May it offers horseback-riding vacations with a three-night minimum. Accommodations are in rustic but comfortable rooms and cabins, and all meals are provided. Rates are about $500 per person for three days and nights, including riding, though kids and families can arrange package discounts.

Of several B&Bs that have blossomed recently, the *Duquesne House* (☎ 520-394-2732), 357 Duquesne St, PO Box 772, Patagonia, AZ 85624, is one of the longest established and is also one of Patagonia's first buildings. Three rather spacious, old-fashioned units with private bath are $70 a double. The visitor center can suggest half a dozen others.

Restaurants in Patagonia include *The Ovens Bakery* (☎ 520-394-2483) and *Marie's* (☎ 520-394-2812), both in the heart of town on Hwy 82. The Ovens, despite calling itself a bakery, serves a variety of Latin-influenced lunches and dinners while Marie's sticks to a small but innovative continental dinner menu. Both are closed on Monday and Tuesday. Daily breakfast, lunch and dinner are available in the restaurant adjoining the Stage Stop Inn.

Sonoita boasts a few remarkable restaurants. *Er Pastaro* (☎ 520-455-5821), 3084 E Hwy 82 (just east of Hwy 83), is one of southern Arizona's better Italian restaurants, owned and operated by a celebrated Italian chef and his friendly wife who got fed up with big-city restaurants. Now they have this little rural place with great food at very reasonable prices. It is open only from 4 to 9 pm, Wednesday to Sunday, and is closed completely in the summer.

Just east is *Karen's Wine Country Cafe* (☎ 520-455-5282), 3266 Hwy 82, serving a limited menu of gourmet meals made with the freshest of ingredients, much of which they grow themselves. It has received rave reviews. Call ahead to make reservations and check its limited hours, recently 11 am to 4 pm, Wednesday to Sunday, and 5 to 8 pm from Thursday to Saturday. Most entrées are in the teens, or you can opt for the four-course dinner, which is accompanied by three glasses of appropriate wines. You can choose meat or fish as an entrée. For $36.50, it's perfect if (like me) you don't really want to hassle with choosing.

If none of these appeal to you, try the *Ranch House* (☎ 520-455-5371), 3520 Hwy 82, for steaks without the music; *Grasslands German Bakery* (☎ 520-457-4770), 3119 Hwy 83 south of town; or *Café Sonoita* (☎ 520-455-5278), 3280 Hwy 82.

ARIZONA

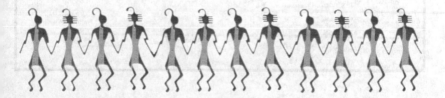

Southeastern Arizona

Whereas the I-19 corridor south of Tucson has Spanish history, the area to the east of it tends to have more Anglo history. This is Cochise County – the land of Indians, cowboys, miners, outlaws, ranchers, gunslingers and Western lore. Today the cattle ranches are still there, but the mining operations have mainly closed down. Two towns, Tombstone and Bisbee, have capitalized upon their Western heritage and turned tourism into a major industry. There are also some very scenic areas here, notably the Huachuca Mountains southwest of the modern town of Sierra Vista and the Chiricahua Mountains in the extreme southeast corner.

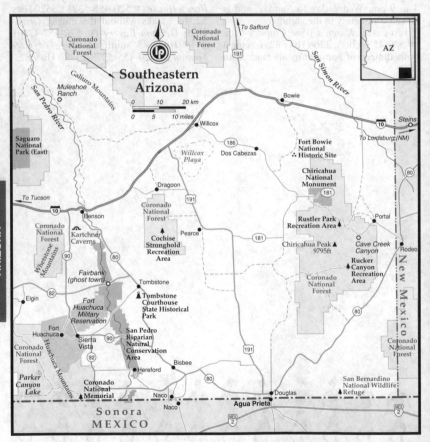

BENSON

This small rural town (population 4200), 45 miles east of Tucson on I-10, grew around a railway stop in the 1880s. Today it is a quiet travelers' stop with some simple places to eat and a few motels. However, the local railroad has generated a solid stream of tourists, and the numbers will grow when the spectacular Kartchner Caverns are opened to the public.

Orientation & Information

The main drag is 4th St, running west-east between exits 303 and 306 on I-10. Ocotillo Ave (which becomes Ocotillo Rd north of I-10) is the main north-south street, leaving I-10 at exit 304.

The chamber of commerce (☎ 520-586-2842, bensonspvchamber@theriver.com), 226 E 4th, is open from 10 am to 4 pm Monday to Friday and sometimes on Saturdays.

The library (☎ 520-586-9535) is at 300 S Huachuca. The post office (☎ 586 3422) is at 260 S Ocotillo Ave. The hospital (☎ 520-586-2261) is at 450 S Ocotillo Ave. The police (☎ 520-586-2211, or 911 in emergencies) are at 360 S Gila St.

San Pedro Valley Arts & Historical Museum

This small local museum (☎ 520-586-3070), at 5th and San Pedro St, is open 10 am to 4 pm Tuesday to Friday and 10 am to 2 pm on Saturday from October to April; it's open from 10 am to 2 pm Tuesday to Saturday in other months except August, when it's closed. Admission is free. The museum has information about historical walking tours in town.

Organized Tours

High Desert Adventures (☎ 520-586-9309, desertjeeptours@theriver.com) arranges custom 4WD tours ranging from 3½ to 6½ hours.

Places to Stay

Camping *Red Barn Campground* (☎ 520-586-2035) and *KOA* (☎ 520-586-3977) are both just off Ocotillo Rd, north of I-10

exit 304. Red Barn charges $14 for tents and $18 for hookups. KOA charges $18 and up and has a pool and recreation area. The campground recently added B&B rooms.

Motels Six basic, old motels along 4th St (Hwy 80) offer cheap rooms, including the *Benson Motel* (☎ 520-586-3346), 185 W 4th St, the *Quarter Horse Motel* (☎ 520-586-3371, 800-527-5025), 800 W 4th St, and the *Sahara Motel* (☎ 520-586-3611), 1150 S Hwy 80.

Several chain hotels have recently opened, mainly at I-10 exit 304, all waiting for Kartchner Caverns crowds. Here, there's the *Super 8 Motel* (☎ 520-586-1530, fax 520-586-1534), 855 N Ocotillo Rd, with a pool and 40 rooms at $43/49 single/double. *Day's Inn* (☎ 520-586-3000, fax 520-586-7000), 621 Commerce Drive, has a pool, spa and 63 rooms mainly in the $40 to $65 range, including continental breakfast. A few mini-suites are slightly pricier. The *Best Western Quail Hollow Inn* (☎ 520-586-3646, fax 520-586-7035), 699 N Ocotillo Ave, has a pool, spa and 90 good rooms with coffeemakers for $44 to $60.

Holiday Inn Express (☎ 520-586-8800), at I-10 exit 302, has a pool, fitness center and rooms with microwaves, refrigerators and coffeemakers for around $52.

Places to Eat

There are plenty of fast-food and chain restaurants, especially along 4th St. If you want more Western character, try the *Horseshoe Cafe* (☎ 520-586-3303), 154 E 4th St, serving American food and some Mexican plates from 6 am to 9 pm daily, till 10 pm on Friday and Saturday. It's been a favorite ranchers' hangout since 1937 and can show you life before the Big Mac.

The *Chute-Out Steakhouse* (☎ 520-586-7297), 161 S Huachuca (a block south of the chamber of commerce), serves steaks and seafood and is locally popular. Its adjoining bar has live music on weekends. At I-10 exit 304, *Denny's* (☎ 520-586-8816), 825 N Ocotillo Rd, is open 24 hours.

Getting There & Away

The Greyhound (☎ 520-586-3141) bus stops at 242 E 4th St on its runs along I-10. Benson Shuttle (☎ 520-586-2429), a subsidiary of Cochise Tours (☎ 520-720-4900), provides van service to all local towns. There is an Amtrak stop on 4th St near Patagonia St, but trains halt only by advance reservation.

AROUND BENSON

San Pedro & Southwestern Railroad

This train follows historic tracks between Benson and the ghost town of Charleston, 27 miles south of Benson, between Tombstone and Sierra Vista. The tracks go along the San Pedro River Valley and do not follow a paved road, so you get to see countryside that you otherwise would have missed. Narration on the four-hour round-trip tour tells of the region's Wild West history and wildlife, and entertainment (cowboy musicians, mystery theater and more) is often provided. The train leaves the Benson station on Country Club Drive (off Hwy 80 a mile south of town); departure times and dates vary but are usually from Thursday to Sunday during most months. Both enclosed and open-air carriages are available. Call the railroad (☎ 520-586-2266, 800-269-6314) for schedules, entertainment and reservations (required). Rates are $26 for adults, $23 for people aged 60 and older, $17 for five- to 17-year-olds, free for younger kids, and $80 for families (two adults and up to four kids).

Vega-Bray Observatory

This astronomy observatory is on a hill a few miles southeast of Benson. It has a classroom, planetarium and eight telescopes from 6 to 20 inches in diameter, the latter controlled by computer. During the day, telescopes with filters are used for solar observations. A 2-mile nature trail goes to the San Pedro River.

At the observatory is *Skywatcher's Inn* (☎/fax 520-745-2390, vegasky@azstarnet.com), a three-room B&B. All rooms have private baths, and guests have the use of two kitchens. Rates are $85 (one or two people). A four-hour guided astronomy session for up to five people is $75, and various other sky-watching packages for beginners to professionals can be arranged. Reservations are necessary.

Amerind Foundation

This excellent museum and archaeology research center (☎ 520-586-3666) is in Dragoon, 15 miles east of Benson. The exhibits of Native American archaeology, history and culture cover many tribes from Alaska to South America, with a special focus on Southwestern Indians. Don't miss the Western Art gallery in a separate building; it features a small but superb collection of artists of the past century including some Indian painters whose works have been exhibited internationally. Hours are from 10 am to 4 pm daily, September to May, closed Monday and Tuesday in summer and all major holidays. The art gallery closes from noon to 1 pm. Admission is $3; $2 for those over 60 and 12- to 18-year-olds. Take I-10 exit 318 and head east 1 mile.

Kartchner Caverns State Park

This spectacular limestone cave was completely undamaged and unexplored when discovered. The moist cave is 2½ miles long and the geological features within it are still growing. Hikers stumbled across it in 1974, but the location of this spectacular spot was kept secret until 1988, when it became a state park and its protection could be assured.

Originally set to open in 1995, the caverns still have not opened to the public, and may not do so until anywhere from early 1999 to mid-2001. The visitor center and parking area have been built, but delays have been caused by the installation of a costly state-of-the-art trail and lighting system designed to protect this unique and fragile living cave. All equipment has to go through air locks to avoid contaminating the cave. More than $25 million has been spent in preparing the cave for visitors. Meanwhile, motel and restaurant owners in

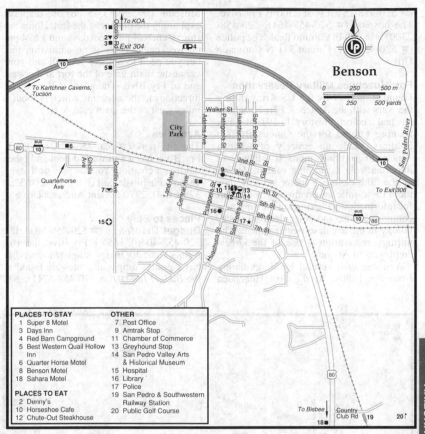

Benson

0   250   500 m
0   250   500 yards

PLACES TO STAY
1 Super 8 Motel
3 Days Inn
4 Red Barn Campground
5 Best Western Quail Hollow
   Inn
6 Quarter Horse Motel
8 Benson Motel
18 Sahara Motel

PLACES TO EAT
2 Denny's
10 Horseshoe Cafe
12 Chute-Out Steakhouse

OTHER
7 Post Office
9 Amtrak Stop
11 Chamber of Commerce
13 Greyhound Stop
14 San Pedro Valley Arts
   & Historical Museum
15 Hospital
16 Library
17 Police
19 San Pedro & Southwestern
   Railway Station
20 Public Golf Course

ARIZONA

Benson are waiting anxiously for the anticipated flood of visitors for what is touted as one of the 10 best caves in the world.

The park is 8 miles south of Benson on Hwy 90. For current information call the chamber of commerce or Arizona State Parks headquarters in Phoenix (☎ 602-542-4174).

SIERRA VISTA
Sierra Vista (elevation 4623 feet) was founded in the 1950s as a service center for Fort Huachuca (see below) and is now a modern town of about 40,000 inhabitants.

It makes a good base from which to visit Cochise County's attractions.

Information
The chamber of commerce (☎ 520-458-6940, 800-288-3861), 21 E Wilcox Drive, is open 8 am to 5 pm, Monday to Friday, and from 9 am to 1 pm on Saturday. The Coronado National Forest Sierra Vista Ranger Station (☎ 520-378-0311) is 7 miles south at 5990 Hwy 92, Hereford, AZ 85615.

The library (☎ 520-458-4225) is at 2950 E Tacoma St. The local newspaper is the *Sierra Vista Herald*. The post office

(☎ 520-458-2540) is at 2300 E Fry Blvd. The hospital (☎ 520-458-4641, 520-458-2300) is at 300 El Camino Real. The police (☎ 520-458-3311) are at 911 N Coronado Drive.

Fort Huachuca Military Reservation
Founded in 1877 by the US Army during the wars with the Apaches, Fort Huachuca has had a colorful history. In 1913 it was a training ground for the famous Buffalo Soldiers, made up entirely of African American fighting men. It played an important role in training soldiers for all of the 20th century's major wars. Today, the 115-sq-mile reservation is important for information gathering, and testing new communications and other electronic technology in the dry desert environment. The military reservation is one of the largest employers in Arizona.

You can visit several buildings dating from the 1880s. At the Fort Huachuca

Museum (☎ 520-533-5736) are displays explaining the history of the fort. Hours are from 9 am to 4 pm weekdays and 1 to 4 pm on weekends. There is no admission fee, but you need to register yourself and your car at the main gate of the fort at the west end of Fry Blvd. The guard will give you directions to the museum, which is about 3 miles west of the main gate.

Activities
The city park (☎ 520-458-6742), 3025 E Fry Blvd, has a **swimming** pool and other outdoor recreation. You can play **golf** at the 18-hole Pueblo del Sol Golf Course (☎ 520-378-6444), 2770 S Saint Andrews Drive.

Places to Stay
Budget The *Motel 6* (☎ 520-459-5035, fax 520-458-4046), 1551 E Fry Blvd, has 103 rooms for $30/36 for singles/doubles. It has a pool. Comparable rates are found at the *Budget Inn* (☎/fax 520-458-6711), 201

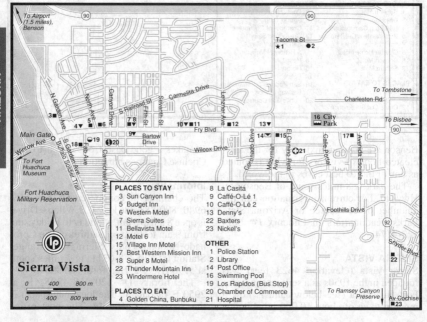

ARIZONA

Sierra Vista

PLACES TO STAY	
3	Sun Canyon Inn
5	Budget Inn
6	Western Motel
7	Sierra Suites
11	Bellavista Motel
12	Motel 6
15	Village Inn Motel
17	Best Western Mission Inn
18	Super 8 Motel
22	Thunder Mountain Inn
23	Windermere Hotel

PLACES TO EAT	
4	Golden China, Bunbuku
8	La Casita
9	Caffé-O-Lé 1
10	Caffé-O-Lé 2
13	Denny's
22	Baxters
23	Nickel's

OTHER	
1	Police Station
2	Library
14	Post Office
16	Swimming Pool
19	Los Rapidos (Bus Stop)
20	Chamber of Commerce
21	Hospital

W Fry Blvd, with a lounge, tiny pool and 67 rooms, and the *Western Motel* (☎ 520-458-4303), 43 W Fry Blvd, with 25 small rooms, but all with a mini-fridge, microwave, TV and clock radio.

Other places with rooms in the $30s and low $40s, all with small seasonal swimming pools, include the clean *Bellavista Motel* (☎ 520-458-6737, fax 520-458-5284), 1101 E Fry Blvd, which has 40 rooms, some with kitchenettes, and the *Village Inn Motel* (☎ 520-458-4315), 2440 E Fry Blvd, which has a simple restaurant and lounge on the premises. It has 52 rooms, as does the *Super 8 Motel* (☎ 520-459-5380, fax 520-459-6052), 100 Fab Ave, which charges $42.88/47.88 single/double (one bed) or $52.88 with two beds and offers free coffee and pastries for breakfast.

Middle The following all have seasonal pools. The *Sun Canyon Inn* (☎ 520-459-0610, fax 520-458-5178), 260 N Garden Ave, has 80 rooms in the $50s and low $60s, all with microwaves and refrigerators. The inn also offers golf packages, a spa, a continental breakfast and a lounge with occasional entertainment. The similar *Thunder Mountain Inn* (☎/fax 520-458-7900), 1631 S Hwy 92, has 102 rooms, a spa, coffee shop and Baxter's Restaurant & Lounge, which provides room service and entertainment. Breakfast is not included.

Sierra Suites (☎ 520-459-4221, fax 520-459-8449), 391 E Fry Blvd, has 100 large rooms with refrigerators and microwaves for about $50 to $60 and a few two-room suites for $70 to $90. There is a spa, and continental breakfast and an evening cocktail are included in the rates. The *Best Western Mission Inn* (☎ 520-458-8500, fax 520 459 3070), 3640 E Fry Blvd, has 40 rooms for $45 to $65, including continental breakfast.

The *Windermere Hotel* (☎ 520-459-5900, 800-825-4656, fax 520-458-1347), 2047 S Hwy 92, has a spa, lounge, restaurant with room service and 149 good-size rooms with coffeemakers. Rates are $60 to $85, including continental breakfast and

complimentary evening cocktails. Two suites are about $150.

Places to Eat
There are plenty of restaurants to choose from along Fry Blvd. Very popular for a variety of coffees, as well as breakfast and lunch, is *Caffé-O-Lé 1* (☎ 520-458-8621), 400 E Fry Blvd (in the Haymore Plaza), open from 6 am to 3 pm, Monday to Saturday, and 8 am to 3 pm on Sunday, and *Caffé-O-Lé 2* (☎ 520-417-0304), 1081 E Fry Blvd, which remains open until 8 pm, Tuesday to Saturday.

Two places recommended as being popular with off-duty base personnel are the *Golden China* (☎ 520-458-8588), 325 W Fry Blvd, which is open daily for inexpensive buffet lunches and fancier dinners from the varied menu, and *Bunbuku* (☎ 520-459-6993), 297 W Fry Blvd, for Japanese lunches and dinners. Decent Mexican food is served at *La Casita* (☎ 520-458-2376), 465 E Fry Blvd, from 11 am to 9 pm, Monday to Thursday, and to 10 pm on Friday and Saturday.

For American steak and seafood, the best place is 7 miles south at *The Mesquite Tree* (☎ 520-378-2758), 6398 S Hwy 92, which is open from 5 to 8 pm Sunday and Monday, and till 9 pm the rest of the week. Dinner entrées range from $11 to $18. Also good, and in a similar price range, are *Baxters* in the Thunder Mountain Inn and *Nickel's* in the Windermere Hotel. The latter both serve lunch as well.

For a more continental menu, the casually elegant *Outside Inn* (☎ 520-378-4625), 4907 S Hwy 92, is open from 11 am to 1:30 pm, Monday to Friday, and 5 to 9 pm, Monday to Saturday. Lunch salads and sandwiches are $6 to $8, and dinner entrées, which cover a wide spectrum of veal, lamb, beef, chicken and seafood, all including a soup or salad, are in the $11 to $19 range.

Getting There & Away
America West Express (☎ 520-459-8575) has several flights a day between Phoenix and Sierra Vista's Fort Huachuca Airport,

ARIZONA

3 miles north of the west end of Fry Blvd. Los Rapidos (☎ 520-458-3471), a Greyhound subsidiary at 28 Fab Ave, has five buses a day on its Douglas-Bisbee-Sierra Vista-Tucson runs, with three continuing to Phoenix. Shuttle Express (☎ 520-458-3330) has vans to Tucson Airport.

Getting Around
Sierra Vista Public Transit (☎ 520-459-0595) has buses along Fry Blvd about every hour during the day from Monday to Saturday.

You can rent cars from Enterprise (☎ 520-458-2425), or try Practical Rent-a-Car (☎ 520-458-4441) or Monty's Motors (☎ 520-458-2665), all in Sierra Vista.

AA Cab (☎ 520-417-0308) and ABC Cab (☎ 520-458-8429) have 24-hour taxi service.

AROUND SIERRA VISTA
Ramsey Canyon Preserve
At an elevation of about 5500 feet in the Huachuca Mountains south of Sierra Vista, this Nature Conservancy-owned preserve is famous throughout the birding world as one of the best places in the USA to see hummingbirds. The highest numbers are seen from April to September (in April, May and August especially), but there are always a few species here year-round. Trogons (colorful tropical birds) and other rarities from Mexico are also seen in the wooded riparian habitat in the canyon. Also protected is the Ramsey Canyon leopard frog, found nowhere else in the world. Visitors are quite likely to see deer, and sightings of coatis, ringtails, javelinas, mountain lions and black bears are reported regularly.

Entrance to the preserve is limited by the small size of the parking lot, at the end of a very narrow and winding road along which parking is illegal. There's no room for RVs or trailers. During the busy months and summer weekends you should make reservations as far ahead as possible for parking spaces at the preserve (☎ 520-378-2785, fax 520-378-1480), 27 Ramsey Canyon Rd, Hereford, AZ 85615. Reservations are

required year-round. (There are plans to enlarge the parking lot in the future.)

The preserve is open from 8 am to 5 pm daily and a $5 donation is requested for non-Nature Conservancy members. At the parking lot there is a visitor center with a gift and book shop, and many hummingbird feeders are hung on the grounds to attract the birds. From the parking lot, two trails lead up into the canyon. The 0.7-mile nature loop is quite easy, and the longer Hamburg Trail climbs high into the Huachucas. You have to register at the visitor center to use the trails.

If you wish to stay on the preserve overnight, the *Ramsey Canyon Inn B&B* (☎ 520-378-3010), 27 Ramsey Canyon Rd, Hereford, AZ 85615, has two housekeeping cabins and six B&B rooms. These are often booked a year ahead for the peak summer season, and reservations are always necessary. Rates range from $105 to $135. Minimum two- or three-night stays may be required in the busy season. If the Inn is full, Sierra Vista is just 10 miles away.

Coronado National Memorial
US history as often taught in US schools tends to begin with the pilgrims and very slowly moves west. Earlier incursions of Spain into the Southwest during the 16th century are generally ignored. The Coronado National Memorial fills in some of those gaps between Native American prehistory and Anglo history. Francisco Vásquez de Coronado, accompanied by hundreds of Spanish soldiers and Mexican Indians, passed through here in 1540 on his way from Mexico City, searching for gold in the Seven Cities of Cibola. This was the first major European expedition into the Southwest, and Coronado is credited with introducing horses to the Indians.

The memorial is at the southern end of the Huachuca Mountains on the Mexican border, 20 miles south of Sierra Vista on Hwy 92. The visitor center (☎ 520-366-5515) is open from 8 am to 5 pm daily except Thanksgiving and Christmas and has exhibits on Coronado's expedition as well as the area's wildlife. The memorial itself is open during daylight hours and admission is free.

The road from Sierra Vista to the visitor center is paved. West from the visitor center (at 5300 feet), an unpaved road climbs over the 6575-foot-high Montezuma Pass, offering great views. A 3.3-mile hiking trail also links these two points. From the pass, a 0.7-mile trail climbs to Coronado Peak (6864 feet) with great views into Mexico and, if the weather is clear, to Baboquivari Peak, 80 miles west. West of the pass, an unpaved road goes through the Coronado National Forest emerging at Nogales, Mexico, about 50 miles away. This road is passable to cars except after rain. A detailed description of the drive is given in Annerino's *Adventuring in Arizona*.

There is no camping in the memorial, but you can camp for free almost anywhere in the Coronado National Forest to the west. *Lakeview* is a developed USFS campground at **Parker Canyon Lake**, reached by driving west from the memorial or south from Sonoita on Hwy 83; both roads are unpaved. At the lake is a marina (☎ 520-455-5847) with boat rentals and fishing supplies. A 5-mile hiking trail encircles the lake. There are 65 camping sites with water but no hookups for $10, available on a first-come, first-served basis. Day use is $5.

San Pedro Riparian National Conservation Area

About 95% of Arizona's riparian habitat has disappeared, victim to poor grazing practices, logging for firewood, dropping water tables and development. Loss of this habitat has endangered many species' existence, and about 10% of the more than 500 species on the Endangered Species List are found along the San Pedro River. Clearly, this is valuable habitat. Almost 400 species of birds, more than 80 species of mammals and about 47 species of reptiles and amphibians have been recorded along the 40-mile stretch of the San Pedro within the conservation area.

This is the healthiest riparian ecosystem in the Southwest and is part of the Nature Conservancy's 'Last Great Places' Program. The San Pedro is also the longest (remaining undammed) river in Arizona, and developers and ranchers have their eyes on it.

The conservation area is currently managed by the BLM (☎ 520-458-3559), 1763 Paseo San Luis, Sierra Vista, AZ 85635, which can give information. Several roads to the area cross the river east of Sierra Vista. Hwy 82 crosses the river at **Fairbank**, a ghost town with a picnic area (railroad passengers from Benson stop here) and a volunteer BLM host who supplies information during daylight hours. Hwy 90 crosses the river at San Pedro House, a 1930s ranch that now houses an information center and bookshop run by the Friends of the San Pedro River (☎ 520-459-2555). It's open daily from 9:30 am to 4:30 pm.

Further south, there's a parking area where Hereford Rd crosses the river. From all three points, hiking trails extend north and south along the river and are ideal for birding. The Southeastern Arizona Bird Observatory (SABO, see Bisbee, later in this chapter) does **birding tours** of the area.

Permits for **backcountry camping** cost $2 per day and are available at self-pay stations at parking areas. You must camp at least 1 mile away from roads and parking areas.

The closest accommodation is at *Casa de San Pedro B&B* (☎ 520-366-1300, fax 520-366-0701, casadesanpedro@theriver .com), 8933 S Yell Lane, Hereford, AZ 85615, near the river off Hereford Road. They have 10 comfortable rooms with private bath for $95 to $115 a double, including full breakfast and homemade pie during the day. SABO workshops are sometimes held here, and the inn is popular with birders; guides can be arranged for about $120 for a full day for two people. Another similarly priced choice is the rustic *San Pedro River Inn* (☎ 520-366-5532), 8326 S Hereford Rd, Hereford, AZ

85615, with four housekeeping cottages about 2 miles east of the river.

TOMBSTONE

Despite being told by friends that all he would find would be his own tombstone, prospector Ed Schieffelin braved the dangers of Apache attack and struck it rich. The year was 1877, and a rip-roaring, brawling, silver-mining town appeared very quickly. In 1881, 110 saloon licenses were sold, and there were 14 dance halls for the entertainment of the get-rich-quick miners. By then the population was 10,000 and Tombstone became the Cochise County seat. The famous shootout at the OK Corral also took place in 1881, during which the brothers Earp and Doc Holliday gunned down three members of the Clanton cowboy gang. This was one of dozens of gunfights in Tombstone, but it so caught people's imagination that it now is perhaps the most famous shootout in history.

Wyatt Earp

Tombstone was typical of southwestern mining towns of the period. Saloons, gambling halls and bordellos made up a good portion of the buildings, but there were, as always, a sprinkling of sober citizens running newspapers, businesses and banks. The silver-mining boom was short-lived and declining silver prices and floods in the mines closed down the last operation in the early 1900s. Most other boomtowns in this situation became ghost towns, but Tombstone, nicknamed the 'Town Too Tough to Die,' continued to be a commercial center and the seat of Cochise County until the seat moved to Bisbee in 1929.

After WWII, the growing population of Arizona gave Tombstone a new vitality; the old county courthouse opened as a museum in the 1950s. Tombstone became a National Historic Landmark in 1962 and now attracts large crowds of tourists who visit the town's old Western buildings, most of which are now gift shops. Reenactments of gunfights and other late 1800s events provide entertainment.

Tombstone is 4539 feet above sea level (usually about 7°F cooler than Tucson) and has 1300 residents, who are often outnumbered by tourists on a busy day.

Information

The Visitor and Information Center (☎ 520-457-3929, 800-457-3423) at the corner of 4th and Allen Sts, and the chamber of commerce (☎ 520-457-9317, 888-471-5588, 888-457-3929, fax 520-457-2458), on 4th St next door to the center, provide tourist information. Both are staffed by volunteers and open from 9 am to some time in the afternoon daily.

The library (☎ 520-457-3612) is at 4th St and Toughnut. The post office (☎ 520-457-3479) is at 516 E Allen St. The police (☎ 520-457-2244) are by the City Hall at 315 E Fremont St.

The OK Corral & Around

The OK Corral, site of the famous gunfight, still stands and is now the heart of both historic and touristic Tombstone, as well as the first stop for most visitors. The

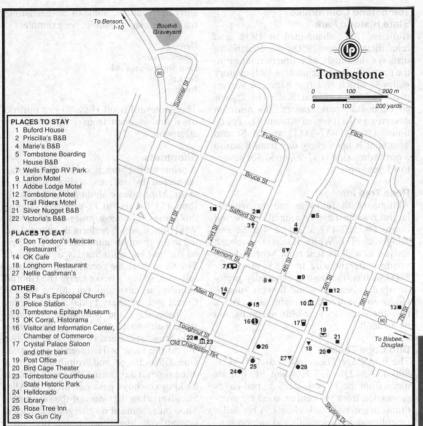

To Benson,
I-10

Boothill
Graveyard

Tombstone

0   100   200 m
0   100   200 yards

PLACES TO STAY
1 Buford House
2 Priscilla's B&B
4 Marie's B&B
5 Tombstone Boarding
   House B&B
7 Wells Fargo RV Park
9 Larion Motel
11 Adobe Lodge Motel
12 Tombstone Motel
13 Trail Riders Motel
21 Silver Nugget B&B
22 Victoria's B&B

PLACES TO EAT
6 Don Teodoro's Mexican
   Restaurant
14 OK Cafe
18 Longhorn Restaurant
27 Nellie Cashman's

OTHER
3 St Paul's Episcopal Church
8 Police Station
10 Tombstone Epitaph Museum
15 OK Corral, Historama
16 Visitor and Information Center,
   Chamber of Commerce
17 Crystal Palace Saloon
   and other bars
19 Post Office
20 Bird Cage Theater
23 Tombstone Courthouse
   State Historic Park
24 Helldorado
25 Library
26 Rose Tree Inn
28 Six Gun City

Summer St

Fulton

Fitch

Bruce St

Safford St

Fremont St

Allen St

Toughnut St

Old Charleston Rd

Skyline Dr

To Bisbee,
Douglas

ARIZONA

OK Corral (☎ 520-457-3456, okcorral@ ok-corral.com), on Allen St between 3rd and 4th Sts, is open from 9 am to 5 pm daily; admission is $2.50 (free for children under six) and you can see models of the gunfighters and numerous other Western exhibits. The most interesting is CS Fly's early photography studio. Next door is **Historama** with 26-minute presentations of Tombstone's history using animated figures, movies and narration (by Vincent Price). There is an additional cost of $2.50, and showings are on the hour between 9 am and 4 pm.

A $5 combined ticket gets you into both attractions plus the **Tombstone Epitaph Museum** (☎ 520-457-2211), 5th and Fremont Sts, which houses the presses of the town's first newspaper. Hours are 9 am to 5 pm daily; admission is $1 (unless you have the combo ticket) and includes a replica of the October 27, 1881 edition of the *Tombstone Epitaph*. This reports the gunfight in detail and also contains various period ads, including one for GF Spangenberg, a gun dealer at 4th and Allen Sts. The business still operates today, selling both modern and antique weapons.

Tombstone Courthouse
State Historic Park
Built in 1882, abandoned in 1931, and rehabilitated in the 1950s, the courthouse displays thousands of artifacts relating to the town's history, including a 19th-century gallows, which will (for better or worse) pique children's interest. Staffed by knowledgeable state park rangers, this museum deserves a visit if you're in town. The courthouse (☎ 520-457-3311) at 3rd St and Toughnut is open every day from 8 am to 5 pm. Admission is $2.50, or $1 for seven-to 13-year-olds.

Rose Tree Inn
Antique 1880s furniture and the world's largest rosebush can be seen at this period house (☎ 520-457-3326) at 4th St and Toughnut. The White Banksia rosebush arrived as a shoot sent from Scotland to a young emigrant wife in 1885; now over 8000 sq feet, the bush is especially pretty in April, when the white flowers bloom. Hours are 9 am to 5 pm; admission is $2, free for under-15-year-olds accompanied by an adult.

Bird Cage Theater
The Bird Cage Theater (☎ 520-457-3421, 800-457-3423), 517 E Allen St, got its name from the 14 bed-sized, draped cages suspended from the ceiling, used by prostitutes to entertain their clients. A bordello, gambling den, dance hall and saloon during the 1880s, this was the wildest place in the West in those days, and you can see it for $3.50 per person, with discounts for children or families/groups. Hours are from 8 am to 6 pm daily.

St Paul's Episcopal Church
Located at the corner of Safford and 3rd Sts, this is Arizona's oldest non-Catholic church, dating from 1881.

Boothill Graveyard
One of the few places you can see for free in this tourist town (though you have to enter through a gift shop!), this cemetery holds the graves of many of Tombstone's early desperadoes. Some of the headstones make interesting reading, for example:

Here lies
Lester Moore
Four slugs from a .44
No Les
No more.

The graveyard is off Hwy 80 just north of town and is open from 7:30 am to late afternoon.

Shootouts
A prime tourist attraction, the shootouts are reenacted by various acting troupes in town. Most charge about $3 or $4 for the show ($1 for six- to 12-year-olds) though this varies. The most professional are the Wild Bunch, which perform the events leading to the shootout at the OK Corral at 2 pm on the first and third Sunday of the month. The show is at the corral itself, and often sells out, so buy a ticket early. The Boothill Gunslingers also shoot it out at the OK Corral at 2 pm every Friday and Saturday.

On Sundays, the Tombstone Vigilantes stage their shootout at 2 pm on the Helldorado Stage at the end of 4th St. Other outfits do the same at Helldorado and at Six Gun City, 5th St and Toughnut, two or three times a day during the week. Rough-looking cowboys pass out fliers on Allen St, advertising the times of the next show. Shootouts, some at no charge, occur spontaneously at other times, especially during the various special events during the year.

Organized Tours
You can ride a stagecoach around town while listening to narration by local guides, many of whom trace their ancestors back to the Old West. Tombstone Stage Coach (☎ 520-457-3191, 800-262-2457, fax 520-457-3097) and Old Tombstone Historical Tours (☎ 520-457-3018) both are easily found downtown.

Special Events
Tombstone's events revolve around weekends of Western fun with shootouts (of course!), stagecoach rides, chili cook-offs,

fiddling contests, 'vigilette' fashion shows, mock hangings and melodramas. The biggest event is Helldorado Days over the third weekend in October. Other events are Territorial Days (variable dates in March), Wyatt Earp Days (Memorial Day weekend), Vigilante Days (second weekend in August) and Rendezvous of the Gunfighters (Labor Day weekend).

Places to Stay – Camping
Tombstone KOA (☎ 520-457-3829), 1½ miles north on Hwy 80, has a pool, playground, showers, laundry and more than 80 tent and RV sites from $19 to $25. Kamping Kabins are $28. *Wells Fargo RV Park* (☎ 520-457-3966), 3rd and Fremont Sts, allows tents and has about 60 sites at $18 for full hookups. Both places fill quickly from October to March; reservations are advised.

Places to Stay – Budget
There are no very cheap motels in Tombstone, and all of them raise their rates during special events, when demand is high and reservations are recommended. Summer rates are usually the lowest.

The recently reconditioned *Larion Motel* (☎/fax 520-457-2272, larianmotel@theriver .com), 410 E Fremont St, has nine very clean rooms with coffeemakers, most with two beds, for $40 to $55 a double. The *Trail Riders Motel* (☎ 520-457-3573, 800-574-0417, fax 520-457-3049), 13 N 7th St, has 14 plain but reasonably sized rooms with two beds for $40 to $55 for one to four people in winter, $5 less in summer. The charge is $70 per room for special event weekends.

The *Adobe Lodge Motel* (☎ 520-457-2241, 888-457-2241), 505 E Fremont St, has 21 adequate rooms for $50 to $60 a double ($70 for special events), including a few larger units for $70 to $125. Nearby, the *Tombstone Motel* (☎ 520-457-3478, 888-455-4578, tombstonemotel@theriver .com), 502 E Fremont St, has 12 decent rooms at $45 to $55 single and $50 to $70 double in winter, $10 less in summer. They have one 'suite.'

Places to Stay – Middle
Motels The most comfortable motel is on Hwy 80 a mile north of downtown at the *Best Western Lookout Lodge* (☎ 520-457-2223, fax 520-457-3870), which has a pool, nice views and 40 good-size rooms for $55 to $80, including continental breakfast.

B&Bs All the following serve a full, hot breakfast unless otherwise indicated. *Priscilla's B&B* (☎ 520-457-3844, prisc@theriver.com), 101 N 3rd St, PO Box 700, Tombstone, AZ 85638, a two-story Victorian clapboard house dating from 1904, has three rooms, each with a sink and shared bathroom for $40/55 for single/double occupancy; one suite (a room with a queen-size bed and another with two singles) with private bath is $69 double.

The 1880 *Buford House* (☎ 520-457-3969, 800-263-6762, bufordbb@primenet .com), 113 E Safford St, Tombstone, AZ 85638, has five antique-filled rooms, three with sinks and shared bathrooms, two with private bathrooms and one with a fireplace, for $65 to $95. No smoking is allowed inside.

Marie's B&B (☎ 520-457-3831, maries@theriver.com), 101 N 4th St, PO Box 744, Tombstone, AZ 85638, is a 1906 adobe house. Two pretty guest rooms are separated by a shared bathroom and both open onto an attractive parlor for guest use. The larger room, with a king-size bed, is $65 and the smaller room, with a double bed, is $55 in winter, with seasonal changes. Breakfast is a choice of American in the B&B or a voucher for a Mexican breakfast at nearby Don Teodoro's Mexican Restaurant.

Victoria's B&B (☎ 520-457-3677, 800-952-8216, vsbb@primenet.com), at 211 Toughnut, PO Box 37, Tombstone, AZ 85368, dates from 1880 and has a checkered past featuring gamblers, judges and ghosts. Nowadays, it has a private wedding chapel (!) and the owner will arrange for a minister if you bring a partner and the wedding license. Three rooms with private bath rent for $65 double, $75 during special events and less if you stay two or more nights.

Silver Nugget B&B (☎ 520-457-9223, fax 520-457-3471), 520 E Allen St, PO Box 268, Tombstone, AZ 85638, is upstairs over the Silver Nugget Ice Cream Parlor and gift shop. From your rocker on the old-fashioned wooden balcony you can watch the busy Allen St activities. Two rooms with shared bath are $60 and two with private bath are $75 double. A common room with TV provides balcony access and one $75 room has private access. Breakfast is continental (pastries, cereal, juice and hot beverage).

Tombstone Boarding House B&B (☎ 520-457-3716, fax 520-457-3038), 108 N 4th St, PO Box 906, Tombstone, AZ 85638, is in two restored 1880s adobe homes. Eight bedrooms with private baths are furnished with period pieces and rent for $65 to $80 double.

Places to Eat
Nellie Cashman's (☎ 520-457-2212), 5th St and Toughnut, dates from 1882. Nellie was a tough Irishwoman who stood no nonsense but helped out many a miner down on his luck. This is a no-alcohol establishment and serves excellent home-style meals from 7 am to 9 pm daily. Huge hamburger plates are around $5 and steaks are in the $11 to $16 range. Chicken, pork, fish and spaghetti are also served in the quietly charming dining room. For something a little wilder, the popular *Longhorn Restaurant* (☎ 520-457-3405), 5th and Allen Sts, serves American and Mexican breakfast, lunch and dinner. Tourists line up outside the door at lunchtime.

For the most authentic Mexican food, *Don Teodoro's Mexican Restaurant* (☎ 520-457-3647), 15 N 4th St, is a hole-in-the-wall kind of place with good, inexpensive food served from 6 am to 9 pm daily. For buffalo, ostrich and emu burgers and other American delights, the *OK Cafe*, 220 E Allen St, opens from 7 am to 2 pm daily.

Entertainment
Several bars along Allen St have old Wild West ambiance. The best kept of these is the *Crystal Palace Saloon*, at 5th and Allen

Sts, which dates from 1879; nearby establishments are pretty similar. There's not much else to do in the evening but go on a pub crawl – or perhaps that should be a saloon stagger.

BISBEE AREA
Bisbee is just 24 miles south of Tombstone. Both towns began in the late 1870s as mining towns, and both share a similar wild early history. The difference between the two lies in what was mined. Tombstone had silver, which fizzled out in the 1890s, while Bisbee had copper, which became Arizona's most important industry. Accordingly, as Tombstone faltered, Bisbee grew. By 1910 Bisbee had 25,000 inhabitants, making it the biggest city between El Paso, Texas, and San Francisco, California. In 1929, the Cochise County seat moved from Tombstone to Bisbee.

Residents built many elegant Victorian brick buildings, reminiscent of the East Coast and reasonably suited to the cooler 5300-foot elevation of Bisbee. The town was built in a narrow canyon, and soon there was no room for more construction. Today, many of the buildings in town date from the heyday of the early 20th century, and Bisbee has more of a Victorian feel to it than any other town in Arizona. Copper mining declined after WWII and the mine closed in 1975, when production became unprofitable. Paradoxically, the mines here produced more gold and silver than any other mine in Arizona, but Bisbee is still thought of as an old copper-mining town.

Bisbee's pleasant climate and old-fashioned ambiance attracted artists and the artistically inclined, and now the town is an intriguing mix of aging miners and gallery owners, ex-hippies and artists. It has more of an upscale air than Tombstone. Whereas Tombstone thrives on gunfight reenactments, Bisbee offers mine tours, which are more relevant and realistic. The population is almost 7000.

Orientation
The steep canyon walls encompassing Old Bisbee make the town's layout rather

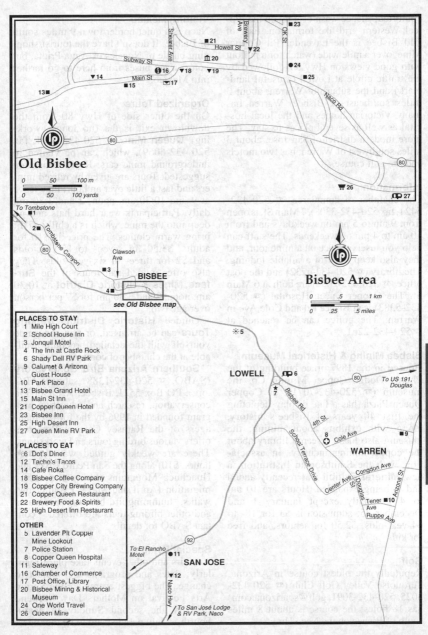

Old Bisbee

```
0    50    100 m
0    50    100 yards
```

To Tombstone

Clawson Ave

BISBEE

see Old Bisbee map

Bisbee Area

```
0    .5    1 km
0    .25    .5 miles
```

LOWELL

To US 191,
Douglas

WARREN

To El Rancho
Motel

SAN JOSE

To San José Lodge
& RV Park, Naco

To Bisbee
Rd

Naco Hwy

School Terrace Drive

Center Ave
Douglas

Congdon Ave

Arizona St

Tener
Ave

Ruppe Ave

4th St

Cole Ave

PLACES TO STAY
1   Mile High Court
2   School House Inn
3   Jonquil Motel
4   The Inn at Castle Rock
6   Shady Dell RV Park
9   Calumet & Arizona
    Guest House
10 Park Place
13 Bisbee Grand Hotel
15 Main St Inn
21 Copper Queen Hotel
23 Bisbee Inn
25 High Desert Inn
27 Queen Mine RV Park

PLACES TO EAT
6   Dot's Diner
12 Tacho's Tacos
14 Cafe Roka
18 Bisbee Coffee Company
19 Copper City Brewing Company
21 Copper Queen Restaurant
22 Brewery Food & Spirits
25 High Desert Inn Restaurant

OTHER
5   Lavender Pit Copper
    Mine Lookout
7   Police Station
8   Copper Queen Hospital
11 Safeway
16 Chamber of Commerce
17 Post Office, Library
20 Bisbee Mining & Historical
    Museum
24 One World Travel
26 Queen Mine

ARIZONA

contorted; Bisbee wasn't set up on the typical Western grid-like formation. East of Old Bisbee is the Lavender Pit Copper Mine, over a mile wide (watch for a pullout with good views on Hwy 80) followed by the traffic circle at Lowell (a useful landmark) and the suburb of Warren, about 3 miles southeast of Bisbee. Warren has many Victorian homes and the local hospital as well as several places to stay. The more modern district of San Jose, about 3 miles southwest of Warren, has two motels and the golf course.

Information
The chamber of commerce (☎ 520-432-5421, fax 520-432-3308), 7 Main St, is open from 9 am to 5 pm on weekdays and from 10 am to 4 pm on weekends. The staff can help you reserve space on a mine tour, and they also keep track of available lodging. The library (☎ 520-432-4232) and the post office (☎ 520-432-2052) are both at 6 Main St. The Copper Queen Hospital (☎ 520-432-5383) is at Bisbee Rd and Cole Ave in Warren. The police can be reached at ☎ 520-432-2261.

Bisbee Mining & Historical Museum
Housed in the 1897 office building of the Phelps Dodge Copper Mining Co, the museum (☎ 520-432-7071), at Copper Queen Plaza, has a fine display depicting the first 40 years of Bisbee's history, along with exhibits about mining; the museum also has a research library about the copper-mining industry. In association with the Smithsonian Institution, a new **Mineral Exhibit** was recently added and is being expanded. Hours are 10 am to 4 pm daily except January 1 and December 25; admission is $3 for 18- to 64-year-olds, $2.50 for seniors, and free for kids.

Golf
Reputedly the oldest course in Arizona, Turquoise Valley Golf Club (☎ 520-432-3025, 520-432-3091, golf@soarizona.com) has 18 holes; the course is about 8 miles south of Bisbee on the Naco Hwy.

Visiting Mexico
Naco is a quiet border town 9 miles south of Bisbee. It doesn't have the tourist/shopping bustle of Nogales or Agua Prieta, but you can get buses from here to go farther into Mexico.

Organized Tours
On the other side of Hwy 80 from the downtown exit is the (no longer working) **Queen Mine** (☎ 520-432-2071, fax 520-432-6069), which can be visited in underground mine cars. Reservations are suggested. Tours are given by retired miners and last a little over an hour; they leave at 9 and 10:30 am, noon, 2 and 3:30 pm daily. Participants wear hard hats and go deep into the mine, which is a chilly 47°F; bring warm clothes. The price is $10 for adults, $3.50 for seven- to 15-year-olds and $2 for three- to six-year-olds. They also offer guided van tours of the **Surface Mines & Historic District** at 10:30 am, noon, 2 and 3:30 pm for $7 per person over age two.

Guided **Historic District Walking Tours** can be arranged, or you can guide yourself with the detailed brochure available at the chamber of commerce.

Southern Arizona Bird Observatory (SABO, ☎ 520-432-1388, sabo@SABO .org), PO Box 5521, Bisbee, AZ 85603, a conservation, research and education program founded in 1996 by the former managers of the Ramsey Canyon Preserve, offers various birding tours and workshops. There are weekly guided walks (three hours, $10) along the San Pedro River and Huachuca Mountains during the spring migration (April and May). Evening owl walks, hummingbird-banding programs and other birding tours are offered – contact SABO for details.

Special Events
Art fairs and other events take place regularly; dates and programs are subject to change. The biggest events are the Spring Arts Festival on Mothers Day weekend (usually the second Sunday in May), Fourth of July parade (said to be the oldest

in the state), a poetry festival in August, Brewery Gulch Days over Labor Day weekend and a Home Tour over Thanksgiving weekend.

Places to Stay
Bisbee, at 5300 feet, is a year-round destination, hot but not baking in summer, cold but not frozen in winter. Therefore there are no high or low seasons; however, most beds are full on weekends and you definitely need reservations for special events or holiday weekends. Most accommodations are historic hotels or B&Bs in older houses; there are no modern chain motels.

Camping Many sites are taken by long-term visitors in winter, when reservations are strongly recommended. *Queen Mine RV Park* (☎ 520-432-5006) next to the Queen Mine, has 25 RV sites with hookups for $16. *Turquoise Valley Golf & RV Park* (☎ 520-432-3091), by the golf course in Naco, has 100 RV sites with hookups for $15.

San Jose Lodge & RV Park (see Hotels & Motels) has 25 RV spaces with hookups for $14. The *El Rancho Motel* also has RV hookups. *Double Adobe RV Park & Campground* (☎ 520-364-4000, 800-694-4242, doubleadobe@theriver.com), 4 miles southeast of Lowell along Hwy 80, then 4 miles on Double Adobe Rd, has showers, trap shooting and a birding list (a list of birds for birders). Tent camping is $7.50/10 for one/two people; RV sites with hookups are $14.

Hotels & Motels The *Jonquil Motel* (☎ 520-432-7371), 317 Tombstone Canyon, is the closest budget place to Old Bisbee with seven older but clean nonsmoking rooms at $35 to $45, and free coffee to enjoy on the little patio in the morning.

Budget motel rooms are also available at the *San Jose Lodge & RV Park* (☎ 520-432-5761, fax 520-432-4226), 1002 Naco Hwy (1½ miles from Hwy 92), with 43 modern rooms, a seasonal pool and a restaurant and lounge serving inexpensive Mexican and American food from 7 am to

Vintage Vacation
One of the most unusual places to stay in Bisbee is the *Shady Dell RV Park* (☎ 520-432-3567, 520-432-4858), 1 Douglas Rd at the Lowell traffic circle, which rents seven antique aluminum camping trailers. Among the lineup is a 1949 Airstream, a 1951 Spartan Royal Mansion and others from the 1940s and 1950s. They have been restored and fitted out with refrigerators and propane stoves; dishes and bedding are provided. Most of them do not have their own showers and bathrooms. Trailers will sleep from one to four people and rent for $25 to $55. If you have your own rig, a few RV hookups are available and tent camping is possible.

Also on the premises is *Dot's Diner* (☎ 520-432-2046), an authentic 1957 Valentine 10-stool dining trailer where you can have a burger or milkshake – it's not fast food. Hours are 6:30 am to 2 pm, Tuesday to Friday, and 7 am to 3 pm on Saturday. ■

9 pm. Rates are $45 to $50 for a double. *El Rancho Motel* (☎ 520-432-2293, fax 520-432-7738), 1104 Hwy 92 (3½ miles from the Lowell traffic circle) has 39 rooms starting at $42 for a double, or more for a kitchenette and sitting area.

Downtown, the *Copper Queen Hotel* (☎ 520-432-2216, 800-247-5829, fax 520-432-4298), 11 Howell St, was built in 1902 and was Bisbee's most famous hotel. It still retains its turn-of-the-century feel throughout. The 45 old-fashioned rooms are furnished with antiques, vary in size and comfort, and rent at $70 to $105. There is an outdoor swimming pool, a saloon that harks back to mining days, and an award-winning dining room.

Also downtown, the *High Desert Inn* (☎ 520-432-1442, 800-281-0510, fax 520-432-1410), 8 Naco Rd, has five comfortable rooms in contemporary European style, though the building itself was the county jail back in 1901. The hotel also

ARIZONA

houses an exclusive restaurant (dinners only). Room rates are $65 to $90.

B&Bs A number of beautiful older homes and hotels offer B&B accommodations in and around town. B&Bs come and go in Bisbee, so call ahead to check. These are generally nonsmoking places.

The *Bisbee Grand Hotel* (☎ 520-432-5900, 800-421-1909), 61 Main St, PO Box 825, Bisbee, AZ 85603, is of the red-velvet and stuffed-peacock school of elegance – definitely Victorian though some rooms have different themes. There is a billiards room and a Western saloon for relaxation. There are eight rooms, all with private baths (though two of them are detached baths) ranging from $69 to $85 double, and three suites are $100 to $125, including full breakfast.

Once an 1888 boarding house for miners, the *Main Street Inn* (☎ 520-432-1202, 800-467-5237), 26 Main St, PO Box 433, Bisbee AZ 85603, is a bit more upscale now, with Southwestern décor and rates in the $49 to $65 range for seven rooms sharing four bathrooms, and $95 to $105 for two rooms with private bath, including continental breakfast buffet.

The *Bisbee Inn* (☎ 520-432-5131, 888-432-5131), 45 OK St, PO Box 1855, Bisbee AZ 85603, is a 20-room hotel built in 1916, when rates were $2 a night or $8 a week. Renovated in 1996, the antique-filled hotel now charges $65 to $75 a double for 15 rooms with private bath, or $50 for five rooms with shared bath. The delicious breakfast is all-you-can-eat.

The *Inn at Castle Rock* (☎ 520-432-4449, 800-566-4449, fax 520-432-7868, castlerock@theriver.com), 112 Tombstone Canyon, PO Box 1161, Bisbee, AZ 85603, is a fire-engine-red building at the edge of downtown. Inside the 1890 building are 14 eclectically decorated rooms, all with private bath as well as a lounge bar with a fireplace, an art gallery, gardens and a restaurant named *Eccentricity's* – a friendly but offbeat place to stay. Rates are $58 to $87 for a double depending on room size (some are 'cozy') and they include full

breakfast. You can eat dinner as well by prior arrangement.

Almost 2 miles from downtown, up a hill, the *School House Inn* (☎ 520-432-2996, 800-537-4333), 818 Tombstone Canyon, PO Box 32, Bisbee, AZ 85603, built in 1918 as a school, now has nine attractive guest rooms following themes such as the Principal's Office and the Writing Room. Rates are $55 to $75 a double with full breakfast. All rooms have private baths. Further up is *Mile High Court* (☎ 520-432-4636), 901 Tombstone Canyon, PO Box 23, Bisbee, AZ 85603, near the upper entrance from Hwy 92. Three large rooms with kitchenettes are $50 to $55 and a regular room is $45, all with private baths and continental breakfast.

In the historical suburb of Warren is the *Calumet & Arizona Guest House* (☎ 520-432-4815), 608 Powell, Bisbee, AZ 85603, a grand house built in 1906 for an official in the Calumet & Arizona Mining Company. Now there are six spacious, old-fashioned but comfortable rooms, two with private bath and four sharing two baths, for $60 to $70 double. Also in Warren, *Park Place* (☎ 520-432-3054, 800-388-4388), 200 East Vista, Bisbee, AZ 85603, has four modern and pretty rooms, three with balconies, two with private baths, for $50 to $70 double. Both these B&Bs serve excellent full breakfasts.

Places to Eat
There are not many places for dinner, especially Monday and Tuesday, so plan ahead.

The popular, airy and modern *Copper City Brewing Company* (☎ 520-432-7787) in Copper Queen Plaza, serves moderately priced ($5 to $9) soups, salads, sandwiches and pastas along with microbrews from 11 am to 6 pm on Wednesday and Thursday, to 10 pm on Friday and Saturday and to 5 pm on Sunday. Also in this plaza, *Bisbee Coffee Company* (☎ 520-432-7879) serves mainly coffees and some sandwiches from 7:30 am to 9 pm daily except Mondays, when they close at 6 pm.

Brewery Food & Spirits (☎ 520-432-3317), 15 Brewery Ave, in a Victorian building, has a fine, mainly meaty menu ranging from mesquite burgers for $7 to 22-ounce porterhouse steaks for $20. It's open daily from 11 am to 3 pm and 5 to 9 pm.

The best restaurant is *Cafe Roka* (☎ 520-432-5153), 35 Main St, whose excellent and innovative dinners are available only from 5 to 9 pm, Wednesday to Saturday. The menu changes often, but it's basically a limited gourmet American selection in the $11 to $19 range, including soup and salad. They have Sunday jazz evenings with a limited light menu.

Good hotel restaurants include the elegant old *Copper Queen Hotel Restaurant*, open daily from 7 am to 2:30 pm and from 5:30 to 9 pm. It serves good American food, with dinner entrées in the $15 to $20 range. The *High Desert Inn Restaurant* has received good reviews for its fine dinners, served only from 5 to 9.30 pm, Thursday to Saturday, and its Sunday brunch.

For Mexican food, the best is said to be *Tacho's Tacos* (☎ 520-432-7811), 115 Naco Hwy, open from 9 am to 9 pm daily (till 8 pm on Sunday). You won't find fast food in Bisbee, though there is a *Burger King* (☎ 520-432 3007) at the Safeway Plaza on Hwy 92. This is the place to buy groceries; for a late-night food emergency, the Circle K store next to the Jonquil Motel is open 24 hours.

Shopping
The best stores are in the center of Old Bisbee, and many exhibit and sell the work of local artists. The quality is mixed, but the discerning eye may discover an as-yet-undiscovered artist here. It's worth a browse if you are looking for Western art, jewelry or crafts.

Getting There & Away
Los Rapidos has five daily buses between Douglas and Tucson (via Sierra Vista), three continuing to Phoenix. Buy tickets at One World Travel (☎ 520-432-5359), 7 OK St.

DOUGLAS & AROUND
James Douglas of the Phelps Dodge Co founded this town on the Mexican border

in 1901 and built a copper smelter here. Production ceased in 1987, and Douglas, along with its much larger sister city of Agua Prieta in Mexico, has become a ranching and manufacturing center. The downtown area looks pre-WWII without the hoopla of Bisbee or Tombstone. The population is about 15,000, but another 100,000 people live across the border in Agua Prieta. Many Mexicans work in Douglas. The elevation here is 4000 feet.

Information
The chamber of commerce (☎ 520-364-2477, 888-315-9999, fax 520-364-6304), 1125 Pan American Ave, is open from 9 am to 5 pm Monday to Friday. The Coronado National Forest Douglas Ranger Station (☎ 520-364-3468, 520-364-3231), Leslie Canyon Rd, is open from 7:30 am to 4:30 pm Monday to Friday.

The library (☎ 520-364-3851) is at 560 10th St. The post office (☎ 520-364-3631) is at 601 10th St. The hospital (☎ 520-364-7931) is 4 miles west of Douglas. The police (☎ 520-364-8422) are at 300 14th St.

Gadsden Hotel
Established in 1907, the hotel (see Places to Stay, below) is on the National Register of Historic Places. The lobby is one of the most opulent turn-of-the-19th-century public areas to be seen in Arizona. A white Italian marble staircase and marble pillars with gold-leaf decorations, a superb 42-foot Tiffany stained-glass Southwestern mural and vaulted stained-glass skylights combine for an elegant surprise. It's well worth a visit even if you aren't staying here.

Other Attractions
The **Douglas/Williams House Museum** (☎ 520-364-7370), 10th St at D Ave, houses local historical exhibits in a 1909 house. Hours are 1 to 4 pm, Tuesday, Wednesday, Thursday and Saturday. Call for tours. This museum is on the corner of **Church Square Park**, unique in the USA for having a church on each corner of this block north of the park. The local **Art Gallery**, 625 10th St, is in a 1902 building and is

ARIZONA

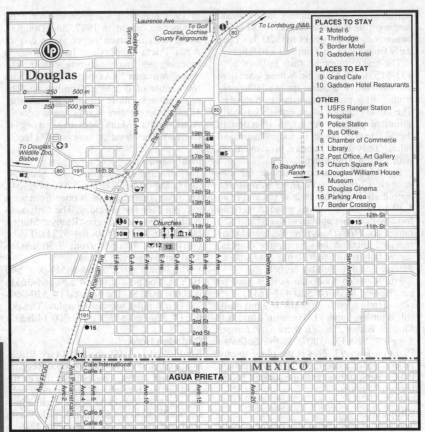

Douglas

0   250   500 m

0   250   500 yards

AGUA PRIETA

MEXICO

PLACES TO STAY
2   Motel 6
4   Thriftlodge
5   Border Motel
10 Gadsden Hotel

PLACES TO EAT
9   Grand Cafe
10 Gadsden Hotel Restaurants

OTHER
1   USFS Ranger Station
3   Hospital
6   Police Station
7   Bus Office
8   Chamber of Commerce
11 Library
12 Post Office, Art Gallery
13 Church Square Park
14 Douglas/Williams House Museum
15 Douglas Cinema
16 Parking Area
17 Border Crossing

open 10 am to 4 pm. The small **Douglas Wildlife Zoo** (☎ 520-364-2515), 4 miles west of town, is open 10 am to 5 pm (closed major holidays); admission is $3 or $2 for three- to 12-year-olds. See Places to Stay, below, for **golf**.

Visiting Mexico

Agua Prieta is a big border town and you can enter from Arizona on foot. The atmosphere is much more leisurely and relaxed than Nogales and you'll find a selection of gift shops (no bargaining) and restaurants. From the international border, walk south six blocks to Calle 6 and turn left for two blocks to the church and plaza, which are pleasant.

The Douglas Chamber of Commerce arranges free walking/shopping/lunch tours into Mexico leaving from the chamber at 10 am – call to reserve a spot. If you go alone, park at 3rd St and Pan American Ave.

Agua Prieta hotels are few in number and not especially cheap. Buses go from here to the rest of Mexico. If you are driving into Mexico, interesting day trips or overnights include visiting Nuevo Casa Grandes (125 miles), where there are decent motels.

Nearby are the 1000-year-old ruins of Paquimé, the largest archaeological site in northern Mexico. Another possibility is a 300-mile-roundtrip drive that passes numerous colonial churches – but there are no hotels. The chamber has details. (See the Crossing the Border sidebar in the Tucson & Southern Arizona chapter.)

John Slaughter Ranch & San Bernardino National Wildlife Refuge

This was one of the largest and most successful ranches of the late 1800s. The ranch buildings have been restored to their original appearance, and the ranch is now on the National Register of Historic Places. Photo exhibits and a movie show what life was like on the property a century ago. The ranch (☎ 520-558-2474) is 16 miles east of Douglas (leave town via 15th St) along a gravel road paralleling the border. Hours are from 10 am to 3 pm, Wednesday to Sunday, and admission is $3 for those over 14.

The former ranchlands are now a wildlife refuge. For information, call the NWR headquarters (☎ 520-364-2104), 7628 N Hwy 191.

Special Events

Cinco de Mayo, celebrated on or near May 5th, and Douglas Fiestas in mid-September, honor the town's Mexican ties, while Fourth of July celebrations include many activities. The Cochise County Fair is held the third week in September in the fairgrounds on Leslie Canyon Rd.

Places to Stay

Camping *Douglas Golf Club RV Park* (☎ 520-364-3722), north of Douglas on Leslie Canyon Rd, off Hwy 80, has 29 RV sites with hookups for $12. The park has an 18-hole golf course and a swimming pool.

Hotels & Motels The rooms are nowhere near as fancy as the lobby in the *Gadsden Hotel* (☎ 520-364-4481, fax 520-364-4005, rgadsden@theriver.com), 1046 G Ave, but they are comfortable enough and the price is right. There are 156 rooms and suites ranging from $38 to $85; most are under

$50. The rooms contain an eclectic grouping of styles and amenities, but just sitting in the lobby makes this a great value.

Other places include the *Motel 6* (☎ 520-364-2457, fax 520-364-9332), 111 16th St, with a pool and 137 rooms at $30/36 for singles/doubles; the more basic 17-room *Border Motel* (☎ 520-364-8491), 1725 A Ave, for $30/34; and the *Thriftlodge* (☎ 520-364-8434, fax 520-364-5687), 1030 19th St, with a pool and 30 rooms for $35/40.

Places to Eat

The restaurants in the Gadsden Hotel are good, or you can eat Mexican and American food across the street in the *Grand Cafe* (☎ 520-364-2344), 1119 G Ave, open from 10 am to 10 pm, Tuesday to Sunday, and to midnight on Friday and Saturday.

There are Mexican restaurants on both sides of the border.

Entertainment

The *Douglas Cinema* (☎ 520-364-5000), 1111 San Antonio Drive, screens movies. The bar in the Gadsden Hotel is a nice place for a refreshing drink.

Getting There & Away

Los Rapidos (☎ 520-364-2233), 538 14th St, has five buses a day to Tucson (via Bisbee and Sierra Vista) with three continuing to Phoenix; they connect with Greyhound. Douglas Shuttle (☎ 520-364-3761) has five vans a day to the Tucson and Phoenix airports.

WILLCOX

Settled in 1880 as a railroad camp, Willcox quickly became a major shipping center for southeastern Arizona's cattle ranches. Although ranching remains important, today Willcox is also famous as a fruit-growing center, and people drive from all over southeastern Arizona for the apple harvest. Willcox is the boyhood home of cowboy singer and movie actor Rex Allen who was born here in 1920 and still lives in the area. Nearby is a playa – a lake that dries in summer – which is the wintering ground of thousands of sandhill cranes, a spectacular sight for bird watchers. The elevation is 4167 feet.

Information
The chamber of commerce (☎ 520-384-2272, 800-200-2272), 1500 N Circle I Rd, northeast of I-10 exit 340, is open from 9 am to 5 pm, Monday to Saturday, and 9 am to 1 pm on Sunday. The small local Museum of the Southwest is here; it's free.

The library (☎ 520-384-4271) is at 207 W Maley St. The post office (☎ 520-384-2689) is at 200 S Curtis Ave. The hospital (☎ 520-384-3541) is at 901 W Rex Allen Drive. The police (☎ 520-384-4673) are at 151 W Maley St.

Rex Allen Arizona Cowboy Museum & Willcox Historic District
This museum (☎ 520-384-4583), 155 N Railroad Ave, is in an 1890s adobe building and presents the life of Rex Allen; opposite the museum is a large bronze statue of the star. Exhibits also interpret the lives of pioneers. Hours are 10 am to 4 pm, and they close on most Sundays and major holidays; admission is $2 per person, $3 for a couple and $5 for a family.

The museum is located in Willcox's most historic area. The Willcox Commercial Store, at the corner northeast of the museum, dates to 1881 and is the oldest

Ratite Farming
Ratites (birds such as ostriches and emus) are commercially farmed in Arizona, and there are ostrich farms near Willcox. Every part of the large bird is put to use: the feathers, the bones, the hide and, of course, the meat! It is said to taste like beef but with a much lower fat and cholesterol level – try some at the Solarium Restaurant. The chamber of commerce museum has a small exhibit about ostrich farming and can help arrange a farm tour. ∎

continuously operating store in Arizona. Also on the block is the rowdy Historic Palace Saloon (☎ 520-384-4712), built in 1905 and featuring pool tables and occasional live weekend entertainment. The art deco Rex Allen Theater (☎ 520-384-4244) was built in 1935 and still shows movies. On the southwest corner is a bright-red 1920s railroad dining car, which served food until recently (it's for sale if you need an antique railroad carriage!). Opposite, the 1880s railway station is being restored and will be the future home of the city hall.

Willcox Playa
South of town, this huge, sometimes dry, lake is the winter home of approximately 10,000 sandhill cranes. To see them, drive southeast on Hwy 186 a few miles and then take the left fork for Kansas Settlement. At dawn, the birds fly out of the playa and land in the corn stubble around Kansas Settlement, where they feed during the day, flying back to the playa at sunset.

Special Events
On the third weekend in January, Wings Over Willcox Sandhill Cranes Celebration has guided tours to good viewing sites near Willcox Playa and offers related birding activities. Rex Allen Days (with a PRCA rodeo, country music and dancing, and local arts and crafts) is the first weekend in October.

In the late summer and fall, there are pick-your-own apple orchards, roadside fruit and vegetable stands, and often an apple harvest festival in December. Stouts Cider Mill (☎ 520-384-3696), next to the chamber of commerce, is famous for HUGE apple pies and other apple-related items. Hours are 8 am to 6 pm daily.

Places to Stay
Camping At *Magic Circle RV Park* (☎ 520-384-3212), at I-10 exit 340, a few tent sites are $13.50 and 80 RV sites with hookups are $18; amenities include a swimming pool, showers and a recreation area. *Lifestyle RV Resort* (☎ 520-384-3303), 622 N Haskell Ave, has a pool, spa

and 60 RV sites with hookups for $20. *Grande Vista* (☎ 520-384-4002), 711 N Prescott Ave, has showers and charges $13.50 for 50 RV sites with hookups.

Hotels & Motels Note that rates increase the third weekend in January and first weekend in October.

The cheapest places are small mom-and-pop establishments along Haskell Ave. The *Royal Western Lodge* (☎ 520-384-2266), 590 S Haskell Ave, and the *Sands Motel* (☎ 520-384-3501), 400 S Haskell Ave, both have small pools and rooms in the $20s.

Others include the *Motel 8* (☎ 520-384-3270), 331 N Haskell Ave, the *Desert Inn of Willcox* (☎ 520-384-3577, fax 520-384-5371), 704 S Haskell Ave, and the *Riteway Budget Motel* (☎ 520-384-4655), 660 N Haskell Ave.

Otherwise, choose from a chain motel at I-10 exit 340. All have pools. The *Motel 6* (☎ 520-384-2201, fax 520-384-0192) has 123 rooms for $31/37 single/double. The *Days Inn* (☎ 520-384-4222, fax 520-384-3785) has 73 large rooms for $40 to $50 a double, including a continental breakfast bar. The *Super 8 Motel* (☎ 520-384-0888,

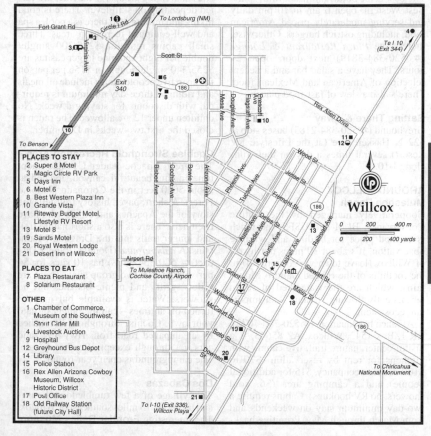

PLACES TO STAY
2 Super 8 Motel
3 Magic Circle RV Park
5 Days Inn
6 Motel 6
8 Best Western Plaza Inn
10 Grande Vista
11 Riteway Budget Motel,
    Lifestyle RV Resort
13 Motel 8
19 Sands Motel
20 Royal Western Lodge
21 Desert Inn of Willcox

PLACES TO EAT
7 Plaza Restaurant
8 Solarium Restaurant

OTHER
1 Chamber of Commerce,
    Museum of the Southwest,
    Stout Cider Mill
4 Livestock Auction
9 Hospital
12 Greyhound Bus Depot
14 Library
15 Police Station
16 Rex Allen Arizona Cowboy
    Museum, Willcox
    Historic District
17 Post Office
18 Old Railway Station
    (future City Hall)

Willcox

ARIZONA

fax 520-384-4485) has an indoor pool and spa and 53 rooms in the $40s (one bed) and $50s (two beds), including continental breakfast.

The most comfortable in town is the *Best Western Plaza Inn* (☎ 520-384-3556, fax 520-384-2679), 1100 W Rex Allen Drive, with a pool, spa, and a restaurant and bar with room service. There are 92 rooms with coffeemakers and refrigerators; six have whirlpool baths as well. Rates are about $70 a double, or $90 with the whirlpool bath, and include full breakfast.

Places to Eat
The best is the *Solarium Restaurant*, in the Best Western, open 6 am to 10 pm daily and serving moderately priced American food, including ostrich burgers. Otherwise, there's the *Plaza Restaurant & Lounge* (☎ 520-384-3819) next door, open 24 hours. They have a salad bar and a decent selection of American and Mexican food. There's also a slew of fast-food places.

Getting There & Away
Greyhound (☎ 520-384-2183) buses stop at 622 N Haskell Ave (at the Lifestyle RV Resort) several times a day on their runs along I-10.

AROUND WILLCOX
Muleshoe Ranch
Cooperatively managed by the Nature Conservancy, BLM and USFS, the ranch is a good place for birding and wildlife observation. It's about 30 miles northwest of Willcox (leave town via Airport Rd) in the foothills of the rugged Galiuro Mountains, which are the watershed of seven permanently flowing streams – an important ecosystem.

At ranch headquarters (☎ 520-586-7072), RR 1, Box 1542, Willcox, AZ 85643, is a visitor center, nature trail, five cabins with kitchens for rent by reservation ($70 to $100 double occupancy, $15 for additional people) and a camping area ($6, cold showers, no RV hookups). Cabins require a two-day minimum stay on weekends and from March through May. Primitive back-country camping is allowed by permit, and there are hiking and horse trails. Call about road conditions – the road here is unpaved.

Pearce
A ghost town about 27 miles south of Willcox, Pearce still has a few inhabitants and some funky old buildings. A few miles west, at 5000 feet in the foothills of the Dragoon Mountains, is the *Grapevine Canyon Ranch* (☎ 520-826-3185, 800-245-9202, fax 520-826-3636), PO Box 302, Pearce, AZ 85625.

This is a working cattle ranch offering horseback rides and cattle roundups. The staff here emphasizes personal attention and small riding groups, so the rides are varied depending on skill level. There is good hiking and birding, and there is a pool, a spa and well-equipped recreation areas. Three small cabins rent for $215/300 single/double per night and nine larger casitas are $255/340 single/double or $155 per person for up to five people. Rates include all meals and riding; a three-day minimum is required, with discounts for staying a week. No children under 12 are allowed. The ranch is closed the first two weeks in December.

Cochise Stronghold Recreation Area
The great Apache leader Cochise spent time in this beautiful canyon, located at about 5000 feet in the Coronado National Forest. A short, paved history trail tells the story of the Apaches and others who have been here. There is also a short nature trail and longer trails into the Dragoon Mountains. A *campground* (Douglas Ranger District, ☎ 520-364-3468) has 10 sites for $6 per vehicle plus two group sites. There are toilets, grills and picnic benches but no showers. Water is available but may be turned off at times – call the ranger or haul your own. Cochise Stronghold is reached by an unpaved road from Hwy 191, and cars get through except after heavy rain. The campground is open year-round.

Dos Cabezas
This village of a few tumbledown houses and trailers is 15 miles southeast of Willcox. The interesting **Frontier Relics Museum**

(☎ 520-384-3481) is a well-organized, one-man exhibit of local artifacts collected over 40 years by Orville Mickens; he knows about every piece. It's on the left side as you drive toward the Chiricahuas and is usually open 9 am to 5 pm, Monday to Saturday.

CHIRICAHUA MOUNTAINS & CHIRICAHUA NATIONAL MONUMENT

The strangely eroded volcanic rocks of the Chiricahua Mountains are unlike any others in Arizona. Geologists aren't exactly sure how these hundreds of standing pinnacles and balanced rocks were formed, but clearly they are the result of millions of years of erosion.

The Chiricahua National Monument contains the wildest and weirdest of the geological formations. This is one of the smaller and more remote NPS areas in the Southwest, but it can be reached easily enough by paved road; the scenery alone makes it a worthwhile trip. It is surrounded to the north, east and south by the Coronado National Forest (see Douglas, Sierra Vista and Safford for the nearest USFS offices), which also has interesting rock formations as well as camping and nature study.

There's a lot more here than just weird geology, however. The remoteness of the area makes it attractive to wildlife. For about 70 years, the Chiricahuas were the last place in the USA where a jaguar had been sighted, way back in 1912, though recently another jaguar was recorded a short way to the east. There is a good chance of seeing deer, coatis and javelinas. Mountain lions, bobcats and bears are sighted many times a year on the hiking trails within the monument. The Chiricahuas are the nearest high mountains to the Mexican mountain ranges, and several Mexican bird species are found here, including the Mexican chickadee and the elegant trogon (although the latter is found east of the monument itself, in the Cave Creek Canyon in the National Forest near Portal). The highest peak is 9795-foot Chiricahua Peak, just south of the monument in the national forest.

History and architecture can be found at Faraway Ranch, built in the early part of the 20th century. Tours of the now-restored ranch are led by monument rangers.

Orientation

The monument is almost 40 miles southeast of Willcox by paved road (no gas along this route). From the south it is 70 miles by paved road from Douglas. Access to the monument from the east is limited to a dirt road to Cave Creek Canyon. This road is passable to ordinary vehicles in good weather and is closed by snow in winter. From the north, the unpaved Apache Pass Rd is normally open all year to all vehicles except after bad weather. Both of these dirt roads have some rough stretches and may be problematic for large RVs and vehicles with trailers, so inquire locally.

Information

The monument is open 24 hours a day. The visitor center (☎ 520-824-3560) is open from 8 am to 5 pm daily (except Christmas) and has a slide show about the Chiricahuas, a small exhibit area and a bookstore. Ranger-led programs are offered from March to October but may be curtailed in midsummer. The monument offers no gas, food or lodging (except camping). Admission is $6 per private vehicle or $3 per bicycle, foot or bus passenger, and

Mountain lion

ARIZONA

Golden Age, Access and Eagle Passes are honored. Further information is available from the Superintendent, Chiricahua National Monument, Dos Cabezas Route, Box 6500, Willcox, AZ 85643.

Climate & When to Go
At the national monument, March, April and May are by far the busiest months, due in part to the pleasant spring climate. By June, daytime highs average around 90°F and the number of visitors drops substantially. July through early September are the wettest months, with frequent summer storms. In August of 1993, a record-setting four inches of rain fell in six hours, although usually that is almost the entire month's rainfall. Beware of flash floods after summer storms. Visitation picks up again after the summer rains, and then drops during the winter. Freezing overnight temperatures are normal from late November through February, and the trails, though open year-round, may be snow-covered.

Scenic Drive
The Bonita Canyon Scenic Drive is a paved 8-mile road climbing from the entrance gate (at a little over 5000 feet) to Massai Point at 6870 feet. The visitor center is 2 miles along this road from the entrance station. There are several scenic pullouts and trailheads along this road. The views from Massai Point are spectacular.

Faraway Ranch
Begun in 1888, the ranch was built during a 30-year period. Originally a pioneer's cattle ranch, it became one of Arizona's earliest guest ranches in the 1920s. The ranch is near the monument entrance and a short hiking trail leads to it and on to a cabin dating from the same period. To enter, you must go on a ranger-led tour ($2; free for those under 12) offered several times a day during the busy season, less often in other months.

Hiking
Numerous hiking trails wind through the monument. These range from easy, flat loops of 0.2 miles to strenuous climbs of more than 7 miles. None are accessible to wheelchairs. A free park map showing the scenic drive and trails is available. A detailed hiking guide costs 25¢. Generally, the short, flat trails west of the visitor center and campground are the easiest and are good for birding and wildlife observation. The trails east of the visitor center lead into rugged mountain country with the most spectacular geology.

A hikers' shuttle bus leaves daily from the visitor center and camping area at 8:30 am, going up to Massai Point for $2. This is not a sightseeing bus. It drops hikers off at the top and allows them to return by hiking downhill.

Places to Stay
Trails are for day use only and no wilderness camping is permitted. A campground with 24 sites about 0.2 miles north of the visitor center has water but no hookups or showers. The sites are too small for large RVs and trailers. During the busy months, the campground is full by noon and may be full earlier on weekends. Sites are available on a first-come, first-served basis for $8.

If the campground is full, there are numerous campgrounds in the Coronado National Forest south of the monument. Rangers will give you a map (there's one outside the visitor center if the center is closed) showing where the campgrounds are. These usually have space available. See Beyond the Monument, below.

Immediately outside the entrance gate, Pinery Canyon Rd goes left, passing the *Chiricahua Foothills B&B* (☎ 520-824-3632), Dos Cabezas Route, Box 6310, Willcox, AZ 85643, a quarter-mile away. Six prettily decorated rooms, four in the main house and two in an adjoining building, all have private baths and rent for $65 double, with full breakfast. Dinner ($25 per couple) is available on request.

Basic food supplies are available at the El Dorado Trading Post, about a mile before the monument entrance.

Beyond the Monument

The Chiricahua Mountains extend north, east and south of the monument and are within the Coronado National Forest land. Pinery Canyon Rd (closed in winter) is an attractive and wild drive southeast of the monument entrance station through the national forest, emerging on paved highways at **Portal**, where food and lodging are available. From Portal, the paved road continues east into New Mexico. A gravel road, open all year, goes north to I-10. Stay at the *Portal Peak Lodge* (☎ 520-558-2223), Portal, AZ 85632, with 16 rooms at $55/65 single/double, including breakfast.

There are several USFS campgrounds along the Pinery Canyon Rd. On the east side of the Chiricahuas, near Portal, is Cave Creek Canyon, which is one of the best places in the USA to see or hear both the elegant and the much-rarer eared trogon, as well as the Mexican chickadee; these birds are normally found in the mountains of Mexico. The elegant trogon nests here from April to June and can occasionally be seen in winter. The eared trogon has been heard or seen only in the fall.

Also near Portal is the **American Museum of Natural History Southwestern Research Station** (☎/fax 520-558-2396, swrs@amnh.org), which has a bird list for the area. Cabins here are usually filled with researchers but are sometimes available for rent, especially in spring and fall. Nature study programs are occasionally offered. Lodging is mainly in simple rooms with five beds and a shower; rooms have no TVs or phones. Rates are $63 single and $55 for each additional adult ($40 for 11- to 18-year-olds and $30 for 2- to 10-year-olds) including three meals. Additional nights get a 5% discount. There's a swimming pool and laundry room.

The dirt Rucker Canyon Rd, further south, also enters the national forest and has several campgrounds along it.

North of the monument is the **Fort Bowie National Historic Site**, with a ranger station (☎ 520-847-2500) and small interpretive exhibit. Only the ruined foundations of the 1862 fort are still standing. It can be reached from the Chiricahuas by taking the unpaved Apache Pass (5115 feet) road to Bowie. A mile or two north of the pass (which can become impassable to ordinary cars after heavy rains), there is a parking lot from which you hike 1½ miles to the historic site. The lot can also be reached from I-25 by a better unpaved road 12 miles south of Bowie. For the 3-mile roundtrip hike, carry water and sun protection in summer, and watch for rattlesnakes and flash floods. Recently, mountain lions were sighted close to the trail, so hiking alone is discouraged. The ranger station is open from 8 am to 5 pm; admission is free.

Finally, you can rent a horse (rates from $18 to $85 for one hour to a full day with lunch) at the *Sunglow Guest Ranch* (☎/fax 520-824-3334, sunglow@vtc.net), a few miles southwest of the monument on Turkey Creek Rd off Hwy 181. You can stay here in 12 rooms with kitchenettes; rates range from $55 to $85 a double, depending on season and room size. Rooms sleep from two to six people; one house will sleep up to 12. Weekly discounts are offered. Guests get horse rental discounts and can either cook on their own or pay extra for ranch meals. The rooms lack TVs, telephones and room/maid service, but bedding and kitchenware are provided.

ARIZONA

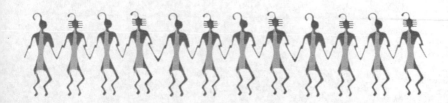

Southeastern Arizona – Chiricahua Mountains

get a 5% discount. There's a swimming pool and laundry room.

The dirt Pinery Canyon Rd, further south, also enters the national forest and has several campgrounds along it.

North of the monument is the Fort Bowie National Historic Site, with a ranger station (☎ 520-847-2500) and small interpretive exhibit. Only the ruined foundations of the 1862 fort are still standing. It can be reached from the Chiricahuas by taking the unpaved Apache Pass (5115 feet) road to Bowie. A mile or two north of the pass, which can become impassable to ordinary cars after heavy rains, there is a parking lot from which you hike 1½ miles of the historic trail. The fort can also be reached from I-20 by a better unpaved road 12 miles south of Bowie. For the family, founding site, fancy waterfowl sun prey during summer, and watch for rattlesnakes and flash floods. Recently, mountain lions were sighted close to the trail, so hiking alone is discouraged. The ranger station is open from 8 am to 5 pm, and small snack bar. Finally, you can rent a horse (rates from $16 to $55 for one hour) or horseback riding at the Southfork Ranch & Kennels (☎ fax 520-823-3334; sun glow turismo), a few miles southwest of the monument on Turkey Creek Rd off Hwy 181. You can stay here in 12 rooms with kitchenettes rated anywhere from $55 to $85, a double depending on the season and room size. Rooms sleep from two to six people; one house will sleep up to 12. Weekly discounts are offered. Guests get horse rental discounts and can either cook on their own or pay extra for ranch meals. The rooms lack TVs, telephones, and room airconditioning; but drug- and smoke-free are provided.

Beyond the Monument

The Chiricahua Mountains extend north and east and south of the monument and are within the Coronado National Forest land. Pinery Canyon Rd (closed in winter) is an attractive and wild drive southeast of the monument entrance station through the national forest, emerging on paved Hwy 181 at Portal, where food and lodging are available. From Portal, the gravel road continues east into New Mexico. A gravel road (east open all year goes northeast) to San Simon on the pavement. From Hwy 181, another route (☎ 520-558-4225) at ☎ 2121 Portal, AZ 85632, with 16 rooms at $55-65 single/double, including a bathroom.

There are several USFS campgrounds along the Pinery Canyon Rd. On the east side of the Chiricahuas, near Portal, is Cave Creek Canyon, which is one of the best places in the USA to observe (and hear) the elegant and rare birds found here, as well as the Mexican chickadee, these birds (normally found in the mountains of Mexico. The elegant trogon, most likely seen in June to August but occasionally be seen in winter. The coral dragon has been seen here or seen only in the fall.

Also near Portal is the American Museum of Natural History Southwestern Research Station (☎ fax 520-558-2396; www.amnh.org), which has a bird list for observers. Cabins here are usually filled with researchers but are sometimes available to tourists, especially in spring and fall. Nature study programs are occasionally offered. Lodging is mainly in simple rooms with fixed beds and bathrooms, have no TVs or phones. Rates are $65 single and $50 for each additional adult, $40 for 11- to 14-year-olds, and $35 for 10-year-olds, including three meals, additional night.

Southwestern Colorado

CHUCK PLACE

Southwestern Colorado

Southwestern Colorado forms the fourth corner of the Four Corners region. Unlike the mountains and plains of other parts of Colorado, the landscape here is the high desert of the Colorado Plateau.

In common with the rest of the four corners, the prime attractions in this area are the numerous sites of the pre-Columbian Ancestral Puebloans. These early inhabitants built elaborate cities at Mesa Verde – first on the mesa tops, later high above the canyon floors in the recesses of cliff faces. Together the Mesa Verde National Park and Ute Mountain Tribal Park, which encircles the southern boundaries of Mesa Verde, protect the archaeological remains at hundreds of these prehistoric communities while providing access to a few of the most spectacular sites for almost a million visitors each year. No road access exists between the two parks.

Nearby towns such as Cortez and Mancos offer places to stay and further information. A bit farther north is the sleepy Dolores River Canyon, which offers untrammeled access to desert backcountry hiking, biking and river rafting. Travelers wanting to visit more of Colorado should check out Lonely Planet's *Rocky Mountains*.

CORTEZ

Cortez (population 8700), is the main lodging spot for visitors to Mesa Verde National Park and other nearby Ancestral Puebloan sites. It's not much more than a place to stay, but people are friendly and there are some reasonably priced motels and a few nice restaurants. Those seeking a more relaxed environment can try Mancos, 17 miles east, or Dolores, 11 miles north.

Orientation

Hwy 160 becomes Main St as it runs east to west through the middle of town, then becomes Broadway where it turns south and joins up with Hwy 666. Main St is where you'll find nearly all the lodging and restaurants, though there are a few motels on Broadway.

Information

The Colorado Welcome Center (☎ 970-565-4048), 928 E Main, is in an adobe-style building at the city park. It has local information plus materials to help you plan your vacation throughout the state. Brochures detailing a self-guided downtown walking tour – the 'Crossroads Culture Walk' – are available there as well. Hours are 8 am to 5 pm (6 pm in summer). The Cortez Chamber of Commerce (☎ 970-565-3414) is also here.

First National Bank (☎ 970-565-3781), 140 W Main, has a 24-hour ATM. The City Market, on the northeast corner of E Main and Harrison, has a Valley National Bank ATM and Western Union service. The post office is at 35 S Beech; the zip code is 81321. Quality Book Store (☎ 970-565-9125), 34 W Main, sells travel books and maps and offers a good selection on local history and Native American cultures.

Southwest Memorial Hospital (☎ 970-565-6666), 1311 N Mildred Rd, has a 24-hour emergency room. A laundry is at the corner of E Main and Mildred Rd, opposite the city park and Colorado Welcome Center. M&M Truckstop (☎ 970-565-6511), south of town at 7006 Hwy 160/666, has showers for $5 plus a $5 key deposit.

Colorado University Center Museum

Throughout the year this museum (☎ 970-565-1151), 25 N Market, offers interpretive exhibits on the Ancestral Puebloans as well as visiting art displays in its gallery.

The **Cultural Park** is an outdoor space where Ute, Navajo and Hopi tribal members share their cultures with visitors through dance, crafts demonstrations, or food preparation in hornos (ovens). Weaving demonstrations and Ute Mountain art are also

COLORADO

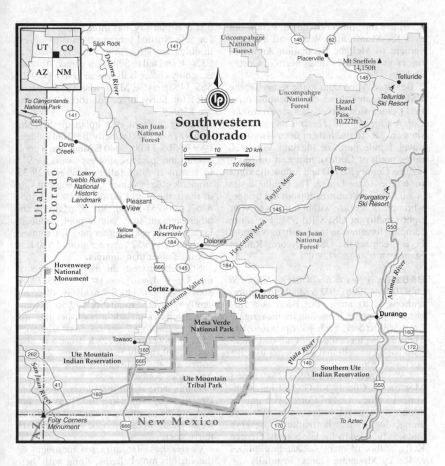

Southwestern
Colorado

shown, and a Navajo hogan and Ute teepee are available for visitors to see.

Summer evening programs feature Native American dances four nights a week at 7:30 pm, followed at 8:30 pm by cultural programs such as Native American storytellers, or occasionally Mexican dances or cowboy poet gatherings. At the time of writing, Native American dances were held in the city park Friday and Saturday nights: they may shift back to the museum. The CU Center Museum is open Monday to Saturday; summer hours are 10 am to 9 pm and winter hours are 10 am to 5 pm.

Places to Stay

Camping Sadly, the only campground in town not next to a highway or dedicated to RVs is the *Cortez-Mesa Verde KOA* (☎ 970-565-9301), located at the east end of town at 27432 E Hwy 160 (there's a big sign). Tent sites are a pricey $18, full RV hookups are $24. It's open from mid-May to mid-September.

Outside of town, there are a few walk-in tent sites for $8 at the USFS *McPhee Campground* (☎ 970-882-9905, 800-280-2267), but most of the 70 reservable campsites are set up for RVs and cost $10, plus

COLORADO

$2 to use the showers. The sites look out over the Montezuma Valley and are convenient to McPhee Recreation Area and reservoir fishing, 14 miles north of Cortez on Hwy 184.

Below McPhee Dam to the reservoir, the USFS operates three campgrounds on a first-come, first-served basis: *Bradfield*, *Cabin Canyon* and *Ferris Canyon*. Tent sites are $8. To reach them from Hwy 666, travel 1 mile north of Pleasant View (20 miles north of Cortez), turn east on Montezuma County Rd DD and follow the signs for 6 miles to the bridge. The Bradfield site is a half mile downstream from the bridge, while the others are within 6 miles to your right (south) on USFS Rd 504. For more camping locations in the San Juan National Forest, contact the USFS Dolores Ranger Station (☎ 970-882-7296).

B&Bs Try *A Bed & Breakfast on Maple St* (☎ 970-565-3906), 102 S Maple. As unpretentious as its name, this B&B is a real home-style place; it has four rooms ranging from $59 to $99, each with private bath. There is also an outdoor hot tub and backyard barbecue grill that guests can use. It's open year-round.

Kelly Place (☎ 970-565-3125), 14663 Montezuma County Rd G (McElmo Canyon), 15 miles west of Cortez, is a unique adobe-style guest lodge on a 100-acre archaeological and horticultural preserve that was founded by the late botanist George Kelly, author of many outstanding guides to Rocky Mountain plants. Tastefully appointed singles/doubles are $59/69 with private bath. Cabins with kitchenettes are $89. Horseback rides, cultural tours and archaeological programs are also offered.

Motels There is a good selection of locally run motels in Cortez, freeing you from patronizing the ubiquitous national chains. Between Memorial Day and Labor Day it's not a good idea to come here without a room reservation – walk-in rates rise to whatever the market will bear.

Summer or winter, the basic but clean *Ute Mountain Motel* (☎ 970-565-8507),

531 S Broadway, has three budget singles for $20. Normal summer rates for singles/doubles are still comparatively cheap at $35/44, and fall to $20/28 in winter. Another economy choice is the *Aneth Lodge* (☎ 970-565-3453), 645 E Main, where high-season rates for fairly large, comfortable rooms are $36/49.

Taking a slight step up in quality, the *Budget Host Inn* (formerly Bel Rau Lodge) (☎ 970-565-3738), 2040 E Main, has a pool, hot tub and spacious, spotless rooms for $45 in summer; rates fall as low as $28/32 single/double in winter. On the western side of town, the *Sand Canyon Inn* (☎ 970-565-8562, 800-257-3699), 301 W Main, is another pleasant spot, with a pool, sundeck, laundry and peak summer rates for singles/doubles of $45/52 – expect around $10 less any time other than summer.

Still farther west, the friendly owners of the *Arrow Motor Inn* (☎ 970-565-7778, 800-727-7692), 440 S Broadway, offer recently renovated rooms for $49/56 in summer. Facilities include a pool, hot tub and laundry. *The Tomahawk Lodge* (☎ 970-565-8521, 800-972-6232), 728 S Broadway, also has a pool, newly redone rooms, 24-hour coffee and tea, and summer rates of $35/47 for singles/doubles.

In this same area is the *Anasazi Motor Inn* (☎ 970-565-3773), 640 S Broadway. It's not bad, but the rooms are overpriced at $55/69 for singles/doubles; even the winter rates are fairly steep.

Cortez has also attracted members of the various motel chains, along with their inflated prices, including two *Best Westerns*, a *Comfort Inn*, a *Super 8* and a *Holiday Inn Express*. They all cost more than they're worth, but if you're stuck, consult the list of toll-free phone numbers in the Motel Chains section of the Facts for the Visitor chapter.

Places to Eat
You can start the day with fresh pastries at the *Belgian Quality Bakery* (☎ 970-565-3753), 44 W Main, or have an espresso and light breakfast dishes next door at the Quality Book Store's *Earth Song Haven*

(☎ 970-565-9125), which also serves tasty lunches with fresh ingredients.

Good lunch specials for $5 are available weekdays at the *Main Street Brewery & Restaurant* (☎ 970-544-9112), 21 E Main. The dinner menu gets more interesting, with a mix of Southwestern, Mexican and Italian dishes, resulting in some unusual items like the 'Bratwurst Burrito.' There are also nightly specials, and entrées range from $7 to $13. The beer they brew here is excellent – reason enough to stop by.

Locals nominate *Francisca's* (☎ 970-565-4093), 125 E Main, as having the best Mexican food in town, and good taste comes at a pretty good price: lunches and dinners range between $4 and $10. It's open Tuesday to Saturday. For standard American family fare, there's *Homesteaders* (☎ 970-565-6253), 45 E Main, open all day, serving barbecue dinners and fresh-baked pies and breads.

At the upper end *Nero's Italian Restaurant* (☎ 970-565-7366), 303 W Main, is another local favorite, winning high marks for its presentation of entrées and its excellent soups. Prices range from $9 to $12 for pasta dishes, $10 to $18 for meat entrées. The *Dry Dock Lounge & Restaurant* (☎ 970-564-9404), 220 W Main, also occupies the higher-end bracket, dishing up steak and seafood platters with a Southwestern flair. Both restaurants have patio dining areas, a nice feature during the warmer months.

Shopping

Native American handicrafts are available at numerous 'trading posts' that line the highway to Mesa Verde National Park. You'll find everything from rubber tomahawks and cheap imported rugs to distinctive handcrafted pottery, jewelry and costly Navajo rugs. Comparison shopping will help identify quality differences and is itself an educational exercise. Prices tend to be competitive – don't be fooled by the '50%-off Sale' signs. Bead and turquoise jewelry-making is a cottage industry practiced by many tribal members soon after leaving the cradle – jewelry offers the best

bargains and most opportunities to buy directly from the artisan.

The Notah Dineh Trading Company (☎ 970-565-9607), 345 W Main, features an outstanding collection of museum-quality goods in the front showroom, a cash/pawn window in the back and a museum downstairs that displays items that are not for sale. To buy directly from Native American artisans and merchants, head south to Towaoc or the numerous stalls at Four Corners where you are certain to find plenty of inexpensive, authentic gifts for your friends back home.

Getting There & Away

Air Cortez Municipal Airport is served by United Express, which offers daily turboprop flights to Denver and Farmington, New Mexico. Most of the Denver flights go via Farmington, though there is usually one direct flight a day. The airport is 2 miles south of town, off Hwy 160/666.

Car In the extreme southwest corner of the state, Cortez is easier to reach from either Phoenix, Arizona or Albuquerque, New Mexico than from Denver, which is 379 miles away by the shortest route. East of Cortez, Hwy 160 passes Mesa Verde National Park on the way to Durango, the largest city in the region, 45 miles away. To the northwest, Hwy 145 follows the beautiful Dolores River through the San Juan Mountains on an old Rio Grande Southern narrow-gauge route over Lizard Head Pass to Telluride, 77 miles away.

Getting Around

U-Save Auto Rental (☎ 970-565-9168) operates out of the Cortez Airport, while Quality Rental (☎ 970-565-2106) is located in town at 410 W Main.

AROUND CORTEZ
Anasazi Heritage Center

One of the largest archaeological projects in the Four Corners region took place along the Dolores River between 1978 and 1981, prior to the flooding of McPhee Reservoir. The Anasazi Heritage Center

COLORADO

(☎ 970-882-4811), at 27501 Hwy 184, 10 miles north of Cortez or 3 miles west of Dolores, offers modern interpretive displays of Ancestral Puebloan artifacts found during this project and other archaeological work in the area. Hands-on exhibits include weaving, corn grinding, tree-ring analysis and an introduction to how archaeologists examine potsherds (pottery fragments).

Between 1 AD and 1300 AD, Ancestral Puebloans inhabited the hilly sites of the Escalante and Domínguez sites, which overlook the Montezuma Valley. A fairly short interpretive nature trail leads to the hilltop Escalante site, which was discovered in 1776 by Father Francisco Atanasio Domínguez and Father Silvestre Vélez Escalante. Archaeologists think that the Escalante site was linked with the Chaco Ancestral Puebloan society, nearly 200 miles south in New Mexico.

Although archaeologists adopted the Navajo term *Anasazi* during the 1930s to refer to the early inhabitants of the American Southwest, they have often mistaken it to mean 'ancient people.' Instead, and much to the chagrin of modern Pueblo peoples of Ancestral Puebloan heritage, it literally means 'enemy ancestors' in the Navajo tongue.

The BLM operates the museum, while a nonprofit museum shop offers a wide variety of books, maps and nature guides that range from professional reports to introductory materials suited for the general public. It's open daily from 9 am to 5 pm, but closes at 4 pm during winter months. Admission is $3.

Crow Canyon Archaeological Center
The Crow Canyon Archaeological Center (☎ 970-565-8975, 800-422-8975), 23390 Montezuma County Rd K, offers an educational day program that visits the Sand Creek Ancestral Puebloan excavation site west of Cortez. Programs teach the sig-

---

Ancestral Puebloan Settlement

Period	Chronology
Hunter-Gatherer	5500 BC
I Basketmaker	1 AD-450 AD
II Modified Basketmaker	450 AD-750 AD
III Developmental Pueblo	Around 750 AD-1100 AD
IV Classic Pueblo	Around 1100 AD-1300 AD

Why the Ancestral Puebloans entered Mesa Verde is a subject of speculation. Habitations in Mesa Verde evolved greatly between 450 AD, when the earliest simple structures were constructed, and 1300 AD when the great cities were mysteriously left behind.

The earliest period of settlement, the so-called Modified Basketmaker phase that extended to about 750 AD, found the Ancestral Puebloans dispersed across the mesa tops in small clusters of permanent pithouse dwellings – semi-subterranean structures with posts supporting low-profile roofs.

During the Developmental Pueblo period, up to 1100 AD, Ancestral Puebloans built surface houses with simple shared walls – like row-house apartments – that formed small hamlets surrounded by fields of maize, beans and squash.

The following Classic Pueblo phase, to 1300 AD, saw the Mesa Verde Ancestral Puebloans elaborate on the earlier structures, using masonry building materials. Their

nificance of found artifacts and are available for adults and children from June to mid-September on Wednesday and Thursday; cost is $45 for adults and $25 for children under 18. This is an excellent way to learn about Ancestral Puebloan culture firsthand.

An adult research program costs $850 and includes Southwestern meals and log cabin lodging for a week. Classroom time culminates with visits to the dig site and active participation in excavation. Reservations are required for both programs.

Fishing

The 11-mile stretch of the lower Dolores River below McPhee Dam to the Bradfield Bridge is a state-designated quality water stream where a catch-and-release program is in effect. To reach the area, turn east off Hwy 666 on to Montezuma County Rd DD, 1 mile north of Pleasant View. Follow the signs for 6 miles to the Bradfield Bridge

and USFS campground; from the bridge, the Lone Dome Rd follows the east bank of the river to the dam.

If trolling is your preference, McPhee Reservoir offers both warm- and cold-water species of fish in the recently flooded Dolores River Canyon. Perhaps to make amends for covering Ancestral Puebloan buildings, burial sites and untold artifacts, the reservoir is kept well stocked for the visiting angler. McPhee Marina (☎ 970-882-2257, 800-882-2038) offers tackle and half-day boat rentals from $65.

Pick up the 'Guide to Fishing in Mesa Verde Country' at the Colorado Welcome Center for additional information.

Biking

The Four Corners area offers some outstanding mountain-bike trails among piñon-juniper woodland and over slickrock mesa trails. The dispersed sites at Hovenweep National Monument (see the Southeastern

efforts housed a peak population of perhaps several thousand in pueblo villages, the precursors to cities. Greater clusters of people created opportunities for united accomplishments and perhaps a rudimentary division of labor, social organization, political control and even organized raids on neighboring villages. Also during this period the Ancestral Puebloans developed subsurface roundrooms, or kivas – for decades thought to be ceremonial by archaeologists, but more recently seen to have more basic uses. At this time they also developed hydraulic schemes to irrigate crops and provide water for villages.

There is mounting evidence of regular communication between Mesa Verdeans and Chaco Canyon peoples in northwestern New Mexico in this period. Some researchers suggest the political, economic and social influences extended from even farther afield in Mesoamerica (present-day Mexico and Central America).

The Puebloans moved to the alcoves of the cliff faces around 1200 AD. Community size depended on available cliff space, so while small cavities may have contained only a few compartments, there were many larger communities with over 200 compartments, including elaborate blocks or rooms, cantilevered balconies, sunken roundrooms and even tower structures – many connected with internal passageways.

Ancestral Puebloans inhabited the cliff dwellings for less than a century before disappearing in accord with a regional demographic collapse that is the greatest unexplained event of the era. Disease, invasion, internal warfare, resource depletion and climatic change are among the hardships these peoples faced. Tree-ring chronologies show a widespread drought lasted from 1276 to 1299 AD, yet this explanation fails to account for the earlier population decline at Chaco Canyon or Mesa Verde's survival of earlier droughts. Population movements did occur, however, and it is probable that many Ancestral Puebloans migrated south to the Pueblos of present-day New Mexico and Arizona. ■

Utah chapter) are ideal riding destinations. In fact, the roads are better suited for bikes than cars. Check at the ranger station for directions and to get suggestions for sites you can visit within 10 miles. Remember, the archaeological sites hold invaluable clues to our heritage and must not be disturbed in any manner.

Another good ride begins at the Sand Canyon archaeological site west of Cortez and follows a downhill trail west for 18 miles to Cannonball Mesa, near the state line. If you're looking for a shorter ride, at the 8-mile mark, the Burro Point overlook of Yellow Jacket and Burro Canyons is a good place to turn back. To get to Sand Canyon, take Hwy 666 north from Cortez, turn left (west) on Montezuma County Rd P and continue 7 miles before making a left (south) turn.

Fat-tire enthusiasts should not miss the 26-mile trail from Dove Creek to Slick Rock along the red-rock Dolores River Canyon. The first 11 miles to the Pyramid offer an easy ride and swimming opportunities. The remainder is a more challenging ride involving a potentially dangerous river ford followed by steep climbs. Stop by the Dove Creek Chamber of Commerce (☎ 970-677-2245) for information on river conditions and a map and description of the route.

Pick up a copy of *Mountain and Road Bike Routes* for the Cortez-Dolores-Mancos area, available at the Colorado Welcome Center in Cortez and at local chambers of commerce. It provides maps and profiles for 11 road- and mountain-bike routes. The booklet *Bicycle Routes on Public Lands of Southwest Colorado* also describes area rides in good detail. It's available for $7 from the USFS Dolores Ranger Station (☎ 970-882-7296), 100 N 6th, Dolores. Contact the Colorado Plateau Mountain Bike Trail Association (☎ 970-241-9561) for even more routes and information.

In Cortez, Kokopelli Bike & Board (☎ 970-565-4408), 30 W Main, rents mountain bikes for $20 per day, including helmet, pump, water bottle and tools. It can also provide information on trails in the area.

River Running

Although the McPhee Reservoir interrupts the Dolores River, the 150-mile stretch from below the dam to the Utah state line offers springtime runs that are unequaled in combining the beauty and solitude of canyon country with occasional technical whitewater challenges. The vegetation along the river changes from ponderosa pines to piñon-juniper and red rock. You can even continue all the way to the Colorado River above Cataract Canyon through Canyonlands National Park.

From the USFS Bradfield Campground (see Camping, earlier in this chapter) it's a 49-mile trip with some Class IV rapids to Slick Rock. From Slick Rock to the historic Bedrock Store in the Paradox Valley it's another 48 miles on Class II-III waters. The 48-mile trip from Bedrock to Gateway passes the historic hanging flume cantilevered from the sheer walls of the Dolores Canyon and includes a few stretches of Class IV white water. By early June, however, the entire excursion may take 10 days due to low water.

If planning your own trip, be sure to buy Ralph DeVries and Stephen Maurer's *Dolores River Guide*. As an alternative, a couple of commercial river guides offer package trips into this desert wilderness. Wilderness Aware (☎ 800-462-7238) offers three-, six- and 10-day trips that explore the cultural and natural history along the river for $325 to $900. Also try Rocky Mountain Adventures (☎ 800-858-6808), which has a good reputation, international rafting experience, and offers three- and six-day trips for $300 and $600, respectively.

Lowry Pueblo Ruins National Historic Landmark

The buildings at Lowry Pueblo, north of Cortez and 9 miles west of Hwy 666 at Pleasant View, underwent heavy stabilization in 1994 to give visitors an opportunity to explore the Ancestral Puebloan site and even enter a central kiva. Near the pueblo, constructed between 1060 and 1170 AD, is one of the largest Great Kivas in the Four Corners region. When researchers from

Chicago's Field Institute first excavated the site during the 1930s, they discovered an elaborate painting in the central kiva – it was removed for display at the Anasazi Heritage Center in 1987.

Note the distinctive Chaco-style masonry using narrow slabs and small dark stones to create a banding effect on the south wall. This and other evidence support the theory that Lowry Pueblo was a Chacoan outlier housing about 100 occupants who were part of the greater network of civilization centered in Chaco Canyon in New Mexico. Self-guided walking tour brochures are available at the site. Picnicking is permitted, but overnight camping is not. For further information contact the BLM San Juan Resource Area (☎ 970-247-4082) in Durango.

Dove Creek

Located on Hwy 666, 35 miles north of Cortez and 2 miles south of Hwy 141, Dove Creek (population 710) claims to be the 'Pinto Bean Capital of the World.' Recently the non-irrigated growers have rediscovered the beans that the 'Anasazi' (Ancestral Puebloans) grew and found that they are sweeter, prettier and – most importantly – cause less flatulence than the high-carbohydrate pinto bean.

Anasazi beans are marketed by Adobe Milling (☎ 970-677-2620, 800-542-3623), which offers gourmet beans and recipes to visitors. Unfortunately, the nearest restaurants serving 'gourmet' beans are in Mesa Verde and Durango, but you can sample a bowl of old-fashioned, gas-inducing pinto beans at the *Blue Mountain Cafe* (☎ 970-677-2261), Hwy 666 at the northern end of town. Rooms at the *Country Inn Motel* (☎ 970-677-2234) start at $34, $28 in winter.

MESA VERDE NATIONAL PARK

Among national parks, Mesa Verde is unique for its focus on preserving cultural relics so future generations may continue to interpret the puzzling settlement, and then abandonment, of the area by its early inhabitants.

History

A US Army lieutenant recorded the spectacular cliff dwellings in the canyons of Mesa Verde in 1849-50. The large number of sites on Ute tribal land, and their relative inaccessibility, protected the bulk of these antiquities from pot-hunters.

The first scientific investigation of the site in 1874 failed to identify Cliff Palace, the largest cliff dwelling in North America. Discovery of the 'magnificent city' occurred only when local cowboys Richard Wetherill and Charlie Mason were searching for stray cattle after a December 1888 snowfall; it is likely that Wetherill had learned about Cliff Palace from Acowitz, a Ute tribal member. The cowboys exploited their 'discovery' for the next 18 years by guiding both amateur and trained archaeologists to the site, particularly to collect the distinctive black-on-white pottery.

Disturbances by casual collectors and the large-scale 'mining' of artifacts by professionals prompted calls to protect the site. The shipping of artifacts overseas motivated Virginia McClurg of Colorado Springs to embark on a long campaign to preserve the buildings and their contents. Along with other members of the Colorado Federation of Women's Clubs, she met with Ute chieftains in 1903 near present-day Towaoc. As a result, the Ute tribe graciously consented to release interest in the canyons containing the cliff houses.

McClurg's efforts led Congress to protect artifacts on federal land with passage of the Antiquities Act and to establish Mesa Verde National Park in 1906. One part of the enabling legislation mandated that, unlike other national parks, the backcountry would be closed to public access.

Orientation

Ancestral Puebloan buildings are present throughout the canyons and mesa tops of Mesa Verde, a high plateau south of Cortez and Mancos. The North Rim summit at Park Point (8571 feet) towers over 2000 feet above the Montezuma Valley. From Park Point the mesa gently slopes southward to the 6000 foot elevation above the

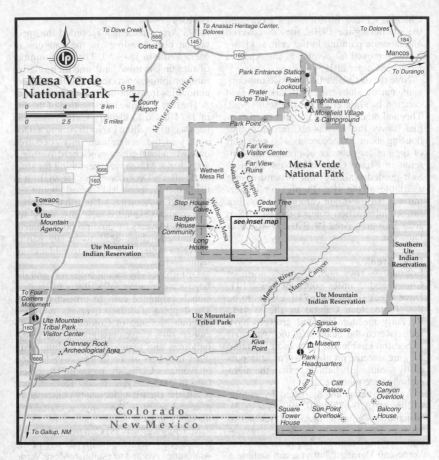

Mancos River in the 195-sq-mile Ute Mountain Tribal Park. The mesa top is dissected by parallel canyons, typically 500 feet below the rim, that serve to carry the drainage southward. Mesa Verde National Park occupies 81 sq miles of the northernmost portion of the mesa and contains the largest and most frequented cliff dwellings and surface structures.

The park entrance is off of Hwy 160, midway between Cortez and Mancos. From the entrance it is 21 miles to park headquarters, Chapin Mesa Museum and Spruce Tree House. Along the way are

Morefield Campground (4 miles), the panoramic viewpoint at Park Point (10 miles) and the Far View Visitor Center opposite the Far View Lodge and Restaurant (15 miles). Towed vehicles are not allowed beyond Morefield Campground.

Chapin Mesa contains the largest concentration of ancient buildings in the area. South from park headquarters, Ruins Rd consists of two one-way circuits. Turn left about a quarter mile from the start of Ruins Rd to visit Cliff Palace and Balcony House on the east loop. Take the west loop by continuing straight to mesa-top sites and many fine cliff-dwelling vantages. Taking the west loop first allows you to roughly follow the Ancestral Puebloan chronology in proper sequence.

At Wetherill Mesa, the second largest concentration of buildings, visitors may enter stabilized surface structures and two cliff dwellings. From the junction with the main road at Far View Visitor Center (see below), the 12-mile mountainous Wetherill Mesa Rd snakes along the North Rim, acting as a natural barrier to tour buses and indifferent travelers. The road is only open from the second week in June to the first week in September.

Information

The Far View Visitor Center (☎ 970-529-4543) is open 8 am to 5 pm from late spring through early autumn. More comprehensive information is available at the Chapin Mesa Museum, but the visitor must also stop at Far View to obtain the required tickets ($1.35) for tours of Cliff Palace or Balcony House. Modestly priced guides to individual sites are available

in French, German and Spanish at the visitor center and the museum.

Park headquarters (☎ 970-529-4461) is open weekdays during park hours. For additional information write Mesa Verde National Park, CO 81330. The Chapin Mesa Museum (☎ 970-529-4475) is open daily from 8 am to 5 pm (6:30 pm in summer) and provides information on weekends, when park headquarters is closed.

Entrance to the park costs $10 for each vehicle passenger and $5 for bicyclists, hikers and motorcyclists; it's valid for seven days. Golden Age, Access and Eagle Passes are accepted. The combined brochure and map handed to each visitor is also available in French, Spanish and German. Park roads are open from 8 am to sunset, except Wetherill Mesa Rd, which closes at 4:30 pm. Winter vehicle travel on Ruins Rd is subject to weather conditions. You may snowshoe or cross-country ski on the roadway when conditions permit.

The post office is at park headquarters on Chapin Mesa; the zip code is 81330.

Note for Mesa Verde National Park Visitors

Preserving the Ancestral Puebloan sites while accommodating ever increasing numbers of visitors continues to challenge the National Park Service. The NPS strictly enforces the Antiquities Act, which prohibits removal or destruction of any artifacts and also prohibits public access to many of the approximately 4000 known sites.

Opportunities for trail hikes are extremely limited. Only a handful of stabilized structures can withstand the trampling and climbing of throngs of visitors. Consider Mesa Verde to be a gigantic outdoor museum; stay on the path or behind the obvious barricades unless guided by an NPS ranger.

Increased visitation and NPS restrictions conspire against casual tourists trying to enjoy the park on a brief visit of only a few hours. Windshield tourists expecting a passive scenic excursion will be disappointed. If you only have time for a short visit, see the Chapin Mesa Museum and try a walk through the crowded Spruce Tree House, where you can climb down a wooden ladder into the cool chamber of a kiva. But Mesa Verde rewards travelers who set aside a day or more to take the ranger-led tours of Cliff Palace and Balcony House, explore Wetherill Mesa, linger in the museum or participate in a campfire program.

If possible, avoid the peak-season crowds from mid-July to September, when the weather may be uncomfortably hot. Late May or mid-September, when most schools are in session, is an ideal time to take advantage of all services but the Wetherill Mesa interpretive tours. ■

The Mesa Verde Museum Association (☎ 970-529-4445), located in the Chapin Mesa Museum, has an excellent selection of materials on the Ancestral Puebloans and modern tribes in the American Southwest.

From May to mid-October, laundry and showers are available 24 hours at Morefield Village, near the Morefield Campground turnoff. Showers are only 10¢, but washers are $1 per load.

Ancestral Puebloan Sites

Chapin Mesa In no other place are so many remnants of Ancestral Puebloan settlement clustered together, providing an opportunity to see and compare examples of all the phases of construction: from pit house to pueblo villages to the elaborate multi-room cities tucked into the cliff recesses. Pamphlets describing most excavated sites are available at either the Far View Visitor Center or Chapin Mesa Museum.

On the upper portion of Chapin Mesa are the **Far View Ruins**, perhaps the most densely settled area in Mesa Verde after 1100 AD. The large, walled pueblo at Far View House encloses a central kiva and room layout that originally was two stories high. To the north is a small row of rooms and an attached circular tower that likely extended just above the adjacent 'pygmy forest' of piñon pine and juniper trees. This tower is one of 57 found throughout Mesa Verde that the Ancestral Puebloans may have built as watchtowers, religious structures or astronomical observatories to decide agricultural schedules. They also built a system to divert stream water to fields and into nearby Mummy Lake Reservoir; a masonry ditch led toward Spruce Tree House.

Near park headquarters, an easy walk without ladders or steps leads to **Spruce Tree House**. This sheltered alcove, measuring over 200 feet in width and almost 90 feet deep, contains about 114 rooms and eight kivas and once housed about 100 people. One kiva has a reconstructed roof and ladder for entry. During the winter, when many portions of the park are closed, site access is by ranger-led tours only.

Square Tower House

You can visit Spruce Tree House daily from 9 am to 5 pm.

South from the park headquarters, the 6-mile Ruins Rd circuit connects 10 excavated mesa-top sites, three accessible cliff dwellings and many vantages of inaccessible cliff dwellings from the mesa rim. The road is open 8 am to sunset. Perhaps the most photographed building in the park, on the west loop of Ruins Rd, is the secluded four-story **Square Tower House**. Among the excellent late-afternoon views of many cliff dwellings from **Sun Point** is the vista of Cliff Palace as sighted by Richard Wetherill in 1888. The mesa-top buildings on the west loop of Ruins Rd also feature the astronomically aligned **Sun Temple**.

On the east loop of Ruins Rd, you must have a ticket to take part in the one-hour guided tours of either **Cliff Palace** or **Balcony House**, open daily from 9 am to 5 pm (closed in winter).

Foot access to Cliff Palace, the largest structure in Mesa Verde, resembles the approach taken by the Ancestral Puebloans – visitors must climb a stone stairway and four 10-foot ladders. This grand representative of engineering achievement, with 217 rooms and 23 kivas, provided shelter for as many as 250 people. However, the inhabitants were without running water – springs across the canyon below Sun Temple were the most likely water sources. Use of small 'chinking' stones between the large blocks is strikingly similar to Ancestral Puebloan construction employed at distant Chaco Canyon.

The residents of Balcony House had outstanding views of Soda Canyon, 600 feet below the sandstone overhang that served as the ceiling for the 35 to 40 rooms. Panoramic views, however, were apparently secondary to either concerns for security (entry was via a narrow tunnel) or the attraction of two reliable springs. Today, the visitor enters the obviously stabilized area by a 32-foot ladder to see the cantilevered balcony and enjoy clambering throughout the tunnel and walls.

Wetherill Mesa The western portion of the park is less frequented, but it also offers a comprehensive display of Ancestral Puebloan relics. From the second week in June to the first week in September, the winding Wetherill Mesa Rd is open daily from 8 am to 4:30 pm. The **Badger House Community** consists of a fairly short trail between four excavated surface sites depicting various phases of Ancestral Puebloan development. For a complete chronological circuit, continue along the trail to **Long House**, the second largest cliff dwelling in Mesa Verde. (For this site you'll first need to purchase a $1.35 ticket at the Far View Visitor Center.) The nearby **Step House**, initially occupied by Modified Basketmaker peoples residing in pit houses, later became the site of a Classic Pueblo period masonry complex of rooms and kivas. Stairways and indentations in the rocks provided access to the partially irrigated crops in the terraces on the mesa top.

Park Point
The fire lookout at Park Point (8571 feet) is the highest elevation in the park and accordingly offers panoramic views. To the north are the 14,000-foot peaks of the San Juan Mountains; in the northeast appear the 12,000-foot crests of the La Plata Mountains; to the southwest, beyond the southward sloping Mesa Verde plateau, is the distant volcanic plug of Shiprock (see the Northwestern New Mexico chapter); and to the west is the prone human-like profile of Sleeping Ute Mountain.

Look for mule deer and wild turkeys in the dense growth of serviceberry and Gambel's oak next to the road. The sturdy hardwood from the Gambel's oak provided the Ancestral Puebloans with handy digging tools and fuel. Near the lookout are yucca plants, indicative of the semi-arid climate, with edible fruits that resemble and taste like cucumber.

Hiking
Backcountry access to the archaeological sites is specifically forbidden within Mesa Verde National Park. However, there are several marked trails open to hikers. From park headquarters and adjacent Chapin Mesa Museum, two trail loops, each under 3 miles in length, are available from the short path to Spruce Tree House. Every hiker must first register at park headquarters before starting. While you're there, pick up pamphlets for the **Petroglyph Point Trail** and the self-guided tour of Spruce Tree House.

From the museum overlook of Spruce Tree House, follow the path to the canyon floor. Return via Petroglyph Point Trail to view the petroglyphs pecked into the naturally varnished rock surface and interpret the uses of native plants. After you climb about 300 feet back to the rim, either return directly to park headquarters or continue to the left on another loop, the **Spruce Canyon Trail**.

From the amphitheater parking area near Morefield Campground, a spur trail climbs to **Point Lookout**, about 2 miles away, where you may witness a fabulous

COLORADO

sunset over Sleeping Ute Mountain (elevation 9884 feet). The 8-mile **Prater Ridge Trail** loop starts at the Hopi group area in Morefield Campground. Neither of these trails requires a permit.

Biking
Finding convenient parking for an automobile at the many stops on Ruins Rd is not a problem for the cyclist. Only the hardiest cyclists, however, will want to enter the park by bike and immediately face the intense 4-mile ascent to Morefield Campground, followed by a narrow tunnel, to reach the North Rim. An easier option is to unlimber your muscles and mount up at Morefield, Far View Visitor Center or park headquarters.

If you choose to cycle, note that the NPS prohibits bicyclists from Wetherill Mesa Rd, and throughout the park secure bicycle parking is rare. Ride *only* on paved roadways.

Organized Tours
ARA Mesa Verde (☎ 970-529-4421), the park concessionaire, offers two guided tours daily from May to mid-October.

Introductory three-hour tours depart from Morefield Campground at 9 am and Far View Lodge at 9:30 am for excavated pit houses, views of cliff dwellings and a tour through Spruce Tree House. Tickets cost $16/8 for adults/children.

A full-day tour costs $21/8 and takes in the morning tour sites. The tour then goes on to examine later architecture and social developments, also taking in the Cliff Palace. For further information contact ARA Mesa Verde at PO Box 277, Mancos, CO 81328.

Places to Stay & Eat
Although there are plenty of mid-range places to stay in Cortez and Mancos, within the national park the visitor must choose between camping or staying at a high-end lodge. An overnight stay in the park allows convenient access to the many ancestral sites during the best viewing hours, participation in evening programs

and the sheer pleasure of watching the sunset over Ute Mountain from the quiet of the mesa top.

With 450 campsites only 4 miles from the park entrance, *Morefield Campground*, open May to mid-October, has plenty of capacity for the peak season. Grassy tent sites at *Navajo Loop* are conveniently near Morefield Village (with a general store, gas station, restaurant, showers and laundry) and cost $10. Full hookups are available for $17. Contact ARA Mesa Verde (☎ 970-529-4421) for information or to reserve group campsites.

Try the *Far View Lodge* (☎ 970-529-4421), 15 miles from the park entrance and perched on the mesa top; it has rooms with private balconies, outstanding views and Southwestern furnishings. Rooms are available from mid-April to the third week in October. The off-peak rate is $73; $93 from Memorial Day to Labor Day. Compared to top-end lodgings in Cortez, the Far View Lodge is a good value and offers a memorable visit.

The *Knife Edge Cafe* in Morefield Village offers breakfast from 7:30 to 10 am and dinner from 5 to 8 pm. The *Far View Terrace*, immediately south of the visitor center, serves reasonably priced meals from 6:30 am to 9 pm, although it closes during the winter months. Near the Chapin Mesa Museum, the *Spruce Tree Terrace* serves sandwiches, salads and the like from 8 am to 5 pm daily.

The *Metate Room* (☎ 970-529-4421) at the Far View Lodge is the nearest restaurant to Dove Creek that serves gourmet Anasazi beans (a variegated pinto bean). Open nightly from 5:30 pm to 9:30 pm, the Metate Room also serves steak, seafood, game specialties and good Mexican dishes for $12 to $20.

Entertainment
Free evening campfire programs are held June to Labor Day nightly at the *Morefield Campground Amphitheater*. For information contact the NPS at the Far View Visitor Center, or call ☎ 970-529-4461 or 970-529-4475.

MANCOS

The historic homes and landmark buildings in Mancos (population 1000), between Cortez and Durango, make for a worthwhile afternoon stop, or a pleasant place to stay while visiting Mesa Verde National Park only 8 miles west.

Historic displays and a walking-tour map are available at the visitor center (☎ 970-533-7434), at the corner of Main and Railroad Ave (Hwy 160). Mancos also offers outdoor activities in the area as well as local ranches that offer horseback rides and Western-style overnight trips.

Places to Stay & Eat

At the east end of Grand Ave, the Mancos River runs beside the town's wooded *Boyle Park*. Tent campsites and restrooms are provided for free; a small donation to help fund park upkeep is appreciated. Please register with the park host, who stays in the trailer at the park entrance.

The best bet in town is the *Old Mancos Inn* (☎ 970-533-9019), 200 W Grand Ave. The hotel's friendly owners, Dean and Greg, have worked hard to renovate the place, and have succeeded in providing very pleasant rooms for reasonable prices. Four rooms with shared bath cost $25 year-round, while those with private bath are $45. An outside deck and a hot tub add yet more value. This is also one of the few truly gay-friendly hotels in Colorado.

Comfortable rooms cost $35/45 a single/double at the *Enchanted Mesa Motel* (☎ 970-533-7729), 862 W Grand Ave. Prices drop to $25/30 in winter. The *Mesa Verde Motel* (☎ 970-533-7741), 191 Railroad Ave, isn't as cozy, but it does have a hot tub. Rooms rates are usually around $40/47.

How about spending the night in a former fire lookout tower? Standing 55 feet above a meadow 14 miles north of Mancos at 9800 feet elevation, the *Jersey Jim Lookout* is on the National Register and is complete with its Osborne fire-finder and topographic map. The tower accommodates up to four adults (bring your own bedding) and must be reserved long in advance; the reservation office opens March 1 and the entire season is usually booked within the next two to three days. (To make reservations call ☎ 970-533-7060.) The nightly fee is $45; the maximum stay is two nights; children under eight are not allowed.

For breakfast or lunch, the *Dusty Rose Cafe* (☎ 970-533-9042), 200 W Grand Ave, offers fresh ingredients at good prices. An upscale steak and seafood dinner choice is *Millwood Junction* (☎ 970-533-7338), at the corner of Main and Railroad Ave. Folks from miles around come to Mancos on Friday night for the $14 seafood buffet.

DOLORES

Dolores (population 1000) enjoys a scenic location in the narrow Dolores River Canyon, 11 miles north of Cortez on Hwy 145. Housed in a replica of the town's old railroad depot, the Dolores Visitors Center (☎ 970-882-4018, 800-807-4712), 421 Railroad Ave (Hwy 145), has information about lodging and outdoor activities in the area. It's open between May and October from 9 am to 5 pm, Monday to Saturday, and 10 am to 4 pm on Sunday. Adjacent to the visitor center is the **Galloping Goose Museum**, which has displays and one example of the rather odd-looking gasoline-powered vehicles used by the Rio Grande Southern Railroad to continue rail service in the San Juan Mountains during the economic troubles of the 1930s.

You can find out about nearby camping and hiking opportunities in the San Juan National Forest at the USFS Dolores Ranger Station (☎ 970-882-7296), at the corner of 6th and Central Ave. Its hours are 8 am to 5 pm weekdays year-round. To clean up after your outings, the Dolores Laundry & Public Showers, 302 Railroad Ave, offers a shower and a towel for about $3.

The first weekend of June is River Raft Days, a playful event that Dolores residents have informally staged on the Dolores River for years in just about anything that floats. Now it also features a strenuous competitive paddle race attracting teams in three classes that start 9 miles upstream from town. To register for the 'fun float'

contact the Dolores Chamber of Commerce
(☎ 970-882-4018).

Places to Stay & Eat

In town, the *Dolores River RV Park*
(☎ 970-882-7761), located about 1½ miles
east of town at 18680 Hwy 145, has nice tent
sites for $11. RV hookups are $18.

At the east end of town, the *Outpost
Motel* (☎ 970-882-7271, 800-382-4892)
has small but clean single/double motel
rooms for $39/49, as well as cabins for
$89. Most of the motel rooms have kitchenettes, and the courtyard features a pleasant
wooden deck overlooking the Dolores
River. The *Dolores Mountain Inn* (☎ 970-882-7203, 800-842-8113), 701 Railroad
Ave (Hwy 145), has immaculate modern
rooms for $54/58 ($40/45 in winter). The
motel's genial owner also offers bike
rentals, shuttle service and guided tours.

Near the visitor center and listed on the
National Register of Historic Places, the
three-story *Rio Grande Southern Hotel*
(☎ 970-882-7527), 101 S 1st, dates from
1893 and has B&B rooms with shared
bath for $35/50; those with private bath
cost $49/65. The restaurant has good breakfasts, including tasty omelets and home
fries for $5, as well as inexpensive lunch
specials. The hotel closes between late
November and early March.

The Outpost Motel, Dolores Mountain Inn
and Rio Grande Southern participate in a
'Half Price Ski Telluride' program, offering
savings for winter visitors who stay in
Dolores before heading to Telluride, 68
miles northeast.

Get started with a good espresso at the
German Stone Oven Bakery Cafe (☎ 970-882-7033), 811 Railroad Ave. The owners
offer delicious Belgian waffles or German
pancake breakfasts for under $5. A fine
Bierliste is available at the *Old Germany
Restaurant* (☎ 970-882-7549), 200 S 8th,
which has tasty German entrées such as
pork tenderloin with potato dumplings,
soup, salad and dessert for $16.

Facts about New Mexico

New Mexico

BONNIE KAMIN

Facts about New Mexico

New Mexico is as much a cultural experience as a place to visit, with its strong Indian, Hispanic and Anglo heritages and influences. The USA prides itself on its multicultural diversity, so what's the big deal about New Mexico's three cultures? The state's triculturalism is simply older and more apparently seamless; many visitors glide almost effortlessly from one culture to another.

Some of the country's most inspiring ancient Indian sites are found in the northwestern corner of the state. Here, the Chaco Culture National Historical Park is my favorite of all the many southwestern archaeological sites. It is more than just a ruin: It has a sense of timelessness and spirituality that is almost palpable. Not far away are more than a dozen centuries-old pueblos (Indian villages constructed permanently in adobe or stone), the most famous of which is the living mesa-top town of Acoma Pueblo, which has been continuously inhabited for about eight centuries. These pueblos provide insight into life here before the continent received its name of America.

Thousands of years before advanced Indian cultures built these massive stone buildings and towns, nomadic hunters and gatherers wandered through the area tracking woolly mammoths and giant sloths and were themselves tracked by saber-toothed tigers. The continent's oldest known Indian sites have been discovered in eastern New Mexico: in Folsom, where the remains of the Folsom man, dating back 10,800 years, were uncovered; and near Clovis, where items from Clovis culture date back 11,000 years.

New Mexico's European history, by comparison, is very recent. Nevertheless, the late-16th- and early-17th-century Spanish buildings are the oldest non-Indian structures in the country, predating the arrival of the Pilgrims in New England. The old center

The roadrunner – New Mexico's state bird

of Santa Fe is as historic a place as any in the country, and it attracts and charms throngs of visitors.

The natural beauty of the state comprises many unique features, not the least of which is the luminescent quality of the light. This has attracted many artists during the 20th century. Georgia O'Keeffe is the best known; her canvases superbly capture the vivid colors of the landscape and sky. The southern part of New Mexico has the huge and empty dunes of the White Sands National Monument as well as one of the most impressive and accessible natural cave systems in the world at Carlsbad Caverns National Park.

With such a combination of culture, light and landscape, it is no wonder that New Mexico hosts travelers from all over the world – and beyond! The area has had among the highest number of UFO sightings anywhere (there's even a museum dedicated to them in Roswell) – maybe the next wave of tourists will be from a different galaxy!

Recent History

The territory of New Mexico included Arizona and some of Colorado when the USA annexed the land from Mexico in 1848. When the territories of Colorado and Arizona were proclaimed in 1861 and 1863, respectively, New Mexico's present borders were defined.

During the American Civil War, the Confederate forces tried to control New Mexico in an effort to keep access to the ports of California, but they were defeated by the Union in the second of two major battles in 1862. After the Civil War came the Indian Wars, particularly against the Navajos and Apaches in western New Mexico and eastern Arizona (see Arizona). Despite the wars with the Indians, settlers in the form of cowboys and miners began to arrive in large numbers in the 1870s. Cattle drives from Texas up the Pecos River Valley into the high plains of eastern New Mexico were some of the largest ever known, with tens of thousands of head of cattle moving across the land. The miners ventured even farther west, especially into the mountains around Silver City.

The arrival of the railroads in the late 1870s opened the state to a period of economic boom, with settlers arriving and cattle and ores being shipped east, where there was a ready market for them. Fortunes were made and lives lost in the lawless days of the Wild West. Most famous among the many violent incidents was the Lincoln County War, which pitted rival ranch factions against one another from 1878 to 1881. A major player in this incident was Billy the Kid, perhaps the West's most famous outlaw even though he was gunned down at the early age of 21. The violence and lawlessness was one factor that dissuaded the federal government from granting statehood to the territory of New Mexico. A second factor was an unfounded distrust of the Hispanic population by the Anglo powers in Washington, DC.

This distrust was partially dispelled by the Hispanic New Mexican soldiers who fought with distinction in the Spanish-American war of 1898. The lawlessness of the late 19th century was brought under control, and by the early 20th century, New Mexico was ready for statehood. After a drawn-out process, New Mexico became the 47th state on January 6, 1912.

As with most of the Southwest, the lack of water greatly limited the state's growth. The construction of the Elephant Butte Dam on the Rio Grande in 1916 began to

New Mexico Trivia
Statehood: January 6, 1912 (47th state)
Area: 121,598 sq miles
(5th largest state)
Highest Point: Wheeler Peak
(13,161 feet)
Lowest Point: Red Bluff Reservoir on the Pecos River (2841 feet)
Population (1996): 1,713,407
(36th most populous state)
Nickname: Land of Enchantment
State Capital: Santa Fe
State Motto: *Crescit eundo*
(It grows as it goes)
State Bird: Roadrunner
State Mammal: Black bear
State Tree: Piñon
State Flower: Soaptree yucca flower
(only commercially viable state flower)
State Gem: Turquoise
State Vegetable: Chile

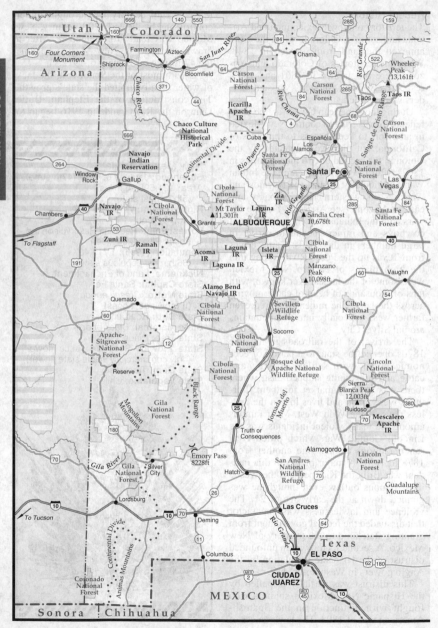

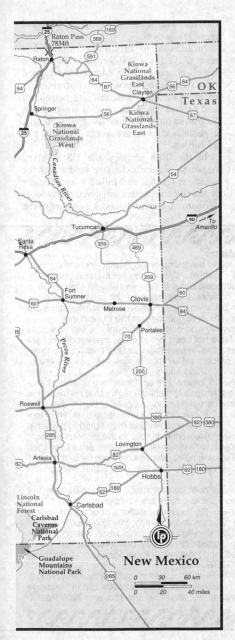

New Mexico

| 0 | 30 | 60 km |
| 0 | 20 | 40 miles |

relieve this. The 1920s were an important decade for New Mexicans. Pueblo Indians gained legal control over their lands after white squatters tried to take them over, and all Indians won US citizenship (although it was not until 1947 that they were allowed to vote). The 1920s also saw the arrival of many artists to the fledgling artist colonies in the Santa Fe and Taos areas.

The Great Depression of the 1930s hit New Mexico hard, although various WPA projects served to alleviate the misery somewhat. WWII revived the state's economy and initiated perhaps the most important project of the war. The Manhattan Project at Los Alamos saw the secret development and testing of the nuclear bomb, which was finally deployed against Japan in 1945 and quickly led to an end to the war. Los Alamos remains an important military research and development center, as does the White Sands Missile Range.

The second half of the 20th century has seen great population growth in New Mexico and throughout the Southwest. This has created pressure on the oldest inhabitants of the state, the Indians and the Hispanic inhabitants who have farmed the land for generations. In 1970, the Taos Pueblo Indians contested the USFS use of their sacred Blue Lake and the surrounding region in the Carson National Forest, and Congress set aside the contested area for sole use of the tribe. Disagreements over the land and resource rights continue today, usually taking the form of lengthy legal wranglings.

Economy
Although the Spanish established missions and haciendas during their first two centuries in New Mexico, agricultural growth was not extensive due to the aridity of the region and Indian opposition to being forced to work Spanish farms. In the 18th century, however, the development of farming, mining and ranching expanded. Not long after Mexico won its independence from Spain, the Santa Fe Trail opened trade with the USA to the east. Despite opposition from Indian tribes,

ranchers and farmers slowly took over the state's extensive grasslands, and in 1879 the Santa Fe Railroad arrived, fueling the growth of the cattle industry during the next decade. Ranching continues to be important to the state's economy today despite extensive overgrazing.

The scarcity of water that had impeded farming efforts and population growth was greatly alleviated by the Elephant Butte Dam on the Rio Grande. Today major crops include hay, sorghum, onions, potatoes, piñon nuts, peppers and pinto beans. However, population growth and agricultural expansion in both New Mexico and Colorado have called into question whether the state will have enough water to support more fast growth.

In addition to agriculture, mining has also played a considerable role in the state's economy. New Mexico has tapped into extensive deposits of potash, uranium, manganese and salt; its petroleum and natural gas production is worth about $3 billion annually; and nonfuel minerals, especially copper, are worth an additional $1 billion.

In the 20th century the US military began to acquire extensive land tracts for weapons testing, and military and nuclear research centers have bolstered many local economies. Currently about a quarter of the

Breaking Stereotypes of Pueblo Indians

People of European heritage have always found the towns of the Pueblo Indians familiar, at least upon first impression. Seeing the organized streets and permanent, multistory buildings, they have inferred that Pueblo cultures parallel European cultures more so than do other Indian cultures. In fact, Spanish conquistadors believed the pueblos were the fabled 'Seven Cities of Gold' and set about pillaging them. However, such inferences are misguided and one-sided, and have had harsh consequences for the Pueblo Indians.

The Pueblo villages have survived physically and culturally throughout the centuries despite barrages of intrusions. Inhabitants have not been forced onto reservations distant and disparate from their original homes, and their leadership remains traditionally theocratic: The religious leaders choose tribal officers rather than acquiescing to the representative system of government that has been forced onto other tribes.

But intrusions have forced Pueblo peoples to forgo some customs for the sake of preserving others. The Hopi, for example, have traditionally placed a high value on the virtue of hospitality, which led them to open many ceremonies to the public. But in the early 1990s, excessive tourism threatened to turn the ceremonies into spectacles. The Hopi could have profited from the tourist interest in their ceremonies, but they opted to preserve their religious integrity by closing most of their ceremonial dances to the general public.

The ceremonies that are open to the public have many restrictions that arise from their spiritual nature. Tribal members participate in ceremonial dances on a prescribed basis – dancers are carefully chosen, and the observers support them and watch with understanding and appreciation.

When non-Indian visitors are allowed to enter pueblos and attend ceremonies, they are often surprised to find that the pueblos and Pueblo culture are unique and distinct from Anglo culture. The pueblos have few or none of the modern trappings of other US towns, such as cars, phones and neon signs. Many areas are off-limits, for no obvious reason. Pueblo Indians rarely offer a hearty handshake or direct eye-contact when welcoming visitors, because eye contact is considered disrespectful. Their conversation can seem muted or limited, but quiet listening is valued, and incessant interjections in conversations such as 'Uh huh' and 'Oh, really?' are considered rude.

Another assumption visitors make about the Pueblo Indians is that only one Pueblo culture exists. The Pueblo groups are united in architecture and theocracy, but in language and dialect, religion and ritual, they differ widely. For instance, the Hopi and Taos Pueblo

state's workers are employed by the federal government, many in military-related jobs.

As in Arizona and Utah, manufacturing industries are experiencing strong growth, and production of electrical goods, food, transportation equipment, machinery and clothing are important. The tourist industry is worth $2.75 billion annually.

The government sector, service and trade industries are the state's major employers, providing about 76% of New Mexico's jobs. Unemployment is 8.1%. Per capita income is $18,770 per year, the third lowest of the 50 states. The US Census Bureau estimates that over 25% of the population lives in poverty, the highest number of any state.

Information

Telephone & Time All of New Mexico uses the 505 area code. The state is on Mountain Time, which is one hour later than the West Coast, two hours earlier than the East Coast, and seven hours behind Greenwich Mean Time.

Driving Laws You must be at least 16 years old, or at least 15 with parental consent, to obtain a driver's license. Drivers and front-seat passengers are required to wear a safety belt. Children under age 11 must use child restraints. You must be over 16 to obtain a motorcycle license. Motorcycle helmets are required for rider and

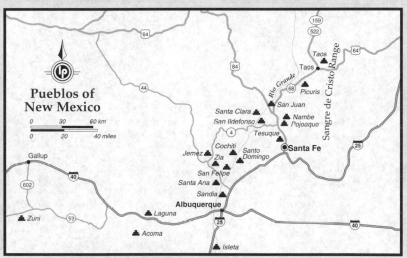

Indians are both Pueblo tribes living in ancient towns, but their languages and customs are very different. The same differences apply to the many pueblos in the Four Corners Area, where several languages and dialects are spoken and customs are distinct. These disparities arose not only from the distances between the pueblos but also from the assimilation of various tribes into many of them, sometimes centuries ago.

Being prepared to encounter and respect these differences will help non-Indian visitors focus on each pueblo's unique traditions. It's also important to remember that each pueblo has its own rules pertaining to acceptable behavior, particularly in the realm of photography, sketching and other forms of recording sights and sounds. ■

passenger if under 18. The blood alcohol concentration over which you are legally considered drunk while driving is 0.10. It is illegal to have an open container of alcohol in your car while driving.

Drinking Laws You must be 21 to buy a drink in a store, bar or restaurant. Beer, wine and spirits are sold in grocery stores and liquor stores from 6 am to midnight, except Sunday, when sales begin at noon. Restaurants must have licenses to serve alcohol; some licenses are limited to beer and wine. Sales of alcohol stop at 1 am and bars close at 2 am except on Sunday, when bars are open from noon until midnight. Alcohol is prohibited on Indian reservations.

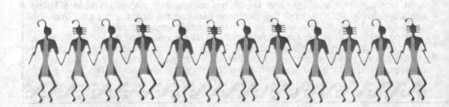

Albuquerque

Although Albuquerque isn't nearly as popular a tourist destination as Santa Fe, the locals don't really mind. At this point they're accustomed to outsiders perceiving their city as a stopover on the way to somewhere else. The largest and most populous city in New Mexico has long been a dot on the map of Route 66, the romantic road that snaked its way from Chicago to Los Angeles in the prehistory of the interstate system.

Indeed, Albuquerque derives part of its identity from its status as a transportation center. Today, more tourists than ever arrive at Albuquerque International Airport before heading north to Santa Fe and Taos. Those pausing long enough to check it out find that Albuquerque has its own appeal and is a convenient base from which to explore the entire region.

At an altitude of 5000 feet and positioned in the valley between the impressive Sandia Mountains to the east and the Rio Grande to the west, Albuquerque exists in a comfortable life zone. Cottonwood trees shade city streets, and the weather is friendly. Winter brings snow to the mountains sufficient for skiers' needs but not enough to make for driving hazards in the valley, and while summer days can reach 100°F, the nights are always forgiving and cool.

Native, Hispanic and Anglo Americans today constitute the bulk of the city's 450,000 residents. The essence of Albuquerque rests in the coexistence of these three cultures as evidenced in the regional art, architecture and food.

HISTORY

The Ancestral Puebloans were the area's first permanent occupants, probably arriving in the sixth century. They planted corn, beans and squash, and constructed dwellings of adobe and brick along the banks of the Rio Grande. The Ancestral Puebloans ultimately abandoned the region around 1300 AD.

In 1540 the Spanish explorer Francisco Vásquez de Coronado arrived in search of riches in the legendary Seven Cities of Cíbola (which he never found). His forces wintered at Kuaua Pueblo on the west bank of the Rio Grande, 20 miles north of present-day Albuquerque. Juan de Oñate's expedition brought settlers in 1598. Farms and ranches sprung up, and a trading center was established at Bernalillo (a few miles north of today's Albuquerque). This was abandoned during the Pueblo Revolt of 1680.

In 1706, provisional governor Don Francisco Cuervo y Valdez established a 'villa' (settlement) south of Bernalillo and named it after the Duke of Alburquerque, viceroy of New Spain. The first 'r' was dropped in the late 19th century, but Albuquerque is still sometimes called the 'Duke City.' During the 18th and much of the 19th centuries, the villa was a dusty trading center along the trail linking Mexico with Santa Fe. Close-knit families of Spanish descent accounted for most of the population. They lived around the central plaza that is today called Old Town.

Albuquerque changed with the arrival of the railroad in 1880. The station, constructed 2 miles east of the plaza, gave rise to a new town reminiscent of the East Coast in design and attitude, and many businesses relocated there. Outsiders soon arrived in numbers enough to change the ethnic makeup of the area. By the time it was incorporated as a town in 1885, Albuquerque had become predominantly Anglo.

Growth continued in the 20th century. Route 66, the easiest way to travel east to west through New Mexico, brought a steady stream of traffic through the town. During the 1930s, motels, restaurants and shops arose along Central Ave to service those motorists.

NEW MEXICO

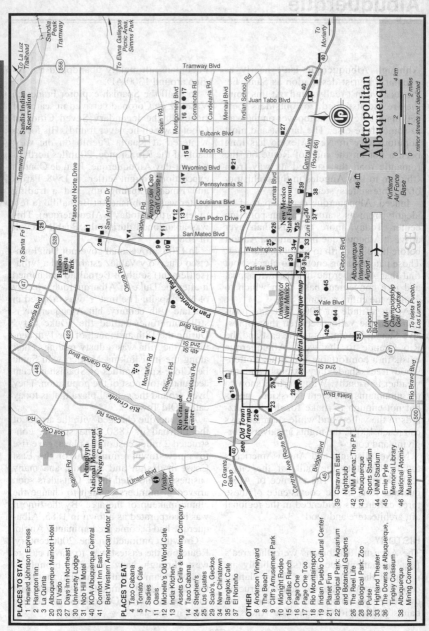

Metropolitan Albuquerque

0   2   4 km
0   1   2 miles
minor streets not depicted

PLACES TO STAY
1 Howard Johnson Express
2 Hampton Inn
3 La Quinta
20 Albuquerque Marriott Hotel
23 El Vado
27 Days Inn Northeast
30 University Lodge
31 Nob Hill Motel
40 KOA Albuquerque Central
41 Comfort Inn East,
Best Western American Motor Inn

PLACES TO EAT
4 Taco Cabana
5 Tomato Cafe
7 Sadies
11 Oasis
12 Michelle's Old World Cafe
13 India Kitchen,
Assets Grille & Brewing Company
14 Taco Cabana
24 Stephen's
25 Los Cuates
29 Scalo's, Geckos
34 New Chinatown
35 Bangkok Cafe
37 El Norteño

OTHER
6 Anderson Vineyard
8 The Beach
9 Cliff's Amusement Park
10 Midnight Rodeo
15 Cadillac Ranch
16 Page One
17 Page One Too
18 Rio Mountainsport
19 Indian Pueblo Cultural Center
21 Planet Fun
22 Biological Park: Aquarium
and Botanical Gardens
26 The Reel Life
28 Biological Park: Zoo
32 Pulse
33 Highland Theater
36 The Downs at Albuquerque,
Tingley Coliseum
38 Albuquerque
Mining Company
39 Caravan East
Nightclub
42 UNM Arena: The Pit
43 Albuquerque
Sports Stadium
44 UNM Stadium
45 Ernie Pyle
Memorial Library
46 National Atomic
Museum

ORIENTATION

Two big interstate highways, I-25 (north-south) and I-40 (east-west), intersect in Albuquerque. An approximate grid surrounds that intersection, the major boundaries of which are Paseo del Norte Drive to the north, Central Ave to the south, Rio Grande Blvd to the west and Tramway Blvd to the east. Central Ave is the main street, passing through Old Town, downtown and the university, Nob Hill and state fairgrounds areas.

Street addresses often conclude with a directional designation, such as Central Ave NE. The center point is where Central crosses the railroad tracks, just east of downtown (see Downtown Albuquerque map). Locations north of Central and east of the tracks would have an NE designation. Any place south of Central and west of the tracks is called SW, and so on.

INFORMATION

The Albuquerque Convention & Visitors' Bureau (☎ 505-842-9918, 800-284-2282, www.abqcvb.org/), 20 First Plaza Building, Suite 601, in the Galleria, is open from 8 am to 5 pm Monday to Friday, and has information on Albuquerque and New Mexico. The Old Town Information Center (☎ 505-243-3215), 303 Romero NW, is open from 9 am to 5 every day. For information on Albuquerque's gay community, call the Albuquerque Lesbian and Gay Chamber of Commerce Information Line (☎ 505-243-6767).

The Cibola National Forest office (☎ 505-842-3292) is on the 5th floor of the Federal Building at 517 Gold Ave SW; it's open 8 am to 4:30 pm Monday to Friday. The main library (☎ 505-768-5140) is downtown at 501 Copper Ave NW. The main newspapers are the *Albuquerque Journal* (morning) and the *Albuquerque Tribune* (evening). The free weekly *Alibi,* published every Tuesday, offers listings of upcoming events in art and entertainment. The University of New Mexico (UNM) publishes the *Daily Lobo,* with entertainment listings as well as alternative perspectives on the news. Two good bookstores are Nob Hill

Books & Music (☎ 505-260-0792), in Nob Hill at 111 Tulane Drive SE, with new and used books, and the huge and comprehensive Page One (☎ 505-294-2026), 11018 Montgomery NE. Page One Too (☎ 505-294-5623), across the street at 11200 Montgomery NE, has used books.

The downtown post office (☎ 505-245-9614) is at 201 5th SW, and the main post office (☎ 505-245-9624) is at 1135 Broadway NE. The Presbyterian Hospital (☎ 505-841-1234 or 505-841-1111 for emergencies) is at 1100 Central Ave SE. For free answers to health-care questions, call ☎ 505-224-7737. The police (☎ 505-768-2020) are at 400 Roma Ave NW.

OLD TOWN AREA

From its founding in 1706 until the arrival of the railroad in 1880, Old Town was the spiritual, social and geographical center of Albuquerque. Many original period structures still stand, making it the city's most popular tourist attraction. Built around a central plaza, Old Town is now a four-block historical and architectural museum, with many art galleries and souvenir shops. The area is bounded by Central Ave, Rio Grande Blvd, Mountain Rd and 19th St.

During April to November, the Albuquerque Museum of Art, History & Science (see below) offers informative and free guided **walking tours** of Old Town. These take about an hour and leave from the main lobby of the museum at 11 am daily except Monday. Call ☎ 505-243-7255 for information. The Old Town Information Center on Romero has a pamphlet called *Old Town: A Walking Tour of History and Architecture* that guides you to 17 of the area's historically significant structures. Also pick up the *Historic Albuquerque Tour Map and Guide* at the Information Center.

San Felipe de Neri Church

At the north end of the plaza, this church is Old Town's most famous sight. Built in 1706, it has undergone several renovations and is much changed from its original

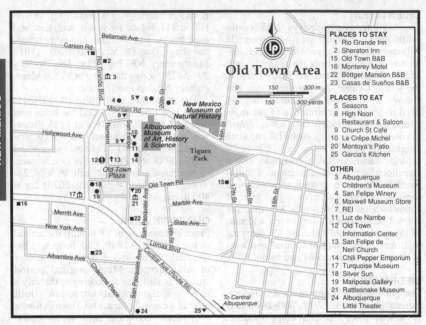

Old Town Area

PLACES TO STAY
1 Rio Grande Inn
2 Sheraton Inn
15 Old Town B&B
16 Monterey Motel
22 Böttger Mansion B&B
23 Casas de Sueños B&B

PLACES TO EAT
5 Seasons
8 High Noon Restaurant & Saloon
9 Church St Cafe
10 Le Crêpe Michel
20 Montoya's Patio
25 Garcia's Kitchen

OTHER
3 Albuquerque Children's Museum
4 San Felipe Winery
6 Maxwell Museum Store
7 REI
11 Luz de Nambe
12 Old Town Information Center
13 San Felipe de Neri Church
14 Chili Pepper Emporium
17 Turquoise Museum
18 Silver Sun
19 Mariposa Gallery
21 Rattlesnake Museum
24 Albuquerque Little Theater

modest adobe form. The humble interior features a balcony reached by a spiral staircase, small wooden pews and an altar decorated with hand-carved statues and icons. Hours are 9 am to noon and 1 to 4:30 pm Monday through Friday, and 9 am to 1 pm Saturday. On Sunday, services begin with Spanish mass at 7 am. Call ☎ 505-243-4628 for further times.

Albuquerque Museum of Art, History & Science

This museum (☎ 505-242-4600), at 2000 Mountain Rd NW, is thematically structured around the city's culturally varied history. Artifact-rich displays lean heavily on the period of Spanish conquest, featuring models of conquistadors in full regalia. A theater presents a film tracing the development of the city from 1875, there's a gallery exhibiting works by New Mexican artists, and exhibits change seasonally. The museum is open from 9 am to 5 pm Tuesday to Sunday; free admission.

New Mexico Museum of Natural History

This excellent museum (☎ 505-841-2800), 1801 Mountain Rd NW, features an interactive walk through Southwestern natural history, taking you back to the dinosaur age, down into an 'active' volcano, into New Mexico's Ice Age and then to the region's saltwater era. The *Evolator* (evolution elevator) transports visitors through 38 million years of New Mexico's geologic and evolutionary history through the use of video technology. Kids love the reconstructed dinosaurs displayed next to replicated skeletons, and the Naturalist Center provides an opportunity for them to get their hands on snakes, frogs and fossils. Its hours are 9 am to 5 pm daily. Admission is $5.20 for adults, $4.20 for seniors and students and $2 for kids under 11.

Visit the **Dynamax Theater** within the museum, with huge-screen 3D 'movies' that give viewers the sensation of physical participation. Admission is $5.20/4.20 for adults/students and $2.10 for seniors and children age three to 11. Combined theater and museum tickets are available at reduced rates.

Turquoise Museum
Less than 10% of New Mexico's $10 billion turquoise business is natural turquoise, and this private museum (☎ 505-247-8650), 2107 Central Ave NW, helps you to recognize the real stuff with specimens from all over the world. It's a small place, but well worth a visit. Hours are 9:30 am to 5:30 pm Monday to Saturday. Admission is $2/1.50 for adults/seniors and kids under 16.

Rattlesnake Museum
This museum (☎ 505-242-6569), 202 San Felipe NW, claims the largest public collection of different species of rattlers in the world, with some 60 snakes on exhibit. The focus is on education, and curator Bob Myers stresses the importance of rattlesnakes to the ecosystem. Hours are 10 am to 6 pm daily. Admission is $2. A gift shop is packed with reptilian curios.

Indian Pueblo Cultural Center
This center (☎ 505-843-7270), 2401 12th NW, is owned and run by an association of New Mexico's 19 pueblos. Anyone planning to visit the pueblos in their travels would benefit from the center's introduction to Pueblo history and culture. A historical museum traces the development of Pueblo cultures from prehistory to the pre-

sent. Exhibits allow for comparison of cultures through examination of languages, customs and crafts. There is also an art gallery with exhibits that change monthly, a children's museum, a gift shop and a restaurant serving Pueblo fare.

The center is north of Old Town, one block north of I-40. It's open from 9 am to 5:30 pm daily except January 1, Thanksgiving and Christmas. Museum admission is $3/1 for adults/students.

DOWNTOWN AREA
This area lies southeast of Old Town and west of the university area.

Rio Grande Biological Park
Rio Grande Biological Park (☎ 505-843-7413) includes the Albuquerque Zoo, the Aquarium and the Botanical Gardens in two locations. The Zoo, 903 10th SW, on 60 shady acres along the river, is home to more than 1300 animals from around the world. On summer evenings the zoo hosts weekly outdoor music events. The Aquarium and Botanical Gardens, 2601 Central NW, feature a 285,000-gallon shark tank, a tropical fish tank depicting the Flower Garden Banks in the northernmost of the Gulf of Mexico, and several conservatories housing an array of desert species from around the world. Hours are 9 am to 5 pm Monday to Friday, till 6 pm on the weekends. Admission to the Aquarium and Botanical Gardens is $4.25 for adults, $2.25 for kids and seniors; it's 25¢ more for the zoo.

KiMo Theater
Built in 1927, the KiMo (☎ 505-848-1370, 505-764-1700 ticket office), 423 Central Ave NW, is a historic landmark. The architect, Carl Boller, created a kind of Pueblo art deco in the KiMo using impressions gathered on visits to Indian pueblos and reservations – including such unique adornments as the steer-skull light fixtures with glowing eyes.

Today, the city-owned KiMo is a community arts center, featuring all types of entertainment (see Performing Arts below). The theater may be toured between 9 am and 5 pm Monday to Friday.

Telephone Pioneer Museum of New Mexico

This museum (☎ 505-842-2937), 110 4th NW, has hundreds of telephones and phone memorabilia from the days of Alexander Graham Bell to the present. Museum hours are 10 am to 2 pm Monday to Friday. Admission is free.

UNIVERSITY OF NEW MEXICO (UNM) AREA

With about 23,000 full-time students in some 125 fields, plus another 40,000 students in the continuing education program, UNM is New Mexico's leading university. There are several museums and many cultural events of interest to the visitor. Further information is available from Public Affairs (☎ 505-277-5813) or from the **Visitor Information Center** (☎ 505-277-1989) on Las Lomas Rd, half a block from the intersection of University Blvd and Campus Blvd (at the northwestern corner of the campus). Redondo Drive is the road that loops around the campus.

Tours are available through Outreach Services (☎ 505-277-2260) and last an hour. Museums are closed on legal holidays.

Maxwell Museum of Anthropology

This UNM museum (☎ 505-277-4404), on University Blvd near the Visitor Information Center on Las Lomas, has a permanent 'People of the Southwest' exhibit, depicting 11,000 years of cultural history in the region. A fabricated dig, complete with tools, demonstrates the painstaking methods of archaeology. There are other changing exhibits, and the gift shop has a selection of scholarly books. Hours are 9 am to 4 pm Tuesday to Friday, with varying weekend hours; closed Monday. An adjunct to the museum, the **Maxwell Museum Gallery and Store** (☎ 505-247-1440) is in Old Town at 2031 Mountain Road NW.

University Art Museum

This collection (☎ 505-277-4001) is in the Center for the Arts Building at Redondo and Cornell Drives on the south side of campus. The smallish space is crammed with paintings, prints and sculptures from a permanent collection of 24,000 pieces, many of which highlight New Mexico's rich Hispanic tradition. The museum is renowned for its ample collection of photographs, and its interesting temporary exhibits change frequently. Hours are from 9 am to 4 pm Tuesday to Friday, 5 to 8 pm Tuesday evenings and 1 to 4 pm Sunday. It is also open during most weekend evening performances at adjoining Popejoy Hall.

The affiliated **Jonson Gallery** (☎ 505-277-4967), 1909 Las Lomas Rd, is in the former home and studio of painter and longtime UNM professor Raymond Jonson; it's open from 9 am to 4 pm Tuesday to Friday, and from 5 to 8 pm Tuesday evenings. The small, modern **University Art Museum Downtown** (☎ 505-242-8244), 516 Central Ave SW, is open 11 am to 4 pm Tuesday to Saturday.

Other UNM Museums

In Northrop Hall you'll find the **Meteorite Museum** (☎ 505-277-2747), run by the Institute of Meteoritics, and the **Geology Museum** (☎ 505-277-4204), run by the Department of Earth and Planetary Sciences. Permanent and changing exhibits feature meteorites from around the world and an extensive display of rocks and fossils. They are open weekdays only; call for hours.

Next door in Castetter Hall, room 167, the **Biology Museum** (☎ 505-277-3411) is for biology buffs. Although more research library than museum, this place nonetheless has a large collection of information on Southwestern plant and animal life. There are no regular hours; call for an appointment.

Tamarind Institute

Highly regarded by lithographers, the Tamarind Institute (☎ 505-277-3901), 108 Cornell Drive SE, features modern lithographs, most of which are for sale. It's open 9 am to 5 pm weekdays, and admission is free.

Ernie Pyle Memorial Library

Once home of the Pulitzer Prize-winning war correspondent, this branch of the city's public library pays tribute to the achievements of Ernie Pyle. Fondly remembered by veterans of WWII for his firsthand accounts of action in Europe and North Africa, Pyle was killed by enemy fire in the Pacific. The library (☎ 505-256-2065) is at 900 Girard Blvd SE. Hours are 12:30 to 9 pm Tuesday and Thursday, and 9 am to 5:30 pm Wednesday, Friday and Saturday. Admission is free.

METROPOLITAN ALBUQUERQUE
Rio Grande Nature Center

The center (☎ 505-344-7240), 2901 Candelaria Rd NE, is a 270-acre reserve on the Rio Grande, with gentle hiking and biking trails winding through meadows and groves of trees. Raccoons, rodents and occasionally coyotes can be spotted. About 260 species of birds have been observed here.

The visitors center displays nature-related exhibits, has a glass-walled library overlooking a wetland home to turtles, ducks and beavers, and offers some weekend educational programs. Admission is $1/50¢ for adults/children under 17. Hours are from 10 am to 5 pm daily except Thanksgiving and Christmas. They stay open until 8 pm on Friday during the summer.

Petroglyph National Monument

This monument, west of the city and 3 miles north of I-40 at 6900 Unser Blvd, is

---

Kids' Stuff

Albuquerque has a number of attractions that are great for kids. Although many of the attractions listed below are suitable for the adults and children, they are primarily aimed at kids.

The **Albuquerque Children's Museum** (☎ 505-842-5525), 800 Rio Grande Blvd NW, has programs and exhibits designed to give free reign to creativity and imagination. The museum's hands-on emphasis makes the puppet theater, cartoon making and science experiments especially fun. Hours are 10 am to 5 pm Monday to Saturday and noon to 5 pm Sunday. Admission is $1 per person over 13 years old, and $3 for those two to 13.

The **Explora Science Center** (☎ 505-842-6188), in the Galleria at 2nd St and Tijeras Ave, is an interactive museum geared toward teaching kids scientific principles. Thirty-five exhibits explore light, electricity, sound, motion, anatomy and more. Explora is open from 10 am to 5 pm Wednesday to Saturday and noon to 5 pm Sunday. Admission is $2/1 for adults/children four to 16. Plans to combine the Explora with the Children's Museum in Old Town are in the works, so call first.

Use **Cliff's Amusement Park** (☎ 505-881-9373), 4800 Osuna NE just off I-25, to reward your kids for being so patient and cooperative in the back seat. The park has about 25 rides, including a roller coaster, Ferris wheel and other traditional favorites. An unlimited-ride pass costs $13. The park is open April to October and is closed Monday and Tuesday.

At **Planet Fun** (☎ 505-294-1099), 2266 Wyoming NE, kids leave their shoes at the door and clamber on a giant jungle gym. The coolest feature is the 2000-sq-foot Laser Storm, where kids play 'laser tag' with beams of light. Daily admission is $5 on weekdays, $6 on weekends (free for adults).

Adults might enjoy **The Beach** (☎ 505-345-6066), 3 Desert Surf Circle, just as much as the kids do. There are seven water slides and a giant pool that creates five-foot swells for body surfers. If you're timid, tired or just a toddler, float down the Lazy River or in one of the kiddie pools. From April to Labor Day you can splash all day for $12.50, from 4:30 to 6:30 pm closing for $4, or on Saturday nights until 11 pm for $7 (kids under three are free). Call to confirm ever-changing times and prices.

Celebrating 35 years in 1997, the **Albuquerque Children's Theater** (☎ 505-888-3644) performs two or three shows a year at the KiMo and has shows throughout the year in various locations. ■

home to about 15,000 sacred rock etchings, predominantly created around 1300 AD by Indians who hunted in the area. The visitor center (☎ 505-899-0205) is open 8 am to 5 pm daily. Petroglyphs and hiking trails are at Boca Negra Canyon, 3 miles past the visitors center. Three numbered trails, all relatively vigorous, take you around the petroglyphs. The most challenging, Mesa Point Trail, climbs to the top of a lava flow and gives good views of the petroglyphs, the surroundings and the abutting housing developments. Hike on your own or pick up a schedule for free ranger-led summertime tours at the visitors center. Boca Negra is open from 9 am to 6 pm in the summer and 8 am to 5 pm in winter. Admission is $1 per car on weekdays, $2 on weekends. There are picnic facilities, drinking water and bathrooms, but no camping.

Sandia Peak Tramway

Albuquerque boasts the world's longest tramway (☎ 505-856-7325 or 6419). The beautiful (especially at sunset) 2.7-mile, 18-minute ride starts in the desert realm of cholla cactus and soars through a variety of vegetation zones, until it reaches the Hudsonian-zone climate at the 10,300-foot summit, where riders can enjoy an observation deck, restaurant (☎ 505-243-9742) and trails for hiking, cross-country skiing and biking. You can't bring your bike on the tram, but you can rent one at the ski basin on the east side of the mountain. The tram is also a convenient way for skiers to reach the Sandia Peak ski area.

In summer, trams run 9 am to 10 pm. Hours are somewhat abbreviated in the winter. Roundtrips cost $14/10 for adults/ seniors and children. Price increases are scheduled in late 1988. To reach the tram, take Tramway Blvd north on the east side of town, or take I-25 exit 234 and head east on Hwy 556.

Elena Gallegos Picnic Area in Albert G Simms Park

In the foothills of the Sandia Mountains, off Tramway Blvd NE, north of Academy Ave, this park offers several miles of biking and hiking trails as well as trailheads for hiking in the Sandia Wilderness. The 5.3-mile Pino Trail leads hikers to the crest. Hours are 7 am to 9 pm in the summer and 7 am to 7 pm in the winter. Admission is $1 per car on weekdays, $2 on weekends. Call ☎ 505-857-8334 for more information.

National Atomic Museum

This museum (☎ 505-284-3243) is on the grounds of Kirtland Air Force Base, south of I-40 on Wyoming Blvd. Depending on your perspective, the museum is either a tribute to good old scientific know-how or a bizarre public relations center, extolling the virtues of nuclear technology. Outside is a full range of atomic weaponry, including replicas of the innocuously named 'Little Boy' and 'Fat Man' – the bombs that destroyed Hiroshima and Nagasaki. Inside, a film theater shows *Ten Seconds That Shook the World*, an hourlong film about the development of the atomic bomb. Hours are 9 am to 5 pm daily (except major holidays), and the film is shown four times daily. Admission is free, but you must identify yourself at the base entrance to be admitted.

Wineries

Spanish priests began making wine from local grapes by the mid-17th century. Flash floods and years of drought almost eliminated wine production by 1900, but since the 1960s the area has seen a revival of the ancient art. The annual Bernalillo Wine Festival occurs on Labor Day weekend. Call the New Mexico Wine Growers Association (☎ 505-892-4178) for further information on regional wine festivals.

Several vineyards in or close to Albuquerque offer tours and wine tasting:

Anderson Valley Vineyards, 4920 Rio Grande
  Blvd NW (☎ 505-344-7266)
Gruet Winery, 8400 Pan American NE
  (☎ 505-821-0055)
San Felipe Winery, 2011 Mountain Rd NW
  (☎ 505-843-8171)
Sandia Shadows Vineyard, 11704 Coronado NE
  (☎ 505-856-1006)
Anasazi Fields, PO Box 712, Placitas
  (☎ 505-867-3062)

ACTIVITIES

The omnipresent Sandia Mountains offer many opportunities for hiking, skiing, picnicking, biking and camping. To reach the top, either drive up the eastern side or take the tram up the western side.

The **Sandia Crest National Scenic Byway** (Hwy 536) passes several picnic areas and trailheads (each with a daily $3 fee) as it winds up the eastern slope of the Sandias to Sandia Peak. From Albuquerque, take I-40 east to exit 175, and drive about 6 miles north on Hwy 14 until it connects with Hwy 536 at San Antonito. An alternative route is to go north on I-25 to exit 242 and take Hwy 165 east past Placitas; this bumpy dirt road through Las Huertas Canyon connects with Hwy 536 just north of the ski base and a few miles south of the peak. Along the way, stop at **Sandia Man Cave**, a prehistoric dwelling site. It's a beautiful drive, with several picnic and camping areas, but closed during winter. Call the helpful Sandia Ranger Station (☎ 505-281-3304), 11776 Hwy 337, about a mile south of I-40 exit 175, for maps and information on the Sandia Wilderness Area. They are open 8 am to 5 pm daily except major holidays and close for lunch on weekends.

Skiing

You can hit the slopes at 200-acre Sandia Peak Ski Area (☎ 505-242-9133) in less than an hour from downtown. Ride the tram from the western base of the Sandias to the top of the ski area, or drive up the eastern side and park at the bottom of the slopes. Full/half-day lift tickets are $32/$22 for adults, and $22/$14 for kids (those under 46 inches in their ski boots ski free) and seniors. Combined ski and tram tickets cost slightly less. Rent downhill skis at the ski base for about $15 a day.

Cross-country trails atop the mountain are maintained by the Cibola National Forest. In town, Rio Mountainsport (☎ 505-766-9970), 1210 Rio Grande Blvd NW, rents cross-country skis and snowshoes for about $15 a day. REI (☎ 505-247-1191), 1905 Mountain Rd NW in Old Town, and

Mountains and Rivers (☎ 505-268-4876), 2320 Central Ave SE, also rent equipment.

Biking

There are extensive mountain biking trails in the Sandia Mountains, as well as in the Rio Grande Bosque. From late May through mid-October, the Sandia Ski operates one summer chair-lift from 10 am to 4 pm, Thursday to Sunday. You can rent bikes at the top of the lift (accessed by the tram) or at the ski base for $35 a day, including unlimited lift rides. With your own bike or just to ride the lift, it is $6 roundtrip or $10 for unlimited rides all day.

Hiking

Albuquerque's most attractive day hike is perhaps the beautiful 8-mile **La Luz Trail** to the top of the Sandias, with spectacular views over Albuquerque, the West Mesa and the mountain ranges beyond. The trail goes from high desert, past a small waterfall and into the pine forests of the peak. You can hike up and take the tram down, but then you'll need to hike 2 miles north from the tram base, along the foothills of the Sandia Mountains on the **Tramway Trail**, to return to your car at the La Luz trailhead. To reach the trailhead, take I-25 north to the Tramway exit and head east. The first road on the left, USFS Rd 444, heads toward the Sandias, and La Luz starts at the end of the road. Follow the signs.

The **Crest Trail** is a 27-mile trail along the top of the Sandias. You'll find three entrances to the trail, one at the northern tip (Tunnel Springs), one in the center (at Sandia Peak) and one at the southern tip just off I-40 (Canyon Estates).

From Simms Park, you can take the 5.3-mile **Pino Trail** to the top of the Sandias; it becomes difficult near the end. There are many shorter hikes throughout the Sandias. Call the Sandia Ranger Station for information.

Other Activities

You can **golf** all year at the UNM Championship Course (☎ 505-277-4546), 3601 University Blvd SE, which charges $57 on the weekdays, $67 on the weekends, for 18 holes. After 4:30 pm, play nine holes for $15. Other popular courses are Arroyo del Oso (☎ 505-884-7505), 7001 Osuna Rd NE, and Paradise Hills (☎ 505-898-7001), 10035 Country Club Ln NW. For more information about these and other courses, call the city's Golf Management Department (☎ 505-888-8115). Santa Ana Pueblo (see that section later in this chapter) has a golf course with spectacular views.

The Tennis Complex of Albuquerque (☎ 505-764-1729) manages **tennis** courts at parks throughout the city.

About 16 companies, including World Balloon Corporation (☎ 505-293-6800, 800-351-9588) and Rainbow Ryders (☎ 505-293-0000, 800-725-2477), offer **hot-air balloon** rides over the city and the Rio Grande for an average of $140 per person. The price usually includes hotel pickup and the traditional champagne breakfast upon landing. The visitors' bureau has a listing for other balloon outfitters.

The Reel Life (☎ 505-268-1693), 1100 San Mateo NE, rents **fly-fishing** equipment and arranges guides.

ORGANIZED TOURS
Numerous companies tour Albuquerque and outlying areas of interest. Gray Line (☎ 505-242-3880) and Rio Grande Super Tours (☎ 505-242-1325) have, among other things, narrated bus tours of the city for $23 per person, of Acoma Pueblo for about $30 and an all-day roundtrip tour to Santa Fe for $36. Seniors and kids pay less.

Southwest Wilderness Trails (☎ 505-867-3442) and Vista Hermosa Llama Farms (☎ 505-898-0864, 800-339-4709) offer day/overnight **llama pack trips** to the Pecos, Sandia and Jemez Wilderness Areas, as well as specialized geology, bird-watching and fly-fishing trips.

New Mexico native Christy Rojas runs Aventura Artistica (☎ 800-808-7352; aven@cerfnet.com), offering customized five-night tours with expert guides focusing on the culture and history of the area. Prices are about $925 per person, double occupancy.

SPECIAL EVENTS
For a complete listing of local and regional events, check with the visitors' bureau. The Friday *Journal* includes a Venue section with an exhaustive listing of festivals and activities, or call ☎ 800-284-2282 for a recorded listing of major events. The following are some of the most notable.

The spectacular **International Balloon Festival** (☎ 505-821-1000, 888-422-7277) attracts almost a million spectators during nine days between the first and second weekends in October. Hundreds of hot-air balloon pilots show their skills in a variety of events and competitions. After sunset, the balloons are internally illuminated and the sky over the festival grounds seems to be filled with giant Chinese lanterns. With so many spectators, parking and accommodations are a big problem, with some hotels booked months in advance.

For 16 days in September, Albuquerque hosts the **New Mexico State Fair**. Attractions include the daily PRCA rodeo, Native American dances, live music by nationally acclaimed bands, thoroughbred horse-racing and midway rides. The ticket prices vary from $1 to $4, and some events require additional admission charges. Fairground entrances are on Central Ave NE and Lomas Blvd NE, between Louisiana Blvd and San Pedro Drive. Call ☎ 505-265-1791 for more information.

The **Gathering of Nations Powwow** features dance competitions, displays of Native American arts and crafts and the 'Miss Indian World' contest. The powwow is held for two days in late April in the UNM Arena, referred to as The Pit (☎ 505-925-5626), at University and Stadium Blvds. In late June, the **New Mexico Arts & Crafts Fair** features works by more than 200 New Mexican artists, with an emphasis on Hispanic and Native American works. This three-day, outdoor exhibit is at the state fairgrounds (☎ 505-265-1791).

During the summer, the city (☎ 505-768-3483) runs two series of weekend outdoor festivals, **Arts in the Parks** and **Summerfest**. Summerfest, in downtown Albuquerque on Saturdays from 6 pm to

11 pm, features different ethnic food and entertainment each weekend.

The **Bernalillo Wine Festival**, held in the village of Bernalillo about 15 minutes north of Albuquerque, takes place every year on Labor Day weekend. The festival has grown into quite a festivity, featuring samples from all the New Mexican wineries, live music, excellent food and crafts booths. Although it can be very crowded, it's a lot of fun and a wonderful way to enjoy the Southwestern sun and relax on the grass. There is an entrance fee of about $10.

PLACES TO STAY – CAMPING

KOA Albuquerque Central (☎ 505-296-2729, 800-562-7781, fax 505-296-3354), 12400 Skyline Rd NE (I-40 exit 166 at Juan Tabo), has more than 200 sites and charges $24 to $31 for electric, water and sewer hookups, all depending on which amenities you want. Tent sites are $22. Kamping Kabins are $37 a double for one room, $47 for two rooms. There's a pool, a hot tub, a miniature golf course, coin laundry and a convenience store on the premises. At the west end of town across the Rio Grande, the *Palisades RV Park* (☎ 505-831-5000), 9201 Central Ave NW, has 109 sites and charges $17/21 for sites without/with hookups and $10 for tent sites. Also along the west side of the river is the *Albuquerque West RV Park* (☎ 505-831-1912), about a half mile north of I-40 at 5739 Ouray Rd NW and Coors Rd. They have 125 sites, mainly for RVs, and charge $13/18 without/with hookups.

You'll find plenty of camping in the Sandia Mountains, though few sites have facilities. You have to pay $3 to park at any of the designated areas. Call the Sandia Ranger Station (☎ 505-281-3304) for specific information on camping in the Sandias.

There's also camping in Bernalillo (see North of Albuquerque) and in the Manzano Mountains State Park (see Southeast of Albuquerque) and south on I-25 at Senator Willie M Chavez State Park (see Belen).

PLACES TO STAY – HOSTELS

There are a few hostels in the Albuquerque area. The *Route 66 Hostel* (☎ 505-247-1813; Ctaylor939@aol.com), 1012 Central Ave SW, offers dormitory bunk beds for $12/14 for HI/AYH members/nonmembers. Private rooms with shared bath are $18/23 for singles/doubles. A room with a private bath is $27. The independent rural *Sandia Mountain Hostel* (☎ 505-281-4117), 12234 Hwy 14, is 20 miles east of the city, on the opposite side of the Sandias; it affords easy access to the Manzano and Sandia Mountains. A dormitory bunk bed and shared bath is $10, plus $2 for linen. Private rooms are $25.

PLACES TO STAY – HOTELS

Albuquerque offers an abundance of hotel lodging possibilities. The least expensive places are along Central Ave. This urban thoroughfare passes Old Town, downtown, the UNM campus, trendy Nob Hill, the state fairgrounds, fine restaurants, sleazy dives and porno stores. While some areas can be rather dangerous and seedy, others have been spruced up in recent years as part of a national effort to preserve and restore historic Route 66.

Rates fluctuate tremendously according to season as well as for seemingly no reason at all – some places even charge up to $15 more for rooms on the ground level than for rooms on the second floor or higher! Many hotels have weekend specials. Summer rates are given below, but prices drop in winter. During the New Mexico State Fair and the International Balloon Festival, rates may be higher and you need to book a room well in advance.

Budget

Motels on Central Ave offer weekly rates and many have kitchens. The following are listed heading east from Old Town. Near to Old Town are two old Route 66 motels, *El Vado* (☎ 505-243-4569), 2500 Central Ave SW, and the *Monterey Motel* (☎ 505-243-3554), 2402 Central Ave SW. El Vado, built with adobe bricks in 1936, claims to be the purest surviving Route 66

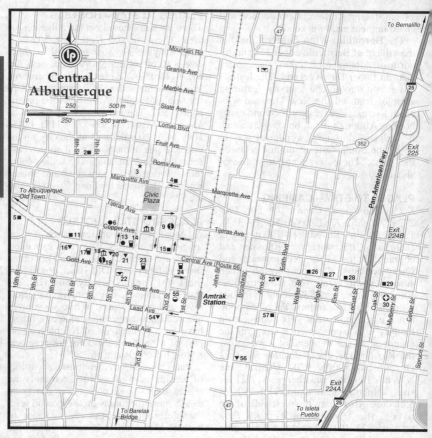

Central Albuquerque

motel in Albuquerque, and it certainly has that Route 66 feel. Clean, simple rooms, many with individual car ports, cost $25/35 for a single/double. The rooms at Monterey are about $48. Continuing east, a great place to stay if you want to be in the downtown area is the Executive Inn (☎ 505-247-1501), 717 Central Ave NW. It's a six-story building with rooms in the $25 to $40 range. Past the central downtown area, clumped together in the blocks just west of I-25, are several nondescript spots with rooms in the $25 to $35 range: *Gaslite* (☎ 505-242-6020), 601 Central

Ave NE, the *Travel Inn* (☎ 505-247-8897), 615 Central Ave NE, the *Imperial Inn* (☎ 505-247-4081), 701 Central Ave NE, the preferable *Lorlodge East* (☎ 505-243-2891), 801 Central Ave NE, and the *Stardust Inn* (☎ 505-243-1321), 817 Central Ave NE.

Conveniently located between downtown and the university area is *Crossroads Motel* (☎ 505-255-7586), 1001 Central Ave NE. East of the University in the trendy Nob Hill district, with many restaurants, bars and two art theaters within blocks, is the *Hiway House Motel* (☎ 505-268-3961),

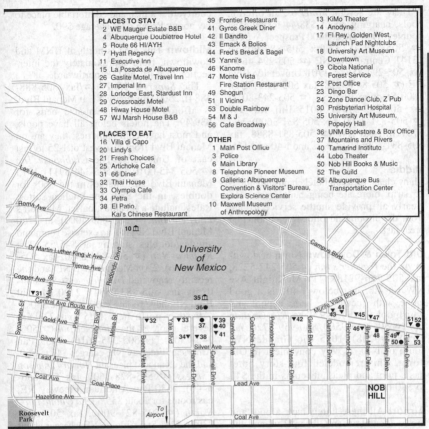

PLACES TO STAY
2 WE Mauger Estate B&B
4 Albuquerque Doubletree Hotel
5 Route 66 HI/AYH
9 Hyatt Regency
11 Executive Inn
15 La Posada de Albuquerque
26 Gaslite Motel, Travel Inn
27 Imperial Inn
28 Lorlodge East, Stardust Inn
29 Crossroads Motel
48 Hiway House Motel
57 WJ Marsh House B&B

PLACES TO EAT
16 Villa di Capo
20 Lindy's
21 Fresh Choices
25 Artichoke Cafe
31 66 Diner
32 Thai House
33 Olympia Cafe
34 Petra
38 El Patio,
      Kai's Chinese Restaurant

39 Frontier Restaurant
41 Gyros Greek Diner
42 Il Bandito
43 Emack & Bolios
44 Fred's Bread & Bagel
45 Yanni's
46 Kanome
47 Monte Vista
      Fire Station Restaurant
49 Shogun
51 Il Vicino
53 Double Rainbow
54 M & J
56 Cafe Broadway

OTHER
1 Main Post Office
3 Police
6 Main Library
8 Telephone Pioneer Museum
9 Galleria: Albuquerque
      Convention & Visitors' Bureau,
      Explora Science Center
10 Maxwell Museum
      of Anthropology

13 KiMo Theater
14 Anodyne
17 FI Rey, Golden West,
      Launch Pad Nightclubs
18 University Art Museum
      Downtown
19 Cibola National
      Forest Service
22 Post Office
23 Dingo Bar
24 Zone Dance Club, Z Pub
30 Presbyterian Hospital
35 University Art Museum,
      Popejoy Hall
36 UNM Bookstore & Box Office
37 Mountains and Rivers
40 Tamarind Instituto
44 Lobo Theater
50 Nob Hill Books & Music
52 The Guild
55 Albuquerque Bus
      Transportation Center

3200 Central Ave SE. At another great location, on the eastern edge of Nob Hill just past Carlisle, is the *Nob Hill Motel* (☎ 505-255-3172), 3712 Central Ave SE, and the *University Lodge* (☎ 505-266-7663), 3711 Central Ave NE. The University Lodge is a cut above the competition, offering free coffee and donuts, a pool and a tidy appearance. Rates at both Nob Hill spots range from $25 to $35.

Nearer to Washington St, *Royal Hotel* (☎ 505-265-3585), 4119 Central Ave NE, *American Inn* (☎ 505-262-1681), 4501 Central Ave NE, and *Zia Motor Lodge*

(☎ 505-265-2896), 4611 Central Ave NE, offer rooms from about $30.

Continuing east on Central Ave, toward the increasingly seedy state fairgrounds area and near San Mateo Blvd, are several spots with doubles in the $30s: the *Riteway Inn* (☎ 505-265-8413), 5201 Central Ave NE, the *Trade Winds Motor Hotel* (☎ 505-268-3333), 5400 Central Ave SE, and the "old Route 66" looking *Tewa Lodge* (☎ 505-255-1632), 5715 Central Ave NE. Directly across from the fairgrounds is the pleasant *Luxury Inn* (☎ 505-255-5900, fax 505-256-4915), with doubles starting at $35.

There are several *Motel 6*s, all offering pools, charging about $38/44 for singles/doubles. They are at 3400 Prospect Ave NE (☎ 505-883-8813, fax 505-883-6056); 13141 Central Ave NE (☎ 505-294-4600, fax 505-294-7564); 1701 University Blvd NE (☎ 505-843-9228, fax 505-842-1757); 1000 Stadium Blvd SE (☎ 505-243-8017, fax 505-242-5137); 6015 Iliff Rd NW (☎ 505-831-3400, fax 505-831-3609); and 5701 Iliff Rd NW (☎ 505-831-8888, fax 505-831-6296), at Coors and I-40 exit 155.

Middle

Many clean, pleasant hotel chains hug the I-25 strip; more are being built every year. Nearly all provide shuttle service to and from the airport and offer free continental breakfast.

Old Town & Downtown North of downtown, the *Traveler's Inn* (☎ 505-242-5228, fax 505-766-9218), 411 McKnight Ave NW (at 4th, just below I-40), is a good value with queen-size beds, a pool and whirlpool for $43/49. The *Rio Grande Inn* (☎ 505-843-9500, 800-959-4726, fax 505-843-9238), 1015 Rio Grande NW, south of I-40, is very convenient to Old Town. This remodeled four-story hotel has a pool and pleasant rooms in the $40 to $70 range.

Airport All these hotels have a pool and are located between Gibson Blvd and the airport. The *Best Western Airport Inn* (☎ 505-242-7022, fax 505-243-0620), 2400 Yale Blvd SE, offers rooms in the $60s. Next door, the *Comfort Inn* (☎ 505-243-2244, fax 505-247-2925), 2300 Yale SE, charges $50 to $80. The *La Quinta Inn – Airport* (☎ 505-243-5500, fax 505-247-8288), 2116 Yale Blvd SE, offers large, comfortable rooms and has rates starting at $75. Also try the *Radisson Inn* (☎ 505-247-0512, fax 505-843-7148), 1901 University Blvd SE, with weekend rates starting at $59, weekdays at $80.

The prominent feature of the *Courtyard by Marriott* (☎ 505-843-6600, fax 505-843-8740), 1920 Yale Blvd SE, is its central courtyard – a lush and comfortable place to lay about. Room rates average $90.

Midtown This area is north of UNM and downtown, from approximately the intersection of I-40 and I-25 northward.

The *Super 8 Motel* (☎/fax 505-888-4884), 2500 University NE at Menaul Blvd, is affordable with queen-size beds for $39/49. The hotels below all have pools, and most have coin laundries; they are on Menaul Blvd from just west of I-25 to just east of University. The *Clubhouse Inn* (☎ 505-345-0010, fax 505-344-3911), 1315 Menaul Blvd NE, charges in the $60s for doubles, in the $80s for kitchen suites. Rates include a breakfast buffet. Marriott's *Fairfield Inn* (☎ 505-889-4000), at 1760 Menaul Blvd NE, has an exercise room and singles/doubles starting at $45/55. The *Rodeway Inn* (☎ 505-884-2480, fax 505-889-0576), 2108 Menaul Blvd NE, and the recently renovated *Travelodge* (☎ 505-884-0250, fax 505-883-0594), 2120 Menaul Blvd NE, have rooms starting in the $50s.

Farther north near I-25 exit 231 are several choices: the *Budgetel Inn* (☎ 505-345-7500, fax 505-345-1616), 7439 Pan American Freeway NE, charges $40 to $60, and the clean and pleasant *Howard Johnson Express* (☎ 505-828-1600, fax 505-856-6446), 7630 Pan American Freeway NE, has rooms for about $55/63. *La Quinta Inn – North* (☎ 505-821-9000, fax 505-821-2399), 5241 San Antonio NE, charges about $75 for attractive Southwestern rooms; across I-25, the *Hampton Inn* (☎ 505-344-1555, fax 505-345-2216), 5101 Ellison NE, has rooms for about $60. Rates for one- and two-room suites, each with a kitchenette, range from $75 to $90 at the full-service *Amberly Suite Hotel* (☎ 505-823-1300, 800-333-9806, fax 505-823-2896), 7620 Pan American Freeway NE. There's a restaurant and a bar with live music.

East Side The accommodations on Albuquerque's east side offer convenient access to the Sandia and Manzano Mountains. The choices below offer standard rooms in the $60 to $80 range.

The *Best Western American Motor Inn* (☎ 505-298-7426, fax 505-298-0212), 12999 Central Ave NE, and the *Comfort Inn – East* (☎ 505-294-1800, fax 505-293-1088), 13031 Central Ave, are near Tramway Blvd. The *Days Inn Northeast* (☎ 505-275-3297, 800-329-7466, fax 505-275-0245), 10321 Hotel Ave NE, is off I-40 exit 165 (Eubank Blvd).

Top End

Old Town & Downtown The *Sheraton Inn* (☎ 505-843-6300, 800-237-2133), 800 Rio Grande Blvd NW, just a stroll away from Old Town, offers Southwestern-style rooms in the $120 to $170 range, with weekend packages available.

Two modern, luxury downtown hotels are full-service establishments, featuring all the amenities. The 20-story *Hyatt Regency* (☎ 505-842-1234, 800-233-1234, fax 505-842-1184), 330 Tijeras NW, has rooms for $100 to $325. A weekend night at the *Albuquerque Doubletree Hotel* (☎ 505-247-3344, fax 505-247-7025), 201 Marquette Ave NW, across from the civic plaza, can be had for as little as $80. Weekday rates start at $115, and suites range from $270 to $470.

La Posada de Albuquerque (☎ 505-242-9090, 800-777-5732, fax 505-242-8664), 125 2nd NW, was built in 1939 by Conrad Hilton, a Socorro-area native, and is registered with Historic Hotels of America. The lobby's relaxed bar, with weekend jazz, tiled fountain, white stucco walls rising to a dark wooded mezzanine, and gaslight-style chandeliers all give La Posada the look of an Old World hacienda. The spacious Southwestern rooms with handmade furniture are in the $70 to $160 range.

Midtown The *Albuquerque Hilton* (☎ 505-884-2500, fax 505-889-9118), 1901 University Blvd NE, has 264 rooms starting at $90, and suites for $375 and up. Facilities include tennis courts, two pools and two restaurants. The *Holiday Inn Mountain View* (☎ 505-884-2511), 2020 Menaul Blvd NE, has a sauna, spa, exercise area, restaurant and coffee shop. They quote rooms as starting at $100, but they can sometimes go down to $75.

The *Residence Inn by Marriott* (☎ 505-881-2661, fax 505-884-5551), 3300 Prospect Ave NE, looks like an apartment complex and offers weekly rates. The hotel's 112 rooms/suites all have kitchenettes, and there is a pool and sauna. Rates start at $115 for a studio. Farther east, the *Albuquerque Marriott Hotel* (☎ 505-881-6800, fax 505-888-2982), 2101 Louisiana Blvd (I-40 exit 162), has all the usual frills with large rooms for about $100.

PLACES TO STAY – B&Bs

Bed and Breakfast Direct (☎ 800-401-2262) or Bed & Breakfast Southwest Reservation Service (☎ 800-762-9704) can assist you in finding and reserving a room at one of the area's many B&Bs. Most B&Bs don't allow smoking.

The friendly *Böttger Mansion* (☎ 505-243-3639, 800-758-3639), 110 San Felipe NW, Albuquerque, NM 87104, is right in Old Town. Built in 1912, it retains its original early Anglo style – no Old West or Southwestern feel here! A full breakfast in the grassy enclosed courtyard and an evening social hour with wine and hors d'oeuvres is included in the $90 to $130 rate.

Old Town B&B (☎ 505-764-9144, 888-900-9144), 707 17th NW, Albuquerque, NM 87104, two blocks from Old Town, is a simple place in a private home with a pleasant garden courtyard and two rooms for about $75.

Also convenient to Old Town, across the street from the country club golf course, is the incredible *Casas de Sueños* (☎ 505-247-4560, 800-242-8987), 310 Rio Grande Blvd SW, Albuquerque, NM 87104. With one and half acres of luscious gardens enclosed within a grassy courtyard and first-class service, this is a special treat. Originally built as an artists' colony in the 1930s, the 19 adobe casitas feature handcrafted furniture and original artwork by the many artists who have used the peaceful spot as a studio over the years. All have a private bath, and some have a kitchenette, fireplace and/or private hot tub (a couple are outside in a private garden). Rates range from $85 to $245 and include a full breakfast (cooked with herbs grown in their gardens). Massages are available, and one casita features a massage room and how-to books for a romantic getaway!

Near downtown, the *WJ Marsh House* (☎ 505-247-1001), 301 Edith Blvd SE, Albuquerque, NM 87102, is an 1895 brick Queen Anne Victorian house. Six rooms with shared baths and the separate Snyder Cottage, which sleeps up to six people with a private bath and kitchen, range from $60 to $120. *WE Mauger Estate* (☎ 505-242-8755), 701 Roma Ave NW, Albuquerque, NM 87102, built in 1897, is another restored Victorian convenient to both Old Town and downtown. It has eight suites with private baths, some with a kitchenette. Rates range from $110 to $130.

In the rural village of Corrales, about 20 minutes north of downtown Albuquerque, you can stay at the warm and friendly *Nora Dixon Place* (☎ 505-898-3662, 888-667-2349, fax 505-898-6430; Noradixon@ aol.com), 312 Dixon Rd, Corrales, NM 87048. Three rooms with private entrances look out on a peaceful courtyard with spectacular views of the Sandias, and the Bosque and Rio Grande is a five-minute walk. One room has an Indian-style fireplace, another is a two-room suite and all have a refrigerator and microwave. The $80 to $90 rate includes a full breakfast on the weekends and fresh fruit, muffins, yogurt and cereal on the weekdays.

PLACES TO EAT

Some hours are listed below, but generally the hours change according to season, so call to confirm. Often restaurants are open later on weekends.

Budget

Budget-conscious travelers will find plenty of cheap, fast-food and all-you-can-eat options in town, including nightly specials at the nearby casinos. The *Frontier* (☎ 505-266-0550), 2400 Central Ave SE, is a famous 24-hour restaurant that attracts students by day and hungry revelers in the wee hours. Cheap breakfasts, burgers and

burritos (try the breakfast burrito or the green chile cheeseburger, but be warned that the chile is hot!) are always delicious at this barn-size Albuquerque favorite.

Grab a tray and stand in line at *Furr's Cafeteria* (☎ 505-265-1022), 6100 Central Ave SE, in the first block west of San Pedro Drive, for all the turkey, mashed potatoes and gravy you can eat for $5 at lunch weekdays and for $6 at dinner and on weekends. Furr's also operates several other Albuquerque locations. *Taco Cabana Patio Cafe*, open 24 hours, serves drive-thru and sit down Mexican and New Mexican food. It's better than most fast-food joints, and serves beer and margaritas. There are two locations, 6500 San Mateo Blvd NE (☎ 505-821-0203) and 8330 Montgomery NE (☎ 505-275-2600). Try the original *66 Diner* (☎ 505-247-1421), 1405 Central Ave NE, a former service station on old Route 66. It burned down recently but was rebuilt as an exact replica. Enjoy low-priced 'blue plate' specials, such as meat loaf or macaroni and cheese, with a thick milkshake.

Downtown, *Lindy's* (☎ 505-242-2582), 500 Central Ave SW, is a true-blue diner with daily specials, hamburgers, chiles and homemade pies all in the $2.50 to $5.75 range. Another good option downtown is the brick-walled *Fresh Choices* (☎ 505-242-6447), 402 Central SW, specializing in a healthy all-you-can-eat soup, salad, pizza and pasta bar for $7. A popular all-you-can-eat spot is the *Tomato Cafe Pizza and Pasta Bar* (☎ 505-821-9300), at Wyoming and Academy NE, with a tasty lunch buffet for $6 and a dinner buffet for $8.

Coffee Shops

There are several good coffee shops in the UNM/Nob Hill areas. *Fred's Bread and Bagel* (☎ 505-266-7323), 3009 Central Ave NE, is a hangout for students and Nob Hill workers who enjoy great coffee, juices, bagels and sandwich specials. It's open from 6:30 am to 10 pm daily. *Emack & Bolios* (☎ 505-262-0103), 3001 Central NE across from UNM, is an ice cream chain that originated in Boston and has thankfully made its way to Albuquerque. The ice cream and frozen yogurt is fantastic, and they serve a light lunch.

Now an Albuquerque institution, *Double Rainbow* (☎ 505-255-6633), 3416 Central in Nob Hill, is the place to go for delicious homemade soups, muffins, breads, desserts and ice cream. They serve a spectrum of hot dishes as well, including innovative daily specials. Bakers arrive every morning at 3 am to work on the day's pastries, herbs are brought in fresh daily and you can get unlimited refills on the gourmet coffee for $1.20. Lines tend to go out the door in the late evening and for Saturday and Sunday brunch. The owners have opened a second location in the Northeast Heights (☎ 505-275-8311), 4501 Juan Tabo NE. Hours are 6:30 am to midnight every day.

Mexican & New Mexican

Pancho's Mexican Buffet (☎ 505-265-5634), 8601 Central Ave NE, in the first block west of Wyoming Blvd, serves all-you-can-eat Mexican food for $5 from 11 am to 9 pm on weekdays. *Adobe Rose* (☎ 505-897-2329) moved before press time to 1011 Ortega Rd. It serves tostadas and enchiladas for about $1. Its 1-pound fajita, served with eight flour tortillas for $11, can feed three people!

Mac's La Sierra Coffee Shop (☎ 505-836-1212), 6217 Central Ave NW, across the Rio Grande and three blocks east of Coors Blvd, is a busy spot that's been catering to local families for 40 years. Dinners are about $6. Mac's is open from 5 am to midnight Monday to Thursday, till 3 am on Friday and Saturday, and till 10 pm on Sunday.

UNM students favor *El Patio* (☎ 505-268-4245), 142 Harvard Drive SE, open 11 am to 9 pm daily, for its tasty dishes (ranging from $4 to $7), relaxed atmosphere and patio dining. *Garcia's Kitchen* (☎ 505-842-0273), 1736 Central Ave SW, closer to Old Town, is a friendly family restaurant that draws crowds of locals with its homemade specialties, carne adobada, fajitas and chile stew. Dinners range from $3 to $7. It's open from 6:30 am to 10 pm, but stays open until midnight on Friday and Saturday.

For $6 to $12 including a frosty beer, get some of the most authentic Mexican food in town at *El Norteño* (☎ 505-256-1431), 6416 Zuni SE, two blocks east of San Pedro Blvd. Leo and Martha Nuñez (both from Mexico) and their children run this family restaurant, focusing on fresh ingredients and traditional Mexican recipes. The pollo norteño is fantastic, as is the carne adobada, the chicken mole and the cabrito al horno (oven-roasted goat). For under $6, you can choose from 12 tacos and 10 burritos. Hours are 11 am to 9 pm daily. Across the street from the university, *Il Bandito* (☎ 505-255-6946), 2720 Central Ave SE, is owned by the oldest son, Leo Nuñez Jr. It also serves Mexican food, but it's open late and is more of a café. Try a refreshing agua fresca (cold fresh-fruit drink).

Sadie's (☎ 505-345-5339), 6230 4th St NW near Montaño Rd, a massive place with a barnlike atmosphere, is a local institution and a favorite with many. Giant dinners run from $5 to $13. There is a big-screen TV in the bar, where you will likely have to wait munching on chips and salsa.

Los Cuates (☎ 505-255-5079), 4901 Lomas Blvd NE at Monroe, open daily from 11 am, serves up huge plates of Southwestern specialties for under $8, but come during lunch or for an early dinner if you want to avoid a wait. This place is not for tender palates, as the salsa and chile are full-strength, but the food is excellent and the locals keep coming! If the tiny place is packed, try the restaurant directly across the street – same name, same owners (☎ 505-268-0974) – at 5016B Lomas NE.

M&J (☎ 505-242-4890), 403 2nd St SW, calls itself both a restaurant and a 'Sanitary Tortilla Factory.' It serves very good New Mexican fare, and you can buy a stack of fresh tortillas to go. It's open from 9 am to 4 pm Monday to Friday.

In Old Town, *Montoya's Patio* (☎ 505-243-3357), 202 San Felipe NW, dishes up low-priced breakfasts, as well as burritos and fajitas. The outdoor patio makes for good summer sitting. It's open daily from 9 am, through dinner, till 'whenever business is bad.' Historic Casa Ruiz, home to one of Albuquerque's founding families for over 250 years, now houses the *Church St*

Cafe (☎ 505-247-8522), 2111 Church St NW. With patio dining and a cozy casual interior, this is a good place for breakfast. Strong coffee complements huevos rancheros, omelets or any of the $4 daily specials. The café is open from 8 am to 4 pm daily, and it stays open until 8:30 pm on Friday and Saturday.

Italian

Convenient to downtown is *Villa di Capo* (☎ 505-242-2006), 722 Central Ave SW. Sit inside on overstuffed chairs or outside among the greenery and the fountain. They serve large portions of reasonably priced standard Italian fare. Closed Sunday.

Il Vicino (☎ 505-266-7855), 3403 Central Ave in Nob Hill, is a small and trendy bistro with sidewalk tables and tasty home-brewed beer. Create your own pizza masterpiece, which will be baked in a wood-burning oven, from a selection of interesting toppings like spinach, feta and fresh herbs. They are open from about 11 am to 10 pm daily. They opened in 1993 and did so well that they now have another location in Santa Fe and two in Colorado.

Scalo's (☎ 505-255-8781), 3500 Central Ave SE, in the first block west of Carlisle Blvd, mixes excellent Northern Italian cuisine with casual elegance. There's a candlelit outdoor patio and a newly expanded bar. Most entrées are in the $10 to $18 range. The bar is open until 1 am daily, till 9 pm Sunday. On Friday and Saturday they serve a full menu until midnight.

With seven drive-through locations in town, *Dion's* is a great choice for fast and delicious pizza, salads and subs.

Mediterranean

Try *Petra* (☎ 505-266-2477), 115 Harvard Drive SE, open daily for lunch and dinner, serving vegetarian, Arabic and other dishes. Dinner specials, like kifta and a Greek salad or soup, are only $6. Sit on the patio and enjoy a Turkish coffee.

Across from the university, *Gyros Greek Diner* (☎ 505-255-4401), 106 Cornell Drive SE, and *Olympia Cafe* (☎ 505-266-5222), 2210 Central Ave SE, specialize in generously portioned and tasty Greek dishes for around $5. Olympia Cafe is closed Sunday. In Nob Hill, the white-walled *Yanni's* (☎ 505-268-9250), 3109 Central Ave NE, is a casual and airy spot with good food.

Michelle's Old World Cafe (☎ 505-884-7938), 6205 Montgomery Blvd, serves an interesting combination of Greek, Lebanese and German cuisine. Entrées such as chicken kebabs and wienerschnitzel with sauerkraut are in the $7 to $14 range. Nestled behind the San Mateo strip is *Oasis* (☎ 505-884-2324), 5400 San Mateo Blvd NE, a rather odd spot in a windowless room with the walls painted to mimic the views of the Greek Islands. The food, however, is delicious. Expect to pay about $20 a person for dinner and an appetizer.

Asian

For a cheap meal, it's hard to beat the $6 all-you-can-eat lunch specials on weekdays and the $8 Sunday brunch buffet at the *New Chinatown* (☎ 505-265-8859), 5001 Central Ave. A few blocks from the university is *Kai's Chinese Restaurant* (☎ 505-266-8388), 138 Harvard Drive SE, open 11 am to 8 pm Monday to Saturday, offering standard Chinese fare in the $5 to $10 range.

India Kitchen (☎ 505-884-2333), 6910 Montgomery Blvd NE, open for dinner only and closed on Sunday, is locally favored for its spicy East Indian cuisine. Tandooris, curries, seafood and vegetarian dishes are custom-made to suit anyone's heat tolerance. Dinner prices average $8.

Thai House (☎ 505-247-9205), 106 Buena Vista Drive SE, has good food. Another good spot is *Bangkok Cafe* (☎ 505-255-5036), 5901 Central Ave, voted best Thai food by the weekly *Alibi*'s annual restaurant poll four years in a row. For Japanese fare, including sushi, try the small and airy *Shogun* (☎ 505-265-9166), in Nob Hill at 3310 Central Ave SE. Down the street, *Kanome* (☎ 505-265-7773), 3128 Central Ave SE, has a spectrum of unique Asian dishes in a bright and modern space. Expect to pay about $30 for two people.

Other Eateries

Albuquerque's first microbrewery was the *Assets Grille and Brewing Company* (☎ 505-889-6400), 6910 Montgomery Blvd NE. It now serves a wide selection of fresh-brewed beer, as well as a broad menu, indoors or on its patio. The bar, often filled with a young-professional crowd, is open until 11 pm except on Sunday. They don't serve the full menu that late, but the pizza chef will stay until no one wants pizza!

A relaxed Nob Hill hangout for good grilled burgers and other American/New Mexican fare is *Geckos* (☎ 505-262-1848), 3500 Central Ave SE. It's a popular bar as well, and a pleasant spot to hang out on the patio and people watch.

The unpretentious service at the *Artichoke Cafe* (☎ 505-243-0200), 424 Central Ave SE, belies the fact that the place has been voted an Albuquerque favorite many times. The creative menu has full meals, including lamb and salmon specialties, salads and interesting appetizers. Dinners can reach $20, but it's certainly possible to dine for much less. The café is in an old brick building around a cozy patio, liberally decorated with works of local painters. Lunch hours are from 11 am to 2:30 pm on weekdays, and dinner is served 5:30 to 10 pm Monday to Saturday.

Several places in Old Town are quite good. The *High Noon Restaurant & Saloon* (☎ 505-765-1455), 425 San Felipe, has a rough-hewn atmosphere in keeping with the 18th-century adobe that houses it. They have excellent margaritas and a wide range of very grilled specialties, everything from a basic steak to wild game. With bright yellow walls, high ceilings, fresh flowers and a creative menu, the contemporary *Seasons* (☎ 505-766-5100), 2031 Mountain Rd NW, is a welcome change from the usual Old Town feel. Eat hearty red-chile-dusted chicken burgers or Baja tacos inside, on the patio or on the rooftop cantina (limited menu, open daily). The romantic *Le Crêpe Michel* (☎ 505-242-1251) on San Felipe features a wide variety of crêpes and other traditional French dishes of beef, veal and fresh fish.

Locals go to the *Monte Vista Fire Station* (☎ 505-255-2424), 3201 Central Ave NE, for crab cake appetizers and ambitious dishes with hints of Southwestern and European influences. Entrées run from $14 to $20. The Pueblo Revival building was home to Fire Engine Company Three for nearly 40 years and still has the brass pole. Upstairs, the popular bar spills onto a balcony overlooking the nighttime scene on Nob Hill. *Stephen's* (☎ 505-842-1773), 1311 Tijeras Ave NW at 14th, offers superb Southwestern nouvelle cuisine in an elegant, comfortable atmosphere. Consistently voted one of the city's top restaurants, Stephen's is open daily for dinner only and is a good choice for a quiet upscale meal.

Cafe Broadway (☎ 505-842-8973), 606 Broadway SE at Iron, housed in a beautifully renovated home with a garden courtyard, is the only place in town for Spanish tapas. Most of them are under $3. If you'd prefer a main course to a selection of tapas, they have a great hamburger and fancier options such as paella, grilled lamb chops and fresh fish. On Saturday night, there is a $6 cover for flamenco dancing. Hours are from 11:30 am to 9:30 pm Monday through Saturday.

For great views, try the *High Finance* (☎ 505-243-9742) at the top of Sandia Peak – take the tramway there or drive up the eastern side of the Sandias and walk about a half mile along the crest to the restaurant. While lunch here is affordable, dinners can range from $14 for the basics to about $30 for steak and lobster tail (diners receive a discount on the tram!). The bar opens for early birds at 9 am; they start serving food at about 11 am and they close at 8 pm.

ENTERTAINMENT
Cinemas

A complete listing of what's showing in Albuquerque's many cinemas can be found in the entertainment section of the daily newspapers.

The *Lobo Theater* (☎ 505-265-4759), 3013 Central Ave NE, just east of the university, used to screen foreign and alternative American movies, but it's currently being

New Mexican Indian Casinos

Despite continuing debates between tribal, state and federal government agencies over the legality of Indian casinos, several of New Mexico's Pueblos and other tribes offer 24-hours-a-day Vegas-style gambling, although the casinos are far less glamorous than in Las Vegas. They all have slots, and most offer blackjack, poker and bingo, while some have one or more of craps, keno, roulette and video poker. Many casinos offer wonderfully inexpensive buffets – inexpensive, that is, if you can withstand the temptation to try your luck on your way to the restaurant. Most casinos also offer free shuttles to and from hotels – simply call the casino to arrange a ride. The biggest downside (apart from losing!) is that most are pretty smoky.

Albuquerque area casinos include Isleta Gaming Palace (☎ 505-869-2614) on I-25 exit 215 just south of Albuquerque; Casino Sandia (☎ 505-897-2173, 505-898-0852) at I-25 and Tramway, exit 234; Santa Ana Star Casino (☎ 505-867-0000) in Bernalillo, just north of the city on I-25 exit 243; Casino Hollywood (☎ 505-867-6700), at San Felipe Pueblo, about 15 minutes north of Bernalillo on I-25 exit 252, and Sky City Casino (☎ 505-552-6017) at Acoma Pueblo.

Between Santa Fe and Española is Tesuque's Camel Rock Casino (☎ 505-984-8414) and Pojaque's Cities of Gold Casino (☎ 800-455-3313). San Juan Pueblo's Ohkay Casino (☎ 800-752-9286) is three miles north of Española. In Taos, the tiny Taos Mountain Casino (☎ 505-758-9430, 888-946-8267) does not offer big buffets and has only slots but is smoke free.

In Dulce, the Apache Nugget (☎ 505-759-3777, 800-294-2234) and near Ruidoso, the Casino Apache (☎ 800-545-6040) are the only two that serve alcohol. ■

---

renovated into a restaurant/bar/theater with plans to somehow link the meals served to the movies screened. Could be interesting! Another art house, the *Guild* (☎ 505-255-1848), is a few blocks east at 3405 Central Ave NE. On the UNM campus, the *Southwest Film Center* (☎ 505-277-5608) runs several series concurrently, though they are closed during the summer. Films are shown in the basement of the Student Union Building in the SUB Theater.

Nightlife

For a comprehensive list of Albuquerque's diverse nightspots and a detailed calendar of events, get the *Alibi*, a free weekly. The entertainment sections of Thursday evening's *Albuquerque Tribune* and the Friday and Sunday *Albuquerque Journal* are helpful, too. You must be 21 to enter most nightclubs.

Albuquerque's downtown has several live music clubs and bars within a concentrated area. *El Rey* (☎ 505-764-2624), 624 Central Ave SW, attracts well-known national rock, blues, jazz and country acts, as well as local favorites. The cavernous former movie theater has two large dance floors, three bars, a Friday blues happy hour and a lively crowd. Next door, and part of El Rey, the *Golden West* (☎ 505-764-2624) showcases local and regional bands. It's got an Old West feel, with a good-size dance floor, a couple of pool tables and a different beer special every night. Cover charges vary from $2 to $11.

The *Launch Pad* (☎ 505-764-8887), 618 Central Ave SW, a rather cozy place with a retro modern look, features alternative sounds (both local and national bands), a full menu at the contemporary diner in the front and a happy hour beer and shots bar. Until 9 pm, people under 21 are allowed in and there is no cover (any later, cover charge is about $5). Three pool tables on the second floor overlook the dance floor and band. The *Dingo Bar* (☎ 505-243-0663), 313 Gold Ave SW, a long-time popular spot, pumps out nightly live music, sometimes by national blues, rock and reggae bands. Covers vary from nothing for local bands to $15 for big names. *Zone* and the *Z Pub* (☎ 505-843-7236), 120 Central Ave SW, a rock-and-roll dance club and bar that'll keep you waiting in line to get in, can be pretty crowded and wild. Frequent special events, including dance contests (like the Baja Beach Party and Bikini Contest) and other giveaways, attract an energetic crowd. Quirky drink specials change nightly. The pub opens at 8 pm nightly and the cover varies from nothing to $8.

In sharp contrast, the genteel hotel lobby of the historic *La Posada* (☎ 505-242-9090), 125 2nd NW, features a locally popular happy hour weeknights from 5 to 7 pm, with a buffet and piano bar. There's a jazz combo every Friday and Saturday night. An excellent spot for a game of pool is *Anodyne* (☎ 505-244-1820), 409 Central Ave NW, open from about 4:30 pm daily. A huge space, with book-lined walls, wooden ceilings, plenty of overstuffed chairs, more than a hundred bottled beers and a long window to sit and watch Central Ave, this comfortable pool hall and bar has a relaxed feel. Come just to hang out, or pay $6 an hour for pool.

You can practice your two-step or line dancing to two live country & western bands nightly at the *Caravan East* (☎ 505-265-7877), 7605 Central Ave NE. The *Midnight Rodeo* (☎ 505-888-0100), 4901 McLeod Rd NE, has live country & western and classic rock bands, a huge buffet, pool tables and a race-track dance floor. Both places offer free line and country & western dance lessons and complimentary happy-hour buffets – call for days and times.

For dancing to live Mexican music on Saturdays and a top-40 deejay on weekdays, go to the *Cadillac Ranch* (☎ 505-298-2113), 9800 Montgomery Blvd NE.

Unlike Santa Fe and Taos, the gay scene in Albuquerque is not as well integrated into the straight scene. Two popular gay bars are the *Albuquerque Mining Company* (☎ 505-255-0925), 7209 Central Ave NE and *Pulse* (☎ 505-255-3334), 4100 Central Ave SE.

Performing Arts
The University of New Mexico Box Office (☎ 505-277-4569), located inside the university bookstore at Central and Cornell, sells tickets for *Popejoy Hall*, the primary place in town to see big-name national acts as well as local opera, symphony and theater. *The Pit* (☎ 505-925-5626), the university's sports arena, and *Tingley Coliseum* (☎ 505-265-1791), in the state fairgrounds, host Albuquerque's major events.

The *Albuquerque Civic Light Opera* (☎ 505-262-9301) stages five Broadway musical productions each year at both Popejoy Hall and Highland Theater, 4804 Central SE; ticket prices start at $9. The *New Mexico Ballet Company* (☎ 505-292-4245) runs from October to April, with ticket prices ranging from $5 to $25. For between $12 and $35, you can watch the *New Mexico Symphony Orchestra* (☎ 505-881-8999) perform at various venues, including four spring performances at the Albuquerque Zoo (live music on summer evenings is often featured at the zoo). On Mother's Day, the second Sunday of May, they play for free at the zoo, but the other zoo shows are $12. The Albuquerque Museum (☎ 505-243-7255) hosts summer jazz in the courtyard during summer weekends.

Built in 1936 by the Depression-era Works Progress Administration (WPA), the *Albuquerque Little Theater* (☎ 505-242-4750), 224 San Pasquale Ave SW, near Old Town, is a long-standing, nonprofit community company that stages about six shows a year from September to May. Something is always happening at the historic *KiMo Theater* (see the description at the beginning of the chapter). The venerable old building plays host to a broad range of cultural activities. There are no performances in August. *La Compañía de Teatro de Albuquerque* (☎ 505-242-7929), a bilingual Hispanic theater group, performs many shows on the road at area community centers, but generally they feature three series of shows at the KiMo every year.

SPECTATOR SPORTS

True, there's no match for a big-league **baseball** game, but the Albuquerque Dukes of the Pacific Coast League come pretty close. The Albuquerque Sports Stadium (☎ 505-243-1791), Stadium Blvd at University, is a friendly, intimate park with a sunken playing field and good views – of both the game and the Sandias! – from the stands. Beyond the outfield, a grassy picnic area has been designated the family section – picnics and grilling are allowed but alcohol is not. Ticket prices range from $3 to $6 – less than you'd pay for parking at major league games.

If you're interested in **horseracing**, the Downs at Albuquerque (☎ 505-266-5555) in the state fairgrounds has races from early September through December. When there are no live races, you can go and bet on simulcast races. Admission is free for the bottom floor. On Friday, Saturday and Sunday $3 tickets for Jockey Club seats are available.

Perhaps because of the city's dearth of professional sports teams, the UNM Lobos draw huge crowds from throughout the city for both college **basketball** and **football** games. Call the UNM Box Office (☎ 505-277-4569) or The Pit (☎ 505-925-5626) for ticket information.

Though **ice hockey** and Albuquerque don't seem like natural partners, the newest addition to the Duke City's sports scene is the Scorpions. They play October through March at Tingley Coliseum (☎ 505-265-1791). Also at Tingley Coliseum is the state **rodeo**, held during the state fair in September. There are plenty of smaller rodeos throughout the year, both in Albuquerque and the surrounding area. For information on rodeo events, call the New Mexico Rodeo Association (☎ 505-873-7770).

SHOPPING

There are many galleries and trading posts around and near the Old Town Plaza. In addition, vendors spread out jewelry and crafts along the sidewalks.

For a wide selection of Native American crafts and informed salespeople, stop by the Palms Trading Post (☎ 505-247-8504), 1504 Lomas Blvd NW. Luz de Nambe (☎ 505-242-5699), 328 San Felipe NW, sells discounted Nambeware (see Santa Fe, Shopping). Unique and contemporary crafts including jewelry, ceramics and wearable art can be found at Mariposa Gallery (☎ 505-842-9097), 113 Romero NW. The Chile Pepper Emporium (☎ 505-242-7538), 328 San Felipe NW, has everything for the chile lover, from salsas to statues of the state vegetable. Silver Sun (☎ 505-242-8265), 2042 South Plaza NW, is a reputable spot for turquoise.

GETTING THERE & AWAY

Air

The Albuquerque International Airport is New Mexico's biggest, but it is still a relatively small, simple and friendly airport. Southwest Airlines, America West and Reno Air often have the most reasonable rates to Albuquerque. Most of the other major American airlines serve Albuquerque. Mesa Airlines (☎ 505-842-4218, 800-637-2247) provides local service to cities within New Mexico, to Durango and Colorado Springs, Colorado, and to Dallas, Texas.

The airport about 4 miles south of downtown, is served by the No 50 SunTran bus weekdays from around 7 am to 6 pm and Saturday from 8 am to 4 pm. There is no Sunday service. A taxi downtown takes 10 minutes and charges about $8. You can get to and from most hotels and some motels via free hotel shuttles. Sunvan (☎ 505-764-6165) offers handicapped transportation free of charge; call up to two weeks in advance to arrange an airport pick up. Shuttlejack (☎ 505-243-3224) runs 10 to 12 shuttles daily to Santa Fe, from 8 am to 5 pm, for $20 one-way.

Bus

The Albuquerque Bus Transportation Center, 300 2nd SW, is home to Greyhound (☎ 505-243-4435, 800-231-2222) and some local carriers. Greyhound has four buses a day to Santa Fe ($11.50 one-way) and two daily to Taos ($22 one-way). It also has several daily buses to various US cities.

Train
Amtrak's (☎ 800-872-7245) *Southwest Chief* makes two daily stops in Albuquerque – the eastbound train departs at 1:24 pm, and the westbound pulls out at 5:18 pm. One-way fare to Los Angeles is $95; the trip takes about 16 hours. Service to Santa Fe, at $37 one-way, is via the 1:24 pm train to Lamy, connecting with a bus to arrive in Santa Fe by 3:15 pm. The station is at 214 1st SW.

GETTING AROUND
Bus
SunTran (☎ 505-843-9200), Albuquerque's bus company, covers the city well enough, but its hours of operation aren't the most convenient. The buses stop running around 6 pm, and only three lines run on Sunday. Bus fare is 75¢, and free transfers are available upon request. Pick up a schedule from the visitors centers, the airport, city shopping malls and at most big hotels. The Sun Trolley (☎ 505-843-9200) is an open-sided red trolley that services Central Ave, with detours through Old Town and downtown. It costs 75¢, 25¢ for students, and runs daily from 6 am to 10 pm.

Taxi
Cabbies patrol the airport, train and bus stations and the major hotels, but are rarely roaming the streets to be hailed down. There are two cab companies with 24-hour service: Albuquerque Cab (☎ 505-883-4888) and Yellow Cab (☎ 505-247-8888, 505-243-7777). Handicapped service is provided, within city limits and as available, by Sunvan (☎ 505-764-6165).

Car Rental
Most major agencies are at the airport. Wheelchair Getaways (☎ 505-247-2626) rents travel wheelchairs and wheelchair-accessible vans.

Bicycle
Rio Mountainsport (☎ 505-766-9970), 1210 Rio Grande Blvd NW just north of I-40, rents mountain bikes ($14 to $25 for a half day and $20 to $35 for a full day, including lock and helmet). It also rents rollerblades for $14 a day. Bike racks for cars are available, as are maps and local information.

NORTH OF ALBUQUERQUE
Sandia Pueblo
This Indian pueblo, 13 miles north of Albuquerque, was established around 1300 AD but is perhaps best known for its modern offerings, including a casino (see the New Mexican Indian Casinos sidebar earlier in this chapter) and the **Bien Mur Indian Market Center** (☎ 505-821-5400). Stop by to peruse arts and crafts from pueblos around the state. Hours are 9 am to 5:30 pm Monday to Saturday and 11 am to 5 pm Sunday.

The **Sandia Lakes Recreation Area** (☎ 505-897-3971), almost 2 miles west of I-25 exit 234, has three lakes well-stocked with trout, catfish and bass for the angler not wanting to come away empty-handed. It costs $8 for a full day, $4 for the evening only. You can rent poles for $4, but they only have three, so it's first-come, first-served. Nearby, **Sandia Trails** (☎ 505-898-6970), 10601 4th NW, offers horse rides along the river and through the Bosque for $15 an hour (make reservations).

Saint Anthony's Day (June 13) is celebrated with ceremonial dancing open to the public. Photography and sketching are prohibited. Other dances are held on January 6 and Christmas.

Take I-25 north to the Tramway exit, then head 4 miles north on Hwy 313 to the entrance. Further information is available from the Governor's Office (☎ 505-867-3317, fax 505-867-9235).

Corrales
Squished between ever-expanding Albuquerque, the developing west mesa and the suburban sprawl of Rio Rancho is the rural village of Corrales along the Rio Grande. The village was Spanish speaking from the time of the 1710 land grant until the late 1800s, when Europeans began moving here. In the 1930s, English-speaking ranchers and farmers arrived. Now horses, llamas, sheep and other animals live side

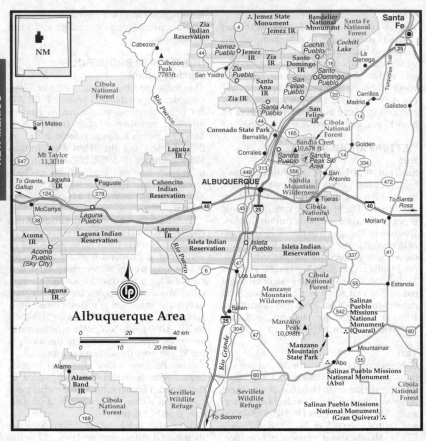

Albuquerque Area

0   20   40 km

0   10   20 miles

by side with million-dollar homes and traditional working farms – you're just as
likely to see a horse trotting up to the
drive-through liquor store as the newest
model jeep pulling into *Roadrunner Coffee*
(☎ 505-898-0767). The main thoroughfare
is Corrales Rd (Hwy 448), and most others
are dirt. Corrales offers easy access to the
Rio Grande and walks along the bosque.

The *Corrales Bosque Gallery* (☎ 505-
898-7203) is a cooperative gallery of local
artisans, with consistently strong, interesting work. Off of Corrales Rd is *Old San
Ysidro Church* (follow the sign). Built in
1776-78, it is a beautiful example of

Spanish colonial architecture. Today it is a
hub of activity and is used as a venue for
concerts, meetings, weddings and whatever
else. Plans are in the works to open *Casa
San Ysidro*, a private, 1740s home across
the street from the church, as a living
museum for guided tours.

Enjoy a drink with summer jazz on the
patio or a winter fire in the cozy adobe bar
at *Casa Vieja* (☎ 505-898-7847). You can
eat here as well, but the food is expensive
and the service shaky. Another great bar,
but with mediocre food, is *Rancho de Corrales* (☎ 505-897-3131). For lunch, try
New Mexican fare at the historic *Perea's*

Tijuana Bar (☎ 505-898-2442) or the pizza buffet at *Village Pizza* (☎ 505-898-0045). Call the village of Corrales (☎ 505-897-0502, www.corrales.org) for information on local businesses and community events, including the annual Harvest Festival and the 4th of July parade.

If you want to spend the night, see Places to Stay – B&Bs earlier in this chapter for information on the *Nora Dixon Place*.

Bernalillo

On the west bank of the Rio Grande, just north of Albuquerque in the town of Bernalillo, **Coronado State Park** (☎ 505-867-5589) has hiking trails and picnic areas that afford splendid views of the river and valley beyond, as well as of the Sandia Mountains. Camping costs $11/7 for an RV hookup/tent site. There is water and bathrooms.

Within the state park is the **Coronado State Monument** (☎ 505-867-5351), the site of multi-tiered Kuaua Pueblo. Home of the Tiwa-speaking people as early as 1300, this is where Coronado decided to spend the winter in 1540. You can climb down into a restored kiva, decorated with a reproduction of the original wall paintings. The visitors center museum displays, among other things, 15 original kiva paintings that date back to 1300. From Albuquerque, take I-25 north to exit 242, then take Hwy 44 west. Hours are from 8:30 am to 5 pm daily. Admission to the park and monument is $3.

The *Prairie Star* (☎ 505-867-3327), a couple miles west off of exit 242, is considered by many to be the best, and one of the most expensive, restaurants in the Albuquerque area. The view of the bosque and mountains is, however, spectacular – if nothing else, it is an ideal spot for a sunset drink on the patio. Construction is under way for an adjacent pub. It is open 5 to 9 pm daily.

The *Range Cafe and Bakery* (☎ 505-867-1700), 925 Camino del Pueblo, serves hearty Southwestern food, burgers and continental fare in the $6 to $13 range. The first location for this jewel burned down

several years back. The second was too close to a school to serve liquor. Let's hope this one sticks – it is an open, airy, bustling place with delicious food and excellent service. To get there, take exit 240 off of I-25 and turn north onto Camino del Pueblo. It is less than a mile on your left.

Next door is *Silva's Saloon* (☎ 505-867-9976), the quintessential Old West bar, a family-run spot 'setting 'em up since '33.' The walls and ceiling are packed with posters, photos, dollar bills, memorabilia and whatever else someone happens to donate, hence its claim to be a 'historical museum.' Stop by for a classic margarita and great conversation – you may have to knock, since it's sometimes locked to keep out ruffians!

San Felipe Pueblo

This conservative Keresan pueblo is best known for the ceremonial Green Corn Dance performed on May 1. Feast day, on February 2, features the Buffalo Dance. Photography, recording and sketching are strictly prohibited. The pueblo runs the Casino Hollywood, which never closes (see the Casinos sidebar earlier in this chapter).

In addition, San Felipe has a growing reputation for its intricate and beautiful beadwork. It's located off I-25 about 10 miles north of Bernalillo. Further information is available from the Governor's Office (☎ 505-867-3381).

Santa Ana Pueblo

Santa Ana Pueblo lies on the west side of the Rio Grande, just north of Bernalillo. The Santa Ana Golf Club (☎ 505-867-9464) is a beautiful 27-hole championship course with panoramic views of the Sandias. Next to the golf course is a gourmet restaurant with a spectacular patio setting (see Prairie Star under Bernalillo, above). Down the road you can gamble at Star Casino. Take I-25 to exit 242, then drive a few miles west and follow the signs. Saint Anne's Feast Day, on July 26, is celebrated with a mass, dancing and food. No photography or sketching is allowed at any time. Call ☎ 505-867-3301 for further information.

NEW MEXICO

Santo Domingo Pueblo

Santo Domingo Pueblo is on Hwy 22, 6 miles northwest from I-25 exit 259, about halfway between Albuquerque and Santa Fe. Juan de Oñate stopped here in 1598 to establish a mission center for the whole area. Long ago destroyed by Rio Grande floods, the original mission was replaced in 1886 by the current church, which contains paintings and frescoes by local artists.

The church and plaza are the center of the pueblo, and some small shops sell both crafts and food. Stop by the funky Santo Domingo Trading Post, which is about 3 miles north of town and dates from the 1880s. The pueblo is known for its jewelry, especially the delicate *heishi* beads that are carved from shells and turquoise, and for its traditional pottery. Near the I-25 exit is a modern cultural center, with a small museum of historical artifacts, photographs, crafts and a gift shop.

The impressive annual Feast and Corn Dance, which is usually held on August 4, but may be held the first weekend in August, involves hundreds of dancers and is open to public viewing. There is also a Corn Dance as part of the Easter and Christmas celebrations. Santo Domingo is open to the public from about 8 am to an hour before sunset every day. No photography, sketching or any other kind of recording is allowed. Further information is available from the Office of the Governor (☎ 505-465-2214), Santo Domingo Pueblo, NM 87052.

Cochiti Pueblo

This pueblo is due north of Santo Domingo. Either continue north on Hwy 22 for about 10 miles or take I-25 exit 264 and head northwest on Hwy 16. The Cochiti Pueblo mission dates from 1628, and although it has changed a great deal since, parts of the original building are still visible. There are no shops or trading posts in the pueblo, but local artisans may post signs on their houses advertising work for sale.

Cochiti is the main center for making the bass drums used in ceremonials. They are usually constructed of hollow sections of aspen log covered with leather and then painted. Also noteworthy are the storyteller ceramic figurines first made famous in the 1960s by Cochiti potter Helen Cordero.

Photography, sketching and other recording are prohibited. The annual feast day is on July 14 and is open to the public. Further information is available from the Office of the Governor (☎ 505-465-2244), Cochiti Pueblo, NM 87072.

Cochiti Lake

This artificial lake, formed by a dam across the Rio Grande, provides water recreation on land leased by the federal government from Cochiti Pueblo. The lake is a few miles north of the pueblo and offers boat ramps, fishing and swimming.

At the dam, the village of Cochiti Lake has a small marina (☎ 505-465-2219). Two miles north is the 18-hole Cochiti Golf Course (☎ 505-465-2239).

You can camp at *Cochiti Lake Campground* and *Tetilla Campground* (☎ 505-465-2300 or 0307), on different sides of the lake. While Cochiti is open year-round, Tetilla is open only from April through October. Hookups and tent sites cost about $12/8. Reach Tetilla via a signed road off Hwy 16, about 4 miles from I-25.

EAST & SOUTH OF ALBUQUERQUE
Moriarty

This small town of 1500 people is the largest town in sparsely populated Torrance County. Thirty-five miles east of Albuquerque along I-40, it's a port in a storm for weary travelers. Moriarty is a bean-growing center and hosts an annual bean festival in August. Most of the town is along Central Ave, paralleling I-40 to the south.

The pleasant *Days Inn* (☎ 505-832-4451, fax 505-832-6464), near I-40 exit 194 at the west end of town, the *Sunset Motel* (☎ 505-832-4234), on Central Ave at the east end of town, and the *Howard Johnson* (☎ 505-832-4457, fax 505-832-4965), 1316 Central Ave, offer standard rooms for about $50 most of the year. Cheaper basic places along the strip include the *Sands Motel* (☎ 505-832-4445), the *Siesta Motel* (☎ 505-832-4565) and the *Ponderosa Motel* (☎ 505-832-4403) in roughly ascending order of price.

For food, try *El Comedor* (☎ 505-832-4442) for Mexican or try *Mamma Rosa's* (☎ 505-832-4966) for Italian; both are on Central Ave.

Isleta Pueblo

This pueblo is 16 miles south of Albuquerque, south of I-25 exit 215. It is best known for its church, **San Agustin Mission** (☎ 505-869-3398), built in 1613 and in constant use since 1692. It is open daily from 9 am to 6 pm. A few shops on the plaza sell local pottery, and there is gambling at the Isleta Gaming Palace (☎ 505-869-2614). Call ☎ 505-881-2223 for free shuttle information. Saint Augustine's Day is celebrated with ceremonial dancing on September 4, and there is also ceremonial

Turquoise Trail

East of Albuquerque, Hwy 14 parallels I-25 heading north, offering a scenic alternative for reaching Santa Fe. This 'trail' passes through three mining towns where silver, gold, turquoise and coal were once excavated. Today, many artists and craftspeople live in the former 'ghost towns,' bringing new life to the historic sites.

The highway bogins at Tijeras, at I-40 exit 175. Take a detour, a few miles on Hwy 536 toward Sandia Crest, to visit the quirky **Tinkertown Museum** (☎ 505-281-5233). Here you'll see over 20,000 hand-carved wooden miniatures of all kinds, including a full circus, surrounded by a wall made of over 40,000 bottles. Return to Hwy 14. After 23 miles, the winding, narrow but paved highway passes through **Golden**, where gold was discovered in 1825 and, later, silver. The town's heyday was in the 1890s, when the population reached about 1500. Today, it's nearly a ghost town with a general store and an old adobe church that provides a great photo opportunity.

About 12 miles farther north sits **Madrid** (pronounced MAH-drid), a thriving coal-mining town from the late 1800s to the mid-1950s. Madrid went bust with the development of alternative energy sources. In 1974 the town was purchased lot by lot in just two weeks and has been experiencing a resurgence ever since. Artists and craftspeople now make up the bulk of the population, opening their studios to the public during the town's 'Christmas in Madrid' celebration in December. You can shop at any of the galleries and boutiques housed in the old storefronts along the rustic main street. During the summer, there's a series of classical, jazz and bluegrass concerts held outdoors at the old ballpark.

Remnants of the town's boom years are now part of the attraction. The **Old Coal Mine Museum** (☎ 505-438-3780) affords access to a mine shaft and all the old mining equipment. There are railroad relics on display as well, including Engine 769, an old steam locomotive. Admission to the museum is $3/1 for adults/kids. Within the museum is the Engine House Theater, with Saturday and Sunday performances.

In front of the museum, the Mine Shaft Tavern (☎ 505-473-0743) proudly features the longest stand-up bar in New Mexico. You see why it's needed when the tour buses drop off about a hundred thirsty tourists for lunch. At other times it's kind of quiet in the 50-year-old bar. The restaurant serves generously portioned lunches and dinners until 8 pm on weekends. The menu includes sandwiches, burgers and burritos for about $7. There's live local music to listen and dance to on weekends. The Tavern opens at 11 am daily, an hour later on Sunday.

Another boom-to-bust town, **Cerrillos** is 3 miles farther north. Built by the Santa Fe Railroad after gold was discovered in 1879, Cerrillos had 21 saloons, four hotels and a peak population of about 2500 miners. Today, the shell of the old town is home to a couple of gift shops, and it occasionally attracts Hollywood directors wanting an authentic Old West atmosphere. The Casa Grande (☎ 505-438-3008), something of a mining museum, is also a petting zoo, gift shop and an information outlet. ■

dancing on August 28. For more information, contact the Governor's Office (☎ 505-869-3111, fax 505-869-4236).

Los Lunas

This small town, located 25 miles south of Albuquerque along I-25 (exit 203), is the Valencia County seat. There is little of interest apart from two clean and pleasant motels and a historic restaurant. The *Comfort Inn* (☎ 505-865-5100, 800-221-5150, fax 505-866-0858,), 1711 Main St SW, has rooms starting at $43 and going up to $87, and the *Days Inn* (☎ 505-865-5995), built in 1996, has an indoor pool with singles/doubles for $55/70. Just east of I-25 is the recommended *Luna Mansion Restaurant* (☎ 505-865-7333), housed in a restored 1881 adobe mansion. Though the à la carte menu can run up to $20, they offer a daily homestyle deal – ribs, green chile chicken pot pie and other family-style meals for about $8.

Belen

Thirteen miles south of Los Lunas is Belen (I-25 exit 195), the largest town in Valencia County. Here you'll find the only railroad museum in New Mexico, the *Harvey House* (☎ 505-861-0581), originally built in 1910 as an eating house for tourists traveling along the Santa Fe Railroad. The museum, located along the tracks at 104 N 1st, features memorabilia from the famous and influential union of entrepreneur Fred Harvey and the Atchison, Topeka, and Santa Fe Railway.

The *P&M Farm Museum* (☎ 505-864-8354) in Jarales (just south of Belen) is a lifelong labor of love. Its several rooms and two huge barns are stuffed with the eclectic personal collection of Pablo and Manuela Chavez (they will personally guide you through), which includes everything from frontier furniture and silver to about 25 beautifully restored, original covered wagons, buggies and antique cars. To get there, cross the railroad tracks in Belen and drive 2.7 miles south at the first light (Reinken Ave) toward Jarales.

You can camp in *Senator Willie M Chavez State Park* (☎ 505-864-3915), next to the Rio Grande 2 miles east of town. Tent sites are $7, hookups are $11. Day use, open 7 am to 9 pm, is $3. The *Super 8 Motel* (☎ 505-864-8188, fax 505-864-0884), 428 S Main St, has rooms in the $40s and a family restaurant next door.

Manzano Mountains

Often overlooked in favor of the Sandias, the Manzano Mountains are easily accessible from Albuquerque and have plenty of opportunities for camping, hiking (including the breathtaking 22-mile crest trail with several access trails), biking and cross-country skiing. The Mountainair Ranger District (see Mountainair below) has information.

The Manzano Mountains State Park (☎ 505-847-2829), nestled in the foothills 12 miles north of Mountainair, affords spectacular views of the distant mountains to the east. There is a $3 day-use fee to park at trailheads and the six developed campgrounds. Sites are $11/7 with/without hookups; there is water but no showers.

A B&B option is the *Three Pine Ranch* (☎ 505-384-2877), with one two-room casita for $75 a night including full breakfast. Surrounded by flat ranchlands and panoramic vistas, this is an excellent place to get away from it all. You can pick your own salad from the garden, play tennis, swim in the indoor lap pool and enjoy the nearby mountains.

To get to the Manzanos from Albuquerque, drive east on I-40 to Tijeras Canyon/Cedar Crest (exit 175) and drive south on Hwy 337, which becomes Hwy 55 after 30 miles. From Belen, take Hwy 47 southeast to Hwy 60, go east till you reach Hwy 55 at Mountainair, and then go north. Both are spectacular scenic drives.

Mountainair

Mountainair is the central town for the Manzano region. Call the chamber of commerce (☎ 505-847-2795), 217 Broadway, for information on activities and local festivals, such as the annual spring **Ranchers' Days**, with a Ranchers' Rodeo, cowboy music and a quilt show, and the **Garlic Fes-**

tival in August. The Cibola National Forest Mountainair Ranger District (☎ 505-847-2990) sells topographical maps of the Manzanos for $5.

Tillies (☎ 505-847-0248) has tent/hookup sites for $9/16, doubles for $36 and rooms with kitchenettes for up to four people for $45. *El Rancho Motel* (☎ 505-847-2577), 901 Hwy 60, offers basic accommodations for $28 a double. Both are friendly and simple places.

The unassuming *Hummingbird Cafe* (☎ 505-847-0270) is run by a New York City transplant who features weekly events such as poetry reading, children's theater and chautauquas (living history performances that used to be held yearly in Mountainair from 1908 to 1917). The café offers delicious home-cooked international food for $4 to $12. It's open from 11 am daily, closed January and February.

Salinas Pueblo Missions National Monument

This monument consists of three separate pueblos and their accompanying 17th-century Spanish missions, which were each abandoned in the late 17th century. The monument headquarters in Mountainair (☎ 505-847-2585) offers a good museum.

Each site has a small visitor center and picnic area. The sites are open from 9 am to 5 pm daily. Admission is free.

Gran Quivira (☎ 505-847-2770), 26 miles south of Mountainair along Hwy 55, is the biggest of the three sites. Around 300 rooms and several kivas have been excavated. The ruins of two churches, dating from 1630 and 1659, can also be visited.

Eight miles north of Mountainair on Hwy 55 is **Quarai** (☎ 505-847-2290). The 40-foot-high remains of a 1630 church are the highlight here. The remains of the Tiwa-speaking Indian Pueblo have not been excavated.

Abo (☎ 505-847-2400), 9 miles west of Mountainair along Hwy 60, features a ruined 1620 church, one of the oldest in the country, and the remains of a large Tompiro Pueblo.

Santa Fe & Taos

The last 30 years have brought extraordinary changes to the land and cultures of Santa Fe and Taos. In the 1970s most roads in Santa Fe were unpaved, and Taos was a dusty mecca primarily for artists and hippies. But land development and an influx of tourism have drastically altered the region's landscape and character. And while tourism has prompted interest in preserving what is unique to the area, savvy marketing has trivialized the very term 'Southwestern.'

Today, Santa Fe and Taos rank among the top tourist destinations in the USA. Santa Fe, especially, offers cosmopolitan conveniences and culinary delights, and movie stars and other wealthy Americans have built adobe mansions in the piñon- and cedar-spotted hills. Hispanic families who have lived in the river valleys for generations and Native Americans who have called them home for even longer find themselves confronting wave after wave of newcomers and tourists. The ensuing sociopolitical problems are complex.

Nevertheless, the national forests and deserts surrounding Santa Fe and Taos are still stunning. The phenomenon of desert light, in part a factor of the high altitude, can only be appreciated through experience. The Chama and Rio Grande Rivers cut through dry hills and form oases of green valleys, whose cottonwood trees turn brilliant yellow in the fall. The incredibly varied landscapes of red rocks, tubular rock formations, desert and high mountain lakes, and ponderosa-pine forests assure a spectacular drive no matter where you go. Take the time to explore beyond the cities. Wander into small Hispanic villages, and follow your nose down dirt roads and through canyons. Despite tourism, which gathers in pockets throughout the area, many places offer unexpected moments of awe.

In addition to simply wandering, you can hike the forests, ski at the world-renowned Taos Ski Valley, cross-country ski, camp, white-water raft, fly-fish, rock climb, mountain bike and swim within minutes of either Santa Fe or Taos, and numerous companies are eager to arrange guided tours or rent you equipment. The surrounding Indian pueblos offer tours, and their feast days and festivals provide a window into the history and spirituality of Native American culture. The history of all the area's peoples – Indians, Hispanic settlers, traders and mountain men – cannot be separated from the landscape. Any visit to Santa Fe and Taos can shed light on this primal relationship, especially if you combine visits to museums, pueblos and ancient dwellings with some outdoor activities.

Today, restaurants and shopping are an integral part of Santa Fe and Taos, and sampling the local flavors and scouring the shops and markets for local pottery and jewelry can be habit-forming. In recent decades, the abundance of artists has supported numerous galleries showcasing contemporary works that rank among the nation's best. Indian art and cultural artifacts have become popular collectibles – at Sotheby's and Christie's in New York City, Native American blankets have been auctioned for as much as $500,000.

Regardless of budget, you can find plenty to do, whether you choose to camp in the national forest or to luxuriate in a $290 room in Santa Fe, whether you feast at some of the best restaurants in the country or dig into beans and green chile with a tortilla for $2. But always remember to wander beyond the standard destinations and seek the local treasures – even minutes from the fast-food joints and tourist traps, you can find yourself strolling into another era.

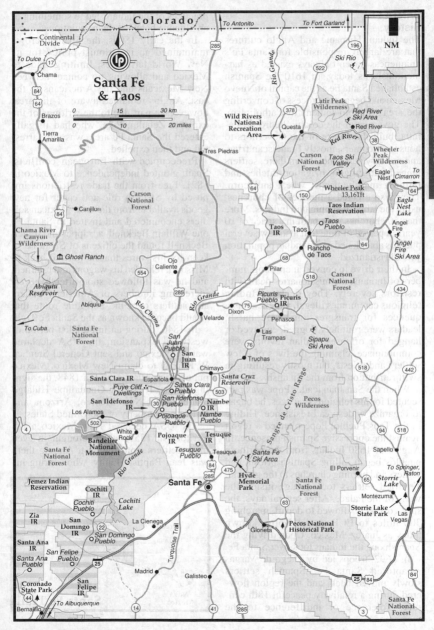

Santa Fe & Taos

SANTA FE
History

The Indian, Hispanic and Anglo cultures that are largely responsible for Santa Fe's uniqueness haven't always existed as harmoniously as today. In 1610 the Spanish established Santa Fe as the capital of Nuevo Mexico and began the process of converting the area's Pueblo Indians to Catholicism. The governor of the colony, Pedro de Peralta, built the Palace of the Governors to house newcomers, mostly Franciscan friars and military personnel. From there, settlers fanned out, digging irrigation ditches and farming mainly beans, wheat and corn. They also erected a number of churches, using the labor of subjugated Indians. More than 50 churches were built in a space of 10 years, a period of time that also saw several pueblos abandoned as the Indian population was Christianized.

In their drive to convert increasing numbers of Indians, the missionaries dealt with resistors severely. They declared Indian religious ceremonies illegal, and the consequences for transgressions were harsh; leaders were routinely flogged, enslaved or hanged for offenses. Indian revolts were commonplace, claiming the lives of a few settlers and priests, but mostly resulting in swift retribution from the Spanish.

When the San Juan leader Popé was persecuted for his religious practices, he began to organize widespread resistance. Hiding in the Taos Pueblo, Popé planned a revolt against the oppressive Spanish presence. In August of 1680 Indians from the northern pueblos began killing Spanish priests and settlers and burning churches to the ground. Terrified settlers took refuge inside the walls of the Palace. After several days, the survivors were allowed to depart, marching 300 miles to El Paso del Norte, known today as Juárez, Mexico. Upon driving the Spanish out, the Indians took over Santa Fe.

In 1692, troops led by Diego de Vargas recaptured Santa Fe. Spanish settlers slowly moved back, and the region flowered during a relatively peaceful 18th century. Tolerance or indifference to the practices of the Indians led to something of an alliance between the populations.

In the early 1800s, the Spanish crown maintained an isolationist policy for its New World territories, limiting trade to Mexico and allowing no contact between New Mexicans and the Americans to the east. Anglos remained aware of the area, however, in part due to the writings of the explorer Zebulon Pike, who had illegally entered the Santa Fe area, was duly arrested and then expelled.

Preoccupied with European conflicts, Spain granted independence to Mexico in 1821. Free from the trade restrictions imposed by Spanish rule and eager for new goods available from the east, Mexican soldiers encountered and invited to Santa Fe one William Becknell, a trapper and trader. Becknell found the citizens of Santa Fe so keen for his wares that he hurried back to Missouri, reloaded his wagons and returned, and he was followed soon after by ever-increasing numbers of American traders and settlers over the 800-mile route that would become known as the Santa Fe Trail.

In 1846, during an imperialist period of westward expansion, the USA declared war on Mexico and sent General Stephen W Kearny to claim New Mexico. Mexico put up no resistance, and in 1848, the signing of the Treaty of Guadalupe Hidalgo made Texas, New Mexico, Arizona and California property of the United States.

The USA declared New Mexico a US territory in 1851, which brought in even more settlers from the east. Among them was Jean Baptiste Lamy, who, during his

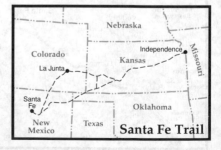

Santa Fe Trail

tenure as Archbishop of Santa Fe, eventually built some 40 churches, including the St Francis Cathedral and the Loretto Chapel, and established a parochial school system. When the railroad arrived in 1879, bringing passengers to the terminal in nearby Lamy, an even larger population boom occurred. In 1912, New Mexico became the 47th state in the union, and Santa Fe changed from being a territorial to a state capital.

Santa Fe's reputation as an art mecca has early roots. Painters intent upon capturing the ethereal essence of the area arrived in the 1920s and established the Santa Fe Art Colony. Central to that group was a quintet known as Los Cinco Pintores, or 'the Five Painters.' These post-impressionists, led by Will Shuster, were the first to take up residence along Canyon Rd, which remains the heart of the local art scene.

A scientific community descended on the area in 1943, establishing a lab at Los Alamos for developing the first atomic bomb. The community, 35 miles northwest of Santa Fe in the Jemez Mountains, was at first wholly secret and travel out of the area was prohibited. But with the completion of the mission and the end of WWII, restrictions on travel were relaxed enough to allow members of the intelligentsia living there to take advantage of Santa Fe's offerings.

The birth and subsequent rise of the tourist industry has had a great impact on the city. By the 1950s, painters, long attracted to the area for its land- and skyscapes, began exhibiting and selling their works locally as art galleries sprang up. The opening of Taos Ski Valley in 1956 added skiers to the list of newcomers. Interest in alternative lifestyles attracted others to the area during the '60s and '70s.

Orientation

Cerrillos Rd, a 6-mile strip of hotels and fast-food restaurants, runs southwest to northeast through town, ending just after Paseo de Peralta joins it from the east. North of Paseo de Peralta, Cerrillos Rd becomes Galisteo. Paseo de Peralta circles the center of town to the east, composing the southern, eastern and northern borders of downtown Santa Fe. Running north south, St Francis Drive (Hwy 285/84) forms the western border of downtown, from Cerrillos Rd to Paseo de Peralta, and it continues north to Española, Taos and Los Alamos. The Plaza, the focal point of downtown Santa Fe, is often used as a base for giving directions. Alameda follows the canal east-west through the center of town, and Guadalupe is the main north-south street through downtown. Most downtown restaurants, galleries, museums and sites are either on or east of Guadalupe.

Information

The Santa Fe Convention and Visitors' Bureau (☎ 505-984-6760, 800-777-2489, www.santafe.org), 201 W Marcy, and the New Mexico Department of Tourism (☎ 505-827-7400, 800-545-2040, www.nets.com/newmextourism/), in the Lamy Building at 491 Old Santa Fe Trail, are open 7 am to 6 pm Monday through Friday. The chamber of commerce (☎ 505-988-3279, fax 505-984-2205), at the north end of De Vargas Mall (at the intersection of N Guadalupe and Paseo de Peralta), is open 8 am to 5 pm Monday through Friday. The Public Lands Information Center (☎ 505-438-7542, www.nm.blm.gov), 1474 Rodeo Rd, is a convenient consolidation that provides camping and recreation information for all public lands in New Mexico; it's open 8 am to 5 pm Monday to Friday. New Mexico State Parks and Recreation Division (☎ 505-827-7173), 2404 Pacheco St at St Michael's Drive, can answer questions about recreation in the state parks. The main library (☎ 505-984-6780) is north of the Plaza at 145 Washington. The New Mexican is Santa Fe's daily newspaper. The free weekly Santa Fe Reporter and the Pasatiempo section of Friday's New Mexican provide thorough listings of upcoming events in the art and entertainment world.

The main post office (☎ 505-988-6351) is at 120 S Federal Place. St Vincent Hospital (☎ 505-983-3361), 455 St Michael's

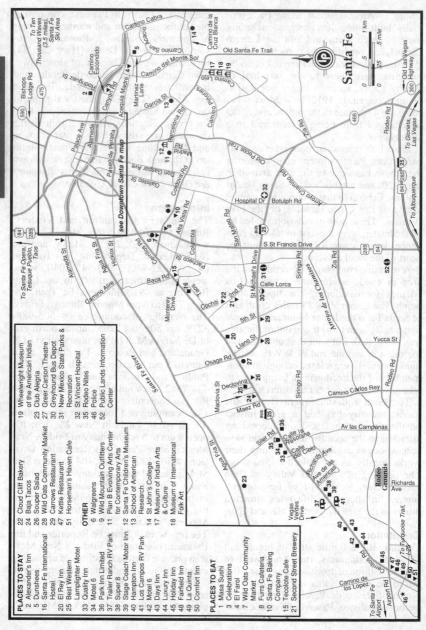

NEW MEXICO

PLACES TO STAY
2   Alexander's Inn
5   Dunshees
16 Santa Fe International Hostel
20 El Rey Inn
25 Best Western Lamplighter Motel
33 Quality Inn
34 Motel 6
36 Park Inn Limited
37 Trailer Ranch RV Park
38 Super 8
39 Stage Coach Motor Inn
40 Hampton Inn
41 Los Campos RV Park
42 Motel 6
43 Days Inn
44 Luxury Inn
45 Holiday Inn
48 Fairfield Inn
49 La Quinta
50 Comfort Inn

PLACES TO EAT
1   Masa Sushi
3   Celebrations
4   El Farol
7   Wild Oats Community Market
10 Santa Fe Baking Company
15 Tecolote Cafe
21 Second Street Brewery

22 Cloud Cliff Bakery
24 Baja Tacos
26 Souper Salad
28 Wild Oats Community Market
29 Carrows Restaurant
47 Kettle Restaurant
51 Horseman's Haven Cafe

OTHER
6   Walgreens
9   Wild Mountain Outfitters
11 Plan B Evolving Arts Center for Contemporary Arts
12 Santa Fe Children's Museum
13 School of American Research
14 Museum of Indian Arts & Culture
17 Museum of International Folk Art

19 Wheelwright Museum of the American Indian
23 Club Alegria
27 Greer Carson Theatre
30 Greyhound Bus Depot
31 New Mexico State Parks & Recreation
32 St Vincent Hospital
35 Rodeo Nites
46 Police
52 Public Lands Information Center

Drive, provides 24-hour emergency care. Walgreens (☎ 505-982-4643), 1096 S St Francis Drive, has a 24-hour pharmacy. The police (☎ 505-473-5000) are at 2515 Camino Entrada. Translators, interpreters and special assistance for foreign travelers is provided through the Santa Fe Council on International Relations (☎ 505-982-4931), room 156 at La Fonda Hotel. The Santa Fe Women's Information Hotline is ☎ 505-438-8503.

The Plaza

The Plaza dates back to the city's beginning in 1610, and from 1821 to 1880, it was the end of the Santa Fe Trail. Traders from as far away as Missouri drove here in their wagons laden with goods. Today, Native Americans sell their jewelry and pottery along the wall of the Palace of the Governors, kids skateboard and play hacky-sack and tourists weighed down with cameras and purchases flock the square. You can buy T-shirts and howling coyotes carved from wood at many of the stores surrounding the square. In the summer the Plaza can be depressingly filled with tour groups, but even then the grass and shade of the trees make it a pleasant place to relax and people-watch!

Museum of New Mexico

The Museum of New Mexico (☎ 505-827-6463 or 6451, www.nmculture.org) administers four museums in Santa Fe; all are open 10 am to 5 pm Tuesday to Sunday. All museums cost $5 for one visit/one museum and $8 for four days of unlimited visits to all four (plus the Georgia O'Keeffe Museum). Friday evenings at the Museum of Fine Arts and Palace of the Governors are free.

The **Palace of the Governors** (☎ 505-827-6483), 100 Palace Ave, on the Plaza, is one of the oldest public buildings in the country. Built in 1610 by Spanish officials, it housed thousands of villagers when the Indians revolted in 1680 and was home to the territorial governors after 1846. Since 1909 the building has been a museum, with more than 17,000 historical objects reflecting Santa Fe's Indian, Spanish, Mex-

ican and American heritage. The Palace conducts daily seasonal walking tours of historic Santa Fe for $10 (children under 17 are free). Call ☎ 505-827-6474 for information.

The **Museum of Fine Arts** (☎ 505-827-4468 or 4455), 107 Palace Ave, on the northwest corner of the Plaza, features works by regional artists and sponsors regular gallery talks and slide lectures. Built in 1918, the architecture is an excellent example of the original Santa Fe-style adobe that has since inundated the area.

The state opened the **Museum of Indian Arts & Culture** (☎ 505-827-6344), 710 Camino Lejo, in 1987 to display artifacts that have been unearthed by the Laboratory of Anthropology, which must confirm that any proposed building site in New Mexico is not historically significant. Since 1931 it has collected over 50,000 artifacts. Rotating exhibits explore the historical and contemporary lives of the Pueblo, Navajo and Apache cultures.

The **Museum of International Folk Art** (☎ 505-827-6350), 706 Camino Lejo, houses more than a hundred thousand objects from more than a hundred countries and is arguably the best museum in Santa Fe. The exhibits aren't simplistically arranged behind glass cases, the historical and cultural information is concise and thorough, and a festive feel permeates the rooms. The Hispanic Wing displays religious art, tin work, jewelry and textiles from northern New Mexico and throughout the Spanish Colonial Empire, dating from the 1600s to the present.

Georgia O'Keeffe Museum

In 1997, Santa Fe proudly celebrated the opening of its newest museum, honoring New Mexico's most famous artist, Georgia O'Keeffe. O'Keeffe first visited New Mexico in 1917 and lived in Abiquiu, a village 45 minutes northwest of Santa Fe, from 1949 until her death in 1986 (see the O'Keeffe sidebar in the Abiquiu & Around section of Northwestern New Mexico). This museum (☎ 505-995-0785, main@okeeffe-museum.org), 217 Johnson, is the

NEW MEXICO

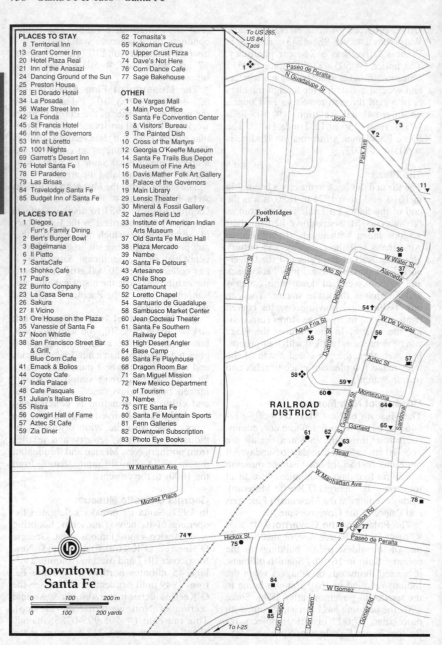

PLACES TO STAY
8 Territorial Inn
13 Grant Corner Inn
20 Hotel Plaza Real
21 Inn of the Anasazi
24 Dancing Ground of the Sun
25 Preston House
28 El Dorado Hotel
34 La Posada
36 Water Street Inn
42 La Fonda
45 St Francis Hotel
46 Inn of the Governors
53 Inn at Loretto
67 1001 Nights
69 Garrett's Desert Inn
78 Hotel Santa Fe
78 El Paradero
79 Las Brisas
84 Travelodge Santa Fe
85 Budget Inn of Santa Fe

PLACES TO EAT
1 Diegos,
    Furr's Family Dining
2 Bert's Burger Bowl
3 Bagelmania
7 Il Piatto
7 SantaCafe
11 Shohko Cafe
17 Paul's
22 Burrito Company
26 La Casa Sena
26 Sakura
27 Il Vicino
31 Ore House on the Plaza
35 Vanessie of Santa Fe
37 Noon Whistle
38 San Francisco Street Bar
    & Grill,
    Blue Corn Cafe
41 Emack & Bolios
47 Coyote Cafe
47 India Palace
48 Cafe Pasquals
51 Julian's Italian Bistro
55 Ristra
56 Cowgirl Hall of Fame
57 Aztec St Cafe
59 Zia Diner

62 Tomasita's
65 Kokoman Circus
70 Upper Crust Pizza
74 Dave's Not Here
76 Corn Dance Cafe
77 Sage Bakehouse

OTHER
1 De Vargas Mall
4 Main Post Office
5 Santa Fe Convention Center
    & Visitors' Bureau
9 The Painted Dish
10 Cross of the Martyrs
12 Georgia O'Keeffe Museum
14 Santa Fe Trails Bus Depot
15 Museum of Fine Arts
16 Davis Mather Folk Art Gallery
18 Palace of the Governors
19 Main Library
29 Lensic Theater
30 Mineral & Fossil Gallery
32 James Reid Ltd
33 Institute of American Indian
    Arts Museum
37 Old Santa Fe Music Hall
38 Plaza Mercado
39 Nambe
40 Santa Fe Detours
43 Artesanos
49 Chile Shop
50 Catamount
52 Loretto Chapel
54 Santuario de Guadalupe
58 Sambusco Market Center
60 Jean Cocteau Theater
61 Santa Fe Southern
    Railway Depot
63 High Desert Angler
64 Base Camp
66 Santa Fe Playhouse
68 Dragon Room Bar
71 San Miguel Mission
72 New Mexico Department
    of Tourism
73 Nambe
75 SITE Santa Fe
80 Santa Fe Mountain Sports
81 Fenn Galleries
82 Downtown Subscription
83 Photo Eye Books

**Downtown
Santa Fe**

0   100   200 m
0   100   200 yards

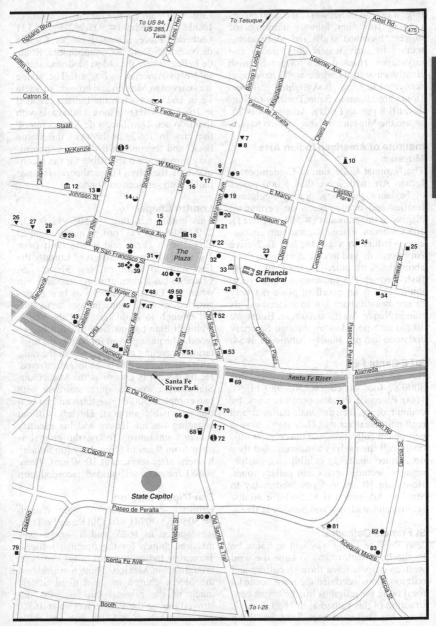

NEW MEXICO

largest exhibit of her work; it has 80 pieces ranging from her famous paintings of flowers, bleached skulls and adobe architecture to early watercolors, nudes and cityscapes. Housed in a former Spanish Baptist church, its adobe walls have been renovated to form 10 skylighted galleries. Hours are 10 am to 5 pm Tuesday to Sunday, till 8 pm on Friday. Admission is $5, or use the Museum of New Mexico pass.

Institute of American Indian Arts Museum

The National Collection of Contemporary Indian Art, with more than 8,000 pieces of basketry, paintings, pottery, sculpture, textiles and beadwork, is on permanent display at this museum (☎ 505-988-6211), 108 Cathedral Place. The museum encourages visitors to view the art as Native Americans do and to take the time to think about the work quietly rather than simply rush through the museum seeing everything. This is an excellent place not only to see beautiful art but to understand its role in Native American culture. Hours are 10 am to 5 pm Monday through Saturday and noon to 5 pm Sunday. Admission is $4.

SITE Santa Fe

Housed in the old Coors Brewery, this 8000-sq-foot space (☎ 505-989-1199), 1606 Paseo de Peralta, presents work by contemporary international, national and regional visual artists. They don't have a permanent collection, and thus cannot officially call themselves a museum, but they do feature changing exhibitions, performances, lectures series and gallery tours. Hours are 10 am to 5 pm Wednesday to Sunday. Admission is $2.50/1 for adults/seniors and students, and Sunday is free.

St Francis Cathedral

Jean Baptiste Lamy was sent to Santa Fe by the Pope with orders to tame the wild western outpost town through culture and religion. Convinced that the town needed a focal point for religious life, he began construction of this cathedral in 1869. Lamy's story has been immortalized in Willa

Cather's *Death Comes for the Archbishop*. Inside the cathedral (☎ 505-982-5619), 131 Cathedral Place, is a small chapel, Capilla de Nuestra Señora la Conquistadora, Reina de la Paz, where the oldest Madonna statue in North America is housed. The statue was carved in Mexico and brought to Santa Fe in 1625, but when the Indians revolted in 1680, the villagers took it into exile with them. When Don Diego de Vargas retook the city in 1692, he brought the statue back, and legend has it that its extraordinary powers are responsible for the reconquest of the city. The cathedral is open daily, with services on Sunday.

Loretto Chapel

This gothic structure (☎ 505-982-0092), 219 Old Santa Fe Trail, is modeled on St Chapelle in Paris, and it was built from 1873 to 1878 for the Sisters of Loretto, the first nuns to come to New Mexico. St Chapelle has a circular stone staircase, but when the Loretto Chapel was being constructed, no local stone masons were skilled enough to build one, and the young architect didn't know how to build one of wood. The nuns prayed for help and a mysterious traveling carpenter, whom the nuns believed afterward to be St Joseph, arrived. He built what is known as the Miraculous Staircase, a wooden spiral staircase with two complete 360-degree turns and no central or visible support. He left without charging for his labors and his identity remains unknown. Today, the chapel is open from 9 am to 5 pm daily (on Sunday it opens after services at 10:30 am). There is a $1 fee and a self-guided, recorded tour.

San Miguel Mission

Original construction of this church (☎ 505-983-3974), 401 Old Santa Fe Trail, was started in 1625, and it served as a mission church for the Spanish settlers' Tlaxcalan Indian servants, who had been brought from Mexico. Though considered the oldest church in the United States, much of the original building was destroyed during the Pueblo Revolt of 1680, and it was rebuilt in 1710, with new walls added to what remained. The current square tower was added in 1887, and the interior was restored in 1955. The chapel and gift shop are open 9 am to 4:30 pm Monday through Saturday and 1 to 5 pm Sunday. On Sunday there is a 5 pm mass. Call for winter hours.

Cross of the Martyrs

At the northeastern end of downtown, a short walk takes you to a cross at the top of a hill; along the way, a series of plaques recounts the city's history. It is an easy walk, and there are views of the city and three mountain ranges – the Sangre de Cristos to the northeast, the Jemez to the west and the Sandias to the south. The cross at the top is a memorial to over 20 Franciscan priests who were killed during the Pueblo Revolt of 1680. The walk begins at Paseo de Peralta between Otero and Castillo Place.

Canyon Road

At one time Canyon Rd, on the east side of downtown, was a dusty street lined with artists' homes and studios, but today most of the artists have fled to cheaper digs, and the private homes have been replaced with a flock of upscale galleries. There are about a hundred galleries and a few restaurants on this small, adobe-lined street, and despite the commercialism and packs of tourists, it's worth a stroll. Come on foot, though – the one-way street provides very little parking.

State Capitol

The Roundhouse, as it is locally known, on Old Santa Fe Trail at Paseo de Peralta, is the center of New Mexico's government and where the governor and legislators have their offices. It is designed after the state symbol, the Zia sign. There are free tours at 10 am and 2 pm Monday through Friday, or private tours can be arranged. Call ☎ 505-986-4589 for information.

Santuario de Guadalupe

This adobe church (☎ 505-988-2027), 100 S Guadalupe, is the oldest extant shrine to Our Lady of Guadalupe, the patroness of the poor in Mexico. It was constructed between 1776 and 1796 near the end of the Camino Real, a 1500-mile trading route from Mexico that ended in Santa Fe. There have been several additions and renovations since. The oil-on-canvas Spanish baroque retablo (altar painting) inside the chapel was painted in Mexico in 1783 by Jose de Alzibar, whose signature appears in the lower-left corner. For the trip to Santa Fe, the painting had to be taken apart and transported up the Camino Real in pieces on muleback. Look closely to see the seams where the painting was put back together. Now there is mass once a month, and the church is used as a venue for performing arts. Hours are 9 am to 4 pm Monday through Saturday.

Santa Fe Southern Railway

You can ride the old Santa Fe Southern Railway train (☎ 505-989-8600), 410 S Guadalupe, to Lamy, 18 miles to the south, and back at 10:30 am on Tuesday, Thursday, Saturday and Sunday. It's a pretty trip through the desert hills. Bring a picnic lunch, or eat at the Legal Tender restaurant in Lamy. The 'scenic excursion' costs $21, less for children. On Friday nights there is a dinner train, including a buffet (eat on your lap), a campfire in Lamy and live music (old railroad songs) for $35.

Santa Fe Children's Museum

This museum (☎ 505-989-8359), 1050 Old Pecos Trail, features hands-on exhibits on science, art and so on for children ages two to nine, but adults will enjoy it as well. Admission is $3/2 for adults/children under 12. It's open 10 am to 5 pm Thursday to Saturday, noon to 5 pm Sunday. Call for special events.

School of American Research

A center for advanced studies in anthropology and archaeological research since 1907, the school (☎ 505-982-3584), 660 E Garcia, has a comprehensive collection of textiles and Indian art in its Indian Arts

Research Center. Tours are given by appointment only. Call for prices.

Santa Fe River Park

With 19 acres of grassy park and towering shade trees along the canal, this is a relaxing place to escape the Santa Fe crowds and summer heat. It runs on both sides of the canal east from Guadalupe to near the end of Canyon Rd and has security lighting.

Wheelwright Museum of the American Indian

In 1937 Mary Cabot established this museum (☎ 505-982-4636), 704 Camino Lejo, to showcase Navajo ceremonial art. While its strength continues to be Navajo exhibits, it now includes contemporary Native American art and historical artifacts as well. There is an extensive collection of sand-painting reproductions taken from Navajo healing ceremonies and notes, photographs and recordings from the ceremonies. It is open 10 am to 5 pm Monday through Saturday, and 1 to 5 pm Sunday. Admission is free.

Ten Thousand Waves

This delightful and relaxing Japanese health spa (☎ 505-982-9304, 505-988-1047, fax 505-989-5077), nestled in the quiet hills 3½ miles outside of town, offers private and public hot tubs, massages, watsu (massage in water), couple's massages, body treatments and facials. The Waterfall Tub, with a private steam room and waterfall into a cold plunge, holds up to 12 people and costs $23 per person, per hour; a regular tub is $18 per person, per hour. The communal tub/sauna and the women's tub are $13 for unlimited time. Massages and all-natural body treatments range from $30 for a half-hour massage to $90 for a 1½-hour East Indian Cleansing Treatment. Spa packages as well as overnight stays in one of their luxury suites (see Places to Stay below) are available. They are open daily except Tuesday; call for hours. To get there, take Hwy 475 toward the Santa Fe Ski Area.

Santa Fe Opera

Opera fans will enjoy seeing a performance at the open-air auditorium in the desert hills north of town. Evening summer storms over Los Alamos sometimes add to the drama on stage, but be prepared with warm clothing and rain gear, since not all seats are protected. The season runs from late June to late August. Tickets range from $20 to $250, with weekday seats being the cheapest and standing-room prices going as low as $6. At the end of August there are two apprentice concerts for $10. Backstage tours are available at 1 pm Monday through Saturday, July through August, and cost $6. You can enjoy a pre-performance buffet, with a guest speaker, for $36 or a gourmet picnic dinner (and drinks) on the grass for $24. Many simply bring their own and eat in the parking lot, everything from pizza on the roof of the car to elegant meals with crystal, linens and candles on folding picnic tables. Tickets go on sale in early May at the El Dorado Hotel or call the box office (☎ 505-986-5900, 800-280-4654) for credit-card orders by phone. The opera grounds are 5 miles north of Santa Fe on Hwy 84/285.

Activities

Several sporting shops in the area give information, sell maps and books, provide guides and rent equipment for outdoor activities. Try *Santa Fe Mountain Sports* (☎ 505-988-3337), 518 Old Santa Fe Trail, *Wild Mountain Outfitters* (☎ 505-986-1152), 541 Cordova Road, or *Base Camp* (☎ 505-982-9707), 322 Montezuma.

Skiing The **Santa Fe Ski Area** (☎ 505-982-4429) is a half hour from the Plaza up Hwy 475. The basin is 12,000 feet high, and there are 39 trails for all levels. (For more advanced skiing, see the Skiing section for Taos.) From the top of the mountain, you can admire 80,000 sq miles of desert and mountains spread out below. Lift tickets are $25/39 for a half/full day, and the season runs from roughly Thanksgiving through Easter. Shuttlejack

(☎ 505-982-4311) and the Santa Fe Ski Shuttle provides shuttle service from Santa Fe to the ski basin for about $10 roundtrip. For a snow report, call ☎ 505-983-9155. During the summer and for a couple weeks during fall foliage, the chair lift is open for $4 one-way and $6 roundtrip, and there is an expansive system of hiking trails.

There are numerous cross-country ski trails in the Jemez Mountains and the Santa Fe National Forest. The Public Lands Information Center (☎ 505-438-7542) can provide a free packet of cross-country ski information. Hyde Memorial State Park (☎ 505-983-7175), on the road to the ski basin, has trails as well. Cross-country skiers will want to locate the useful *Skiing in the Sun: Ski Touring in New Mexico's National Forests* by Jim Burns and Cheryl Lemanski.

River Running Busloads of people head up to the Taos Box for white-water river running, but there are also mellow float trips throughout New Mexico and overnight guided rafting trips. For thorough information on white-water rafting as well as more leisurely float trips, call White Water Information and Reservations (☎ 505-983-6565). Santa Fe Rafting Company (☎ 505-988-4914) offers many trips beginning at $47 for a half day.

Hiking Just walking around Santa Fe can be quite strenuous because of the 7000-foot elevation. Spend a day or two here to acclimatize before rushing off into the mountains of the Santa Fe National Forest, immediately to the east of town. The heart of the national forest is the undeveloped Pecos Wilderness, with trails leading to several peaks over 12,000 feet. Nearly a thousand miles of trails, forming a complex web, are suitable for short hikes and multiday backpacks.

Weather changes rapidly in the mountains and summer storms are frequent, especially in the afternoons, so check weather reports and hike prepared. Permits are not required. The trails are usually closed by snow in winter, and the higher trails may be closed through May. These are then used by cross-country skiers.

Maps and thorough information on hiking throughout the area are available from the Public Lands Information Center (☎ 505-438-7542), 1474 Rodeo Rd; New Mexico State Parks (☎ 505-827-7173); and the Pecos/Las Vegas Ranger Station in Pecos (☎ 505-757-6121, 505-438-7699, fax 505-757-2737). Local bookstores carry New Mexico hiking guides, including the useful *Day Hikes in the Santa Fe Area* by the Sierra Club.

The most immediately accessible trailheads, offering day hikes or entrance into a host of longer hikes, are northeast of Santa Fe along Hwy 475, within Hyde Memorial State Park (☎ 505-983-7175) and at the ski base. Short loops are possible – the 4-mile Tesuque Creek Loop leaving from the north end of Hyde Memorial State Park is a good one. These trails connect with the popular Winsor Trail (Trail 254), which gives access to a huge network of trails in the Pecos Wilderness. North of the Pecos National Historical Park in the Santa Fe National Forest, good places to start are either the Holy Ghost or Iron Gate Campgrounds (see Places to Stay – Camping below).

Fishing Local fish include bass, perch, Kokanee salmon and five species of trout. Lake fishing is possible at various pueblo lakes (see individual pueblos) and at Abiquiu Reservoir (75 miles northwest), as is fly-fishing in streams and rivers throughout northern New Mexico. High Desert Angler (☎ 505-988-7688), 435 S Guadalupe, and the Santa Fe Flyfishing School (☎ 505-986-3913) rent and sell rods, reels, flies and other fishing gear, give classes for all levels and provide guide services for the area. Expect to pay $250 for a day of fishing for two people. A fishing license for nonresidents costs $9 to $14 for one day and $17 to $22 for five days. For regulations and licenses, either ask at the companies above or call the New Mexico Department of Game and Fish (☎ 505-827-7911).

Other Activities The Downs at Santa Fe (☎ 505-471-3311), about 15 minutes south on I-25, runs **horseraces** from June through Labor Day. You have a choice of free general admission seats, $4 Turf Club seats (with access to a concession stand and cocktail service) and $8 Jockey Club seats (with a $12 buffet). If you'd rather ride horses than watch them race, several stables in and around Santa Fe offer **horseback riding** trips. Ask the visitors bureau for a complete listing.

You can play **golf** at Cochiti Lake (☎ 505-465-2230), southwest of town. It's a beautiful high-desert course, surrounded by cedars and piñons. Closer to town is the Santa Fe Country Club (☎ 505-471-0601) and the Santa Fe Golf and Driving Range (☎ 505-474-4680).

There is plenty of **mountain biking** in the area. Mountain Bike Adventures (☎ 505-474-0074) rents bikes and offers one- to six-day tours for all levels. If you want to learn how to **rock climb** or if you are an experienced climber and want a guide, Southwest Climbing Resource (☎ 505-983-8288, fax 505-982-5884) has one- to five-day seminars for all abilities and ages.

Call the City Recreation Department (☎ 505-438-1485) for information on Santa Fe's three public indoor **swimming** pools and one outdoor pool and its 44 public **tennis** courts (see Abiquiu for information on swimming at the dam).

A popular pastime in northern New Mexico is **hunting** for deer, elk, squirrels, waterfowl, turkey and antelope. For regulations and licenses, call the New Mexico Department of Game and Fish (☎ 505-827-7911).

If you develop a love for New Mexican food, as many do, try **cooking lessons** at the Santa Fe School of Cooking (☎ 505-983-4511, fax 505-983-7540). Classes, with 18 options including traditional New Mexican, Mexican light and Southwestern breakfast, are 2½ hours long and range from $30 to $70, including the meal.

Tesuque, Pojaque and San Juan Pueblos (as well as several pueblos in and around Albuquerque) offer 24-hour Las Vegas-style **gambling**. Many have free shuttle service and cheap buffet meals.

Organized Tours

Several companies offer bus tours of Santa Fe and northern New Mexico, and others organize guided trips to the pueblos, as well as air tours and biking, hiking, rafting and horseback riding trips. Ask the visitors bureau for a complete listing. The Gray Line (☎ 505-983-9491) offers a three-hour lecture tour of the city for $17 per person. Aboot About Santa Fe Walks (☎ 505-988-2774), at the El Dorado Hotel, features walking tours daily for $10, as well as a variety of historical, cultural, outdoor activity and foreign-language tours.

Santa Fe Detours (☎ 505-983-6565), 54½ E San Francisco, on the plaza, offers a wide selection of trips and tours, including horseback riding. If you want to try some back roads, Outback Tours (☎ 505-820-6101, 800-800-5337, fax 505-820-0830) focuses on the region's geology, ecology and history on 4WD day and evening tours. Costs range from $60 to $100. For $100, take a one-hour 'soar' in a glider over Santa Fe and the surrounding mountains with Santa Fe Soaring (☎ 505-424-1928).

Special Events

Indian Market On the third weekend in August, more than a thousand Indian artists from around the country show their works in booths on and around the Plaza. This is a judged show, and the quality of the work presented here is phenomenal. Collectors arrive in town as early as dawn on Saturday, and often the best items are gone by Saturday afternoon. Downtown hotels as well as the motels on Cerrillos Rd are usually booked months in advance for Indian Market, so plan ahead. The Southwestern Association for Indian Arts (☎ 505-983-5220) has more information.

Santa Fe Fiesta Every year on the weekend after Labor Day this fiesta commemorates Don Diego de Vargas' reconquering of the city in 1692. Various religious and

Pueblo Languages

From 1539, when the Spanish explorers first encountered the Zuni, until 1847, when the Taos Indians rebelled against the US government, the Pueblo Indians were harassed by invading foreign armies and missionaries. In spite of the 300 years of turmoil, they have successfully maintained their lifestyles, ceremonies and languages.

The languages spoken by the Pueblo peoples include Keresan and Tanoan. Tanoan includes dialects of Tewa, Tiwa and Towa. Many Pueblo Indians describe their language as an ancient tongue, and their elders say that the language was constructed according to the different vibratory levels of Mother Nature. According to their ancient wise ones, the sounds of all native tongues are in an enormous ball of whirling energy that comes from an existence of goodness. Out of this whirling ball the Creator fashioned the different tongues, each with unique elements and each made from resonating qualities of goodness. Every tongue has its own vibration.

In Pueblo thought, the answer 'yes' is what created the blood of life. Their people were vibrations constructed by four processes described as descending, arising, purifying and relativity. Their language is the sound that fuses the descending and arising light in the crystallized meaning of time. Beyond the tongue, and beyond all sound, is silence. Silence is the root of all languages, because it is the pathway to the materialization of all concepts.

The Creator made us when He found that form could exist from sound. He made vibration, He made form, and He made our Mother and Father, the living universe.
– *Eagle/Walking Turtle*

---

historical festivities are scheduled, and food booths are set up on the Plaza, where music plays from morning until past midnight. The highlight of the weekend is the **Burning of Zozobra** on Friday night at Fort Marcy Park. Old Man Gloom, a 40-foot-high papier-mâché doll dressed in black and white, is burned to symbolize the end of last year's problems. Up to 40,000 people gather in the ballfield as the evening progresses, and when darkness falls, a firedancer touches Zozobra with a torch. As it goes up in flames, the crowd goes wild. The whole weekend is characterized by drunken revels. Call the Santa Fe Fiesta Council (☎ 505-988-7575) for specific information.

Eight Northern Indian Pueblos Artist & Craftsman Show Every summer a different pueblo hosts a huge celebration, with all kinds of food, dances and music as well as a comprehensive craft show. Eight Northern Indian Pueblos (☎ 800-793-4955) has information.

Other Events Another, far less crowded market is **Spanish Market** (☎ 505-983-4038) on the last weekend of July. Traditional and Hispanic crafts are sold at booths set up on and around the Plaza. A winter market is held the first weekend in December at the Sweeny Convention Center.

The **Rodeo of Santa Fe** (☎ 505-471-4300) is a four-day regional rodeo held on the second weekend of July. A rodeo parade marches through the downtown Plaza on Wednesday morning, and competitions run through Saturday night. There are two annual New Mexican wine festivals in or near Santa Fe, the **New Mexico Wine and Chili War Festival** (☎ 505-982-8686) on Memorial Day weekend and the **Santa Fe Wine Festival** at El Rancho de las Golondrinas (see Around Santa Fe below) on Fourth of July weekend.

Places to Stay

When looking for accommodations in Santa Fe, remember that rates vary from week to week, day to day and mood to mood, so always ask if a hotel will lower its rates. One traveler arrived in town looking for a place to stay, and the hotel quoted $440 for a double. By the end of a three-minute conversation, the rate had been reduced to $135! Generally, January and February have lower rates; prices listed here are summer rates, but use them only as a rough guide. Cerrillos Rd, the 6-mile main strip of motels and fast-food restaurants, is southwest of downtown, and it can be very inconvenient without a car. However, rates closer to the Plaza and at the big hotels can be excruciatingly high. Always ask for specials, discounts and best offers!

Alternative Accommodations (☎ 505-820-2468, 800-995-2272, fax 505-989-1079) specializes in home stays, ranch resorts, casitas and other places beyond hotels and B&Bs. Santa Fe Central Reservations (☎ 505-983-8200, 800-776-7669) and the Accommodations Hotline (☎ 505-986-0038, 800-338-6877) can help find short-term rooms and condos within your budget. They are especially helpful during special events, when finding any room is difficult. Many hotels offer reasonably priced winter ski packages, which include four nights lodging and three all-day lift tickets. Santa Fe Central Reservations has information.

Places to Stay – Camping

The Santa Fe National Forest and the Pecos Wilderness have numerous camping sites. The helpful Public Lands Information Center (☎ 505-438-7542), 1474 Rodeo Rd, has maps and detailed information. The *New Mexico Recreation and Heritage Guide*, from the New Mexico Department of Tourism, is a good map for an overview of camping in the area.

The nearest USFS campgrounds, open April to October, are northeast of Santa Fe along Hwy 475 on the way to the ski basin. They are administered by the Española Ranger Station (☎ 505-753-7331), none have showers or hookups, and most are first-come, first-served, with honesty boxes charging about $5 per night. If you are

desperate to clean up thoroughly, consider a splurge at Ten Thousand Waves, which is along Hwy 475 closer to town (see above). Seven miles from Santa Fe on Hwy 475 is *Black Canyon* (☎ 505-982-8674), which has 45 sites for $8 each. This is one of the few places in which you can reserve ahead of time. Just past Black Canyon, *Hyde Memorial State Park* (☎ 505-983-7175) has seven sites with hookups ($11) and many more tent sites ($7), some with three-sided wooden shelters. There are no showers. The park has hiking and skiing trails and is open year-round, weather permitting. Day use is $3.

Los Campos RV Park (☎ 505-473-1949), 3574 Cerrillos Rd, offers hot showers and laundry facilities for $11/23 for tents/hookups. *Trailer Ranch RV Park* (☎ 505-471-9970), 3471 Cerrillos Rd, is basically just a parking lot; it has full hookups for $18/108 a day/week.

Numerous RV parks on the outskirts of Santa Fe are more pleasant than the ones on Cerrillos Rd. Most are closed from November to March; all have hot showers and laundry facilities. In Tesuque, 10 miles north of town, *Camel Rock RV Campground* (☎ 505-455-2661) has full hookups for $17/102/305 a day/week/month, and campsites for $14/82/250. Eleven miles southeast of town at I-25 exit 290 is a *KOA* (☎ 505-466-1419), with RV hookups for $19 to $23, tent sites for $17 and cabins for $28. There's a convenience store and nightly movies. Also at exit 290 is *Rancheros de Santa Fe Camping Park* (☎ 505-466-3482), with a convenience store and tent sites/hookups for $17/23. *Piñon RV Park* (☎ 505-471-9288), 10 miles south of Santa Fe at I-25 exit 276, has tent sites/hookups for $12/19.

Just north of Pecos National Historical Park (see below) along Hwy 63, are five campgrounds, open May through October, administered by the Pecos/Las Vegas Ranger District (☎ 505-757-6121, 505-438-7699, fax 505-757-2737). Showers and hookups are not available. *Jack's Creek* ($10) has water, grills and fishing. *Holy Ghost* costs $6, and *Field Tract* is $7.

Sixteen miles north of Pecos and 1 mile on Forest Rd 646 is *Links Track*, with 20 free sites. *Iron Gate*, 23 miles north of Pecos on Forest Rd 223, has 14 free sites and horse corrals; however, the last portion of the road to Iron Gate is not publicly maintained and is particularly bad, especially after rain.

Places to Stay – Budget

Santa Fe International Hostel (☎ 505-988-1153, hostel@trail.com), 1412 Cerrillos Rd, has dorm rooms for $15. Private rooms with shared bath/private bath are $25/$33 for one person, $10 for each additional person. There are two *Motel 6*s, one at 3695 Cerrillos Rd (☎ 505-471-4140, fax 505-474-4370) and the other at 3007 Cerrillos Rd (☎ 505-473-1380, fax 505-473-7784). Both have pools and rooms for about $46/52.

Other options include the *Super 8* (☎ 505-471-8811, fax 505-471-3239), 3358 Cerrillos Rd, with doubles for about $50 and the pleasant *Stage Coach Motor Inn* (☎ 505-471-0707), 3360 Cerrillos Rd, with doubles starting at $55. The *Park Inn Limited* (☎ 505-473-4281, 800-279-0894, fax 505-473-4281), 2900 Cerrillos Rd, is a nice place, with rooms starting at $60.

Places to Stay – Middle

Hotels The *Quality Inn* (☎ 505-471-1211, fax 505-438-9535), 3011 Cerrillos Rd, offers good rooms for $90 in August and September and substantially less in other months. Closer to downtown and off the main strip, but within walking distance to most sites and restaurants, *Travelodge Santa Fe* (☎ 505-982-3551, fax 505-983-8624), 646 Cerrillos Rd, and the *Budget Inn of Santa Fe* (☎ 505-982-5952, 800-288-7600, fax 505-984-8879), 725 Cerrillos Rd, have doubles in the $60 to $80 range.

Conveniently located only a few blocks from the Plaza, *Garrett's Desert Inn* (☎ 505-982-1851, 800-888-2145, fax 505-989-1647), 311 Old Santa Fe Trail, has a French American restaurant, a lounge with a big screen TV and pool tables, an outdoor

pool and standard rooms from $90/70 during the high/low season.

An interesting place on the Cerrillos Rd strip is the *El Rey Inn* (☎ 505-982-1931, 800-521-1349, fax 505-989-9249), 1862 Cerrillos Rd, situated on 3.5 grassy acres with a playground, picnic area and pool. Southwest-style rooms and suites, some with fireplace, patio and kitchenette, range from $60 to $155. It's a pleasant spot and is fairly close to downtown Santa Fe. The recently built *Hampton Inn* (☎ 505-474-3900, fax 505-474-4440), 3625 Cerrillos Rd, has an indoor swimming pool, hot tub and exercise room, with rooms starting at $75. Another good option is the relatively new *Fairfield Inn* (☎ 505-474-4442, fax 505-474-7569), 4159 Cerrillos Rd, with an indoor pool and rooms starting at $90. All three include continental breakfast, as do most of the following.

At *La Quinta* (☎ 505-471-1142, 800-531-5900, fax 505-438-7219), 4298 Cerrillos Rd, good-size rooms are about $80. The motel-style *Best Western Lamplighter Motel* (☎ 505-471-8000, fax 505-471-1397), 2405 Cerrillos Rd, offers rooms with kitchens for about $90 and standard rooms for about $75. Rooms at the *Days Inn* (☎ 505-438-3822, fax 505-438-3795), 3650 Cerrillos Rd, and the *Comfort Inn* (☎ 505-474-7330), 4312 Cerrillos Rd, are in the $55 to $110 range. The *Luxury Inn* (☎ 505-473-0567, 800-647-1346, fax 505-471-9139), 3752 Cerrillos Rd, charges about $80 and has a pool and spa. Rooms at the *Holiday Inn* (☎ 505-473-4646, fax 505-473-2186), 4048 Cerrillos Rd, start at about $100. There are indoor/outdoor pools; a spa, sauna; exercise area; and a restaurant and lounge.

Condominiums *Las Brisas* (☎ 505-982-5795, fax 505-082-7900) provides fully equipped condos, with pleasant Southwestern-style furnishings, fireplaces and enclosed courtyards, conveniently located downtown. Prices range from about $150 for a one-bedroom during low season to about $215 for a two-bedroom during high season.

B&Bs *Alexander's Inn* (☎ 505-986-1431, 888-321-5123, fax 505-982-8572, AlexandInn@aol.com), 529 E Palace Ave, Santa Fe, NM 87501, is a turn-of-the-19th-century Victorian house with five doubles, plus one casita and one cottage, from $75 to $160. Though located in a quiet, tree-lined residential neighborhood with grassy grounds and lilac trees, both Canyon Rd and the Plaza are within easy walking distance. There is no attempt at Southwest style here, and no cutesy feel either. Breakfast is family style and includes fresh fruit, cereal and pastries.

Grant Corner Inn (☎ 505-983-6678, 800-983-1526, fax 505-983-1526), 122 Grant Ave, Santa Fe, NM 87501, is a Cape Cod-style home with a picket fence and flower gardens two blocks from the Plaza. Lovely rooms range from $80 to $155, with a big breakfast. The award-winning adobe restoration of *Water Street Inn* (☎ 505-984-1193), 427 W Water, Santa Fe, NM 87501, features a variety of rooms, some with fireplaces, four-poster beds and patios. New Mexican wine and hot hors d'oeuvres are served nightly, and breakfast includes fruit, pastries and cereal.

The relaxed and friendly *El Paradero* (☎ 505-988-1177), 220 W Manhattan Ave, Santa Fe, NM 87501, is a mishmash of mission-, territorial- and Victorian-style architecture, some with skylights, fireplaces, tiled floors, woven textiles and folk art. Rooms also vary in size. Doubles range from $65 to $135 and include a hot breakfast.

1001 Nights, 147 E De Vargas, Santa Fe, NM 87501, is a lovely, cozy adobe with a peaceful grass courtyard that seems to instantly remove you from the bustle and dust of Santa Fe. Rooms are richly decorated, and all have a fireplace, kitchen and living room. Unfortunately, you have to go to their main office in town for breakfast. Rates are $80 to $180. The *Territorial Inn*, 215 Washington Ave, Santa Fe, NM 87501, is a territorial home centrally located one and a half blocks from the Plaza. Complimentary wine and cheese are served in the early evening, and brandy and cookies are put out by the fire at bedtime. Rooms range from $90 to $160. Reservations for both can be made at ☎ 505-989-7737, 800-745-9910, or reservations@santafehotels.com.

All five casitas at *Dancing Ground of the Sun* (☎ 505-986-9797, 800-645-5673, fax 505-986-8082), 711 Paseo de Peralta, Santa Fe, NM 87501, feature a fully equipped, Mexican-tiled kitchen. Most are spacious two-room suites, with a dining/living room where continental breakfast is provided. Some have a fireplace and/or a washer and dryer, and all are tastefully done in Southwest style. Rates range from $130 to $160.

Dunshees (☎ 505-982-0988, sdunshee@aol.com), 986 Acequia Madre, Santa Fe, NM 87501, offers a one-unit guest house with a living room, two fireplaces, Mexican tile in the bath, a TV, VCR and stereo for $125. There is also a casita on the grounds, with a private kitchen, that is $125/800 a day/week. Rates include a full hot breakfast at the guest house and a stocked refrigerator for breakfast in the casita. This friendly place in a residential area of Santa Fe, off the east end of Canyon Rd, can be difficult to find.

The *Preston House* (☎ 505-982-3465), 106 Faithway, Santa Fe, NM 87501, offers various size rooms from $80 to $150, including a full hot breakfast. Built in 1886, this Queen Anne Victorian with a dark wood stair railing and leaded stained-glass windows is another place that avoids Southwest style.

Places to Stay – Top End
Top-end accommodations are predominantly located in downtown, where you can park at your hotel and walk to most of the sites, museums, restaurants and galleries.

One block from the Plaza and directly across from the St Francis Cathedral is *La Fonda* (☎ 505-982-5511, 800-523-5002, fax 505-988-2952), 100 E San Francisco. A hotel has existed on the site since 1610, and the guest list includes Kit Carson, General and Mrs Ulysses S Grant, President and Mrs Rutherford B Hayes, and more recently, Errol Flynn, John Travolta,

Shirley MacLaine and Ross Perot. The current hotel, built in 1920, is a huge adobe with stores, a pool, a courtyard restaurant and a cozy bar lounge with great local entertainment. The dark lobby of heavy vigas, overstuffed armchairs and Mexican tile is always bustling with activity. There is a tour service desk in the lobby that will help book rafting trips, Pueblo tours and other outings, and the staff can answer any questions about things to do in the area. Southwest-style rooms, some with fireplaces and balconies, range from $119 for an 'economy room' to $260 for a suite.

The *Inn at Loretto* (☎ 505-988-5531, 800-727-5531, fax 505-984-7988), 211 Old Santa Fe Trail, is a sprawling adobe inspired by Taos Pueblo. It has a pool, bar, restaurant, galley full of shops, hair salon and wine-tasting room. Rooms range from $145 to $275. Rooms and suites at the *Inn of the Governors* (☎ 505-982-4333, 800-234-4534, fax 505-989-9149, info@inn-gov.com), 234 Don Gaspar Ave, start at $157. This is really no more than a glorified motel, and some rooms are rather small and nondescript, though many have a fireplace or terrace. Inside, Mañana the Bar is a popular and cozy piano bar, and the restaurant serves breakfast, lunch and dinner either inside by the fire or outside in the shady courtyard. *St Francis Hotel* (☎ 505-983-5700, 800-529-5700, fax 505-989-7690), 210 Don Gaspar Ave, was built in 1924 on the spot of another hotel destroyed in a fire, and it was renovated in the 1980s. This is one of the few hotels that does not strive for Southwest style, but instead has the feel of a small European hotel with an elegant lobby, afternoon tea, a courtyard restaurant and a busy bar. All 82 rooms have a refrigerator; rates range from $118 to $188.

Hotel Santa Fe (☎ 505-982-1200, 800-825-9876, fax 505-984-2211), 1501 Paseo de Peralta, which opened in 1991, is majority-owned by the Picuris Pueblo. A sprawling adobe off Cerrillos Rd, this hotel is more low-key than most of the other upper-end accommodations. The excellent restaurant, Corn Dance Cafe, serves a Native American menu. The rooms are spacious and tastefully done, some with a terrace and all with a refrigerator. There is an outdoor pool and hot tub. Rates range from $139 to $199 in the high season, and start at $89 in the winter.

Perhaps the most elegant and coziest place in town is *Inn of the Anasazi* (☎ 505-988-3030, 800-688-8100, fax 505-988-3277), 113 Washington Ave, located a half block from the Plaza. It opened in 1991 and achieves an Old World feel with heavy wood, textiles, stone floors and leather furniture. Compared to most of the huge, busy hotels in town, the Inn of the Anasazi is a quiet retreat. The public rooms – the little bar, restaurant and lounges – are gorgeous, with hand-carved furniture, overstuffed chairs, wood floors and throw rugs, but the bedrooms are rather small. Prices reflect its worldwide reputation for luxury and personal service: rooms start at $199 in low season, $235 during high season.

Next door is *Hotel Plaza Real* (☎ 505-988-4900, 800 279-7325, fax 505-983-9322, plazareal@unix.nets.com), at 125 Washington Ave. This territorial-style hotel is a light and cheerful place, with a brick courtyard and a street café. Most rooms have a fireplace and balcony, and continental breakfast is complimentary. Doubles range from $150 to $220.

The *El Dorado Hotel* (☎ 505-988-4455, 800-955-4455, fax 505-982-0713), 309 W San Francisco, is Santa Fe's largest hotel, with 218 rooms and suites, a huge bar and lobby, two restaurants, shops, a pool and a sauna. There is no escaping the big city feel of this place, and its massive five-story structure is a sore point with locals. Rates range from $220 to $350.

La Posada (☎ 505-986-0000, 800-727-5276, fax 505-982-6850), 330 E Palace Ave, with 6 acres of grass and fruit trees only blocks from the Plaza, is reminiscent of an English country hotel with a pool, a Victorian-style bar and a peaceful patio in the grassy courtyard. Lovely rooms, some with a fireplace, range from $110 to about $380 for a deluxe suite. All but five rooms are casitas with private entrances.

Eight miles north of Santa Fe in the hills around Tesuque is *Rancho Encantado* (☎ 505-982-3537, 800-722-9339, fax 505-983-8269), a 168-acre resort offering tennis, horseback riding and swimming. The original lodge was built in 1932, and today you can stay in a beautifully decorated double or in a personal cottage with a private kitchen. Though this is an expensive place, it is relaxed and casual. Anyone can stop by for a drink on the patio to escape the Santa Fe crowds and watch the sun set peacefully over the desert. Rates range from $175 to $320.

You can also stay at the *Ten Thousand Waves* spa (☎ 505-982-9304, 505-988-1047, fax 505-989-5077), on Hwy 475 on the way to the Santa Fe Ski Area (see above for complete description). Eight luxurious private suites are available, most accommodating up to four. Some have kitchens, fireplaces and patios. Single or double occupancy rates range from $115 to $200, $10 less per night for two nights or more and add $10 for each additional person. Rates include unlimited access to the communal tub and 10% discount on all other services.

Places to Eat

The Plaza The number of restaurants within a three-block radius of the Plaza is staggering, and among them you'll find a meal to match any budget and most gastronomic desires. A convenient spot for a quick, cheap meal is the *Burrito Company* (☎ 505-982-4453), 111 Washington Ave, where you can get hot dogs and New Mexican fare for under $5. It has great breakfast burritos. Hours are 7:30 am to 7 pm Monday through Saturday, 11 am to 5 pm Sunday.

In the Plaza Mercado on San Francisco just west of the Plaza, the *San Francisco Street Bar and Grill* (☎ 505-982-2044), open 11 am to 11 pm, serves 'first-rate hamburgers and fries,' according to the *New York Times*. It also has a broiled fish sandwich on a baguette, yummy salads and grilled fare for under $10. The only drawback to this place is that it's in the basement. For ice cream and frozen yogurt, the best place in town is *Emack & Bolios* (☎ 505-989-4002) in the Plaza Galleria on the south side of the Plaza.

Josie's Casa de Comida (☎ 505-983-5311), 225 E Marcy, is a simple mom-and-pop place serving a limited menu of home-style New Mexican fare and famous fruit cobblers and pies for under $6. You can also get pints or gallons of chile and salsa, Southwestern casseroles and pies to go.

Go to *Upper Crust Pizza* (☎ 505-982-0000), 329 Old Santa Fe Trail, for unbeatable traditional or whole-wheat crust pizza, with interesting toppings like feta cheese and broccoli, Italian sandwiches and calzones. Eat on the front porch, or they deliver. Try *Il Vicino* (☎ 505-986-8700), 321 W San Francisco, for excellent wood-oven pizza with a wide selection of gourmet toppings. This is the second location of the popular Albuquerque restaurant.

Cafe Pasquals (☎ 505-983-9340), 121 Don Gaspar Ave, is famous for its breakfasts, which are served all day, but lunch is excellent as well. The menu incorporates fresh herbs, whole grains and high-quality meats and includes chorizo, salmon or free-range chicken burritos and pancakes with apple-smoked bacon. There is almost always a wait, but it's not long if you're willing to sit at the community table – and it's definitely worth it! Hours are 7 am to 3 pm Monday through Saturday, 8 am to 2 pm Sunday, and 6 to 10:30 pm daily.

Good Indian food, including a $7 lunch buffet and a wide selection of vegetarian dishes, can be found at *India Palace* (☎ 505-986-5859), 227 Don Gaspar Ave. Dinners are in the $7 to $25 range. It's open 11:30 am to 2:30 pm and 5 to 10 pm daily.

Choose from a hundred margaritas and watch the mingling Plaza crowds from the 2nd-story balcony of the *Ore House on the Plaza* (☎ 505-983-8687), 50 Lincoln Ave. Readers have recommended the *Blue Corn Cafe* (☎ 505-984-1800), 133 Water in the Plaza Mercado, as another spot for great margaritas and big plates of New Mexican fare.

Paul's (☎ 505-982-8738), 72 W Marcy, features imaginative dishes like stuffed pumpkin bread, and it won first place in a local restaurant cook-off for its baked salmon with pecan-herb crust. It's a small, whimsical place, with folk art on the walls and impeccable service; dinner entrées are between $13 and $19. A less-expensive option across the street is *Il Piatto* (☎ 505-984-1091), a casual, unpretentious spot with first-class, friendly service and tasty Italian food in the $8 to $13 range. In the summer, eat at one of the few sidewalk tables and people-watch. It's open daily for dinner and weekdays for lunch. For a quiet, romantic meal, try *Julian's Italian Bistro* (☎ 505-988-2355), 221 Shelby, a cozy, adobe restaurant serving excellent duck, pasta and veal in the $12 to $23 range.

Santa Fe boasts two world-famous restaurants, and though they are expensive, the menus are creative and the food first-rate. *SantaCafe* (☎ 505-984-1788), 231 Washington Ave, has enjoyed well-deserved critical acclaim in *Condé Nast Traveler, Gourmet Magazine* and the *New York Times* for its eclectic blending of Asian and Southwestern cuisine. The menu changes seasonally, and expect to pay between $10 and $25 for an entrée – try the generous grilled filet mignon with roasted garlic/green chile mashed potatoes. The décor is simple white-walled adobe with white tablecloths, and in warm weather you can eat in the brick courtyard. Celebrities and out-of-towners head for the cowhide barstools at the *Coyote Cafe* (☎ 505-983-1615), 132 W Water. The hype about this place has become almost comical, and the food, at $10 to $25, doesn't always live up to its reputation. The outdoor rooftop cantina in the summer, however, is an excellent spot to watch the street activity and enjoy fresh Southwestern cooking for half the price of the main restaurant.

La Casa Sena (☎ 505-988-9232), 125 E Palace Ave, is actually two restaurants; one is a formal, territorial-style adobe home serving continental cuisine with a Southwestern accent, and the other is a casual cantina, where the waitstaff sings Broadway hits and serves consistently good food. Shows run from 6 to 11 pm. In the summer, eat in the pleasant courtyard.

Another option for a high-end meal is *Anasazi* (☎ 505-988-3236), inside the Inn of the Anasazi (see Places to Stay above). Though the food can be very good, it is inconsistent. The primary reason to come here is to enjoy the dramatic and cozy interior of heavy wood and hand-woven textiles. The New Mexican and Native American dishes, emphasizing fresh, local ingredients and creative combinations, are in the $10 to $25 range, but you can have something less expensive at the bar.

An excellent spot for a sunset drink is the *Belltower*, the rooftop bar at La Fonda (☎ 505-982-5511), 100 E San Francisco. It's the only spot in town where you get far enough above the rooftops to watch the desert sky.

Guadalupe St Guadalupe runs roughly north/south along the western edge of downtown. Most of the establishments described below are either on or near Guadalupe, and all are within walking distance of the Plaza. At the southern end, *Tomasita's* (☎ 505-983-5721), 550 S Guadalupe, is housed in a former rail-yard warehouse. It has become a loud and crowded tourist hangout (Hillary Clinton ate here!), but the New Mexican food is good, and prices are in the $6 to $12 range. Hours are 11 am to 10 pm Monday to Saturday.

The *Zia Diner* (☎ 505-988-7008), 326 S Guadalupe, serves reasonably priced, upscale diner food like meatloaf and hot turkey sandwiches, as well as daily specials, Southwestern fare and homemade pies. The blue corn chicken enchiladas are fantastic. This popular local hang out, an old stand-by for many, is always busy, but you're guaranteed a great meal at a great value. Prices range from $5 to $15. They're open 11:30 am to 10 pm daily.

The small and busy *Cowgirl Hall of Fame* (☎ 505-982-2565), 319 S Guadalupe, has tasty all-you-can-eat specials for under

$10. They serve hearty Texan specialties with a Cajun twist such as a honey fried chicken picnic and a fried catfish and barbecued chicken meal on Monday. The décor is relaxed Old West – eat inside or on the patio. It's a fun place, open daily for lunch and dinner, and the bar has live music nightly.

Inside Hotel Santa Fe is *Corn Dance Cafe* (☎ 505-982-1200), 1501 Paseo de Peralta, the only place in town that specializes in Native American fare. The food is very good and interesting. Across the street, the *Sage Bakery* (☎ 505-820-7243) has great bread, hearty sandwiches and breakfast treats. This bakery coffee shop is open 7 am to 7 pm, Monday to Friday, with shortened hours on the weekend. A popular hangout for the black-turtleneck crowd is the *Aztec St Cafe* (☎ 505-983-9464), 317 Aztec, serving coffee drinks, pastries and a light food menu. Just east of Guadalupe, *Kokoman Circus* (☎ 505-983-7770), 301 Garfield, has a huge wine selection, an excellent deli with all kinds of unique food and a low-key bar and restaurant.

Just north of the canal, you can escape the tourist crowds and enjoy a good sandwich for under $5 at the *Noon Whistle* (☎ 505-988-2636), at 451 W Alameda. *Vanessie of Santa Fe* (☎ 505-982-9966), 434 W San Francisco, a massive place with a high-beamed ceiling, 12-foot adobe doors and big fireplaces, is a popular, fun spot. The menu includes only the basics, like a whole rotisserie chicken for $11 and an 18-oz ribeye for $22; everything is à la carte, and everything is huge. The lounge is open from 4:30 pm to 2 am, and a piano bar gets going at about 9 pm nightly. Dinner is served from 5:30 to 10:30 pm.

For sushi and other Japanese dishes, try *Sakura* (☎ 505-983-5353), 321 W San Francisco, where you can dine in the grassy courtyard or in a private tatami room. It's open for lunch from 11:30 am to 2 pm Tuesday through Friday, and for dinner from 5:30 to 9 pm Tuesday through Sunday. Another spot for Japanese fare is *Shohko Cafe* (☎ 505-983-7288), a couple of blocks north at 321 Johnson.

A great spot for a legendary burger is *Bert's Burger Bowl* (☎ 505-982-0215), 235 N Guadalupe. There are no tables inside, and only a few out, but don't worry about sitting – just get a green chile cheeseburger for $3 to go. *Bagelmania* (☎ 505-982-8900), 420 Catron, behind Bert's Burger Bowl, has bagels and lox, pastrami and other deli goodies from 7 am to 6 pm Monday through Saturday, and until 3 pm on Sunday.

At the north end of Guadalupe in De Vargas Mall, *Diegos* (☎ 505-983-5101) is considered by many to be Santa Fe's best bargain, and judging from the crowds, the New Mexican fare is excellent. Hours are 11 am to 9 pm Monday to Saturday, noon to 7 pm Sunday. Also in De Vargas Mall is *Furrs Cafeteria* (☎ 505-988-4431), open 11 am to 8 pm daily. It has all-you-can-eat meals for under $6. There is also a Furrs at 522 Cordova Rd (☎ 505-982-3816).

Dave's Not Here (☎ 505-983-7060), off the far south side of Guadalupe on Hickox, has a legendary reputation for cheap, delicious New Mexican fare.

Canyon Rd *El Farol* (☎ 505-983-9912), 808 Canyon Rd, specializes in a delicious variety of Spanish tapas, including grilled cactus, chorizo and mussels. The restaurant serves from 11:30 am to 4 pm and 6 to 10 pm daily, and the bar is open from 2 pm to 1:30 am.

Celebrations (☎ 505-989-8904), 613 Canyon Rd, offers a pleasant place to relax on its patio or inside by the fire. Big salads, burgers, interesting sandwiches and Southwestern dishes range from $5 to $9, and hearty breakfasts are $4 to $7. It's open from 7:30 am to 2:30 pm daily and for dinner 5:30 to 9 pm Wednesday through Saturday.

Cerrillos Rd An excellent spot for a hearty and relatively cheap breakfast or lunch is the *Tecolote Cafe* (☎ 505-988-1362), 1203 Cerrillos Rd. This bright, unpretentious breakfast spot is popular with the locals. Atole piñon hotcakes and a carne adobada burrito, as well as the homemade bakery items, fresh fruit and standard fare, are delicious, and the portions are generous. Hours are 7 am to 2 pm Monday to Saturday. *Baja Tacos* (☎ 505-471-8762), 2621 Cerrillos Rd, is another popular hangout. It's just a drive-through, but prices are cheap, the food is good and lunch lines can be long.

Inside the Texaco Station at 6500 Cerrillos Rd is a little jewel, the family-run *Horseman's Haven Cafe* (☎ 505-471-5420). The tiny space is busy with locals and free of Santa Fe frills, and it serves up some of the best green chile in town and a huge burger for $4.25. Carne adobada and eggs, with fried potatoes and a warm tortilla, is the most expensive breakfast choice at $6, lunch is about $5 and dinner is about $6, except for the 'Gringo Steak,' which will run you $9.45. If there is a quintessential New Mexican diner, this is it. It's open 8 am to 8 pm Monday to Saturday, 8:30 am to 2 pm Sunday.

Just off of Cerrillos Road are two excellent spots. The *Cloud Cliff Bakery* (☎ 505-983-6254), 1805 2nd, serves all kinds of breads, scones, muffins and other baked goods as well as hearty breakfasts (including frittatas and blue corn pancakes) and scrumptious lunch sandwiches daily. For locally brewed beer and reasonably priced pub fare, far from the Santa Fe tourist crowd, stop by the unpretentious *Second Street Brewery* (☎ 505-982-3030), 1814 2nd.

The *Kettle Restaurant* (☎ 505-473-5840), 4250 Cerrillos Rd, and *Carrows Restaurant* (☎ 505-471-7856), 1718 St Michael's Drive, are open 24 hours. *Souper Salad* (☎ 505-473-1211), 2428 Cerrillos Rd, offers an extensive all-you-can-eat soup and salad bar as well as sandwiches. Hours are 11 am to 9 pm Monday through Saturday and noon to 8 pm Sunday.

Other Eateries Owned by a Japanese sushi chef, *Masa Sushi* (☎ 505-982-3334), 927 W Alameda in Solana Center, is a delight! The food is authentic, delicious and fresh, the prices reasonable, the portions generous and the menu varied – you'll find

the usual Japanese fare, as well as some exotic options and Korean dishes. Removed from the tourist bustle of the Plaza, this place is worth finding. It's open for lunch Monday through Friday and for dinner daily.

You can enjoy the spectacular desert landscape at several rural restaurants just out of Santa Fe. The *Tesuque Market* (☎ 505-988-8848) in the trendy valley village of Tesuque, 7 miles north of town, has great breakfasts and sandwiches, from 7 am to 9 pm daily. The bar at *Rancho Encantado* (☎ 505-982-3537), nestled in the foothills to the north of town, offers a fantastic view to the west over the Rio Grande Valley (see Places to Stay above). Two other restaurants that are worth the drive are *Rancho de Chimayo* (☎ 505-351-4444; see Chimayo below) and the tranquil, first-rate *Rancho de San Juan* (☎ 505-753-6818; see Española below).

The *Wild Oats Community Market*, at St Francis Drive and Cordova Rd (☎ 505-983-5333) and at St Michael's and Llano (☎ 505-473-4943), sells all kinds of health foods, including organic produce, free-range chicken and fresh bread. They also have a deli, with delicious sandwiches and gourmet takeout, a salad and juice bar and pastries. Hours are 8 am to 11 pm daily. On Cordova Rd, a half block east of the Wild Oats market, is the *Santa Fe Baking Company and Cafe* (☎ 505-988-4292), a great spot for a hearty and earthy breakfast. *Downtown Subscription* (☎ 983-3085), 376 Garcia St, is a small but busy spot and has a wide range of newspapers and magazines, as well as light meals and desserts.

Entertainment
Check the free weekly *Santa Fe Reporter* for the calendar of weekly events. The *Pasatiempo* section of the Friday edition of the *New Mexican* includes a thorough listing of what's going on in and around Santa Fe as well as reviews of shows, galleries and restaurants.

Cinemas The daily newspapers have a complete listing of what's showing.

The *Lensic Theater* (☎ 505-982-0301), 211 W San Francisco, was built in 1930 and remains as it looked then, with minor renovations. It is one of the few traditional movie theaters in the country, with a huge screen, red velvet curtains and intricately painted walls and high ceiling. The Lensic plays modern releases, as well as old favorites like *Casablanca*, but regardless of the film, the theater's worth the trip.

The *Jean Cocteau Theater* (☎ 505-988-2711), 418 Montezuma, and the *Plan B Evolving Arts Center for Contemporary Arts* (☎ 505-982-1338), 1050 Old Pecos Trail, play foreign and alternative films. For $3.25 a person (on top of the film ticket price) up to four people can bring their own food and relax in love seats in the Jean Cocteau's private screening room.

Nightlife The *Cowgirl Hall of Fame* (☎ 505-982-2565), 319 S Guadalupe, is a small but popular venue for nightly blues, jazz, folk, Latino and Dixie music. There may be a $2 to $6 cover charge. *Catamount* (☎ 505-988-7223), 125 E Water, has pool tables, comfortable chairs, a busy bar and weekend rhythm and blues. The lounge at *La Fonda* (☎ 505-982-5511), 100 E San Francisco, has surprisingly good country and folk music, among other draws. The piano bar at *Vanessie of Santa Fe* (☎ 505-982-9966), at 434 W San Francisco, is another busy spot. *La Casa Sena* (☎ 505-988-9232), 125 E Palace, features waiters and waitresses singing Broadway show tunes. It sounds cheesy, but it's a hopping place! The *Dragon Room Bar* (☎ 505-983-7712), 406 Old Santa Fe Trail, has live entertainment nightly. It's a dark, cozy place, with free popcorn and bar food.

For live country music and free dance lessons on Monday nights, try *Rodeo Nites* (☎ 505-473-4138), 2911 Cerrillos Rd. Covers at *Club Alegria* (☎ 505-471-2324), Lower Agua Fria, vary from nothing to $20 for everything from salsa to blues by local musicians to big-name national bands. This lively spot is open on weekends and during the week only if something is scheduled. On Friday nights, catch salsa with Pretto

(known as the 'salsa priest' because his day job is with the church) and Parranda. There is plenty of dancing and two bars.

While there are no exclusively gay bars or nightclubs, Santa Fe is a relatively gay-friendly town and there is a low-key, mixed scene at most of the bars listed above.

Performing Arts Santa Fe enjoys an incredible variety of music programs, many of them recognized internationally. It is not only the quality of the performances but the variety of venues – cathedrals, chapels and outdoor theaters – that make them particularly interesting. Protix (☎ 800-905-3315) sells tickets for many performances.

The *Santa Fe Symphony* (☎ 505-983-1414, 800-480-1319) has about seven concerts annually and seven special event performances. Chamber music performed by the *Ensemble of Santa Fe* (☎ 505-984-2501) in the Loretto Chapel and the Santuario de Guadalupe can be heard October through May.

The *Santa Fe Chamber Music Festival* (☎ 505-983-2075), which runs from mid-July through late August, brings internationally renowned classical and jazz musicians to Santa Fe. Another seasonal event is the *Desert Chorale* (☎ 505-988-7505, 800-244-4011), with six eclectic programs, at various venues, from early July through mid-August. They also perform Christmas concerts at the Santuario de Guadalupe. New Mexico's only fully professional theater company, *Santa Fe Stages* (☎ 505-982-6683, fax 505-982-6682) presents international companies and stages its own productions from June through August, as well as some winter shows, at the Greer Garson Theatre Center (☎ 505-473-6511), 1600 St Michael's Dr. *Summerscene* (☎ 505-438-8834), sponsored by the City of Santa Fe Arts Commission, features a series of free noon and evening concerts twice a week on the Plaza from June to August.

Poetry readings, dance concerts and other performances are presented at the *Plan B Evolving Arts Center for Contemporary Arts* (☎ 505-982-1338), 1050 Old

Pecos Trail. The *Maria Benitez Spanish Dance Company* (☎ 505-982-1237) performs flamenco and other Spanish dances from June through September. *Santa Fe Playhouse* (☎ 505-988-4262), on E De Vargas, the state's oldest theater company, performs avant-garde and traditional theater and musical comedy year-round. During July and August, the free *Shakespeare in the Park* program (☎ 505-982-2910) takes place every Friday, Saturday and Sunday at St John's College. There is seating for 350 and space for blankets, food is available and admission is free. The *Old Santa Fe Music Hall* (☎ 505-983-3311), 100 N Guadalupe, has adobe-style dinner theater consisting of an original off-Broadway Western musical. Tickets, which include dinner, run $28 to $35.

There are numerous other smaller companies performing a variety of shows. Check weekly newspaper listings.

Shopping

You can spend weeks shopping in Santa Fe, and some people do. During the summer, the stores can be annoyingly crowded, but if you have the patience and the pocketbook, you'll find many beautiful things to buy. Native American jewelry, predominantly of silver and turquoise, basket work, pottery and textiles are for sale at about every other store, as well as along the Palace of the Governors and in the Plaza. Quality and prices vary considerably from store to store, and though the choices can be overwhelming, it is worth shopping around before buying. If you browse in the nicest shops first, you'll learn what distinguishes the best-quality items. Even shops with mediocre stock often have a few good-quality gems among the dross, if you can recognize the difference. The *Wingspread Collectors Guide* provides specific information and maps for all the galleries in town; you can pick one up at most of the big hotels. Store hours vary according to the season, but generally stores are open from 9 am to 5 pm Monday through Saturday, with many staying open on Sunday.

Coyote Cafe General Store (☎ 505-982-2454), 132 W Water, stocks an incredible variety of Southwestern salsa, hot sauces, chiles, tortilla and sopaipilla mixes and other local food items, as well as cookbooks. Another place for Southwestern culinary delights is the Chile Shop (☎ 505-983-6080), 109 E Water. You can also get chile pepper ceramics, chile pepper placemats, chile pepper door handles . . . you get the idea!

A unique metal alloy that contains no silver, lead or pewter but looks like silver was discovered in 1951 to the north of Santa Fe near Nambe. As durable as iron and able to retain heat and cold for hours, the alloy is ideal for cookware. Nambeware capitalizes on this idea. Each piece is individually sandcast in designs that have won national and international recognition, including being selected for the Museum of Modern Art's exhibition entitled *US Design at Its Best*. There are two Nambe foundry outlets in Santa Fe, one at 104 W San Francisco (☎ 505-988-3574) and the other at 924 Paseo de Peralta (☎ 505-988-5528).

If you're looking for Mexican-style tiles, go to Artesanos (☎ 505-983-1743), 222 Galisteo, which has a wide variety of tile by the piece, as well as tile sinks, door knobs, bathroom objects and other Mexican folk art. In the fall, you can also send *ristras* (wreaths of chile peppers) directly from the store. They also have a tile warehouse showroom (☎ 505-471-8020), 1414 Maclovia, off Cerrillos Rd. James Reid Ltd (☎ 505-988-1147), 114 E Palace Ave, has some beautiful hand-crafted silver jewelry and an exceptional collection of belt buckles.

You can buy what has become known as Santa Fe-style folk art, including brightly painted snakes, coyotes and rabbits, at the Davis Mather Folk Art Gallery (☎ 505-983-1660), 141 Lincoln. If you'd rather make your own Santa Fe style, or avoid it altogether, The Painted Dish (☎ 505-995-1165), 105 E Marcy, provides all the material to paint your own ceramic dishes. They fire your work within a few days and will ship it home. For photography books, including first editions and out-of-print books, go to Photo Eye Books (☎ 505-988-4955), 376 Garcia. The Mineral and Fossil Gallery (☎ 505-984-1682, 800-762-9777), 127 San Francisco, has an excellent collection of, of course, minerals and fossils.

The Farmers Market at Sambusco Market Center features local produce, fresh salsas and chile and baked goods from 7 am to noon on Tuesdays and Saturdays from June through April.

Trader Jack's Flea Market, next to the opera north of town, runs from Easter through Thanksgiving, from 8 am to 4 pm Friday through Sunday. In a dusty parking lot, hundreds of vendors sell everything from cast-iron pots to Indonesian textiles to old hinges and doorknobs. You never know what you'll find here, and it's a great place to poke around. Remember to bargain!

Perhaps more of a museum than a gallery, Fenn Galleries (☎ 505-982-4631), 1075 Paseo de Peralta, is one of Santa Fe's best known. The outdoor garden features larger-than-life bronze sculptures, and the low-ceilinged adobe interior is filled with masterpieces. Even if you can't afford to buy anything here, it's worth a stop just to admire the work.

Getting There & Away
Air Two airlines fly regularly in and out of Santa Fe: United Express (☎ 800-241-6522, 800-822-2746) flies from Denver, and Aspen Mountain (☎ 800-877-3932, or call American Airlines) flies from Dallas. Roadrunner (☎ 505-424-3367) at the airport has transportation to local hotels for about $10 per person.

Bus TNM&O-Greyhound (☎ 505-471-0008), St Michael's Drive and Calle Lorca, runs four buses daily to/from Albuquerque for $12 and two daily to/from Taos for $17. Some Greyhound buses stop here as part of their national route. Shuttlejack (☎ 505-982-4311) runs 10 to 12 times daily to/from Albuquerque International Airport for $20 each way. Hotel pick-up/drop-off can be arranged in advance.

Train Amtrak (☎ 800-872-7245) stops every afternoon at Lamy; from here, buses continue 17 miles to Santa Fe. Trains go to Los Angeles or Chicago.

Getting Around
Bus Santa Fe Trails (☎ 505-438-1464) is the country's first natural-gas city bus system. Fares are 50¢, and daily/monthly passes are $1/5. The bus drivers sell daily passes, and various outlets, including Wild Oats Community Market (☎ 505-983-5333), 1090 St Francis Drive, sell monthly passes. The bus depot is on Sheridan Ave between Palace and Marcy.

Taxi Capital City Cab (☎ 505-438-0000) provides service throughout town.

Car Rental Most major agencies have offices in Santa Fe. Major hotels can help arrange car rentals. Wheelchair Getaways of New Mexico (☎ 800-408-2626) rents wheelchair-accessible transportation.

AROUND SANTA FE
Shidoni Foundry
Located 5 miles north of Santa Fe on Bishop's Lodge Rd in Tesuque, the Shidoni Foundry (☎ 505-988-8001) is an 8-acre apple orchard devoted to bronze sculptures. Founded in 1971, it has evolved into a world-renowned fine-art casting facility and showplace. A gallery hosts changing exhibits, and there is a year-round outdoor sculpture garden on the lawn. Every Saturday, and periodically throughout the week, you can watch 2000°F molten bronze being poured into ceramic shell molds, one of several steps in the complex lost-wax casting technique. The artists practice mold-making and sand-casting on the premises as well, and will explain the processes and answer questions. There are daily demonstrations of glass-blowing at *Tesuque Glass Works* (☎ 505-988-2165), located on the grounds.

El Rancho de las Golondrinas
El Rancho de las Golondrinas (☎ 505-471-2261), a 200-acre ranch with 70 restored

and original buildings in the town of La Cienega, is a living-history museum that shows what life was like for Spanish settlers in the 18th and 19th centuries. There are festivals in the spring, summer and fall, when volunteers dressed in period costumes demonstrate traditional domestic and farming activities such as making bread and soap or drying chiles. To get there, take I-25 16 miles southwest to exit 276 and follow the signs. It is closed November through March and costs vary. Call for information on festivals and special events.

Pecos National Historical Park

When the Spanish arrived, Pecos Pueblo, five stories high with almost 700 rooms, was an important center for trade between the Pueblo Indians of the Rio Grande and the Plains Indians to the east. The Spaniards completed a church here in 1625, but it was destroyed in the Pueblo Revolt of the 1680s. The remains of the rebuilt mission, completed in 1717, are the major attraction. The pueblo itself declined, and in 1838 the 17 remaining inhabitants moved to Jemez Pueblo. Today the pueblo structures are nothing but grassy mounds.

The visitor center (☎ 505-757-6414 or 6032) is open daily (except Christmas) from 8 am to 5 pm, till 6 pm in summer. A museum and short film explain the area's history. A 1¼-mile self-guided trail goes through the site. Admission is $4 per car or $2 per bus passenger or bicycle; Golden Age, Access and Eagle Passes are honored. Pecos is about 25 miles southeast of Santa Fe. Take I-25 east to exit 299, and continue east for 8 miles, or take I-25 east to exit 307 and head north for 3 miles.

There are no facilities in the park, but you can camp in the Santa Fe National Forest to the north along Hwy 63. (See Santa Fe, Places to Stay – Camping, earlier in this chapter.)

SANTA FE TO ESPAÑOLA
Tesuque Pueblo

Nine miles north of Santa Fe along Hwy 285/84 is Tesuque Pueblo, whose members played a major role in the Pueblo Revolt of 1680. Offices are closed on August 10 to commemorate their first strike against the Spanish. Today, the reservation encompasses more than 17,000 acres of spectacular desert landscape, including Aspen Ranch and Vigil Grant, two wooded areas in the Santa Fe National Forest. There is a small plaza with a Catholic church, and you can buy local crafts. The pueblo runs the Camel Rock Casino (☎ 505-984-8414) and an RV park at Camel Rock (see Santa Fe Places to Stay above). You can purchase permits to camp or fish at the local lake or in the mountains nearby. San Diego Feast Day on November 12 features dancing, but no food booths or vendors are allowed. Photography may or may not be allowed. The Governor's Office (☎ 505-983-2667) has information.

Pojoaque Pueblo

Although this pueblo's history predates the Spaniards, a smallpox epidemic in the late 19th century killed many inhabitants and forced the survivors to evacuate. No old buildings remain. The few survivors intermarried with other Pueblo people and Hispanics, and their descendants now number about 200. In 1932, a handful of people returned to the pueblo and they have since worked to rebuild their people's traditions, crafts and culture.

The Poeh Cultural Center and Museum is scheduled to be completed by the year 2000. Though it will eventually feature a permanent collection of traditional arts and serve to educate visitors on the history and culture of the Tewa-speaking people, at this point it exhibits work by students enrolled in its numerous craft classes. Call ☎ 505-455-3334 to find out what's open and to arrange a tour. *Po suwae geh* (☎ 505-455-7493), serving Spanish, Native American and American fare, is open 7 am to 8 pm daily. A large selection of top-quality crafts from the Tewa pueblos is for sale at the visitor center and gift shop (☎ 505-455-3460). The Cities of Gold Casino (☎ 800-455-3313) has 24-hour gambling and buffet dinner specials.

The pueblo public buildings are 16 miles north of Santa Fe on the east side of Hwy 84/285 just south of the Hwy 502 intersection. The annual feast day, December 12, is celebrated with ceremonial dancing. Call ☎ 505-455-2278 for more information.

San Ildefonso Pueblo

Eight miles west of Pojoaque along Hwy 502, the ancient pueblo of San Ildefonso was the home of Maria Martinez, who in 1919, along with her husband, Julian, revived a distinctive traditional black-on-black pottery style. Her work, now valued at tens of thousands of dollars, has become world famous and is considered some of the best pottery ever produced.

Several other exceptional potters (including her direct descendants) work in the pueblo, and many different styles are produced, but black-on-black remains the hallmark of San Ildefonso. Several gift shops and studios, including Sunbeam Indian Arts (☎ 505-455-7132) and Juan Tafoya Pottery (☎ 505-455-2469), have original Martinez pieces and sell the pueblo's pottery. For a wide selection of quality crafts, including pottery, moccasins, Kachina dolls and rugs, stop by Babbitt's Cottonwood Trading Post (☎ 505-455-7569, 800-766-6864), nestled under cottonwoods at the foot of desert hills. The San Ildefonso Pueblo Museum, with exhibits on the pueblo's history and culture, is open 8 am to 4 pm Monday to Friday. A fishing lake is stocked during the summer, and visitors can purchase permits on site.

Admission to the pueblo is $3 per car. Camera permits are $5, or $15 for sketching and videotaping. No photography or sketching is allowed during ceremonial dances. Pueblo hours are 8 am to 5 pm daily, shop hours vary. Ceremonial dances take place on the annual January 23 feast day. Other ceremonies include Matachine Dances around Christmas, Easter dances and Corn Dances in June, August and September. Obtain information from the visitor center (☎ 505-455-3549) or the Governor's Office (☎ 505-455-2273).

Nambe Pueblo

Set in the agricultural river valley east of Española on Hwy 503 and surrounded by piñon and juniper, Nambe Pueblo encompasses 30 sq miles and is home to some 600 members. Inhabited since around 1300 AD, the pueblo still has a few precolonial structures.

Nambe Falls Recreational Site, in the hills above the pueblo, has one of the few waterfalls in New Mexico, and you can camp along the river and hike through the canyon to the falls. There is a $2 entrance fee per person. Fishing and paddle boats are also available at Nambe Reservoir, a desert lake surrounded by sand and cedar. There is $6 fee for fishing, with a 10-fish limit, and a $7 fee for boating. A tent/hookup site is $8/15. The falls are open from March to October. **Nambe Buffalo Range**, with 27 animals, can be viewed free of charge.

St Francis of Assisi Feast Day, celebrated on October 4 with evening vespers at sundown October 3, is open to the public, but no photography is allowed. On the Fourth of July, the pueblo celebrates with dancing, craft booths and food at the falls.

There is a $10 fee to sketch, $25 for video cameras and $5 to use still cameras. The Governor's Office (☎ 505-455-0526) has information. (Ask about tours; they are occasionally offered.)

Santa Clara Pueblo

The well-marked pueblo entrance is 1.3 miles southwest of Española on Hwy 30. The Santa Clara Tourism Office (☎ 505-753-7326, fax 505-753-8988), in the main tribal building just north of the pueblo entrance, is open from 8 am to 4:30 pm daily in the summer and from 9 am to 4:30 pm in the winter. A camera permit is $5, video cameras $15. Private tours of the pueblo, which take you to see artists at work on intricately carved pottery, can be arranged with five days' notice.

On the reservation at the entrance to Santa Clara Canyon, 5.7 miles west of Hwy 30 and southwest of Española, are the **Puye Cliff Dwellings**. Ancestors of today's Santa Clara Indians lived here until about 1500. The original carvings were cut into the Puye Cliffs on the Pajarito Plateau, and structures were later added on the mesas and below the cliffs. You can climb around in the 740 apartmentlike rooms on the top and enjoy a spectacular view of the Rio Grande Valley. Take a self-guided tour for $5, or arrange a private tour (☎ 505-753-7326). Hours are 8 am to 5 pm or later in summer.

Continuing past the cliff dwellings about 4 miles is the **Santa Clara Canyon Recreation Area**, with camping and four stocked lakes. Fees arc $15 for fishing or $10 per vehicle for picnicking and sightseeing. It is open from April through October.

Santa Clara Feast Day (August 12) and St Anthony's Feast Day (June 13) feature the Harvest and Blue Corn Dances, and are open to the public. Sketching and videotaping are not allowed. Photography may or may not be allowed – ask beforehand.

ESPAÑOLA & AROUND

In some ways Española is the gateway to the real New Mexico, separating the tourist-infested wonderland of Santa Fe from the reality of the rural state. As late as 1993, residents in the area did not have official addresses. The Rio Grande, Rio Chama and Santa Cruz River converge near the city, and the surrounding area is farmland, much of which has been deeded to Hispanic land-grant families since the 1600s. Though the town itself doesn't offer much beyond a disproportionate number of hair salons, its central location and abundance of good budget restaurants make it a convenient place from which to explore northern New Mexico. Instead of Santa Fe's quaint plaza, adobe buildings and expensive restaurants only 24 miles away, Española is predominantly made up of trailer homes and a small strip of motels and fast-food restaurants. There has been an increase in violent crime in the area, so be careful walking late at night and lock up your valuables.

Orientation

Hwy 84/285 runs through Española and is the main north/south road, splitting north of town into Hwy 84 heading northwest toward Abiquiu and Hwy 285 heading north toward Ojo Caliente. Hwy 30 runs southwest toward Los Alamos. Española is 24 miles north of Santa Fe and 44 miles south of Taos.

Information

The chamber of commerce (☎ 505-753-2831) is in the Big Rock Shopping Center next to Walgreens; hours are 9 am to 5 pm Monday through Friday. The Santa Fe National Forest Supervisor's Office (☎ 505-753-7331) is on the Los Alamos Hwy. The police (☎ 505-753-5555) are at 408 Paseo de Oñate. The hospital (☎ 505-753-7111) is at 1010 Spruce.

San Juan Pueblo

Drive 1 mile north of Española on Hwy 68 and 1 mile west on Hwy 74 to get to San Juan Pueblo (☎ 505-852-4400), which is no more than a bend in the road with a compact main plaza surrounded by cottonwoods. The pueblo was visited in 1598 by Juan de Oñate, who named it San Gabriel and made it the short-lived first capital of New Mexico. The original Catholic mission, dedicated to St John the Baptist, survived until 1913 but was replaced by the adobe, New England-style building that faces the main plaza. Adjacent to the mission is the **Lady of Lourdes Chapel**, built in 1889. The kiva, shrines and some of the original pueblo houses are off-limits to visitors. There is a $5 fee for photography and a $10 fee for video cameras.

Stop in at *Tewa Restaurant*, open 9 am to 2:30 pm, for traditional Indian foods such as pozole, bread pudding and red and green chile stews. The arts and crafts cooperative **Oke Oweenge** (☎ 505-852-2372) has a good selection of traditional red pottery, seed jewelry, weavings and drums; it's open 9 am to 4:30 pm Monday through Saturday. San Juan Feast Day is celebrated June 23 and 24 with Buffalo and Comanche Dances from late morning until mid-afternoon, as well as food booths and arts and crafts.

The tribe operates the **Ohkay RV Park & San Juan Tribal Lakes** (☎ 505-753-5067), which has RV and tent camping and is open for fishing at $7 per day with an eight-fish limit. The **Ohkay Casino** (☎ 505-747-1668, 800-752-9286), 3 miles north of Española, offers 24-hour gambling.

Ojo Caliente

Billed as America's oldest health resort, Ojo Caliente (☎ 505-583-2233, 800-222-9162, fax 505-583-2464) draws therapeutic mineral waters from five springs. The waters have traces of arsenic, iron, soda, lithium and sodium, each with unique healing powers. Massages, facials and herbal wraps are $35 to $90. Rates at the hotel range from $84 for a double to $125 for a cottage with a kitchen, including unlimited use of the mud pool, mineral pool and body wraps. Nonguests pay $9/11 for the mineral pool and $12/15 for a private bath during the week/weekend. Hours are 8 am to 9 pm Sunday through Thursday, till 10 pm Friday and Saturday. You can hike in the surrounding hills, and though this place is nothing fancy, it's relaxing. A casual restaurant serves tasty food for breakfast, lunch and dinner, seven days a week; there is an outdoor pool; and horses are available for riding.

Places to Stay

Nambe Pueblo, Santa Clara Pueblo and San Juan Pueblo have camping and RV facilities (see individual pueblos). South of town on Hwy 84/285, the *Cottonwood RV Park* (☎ 505-753-6608, fax 505-753-3858) at Cottonwood Plaza has nothing to do with cottonwoods; it is basically a parking lot with hookups. It operates Martinis Restaurant and Lounge, open daily for lunch and dinner. Rates are $17/19 for a full hookup in the winter/summer and $12/15 for a tent. Ten miles east of Española outside Chimayo is **Santa Cruz Lake**, which has BLM camping for $7 to $9, with a shelter and a grill. Day use costs $5. Follow signs down a winding road off

Hwy 503 to the desert lake. Swimming is not allowed, due to underwater currents, but you can fish.

Rooms in Española are cheaper than in nearby Santa Fe. As everywhere in New Mexico, rates vary both by the month and according to demand. Always ask for a discount! A couple of small, basic places on Riverside Drive are the eight-room *Arrow Motel* (☎ 505-753-4095), with triples only for $48, and the *Travelers Motel* (☎ 505-753-2040), with doubles for $40. On the Taos Hwy, heading north of town, is the *Ranchero Motel* (☎ 505-753-2740) with rooms for about $33.

The *Comfort Inn* (☎ 505-753-2419), 247 S Riverside Drive, has an indoor pool, with rooms ranging from $55 to $76. Built in 1995, the *Days Inn* (☎ 505-747-1242, fax 505-753-8089), 292 S Riverside Drive, has rooms for about $70, and the *Super 8* (☎ 505-753-5374), 298 S Riverside Drive, has doubles for about $55.

The most upscale place in town is the newly constructed adobe *Inn at the Delta* (☎ 505-753-9466, 800-995-8599, fax 505-753-5057), 304 Paseo de Oñate. All the rooms are lovely and huge, with hot tubs in the bathroom, Mexican tile, a fireplace, high ceilings with vigas and locally carved Southwestern furniture. Rates are $100 to $150 for a double, plus $10 for each additional person, and include a hot buffet breakfast.

Places to Eat

Run by the same family that runs the Inn at the Delta, *Anthony's at the Delta* (☎ 505-753-4511), 228 Oñate NW, is open every day from 5 to 9 pm. It is a two-story adobe with trees in the indoor courtyard, a garden patio, a friendly and cozy bar with a roaring fire and local weavings and pottery on the walls. This is the fanciest place in town, specializing in steak and seafood; entrées range from $12 for barbecued ribs to $24 for lobster. *Angelina's* (☎ 505-753-8543), 1226 North Railroad Ave, is a great place for simple New Mexican fare, serving some of the best sopaipillas in the area and delicious beans and green chile. Hours are 7:30 am to 9 pm daily, and prices are under $8. Whereas Angelina's is popular with locals, *El Paragua* (☎ 505-753-3211), a two-story adobe home on the corner of Hwys 285 and 76, draws the tourist crowd. It enjoys a reputation for authentic, home-cooked New Mexican food, but it's nothing spectacular. The restaurant is open from 11 am to 9 pm daily.

Just north of Española is the tranquil *Rancho de San Juan* (☎ 505-753-6818), a first-class gourmet restaurant nestled into the hillside. A set menu of soup, salad, appetizer and main course is $35; reservations are necessary since there are only a handful of tables.

There are several other roadside spots serving basic beans, burritos, enchiladas and other regional dishes. You won't find Santa Fe style, but you'll get some good food for little money.

Getting There & Away

TNM&O-Greyhound (☎ 505-753-8617, 800-231-2222) offers service from Albuquerque for $20/38, from Santa Fe for $6.30/13 and from Taos for $10.50/21 one-way/roundtrip. Buses stop at Box Pack Mail (☎ 505-753-4025), 1114 N Riverside Drive.

ESPAÑOLA TO TAOS

Taos is northeast of Española. Off Hwy 84/285, you can take either Hwy 68 (known as the Low Road) or Hwy 76 (the High Road). Hwy 76 dead ends at Hwy 75. From there, drive east to Hwy 518 and north to Rancho de Taos, where the Low and High Roads meet just south of Taos. Another option is to take Hwy 503 east, about 15 miles south of Española, go through Nambe Pueblo and Santa Cruz Lake, and connect with Hwy 76 in Chimayo.

High Road to Taos

Generally considered the scenic route, the High Road, Hwy 76, winds through a spectrum of landscapes including river valleys, hundred-foot-high sandstone cliffs reminiscent of Roadrunner cartoons and high mountain pine forests. There are numerous galleries and small villages along the way. Plan on spending at least an afternoon, but if you don't stop at all, you can make it to Taos in 2½ hours.

From Hwy 503, follow signs for the **Nambe Trading Post** (☎ 505-455-2513), where you can find Navajo rugs, painted gourds and other crafts. Surrounded by farmland and woods, it's a welcome change from the hectic pace of Santa Fe.

Chimayo If you're not going on to Taos, make the drive to Chimayo during sunset – the light on the high desert hills is simply spectacular. Originally established by Spanish families with a land grant, Chimayo is famous for its **Santuario de Chimayo**, built in 1816. Legend has it that the dirt from the church has healing powers, and the back room is a shrine to its miracles, with canes, wheelchairs, crutches and other medical aids hanging from the wall. Kneel into a hole in the ground and smear dirt on the parts of your body that are ailing. As many as 30,000 people make an annual pilgrimage to the church every spring on Good Friday.

For an excellent meal anytime, go to *Rancho de Chimayo* (☎ 505-351-4444) on Hwy 520 in Chimayo, an old ranch house backing up to the hills, and enjoy New Mexican food in the courtyard or by the fire in the winter. The ranch (☎ 505-351-2222) also has seven attractive rooms with private bath for $70 to $110 a night.

Another option for accommodations is *La Posada de Chimayo B&B* (☎ 505-351-4605), PO Box 463, Chimayo, NM 87522. It's at the end of a quiet dirt road – call for directions. There are two unpretentious suites each with a private bath and Indian-style fireplace, and four rooms with a private bath. Rates are $80 to $100. *Casa Escondida* (☎ 505-351-4805, fax 505-351-2575) has eight rooms and a hot tub, with rates from $75 to $150. Both serve a full breakfast.

Stop in at the Oviedo Gallery (☎ 505-351-2280) on Hwy 76. The Oviedo family has been carving native woods since 1739, and today the gallery is housed in the 270-year-old family farm. Marco Oviedo, a donkey breeder with a PhD, was the first in the state to freeze donkey semen, and he conducts research on artificial insemination in donkeys when he's not working on his art. His carvings have consistently won awards at the Indian Market in Santa Fe. If you're interested in handloomed weaving, you're better off avoiding the tourist-infested Ortegas (☎ 505-351-4215) and stopping instead at Centinela Traditional Arts (☎ 505-351-2180). Irvin Trujillo, a seventh-generation Rio Grande weaver, whose carpets are in collections at the Smithsonian in Washington, DC, and the Museum of Fine Arts in Santa Fe, works out of and runs this cooperative gallery of 20 weavers. Naturally dyed blankets, vests and pillows are sold, and you can watch the artists weave on handlooms in the back.

Quaint-looking Chimayo has developed a reputation for drug and gang problems. Don't be fooled into thinking it's a safe rural village. Be careful walking around after dark, and always lock your car.

Truchas Continue up Hwy 76 to Truchas, originally settled by the Spaniards in the 1700s. Robert Redford's *Milagro Beanfield War* was filmed here, and with its dusty New Mexican feel, small farms and spectacular views, it is easy to see why. On a clear day you can see across the Rio Grande Valley to the Jemez Mountains, Los Alamos and the flat-topped Pedernal, and south to the Sandia Mountains by Albuquerque. Eight galleries, including the Cordovas' Handweaving Workshop (☎ 505-689-2437), are nestled in the village. Private rooms or casitas for $60 to $110 a night are available at the *Truchas Farmhouse* (☎ 505-689-2245), PO Box 410, Truchas, NM 87578. If you drive through town, rather than taking the turn for Taos, you'll find yourself winding into a mountain river valley with fields of daisies in the summer, a creek and the trailhead to Truchas Peak (at 13,101 feet, the second-highest peak in New Mexico)

and the Carson Wilderness Area. Two miles past Tafoya's General Store, nestled in a meadow with views of the peaks, is *Casa Milagro B&B* (☎ 505-689-2526), with two rooms for $45 to $65, including full breakfast. The owner is a licensed massage therapist.

Las Trampas Built in 1760, constantly defended against Apache raids and considered one of the finest surviving 18th-century churches, the **Church of San José de Gracia** is well worth a stop. Original paintings and carvings remain in excellent condition and bloodstains from the Los Hermanos Penitentes (a secretive religious order with a strong following in the northern mountains of New Mexico) are still visible. The church is open from 9 am to 5 pm daily in June, July and August. It is open for mass at noon on the first and third Sunday of the month.

Picuris Pueblo Just west of **Peñasco** village near the junction of Hwys 75 and 76 lies the picturesque Picuris Pueblo. Though the smallest of the pueblos, Picuris played a major role in the Pueblo Revolt of 1680, and when the Spanish retook control, the Picuri fled their pueblo. In 1706 they returned, with only about 500 of the original 3,000 members, and today that population has fallen to 250. Few original mud and stone houses remain at Picuris, but the pueblo is working to restore its church, and newer adobes dot the rolling hills.

There is a $5 fee to use still cameras, a $10 fee for sketching and movie or video cameras. During celebrations, photography may or may not be allowed. Permits, as well as $2 self-guided tours explaining significant points of interest, can be purchased at Hidden Valley restaurant. Write or call Picuris Pueblo (☎ 505-587-2957), PO Box 487, Peñasco, NM 87553, for further information.

Pottery, beadwork and weaving, as well as historical artifacts, are on display at the **Picuris Pueblo Museum**. There is no charge. In the same building, the *Hidden Valley Shop and Restaurant*, overlooking

Tu-Tah Lake, is open for lunch and dinner daily. The Tribal Game and Fishing Ranger sells fishing permits for Pu-Na and Tu-Tah Lakes for $6 and primitive camping passes for $7.

The ceremonies celebrating San Lorenzo Feast Day commence on the evening of August 9, with mass at San Lorenzo Mission, native rituals and a procession along the shrine path through the northern part of the village. There are foot races and dances the following day. Be sure to ask at the restaurant exactly when photography is allowed, as it changes throughout the celebration.

On the first weekend of July, there is an arts and crafts fair with food booths and a fishing derby to raise money for the restoration of San Lorenzo Church.

From Picuris Pueblo, follow Hwy 75 east and go north on Hwy 518 to connect with Hwy 68, the main road to Taos.

Low Road to Taos

Hwy 68 out of Española turns into a winding, two-lane road that follows the Rio Grande 37 miles to Taos. Though the High Road is pushed as the scenic route, the Low Road is equally beautiful and gets you to Taos more quickly. Much of the road cuts through the river valley, with steep sides of rock to one side and the river on the other, and it's crowded with impatient drivers in both summer and winter. There are numerous spots to pull over and fish, fruit stands with ristras and local apples, and several art galleries, wineries and cafés.

Velarde Fifteen miles north of Española is **Black Mesa Winery** (☎ 505-852-2820, 800-852-6372), 1502 Hwy 68 in Velarde, where you can stop and taste the local vintage. The winery sometimes runs a B&B, with two rooms, each for $75 including a bottle of wine and full breakfast. The highway then cuts through the apple orchards of Velarde and into the Rio Grande Canyon.

Eight miles farther down the road is *Embudo Station* (☎ 505-852-4707), a brew-

ery and café that make a pleasant place to enjoy a freshly brewed beer under the cottonwoods along the Rio Grande. The rather expensive restaurant offers standard New Mexican fare and sandwiches, and it specializes in fresh smoked ham and trout. It is closed in the winter, but it offers a weekend deli. You can rent a river-view cabin behind the restaurant for $75 for two ($125 for four) including full breakfast.

A detour a few miles east on Hwy 75 takes you to the farming community of **Dixon**. There are a couple of galleries here, as well as **La Chiripada Winery** (☎ 505-579-4437), which offers tasting from 10 am to 5 pm Monday through Saturday.

Pilar Seven miles farther north, Pilar is comprised of about four buildings, but it's the regional center for summer whitewater rafting.

Camping is possible at the *Orilla Verde National Recreation Site* (☎ 505-758-4060). To get there, take Hwy 570 west at the Pilar Yacht Club. The BLM runs five campgrounds with shelter, grills, toilets and drinking water, and three are right on the Rio Grande. With great fishing and a spectacular high desert/river valley landscape, this is a convenient and beautiful place to camp, but it tends to be busy in the summer. There is a $6 to $8 charge per vehicle, per night; $3 for day use. The Orilla Verde Contact Station (☎ 505-758-4060) is on Hwy 68.

The Greyhound bus will drop you off at the front step of the *Rio Grande Gorge Hostel* (☎ 505-758-0090), a friendly, relaxed place next door to the Pilar Yacht Club. Eva Behrens, the owner, runs Rio Grande Reservations and can help arrange rafting trips, horseback riding and B&B accommodations in the area. Rates are $11 for a dorm, $29 for a room with a private bath. Also available are two dome houses, which sleep one or two people in a loft bed, by the orchards in the back of the hostel. Though you have to walk to the main house for the bathroom, they're very quiet, private and only $23. Weekly and monthly rates are negotiable.

The *Pilar Yacht Club* (☎ 505-758-9072), more of a café than 'yacht club,' sells great burritos and pastries in the summer and arranges raft trips.

TAOS
History

The first permanent residents of the area were descendants of the Ancestral Puebloans from the Four Corners area. The Taos Pueblo, a spectacular example of Indian architecture dating back to 1440 AD, was a thriving community by the time conquistador Hernando de Alvarado came to the area in 1540. By 1598, Padre de Zamora had established the first mission, and in 1617 Fray Pedro de Miranda led the first flock of Spanish colonists to the area we now know as Taos, a Tewa phrase meaning 'place of the red willows.' After a hundred years of Spanish rule and shaky tolerance between the Indians and the Spanish colonists, the Pueblo peoples rebelled in the Great Pueblo Revolt of 1680. All the Spaniards in the area were either killed or forced to flee, and many ended up in what is now El Paso, Texas. The next influx of Spanish settlers began in 1692, when Don Diego de Vargas arrived with orders to reconquer the Indians. After four years of violence, colonists came to live in areas around the pueblo and in Rancho de Taos and Taos Plaza.

French trappers came in 1739 to hunt in the rich beaver ponds of the surrounding area, and the second phase of Taos history began. The town soon became a trading center for British and American mountain men and Indians in surrounding pueblos. Its reputation spread, and traders from as far away as Missouri and Mexico came with wagon trains full of goods to the famous Taos trade fairs. Kit Carson, the most prominent name in the westward expansion, first came to Taos in 1826 and continued to come sporadically between expeditions. In 1843 he married the 14-year-old daughter of a wealthy Taos family and settled here as a permanent resident.

In 1847 Taos was involved in another uprising after the American victory in the 1846 Mexican War. Hispanics and members of the Taos Pueblo fought against American rule, and Governor Charles Bent died in the massacre that followed. Except for occasional disputes during the Civil War and Indian skirmishes, Taos remained a relatively quiet outpost through the rest of the 19th century.

The third phase of Taos' history began with the arrival of Anglo artists and writers at the end of the 19th century. In 1898, the painter Ernest Blumenschein and Bert Phillips were on a sketching expedition that took them 30 miles north of Taos, but a broken wagon wheel forced them to stay for an extended period in town. Blumenschein returned for many summers, and he and his family took up permanent residence in 1919. He was one of six artists to establish the Taos Society of Artists in 1915 and he is recognized as the founding father of Taos' artists' colony. Attracted to the striking landscape and brilliant colors as well as to the Indian history, spirit and lifestyle, Anglo artists thrived in Taos in the early 20th century. Bert Harwood, Nicholai Fechin, Leon Gaspard and later DH Lawrence, Georgia O'Keeffe and Ansel Adams all contributed to Taos' reputation as a center for artists and writers.

In 1957, Ernie Blake transformed the tiny mining village of Twining, north of Taos, into a thriving ski resort. Thus began the fourth phase of Taos history. Despite Taos' current international reputation as an expert ski area, Taos Ski Valley is rather low key.

Today, visitors flock to Taos year-round to enjoy the Carson National Forest, the plethora of art galleries and Taos Pueblo. Many of the historic adobe buildings are intact, and except for the Hwy 68 strip as you enter from the south, Taos has maintained a feeling of the old Southwest. White-water rafting in the summer and skiing in the winter are the primary outdoor activities, and restaurants and galleries are busy all year. A popular excursion is to drive the Enchanted Circle road. Though Taos can get thick with tourists, the crowds tend to stick to the Plaza area. Remnants of hippie culture are evident, and the predominant feel is casual – you won't find minks and limos here. The Santa Fe scene has thankfully not yet found its way to Taos.

Orientation

The town is bordered by the Rio Grande and the Taos Plateau to the west, and the Sangre de Cristo Mountains to the north. Entering from the south, Hwy 68 turns into Paseo del Pueblo Sur, the main strip of motels and fast-food chains. It changes

briefly into Santa Fe Rd and then into Paseo del Pueblo Norte, the main north-south street in the town. One mile north of town, Paseo del Pueblo Norte forks: to the northeast it becomes Camino del Pueblo and heads toward Taos Pueblo, and to the northwest it becomes Hwy 64 and goes toward the ski valley. Kit Carson Rd begins at Paseo del Pueblo Sur near the center of town at the Taos Plaza and runs east, turning into Hwy 64 as it heads toward Angel Fire. El Prado is the town directly north of Taos, though it is generally considered part of Taos. 'The blinking light'

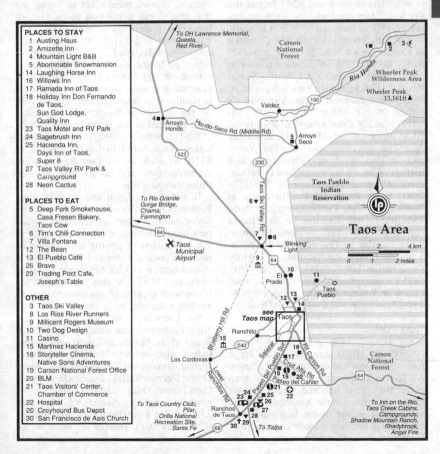

PLACES TO STAY
1   Austing Haus
2   Amizette Inn
4   Mountain Light B&B
5   Abominable Snowmansion
14 Laughing Horse Inn
16 Willows Inn
17 Ramada Inn of Taos
18 Holiday Inn Don Fernando
    de Taos,
    Sun God Lodge,
    Quality Inn
23 Taos Motel and RV Park
24 Sagebrush Inn
25 Hacienda Inn,
    Days Inn of Taos,
    Super 8
27 Taos Valley RV Park &
    Campground
28 Neon Cactus

PLACES TO EAT
5   Deep Fork Smokehouse,
    Casa Fresen Bakery,
    Taos Cow
6   Tim's Chili Connection
7   Villa Fontana
12 The Bean
13 El Pueblo Cafe
26 Bravo
29 Trading Post Cafe,
    Joseph's Table

OTHER
3   Taos Ski Valley
8   Los Rios River Runners
9   Millicent Rogers Museum
10 Two Dog Design
11 Casino
15 Martinez Hacienda
18 Storyteller Cinema,
    Native Sons Adventures
19 Carson National Forest Office
20 BLM
21 Taos Visitors' Center,
    Chamber of Commerce
22 Hospital
26 Greyhound Bus Depot
30 San Francisco de Asis Church

To DH Lawrence Memorial,
Questa,
Red River

Carson
National
Forest

Rio Hondo

Wheeler Peak
Wilderness Area

Wheeler Peak
13,161ft ▲

Valdez

150

Arroyo
Hondo

Hondo-Seco Rd (Middle Rd)

Arroyo
Seco

522

230

Taos Pueblo
Indian
Reservation

Taos Area

0   2   4 km

0   1   2 miles

To Rio Grande
Gorge Bridge,
Chama,
Farmington

64

Taos
Municipal
Airport

'Blinking'
Light

64

El
Prado

Taos
Pueblo

see
Taos map   Taos

Ranchito

240

Los Cordovas

Blueberry Hill Rd

Salazar

Kit Carson Rd

Carson
National
Forest

64

Cruz Alta Rd

Paseo del Pueblo Sur

Paseo del Cañon

To Taos Country Club,
Pilar,
Orilla National
Recreation Site,
Santa Fe

Ranchos
de Taos

To Talpa

68

Lower Ranchos Rd

To Inn on the Rio,
Taos Creek Cabins,
Campgrounds,
Shadow Mountain Ranch,
Shadybrook,
Angel Fire

north of town is a focal point for directions (though it now functions as a regular traffic light); from it, Hwy 64 heads west to the Rio Grande Gorge Bridge, Hwy 522 heads northwest to Arroyo Hondo and Questa, and Hwy 150 heads northeast to Arroyo Seco and the Taos Ski Valley. Going clockwise from Taos, the Enchanted Circle begins by taking Hwy 522 north, then Hwy 38 east, then Hwy 64 south and west back to Taos.

Information

About 4500 people live here. The elevation is 6967 feet in town and 9207 feet at the ski base. Average high/low temperatures are 82/45°F in June and 40/9°F in January.

The Taos Visitors' Center and Chamber of Commerce (☎ 505-758-3873, 800-732-8267, fax 505-758-3872, www.taoswebb.com/TAOS), on Paseo del Pueblo Sur at Paseo del Cañon, is open 9 am to 5 pm daily. The Carson National Forest Supervisor's Office (☎ 505-758-6200, fax 505-758-6213) is at 208 Cruz Alta. Next door is the BLM office (☎ 505-758-8851), 224 Cruz Alta. The main newspaper is the *Taos News*, and the Thursday Tempo section provides listings of upcoming events and entertainment. The main post office (☎ 505-758-2081) is on Paseo del Pueblo Norte at Brooks. The Taos Public Library (☎ 505-758-3063), 402 Camino de la Placita behind the Town Hall, is open 10 am to 8 pm Tuesday to Thursday and 10 am to 5 pm on Friday and Saturday. The Holy Cross Hospital (☎ 505-758-8883, 505-751-5895 for emergencies) is just off Paseo del Cañon on Weimar Rd. The police (☎ 505-758-2216) are at 107 Civic Plaza Drive.

Taos Pueblo

Built around 1450 AD, Taos Pueblo (☎ 505-758-1028) consists of two large four- to five-story adobe communal houses. An Indian community lived in the area more than five hundred years before Columbus arrived in the Americas, and the architecture is one of the best surviving examples of traditional adobe construction. Continuously inhabited for centuries, Taos Pueblo is today the largest existing multistoried pueblo structure in the USA and the forerunner of modern apartment buildings. For this alone, it is well worth a visit.

Even after the southern pueblos were subjugated by Don Diego de Vargas in 1692, the people of Taos Pueblo continued to revolt. Today, about 1500 Taos Indians, who speak the native Tewa language, reside here. Sensing that Taos residents both welcome and resent tourists, visitors may be disconcerted and saddened to walk around the ancient complex with its various tourist shops. The pueblo is open to visitors from 8 am to 5 pm, but it is best to call to confirm times. Guided tours are sometimes offered. The Tewa Kitchen (☎ 505-751-1020) serves traditional feast day foods. For 24-hour gambling, go to the pleasant Taos Mountain Casino (☎ 505-758-9430, 888-946-8267). Housed in a one-room adobe building, it is smaller than other pueblo casinos, with no big buffets or bingo, and is smoke-free. The Taos Indian Horse Ranch (☎ 505-758-3212, 800-659-3210) offers horseback riding through Indian lands, for $32 to $110, as well as an evening campfire dinner/hayride and a 24-hour rafting/riding/camping trip.

In February, March and August, Taos Pueblo may be closed for sacred ceremonial dances. Visitors are charged $5 for parking, though rates vary. Remember to ask permission to photograph, sketch or paint the pueblo. There is a $5 fee to use a still camera, a $10 fee for movie or video cameras, a $15 fee to sketch and a $35 fee if you want to paint. If you use residents as models, remember to tip them.

San Geronimo Day, September 29 and 30, is celebrated with dancing and food. It is one of the largest and most spectacular Indian celebrations in New Mexico. Other special days are the Turtle Dance (January 1), the Deer or Buffalo Dance (January 6), Corn Dances (May 3, June 13 and 24), the powwow (in July), Santiago's Day (July 25) and the Deer Dance or Matachines (Christmas Day). Dances are open to the public, but cannot be photographed. Six kivas (ceremonial chambers) are closed to the public.

Historical Homes

The historic homes of three influential local figures reflect three distinct elements of Taos history – the mountain man, the artist and the trader. Small and compact, these homes offer a great way to get a feel for Taos history, and it's well worth visiting at least one. They are run by the same management (☎ 505-758-0505), and tickets for one or all can be purchased at any of the three museums – $4 for one museum, $6 for two and $8 for all three. There is no expiration limit on the tickets. Another option is to buy a museum pass for $20, which is good for one year of unlimited visits to most of Taos' museums. The homes are open from 9 am to 5 pm in the winter, with slightly longer summer hours.

The **Kit Carson Home & Museum** (☎ 505-758-4741), located a block from the Plaza on Kit Carson Rd, houses such artifacts as Carson's rifles, telescope and walking cane. Kit Carson (1809-1868) was the Southwest's most famous mountain man, guide, trapper, soldier and scout, and his home and life serve as an excellent introduction to Taos in the mid-19th century. Built in 1825 with 30-inch adobe walls and traditional territorial architecture, the home's 12 rooms are today furnished as they may have been during Carson's days, with exhibits on all periods of Taos history and mountain man lore. There is a great gift shop, with a variety of books on outlaws, old-time trapping and farming and traditional remedies, as well as on local biking, skiing and hiking.

The **Blumenschein Home & Museum** (☎ 505-758-0505), 222 Ledoux, dates back to 1797. In the 1920s it was the home of artist Ernest Blumenschein and his wife and daughter. It is today maintained much as it would have been when they lived here. Use the free written guide as you walk through the home.

Resembling an adobe fortress, with no exterior windows and massive walls, the

Martínez Hacienda (☎ 505-758-1000) on Ranchitos Rd (Hwy 240), 2 miles southwest of Taos, served as a refuge for neighbors and valuable livestock during the Comanche and Apache raids of the late 18th century. Don Antonio Severino Martínez bought it in 1804 and enlarged it to accommodate his flourishing trade business. By his death in 1827, there were 21 rooms and two interior courtyards, and today the museum focuses on the life of a colonial family in New Mexico. There are daily craft demonstrations and an annual trade fair.

Governor Bent Museum

When New Mexico became a US territory after the Mexican War in 1846, Charles Bent was named as the first governor. Hispanics and Indians did not appreciate being forced under US rule, and on January 19, 1847, they attacked the governor in his home. Bent's family was allowed to leave, but he was killed and scalped. Today, his home is a small museum with memorabilia from his early days as a trader along the Santa Fe Trail and his life as governor; it also recounts the historical circumstances that led to his death. The museum (☎ 505-758-2376), 117 Bent, is open from 9 am to 5 pm in the summer (from 10 am in the winter). Admission is $1.

Harwood Foundation Museum

The Harwood Foundation Museum (☎ 505-758-9826), 238 Ledoux, is housed in a historic mid-19th-century adobe compound and features paintings, drawings, prints, sculpture and photography by northern New Mexico artists, both historical and contemporary. Founded in 1923, the museum has been run by the University of New Mexico since 1936, making it the second-oldest museum in the state. After extensive renovations and expansion in 1996, the museum is now able to show its permanent collection, including 19th-century *retablos* (religious paintings on wood) and works by many of Taos' best-known artists. Hours are 10 am to 5 pm Tuesday to Saturday, noon to 5 pm Sunday (hours may change in winter; call for revised winter schedule). Admission is $4.

Van Vechten-Lineberry Taos Art Museum

Built in memory of Edwin Lineberry's first wife, the late Taos artist Duane Van Vechten, this museum (☎ 505-758-2690), on Camino del Pueblo, displays Lineberry's private art collection featuring works by the founding fathers, active members and associate members of the Taos Society of Artists. Despite the short-lived society's incredible influence on the history and perception of the region, the members are better known for their individual work than as a group; this is an effort to unify them. Hours are 11 am to 4 pm Wednesday through Friday, from 11:30 am Saturday and Sunday. Admission is $5.

Fechin Institute

This museum (☎ 505-758-1710), 227 Paseo del Pueblo Norte, was home to Russian artist Nicolai Fechin, who emigrated to New York City in 1922 at age 42 and moved to Taos in 1926. Today his paintings, drawings and sculpture are in museums and collections worldwide. Between 1927 and 1933, Fechin completely reconstructed the interior of his adobe home, adding his own distinctly Russian wood carvings. The Fechin House exhibits the artist's private collection, including much Asian art, and hosts occasional chamber music events. It is open 10 am to 5 pm Wednesday through Sunday, with shortened winter hours. Admission is $4 for adults; children are free. Tours are available and the institute runs art workshops from May through October.

San Francisco de Asis Church

Four miles south of Taos is the San Francisco de Asis Church (☎ 505-758-2754), St Francis Plaza in Ranchos de Taos. Built in the mid-1700s and opened in 1815, it has been memorialized in numerous Georgia O'Keeffe paintings. The history of the church is summarized in a slide show. It's open 9 am to 4:30 pm daily. Mass is held at 6 pm on the first Saturday of the month, and at 7 (in Spanish), 9 and 11:30 am every Sunday (call to confirm times).

Millicent Rogers Museum

This museum (☎ 505-758-2462), on Millicent Rogers Museum Rd about 4 miles from the Plaza, is predominantly filled with pottery, jewelry, baskets and textiles from the private collection of Millicent Rogers, a model and oil heiress who moved to Taos in 1947 and acquired one of the best collections of Indian and Spanish colonial art in the USA. Also displayed are contemporary and traditional Hispanic (both Spanish and Mexican) and Native American art forms, annual invitational shows of Hispanic and Native American artwork, and prehistoric and contemporary Pueblo pottery and paintings. A research library with over three thousand books and pamphlets is open by appointment. The hours are 10 am to 5 pm daily, but call to confirm. Admission is $6/5 for adults/students.

Rio Grande Gorge Bridge

On Hwy 64 about 12 miles northwest of Taos, this bridge is the second-highest suspension bridge in the USA and is well worth a stop. Built in 1965, the vertigo-inducing steel bridge spans 500 feet across the gorge and 650 feet above the river below. The views west over the emptiness of the Taos Plateau and down into the jagged walls of the Rio Grande are awe inspiring.

Earthships

Earthships (☎ 505-751-0462) are the brainchild of architect Michael Reynolds, whose idea was to develop a building method that 'eliminates stress from both the planet and its inhabitants.' The Earthships are constructed of used automobile tires and cans into which earth has been pounded. Buried on three sides by earth, they are designed to heat and cool themselves, make their own electricity and catch their own water. Sewage is decomposed naturally and dwellers grow their own food. About 400 Earthships have been built around the world, at an average of $85 per square foot, and the Taos Plateau is home to three prototype communities for Earthship dwellers. Three Earthships are available for rental (see Places to Stay). Call for tour information.

Skiing

Founded by Ernie Blake, the **Taos Ski Valley** embodies his vision of a skier's mountain, preserving the alpine experience that he had enjoyed in the Swiss Alps. This is a small, low-key, no-frills ski valley, with everything from winding trails to double diamond expert runs. You can see all the hotels and restaurants from the parking lot, and the condominiums are nestled tastefully in the woods.

With all the ski and lodging packages available, it can be confusing to arrange your own trip. If you're interested in a ski trip, your best bet is to work through the Taos Valley Resort Association (see Places to Stay), which can arrange complete packages, including roundtrip flight to Albuquerque and transfer to Taos, plus lodging, lifts and lessons. The association offers custom packages for all interests, including all types of accommodations. In addition to Taos Ski Valley, less-challenging downhill skiing can be found at Red River, Angel Fire and Ski Rio (see the Red River and Angel Fire sections). See Mora in Northeastern New Mexico for the nearby Sipapu Ski Area.

Though skiing is its primary focus, Taos Ski Valley is trying to develop a summer clientele. In summer, lifts run from 10 am to 4 pm Thursday to Sunday and cost $6 roundtrip. No mountain bikes are allowed, but you can take the lift up and hike down or vice versa. Call the Taos Ski Valley for information on summer festivals and special events. If you are coming when the ski slopes are closed, be sure to call in advance to find out what is open, and plan on having a car or getting a ride. Shuttle service is sporadic and undependable.

Information With a peak elevation of 11,819 feet and a 2612-foot vertical drop,

Taos offers some of the most challenging skiing in the USA. The 72 slopes (36 expert, 19 intermediate and 17 beginner) are serviced by 11 lifts. Snowboards are not allowed. The ski season runs from Thanksgiving through Easter, and rates for lift tickets and ski packages vary during the season.

In the low season – generally Thanksgiving to the week before Christmas and from the end of March to closing – a full-day lift ticket is $27, and a half day is $24. During prime time skiing – that is, during Christmas/New Year's and generally all of February and March – full-day lift tickets cost $40, and a half day is $27. The lifts are open 9 am to 4 pm. Half-day rates start at 12:30 pm.

Taos Ski Valley does not offer the amenities of a real town. There is no grocery store, and unless meals are included in a ski package, most of the restaurants tend to be pricey. You are pretty isolated in the valley, and it is important to remember to bring any supplies or groceries from the town of Taos. There isn't even a gas station anywhere in the vicinity! If you are staying in one of the hotels at the base, you don't need a car, but if you are staying in one of the lodges on the way from Taos, check to see if shuttle service is included.

Taos Ski Valley, Inc (☎ 505-776-2291, 800-776-1111, fax 505-776-8596, tsv@ taoswebb.com,www.taoswebb.com/nmusa/ skitaos/), can answer all questions about the valley, including special events. The 24-hour number for snow conditions is ☎ 505-776-2916. There is a local sheriff (☎ 505-758-3361). Any medical questions or problems should be directed to the Taos Ski Valley or to someone at the desk of any of the hotels.

To reach the valley, take Hwy 64 north out of Taos to the blinking light, and veer right on Hwy 150 toward Arroyo Seco. The whole trip, a beautiful winding drive along a mountain stream, is about 20 miles.

Ernie Blake Ski School This ski school (☎ 505-776-2291) claims to be the best in the country and offers an incredible variety of ski packages. If you're only interested in skiing, this is the way to go. The packages are coordinated with hotels in the valley, but they can also be arranged independently if you choose to camp in the area or to stay anywhere beyond the ski valley.

The quintessential Taos ski-school experience is the traditional Learn to Ski Better Week, in which you participate in a five- or six-day program that includes five days of ski lessons, accommodations and meals. They are offered all season, with reduced prices during low season. Other options

include weekends of lessons for women by female instructors; mogul/extreme skiing weekends for $140; a $50 beginners' program including ski rental, tickets and two lessons; and ski guides who take 10 skiers into the high mountain ridges for two hours at a cost of $130. Call the ski valley for more options.

Other Activities

The variety of outdoor activities in the Taos area is exhaustive. Native Sons Adventures (☎ 505-758-9342, 800-753-7559, fax 505-751-4610), 1033-A Paseo del Pueblo Sur,

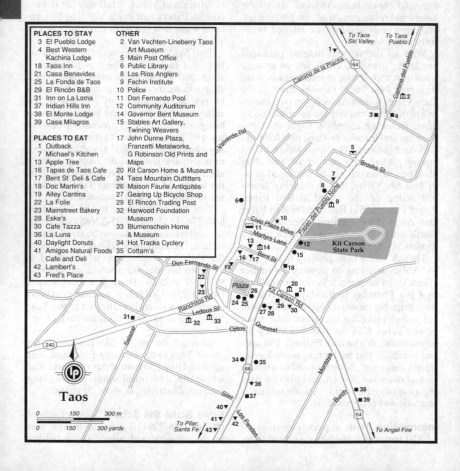

PLACES TO STAY
3 El Pueblo Lodge
4 Best Western Kachina Lodge
18 Taos Inn
21 Casa Benavides
25 La Fonda de Taos
29 El Rincón B&B
31 Inn on La Loma
37 Indian Hills Inn
38 El Monte Lodge
39 Casa Milagros

PLACES TO EAT
1 Outback
7 Michael's Kitchen
13 Apple Tree
16 Tapas de Taos Cafe
17 Bent St Deli & Cafe
18 Doc Martin's
19 Alley Cantina
22 La Folie
23 Mainstreet Bakery
28 Eske's
30 Cafe Tazza
36 La Luna
40 Daylight Donuts
41 Amigos Natural Foods Cafe and Deli
42 Lambert's
43 Fred's Place

OTHER
2 Van Vechten-Lineberry Taos Art Museum
5 Main Post Office
6 Public Library
8 Los Rios Anglers
9 Fechin Institute
10 Police
11 Don Fernando Pool
12 Community Auditorium
14 Governor Bent Museum
15 Stables Art Gallery, Twining Weavers
17 John Dunne Plaza, Franzetti Metalworks, G Robinson Old Prints and Maps
20 Kit Carson Home & Museum
24 Taos Mountain Outfitters
26 Maison Faurie Antiquités
27 Gearing Up Bicycle Shop
29 El Rincón Trading Post
32 Harwood Foundation Museum
33 Blumenschein Home & Museum
34 Hot Tracks Cyclery
35 Cottam's

Taos

0   150   300 m
0   150   300 yards

Kit Carson State Park

To Taos Ski Valley
To Taos Pueblo
To Pilar, Santa Fe
To Angel Fire

is a good source for information, and they rent equipment and offer various guided trips. Taos Mountain Outfitters (☎ 505-758-9292), on the Plaza, and Cottam's (☎ 505-758-2822), at 207-A Paseo del Pueblo Sur, sell gear, maps and guidebooks. The Convention and Recreation Service (☎ 505-758-4160) can answer questions about local recreation programs.

River Running The major attraction in the summer is white-water rafting in the Taos Box, the steep-sided cliffs that frame the Rio Grande. Busloads of rafters from Santa Fe go up to Pilar, which can become a flurry of sunburned and screaming tourists, but you can also enjoy quiet float trips away from the masses. There are several rafting companies offering day and overnight trips, so it helps to shop around. Be sure that you raft with a licensed company; there have been deaths due to inexperienced guides.

Some companies to try are Los Rios River Runners, Inc (☎ 505-776-8854, 800-544-1181), a quarter mile northeast of the blinking light on Ski Valley Rd, the friendly Pilar Yacht Club & Cafe (☎ 505-758-9072) in Pilar just south of town, and Big River Raft Trips (☎ 505-758-9711), also in Pilar. Rafting trips run around $30 to $40 for a half day and $70 to $85 for a full day. If you're not interested in white-water or want to avoid any kind of group activity, the Pilar Yacht Club rents one-person inflatable kayaks for $55; they're a great way to relax down the river.

Hiking There is no shortage of nearby hiking trails, ranging from easy day hikes to overnight backcountry trips, from alpine mountain trails along rivers to awesome hikes along and through the Rio Grande Gorge. Stop at the Carson National Forest Service, the BLM or an outdoors shop (see above) for guides and maps. Several trailheads are along Hwy 150 to Taos Ski Valley and at the northern end of the ski valley parking lot. Before setting out on any kind of hike, be sure to check

weather forecasts, let someone know where you're going and bring raingear. New Mexico is infamous for its volatile weather patterns, and the northern mountain ranges can be dangerous in sudden rain- or snowstorms.

Fishing Los Rios Anglers (☎ 505-758-2798, 800-748-1707), 226 Paseo del Pueblo Norte, has guided fly-fishing trips. If you're a hard-core angler, know what you're doing and are willing to pay $250 for a local guide, this is a fine place, but it's not for beginners. Doug Camp at Willows Inn (see Places to Stay – B&Bs) offers a more relaxed but no less professional experience. A full day of fishing, including flies, a rod, waders, lunch and drinks, costs $150 for one, $50 for each additional person.

Horseback Riding Shadow Mountain Ranch (☎ 505-758-7732, 800-405-7732) arranges rides through the Sangre de Cristo Mountains for $25 an hour. This is a friendly and relaxed spot, 6 miles east of Taos on Hwy 64 and 3 miles north on a rough dirt road. Cabin and lodge accommodations are available (see Places to Stay). South of town in Peñasco, Llano Bonito Ranch (☎ 505-587-2636) offers rides ranging from $15 for a half hour to $720 for three-day, all-inclusive pack trips to an altitude of 12,500 feet (four person minimum).

Golf The 18-hole golf course and driving range at Taos Country Club (☎ 505-758-7300), Hwy 570 W south of Rancho de Taos, is open from May to October. With 360-degree views of the plateau and surrounding mountains, this is a beautiful spot even if you don't play golf!

Swimming The Don Fernando Pool (☎ 505-758-9171), 124 Civic Plaza Drive, is open to the public all year for $2.

Ice Skating Skate for $1 on the pond in the Kit Carson State Park (☎ 505-758-8234) in the middle of town. It has been undergoing renovations, however, and it isn't clear when they'll reopen. Skate rental is $1.

Special Events

There are numerous athletic and cultural events all year, as well as workshops in the visual arts. For details on seasonal events, call the Taos Visitors' Center.

Big annual events include Taos Pueblo dances and celebrations (see Taos Pueblo above), as well as the **Taos Film Festival** in April and the **Taos Mountain Balloon Rally** (☎ 505-758-8321) over the last full weekend in October. This last is a smaller version of the Albuquerque International Balloon Festival, which tends to be overwhelmingly crowded. There are three mass ascensions of balloons, as well as parades, parties and community events. In Taos and Angel Fire, the **Summer Chamber Music Festival** draws crowds to outdoor concerts.

Places to Stay

Taos offers a wide variety of accommodations, ranging from free camping in national forests to gourmet B&Bs in historic adobes. Driving in on Paseo del Pueblo Sur, you'll find standard motel chains. High season for the village of Taos is summer, holidays and ski season, while high season for the ski valley is winter and holidays. There are two hostels in the nearby towns of Pilar and Arroyo Seco (see Pilar above and Places to Stay – Budget below).

In typical New Mexico style, prices vary according to how busy an establishment is, the season and the day of week. Call before assuming that the rates below are accurate, and always ask if they are willing to go lower! Most places offer reduced weekly rates, and many have self-contained suites with a kitchen and hot tub. All rates listed are high-season rates and do not include the 11% tax. The ski valley hotels generally offer only week-long packages, and these should be booked months in advance (see Taos Ski Valley at the end of this section).

The Taos Valley Resort Association (☎ 505-776-2233, 800-776-1111, res@ taoswebb.com), PO Box 85, Taos Ski Valley, NM 87525, is an excellent general source for booking hotels, B&Bs, condominiums and private homes. If you let them know your budget and what you're looking for, they'll do the legwork and save you the hassle for no charge. They also arrange vacation packages that include car rental and airfare, as well as rafting, snowmobiling, horseback riding – whatever you're looking for – for less than you would pay if you worked it out on your own. Other reservation companies include Taos Central Reservations (☎ 505-758-9767, 800-821-2437, fax 505-758-1875, central@taos.newmex.com), Ski Central Reservations (☎ 505-758-9550, 800-238-2829, fax 505-758-9559, skicentral@ newmex.com) and Affordable Accommodations and Tours (☎ 505-751-1292, 800-290-5384, fax 505-751-4610, nsa@laplaza .org). For information on more than 50 accommodation options, access www. taoswebb.com/TAOS/lodging.html.

Places to Stay – Camping

The *New Mexican Recreation and Heritage Guide*, available at the chamber of commerce, the USFS and the BLM, is a map noting official camping sites. For a complete detailed listing of camping in the area, stop at the USFS and the BLM offices or contact the Public Lands Information Center in Santa Fe (see Places to Stay – Camping in Santa Fe). If you are planning on backcountry camping, be prepared and remember that summer storms develop quickly, and winter weather can be treacherous and unpredictable.

There is no shortage of camping in the Carson National Forest, under the jurisdiction of the USFS (☎ 505-758-6200) or the BLM (☎ 505-758-8851). Most campgrounds are open April through October, depending on the weather, and none have showers. Some charge a daily fee of $6 to $8; all fee sites have drinking water. The closest campgrounds, maintained by the Camino Real Ranger District in

Peñasco (☎ 505-587-2255), are east of Taos nestled between Hwy 64 and a beautiful fishing creek. Three free sites, *El Nogal, La Vinateria* and *Las Petacas* are within 5 miles of town and the first fee site, *Capulin,* is about 7 miles from town. The Questa Ranger Station (☎ 505-586-0520) maintains five small, free campgrounds along the stream on the road to Taos Ski Valley.

There are two relatively close places to camp along the Rio Grande Gorge: either north of Taos at the beautiful Wild Rivers National Recreation Area (see below) or south in Pilar, near rafting and river access (see above).

The *Taos Motel and RV Park* (☎ 505-758-2524, 800-323-6009, fax 505-758-1989), 1799 Paseo del Pueblo Sur, has seven grassy camping sites for $12 and full RV hookups for $18. The *Taos Valley RV Park & Campground* (☎ 505-758-4469, 800-999-7571), 120 Estes Rd, Ranchos de Taos, has 92 sites open from April 15 until October. Tent/RV sites are $15/20 to 25. Facilities include hot showers, convenience store, lounge, coin laundry and a playground.

Places to Stay – Budget

Taos' budget motels line the strip along Paseo del Pueblo Sur as you enter town from the south, and there are more along Kit Carson Rd.

Ten minutes north of Taos in the tiny town of Arroyo Seco is *Abominable Snowmansion* (☎ 505-776-8298, fax 505-776-2107), which provides bunk-style lodging, as well as teepees and camping in the summer. Dorm beds are $16 in the summer, $22 in the winter, and private double rooms are $45 to $60 all year. Teepees cost $13 and camping is $8, including the use of showers and bathrooms. Winter rates include a hearty ranch-style breakfast and summer rates include full use of the kitchen. A two-story lodge room with a circular fireplace provides a cozy spot to relax. This is a clean, spacious hostel, popular with skiers and backpackers. A coffee shop deli, a reasonably priced and tasty

barbecue spot and an ice cream store are all right next door.

The *Taos Motel and RV Park* (☎ 505-758-2524, 800-323-6009, fax 505-758-1989) 1799 Paseo del Pueblo Sur, has standard rooms for about $49. The *Super 8 Motel* (☎ 505-758-1088, fax 505-758-2684), 1347 Paseo del Pueblo Sur, has singles/doubles for $57/62, with doubles going down to $42 during low season. The *Days Inn of Taos* (☎ 505-758-2203, fax 505-758-8929), 1333 Paseo del Pueblo Sur, offers rooms in the $55 to $70 range. Rooms at the *Hacienda Inn* (☎ 505-758-8610), 1321 Paseo del Pueblo Sur, are about $65.

Closer to the center of town, the pleasant, adobe-style *El Pueblo Lodge* (☎ 505-758-8700, 800-433-9612, fax 505-758-7321), 412 Paseo del Pueblo Norte, has singles/doubles for $50/63, including continental breakfast, and there is a pool and hot tub. Rooms with fireplaces and kitchenettes are available. Another option close to town is the *Indian Hills Inn* (☎ 505-758-4293, 800-444-2346), 233 Paseo del Pueblo Sur, with rooms from $50 to $75 and a pool.

Places to Stay – Middle

Hotels Rooms at the *Sun God Lodge* (☎ 505-758-3162, 800-821-2437, fax 505-758-1716), 909 Paseo del Pueblo Sur, are in the $50 to $90 range. The Southwestern-style décor is well done, some rooms have fireplaces, and there is a grassy courtyard and a pleasant hot tub in the back with views of the mountains. *El Monte Lodge* (☎ 505-758-3171, 800-828-8267, fax 505-758-1536), 317 Kit Carson Rd, offers rooms with refrigerators for about $75.

One and a half miles east of the Plaza on Hwy 64, in a quiet residential setting with a small pool and a peaceful grass area, is the *Inn on the Rio* (☎ 505-758-7199, 800-859-6752, fax 505-751-1816). Bright Southwestern rooms at this adobe motel are in the $70 to $90 range, including a hearty continental breakfast.

The nice *Best Western Kachina Lodge* (☎ 505-758-2275, fax 505-758-9207, kachina@newmex.com), 413 Paseo del Pueblo Norte, a big complex with an outdoor pool, coffee shop, restaurant, entertainment and conference facilities for up to 500, is walking distance from the Plaza. Rates range from $95 to $110. On Sunday morning it has a breakfast buffet for $6, and during the summer it hosts evening Indian dances.

Along the strip just south of town there are several hotels. The *Sagebrush Inn* (☎ 505-758-2254, 800-428-3626, fax 505-758-5077), 1508 Paseo del Pueblo Sur, has a great long bar offering nightly live music and two-steppin' on the weekends. It's a huge 1929 mission-style building with giant wooden portals, an outdoor patio and a swimming pool. Rates are in the $85 to $140 range, including a full hot breakfast. The *Holiday Inn Don Fernando de Taos* (☎ 505-758-4444, 800-759-2736, fax 505-758-0055), 1005 Paseo del Pueblo Sur, has a pool, tennis courts, a bar and a restaurant. It offers a complimentary hors d'oeuvres buffet 5 to 7 pm Monday through Friday that can serve as a cheap alternative for dinner. Rates are about $110. The *Quality Inn* (☎ 505-758-2200, 800-845-0648, fax 505-758-9009), 1043 Paseo del Pueblo Sur, has rooms in the $65 to $100 range, an indoor hot tub and an outdoor pool. Closer to town is the *Ramada Inn of Taos* (☎ 505-758-2900, 800-659-8267, fax 505-758-1662), on the corner of Frontier Rd and Paseo del Pueblo Sur, with an indoor pool and rooms for about $95.

Each of the five rooms and suites at the *Neon Cactus* (☎ 505-751-1258), 1523 Paseo del Pueblo Sur, is decorated in a particular movie-star theme. Four months of the year are considered high season, and prices range from $50 for a single with a shared bath in the Casablanca room to $85 for a double, to suites for $105 to $145. Low-season rates drop to $35 to $105.

Centrally located right on the Taos Plaza, *La Fonda de Taos* (☎ 505-758-2211, 800-833-2211, fax 505-758-8508, lafonda@ silverhawk.com), 108 South Plaza, is a late 1930s hotel that looks lost in a time

warp. Though big, the lobby is eerily quiet, dark and dusty. It has great character and is a good alternative to comparably priced chains on the strip. Even if you're not staying there, you might want to pay $3 to see a locked side room containing erotic paintings by DH Lawrence that were banned in England in 1929. Doubles are about $65, and two-room suites sleeping four to six people are about $100.

Several rural options, relatively close to town, hug the Carson National Forest along Hwy 64. Six miles east from Taos Plaza, *Taos Creek Cabins* (☎ 505-758-4715, tcc@newmex.com) rents five cabins with decks overlooking the creek. One/ two bedrooms sleeping two/four rent for $85/100 (down to $60 off-season), $10 for each additional person. Across the street and a few miles up a rough dirt road through the national forest, the quiet *Shadow Mountain Ranch* (☎ 505-758-7732, 800-405-7732, fax 505-758-1725, wenom@kensco.net) offers standard rooms for $50, a kitchen suite for $70 and cabins for $100 a double. Just outside your door, you can fish in a stocked pond, hike and cross-country ski for miles and ride horseback ($25 an hour). A mile and a half farther down Hwy 64 is *Shadybrook* (☎ 505-751-1315, 800-574-2395, fax 505-751-3088), where you can rent an adobe casita with a fireplace, microwave and refrigerator for $75 to $130 a night, fourth night free. They have a little restaurant where the chef will cook up anything you want; it's open from 8 am to 9 pm. *Suncatcher Earthship* (☎ 505-758-8745), a 700-sq-foot Earthship 3½ miles west of Rancho de Taos, can be rented for $70 per night for two people. Call ☎ 505-751-0462 for information on other Earthships; double occupancy rates range from $105 to $120 (see Earthships above).

B&Bs There is a plethora of B&B accommodations in Taos and the surrounding area, and the differences among them are significant. Don't assume that a B&B is more expensive than a hotel. Most of the ones listed here are comparably priced to a strip motel. The Taos Bed and Breakfast Association (☎ 505-758-4747, 800-876-7857, fax 505-758-7875, tbba@taos .newmex.com) and the Traditional Taos Inns Association (☎ 800-939-2215) can help find a place in advance. Taos Vacation Rentals (☎ 505-758-5700, 800-788-7267, fax 505-758-7875) provides personal service and specializes in finding unique accommodations, from historic adobes in town to mountain casitas. Rates range from $100 to $500 nightly.

If you're looking for a unique, friendly and relaxed spot with reasonable rates, try the *Laughing Horse Inn* (☎ 505-758-8350, 800-776-0161, fax 505-751-1123, laughors@laplaza.org), 729 Paseo del Pueblo Norte, Taos, NM 87571, a half mile north of the Taos Pueblo turnoff. In the '20s and '30s it was the home of Spud Johnson, publisher of a local magazine featuring work by DH Lawrence, Gertrude Stein and Georgia O'Keeffe, who were frequent guests. His quirky home, now more than a hundred years old, has expanded to 10 rooms of various sizes plus a huge penthouse, most with shared bathrooms and some with a fireplace. The smaller ones have loft beds with the TV/VCR affixed to the ceiling. Singles are $42 to $75, and doubles are $49 to $95. A guest house with kitchen and fireplace is $140 a double, $10 for each additional person. Rooms have VCRs, and the inn features a free video library, an outdoor hot tub and loaner bikes. The kitchen is open to anyone who needs it, and there is an honor system for beer, wine, juice, snacks and breakfast.

El Rincón Bed & Breakfast (☎ 505-758-4874, fax 505-758-4541), 114 Kit Carson Rd, Taos, NM 87571, is run by the daughter of Ralph Meyers, a well-known Taos figure from the early 20th century. The family still runs the oldest trading post in town, now a store and an eclectic museum of old Taos, 50 feet from the 100-year-old adobe home. Each room has a VCR and stereo, and many have fireplaces, spas and refrigerators. They range from $59 for a double to $125 for a suite. Some of the rooms have waterbeds, and each one is done in antique furniture and Mexican tile. Breakfast is fruit, muffins and cold cereal – by the fireplace in the winter or in the courtyard in the summer. There are no pretensions to this place, and you won't be disappointed by a generic bedroom at an exorbitant rate. The central location makes it easy to walk to nearby restaurants and galleries.

The *Willows Inn* (☎ 505-758-2558, 800-525-8267, fax 505-758-5445, willows@ newmex.com), 412 Kit Carson Rd and Dolan, Box 6560 NDCBU, Taos, NM 87571, is run by Arkansas transplants Janet and Doug Camp, whose warmth and sincerity work to make this more like a home than an inn. A family-style hot breakfast and evening appetizers of wine and smoked trout, or something comparable, are included in the price, and Doug, an avid fisherman and guide, can direct you to local fishing and lend you his portable fly-tying table and tools. Listed on the National and State Registers of Historic Places, the property was once the home and art studio of the late E Martin Hennings, a member of the Taos Society of Artists in the 1920s. The large adobe walls enclose an expansive lawn, towered over by two of the largest willows in North America, where Doug will snap your photo before you leave and then send it to you a few weeks later. There are five rooms, all with private baths, a fireplace and private entrance, for $95 to $130. Located a half mile from the Plaza, this is an especially nice place to stay in the summer, when the quiet gardens and grass are a welcome change from the high desert.

Casa Milagros (☎ 505-758-8001, 800-243-9334), 321 Kit Carson Rd, Taos, NM 87571, has five rooms for between $85 and $120, and a two-bedroom suite with kitchen, fireplace and double shower for $125 to $175, including breakfast for two. Most rooms have a fireplace, and all have a down comforter and tasteful Southwestern décor. Closer to town, *Casa Benavides* (☎ 505-758-1772, 800-552-1772, fax 505-758-5738), 136 E Kit Carson Rd, Taos, NM 87571, run by two Taos natives, consists of six individual historic buildings on five acres. All rooms, some in adobe Southwestern style and some in a historic Victorian home, have a private bath and antique furnishings, and some have a fireplace. Rates range from $80 for a double to $195 for a two-bedroom kitchen suite, including afternoon tea and full breakfast.

An inexpensive rural option is *Mountain Light B&B*, (☎ 505-776-8474, fax 505-776-8050, mtnlightbb@aol.com), PO Box 241, Taos, NM 87571. The two rooms are small and simple, but the house is perched on top of a hillside near Arroyo Hondo, 12 miles north of Taos, with an incredible 80-mile view over the valley and the Sangre de Cristo Mountain Range from the breakfast porch. Rooms are from $45 to $52 for one person and $62 to $75 for two. A full breakfast of blue corn pancakes and eggs and use of a communal kitchen is included, but don't expect anything fancy here. It's about one winding mile off the main road in Arroyo Hondo; call for directions.

Places to Stay – Top End

Hotels Parts of the *Taos Inn* (☎ 505-758-2233, 800-826-7466, fax 505-758-5776), 125 Paseo del Pueblo Norte, date to the 1600s, which is why it's on the National Register of Historic Places. The inn is probably the most upscale place in town, though it certainly isn't fancy. The cozy lobby – with adobe archways, heavy wood furniture and a sunken fireplace – is always busy, and there is live local music, from jazz and pop to classical, several nights a week. The Adobe Bar, and the streetside patio in the summer, is packed on the weekends with locals and tourists alike. Stop for a drink or a snack. The rooms are, of course, decorated in a Southwestern motif, and the more expensive ones have a fireplace. Rates range from $85 to $160 all year long, except November and April, when they drop to between $75 and $115.

Inn on La Loma (☎ 505-758-1717, 800-530-3040, fax 505-571-0155, laloma@taosweb.com), 315 Ranchitos Rd, is a beautiful rambling hacienda with several rooms dating back to the early 19th century and huge cottonwoods in the courtyard. It's completely enclosed by an adobe wall and perched on a bit of a hill, so you feel like you're far from town even though you're only a few blocks from the Plaza. The owners are from Aspen, and their focus is on luxury, but their efforts come across as a bit aloof and snobby. The public rooms are spacious, including a huge glassed-in breakfast room, but the bedrooms are rather small. Rates range from $85 to $185, including a full breakfast and snacks.

Taos Ski Valley There are about 20 lodges in and around the ski valley. Condominium rentals are available as well, and the easiest way to book one is through the Taos Valley Resort Association (see Places to Stay above). Most places offer weekly rates and reasonably priced ski packages.

The lodges along the drive to the ski valley back up to the national forest. The *Amizette Inn* (☎ 505-776-2451, 800-446-8267, fax 505-776-2451), a half mile from the ski base, offers nightly rates that include a full breakfast, ranging from $95 for one person to $195 for six people in the winter, and from $45 to $75 in the summer. Two miles from the slope, the pleasant *Austing Haus* (☎ 505-776-2649, 800-748-2932, fax 505-776-8751, austing@newmex.com), with exposed beams and a winter-only continental restaurant, has rooms for $45 to $95 in summer, $100 to $190 in winter. Rates include a continental buffet breakfast.

There are three ski lodges at the ski base, and the differences between them are several. They all offer ski week packages, which include seven nights, six days of lift tickets, six morning lessons and three meals daily (prices are quoted per person). Though all will have better than generic rooms, many with fireplaces and refrigerators, the ambiance varies significantly. *Hotel*

Edelweiss (☎ 505-776-2301, 800-458-8754, fax 505-776-2533, edelweiss@taosnm.com) is a small, cozy European-style hotel with newly renovated rooms. Doubles start at $65 in the summer, and ski week packages in the hotel or in condos start at $1470. The *Inn at Snakedance* (☎ 505-776-2277, 800-322-9815, fax 505-776-1410, snakednc@taos.newmex.com) is the biggest of the three and is more like a big hotel than a ski lodge. Facilities include a minispa with exercise equipment, a hot tub, a sauna and massage facilities, as well as a dining room and a bar overlooking the ski lifts. A double in the summer is $75, including a full breakfast, but in the winter they start at $195. Ski week packages start at $1160. *Hotel St Bernard* (☎ 505-776 2251) generally offers only ski week packages, starting at $1390, but if it's slow they'll rent a room by the night. Call for further rates.

Places to Eat

Eating out in Taos can be pricey. Try any of the open trailers along the road for a cheap, fast burrito or burger. Even the fanciest of places is casual, and restaurants are generally open until 9 or 10 pm.

Coffee Shops For an early cup of coffee and a donut, stop by *Daylight Donuts* (☎ 505-758-1156), 312 Paseo del Pueblo Sur. It's open 4 am to 1 pm Monday through Friday and until noon on Saturday, offering nothing but donuts, bagels and sausage gravy and biscuits.

Michael's Kitchen (☎ 505-758-4178), 304C Paseo del Pueblo Norte, is a busy breakfast spot for skiers and tourists, despite their claims that this is where the locals hang out. You're likely to find an early morning wait. Stop in for the biggest cinnamon roll you'll ever see and a wide selection of other hefty pastries. Breakfast includes the standard fare for between $4 and $8. Lunch and dinner offerings include sandwiches, burgers, New Mexican dishes, steaks and fish, with lunch in the $4 to $8 range and dinner under $13. Though the menu is extensive and portions hearty, the food is nothing special. It's open from 7 am to 8:30 pm.

The outdoor patio and grassy courtyard at *Cafe Tazza* (☎ 505-758-8706), 122 E Kit Carson Rd, is a pleasant place to enjoy an espresso and pastry. Menu items include homemade soups and tamales and a wide selection of coffee drinks in a bohemian atmosphere. Live entertainment, including locals playing acoustic folk-pop and reading poetry, takes place on weekend evenings. It's open 8 am to 6 pm daily, but generally stays open until 10 pm Wednesday through Sunday. On the north end of town, *The Bean* (☎ 505-758-7711), 900 Pasco del Pueblo Norte, roasts its own beans. It's a popular spot for locals to hang out over coffee and pastries, and the little outdoor patio can get pretty crowded.

For an interesting menu of freshly made sandwiches, try eating inside or on the patio at the *Bent St Deli & Cafe* (☎ 505-758-5787), 120 Bent. With 21 sandwiches, including the Blue Ribbon BBQ and the Taos (turkey, green chile, bacon, salsa and guacamole rolled in a flour tortilla), and salads ranging from hummus and tabbouleh to caesar, it offers something for everyone. Lunches are under $8. For dinner there's pasta and a variety of unique entrées for $10 to $12. Hours are 8 am to 9 pm Monday through Saturday. Another good spot for sandwiches and burgers, more popular with locals than tourists, is the casual café, store and bar *Bravo* (☎ 505-758-8100), next door to the Fina station on Paseo del Pueblo Sur. They also have a wide selection of beer, wine and gourmet snacks to go. It's open 11 am to 9 pm Monday to Saturday.

Just west of the Plaza but far from the tourist crowds, the *Mainstreet Bakery* (☎ 505-758-9610) on Guadalupe Plaza bakes bread for grocery stores in Santa Fe and Albuquerque. 'All organic – all natural . . . almost' is the motto in this simple place. It serves such fare as scrambled tofu and oatcakes, as well as a huge plate of eggs, beans and potatoes, for about $5. Lunch is a gardenburger or sandwich for $4 to $7 or the special – a bowl of black beans, green chile, red onions, tomatoes and cornbread for $4. Hours are 7:30 am to 6 pm Monday to Friday, 11:30 am to 2 pm Saturday and Sunday.

Mexican & New Mexican Popular among locals is *Fred's Place* (☎ 505-758-0514), 332 Paseo del Pueblo Sur. Before opening his restaurant, Fred spent months researching traditional recipes for standard New Mexican dishes. After talking to old Hispanic families in the area, as well as old-timers of Taos Pueblo, and writing down their hints about not only what to cook but how to cook, Fred opened his restaurant. His simple one-room place, reminiscent of old Mexico, has a limited menu of excellent dishes. Everything is fresh and hearty. Try the carne adobada, slowly simmered pork in spicy red chile. Prices range from $4 to $8. It's open for dinner only, 5 to 9:30 pm Monday through Saturday.

On Hwy 150 to the ski valley, the friendly and relaxed *Tim's Chili Connection* (☎ 505-776-8787), started by the same Tim of Tim's Stray Dog at the ski base (who was tragically killed in a Taos avalanche in 1996), serves up delicious green chile, huge margaritas and other hearty New Mexican fare, ranging from $5 for nachos to $16 for a cowboy steak. Eat inside the rambling adobe or, in the summer, enjoy the mountain views from the spacious, open grass and garden courtyard. Local bands play here weekly.

The *Alley Cantina* (☎ 505-758-2121), 121 Terracina Lane, is housed in the oldest building in Taos, which was built in the 1500s by Pueblo Indians and once served as the Taos Pueblo trading post. It serves good New Mexican and American fare as well as late-night pizza and burgers. It's a cozy place, with a pool table in one room, a shuffleboard in another and live music either on the patio or occasionally inside.

El Pueblo Cafe (☎ 505-758-2053), 625 Paseo del Pueblo Norte, is a no-frills café and one of the few places in town open until 2:30 am on the weekends. Food is standard New Mexican fare, including traditional menudo and pozole, in the $3 to $9 range. Beer and wine is available. Hours are 6 am to 11:30 pm Sunday through Thursday, 6 am to 2:30 am Friday and Saturday. Another no-frills option is *Rita's* (☎ 505-751-9803) in El Prado. This isn't much more than plywood floors, a few tables and a walk-up window with a grill, but the food is good and nothing is more expensive than $6.

Italian One of the best restaurants in town is the *Trading Post Cafe* (☎ 505-758-5089), 4179 Hwy 68. The chefs use only the freshest ingredients in their northern Italian dishes; sit at the counter and dip your bread in seasoned olive oil while you wait. If you're looking for an upscale but relaxed meal, this is one of those places where all the pieces fall together, but you pay for it. Housed in an old trading post, the décor is contemporary and lively, and it's a favorite with locals. The lunch menu runs in the $5 to $9 range, but expect to pay about $25 a person for a dinner with dessert and wine. It's open from 11:30 am to 2:30 pm for lunch and 5 to 9:30 pm for dinner.

The *Outback* (☎ 505-758-3112), 712 Paseo del Pueblo Norte, just north of town behind a secondhand sports store, is a local favorite for pizza by the slice or whole. The menu includes calzones and unique pizza toppings like honey-chipotle chile sauce, Thai chicken and, of course, green chile. A slice costs between $2.60 and $5, and expect to pay $14 for a whole plain cheese pizza and up to $21 for some of the quirky gourmet pizzas. Salads and sandwiches, as well as beer and wine, are also available. Open from 11 am to 9 pm daily, until 10 pm Friday and Saturday.

La Luna (☎ 505-751-0023), on Paseo del Pueblo Sur in the Pueblo Alegre Mall, serves traditional Italian specialties, including antipasto, various pastas, marinated shrimp, fresh mussels and pizzas baked in a wood-burning oven. Prices are in the $9 to $18 range, but the food is consistently fresh and tasty. It's open for dinner only, closed Wednesday.

One of the most elegant restaurants in town is *Villa Fontana* (☎ 505-758-5800), housed in an old home 5 miles north of Taos on Hwy 522. The northern Italian dishes focus on locally picked mushrooms and seasonal game and range from $14 to $25. It opens for cocktails at 5:30 pm Monday through Saturday, and dinner service begins at 6 pm.

Continental Centrally located and busy, with impeccable service, a creative menu and ample servings, the *Apple Tree* (☎ 505-758-1900), 123 Bent, is a good bet. Sit in one of the rooms of the large historic adobe or under the stars in the courtyard and enjoy smoked trout, mango chicken enchiladas, steak, lamb, curry and pasta specialties. The food is consistently excellent, but expect to pay about $80 for a dinner for two, including appetizer, a bottle of wine and dessert. Lunch is considerably less. Brunch in the $5 to $12 range is served 10 am to 3 pm Sunday. Lunch is 11:30 am to 3 pm, and dinner is 5:30 to 9:30 pm, Monday through Saturday. Dinner reservations are recommended.

The brightly colored, contemporary bistro *La Folie* (☎ 505-758-8800), 122 Dona Luz, offers a spectrum of unique dishes and international flavors, including salmon, duck and ostrich for $8 to $15. In the summer the peaceful courtyard, with sculptures and a fountain, has an outdoor grill. The feel is relaxed, friendly and intimate. It's closed Monday. Another cozy bistro is *Joseph's Table* (☎ 505-751-4512) on Paseo de Pueblo Sur in Rancho de Taos. With rough-painted yellow walls, a low beamed ceiling, a huge chalkboard listing specials, about seven tables and a little patio overlooking the Taos Plateau, this is a lovely, quiet spot with delicious food. For lunch, polenta, specialty pizzas and sandwiches are about $7, but dinner, including dishes such as dijon-crusted pork, mahi mahi and steak au poivre, runs about $18.

Lambert's (☎ 505-758-1009), 309 Paseo del Pueblo Sur, is fancy by Taos standards. It features American 'contemporary'

gourmet dishes and specializes in grill fare such as roast duck, salmon, halibut with green chile and pepper-crusted lamb. Prices range from $9 to $24. With its whitewashed walls and formal waitstaff, this place tends to be a bit stuffy, but the food is very good. It's open for lunch 11 am to 2 pm Monday through Friday and for dinner from 5:30 to 9 pm nightly.

Isolated in the hills 9 miles south of town and offering absolutely incredible views of Taos Valley, *Stakeout Grill & Bar* (☎ 505-758-2042), 101 Stakeout Drive, is reminiscent of the cowboy West and specializes in steaks, including a New York strip for $17 and a 20-oz 'real cowboy steak' for $27. A vegetarian kabob at $10 and pasta at $13 are the cheapest items on the menu, with appetizers going for $7 to $9. The meat-and-potato meals include excellent quality beef, but stay away from anything that sounds too fancy. If nothing else it's well worth stopping by for a drink to enjoy the quiet views; it's open nightly from 5 to 10 pm. Drive south from the Plaza on Hwy 68 for 8 miles, keeping an eye out for the Stakeout sign. The restaurant is about a mile up on a dirt road.

Inside the Taos Inn is *Doc Martin's* (☎ 505-758-2233), with an extensive wine list and a creative menu of continental and New Mexican cuisine, including seafood and game dishes. This is one of the most expensive restaurants in town, and reservations are recommended for dinner. It is open from 7:30 am to 2:30 pm and 5:30 to 10 pm daily.

Other Eateries Offering six daily beer specials, each brewed on the premises, *Eske's* (☎ 505-758-1517), at 106 Des Georges Lane, a half block south of Taos Plaza, is a crowded hangout catering to locals and ski bums alike. A casual, two-room adobe, this is not only an excellent place for a nice cold beer ($3 a pint for such specialties as green chile beer and Dead Presidents Ale) but for cheap, fresh, hearty pub fare as well. Bangers and mash, served with warm applesauce and bread, is $7, and a huge burrito with whole-wheat tortilla, two kinds of beans and salsa is $4.50. For $1 extra, get it smothered in vegetarian green chile brimming with zucchini and potatoes, also available by the cup for $3. Tuesday is sushi night. There is often live music, such as banjo, acoustic guitar, jazz or conga drums. Hours vary, but they're generally open for lunch and dinner every day.

The only tapas place in town, *Tapas de Taos Cafe* (☎ 505-758-9670), 136 Bent, is not limited to the standard Spanish fare. A quirky little place, with a casual cozy interior and patio dining in the summer, it serves an eclectic menu of Mexican dishes. You can get an interesting variety of appetizer portions for $4 to $7 each or a full dinner for $6 to $13. Lunch costs a bit less. It's open daily for lunch and dinner.

Amigos Natural Foods Cafe and Deli (☎ 505-758-8493), 326 Paseo del Pueblo Sur, has tofu burgers, salads and stir-fry in the $3 to $6 range. Hours are 9 am to 7 pm Monday through Saturday, and 11 am to 5 pm Sunday.

Taos Ski Valley On the way to Taos Ski Valley, the town of Arroyo Seco offers three excellent reasons to stop. *Taos Cow Ice Cream* (☎ 505-776-5640) serves famous all-natural ice cream, bagel sandwiches and coffee. Prices range from $1 to $5. Offering such treats as smoked trout, pâté and tiny bottles of extra virgin olive oil, as well as a wide selection of breads and pastries, imported cheeses and fruit, *Casa Fresen Bakery* (☎ 505-776-2969) is a gourmet deli in the middle of nowhere! Tasty and creative sandwiches (a bit pricey at $5 to $8), as well as a few hot entrées like green chile chicken pot pie and grilled panini sandwiches with gorgonzola, smoked salmon and sun-dried tomatoes, are available all day. Stop in here for a coffee jolt, and put together a picnic for a day on the ski slopes or the hiking trails of the Carson National Forest. It's open 7:30 am to 6 pm.

Another notable Arroyo Seco restaurant is the *Deep Fork Smokehouse* (☎ 505-776-1306), with red-checkered tablecloths,

dark wood and huge portions of delicious smoked meats like ribs and turkey for under $11.

Food at the ski valley itself tends to be expensive. *Rhoda's* (☎ 505-776-2005) operates outdoor grills right at the base, offering burgers and chicken; sandwiches and pasta are available inside. Expect to pay $5 to $15 for lunch. *Tim's Stray Dog Cantina* (☎ 505-776-2894) serves up some of the best green chile in New Mexico, as well as other pub fare, and is always busy with the ski crowd. Beans with green chile and a tortilla with a soda will run you $5, and Southwestern basics range from $4 to $7. It's open for breakfast at 7:30 am and serves until 9 pm during ski season, from 11 am to 9 pm during the rest of the year. Stop by for an aprés-ski beer or sit on the outdoor patio in the summer.

The lodges offer comparable continental gourmet cuisine, but they haven't generally been known for delicious food or creative menus. Unfortunately, the excellent kitchen at Hotel Edelweiss burned down, but plans are in the works to open a new one.

Entertainment

The *Storyteller Cinema* (☎ 505-758-9715) is at 110 Old Talpa Canon Rd, near the Holiday Inn. The *Taos Community Auditorium* (☎ 505-758-4677), 145 Paseo del Pueblo Norte, runs a film series featuring old and independent films and hosts a variety of theater and concert productions. Tickets are generally $10. Several restaurants and bars offer live music (see Places to Eat).

Shopping

Taos has historically been a mecca for artists, and the huge number of galleries and studios in and around town are evidence of this. Unfortunately, there is also a lot of junk as well as a bustling tourist industry of T-shirt and coffee-mug shops, which is generally focused around the Plaza. You could easily spend an entire day wandering the streets, and a good rule to follow is that the places that look the least inviting – a little dilapidated, with a handwritten sign tacked to the door – often have the most interesting work. The best way to explore the art community of Taos is to take the time to poke around, but if you'd like more direction or have specific interests, the visitor center has a helpful Collectors' Guide with maps and information on galleries.

The Stables Art Gallery (☎ 505-758-2036), 133 Paseo del Pueblo Norte, managed by the Taos Art Association, is next to the Community Auditorium and shows works by Taos artists. The building itself has a mysterious past. Arthur Manby, a wealthy entrepreneur and land developer, once lived here. He apparently made many enemies in his acquisition of over 60,000 acres of land in the early 20th century, and his decapitated body was found in the house in 1929. His murder remains unsolved. The Taos Art Association bought the property in 1953, and today it is a great source of information about the local art scene. Shows change monthly. The center is open from 10 am to 5 pm in the winter, with longer summer hours.

Twining Weavers (☎ 505-758-9000), 135 Paseo del Pueblo Norte, has two stores right next to each other, one in the long, low adobe stables behind the Stables Art Gallery and another smaller one on the street. It features handwoven rugs, tapestries and pillows, as well as work in fiber, basketry and clay. Hours are 10 am to 5 pm Monday through Saturday, 11 am to 4 pm Sunday.

El Rincón Trading Post (☎ 505-758-9188), 114 E Kit Carson Rd, features a great selection of Indian crafts and jewelry and Old West memorabilia. The store dates back to 1909 when German Ralph Meyers arrived, one of the first traders in the area, and it is still run by his widow. Even if you're not looking to buy anything, stop in here just to browse through the dusty museum of artifacts. It's open from 9 am to 5 pm daily.

If you're in the market for old medical objects, US military memorabilia or Art Deco lamps, stop in at Maison Faurie

Antiquités (☎ 505-758-8545), 1 McCarthy Plaza. This eclectic mix of antiques – basically anything that intrigues owner Robert Faurie – is crammed into cabinets and shelves and makes a great place to poke around. It's open from 8 am to 9 pm daily.

In the John Donn Plaza, across from the Apple Tree on Bent, there are several shops. Franzetti Metalworks (☎ 505-758-4784) was the first store to sell the light switch and plug covers, as well as toilet paper holders, that are now ubiquitous throughout New Mexico. This place has a great variety of shapes, like wolves, cats, cows and pigs, and ones that you won't find elsewhere. Another interesting stop, if for nothing else but to check out original maps of the American West including railroad, geological and army surveys, is G Robinson Old Prints and Maps (☎ 505-758-2278, fax 505-758-1606). He sells antique maps and prints from the 16th to the 19th century. Nambe Mills (☎ 505-758-8221), 216 Paseo del Pueblo Norte, sells a large selection of Nambeware, both first quality and seconds (see Santa Fe, Shopping for a description of Nambeware).

If you find yourself creatively inspired by the Southwest and the galleries (but frustrated with the prices!), or in need of a rest from outdoor activities, stop by Two Dog Design Company (☎ 505-751-9097) on Paseo del Pueblo Norte in El Prado. This friendly spot provides unpainted ceramics, brushes and paints for you to paint your own pottery. They'll fire it for you within a few days. Tile making, tinsmithing, papermaking and other workshops are offered for between $25 and $125.

Getting There & Away
Car Beware of crazy drivers on the two 75-mile routes from Santa Fe, both of which are winding. Elevation changes can result in dramatic differences in weather conditions.

Bus TNM&O-Greyhound (☎ 505-758-1144, 800-231-2222), in the Fina station on Paseo del Pueblo Sur, has daily bus service to/from Albuquerque ($22) and Santa Fe ($17), with stops at Pilar and Española. Buses leave Albuquerque at 6:30 am and 11:15 am; they leave Santa Fe at 7:40 am and 12:50 pm.

Shuttle Faust (☎ 505-758-3410, 800-535-1106) and Pride of Taos (☎ 505-758-8340, 800-273-8340, fax 505-758-0713) offer two to three daily shuttles from Albuquerque Airport to Taos for $35/65 and from Santa Fe to Taos for $25/45 one-way/roundtrip. Faust has a $45/85 shuttle to Angel Fire and a $55/95 shuttle to Red River. Pride of Taos charges $45 one-way to either Red River or Angel Fire. Three daily shuttles to Taos Ski Valley (winter only) cost $10 roundtrip. Schedules vary.

Getting Around
Taxi Faust runs an on-call taxi service, from 7 am to 9 pm, with costs ranging from $7 for one to two people within the city limits to $30 one-way to Taos Ski Valley and $125 one-way to Santa Fe.

Bus The Chile Line (☎ 505-751-2000) is Taos' local bus service, though financial difficulties may force it to close down. It runs on the half hour, starting at 7 am southbound from the Kachina Lodge and northbound from the post office in Rancho de Taos, and costs 50¢ per ride, $1 for a daily pass, or $5 for a seven-day pass.

Car Rental At the Taos Municipal Airport (☎ 505-758-4995), on Hwy 64 just west of town, is Dollar Rent A Car (☎ 505-758-4995), with jeeps and other options. Major rental car agencies are located in Santa Fe and Albuquerque.

Air Air Taos (☎ 505-758-9501 or -4995) offers charter flights from Albuquerque for $230. Plans are in the works to take up to five people, at a rate of $80, when they fly in supplies twice a week. Call to see if this is available.

Bicycle Mountain bikes, road bikes and bike racks can be rented through Gearing

Up Bicycle Shop (☎ 505-751-0365), 129 Paseo del Pueblo Sur, Hot Tracks Cyclery (☎ 505-751-0949), 729 Paseo del Pueblo Sur, Cottam's (☎ 505-758-2822), 207-A Paseo del Pueblo Sur, and Native Sons Adventures (☎ 505-758-9342, 800-753-7559), 1033-A Paseo del Pueblo Sur. Costs range from about $20 to $35 daily, with weekly discounts.

Hitchhiking Though hitchhiking is dangerous anywhere, it is common to see people hitching to and from Taos Ski Valley. Use caution hitchhiking; women should not hitchhike alone.

THE ENCHANTED CIRCLE
This 84-mile loop around Wheeler Peak, New Mexico's highest mountain at 13,161 feet, is a beautiful drive through the Carson National Forest. It passes a few small towns along the way, as well as a spectrum of hiking trails and lakes and two ski basins. The Taos Visitors' Center sells a USFS guidebook ($2) outlining everything to see and do along or near the Enchanted Circle. Storms arise quickly in both the summer and winter, and parts of this drive are at 10,000 feet. Be sure to check road conditions before heading out (☎ 800-432-4269).

Begin by taking Hwy 522 north out of Taos, stopping by the DH Lawrence Memorial, and head to Questa. Take a detour west on Hwy 378 to one of the most spectacular camping and hiking sites in the area, Wild Rivers National Recreation Area.

Retrace your steps back to Questa and continue east on Hwy 38 to Red River, which has both downhill and cross-country skiing. The next stretch is rather barren high-mountain terrain, with Eagle Nest Lake, good for boating and stocked for fishing, set in the desolate grasslands of the Moreno Valley. In the 1800s, the Moreno Valley boomed with gold seekers, but today Eagle Nest is quiet.

Continue south on Hwy 38 toward Angel Fire, which is a ski resort. Then take Hwy 64 west through the winding roads of the

DH Lawrence Memorial

Like so many artists in the early 20th century, DH Lawrence found inspiration in the land and lifestyle of northern New Mexico. Three of his books, *The Plumed Serpent*, *David* and *Mornings in Mexico*, were influenced by his two-year stay at the Kiowa Ranch, just north of Taos. Mabel Dodge Luhan had tried to give the ranch to Lawrence in the 1920s, but he didn't want to be indebted to her. His wife, Frieda, later accepted it in exchange for the original manuscript of *Sons and Lovers*.

When Lawrence died in France in 1930, Frieda brought his ashes back to Kiowa Ranch. She was so afraid that Mabel would try to steal them that, as the story goes, she had them mixed into the cement of a small shrine in the shape of a cabin. Frieda was eventually buried outside the memorial.

Today, the ranch is owned by the University of New Mexico, which uses it for academic research. To get to the DH Lawrence Memorial (☎ 505-776-2245), drive past the farming village of Arroyo Hondo on Hwy 522 and follow signs down a dirt road on the right. There is no museum, but you can come here to pay your respects to the Lawrences. Admission is free. ■

Carson National Forest, following the stream, back to Taos.

QUESTA

This tiny community is at the turnoff from Hwy 522 onto Hwy 38 to Red River.

The USFS Questa Ranger Station (☎ 505-586-0520, 505-758-6230), PO Box 110, Questa, NM 87556, 1 mile east of Questa on Hwy 38, has information about campgrounds in the Carson National Forest, which are open mid-May through mid-October. Most are small and available on a first-come, first-served basis. Those with fees, ranging from $6 to $8, have drinking water. Nearby is the Wild Rivers National Recreation Area (see below) and

the 20,000-acre Latir Peak Wilderness Area (☎ 505-758-6200), which offers scenic camping, picnicking, hiking and fishing. To get to the Latir Peak Wilderness Area from Questa, take Hwy 522 north toward Costilla.

The *Sangre de Cristo Motel* (☎ 505-586-0300) has standard doubles for about $50. Family-run *El Seville Restaurant* (☎ 505-586-0300) serves New Mexican and American dishes for about $8; it's open from 6:30 am to 8 pm daily. *Louie's Cafe* (☎ 505-586-0590), closed in the winter, has great green-chile cheeseburgers.

WILD RIVERS NATIONAL RECREATION AREA

Awe-inspiring camping and hiking are available year-round at the beautiful and desolate Wild Rivers National Recreation Area, 26 miles north of Taos along Hwy 522 and then west on Hwy 378. Flat mesas covered in sagebrush surround the deepest part of the Rio Grande Gorge. Though it can be relatively busy in the summer, it is easy to get away from the crowds. La Junta and Big Arsenic Springs Trails go about 1 mile into the gorge at the junction of the Red River and the Rio Grande, where you can fish in designated fly-fishing water. There are other trails for all levels, including one which tracks through an extinct volcano. The small museum at the visitor center (☎ 505-239-7211) explains local geology, and staff offer interpretive hikes and evening campfire programs. There is a $3 fee per vehicle for day use.

You can camp and/or grill at the piñon-studded sites overlooking the Rio Grande Gorge, or hike down the gorge to backcountry sites by the river. Roadside sites are $7 per vehicle, backcountry sites are $5. There are no showers or hookups.

RED RIVER

In the 19th century, gold was discovered in the hills surrounding Red River, and by 1905 there were 3,000 people, four hotels, 15 saloons and a thriving red-light district. The town developed a wild reputation, but by 1925 miners had left for golder pastures. Today the population of 350 survives predominantly on tourism. Fortunately, the national forest prevents sprawling development and protects its Old West feel. The buildings look like they're out of a movie set. Small-town family fun and outdoor recreation are the focus here, though there are a couple of bars with live country music. You won't find a wild nightlife or the post-hippie and ski clientele characteristic of Taos. At an elevation of 8,750 feet, the weather can be pretty cold even in the summer.

Orientation & Information

There are three streets running parallel to the river at the base of the ski slope – Rivers, Main and High – and you can walk anywhere within town. The chamber of commerce (☎ 505-754-2366, 800-348-6444, fax 505-754-2944, www.taoswebb .com/RedRiverInfo) is on the second block of Main. The police can be reached at ☎ 505-754-6166. A trolley service runs through the town, with free pickups at all the accommodations. Enchanted Circle Tours & Coaches (☎ 505-754-3154) offers taxi service within town and roundtrip shuttles to Santa Fe for $85, Taos Ski Valley for $65, Taos for $45 and Albuquerque for $95.

Tumbleweeds

Huge twiggy balls rolling across the desert seem as much a part of the Southwestern landscape as the cowboy. However, both are recent imports to the Southwestern scene. The tumbleweed, also called the Russian thistle (*Salsola kali*), arrived in the 19th century with immigrant farmers from Eastern Europe.

The tumbleweed is an annual that grows quickly in disturbed areas and soon becomes a large ball of tough branches attached to the ground by a single stem. Summer winds uproot the dried plants and send them tumbling eerily across the desert. ■

Activities

Red River can be a less-expensive base from which to explore the natural splendors of the area. The Williams Trading Post (☎ 505-754-2217) is a local institution and a general source of information on fishing and hiking.

Hiking & Biking The area around Red River offers great hiking through the Carson National Forest's mountain meadows, lakes and streams. You can pick up trail maps at the chamber of commerce. Trails of 2 to 16 miles at all levels of difficulty weave through Columbine Canyon, including one to the top of Wheeler Peak. The trailhead for Red River Nature Trail, an easy 2-mile trail along the stream that hugs the town, is at the ski base. In the summer you can take a **mountain bike** up in the chair lift and ride down. Beaver Ponds and Middle Fork Lake Trails start at the end of Upper Valley Rd. You can either take an easy half-day hike to the Beaver Ponds, or park at the Middle Fork Trail lot and hike 2 miles, ascending 2000 vertical feet, to a high mountain lake.

Skiing The *Red River Ski Area* (☎ 505-754-2223, fax 505-754-6184, redriver@ newmex.com) has predominantly intermediate runs; you won't find the high-terrain mountain trails that you do in Taos. It's a great place to come if you're just learning or if you find the intensity of Taos intimidating. Lift tickets are $37 for a full day, $27 for a half day. Call for package rates, which include lifts and lesson. *Ski Rio* (☎ 505-586-9949) is north of Red River outside Costilla. With 1400 acres and 30 kilometers of groomed trails through national forest and alpine fields, the *Enchanted Forest* (☎ 505-754-2374) is New Mexico's biggest cross-country ski area. An all-day pass costs $11, ski rentals are $10.50 and snowshoes are $9. Learn to Ski packages, private and group lessons and multiday passes are available. For the three days before the full moon, they offer Moonlight Ski Tours. Go to *Miller's Crossing* (☎ 505-754-2375), 212 Main, to book trips and arrange drop-offs. The Just Desserts Eat & Ski Festival is at the end of February; restaurants in town set up tables of desserts all along the trail system, and you can eat your way along.

Fishing The fishing in Red River is great, due to the 20,000 German brown, cutthroat and rainbow trout that are annually stocked in the river and surrounding lakes. A half-day license is $9 to $14, a five-day license is $17 to $22. Talk to staff at Williams Trading Post for information.

Organized Tours

There is no shortage of outdoor adventure organizations in Red River, and they'll arrange any kind of trip you're looking for. Two that enjoy a good reputation are *Red Dawg* (☎ 505-754-2721) for snowmobiling trips and *Bitter Creek Guest Ranch* (☎ 505-754-2587) for horseback riding. *New Mexico Adventure Co* (☎ 505-754-2437) rents bikes and jeeps and offers guided trips of all kinds.

Special Events

Red River hosts Mardi Gras in the Mountains a half hour north of town to coincide with New Orleans' street festival, and on Memorial Day weekend, 6000 motorcyclists converge on the small town for one of the biggest biking weekends in the country.

Places to Stay

Accommodations in Red River generally consist of motel-type lodges in town, condominiums, cabins in the mountains and camping out. *Bandanna Properties* (☎ 505-754-2949), *Reservations Unlimited* (☎ 505-754-6415, 800-545-6415, fax 505-754-6679, reserve@newmex.com) and *Red River Real Estate* (☎ 505-754-2459) can arrange the rental of a private home, or any other accommodation. The chamber of commerce has a visitors guide with a complete listing.

Camping There is plenty of seasonal camping in and around Red River. The following are RV campgrounds in town,

with fees averaging $23 for hookups: *Roadrunner Campground* (☎ 505-754-2286, 800-243-2286), *Mayes Triangle M* (☎ 505-754-2305), *Red River RV Park* (☎ 505-754-6187, 800-670-3711), *River Branch* (☎ 505-754-2293), and *Silver Spur* (☎ 505-754-2378, 800-545-8372). See Questa, above, for information about campsites in the national forest along Hwy 38.

Hotels/Lodges/B&Bs The *Lodge at Red River* (☎ 505-754-6280, 800-915-6343, fax 505-754-6304) is probably the nicest place in town. This centrally located landmark hotel has a cozy European feel, which is lacking in the others. There is a bar and restaurant, with home cooking for breakfast and dinner only. Doubles range from $68 to $96 in the summer, $78 to $106 in the winter. The *Copper King Lodge* (☎ 505-754-6210), 307 E River, has doubles and private cabins for $59 to $140. Rooms at the *Ponderosa Lodge* (☎ 505-754-2988) are in the $55 to $116 range. *Lifts West* (☎ 505-754-2778, 800-221-1859), 201 Main, is a hotel complex in the center of town.

On 2 acres outside of town, the *Riverside* (☎ 505-754-2252, 800-432-9999) offers quiet cabins with kitchens as well as double rooms for $60 to $77. Nestled up in the mountains, with a private fishing pond, snowmobiles for rent and stables, *Bitter Creek Guest Ranch* (☎ 505-754-2587) offers doubles and cabins ranging from $65 to $125, more on holidays. It's closed for November.

If you're looking for a B&B, try the *Sundance* (☎ 505-754-2321), 1301 E Hwy 38, Red River, NM 87558, which overlooks the town. All rooms have private baths, down comforters and feather beds, and rates include a full breakfast. Doubles are $75 to $120. There's a two-night minimum stay requirement.

Places to Eat

At *Shotgun Willie's* (☎ 505-754-6505), across the street from Lifts West, all-you-can-eat mountain man breakfasts are

$4, and fast-food burgers and barbecue are up to $7. *Sundance Mexican Restaurant* (☎ 505-754-2971) serves plates of beans and burritos and the like for under $10.

Waits are sometimes four hours long at the local steak saloon, *Texas Red's Steakhouse* (☎ 505-754-2964), but you can call the 'hostess hotline' at ☎ 505-754-2922 to find out. It's a favorite with tourists looking for that taste of the Old West and worth a stop. Expect to pay $10 to $20 for a steak, but they also have buffalo burgers and chicken fajitas for $7.50 and an extensive beer list. At the far end of town, *Brett's Homestead Steakhouse* (☎ 505-754-6136) is the locals' alternative to Texas Red's. Go to the *Black Crow Coffee House* (☎ 505-754-3150), 500 E Main, for a strong cup of coffee and pastries, with pasta and live music on the weekends. The owner, Nancy, always has time to chat and give tips on local things to do and places to stay and eat. Stop in *Lonesome Pine Pub*, 500 W Main, for a microbrewed beer, sandwiches and snacks under $6.

For boot-scooting to live country & western music Thursday through Sunday, go to the *Motherlode Saloon* (☎ 505-754-6280). Another bar popular with locals is the *Bull O' the Woods* (☎ 505-754-2593), next door to Motherlode, with a happy hour from 3 to 6 pm. Both places are hopping, casual saloons.

EAGLE NEST

Little more than windswept high desert, Eagle Nest is at best a cheap base from which to explore the area. *D & D Motel* (☎ 505-377-2408, 800-913-9548) offers clean, simple rooms from $32 for a single to $54 for a two-bedroom suite with a full kitchen. They can also arrange boat rentals. *Gold Pan Motel Ski Lodge, Steakhouse, and RV Park* (☎ 800-388-2286) has motel rooms ranging from $30 to $67 for a kitchenette and RV hookups for $10. Rates are higher in winter. In the restaurant, a steak will run you about $10. For more information, call the Eagle Nest Chamber of Commerce (☎ 800-494-9117).

ANGEL FIRE

Twenty-two miles east of Taos, the ski resort of Angel Fire has gained a reputation as condominium heaven. Though locals are making a great effort to develop a tourist clientele, the town grew too quickly, and there is no sense of history or even a quaint village. It just sprawls on the edge of a plateau, and a few monotonous restaurants and hotels and condos dot the hillside.

The chamber of commerce (☎ 505-377-6661, 800-446-8117, www.angelfirenm.com/visit) is on the right as you drive into town. Bookings at houses, condos and B&Bs can be made through Angel Fire Central Reservations (☎ 800-323-5793). Roadrunner Tours (☎ 505-377-6416, 800-377-6416) rents skis and bikes and arranges outdoor trips, including snowmobile tours, sleigh rides and overnight horseback riding trips.

Places to Stay & Eat

The primary gig in town is the *Angel Fire Resort* (☎ 505-377-6401, 800-633-7463), at the base of the slopes, a huge hotel with a pool, restaurant and bar that is trying hard to develop Angel Fire as a year-round, family-oriented vacation spot. Eighteen-hole golf (☎ 505-377-3055) is available for $40, $23 after 4 pm; tennis courts are free. River rafting (through Taos-based companies), horseback riding through on-site stables, bike rental, guided hiking, mountain biking, fishing trips and hot-air balloon or helicopter trips can be arranged through the 'summer adventure desk' (☎ 505-377-4282). Double rooms in the spring, fall and summer range from $70 to $99 and condos from $60 to $105. Ski packages are available in the winter, at higher daily rates.

The *Inn at Angel Fire* (☎ 505-377-2504, 800-666-1949) is an unpretentious and informal ski lodge. Doubles are $90; a dorm room sleeping up to 12 is $90 for the first four occupants and $20 for each additional one. Ski packages range from $100 to $130 nightly per person and include breakfast, dinner and lift tickets. Call for summer rates.

A three-bedroom, two-bath guest house, with a private fly-fishing lake nestled high in the Sangre de Cristo mountains, is available for $250 per person at the *Blackfire Flyfishing Guest Ranch* (☎ 505-377-6870). Rates include all meals, two nights lodging and fishing.

Zebadiah's (☎ 505-377-6358), Hwy 434, has a choice of eight half-pound burgers for under $5, barbecue for $7 to $11, New Mexican fare and steaks. With pool tables and occasional live music, this is the best place in town to hang out over a beer. It's open daily for breakfast, lunch and dinner.

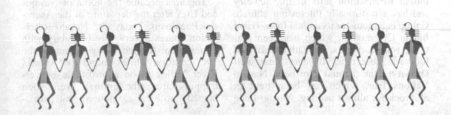

Northwestern New Mexico

Much of northwestern New Mexico is high desert, with starkly beautiful buttes and badlands pushing up against startlingly blue skies. As the visitor heads east from the Arizona state line, across the Continental Divide and toward the Rio Grande, the bare scenery eases into softer forest-clad mountains. The area is slashed by I-40, which carries traffic from Arizona to Albuquerque and beyond.

The area showcases some of the Southwest's most fabulous ancient Indian sites. Much of the land remains in the hands of Native Americans, with the Navajo, Zuni, Acoma and Jicarilla Apache Indian Reservations among those of most interest to visitors.

Within this scenic land, the juxtaposition of the ancient and traditional with the modern and technological can be startling and thought-provoking. The fascinating 900-year-old Acoma Pueblo (also called 'Sky City'), one of the oldest continuously inhabited communities in North America, is visible from your car as you speed along I-40. At Bandelier National Monument, important archaeological sites and barely accessible ancient cliff dwellings lie a few miles away from the town of Los Alamos, famous as the site where the first atomic bomb was developed. And Shiprock, a huge, strangely shaped butte of legendary religious importance to the Navajos is just 20 miles west of the tribally operated Navajo Mine, the largest open-pit mine in New Mexico.

Other attractions abound. The Zuni Indian Reservation sells unique jewelry and has a historically interesting church. Gallup is famous for its annual Inter-Tribal Indian Ceremonial, which has been featuring rodeos, dances, and native crafts and food for more than 70 years. Less well known is the annual Northern Navajo Nations Fair, which has been held in Shiprock for almost as long. Navajo Lake State Park features one of New Mexico's largest artificial lakes, which is excellent for fishing and other water sports. People enjoying rod and gun find good sport farther east in the Chama area, where both Apache and non-Indian guides take customers to the best fishing and hunting spots. Railroad buffs revel in a nostalgic steam-engine trip out of Chama on the Cumbres & Toltec Scenic Railroad. South of there is the wide-open, crystal clear, dramatic country made famous by the paintings of Georgia O'Keeffe.

From cultural, scenic, archaeological and historical perspectives there is much to interest the visitor. The chapter begins in the far northwest and goes from Farmington to Chama, Los Alamos and the Rio Grande. Then it traces the more frequently traveled I-40 corridor west of Albuquerque as it passes 'Sky City' and Gallup en route to the Navajo Indian Reservation and Arizona.

The Farmington Area

Ancestral Puebloans left some magnificent sites here – foremost among them is Pueblo Bonito in the Chaco Culture National Historical Park, about two hours' drive south of Farmington. Many other Indian sites called 'outliers' dot the surrounding area. Aztec Ruins National Monument and Salmon Ruin are both a few miles from Farmington.

The area became the home of Navajos and Utes after the departure of the Ancestral Puebloans. Today, the Navajo Reservation shares a very tiny boundary with Farmington. Around the beginning of the 19th century, whites found the Animas River Valley to be a profitable beaver-trapping area (the animals were soon hunted into local extinction), but perma-

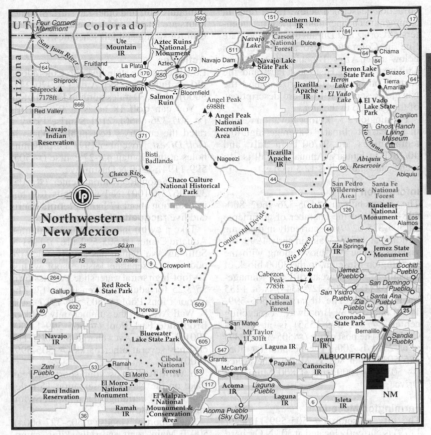

Northwestern New Mexico

nent Anglo settlement didn't happen until 1876, when ranchers arrived at the confluence of the Animas, San Juan and La Plata Rivers. The site became known as Farmingtown (the 'w' was later dropped), and the town developed into an agricultural center. The nearby towns of Aztec and Bloomfield were settled soon after. Aztec became the seat of San Juan County in 1891, but Farmington has since eclipsed it in size and economic importance.

The population was largely rural until the 1950s, when oil, gas and coal extraction began. Currently, mining, agriculture and

tourism all play an important part in Farmington's economy.

FARMINGTON

Farmington boomed from a sleepy agricultural town of less than 4000 inhabitants in the 1950s to a mining center of about 25,000 by the 1960s. Today, with a population of around 40,000, Farmington is the largest town in northwestern New Mexico (and the Four Corners area) and offers plenty of facilities for the visitor – you could spend several nights here using the town as the base for excursions to the attractions described below. Hotel rates in summer are cheaper than in the tourist centers of Cortez and Durango across the state line in Colorado. Also see the entries below under Aztec, Bloomfield and Chaco Culture National Historical Park and the section on northeastern Arizona and the Navajo Reservation for more descriptions of things to do in the area.

Farmington's 5300-foot elevation results in a pleasant climate – average high/low temperatures are 91/60°F in July and 40/18°F in January. Annual rainfall is 7½ inches and snowfall is 12.3 inches.

Information
The visitors bureau (☎ 505-326-7602, 800-448-1240) and the chamber of commerce (☎ 505-325-0279) are currently in the same building at 203 W Main; in early 1999, the visitors bureau will move, along with the Farmington Museum, to the 3000 block of E Main St. The Bureau of Land Management (BLM; ☎ 505-327-5344) is at 1235 La Plata Hwy. The library (☎ 505-599-1270) is at 100 W Broadway. A recycling center (☎ 505-599-1555) is at 400 S Orchard. The post office (☎ 505-325-5047) is at 2301 E 20th. The hospital (☎ 505-325-5011) is at 801 W Maple. The police (☎ 505-599-1000) are at 800 Municipal Drive.

Farmington Museum
The city museum (☎ 505-599-1174 or 1179) is currently located at 302 N Orchard Ave, though it will move with the visitors bureau to the 3000 block of E Main St in early 1999. The museum showcases the pioneer history and the geology of the area. There is a children's gallery (which will remain in this location) with fun hands-on exhibits and a variety of changing shows. Ask for a brochure describing some of Farmington's earliest buildings. Hours are noon to 5 pm Tuesday to Friday and 10 am to 5 pm on Saturday. Admission is free.

Family Funland
This amusement park (☎ 505-324-0940), 200 Scott Ave, has carnival rides, go-carts, miniature golf and other kid stuff. Summer hours are 3 to 10 pm daily except Tuesday. Call for spring and fall schedules.

Activities
Locals cross the state line into Colorado to **ski** at Purgatory Ski Area (☎ 970-247-9000), about 80 miles north of Farmington.

You can **golf** 18 holes at Piñon Hills (☎ 505-326-6066), 2101 Sunrise Pkwy – rated the country's best public course in *Golf Digest*, November 1995. Or play nine holes at the Civitan par-27 course (☎ 505-599-1194), 2200 N Dustin Ave.

Farmington Recreation Center (☎ 505-327-9673), 1001 N Fairgrounds Rd, has information about 17 lighted **tennis** courts and five **racquetball** courts.

Take a **swim** indoors at the Farmington Aquatic Center (☎ 505-599-1167), 1151 N Sullivan Ave, which has an Olympic-size pool and a separate leisure pool with a 20-foot-high spiral water slide. Admission is $5/3.25 for adults/children under 13. The indoor Lions Pool (☎ 505-599-1187), 405 N Wall Ave, and the summer-only outdoor Brookside Park Pool (☎ 505-599-1188), 1901 N Dustin Ave, charge $1.50/1. The city has several other parks (☎ 505-599-1400).

If **windsurfing** is your sport, Morgan Lake on the Navajo Reservation 15 miles southwest of Farmington is popular. Swimming is not allowed.

Zia's Sporting Goods (☎ 505-327-6004), 500 E Main, rents and sells skiing, camping and fishing gear.

Special Events
Call the chamber of commerce for exact dates of all events. Rodeos are popular in Farmington. The biggest is the San Juan County Sheriff Posse Rodeo, held in early June at the County Rodeo Ground (☎ 505-326-4007) on Hwy 550 northeast of town. Locals say that the San Juan County Fair, with a rodeo, chile cook-off, fiddlers' contest and plenty of other attractions, is New Mexico's largest county fair. It is held in mid-August at McGee Park (☎ 505-326-2693), southeast of town on Hwy 64.

McGee Park is also the site of the Pro-Rodeo Roundup in early April.

Over Memorial Day weekend, the Invitational Balloon Festival features a balloon splash (hot-air balloonists dip their baskets in Farmington Lake), tractor-pulls, river rafting, arts and crafts, entertainment and more. Freedom Days sees extensive celebrations on and around the Fourth of July. The Connie Mack World Series Baseball Tournament in mid-August features top amateur ballplayers and attracts scouts from college and professional teams. The seven-day event is held at Ricketts Ball Park (☎ 505-327-9673), 1101 N Fairgrounds Rd. The Totah Festival, held in the Civic Center over Labor Day weekend, has top-quality Native American arts and crafts both in juried competition and for sale by auction. Native American Days is held at the Animas Valley Mall, 4601 E Main, in late September. You can see Indian dances and browse the arts and crafts. A Holiday Arts & Crafts Fair is held in the first weekend in December. Over 100,000 luminarias (candle lanterns) illuminate the San Juan College campus beginning the first weekend in December.

Places to Stay – Camping

Mom & Pop RV Park (☎ 505-327-3200), 901 Illinois Ave (just off Hwy 64), has showers and charges $14 for sites with RV hookups and $5 per person in tents. There are 43 sites. The smaller *River Grove RV Park* (☎ 505-327-0974), 801 E Broadway, charges $11 for sites with RV hookups. The *Downs RV Park* (☎ 505-325-7094), 5701 Hwy 64, has showers, a laundry and RV sites with hookups for $14 and cheaper tent sites. There is free primitive camping at Morgan Lake.

Places to Stay – Budget

Hotel rates stay about the same year-round, with a slight increase during summer.

The cheapest places have simple but clean rooms in the upper $20s for a double. These include the *Journey Inn* (☎ 505-325-3548), 317 Airport Drive, which has a pool; the *Sage Motel* (☎ 505-325-7501), 301 Airport Drive; and the nearby *Basin Lodge* (☎ 505-325-5061), 701 Airport Drive, with large rooms. The *Redwood Lodge* (☎ 505-326-5521), 625 E Main, is also a decent choice.

There is a *Motel 6* at 1600 Bloomfield Hwy (☎ 505-326-4501, fax 505-326-3883), with singles/doubles for $28/33, and another at 510 Scott Ave (☎ 505-327-0242, fax 505-327-5617), with prices at $30/36. Both have swimming pools and between them offer well over 200 rooms. The *Super 8 Motel* (☎/fax 505-325-1813), 1601 Bloomfield Hwy, has a game room and 60 good-size rooms for $33.88/39.88, continental breakfast included.

The *Farmington Lodge* (☎ 505-325-0233, fax 505-325-6574), 1510 W Main, has very clean rooms, some with microwave or refrigerator. There is a pool, and the place is a good value with rooms in the $30s including continental breakfast.

With the exception of the Motel 6s and Super 8 Motel, all the bottom-end places are quite small with 40 or fewer rooms and offer cheap weekly rates.

Places to Stay – Middle

Hotels The hotels in this section are all quite large, with anywhere from about 70 to almost 200 rooms. Most offer free transportation to and from the airport or bus station.

The *Villager Lodge* (☎ 505-327-4433), 2530 Bloomfield Hwy, has a pool, spa, restaurant and bar on the premises. Rooms are reasonably sized and there are some suites; rates are $40 to $60. The *Anasazi Inn* (☎ 505-325-4564), 903 W Main, also has good rooms and a few suites in the same price range. There is a restaurant and bar but no pool.

Most of the town's best hotels are clustered around Scott Ave and Broadway. *La Quinta Inn* (☎ 505-327-4706, fax 505-325-6583), 675 Scott Ave, has a pool, a picnic and barbecue area and free coffee and continental breakfast. A 24-hour restaurant is next door. Attractive, large rooms are in the $60s. The similarly priced *Comfort Inn*

NEW MEXICO

NEW MEXICO

PLACES TO STAY
16 Basin Lodge
17 Journey Inn
   & Sage Motel
18 Farmington Lodge
19 Anasazi Inn
22 Casa Blanca Inn
25 Redwood Lodge
27 Motel 6
28 Comfort Inn
29 La Quinta Inn
30 Holiday Inn
32 River Grove RV Park
33 Best Western Inn
   & Suites
35 Super 8 Motel
36 Motel 6
37 Mom & Pop RV Park
38 Holiday Inn Express
40 Villager Lodge

PLACES TO EAT
6 K-Bob's Steak House
8 Clancy's Pub
11 Señor Pepper's Airport
   Restaurant
14 La Fiesta Grande
20 El Charro Cafe
29 Kettle Restaurant
31 Rocky Mountain Rib
   Company
39 Sonya's Cookin' USA
44 Something Special
49 Three Rivers Eatery
   & Brewhouse
50 KB Dillon's

OTHER
1 San Juan College
2 Piñon Hills Golf Course
3 Civitan Golf Course
4 Brookside Park Pool
5 Allen 8 Cinema
7 Post Office
9 New Visitors Bureau,
   Farmington Museum

10 BLM
12 Police
13 Farmington Aquatic
   Center
15 Ugly Duckling
   (Car Rental)
21 Cameo Theater
23 Top Deck Lounge
24 Zia's Sporting Goods
26 Family Funland
34 Hospital
41 Farmington Children's
   Museum
42 Lions Pool
43 Civic Center
45 Allen Theater
46 Totah Theater
47 Visitors Bureau
   Chamber of Commerce
48 Library
51 TNM&O Bus Depot
52 Farmington Indian
   Organization (Bus Stop)
53 Recycling Center

Farmington

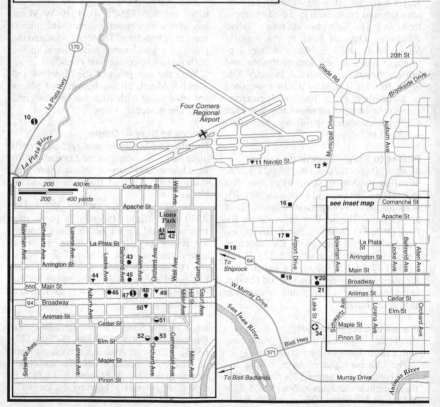

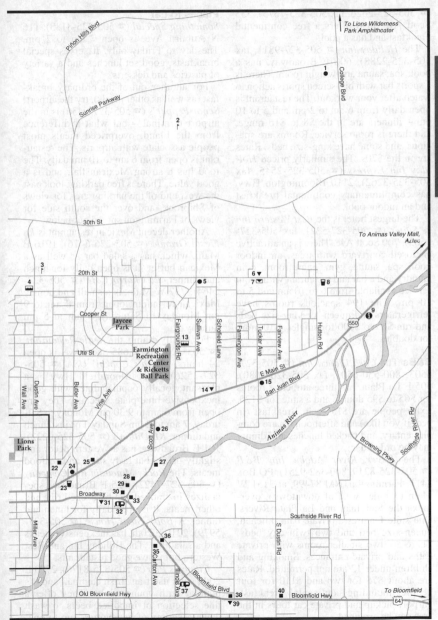

To Lions Wilderness
Park Amphitheater

Piñon Hills Blvd

College Blvd

1

Sunrise Parkway

2

30th St

To Animas Valley Mall,
Aztec

3

20th St

4

6

7

8

5

Cooper St

Jaycee
Park

Fairgrounds Rd

Sullivan Ave

Schofield Lane

Farmington Ave

Tucker Ave

Fairview Ave

Hutton Rd

9

550

13

Ute St

Farmington
Recreation
Center
& Ricketts
Ball Park

14

E Main St

15

San Juan Blvd

Animas River

Browning Pkwy

Southside River Rd

Wall Ave

Dustin Ave

Butler Ave

Vine Ave

Scott Ave

26

Lions
Park

22

24

25

27

23

28

29

30

33

Broadway

31

32

Miller Ave

Southside River Rd

S Dustin Rd

36

35

Carlton Ave

Illinois Ave

Old Bloomfield Hwy

Bloomfield Blvd

37

38

39

40

Bloomfield Hwy

To Bloomfield

64

(☎ 505-325-2626, fax 505-325-7675), 555 Scott Ave, also offers a free continental breakfast and has a pool.

The *Holiday Inn* (☎ 505-327-9811, fax 505-325-2288), 600 E Broadway, has a pool, spa, sauna and weight room. There is a sports bar with big-screen sports action to watch after your workout. The restaurant is open daily from 6 am to 2 pm and 5 to 10 pm – dinners are in the $8 to $16 range, and there is room service. Rooms are spacious, and some have king-size beds. Rates are in the $70s. The similarly priced *Holiday Inn Express* (☎ 505-325-2545, fax 505-325-3262), 2110 Bloomington Hwy, has complimentary continental breakfast and an indoor pool.

The largest hotel is the *Best Western Inn & Suites* (☎ 505-327-5221, fax 505-327-1565), 700 Scott Ave. There is an attractive enclosed courtyard with trees, an indoor pool, spa, sauna, gym, game room, coin laundry and a bar and restaurant with room service available from 6 to 10 am and 5 to 10 pm. The 194 spacious rooms have refrigerators and queen- or king-size beds and run $65 to $100 for singles, $10 more for doubles.

B&Bs The *Casa Blanca Inn* (☎ 505-327-6503, 800-550-6503, fax 505-326-5680), 505 E La Plata, has three attractive rooms for $65 to $95 double and a suite for $125. Extra people are $15 each. Breakfast (in bed, if you like) and afternoon tea are complimentary, and packed lunches and dinner may be ordered.

The *Silver River Adobe Inn B&B* (☎ 505-325-8219, 800-382-9251), PO Box 3411, Farmington, NM 87499, at 3151 W Main (3 miles west of downtown), overlooks the San Juan and La Plata Rivers. One suite features a private bath, kitchen, queen-size bed and two twin day beds. There are two smaller rooms with private baths and private entrances. Smoking and children under 12 are not permitted. Rates are about $75 for two and $110 for four people, including continental breakfast. Airport pickup and private car tours in the area can be arranged.

Places to Eat

Something Special (☎ 505-325-8183), 116 N Auburn Ave, is open 7 am to 2 pm, Tuesday to Friday only. It serves special breakfasts, good set lunches and a variety of pastries and desserts.

For another out-of-the-ordinary breakfast (as well as other meals), try the airport! *Señor Pepper's* (☎ 505-327-0436) is in the airport terminal – but what a difference from the bland, overpriced meals most people associate with airports. The restaurant is open from 6 am to 10 pm daily. The food has a strong Mexican flair and is a good value. There is free parking; look past the west end of the parking area for views of Shiprock, and over the south side for views of Farmington spread out below.

Another decent Mexican restaurant is *La Fiesta Grande* (☎ 505-326-6476), 1916 E Main, which has a salad bar as well as a Mexican buffet. It is open daily for lunch and dinner. *El Charro Cafe* (☎ 505-327-2464), 737 W Main, is a small and homey Mexican restaurant open from 8 am to 9 pm Monday to Saturday, 9 am to 5 pm Sunday.

For family dining, the *Kettle Restaurant*, (☎ 505-326-0824), 685 Scott Ave, is open 24 hours. *Sonya's Cookin' USA* (☎ 505-327-3526), 2001 Bloomfield Hwy, is a pleasant, locally popular diner with good inexpensive blue-plate specials. They are open from 6 am to 9:30 pm Monday to Saturday, 7 am to 2 pm Sunday. For just lunch and dinner, *KB Dillon's* (☎ 505-325-0222), 101 E Broadway, has a Western decor and slightly pricey but tasty steak and seafood meals. The *Rocky Mountain Rib Company* (☎ 505-327-7422), 525 E Broadway, specializes in smoked and barbecued ribs and other meats. It is open daily for lunch and dinner. *K-Bob's Steak House* (☎ 505-327-5979), 2210 E 20th, has inexpensive steaks and a salad bar. The Holiday Inn and Best Western both have good restaurants.

Clancy's Pub (☎ 505-325-8176), 2703 E 20th, calls itself an 'Irish cantina,' and it's popular with young adults. They offer a fine selection of imported beers to wash down a variety of hamburgers (up to one-pounders!), sandwiches, Mexican food and pub grub. You can dine inside, where it's loud with rock music and interesting art covers the walls, or outside on their patio. Hours are 11 am to 2 am daily, and prices are low to moderate.

Locally popular, especially for lunch, is the *Three Rivers Eatery & Brewhouse* (☎ 505-324-2187), 101 E Main, with sandwiches, salads, appetizers, dinner entrées and their own microbrewed beers.

Entertainment
The big annual entertainment event is *Anasazi, the Ancient Ones* – a musical pageant performed from late June to late August several nights each week. The show is at the outdoor amphitheater at Lions Wilderness Park about 3 miles north of downtown along College Blvd. Some years, they alternate the pageant with a different performance – call the visitors bureau for an exact schedule. Shows are at 8 pm, and tickets are $10 for adults and $5 for children up to 18. For an extra $7, a Southwestern buffet dinner is served at 6:30 pm before the show. Tickets are available at the door or call ☎ 505-599-1145, 800-448-1240.

The local San Juan Stage Company (☎ 505-327-7477) presents occasional plays and musicals at the *Totah Theater*, 315 W Main. The Civic Center Foundation for the Performing Arts (☎ 505-599-1145) presents off-Broadway performances at the *Civic Center*, 200 W Arrington.

If you want to see a movie, check the four screens at the *Animas Cinema 4* (☎ 505-327-7856) in the Animas Valley Mall, 4601 E Main; the eight screens at the *Allen 8 Cinema* (☎ 505-324-8665, 505-326-0000), 1819 E 20th; the *Allen Theater* (☎ 505-325-9313), 208 W Main; or the *Cameo Theater* (☎ 505-325-1565), 734 W Broadway.

For bar-oriented nightlife, *Clancy's Pub* (see Places to Eat) is popular. The busiest place in town is the *Top Deck Lounge* (☎ 505-327-7385), 515 E Main, usually with dancing to country or rock music and a cover charge.

Shopping
Several trading posts in the Farmington area offer a variety of high-quality Indian crafts – the Navajo rugs are particularly good, but silver and turquoise jewelry, kachinas, basketware, sand paintings, ceramics and art are also popular buys.

Trading posts can teach you about the historical and cultural significance of these often expensive pieces. A top-quality Navajo rug can fetch several thousand dollars – do a little research before you buy (see the Navajo Weaving sidebar in the Northeastern Arizona chapter). The best trading posts have museum-quality displays and, sometimes, demonstrations of how rugs or jewelry are made. The visitors bureau can tell you about dates of these.

Reliable trading posts are found along Hwy 64 west of town and include the Hogback Trading Company (☎ 505-598-5154), 3221 Hwy 64 (15 miles west of Farmington); the nearby Bob French's Navajo Rugs (☎ 505-598-5621), 3459 Hwy 64; and Foutz Trading Company (☎ 505-368-5790) on Hwy 64 in Shiprock. Downtown, Fifth Generation Trading Company (☎ 505-326-3211), 232 W Broadway, was founded in 1875 and has a big selection. Other good stores are nearby on Main or Broadway.

For sporting goods, see Zia's under Activities, earlier in this chapter.

Getting There & Away
Air The Four Corners Regional Airport at the west end of town is New Mexico's second busiest. Mesa Airlines (☎ 505-326-3338, 800-637-2247) has several daily flights to and from Albuquerque, with connections to other New Mexican towns. America West Express (☎ 505-326-4495, 800-235-9292) has several flights a day to and from Phoenix (via Gallup), with connections to other Arizona towns and nationwide. United Express (☎ 800-241-6522) flies to Denver, Colorado. Four Corners Aviation (☎ 505-325-2867) provides local charter flights.

Bus TNM&O/Greyhound (☎ 505-325-1009), 101 E Animas, has two or three daily buses to Albuquerque (a four-hour trip) with connections to the rest of New Mexico, Texas and Arizona. There are also two or three daily buses to Durango, Colorado, some continuing to Grand Junction and connecting with a Greyhound bus to Salt Lake City, Utah.

Navajo Transit System (☎ 520-729-5449 or 5457) has a 7 am bus to Window Rock (on the Navajo Reservation in Arizona) from Monday to Friday leaving from the Farmington Indian Organization (☎ 505-327-6296), 100 W Elm.

Getting Around

KB Cab (☎ 505-325-2999) has 24-hour taxi service in and around Farmington.

The following companies rent cars (and vans or 4WDs) at the airport: Avis (☎ 505-327-9864); Budget (☎ 505-327-7304); Hertz (☎ 505-327-6093); and National (☎ 505-327-0215). Car rental is also available from Ugly Duckling (☎ 505-325-4313), 2307 E Main. RVs are available at London's RV Rental (☎ 505-598-5177), 4253 Hwy 64, Kirtland (8 miles west of Farmington).

AROUND FARMINGTON
Mine Tours

Navajo Mine (☎ 505-598-5861), 25 miles southwest on the Navajo Reservation, is the largest open-pit mine in the western USA. Free tours are offered at 10 am on Monday. If mine tours interest you, the San Juan Mine (☎ 505-598-2000), 15 miles west of Farmington, has a 10 am tour on Wednesday, and the La Plata Mine (☎ 505-599-4100), 20 miles north of Farmington, has a 10 am tour on Friday. All three mines produce coal used to fire the Four Corners Power Plant (☎ 505-598-8201) near Morgan Lake on the Navajo Reservation. The plant produces much of the energy for the Southwest and can be toured with two weeks' notice.

Shiprock

This 1700-foot-high volcanic plug rises eerily over the landscape and was an early landmark for Anglo travelers, who named it after a fancied resemblance to a ship

under sail. The rock lies 35 miles west of Farmington in Navajoland, and the Navajos, who didn't have much use for sailing ships, had a better name for it: *Tse Bitai*, meaning 'winged rock.' The rock figures in several Navajo legends and is sacred to the tribe, which is why climbing it is prohibited. You can see Shiprock from Hwy 64, but better views are had from Hwy 666 and Indian Hwy 13, which goes almost to the base of it.

The Navajo community of **Shiprock**, 25 miles west of Farmington, is named after the rock. Shiprock hosts an annual Navajo Fair with a rodeo, powwow, parade, contests and arts and crafts, as well as traditional dancing, singing and food. This is perhaps the most traditional of the large Indian fairs and begins with the Night Way, a complex Navajo healing ceremony and *Yei Bei Chei* chant that lasts for several days. Parts of the ceremony are open to the general public, but photography and recording are strictly prohibited. (Photography is permitted at the nonceremonial events such as the rodeo.) The fair is held in late September or early October, and information is available from the fair office (☎ 505-368-5108), the Farmington Chamber of Commerce and the Navajo Tourism Department in Window Rock, Arizona. Fair-goers should stay in Farmington – there are no motels in Shiprock.

Bisti Badlands

'Bis-ti' is Navajo for 'badlands,' so the full name is redundant. Some maps refer to this area, about 35 miles south of Farmington along Hwy 371, as the Bisti Wilderness. The scenery here is barren but geologically interesting, with many eroded and colorfully pigmented formations; the best sights are along trails a couple of miles from the roads. The site is undeveloped BLM wilderness. Dirt roads lead a few miles east to the even more remote **De-Na-Zin Wilderness**. The Farmington BLM office has information (see Orientation & Information, above).

AZTEC

When early pioneers found extensive Indian remains here, they mistakenly thought the site was related to the Aztec civilization in Mexico. Though the ruins proved to be Ancestral Puebloan, the name stuck. The present town was founded in 1890 across the river from the pueblo, and the old downtown sector has several interesting turn-of-the-19th-century buildings, many listed in the National Register of Historic Places. The Aztec Museum and the chamber of commerce have a leaflet describing the most important buildings.

Aztec (population 5500) is the San Juan County seat. The nearest public transport is 14 miles southwest in Farmington.

Information

The chamber of commerce (☎ 505-334-9551), at 110 Ash, is open on weekdays from 10 am to noon and 1 to 5 pm. The library (☎ 505-334-3658) and the police (☎ 505-334-6101) are both in the Aztec City Offices at 201 W Chaco. The post office (☎ 505-334-6181) is on Llano at S Main Ave.

Aztec Ruins National Monument

This small 27-acre national monument tucked away on the north side of town contains important and unique Ancestral

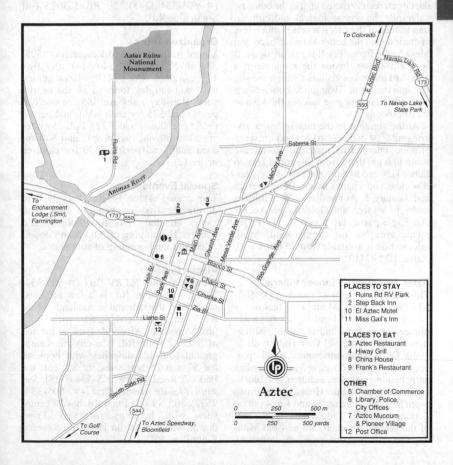

PLACES TO STAY
1 Ruins Rd RV Park
2 Step Back Inn
10 El Aztec Motel
11 Miss Gail's Inn

PLACES TO EAT
3 Aztec Restaurant
4 Hiway Grill
8 China House
9 Frank's Restaurant

OTHER
5 Chamber of Commerce
6 Library, Police, City Offices
7 Aztec Museum & Pioneer Village
12 Post Office

Aztec

0   250   500 m
0   250   500 yards

Puebloan sites. The main site was built in the early 1100s by a Chacoan group in a style similar to that at Chaco Culture National Historic Park (see later in this chapter). This was abandoned in the late 1100s, only to be reinhabited a few decades later by people from the Mesa Verde area who added their own style of architecture to the site before they, too, abandoned it in the late 1200s. The main site is about 360 feet by 280 feet and includes some 400 rooms, of which the most important is the fully reconstructed Great Kiva. This has an internal diameter of almost 50 feet and is the largest reconstructed kiva in the country.

Despite the archaeological and cultural importance of the site, it receives much less visitation than the better-known Chaco and Mesa Verde Parks. For this reason alone, it is worth a stop. Inside the monument, a 400-yard trail takes visitors through the site and into the Great Kiva; guide booklets are available. Rangers give talks in the kiva in the afternoons.

At the entrance to the monument, a visitor center (☎ 505-334-6174) and museum provide interpretive material. Hours are 8 am to 6 pm daily from Memorial Day to Labor Day and to 5 pm the rest of the year. It is closed on Thanksgiving, December 25 and January 1. Admission is $4; children under 17 are free; and Golden Age, Access and Eagle passes are honored. There is a picnic area but no campground. More information is available from PO Box 640, Aztec, NM 87410.

Aztec Museum & Pioneer Village

This small but excellent museum (☎ 505-334-9829), 125 N Main Ave, features a varied collection of local Indian and early pioneering artifacts and is worth visiting. It is housed in the old City Hall, built in 1940. Outside the museum, a small 'pioneer village' has a dozen original or replica early buildings, such as a church, jail, blacksmith shop and bank. Hours are 9 am to 5 pm Monday to Saturday and 1 to 4 pm on Sunday from May 1 to Labor Day; the rest of the year hours are 10 am to 4 pm Monday to Saturday. Admission is by donation.

Car Racing

Aztec Speedway (☎ 505-334-2023) resounds with the roar of automobile engines on Saturdays from April to September. Cars include hobby stock, street stock, mini sprints, winged 360, ASCS sprint cars and IMCA modifieds. I haven't a clue what these are, but if you are a stock-car racing fan, I'm sure no explanation is needed. The track is half a mile south of town off Hwy 544.

Golf

Play nine regulation holes at Hidden Valley (☎ 505-334-3248), 29 Road 3025 (off South Side Rd).

Organized Tours

Moore Anthropological Research (☎ 505-334-6675, fax 505-334-6514), PO Box 1156, Aztec, NM 87410, offers guided half- and full-day tours to all the nearby sites. Half-day rates are $85 for one/two people and $25 for each additional person ($15 for children under 12). Full-day rates are $180 for one/two people and $40 for each additional person ($30 for children under 12).

Special Events

The annual Aztec Fiesta Days is held during the first weekend in June with games, arts and crafts, food booths and a bonfire. The burning of 'Old Man Gloom' celebrates the beginning of summer.

Places to Stay

Camping *Ruins Rd RV Park* (☎ 505-334-3160), 312 Ruins Rd, is a few minutes' walk from the national monument. There are 30 campsites, costing $10 with hookups, $6 without. *Riverside Park*, at the end of S Light Plant Rd, is a city-run campground with 12 campsites with hookups for $7 and 25 tent sites for $5; call the Parks & Rec Dept (☎ 505-334-6725). *San Juan Mobile Home Park* (☎ 505-334-9532), 305 N Light Plant Rd, has 12 campsites with hookups for $10. From downtown, go west on Hwy 550 to reach Light Plant Rd.

Hotels The *Enchantment Lodge* (☎ 505-334-6143, fax 505-334-6144), 1800 W Aztec Blvd, has 20 modern rooms at the west end of town. The lodge has a pool, picnic areas, coin laundry and free morning coffee. Rooms are in the $30s for a single, $38 to $44 for a double. Downtown, *El Aztec Motel* (☎ 505-334-6300), 221 S Main Ave, is similarly priced and has seven rooms with microwaves and refrigerators.

The historic *Miss Gail's Inn* (☎ 505-334-3452), 300 S Main Ave, 87410, is a brick structure that was built in 1907 as 'The American Hotel.' It is decorated with early photographs and period pieces. There are eight rooms with private baths, half of them with kitchenettes. Rates are $60 to $75 for a double with breakfast, but a room for a week, no breakfasts, is much less. They plan to open a restaurant in 1998.

The 40-room *Step Back Inn* (☎ 505-334-1200, 800-334-1255, fax 505-334-9858, stepback@cyberport.com), 103 W Aztec Blvd, charges $64 a room, including continental breakfast. Rooms are decorated in Victorian style and named after local pioneering families; each have two queen-size beds and sleep up to four. Low-season discounts are offered.

Places to Eat

Frank's (☎ 505-334-3882), 116 S Main Ave, serves a pretty good breakfast for $2 or $3, or you can get pancakes for about $1 – a good deal. They serve diner-style lunches as well. The *Aztec Restaurant* (☎ 505-334-9586), 107 E Aztec Blvd, serves decent, reasonably priced Mexican and American fare from 5 am to 9 pm. The *Hiway Grill* (☎ 505-334-6533), 401 E Aztec Blvd, is a '50s-style full-service restaurant – check out the big-finned powder-blue sedan stuck on top of the sign outside. They're open from 11 am to 10 pm daily, till 11 pm on Friday and Saturday. *China House* (☎ 505-334-8838), 104 S Main Ave, serves Italian food (just checking to see if you're paying attention!).

BLOOMFIELD

Settled in the 1870s, Bloomfield was notorious as a haunt of cattle rustlers and gunslingers. In the early 20th century, Bloomfield began developing irrigation projects and became a small but modestly thriving farming community with almost 6000 inhabitants.

Orientation & Information

Bloomfield is 13 miles east of Farmington, and in town Hwy 64 becomes Broadway Ave (the main drag).

The chamber of commerce (☎ 505-632-0880), 224 W Broadway, is open from 9 am to 4 pm weekdays. The Carson National Forest Ranger Station (☎ 505-632-2956) is at 644 E Broadway. The post office (☎ 505-632-3050) is at 1108 W Broadway. The police (☎ 505-632-8096) are at 915 N 1st. Fish'n Stuff (☎ 505-632-0952), 202 W Broadway, has fishing information and licenses.

Salmon Ruin & Heritage Park

Salmon Ruin is an ancient pueblo similar to the Aztec Ruins: a large village built by the Chaco people in the early 1100s, abandoned, resettled by people from Mesa Verde and again abandoned before 1300. The site is named after George Salmon, an early settler who protected the area.

A self-guided trail winds through the site, which includes a large but unrestored kiva. There is a visitor center, museum, gift shop and picnicking area. The adjoining Heritage Park has the remains of the Salmon homestead and a variety of Indian cultural artifacts, including petroglyphs, a Navajo hogan, an early Puebloan pithouse, a *teepee* (a conical tent used by Plains Indians) and a *wickiup* (a rough brushwood shelter).

Information is available from Salmon Ruin (☎ 505-632-2013), PO Box 125, Bloomfield, NM 87413. Hours are 9 am to 5 pm daily; closed January 1, Thanksgiving and December 25. Admission is $3/2/1 for adults/senior/children six to 16.

Angel Peak National Recreation Area

Along with Shiprock and Bisti, Angel Peak is another area known for its desolate geological formations. There is a free campground with pit toilets but no water. The area is uncrowded and often empty. The turnoff for Angel Peak is 15 miles south of Bloomfield, then 7 miles east along an unpaved road passable to cars.

Places to Stay & Eat

For more comfortable camping than the free sites at Angel Peak, try Bloomfield's *KOA* (☎ 505-632-8339) at 1900 E Blanco Blvd. This campground has a few tent sites at $14, 70 RV sites for $18 and three Kamping Kabins for $23 double. There is a pool, playground, coin laundry and grocery store.

The simple *Bloomfield Motel* (☎ 505-632-3383), 801 W Broadway, offers standard rooms in the $20s. The *Super 8 Motel* (☎ 505-632-8886), 525 W Broadway, is $39.88/43.88 for singles/doubles including continental breakfast.

The best place to eat is the *Five Seasons Restaurant & Lounge* (☎ 505-632-1196), 1100 W Broadway, which serves American and Mexican lunches and dinners daily. Inexpensive *Mary's Café* (☎ 505-632-5420), 109 Salmon Drive, serves home-style breakfasts, lunches and dinners.

Getting There & Away

TNM&O buses (☎ 505-632-8678) stop at 100 E Blanco Blvd; see Farmington for details.

NAVAJO DAM & NAVAJO LAKE STATE PARK

Built on the San Juan River, the Navajo Dam created Navajo Lake, which stretches over 30 miles northeast and across into Colorado. The lake offers excellent boating and fishing (for trout, bass, crappie and pike), and the San Juan River at the base of the dam has trout fishing that the locals call 'world class.'

Orientation & Information

The state park is 23 miles east of Bloomfield and 25 miles east of Aztec. Information is available from Navajo Lake State Park (☎ 505-632-2278), 1448 NM 511 No 1, Navajo Dam, NM 87419. There is a

visitor center at the park entrance, and day use is $3.

Fishing

The tiny community of Navajo Dam (a few miles west of the park entrance at the intersection of Hwys 173 and 511) has several outfitters that provide fishing equipment and information and guide fishing trips. These include Born-n-Raised on the San Juan River, Inc (☎ 505-632-2194), Rizuto's Fly Shop (☎ 505-632-3893, 800-525-1437) and Four Corners Guide Service (☎ 505-632-3566, 800-669-3566). There are also outfitters and tackle shops in Farmington and Aztec – the chambers of commerce have lists. Note that the community of Navajo Dam is not synonymous with the dam itself, which is right by the park entrance on Hwy 539/511.

Fishing is year-round by permit only, and there are catch-and-release and other regulations to protect the high quality of the fishing. Permit and regulation information is available from the state park, local outfitters, Abe's Motel & Fly Shop in Navajo Dam and the New Mexico Department of Game and Fish (☎ 505-827-7911).

Places to Stay & Eat

Navajo Dam *Abe's Motel & Fly Shop* (☎ 505-632-2194), 1791A Hwy 173 in the center of town, has standard double rooms for $50, or $58 with a kitchenette. The place has 50 rooms, but they're often full with anglers – book well ahead. Abe's has RV campsites with hookups for about $10. Next door, *Izzy's* (☎ 505-632-5895) offers 'Dam' good Mexican and American food daily.

The eight-room *San Juan River Lodge* (☎ 505-632-1411), 1796 Hwy 173, also has *Rizuto's Fly Shop*. Rooms with two queen-size beds are $75 and are sometimes booked up weeks ahead.

Navajo Lake The state park (☎ 505-632-2278) operates three campgrounds on the shores of the lake. The biggest is *Pine River*, which has tent sites for $7 and RV sites with hookups for $11. There is a visitor center, a marina and boat launch, grocery store, playground and showers. Waterskiing is popular. Pine River is on the west shore of the lake just past the dam on Hwy 539/511.

San Juan River Campground has sites without hookups for tents or RVs for $7, and a boat launch area for canoes – this is the best place for river trout fishing. Fishing platforms designed for wheelchair access are available. There is drinking water but no showers. The campground is reached by crossing the San Juan River in the village of Navajo Dam and heading east. The lake is 3 miles downstream.

Sims Mesa has sites both with and without hookups for $11 and $7. There are showers, a small visitor center, a boat launch and hiking trails. Sims Mesa is on the east shore of the lake and is reached by 18-mile-long, paved Hwy 527, which goes north from Hwy 64 32 miles east of Bloomfield. A shorter route by unpaved roads leaves Hwy 539 just south of the dam. This is the least-crowded campground.

CHACO CULTURE NATIONAL HISTORICAL PARK

This park contains massive and spectacular Puebloan buildings set in a remote high desert environment. All routes to the park involve rough and unpaved dirt roads, which can become impassable after heavy rains or snow. You need a whole day for a trip here. Although the access is difficult, the rewards are many for those interested in the legacy of the Ancestral Pueblo people.

Chaco Canyon contains evidence of 5000 years of human occupation, from archaic hunters and gatherers to historic Navajo and Anglo settlers. The ancestors of the modern Pueblo people built the impressive Chacoan Great Houses between AD 850 and 1150. Chacoan population estimates vary greatly, and many archaeologists believe the Great Houses were primarily used seasonally during periods of trading, ceremonies and food distribution. After AD 1150, Chaco's importance as a regional center waned, but its influence lingered on in other areas of the Four Corners.

Respecting Ancient Sites

Some sites in Chaco Culture National Historical Park have been severely damaged. One is the 'Sun Dagger,' which consisted of three sandstone slabs arranged so that the sun shone through them to illuminate petroglyphs carved on nearby rocks – researchers found that solstice dates can be determined from the position of the sun on the petroglyphs. Unfortunately, visitation by researchers and others caused the slabs to shift, destroying their value as a calendar. The Sun Dagger is now closed to the public (though a film of it can be seen in the visitor center).

The structures are fragile, and visitors are asked to refrain from climbing on them. Vandals and souvenir hunters are also a problem – leave pottery fragments and stones where they lie. ■

The largest building, Pueblo Bonito, towers four stories tall and may have had 600 to 800 rooms and kivas. The stonework is exceptional, and this is the 'type site' for the classic period of Chacoan architecture.

The excavated great kiva, Casa Rinconada, is one of the largest in the Southwest, larger than the reconstructed great kiva at Aztec Ruins (described above). In addition to these sites, many other excavated and unexcavated sites are accessible along the loop drive.

None of Chaco's sites have been reconstructed or restored. Some have been excavated and stabilized to prevent their deterioration when exposed to wind, rain and freeze-thaw cycles. Many more remain unexcavated and await investigations in the future.

Chaco was the center of a culture that extended far beyond the immediate area. Aztec and Salmon Ruins (see earlier in this chapter) are among the best known of the Chaco 'outliers,' but there are over one hundred others throughout the Four

Corners. These sites were linked to the Great Houses of Chaco Canyon by carefully engineered roads 30 feet wide. Very little of the road system is easily seen today, but about 450 miles have been identified from aerial photos and ground surveys. Clearly, this was a highly organized and integrated culture.

Orientation & Information

Many visitors arrive from the north (Hwy 44), pass by the campground and arrive at the visitor center (☎ 505-786-7014), which is open from 8 am to 5 pm daily year-round except Christmas, and until 6 pm from Memorial Day weekend until Labor Day. There are orientation films, a museum, free backcountry hiking permits and books for sale.

Beyond the visitor center, a paved, one-way 8-mile loop road passes near six of the largest Great Houses, where self-guided trails begin.

Note that facilities within the park are minimal – no food, gas or supplies are available. The nearest provisions are along Hwy 44, 21 miles from the visitor center.

The archaeological sites are open from sunrise until sunset. Park admission is $8 per vehicle, or $4 for bikes. Golden Eagle, Age and Access Passes are honored.

Climate & When to Go

Late summer rains and winter snows may temporarily close the roads to the park; call the visitor center for road conditions. The 6200-foot elevation provides hot summer days and cool nights. Winter nights commonly drop below freezing and occasionally below 0°F.

Things to Do

Apart from the self-guided loop tour, you can hike **backcountry trails** to remote sites or to view the Great Houses from overlooks on the cliffs above. Free backcountry hiking permits are available at the visitor center. No backcountry camping is permitted in the park. Watch your step, as rattlesnakes are commonly seen in the summer. Inquire at the visitor center for

ranger-conducted **tours** and evening campfire programs in summer.

Places to Stay

There are no lodges in the park. The *Gallo Campground*, 1½ miles from the visitor center, is open year-round on a first-come, first-served basis. It can fill by noon in the summer. Camping is $10 per site. Toilets, grills and picnic tables are available. Bring your own wood or charcoal. Trailers over 35 feet cannot easily be accommodated. There are no hookups. Water is available at the visitor center parking lot only.

The nearest lodging is at the *Inn at the Post B&B* (☎ 505-632-3646) at Nageezi Trading Post on Hwy 44. Two rooms with shared bath are $59 double and a third room with private bath is $69 double. Kitchen privileges are available (no restaurant).

Getting There & Away

The roads below are signed. Note that many maps do not show the current road access from the north.

From the North Three miles south of the Nageezi Trading Post on Hwy 44, turn right (south) on CR 7900, which is paved for 5 miles. Continue on the marked unpaved county road for 16 miles to the park entrance. This road is usually the preferred access route.

From the South Turn off I-40 at Thoreau and go north on Hwy 371 to Crownpoint (24 miles). Four miles north of Crownpoint, turn right/east on Hwy 9 (also marked 57) for 14 miles, then turn north for 20 miles on unpaved Hwy 57 to the park entrance.

JICARILLA APACHE INDIAN RESERVATION

The Apaches were comparatively late arrivals in the Southwest, migrating from the north in the 14th century. They were a hawkish group, taking advantage of the more peaceful Pueblo peoples who were already living here. Indeed, the Zuni Indian word for 'enemy,' *apachu*, led to the Apaches' present name. Jicarilla (pronounced hic-a-REE-ya) means 'little basket,' reflecting their skill in basket weaving and other crafts.

Today, various Apache communities in the Southwest provide tourist attractions for visitors, although ranching, logging and mining are economically more important. In the case of the Jicarilla Reservation, Apache crafts, a casino and outdoor pursuits such as hunting, fishing and skiing all draw visitors. About 3000 Jicarilla Apaches live on the 1360-sq-mile reservation.

Orientation & Information

The tiny town of **Dulce** on Hwy 64 in the northern part of the reservation is the tribal capital. The tribal administration office (☎ 505-759-3242, fax 505-759-3242), PO Box 507, Dulce, 87528; the Game & Fish Department (☎ 505-759-3255, fax 505-759-3457), PO Box 313; and the tourism department (☎ 505-759-3442) all have tourist information. For the tribal police, call ☎ 505-759-3222.

Unlike at most reservations, alcohol is available at the hotel and in the Apache House of Liquor. No permits or fees are needed to drive through the reservation. Photography is usually permitted.

Things to See & Do

The **Jicarilla Arts & Crafts Museum** on Hwy 64 near the hotel has exhibits of various local crafts, including baskets, beadwork, leather and feather work. There are occasional demonstrations. Many items are for sale – baskets range from $150 to $1000. The museum's hours are erratic, but admission is free.

The **Apache Nugget Casino** (☎ 505-759-3777, 800 294-2234) has slots, blackjack and roulette.

The reservation's eight lakes and the Navajo River are stocked with trout and provide good **fishing**. Hunters go after mule deer and elk from September to December. The Game & Fish Department requires that anglers and hunters obtain tribal licenses in addition to the more

expensive state licenses. Tribal licenses are easily available at the Game & Fish office in Dulce. Staff there can also advise you about the best sites and arrange guided hunting and fishing trips.

Trails for **cross-country skiing** are maintained in winter, and ski rentals are available.

Special Events

The Little Beaver Roundup features a rodeo, dances and other events on the third weekend in July. The Gojiiya Harvest Festival, held on September 14 and 15 at Stone Lake (19 miles south of Dulce on Tribal Hwy J8), has a powwow and rodeo. The public is welcome. Other ceremonials are held throughout the year – call the tribal tourism department for details.

Places to Stay & Eat

There are campgrounds by most of the fishing lakes. Several are easily accessible by car from Dulce.

The only hotel is a good one. The *Best Western Jicarilla Inn* (☎ 505-759-3663, fax 505-759-3170) has 42 pleasant rooms for $55 to $90. Rates are higher for the Little Beaver Roundup in July and lower from January to May. The hotel has a restaurant, bar and big-money bingo as well as tourist information and a gift shop selling local crafts. They will make arrangements for you to ride on the Cumbres & Toltec Scenic Railroad (see Chama) and offer package rates.

There is also a café in town – I didn't see it, but ask around.

Chama to Española

East of the Jicarilla Apache Indian Reservation (see above), Hwy 64 joins Hwy 84, crosses over the Continental Divide and drops into the small community of Chama. This is the base for one of the most scenic train trips in the Southwest as well as being a mecca for anglers, hunters and cross-country skiers.

South of Chama, the countryside becomes more characteristic of the classic, luminously lit landscapes favored by artists such as Georgia O'Keeffe, who lived in Abiquiu.

CHAMA

This small town of 1250 inhabitants lies at a cool 7880 feet. Indians lived and hunted in the area for centuries, and Spanish farmers settled the Chama River Valley in the mid-1700s, but it was the arrival of the Denver & Rio Grande Railroad in 1880 that really put Chama on the map. Eventually, the railroad closed, but the prettiest part later reopened as the Cumbres & Toltec Scenic Railroad.

Orientation

Downtown Chama is on Hwy 17, 1½ miles north of the so-called Y junction (which is actually more like a T on its side) of Hwy 84/64 with Hwy 17. The main street is variously called Main, Terrace Ave or Hwy 17. The area's attractions are spread out along Hwy 17 and along Hwy 84/64 for several miles south of the Y.

Information

The New Mexico Welcome Center (☎ 505-756-2235) at the Y has general tourism information and maps for the whole state. The chamber of commerce (☎ 505-756-2306, 800-477-0149), 499 Main, is open daily for local information. The post office (☎ 505-756-2240) is at 199 W 5th. The police (☎ 505-756-2319) are at 299 W 4th.

The high elevation makes the climate cool. July temperatures range from 75°F in the daytime to 40°F at night. January temperatures are about 32°F in the day with overnight lows well below 0°F. Snowfall usually begins in October.

Cumbres & Toltec Scenic Railroad

The coal-fired steam engine belches smoke and cinders, and some of the old semi-open carriages offer little protection from the elements, but this is part of the attraction. This is both the longest (64 miles) and highest (over the 10,015-foot-high Cum-

bres Pass) authentic narrow-gauge steam railroad in the USA. Some carriages are fully enclosed, but none are heated. Railroad buffs enjoy the history, and others enjoy the magnificent scenery – it's a worthwhile train trip. Learn more at the Narrow Gauge Railway Museum (☎ 505-756-1850), three blocks south of the Chama Railroad Depot.

The train runs between Chama and Antonito, Colorado, every morning from mid-May to mid-October. You can take the full trip (about eight hours) in either direction and return by van, or go by van and return by train. This costs $52 for adults and $27 for children under 12. Or take the full trip and arrange your own return for $45 adults, $21 children, or only go to the midpoint of Osier, Colorado, then return to your starting point for $34 adults, $17 children. Ask about occasional Moonlight Train Rides and Winter Weekend Excursions.

People over 60 receive a 10% discount, and advance reservations are recommended. To make reservations, call ☎ 505-756-2151 or write to PO Box 789, Chama, NM 87520, or contact the Colorado end at ☎ 719-376-5483, PO Box 668, Antonito, CO 81120. Carriages with wheelchair lifts are available with seven-day advance notice.

Drinking alcohol and smoking are not allowed on the trains. There is a snack bar and restroom on board, and the train makes a lunch stop in Osier, where you can buy lunch. Or, bring your own picnic.

It is possible to get off at Osier and be picked up at a later date. This allows the option of backpacking and fishing in the San Juan Mountains. About 15 or 20 miles away (on foot) is the HI/AYH *Conejos River Hostel* (☎ 719-376-2518), which is remote and uncrowded, except in July and for holiday weekends. Beds are $9 for hostel members.

Antonito, Colorado, is smaller than Chama and offers fewer lodging possibilities. The basic *Park Motel* (☎ 719-376-5582) is near the station and has rooms for $23/33 for singles/doubles. Only a short

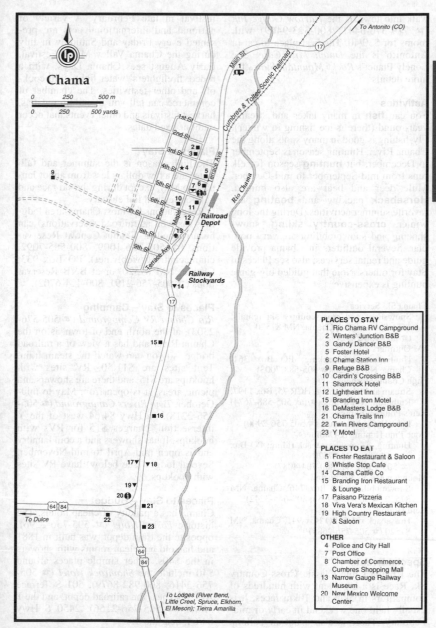

Chama

0   250   500 m
0   250   500 yards

To Antonito (CO)

Main St

Cumbres & Toltec Scenic Railroad

1st St
2nd St
3rd St
4th St
5th St
6th St
7th St
8th St
9th St

Terrace Ave

Rio Chama

Pine St
Maple St

Railroad
Depot

Terrace Ave

Railway
Stockyards

To Dulce

64 84

64

84

To Lodges (River Bend,
Little Creel, Spruce, Elkhorn,
El Meson); Tierra Amarilla

PLACES TO STAY
1   Rio Chama RV Campground
2   Winters' Junction B&B
3   Gandy Dancer B&B
5   Foster Hotel
6   Chama Station Inn
9   Refuge B&B
10 Cardin's Crossing B&B
11 Shamrock Hotel
12 Lightheart Inn
15 Branding Iron Motel
16 DeMasters Lodge B&B
21 Chama Trails Inn
22 Twin Rivers Campground
23 Y Motel

PLACES TO EAT
5   Foster Restaurant & Saloon
8   Whistle Stop Cafe
14 Chama Cattle Co
15 Branding Iron Restaurant
    & Lounge
17 Paisano Pizzeria
18 Viva Vera's Mexican Kitchen
19 High Country Restaurant
    & Saloon

OTHER
4   Police and City Hall
7   Post Office
8   Chamber of Commerce,
    Cumbres Shopping Mall
13 Narrow Gauge Railway
    Museum
20 New Mexico Welcome
    Center

walk into town is the *Narrow Gauge Inn* (☎ 719-376-5441, 800-323-9469) with rooms for $30/40. The best place to eat in Antonito is the *Dutch Mill Cafe*. See Lonely Planet's *Rocky Mountain States* for more details.

Activities

You can **fish** in many lakes and streams year-round (there is ice fishing in winter). Fly-fishing is good in many spots along the Chama River. Hunting season is September to December, but **hunting** season for elk runs from mid-September to mid-October. Mule deer and bear are also hunted. **Horseback** packing and **boating** are favorite summer activities. During the long winter, **cross-country skiing**, snowshoeing and snowmobiling are very popular. Several outfitters in Chama provide guide and rental services; also see Places to Stay for others. Note that guided big-game hunting is expensive.

Chama Ski Service
    Snowshoes and cross-country ski rentals; 1551 S Alamo Rd, Chama, NM 87520 (☎ 505-756-2492)
5M Outfitters
    Hunting, horse packing; PO Box 361, Chama, NM 87520 (☎ 505-588-7003)
High Country Fishing
    Stream and lake fishing; HCR 75, Box 1197, Rutheron, NM 87551 (☎/fax 505-588-7674)
Ken's Pontoon Express
    Lake Heron boat tours (☎ 505-756-2900)
Lone Pine Hunting & Outfitters
    Hunting, fishing, horseback riding; PO Box 314, Chama, NM 87520 (☎ 505-756-2992, 800-704-4087)
Mountain Mike's Recreation
    Snowmobiling; PO Box 746, Chama, NM 87520 (☎ 505-756-9154, 800-645-3242)
Reid Hollo
    Horseback rides; PO Box 941, Chama, NM 87520 (☎ 505-756-2685)

Special Events

The Chama Chile Classic Cross-Country Ski Race is a big event with hundreds of competitors in 5km and 10km races. It is usually held one weekend in early or mid-February. There is also a hot-air balloon festival in late February. A variety of national and international acts are presented every Friday and Saturday in July during the Chama Valley Music Festival. Early August sees Chama Days, with a rodeo, firefighters' water fight, chili cook-off and other festivities. The chamber of commerce can tell you of sailing regattas, harvest festivals and other events that occur without fixed dates.

Places to Stay

The high season is the summer and fall. Rates are a few dollars less from about January to May, except during the ski race and balloon festival in February.

Reservations for most Chama-area lodgings (as well as railroad reservations) can be arranged at Chama Central Reservations (☎ 505-756-1009, 800-585-7092, chamacentral@webtv.net), PO Box 933, Chama, NM 87520, or at B&B Reservations (☎ 505-756-2191, 800-424-6702).

Places to Stay – Camping

Rio Chama RV Campground (☎ 505-576-2303), at the north end of town, is on the Chama River and has a view of a railroad bridge, so you can watch the steam train. Tent sites are $11.50, RV sites with hookups are $15, and there are showers and picnic areas. It is open from May to mid-October. *Twin Rivers Campground* (☎ 505-756-2218), on Hwy 84/64 west of the Y intersection, charges $15 for RVs with hookups. It has showers and a coin laundry and is open mid-April to mid-November. Several lodges (see below) have RV sites with hookups.

Places to Stay – Budget

Chama has a paucity of cheap hotels. The historic *Foster Hotel* (☎ 505-756-2296), opposite the train depot, was built in 1881 and has old but clean rooms with showers in the $40s. Other simple places around $40 include the *Shamrock Hotel* (☎ 505-756-2416, 800-982-8679), 501 S Terrace Ave, also near the railroad depot, and the *Y Motel* (☎ 505-756-2166), 2450 S Hwy 84/64, near the Y.

Places to Stay – Middle to Top End

Motels & Lodges The *Chama Trails Inn* (☎ 505-756-2156, 800-289-1421), 2362 S Hwy 17 by the Y, has 16 attractive rooms, each with New Mexican decor, a refrigerator and TV. There is a sauna. Rooms with one bed are $43, with two beds $51, and the honeymoon suite with spa is $55. Closer to town, the *Branding Iron Motel & Restaurant* (☎ 505-756-2162, 800-446-2650), 1511 S Hwy 17, has over 40 large motel rooms in the $60s and $70s. The *Chama Station Inn* (☎ 505-756-2315), 423 S Terrace Ave, 85720, is opposite the railroad depot and one of Chama's earliest lodges. Renovated in 1993, it offers eight attractive rooms including standard doubles from $46 and two doubles with a queen-size bed and fireplace for $69.

The following places are found along the Rio Chama on Hwy 84/64 about a mile south of the Y, and all are within a short walk of good river fishing. The *Spruce Lodge* (☎ 505-756-2593), 2643 S Hwy 84/64, has a dozen rustic cabins starting at $45 (one bed, no kitchen), $65 (two beds, some with kitchenettes) and $71/77 for three/four people in singles/doubles; each extra person is $6. There are also RV sites. Nearby, the *Little Creel Lodge* (☎ 505-756-2382, 800-242-6259), 2631 S Hwy 84/64, has 64 RV sites and 13 cabins starting around $50. Cabins have one to four rooms, some with kitchens and/or fireplaces, and are popular with outdoorspeople. Corrals for your horses are provided (the Lone Ranger stays here). The *Elkhorn Lodge & Cafe* (☎ 505-756-2105, 800-532-8874), 2663 S Hwy 84/64, has 22 pleasant motel rooms for $50/60 a single/double and 11 cabins with kitchenettes in the $70 to $100 range.

There are several others that can be booked through the reservations agencies listed above. Also see Tierra Amarilla below.

B&Bs The recommended *Gandy Dancer B&B* (☎ 505-756-2191, 800-424-6702), 299 Maple, PO Box 810, Chama, NM 85720, has seven attractive nonsmoking rooms in an early 1900s house with antiques. There is an outdoor hot tub. The helpful hosts provide local information, reservations and dinners or box lunches on request (in addition to a full breakfast). Rates are about $100 a double. But 'Gandy Dancers'? This was the nickname for laborers who built the 19th-century railroads.

The two-room *Lightheart Inn* (☎ 505-756-2908), PO Box 223, Chama, NM 87520, is run by a woman who is a certified masseuse and Reiki Master. Vegetarian breakfasts are available, and rooms have a spa. Other two- to four-room downtown B&Bs are shown on the map and can be reserved through B&B Reservations, listed above.

Places to Eat

For inexpensive meals, I like *Viva Vera's Mexican Kitchen* (☎ 505-756-2557), 2202 S Hwy 17 (400 yards north of the Y), with Mexican and American food, beer and wine, from 7 am to 8 pm daily (till 10 pm in summer). Opposite is *Paisano Pizzeria* (☎ 505-756-2674). *Whistle Stop Cafe* (☎ 505-756-1833) in the Cumbres Shopping Mall is convenient to the railroad depot. It is open from 7:30 am to 7:30 pm Monday to Saturday and serves American food; dinners are $8 to $14 and lunch sandwiches are $3 to $5. The *High Country Restaurant & Saloon* (☎ 505-756-2384), 2289 S Hwy 17, is one of the better places; it has a saloon out of the Wild West. They serve breakfast, lunch and dinner. The budget-conscious will find burgers and Mexican food – others may opt for steak and seafood with entrees up to $18. There is also a salad bar. Newer is the *Chama Cattle Co* (☎ 505-756-2808), 1128 S Hwy 17, which has good steaks and the 'Blue Duck Microbrewery.'

Otherwise, your best bet is the hotel restaurants. Inexpensive and old-fashioned, *Foster Restaurant & Saloon* is open from 6 am to 10 pm in summer. The *Elkhorn Cafe* (☎ 505-756-2229), next to the Elkhorn Lodge, also offers moderately priced breakfasts, lunches and dinners.

The *Branding Iron Restaurant & Lounge* (☎ 505-756-2808), next to the Branding Iron Motel, is another reasonable choice.

Getting There & Away
There is no public transport (apart from the scenic railroad).

TIERRA AMARILLA & AROUND
Tiny Tierra Amarilla, 15 miles south of Chama on Hwy 84/64, is the Rio Arriba County seat and has several old buildings, but Chama offers many more visitor services. From TA (as it is locally known), scenic Hwy 64 heads east over a 10,000-foot pass in the Tusas Mountains to Taos, 80 miles away. This road is closed in winter.

Just north of TA and slightly west of Hwy 84/64 is the tiny village of Los Ojos. Here, visit **Tierra Wools** (☎ 505-588-7231), a weaving cooperative in a rustic, century-old building. Watch traditional weavers at work, hand spinning, dying and weaving rugs, hangings, ponchos and clothes. All the products are for sale.

Three miles north of TA, Hwy 512 heads east of Hwy 84/64 to scenic **Brazos Canyon**, with spectacular cliffs and several B&Bs.

Heron Lake State Park
Eleven miles west of TA on Hwy 95, this attractive lake park offers fishing, boating, camping and hiking. The fishing is excellent (a record-breaking 21-pound lake trout was caught in 1993). Motorboats are limited to trolling speed, and sailing, canoeing and windsurfing are popular. Heron Lake Store (☎ 505-588-7436) has fishing gear, boat rental, a café and a grocery and liquor store. There is a short nature trail and a 6-mile trail to El Vado Lake State Park (see below). In winter, locals ice fish and cross-country ski (along the El Vado Lake Trail). There are picnic areas and a visitor center. Day use is $3; for the campground, see Places to Stay. Call or write the park for further information (☎ 505-588-7470), PO Box 31, Rutheron, NM 87563.

El Vado Lake State Park
This park, 14 miles southwest of TA on Hwy 112, is similar to Heron Lake, but water-skiing is allowed in addition to fishing, boating, camping and hiking. There are bathrooms, drinking water, picnic areas and a playground. Day use is $3; for the campground, see Places to Stay. For more information, call or write the park (☎ 505-588-7247), PO Box 29, Tierra Amarilla, NM 87575.

The Rio Chama can be rafted from the park south to the Abiquiu Dam. Outfitters in Taos offer one- to three-day white-water rafting trips on this river.

Places to Stay
Camping *El Vado Lake* campground has 54 sites with no hookups or showers for $7. The campground at *Heron Lake* has eight sites with partial hookups for $11 and about 200 sites without hookups for $7. There are bathrooms (no showers) and drinking water.

Lodges & B&Bs *Stone House Lodge* (☎ 505-588-7274), between Heron Lake and El Vado Lake, has cabins with one/two bedrooms sleeping two/four for $45/70, mobile homes and apartments sleeping up to eight for $90 and the Stone House, which sleeps 20 people for $250. All have kitchens. Campsites are $8/14 without/with hookups. There is a café, laundromat, showers, gas station and a grocery and tackle shop. Canoes and various boats can be rented ($5 to $25 per hour), and fishing guides are available ($125 minimum).

Several small but attractive B&Bs and lodges are found along Hwy 512 to Brazos. Doubles are about $100 or more. For details, call the reservations agencies listed in Chama Places to Stay.

CARSON NATIONAL FOREST
Hwy 64 between Tierra Amarilla (TA) and Taos crosses this forest, passing *Hopewell Campground* at 9800 feet, about 28 miles east of TA. This small campground is open from May to October and has toilets but no drinking water. There is no fee, but

improvements may change this. In Tres Piedras, 50 miles east of TA, there is a ranger station (☎ 505-758-8678).

Canjilon, 3 miles east of Hwy 84 on Hwy 115 and about 17 miles south of TA, has another ranger station (☎ 505-684-2486), PO Box 488, Canjilon, NM 87515. The *Canjilon Lakes Campgrounds* are about 12 miles northeast of Canjilon along dirt roads at 9800-feet elevation. There are 40 sites ($5) with drinking water, toilets and fishing. It is open from May to September. Some 12 miles south of Canjilon, just off Hwy 84, is the *Echo Amphitheater Campground*, named after the natural red rock bowl in which it is located. The campground is open all year, and it has a free picnic site, a short nature trail, drinking water, pit toilets and 20 campsites for $5.

Further information about the Carson National Forest is available from the Supervisor (☎ 505-758-6207), PO Box 558, Taos, NM 87571.

ABIQUIU & AROUND
The tiny community of Abiquiu is famous as the place where renowned artist **Georgia O'Keeffe** lived during most of her productive years. She died in 1986, aged 98, and her adobe house has recently been opened to limited visitation. One-hour tours several times a week are by reservation only (☎ 505-685-4539), cost $15, and may be booked-up weeks ahead. Try to imagine the surrounding countryside through her perceptive eyes.

The attractive village plaza, which has a nice church and other old buildings, is also worth a stop.

About 3 miles away is **Dar Al Islam** (☎ 505-685-4515), an adobe mosque that welcomes visitors. It comes as a surprise in this predominantly Native American and Christian land. From Hwy 84, cross Rio Chama (south side of Abiquiu) on Hwy 554, take your first left (unpaved Hwy 155) and follow it for 3 miles.

Seven miles west of town is **Abiquiu Dam & Reservoir** (☎ 505-685-4371). Surrounded by red rock and high-desert

terrain, the reservoir is a beautiful spot for a swim. It also has a boat ramp, fishing for crappie, bass and trout, water-skiing, picnicking and a **campground** with showers; it's open from mid-April to October. Campsites are $3, and RV sites are $6. Story Book Tours (☎ 505-685-4808, 800-239-2865) operates boat tours on the reservoir.

About 9 miles northwest of the dam lies the **Ghost Ranch Living Museum** (☎ 505-685-4312). Operated by the USFS, it is a living collection of indigenous plants and animals that have been hurt or abandoned. If they recover enough to survive on their own, they are returned to the wild. An excellent geological exhibit explains the evolution of the nearby rock formations. Interpretive trails are designed to teach you about the area's natural and cultural history – it's a worthwhile stop. The museum is 4 miles south of Echo Amphitheater on Hwy 84, or about 15 miles northwest of Abiquiu. Hours are 8 am to 4:30 pm Tuesday to Sunday. Suggested donations are $3/2 for adults/seniors and students.

Ghost Ranch Conference Center (☎ 505-685-4333, fax 505-685-4519), just before the Living Museum, is a conference center with an ongoing dinosaur excavation, and you can watch scientists painstakingly excavate dinosaur bones from locally quarried rock. There is also a small museum on local history and archaeology. This is where *City Slickers* was filmed, and it is a spectacular spot with hiking trails among the red rocks and grassy fields. Suggested donations are $2/1 for adults/students.

Places to Stay & Eat
The nice-looking Southwestern-style *Abiquiu Inn* (☎ 505-685-4378, 800-447-5621), Box A, Hwy 84, Abiquiu, NM 87510, has 19 units ranging from rooms with one bed to rooms with two beds and a kitchen, all with private bath, TV, telephone and air-conditioning. Rates are $55 to $90 a double and advance reservations are advised. Two casitas with two bedrooms, living room with fireplace, eat-in kitchen and bathroom

are $110 to $125 for up to four people. The adjoining reasonably priced and well-recommended *Café Abiquiu* has a tasty selection of New Mexican, Middle Eastern and Asian Indian dishes. Both are on Hwy 84.

La Cocinita (☎ 505-685-4609), on Hwy 84 across from the Trujillo General Store, serves tasty homemade New Mexican food, burgers and fresh fry bread from 10 am to 8 pm daily March through December. It doesn't look like much from the outside, but it's the spot for a good, inexpensive meal. You can buy food to go at the walk-up window or eat inside.

A few tiny B&Bs, most with just two rooms, are also available. Call for rates and directions: *Casablanca* (☎ 505-685-4505), *Old Abiquiu B&B* (☎ 505-685-4784) or *Casa del Rio* (☎ 505-753-2035).

Pajarito Plateau & Jemez Mountains

This area contains some of New Mexico's most rugged topography, and it's tough to get around in quickly. A series of massive volcanic explosions occurred more than one million years ago and blew an estimated 100 cubic miles (some authorities suggest 450 cubic miles) of ash and pumice into the air. (Compare this to the paltry .25 cubic miles ejected by the famous 1980 eruption of Mt St Helens in Washington State.)

Eventually, the volcano collapsed in upon itself, leaving behind the tortured landscape of a massive caldera surrounded

Georgia O'Keeffe

One of the 20th century's most admired American artists and certainly the Southwest's most internationally famous painter, Georgia O'Keeffe (1887-1986) was born and raised on a Wisconsin farm before moving to Chicago and later New York to study art. She taught art in several southern states and in Texas from 1912 to 1916. Then her work was shown to photographer and gallery owner Alfred Steiglitz, whose '291' was New York's foremost avant-garde gallery of the time (where Europeans such as Rodin, Cézanne and Picasso had their works introduced to America). Steiglitz called O'Keeffe's drawings 'the purest, most sincere work that has entered 291 in a long while.'

So began a long and often complicated relationship between O'Keeffe and Steiglitz, who was 23 years her senior. In 1918 she moved in with him, causing a scandal because Steiglitz was married. Over the next two decades, she posed for his camera hundreds of times, forming one of the most remarkable series of photographic portraits ever made. They married in 1924, but their relationship remained enigmatic with both partners having affairs with other men and women.

O'Keeffe often left Steiglitz and New York City to seek inspiration elsewhere – upstate New York and Maine were favorite places. During this period she painted pictures of city skyscrapers and began painting the sensual enlargements of flowers (such as *Black Iris*, 1926) for which she is especially remembered. But she frequently hankered after the wide-open spaces of the West, recalling her teaching experiences in Texas and a 1917 vacation in New Mexico. Her opportunity came in 1929, when she was invited to Santa Fe and Taos by Mabel Dodge Luhan, New Mexico's leading patron of the arts.

New Mexico enchanted and influenced the artist. She began collecting bleached bones from the desert and incorporating them into her landscapes or painting them as close-ups; bones are another of her most recognizable trademarks. Her works were imbued by her own mixed emotions, lending the paintings abstractly suggestive and subtly symbolic qualities that made them uniquely her own. Although she returned to New York after several months in New Mexico, she continued to visit year after year until Steiglitz's death

by fingerlike plateaus kicking off into what are now called the Jemez Mountains.

Hunter-gatherers lived in the area for thousands of years. The Rio Grande Ancestral Puebloan Indians arrived by about 1200 AD and stayed for almost 400 years, leaving many ancient buildings in the area – 7000 by one account. The most spectacular and important of these are preserved in Bandelier National Monument.

The rugged, out-of-the-way Pajarito Plateau area was the site chosen to develop the US atomic bomb, and interested visitors can tour a fine museum explaining the history and research involved. In addition, the wild countryside provides challenging outdoor activities such as backpacking, cross-country skiing, fishing and hunting. Hwy 4, south of Los Alamos, gives a scenic view of the collapsed caldera.

LOS ALAMOS

Los Alamos is named after a ranch built on the Pajarito Plateau by homesteaders in 1911. Seven years later, this became the Los Alamos Ranch School, an innovative place where rich young men were given a rounded education ranging from Homer to horseback riding.

In 1943, the US government took over the school and turned it into the top-secret headquarters of the Manhattan Project – and the race to build the first atomic bomb was on. Over the next two years, the government poured $2 billion into the project headed by nuclear physicist J Robert Oppenheimer, who was assisted by many other brilliant scientists and the US military. On July 16, 1945, project scientists stood on a hillside near Trinity Site (see the Southeastern New Mexico chapter) and

in 1946. After settling her husband's affairs, she moved permanently back to New Mexico in 1949, where she had renovated an adobe home in the tiny village of Abiquiu.

By this time she had completed her most famous works, but continued to paint until she lost her sight in the 1980s. Some of the best-known work of her later life was inspired by world travel, especially the airplane flights that provided her with vistas of clouds, which led to the painting of a 24-foot-wide mural, *Sky Above the Clouds* (1965). Throughout her life she was an intensely private person, but she did write an autobiography, published in 1976. Failing health caused her to move to Santa Fe, where she died in 1986 at the age of 98.

Today, O'Keeffe's work is exhibited in major museums throughout the world and she is considered one of the best painters of the 20th century. Her home in Abiquiu can now be visited by advance appointment, but for most visitors the best opportunity to come into contact with her iconic work is at the newly opened Georgia O'Keeffe Museum in Santa Fe. (See that chapter for information on the museum.) ∎

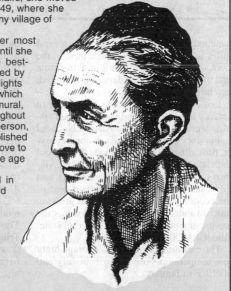

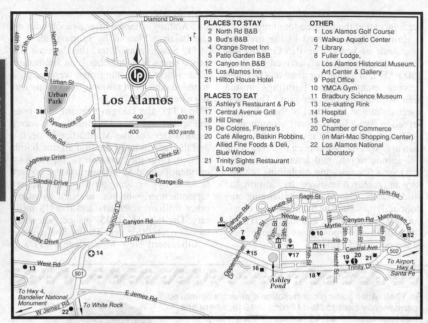

PLACES TO STAY
2 North Rd B&B
3 Bud's B&B
4 Orange Street Inn
5 Patio Garden B&B
12 Canyon Inn B&B
16 Los Alamos Inn
21 Hilltop House Hotel

PLACES TO EAT
16 Ashley's Restaurant & Pub
17 Central Avenue Grill
18 Hill Diner
19 De Colores, Firenze's
20 Café Allegro, Baskin Robbins,
     Allied Fine Foods & Deli,
     Blue Window
21 Trinity Sights Restaurant
     & Lounge

OTHER
1 Los Alamos Golf Course
6 Walkup Aquatic Center
7 Library
8 Fuller Lodge,
     Los Alamos Historical Museum,
     Art Center & Gallery
9 Post Office
10 YMCA Gym
11 Bradbury Science Museum
13 Ice-skating Rink
14 Hospital
15 Police
20 Chamber of Commerce
     (in Mari-Mac Shopping Center)
22 Los Alamos National
     Laboratory

watched the first atomic explosion several miles in the distance. Within a month, the USA dropped atomic bombs on Hiroshima and then Nagasaki, and Japan surrendered, essentially ending WWII.

Los Alamos continued to be clothed in secrecy until 1957, when restrictions on visiting were lifted. The Los Alamos National Laboratory continues to be a major employer, providing some 13,000 jobs throughout the state. The town is the seat of Los Alamos County (New Mexico's smallest), and government jobs are an important part of the economy. There is a small but growing tourism industry, and Los Alamos has the lowest unemployment rate in the state. About 19,000 people live here.

The elevation is 7400 feet. Average high/low temperatures are 80/56°F in July and 40/19°F in January.

Orientation

Built on long thin mesas separated by steep canyons, Los Alamos has a confusing lay-out that takes some getting used to. The main entrance from the east is Hwy 502, which branches into the east-west streets of Canyon Rd, Central Ave and Trinity Drive – these are the main streets of town.

Information

The chamber of commerce (☎ 505-662-8105, 800-444-0707), 800 Trinity Drive, is open 8 am to 5 pm Monday to Friday. The library (☎ 505-662-8240) is at 2400 Central Ave. The local newspaper is the *Los Alamos Monitor*. The post office (☎ 505-662-2071) is at 1808 Central Ave. The hospital (☎ 505-662-4201) is at 3917 West Rd. The police (☎ 505-662-8222) are at 2500 Trinity Drive. A pamphlet for a self-guided downtown walking tour is available free from the chamber of commerce and the historical museum.

Bradbury Science Museum

After the development of the atomic bomb, J Robert Oppenheimer, troubled by ethical

ANN NEET

CHUCK PLACE

STEPHEN TRIMBLE

Top Left: St Francis Cathedral, Santa Fe, New Mexico
Bottom: Church and hornos (ovens), Zuni Pueblo, New Mexico

Top Right: San José Mission, Laguna Indian Pueblo, New Mexico

Top: Lightning strike, White Sands National Monument, New Mexico

Bottom: Church & kiva, Pecos National Historical Park, New Mexico

issues raised by further development of nuclear weapons, left his post as director of the Manhattan Project and was succeeded by Norris E Bradbury, after whom this museum is named. The well-organized displays, hands-on exhibits and audiovisual interpretations describe not only the history of the Manhattan Project but also nuclear research and defense technology up to the present. The national lab itself is not open to tours.

The museum (☎ 505-667-4444), Central Ave at 15th, is open from 9 am to 5 pm Tuesday to Friday and from 1 to 5 pm Saturday to Monday, except January 1, Thanksgiving and December 25. Admission is free. Next door to the museum is the Otowi Station Museum Shop and Bookstore, which has a fine selection of science books and gifts.

Fuller Lodge
This rustic log building was once the dining/rec room for the Los Alamos Ranch School and later for the scientists of the Manhattan Project. The lodge is now a national historic landmark and has two adjoining museums in the complex at 2132 Central Ave. It was a set for Robert Redford's movie *The Milagro Beanfield War*.

The **Los Alamos Historical Museum** (☎ 505-662-4493), on the north side of the lodge, has exhibits on the area's archaeological, social and nuclear history. Lectures and changing exhibits are featured, and there is a bookstore. Summer hours are 9:30 am to 4:30 pm Monday to Saturday, and 11 am to 5 pm Sunday. Winter hours are 10 am to 4 pm Monday to Saturday and 1 to 4 pm Sunday. Admission is free.

The **Art Center & Gallery** (☎ 505-662-9331) has well-reviewed mixed-media shows of local and national artists. Some work is for sale. Hours are 10 am to 4 pm Monday to Saturday year-round, and 1 to 4 pm Sunday from April to November. Admission is free.

Swimming
The Walkup Aquatic Center (☎ 505-662-8170), 2760 Canyon Rd, is the nation's highest Olympic-size pool. It has been the training ground of several Olympic medal-winning swimmers, who claim the elevation helps them build endurance. The pool has daily public swimming (call for hours). Entrance is $2.50 for adults, less for students and seniors. Multi-visit and other discounts are available.

Skiing
Pajarito Ski Mountain (☎ 505-662-5725), about 7 miles west of downtown, has five chair lifts servicing more than 40 runs of which 40% are for experts and 45% are for intermediate skiers. Peak elevation is 10,440 feet, dropping to 9200 feet at the base. The resort is open on weekends, Wednesdays and holidays. Lift tickets are $35 for adults and $22 for seniors and children. Hours are 9 am to 4 pm. The mountain is quite challenging and not very crowded; there are no accommodations. For a snow and road report (chains may be required), call ☎ 505-662-7669.

Other Activities
The Los Alamos Golf Course (☎ 505-662-8139), 4250 Diamond Drive, offers the opportunity to **golf** an 18-hole round. The popular course is often busy – call by Wednesday for weekend tee times. Snow closes the course from mid-November to mid-March.

Call the Parks Department (☎ 505-662-8170) for **tennis** information. The court at Urban Park on North Rd and 42nd is open until 11 pm daily – there are basketball and handball courts and a playground here as well.

An outdoor **ice skating** rink (☎ 505-662-4500 or 8174), 4475 West Rd, is open from Thanksgiving through February.

The YMCA **gym** (☎ 505-662-3100), 900 15th, offers use of its squash and racquetball courts and exercise equipment for $10 a day (local hotels can arrange discounts).

The chamber of commerce can tell you about bowling, archery and other sporting activities.

Organized Tours

Buffalo Tours (☎ 505-662-3965) offers 1½-hour van tours of the 'Atomic City' at 10:30 am and 2 pm in summer for $8. Children with adults are $4.25. Tickets, information and winter hours are available at the Otowi Station Bookstore next to the Bradbury Science Museum. Other tours are available on request.

Special Events

The main annual event is the Los Alamos County Fair & Rodeo held during 10 days in early August. The chamber of commerce lists other events.

Places to Stay

Hotels There are no cheap motels in town. The *Los Alamos Inn* (☎/fax 505-662-7211, 800-279-9279), 2201 Trinity Drive, has a good restaurant, a lounge with pool tables and occasional live music, a pool and spa. Over a hundred pleasant standard and executive rooms (with data-port terminals, refrigerators and coffeemakers) are in the $70s and $80s. The *Hilltop House Hotel* (☎ 505-662-2441, 800-464-0936, fax 505-662-5913, hilltop@unix.nets.com), 400 Trinity Drive, has a restaurant, lounge and indoor pool. Some of the 82 rooms have kitchenettes, and there are 18 suites. Rates start at $68/78 a single/double and suites range from $100 to $275, including breakfast.

B&Bs The *Orange Street Inn* (☎ 505-662-2651, 800-279-2898, ORANGE4767@aol.com), 3496 Orange, Los Alamos, NM 87544, is the best-established of the town's B&Bs. It has four rooms sharing two baths for $54, two larger rooms with private bath for $65, a mini-suite for $75 and a 'treehouse room' with private entrance and deck for $75; all rates are for two people. The friendly owners know the area and will even give you breakfast in bed. Smoking is allowed outside only.

Bud's B&B (☎ 505-662-4239, 800-581-2837, BudsBB@aol.com), 1981 B/C North Rd, Los Alamos, NM 87544, has six nonsmoking rooms with shared bath for $50/60 a single/double and two rooms with private bath for $60/70. The owner is a poet and a professional cook who offers homemade vegetarian breakfasts – he even grinds his own wheat for his waffles! There are kitchen and laundry privileges. *Canyon Inn B&B* (☎ 505-662-9595, 800-662-2565), 80 Canyon Rd, Los Alamos, NM 87544, is a nonsmoking establishment with four rooms. Rates are $45/55 with shared bath and $50/60 with private bath, including a continental buffet breakfast. *Patio Garden B&B* (☎ 505-662-9581, BetsyBnB@aol.com), 4756 Trinity Drive, Los Alamos, NM 87544, has two rooms sharing one bath for $50/65 a single/double including full breakfast. *North Rd B&B* (☎ 505-662-3687, 800-279-2898), 2127 North Rd, Los Alamos, NM 87544, has two rooms and three two-room suites, most with private bath, for $50 to $60. Smoking is allowed outside only. All of these places give weekly discounts.

Places to Eat

Ashley's Restaurant & Pub in the Los Alamos Inn is open from 6:30 am to 2 pm and 5 to 9 pm daily, with dinner entrées in the $10 to $15 range. The slightly pricier *Trinity Sights Restaurant & Lounge* in the Hilltop House Hotel has good views and is open from 6:30 to 9:30 am, 11:30 am to 2 pm and 5 to 9 pm.

For a morning espresso jolt, head over to the *Cafe Allegro* (☎ 505-662-4040), 800 Trinity Drive (in the Mari-Mac Shopping Center). It has espresso, sandwiches, pastries and newspapers from 9:30 am to 6 pm Monday, from 8 am to 6 pm Tuesday to Friday and from 9 am to 2 pm on weekends. Also in the shopping center is a *Baskin Robbins* ice-cream parlor and *Allied Fine Foods & Deli* (☎ 505-662-2777) for sandwiches and carry-outs from 7:30 am to 6 pm Monday to Friday (till 4 pm Saturday). Upstairs, the *Blue Window* (☎ 505-662-6305) serves good, if slightly pricey, continental cuisine from 11 am to 2:30 pm and 5 to 8:30 pm Monday to Friday.

Next door, good New Mexican fare is offered at *De Colores* (☎ 505-662-6285),

820 Trinity Drive. It is open from 11 am to 2 pm and 5 to 8 pm Monday to Saturday. Upstairs, *Firenze's* (☎ 505-662-2324), serves good Italian food from 11 am to 2 pm and 5 to 8 pm Tuesday to Friday, with dinner also on Saturday.

The popular and inexpensive *Hill Diner* (☎ 505-662-9745), 1315 Trinity Drive, is open 11 am to 8 pm weekdays and 8 am to 8 pm weekends. A fine array of American diner fare – tasty soups, salads, sandwiches, burgers, desserts and blue-plate specials – are served daily, plus breakfasts on weekends. The equally popular *Central Avenue Grill* (☎ 505-662-2005), 1789 Central Ave, is open from 11 am to 8 pm daily (9 pm in summer) and serves a slightly more upscale version of American food at moderate prices.

Getting There & Away

Public transport to Los Alamos is limited and liable to change. The airport (☎ 505-662-8420) may have flights with local carriers like Ross Aviation (☎ 505-667-4521) to and from Albuquerque.

Bus service between Los Alamos, Española and Santa Fe is set to begin in November 1998. Call the chamber of commerce for more information.

Getting Around

Los Alamos Bus (☎ 505-662-2080) offers local bus service.

WHITE ROCK

This small town is 7 miles southeast of Los Alamos. It lies between the Tsankawi Ruins sector and the main section of Bandelier National Monument.

The *Bandelier Inn* (☎ 505-672-3838, 800-321-3923, fax 505-672-3537, bi@unix.nets.com), in the White Rock Shopping Center just off Hwy 4, has about 50 pleasant rooms for $59/66 a single/double, including continental breakfast. Most rooms have a microwave and refrigerator. Two-bedroom, two-bathroom suites with kitchen and living room are about $125.

For a meal, a few fast-food and other simple places are easily found. *Katherine's*

(☎ 505-672-9661), 121 Longview Drive, is considered the best restaurant. It is open for lunch 11:30 am to 2:30 pm Tuesday to Friday and dinner 5:30 to 10 pm Tuesday to Saturday.

BANDELIER NATIONAL MONUMENT

This monument is named after the Swiss-American explorer Adolph Bandelier, who surveyed the area in the 1880s. Almost 50 sq miles of rugged canyons are protected within the monument, and apart from a short entrance road, Bandelier can be visited only on foot or horseback.

Unlike the Ancestral Puebloans in the Four Corners region who moved on by about 1300 AD, the Rio Grande Puebloans inhabited Bandelier until about the mid-1500s, perhaps because of the moister climate. Several sites in Frijoles Canyon have been studied by archaeologists, including the large, oval-shaped Tyuonyi, which contained almost 400 rooms, and several ceremonial kivas. Many others are found scattered in the backcountry, and Bandelier provides a fine destination for those interested in ancient pueblos, backpacking or both. None of the pueblos have been restored to original condition.

Orientation & Information

Hwy 4 follows the northern border of the monument to the entrance at the northeast corner. The road continues about 3 miles to the visitor center (☎ 505-672-3861, ext 517, or 505-672-0343 for a 24-hour recording) in Frijoles Canyon. It is open from 8 am to 5 pm daily and to 6 pm from Memorial Day to Labor Day; closed January 1 and December 25. The visitor center has a slide show and a small museum. There is a bookshop, gift shop, snack bar and a nearby picnic area. Restrooms are open 24 hours.

The bookshop sells trail maps and guidebooks, which can be obtained in advance from the Southwest Parks and Monuments Association (☎ 505-672-3861, ext 515), HCR 1, Box 1, Suite 2, Los Alamos, NM 87544-9701. You can also write to the Superintendent, Bandelier National Monument, at Suite 15 at the same address.

NEW MEXICO

Several trails leave from the visitor center through Frijoles Canyon. Ranger-led walks and talks are offered during the summer.

The monument trails are open from dawn to dusk. Admission to the visitor center is free. Admission to the monument is $10 per car or $5 per individual; Golden Eagle, Access and Age Passes are honored.

Frijoles Canyon Trail

This 1-mile (one-way) trail heads north from the visitor center and passes the major sites. The first section is wheelchair accessible. A trail guidebook from the visitor center is $1 (free loans are available). Sites along the first half mile of the trail, which is fairly flat, include a big kiva, Tyuonyi and Long House, and cliff dwellings. The second half mile continues to the Ceremonial Cave, which is 140 feet above the canyon floor and reached by climbing four ladders – not recommended for people with a fear of heights. The Ceremonial Cave, which contains a kiva that may be entered, is a highlight of a visit to Bandelier.

Falls Trail

This heads south from the visitor center, reaches two waterfalls, 1½ and 2 miles away, and continues to the Rio Grande, 2½ miles away. A trail-guide booklet is available.

Tsankawi

This unexcavated site is a separate sector of the park, 13 miles north of the visitor center on Hwy 4 and 2 miles north of White Rock. There is a small sign and parking area. Mesa-top Tsankawi provides good views, but the highlight is the steep, 2-mile trail itself, which had been walked for centuries by the early inhabitants. Their feet wore a trench into the soft rock more than knee deep in places.

Backpacking

About 70 miles of trails meander up, down and through the canyons of Bandelier. Elevations range from 6000 to over 8000 feet, and the trails are steep. You should be in reasonable shape to hike them. Backpacking is allowed with a free permit available from the visitor center. No open fires are permitted. The trails are open year-round but may be snow-covered in winter. Thunderstorms and heat are summer hazards, so spring and fall are considered the best backpacking seasons. Some areas may be closed because of forest fires in 1996 and 1997.

Places to Stay

There are no lodges. *Juniper Campground*, near the monument entrance, offers about a hundred sites, drinking water, toilets, picnic tables and fire grates, but no showers. The sites are open on a first-come, first-served basis from March to November and cost $10.

Ponderosa Group Campground (☎ 505-672-3861 ext 534), 6 miles west of the entrance station on Hwy 4, has two sites open from mid-April to October for $35 for 10 to 50 persons. Early reservations are necessary.

JEMEZ SPRINGS & AROUND

Southwest of Los Alamos and west of Bandelier National Monument, the Jemez (pronounced HAY-mez) Mountains provide outdoor recreation opportunities, beautiful scenery, Jemez State Monument, Jemez Pueblo and more. Much of the land is within the Santa Fe National Forest. All these places are reached via Hwy 4, which goes west then south from Bandelier.

The tiny town (population 456) of Jemez Springs has an eclectic and esoteric mix of visitor services squeezed into a beautiful narrow valley watered by the trickling Jemez River, which supports a slash of lush green trees flanked by steep red cliffs. Services include several B&Bs, a few churches and monasteries (with slightly ominous names like Servants of the Paraclete), a Zen Buddhist center and shops and galleries selling homemade chocolate, herbs, crystals and local arts and crafts. A Santa Fe National Forest Ranger Station (☎ 505-829-3535), a mile north of town, has information about camping, hiking, fishing, hunting and other activities in the national forest. Several fishing access pullouts south of Jemez Springs provide convenient parking for the Jemez River.

There are natural hot springs – you can take a dip at the **Bath House** (☎ 505-829-3303), which dates back to 1870 but has been modernized. Entrance is $8/12 for a 30/60-minute soak. Massages ($30/45 for 30/60 minutes), herbal wraps, facials and acupuncture are offered by reservation (and can be booked solid for days ahead!). Hours are 9 am to 9 pm in summer and 10 am to 8 pm at other times. The Forest Service rangers know of other natural hot spring sites that can be visited for free.

Just over 2 miles north of the town, look for **Soda Dam** – strange mineral formations across Jemez Creek on the right side of the highway. The natural dam was formed by spring water heavily laden with minerals.

Note that the 25mph speed limit through town is strictly enforced.

Jemez State Monument

Once called Giusewa by the original inhabitants, the Jemez Pueblo Indians (see below), the monument now houses both Indian sites and the ruins of a Spanish colonial church completed in 1622 – these are the main sights here. A worthwhile museum explains the significance and history of the area.

The monument is open daily from 8:30 am to 5 pm – inclement weather may alter this. Admission is $3 for adults. The monument is off Hwy 4 just north of Jemez Springs. Call ☎ 505-829-3530 for further information.

Jemez Pueblo

The Jemez were among the most active opponents of the Spanish during the Pueblo Revolt of the 1680s and 1690s, and they are the only people who speak the Towa language. Today, their pueblo, about 12 miles south of Jemez Springs, is more conservative than most and is generally closed to visitors.

However, the pueblo operates the Walatowa Visitor Center (☎ 505-834-7235, fax 505-834-7331), off Hwy 4, open 10 am to 5 pm on weekdays, till 4 pm on weekends. It has information, a small photo exhibit and local arts and crafts for sale. The Jemez are good potters and make storyteller doll pots and tan background animal ceramics. Some potters have signs on Hwy 4 inviting visitors to stop into their houses. Entrance to the rest of the pueblo requires a permit. The visitor center can arrange tours (advance arrangements necessary).

Jemez Pueblo has several public events, including the Red Rock Arts Show on the second weekend in June, a Fall Art Fiesta on the second weekend in October and a Winter Arts & Crafts Show on the first weekend in December. Traditional food and art and dance demonstrations are part of the proceedings. In addition, there are several feast days with ceremonial dances that the pueblo does not care to publicize to maintain the privacy of the tribe. Call the visitor center for information about which ones may be open to the general public. Photography, recording and sketching are prohibited.

The scenery around and south of the pueblo is spectacular and intensely red. Red Rock, about 3 miles north of the pueblo, is the site of stalls selling local arts and crafts and food, especially on summer weekends.

The pueblo is in the middle of the extensive Jemez Indian Reservation, which the people use for agriculture, hunting and fishing. Two fishing areas open to the public are Holy Ghost Spring and Dragonfly, about 18 and 24 miles north of San Ysidro on Hwy 44. Local rangers sell tribal permits, and the trout fishing is good. Further information is available from the visitor center.

Places to Stay

Camping The Santa Fe National Forest operates several campgrounds in the area, most charging $8 a site and providing drinking water, toilets, grills and picnic tables but no showers or RV hookups. They are open from May to October. Free dispersed camping (no facilities) is also possible. Information is available from the ranger stations in Jemez Springs, Cuba, Española or Santa Fe.

USFS campgrounds along Hwy 4 include *Vista Linda*, 4½ miles south of Jemez Springs, with 14 sites; *Redondo*, 11 miles north of Jemez Springs, with 60 sites; and *Jemez Falls*, 15 miles north of Jemez Springs, with 52 sites and various hiking trails, including a steep 1-mile trail to a 50-foot waterfall.

At La Cueva, 9 miles north of Jemez Springs, Hwy 4 intersects with Hwy 126, and gas and food are available here. Two miles west on Hwy 126 is the USFS *San Antonio* campground with 47 sites. Six miles farther west along Hwy 126, *Fenton Lake* (☎ 505-829-3630) is state-operated and provides year-round camping in 30 sites ($7), fishing and, in winter, cross-country skiing. Five sites have RV hookups ($11).

Motels & B&Bs The popularity of this area is growing and several new accommodations have opened in recent years. Most have a no-smoking policy in their rooms.

In town, the *Laughing Lizard Inn & Cafe* (☎ 505-829-3108, 888-532-5290, lizard@ jemez.com), PO Box 263, Jemez Springs, NM 87025, has four rooms, each decorated differently, in the $60s. The *Jemez Mountain Inn* (☎ 505-829-3926), 17555 Hwy 4, Jemez Springs, NM 87025, is a restored turn-of-the-19th-century adobe with seven rooms, three with kitchenettes, for $105 a double. The *Giggling Star* (☎ 505-829-9175), PO Box 60, Jemez Springs, NM 87025, rents three rustic cabins, two with kitchens, for $79 to $125.

Half a mile south of town on Hwy 4 is the *Jemez Canyon Inn* (☎ 505-829-3254), PO Box 158, Jemez Springs, NM 87025, with six rustic rooms, three with kitchenettes, in the $40s and $50s. Weekly discounts are available. A mile south is the *Jemez River B&B* (☎/fax 505-829-3262, 800-809-3262), 16445 Hwy 4, Jemez

Springs, NM 87025. It has six rooms decorated in Southwestern style with TV, telephone and air-conditioning for $99 to $109 a double; a three-room casita sleeping four to eight is $129 to $179. Healing arts and massages can be arranged in advance. Almost 3 miles south, the *Dancing Bear B&B* (☎ 505-829-3336, 800-422-3271), PO Box 128, Jemez Springs, NM 87025, has four different attractive rooms, one with a fireplace, for $65 to $115.

La Cueva Lodge (☎ 505-829-3814), 9 miles north of Jemez Springs, has 15 motel rooms for $50/55 a single/double. There's a restaurant next door.

Places to Eat

The *Laughing Lizard Cafe*, by the motel, serves good sandwiches, salads, burritos and pizzas in the $6 to $9 range, and it has espresso drinks. They are closed Monday. The *Los Ojos Saloon* (☎ 505-829-3547) is an Old West-style saloon that serves decent food. Also try *Deb's Deli* (☎ 505-829-3829) for breakfasts and coffee.

CUBA

The scenic 40-mile drive north of San Ysidro along Hwy 44 to Cuba has good views of red-rock scenery and 7785-foot Cabezon Peak – a volcanic plug rising over 2000 feet above the countryside. The base of the mountain can be reached by a dirt road leaving Hwy 44 to the west from near the Holy Ghost Spring in the Jemez Reservation. It's about a 10-mile drive passable to cars.

Settled over 200 years ago, Cuba is now a small agricultural center (population 750) and a pleasant stop on the way to or from Chaco Culture National Historical Park. It's about another 50 miles to the turnoff to Chaco.

The chamber of commerce (☎ 505-289-3705) is on the main street. The Santa Fe National Forest Ranger Station (☎ 505-289-3265), PO Box 130, Cuba, NM 87103, is on the right side of Hwy 44 as you arrive from the south.

The Sandoval County Fair & Rodeo is held annually in early August.

Places to Stay & Eat

Hwy 126 east of Cuba leads 11 miles to *Clear Creek* campground, operated by the USFS. There are pit toilets and fire grills but no drinking water. The 10 sites are open from May to October and are free. A couple of miles farther on Hwy 126, *Rio Las Vacas* offers 15 sites with similar facilities. Hwy 126 continues 15 miles to Fenton Lake (see Jemez Springs), but the dirt road is impassable after bad weather. It's a beautiful drive if you can get through. There are other campgrounds along the way, plus backpacking opportunities. Details are available from the forest ranger in Cuba.

Formerly a hunting lodge set in 330 acres in the Nacimiento Mountains, the friendly *Circle A Ranch Hostel* (☎ 505-289-3350), PO Box 2142, Cuba, NM 87013, calls itself 'rustic yet elegant' and is a favorite with many looking for a quiet retreat. Dorms cost $10; private rooms range from $20 to $35. The hostel is open May 1 to October 15. You can take the TNM&O/Greyhound bus to Cuba (there's no official stop) and call for a pick up.

From south to north, you'll find the *Cuban Lodge Motel* (☎ 505-289-3269), the *Del Prado Motel* (☎ 505-289-3475) and the *Frontier Motel* (☎ 505-289-3474). Rooms start in the mid-$20s. The *Cuban Cafe* (☎ 505-289-9434), opposite the Cuban Lodge Motel, serves home-style meals all day long, and the *Del Prado Restaurant* (☎ 505-289-3888), next to the motel, has cheap Mexican food. The well-recommended *El Bruno's Cantina y Restaurante* (☎ 505-289-9429), in the middle of town, is one of the best Mexican restaurants in northwestern New Mexico.

ZIA PUEBLO

Once home to some 6000 people, Zia Pueblo was destroyed during the Pueblo Revolt of the 1680s. Now, only a few hundred people live here, and they are famous for their pottery. A stylized red sun motif on a yellow background, found on a Zia pot, has been incorporated into the state flag and is a well-known symbol of New Mexico. Zia pottery includes many other designs, such as a stylized roadrunner (bird) and a double rainbow, and is available in the Zia Cultural Center and at many other outlets in New Mexico.

The annual ceremonial is on August 15, and the public may attend, but no photography, recording or sketching is allowed. The pueblo is about 6 miles southeast of San Ysidro off Hwy 44 (or 17 miles northwest of Bernalillo). Further information is available from the Zia Pueblo Governor's Office (☎ 505-867-3304, fax 505-867-3308).

SANTA ANA PUEBLO

This pueblo, about 8 miles southeast of Zia and 8 miles northwest of Bernalillo, is reached by a 2-mile gated road off Hwy 44. The gate is opened to the public only on the following feast days (subject to change): January 1 and 6, Easter, June 24 and 29, July 25-26 and December 25-28. Most of the tribe lives outside the pueblo in a modern village a couple of miles out of Bernalillo on Hwy 313. The tribe also operates the 27-hole Valle Grande Golf Course (☎ 505-867-9464) north of Bernalillo and a 24-hour casino.

Further information is available from the Governor's Office (☎ 505-867-3301, fax 505-867-3395).

I-40 Corridor West of Albuquerque

You can drive the 150 miles from Albuquerque to the Arizona border in a little over two hours, but don't. There is much to see along the I-40 corridor, and it's worth a couple of days at least. Two Indian pueblos are within sight of the freeway, and a third is a short drive away. The scenery is a mixture of red rock and black lava, with a couple of national monuments to showcase the highlights. Indian villages welcome tourists searching for unique arts and crafts. Anglo-Hispanic towns offer museums, lodging and a taste of the Wild West. And a national forest gives ample camping opportunities on tree-clad mountain slopes.

LAGUNA PUEBLO
This Indian reservation (about 40 miles west of Albuquerque or 30 miles east of Grants) consists of six small villages. Although it was founded in 1699, it is the youngest of New Mexico's pueblos. The founders were escaping from the Spaniards and came from many different pueblos, and so the Laguna people have a very diverse ethnic background.

Laguna Pueblo was built on uranium-rich land, and most inhabitants were involved in the local post-WWII mining boom. Now, they are involved in a cleanup and reclamation program.

The pueblo is open daily from dawn to dusk. Information about feast days and other matters is available from Laguna Pueblo (☎ 505-552-6654, 505-243-7616, fax 505-552-6007).

The **San José Mission** (☎ 505-552-9330) is visible from I-40 and reached from exit 114. The stone and adobe church was completed in 1705 and houses fine and interesting examples of early Spanish-influenced religious art painted by the Laguna people. Hours are 9 am to 3 pm on weekdays.

There is a growing Acoma-style ceramic pottery industry. Contact the tribal office about purchases.

Special Events
Feast days are celebrated with dances, ceremonies, parades and sales of arts and crafts. The public may attend, but no photography, sketching or recording is permitted. The main feast days are two St Joseph's (San José's) Days on March 18 and September 19, St John's (San Juan's) Day on June 24, St Laurence's (San Lorenzo's) Day on August 10 and Christmas Eve. These are held in Old Laguna, and some lesser feasts may be held in other pueblo villages on other dates.

ACOMA PUEBLO
Also known as 'Sky City' because of its fantastic mesa-top location, Acoma (pronounced AHK-oh-ma) is one of the most historic places on the continent. It vies with Taos Pueblo and Oraibi (on the Hopi Reservation in Arizona) for the title of oldest continuously inhabited settlement in North America. People have lived here since the 12th century, and local legend claims that the first inhabitants arrived centuries earlier. Acoma Pueblo has had a long and often terrible history.

Several dozen residents live in Acoma year-round, although the village lacks electricity and running water. Most residents are elders who don't have to worry about getting their children off to school. Many other people have temporary homes on the mesa, and hundreds more show up on ceremonial days. Most of the several thousand Keresan-speaking Acoma people live in one of the modern villages below the mesa, such as McCartys, Anzac and Acomita, all on the Acoma Indian Reservation.

The famous Acoma pottery is made from a very fine gray clay dug on the reservation. This clay enables ceramics to be made with extremely thin yet very strong walls, and Acoma pots are sought after by collectors. Good pots cost hundreds of dollars, and top-quality pieces run into the thousands. Note that some pots sold on the reservation are made from different clays, and although they have Acoma designs on them, they are cheaper and of inferior quality. Ask the salesperson what kind of clay has been used.

Visitor Center & Museum
The visitor center (☎ 505-252-1139, 800-747-0181) is at the base of the Sky City mesa. A permanent museum exhibit called *One Thousand Years of Clay: Pottery, Environment and History* highlights the history of Acoma and showcases the local pottery. There's a snack bar with Indian and American food, restrooms, a parking lot, tour office and arts and crafts stalls. Hours are 8 am to 7 pm April to October

and 8 am to 4:30 pm the rest of the year. Admission is free.

Organized Tours

To reach Sky City, 7000 feet above sea level and 367 feet above the surrounding plateau, you must go on a guided tour; these leave from the visitor center frequently throughout the day. The last tour is one hour before closing. Each is led by a knowledgeable Acoma guide who provides interesting narration and answers questions. The ascent of the mesa is made by bus and the descent is by bus or foot. The walking tour at the top lasts about an hour.

Apart from the ancient pueblo dwellings, tours visit the fortresslike **San Esteban del Rey Mission** built on the mesa top in the early 1600s with construction materials carried up (!) to the site. The views from here are seemingly endless.

Tours go daily except for July 10-13 and either the first or second weekend in October, when the pueblo is closed to visitors. Tour fees are $6 for adults, $5 for seniors and $4 for children 17 and under. Still photography is permitted for a $10 fee (but not during special events). Video and movie cameras are not allowed.

Special Events

Ceremonial dances and events should be observed respectfully – please don't join in. No photography or recording of any kind is permitted. For precise dates or information, call the visitor center. Sky City events include a Governor's Feast in February. There is a Harvest Dance on San Esteban Day (September 2) and festivities at the San Esteban Mission on December 25-28.

In addition, outside of Sky City, there are celebrations at Acomita and McCartys on Easter, at McCartys on Santa Maria Day (the first Sunday in May) and at Acomita on San Lorenzo's Day (August 10).

Getting There & Away

The visitor center is 13 miles south of I-40 exit 96 (15 miles east of Grants) or I-40 exit 108 (50 miles west of Albuquerque). McCartys is near exit 96, and Acomita is near exit 102. There is no public transport.

GRANTS & AROUND

Originally an agricultural center and railway stop founded in the 1880s, Grants experienced a major mining boom when uranium was discovered in 1950. After about 30 years, the boom went bust, but Grants discovered a new industry – tourism. The town has a fine mining museum and makes a good center for visits to, among other places, the El Morro and El Malpais National Monuments and the Acoma and Laguna Pueblos.

Orientation & Information

Santa Fe Ave (Business I-40 or Old Hwy 66) is the main drag through town and runs parallel and north of I-40 between exits 81 and 85.

The chamber of commerce (☎ 505-287-4802, 800-748-2142), 100 Iron, is open 8 am to 5 pm on weekdays. The Cibola National Forest Mount Taylor Ranger Station (☎ 505-287-8833), 1800 Lobo Canyon Rd, Grants, NM 87020, is open from 8 am to noon and 1 to 5 pm Monday to Friday. The library (☎ 505-287-6024) is at 525 W High St. The post office (☎ 505-287-3143) is at 120 N 3rd. The hospital (☎ 505-287-4446) is at 1212 Bonita Ave. The police (☎ 505-287-4404) are on Roosevelt Ave near 1st.

New Mexico Mining Museum

Sharing the chamber of commerce building (see above), this is the only uranium-mining museum in the world (they say), and you can go underground and see what it was like to be a miner. Although the mine no longer operates because of decreased demand for this mineral, it remains America's largest uranium reserve.

On the ground floor is a free museum of local Indian artifacts. Going below ground (by elevator in a miners' cage) costs $3 for ages 9 to 59, free for younger kids and $2 for seniors. Admission includes use of a 'sound stick,' which provides a self-guided

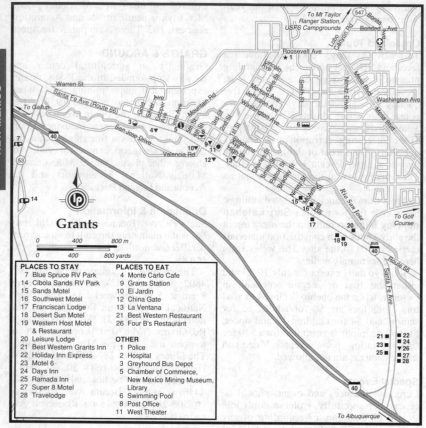

Grants

PLACES TO STAY
7 Blue Spruce RV Park
14 Cibola Sands RV Park
15 Sands Motel
16 Southwest Motel
17 Franciscan Lodge
18 Desert Sun Motel
19 Western Host Motel
    & Restaurant
20 Leisure Lodge
21 Best Western Grants Inn
22 Holiday Inn Express
23 Motel 6
24 Days Inn
25 Ramada Inn
27 Super 8 Motel
28 Travelodge

PLACES TO EAT
4 Monte Carlo Cafe
9 Grants Station
10 El Jardin
12 China Gate
13 La Ventana
21 Best Western Restaurant
26 Four B's Restaurant

OTHER
1 Police
2 Hospital
3 Greyhound Bus Depot
5 Chamber of Commerce,
   New Mexico Mining Museum,
   Library
6 Swimming Pool
8 Post Office
11 West Theater

tour at your own pace. Groups can arrange live tour guides (ex-miners) by calling the chamber of commerce in advance. Tour hours are 9 am to 5 pm Monday to Saturday and 9 am to 3 pm Sunday, May to September, and 9 am to 3 pm Monday to Friday in winter.

Bluewater Lake State Park
Camping and fishing for rainbow trout and catfish are the main attractions here. The 7400-foot elevation causes the lake to freeze hard in winter, when there is ice fishing. There is also a small playground, grocery store, boat rental and water-skiing.

Day use is $3; see Places to Stay for the campground. Information is available from Bluewater State Park (☎ 505-876-2391), PO Box 3419, Prewitt, NM 87045. The park is off exit 63 on I-40 (18 miles west of Grants) and then 6 miles south.

Mt Taylor
This 11,301-foot peak is the highest in the area and is the southernmost of the four sacred mountains of the Navajo. Head northeast on Lobo Canyon Rd (Hwy 547) for about 13 miles to where it changes into gravel USFS Rd 239. Follow 239 and then USFS Rd 453 for another 3.3 miles to La

Mosca Lookout at 11,000 feet, about a mile northeast of Mt Taylor's summit. It's possible to hike to the top of Mt Taylor, but check with the ranger station in Grants about trail conditions.

Activities

Play **golf** at the 18-hole Coyote del Malpais course (☎ 505-285-5544), 2001 Camino del Coyote. **Swim** at the public pool (☎ 505-287-7636), 551 Washington, open afternoons daily for $1.50. Call the parks department (☎ 505-287-7927) for **tennis** court information.

Special Events

The Mt Taylor Quadrathlon, held the second week in February, goes from Grants to Mt Taylor and combines cycling, running, cross-country skiing and snowshoeing. Individuals and teams of two to four athletes compete. Wild West Days features a PRCA rodeo, parade, dancing, arts and crafts, food and fireworks on the Fourth of July or the closest weekend. The Chili Fiesta, on the first Saturday in October, has a chile cook-off and various other foods and fun events.

Places to Stay

The uranium boom produced many hotels – the bust left Grants with a surfeit of cheap lodging that will delight the budget-conscious. Summer rates given here may drop out of season or rise over holiday weekends.

Places to Stay – Camping

Cibola Sands RV Park (☎ 505-287-4376), on Hwy 53 half a mile south of I-40 exit 81, has a playground, store, showers and a coin laundry. The 54 sites are $12 for tents or $16 with RV hookups. Next to I-40, the similarly priced *Lavaland RV Park* (☎ 505-287-8665) at exit 85 and the cheaper and smaller *Blue Spruce RV Park* (☎ 505-287-2560) at exit 81 both have tent and RV facilities and showers. There is tent and RV camping 20 miles west along I-40 at *Grants-West RV Park* (☎ 505-876-2662) at exit 63 in Prewitt for $9/12 and

at *St Bonaventure RV Park* (☎ 505-862-7885) 30 miles west at exit 53 in Thoreau for $11/15.

The USFS (☎ 505-287-8833) operates the *Lobo Canyon Campground*, 8 miles northeast on Lobo Canyon Rd and then 1½ miles east on unpaved USFS Rd 193. There are pit toilets and picnic facilities, but no water. The pleasantly wooded *Coal Mine Campground*, 10 miles northeast on Lobo Canyon Rd, has a nature trail, drinking water and flush toilets but no showers; it costs $5. Both are open from mid-May to late October. The free, waterless *Ojo Redondo Campground* is about 20 miles west of town along unpaved USFS Rd 49 and USFS Rd 480. This is open all year, unless snow closes the road.

Eighteen miles west of Grants, *Bluewater Lake State Park* runs a campground with laundry and showers; tent sites are $7 and sites with RV hookups are $11.

Places to Stay – Budget

The cheapest motels include the *Franciscan Lodge* (☎ 505-287-4424), 1101 E Santa Fe Ave, which charges $18/20 for singles/doubles and is a Route 66 original; the *Southwest Motel* (☎ 505-287-2935), 1000 E Santa Fe Ave, with rooms from $20; the *Western Host Motel* (☎ 505-287-4418), 1150 E Santa Fe Ave, which has a pool and restaurant and charges $20/25; and the similarly priced *Desert Sun Motel* (☎ 505-287-4426), 1121 E Santa Fe Ave, which has larger rooms than most of the cheapest hotels. There are some others.

The well-recommended *Leisure Lodge* (☎ 505-287-2991), 1204 E Santa Fe Ave, has decent-looking rooms for $24/28 (one bed) or $36 (two beds). There is a pool.

The *Motel 6* (☎ 505-285-4607), 1505 E Santa Fe Ave, has a pool and officially charges $34/40 for standard rooms, but in practice is often $30/36 in summer or less in winter.

Places to Stay – Middle

Several other less basic chain hotels advertise a few rooms with prices to match the Motel 6 if business is slow, but charge $40 to $80 when they can. These include the *Days Inn* (☎ 505-287-8883, fax 505-287-7772), 1504 E Santa Fe Ave, which has spacious, well-kept rooms with queen- and king-size beds; the *Ramada Inn* (☎ 505-287-7700, fax 505-285-4125), 1509 E Santa Fe Ave, with a pool, restaurant and lounge with live entertainment; and the *Travelodge* (☎/fax 505-287-7800), 1608 E Santa Fe Ave, with an indoor pool and spa and continental breakfast.

The independent *Sands Motel* (☎ 505-287-2996), 112 McArthur, has good-size rooms, many with a queen- or king-size bed and refrigerator, in the low $40s for a double. The *Super 8 Motel* (☎/fax 505-287-8811), 1604 E Santa Fe Ave, has a pool, hot tub, exercise room and complimentary continental breakfast; rates are $39.88/43.88 for one bed and $47.88 for two beds. The *Holiday Inn Express* (☎ 505-285-4676, fax 505-285-6998), 1496 E Santa Fe Ave, has an indoor pool and hot tub, coin laundry, exercise room and complimentary continental breakfast; rooms run $60 to $90.

The best hotel is the *Best Western Grants Inn* (☎ 505-287-7901, fax 505-285-5751), 1501 E Santa Fe Ave. Facilities include an indoor pool, hot tub, sauna, game room, coin and valet laundry, restaurant with room service and lounge with weekend entertainment and dancing. Large rooms have a queen- or king-size bed, double wash basin and coffeemaker. Rates are $65 to $89 a single, $73 to $99 a double. Kitchenette suites are a little more.

Places to Eat

Locally popular *Grants Station* (☎ 505-287-2334), 200 W Santa Fe Ave, has American and Mexican meals from 6 am to 11 pm daily. A self-serve soup- and-salad bar is $5 and meals are $4 to $12. Alcohol isn't served. The 'Station' refers to the railroad (no longer a passenger stop), and there's plenty of railroad memorabilia.

The *Monte Carlo Cafe* (☎ 505-287-9250), 721 W Santa Fe Ave, serves reasonably priced and tasty Southwestern food in a traditional setting. Menu items range

from stuffed chiles to Navajo tacos to steaks. Hours are 8 am to 10 pm Monday to Saturday, 9 am to 9 pm Sunday. Homey and pleasant *El Jardin* (☎ 505-285-5231), 319 W Santa Fe Ave, offers a very good value, with well-prepared Mexican food from 11 am to 2:30 pm and 5 to 9 pm Monday to Friday (dinner also on Saturday).

The 24-hour *Four B's Restaurant* (☎ 505-285-6697), on Santa Fe Ave just north of I-40 exit 85, features inexpensive American fare but no alcohol, and is convenient to the cluster of motels near that exit. Travelers with large appetites and slim budgets can try the *China Gate* (☎ 505-287-8513), 105 W Santa Fe Ave, with all-you-can-eat buffet lunches and dinners for about $5 and $6.

Decent steak and prime rib is served at *La Ventana* (☎ 505-287-9393), 110½ Gies. Prices are around $15, although there are cheaper Mexican and chicken items. Seafood is also offered. Hours are 11 am to 10:30 pm daily except Sunday. The restaurant in the Best Western Grants Inn (☎ 505-287-7901) is also good. It's open from 6 to 10 am for breakfast and 5 to 9 pm for dinner.

Entertainment

Catch a movie at the *West Theater* (☎ 505-287-4692), 118 W Santa Fe Ave.

Getting There & Away

Greyhound (☎ 505-285-6268), 1011 W Santa Fe Ave, has about five buses a day to Albuquerque (2½ hours), Flagstaff, Arizona (three hours) and beyond.

EL MALPAIS NATIONAL MONUMENT

El Malpais (pronounced el mahl-pie-ees and meaning 'bad land' in Spanish) is almost 200 sq miles of lava flows abutting adjacent sandstone. Five major flows have been identified, with the most recent 2000 to 3000 years old. Local Indian legend tells of 'rivers of fire,' and prehistoric Native Americans may have witnessed the final eruptions.

The landscape is harsh but interesting and unique. There are cinder cones and spatter cones, smooth *pahoehoe* lava and jagged *aa* lava, and a 17-mile-long lava tube system. Some lava caves contain permanent ice. Around the edges of the lava flows are sandstone formations, including New Mexico's largest accessible arch, and signs of previous dwellers in the area – petroglyphs, ruins and homesteaders' cabins.

Information

El Malpais is a hodgepodge of NPS land, conservation areas and wilderness areas administered by the BLM, and private lands. Each area has different rules and regulations, and these change from year to year. There are no developed campsites or lodges. Backcountry camping is allowed, but a free permit is required.

The BLM Ranger Station (☎ 505-240-0300) on Hwy 117, 9 miles south of I-40 exit 89, is open from 8:30 am to 4:30 pm daily, as is the NPS Information Center (☎ 505-783-4774), 22 miles southwest of Grants on Hwy 53. The area is open year-round, and admission is free (fees may be charged in future). Further information is available from the NPS (☎ 505-285-4641), PO Box 939, or the BLM, PO Box 846, Grants, NM 87020.

Things to See

On the east side of the monument, Hwy 117 passes **Sandstone Bluffs Overlook** about 11 miles south of I-40. There is a picnic area with fine views of the lava flow. An interesting but rough hike (wear heavy shoes or boots) is the 7½-mile (one way) **Zuni-Acoma Trail**, which leaves from Hwy 117 a few miles farther south. The trail crosses several lava flows and ends at Hwy 53 on the west side of the monument. **La Ventana Natural Arch** is visible from Hwy 117, 18 miles south of I-40. Just beyond is another hiking trail.

County Rd 42 leaves Hwy 117 about 34 miles south of I-40 and meanders for about 40 miles through the BLM country on the west side of El Malpais. It passes several craters and lava tubes (reached by signed trails) and emerges at Hwy 53 near Bandera Crater. The road is unpaved, and high-clearance 4WD is recommended. Hikers

need good boots on the rough lava and should carry a gallon of water per person per day. If entering lava tubes or caves beyond where daylight penetrates, you should carry three sources of light. The Park Service recommends wearing a hard hat. Go with a companion – this is an isolated area.

Bandera Crater/Ice Cave is 25 miles southwest of Grants on Hwy 53. The area is private property (☎ 505-783-4303) surrounded by the national monument and costs $6.50 to visit, or $3 for children five to 11 years old. A quarter-mile trail leads to the Ice Cave, and a 1½-mile trail leads part of the way up the Bandera Volcano. Both trails are rough.

EL MORRO NATIONAL MONUMENT

El Morro (Spanish for 'the headland') is a 200-foot-high sandstone outcropping with a permanent pool of water at its base. This has made it a travelers' stopping place for thousands of years. In the 1200s, the Zuni people built a small pueblo on top of El Morro; the pueblo was abandoned around 1300. Today's Zuni call it *A'ts'ina* or the 'place of rock carvings.' The ancient inhabitants left many petroglyphs carved into the soft sandstone.

In 1605, Don Juan de Oñate left his name inscribed on El Morro – the first non-Native American carving – and Spaniards following him did the same. Anglos in the 1800s also carved evidence of their passing here until carving became illegal in 1906. Visitors today can see the pueblo, the petroglyphs and the historical inscriptions.

Orientation & Information

El Morro, 43 miles southwest of Grants on Hwy 53, is open daily from 9 am to 7 pm from Memorial Day to Labor Day and to 5 pm the rest of the year. It is closed January 1 and December 25. A visitor center has audiovisual and other displays, information, a bookshop and a picnic area. Rangers give talks during summer weekends. Admission is $4 per vehicle or $2 per person, and Golden Eagle, Age and Access Passes are honored.

Two self-guided trails leave the visitor center. The paved, half-mile-loop Inscription Rock Trail is wheelchair accessible and the unpaved, 2-mile-loop Mesa Top Trail requires a steep climb to the pueblos. Guide booklets are available. Trail access stops one hour before closing.

Further information is available from the Superintendent, El Morro (☎ 505-783-4226), Route 2, Box 43, Ramah, NM 87321-9603.

Places to Stay & Eat

A nine-site NPS campground is a mile before the visitor center. Drinking water and pit toilets are available. Fees are $5 per site on a first-come, first-served basis. The campground usually fills during summer weekends but rarely midweek. It closes from October to April.

El Morro RV Park and Cabins (☎ 505-783-4612) is on Hwy 53, about a mile east of El Morro. From mid-March through November, six tents sites are $7 and 27 RV sites with hookups are $10. There are showers, and a snack bar is open from 7 am to 8 pm. Two cabins rent year-round for $35/45 for one/two beds, and two larger cabins with TV are $50/60. Reservations are recommended. Hiking trails are nearby. A couple of miles farther east is *Tinaja RV Park & Trading Post* (☎ 505-783-4349) which has RV sites with hookups for $10.50 from May to September.

The *Stagecoach Cafe* (☎ 505-783-4288) is in Ramah, a few miles west of El Morro. They open from 8 am to 9 pm Monday to Saturday as well as Sunday in summer. On the west side of Ramah is the acclaimed *Blue Corn Restaurant* with nouvelle Southwestern cuisine (blue corn crab enchiladas!) and daily specials in the $10 to $13 range. Hours are 7 am to 9 pm Wednesday to Sunday, and reservations are recommended. An adjoining gallery sells local art.

ZUNI PUEBLO

The Zuni people speak a language different from all other Indian groups. The early Spaniards thought the pueblo was one of the legendary 'seven cities of gold.'

Although it was not a city of gold, today it is a premier jewelry-making center. The pueblo is 35 miles south of Gallup and has about 8500 inhabitants.

Zuni Pueblo

Orientation & Information

Most main public buildings are stretched along Hwy 53, with side streets curving away into the pueblo. Photography is by permit only and is prohibited in some areas and for special events. Primitive camping requires a $3 permit from the tribal office. Zuni has a couple of cafés, grocery stores and gas stations but no hotels. Information is available from the Zuni Tribal Office (☎ 505-782-4481, fax 505-782-2700).

Our Lady of Guadalupe Mission

Walking from Hwy 53 to the mission (☎ 505-782-4477) takes five minutes, and you pass Zuni stone houses and beehive-shaped mud ovens used for baking. The church dates from 1629, although it has been rebuilt twice since then. With its massive adobe walls and vigas, it is typical of Southwestern missions except that the interior features two murals (running the length of the church) with about 30 superb, life-size paintings of kachinas by local artist Alex Seowtowa and sons Kenneth and Edwin. They began this project in 1970 and plan to finish by the year 2000. Photography is not allowed inside.

The church is open during the day (no fixed hours) from Monday to Friday and for 10 am mass on Sunday.

A:shiwi A:wan Museum & Heritage Center

This small historical museum (☎ 505-782-4403) on Hwy 53 displays early photos and other tribal artifacts. Hours are 9 am to 4 pm weekdays, and admission is by donation.

Special Events

This pueblo continues to allow non-Native Americans to its ceremonies, although they must adhere to appropriate etiquette, especially the no-photography rule. The most famous is the all-night *Sha:lak'o* ceremonial dance held in late November or early December.

In late August, the Zuni Tribal Fair features a powwow, local food and arts and crafts stalls. Other ceremonials occur on varying dates – ask at the tribal office.

GALLUP

The Gallup Convention and Visitors Bureau proudly proclaims their town to be 'The Heart of Indian Country,' and indeed, Gallup is arguably the most 'Indian' of all off-reservation towns. It serves as the Navajo and Zuni peoples' major trading center, both for buying and selling. The supermarkets and shopping malls are crowded with Native Americans, and in turn, the many trading posts and arts and crafts galleries attract people from all over the world searching for the best of the local Indian rugs, jewelry, silverware, pottery, fetishes, kachinas, baskets, sand paintings and various other art forms. The visitor center estimates that 80% of Southwestern silver jewelry sold in the USA passes through Gallup.

Apart from fine shopping opportunities, visitors are attracted by the Inter-Tribal Indian Ceremonial – an annual six-day event that draws both Native American and non-Indian visitors. This is the biggest such affair in the Southwest and is well worth attending. And if you miss the Ceremonial, you can still see Indian dances performed nightly during the summer.

The Navajo Indian Reservation is the largest in the USA. The tribal capital at Window Rock, Arizona, is just 24 miles to the northwest, and so Gallup makes a good base from which to visit Navajoland. Although small areas of the reservation lie in Utah and New Mexico, the bulk is within Arizona.

As a town, Gallup dates back to 1881, when the Atchinson, Topeka & Santa Fe Railroad (then called the Atlantic and Pacific Railroad) reached that point. Before the railroad was built, there was a Wild West saloon here, a stopping place on the Overland Stagecoach route. The railroad workers used to come by here to pick up their paychecks – the story is that the paymaster's name was David Gallup, and the town took its name from him. Coal was discovered soon after the railroad arrived, and Gallup remained an important mining town until the middle of this century.

Today, Gallup (population about 20,000 inhabitants) is the seat of McKinley County. Its economy relies on trade and tourism.

Orientation & Information

The famous old Hwy 66 is the main drag through town and runs east-west, parallel to and south of I-40, the Rio Puerco and the railway line.

The Welcome Center (☎ 505-863-4902), 701 Montoya Blvd, has information about the whole state from 8 am to 5 pm daily in summer and Monday to Friday in winter. The Convention and Visitors Bureau (☎ 505-863-3841, 800-242-4282) is at the same address. Local information is also available from 8:30 am to 5 pm Monday to Friday at the chamber of commerce (☎ 505-722-2228), 103 E Hwy 66, next to the Amtrak station. The library (☎ 505-863-1291) is at 115 W Hill. The local newspaper is the *Independent*. The post

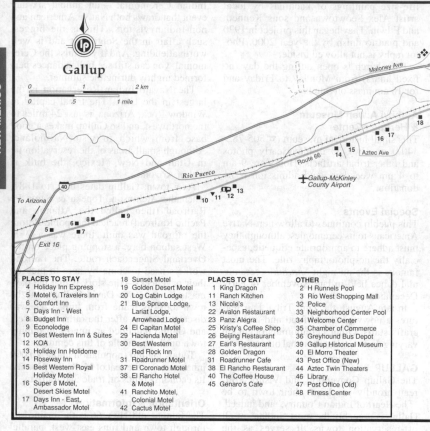

Gallup

0   1   2 km
0   .5   1 mile

To Arizona

Exit 16

Rio Puerco

Route 66

Maloney Ave

Gallup-McKinley
County Airport

Aztec Ave

PLACES TO STAY		PLACES TO EAT	OTHER
4 Holiday Inn Express	18 Sunset Motel	1 King Dragon	2 H Runnels Pool
6 Motel 6, Travelers Inn	19 Golden Desert Motel	11 Ranch Kitchen	3 Rio West Shopping Mall
6 Comfort Inn	20 Log Cabin Lodge	13 Nicole's	32 Police
7 Days Inn - West	21 Blue Spruce Lodge,	22 Avalon Restaurant	33 Neighborhood Center Pool
8 Budget Inn	Lariat Lodge,	23 Panz Alegra	34 Welcome Center
9 Econolodge	Arrowhead Lodge	25 Kristy's Coffee Shop	35 Chamber of Commerce
10 Best Western Inn & Suites	24 El Capitan Motel	26 Beijing Restaurant	36 Greyhound Bus Depot
12 KOA	29 Hacienda Motel	27 Earl's Restaurant	39 Gallup Historical Museum
13 Holiday Inn Holidome	30 Best Western	28 Golden Dragon	40 El Morro Theater
14 Roseway Inn	Red Rock Inn	31 Roadrunner Cafe	43 Post Office (New)
15 Best Western Royal	31 Roadrunner Motel	38 El Rancho Restaurant	44 Aztec Twin Theaters
Holiday Motel	37 El Coronado Motel	40 The Coffee House	46 Library
16 Super 8 Motel,	38 El Rancho Hotel	45 Génaro's Cafe	47 Post Office (Old)
Desert Skies Motel	& Motel		48 Fitness Center
17 Days Inn - East,	41 Ranchito Motel,		
Ambassador Motel	Colonial Motel		
	42 Cactus Motel		

office (☎ 505-863-3491) is at 500 S 2nd, and a new one is under construction at Aztec and 9th. The hospital (☎ 505-863-7000) is at 1901 Red Rock Drive. The police (☎ 505-722-2231) are at 451 State Rd 564.

Historical & Cultural Sites

The small Gallup Historical Museum, 300 W Route 66, is open from 9 am to 4 pm Monday to Saturday and is in the renovated turn-of-the-19th-century Rex Hotel. This and 18 other downtown structures of historic and architectural interest, built between 1895 and 1938, are described in a free brochure available at the Welcome Center or chamber of commerce. Most of these buildings are mainly along 1st, 2nd and 3rd Sts between Hwy 66 and Hill Ave.

A cultural center is under construction in the Amtrak Building.

Red Rock State Park

Six miles east of town, this park features a museum and campground and is also the site of the annual Inter-Tribal Ceremonial and many other events (see below). The

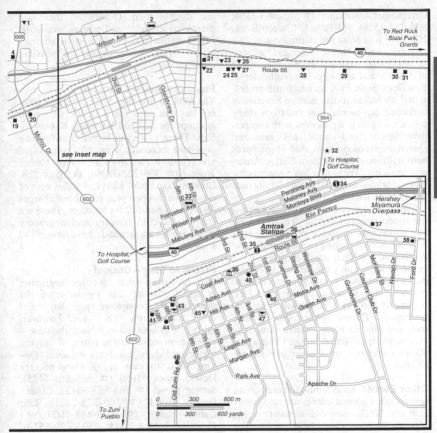

museum (☎ 505-863-1337) features both modern and traditional arts and crafts from several tribes, and it's open from 8:30 am to 4:30 pm Monday to Friday (hours are extended in summer). A $1 donation is suggested for adults. There are hiking trails within the park.

Activities

Golf 18 holes at the Gallup Municipal Golf Course (☎ 505-863-9224), 1109 Susan Drive, on the southeastern outskirts of town. **Swim** at the Neighborhood Center Pool (☎ 505-863-1328), 400 W Princeton

Ave, or H Runnels Pool (☎ 505-722-7107), 720 E Wilson Ave. The Fitness Center (☎ 505-722-7271), 700 Old Zuni Rd, has **tennis** and **racquetball** courts, a gym and other equipment.

Special Events

Inter-Tribal Indian Ceremonial Gallup celebrates its 78th annual Indian Ceremonial in 1999 – dates are normally six days in mid-August. This is a huge event, and all hotel rooms and campgrounds should be booked as far ahead as possible. Information is available from the Indian

Ceremonial Association (☎ 505-863-3896, 800-233-4528), PO Box 1, Church Rock, NM 87311, or from the visitor center.

Thousands of Native Americans as well as non-Indian tourists throng the streets of Gallup and the huge amphitheater at Red Rock State Park to watch the professional all-Indian rodeo, admire beautifully bedecked ceremonial dancers from many tribes, take part in a powwow with competitive dancing and choose a Ceremonial Queen in a competition that emphasizes both traditional and modern Native American customs. There is a huge nonmechanized parade, arts and crafts stalls and plenty of native food.

Costs of the events are very reasonable – the rodeo is about $6 for the afternoon, and an evening of dance performances is $12 in reserved seating or less for general admission. Children are half price. A $2 grounds admission (waived for rodeo and dance performance-goers) gets you into the powwow and the arts and crafts and food booths, as well as a variety of other performances. Photographers should note that, contrary to many Native American events, the Inter-Tribal Indian Ceremonial allows cameras – no fees or permits are needed.

Other Events Apart from the ceremonial, several other annual events attract visitors and fill hotel rooms. Foremost is the Navajo Nation Fair, held in nearby Window Rock, Arizona, during the first weekend in September. The Lions Club Rodeo, held in the third week in June, is the most professional and prestigious of several rodeos held throughout the year in the Gallup area. A Balloon Rally is held at Red Rock State Park during the first weekend in December – over a hundred colorful hot-air balloons take part in demonstrations and competitions. Square dancers converge on Gallup in mid-April for their annual Fest-i-Gal.

Places to Stay

It's a seller's market during Ceremonial week and other big events, and hotel prices

can double then. Otherwise, there are plenty of cheap hotel rooms available. Prices below reflect the normal summer rates – further discounts are possible during winter.

Places to Stay – Camping

The *KOA* (☎ 505-863-5021), 2925 W Hwy 66, has tent sites for $20, RV sites with hookups for $24 and Kamping Kabins for $30. There is a coin laundry, swimming pool and recreation area, playground and grocery store. *Red Rock State Park Campground* (☎ 505-722-3839), PO Box 328, Church Rock, NM 87311, 6 miles east of downtown, is open year-round and charges $8 for tents and $12 for hookups. There are showers, a coin laundry and a grocery store. Both campgrounds have about 140 sites each.

Places to Stay – Budget

The following offer doubles beginning at about $20 or less for most of the year, and the rooms are quite basic and often well worn. They are, however, fairly clean and provide hot showers – some even have kitchenettes. If staying for several days, ask for a discount. Driving west to east along Hwy 66, try Desert Skies Motel (☎ 505-863-4485), Sunset Motel (☎ 505-863-3012), Golden Desert Motel (☎ 505-722-2231), Log Cabin Lodge (☎ 505-863-4600), El Coronado Motel (☎ 505-722-5510), Lariat Lodge (☎ 505-722-5496), Arrowhead Lodge (☎ 505-863-5111), Hacienda Motel (☎ 505-722-5900) and numerous others. Along Coal Ave just off Hwy 66, the Ranchito Motel (☎ 505-863-6845) and the Cactus Motel (☎ 505-863-6112) both advertised $14 singles recently, and there is the Colonial Motel (☎ 505-863-6821).

If you're willing to spend a little more, the best of the cheaper places are the following. The popular (and often full) 20-room *Blue Spruce Lodge* (☎ 505-863-5211, fax 505-863-6104), 1119 E Hwy 66, is very clean, has free coffee and some rooms have microwaves. Rates are in the

Rug Auction

The eastern Navajo community of Crownpoint, 25 miles north of Thoreau (exit 53 on I-80), is a great place to seek out Navajo rugs. On the third (occasionally fourth) Friday of the month, a rug auction in the Crownpoint Elementary School attracts several hundred buyers, sellers and visitors. Rug previewing is from 3 to 6 pm and bidding is from 7 to 11 pm. It's standing room only – arrive early.

Admission is free, and the several hundred available rugs sell anywhere from under $100 to over $3000. Prices are better than in stores – bring cash or checks for purchase. Many Navajos, often traditionally dressed, are in attendance, and other Native Americans sell crafts outside the school.

Information and dates are available from the Rug Weavers Association (☎ 505-786-5302, 505-786-7386), PO Box 1630, Crownpoint, NM 87313.

There is food and gas in Crownpoint, but nowhere to stay. Gallup and Grants are each about a 75-minute drive away. ■

upper $20s. The larger *Ambassador Motel* (☎ 505-722-3843), 1601 W Hwy 66, has a pool and is similarly priced. The *Budget Inn* (☎ 505-722-6631), 2806 W Hwy 66, has decent rooms around $30.

The *El Capitan Motel* (☎ 505-863-6828, fax 505-722-7580), 1300 E Hwy 66, has decent rooms with coffeemakers in the $30s; a 24-hour restaurant is on the same block. Similar rooms are offered at the *Roadrunner Motel* (☎ 505-863-3804), 3012 E Hwy 66, which has a café and pool.

Places to Stay – Middle

The *Motel 6* (☎ 505-863-4492), 3306 W Hwy 66, is convenient to the freeway and has a pool. Rooms are $37/43 for a single/double in summer. Next door, the *Travelers Inn* (☎ 505-722-7765, fax 505-722-4752), 3304 W Hwy 66, has similar facilities and

prices. The *Econo Lodge* (☎ 505-722-3800, 800-424-4777), at 3101 W Hwy 66, has slightly nicer rooms at comparable prices. Also in the $30s and $40s, the *Roseway Inn* (☎ 505-863-9385, 800-454-5444, fax 505-863-6532), 2003 W Hwy 66, seems a reasonable deal and features a pool, spa, sauna, adjoining restaurant and bar.

Gallup's most interesting hotel is the historic *El Rancho* (☎ 505-863-9311, 800-543-6351, fax 505-722-5917), 1000 E Hwy 66. Opened in 1937, it quickly became known as the 'home of the movie stars.' Many of the great actors of the '40s and '50s stayed here – Humphrey Bogart, Katharine Hepburn and John Wayne to name just a few of dozens. The hotel fell on hard times in the '70s but was completely renovated and expanded in the late '80s. It now features a superb Southwestern lobby, classy gift shop with top-quality arts and crafts, a reasonably priced restaurant and bar, and an eclectic selection of 102 rooms, many with Western decor and named after the stars who stayed there. Rates range from $35 to $50 a single and $43 to $55 a double, and a few suites (sleeping up to six) go for $71 – a good deal, especially for those searching for a little nostalgia. Next door is a modern 24-room motel under the same ownership with rooms for a few dollars less.

Other places with rooms in the $40s and $50s include the *Super 8 Motel* (☎ 505-722-5300, fax 505-722-6200), 1715 W Hwy 66, which has an indoor pool, sauna, spa and coin laundry. The *Days Inn – West* (☎/fax 505-863-6889), 3201 W Hwy 66, has similar amenities, and the cheaper *Days Inn – East* (☎/fax 505-683-3891), 1603 W Hwy 66, has a seasonal pool. The *Comfort Inn* (☎ 505-722-0982, fax 505-722-2404), 3208 W Hwy 66, has an indoor pool. All of these hotels include continental breakfast and have rooms with coffeemakers.

Places to Stay – Top End

Hotels Two Holiday Inns and three Best Westerns have the top-end wrapped up in Gallup – though, for my money, the El

Rancho (above) is much more fun if not quite as modern amenity-laden. Each of the hotels below has an indoor pool, sauna, spa, exercise area, coin laundry and comfortable, spacious rooms.

The *Holiday Inn Holidome* (☎ 505-722-2201, 800-432-2211, fax 505-722-9616), 2915 W Hwy 66, is the biggest place in town with over 200 rooms. The hotel has two restaurants, room service, lounge bar with entertainment and country & western dancing, and a game room. Open from 6 am to 10 pm, the restaurant is good and not overly expensive. Most rooms are $60 to $80. The new and slightly cheaper *Holiday Inn Express* (☎/fax 505-726-1000), 1500 W Maloney Ave, includes a continental breakfast.

The *Best Western Royal Holiday Motel* (☎ 505-722-4900, fax 505-722-6200), 1903 W Hwy 66, has about 50 spacious rooms from $60 to $90, with coffeemakers and some with microwaves and refrigerators. The *Best Western Red Rock Inn* (☎ 505-722-7600, fax 505-722-9770), 3010 E Hwy 66, has rooms from $65 to $80, some with balconies, and a few suites for up to $145. Both these hotels include continental breakfast. The *Best Western Inn & Suites* (☎ 505-722-2221, fax 505-722-7442), 3009 W Hwy 66, has a restaurant and bar with room service; its large rooms are $65 to $110 during summer, somewhat less at other times. The suites run up to $140. This and the Holidome are considered the best in town.

B&Bs About 20 miles east of town at exit 44 on I-40 is *Stauder's Navajo Lodge B&B* (☎ 505-862-7553), HC32-Box 1, Continental Divide, NM 87312. They rent two cottages, each with kitchen, living room and bathroom, for $85 to $95 a double including continental breakfast.

Places to Eat

Food in Gallup is pretty much standard Western fare – steak and seafood, burgers and fries, and a sprinkling of Italian, Chinese, Mexican and New Mexican cooking. There are no restaurants specializing in Native American food, though you find Navajo tacos offered on many menus.

Almost everybody seems to stop by the *Ranch Kitchen* (☎ 505-722-2537), 3001 W Hwy 66, open from 6 am to 9 pm daily (except Christmas) and till 10 pm in summer. It's been serving Mexican and American food since the 1950s, prices are reasonable, and the food is good. Beer and wine are available. Another good and slightly cheaper family restaurant that has been operating for almost half a century is *Earl's Restaurant* (☎ 505-863-4201), 1400 E Hwy 66, with a salad bar but no alcohol. If you prefer a smaller, mom-and-pop type place, try the inexpensive *Roadrunner Cafe* (☎ 505-722-7309), 3014 E Hwy 66. Both these serve breakfast, lunch and dinner daily except some major holidays.

Very hungry travelers on a tight budget can try the $4.99 all-you-can-eat specials offered from 11 am to 3 pm Monday to Saturday at the *King Dragon* (☎ 505-863-6300), 828 N Hwy 666. They are open from 11 am to 9 pm daily, till 10 pm on Friday and Saturday. Several other Chinese restaurants such as the *Golden Dragon* (☎ 505-722-5652), 1800 Zecca Plaza, and the *Beijing Restaurant* (☎ 505-863-2654), 1321 E Hwy 66, offer cheap lunch buffets. Fancier Chinese food is served at the locally popular *Avalon Restaurant* (☎ 505-863-5072), 1104 E Hwy 66.

For more upscale dining, *Panz Alegra* (☎ 505-722-7229), 1201 E Hwy 66, is a good choice. The food is Mexican and tasty; the carne adobada (pork in spicy sauce) is the house specialty. Italian and American meals are also served. It's not a fancy place, but it is locally popular and a good value. *Genaro's Cafe* (☎ 505-863-6761), 600 W Hill Ave, is a smaller place serving fine cheap Mexican food but no alcohol.

The better hotels offer good dining, especially the *El Rancho*, which is open from 6:30 am to 10 pm daily and offers good daily specials as well as à la carte meals in the $10 to $15 range. The menu is a decent selection of Mexican and American fare. Similarly priced meals are served in *Nicole's* at the Holiday Inn Holidome, and at the Best Western Inn & Suites.

For specialty coffees, stop by *The Coffee House* (☎ 505-726-0291), 203 W Coal Ave, open 7 am to 10 pm daily and till midnight on weekends. They also do soups, salads, sandwiches and desserts.

Night owls can grab a bite at *Kristy's Coffee Shop* (☎ 505-863-4742), 1310 E Hwy 66, or at the *Country Pride* (☎ 505-863-6801), in the Truckstops of America Plaza by exit 16 on I-40 west of town. Both are open 24 hours.

Entertainment

Local Native Americans perform social Indian dances at 7 pm nightly from Memorial Day to Labor Day by the Amtrak Station. Admission is free and photography is allowed.

Catch a movie at the *Aztec Twin Theaters* (☎ 505-863-4651), 911 W Aztec Ave, or at the *El Morro Theater* (☎ 505-722-7469), 207 W Coal Ave.

Shopping

Gallup has one of the country's biggest selection of stores selling Indian jewelry and other arts and crafts. The chamber of commerce provided me with a list of over 60 arts and crafts shops, galleries, trading posts and pawnbrokers, and there are others. Check out as many as you can if you are seriously interested in getting top-quality goods at fair prices. Many stores

are found downtown in the Historic District on Hwy 66.

Getting There & Away

Air America West Express (☎ 800-235-9292) has direct flights to Farmington and Phoenix, Arizona, several times a day from the Gallup Airport at the west end of town. City Cab (☎ 505-863-6864) goes there for about $5.

Bus The Greyhound Bus Station (☎ 505-863-3761), 225 E Hwy 66 (in the Amtrak building), has four daily buses to Flagstaff, Arizona (three hours 20 minutes), and Albuquerque (two and a half hours) with connections to other cities.

The Navajo Transit System (☎ 520-729-4115, 520-729-4002 in Window Rock, Arizona) has four buses Monday to Friday and three buses on Saturday from the Gallup Greyhound Station to Window Rock (45 minutes). Schedules change, so call the numbers above to find the best connections.

Train The Amtrak Station, 201 E Hwy 66, has a daily evening train to Flagstaff, Arizona, continuing to Los Angeles, California, and a morning train to Albuquerque continuing on to Chicago, Illinois. Book tickets in advance through Amtrak (☎ 800-872-7245). There is no ticket agent at the Gallup station. Amtrak provides an 'Indian Country Guide' who gives informative narration for the journey to or from Gallup.

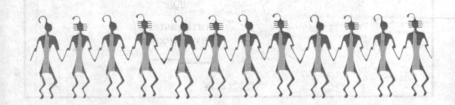

Northeastern New Mexico

Northeastern New Mexico is high plains country: grasslands stretching to infinity. Many travelers speed through along I-40 or I-25 on their way to or from Albuquerque, oblivious to the area's fascinating history or geological landmarks. Some of the oldest Paleo-Indian artifacts have been found at Folsom. The Santa Fe Trail provided a pioneering route through the area that would change Indian country forever.

Here, 19th-century towns with period architecture evoke a real feel of the Wild West. And the vastness of the rolling plains hides surprises: volcanoes, the best scuba diving in the Southwest, superb fishing, dinosaur footprints, hot springs and the best chances to see pronghorn antelopes in the Southwest.

I begin by describing the area along I-40, continue north from Las Vegas along I-25

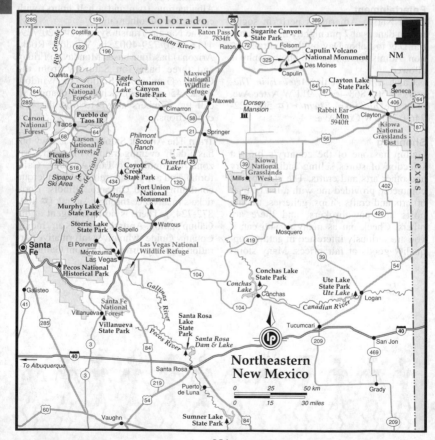

to the Colorado border and then move to the northeast corner of the state, abutting Colorado, Oklahoma and Texas.

I-40 Corridor East of Albuquerque

Santa Rosa, due east of Albuquerque, and Tucumcari, near the Texas state line, were once key stops along old Route 66, though today many travelers simply set their sights on the major cities. But they're bypassing many historical buildings as well as a surprising number of small lakes ideal for boating, fishing and other water activities.

SANTA ROSA

Santa Rosa's claim to fame is as the scuba diving capital of the Southwest. Admittedly, scuba diving is not a major Southwest attraction, and most travelers won't be carrying their diving gear with them. Nevertheless, Santa Rosa is locally called 'The City of Natural Lakes,' and these lakes interest divers seeking unusual dive sites.

Santa Rosa is on I-40, 114 miles east of Albuquerque. It is also 45 miles northwest of (and the nearest city to) Fort Sumner and the grave of Billy the Kid (see Southeastern New Mexico). Santa Rosa is the seat of sparsely populated Guadalupe County, which has less than 6000 inhabitants, about half of whom live in Santa Rosa.

Settled in the mid-19th century by Spanish farmers, the town is named after the chapel of Santa Rosa, built in 1879 by Don Celso Baca, one of the early settlers, in memory of his mother, Rosa. The roofless walls of the original chapel can be seen a quarter mile southeast of the newer church on the road to Puerto de Luna. Although it lies in ruins, the cemetery around it is still very much a part of the community.

Orientation

Santa Rosa lies on the Pecos River at the point where it's crossed by I-40. There are three freeway exits. From the western exit

273, the main street begins as Coronado St, then becomes Parker Ave through downtown, and then becomes Will Rogers Drive as it passes exits 275 and 277. This main thoroughfare is part of the celebrated Route 66, and most hotels and restaurants lie along it.

Information

The chamber of commerce (☎ 505-472-3763, 800-450-7084), 486 Parker, has tourist information and is open 8 am to 5 pm Monday to Friday. The library (☎ 505-472-3101) is at 208 5th. The local newspapers are the *Santa Rosa News* and the *Guadalupe County Communicator*. The post office (☎ 505-472-3743) is at 120 5th. The hospital (☎ 505-472-3417) is at 535 Lake Drive. The police (☎ 505-472-3605) are by the city hall on 4th.

Blue Hole

This hole in the sandstone is fed by a natural spring flowing at 3000 gallons a minute, which keeps the water both very clear and pretty cool (about 61° to 64°F). The hole, a favored destination for scuba divers and swimmers, is 80 feet in diameter at the surface and is bell-shaped, with a diameter reaching 130 feet below the surface. It is about 81 feet deep. Divers need a permit from the city hall; they also must use their dive tables with care, since the 4600-foot elevation changes atmospheric pressure considerably and makes the bottom equivalent to almost 100 feet at sea level.

Another dive site is **Perch Lake**, a short way south on Hwy 91, where a plane wreck lies submerged at 55 feet.

Not far west of Blue Hole, **Park Lake** offers a playground, tennis court, swimming, picnicking and fishing.

Puerto de Luna

This tiny village, 9 miles south of town, was founded in the 1860s and is one of the oldest settlements in New Mexico. It was the county seat from 1891 to 1903. Attractions include the old county courthouse, village church and various weathered adobe buildings. The drive there is pretty, winding through arroyos surrounded by eroded sandstone mesas. It is said that Billy the Kid used to hang out here.

Santa Rosa Lake State Park
This state park (☎ 505-472-3110), Box 384, Santa Rosa, NM 88435, about 8 miles north of Santa Rosa, offers boating, water-skiing, windsurfing, fishing, picnicking, camping (see Places to Stay) and a short nature trail to the visitor center. The lake, formed by a small dam across the Pecos River, attracts anglers from afar who fish for channel catfish, bass, walleye and crappie. Day use is $3 per vehicle.

From downtown Santa Rosa, turn north on 2nd and follow the signs.

Special Events
Santa Rosa Days, celebrated annually over Memorial Day weekend, features a parade, entertainment, many food booths, a softball tournament, a raft race and other sporting events.

The Annual Custom Car Show is held in August (usually the second weekend) and attracts vintage and classic car enthusiasts as well as folks driving strange things on wheels. There's a parade as well as live music and street dancing in the evening.

The third week in August sees Santa Rosa Fiestas, with local entertainment, a beauty-queen contest and crowning, and the bizarre annual Duck Drop, for which contestants buy squares and then wait for a duck suspended over the squares to poop – if the poop lands on your square, you win a cash prize.

Places to Stay
Camping The *KOA* (☎ 505-472-3126), 2136 Will Rogers Drive, has tent sites for $17 and RV sites with hookups for $24 or less according to season and which hookups you need. Kamping Kabins are $26.50 a double. Facilities include a coin laundry, showers, a café, playground and swimming pool. The small and much

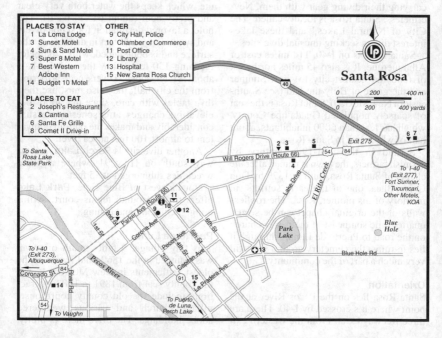

PLACES TO STAY
1 La Loma Lodge
3 Sunset Motel
4 Sun & Sand Motel
5 Super 8 Motel
7 Best Western Adobe Inn
14 Budget 10 Motel

PLACES TO EAT
2 Joseph's Restaurant & Cantina
6 Santa Fe Grille
8 Comet II Drive-in

OTHER
9 City Hall, Police
10 Chamber of Commerce
11 Post Office
12 Library
13 Hospital
15 New Santa Rosa Church

Santa Rosa

0   200   400 m
0   200   400 yards

To Santa Rosa Lake State Park

Will Rogers Drive (Route 66)

Exit 275
To I-40 (Exit 277), Fort Sumner, Tucumcari, Other Motels, KOA

Lake Drive
El Rito Creek

Park Lake
Blue Hole

Blue Hole Rd

To I-40 (Exit 273), Albuquerque

Pecos River
Coronado St
River Rd
Parker Ave
2nd St
1st St
Corona Ave
Pecos Ave
Capitan Ave
3rd St
4th St
5th St
6th St
La Pradera Ave

To Vaughn

To Puerto de Luna, Perch Lake

more basic *Donnie's RV Park* (☎ 505-472-3942), 2100 Will Rogers Drive, is just $10 with hookups. *Ramblin' Rose RV Park* (☎ 505-472-3820) on Hwy 54 and Black, southwest of town, has showers and is $12 with hookups.

Seven miles away at *Santa Rosa Lake State Park* (☎ 505-472-3110), there are tent sites for $7 and RV sites with partial hookups for $11. Showers are available.

Hotels Santa Rosa has many inexpensive motels catering to I-40 traffic. Summer rates are given – expect discounts at other times.

The cheapest is the basic family-operated *La Mesa Motel* (☎ 505-472-3031), 2415 Will Rogers Drive, which charges $17 a single. Other mom-and-pop motels in the $20s for two people include the friendly *Budget 10 Motel* (☎ 505-472-3454 or 3898), 120 Hwy 54; *La Loma Lodge* (☎ 505-472-3379), 736 Parker Ave; *Sunset Motel* (☎ 505-472-3762), 929 Will Rogers Drive; and *Sun & Sand Motel* (☎ 505-472-5268), 1120 Will Rogers Drive, with a restaurant. There are several others that look OK. The *Shawford Motel* (☎ 505-472-3494), 1819 Will Rogers Drive, has a decent restaurant and nicer rooms in the $30s.

Mid-priced chains include the *Motel 6* (☎ 505-472-3045, fax 505-472-5923), 3400 Will Rogers Drive, at $36/42 and with a pool; *Super 8 Motel* (☎ 505-472-5388, fax 505-472-5388), 1201 Will Rogers Drive, at $38.88/46.88 with continental breakfast; *Days Inn* (☎ 505-472-5985, fax 505-472-5989), 1830 Will Rogers Drive, with rooms in the $50s with continental breakfast; *Best Western Adobe Inn* (☎ 505-472-3446, fax 505-472-5759), 1501 Will Rogers Drive, and *Best Western Santa Rosa Inn* (☎ 505-472-5877, fax 505-472-5800), 3022 Will Rogers Drive, both with continental breakfast, seasonal outdoor pool and rooms in the $50s; *Comfort Inn* (☎ 505-472-5570, fax 505-472-5575), 3343 Will Rogers Drive, with standard rooms in the $60s and $70s with continental breakfast and a year-round indoor pool; and *Holiday Inn Express* (☎ 505-472-

5411, fax 505-472-3537), at 3202 Will Rogers Drive, with an indoor pool, spa, continental breakfast and nicer rooms in the $50s, $60s and $70s.

Places to Eat

The town's Hispanic heritage is evident – almost all the restaurants advertise 'Mexican and American food.' Some claim to be a 'Historic Route 66 Restaurant' and back this up with nostalgia on the walls. The following are in this category. *Joseph's Restaurant & Cantina* (☎ 505-472-3361), 865 Will Rogers Drive, is the most popular place for inexpensive Mexican and American food. The *Comet II Drive-in* (☎ 505-472-3663), 239 Parker Ave, has decent, reasonable food with choices beyond the usual burgers and fries. The *Route 66 Restaurant* at the Shawford Motel is also OK. All are open for breakfast, lunch and dinner.

The most upscale place in town (though moderately priced and far from fancy) is the *Santa Fe Grille* (☎ 505-472-5689), 1429 Will Rogers Drive, with Southwestern food from 11 am to 9 pm daily.

Getting There & Away

Greyhound (☎ 505-472-5720) stops at Mateo's restaurant, 500 Coronado W (which has OK cheap food). However, the Greyhound stop has moved several times in recent years. There are buses west to Albuquerque and east to Tucumcari and Amarillo, Texas, four times daily.

VAUGHN

This small town, about 40 miles southwest of Santa Rosa, is near the intersections of Hwys 60, 54 and 285 and serves a large rural area. There's not much to do here, but there are half a dozen simple motels, of which the best is the *Bel-Air Motel* (☎ 505-584-2241) with rooms in the $30s. Among the others are the *Ranch View Motel* (☎ 505-584-2264), *Sands Motel* (☎ 505-584-2522), *Skyline Motel* (☎ 505-584-2981) and *Western Motel* (☎ 505-584-2391), all along Hwy 60.

TUCUMCARI

The origin of the name Tucumcari is unknown, though locals suggest a legend of love between Apache Indians named Tocom and Kari. As the biggest town on I-40 between Albuquerque (173 miles west) and Amarillo, Texas (114 miles east), Tucumcari (population 7000) caters to travelers – tourism is a mainstay of the local economy. Founded in 1901 as a railway town, it soon became the seat of Quay County. When Route 66 was opened in the 1920s, Tucumcari became an obligatory stop for travelers; today, with faster freeway speeds, many travelers simply drive on through. Nevertheless, there still are many inexpensive motels here, and signs advertise 'Tucumcari Tonight' for 300 miles in either direction along the interstate. This is a good, economical place to rest up.

Orientation

Tucumcari lies to the north of I-40 between exits 329 and 335. The main west-east thoroughfare between these exits is old Route 66, called Tucumcari Blvd through downtown. The principal north-south artery is 1st, which intersects I-40 at exit 332. The old downtown area around 1st and Main is slowly being restored.

Information

The chamber of commerce (☎ 505-461-1694), 404 W Tucumcari Blvd, is open 9 am to noon and 1 to 5 pm Monday to Friday. The library (☎ 505-461-0295) is at 602 S 2nd. The *Quay County Sun* is the local newspaper, published biweekly. The post office (☎ 505-461-0370) is at 222 S 1st. The hospital (☎ 505-461-0141) is at 301 Miel de Luna. The police (☎ 505-461-2160) are at 215 E Center.

Tucumcari Historical Museum

This museum (☎ 505-461-4201), 416 S Adams, displays an eclectic mixture of local memorabilia, including thousands of items ranging from Indian artifacts to a barbed-wire collection. Several rooms are reconstructions of early Western interiors, such as a sheriff's office, classroom and hospital room. Admission is $2 for adults and 50¢ for six- to 15-year-olds. Summer hours are 9 am to 6 pm Monday to Saturday and 1 to 6 pm Sunday. During the rest of the year, they close one hour earlier and take Monday off.

Mesalands Dinosaur Museum

This new museum (☎ 505-461-4413), 222 E Laughlin, is due to open in the spring of 1999, with replicas, dioramas, hands-on exhibits and lectures on paleontology and geology. Call for details.

Ladd S Gordon Wildlife Preserve

At the east end of town off Tucumcari Blvd, the 770-acre preserve encompasses Tucumcari Lake, which attracts many overwintering ducks, geese and other water birds. The preserve is recommended for bird watchers. Ducks begin arriving in mid-October, and geese a month later. Though still under development, the preserve is open to visitors, who can reach it by taking a gravel road north of the Motel 6.

Activities

Cool off at the municipal **pool** (☎ 505-461-4582), 415 W Hines. You can also **golf** at the City Golf Course (☎ 505-461-1849), is on the west side of town.

Special Events

The Quay County Fair and Route 66 Festival & Crafts Fair happen together over several days in mid-August. Arts & Crafts Fairs are held during weekends in early June and early December.

Places to Stay – Camping

The *KOA* (☎ 505-461-1841), a quarter mile east of exit 355, has tent sites for $15.50, RV sites with hookups for $20 and Kamping Kabins for $25 a double. Facilities include showers, a coin laundry, pool, game room and playground. The *Mountain Rd RV Park* (☎ 505-461-9628), 1700 Mountain Rd, offers RV sites with hookups for $15 and tent sites for $9. There are

NEW MEXICO

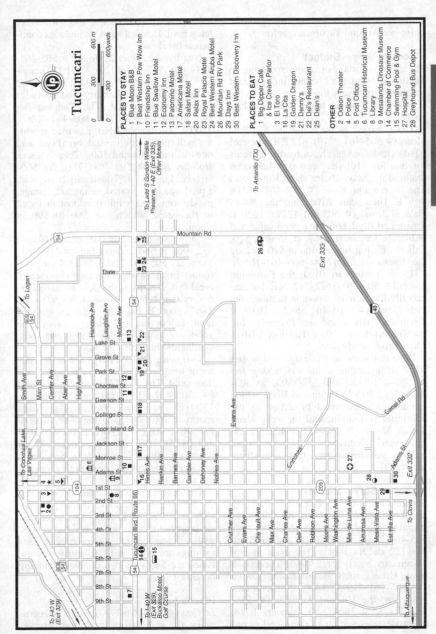

Tucumcari

0   300   600 m
0   300   600 yards

To Ladd S Gordon Wildlife
Preserve, I-40 E (Exit 335)

To Amarillo (TX)

Mountain Rd

Exit 335

To Logan

To Conchas Lake,
Las Vegas

To I-40 W
(Exit 329)

To I-40 W
Buckaroo Motel,
Golf Course

To Clovis

To Albuquerque

Exit 332

PLACES TO STAY
1   Blue Moon B&B
7   Best Western Pow Wow Inn
10 Friendship Inn
11 Blue Swallow Motel
12 Economy Inn
13 Palomino Motel
17 Americana Motel
18 Safari Motel
20 Relax Inn
23 Royal Palacio Motel
24 Best Western Aruba Motel
26 Mountain Rd RV Park
29 Days Inn
30 Best Western Discovery Inn

PLACES TO EAT
1   Big Dipper Café
    & Ice Cream Parlor
3   El Toro
16 La Cita
19 Golden Dragon
21 Denny's
22 Del's Restaurant
25 Dean's

OTHER
2   Odeon Theater
4   Police
5   Post Office
6   Tucumcari Historical Museum
8   Library
9   Mesalands Dinosaur Museum
14 Chamber of Commerce
15 Swimming Pool & Gym
27 Hospital
28 Greyhound Bus Depot

showers, coin laundry and playground. (Also see Around Tucumcari, below.)

Places to Stay – Budget

There is no shortage of accommodations in Tucumcari, and the cheaper independent hotels advertise very low prices most of the year – don't expect luxury and do shop around.

The cheapest is the old *Blue Swallow Motel* (☎ 505-461-9849), 815 E Tucumcari Blvd, which for years has advertised rooms for two for $10! (Its neon sign has been featured in many articles about Route 66.) The *Americana Motel* (☎ 505-461-0431), 406 E Tucumcari Blvd, and the *Royal Palacio Motel* (☎ 505-461-1212), 1620 E Tucumcari Blvd, both are a good value and publicize rooms starting at around $20. Others offering rooms around $20 include the *Buckaroo Motel* (☎ 505-461-1650), 1315 W Tucumcari Blvd; the *Palomino Motel* (☎ 505-461-3622), 1215 E Tucumcari Blvd, which has a pool in summer; the *Relax Inn* (☎ 505-461-3862), 1010 E Tucumcari Blvd; and the *Economy Inn* (☎ 505-461-1340), 901 E Tucumcari Blvd. There are several others.

Decent rooms in the mid- and upper $20s are available at the *Friendship Inn* (☎ 505-461-0330, 800-537-3893, fax 505-461-0330), 315 E Tucumcari Blvd, which includes a continental breakfast in the adjoining restaurant, and the very clean *Safari Motel* (☎ 505-461-3642), 722 E Tucumcari Blvd. Both these have a pool open in summer. Again, there are others under $30.

Places to Stay – Middle

Several chain hotels are near I-40 exit 335 at the east end of Tucumcari Blvd. The old standby, *Motel 6* (☎ 505-461-4791, fax 505-461-2283), 2900 E Tucumcari Blvd, has 122 decent rooms (the most in any Tucumcari hotel) for $34/40. There is a pool. Others such as the *Econo Lodge* (☎ 505-461-4194), 3400 E Tucumcari Blvd, and the *Howard Johnson* (☎ 505-461-2747), at 3604 E Tucumcari Blvd, advertise rates similar to the Motel 6 and

have less spartan rooms, though neither has a pool. Howard Johnson includes continental breakfast.

Nearby, the *Super 8 Motel* (☎ 505-461-4444, fax 505-461-4320), 4001 E Tucumcari Blvd, charges $41/45 and has an indoor pool, coin laundry and includes continental breakfast. The *Comfort Inn* (☎ 505-461-4094, fax 505-461-4099), 2800 E Tucumcari Blvd, has nice rooms, a small pool, continental breakfast and rates in the $50s and $60s. There's also a *Holiday Inn* (☎ 505-461-3780, fax 505-461-3931), 3716 E Tucumcari Blvd, with a pool, spa, playground, restaurant, lounge, good rooms and a full breakfast included in the rates, which run $60 to $90 in summer.

At the south end of 1st, near I-40 exit 332, you'll find a *Days Inn* (☎ 505-461-3158, fax 505-461-2205), 2623 S 1st, with rooms in the $40s including continental breakfast. Nearby is the *Best Western Discovery Inn* (☎ 505-461-4884, fax 505-461-2463), 200 E Estrella, with an outdoor pool, indoor spa and exercise room. The good-size rooms are in the $50s and $60s, continental breakfast included.

Two more Best Westerns are in the center of town and both have a seasonal outdoor pool. The *Best Western Aruba Motel* (☎ 505-461-3335, fax 505-461-6269), 1700 E Tucumcari Blvd, has standard rooms in the $40s, and the *Best Western Pow Wow Inn* (☎ 505-461-0500, fax 505-461-0135), 801 W Tucumcari Blvd, charges in the $50s and $60s and has a restaurant and lounge bar with live music – the nicest bar in town.

The recently opened *Blue Moon B&B* (☎ 505-461-4430), above the Big Dipper Café at 101 S 2nd in the historic area, has six large bedrooms sharing two bathrooms, with kitchen and laundry privileges. Furnishings are from the 1930s and 1940s era. Rates are $45 to $75 a double, including breakfast.

Places to Eat

La Cita (☎ 505-461-3930), 812 S 1st, earns praise for its Mexican food. It also serves inexpensive American food from 11 am to 9 pm daily. Another good, low-budget Mexican/American café is *El Toro* (☎ 505-461-3328), 107 S 1st, open from 11 am to 7 pm daily. The *Golden Dragon* (☎ 505-461-2853), 1006 E Tucumcari Blvd, has served decent Chinese food since 1966. Hours are 11 am to 2:30 pm and 4 to 9:30 pm daily.

Denny's (☎ 505-461-3094), 1102 E Tucumcari Blvd, and the *Terminal Cafe* (☎ 505-461-9649), at the truck stop at the west end of town, are both open 24 hours. *Dean's* (☎ 505-461-3470), 1806 E Tucumcari Blvd, is one of those fairly bland family restaurants that serves a little of everything – American, Mexican and Italian food for breakfast, lunch and dinner. *Del's Restaurant* (☎ 505-461-1740), 1202 E Tucumcari Blvd, is open 6 am to 9 pm, with good Mexican/American food and one of the town's best salad bars.

Note that most of these places don't serve alcohol. For a drink, eat at one of the hotel restaurants – the one at the Best Western Pow Wow Inn is one of the town's best.

For light meals and excellent ice cream treats, head over to *The Big Dipper Café & Ice Cream Parlor* (☎ 505-461-4430), 101 S 2nd, in a turn-of-the-19th-century building with art deco embellishments. They open at 9 am during the week, noon on Saturday and 2 pm on Sunday and close at 7 pm (later in summer). The Big Dipper also has the largest selection of vitamins, herbs and health supplies in northeastern New Mexico.

Entertainment

The renovated old *Odeon Theater* (☎ 505-461-0100), 123 S 2nd, shows movies. The *Pow Wow Inn* has live music most nights and dancing on weekends.

The *Caprock Amphitheater* (☎ 505-576-2519), 21 miles east of Tucumcari (8 miles south of San Jon), is where the New Mexico Outdoor Drama Association (☎ 505-576-2455) presents historical Western performances during summer weekends (Billy the Kid shows are the most popular). Some shows include a BBQ dinner.

Getting There & Away

Buses to Albuquerque and Amarillo, Texas, depart four times daily from the Greyhound Bus Terminal (☎ 505-461-1350), 2618 S 1st (behind McDonald's).

AROUND TUCUMCARI
Ute Lake State Park

This park (☎ 505-487-2284), Box 52, Logan, NM 88426, is 26 miles northeast of Tucumcari or 3 miles west of the small village of Logan.

The 12-sq-mile lake is reportedly the second largest in New Mexico, and the fishing is noted for crappie and walleye. There is also boating, hiking, picnicking and camping. The Mine Canyon Entrance, a few miles southwest of Logan, leads to a boat ramp with no other facilities. The South Entrance (the main entrance) is via Hwy 540, which leaves Hwy 54 at the southwest side of Logan. This leads to *two campgrounds* with tent and RV sites for $7/11.

If you don't want to camp in the state park, the village of **Logan**, 23 miles northeast of Tucumcari on Hwy 54, is the nearest settlement. Stay at *Ute Lake Motor Inn* (☎ 505-487-2245), off Hwy 540 west of Logan, which is near a boat ramp. In town, there is the *Village Inn Motel* (☎ 505-467-2247 or 2147) and the basic *Yucca Motel* (☎ 505-487-2272).

The *Fireside Cafe* (☎ 505-487-9696) offers inexpensive American food.

Conchas Lake State Park

This park (☎ 505-868-2270), Box 976, Conchas Dam, Logan, NM 88416, is 32 miles northwest of Tucumcari on Hwy 104. The main attraction is excellent fishing, especially for walleye, crappie, bass and catfish. Swimming, boating, golf, a children's playground, picnicking and camping are other attractions. *Conchas Lodge*, at the south end of the lake, has a restaurant and lounge (weekend entertainment in summer), groceries and rooms in the low-to mid price range. At the north end of the lake is a marina with boat rentals. Camping is available in more than 100 developed sites in four areas for $7, or $11 with RV hookups. There are more undeveloped sites.

The park is very popular, with fishing competitions drawing hundreds of entrants. On busy summer weekends there may be up to 400 boats on the lake and many thousands of visitors.

Las Vegas to Colorado

This stretch of I-25 largely traces the route of the Santa Fe Trail. Las Vegas and Raton were both important centers of trade in the late 1800s, and both towns retain the flavor of that era in their many well-preserved buildings. The area is dotted with small lakes and canyons of breathtaking beauty. If you're looking for a bit of the Old West without a patina of consumer hype, this is the place.

LAS VEGAS

Las Vegas is the largest and oldest New Mexican town east of the Sangre de Cristo Mountains. The area was inhabited mainly by Comanches until 15 Hispanic families received a grant from the Mexican government to found Las Vegas in 1835. The importance of the town grew with the Santa Fe Trail, and when the US assumed possession in 1846, there were 1500 Hispanic inhabitants.

The building of nearby Fort Union in 1851 and the arrival of the railroad in 1879 both spurred progress. Las Vegas was a rough and booming town, attracting cattle barons and cattle rustlers, outlaws and gunslingers, as well as honest pioneers trying to make a living. During the late 1800s, Las Vegas was the most important city in New Mexico, and many buildings were constructed. Historians claim that there are more than 900 19th-century buildings in Las Vegas listed on the National Register of Historic Places.

Today, a majority of the inhabitants claim Hispanic heritage, and Las Vegas remains an important center for transportation, commerce and ranching. Tourism is playing an ever-bigger role in the town's economy. Visitors come to savor the historic but uncrowded streets and to take advantage of the area's outdoor recreational opportunities.

Orientation & Information

Las Vegas is on I-25, 64 miles east of Santa Fe and 109 miles south of Raton. The main street is Hwy 85 or Grand Ave, which runs north-south, paralleling the interstate.

With a population of around 16,000, Las Vegas is 6436 feet above sea level, and it's the San Miguel County Seat. Average high/low temperatures in January are 46°/18°F and in July are 83°/54°F. The chamber of commerce (☎ 505-425-8631), 727 Grand Ave, is in the same building as the City Museum. Tourist information is available from 9 am to 5 pm Monday to Thursday, and 9 am to 4 pm Friday.

The Santa Fe National Forest Ranger Station (☎ 505-425-3534) is at 1926 7th. The library (☎ 505-454-1403) is at 500 National. The local newspaper is the *Las Vegas Daily Optic*. The main post office (☎ 505-425-9387) is at 1001 Douglas. The hospital (☎ 505-425-6751) is at 1235 8th. The police (☎ 505-425-7504) are at 318 Moreno.

Historical Buildings

The chamber of commerce has brochures describing walks in various historical districts. The historical center is the Old Plaza, at the intersection of S Pacific and Bridge. The **Plaza Hotel** (built in 1880) is still in use. To the right are the **Ilfeld Buildings** (where the Los Artesanos Bookstore is), which were built and improved upon between 1867 and 1921. Next to the bookstore are the adobe **Dice Apartments**, parts of which predate the annexation by the USA in 1846. The **First National Bank** at the southeast corner of the plaza dates from 1880. Several more historical buildings are on and near the plaza and along Bridge.

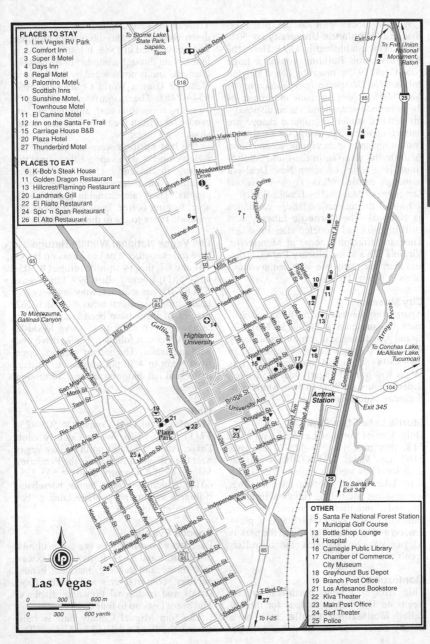

PLACES TO STAY
1 Las Vegas RV Park
2 Comfort Inn
3 Super 8 Motel
4 Days Inn
9 Regal Motel
9 Palomino Motel,
   Scottish Inns
10 Sunshine Motel,
   Townhouse Motel
11 El Camino Motel
12 Inn on the Santa Fe Trail
15 Carriage House B&B
20 Plaza Hotel
27 Thunderbird Motel

PLACES TO EAT
6 K-Bob's Steak House
11 Golden Dragon Restaurant
13 Hillcrest/Flamingo Restaurant
20 Landmark Grill
22 El Rialto Restaurant
24 Spic 'n Span Restaurant
26 El Alto Restaurant

OTHER
5 Santa Fe National Forest Station
7 Municipal Golf Course
13 Bottle Shop Lounge
14 Hospital
16 Carnegie Public Library
17 Chamber of Commerce,
   City Museum
18 Greyhound Bus Depot
19 Branch Post Office
21 Los Artesanos Bookstore
22 Kiva Theater
23 Main Post Office
24 Serf Theater
25 Police

Las Vegas

NEW MEXICO

A few blocks east of the plaza on Bridge is **Highlands University** (☎ 505-425-7511), established in 1893. Here, the Administration Building houses a huge New Deal (1930s) mural by Lloyd Moylan entitled *The Dissemination of Education in New Mexico*. Moylan made clever use of the rather odd-shaped walls at his disposal – his detailed studies of cultural change are painted on three high walls over a stairway, continuing up to arches on the second floor. Also on the campus, in the Ilfeld Auditorium, is a series of seven New Deal-era paintings entitled *Music Is the Universal Language of Mankind* by Brooks Willis.

East of the university, Bridge continues as National. The **Carnegie Library** was built in 1903 and modeled after President Thomas Jefferson's home at Monticello, Virginia. This is the **Library Park** district, and there are many late-19th-century mansions in nearby blocks.

City Museum

Apart from the usual local historical artifacts, this museum (☎ 505-425-8726), 729 Grand Ave, features an exhibit about Teddy Roosevelt's Rough Riders, who fought in the 1898 Spanish-American War. Las Vegas was home to nearly half the Rough Riders. Hours are 9 am to 4 pm Monday to Saturday. Admission is free.

Storrie Lake State Park

Only 4 miles north of Las Vegas on Hwy 518, this park (☎ 505-425-7278), Box 3167, Las Vegas, NM 87701, is popular with locals as well as visitors. The 1100-acre lake offers boating, windsurfing, water-skiing and fishing (rainbow trout are stocked), and there are picnic grounds, campsites (see Places to Stay), a playground and showers. Day use of the park is $3 per vehicle; walk-ins and bicyclists aren't charged.

Montezuma

This village, 5 miles northwest of Las Vegas on Hwy 65, is famous for the so-called **Montezuma Castle**, built as a luxury hotel near the local hot springs.

There were several hotels on the site, all destroyed by fire, and the present building was constructed in 1886. It lost money as a hotel, went through a number of ownership changes, and is now owned by the Armand Hammer United World College (☎ 505-454-4248). The magnificent building is awaiting restoration and, although closed, can be seen from the road. Tours are occasionally arranged.

The **hot springs** were named after the Aztec emperor who supposedly visited the springs in the early 1500s. The waters reputedly have curative and therapeutic powers. There are changing rooms available; bathing is free. Look for holes in the roadside fence to get to the best pools.

Las Vegas National Wildlife Refuge

Five miles southeast of Las Vegas on Hwys 104 and 67, this 14-sq-mile refuge (☎ 505-425-3581), Route 1, Box 399, Las Vegas, NM 87701, has marshes, woodlands, grasslands and agricultural areas on which 262 species of birds have been recorded. The refuge is open daily from dawn to dusk, and visitors can follow a 7-mile drive and walking trails. The ranger station, open from 8 am to 4:30 pm Monday to Friday, has a bird list and information. Admission is free.

Golf

The Municipal Golf Course (☎ 505-425-7711) is off Mills Ave at Country Club Drive. About 20 miles north of Las Vegas near the village of Rociada is the Pendaries Village Golf & Country Club (☎ 505-425-6018), which also offers tennis, horseback riding, a swimming pool, restaurant, bar and accommodations.

Special Events

Las Vegas Fourth of July is a colorful mix of Hispanic and Anglo festivities: Mexican folk music and dancing, mariachi bands, parades, contests, arts and crafts, food stands and traditional fireworks displays. The event lasts up to four days.

The San Miguel County Fair is held around the third weekend in August. The

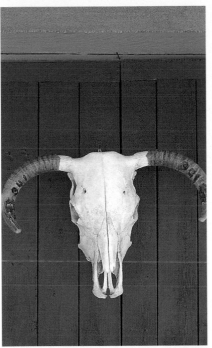

BONNIE KAMIN

BONNIE KAMIN

CHUCK PLACE

Top Left: Taos, New Mexico
Bottom: San Juan Deer Dance, Gallup Inter-Tribal
   Indian Ceremonial, Gallup, New Mexico

Top Right: Standing Deer, Taos Pueblo, New Mexico

Top Left: Ristra, Old Town, Albuquerque, New Mexico
Bottom: Fort Union National Monument, New Mexico

Top Right: Inter-Tribal Rodeo, Gallup, New Mexico
Middle Right: Southwestern sun

People's Faire, sponsored by the Arts Council, has both performing and mixed-media arts and crafts in the Carnegie Library Park on the last weekend in August. A Christmas lights parade is held after sunset on the first Saturday of December.

Rails 'n Trail Days and Santa Fe Heritage Days, with changing dates from year to year, celebrate the town's history with train rides, a rodeo, country dancing, barbecue, historical reenactments (from shootouts to sheep-shearing) and old-fashioned fun.

The chamber of commerce has information about these and other events.

Places to Stay – Camping
The *KOA* (☎ 505-454-0180) is 4 miles south of downtown off I-25 exit 339. Rates start at $15 for tent campers, $20 for RV hookups. Kamping Kabins are $26 a double. There are showers, a laundry, playground, pool and recreation area. It is open from March to mid-November.

Las Vegas RV Park (☎ 505-425-5630), 504 Harris Rd (north of town off 7th), is open year-round with tent and RV sites for $10 to $16. There are showers.

At Storrie Lake State Park, tent sites are $7, and sites with RV hookups are $11. The campground fills up on summer weekends. Also see Around Las Vegas below.

Places to Stay – Budget
Summer rates are given; rates the rest of the year are marginally lower.

Several places on Grand Ave near Baca Ave charge in the high $20s for singles and the low to mid $30s for doubles (one bed). These motels include: the *Sunshine Motel* (☎ 505-425-3506), 1201 Grand Ave; the *Palomino Motel* (☎ 505-425-3548), 1330 Grand Ave; *Scottish Inns* (☎ 505-425-9357), 1216 Grand Ave; the *Townhouse Motel* (☎ 505-425-6717), 1215 Grand Ave; and the *Regal Motel* (☎ 505-454-1456), 1809 Grand Ave. The last two have larger than average rooms. The *El Camino Motel* (☎ 505-425-5994), 1152 Grand Ave, and the *Thunderbird Motel* (☎ 505-454-1471), at the south end of Grand Ave near I-25, are a few dollars

more. All of these appear to be reasonably well-kept budget motels.

Places to Stay – Middle
Hotels The *Super 8 Motel* (☎ 505-425-5288, fax 505-425-8481), 2029 Grand Ave, charges $41.88/46.88 for singles/doubles with one bed or $49.88 with two beds. Rates are $4 less off-season. The *Days Inn* (☎ 505-425-1967, fax 505-454-8130), 2000 Grand Ave, charges about $50/60, including continental breakfast, and has a small indoor pool and spa. The *Comfort Inn* (☎ 505-425-1100, fax 505-454-8404), 2500 Grand Ave near I-25 exit 347, has similar amenities and prices; it's the biggest place in town with over a hundred rooms.

The *Inn on the Santa Fe Trail* (☎ 505-425-6791, fax 505-425-0417), 1133 Grand Ave, is set in tree-filled grounds and has attractive rooms with Southwestern décor. They have a heated outdoor pool and spa and charge in the $50s and $60s, including continental breakfast.

Las Vegas' most celebrated lodging is the *Plaza Hotel* (☎ 505-425-3591, 800-328-1882, fax 505-425-9659, plazanewmex@nmhu.campus.mci.net), 230 Old Town Plaza. Opened in 1882, the elegant building overlooking the historical town plaza was then the best in New Mexico. The hotel was carefully remodeled a century later and now offers comfortable accommodations in antique-filled rooms. Rates are a good value at about $59/65 for most singles/doubles and up to about $110 for suites – reservations are advised. There is a good restaurant and bar, and room service is available.

B&Bs The *Carriage House B&B* (☎ 505-454-1784), 925 6th, Las Vegas, NM 87701, is a house dating from the 1890s. Its six rooms are charmingly decorated with period pieces and some have private bathrooms. Rates are $55/75 with shared/private bathroom and include a full breakfast for two.

Places to Eat
Open daily from 7 am to 6 pm, the *Spic 'n Span* (☎ 505-425-6481), 713 Douglas, is a

NEW MEXICO

good, locally popular choice for breakfast and lunch. It is especially busy at breakfast time, when half the town seems to stop by for the Mexican and American fare. Another good place is the *Hillcrest/ Flamingo Restaurant* (☎ 505-425-7211), 1106 Grand Ave, which serves breakfasts and Mexican and American food at low to moderate prices from 6 am to 8:45 pm daily. Nearby is the *Golden Dragon* (☎ 505-425-8522), 1336 Grand Ave, with reasonably priced Chinese food served from 11 am to 2:30 pm Monday to Friday and 4:30 to 9 pm daily.

El Alto Restaurant (☎ 505-454-0808), at the western end of Sapello overlooking the city, is also called the 'supper club' because it's open only from 6 to 9 pm Tuesday through Saturday. A Las Vegas institution, this restaurant is famous for its steak meals. Cheaper Mexican food is available, and there is a bar with music on some nights. Steaks are also served at the more moderately priced *K-Bob's* (☎ 505-425-6322), 1803 7th, which is open from 11 am to 8:45 pm daily and has a good salad bar.

A good choice is *El Rialto Restaurant* (☎ 505-454-0037), 141 Bridge, which is in a late Victorian building in the historic center. It is locally popular and serves a wide range of meals from 10:30 am to 9 pm daily except Sunday. Also on this same block are a couple of erratically open cafés serving espresso and other coffees.

The historic Plaza Hotel has the elegant *Landmark Grill* (☎ 505-425-3591), which is considered the best restaurant in town. It serves a reasonably priced breakfast and lunch from 7 am to 2 pm and a fine dinner menu from 5 to 9 pm daily. Dinner reservations are a good idea.

Entertainment
The *Serf Theater* (☎ 505-425-1188), 707 Douglas Ave, and the historic *Kiva Theater* (☎ 505-454-0152), 109 Bridge, show nightly movies. The *Bottle Shop Lounge* (☎ 505-454-0373), 1130 Grand Ave, sometimes has live country & western music and dancing. The *Plaza Hotel Bar* has occasional entertainment. Cafés and coffee shops on Bridge St may have poetry readings or folk music.

Shopping
Los Artesanos Bookstore (☎ 505-425-8331), 220 Old Town Plaza, has an excellent selection of used and rare books on Las Vegas and the Southwest. Other bookstores are found along historic Bridge St, tucked away among funky art galleries and antique stores – a fun place to browse and shop.

Getting There & Away
Bus Greyhound and TNM&O buses (☎ 505-425-8689) go to Raton, Santa Fe and beyond. The bus stop is outside Classic Travel & Tours (☎ 505-454-1415), 834 Grand Ave, which sells bus, train and plane tickets.

Train Amtrak (☎ 800-872-7245) runs a daily train to Chicago, Illinois, and to Los Angeles, California.

AROUND LAS VEGAS
Gallinas Canyon
Beyond Montezuma, Hwy 65 climbs up to the attractive scenery of Gallinas Canyon in the Santa Fe National Forest. Six miles beyond Montezuma is the village of **El Porvenir**, where there is the *Mountain Music Guest Ranch* (☎ 505-454-0565), with five cabins for rent for about $100, or *El Rito de San José* (☎ 505-425-7027), with 10 cabins for about $60. In Gallinas Canyon, beyond El Porvenir, you can throw up a tent at the *El Porvenir* and *EV Long* USFS campgrounds, where sites go for $6 per night. The campgrounds are open from May to October, water is available, and there is hiking and fishing nearby. Free dispersed camping is also possible. During the winter, the Gallinas River freezes, and there is ice-skating and cross-country skiing.

Sapello
This tiny village, 13 miles north of Las Vegas on Hwy 518, has the *Star Hill Inn* (☎ 505-425-5605), which calls itself 'an

astronomers' retreat in the Rockies.' Set at 7200 feet, the inn is far from interference from city lights. Various telescopes are available for rent, and astronomy and bird-watching workshops are offered several times a year. Seven comfortable cottages with fireplaces and kitchens rent from $70 to $120, and a two-night minimum is required. The inn is on 195 acres, and hiking and cross-country skiing trails are available. There are no stores nearby, so bring food for the kitchens.

Fort Union National Monument
Fort Union was established in 1851 to protect both Santa Fe and the Santa Fe Trail from Indian attack. It was the largest fort in the Southwest and was critical in mounting a defense against Confederate soldiers during the Civil War. It remained very important until the railway arrived in 1879. By 1891, the fort had been abandoned, and today nothing remains except for a surprisingly large area of crumbling walls in the middle of the grasslands. A visitor center provides an informative exhibit and display of area artifacts, and there is a self-guided tour of the ruins.

Fort Union National Monument (☎ 505-425-8025), Watrous, NM 87753, is 26 miles north of Las Vegas. Take I-25 to Watrous and then Hwy 161 to Fort Union. Hours are 8 am to 5 pm daily (except December 25 and January 1) and extend to 6 pm in summer. Admission is $4 per vehicle, $2 for bicyclists or bus passengers and free with Golden Eagle, Age and Access Passes. There are picnic sites but nowhere to stay or camp.

Villanueva State Park
This park (☎ 505-421-2957), Villanueva, NM 87583, lies in a red rock canyon on the Pecos River valley. The valley was a main travel route for Indians and, in the 1500s, for the Spanish conquistadors. A small visitor center and self-guided trails explain the history. Other attractions include trout fishing on the Pecos River, a playground, picnicking and camping (with showers).

The park is 35 miles south of Las Vegas. Take I-25 south for 22 miles to Hwy 3; follow Hwy 3 south for 12 miles to the park entrance. Day use is $3. Camping is $7, and RV sites with hookups are $11.

En route to the park along Hwy 3 are the Spanish colonial villages of **Villanueva** and **San Miguel** (the latter with a fine church built in 1805). All around are the vineyards of **Madison Winery**; the tasting room (☎ 505-421-8028) is on Hwy 3 just north of I-25 (follow the signs).

MORA & AROUND
This small Hispanic village is the Mora County seat. The beautiful rural area was once an important wheat-farming region, but is now economically depressed. Driving through, you'll see tumbledown adobe buildings and a variety of farm animals including alpacas (just east of town on Hwy 434).

Accommodation is limited to the simple *Motel Almanzar* (☎ 505-387-5230) and the little *St Vrain B&B* (☎ 505-387-2471).

Cleveland Roller Mill Museum
Two miles north of Mora on Hwy 518, there's a local history museum inside the Cleveland Roller Mill (☎ 505-387-2645), which was one of the county's major flour mills around 1900. Hours are 10 am to 5 pm, Memorial Day to October 31, and by appointment at other times. Admission is $2 for adults, $1 for seven- to 18-year-olds.

Morphy Lake State Park
This park (☎ 505-387-2328) is 6 miles southwest of Mora along Hwy 94. The last 2 miles to the lake are very narrow, steep, rutted and unsuitable for motor homes, trailers or ordinary cars.

The pretty lake is set at over 8000 feet in conifer forests. There is trout fishing and a small boat ramp for self-powered or electric motor boats. Primitive camping is $6. There are pit toilets but no drinking water.

Coyote Creek State Park
Coyote Creek also offers fishing, as well as a children's playground, visitor center and

developed camping. Sites are $7/11 without/with RV hookups. The park is 17 miles north of Mora on Hwy 434. Call ☎ 505-387-2328 for more information.

Sipapu Lodge & Ski Area

Sipapu is 25 miles northwest of Mora on Hwy 518, halfway between Mora and Taos. It is the oldest and one of the smallest and least known of the ski areas in northern New Mexico. There is a triple chair and a poma lift, each gaining about 800 feet of elevation and giving access to mainly more difficult runs, and a small poma, which gains 100 vertical feet with access to two easy runs. Lift rates are $27 for adults, $20 for six- to 12-year-olds and 65- to 69-year-olds, and free to those five and under or 70 and older. Rates for the small poma only are $10. Half-day rates are $19/15 for adults/kids, and skiing and snowboarding lessons and rentals are available.

During the summer the area is used for hiking, fishing, hunting and motorcycling. A variety of accommodations are offered year-round, ranging from camping ($8/18 for tents/RVs with hookups); eight-bed dorms ($10 per bed; bring a sleeping bag); camping cabins with bath and kitchenette ($26 a double; bring bedding); cabins ($40 a double); motel rooms and apartments ($50 a double); and larger suites and duplexes ($65 to $75 a double). Many have fireplaces. All cabins and rooms sleep up to four, and larger units sleep six to 10 people at $8 extra per person. Call the lodge (☎ 505-587-2240, 800-587-2240) for reservations and snow conditions.

SPRINGER & AROUND

This small town (population 1500) was founded in 1879. It was the Colfax County seat from 1882 to 1897, when the seat was moved to Raton. Its main importance is as a center for the surrounding ranches, but there are some historical buildings and a museum worth visiting. Watch for herds of pronghorn antelope in this area.

Springer is off I-25, 67 miles north of Las Vegas and 39 miles south of Raton. The tourist information center is the Santa Fe Trail Museum in summer and the chamber of commerce (☎ 505-483-2998) at other times.

Santa Fe Trail Museum

Housed in the 1882 building that used to be the Colfax County courthouse, this museum (☎ 505-483-2341 for the curator) displays the usual historical artifacts plus the only electric chair ever used in New Mexico. Hours are 10 am to 4 pm Monday to Saturday, from Memorial Day to Labor Day. Admission is $1.50/1/75¢ for adults/seniors/children under 12.

Dorsey Mansion

This two-story log-and-stone mansion was built in 1878-86 by cattle rancher and then Arkansas senator Stephen Dorsey. It was the most opulent Southwestern residence of its time, and today it's still impressive. After a turbulent history as a home, hospital and hotel (not to mention post office, store and state monument), it is now privately owned – call ahead (☎ 505-375-2222) if you are interested in touring this grand historical building in the middle of nowhere. Tours are $2/1 for adults/children under 12, with a $5 minimum. The mansion is 24 miles east of Springer on Hwy 56, then 12 miles north on a dirt road.

Fishing

Five miles west of Springer, Springer Lake is famous for producing sizable pike and rainbow trout. Charette Lake, known for trout, is about 12 miles southwest of town (take the Hwy 569 exit from I-25).

Places to Stay & Eat

There's free camping at *Charette Lake* from March through October, with latrines but no drinking water. Free camping is also permitted at *Springer Lake*. In Springer, the *Sportsman's Supply RV Park* (☎ 505-483-5020), next to the Texaco Station, has 15 RV sites with hookups for $10.

Basic motel rooms are available at the *Broken Arrow Motel* (☎ 505-483-5555) or at the slightly pricier *Oasis Motel* (☎ 505-483-2777). The old-fashioned *Brown Hotel*

Doc Holliday

& *Café* (☎ 505-483-2269, 800-570-2269), 302 Maxwell, PO Box 927, Springer, NM 87747, offers bed & breakfast for $40/50 a single/double. There are 12 rooms decorated in simple late-19th-century style – no TVs or telephones, though a downstairs living room provides these amenities. Most rooms share one bathroom between two rooms and could thus make a two-room unit for families. The homey café serves a small selection of inexpensive Mexican and American meals.

There are a few other places to eat, of which the best is *El Taco Café* (☎ 505-483-9924). All of these are along the main road in Springer.

Getting There & Away
Greyhound (☎ 505-483-2379), 825 4th St, has two buses a day on the Raton to Las Vegas and Albuquerque runs.

CIMARRON
Cimarron is a historic Wild West town set in lovely country at the eastern base of the

Sangre de Cristo Mountains. The area was the home of Ute and Apache Indians prior to being settled in the 1840s by cattle baron Lucien Maxwell (see Fort Sumner State Monument in Southeastern New Mexico). Cimarron became a stop on the Santa Fe Trail as well as being the first Colfax County seat.

During the town's early decades, it was home to various gunslingers, train robbers, desperadoes, lawmen and other notable Western figures. Kit Carson, Buffalo Bill Cody, Annie Oakley, Clay Allison, Black Jack Ketchum, Wyatt Earp, Jesse James and Doc Holliday are just a few who passed through here. It was a wild town, with gunfights and murders commonplace. The old St James Hotel alone saw the deaths of 26 men within its walls.

Today, Cimarron is a quiet village of less than a thousand inhabitants. Several early buildings still stand and warrant a visit.

Orientation & Information
Cimarron is on Hwy 64, 41 miles southwest of Raton and 54 steep and mountainous miles east of Taos.

The chamber of commerce (☎ 505-376-2417, 800-700-4298), Box 604, Cimarron, NM 87714, on the main highway, has local information. Hours are 9 am to 6 pm daily in summer, and 9 am to 5 pm except Wednesday and Sunday during the rest of the year. There is a post office (☎ 505-376-2548), a clinic (☎ 505-376-2402) and police (☎ 505-376-2351).

Historical Buildings
Most of the historical buildings lie south of the Cimarron River on Hwy 21, which heads south from Hwy 64 near the middle of town. Everything is within walking distance of the chamber of commerce.

The **Old Mill Museum** (☎ 505-376-2913) is in the Aztec Mill, built in 1864; it houses historical photographs and local memorabilia, annotated by more informative signs than in most small county museums. Hours are 10 am to 4 pm daily except Thursday from June to August, and on weekends in May and September.

Admission is $2/1 for adults/seniors, uniformed scouts and children under 12.

Nearby is the historic St James Hotel (see Places to Stay). Behind the St James is the Santa Fe Trail Inn, built in 1854, the old town plaza and well, and the Dold Trading Post. South of the St James is Schwenk's Gambling Hall, the Wells Fargo Station and the old jail built in 1872.

Philmont Scout Ranch
A working ranch (☎ 505-376-2281) about 4 miles south of Cimarron, this huge property (almost 220 sq miles) was donated to the Boy Scouts of America (BSA) by Waite Phillips, an Oklahoma oilman. Since 1938, over 500,000 scouts have stayed here – camping, backpacking and learning outdoor skills.

The ranch headquarters is in **Villa Philmonte**, a Spanish Mediterranean-style mansion completed in 1927. Guided tours ($4 for adults) are offered in the summer; call for hours. Nearby, **Seton Memorial Library & Museum** features local frontier history and exhibits the works of ET Seton, first Chief Scout of the BSA. Hours are 8 am to 5 pm daily from June to August, and Monday to Saturday in other months. Admission is free.

Seven miles farther south in the village of Rayado is the free **Kit Carson Museum**. Furnished in 1850s style, it has interpreters in period costumes giving guided tours daily from June to August.

Special Events
Working cowboys compete in the annual the Fourth of July Rodeo. There are also fireworks and a parade. Cimarron Days is held in late July (dates vary) and features arts and crafts, music and entertainment.

Places to Stay
Camping *Apache Ridge RV Park* (☎ 505-376-2109), near the St James Motel, has RV sites with hookups for $14 and tent sites for $5. There are showers. The *Ponil Campground* (☎ 505-376-2700), a mile north of town, has shaded RV and tent sites for about the same price. There is a laundry and showers. Near the chamber of commerce, *Cimarron Inn & RV Park* (☎ 505-376-2268, 800-546-2244) has RV sites with hookups for $13.50 and inexpensive tent spaces and showers. All offer weekly discounts. *Johnson's Cabins* (☎ 505-376-2210) allows tents for $3 per camper.

Also see Around Cimarron, below.

Hotels Cimarron is small and street signs are few. When you get to town, stop by the very helpful chamber of commerce for directions to these hotels.

The cheapest place is the simple but clean and friendly *Cimarron Inn & RV Park* (☎ 505-376-2268, 800-546-2244), with 12 rooms for $34/36 for singles/doubles. Some rooms have microwaves and refrigerators. Also very friendly, the *Kit Carson Inn* (☎ 505-376-2288, 800-293-7961, fax 505-376-9214) has 40 clean motel rooms, a good inexpensive restaurant open from 6 am to 8 pm, and a very lively bar with occasional live bands. Rates are $38/42 in summer, less in winter. *Johnson's Cabins* (☎ 505-376-2210) has small cabins, each with an equipped kitchenette and queen-size bed, for $38 a double. You can fish in the little Cimarron River by the cabins.

The best-known place is the recommended *St James Hotel* (☎ 505-376-2664, 800-748-2694, fax 505-376-2623). It was first a saloon in 1873, a hotel in 1880 and then renovated in 1985. The 13 historical rooms are named after the many famous Westerners who have stayed here. They are furnished with antiques and decorated in turn-of-the-19th-century style; no TVs or phones. Rates vary from $55 for three rooms with shared hall baths to between $80 and $100 for rooms with private baths. Most of the antique beds are doubles or twins; two rooms have modern queen-size beds. Visitors can see some of the rooms if they are not in use. A modern annex has 10 new rooms with TVs and phones for $55 to $70. Most have two double beds, and a couple have two double and two twin beds.

There is a coffee shop, a good restaurant and a cozy bar with a pool table. Dinner entrees in the restaurant fall in the $10 to

$20 range; while waiting for your food, see how many bullet holes you can count in the period pressed-tin ceiling.

B&Bs The *Cimarron House* (☎ 505-376-2616, 800-637-3354), Route 1, Box 13A, Cimarron, NM 87714, is a modern house offering five no-smoking rooms with king-size beds. Four rooms share two bathrooms and cost $65 and one has a private bathroom for $85, all including a full breakfast. There is an impressive indoor pool.

The *Casa del Gavilan* (☎ 505-376-2246, 800-428-4526, fax 505-376-2247), PO Box 518, Cimarron, NM 87714, is a comfortable B&B in a 1908 white adobe house decorated with Southwestern antiques and art. Four individually decorated and variously sized rooms with private bath are $70, $80, $90 or $100 a double. A two-room guest house with one bathroom is $125 for four people. Full breakfasts are served and no smoking is permitted.

Places to Eat
Heck's Hungry Traveler (☎ 505-376-2574) serves inexpensive Italian, Mexican and American food. The *Cimarron Art Gallery* (☎ 505-376-2614) sells Southwestern art, souvenirs and fishing licenses; it also has an old-fashioned ice cream shop. There are a few other simple eateries in addition to the hotel restaurants.

Getting There & Away
TNM&O buses run between Denver (via Raton) and Albuquerque (via Taos and Santa Fe) and stop once a day in each direction. Information is available from Bet-R-Dun Sporting Goods (☎ 505-376-9005) or the White Buffalo Gallery next door, both near the chamber of commerce.

AROUND CIMARRON
Cimarron Canyon State Park
This scenic steep-walled canyon begins 13 miles west of Cimarron and continues for 7 miles along Hwy 64. Several hiking trails leave from the three campgrounds (☎ 505-377-6271), Box 147, Ute Park, NM 87749, nestled along the Cimarron River. The trout

fishing is excellent. Campsites with water but no showers or RV hookups are $7 and fill quickly on weekends.

Valle Vidal
This mountainous and forested area in the northeastern corner of the Carson National Forest is the nearest national forest to Cimarron. Gravel roads wind through remote countryside, which contains a 2000-head elk herd, bears, mountain lions, deer, turkeys and other wildlife. This is a good opportunity to see the fantastic scenery of the Sangre de Cristo Mountains without encountering much traffic.

Two campgrounds, *McCrystal Creek* (8100 feet) and *Cimarron* (9400 feet), charge $7 per night and have drinking water but no showers or RV hookups. (Cimarron is closed in winter.) Dispersed and wilderness camping and backpacking are permitted. The nearest ranger stations are in Taos and Questa.

Go east of Cimarron 7 miles on Hwy 64 and turn northwest on graveled USFS Rd 1950. It is about 20 miles to Valle Vidal, a farther 20 through the area and a final 20 to Costilla (on Hwy 522, north of Questa). To protect the elk, parts of the area may be closed from January to June.

RATON
One of the most difficult sections of the Santa Fe Trail was the Raton Pass (7834 feet) in the foothills of the Rockies, near what is now the Colorado-New Mexico state line. The rocky pass had been known to Indians and Spanish explorers for centuries before its increasingly frequent use by traders' wagons prompted local mountain man 'Uncle Dick' Wooton to make improvements. In 1866, Wooton dynamited a rough 'road' through the pass and set up a toll booth. Just south of the pass, wagon trains would rest and water at Willow Springs.

The arrival of the railroad in 1879 prompted the founding of Raton (at Willow Springs), and it quickly grew into an important railway stop and mining and ranching center. Many turn-of-the-19th-century buildings have been preserved and can be visited. Today, ranching and mining continue to be important, and the railway, along with the construction of I-25, has maintained Raton as a transport center. In addition, tourism is a growing industry. Travelers come to experience Raton's early Western ambiance and to visit the surrounding natural recreation areas.

Raton (population about 8000) is 6668 feet above sea level and is the Colfax County seat. The elevation makes for pleasant summers and cool winters, with average overnight lows of 18°F in January and highs of 82°F in July.

Orientation

Raton lies along I-25, 8 miles south of Raton Pass and the Colorado state line. The main north-south thoroughfare is 2nd St, which runs parallel to and just west of I-25. The main east-west street is Hwy 64/87, called Tiger Drive west of 2nd St and Clayton Rd east of 2nd St.

Information

The visitor center (☎ 505-445-3689, 800-638-6161), 100 Clayton Rd, is open from 8 am to 5 pm daily and has state-wide information for visitors arriving from Colorado. The library (☎ 505-445-9711) is at 244 Cook Ave. The post office (☎ 505-445-2681) is at 245 Park Ave. The local newspaper is the *Raton Daily Range*. The hospital (☎ 505-445-3661) is on Hospital Drive at the south end of town. The police (☎ 505-445-2704) are at 224 Savage Ave.

Historical District

The historical district lies along 1st, 2nd and 3rd Sts between Clark and Rio Grande Aves. This small area harbors over two dozen interesting buildings and a detailed brochure is available from the visitor center or the Raton Museum.

From the Raton Museum (see below), begin at the **Railway Station**, at 1st and Cook, which was built in 1903. Opposite the railway are several attractive buildings dating from the 1880s and 1890s. The yellow-painted brick **Marchiondo Building**, constructed in 1882, housed a dry

goods store and post office. A block to the north, on 1st between Park and Clark, are the Veterans of Foreign Wars and Bennett's Transportation Buildings, which are the oldest in the district.

The **Shuler Theater** (☎ 505-445-5520), 131 N 2nd, was completed in 1915, and the elaborate European Rococo interior boasts excellent acoustics. In the foyer, eight New Deal (1930s) murals painted by Manville Chapman depict area history from 1845 to 1895. The theater is still in operation. Other New Deal murals can be seen in the **library**, which was built in 1917 and was originally the post office, and in the present post office a block away. More New Deal art graces the historic **El Portal Hotel**, originally the Seaburg European Hotel, constructed in 1904.

Raton Museum

This museum of local history (☎ 505-445-8979), 218 S 1st St, is housed in the 1906 Coors Building. Hours (subject to change) are 9 am to 5 pm from Tuesday to Saturday during the summer and on weekends in winter. Admission is free.

Sugarite Canyon State Park

This park (☎ 505-445-5607), Box 386, Raton, NM 87740, has a visitor center with exhibits about nature and local history. There was an important early-20th-century coal mine here, and some of the old buildings can be seen. Two lakes stocked with rainbow trout (fishing license required) allow boating with oars or electric motors only.

The park lies in pretty meadows and forests in the foothills of the Rockies 10 miles northeast of Raton. Wild turkey and deer are sometimes seen in the area. The 7800-foot elevation provides cross-country skiing, skating and ice fishing in winter. Day use is $3 per vehicle, and there is a picnic area and campground (see Places to Stay – Camping, below).

Whittington Center

This 33,000-acre facility has shooting ranges operated by the National Rifle

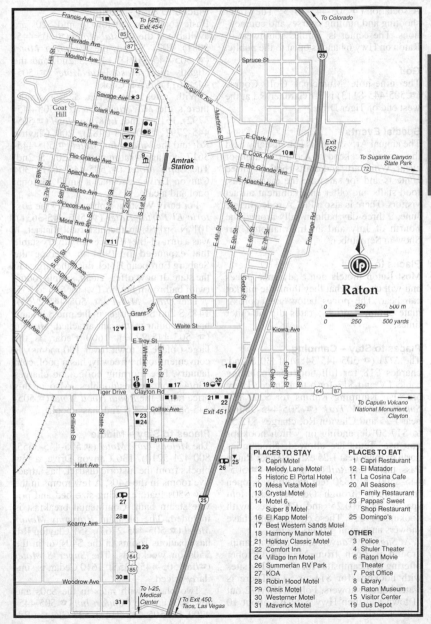

Raton

| 0 | 250 | 500 m |
| 0 | 250 | 500 yards |

To Colorado

To Sugarite Canyon
State Park

To Capulin Volcano
National Monument,
Clayton

To I-25,
Exit 454

Exit 452

Exit 451

To I-25,
Medical Center

To Exit 450,
Taos, Las Vegas

Amtrak
Station

Goat
Hill

PLACES TO STAY
1 Capri Motel
2 Melody Lane Motel
5 Historic El Portal Hotel
10 Mesa Vista Motel
13 Crystal Motel
14 Motel 6,
   Super 8 Motel
16 El Kapp Motel
17 Best Western Sands Motel
18 Harmony Manor Motel
21 Holiday Classic Motel
22 Comfort Inn
24 Village Inn Motel
26 Summerlan RV Park
27 KOA
29 Oasis Motel
30 Westerner Motel
31 Maverick Motel

PLACES TO EAT
1 Capri Restaurant
12 El Matador
11 La Cosina Cafe
20 All Seasons
   Family Restaurant
23 Pappas' Sweet
   Shop Restaurant
25 Domingo's

OTHER
3 Police
4 Shuler Theater
6 Raton Movie
   Theater
7 Post Office
8 Library
9 Raton Museum
15 Visitor Center
19 Bus Depot

Association (☎ 505-445-3615). They offer shooting and hunting courses and competitions. The center is 7 miles southwest of Raton on Hwy 64 and is open to the public.

Golf
The nine-hole Municipal Golf Course (☎ 505-445-8113) is off Gardner Rd at the west end of Tiger Drive.

Special Events
The annual Arts & Crafts Fair, usually held the second weekend of August, is a major event. While arts and crafts (both in juried contests and for sale) are the main focus, food stalls and other entertainment attract visitors. There is also a PRCA rodeo in late June, a three-day balloon rally around the Fourth of July and an International Art Show in September.

Places to Stay
Most Raton motels don't advertise prices and will charge what they think the market can bear. The prices below are approximate summer prices; rates dip at other times.

Places to Stay – Camping
The *KOA* (☎ 505-445-3488), 1330 S 2nd, charges $18 for full hookups including cable TV and $13 for a tent space. There are also Kamping Kabins for $22. The *Summerlan RV Park* (☎ 505-445-9536), near I-25 and Clayton Rd, charges $12.50 to $17.50 depending on which hookups you use. Tents are allowed. Nine miles north of town near I-25 exit 460 near Raton Pass, the *Cedar Rail Campground* (☎ 505-445-8500), at 7830 feet elevation, is open from April through October with tent spaces for $10.25 and RV sites with hookups for $15. These campgrounds have showers and small grocery stores.

At *Sugarite Canyon State Park*, a campground is open from May to October offering tent campsites for $7 and RV sites with hookups for $11 or $13. There is water but no showers. Follow Hwy 72 out of town and then Hwy 526; it's about 10 miles and signed.

Places to Stay – Budget
Basic rooms in the low to mid $20s are available at the *Crystal Motel* (☎ 505-445-3681), 1021 S 2nd; the *Westerner Motel* (☎ 505-445-3101), 1460 S 2nd; and the slightly nicer *Mesa Vista Motel* (☎ 505-445-3611), 726 E Cook.

With rates starting at $28 a single, there's the *Maverick Motel* (☎ 505-445-3792), 1510 S 2nd; *El Kapp Motel* (☎ 505-445-2791, 800-748-2482), 200 Clayton Rd; and the *Village Inn Motel* (☎ 505-445-3617, village@raton.com), 1207 S 2nd. The *Capri Motel* (☎ 505-445-3641), 304 Canyon Drive, also has a small seasonal pool and a café.

For early Western ambiance, try the *Historic El Portal Hotel* (☎ 505-445-3631), 101 N 3rd St, in the historical district. It was a turn-of-the-19th-century livery stable that expanded in 1904 to become the Seaburg European Hotel, once the largest in the state. It now offers clean, simple rooms (with bathroom but no TV) for $25 to $35.

The *Oasis Motel* (☎ 505-445-2766), 1445 S 2nd St, charges in the mid $30s and has a popular restaurant attached. *Motel 6* (☎ 505-445-2777), 1600 Cedar, is the largest place in town (over 100 rooms), is convenient to the freeway, has a pool, coin laundry, free morning coffee and charges $36/42 for singles/doubles. Also in this price range, the *Robin Hood Motel* (☎ 505-445-5577), 1354 S 2nd, has a pool.

Places to Stay – Middle
The *Melody Lane Motel* (☎ 505-445-3655, 800-421-5210), 136 Canyon Drive, a few blocks from the historic district, has attractive rooms in the $40s. A few rooms in the low $50s feature a king-size bed and private steam bath. Continental breakfast is included. The pleasant *Harmony Manor Motel* (☎ 505-445-2763), 351 Clayton Rd, has spacious rooms in the $40s, or in the $50s on weekends. The *Super 8 Motel* (☎/fax 505-445-2355), 1610 Cedar, is similarly priced.

Two places with rates in the $50s and low $60s are the *Comfort Inn* (☎ 505-445-4200, fax 505-445-7144), 533 Clayton Rd, which has comfortable rooms, some with microwaves and refrigerators, and includes continental breakfast, and the *Holiday Classic Motel* (☎ 505-445-5555, 800-255-8879), 473 Clayton Rd, which has an indoor pool, game room, coin laundry and a good restaurant and lounge. The *Best Western Sands Motel* (☎ 505-445-2737, 800-528-1234, fax 505-445-4053), 300 Clayton Rd, has a seasonal heated pool, playground and restaurant. Spacious rooms with a queen- or king-size bed are $75 to $95. The larger rooms have a coffeemaker and refrigerator.

Places to Stay – Top End
The *Vermejo Park Ranch* (☎ 505-445-3097 or 5028, fax 505-445-3474), PO Drawer E, Raton, NM 87740, owned by Ted Turner and Jane Fonda, is a hunting and fishing lodge near the end of Hwy 555, 40 miles west of Raton. Fly-fishing clinics are held during the June to August season. Elk and deer are hunted from October to December, and wild turkey in April and May. Rates start around $300 per person per day, including all meals and activities; private guides are extra.

Places to Eat
Pappas' Sweet Shop Restaurant (☎ 505-445-9811), 1201 S 2nd, has been around since 1923 and is one of the best restaurants. Food is mainly American, with some Mexican dishes. The fanciest dinner plates are in the $20s, but many cheaper options are available. Hours in the antique-filled dining room are 9 am to 2 pm and 5 to 9 pm daily (except Sunday in winter). Alcohol is served.

For New Mexican food, *La Cosina Cafe* (☎ 505-445-9675), 745 S 3rd, has a homey atmosphere; it's closed Sunday. The Mexican food is good at *El Matador* (☎ 505-445-9575), 1012 S 2nd, open from 7 am to 8:30 pm, closed Monday. Both places are reasonably priced but neither serve beer.

Domingo's (☎ 505-445-2288), 1903 S Cedar, is open daily and encourages you (and your children!) to enjoy the unusual décor of waterfall, bridge and caves in the restaurant. They serve Mexican meals in the $5 to $7 range, and burgers and steaks (up to $15) are also available. Beer and wine are served.

The Capri Motel and Oasis Motel have inexpensive cafés, and the Best Western Sands and Holiday Classic Motels have more upscale restaurants.

For early breakfasts, the Oasis Motel café and the *All Seasons Family Restaurant* (☎ 505-445-9889), Clayton Rd by I-25, both open at 6 am.

Entertainment
Movies play at the *Raton Movie Theater* (☎ 505-445-3721), at 2nd and Park. On the same block, the historic *Shuler Theater* presents plays.

Getting There & Away
Bus Greyhound (☎ 505-445-9071) and TNM&O stop behind McDonald's on Clayton Rd. Several buses a day serve the route from Denver, Colorado, to Santa Fe (via both Taos and Las Vegas) and on to Albuquerque. A bus leaves in the middle of the night for Clayton and Amarillo, Texas.

Train Amtrak (☎ 800-872-7245) stops at the historic railway station on 1st St. One daily train goes to Chicago and one to Los Angeles.

AROUND RATON
Maxwell National Wildlife Refuge
This refuge (☎ 505-375-2331), Box 276, Maxwell, NM 87728, is 28 miles south of Raton along I-25 and 3 miles west of Maxwell along Hwys 445 and 505. A visitor center is open from 7:30 am to 4 pm Monday to Friday.

The refuge encompasses 2800 acres of grassland and farmland around three lakes. It is managed for wintering waterfowl and upland game birds, and birding is good from October through the winter. The burrowing owl and many other birds nest here in summer.

Free camping is permitted (with toilets but no water), but call ahead because portions of the refuge are closed in winter for waterfowl protection. Fishing is allowed during the March to October season.

NEW MEXICO

The Northeast Corner

Ranching is a mainstay of the economy in the sparsely populated northeast corner of New Mexico. On many stretches of road, you'll see more cattle than people or cars. Near Capulin Volcano, the discovery of ancient bison bones and associated arrowheads more than doubled estimates of how long humans have lived on this continent (see the Folsom Man sidebar). And not far from that discovery, footprints of at least eight species of dinosaur have been found.

As you drive, keep your eyes peeled for wildlife, especially pronghorn antelope, which are common in this area.

CAPULIN VOLCANO NATIONAL MONUMENT

Fifty or sixty thousand years ago, huge volcanic explosions spewed molten lava over the high plains. Cinders, ash and other debris piled up around the main vent, resulting in a symmetrical cone-shaped volcano rising 1300 feet above the surrounding plains. This is Capulin Volcano, the easiest to visit of several volcanoes in the area. It became a national monument in 1916.

The entrance to the Capulin Volcano National Monument (☎ 505-278-2201), Box 40, Capulin, NM 88414-0040, is 3 miles north of the village of Capulin. (The village is 58 miles west of Clayton and 30 miles east of Raton on Hwy 64/87.) Near the entrance is a visitor center, open 7:30 am to 6:30 pm from Memorial Day to Labor Day and 8 am to 4 pm during the rest of the year. Admission is $4 per vehicle (free with Golden Eagle, Age or Access Passes). Informative audiovisual presentations are shown on request. Behind the visitor center, there is a short nature trail and picnic area.

From the visitor center, a 2-mile road spirals up the mountain to a parking lot at the crater rim. A 1-mile trail (some steep

---

Folsom Man

A few miles north of Capulin Volcano is **Folsom**, the village near which the most important archaeological discovery in America was made. In 1908, George McJunkin, a local African American cowboy, noticed some strange bones in Wild Horse Arroyo. Cowboy that he was, he knew that these were no ordinary cattle bones, and so he kept them, suspecting correctly that they were bones of an extinct form of bison. McJunkin told various people of his find, but it was not until 1926 to 1928 that the site was properly excavated, first by fossil bone expert Jesse Figgins and then by others.

Until that time, scientific dogma stated that humans had inhabited North America for, at most, 4000 years. Suddenly, facts about the continent's ancient inhabitants had to be completely revised. The 1926 to 1928 excavations showed stone arrowheads in association with extinct bison bones dating from 8000 BC, thus proving that people have lived here for at least that long. These Paleo-Indians became known as Folsom Man.

Thus the era of modern American archaeology began in Folsom in the late 1920s. More recent dating techniques have shown these artifacts to be 10,800 years old, among the oldest discovered on the continent, although it is clear that people have lived in the Americas for even longer.

To learn more about George McJunkin and his incredible find, stop by the Folsom Museum (☎ 505-278-2122) in the village of Folsom. It's open 10 am to 5 pm daily, Memorial Day to Labor Day, and during weekends in May and September. On other days, call the director (☎ 505-278-2477, 505-278-3616) for an appointment. Admission is $1, or 50¢ for children under 12. ∎

sections) loops around the entire crater, which is 8182 feet at its highest point. Great views! A quarter-mile trail drops into the volcanic crater to the vent. Off-trail hiking is not allowed.

Places to Stay & Eat
There is no camping in the monument. In the village of **Capulin**, the *Capulin Camp* (☎ 505-278-2921) has RV hookups ($12.50), tent spaces and showers. Opposite is a grocery store and restaurant.

Des Moines, 9 miles east of Capulin, has the *Central Motel* (☎ 505-278-2111) with five clean rooms from $21. Nearby, the *Sierra Grande Restaurant* (☎ 505-278-2721) is OK.

CLAYTON
Dinosaur tracks and the tracks of the Santa Fe Trail both contribute to the ancient and historical allure of the Clayton area. This high-plains region was the home of the Comanches and saw several Spanish expeditions, followed by intense Comanche-Spanish battles. It was part of the Spanish Empire until 1821, then part of Mexico, and it was finally annexed by the USA in 1848. Throughout this time, the Comanches retained a great amount of control in the area.

Clayton was founded in 1888 as a railway stop and became the Union County seat in 1984. Several turn-of-the-19th-century buildings remain in the historical downtown area. The Eklund Dining Room & Saloon (see Places to Eat) is especially attractive. The infamous train robber Black Jack Ketchum was caught near Clayton and hanged here in 1901; the gruesome story is documented in the local museum.

Clayton (population about 2500), at 5050 feet above sea level, is the center of Union County's cattle ranches and feedlots, and corn, wheat and sorghum are important crops. It is also near the Bravo Dome CO_2 Field, the world's largest natural deposit of carbon dioxide gas. The underground carbon dioxide deposit is injected into nearby oil fields, thus increasing oil production by up to 50%.

Orientation & Information
The major thoroughfare is 1st, which runs northwest-southeast as Hwy 87. Hwy 56 intersects it as Monroe to the west and Main to the east.

The chamber of commerce (☎ 505-374-9253), 1103 S 1st, flanked by huge dinosaur monuments, is open 8 am to 5 pm Monday to Friday. The Kiowa National Grasslands Headquarters (☎ 505-374-9652) is at 714 Main. The library (☎ 505-374-9423) is at 17 Chestnut. The local newspaper is the *Union County Leader*. The post office (☎ 505-374-9541) is at 1 Walnut. The hospital (☎ 505-374-2585) is at 301 Harding. The police (☎ 505-374-2504) are at 112 N Front.

Herzstein Memorial Museum
This free museum (☎ 505-374-2977), 2nd and Walnut, displays local artifacts in the renovated Methodist Episcopal Church, dating from 1919. The museum was dedicated in 1989, and exhibits are slowly expanding. The museum is open Tuesday to Sunday afternoons in summer and weekend afternoons year-round.

Golf
Clayton Golf Club (☎ 505-374 9957) is at the Air Park.

Places to Stay
Camping *KOA* (☎ 505-374-9508), 903 S 5th, has a coin laundry, showers, playground, recreation area, tent spaces for $14, RV sites with hookups for $16 and Kamping Kabins for $22.50. It operates from March through October.

Hotels The *Mission Motel* (☎ 505-374-9890), 214 N 1st, and *Allen's Motel* (☎ 505-374-8099), 412 N 1st, both have basic rooms in the low $20s. The *Clayton Motel* (☎ 505-374-2544), 422 Monroe, charges $25/31 for singles/doubles. The *Clayton Holiday Motel* (☎ 505-374-2558, fax 505-374-8100), 1 mile northwest on Hwy 87, offers clean rooms with queen-size beds for $28/33. The *Super 8 Motel* (☎ 505-374-8127, fax 505-374-2598),

NEW MEXICO

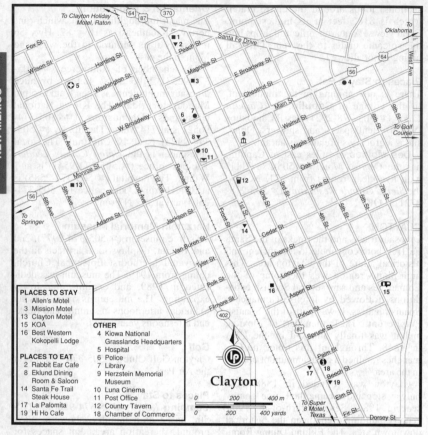

Clayton

PLACES TO STAY
1   Allen's Motel
3   Mission Motel
13 Clayton Motel
15 KOA
16 Best Western
    Kokopelli Lodge

PLACES TO EAT
2   Rabbit Ear Cafe
8   Eklund Dining
    Room & Saloon
14 Santa Fe Trail
    Steak House
17 La Palomita
19 Hi Ho Cafe

OTHER
4   Kiowa National
    Grasslands Headquarters
5   Hospital
6   Police
7   Library
9   Herzstein Memorial
    Museum
10 Luna Cinema
11 Post Office
12 Country Tavern
18 Chamber of Commerce

0   200   400 m
0   200   400 yards

1425 S 1st, has good rooms with queen- or king-size beds for $38.88/44.88, including continental breakfast.

The *Best Western Kokopelli Lodge* (☎ 505-374-2589, 800-392-6691, fax 505-374-2554), 702 S 1st, in operation since the 1940s, has been well maintained. Rooms vary in size, and prices range from $50 to $75 including continental breakfast. Some units have a king-size bed; others have two bedrooms. A swimming pool is open in summer.

Places to Eat

For breakfast, *La Palomita* (☎ 505-374-2127), S 1st and Palm, is open at 7 am and

very popular; it serves Mexican and American food till 10 pm. The *Rabbit Ear Cafe* (☎ 505-374-9912), 402 N 1st, is open 6 am to 10 pm in summer. The *Hi Ho Café* (☎ 505-374-9515), 1201 S 1st, is popular for lunch. The *Santa Fe Trail Steak House* (☎ 505-374-8585), 22½ Pine, has decent, reasonably priced steaks but lacks a beer license.

The *Eklund Dining Room & Saloon* (☎ 505-374-2551), 15 Main, is the best place for lunches and dinners. It's in the historic Eklund Hotel, built in the 1890s but no longer functioning (though there are plans to restore the hotel). The dining/saloon area is restored to the original

Victorian style. Mexican dinners and sandwiches are $4 to $9, and American dinner entrées (steaks and trout) fall in the $9 to $18 range.

Entertainment
The *Luna Cinema* has movies. The *Country Tavern* (☎ 505-374-2413), 201 S 1st, has a country & western band and dancing on weekends.

Getting There & Away
Greyhound and TNM&O buses stop at the Phillips 66 Truck Stop (☎ 505-374-9300) on Hwy 87, south of town, on the daily run from Raton to Amarillo, Texas.

AROUND CLAYTON
Clayton Lake State Park
This park (☎ 505-374-8808), Seneca, NM 88437, contains over 500 footprints of eight different species of dinosaur. A half-mile trail leads to the prints and a walkway with interpretive signs. The low angles of early morning or late afternoon sunlight provide the best viewing.

Other attractions include fishing (especially trout and catfish from April 1 to October 31), boating and swimming in summer, watching migratory waterfowl in winter, picnicking and camping. Tent sites are $7; sites with RV hookups are $11. There are showers and a playground. Day use is $3.

The park is 12 miles northwest of Clayton on Hwy 370.

Kiowa National Grasslands
These grasslands were farmed throughout the early 20th century until poor agricultural techniques led to the soil becoming useless and blowing away during the dust bowl years of the 1930s. This is documented in photos in Clayton's museum. Four different areas are now managed by the US Department of Agriculture and comprise the Kiowa National Grasslands. Two areas are in northeastern New Mexico and the others are in Texas and Oklahoma.

One New Mexican unit lies between Clayton and the Oklahoma and Texas state lines to the east. The other New Mexican unit is southwest of Clayton in Harding County, the most sparsely populated county in New Mexico. This is high-plains ranch land – open, vast and lonely. The Grasslands Headquarters is in Clayton (see above).

The grasslands are no longer farmed but are managed for grazing and wildlife habitat protection. In the Harding County unit I saw dozens of pronghorn antelope on a recent visit, while the unit east of Clayton had more desert tortoises than I have seen anywhere in the Southwest. Several, unfortunately, were roadkill, so keep your eyes open and try to avoid them. They are becoming increasingly rare and are protected.

The most visited section (though visitors are scarce) is north of the village of **Roy** (with a gas station and grocery store).

Nine miles northeast of Roy on Hwy 120 is Chicosa Lake, which was once a watering site for cowboys driving huge cattle herds along the famous Goodnight-Loving Trail in the 1860s and 1870s. Now, the lake has dried out, and the visitor center and camping area here are closed.

About 10 miles northwest of Roy on Hwy 39, a signed dirt road (not suitable for trailers) heads west another 10 miles to the *Mills Camping Area* near the Canadian River, where there is free primitive camping with pit toilets, but no drinking water. The river forms a small gorge here, and the area is quite scenic.

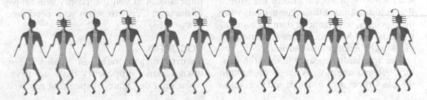

Southwestern New Mexico

This chapter covers the Rio Grande Valley south of Albuquerque down to the Texas border, and the area west of there to the Arizona state line. The Rio Grande Valley is, and always has been, the main thoroughfare through the area, and I-25 parallels it from Albuquerque south to Las Cruces, the largest city in southwestern New Mexico. At Las Cruces, I-25 joins I-10, which continues south into Texas or heads west into Arizona. Most travelers along these routes cruise through the region as quickly as possible, bent on visits to the more famous parts of New Mexico such as Santa Fe and Taos. Nevertheless, southwestern New Mexico offers much to travelers.

The first inhabitants of the area were hunter-gatherers of the Cochise Culture, which dates from about 7000 BC. The Cochise gave rise to the Mogollon Culture, which began to appear about 200 BC. The people lived in the mountains and valleys and relied more on hunting and gathering than their Hohokam and Puebloan contemporaries, but eventually the latter strongly influenced the Mogollon culture. This left us with a number of archaeological sites, of which the Gila (pronounced 'HEE-la') Cliff Dwellings north of Silver City are the best known and most spectacular. They also left us with superb Mimbres black-on-white pottery that can be examined in several museums in the area. The Mogollon culture died out in the early 14th century.

The Pueblo Indians of the northern Rio Grande had a few southern outposts in the area. Late arrivals on the scene, Athapaskan-speaking Indians arrived from the north soon after the disappearance of the Mogollon culture. Among these late arrivals were the Apaches, who came to dominate southwestern New Mexico. The most famous of the Apache leaders was Geronimo.

The Spaniards appeared in the 16th century. Álvar Cabeza de Vaca went through the Las Cruces area in 1535, and Coronado marched north along the Rio Grande in 1540. By the 17th century, many of the pueblos had fallen under Spanish mission control, but the more nomadic Apaches remained free. The arrival of the Anglos in the 19th century changed that forever.

Today, with the exception of Las Cruces and Socorro, most of the towns in southwestern New Mexico are relatively young, dating to the late 19th century. Much of the southernmost part, around I-10, is part of the Chihuahua Desert, where yucca and agave plants dominate the scene. This is ranching country, though the cattle are sparse. North of the desert, the countryside rises to the rugged mountains encompassed by the Gila National Forest. This is also wild country where opportunities for adventurous backpacking, fishing and hunting abound. The residents are few, and their livelihoods tend toward ranching, logging and some mining in the Silver City area.

The very wildness of the area is perhaps its greatest attraction, but visitors will also enjoy the Gila Cliff Dwellings National Monument, the Spanish architecture in the Las Cruces suburb of Mesilla, the quaint Victorian buildings in Silver City and the remnants of ghost towns near Lordsburg. The Bosque del Apache National Wildlife Refuge near Socorro offers unique birding opportunities.

Many of southwestern New Mexico's small towns have annual country fairs and festivals, some of which are quite peculiar, such as the duck races in Deming. Most of these towns have small but interesting museums. And you'll certainly avoid most of the tourist crowds when you spend time in this area.

SOCORRO

Socorro means 'help' in Spanish. The town's name supposedly dates to 1598, when Juan de Oñate's expedition received

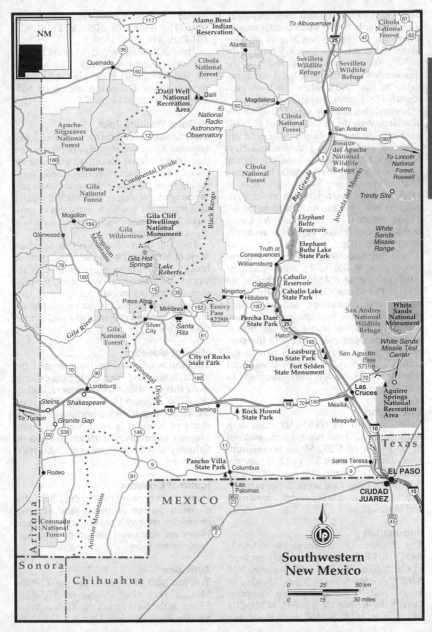

NEW MEXICO

Southwestern
New Mexico

0	25	50 km
0	15	30 miles

help from Pilabo Pueblo (now defunct). The Spaniards built a small church nearby, expanding it into the San Miguel Mission in the 1620s. After the Pueblo Revolt of the 1680s, Socorro was abandoned and the mission fell into disrepair, but it was renovated in the 1820s when the town was resettled by mainly Hispanic pioneers.

Socorro became an agricultural center and later, with the introduction of the railroad in 1880 and the discovery of gold and silver, a major mining center and New Mexico's biggest town – the population grew from 500 in 1880 to 4000 by the late 1880s. The mining boom went bust in 1893, and the town returned to its agricultural base, but the growth surge of the 1880s resulted in the many Victorian buildings that make the town architecturally interesting.

Now the Socorro County seat, Socorro (population 9000) is 75 miles south of Albuquerque and 4585 feet above sea level. The New Mexico Institute of Mining and Technology (locally referred to as Tech) offers post-graduate education and advanced research facilities, runs a mineral museum and, along with the government sector, plays a major part in the county's economy. The nearby Bosque del Apache refuge draws birders, especially in winter.

Orientation

California St (Hwy 60/85), the main drag through town, runs north-south, parallel to and west of I-25. Major north-south streets are designated SW or SE if they are south of Manzanares Ave and the plaza, NW or NE if they are north. Some mapped streets, even close to the center, are narrow and unpaved.

Information

The chamber of commerce (☎ 505-835-0424), 103 Francisco de Avondo (just west of California), PO Box 743, Socorro, NM 87801, is open 9 am to 5 pm, Monday to Friday and 10 am to 1 pm on Saturday. Dana's Book Shop (☎ 505-835-3434), 203 Manzanares in the old Val Verde Hotel, has a good selection of books about the Southwest. The library (☎ 505-835-1114) is at 401 Park SW.

The post office (☎ 505-835-0542) is on the west side of the plaza. The hospital (☎ 505-835-1140) is on Hwy 60, southwest of town. The police station (☎ 505-835-1883) is at 404 Park SW.

Historic Walking Tour

The chamber of commerce publishes a free biannual *Socorro County Guidebook* with a map of the historic downtown area near the plaza. Sixty sites are described, most dating from the late 19th century. An early morning or evening stroll around the plaza area transports you back to the era of territorial New Mexico with no tourist throngs breaking the illusion.

The highlight of the walk is the **San Miguel Mission** (☎ 505-835-1620), three blocks north of the plaza. Although restored and added to several times, the mission still retains its colonial feel and parts of the walls date back to the original building. The mission is open daily, and admission is free.

Mineral Museum

Thousands of minerals from around the world, fossils and other geological exhibits make this the state's largest mineral collection. The museum (☎ 505-835-5420) is on the Tech campus on the northwestern outskirts of town; it is open 8 am to 5 pm, Monday to Friday, and 10 am to 3 pm on Saturday and Sunday; museum admission is free.

Hammel Museum

Housed in a brewery built in the 1880s, this museum on the northeast side of town chronicles the city's growth in those years. Hours are 9 am to 1 pm on the first Saturday of the month.

Activities

You can **golf** 18 holes at the par-72 New Mexico Tech Golf Course (☎ 505-835-5335), at the west end of the Tech campus. Sedillo Park, 1004 El Camino Real NW, has a **swimming pool** (☎ 505-835-3091) open summer afternoons, and **tennis** courts and playground equipment.

Special Events

The Hilton Golf Tournament held the first week in June features a unique one-hole event on the last day: the players tee off from the top of a mountain and then golf through a makeshift course in the desert to the hole, about 5 miles away and 3000 feet below. The usual 18-hole tournament games are also held.

The San Miguel Fiesta during the first weekend in August features games, dances,

food and crafts stalls outside the mission. The Socorro County Fair & Rodeo takes place over Labor Day weekend. The Festival of the Cranes on the third weekend in November features special tours of Bosque del Apache, wildlife workshops, and arts and crafts.

Places to Stay – Camping

Socorro RV Park (☎ 505-835-2234), S Frontage Rd by exit 147 of I-25, has a pool, showers and coin laundry. Rates are $15 without hookups and $19 with.

Along Hwy 1 en route to Bosque del Apache refuge, the *Birdwatchers RV Park*

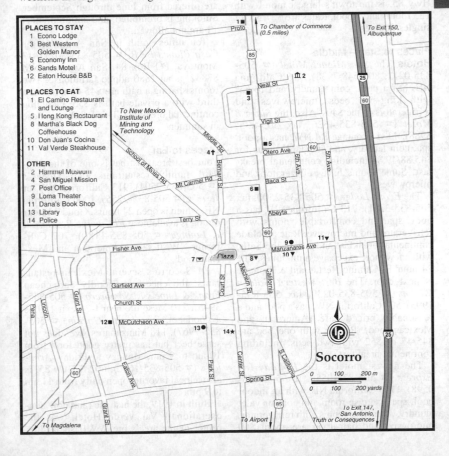

PLACES TO STAY
1 Econo Lodge
3 Best Western
   Golden Manor
5 Economy Inn
6 Sands Motel
12 Eaton House B&B

PLACES TO EAT
1 El Camino Restaurant
   and Lounge
5 Hong Kong Restaurant
8 Martha's Black Dog
   Coffeehouse
10 Don Juan's Cocina
11 Val Verde Steakhouse

OTHER
2 Hammel Museum
4 San Miguel Mission
7 Post Office
9 Loma Theater
11 Dana's Book Shop
13 Library
14 Police

To Chamber of Commerce (0.5 miles)

To Exit 150, Albuquerque

To New Mexico Institute of Mining and Technology

Neal St
Vigil St
Otero Ave
Baca St
Abeyta
Manzanares Ave
Fisher Ave
Garfield Ave
Church St
McCutcheon Ave
Terry St
Proto
Middle Rd
School of Mines Rd
Mt Carmel Rd
Bernard St
Plaza
1st St
Court St
McLean St
California
Center St
Park St
Spring St
Grant St
Pena
Lincoln
Grant St
Eaton Ave
Garfield Ave
Neal St
5th Ave
6th Ave

Socorro

0   100   200 m
0   100   200 yards

To Magdalena

To Airport

To Exit 147, San Antonio, Truth or Consequences

(☎ 505-835-1366) has sites with hookups for $14.50.

Also see Socorro to Quemado (below).

Places to Stay – Budget

Rooms starting in the low $20s are available at the following, all of which are clean and reasonably well kept: the *Sands Motel* (☎ 505-835-1130), 205 California NW; the *Economy Inn* (☎ 505-835-4666), 400 California NE; and the *Vagabond Motel* (☎ 505-835-0276), 1009 California NW. The latter two have small pools and adjoining restaurants.

The *Motel 6* (☎ 505-835-4300), 807 S Hwy 85, is the town's largest motel with 123 rooms and a pool. Rates are $27/33 for singles/doubles.

Places to Stay – Middle

Hotels The *San Miguel Motel* (☎ 505-835-0211, 800-548-7938), 916 California NE, has a pool, coin laundry and rooms with king-size beds, microwaves and refrigerators in the $40s. Also, the *Super 8 Motel* (☎ 505-835-4626, fax 505-835-3988), 1121 Frontage Rd NW, has a pool, spa, coin laundry, and standard rooms for $45.88/49.88 including continental breakfast. Some rooms have refrigerators and microwaves.

The *Econo Lodge* (☎ 505-835-2500, fax 505-835-3261), 713 California NW, has a pool, spa, and comfortable rooms with refrigerator and microwave. Rates include continental breakfast and run in the $40s, with a few more expensive mini-suites. The 24-hour El Camino Restaurant & Lounge is next door. The *Best Western Golden Manor* (☎ 505-835-0230, fax 505-835-1993), 507 California NW, has a pool and a reasonably priced café (American and Mexican food). Rooms with one bed are $45/47 or $52 with two beds, including continental breakfast.

The newest motel is the *Holiday Inn Express* (☎ 505-838-0556, fax 505-838-0598), 1100 California NE, with an indoor pool, spa, exercise room and coin or valet laundry. Attractive rooms with refrigerator, microwave and hair-dryer are about $60

double, and a few mini-suites are up to $100. Continental breakfast is included.

B&Bs The *Eaton House B&B* (☎ 505-835-1067), 403 Eaton Ave, Socorro, NM 87801, is an 1880s adobe house furnished with antiques. Rooms range in decor from Victorian to Southwestern. The owners are birders and will arrange take-out breakfasts for predawn departures. Five rooms with private baths are $85 to $110; two have a fireplace and a spa. Two separate casitas (one is wheelchair accessible) rent for $120 and have fireplaces. Rates are for two people, including breakfast. Discounts are offered from June through September. Smoking is prohibited, and children under 14 are not allowed.

Ten miles south in San Antonio, the *Casa Blanca B&B* (☎ 505-835-3027), 13 Montoya, PO Box 84, San Antonio, NM 87832, is an 1880 adobe farmhouse. Two rooms sharing a bath are $45 double and a third with a private bath is $55, including continental breakfast. This B&B may close in summer.

Places to Eat

Your best breakfast bet is one of the standard family restaurants like *Denny's* (☎ 505-835-2504), 913 California NW, or *Jerry's* (☎ 505-835-2255), 1006 California NE, which is open 24 hours. Good 24-hour dining is available at *El Camino Restaurant & Lounge* (☎ 505-835-1180), 707 California NW. It serves American and Mexican food.

Of Socorro's several Mexican restaurants, the cheerful, friendly and cheap *Frank & Lupe's El Sombrero* (☎ 505-835-3945), 210 Mesquite near I-25 exit 150, is a good bet. *Don Juan's Cocina* (☎ 505-835-9967), 118 Manzanares Ave, does not serve beer but has pretty good food from 10 am to 9 pm, Monday to Friday. *Armijos's* (☎ 505-835-1686), 602 S Hwy 85, is also a local favorite, open daily from 11 am to 9 pm.

Built in 1919, the historic (and now non-operational) Val Verde Hotel, was the center of the area's pre-WWII social life.

Today it houses the *Val Verde Steakhouse* (☎ 505-835-3380), 203 Manzanares Ave. The restaurant is pleasantly old-fashioned and serves good steak and seafood dinner entrées in the $10 to $17 range, more for lobster. It's open from 12 noon to 9 pm on Sunday, 11 am to 2 pm from Monday to Friday for inexpensive lunches, and 5 to 9:30 pm Monday to Saturday.

The unpretentious *Hong Kong Restaurant* (☎ 505-835 2338), 400 California NE, serves decent Chinese food but they do not serve alcohol. *Martha's Black Dog Coffeehouse* (☎ 505-838-0311), 110 Manzanares Ave, serves a variety of coffees and snacks.

Entertainment

The *Loma Theater* (☎ 505-835-0965), 107 Manzanares Ave, shows movies in a remodeled Victorian store.

The *Val Verde Bar* next to the steakhouse is an attractive drinking hole. The *Sports Page Night Club* (☎ 505-835-3556), 105 Francisco de Avondo, has live bands and dancing (with cover charge) on Thursday to Saturday nights.

The New Mexico Institute of Mining and Technology (☎ 505-835-5616) arranges a varied concert series with performances several times a year.

Getting There & Away

Greyhound (☎ 505-835-1767), in the Chevron Service Station at Hwy 85 near I-25 exit 147, runs two daily buses to Albuquerque and two to Las Cruces and El Paso, Texas. The bus stop location changes.

Socorro Taxi (☎ 505-835-4276, 800-991-4276, fax 505-835-2677) offers several vans a day between Socorro and Albuquerque airport for $45 each way, half price for children. They also have local taxi service and car rental.

AROUND SOCORRO
Bosque del Apache National Wildlife Refuge

This refuge protects almost 90 sq miles of fields and marshes that are a major wintering ground of many migratory birds,

notably the very rare and endangered whooping cranes of which about a dozen winter here. Tens of thousands of snow geese, sandhill cranes and various other waterfowl are also seen. The migration lasts from late October to early April, but December and January are the peak viewing months and offer the best chance of seeing whooping cranes. Year-round, approximately 325 species of birds and 135 species of mammals, reptiles and amphibians have been recorded here.

The visitor center (☎ 505-835-1828), PO Box 1246, Socorro, NM 87801, is open from 7:30 am to 4 pm, Monday to Friday, plus weekends in winter. From the center, there's a 15-mile loop drive around the refuge. There are also hiking trails, viewing platforms and towers. The refuge is open from one hour before sunrise to one hour after sunset, and admission is $3 per car. Golden Eagle, Access and Age Passes are accepted, as are duck stamps (for duck hunters).

Leave I-25 at **San Antonio** (10 miles south of Socorro) and drive 8 miles south on Hwy 1, or take the San Marcial exit and drive 10 miles north on Hwy 1.

Visitors to the refuge often stop by the *Owl Bar Cafe* (☎ 505-835-9946), half a mile east of Hwy 25 exit 139 at the main intersection in San Antonio. It's the childhood home of Conrad Hilton, founder of the well-known hotel chain. The café's green chile cheeseburger is acclaimed. Hours are 8 am to 9:30 pm, Monday to Saturday.

SOCORRO TO QUEMADO

Hwy 60 west of Socorro goes through forests and high plains on its remote way to the Arizona state line, 140 miles away.

Magdalena

In the 1880s, Magdalena was the end of the trail for thousands of range animals herded into town to be shipped on the railroad (now defunct). In 1919, a record-breaking 150,000 sheep and more than 20,000 head of cattle were herded along the trail, which saw its last roundup in 1971.

Magdalena is 26 miles west of Socorro and has a small museum on the main road.

The Cibola National Forest Magdalena Ranger Station (☎ 505-854-2281) is on the left of Hwy 60 coming from Socorro. Three miles south of the ranger station is the ghost town of **Kelly** with a church and some mine-workings still visible. The USFS *Water Canyon Campground* is 11 miles east of Magdalena, then 5 miles south of Hwy 60 along USFS Forest Rd 235. The campground is free, but there is no water. *Montosa Ranch Campground* (☎ 505-854-2235) is 14 miles west of town and has about 60 sites for tents ($5) and RVs with hookups ($15) and has hot showers.

The *High Country Lodge* and *Western Motel* (both ☎ 505-854-2415) have rooms in the $30s. Grab a bite at the locally popular *Evett's Café & Grill* (☎ 505-854-2449) or the *Ponderosa Cafe* (☎ 505-854-9916).

The Very Large Array (VLA) Telescope
About 20 miles west of Magdalena, the National Radio Astronomy Observatory houses the VLA, 27 huge antenna dishes sprouting like giant mushrooms in the high plains. The antennae combine to form an extremely powerful radio telescope used to probe the outer edges of the universe. A sign indicates the visitor center, 4 miles south of the highway, open from 8 am to sunset daily; there is no fee.

Datil
Hwy 60 intersects with Hwy 12 at Datil (43 miles from Magdalena), once a major stop on the herding trail, now an intersection with a gas station and café.

Just beyond is the signed *Datil Well National Recreation Area*, with $5 camp sites, water and several miles of nature trails on BLM lands.

Quemado
From Datil, Hwy 60 continues west 21 miles through the tiny settlement of Pie Town (where the *Pie-o-neer Café* sells pies) and then a further 22 miles to Que-

mado. This ranching town of several hundred inhabitants has an Apache National Forest Ranger Station (☎ 505-773-4678).

Inexpensive rooms and meals are provided by the simple *Largo Motel and Cafe* (☎ 505-773-4686), *Allison Motel* (☎ 505-773-4550) and *Alegre Motel & Game Room* (☎ 505-773-4520). The funky and old-fashioned *El Sarape Cafe* (☎ 505-773-4620) serves Mexican and American food.

TRUTH OR CONSEQUENCES
Originally called Hot Springs and built on the site of natural hot mineral springs in the 1880s, the town voted in 1950 to change its name to that of a famous 1940s radio and TV comedy program as a publicity and fund-raising gimmick, and it has been called Truth or Consequences (locally, T or C) since. The chamber of commerce or museum will fill you in on all the details of the name change.

T or C (population 7500) is the Sierra County seat and a resort town for those wishing to use the hot springs or camp and fish in the three lakes/state parks nearby. T or C is also one of New Mexico's funkiest towns, with a lot of character. Wander around the little hole-in-the-wall cafés downtown, and check out the antique, thrift and junk shops. The elevation is 4260 feet above sea level.

Information
The chamber of commerce (☎ 505-894-3536, 800-831-9487), 201 Foch St, is open from 9 am to 5 pm, Monday to Friday and 9 am to 1 pm on Saturday. The Gila National Forest Ranger Station (☎ 505-894-6677) is at 1804 N Date St. The library (☎ 505-894-3027) is at 325 Library Lane. *The Herald* is the local newspaper. The two post offices (☎ 505-894-3137) are at 1507 N Date St and 300 Main St. The hospital (☎ 505-894-2111) is at 800 E 9th St. The police station (☎ 505-894-7111) is at 401 McAdoo.

Geronimo Springs Museum
This impressive museum (☎ 505-894-6600), 325 Main St, has plenty of local

historical artifacts ranging from prehistoric Mimbres pots to beautifully worked cowboy saddles. Exhibits clarify the details of the famous 1950 name change. There are also mineral displays and local art. Hours are 9 am to 5 pm, Monday to Saturday. Admission is $2; $1 for those under 18.

Callahan's Auto Museum

Cars from the 1920s to the 1960s are displayed here, along with automobile memorabilia. The museum (☎ 505-894-6900), 410 Cedar St, is open from 10 am to 5 pm daily. Admission is $3; $5 for two people.

Hot Springs

A gazebo outside the Geronimo Springs Museum shelters a natural spring in which Geronimo is said to have bathed. Certainly, Indians have bathed in the area's hot springs for centuries. The mineral-laden waters have therapeutic properties, range in temperature from 98° to 115°F and have a pH of 7 (neutral). The commercial hot baths in town date from the 1920s and 1930s and look a little the worse for wear from the outside, though they are acceptably clean inside. Most places charge about $3 to $5 for a hot bath (private, couple and family

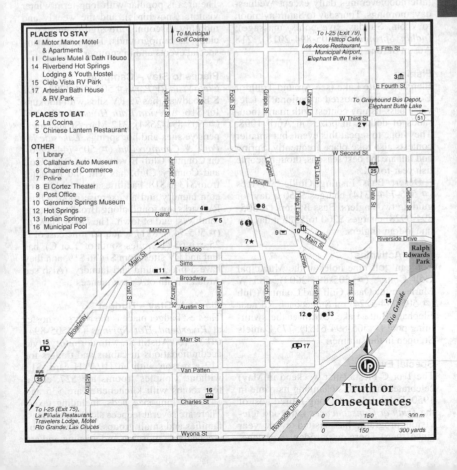

PLACES TO STAY
4 Motor Manor Motel
   & Apartments
11 Charles Motel & Bath House
14 Riverbend Hot Springs
   Lodging & Youth Hostel
15 Cielo Vista RV Park
17 Artesian Bath House
   & RV Park

PLACES TO EAT
2 La Cocina
5 Chinese Lantern Restaurant

OTHER
1 Library
3 Callahan's Auto Museum
6 Chamber of Commerce
7 Police
8 El Cortez Theater
9 Post Office
10 Geronimo Springs Museum
12 Hot Springs
13 Indian Springs
16 Municipal Pool

To Municipal Golf Course

To I-25 (Exit 79),
Hilltop Café,
Los Arcos Restaurant,
Municipal Airport,
Elephant Butte Lake

To Greyhound Bus Depot,
Elephant Butte Lake

Ralph Edwards Park

Rio Grande

Truth or Consequences

To I-25 (Exit 75),
La Piñata Restaurant,
Travelers Lodge, Motel
Rio Grande, Las Cruces

0   150   300 m
0   150   300 yards

tubs available) or $25 and up for a massage. Either bring your own towels or rent them.

Try the following: *Charles Motel & Bath House* (☎ 505-894-7154), 601 Broadway, open 8 am to 5 pm daily (supposedly the hottest water in town, nine indoor tubs, massage, sauna, reflexology, holistic healing available); *Riverbend Hot Springs* (☎ 505-894-6183), 100 Austin St (morning and evening sessions, three outdoor tubs by the river, massage, hostel on premises); *Artesian Bath House* (☎ 505-894-2684), 312 Marr St (eight tubs, RV hookups); *Hot Springs* (☎ 505-894-2228), 300 Austin St (afternoon/evenings daily except Wednesday; mornings, Thursday to Saturday; noon to 7 pm, Sunday, five pools, massage); *Indian Springs* (☎ 505-894-2018), 218 Austin St (one pool).

Fishing
Elephant Butte Lake (see Around Truth or Consequences) hosted a nationally televised bass-fishing contest with many thousands of dollars in prizes in April 1998. They hope to repeat this event, but smaller contests also take place frequently. Spring and fall are the best seasons, though people fish year-round.

Desert Bass Fishing Guide Services (☎ 505-744-5314) charges $250 a day for guiding two anglers. Bass Busters (☎ 505-894-0928) charges $200 to $325 a day for one to four anglers.

Other Activities
You can **golf** nine holes at the Municipal Golf Course (☎ 505-894-2603), 685 W Marie, or the Oasis Golf and Country Club (☎ 505-744-5224) on Stagecoach Rd near Elephant Butte Lake. **Swim** at the swimming pool (☎ 505-894-6151), 775 Daniels St, open in the summer.

Special Events
The T or C Fiesta (first weekend in May) celebrates the town's changing its name in 1950; Ralph Edwards, long-retired host of the *Truth or Consequences* radio and television program, has visited every year since then. There is a rodeo, barbecue,

parade and other events. The Sierra County Fair has livestock and agricultural displays during early September. Geronimo Days, held the weekend before Columbus Day, features Native American dancers; cowboy poetry; fiddlers contests; gunfights and historical reenactments; cloggers and other dancers; country & western, bluegrass and mariachi music; a procession and a bunch of other Western stuff. The Old Time Fiddlers State Championship is held the following weekend. (See also Fishing, above.)

Places to Stay
The area is popular with long-term winter visitors (snowbirds), and the weekly and monthly discounts are significant, especially in campgrounds. Rates rise during special events and in summer.

Places to Stay – Camping
Cielo Vista RV Park (☎ 505-894-3738), 501 S Broadway, has 72 RV sites with hookups for $16. *Artesian Bath House & RV Park* (☎ 505-894-2684), 312 Marr St, has inexpensive sites and hot springs. *Lakeside RV Park & Campground* (☎ 505-744-5996), on Country Club Blvd near the Oasis Golf and Country Club, has tent and RV sites from $13 to $18. Facilities include showers, coin laundry and an exercise room. Other RV parks are found along Broadway at the southwest end of town. The *Lakeview KOA* (☎ 505-743-2811), a quarter mile east of I-25 exit 63 (16 miles south of T or C), has tent and RV sites from $14 to $19, and they have a playground and laundry. (Also see Around Truth or Consequences.)

Places to Stay – Budget
The best budget place is the riverside hostel at *Riverbend Hot Springs* (☎ 505-894-6183), 100 Austin St, with dormitory-style accommodations in cabins and trailers for $12 a person with an HI/AYH card, $13 without. Couples' rooms are $27, and a few rooms with kitchenettes are $35 and $45 with king-size beds, including taxes. There are several teepees sleeping couples, families and small groups. Hot-spring tubs are available morning and evening and are

free for guests ($5 for drop-ins). The owners are friendly and helpful to budget travelers, providing free pastries, local information and discounts at local restaurants and other places.

The cheapest motels start in the $20s for a double room; they're basic and worn, although adequate for those on a tight budget. There are seven or eight cheapies along Date St between Sixth and Ninth Sts, including the *Trail Motel* (☎ 505-894-3106), *Chateau Courts* (☎ 505-894-7049) (some with kitchenettes) and the *Sunland Motel* (☎ 505-894-3571). At the south end is the *Travelers Lodge* (☎ 505-894-6527), 1603 S Broadway.

Better motels start in the low $30s and include the *Motel Rio Grande* (☎ 505-894-9769), 720 S Broadway (in the suburb of Williamsburg at I-25 exit 75), with a pool and some rooms with a kitchenette. The *Ace Lodge* (☎ 505-894-2151), 1302 N Date St, has a pool, play area and decent rooms in the $30s. The *Desert View Motel* (☎ 505-894-3318), 906 N Date St, has OK rooms with refrigerators and free morning coffee. The *Oasis Motel* (☎ 505-894-6629, 800-847-7891), 819 N Date St, is popular with local government workers. The *Motor Manor Motel & Apartments* (☎ 505-894-3648), 595 Main St, has doubles starting in the mid-$30s. The *Charles Motel & Bath House* (☎ 505-894-7154), 601 Broadway, charges from $35 for a single and has its own hot springs.

Places to Stay – Middle
The *Super 8 Motel* (☎ 505-894-7888, fax 505-894-7883), 2151 N Date St (at I-25 exit 79), offers reasonable rooms for around $43/49 for singles/doubles, or $52 with two beds. Opposite, the *Best Western Hot Springs Motor Inn* (☎/fax 505-894-6665), 2270 N Date St, has a seasonal pool, free coffee in the lobby and K-Bob's Restaurant next door. Large, pleasant rooms with queen- and king-size beds and double sinks run $47 to $57 for singles and $5 more for doubles.

Out by Elephant Butte Lake, the *Marina Suites Motel* (☎ 505-744-5269), Country Club Rd, charges $40 to $70 depending on the season. All units have kitchens. The *Inn at the Butte* (☎/fax 505-744-5431), near the lake, has a pool, tennis court, restaurant and bar, and nice rooms (many with lake views) for about $50 to $80. (Also see Elephant Butte Lake State Park, below.)

Places to Eat
The locally popular *Hilltop Cafe* (☎ 505-894-3407), 1301 N Date St, serves inexpensive 'home cooking' from 6 am to 9 pm daily. *K-Bob's* (☎ 505-894-2127), I-25 exit 79, serves reasonably priced family-style meals and steaks from 7 am to 8 pm daily, with longer weekend and summer hours.

Two excellent choices for Mexican food are *La Cocina* (☎ 505-894-6499), 280 N Date St, from 11 am to 9 pm daily, and *La Piñata* (☎ 505-894-9047), 1990 S Broadway, from 7 am to 8 pm, Monday to Saturday. Neither serves alcohol. For Chinese food, try *Chinese Lantern* (☎ 505-894-6840), 414 Main St, open from 11 am to 9 pm daily except Monday. The most upscale place in town is *Los Arcos* (☎ 505-894-6200), 1400 N Date St, serving steaks, lobster, salad bar and local fish dinners from 5 to 10:30 pm daily, plus Sunday brunch from 11 am to 2 pm. Prices vary considerably – there's something for most budgets.

The restaurants at the Inn at the Butte and Dam Site Recreation Area are also good choices.

Entertainment
The old-fashioned *El Cortez Theater* (☎ 505-894-5023), 415 Main St, shows first-run movies.

Getting There & Away
Greyhound/TNM&O (☎ 505-894-3649), 800 N Hwy 51 (at Jerry's RV Center, 1.2 miles from Date and Third Sts), runs several daily buses north and south along I-25.

AROUND TRUTH OR CONSEQUENCES
Elephant Butte Lake State Park
This 60-sq-mile artificial lake is New Mexico's largest, formed in 1916 by

damming the Rio Grande. The state park is on the west shore of the lake, 5 miles east of Truth or Consequences (along Third St). The lake is very popular for fishing and camping. Water-skiing and wind-surfing are big from April to September. Anglers go for bass, stripers and other species.

A visitor center (☎ 505-744-5421), PO Box 13, Elephant Butte, NM 87935, has information, a 1½-mile-loop nature trail and a nearby marina with boat rentals. Several campgrounds provide more than 100 sites with RV hookups, and more than 200 more sites with hookups are planned. There are hot showers, a playground, and picnic and barbecue areas. North along the lake are hundreds of undeveloped sites and other boat launch sites. Day use is $3; undeveloped camping (pit toilets, no water) is $6; developed camping is $7 or $11 with hookups.

At the lake's south end is *Dam Site Recreation Area* (☎ 505-894-2073, fax 505-894-0776, damsite@riolink.com), on state land but privately operated. Seventeen clean, rustic cabins, some with kitchenettes, are $60 to $85 double; 40% off in winter. A B&B is planned for 1999. RV sites (☎ 505-894-3177) are $15 and up. A restaurant and bar (☎ 505-894-2073) is open every day for lunch and dinner from March to October, and from Thursday to Monday in winter. Breakfast is available from Memorial Day to Labor Day. A marina (☎ 505-894-2041) has tackle, gas, basic groceries and supplies, and boat rentals (fishing, pontoon and skiing) from $40 to $90 for two hours, $110 to $220 per day, plus fuel.

Caballo Lake State Park

This park (☎ 505-743-3942), PO Box 32, Caballo, NM 87931, is another artificial lake resulting from a dam on the Rio Grande and offers fishing, boating, skiing and windsurfing. A few dozen bald eagles overwinter around the lake and can often be seen between October and February. Fishing (especially white bass and walleye) is best from mid-March to mid-June.

There are boat ramps, a playground and several campgrounds with hot showers, 64 RV hookups and 250 sites without hookups. The park is a mile northeast of exit 59 on I-25, 17 miles south of Truth or Consequences. The ranger station is at the northernmost park entrance, and there is a bait and tackle shop (☎ 505-743-0409) opposite.

Percha Dam State Park, about 3 miles south of Caballo Lake State Park and administered by it, has a further 80 sites, six with hookups, hot showers and a playground. There is no boat ramp. Fees are $3 per vehicle for day use, $7 for camping and $11 with hookups.

Ghost Towns

Several Sierra County ghost towns, with numerous standing though empty or dilapidated buildings and a few restored ones, are west of I-25 exit 83. In **Cuchillo**, about 8 miles west of I-25, buy a beer or snack at the *Cuchillo Bar & Store* (☎ 505-743-2296), which has been here since about 1850 and hasn't changed much. Or grab a bite at the *Cuchillo Café* (☎ 505-743-2591), open from noon to 7 pm, Friday to Sunday, serving good homemade New Mexican food. (They even grind their own blue-corn flour, I'm told.)

About 29 miles farther west is **Winston**, once a mining town of more than 3000 inhabitants and now home to a few families. Stay at the century-old, two-room *Winston B&B and Cafe* (☎ 505-743-0208). The simple rooms are unpretentiously old-fashioned and share a bath and phone; rates are $50 to $65 a double (depending on season) with a full breakfast, $15 less without. The café is open 9 am to 8 pm, Wednesday to Sunday, closed Monday and Tuesday. Winston also has a store (☎ 505-743-6915) and the *Diamond Bar* (☎ 505-743-3446), closed Sunday.

Two miles beyond Winston is **Chloride**, the end of the road as far as ordinary cars go. The Pioneer Store Museum (☎ 505-743-2736) has historical artifacts housed in the restored Pioneer Store, which operated from 1881 to 1921.

HATCH

Hatch is 2 miles west of I-25 exit 41, at the junction of Hwys 26 and 185/187, 41 miles north of Las Cruces. Drivers rushing from Arizona to Albuquerque can take Hwy 26 between Deming and Hatch, thus avoiding Las Cruces and cutting about 55 miles from the trip.

Hatch is famous for being the center of New Mexico's (and hence the USA's) chile-growing region, and you can buy chiles, salsas, *ristras* (decorative strings and wreaths of chiles) and other chile products in one of several stores in this small town.

The chamber of commerce (☎ 505-267-5050), 112 W Hall (just north of Hwy 26 on Hwy 187), open 9 am to 2 pm, Monday to Friday, has a tiny museum. The police station (☎ 505-267-3021) is at 104 Franklin (Hwy 26).

An annual **chile festival** is held over Labor Day weekend. Delicious meals and fresh and prepared chiles of all levels of spiciness are sold, and various country-fair-type events take place. Food lovers could combine this festival with the nearby Hillsboro Apple Festival, held the same weekend.

The only hotel is the small and inexpensive *Village Plaza Motel* (☎ 505-267-3091), 608 Franklin. *Happy Trails RV Park* (☎ 505-267-4522) is at 508 Franklin. There are also a couple of cafés in the area.

LAS CRUCES

The city of Las Cruces is at 4200 feet, in an attractive setting between the Rio Grande Valley and the strangely fluted Organ Mountains rising to the east. To the north lies the remains of Fort Selden and the adjacent Leasburg Dam State Park, where a small lake offers respite on hot days. To the east, two recreation areas lure bird watchers and outdoor enthusiasts. Despite several rather interesting annual events, there is no high/low season for hotels.

History

In 1535, Spanish explorers heading north from Mexico along the Rio Grande Valley passed through this area, recording that there were Indian villages nearby. Today there is little trace of those villages and of the many early travelers who had passed through and camped in the area. In 1787 and again in 1830, Apaches killed bands of travelers camping here, and their graves were marked by a collection of crosses – hence the Spanish name of Las Cruces. There was no permanent settlement here until 1849, however. Several of the town's original buildings are still standing.

Adjacent to Las Cruces, the historic village of Mesilla was established in 1850 for Mexican settlers who wished to avoid becoming part of the USA after the Mexican-American War. Their hopes were short-lived, however; in 1853, the USA bought Mesilla and many miles of land to the south and west in what became known as the Gadsden Purchase. Initially, Mesilla was a larger and more important town than Las Cruces, and Mesilla's Hispanic plaza and surrounding streets contain many buildings from those early years, including a stagecoach stop for the Butterfield Overland Mail Company.

Today, Las Cruces is booming with 74,000 inhabitants (a sixfold growth since 1950), while Mesilla has fewer residents than it did in the 19th century. Las Cruces is the Doña Ana County seat and New Mexico's second largest town. It is an important agricultural, industrial and academic center. Most farms are small and family-owned, and major crops are chiles, pecans and apples. The nearby White Sands Missile Range provides thousands of jobs. The New Mexico State University (NMSU) has some 15,000 students attending undergraduate, graduate and post-graduate programs.

Orientation & Information

The city lies roughly northwest of the intersection of I-25 and I-10 linking Arizona and Texas.

The Convention and Visitor's Bureau (☎ 505-541-2444, 800-343-7827), 211 N Water, Las Cruces, NM 88001, and chamber of commerce (☎ 505-524-1968), 760 W Picacho Ave, Las Cruces, NM 88005, both provide visitor information from 8 am to 5 pm, Monday to Friday. The BLM

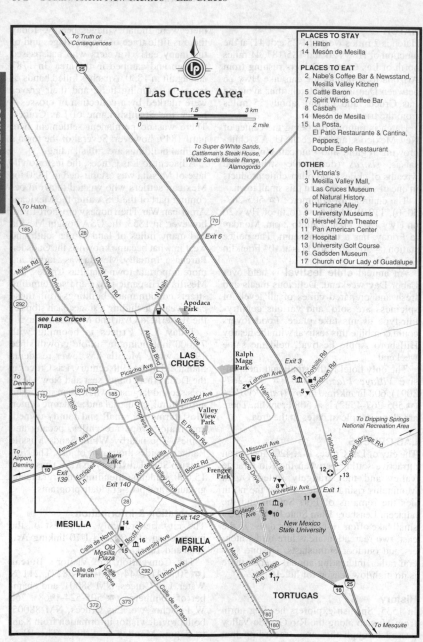

Las Cruces Area

To Truth or
Consequences

0   1.5   3 km
0   1   2 mile

To Super 8/White Sands,
Cattleman's Steak House,
White Sands Missile Range,
Alamogordo

PLACES TO STAY
4   Hilton
14   Mesón de Mesilla

PLACES TO EAT
2   Nabe's Coffee Bar & Newsstand,
     Mesilla Valley Kitchen
5   Cattle Baron
7   Spirit Winds Coffee Bar
8   Casbah
14   Mesón de Mesilla
15   La Posta,
     El Patio Restaurante & Cantina,
     Peppers,
     Double Eagle Restaurant

OTHER
1   Victoria's
3   Mesilla Valley Mall,
     Las Cruces Museum
     of Natural History
6   Hurricane Alley
9   University Museums
10   Hershel Zohn Theater
11   Pan American Center
12   Hospital
13   University Golf Course
16   Gadsden Museum
17   Church of Our Lady of Guadalupe

To Hatch

To Deming

To Airport,
Deming

see Las Cruces
map

LAS
CRUCES

Apodaca
Park

Ralph
Magg
Park

Valley
View
Park

Burn
Lake

Frenger
Park

To Dripping Springs
National Recreation Area

MESILLA

MESILLA
PARK

Old
Mesilla
Plaza

New Mexico
State University

TORTUGAS

To Mesquite

(☎ 505-525-4300) is at 1800 Marquess St. The library (☎ 505-528-4000) is at 200 E Picacho Ave. The local newspapers are the daily *Las Cruces Sun-News*, which runs both international and local news, and *The Bulletin*, a free weekly covering local community news. The main post office (☎ 505-524-2841) is at 201 E Las Cruces Ave. Las Cruces Recycling (☎ 505-528-3590) has information; bins are at Smith's, 2200 E Lohman Ave, K Mart, 1240 El Paseo Blvd and other locations. The main hospital (☎ 505-522-8641) is at 2450 S Telshor Blvd. The police station (☎ 505-526-0795) is at 217 E Picacho Ave.

Historic Buildings

Check at the chamber or visitor's bureau for brochures about local historical self-guided walks. Highlights include the old **Amador Hotel**, built in 1853 at Amador Ave and Water St, once the best hotel for many miles around and now a county office building. Built in 1877, the **Armijo House**, at Lohman Ave and Church St, was the home of one of Las Cruces' most important

families and now houses a law firm. You can see a variety of turn-of-the-century buildings in the **Mesquite District** and the **Alameda District**, a few blocks east and west of the Downtown Mall.

Branigan Cultural Center

In the Downtown Mall at 490-500 N Water St, the center (☎ 505-541-2155) houses both the **Museum of Fine Art & Culture** and the **Las Cruces Historical Museum**, slated to open in 1998. There are small collections of local art, sculpture, quilts and historic artifacts, and changing art shows. The center also arranges tours of the late 1800s **Log Cabin Museum** at Lucero Ave and Main St at the north end of the Downtown Mall. Hours are 10 am to 5 pm, Monday to Friday, 9 am to 3 pm on Saturday and 1 to 5 pm on Sunday, but hours are subject to change. Admission is free.

University Museums

The **NMSU Museum** (☎ 505-646-3739), in Kent Hall at Solano Drive and University Ave, houses changing exhibits focusing on

---

Downtown Mall

Las Cruces, like many US cities, has suffered from economic depression in the downtown area as new homes are built in the suburbs and many businesses move there to service the growing population. In an attempt to revitalize the old central area, the Downtown Mall was built, but it has been unsuccessful in drawing people back. After all, most people live on the east side where the huge Mesilla Valley Mall is both larger and more convenient to shoppers.

Faced with what looked like an expensive white elephant, the city decided that instead of trying to make it a shopping mall, it would make the Downtown Mall more of a community center. As such, the mall has been moderately successful and is now the site of many of the city's most important annual special events. In addition, every Wednesday and Saturday from 8 am to 12:30 pm, it is the site of the popular Las Cruces Farmers & Crafts Market, where anywhere from 80 to 250 vendors set up stalls to sell fresh produce (including chiles, of course) and all kinds of Southwestern arts and crafts.

The Branigan Cultural Center in the mall was expanded in 1997-98 to house two museums. There are a couple of theaters, a large used bookstore (☎ 505-524-8471), some restaurants and the Convention & Visitor's Bureau across the street. So, apart from the bookstore and the Wednesday and Saturday markets, this isn't a mall for shopping, but it does have plenty of cultural interest. And a short walk east or west of the mall takes you into the Mesquite and Alameda districts, where many of the city's oldest buildings still stand. ■

local art, history and archaeology. It's worth a look. Hours are 1 to 4 pm, Tuesday to Friday, and the museum is closed when school is not in session. The **NMSU Art Gallery** (☎ 505-646-2545), in Williams Hall just east of Kent Hall, has changing exhibits almost every month and a large permanent collection of contemporary art. Hours are 10 am to 4 pm, Monday to Friday. Admission is free.

Las Cruces Museum of Natural History
In an improbable location within the Mesilla Valley Mall, 700 S Telshor Blvd, this museum (☎ 505-522-3120) has both live and stuffed wildlife as well as other items loosely connected with natural history and free Internet access. Kids like the interactive exhibits. Admission is free and hours are noon to 5 pm Monday to Thursday, noon to 9 pm Friday, 10 am to 6 pm Saturday and noon to 6 pm Sunday.

Mesilla
For many visitors, a stop in Mesilla is the highlight of their time in Las Cruces. Despite the souvenir shops and tourist-oriented restaurants, the Mesilla Plaza and surrounding blocks are a step back in time. The plaza is the obvious center of things, but wander a few blocks around to get a feeling of an important mid-19th-century Southwestern town of Hispanic heritage.

Formerly a Mexican town, Mesilla became part of the USA after the Gadsden Purchase. For the story, visit the private **Gadsden Museum** (☎ 505-526-6293), on Boutz Rd just off Hwy 28, a few hundred yards east from the plaza. Mesilla is about 3 miles southwest of downtown Las Cruces.

Dripping Springs National Recreation Area
Once called the Cox Ranch and now jointly managed by the BLM and the Nature Conservancy, this area is a good place for bird-watching in the Organ Mountains. There is a nature trail and picnic area. Deer, coyotes and rock squirrels are often seen, and

mountain lions are occasionally reported. To get there, head east on University Ave, which becomes unpaved Dripping Springs Rd (it's about 9 miles). Hours are 8 am to sunset; the Cox Visitor Center (☎ 505-522-1219) is open from 9 am to 5 pm. Admission is $3 per vehicle.

En route to the area is the **New Mexico Farm & Ranch Heritage Museum** (☎ 505-522-4100), 4100 Dripping Springs Rd, the largest farm and ranch museum in the country.

Activities
You can **golf** at the 18-hole NMSU course (☎ 505-646-3219) at University Ave and Telshor Blvd.

Special Events
Whole Enchilada Fiesta The city's best-known event is their Enchilada Fiesta (☎ 505-647-1228), held the first Friday to Sunday in October, which features a big variety of live music, food booths, arts and crafts, sporting events, a chile cookoff, carnival rides and a parade, all of which culminate in the cooking of the world's biggest enchilada on Sunday morning. Events are held in the Downtown Mall.

Fiesta of Our Lady of Guadalupe Held December 10 to 12 in the Indian village of Tortugas at the south end of Las Cruces, this fiesta involves drummers and masked dancers who accompany a statue of Mary in a procession from the church late into the first night. On the following day, participants climb several miles to 4914-foot Tortugas Mountain for mass; dancing and ceremonies continue in the village into the night. The Church of Our Lady of Guadalupe (☎ 505-526-8171) is on Emilia St south of Tortugas Drive. The public is welcome.

Other Events The Mesilla Balloon Rally (☎ 505-524-1968) is held in mid-January. The Border Book Festival (☎ 505-524-1499), held in the Branigan Cultural Center around mid-March, features writing workshops, discussions with famous writers and, of course, books. The Southern New

Mexico State Fair (☎ 505-524-6897), held for five days in late September at the fairgrounds west of town, features a rodeo and other Western events. The Renaissance Arts and Crafts Fair (☎ 505-523-6403), held the first weekend in November, features performers in 16th-century English garb and is the biggest crafts fair of the year. An International Mariachi Conference (☎ 505-523-2681) is held in mid-November.

Places to Stay
Most hotels have small outdoor pools open in summer; assume they do unless I state otherwise. The rates are slightly higher in summer, but seasonal variation is small, except for the occasional special event.

Places to Stay – Camping
In town, there's Siesta RV Park (☎ 505-523-6816), 1551 Avenida de Mesilla, with showers and a coin laundry. It charges $17 with full hookups and has a few less expensive tent sites. Nearby, RV Doc's (☎ 505-526-8401), 1475 Avenida de Mesilla, is a newer, cheaper RV park. Other cheaper places include Coachlight Inn RV Park (☎ 505-526-3301), 301 S Motel Blvd (no tents), and Dalmonts RV Trailer Corral (☎ 505-523-2992), 2224 S Valley Drive.

The Best RV Park (☎ 505-526-6555, 800-526-6555), 814 Weinrich Rd, 5 miles west of the Rio Grande along Picacho Ave, has a pool, laundry, recreation room, playground, grocery store and showers. RV sites are $20 with hookups, tents are $15 and four camping cabins are $23 each. (Also look under Around Las Cruces and Aguirre Springs National Recreation Area, later in this chapter.)

Places to Stay – Budget
A number of cheap places are clustered along Picacho Ave east of Hwy 292. Most have doubles in the $20s, some in the teens. The nicest of these is the Royal Host Motel (☎ 505-524-8536), 2146 W Picacho Ave, at $28/32 for singles/doubles. Others include the Western Inn (☎/fax 505-523-5399), 2155 W Picacho Ave, with singles from $25; Economy Inn (☎ 505-524-8627),

2160 W Picacho Ave, with 100 rooms from $24/28; Desert Lodge (☎ 505-524-1925), 1900 W Picacho Ave, for $20/24 (no pool); Budget Inn (☎ 505-523-0365), 2255 W Picacho Ave with doubles around $20 (no pool); the less expensive Townhouse Motel (☎ 505-524-7733), 2205 W Picacho Ave, and a few others.

Other basic hotels with rooms starting in the $20s are scattered around town. These include the Coachlight Inn (☎ 505-526-3301), 301 S Motel Blvd, which is clean and has a pool and RV sites; Sands Motel (☎ 505-524-7791), 1655 S Main St, also with a pool; and several others listed by the visitor's bureau.

The reliable Motel 6 (☎ 505-525-1010, fax 505-525-0139), 235 La Posada Lane, charges $34/40 in summer and $30/36 the rest of the year. Also, the pleasant Day's End Lodge (☎ 505-524-7753, fax 505-523-2127), 755 N Valley Drive, has rooms for about $35/40.

Places to Stay – Middle
Motels The Super 8 Motel/White Sands (☎ 505-382-1490, fax 505-382-1849), 4411 N Main St, northeast of town, is one of the few Super 8s with a pool. Standard rooms have coffeemakers, a few have refrigerators or microwaves, and rates are in the $40s with continental breakfast. Super 8 Motel/La Posada (☎/fax 505-523-8695), 245 La Posada Lane, lacks a pool and has rooms for $38.88/44.88. The new Budgetel (☎ 505-523-0100, fax 505-523-0707), 1500 Hickory Drive, is also in this price range, though recently had discounts to $30, including continental breakfast. Rooms are quiet, bright and comfortable, with coffeemakers and clock radios, and there's a coin laundry and year-round outdoor pool.

The Days Inn (☎ 505-526-4441, fax 505-526-1980), 2600 S Valley Drive, has a restaurant (breakfast and dinner only), bar, indoor pool, sauna and coin laundry. Decent rooms, some with microwaves or coffeemakers, are $45/55 (though $39 rooms were offered recently). Nearby, the Comfort Inn (☎ 505-527-2000, fax

505-527-0966), 2585 S Valley Drive, has rooms with microwaves and refrigerators, free continental breakfast, and a year-round outdoor pool and spa. Rates are around $55/60.

The *Hampton Inn* (☎ 505-526-8311, fax 505-527-2015), 755 Avenida de Mesilla, is one of the closest hotels to Mesilla; it has nice rooms for $55 to $65 (discounts for long stays). Full continental breakfast is included, and there are coffeemakers in each room. Nearby is *La Quinta* (☎ 505-524-0331, fax 505-525-8360), 790 Avenida de Mesilla, which offers an exercise room and comfortable rooms from $50 to $65, including continental breakfast. Opposite is the *Best Western Mesilla Valley Inn* (☎ 505-524-8603, fax 505-526-8437), 901 Avenida de Mesilla. It has a restaurant open from 6 am to 10 pm, room service, a bar with occasional entertainment, a pool and spa, a game room, coin laundry and health club privileges. Double rooms are in the $50s and $60s.

The slightly cheaper *Best Western Mission Inn* (☎ 505-524-8591, fax 505-523-4740), 1765 S Main St, has spacious rooms and includes a full breakfast. There is a restaurant and lounge and pleasant grounds with a playground.

B&Bs *Lundeen Inn of the Arts* (☎ 505-526-3327, 888-526-3326, fax 505-647-1334, lundeen@innofthearts.com), 618 S Alameda Blvd, Las Cruces, NM 88005, is a large, turn-of-the-19th-century adobe house owned by architects, with 20 guest rooms and an art gallery. Some rooms have kitchenettes and all have private baths and phones. Rates range from $72 to $100, including full breakfast.

The *TRH Smith Mansion B&B* (☎ 505-525-2525, 800-526-1914, fax 505-524-8227, SmithMansion@zianet.com), 909 N Alameda Blvd, Las Cruces, NM 88005, is in a historic 1914 mansion. Four guest rooms have phones and cassette/radios. Two rooms share a bath ($60) and two have private baths, one with a fireplace ($70 or $80), including a full German-style breakfast. A game room includes a pool table,

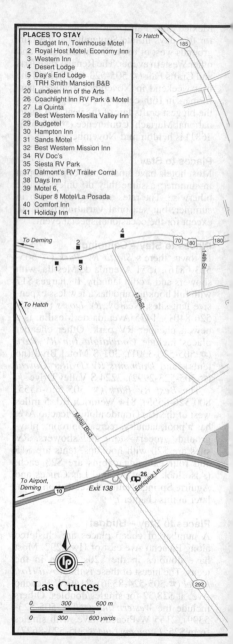

PLACES TO STAY
1 Budget Inn, Townhouse Motel
2 Royal Host Motel, Economy Inn
3 Western Inn
4 Desert Lodge
5 Day's End Lodge
8 TRH Smith Mansion B&B
20 Lundeen Inn of the Arts
26 Coachlight Inn RV Park & Motel
27 La Quinta
28 Best Western Mesilla Valley Inn
29 Budgetel
30 Hampton Inn
31 Sands Motel
32 Best Western Mission Inn
34 RV Doc's
35 Siesta RV Park
37 Dalmont's RV Trailer Corral
38 Days Inn
39 Motel 6,
   Super 8 Motel/La Posada
40 Comfort Inn
41 Holiday Inn

To Hatch
185

To Deming
4
2
70 80 180
1 3
14th St

To Hatch

17th St

To Deming

26
Enriquez Ln

To Airport,
Deming
10   Exit 138

Las Cruces

0   300   600 m

0   300   600 yards

292

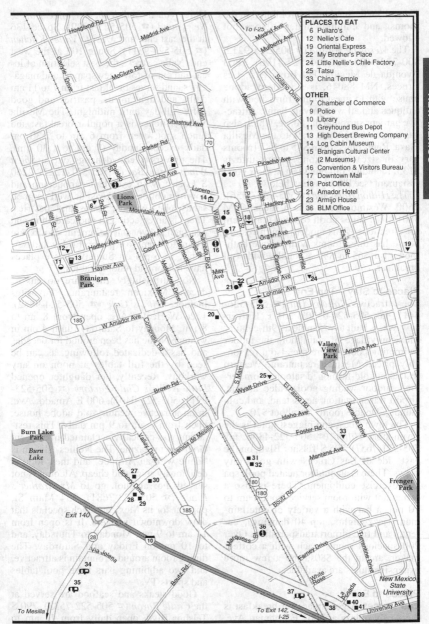

PLACES TO EAT
- 6 Pullaro's
- 12 Nellie's Cafe
- 19 Oriental Express
- 22 My Brother's Place
- 24 Little Nellie's Chile Factory
- 25 Tatsu
- 33 China Temple

OTHER
- 7 Chamber of Commerce
- 9 Police
- 10 Library
- 11 Greyhound Bus Depot
- 13 High Desert Brewing Company
- 14 Log Cabin Museum
- 15 Branigan Cultural Center (2 Museums)
- 16 Convention & Visitors Bureau
- 17 Downtown Mall
- 18 Post Office
- 21 Amador Hotel
- 23 Armijo House
- 36 BLM Office

TV and VCR. Smoking is prohibited in the rooms, and children under 10 are not allowed.

The *Mesón de Mesilla* (☎ 505-525-9212, 800-732-6025, fax 505-527-4196), 1803 Avenida de Mesilla, PO Box 1212, Las Cruces, NM 88046, is a modern adobe house with 15 guest rooms furnished with antiques and all with private baths. Attractive gardens surround the house, which also has a pool. It's a short walk to the Mesilla Plaza. Rates range from $45 to $87 (rooms vary in size) and a honeymoon suite is $135, including full breakfast in their good restaurant (see Places to Eat, below).

The *Hilltop Hacienda* (☎ 505-382-3556), 2600 Westmoreland, Las Cruces, NM 88012, is 7 miles north of town (call them for directions). This modern Southwestern house has three rooms with private bathrooms for $65 to $85 a double, with full breakfast.

Places to Stay – Top End

The attractive *Holiday Inn* (☎ 505-526-4411, fax 505-524-0530), 201 E University Ave, is built to resemble a 19th-century Mexican village (if you ignore the indoor swimming pool). There are also a reasonably priced Mexican restaurant, Western restaurant, old-fashioned saloon, room service, indoor wading pool, video arcade, airport transportation, newsstand and coin laundry. Double rooms are about $70.

The town's best and biggest hotel is the seven-story *Hilton* (☎ 505-522-4300, fax 505-521-7657), 705 S Telshor Blvd, on the east side of Las Cruces with good city views. There is an outdoor heated pool, spa and exercise equipment. There is also a restaurant with room service from 6 am to 10 pm, a bar with a variety of entertainment (jazz nights, top-40 dancing), car rental and free airport transportation. Over 200 spacious rooms, each with a coffee-maker, are in the $80s, and a few more expensive suites are available.

Places to Eat

Las Cruces A good place for breakfast is the Arroyo Plaza at 2001 E Lohman Ave.

Here, you'll find *Nabe's Coffee Bar & Newsstand* (☎ 505-523-9339), Space 136 at the east end, and *Mesilla Valley Kitchen* (☎ 505-523-9311), Space 102 at the west end. Nabe's stocks the best selection of local and out-of-town newspapers and magazines, and serves breakfast from 7 to 11 am daily, and light meals, pastries and good coffee all day until midnight. The Mesilla Valley Kitchen is a popular breakfast and lunch spot, open from 6 am to 2:30 pm daily except Sunday (7 am to 1:30 pm). The university crowd hangs out at *Spirit Winds Coffee Bar* (☎ 505-521-1222), 2260 S Locust, with excellent cappuccino and gourmet coffees and teas, as well as good sandwiches, salads, soups and pastries. There is an eclectic gift and card shop and occasional live entertainment. Hours are 11 am to 8 pm, to 9 pm on Friday and Saturday, to 6 pm on Sunday. These places have indoor and outdoor tables.

Not surprisingly, there are dozens of decent Mexican restaurants. Favorites include *Nellie's Cafe* (☎ 505-524-9982), 1226 W Hadley Ave, open from 8 am to 8 pm, Monday to Saturday (until 4 pm in winter). Nellie has been around for decades and has a dedicated following, as can be seen by the full tables at noon on any workday. Recently, her daughter opened *Little Nellie's Chile Factory* (☎ 505-523-9911, 505-523-6407), 600 E Amador Ave, in an attractive, century-old adobe house, open from 7 am to 9 pm daily. This restaurant was critically acclaimed in a recent *Gourmet* magazine. The Nellies' slogan is 'Chile with an Attitude' and their food is deliciously spicy and cheap. Alcohol is not served. For alcohol, go to *My Brother's Place* (☎ 505-523-7681), 334 Main St, popular for its Mexican lunch specials that draw downtown workers. It is open from 11 am to 9 pm, Monday to Thursday, and to 10 pm on Friday and Saturday. The dining room around a fountain is attractive, and two adjoining bars have pool tables and sports TV.

Good steaks and seafood are served at the *Cattle Baron* (☎ 505-522-7533), 790 S Telshor Blvd, open daily from 11 am to

9:30 pm, Friday and Saturday to 10 pm. Most dinners cost from $10 to $20, and a kids' menu is available. *Cattleman's Steak House* (☎ 505-382-9051), 4401 N Main St, is cheaper and convenient to the Super 8 Motel/White Sands. It is open from 11 am to 2 pm, Monday to Friday, 5 to 10 pm, Monday to Saturday and from 11 am to 10 pm on Sunday. This restaurant features a variety of entertainment, ranging from musicians to dinner theater.

For Chinese food, *China Temple* (☎ 505-522-8770, 505-526-5210), 1401 El Paseo Rd, is open from 11 am to 9:30 pm daily, with an all-you-can-eat lunch buffet until 2:30 pm daily except Sunday. All you-can-eat lunches and dinners for about $5 and $6 are also featured at *Oriental Express* (☎ 505-524-7423), 1413 E Amador Ave, open from 11 am to 9 pm daily, till 10 pm on Friday and Saturday. For reasonably priced Japanese and 'New Oriental' dining, try unpretentious *Tatsu* (☎ 505-526-7144), 930 El Paseo Rd, open daily from 11 am to 9 pm, till 10 pm on Friday and Saturday. A good choice for Italian food is *Pullaro's* (☎ 505-523-6801), 901 W Picacho Ave, open daily from 11 am to 2 pm and 5 to 9 pm. *Casbah* (☎ 505-522-8530), 2404 S Locust, has a small menu of authentic Arabic cuisine in the $8 to $10 range.

Mesilla The *Mesón de Mesilla* (☎ 505-525-2380) restaurant (in the B&B) is a good one, serving daily dinner from 5:30 to 9 pm. The small but varied continental gourmet menu has entrées between $20 and $30. Sunday brunch is $17. Reservations are requested.

For Mexican and New Mexican cuisine, traditional Mesilla provides the appropriate setting. The most famous place is *La Posta* (☎ 505-524-3524), which is in an early-19th-century adobe house (predating the founding of Mesilla) on the east corner of the plaza. Once a Butterfield stagecoach stop in the 1850s, the restaurant is now full of character. The current restaurant, which has been on the premises since the 1930s, is open from 11 am to 9 pm (9:30 pm on Fridays and Saturdays) daily except Mon-

day. You can get a good Mexican or steak dinner here for about $5 to $14, depending on your appetite.

Several other restaurants on the plaza serve equally good food – some people say even better, but in my mind, they are all good. *El Patio Restaurante & Cantina* (☎ 505-524-0982), a Mexican restaurant also housed in an early adobe building and in operation since the 1930s, has prices a touch lower than La Posta, and the bar attracts local jazz lovers. Hours are 11 am to 2 pm, Monday to Friday, 5:30 to 9 pm daily (9:30 on Friday and Saturday); closed Sunday. Plant-filled *Peppers* (☎ 505-523-4999), in modern pink and green pastels set off by old beams, serves a varied New Mexican cuisine in the $10 to $15 range. It is open from 11 am to 10 pm daily (9 pm on Sunday). Next door, the *Double Eagle Restaurant* (☎ 505-523-6700) is Mesilla Plaza's most upscale restaurant, offering continental and Southwestern cuisine in an elegant Victorian setting. It is open from 11 am to 10 pm Monday to Saturday (call for Sunday hours) and has dinner entrées in the $14 to $30 range.

Entertainment

The Bulletin (appearing Thursdays for free) is a good source for local entertainment. *Las Cruces Sun-News* runs daily cinema listings and a nightlife guide in its Friday edition. The main cinema complexes are *Cinema 8* (☎ 505-521-9355), in the Mesilla Valley Mall; *Rio Grande Twin Theater* (☎ 505-526-2321), 213 N Main St (Downtown Mall); and *Video 4* (☎ 505-523-6900), 1005 El Paseo Rd. Foreign and art films are screened at the *Fountain Theater* (☎ 505-524-8287), 2469 Calle de Guadalupe, half a block south of the Mesilla Plaza.

The reputable American Southwest Theater Company presents plays at the *Hershel Zohn Theater* (☎ 505-646-4515) on the NMSU campus. The Las Cruces Symphony (☎ 505-646-3709) plays at the NMSU *Pan American Center* (☎ 505-646-1420). Other cultural events take place here; call the special events director (☎ 505-646-4413) for information. The Las Cruces Community

Theater (☎ 505-647-2060) performs in the *Downtown Mall* with five shows a year.

For the bar scene, check out *El Patio* (☎ 505-526-9943), next to the restaurant in Mesilla, with jazz acts midweek and rock or blues on weekends. *High Desert Brewing Company* (☎ 505-525-6752), 1201 W Hadley Ave, is a microbrewery with good beer and live music on weekends. *Hurricane Alley* (☎ 505-532-9358), 1490 Missouri Ave, also has live rock music and dancing on weekends. *Victoria's* (☎ 505-523-0440), 2395 N Solano Drive, features mariachi and Latin bands on weekends.

Local acts to catch include slide-guitarist/singer Bugs Salcido (tell me who he reminds you of for my informal survey) and Last Men On Earth (Roots Rock de Nuevo Mexico) with Eddy doing covers in his own style – you might not recognize the song unless you know the words. Nice folks.

Shopping
The Mesilla Plaza area has more than 30 stores selling anything from Navajo rugs to the latest novels. Mainly, the stores sell souvenirs ranging from cheap and kitsch to expensive and excellent. Shoppers should allow several hours – good restaurants provide a respite from the consumer frenzy.

The huge Mesilla Valley Mall, near I-25 exit 3, has department stores and many other establishments, including the Mesilla Valley Fine Arts Gallery (☎ 505-522-2933) with an excellent ever-changing display of local artists. This is a cooperative, and though pieces are for sale, the artists encourage browsing.

Visit the Downtown Mall on Wednesday and Saturday mornings. (See the Downtown Mall sidebar.)

Getting There & Away
Air Las Cruces has a small airport about 8 miles west of downtown. Mesa Airlines (☎ 505-526-9743) runs three flights on weekdays, two on weekends, straight to Albuquerque.

El Paso International Airport, less than an hour away, has flights to all over the USA. See Bus (below) for transport to El Paso.

Bus Greyhound/TNM&O (☎ 505-524-8518), 490 N Valley Drive, has two daily buses east to Roswell and beyond, 12 daily south to El Paso, six daily west to Tucson, Phoenix and California, and four daily north to Albuquerque and Denver, Colorado.

Las Cruces Shuttle Service (☎ 505-525-1784, 800-288-1784) has 13 vans a day from Las Cruces to the El Paso Airport. The one-way fare is $23 for one person and $10 for each additional person in your group. The service also runs four vans a day to Deming and Silver City ($25 one-way and $14 for each additional person). Roundtrip discounts are available. There is an extra $6 charge for pickup at your address, or call them for the nearest designated stop. Reservations are required.

Getting Around
Bus Roadrunner Transit (☎ 505-525-2500) operates eight bus routes in Las Cruces (but not Mesilla). Buses run every 40 minutes from 6:30 am to 7:10 pm, Monday to Friday, and every 30 minutes from 9 am to 6 pm on Saturday. There is no Sunday service. Call the company from 8 am to 5 pm, Monday to Friday, ask any bus driver or look in the telephone directory for route maps.

There is no bus service to Las Cruces Airport.

Taxi Checker Cab/Yellow Cab (☎ 505-524-1711) will take reservations and pick you up 24 hours a day.

Car Rental Enterprise (☎ 505-525-1778), 121 Wyatt Drive; Hertz (☎ 505-521-4807), in the Hilton; and Toyota (☎ 505-523-5566), 935 S Valley Drive, all rent cars.

AROUND LAS CRUCES
Fort Selden State Monument
Fort Selden was built in 1865 to protect travelers. Buffalo soldiers (African American army units) were stationed here, and US General Douglas MacArthur spent some of his childhood at the fort. Closed in 1891, Fort Selden is now in ruins, but a small museum presents memorabilia, and an interpretive trail winds through the

NEW MEXICO

remains. Park rangers in period dress give demonstrations during summer weekends.

The monument (☎ 505-526-8911) is 15 miles north of Las Cruces (near I-25 exit 19). Daily hours are 8:30 am to 5 pm; later in summer and closed on major holidays. Admission is $2 for those over 16.

Adjacent to Fort Selden, **Leasburg Dam State Park** offers camping and picnicking in desert scrub scenery. Leasburg Dam impounds a small lake offering limited boating, swimming and fishing, and there is a playground and play fort for kids. Water and showers are available.

The park (☎ 505-524-4068), PO Box 61, Radium Springs, NM 88054, is open year-round. Day use is $3; camping is $7 or $11 with partial hookups. The 45 sites sometimes fill on weekends.

Aguirre Springs National Recreation Area

About 20 miles east of Las Cruces, this BLM-managed scenic area on the east side of the Organ Mountains offers good bird-watching, strenuous mountain hiking, horse trails and primitive camping. Drive east on Hwy 70, over the scenic **San Agustin Pass** (5719 feet; there is a view-point) to the signed Aguirre Springs road 2 miles beyond the pass. It's about 5 miles to the campground along the steep and winding road (trailers over 22 feet not recommended), and the mountain views are worthwhile. Day use is free; the primitive campground costs $3 and has pit toilets and picnic tables but no drinking water.

White Sands Missile Range Museum

The White Sands Missile Test Center is some 27 miles east of Las Cruces along Hwy 70. It is the heart of the White Sands Missile Range, a major military testing site since 1945 that has also become an alternate landing site for the space shuttle. The museum (☎ 505-678-2250), at the Test Center's entrance gate, describes the development of these activities, and has a gift shop. Hours are 8 am to 4:30 pm, Monday to Friday; admission is free. Outside the museum is Missile Park, where many missiles are on display daily. At the entrance gate to the Test Center, tell the guard you are visiting the museum/park; be prepared to show your drivers license and car documents.

War Eagles Air Museum

Located in Santa Teresa, on the Texas border about 30 miles south of Las Cruces, this museum (☎ 505-589-2000) features many of the aircraft used during WWII and the Korean War, especially the fighters. Most are in flying condition. Hours are 10 am to 4 pm, Tuesday to Sunday. Admission is $4, $3 for seniors and free for children under 12. Take I-10 south into Texas, take exit 11 and head back into New Mexico, following museum signs.

DEMING

Deming is on the northern edge of the Chihuahua Desert, midway between Lordsburg and Las Cruces along I-10. Founded in 1881 as a railway junction town, it is now an agricultural center and the Luna County seat. Water for the farms and ranches comes from the invisible Mimbres River, which disappears underground about 20 miles north of town and emerges in Mexico. With over 14,000 inhabitants, Deming is the second largest town in southwestern New Mexico. A good museum, nearby state parks and a pleasant climate at 4335 feet above sea level are the main year-round attractions for visitors. Deming has some unusual annual events, described below.

Orientation & Information

The main west-east street is Pine St, also called Motel Drive. The chamber of commerce (☎ 505-546-2674, 800-848-4955), 800 E Pine St, is open from 8 am to 5 pm, Monday to Friday and 9 am to 5 pm on Saturday. Drop-off recycling (closed Monday) is across the street. The library (☎ 505-546-9202) is at 301 S Tin St. The local newspaper is *The Deming Headlight*. The post office (☎ 505-546-9461) is at 209 W Spruce St. The hospital (☎ 505-546-2761) is at 900 W Ash St. The police station (☎ 505-546-3011) is at 700 E Pine St.

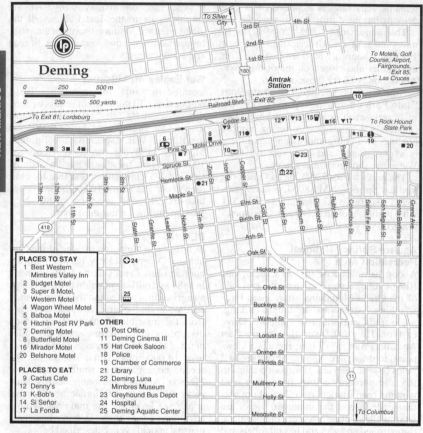

Deming Luna Mimbres Museum

Run by the Luna County Historical Society (☎ 505-546-2382), the museum is housed in what was once the National Guard Armory, built in 1916 at 301 S Silver St. Exhibits are varied, interesting and well displayed. See a superb doll collection, many Mimbres pots, several vintage cars, 1200 liquor decanters, beautiful homemade quilts, a Braille edition of *Playboy* and much more. Hours are 9 am to 4 pm daily except Sunday (1:30 to 4 pm); closed January 1, Easter, Thanksgiving and Christmas. Admission is free, but I encourage contributions and a purchase at the gift shop.

Historic Buildings

Four buildings on the National Register of Historic Places and a further dozen on the State Register can be examined, mainly from the exterior. They date from the 1880s to the early 20th century. Pick up a *Historic Landmark Walking Tour* brochure from the chamber and start the tour at the museum; most buildings are within four blocks.

Activities

You can **golf** 18 holes at the Rio Mimbres Country Club (☎ 505-546-3023, 505-546-9481) at the east end of town. **Swim** at the new Deming Aquatic Center (☎ 505-546-

7958), 815 W Buckeye, open afternoons Tuesday to Sunday with a water slide, spa and other attractions.

Special Events
Great American Duck Races (GADR)
This is one of the most whimsical and popular festivals in the state, attracting tens of thousands of visitors every fourth weekend in August; 1999 will be the 20th anniversary. The main events are the duck races themselves, with thousands of dollars in prizes. Anybody can enter for a $10 fee ($5 for kids), which includes 'duck rental.' By strange coincidence, the surname of some of the best duck trainers is Duck. (Robert and Bryce Duck's ducks took first and second place in the 1994 races.) Other events during the GADR include the Tortilla Toss (winners toss tortillas over 170 feet), Outhouse Races, Best Dressed Duck contest and many sporting events. There is also entertainment ranging from cowboy poets to local musicians, a parade, hot-air balloons and food.

Other Events Additional local events include the Southwestern New Mexico State Fair, held for five days in early October, which features livestock and produce judging, an auction, rodeo events, a carnival and arts and crafts. The rodeo and fairgrounds are at the east end of town. The Rock Hound Round-Up has been held annually in mid-March for more than 30 years; your chance to buy, sell and learn more about the local gems, minerals and rocks. Sausage lovers won't want to miss the Czechoslovakian Klobase Festival held the third Sunday in October.

Places to Stay
Rooms are at a premium and prices rise during the duck races and the state fair, when you need reservations. Otherwise, there is a good selection of reasonably priced accommodations in Deming.

Places to Stay – Camping
All campgrounds are popular and often full in winter, so call ahead.

There are plenty of inexpensive RV parks in town, charging $8 to $15 and geared to RVs rather than tents. The best are the *Roadrunner RV Park* (☎ 505-546-6960, 800-226-9937), at 2849 E Pine St, which allows tents, and the *Little Vineyard RV Park* (☎ 505-546-3560), 2901 E Pine St. Both have an indoor pool, spa, recreation area and coin laundry. Cheaper places include the *Hitchin Post RV Park* (☎ 505-546-9145), 611 W Pine St; the *Wagon Wheel RV Park* (☎ 505-546-8650), 2801 E Pine St; and the *Sunrise RV Park* (☎ 505-546-8565), 2601 E Pine St; none allow tents.

Also see Around Deming, below.

Places to Stay – Budget
The *Belshore Motel* (☎ 505-546-2717), 1210 E Pine St, has a small pool and inexpensive restaurant; it doesn't look too bad for about $20 a double. With 30 rooms, it is the largest of the cheap motels. Some even cheaper basic places include the *Hacienda Motel* (☎ 505-546-0817), 2909 E Pine St, and the *Balboa Motel & Restaurant* (☎ 505-546-6473), 708 W Pine St.

The following look reasonable with rooms in the mid-$20s to low $30s. The *Budget Motel* (☎ 505-546-2787), 1309 W Pine St, and the *Wagon Wheel Motel* (☎ 505-546-2681, fax 505-546-7020), 1109 W Pine St, both have a small seasonal pool, and the Wagon Wheel has a coin laundry and free morning coffee. The *Mirador Motel* (☎ 505-546-2795), 501 E Pine St, lacks a pool but is OK otherwise. Others at this price include the *Western Motel* (☎ 505-546-2744), 1207 W Pine St, which has a café attached; the *Deming Motel* (☎ 505-546-2737, fax 505-546-8556), 500 W Pine St, with free morning coffee; and the *Butterfield Motel* (☎ 505-544-0011), 309 W Pine. Each of these places has a small pool.

The *Motel 6* (☎ 505-546-2623, fax 505-546-0934), exit 85 off I-10, is Deming's largest motel with 102 rooms at $30/36 for singles/doubles. It has a pool and coin laundry.

Places to Stay – Middle

All motels in this section have pools. The independent *Grand Motor Inn* (☎ 505-546-2631, fax 505-546-4446), 1721 E Pine St, charges in the $40s, often gives discounts and has 62 nice rooms. The grassy grounds have both adult and children's pools. Its restaurant (☎ 505-546-2632), one of the best in town, is open from 6 am to 9 pm, or 10 pm in summer. It serves steak, seafood and Mexican meals and has a salad bar and lounge. Dinner entrées are in the $8 to $16 range.

The *Super 8 Motel* (☎ 505-546-0481, fax 505-544-0057), 1217 W Pine St, has standard rooms in the $40s, including continental breakfast. There is also a year-round indoor pool and spa. The *Days Inn* (☎ 505-546-8813, fax 505-546-7095), 1709 E Pine St, is slightly cheaper, includes breakfast and has an inexpensive restaurant open from 5:30 am to 9 pm. The *Best Western Mimbres Valley Inn* (☎ 505-546-4544, fax 505-546-9875), 1500 W Pine St, has good-sized rooms for $45 to $54 and free continental breakfasts. The nicely renovated *Holiday Inn* (☎ 505-546-2661, fax 505-546-6308), exit 85 off I-10, has more than 80 spacious rooms for around $60, coin laundry, lounge and the recommended Fat Eddie's Restaurant open from 6 am to 2 pm and 4 to 9 pm, with room service available. The menu is American and Mexican with main courses from $5 to $17.

Places to Eat

Apart from the hotel restaurants, Deming has a handful of good Mexican-American restaurants, including *La Fonda* (☎ 505-546-0465), 601 E Pine St, open from 9 am to 8 pm daily, with longer hours weekends and in summer, and the popular *Cactus Cafe* (☎ 505-546-2458), 218 W Cedar St, open 7 am to 9 pm daily. They have a Mexican buffet most days. For straightforward Mexican food, the locally popular *Sí Señor* (☎ 505-546-3938), 200 E Pine St, is cheap and is a good value. Inexpensive family dining is available at *K-Bob's* (☎ 505-546-8883), 316 E Cedar St, which is open from 10:30 am to 10 pm daily, features a $2.99

chicken-fried steak special, a big salad bar, sandwiches, seafood and steak, up to about $16. *Denny's* (☎ 505-546-2258), 120 N Platinum St, is open 24 hours.

Entertainment

Watch movies at the *Deming Cinema III* (☎ 505-546-8188) on Pine St at Gold St. The *Hat Creek Saloon* (☎ 505-546-2002), 122 N Ruby St, has country & western dancing on weekends.

Getting There & Away

Bus Greyhound (☎ 505-546-3881), 300 E Spruce St, has three or four daily buses westbound and eastbound along I-10. Las Cruces Shuttle Service (☎ 505-525-1784, 800-288-1784) runs four daily van trips between El Paso and Silver City. Several Deming stops are available, and reservations are required.

Train Amtrak stops at Deming three times weekly on the Los Angeles-Tucson-El Paso-New Orleans run.

AROUND DEMING
Rock Hound State Park

This park is known for semiprecious or just plain pretty rocks that can be collected (there's a 15 pound limit). The best rocks have been picked up, so you need a shovel and some rockhounding experience to uncover anything special, but beginners can try their luck. The best advice is to walk into the Little Florida Mountains for a while before beginning to look for rocks bearing (perhaps) agate, opal, jasper or quartz crystals.

The park is 14 miles southeast of Deming via Hwys 11 and 141. Two miles before the park is the **Museum and Rock Shop**, open from 9 am to 5 pm, Thursday to Tuesday. There is a $1 admission to the museum. The park has a 29-site campground ($7 or $11 with RV hookups), picnic areas, drinking water, showers and a playground. Day use is $3 per vehicle. About 2 miles southeast of the main area is **Spring Canyon**, known for an introduced herd of wild Persian ibex (wild goats), which you may catch a glimpse of if you are lucky. Other wildlife such as lizards, birds, rock squirrels and deer are often spotted here. Information is available from Rock Hound State Park (☎ 505-546-6182), PO Box 1064, Deming, NM 88030.

City of Rocks State Park
This park is 27 miles northwest of Deming along Hwy 180, then about 4 miles northeast on Hwy 61. Rounded volcanic towers make up this 'city,' and the landscape is quite dramatic. You can camp among the towers in secluded sites with tables and firepits. Most sites are $7, a few with electrical hookups are $11. A nature trail, drinking water and showers are available. The park (☎ 505-536-2800), PO Box 50, Faywood, NM 88034, is open year-round and charges $3 for day use.

PANCHO VILLA STATE PARK
On March 9, 1916, the Mexican revolutionary and outlaw Pancho Villa, unhappy with the US government's support of his enemies, stormed across the border with between 500 and 1000 troops. He attacked US Army Camp Furlong and the town of **Columbus** (3 miles north of the Mexican border), killing 18 people and burning several buildings before being pushed back into Mexico, having lost over 100 men. He was chased deep into Mexico by General John 'Black Jack' Pershing, who led US troops using aircraft and motor vehicles – the first time the USA used both in warfare. Villa succeeded in eluding capture, however, and the USA hasn't undergone an invasion since.

Camp Furlong is long gone, and once-bustling Columbus is now a village of some 600 inhabitants, but visitors head there because of its unique history. The story of the invasion is described in a small museum housed in the restored 1902 US Customs House, which also serves as the park office. It's open from 8 am to 5 pm daily. A short film can also be viewed, as can several buildings dating back to Camp Furlong days. There is also a desert botanical garden, picnic area, playground, camp-

ground with about 60 sites and showers, drinking water and fire pits. Rates are $3 for day use, $7 for camping or $11 with electrical hookups year-round. The park is off Hwy 11 in 'downtown' Columbus. Further information is available from Pancho Villa State Park (☎ 505-531-2711), PO Box 224, Columbus, NM 88029.

Columbus Historical Museum
This small museum (☎ 505-531-2620) is opposite the state park in the 1902 railway depot. Hours are 10 am to 4 pm daily, with shorter hours in the heat of summer. Admission is free; donations accepted.

Visiting Mexico
Walk across to Las Palomas, a village on the Mexican side. Curio shops and restaurants provide a taste of Mexico, and proprietors are happy to accept US dollars. The border is open 24 hours.

Special Events
In town, the Columbus Festival features a parade, street fair and entertainment on the second Saturday in October. A commemorative ceremony is held on March 9 for those killed in the 1916 raid. Obtain information from the Columbus Chamber of Commerce (☎ 505-531-2307, fax 505-531-2630).

Places to Stay & Eat in Columbus
Martha's Place Bed & Breakfast (☎ 505-531-2467, fax 505-531-2376), PO Box 587, Columbus, NM 88029, is at Main and Lima Sts, two blocks east of Hwy 11. Five modern rooms with private bath, TV and balcony rent for $55 a double, including full breakfast. Rooms for $30 are available at the *Sun Crest Inn* (☎ 505-531-2323, 505-531-2275), just off of Hwy 11 in the center of Columbus. There are three small restaurants.

SILVER CITY
At 5938 feet, Silver City is on the southern edge of the mountainous Gila National Forest, 44 miles away from and almost 2000 feet above Lordsburg and the Chihuahua

Desert. Summer high temperatures in the upper 80°s F and winter lows in the 20°s F attract outdoors-people to the area. The weather is generally sunny and fairly dry; July is the wettest month and May is the driest.

The city's name tells its story: a mining town founded in 1870 after the discovery of silver. Silver prices crashed in 1893, leading to the demise of that industry. But, instead of becoming a ghost town like many others, Silver City tapped another mineral wealth, copper, which is still mined today. Ranching is of some importance, and the city is the part-time home to more than 2000 students at Western New Mexico University.

History is in evidence in the downtown streets, with their Victorian brick buildings and Wild West air. Billy the Kid spent some of his boyhood here, and a few of his haunts can be seen.

Today, Silver City (population more than 12,000) is the Grant County seat and gateway to outdoor activities in the Gila National Forest. Locals sometimes call the town, simply, Silver.

North of Silver City, Hwy 15 heads through Pinos Altos and dead ends at the Gila Cliff Dwellings National Monument, 42 miles away. The road is scenic, mountainous, narrow and winding – allow a couple of hours to drive it.

To the east, Hwy 152 breaks off from Hwy 180 and heads to Emory Pass, beyond which you can take in good views of the Rio Grande country to the east. This route is scenic, but expect lots of hairpin bends.

Orientation

Hwy 180, the main east-west route, is sometimes called Silver Heights Blvd. Hwy 90 (Hudson St) enters from the south and intersects Hwy 180 north of downtown. The historic district lies west of Hudson St.

Information

The chamber of commerce (☎ 505-538-3785, 800-548-9378), 1103 Hudson St, is open from 9 am to 5 pm, Monday to Saturday. (A new chamber is planned on Hudson St near Broadway.) The Gila National Forest Ranger Station (☎ 505-538-2771, 505-388-8201) is at 3005 E Camino del Bosque (behind Wal-Mart, 3031 E Hwy 180). The library (☎ 505-538-3672) is at 515 W College Ave. Grant County Recycling (☎ 505-538-2560), 1510 W Market St, is open 8 am to 4 pm, Tuesday to Saturday. The local newspaper is the *Silver City Sun-News*. The post office (☎ 505-538-2831) is at 500 N Hudson St. The medical center (☎ 505-538-4000) is at 1313 E 32nd. The police station (☎ 505-538-3723) is at 1011 Hudson St.

Historic Downtown

Bullard, Texas and Arizona Sts between Broadway and 6th St is the heart of Victorian Silver City. (John Bullard opened the first silver mine here in 1870 but died the next year in a fight with Apaches.) The former Main St, one block east of Bullard St, was washed out in a series of massive floods, some up to 12 feet deep, beginning in 1895. Caused by runoff from logged and overgrazed areas north of town, the floods eventually cut 55 feet down below the original height of the street. Consequently, this gouged-out area has been turned into **Big Ditch Park**. Brochures at the chamber of commerce describe self-guided tours of the historic downtown area as well as driving tours in the surrounding countryside.

Silver City Museum

The city museum (☎ 505-538-5921), 312 W Broadway, is in an elegant Victorian house built in 1881. Exhibits display Mimbres pottery and mining and household artifacts from Silver City's Victorian heyday. There are also changing exhibits, occasional lectures and a store selling Southwestern books and gifts. Hours are 9 am to 4:30 pm, Tuesday to Friday, and 10 am to 4 pm on weekends. Admission is free.

Western New Mexico University Museum

The WNMU Museum (☎ 505-538-6386) houses the world's largest collection of

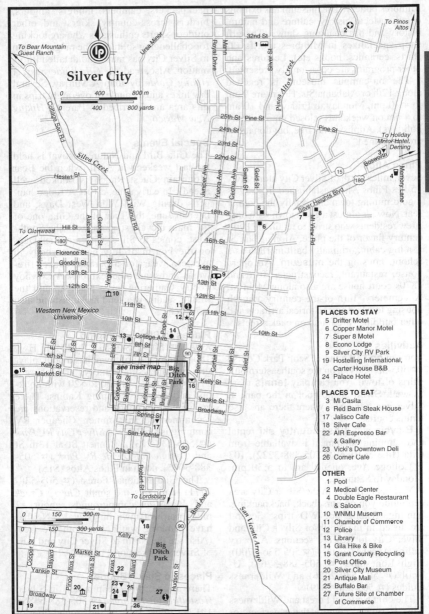

NEW MEXICO

Silver City

To Bear Mountain Guest Ranch

To Glenwood

To Lordsburg

To Pinos Altos

To Holiday Motor Hotel, Deming

Western New Mexico University

Big Ditch Park

see inset map

0   400   800 m
0   400   800 yards

0   150   300 m
0   150   300 yards

PLACES TO STAY
5 Drifter Motel
6 Copper Manor Motel
7 Super 8 Motel
8 Econo Lodge
9 Silver City RV Park
19 Hostelling International,
   Carter House B&B
24 Palace Hotel

PLACES TO EAT
3 Mi Casita
6 Red Barn Steak House
17 Jalisco Cafe
18 Silver Cafe
22 AIR Espresso Bar
   & Gallery
23 Vicki's Downtown Deli
26 Corner Cafe

OTHER
1 Pool
2 Medical Center
4 Double Eagle Restaurant
   & Saloon
10 WNMU Museum
11 Chamber of Commerce
12 Police
13 Library
14 Gila Hike & Bike
15 Grant County Recycling
16 Post Office
20 Silver City Museum
21 Antique Mall
25 Buffalo Bar
27 Future Site of Chamber
   of Commerce

Mimbres pottery. The museum has exhibits detailing local history, culture and natural history and has changing shows. The gift shop specializes in Mimbres motifs (T-shirts, ceramics, books etc). Lectures and other programs are occasionally presented.

The on-campus museum is reached along 12th or Alabama Sts. Hours are 9 am to 4:30 pm, Monday to Friday, and 10 am to 4 pm on weekends (closed on university holidays). Admission is free, but donations are welcomed.

Pinos Altos

Seven miles north of Silver City along Hwy 15 lies Pinos Altos, established in 1859 as a gold mining town and briefly the county seat. Now it's almost a ghost town with only a few residents who strive to retain the 19th-century flavor of the place. Along Main St is a log cabin, originally built in 1866 as a school, housing the **museum**. An opera house, restaurant, reconstructed fort and 1870s court house are also along Main St. A cemetery, turn-of-the-century church housing local art and historical artifacts and other buildings are found on back streets.

Activities

You can **golf** 18 holes at Scott Park Course (☎ 505-538-5041), on the southeastern outskirts of town. You can play **tennis** there as well. **Swim** at the pool in the park at Silver and 32nd Sts, where there are also tennis courts.

Bicycle and **cross-country ski** rental and camping equipment is available from Gila Hike & Bike (☎ 505-388-3222), 103 E College Ave, open 9 am to 5:30 pm, Monday to Saturday.

Various outfitters in the Silver City area can guide you on horseback, backpacking, hunting, fishing or 4WD trips. Several are listed in the North of Silver City and Silver City to Reserve sections. Also try calling Apache Country (☎ 505-536-3700), High Lonesome (☎ 505-388-3763), U-Trail (☎ 505-539-2426) and Wilderness Guides (☎ 505-536-2879).

The Gila National Forest and Wilderness Area is rugged country that's perfect for backpackers, campers, hunters, anglers, birders, cross-country skiers and other outdoor-sports enthusiasts who are looking for challenging solitude. The ranger station in Silver City has maps and detailed information. Also, read *The Gila Wilderness: A Hiking Guide* by John A Murray. Several day hikes and a couple of overnight trips in this area are described in Parent's *Hiking New Mexico*.

Special Events

The Gila Bird and Nature Festival is held the last weekend in April (when the Bear Mountain Guest Ranch is booked well ahead). In early June, a PRCA rodeo happens during Wild Wild West Days, and later in June, the Tour of the Gila, one of the main bicycle stage races in the Southwest, comes to Silver City. Frontier Days on the Fourth of July has everybody in Western wear for a parade, dance, fireworks and some other exhibits. A Cowboy Poetry Gathering takes place around the first or second weekend in August and also in March.

Places to Stay – Camping

KOA (☎ 505-388-3351), 11824 E Hwy 180, 5 miles east of town, has a pool, playground and coin laundry, and charges $14.50 for tents, $17.50 to $20 with hookups and $28 for Kamping Kabins. There are winter discounts, and reservations are recommended in summer. Cheaper RV camping is available at *Silver City RV Park* (☎ 505-538-2239), Bennett St at 13th St and *Continental Divide RV Park* (☎ 505-388-3005), north in Pinos Altos ($15).

The Gila National Forest (☎ 505-538-2771) maintains the small *Cherry Creek* and *McMillan* campgrounds, about 12 miles north of town on Hwy 15. Neither have drinking water, but both are free. (Also see the North of Silver City and East of Silver City sections, below.)

Places to Stay – Budget

There are no truly cheap motels in Silver. *Hostelling International* (☎ 505-388-5485), 101 N Cooper St, is on the ground floor of the Carter House B&B (see below) and offers two clean, 10-bed dormitories for $12.50 per member and a private room for $25 (double). Nonmembers add $3. TV room, kitchen and laundry facilities are available. Reservations can be made with a credit card over the phone. Office hours are 8 to 10 am and 4 to 9 pm daily.

Places to Stay – Middle

Motels To experience a little of Silver City's history, stay at the restored *Palace Hotel* (☎/fax 505-388-1811), at 106 W Broadway, Silver City, NM 88061-5093. This hotel dates from 1882, and the 21 rooms vary from small rooms with a double bed for $30 to two-room suites with king- or queen-size beds for $48 to $55, including continental breakfast. Rooms may have a shower, a bath tub or both. Some rooms have a refrigerator and all have old-fashioned decor, though there are phones and TV. One small room has a bathroom down the hall for $26. The downtown location can be a little noisy on weekends.

The *Drifter Motel* (☎ 505-538-2916, 800-853-2916), 711 Silver Heights Blvd, faces the *Copper Manor Motel* (☎ 505-538-5392, 800-853-2916), at 710 Silver Heights Blvd. Both are under the same ownership and have a pool, restaurant and lounge. Adequate rooms are about $38 to $48 at the Drifter and $40 to $55 at the Copper Manor, which has a spa and indoor pool. The Drifter Lounge has live music (country & western, mainly) and dancing most nights.

The *Super 8 Motel* (☎/fax 505-388-1983), 1040 E Hwy 180, charges around $47/52 for one/two people in standard rooms with one bed or $55 with two beds in summer, from about $40 a single in winter. The *Holiday Motor Hotel* (☎ 505-538-3711, 800-828-8291), 3420 E Hwy 180, has 80 decent rooms from $46 in winter, $56 in summer. It also has a pool, coin laundry and Michael's Restaurant. The similarly priced *Econo Lodge* (☎ 505-534-1111, fax 505-534-2222), 1120 E Hwy 180, has an indoor pool and spa, and free continental breakfast.

The *Bear Creek Motel & Cabins* (☎ 505-388-4501, fax 505-538-5583) in Pinos Altos has 13 cabins, all with fireplaces and wood, some with kitchenettes and balconies. The managers will lend you a gold pan if you want to try your luck in nearby Bear Creek. The rates are $99 to $129 in summer, $10 less in spring and fall and $20 less in winter.

B&Bs Built in 1906, the *Carter House B&B* (☎ 505-388-5485), 101 N Cooper St (near Broadway), Silver City, NM 88061, houses a youth hostel downstairs (see Places to Stay – Budget, above) and five attractive rooms upstairs with private bath. Rates range from $57/65 to $67/75 for singles/doubles, with a buffet-style full breakfast. There is a library, large porch, and TV lounge (no TVs or telephones in the rooms).

Bear Mountain Guest Ranch (☎ 505-538-2538, 800-880-2538, innkeeper@ BearMtGuestRanch.com), 2251 Cottage San Rd, PO Box 1163, Silver City, NM 88062, is a large ranch house built in 1928 on 160 acres about 3 miles northwest of town (leave along Alabama and follow the signs). A B&B since 1959 (the owner says 'It was New Mexico's first B&B with guests in 6000 BC!'), it has gained a well-deserved reputation among bird watchers and nature lovers as *the* place to stay in southwestern New Mexico. Rates start at $40/67 for singles/doubles with breakfast or $54/105 with all meals. There are suites sleeping five people ($125 with breakfast, $195 with all meals). One cottage has a kitchenette. All have private baths. They also have six-day, five-night 'Lodge & Learn Programs' for $275 per person with all meals and classes on topics such as bird and plant identification, photography, local archaeology and history.

Places to Eat

For some good breakfasts and light meals throughout the day, the *Corner Cafe* (☎ 505-388-2056) at 200 N Bullard St is a good choice. It is open from 7 am to 4 pm, Monday to Saturday, and 8 am to 2 pm on

Sunday. *AIR Espresso Bar & Gallery* (☎ 505-388-5952), 106 W Yankie St, is the place to go for a gourmet coffee and easy conversation. AIR? That's 'Artist in Residence' – enjoy the local art on the walls. It is open from 8 am to 5:30 pm daily except Sunday. *Vicki's Downtown Deli* (☎ 505-388-5430), 107 W Yankie St, serves good sandwiches from 9 am till 4 pm on Monday, till 7 pm Tuesday to Thursday and to 8 pm on Friday and Saturday.

You have a few choices for good Mexican food in town. For a tasty breakfast or other meal with a New Mexican flavor, try the funky and locally popular *Silver Cafe* (☎ 505-388-3480), 514 N Bullard St, open 7:30 am to 7:30 pm daily except Sunday. The unpretentious but good *Jalisco Cafe* (☎ 505-388-2060), 100 S Bullard St, is a local favorite; it is open 11 am to 8:30 pm, Monday to Saturday. (They don't serve alcohol.) Another local favorite is *Mi Casita* (☎ 505-538-5533), 2340 Bosworth Drive, which serves huge plates for about $4 or $5 from 11 am to 8 pm, Monday to Friday.

This is cattle country. For a good steak, head over to the *Red Barn Steak House* (☎ 505-538-5666), 708 Silver Heights Blvd (adjoining the Copper Manor Motel). Most steaks are in the $10 to $20 range; the restaurant serves seafood and has a salad bar as well. *Michael's* (☎ 505-538-3711), in the Holiday Motor Motel, is considered by many locals to be the best fine-dining experience in town.

The *Buckhorn Saloon* (☎ 505-538-9911), on Main St in Pinos Altos, offers fine dinners daily except Sunday from 6 to 10 pm (the saloon opens at 3 pm). Steaks, seafood and more are served in 1860s Wild West decor, and there is often live country music on Friday and Saturday. Most entreés are in the $10 to $20 range.

Entertainment
The *Real West Cinema II* (☎ 505-538-5659) is at 11585 E Hwy 180 (on the north side, 5 miles east of town; look hard for the sign).

The *Buffalo Bar* (☎ 505-538-3201), 201 N Bullard St, has occasional dances with live or recorded music in the adjacent nightclub. Otherwise, it's your basic, not especially salubrious, Western bar. Underage students frequent the nightclub because it has nondrinking nights – you can get a drink in the bar next door but can't bring it back into the nightclub. The *Double Eagle Restaurant & Saloon* (☎ 505-538-0100), 1740 E Hwy 180, has pool tables and a small dance floor with Friday/Saturday night dancing. (Also see the Buckhorn Saloon and Drifter Motel, above.)

Shopping
Many artists work in the area and the chamber of commerce has a map with 26 galleries in Silver City. Also stop by the Antique Mall on Broadway at Texas.

Getting There & Away
Air The airport is 11 miles southeast of Silver City off Hwy 180. Mesa Air (☎ 505-388-4115) has two daily flights from Monday to Friday, to and from Albuquerque.

Bus Las Cruces Shuttle Service (☎ 800-288-1784) has vans leaving Silver City four times a day for El Paso via Deming and Las Cruces (see Las Cruces for details). Silver Stage Lines (☎ 800-522-0162) has vans leaving Silver City at 7 am and 2 pm for El Paso Airport ($35 one way or $50 roundtrip). They'll also do charter trips elsewhere (for example, $125 to Tucson for one to four people).

Getting Around
Grimes Car Rental (☎ 505-538-2142) is at the Silver City Airport. In town you can try Taylor Car Rental (☎ 505-388-1800, 505-388-4848), 808 N Hudson St, or Amigo Car Rental (☎ 505-388-9207).

NORTH OF SILVER CITY
Lake Roberts Area
Lake Roberts, 25 miles north on Hwy 15 and 4 miles east on Hwy 35, offers boating facilities and opportunities to fish for rainbow trout, catfish and smallmouth bass. (Hwy 15 from Pinos Altos to Hwy 35 is not recommended for trailers over 22 feet.)

At the Hwy 15 and 35 intersection is *Sapillo Crossing Lodge* (☎ 505-536-3206, fax 505-536-3207), which has RV sites, a decent restaurant open at 7 am, a good gift shop, and 16 rustic nonsmoking rooms with Western decor and private baths for $45/55. The guided trail rides, suitable for novices as well as experienced riders, are $15 an hour ($65 for six hours) including lunch. Longer pack trips and other rides (including women-only) can be arranged in advance.

The Gila National Forest (☎ 505-536-2250) maintains *Mesa* and *Upper End* campgrounds ($7) at the east end of the lake, both with drinking water but no showers. One campground may close in winter. Nearby, Lake Roberts Picnic Area has a boat ramp.

At the lake's west end, the *Lake Roberts General Store & Cabins* (☎ 505-536-9929), Route 11, Box 195, Lake Roberts, NM 88061, has nine cabins ranging from $30 a double to $80 for a trailer sleeping ten. All are fully furnished with bathrooms and kitchens but no TV. There are boat rentals, and guided hunting and pack trips are arranged with Gary Webb (505-536-9368).

Hwy 35 provides an alternate (trailer accessible) but longer scenic route between the Gila Cliff Dwellings and Silver. It continues east from the lake through the Mimbres Valley, passing the small *Rio Mimbres Lodge & RV Park* (☎ 505-536-3777) after about 15 miles and joining Hwy 152 about 10 miles farther.

Gila Hot Springs

Used by Indians since ancient times, the hot springs are 39 miles north of Silver City within the *Gila Hotsprings Vacation Center* (☎ 505-536-9551, 505-536-9314), Route 11, Silver City, NM 88061. The center has a coin laundry, snack bar, gift shop and doll museum ($1 fee). Simple rooms with kitchenettes are $40/45 with one/two beds. Advance reservations are recommended. An RV park with a spa and showers fed by hot springs has sites for $12 with hookups and $9 without. A primitive campground next to hot pools has

drinking water and toilets but no showers. Day use is $2 per person; camping is $3 per person age six and over. Horses can be rented for $27.50 a day, plus $55 if you want a guide. Guided fishing and wilderness pack trips can be arranged in advance for $75 to $110 per person per day, depending on group size. Trout fishing for hatchery-raised fish is best in spring on the Middle and West Forks of the Gila River, or year-round for wild fish in the backcountry. The East Fork and main river offer good bass fishing. Guided hunting trips and other outfitting services are also available.

The *Wilderness Lodge* (☎ 505-536-9749), Route 11, Box 85, Silver City, NM 88061, is a rustic B&B in a converted century-old schoolhouse. Five rooms with shared bath are $40/45 single/double and a two-bedroom suite with private bath is $55 double, including breakfast. Other meals can be arranged. The lodge is on an access road 1/4 mile south of the Vacation Center.

The Gila River is 2 miles south of the hot springs. Two free Gila USFS *campgrounds* (no drinking water) are available on the north and south sides of the river where Hwy 15 crosses it. It is possible to float down the river from here to Turkey Creek, 45 miles away – contact the USFS for details. March and April are the best months.

Gila Cliff Dwellings National Monument

The influence of the Ancestral Puebloans on the Mogollon culture can clearly be seen in these cliff dwellings, occupied in the 13th century and reminiscent of ones in the Four Corners area. Aside from their historical value, the best thing about the dwellings is their relative isolation, which dissuades visitors who crowd many other Southwestern archaeological sites. A one-mile roundtrip self-guided trail climbs 180 feet to the dwellings, set in cliffs overlooking a lovely forested canyon. Parts of the trail are steep and involve ladders.

The trail begins at the end of Hwy 15, 2 miles past the visitor center (☎ 505-536-9461), which is a joint NPS/USFS operation and has displays, a gift shop and information about the monument and surrounding forest lands. From Memorial Day to Labor Day weekends, the visitor center is open from 8 am to 5 pm and the trail from 8 am to 6 pm. At other times, the visitor center is open from 8 am to 4:30 pm and the trail from 9 am to 4 pm. The monument is closed January 1 and Christmas. Admission is $3 per person age eight and above. If you arrive any time other than the busy summer season, you may have the site to yourself, as I did one lovely October morning.

Between the visitor center and trailhead are two small campgrounds with drinking water, picnic areas and toilets. They are free on a first-come, first-served basis and may fill on summer weekends. A short trail behind the campground leads to other, older dwellings.

Further information is available from Gila Cliff Dwellings, Route 11, PO Box 100, Silver City, NM 88061.

EAST OF SILVER CITY

Hwy 152 takes off from Hwy 180 about 8 miles east of Silver City. The Santa Rita Chino Open Pit Copper Mine is seen a few miles east on Hwy 152; there is an observation point on the highway. Worked by Indians and Spanish and Anglo settlers, it is the oldest active mine in the Southwest. It became an open pit in 1910 and is now a staggering 1½ miles wide, 1800 feet deep and produces 150,000 tons of copper annually.

Hwy 152 crests the Black Range at Emory Pass, about 36 miles east of Silver City. At the 8228-foot pass, a lookout gives views of the drier Rio Grande country to the east. This is a scenic but slow road with plenty of hairpin bends. Four miles west of the pass, *Iron Creek Campground*, in the Gila National Forest, has a few free sites with no water.

Kingston

The almost-ghost town of Kingston is a few miles beyond Emory Pass. Once a booming silver-mining town (7000 people in the 1880s), it now has a few dozen full-time residents. The *Black Range Lodge* (☎ 505-895-5652, fax 505-895-3326), Star Rte 2, Box 119, Kingston, NM 88042, offers B&B accommodations in seven rooms, all with a private bath and balcony access. The rates are $50/60 for singles/doubles, with discounts for multinight stays. A game room and kitchen privileges are available.

Hillsboro

Another late-19th-century mining town, Hillsboro was revived by local agriculture after mining went bust. Some of the story is told at the **Black Range Historical Museum** (☎ 505-895-5233, 505-895-5685) in a century-old building on Hwy 152 at the east end of town. Hours vary, but the museum is open most afternoons from March to December. Hillsboro is known for its **Apple Festival** over Labor Day weekend when fresh-baked apple pies, delicious apple cider, street musicians and arts and crafts stalls attract thousands of visitors.

Many old buildings are still in use. Have a drink or stay in the *S Bar X Motel & Saloon* (☎ 505-895-5222), which has seven rooms at $30 to $40. The old saloon has been here since 1877 and has live music on some weekends. Food is served in the café next door. The more recent *Enchanted Villa B&B* (☎ 505-895-5686), PO Box 456, Hillsboro, NM 88042, has three rooms and a two-bedroom suite, all with baths. Rates range from $40 to $70 with full breakfast. *Hillsboro General Store and Cafe* serves breakfast and lunch. The *Hillsboro Orchard Bar-B-Q* (☎ 505-895-5642, 800-447-2486), at the west end of town, has good food but odd hours.

SILVER CITY TO RESERVE

Hwy 180 northwest of Silver goes through remote and wild country dotted with a few tiny communities. The Gila National Forest and Mogollon Mountains offer excellent opportunities for remote and primitive backpacking, hiking, camping and fishing.

Glenwood & Mogollon

The village of Glenwood is 62 miles north-west of Silver. A Gila National Forest Ranger Station (☎ 505-539-2481) is a half mile south of town. Mogollon is a semi-ghost town, 4 miles north of Glenwood and then 9 miles east on steep and narrow Hwy 159 – expect plenty of switchbacks. Tire chains may be needed on this road in winter.

Hwy 174 goes east from Glenwood passing the **trout hatchery** (☎ 505-539-2461) after a half mile. Visitors are welcome. The **Catwalk** is 4½ miles farther – a trail enclosed by a wire cage hugs the cliff up narrow Whitewater Canyon. It follows water pipes built by miners in 1893. When the pipes needed repair, the miners walked along them (the 'Catwalk'). It's a short but worthwhile hike with some steep spots. There is a USFS picnic area here.

Mogollon, once an important mining town, still has a few people living there, offering 'antiques,' snacks and various services such as licensed massage and hypnotherapy. Many buildings lie deserted and empty – it's a slightly spooky place.

Gila Wilderness Tours (☎ 505-388-5866, 800-991-8687) offers various tours of the area.

Places to Stay & Eat The USFS maintains the *Bighorn* campground in Gila National Forest, one mile north of Glenwood, with no drinking water or fee. It is open all year.

In Glenwood, stay at the *Whitewater Motel* (☎ 505-539-2581), the *Lariat Motel* (☎ 505-539-2361) or the *Crab Apple Cabin Motel* (☎ 505-539-2400), all small places charging in the $30 to $50 range. The *Los Olmos Guest Ranch* (☎/fax 505-539-2311) offers a swimming pool, playground, local travel information and horseback riding. The ranch has 13 stone cabins open from March to November. True to the area's remote location, rooms have no telephones or TVs (though all have private baths). Rates start around $50/60 for singles/doubles with breakfast, and dinners can be arranged.

Opposite the Lariat Motel is the *Blue Front Bar & Restaurant* (☎ 505-539-2561), which sells steaks and Mexican food. *Ellie's Country Kitchen* (☎ 505-539-2242) serves food from 7 am to 8 pm.

Reserve

Reserve is on Hwy 12, 7 miles east of Hwy 180 and 100 miles northwest of Silver. Founded in the 1870s, Reserve now has 600 residents and is the seat of Catron County, which only has some 3000 inhabitants itself – mainly ranchers, cowboys and loggers who particularly loathe federal government interference and environmentalists. Recently, county officials passed a resolution urging every family to own a gun. This is about as close to the old Wild West as you'll get.

Information is available from the Catron County Chamber of Commerce (☎ 505-533-6458) or the Reserve Area Chamber of Commerce (☎ 505-533-6211). A Gila National Forest Ranger Station (☎ 505-533-6231) is south of town. Call the Catron County sheriff's office (☎ 505-533-6222) in emergencies.

The Catron County Fair and Rodeo is held in late August.

Places to Stay & Eat The decent *Rode Inn Motel* (☎ 505-533-6661, fax 505-533-6642) charges $45/50 for singles/doubles. Some rooms have kitchenettes. The cheaper *Elk Country Café & Village Motel* (☎ 505-533-6600, 505-533-6615) has very basic rooms and some RV sites. The *Riverbend RV Park* has six sites behind the Black Gold Service Station (☎ 505-533-6538). Ask at the ranger station about the forest campgrounds. *Grandma T's* (☎ 505-533-6230) serves good Mexican and American meals, or head over to *Uncle Bill's Bar* for a beer and burger.

LORDSBURG & AROUND

Lordsburg was founded in 1880 as a railroad town during the construction of the Southern Pacific Railroad. Today, the small town (population 3200) is a minor ranching center and the seat of empty and arid

Hidalgo County. Of particular interest to travelers are the three nearby ghost towns and the surrounding desert.

Orientation & Information

The main drag through town is Motel Drive, which runs east-west, parallel to and north of I-10.

The chamber of commerce (☎ 505-542-9864) is at 208 Motel Drive. At I-10 exit 20 at the west end, a New Mexico Welcome Center (☎ 505-542-8149) gives statewide information 8 am to 5 pm daily except January 1, Thanksgiving and Christmas. The library (☎ 505-542-9646) is at 208 E 3rd St. The local weekly newspaper is the *Lordsburg Liberal*. The post office (☎ 505-542-9601) is at 401 Shakespeare St. The police (☎ 505-542-3505) are in City Hall at 206 S Main St.

Shakespeare Ghost Town

Dating to 1856, Shakespeare was a military commissary, a stagecoach stop and a boom-and-bust mining town that housed nearly 3000 inhabitants (almost as many as Lordsburg today). Of course, Billy the Kid stopped by, as did other Western characters. Since 1935, Shakespeare has belonged to the Hill family who have preserved some of the old buildings. The town is, therefore, private property, and visitors can enter only with educational guided tours, which are interesting and enthusiastic.

Tours (90 minutes) begin at 10 am and 2 pm on the second weekend of each month and visit the interiors of six buildings (formerly eight were visited, but fire closed two in late 1997). Tours are $3, or $2 for kids six to 12 (moneys go to preservation). Private tours can be arranged. On the fourth weekend of April, June, August and October, shootouts and other reenactments are held and cost $1 more.

Shakespeare Ghost Town (☎ 505-542-9034), PO Box 253, Lordsburg, NM 88045, is 2½ miles south of Lordsburg.

Steins Railroad Ghost Town

In 1858, Steins was a stagecoach stop. In 1880, the Southern Pacific Railroad built a depot here, and in the early 20th century, Steins had about 1000 residents. With the advent of diesel trains, Steins lost its importance, and Southern Pacific left in 1958. Many of the buildings were burned down.

In 1988, Larry and Linda Links purchased the town, and they have been restoring it since. They give guided tours and run a gift/snack shop. You can walk around outside or ask in the store for a tour of 10 buildings filled with curios. Tours cost $2.50 for those 13 and older. Their hours are 9 am to 6 pm daily except Thanksgiving and Christmas. Ask about stagecoach and horseback rides. Steins (☎ 505-542-9791), PO Box 2185, Road Forks, NM 88045, is 17 miles west of Lordsburg at I-10 exit 3.

Granite Gap

Formerly a mining town, Granite Gap's main attraction is the old mines; you can even camp in them. Guided mine tours are $10 ($5 for children), and donkey riding and gold panning starts at $5. You can also hunt for treasure. (Some gold bars were reputedly buried here after a stagecoach robbery; the owners keep 20% royalty of whatever you find worth over $500 – good luck!) Camping (no water) is $5 per tent or RV. The site is on Hwy 80, 11 miles south of I-10 exit 5.

Special Events

Land Sail Races are held on a dry lakebed 6 miles west of town in early April. The County Fair and Rodeo happens in August.

Places to Stay – Camping

KOA (☎ 505-542-8003), 1501 Lead St, charges $13.50 for tent sites and $17 with full hookups. It has a pool, playground and coin laundry. There are a couple of cheaper RV parks along Motel Drive that have seen better days.

Places to Stay – Budget

The *Holiday Motel* (☎ 505-542-3535), 600 E Motel Drive, charges $20.50/26 for spacious but spartan singles/doubles. It has a pool, a playground and a restaurant. The

Budget Motel (☎ 505-542-3567), 816 E Motel Drive, charges $18/20. There are two *Motel 10*s. The one at 624 E Motel Drive (☎ 505-542-8850) charges $23/26 for basic but adequate rooms, while the one at 1202 S Pyramid St (☎ 505-542-8872) has nicer rooms at $27.95 and up.

Places to Stay – Middle
The *Super 8 Motel* (☎ 505-542-8882), 110 E Maple St, offers standard rooms for $38.88/44.88 for singles/doubles or $47.88 with two beds. The *Best Western American Motor Inn* (☎ 505-542-3591, fax 505-542-3572), 944 E Motel Drive, has a pool, playground, lounge and restaurant open from 6:30 am to 9:30 pm. Rates are from $39/44 for singles/doubles with one bed, $49 with two beds. The *Best Western – Western Skies Inn* (☎ 505-542-8807, fax 505-542-8895), 1303 S Main St, has a pool and free morning coffee. It charges $46 to $58 for large rooms with two queen-size beds.

Places to Eat
El Charro (☎ 505-542-3400), 209 Southern Pacific Blvd, here for over 50 years under the same owners, serves inexpensive Mexican and American food, has an adjoining lounge and is open 24 hours. *Kranberry's Family Restaurant* (☎ 505-542-9400), 1401 S Main St, serves standard American breakfasts, lunches and dinners.

The *Soda Shoppe* (☎ 505-542-9142), 330 E Motel Drive, is an old-fashioned soda fountain serving ice cream shakes, sundaes, malts, floats, splits and sodas – a nostalgic treat. It's in the Medicine Shoppe of Lordsburg, built in 1929 on the location of Eagle Drug (built in 1889). Hours are 9 am to 6 pm (later in summer), Monday to Saturday.

Getting There & Away
Bus Greyhound (☎ 505-542-3412), 112 Wabash Ave (behind McDonald's) runs three or four daily buses along I-10.

Train Amtrak trains stop downtown three times a week on the run between Los Angeles and New Orleans.

THE SOUTHWEST CORNER
The area south of Lordsburg is known as 'the boot heel' – look at the outline of the state map and you'll see why. The remoteness of this desert country is its own

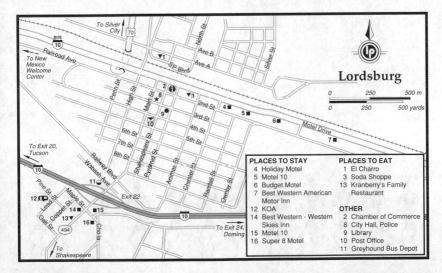

PLACES TO STAY	PLACES TO EAT
4 Holiday Motel	1 El Charro
5 Motel 10	3 Soda Shoppe
6 Budget Motel	13 Kranberry's Family
7 Best Western American	Restaurant
Motor Inn	
12 KOA	OTHER
14 Best Western - Western	2 Chamber of Commerce
Skies Inn	8 City Hall, Police
15 Motel 10	9 Library
16 Super 8 Motel	10 Post Office
	11 Greyhound Bus Depot

attraction for some people. A few tiny communities dot the landscape – Hachita, Animas and Rodeo. **Hachita** has *The Egg Nest* (☎ 505-436-2666) with RV hookups and restaurant, and unique souvenirs made of decorated ostrich eggs! **Rodeo** has a

small historic church, which houses the **Chiricahua Art Gallery** (☎ 505-557-2225), open from 10 am to 4 pm, Monday to Saturday, exhibiting regional artists' work. The cheap *Rodeo RV Park* (☎ 505-557-2266) has RV hookups.

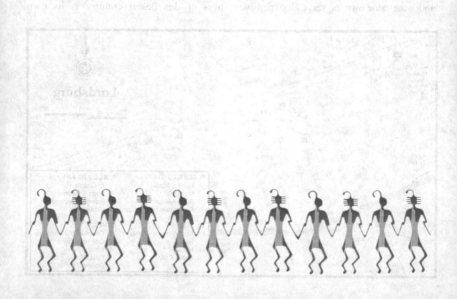

Southeastern New Mexico

This chapter covers the southern portion of New Mexico east of the Rio Grande Valley. I begin at the stunning scenery of the world's largest gypsum sand dunes at White Sands National Monument, near the town of Alamogordo. Then I describe the area north of Alamogordo through the lava fields of the Tularosa Valley to the village of Carrizozo. Next I head into the Sacramento Mountains east of Alamogordo. The mountains provide a cool contrast to the searing desert sands, and the popular highland resorts of Cloudcroft and Ruidoso are described in detail. Then it's northeast to small historical villages – Billy the Kid country.

East of the Sacramento Mountains, the scenery flattens into the desolate tablelands of the *Llano Estacado* (Staked Plains) – no one can remember where the name comes from, though various suggestions are bandied about. Roswell, the largest town in the area and home to a superb museum (and a thriving UFO culture!), is on the western edge of the Llano Estacado. From Roswell, we go south to Carlsbad Caverns National Park, the most magnificent attraction in the area. Then it's northeast, through Hobbs to Clovis, famous as the center of one of the oldest Paleo-Indian cultures on the continent, and the historic Fort Sumner.

WHITE SANDS NATIONAL MONUMENT

The white sands are huge dunes of gypsum covering 275 sq miles. About 110 sq miles of dunes lie within the park. Gypsum is a chalky mineral used in making plaster of Paris and cement; the surrounding mountains contain vast quantities of the stuff. It gets dissolved by snowmelt and rainfall and washed down to Lake Lucero, in the southwest part of the monument. Here, the water evaporates, leaving solid gypsum that is blown northeast in dunes moving as fast as 20 feet per year. The landscape is a dazzling white sea of sand that visitors are encouraged to explore by vehicle or on foot.

Struggling for survival in this otherworldly environment are desert dwellers such as kangaroo rats, snakes and even toads. Some have evolved a lighter color to blend better with the background. Plants have a hard time growing in the shifting sands; a few that manage the trick of holding on include the yucca, the fourwing saltbush and the endearingly named rubber rabbitbush. These botanical acrobats tend to grow near the edges of the dunes – huge areas in the center of the dunes appear devoid of life.

Information

White Sands National Monument (☎ 505-679-2599), Box 1086, Holloman AFB, NM 88330, is 16 miles southwest of Alamogordo. At the entrance you'll find a visitor center, open 8 am to 7 pm from Memorial Day to mid-August and until sunset the rest of the year except Christmas. Inside there is an informative museum, book and gift shop and refreshments. There are ranger-led activities (talks, walks and audiovisual displays) several times daily in the summer. Rangers lead car tours to Lake Lucero on the last weekend of every month.

From beyond the visitor center, a 16-mile loop road (Dunes Drive) leads into the heart of the dunes. The road is open from 7 am to sunset, till 11 pm on full-moon summer nights when there are special programs. There are many parking areas and you are encouraged to climb and play in the dunes – but don't get lost! Trails leaving from parking areas include the Alkali Flat (4½ miles roundtrip backcountry trail through the heart of the dunes), a 1-mile loop nature trail, a 600-yard wheelchair-accessible Interdune Boardwalk and a 500-yard trail leading to a backcountry campsite.

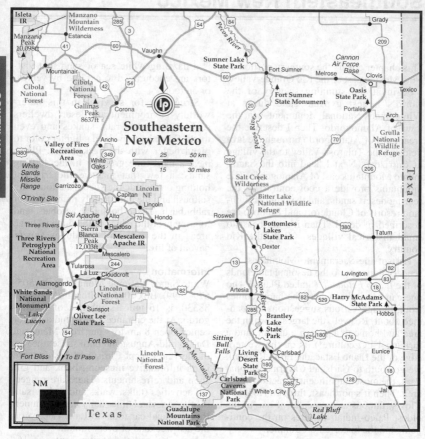

Southeastern New Mexico

Backcountry camping permits are $3 for adults; $1.50 for children under 17 and all holders of Golden Age or Access Passes. Permits are sold at the entrance to Dunes Drive. You must carry water as none is available here. There is no developed camping or other overnighting allowed in the monument. Picnic sites are at the end of the road.

Because of tests at the nearby White Sands Missile Range, the road into the national monument is closed occasionally for a couple of hours – call ahead if your schedule is tight. Entrance fees are $3 per

person over 17; Golden Eagle, Golden Age and Access Passes are honored.

ALAMOGORDO
This pleasant town of more than 31,000 inhabitants lies at 4350 feet in the Tularosa Basin, with the Sacramento Mountains looming to the east. It is 207 miles south of Albuquerque and 68 miles northeast of Las Cruces. Alamogordo (Spanish for 'fat cottonwood tree') is a ranching and agricultural center and the Otero County seat. It is also the center of one of the most historically important space and atomic

research programs in the country. A branch of New Mexico State University is found here. The town is the best base from which to visit White Sands National Monument.

History

Nomadic Indians began living in this area some 7000 years ago. Their descendants were the Jornada Mogollon people, whose village remains, about 1000 miles old, can be seen at the Three Rivers Petroglyph National Recreation Area, 35 miles north of Alamogordo. The Mogollon people left mysteriously around the 13th century, and soon after the Mescalero Apache settled here and became the dominant inhabitants. The area around what is now Oliver Lee State Park, 10 miles south of Alamogordo, was one of the Apache strongholds.

Spanish settlers founded La Luz, a village 4 miles north of Alamogordo, in 1705. Tularosa is 10 miles farther north and was founded in 1863. The Spanish settlers and Apache Indians were constantly skirmishing throughout these years. An 1868 battle at Round Mountain (a few miles east of Tularosa) was one of the last major conflicts in the Alamogordo area, and led to the establishment of the nearby Mescalero Apache Indian Reservation, where many Apaches now live.

Founded in 1898, Alamogordo was an important railroad town, although there are no longer train services here. The population, only 3000 in 1940, boomed with the development of local military bases, climaxing with the July 16, 1945 test explosion of the world's first atom bomb at Trinity Site. The nearby military sites such as Holloman Air Force Base, White Sands Space Harbor (a space shuttle landing site) and White Sands Missile Range continue to be an economic mainstay in the area.

Orientation

White Sands Blvd (also called Hwy 54, 70 or 82) is the main drag through town and runs north-south. I abbreviate this important thoroughfare to WSB below. Addresses on North WSB correspond to numbered cross streets (thus 1310 N WSB is just north of 13th); addresses from one block south of 1st are South WSB.

Information

The chamber of commerce (☎ 505-437-6120), 1301 N WSB, is open 8:30 am to 5 pm Monday to Friday and till 3:30 pm on Saturday. The Lincoln National Forest Ranger Station in the Western-style former federal building (☎ 505-434-7200), 11th and New York Ave, is open from 7:30 am to 4:30 pm Monday to Friday. The library (☎ 505-439-4140) is at 10th and Oregon Ave. The local newspaper is the *Alamogordo Daily News*. The post office (☎ 505-437-9390) is at 900 Alaska Ave. Drop-off recycling bins are on Florida Ave at Indian Wells Rd. The hospital (☎ 505-439-2100) is at 1209 9th. The police (☎ 505-439-4300) are at 700 Virginia Ave.

International Space Hall of Fame

This four-story-high glass museum (☎ 505-437-2840, 800-545-4021), nicknamed 'the golden cube,' looms over the northeast side of the town and is its most important attraction. Inside are exhibits about space research and flight – a must for anyone interested in the USA's research on the cosmos, although the exhibits stop at the late 1980s. There are good views of White Sands National Monument from the museum. The space center is open from 9 am to 5 pm daily (to 6 pm in summer).

The **Tombaugh Space Theater** is inside, with excellent films, laser shows and multimedia presentations presented on a huge wraparound screen. Changing shows feature anything from the Grand Canyon to the dark side of the moon – there are several shows a day and a triple feature at 7 pm daily in summer and weekends in winter. Call the Hall of Fame for current showings. Adult admission is $4.50 for the theater, $2.50 for the Space Hall of Fame, or $6 for both. Children six to 18 years old and seniors receive discounts, as do family groups.

Around the complex are gardens displaying various rockets and astro-artifacts, including the grave of Ham, the first chimp in space. The center is reached from either Scenic Drive or Indian Wells Rd – there are many signs.

Alameda Park & Zoo

The entrance to the Alameda Park & Zoo (☎ 505-439-4290) is south of the chamber of commerce at 1021 N WSB. The zoo was established in 1898 as a diversion for railway travelers – it is the oldest zoo in the state. Small but well run, the zoo features exotics from all over the world, among them the endangered Mexican gray wolf. Hours are from 9 am to 5 pm daily; admission is $2 for adults and $1 for both children and seniors. The park has picnic facilities.

Toy Train Depot

At the north end of Alameda Park, the Toy Train Depot (☎ 505-437-2855), 1991 N WSB, is an 1898 railway depot that now houses hundreds of toy trains running on a quarter-mile of model railway track, as well as other railroad memorabilia and a gift shop. Hours are noon till 5 pm daily except Tuesdays and holidays. Admission is $2; $1.50 for children.

Kids Kingdom

On Oregon Ave south of Indian Wells Rd, this is a well-designed children's adventure playground that will keep younger travelers amused for hours.

Historical Museum

This small museum (☎ 505-437-6120), 1301 N WSB, focuses on local history. Hours are from 10 am to 4 pm daily except Sunday. Admission is free.

Historical Buildings

The historical center of town, east of N WSB along and just off 10th, has many interesting buildings. Go to the attractive USFS building (formerly the federal building) at 11th and New York to see Peter Hurd's *Sun and Rain* frescoes, painted in the early 1940s as part of the New Deal's WPA art program.

Activities

You can play 18 holes of **golf** at Desert Lakes Municipal Golf Course (☎ 505-437-0290), 2351 Hamilton Rd (south of town off Hwy 54). Call the city Parks & Recreation Office (☎ 505-439-4142) for other suggestions.

Places to Stay – Camping

The *KOA* (☎ 505-437-3003), 412 24th, charges $16 for tents, $19 for RV hookups and $25 for Kamping Kabins. Cheaper camping is at Oliver Lee State Park, 13 miles south, or Three Rivers, 35 miles north (see Around Alamogordo, below). Both developed and free dispersed camping are available in the Lincoln National Forest – get USFS maps showing forest roads branching off from Hwy 82 east of Alamogordo.

Places to Stay – Budget

There is an abundance of motels and hotels stretching out along White Sands Blvd for approximately 5 miles. Rates are fairly constant year-round.

One of the cheapest places is the *Alamo Inn* (☎ 505-437-1000), 1450 N WSB, with a small seasonal pool and 40 basic rooms for $21/27. Other adequate budget motels include the *Townsman Motel* (☎ 505-437-0210), 710 N WSB, and the *Budget 7 Motel* (☎ 505-437-9350), 2404 N WSB.

A decent budget motel is the *Western Motel* (☎ 505-437-2922), 1101 S WSB, which charges $26/30 for queen-size beds, $3 or $4 more for king-size. The *All American Inn* (☎ 505-437-1850, 800-224-1850), 508 S WSB, has a pool, and rooms with coffeemakers. It's fair value at $28/30. The *Motel 6* (☎ 505-434-5970), 251 Panorama Blvd (behind the Holiday Inn), has a small pool and charges $29/35.

Places to Stay – Middle

The clean *Satellite Inn* (☎ 505-437-8454, 800-221-7690), 2224 N WSB, has a pool and is a decent value at $32/36. Most rooms have refrigerators and some have microwaves. The *Super 8 Motel* (☎/fax 505-434-4205), 3204 N WSB, looks nice

NEW MEXICO

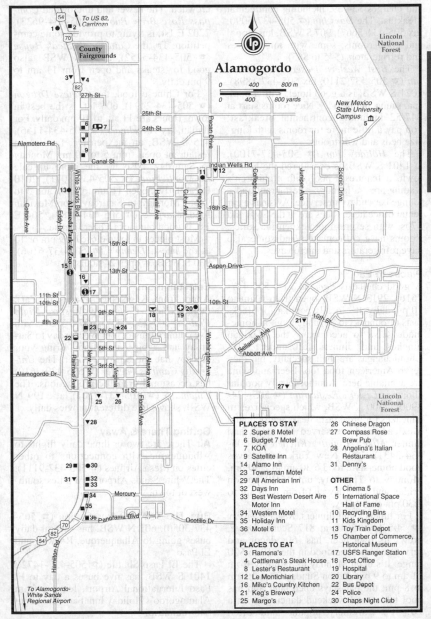

Alamogordo

To US 82, Carrizozo

County Fairgrounds

Lincoln National Forest

New Mexico State University Campus

Lincoln National Forest

To Alamogordo-White Sands Regional Airport

PLACES TO STAY
2 Super 8 Motel
6 Budget 7 Motel
7 KOA
9 Satellite Inn
14 Alamo Inn
23 Townsman Motel
29 All American Inn
32 Days Inn
33 Best Western Desert Aire Motor Inn
34 Western Motel
35 Holiday Inn
36 Motel 6

PLACES TO EAT
3 Ramona's
4 Cattleman's Steak House
8 Lester's Restaurant
12 Le Montichiari
16 Miko'o Country Kitchen
21 Keg's Brewery
25 Margo's
26 Chinese Dragon
27 Compass Rose Brew Pub
28 Angolina's Italian Restaurant
31 Denny's

OTHER
1 Cinema 5
5 International Space Hall of Fame
10 Recycling Bins
11 Kids Kingdom
13 Toy Train Depot
15 Chamber of Commerce, Historical Museum
17 USFS Ranger Station
18 Post Office
19 Hospital
20 Library
22 Bus Depot
24 Police
30 Chaps Night Club

and charges $34/39, including continental breakfast. The *Days Inn* (☎ 505-437-5090, fax 505-434-5667), 907 S WSB, has a pool and good rooms, some with microwaves and refrigerators ($45 to $65).

The *Best Western Desert Aire Motor Inn* (☎ 505-437-2110, fax 505-437-1898), 1021 S WSB, is a good hotel, with a pool, spa, sauna and laundry. Nice rooms start at $47/52 including continental breakfast; you pay a little more for rooms with king-size beds and whirlpools.

The *Holiday Inn* (☎ 505-437-7100), at 1401 S WSB, is considered the best in town. It features a pool with a children's wading area, a laundry, a restaurant and a lounge bar and room service. Avis has a car rental office here. Rates are in the $60s and $70s, with several more-expensive suites. Rooms have coffeemakers and some also have refrigerators and microwaves.

Places to Eat

A good choice is *Ramona's* (☎ 505-437-7616), 2913 N WSB, open from 6 am to 10 pm daily. It's locally popular for breakfasts (around $3 to $6) and has good home-made salsa to accompany the Mexican lunches and dinners (all under $10). Chimichangas are their specialty, but they serve American food too. Beer and wine are available here. Another locally popular choice is *Lester's Restaurant* (☎ 505-434-3900), 2300 N WSB, which specializes in pancakes for breakfast. Steak, seafood, and Mexican food are served for lunch and dinner. *Mike's Country Kitchen* (☎ 505-434-3431), 1201 New York Ave, serves good home-style food 6:30 am to 2:30 pm, Monday to Thursday, until 6:30 pm on Friday and Saturday and from 8:30 am to 2:30 pm on Sunday.

For lunches and dinners, *Keg's Brewery* (☎ 505-437-9564), at 817 Scenic Drive, brews its own beer, has '60s décor and serves steak and seafood in the $10 to $20 range. It's open Monday to Saturday from 11 am to 9 pm and on Sunday from 10 am to 8 pm; the bar stays open later and has pool tables and weekend dancing, with a DJ. It's extremely popular and often crowded. The newer and uncrowded *Compass Rose Brew Pub* (☎ 505-434-9633), 2202 E 1st, is trying to provide some competition. Try the *Cattleman's Steak House* (☎ 505-434-5252), 2904 N WSB, also good for steaks and open from 11 am to 9 pm daily.

For Chinese food, the *Chinese Dragon* (☎ 505-434-2494), 606 1st, is the best in town. Hours are 11 am to 10 pm daily. For Italian, try *Angelina's* (☎ 505-434-1166), 415 S WSB, an inexpensive, family-run restaurant open from 5 to 10 pm Monday to Saturday. Also try the more upscale *Le Montichiari* (☎ 505-439-8071), 2010 Pecan Drive, open 11 am to 3 pm and 5 to 9 pm Monday to Saturday. For Mexican food, *Margo's* (☎ 505-434-0889), 504 E 1st, is good but lacks a beer license.

Most places in town close by 9 pm or 10 at the latest. *Denny's* (☎ 505-437-6106), 930 S WSB, is open 24 hours.

Entertainment

Apart from Keg's (see Places to Eat), there's *Chaps Country & Western Night Club* (☎ 505-434-3757), 607 S WSB, with live country music from Wednesday to Saturday and a big dance floor. Bring your cowboy hat and $5 for a cover. The *University Campus Theater* (☎ 505-439-3619) has occasional dramatic productions. The *Cinema 5* (☎ 505-437-9301), at 3199 N WSB, shows five different movies daily.

Getting There & Away

Air There are two or three daily flights to Albuquerque with connections to other cities on Mesa Airlines (☎ 505-437-9111). The White Sands Airport is 3 miles southwest of town.

Bus The TNM&O Bus Station (☎ 505-437-3050), 601 N WSB, has several daily buses going to Albuquerque, Roswell and El Paso.

The El Paso Shuttle (☎ 505-437-1472), 1401 S WSB, has five buses a day to El Paso International Airport, leaving from Alamogordo's Holiday Inn. Fares are about $40 roundtrip.

Getting Around

Avis, Alamo and Enterprise rent cars at the airport.

AROUND ALAMOGORDO
Oliver Lee State Park

This park (☎ 505-437-8284) is 10 miles south on Hwy 54, then 4 miles east. A visitor center details prehistoric and historic Indian inhabitants of the area, as well as more recent ranchers. Hiking trails provide good views. Park entrance fee is $3 per vehicle. Campsites are $7; $11 with RV hookups. Showers are available.

La Luz & Tularosa

Four miles north (just east of Hwy 54) is La Luz, which is the oldest village in the area and unspoiled by tourism. Ten miles farther north on Hwy 54 is the attractive village of Tularosa, with its St Francis de Paula Church built in 1869 in simple New Mexican style. It's quiet for most of the year, except during the annual Tularosa Rose Festival held during the first full weekend in May. (Call ☎ 505-585-9858 for information.) Tularosa Vineyards (☎ 505-585-2260) is a small local winery 2 miles north of town on Hwy 54 that has daily afternoon tours and tastings. A small historical museum (☎ 505-585-9597) on the south side of Hwy 70 is open from 1 to 4 pm Monday to Saturday.

Three Rivers Petroglyph National Recreation Area

About a thousand years ago, the Jornada Mogollon people inscribed some 20,000 petroglyphs (rock carvings) into boulders scattered around a rocky outcrop. A variety of animals, faces and other symbols can still be seen as you scramble along a stony hiking trail winding for almost a mile through the area. The elevated site gives good views of mountains to the east and the White Sands Monument glistening on the western horizon. Nearby is a pit house in a partially excavated village. Although the site is not as spectacular as other Southwestern archaeological sites it is quiet, uncrowded and worthwhile.

There are six picnic areas, water and restrooms; admission is $2, and overnight camping is permitted. There is no ranger station; call the Bureau of Land Management in Las Cruces (☎ 505-525-4300) for further information or to report vandalism or other problems.

The site is 17 miles north of Tularosa on Hwy 54, then 5 miles east on a signed road. A dirt road continues for about 10 miles beyond the petroglyph area to the Lincoln National Forest, where there is the Three Rivers Campground and trailhead.

CARRIZOZO

This small crossroads town at Hwys 380 and 54, just west of the Sacramento Mountains and 58 miles north of Alamogordo, has 1500 inhabitants and is the Lincoln County seat. Established in 1899, it was briefly an important railway town. Carrizozo lies at 5425 feet, surrounded by high desert and with Carrizo Peak (9650 feet) looming about 9 miles to the east.

Valley of Fires Recreation Area

Four miles west of Carrizozo is the most interesting place to see in the area. Visitors can walk over a flow estimated to be 1500 years old, 47 miles long and up to 160 feet thick. Slowly, pioneering plants and animals have colonized this inhospitable terrain. It is thought-provoking to realize that some of the same lizard, snake and mouse species that exhibit melanism (dark coloration) here, where the lava is black, have adapted light coloration in response to the white gypsum of White Sands.

There is a three-quarter-mile self-guiding nature trail, as well as restrooms, picnic areas and campsites. The trail and restrooms are wheelchair accessible. Entrance is $3 per person or $5 per vehicle for day use. The area is administered by the BLM (☎ 505-624-1790), Box 1857, Roswell, NM 88202.

Places to Stay & Eat

Camping sites at Valley of Fires Recreation Area cost $5 to $11 for primitive sites to RV sites with hookups.

Most of the accommodations are clustered around the main highway intersection and all offer rooms in the $20s or $30s. They include the *Carrizozo Inn* (☎ 505-648-4006), the *Crossroads Motel* (☎ 505-648-2373) and the *Four Winds Motel* (☎ 505-648-2356). Seven blocks south of the intersection is the *Sands Motel & RV Park* (☎ 505-648-2989).

The *Four Winds Restaurant & Lounge* (☎ 505-648-2964) is at the intersection and serves meals from 6:30 am to 9:30 pm every day.

Try the *Oscuro High Desert Hostel* (☎ 505-648-4007, Ctaylor939@aol.com), 1½ miles east of Hwy 54 mile marker 108, 15 miles south of Carrizozo, with dorm beds for $14 and private rooms for $27. A laundry and a guest kitchen (with tea, coffee and food from the ranch) are all available at no extra charge. The hostel provides pickup at the bus stop in Carrizozo, offers inexpensive local tours and has a weekly shuttle to the Route 66 Hostel in Albuquerque.

Getting There & Away
TNM&O buses (☎ 505-648-2964) stop near the Four Winds Restaurant twice daily northbound and twice daily southbound on the Albuquerque to El Paso run.

WEST OF CARRIZOZO
Trinity Site
Thirty-five miles west of Carrizozo, Trinity Site is where the first atom bomb was exploded. The test was carried out above ground and resulted in a quarter-mile-wide crater and an 8-mile-high cloud mushrooming above the desert. This desolate area is fittingly called Jornada del Muerto (Journey of Death) and is overlooked by 8638-foot Oscura Peak (Darkness Peak on state maps). If you want to visit the remnants of this devastation (radiation levels are supposedly safe for brief visits), call the Alamogordo Chamber of Commerce (☎ 505-437-6120). Only two public visits are allowed annually – on the first Saturdays in April and October.

NORTH OF CARRIZOZO
White Oaks
This was a gold-mining center in the 1880s; now it's a ghost town with a small population and some interesting old buildings. It's 11 miles northeast of Carrizozo on Hwy 349. Don't forget to look at the historic tombstones in the cemetery.

Ancho
This village is 22 miles north of Carrizozo (2½ miles east of Hwy 54) and has **My House of Old Things** (☎ 505-648-2456), a small historical museum housed in eight rooms in the 1902 railway depot. It is open from 9 am to 5 pm daily, May to mid-October; adult admission is $3 and kids get in for $1.

Corona
This village is 47 miles north of Carrizozo on Hwy 54, at the northern boundary of Lincoln County. There is a cheap motel and café. Corona is the nearest village to the Roswell UFO crash site.

A few miles south of Corona, USFS Rd 161 and USFS Rd 144 lead nine and 11 miles respectively to primitive, eight-site *Red Cloud Campground* in the Cibola National Forest. This is at 7600 feet on the slopes of isolated **Gallinas Peak** (8637 feet), where there is a lookout. A small elk herd roams the Gallinas Range. The free campground is open all year but has no drinking water. It may fill in the fall hunting season.

CLOUDCROFT
As you drive east of Alamogordo on Hwy 82, a road sign warns drivers to check brakes and gears because the road climbs 4315 feet in the next 16 miles. Cloudcroft is at a cool 9000 feet and provides welcome relief from the heat of the lowlands to the east. This is a village of about 650 people, many of whom work in tourism-related jobs.

Founded in 1898 as a railroad town, Cloudcroft soon became a vacation center for railroad employees because of its cool elevation. The railroad is long gone, but the vacationers remain. Turn-of-the-19th-century buildings make walking around the small downtown area very similar to walking onto a Western movie set, and the town offers several gift shops and galleries. The main attractions, however, are good skiing in the winter and hiking and camping in the cool pine forests during the summer.

Hunting is popular in the fall, as are tours to see the pretty fall colors. High up in the Sacramento Mountains, you may find yourself forgetting that you are in the American Southwest.

Orientation & Information

Hwy 82 is the main drag through town, and most places are on this road or within a few blocks of it.

The chamber of commerce (☎ 505-682-2733), Box 1290, Cloudcroft, NM 88317, is on Hwy 82 and provides excellent tourist information. Summer hours are from 9 am to 5 pm daily except Sunday, when hours are 11 am to 3 pm. Nearby is a drop-off recycling center. The Lincoln National Forest Cloudcroft Ranger Station (☎ 505-682-2551), Box 288, Cloudcroft, NM 88317, is at the western end of Chipmunk

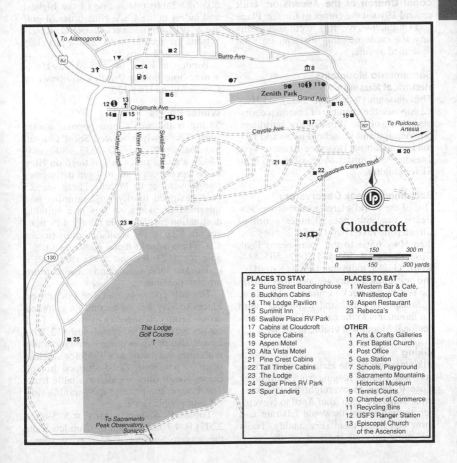

Cloudcroft

PLACES TO STAY	PLACES TO EAT
2 Burro Street Boardinghouse	1 Western Bar & Café,
6 Buckhorn Cabins	Whistlestop Cafe
14 The Lodge Pavilion	19 Aspen Restaurant
15 Summit Inn	23 Rebecca's
16 Swallow Place RV Park	
17 Cabins at Cloudcroft	**OTHER**
18 Spruce Cabins	1 Arts & Crafts Galleries
19 Aspen Motel	3 First Baptist Church
20 Alta Vista Motel	4 Post Office
21 Pine Crest Cabins	5 Gas Station
22 Tall Timber Cabins	7 Schools, Playground
23 The Lodge	8 Sacramento Mountains
24 Sugar Pines RV Park	Historical Museum
25 Spur Landing	9 Tennis Courts
	10 Chamber of Commerce
	11 Recycling Bins
	12 USFS Ranger Station
	13 Episcopal Church
	of the Ascension

NEW MEXICO

Ave. The post office (☎ 505-682-2431) is at 20 Curlew Place, just north of Hwy 82. The nearest hospital is in Alamogordo. In an emergency, call the Cloudcroft police (☎ 505-682-2101).

Historic Buildings
Early-20th-century Western architecture lines the west end of Burro Ave, where you will find the old wooden **First Baptist Church** and various other buildings, including a small shopping area for arts and crafts.

Cloudcroft's oldest church is the **Episcopal Church of the Ascension**, built around 1910 at the corner of Curlew Place and Chipmunk Ave. It is worth seeing this tiny log-cabin building that can only be described as cute.

Sacramento Mountains Historical Museum
This museum (☎ 505-682-2932), on Hwy 82 opposite the chamber of commerce, displays turn-of-the-19th-century buildings, farm equipment, household items and railroad memorabilia. Hours are 10 am to 4 pm Tuesday to Saturday. Admission is $2.50; $1 for children.

Sacramento Peak Observatory
One of the world's largest solar observatories is near Sunspot, 20 miles south of Cloudcroft. Take Hwy 130 for 2 miles and then Hwy 6563 to the Sacramento Peak Observatory (☎ 505-434-7000, 505-434-1390). Guided tours are given on Saturdays and self-guided tours are available during the rest of the week in summer. The drive to Sunspot is a high and scenic one, with the mountains to the east and White Sands National Monument visible to the west.

Hiking
Hiking is one of the main summer activities, with outings ranging from short hikes close to town to overnight backpacking trips. Trails are open from April to November, though spring thaw and fall rain and snow can make them very muddy. Trails are snow-covered the rest of the year.

Although trails are often fairly flat and easy, the 9000-foot elevation can make hiking strenuous if you are not acclimatized.

The most popular easy hike is the 2.6-mile Osha Loop Trail, which leaves Hwy 82 from a small parking area opposite the old railroad trestle, 1 mile west of Cloudcroft. Both the chamber of commerce and the USFS can provide descriptions and/or maps of this and other hikes.

Golf
The Lodge (see Places to Stay) has a popular nine-hole course (☎ 505-682-2098, 505-682-2566) that is one of the highest and oldest in the USA. Nine holes of golf are $10/14 for midweek/weekend. Reservations are recommended and a pro shop rents carts and clubs.

Ponderosa Pines (☎ 505-682-2995) is a nine-hole course 9 miles southeast of Cloudcroft on Hwy 130.

Winter Sports
Skiing is the area's most popular winter sport. The newly renovated Snow Canyon Ski Area (☎ 505-682-2333, 800-333-7542), about 2 miles east of town on Hwy 82, is open from 9 am to 4 pm daily from mid-November to March. There are 25 runs designed mostly for beginning and intermediate skiers, so this is a suitable destination for the whole family. Lift tickets are $25/16 for adults/children (under 12). There are ski-rental packages (available for $12), lessons, a ski shop and a restaurant. Inner-tubing and snowboarding are also possible.

The golf course behind The Lodge (see Places to Stay, below) becomes a groomed cross-country skiing area in winter. Trail passes are $4 and ski rentals are $12. The Lodge also provides guided snowmobiling with rates beginning at $30/45 for singles/doubles per hour. Old-fashioned horse-drawn sleigh rides are also available from The Lodge; the price of a 30-minute ride for four people is $50.

Triple M's Snowplay Area (☎ 505-682-2205) is 4.7 miles south of Cloudcroft on the way to Sunspot. The area has snowmobile tours ($30/40 per hour for single/double machines), horse-drawn sleigh rides ($11 per person), and slopes with a lift for inner-tubing (weekends and holidays, $16 per day for lift and tube rental).

Special Events

The chamber of commerce sponsors a full calendar of events ranging from the Full Moon Skating Party on the night of a February full moon to an Oktoberfest during the first weekend in October. The Oktoberfest features guided tours of the beautiful fall foliage and a juried arts and crafts show. Call the chamber of commerce about various other events throughout the summer.

Cherries are produced in nearby High Rolls (between Cloudcroft and Alamogordo), and there is an annual Cherry Festival with cherry desserts being the major enticement. This is held on the third Sunday of June (Father's Day).

Places to Stay

Camping *Swallow Place RV Park* (☎ 505-682-6014), 104 Swallow Place, has full hookups for two RVs only. A larger and more developed place is *Sugar Pines RV Park* (☎ 505-682-2677) at the southeast end of town, with showers and 10 RV sites with hookups for $15. Tent camping is permitted. Five miles north of town on Hwy 244 is the *Silver Springs RV Park* (☎ 505-682-2803), with 32 sites with hookups for $12.50 and a stocked fish pond where you can catch trout for dinner.

The USFS (☎ 505-682-2551) has several tent/RV campgrounds that, because of the elevation, are open summer only (May to mid-September), though some may open earlier or later with no services or fees, weather permitting. Fees are $6 to $7, vehicles are limited to 32 feet or less in length and there are no RV hookups. During the summer, The Blake Company (☎ 505-682-2054) has information about these USFS campgrounds. A half mile north from the intersection with Hwy 82, just east of Cloudcroft, is *The Pines* with 48 sites and water but no showers. About 1.4 miles farther north along Hwy 244 is

the turnoff to the USFS's *Silver*, *Saddle* and *Apache* campgrounds. Silver, in particular, has good flat sites suited to RVs, and hot showers are available at all three.

About a mile southeast of town on Hwy 130 is the USFS *Deerhead* campground with water but no showers. There are also several campgrounds for groups by reservation only. Free dispersed camping is also available.

The *James Canyon* USFS campground, which doesn't have water and has six free sites, is 16 miles east of Cloudcroft and 2 miles west of the small village of Mayhill.

The *Rio Penasco RV Park* (☎ 505-687-3715) is in Mayhill, at the junction of Hwy 82 and 130. There are showers, a laundry, tent sites ($8) and RV hookups ($12). Mayhill has little more than a store, gas station and 'the last bar for 72 miles.'

Cabins The most popular accommodations in Cloudcroft are cabins, which vary in size and can accommodate up to eight people. Cabins usually include an equipped kitchen, fireplace with wood and the usual bed and bathroom facilities. These places are designed for families spending a few days in the mountains, and minimum stays of two nights are often required on weekends; longer minimum stays might be required during holiday periods, especially around Christmas. Rates vary depending on the number of guests, time of year, size of cabin and length of stay. Average rates for a cabin sleeping four people are $50 to $75 a night. Weekend reservations are a good idea. A selection is given below but there are several other small places.

Buckhorn Cabins (☎ 505-682-2421) is close to downtown at the corner of Hwy 82 and Swallow Place. There are 16 rooms, most with a kitchen and fireplace.

Spruce Cabins (☎ 505-682-2381) is one of the biggest complexes, with 32 cabins in the woods behind the chamber of commerce. Most cabins sleep four or six and have a kitchen and fireplace; a few smaller units for two people are available, with a choice of kitchen or fireplace. Near this complex is *Cabins at Cloudcroft*

(☎ 505-682-2396, 800-248-7967, fax 505-682-2399) with 12 cabins with a fireplace. A few have two bedrooms and one has four bedrooms.

Pine Crest Cabins (☎ 505-682-2631, 800-682-2631), at the east end of town away from the main highway, has five units sleeping five or six people, all with kitchens and fireplaces. Nearby is the similar *Tall Timber Cabins* (☎ 505-682-2301, 800-682-2301). There are several other small places.

Hotels The *Aspen Motel & Restaurant* (☎ 505-682-2526) is a clean and simple motel at the east end of town with 22 rooms at $50 double. The small *Alta Vista Motel* (☎ 505-682-2221) is at the far east end of town and has seven spacious rooms, some with fireplaces.

The *Summit Inn* (☎ 505-682-2814) is near the center of things and has pleasant rooms with kitchenettes for about $40/60/90 for two/four/six people. It also has cottages (or duplexes) with fireplaces and kitchens at about $75 for five people, $95 for eight people. *Burro Street Boardinghouse* (☎ 505-682-3601), in the historic district, has old-fashioned rooms with private baths and antiques for $68 double, including breakfast.

Spur Landing (☎ 505-682-2700, 800-426-3365) has well-appointed one- and two-bedroom townhouses next to the golf course from $100 a night double, with weekly discounts.

The Lodge (☎ 505-682-2566, 800-395-6343, fax 505-682-2715) stands out as one of the best historic hotels in the state and, indeed, the entire Southwest. Built in 1899 as the original vacation lodge for railroad employees, it was destroyed by fire and rebuilt in 1911. Rooms in this antique, three-story hotel are filled with period furnishings and all have private baths; some have fireplaces or whirlpool tubs. A 4th floor features an observatory with a copper dome and great views.

Lodge rooms are about $80 to $100, and pavilion rooms (a few blocks away in a separate, less attractive building) are $65 to

$90. The Honeymoon Suite (mirror-topped bed, whirlpool, champagne and antiques) and the Governor's Suite (the most elegant, where the rich and famous stay) go for about $185. There is also the Retreat, a complete four-bedroom mountain home for $300. Low season discounts are offered.

The Lodge has a pool, sauna, hot tub, restaurant and bar, gift shop, game room and a nine-hole golf course.

Places to Eat

Many people stay in places with kitchens, and there aren't many restaurants. The *Western Bar & Cafe* (☎ 505-682-2445) on historic Burro Ave is a popular place that looks like something out of the Wild West. Inexpensive Mexican and American breakfasts, lunches and dinners are served. Nearby, the *Whistlestop Café* (☎ 505-682-2040) serves sandwiches, ice cream and coffees from 9 am to 5 pm daily. The *Aspen Motel* has a reasonable restaurant with German specialties.

By far the best (and most expensive) food is served at the historic *Rebecca's* (☎ 505-682-3131) in The Lodge. The restaurant is named after a beautiful chambermaid who died during a lovers' dispute in the 1930s; her ghost supposedly haunts The Lodge. Daily dining is from 7 am to 9:30 pm (closed late morning and afternoon) and there is a Sunday brunch. Rebecca's features an outside deck and attractive mountain views; inside there is often piano music or other entertainment. Dining is continental, dinner entrées run from $12 to $25 (cheaper lunches) and reservations are recommended.

Entertainment

The *Red Dog Saloon* in The Lodge is great for a drink; hours are 5 pm to midnight Wednesday to Saturday, and there is live weekend entertainment. There is also the *Western Bar* on Burro Ave.

MESCALERO APACHE INDIAN RESERVATION

The Apaches were a nomadic people who arrived in this area about 800 years ago and soon became the enemies of the local Pueblo Indians. This enmity was exacerbated by the arrival of the Europeans. The Apaches, under pressure from European settlement and with their mobility greatly increased by the introduction of the horse, soon became some of the most feared raiders of the West. Many of the descendants of Geronimo, the most famous of the Apache warrior leaders, live in Mescalero.

Today, about 3000 Native Americans live on the 719-sq-mile reservation, which lies in attractive country south and west of Ruidoso. Despite the name of the reservation, the Apaches here are of three tribes: the Mescalero, the Chiricahua and the Lipan. Residents make a living on logging, ranching and tourism. The Ski Apache resort, lying just outside the reservation, is managed by the tribe (see Skiing, in the Ruidoso section below).

Information
The Tribal Council (☎ 505-671-4494/ 4495), Box 176, Mescalero, NM 88340, is the best information source. The Tribal Cultural Center (ext 254) is also here, with a small but interesting exhibit about the peoples and customs. Hours are 8:00 am to 4:30 pm Monday to Friday. Call for information about dancing and other cultural demonstrations. The village of Mescalero is 17 miles southwest of Ruidoso on Hwy 70.

Special Events
The annual Apache Maidens' Puberty Ceremony takes place for about five days around the Fourth of July and attracts Indians and non-Indians. The traditional rites are held in Mescalero; photography is prohibited, and you should check with the tribal council about what you can actually see. Apart from the sacred rites of the Puberty Ceremony, there is a powwow, a rodeo, and arts and crafts demonstrations to which the public is welcome.

Dancing by other Indian tribes often takes place in Ruidoso on the Fourth of July, and photography is allowed there.

The Inn of the Mountain Gods
This Apache-owned and operated conference center and resort is the most luxurious place to stay in southern New Mexico. Almost every imaginable activity is offered – for a price: golf, tennis, swimming, fishing, hunting, boating, horseback riding, bicycling, shooting, archery, skiing, lawn games and a children's playground. Indoors, guests find more swimming and tennis, saunas and whirlpools, gambling (poker and bingo), video games, a fine and recommended restaurant and a lounge serving alcohol, with live entertainment and dancing.

More than 200 large guest rooms, most with either balconies or patios and with great views, rent for a surprisingly modest $130 during the Memorial Day to Labor Day summer season. Rates are substantially less the rest of the year. An 18-hole round of golf costs $30; a fishing permit is $8; guided hunting trips cost several hundred dollars. Package deals are available for skiing, hunting, tennis and golf. Call the Inn (☎ 505-257-5141, 800-545-9011, fax 505-257-6173) for details or write Box 269, Mescalero, NM 88340. The Inn is about 3 miles southwest of Ruidoso on Carrizo Canyon Rd.

If you are staying in Ruidoso, you are welcome to visit the inn to admire and use the facilities.

RUIDOSO
This resort town of almost 5000 inhabitants lies at 6900 feet in the Sacramento Mountains. Its pleasant climate and forested surroundings attract people escaping the summer heat of Alamogordo 46 miles to the southwest, and Roswell 71 miles to the east, as well as many visitors from Texas.

During the summer, camping, hiking, horseback riding and fishing are the attractions. From early May to early September, the racetrack in nearby Ruidoso Downs has top-notch horseracing. During winter, the excellent Ski Apache resort attracts skiers from afar. Nearby is the Mescalero Apache Indian Reservation. Ruidoso capitalizes on these attractions; there are plenty of places

NEW MEXICO

to stay, many restaurants and gift stores – yet somehow the town manages to avoid the air of being a tourist trap.

Orientation

Ruidoso is a very spread-out town, with vacation homes tucked away on narrow streets sprawling into the surrounding mountains. Hwy 48 from the north is the main drag through town. This is called Mechem Drive until the small downtown area where it becomes Sudderth Drive heading east to the Y-intersection with Hwy 70. Six miles north on Mechem Drive is the community of Alto, with more accommodations. The community of Ruidoso Downs (named after its racetrack) is a separate village just east of Ruidoso on Hwy 70. Both Ruidoso Downs and Alto are included under this Ruidoso section.

Information

Tourist information is available at the chamber of commerce (☎ 505-257-7395,

800-253-2255), Box 698, Ruidoso, NM 88345. It is at 720 Sudderth Drive. Summer hours are from 8:30 am to 5 pm Tuesday to Friday, from 9 am to 5 pm on Monday and Saturday and 1 to 4 pm on Sunday.

The Lincoln National Forest Smokey Bear Ranger Station (☎ 505-257-4095) is at 901 Mechem Drive. The library (☎ 505-257-4335) is at 501 Sudderth Drive. The post office (☎ 505-257-7120) is at 2959 Sudderth Drive. The Medical Center & Hospital (☎ 505-257-7381) is at 211 Sudderth Drive. The police (☎ 505-257-7365) are at 421 Wingfield.

Ruidoso Downs Racetrack

The Ruidoso Downs Racetrack (☎ 505-378-4431, 505-378-4140) is on Hwy 70 about 4½ miles east of downtown Ruidoso. Ruidoso Downs is one of the major racetracks in the Southwest and operates from late May to early September Friday to Sunday (and Monday holidays). The All American Futurity is held at the end of the

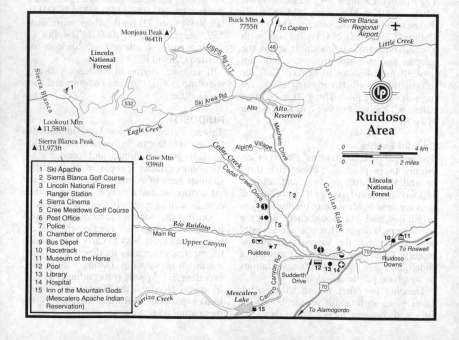

1   Ski Apache
2   Sierra Blanca Golf Course
3   Lincoln National Forest
    Ranger Station
4   Sierra Cinema
5   Cree Meadows Golf Course
6   Post Office
7   Police
8   Chamber of Commerce
9   Bus Depot
10 Racetrack
11 Museum of the Horse
12 Pool
13 Library
14 Hospital
15 Inn of the Mountain Gods
    (Mescalero Apache Indian
    Reservation)

Ruidoso Area

season on Labor Day – this is the world's richest quarterhorse race and is worth over $2,000,000. Post time is 1 pm (call to confirm). General admission is free, parking is $3 and grandstand seats and boxes are available for $2.50 to $8.50. Out of season, pari-mutuel betting is available for races across the USA, which are broadcast live to the sports theater. Good luck!

The Museum of the Horse

This museum (☎ 505-378-4142, 800-263-5929, moth@lookingglass.net), at the east end of the racetrack, has a fine display of more than 10,000 horse-related items. Featured items range from ancient Greek statues through Old West stagecoaches to modern art, including artists such as Frederic Remington and Charles M Russell. Hours are 9 am to 5:30 pm daily from May 1 to Labor Day; 10 am to 5 pm daily September and October; 10 am to 5 pm Tuesday to Sunday in other months (closed Thanksgiving and Christmas). Admission is $5 for adults ($4 for age 60 and up); $3 for five- to 17-year-olds.

Skiing

The best ski area south of Albuquerque is **Ski Apache** (☎ 505-336-4356, snow conditions 505-257-9001). It is 18 miles northwest of Ruidoso and is open daily from 8:45 am to 4 pm, late November to Easter. The S&S Ski Shuttle (☎ 505-378-4456) will pick you up from any spot on Sudderth Drive or Mechem Drive if you call before 7:30 am.

Ski Apache is in the Lincoln National Forest and is operated by the Mescalero Apache Tribe. There are 55 runs between 9600 and 11,500 feet on the slopes of beautiful Sierra Blanca Peak (11,973 feet on some maps and 12,003 on others), the highest mountain in southern New Mexico. Novice runs comprise 20% of the mountain, intermediate 35% and advanced 45%. Ski rental and instruction are available, and there are several snack bars. With the state's only four-passenger gondola, plus eight chair lifts and a surface lift, there is a capacity for a stunning 16,550 skiers per hour, which means short lift lines. All-day passes are $39 for adults; $24 for children 12 and under ($3 more on holidays). There are many ski rental stores open on Mechem and Sudderth – shop around for the best deals.

Hiking

Hiking is a popular summertime activity, with the 4.6-mile day hike from the Ski Apache area to the summit of Sierra Blanca Peak being especially popular. The summit, which lies within the Mescalero Apache Reservation, is more than 2000 feet higher than the Ski Apache parking lot and can only be reached by foot. Take Trail 15 from the small parking area just before the main lot and follow signs west and south along trails 25 and 78 to Lookout Mountain (11,580 feet). From there an unnamed but obvious trail continues due south for 1¼ miles to Sierra Blanca Peak.

Also from Ski Apache you can hike to Monjeau Lookout, 5.6 miles away. Begin with Trail 15 and then take Trail 25 (the Crest Trail) north until you reach USFS Rd 117 – the lookout is less than a mile away. The Crest Trail offers superb views and some sheltered camping areas (carry water). The ranger station in Ruidoso has maps and information for more adventurous trips.

Other Activities

During the nonskiing season, Sierra Blanca Peak offers several lookouts with stunning views, especially in the fall – just drive up Ski Area Rd (532) from Alto. Along this road, you'll see signs for the Monjeau Lookout via USFS Rd 117. This rough road (often impassable in bad weather) also offers exceptional views to motorists.

Horseback riding is another option. Grindstone Stables (☎ 505-257-2241) on Grindstone Resort Drive near downtown rents horses.

Fishing is popular in season. The Rio Ruidoso runs through town and offers some good fishing opportunities, as do several lakes in the national forest.

You can play some **golf** at Cree Meadows (☎ 505-257-5815), 301 Country Club Drive, Ruidoso's oldest golf course. The new links at the Sierra Blanca course (☎ 505-258-5330, 800-854-6571) at 105 Sierra Blanca Drive opened in 1991 and have already gained a reputation as the best course in southern New Mexico. Reservations are recommended.

Go **swimming** at the town pool (☎ 505-257-2795), which features a water slide and is next to the library on Sudderth Drive.

Special Events

The annual Ruidoso Art Festival, held during the last full weekend in July, attracts several hundred applicants, of whom only about 25% are selected. This is a top-quality juried event attended by thousands of browsing and buying visitors from all over the Southwest and beyond. There is a $3 admission.

The Aspenfest in the first weekend in October has a chili cook-off, a street festival and arts and crafts, all among the glorious colors of early fall. Over the second weekend in October, the Lincoln County Cowboy Symposium is held at the Museum of the Horse with events ranging from cowboy poetry to chuckwagon cooking to horse breaking; this is said to be the nation's best cowboy cultural event. Admission is $5. The fun continues with the Oktoberfest during the third weekend. This has a strong Bavarian theme with German food, beer and wine as well as professional polka and other dancing, oompah bands and public revelry. Admission is $5. The chamber of commerce has dates of other events.

Places to Stay

There are many places catering to most budgets, though accommodations in the $20s are hard to find in the high season. Travelers on a budget should avoid racing and holiday weekends, as well as weekends in the ski season, when even the cheaper hotels raise their prices by $5 or more. Reservations are recommended for these weekends if you want your choice of places to stay. Alternatively, form a group and rent a cabin or condo. The lowest rates are from after the Oktoberfest until Thanksgiving and from Easter to early May – when there isn't much

going on. Approximate high-season rates are given below.

Places to Stay – Camping

Commercial campgrounds in Ruidoso include *Blue Spruce RV Park* (☎/fax 505-257-7993), 302 Mechem Drive, where RV sites with hookups are $15. Another RV park is *Tall Pines* (☎ 505-257-5233), 1800 Sudderth Drive, which is $19. Neither has tenting facilities.

The *River Ranch Campground* (☎ 505-378-4245), northeast of Ruidoso on Hwy 70, has RV sites with full hookups for $21.50 and tent sites for $12.50. The *Circle B Campground* (☎ 505-378-4990), 2½ miles northeast of Ruidoso Downs on Hwy 70, offers tent and RV sites with hookups for about $15. In Alto, the *Bonito Hollow Campground* (☎ 505-336-4325), has RV sites with hookups for $14 to $16 and tent sites for $12 as well as bunkhouse rooms and cabins for $25 to $40. These places have showers available.

The Lincoln National Forest (☎ 505-257-4095) operates several campgrounds north of Ruidoso. All are open from May to September and none have showers. *South Fork Campground* is near Bonito Lake and has fishing, hiking trails and drinking water. Take Hwy 48 11 miles north from Ruidoso and turn left on USFS Rd 107 for 5 miles. There is a $6 fee.

The *Oak Grove*, *Skyline* and *Monjeau Campgrounds* all have pit toilets but no drinking water and all are free (though this may change). Oak Grove is 5 miles west of Alto on the Ski Area Rd. Skyline is 4 miles along USFS Rd 117, which heads north a mile along Ski Area Rd. A mile beyond is the Monjeau Campground with four sites. These last three campgrounds are at 9000 feet or higher, so be prepared for cold camping. RVs longer than 16 feet are not recommended. Call the ranger for other campgrounds. Free dispersed camping is also allowed.

Places to Stay – Budget

The *Villa Inn Motel* (☎ 505-378-4471, 800-447-8455) is one of the better budget hotels. It is on Hwy 70 just west of the Y-junction with Sudderth Drive. It has 60 rooms beginning in the $30s midweek, higher on weekends. Also good are the much smaller *Apache Motel* (☎ 505-257-2986, 800-426-0616, apache@lookingglass .net), 344 Sudderth Drive, which offers rooms, some with kitchenettes, from $26 to $68, or the *Innsbruck Lodge* (☎ 505-257-4071), 601 Sudderth Drive, with 47 rooms starting at around $35. Also along Sudderth Drive, you'll find other reasonably priced places, such as the *Winners Inn Motel* (☎ 505-257-5886) and the *Alpine Lodge* (☎ 505-257-4423). Also try the *Stagecoach Motel* (☎ 505-257-2610), and *The Holiday House* (☎ 505-257-4003).

Places to Stay – Middle to Top End
Many of the establishments below have units ranging from simple rooms to comfortable suites. Descriptions begin with motel/hotel accommodations and segue into condos and cabins with some overlap. (The superb Inn of the Mountain Gods is described in the Mescalero Apache Indian Reservation section earlier in this chapter.)

Hotels The *Super 8 Motel* (☎/fax 505-378-8180), on Hwy 70 just west of the Y-junction with Sudderth Drive, offers 63 single/double rooms for $38.88/42.88 (more on weekends) and has a sauna and continental breakfast. The *Pines Motel* (☎ 505-257-4334), 620 Sudderth Drive, is nicely situated by the river and has 10 small but spotless rooms in the $40s. The *Sitzmark Chalet* (☎ 505-257-4140, 800-658-9694, sitzmark@earthlink.com) at 627 Sudderth Drive, has rooms with refrigerator and microwave starting from $40 to $60 in summer and has larger kitchen units for $90. Also, the *Enchantment Inn* (☎ 505-378-4051, 800-435-0280, fax 505-378-5427, magical@lookingglass.net), near the Super 8, has 80 standard rooms around $70 and some suites with kitchens for $85 to $150; a pool and spa are available. The *Best Western Swiss Chalet Inn* (☎ 505-258-3333, fax 505-258-5325), on a hill overlooking Hwy 48 in Alto, halfway between

Ruidoso and Ski Apache, has good rooms for $56 to $100; a pool, sauna and good restaurant are on the premises. A few more-expensive suites are available.

The *Carrizo Lodge* (☎ 505-257-9131, 800-227-1224, fax 505-257-5621), on Carrizo Canyon Rd in the forest south of town, is in a building constructed in 1874. This historic hotel has long been an art center; it continues to host summer art schools and features a Southwestern art gallery. Rooms are $60 to $90; modern condos with fireplaces are slightly more expensive. There is a pool.

The *Village Lodge* (☎ 505-258-5442, 800-722-8779, fax 505-258-3127), 1000 Mechem Drive, has modern suites with king-size beds, kitchenettes and living rooms with fireplaces. These are $89 a double during most racing and skiing season weekends and much less midweek or out of season. Children stay free and additional adults are $10 extra – the suites can sleep up to six in a pinch. The lodge has adjoining pool, spa, tennis courts and golf facilities.

The *Cree Manor Inn* (☎ 505-257-4058), 110 Starlite Rd, is on a quiet side road near the golf course. *Cro's Nest* (☎ 505-257-2773), 143 Upper Terrace Drive, is just east of Mechem Drive. Both places have either simple rooms or apartments for about $40 to $120.

The following are in the Upper Canyon area of Ruidoso. The *Shadow Mountain Lodge* (☎ 505-257-4886, 800-441-4331, fax 505-257-2000, lodge@lookingglass .net), 107 Main Rd, has 19 comfortable rooms, all with king-size beds, fireplaces and kitchenettes. Wooden balconies give it a rustic look, but the lodge is modern and recommended for adults looking for a quiet getaway. Children are not encouraged – distinctive lodging for couples is their theme. Rates are around $90 for racing season weekends and lower at other times.

The *Upper Canyon Inn* (☎ 505-257-3005, 888-478-4367, ucinn@lookingglass .net), 215 Main Rd, has one-bedroom suites or two-bedroom cabins, some with kitchens and/or fireplaces. They'll lend you a fishing pole for use in the nearby river. Rates are $60 to $90.

B&Bs In the Upper Canyon is *Kearny's R&R B&B* (☎ 505-257-2940, 800-854-0697), 404 Main Rd. This is a home built from rocks, unusual among the mainly wooden structures of the Upper Canyon. They'll serve breakfast in bed if you ask.

The *Sierra Mesa Lodge* (☎ 505-336-4515), Box 463, Alto, NM 88312, 6 miles north of Ruidoso, has five rooms with different themes – the Victorian, French Country, Oriental, Country & Western and Queen Anne. All have queen-size beds. Rates are $100 double, including breakfast (in bed if you wish) and afternoon tea. There is a hot tub, and the living room has a fireplace where guests and hosts gather. Children must be over 14 and smoking is not allowed.

Monjeau Shadows (☎ 505-336-4191), Bonito Rd, Nogal, NM 88341, is 15 miles north of Ruidoso. This Victorian-style B&B has six rooms, four with private bath. The building is on several levels with a deck, a porch, bird feeders, a game room, a library and a pleasant 10-acre garden for walks. Rates are $75 to $100 double including breakfast; dinner can be arranged. Higher rates may prevail on holidays.

Condos The *West Winds Lodge & Condos* (☎ 505-257-4031, 800-421-0691, ww@usa.net), 208 Eagle Drive, has accommodations ranging from simple motel rooms to luxury condos. It is close to the town center and a golf course, and has a hot tub and pool. In high season, motel rooms with king-size (or two double) beds are $47 to $55, $59 to $74 with kitchenettes and fireplaces. Condos with one to three bedrooms, up to three baths and sleeping two to eight people, are $85 to $185 in season. All the condos have fireplaces and full kitchens. Ask for extended-stay discounts.

Pi-on Park Condominiums (☎ 505-258-4129, 800-457-4666), at 100 Jack Little Drive, has luxurious, fully equipped and well-kept condos with two to five bedrooms, kitchen, fireplace, laundry and private decks. Most have a game room and the largest ones have a hot tub. The condos are next to the links at Sierra Blanca Golf Course. Two-day minimum stays or four-day stays during holidays are required. These condos are among the best in town. Rates range from $85 to over $200.

Champions Run Condominiums (☎ 505-378-8080) has fully equipped condos right next to the racetrack. There is a swimming pool and spa. *Fairway Meadows* (☎ 505-257-4019, 800-545-9013), 120 Lower Terrace Drive, offers 24 condos with two bedrooms and two bathrooms, kitchens, fireplaces and laundry. It is next to the Cree Meadows Golf Course.

Many other condominium places in town charge from $60 to $200 depending on size and season. Many of them are most easily booked by reservation services whether you're staying for one night or an entire season. Condos and houses are the main offerings, though cabin rentals can also be arranged. Most of the following realtors can sell you a holiday home, too: Central Reservations of Ruidoso (☎ 505-257-7477, 888-257-7577, reservations@usa.net), *Four Seasons* (☎ 505-257-9171, 800-822-7654), *Gary Lynch Realty* (☎ 505-257-4011), *Century 21* (☎ 505-257-9057, 800-657-8980), *Lela Easter* (☎ 505-257-7313, 800-530-4597), *Coldwell Banker* (☎ 505-257-5111, 800-626-9213), *Professional Property Management* (☎ 505-258-5599, fax 505-258-3962, rwright@lookingglass.net) and *Condotel* (☎ 505-258-5200, 800-545-9017, condotel@ruidosoreservations.com).

Cabins Popular with skiers, *A-Frame Cabins* (☎ 505-258-5656, 800-333-7079, aframe@lookingglass.net), 1016 Mechem Drive, has a hot tub, pool and ski rental shop. Two- and three-bedroom cabins with fireplaces and kitchens rent for $65 to $120 for two to eight people. *Ponderosa Courts* (☎ 505-257-2631), 104 Laurel (just off Sudderth Drive), has cabins of various sizes from $40 to $90.

The *Sierra Blanca Cabins* (☎ 505-257-2103, 505-258-4006), 217 Country Club Rd, are on the north side of the river a few blocks away from Sudderth Drive. These are 12 simple cabins with kitchenettes and fireplaces; there are picnic and children's play areas. Summer weekend and holiday rates in one-bedroom cabins are in the $70s; two-bedroom cabins are in the $80s.

Casey's Cabins (☎ 505-257-6355), 2640 Sudderth Drive, has 16 simple cabins with one to four bedrooms, some with fireplaces. Rates are $50 and up. *Apache Village* (☎ 505-257-2435), at 311 Mechem Drive, has cabins with kitchens, fireplaces and some king-size beds from the $40s. Another reasonably priced choice is the *Idlehour Cabins* (☎ 505-257-2711, 800-831-1186), 100 Lower Terrace, one block away from Mechem. They have 12 two-bedroom cabins with kitchens and fireplaces. *El Alto Lodge* (☎ 505-257-2521), 404 Mechem Drive, has cabins with fireplaces and kitchens for $55 to $90.

High Country Lodge (☎ 505-336-4321, 800-845-7265), Box 137, Alto, NM 88312, is on Hwy 48 a little south of the turnoff to Ski Apache. It has 32 two-bedroom cabins, each with kitchen, fireplace and porch. There is a pool, spa, sauna, game room and children's play area on the grounds. Rates are $99 to $125 for two to six people during weekends in season, substantially less at other times. Ask about discounts for extended stays.

The following are in the Upper Canyon area. *Riverside Cottages* (☎ 505-257-4753, 800-328-2804, cottage@lookingglass.net), 100 Flume Canyon Drive, just south of Main Rd, has six rustic cottages by the river. All are self-contained and have one or two bedrooms and a fireplace. Rates range from $60 to $150. *Ruidoso Lodge Cabins* (☎ 505-257-2510, 800-950-2510, ruicabins@usa.net), 300 Main Rd, has eight cabins with one, two or three bedrooms. All come with kitchens, fireplaces, queen-size beds and no phones. Rates are about $85 to $130 for two to six people.

The *Dan Dee Cabins* (☎ 505-257-2165, 800-345-4848, dandee@southwest-mall .com), 310 Main Rd, has 12 cabins with one, two or three bedrooms. They are nicely spread out over 5 acres and all have kitchens, fireplaces, queen-size beds and porches with charcoal grills. These cabins were constructed at various times beginning in the 1940s and each one is unique. There is a small children's playground. Rates are $82 to $122 for two to seven people in summer, $76 to $116 in winter and $66 to $99 out of season. Ask about multi-day discounts.

Storybook Cabins (☎ 505-257-2115, 888-257-2115, fax 505-257-7512, cabins@ usa.net), 410 Main Rd, has 10 spacious, well-maintained cabins, which are some of the better ones in the area. They have one to three bedrooms, queen- or king-size beds, fireplaces, kitchens, porches or decks and are set in attractive gardens. Summer and winter rates are $89 to $159 for one to three bedrooms. *Canyon Cabins* (☎ 505-257-2076), 416 Main Rd, has one- to three-bedroom cabins, some with king-size beds and all with the usual amenities. The largest cabin can supposedly sleep up to 14! Rates are $58 to $150 depending on occupancy.

Forest Homes Cabins (☎ 505-257-4504, 800-678-7647, fax 505-257-4488, forest@ lookingglass.net), 436 Main Rd, offers one- to three-bedroom cabins with the usual amenities for $68 to $135 in season. *Sherwood Forest Cabins* (☎ 505-257-2424, 800-676-9515), 496 Main Rd, has 14 cabins renting from $70 to $120 in season. Apart from the usual amenities, there is a small indoor pool.

Places to Eat

In accordance with its popularity as a year-round resort, Ruidoso has a large and varied selection of restaurants. A reasonable choice for breakfast is the *Log Cabin Restaurant* (☎ 505-258-5029), 1074 Mechem Drive, which is open from 6 am to 2 pm daily except Tuesday and 5 to 9 pm from Thursday to Monday. For New Mexican breakfasts and lunches, the popular *Deck House* at 202 Mechem Drive is recommended for both food and décor. It is open from 7 am to 10 pm daily except Wednesday. *K-Bob's* (☎ 505-378-4747),

Hwy 70 at the Y-junction with Sudderth Drive, is an inexpensive steak house open for breakfast, lunch and dinner. For Mexican breakfast, lunch and dinner, try *Terraza Campanario* (☎ 505-257-4227), 1611 Sudderth Drive.

A couple of small restaurants cater to the light-lunch crowd. The *Hummingbird Tearoom* (☎ 505-257-5100), 2306 Sudderth Drive, is open for soup, salad and sandwich lunches from 11 am to 2:30 pm, Monday to Saturday. It stays open to 4 pm serving delectable desserts and of course afternoon tea. The *Blue Goose* (☎ 505-257-5271), 2693 Sudderth Drive, is behind the fashionable J Roberts clothing store. It is open daily in the summer from 11 am to 4 pm (3 pm on Sundays) and serves sandwiches and lunch specials in a pleasant setting.

There are many more choices for lunch and dinner. The *Casa Blanca* (☎ 505-257-2495), 501 Mechem Drive, is open daily from 11 am to 10 pm. It serves Mexican food and hamburgers in a renovated Spanish-style house with a pleasant beer garden outside – musicians sometimes provide entertainment and the crowd is lively. Happy hour runs from 2 to 6 pm. Prices for dinner entrées are under $10.

The *Flying J Ranch* (☎ 505-336-4330) is on Hwy 48 about 1½ miles north of the Ski Apache turnoff in Alto. The Ranch is as popular for entertainment as for dining and features a 'Western village' with gunfights and pony rides for children. Doors open at 6 pm and a cowboy-style chuckwagon dinner is served at 7:30 pm sharp (!) followed by a stage show of early Western music and melodrama at 8:15 pm. Reservations are requested – though if you have just pulled into town, you can probably mosey on down. The dinner is beef, beans, potatoes, biscuits and cake – cowboys didn't get menus on the trail and you won't either. On the other hand, there's plenty of food – and plenty of coffee or lemonade to wash it all down. The cost is $14 for adults, less for small children and includes the entertainment. The Ranch is open Monday to Saturday from June 1 to Labor Day and on Saturdays (dinner at 7 pm) after Labor

Day till mid-October. Private groups can make reservations from spring to fall.

OK – so you want something more elegant than beef and beans. At the opposite extreme is *Victoria's Romantic Hide-a-Way* (☎ 505-257-5440, 800-959-1328), 2103 Sudderth Drive in the Gazebo Shopping Center. This restaurant serves a fine Sicilian dinner in a romantic setting; there are lace-curtained booths and a pleasant garden area as well as a special honeymoon section. Reservations are required for the eight-course dinner which costs $65 per person and includes wine. Children are not allowed, and the café is no-smoking throughout. Another good choice for Italian food, as well as pizza and giant sandwiches, is *Michelena's* (☎ 505-257-5753), 2703 Sudderth Drive. This is the place to bring the kids or order takeout – it has a deck for dining. Prices are low to moderate. Hours are from 11 am daily – closing hours vary depending on demand. Nearby, *Che Bella!* (☎ 505-257-7540), 2823 Sudderth at Mechem Drive, has received good reviews for its fine Northern Italian lunches and dinners. They close on Tuesdays except in summer. Also good is *Café Rio* (☎ 505-257-7746), 2547 Sudderth Drive, with well-prepared pizza and international food in a low-key setting. Espresso and ice cream are also served. They open from 11 am till about 8 pm but close for three weeks before Christmas and three weeks after Easter.

The *Inncredible Restaurant & Saloon* (☎ 505-336-4312), Hwy 48 in Alto, on the right just before the Ski Apache turnoff, is popular. The skylights and stained glass, cowboy art and a saloon all contribute to the Western ambiance. Steak, prime rib, seafood and pasta dishes are the main offerings, and there is a kids' menu. Dinner entrées run from about $8 to $20. Hours are 5 to 10 pm daily – the lounge stays open later and features live entertainment on some nights. The *Cattle Baron* (☎ 505-257-9355), 657 Sudderth Drive, is the best steak house in town and has excellent seafood as well. The décor is elegant but Southwestern – so you can wear your best finery or cowboy boots and hat and you'll fit in. The Western lounge is popular and deservedly so. Dinner entrées range from about $8 to $22 – lunches are much cheaper. Reservations are a good idea at both these restaurants.

The fanciest place in town is *La Lorraine* (☎ 505-257-2954), 2523 Sudderth Drive. The cuisine is French and well recommended. The décor is also French and there is a courtyard for outdoor dining. Dinner entrées are in the $12 to $22 range; lunches cost about half that. Hours are 11 am to 2 pm for lunch Tuesday to Saturday and 6 to 9 pm for dinner Monday to Saturday.

Entertainment
Going to the races is what Ruidoso is famous for, but there are plenty of other things to do. See also the Flying J Ranch (Places to Eat, above) and the Inn of the Mountain Gods (in the Mescalero Reservation, above).

Sierra Cinema (☎ 505-257-9444) is at 721 Mechem Drive. *Win, Place & Show* (☎ 505-257-9982), 2516 Sudderth Drive, has country & western music and dancing every night. Numerous other bars, coffee-houses and lounges have weekend entertainment.

Shopping
Shopping is a big attraction and not without reason; the various galleries and gift shops along Sudderth Drive and Mechem Drive have a wide selection of items ranging from cheap souvenirs to fine art. You may even find original work by some of the big names in New Mexican art such as Peter Hurd and Henriette Wyeth.

Getting There & Away
Air The nearest airport is Sierra Blanca Regional Airport (☎ 505-336-8111, 505-336-8455) about 12 miles north. Lone Star Airlines (☎ 505-336-4893, 800-877-3932) has two daily flights from Dallas-Fort Worth in summer and one in winter. Mesa Air (☎ 800-637-2247) has flown there in the past but wasn't doing so recently. They do fly into Alamogordo and Roswell.

The nearest major airport is El Paso, 125 miles away.

Bus The bus station (☎ 505-257-2660), 138 Service Rd, is just north of the 300 block of Sudderth Drive. TNM&O and Greyhound have buses headed to Alamogordo, Roswell and El Paso, Texas, several times a day.

Getting Around
Sierra Blanca Motors (☎ 505-336-7933, 800-626-6867 at the airport, 505-257-4081 in Ruidoso) will rent cars if arranged in advance.

SMOKEY BEAR HISTORICAL STATE PARK
This park is set in the village of **Capitan**, 20 miles east of Carrizozo and 20 miles north of Ruidoso. Capitan (population 800) has one claim to fame: Smokey Bear (see sidebar below).

Visitors can see the bear's grave and watch audio-visual programs about fire prevention in the visitor center (☎ 505-354-2748). There is also a small botanical garden, children's playground, picnic area and gift shop. Overnight camping is not allowed; day use is 25¢ for ages five and

NEW MEXICO

> #### The Bear Facts
> In 1950, a nearby fire burned 26 sq miles of forest. Firefighters found a burned black bear cub in the aftermath. They put the cub on a plane to Santa Fe, where he received medical care and recovered. Named Smokey, he became the focus of the USFS's highly visible anti-fire campaign. Slogans such as 'Smokey's ABCs – Always Be Careful . . . with fire!' have been seen throughout national forests for decades. Smokey spent the rest of his life in Washington Zoo, where he died in 1976. He is buried in the Smokey Bear Historical State Park. ■

NEW MEXICO

The Lincoln County War
In the mid-1870s, Lincoln's 400 inhabitants lived in adobe houses and shopped at Murphy's General Store, the only store in the region. Murphy's made large profits by also providing supplies to nearby Fort Stanton. In 1877, competition arrived in the form of John Tunstall, an English merchant who built another general store.

To say that the merchants did not get along is an understatement. Within a year of his arrival, Tunstall was shot dead, allegedly by Murphy and his boys. Supporters of Tunstall wanted revenge, and the entire region erupted in what became known as the Lincoln County War. Tunstall's most famous follower was a wild teenager named Henry McCarty, alias William Bonney, soon to become known as Billy the Kid. Over the next months the Kid and his gang gunned down any of the Murphy faction that they could find, including Sheriff Pat Brady and other lawmen. The Kid was captured or cornered a couple of times but managed some brazen and lucky escapes before finally being shot by Sheriff Pat Garrett near Fort Sumner in 1881.

The story has since been romanticized and retold many times in books, movies and songs. The consummate American outlaw, Billy the Kid has captured the imagination of the nation for more than a century – often as a gunslinger fighting for what he thought was right rather than as a criminal desperado. ■

up. Hours are 9 am to 5 pm daily. The park is on the main street through town.

Every Fourth of July there is a Smokey Bear Stampede with a parade, a rodeo, cookouts and other festivities.

Places to Stay & Eat
The Lincoln National Forest nearby has campgrounds (see Ruidoso).

In Capitan, the *Smokey Bear Motel* (☎ 505-354-2253) on the main road is the only place to stay. It is inexpensive but often full – call ahead. Carrizozo (20 miles west), Lincoln (13 miles east) and Ruidoso (22 miles south) offer hotels. The town has several restaurants, of which the best is the acclaimed *Chango's* (☎ 505-354-4213), with a small selection of gourmet dinners priced in the teens and served from Tuesday to Saturday. With only about eight tables, reservations are necessary.

LINCOLN
The tiny village of Lincoln (about 12 miles east of Capitan) was the scene of the Wild West gunfights that put Billy the Kid into legend and history books (see sidebar above). If you are a fan of Western history, a visit to Lincoln is a must.

Lincoln was Mescalero Apache territory when Spanish settlers took control of it in the mid-1800s. Twenty years later the settlement had grown from the simple tower (or *torreón)* of rocks settlers had erected to defend themselves to the small but booming town of Lincoln, the seat of Lincoln County.

By the end of the century, the railway had come to nearby Carrizozo. Lincoln lost its county seat status and soon declined in political importance. Today the few remaining inhabitants of Lincoln have preserved the buildings of the 1880s and the main street of town is part of Lincoln State Monument (☎ 505-653-4372).

A visit is a walk through time; no modern influences, such as neon-lit motels, souvenir stands and fast-food joints, are allowed to spoil the setting. You can walk through and visit the torreón, the Tunstall Store (with a remarkable display of late-19th-century merchandise), the courthouse where the Kid escaped imprisonment, the San Juan Mission and other buildings. Monument information and brochures are available at the courthouse and Tunstall Store; the latter also has a slide show about Lincoln and Billy the Kid. These places are open from 8:30 am to 5 pm year-round. Admission from April through October is $2.50 for those over 16. In winter, when the Tunstall Store is closed, admission is $2.

At the east end of town is a museum and gift shop run by the Lincoln County Heritage Trust (☎ 505-653-4025), which also operates Dr Woods' house, built in 1882. At time of writing, hours and admission fees to these places had not been decided.

Special Events
Old Lincoln Days are held during the first full weekend in August. Musicians and mountain men, doctors and desperadoes wander the streets in period costume, and there are many activities and demonstrations of spinning, blacksmithing and other common frontier skills. In the evening there is a folk pageant, 'The Last Escape of Billy the Kid.' A small admission fee is charged.

Places to Stay & Eat
Accommodations in town are limited and reservations are suggested. The popular and recommended *Casa de Patrón B&B* (☎ 505-653-4676, 800-524-5202, fax 505-653-4671, patron@pvtnetworks.net), PO Box 27, Lincoln, NM 88338, is in a house built around 1860 and purportedly slept in by the Kid. Seven rooms, all with private baths, are in either the historic main house, in adjoining casitas or in a newer addition. Rates are $79 to $107, including breakfast, and dinner is available by prior arrangement, mainly in winter. The owners sometimes arrange musical evenings and can help with alternative accommodations.

The *Ellis Store Country Inn* (☎ 505-653-4609, 800-653-6460, fax 505-653-4610, ellis@pvtnetworks.net), in a 19th-century adobe house, has three rooms with private bath for $79 to $99. Four more rooms are in a historic mill on the property; two with shared baths are $69, two with private bath are $79. Rooms are decorated with quilts and antiques and feature wood-burning stoves or fireplaces for heating. A cooked-to-order breakfast is included, and a six course gourmet dinner (about $40, wine is extra) can be ordered from Wednesday to

Saturday. Diners can choose from meat, seafood or game entrées. The public is welcome by reservation only.

Another possibility is the *Wortley Hotel & Restaurant* (☎ 505-653-4300, ☎/fax 505-653-4425), an adobe hotel built in 1872 and restored in 1960 after fire damage. Seven rooms with private bath are about $60. The restaurant hours are 7 am to 10 pm in summer, 10 am to 4 pm in winter. Ownership changes have caused erratic closures in recent years.

Snacks and sandwiches are available in the village during the day. For dinner, you can head west to Capitan or 14 miles east to the town of Tinnie, where there is the old-fashioned *Silver Dollar* (☎ 505-653-4425), serving steak and seafood.

ROSWELL
Roswell is at the western edge of the dry plains known as the Llano Estacado. If you're driving east on Hwy 70/380 out of the Sacramento Mountains, enjoy the view. These are the last big mountains you'll see for a while. The Llano Estacado is 3000 to 4000 feet in elevation and Roswell is at 3649 feet.

The 'Staked Plains' extending east through Texas were once home to millions of buffalo and many nomadic Native American hunters. White settlers and hunters moved in throughout the late 19th century. Between 1872 and 1874, some 3,700,000 buffalo were killed, an estimated 3.5 million by whites. Within a few years, the Llano Estacado became desolate and empty, with only a few groups of Comanche mixed with the other tribes roaming the plains, hunting and trying to avoid confinement on reservations.

Roswell was founded in 1871. It became a stopping place for cowboys driving cattle along the Goodnight-Loving Trail from Texas to Colorado and the Chisholm Trail to the west. The discovery of artesian water in 1890 caused the town to boom and now the city is an important crossroads serving the ranching communities of southeastern New Mexico. Roswell sells more wool than any community in the country. It is also an important industrial center, with nearby gas and oil exploration and factories producing buses, clothing (Levi Strauss is here) and other items.

Roswell is the largest town in this part of the state and the seat of Chaves County. The county has a population of some 62,000, of which 50,000 live in Roswell, which suggests how empty the surrounding areas are.

Summers are fairly hot, with many 90°F days, but it's a dry heat. Evenings cool down to pleasant temperatures. Winters can see an occasional snowfall that rarely lasts more than a day or two (it averages 3.3 inches per year, though a freak 12-inch snowfall closed all roads out of town just before Christmas 1997). For many travelers, Roswell is simply a convenient place to stop for a meal or a bed; however, excellent museums and thriving cultural life combined with the nearby wildlife refuge give ample reason to stop and explore.

Orientation
The main west-east drag through town is 2nd and the main north-south thoroughfare is Main St; their intersection is the heart of downtown. Accommodations are on these two streets.

Information
The convention and visitors bureau (☎ 505-624-6860, 888-767-9355, fax 505-624-6863), 912 N Main, is the best source of tourist information. Hours are 9 am to 5 pm on weekdays, with brochures available in the lobby after hours. The chamber of commerce (☎ 505-623-5695, 800-295-7611, fax 505-624-6870) is at 131 W 2nd.

The BLM office (☎ 505-627-0272) is at 2909 W 2nd. The library (☎ 505-622-7101) is at 301 N Pennsylvania Ave. The local *Roswell Daily Record* has been published since 1891. The main post office (☎ 505-622-3741) is at 415 N Pennsylvania Ave. The Eastern New Mexico Medical Center (☎ 505-622-8170) is at 405 W Country Club Rd. The police (☎ 505-624-6770) are at 128 W 2nd. Roswell Recycles (☎ 505-623-0535) is at 3601 E 2nd.

Roswell Museum & Art Center
The excellent and well-organized Roswell Museum and Art Center (☎ 505-624-6744), 100 W 11th St, definitely deserves a visit. With 17 galleries, there is something here for everyone. Art galleries present changing exhibits of works by Peter Hurd, the famous Roswell painter, as well as many other Southwestern artists including Georgia O'Keeffe. Hispanic and Chicano art is also exhibited, and there are fine bronzes on display. Some Native American exhibits feature clothing, ceremonial items, pottery, basketwork and a growing collection of other artwork.

A major focus is space research. Robert H Goddard, who launched the world's first successful liquid fuel rocket in 1926, spent more than a decade carrying out rocket research in Roswell. His laboratory has been reconstructed at the museum, and a variety of early rocketry paraphernalia is on display. Also on display is the space suit that Harrison Schmitt, the New Mexican astronaut, wore on the moon during the Apollo XVII mission in 1972. Adjoining the museum is the **Goddard Planetarium**, with various multimedia shows – call for current events.

Shows change regularly and the museum sponsors a variety of cultural events throughout the year; call for current information. The museum is open from 9 am to 5 pm daily except Sunday, when hours are 1 to 5 pm. Admission is free; donations welcomed. There is a museum store.

Historical Center for Southeast New Mexico
The center (☎ 505-622-8333), 200 N Lea, housed in the 1910 mansion of local rancher James Phelp White, is in the National Register of Historic Places. The building is worth seeing; the inside has been carefully restored to its original early-20th-century décor with period furnishings, photographs and art. The changing exhibits include clothing, toys, crafts, typewriters, telephones and other memorabilia of the early 20th century. The museum is open from 1 to 4 pm Friday to Sunday,

PLACES TO STAY
3 Hacienda Motel
4 Best Western
  El Rancho Palacio
6 Best Western
  Sally Port Inn
7 National 9 Inn
8 Roswell Inn
11 Days Inn
12 Zuni Motel
21 Ramada Inn
22 Leisure Inn
23 Budget Inn West
24 Belmont Motel
25 Mayo Lodge
26 Crane Motel

PLACES TO EAT
5 Nuthin' Fancy Cafe
13 The Cattle Baron
20 Martin's Capitol
  Café
29 Denny's
32 Mario's
33 El Toro Bravo

OTHER
1 Del Norte Twin Cinema
2 Hospital
9 General Douglas L McBride
  Museum, New Mexico
  Military Institute
10 Anderson Museum of
  Contemporary Art
14 Bus Depot
15 Roswell Community
  Little Theater
16 Roswell Museum
  & Art Center,
  Goddard Planetarium
17 Convention & Visitors
  Bureau
18 Post Office
19 Library
27 Historical Center for
  Southeast New Mexico
28 Chamber of Commerce
30 Police
31 UFO Museum &
  Research Center

though special tours can be arranged. Admission is $2 for those over 12.

General Douglas L McBride Museum

This museum (☎ 505-624-8220), 101 W College Blvd, is on the campus of the New Mexico Military Institute. Home to about 1000 high school and junior college cadets, the coed campus is considered one of the best military academies in the country. The institute was established in 1891 and the military Gothic architecture is impressive. The museum has displays on US military history with a focus on

the contributions of New Mexicans and alumni. The campus is open to visitors and tours are offered by appointment. Admission to the museum is free; hours are 9 am to 4 pm Monday to Friday, except holidays.

Anderson Museum of Contemporary Art

This small free museum (☎ 505-623-5600), 409 E College Blvd, exhibits work by past and present artists-in-residence in Roswell. Hours are 9 am to noon and 1 to 4 pm Monday to Friday.

Spring River Park & Zoo

The Zoo (☎ 505-624-6760), College and Atkinson, is a good place for younger kids. Apart from the animals, there is a petting zoo, prairie-dog town, miniature train, antique carousel, kids' fishing pond, playground and picnic area. Hours are 10 am till 8 pm daily; the concessions open from 1 to 6 pm daily during the summer and on weekends in spring and fall. Admission is free.

Golf

The New Mexico Military Institute Golf Course (☎ 505-622-6033), 201 W 19th, is open to the public, as is the Spring River Golf Course (☎ 505-622-9506), 1612 W 8th. Both have 18 holes.

Special Events

The main annual event is the Eastern New Mexico State Fair (☎ 505-623-9411) held in the fairgrounds on Main and Poe. The fair is usually in early October (occasionally late September) and features rodeo, carnival, livestock and agricultural competitions, arts and crafts, chile-eating contests, music and fun.

Also fun is New Mexico Dairy Day in early June. This features the Great Milk Carton Boat Race on Lake Van, 20 miles south of Roswell, as well as cheese sculpting contests, 36-foot-long ice cream sundaes, games and sporting events. Start saving your milk cartons.

Roswell hosts many other events throughout the year, including the UFO Encounter. Call the chamber of commerce for exact dates.

Places to Stay – Camping

Trailer Village Campgrounds (☎ 505-623-6040), 1706 E 2nd, has RV sites with hookups for $14. There are showers, laundry and tent sites. *Town & Country RV Park* (☎ 505-624-1833), 333 W Brasher Rd (south end of town), has tent and RV sites in the $11 to $16 range. Showers are available. The small *Spring River RV Park* (☎ 505-623-8034), 1000 E College Blvd, has RV sites only for $13 with hookups.

Reservations are needed for the last two. See also Bottomless Lakes State Park and Dexter National Fish Hatchery, later in this chapter.

Places to Stay – Budget

Cheap motels charge in the $20s for two people and give weekly discounts, but are sometimes full by early evening. These include the *Belmont Motel* (☎ 505-623-4522, 800-873-0013, fax 505-623-2974), 2100 W 2nd; the *Hacienda Motel* (☎ 505-623-9425), 2331 N Main, which has a pool, as does the *Mayo Lodge* (☎ 505-622-0210), 1716 W 2nd. Others in this price range include the *Crane Motel* (☎ 505-623-1293), 1212 W 2nd, and the *Zuni Motel* (☎ 505-622-1930), 1201 N Main, which also advertises a seasonal pool.

A good choice for budget travelers is the *Budget Inn West* (☎ 505-623-3811, 800-806-7030, fax 505-623-7030), 2200 W 2nd, with simple but clean rooms (some with kitchenettes), a pool and hot tub and free coffee in the lobby. Rooms are about $28/36 for singles/doubles, but discounts are sometimes offered.

Expect price increases during special events and holidays.

Places to Stay – Middle

The independent *Frontier Motel* (☎ 505-622-1400, 800-678-1401, fax 505-622-1405), 3010 N Main, has good rooms with queen-size beds starting around $30/35 for smaller singles/doubles and in the $40s for larger rooms. Continental breakfast is included and there is a pool. The *National 9 Inn* (☎ 505-622-0110, 800-423-3106, fax 505-622-6011), 2001 N Main, is similar and has a kids' playground. Both hotels are a good value.

The *Days Inn* (☎ 505-623-4021, fax 505-623-0079), 1310 N Main, has large rooms, a pool, a hot tub, a restaurant and a lounge. Rates are $38 to $48 single and $42 to $52 double ($48 to $58 with two beds) and include a continental breakfast. The less-expensive *Leisure Inn* (☎ 505-622-2575, 800-990-6888), 2700 W 2nd, has 100 spacious rooms, a pool and

Tourists from Afar

In July 1947 the Roswell newspaper reported a UFO crash near town. The military quickly closed the area and allowed no more information for several decades (although recently they claimed it was a balloon). Was it a flying saucer? The local convention and visitors bureau suggests that Roswell's special blend of climate and culture attracted touring space aliens who wanted a closer look! Keep one eye on the sky.

Serious followers of UFO phenomena (not to mention skeptics or the merely curious) will want to check out the **UFO Museum & Research Center** (☎ 505-625-9495, iufomrc@lookingglass.net), 114 N Main, open 11 am to 5 pm daily. There are a variety of exhibits dealing with the Roswell Incident in particular and UFOs in general, a film-screening room, a research library, a gift/book store with a wide range of UFO-related books and the *Alien Caffeine Espresso Bar*. Admission is free.

Also visit the **UFO Enigma Museum** (☎ 505-347-2275), 6108 S Main, next to the old Roswell Army Air Field where crash debris and aliens' bodies were reportedly taken. More UFO-related exhibits and films can be seen here, and there is a souvenir shop. Hours are 9:30 am to 5 pm, Monday to Saturday, and noon to 5 pm on Sunday. Admission is $1; 50¢ for children.

During the first week of July 1997, on the 50th anniversary of the incident, Roswell hosted a 'UFO Encounter' with lectures, films, workshops, laser shows, tours of the alleged crash site, a trade show of UFO-related items, and various races and entertainment. This is planned to be an annual event (though on a lesser scale in future years).

The crash site is on private property owned by Hub and Sheila Corn (☎ 505-623-4043). With a day's notice, they will give you a guided tour of the site (there's no wreckage!) and tell you about the history of the Roswell Incident. Tours are $15 per person over 13. ■

includes continental breakfast. The *Best Western El Rancho Palacio* (☎ 505-622-2721, fax 505-622-2725), 2205 N Main, has a pool and spa, and a restaurant next door. Standard singles are $38 to $48; doubles are $42 to $56. The *Super 8 Motel* (☎ 505-622-8886, fax 505-622-3627), 3575 N Main, has an indoor pool and spa and large modern rooms with coffee-makers for about $50. Some rooms have microwaves and refrigerators.

The *Ramada Inn* (☎ 505-623-9440, fax 505-622-9708), 2803 W 2nd, has a pool and restaurant and good rooms in the $50s. The *Roswell Inn* (☎ 800-426-3052 in New Mexico, or 800-323-0913, ☎/fax 505-623-4920) 1815 N Main, is an older hotel decorated with Southwestern art and with 121 large rooms. There is a pool and spa. A coffee shop is open from 6 am to 10 pm and there is a dining room and lounge. Rates are in the $60s; suites with king-size beds, coffeemakers and refrigerators start at $90.

The *Best Western Sally Port Inn* (☎ 505-622-6430, fax 505-623-7631), 2000 N Main, is one of Roswell's best. There is an indoor pool, spa, sauna, exercise room and game room. Both coin and valet laundries are available and there is a gift shop and hair salon. The restaurant offers room service and the lounge bar has sports TV. Pleasant rooms with queen-size or king-size beds range from $65 to $100, with most under $80.

Places to Eat

Fast-food, pizza and chain restaurants predominate. The restaurants at the Sally Port and Roswell Inns attract diners who aren't staying at the hotels.

For good American diner food, there's the *Nuthin' Fancy Café* (☎ 505-623-4098), 2103 N Main, open from 6 am to 9 pm and featuring blue-plate specials, an espresso bar, 16 beers on tap and good home cooking.

Several Mexican restaurants stand out. One of the cheapest and best is *Martin's Capitol Café* (☎ 505-624-2111), 110 W 4th, where you can eat a great dinner for

just $4 to $6. They are open from 6 am to 8:30 pm, Monday to Saturday, and 9 am to 2 pm on Sunday. *Los Ranchos* (☎ 505-622-9545), 911 E 2nd, is inexpensive and good. It is open 11 am to 9 pm Monday to Saturday.

El Toro Bravo (☎ 505-622-9280), 102 S Main, has several regional New Mexican dishes mixed in with the mainly Mexican offerings. Prices are low to moderate. They are open for lunch from Monday to Friday and for dinner (until 9 pm) from Monday to Saturday. *Mario's* (☎ 505-623-1740), 200 E 2nd, is good and a bit more upmarket. It serves steaks, seafood, Mexican and Southwestern meals (including ostrich) and has a lounge bar with complimentary hors d'oeuvres from 2 to 7 pm on weekdays. Dinners are in the $6 to $14 range and most include a visit to the salad bar.

For moderately priced steaks and seafood, try the *Cattle Baron* (☎ 505-622-2465), 1113 N Main, or *Cattleman's Steak House* (☎ 505-623-3500), 2010 S Main. The best Italian restaurant is considered to be the *Pasta Café* (☎ 505-624-1111), 4501 N Main in the Roswell Mall.

If you are hungry at 3:49 am, try *Denny's* (☎ 505-623-5377), 200 N Main, open 24 hours. There's another Denny's at 2200 N Main (☎ 505-622-9960).

Entertainment

The *Roswell Symphony Orchestra* (☎ 505-623-5882), 3201 N Main, has been performing since 1960. The main season is October to April, but other concerts may be scheduled throughout the year. Other orchestras play here by invitation. Call for dates.

The *Roswell Community Little Theater* (☎ 505-622-1982), 1101 N Virginia Ave, has also been around for many years and performs several plays throughout its September to June season.

The *Del Norte Twin* (☎ 505-623-5139), 2800 N Main; *Cinema 4* (☎ 505-623-9139), 4501 N Main in the Roswell Shopping Mall; and *Park Twin* (☎ 505-623-8016), 1717 S Union, show movies.

Getting There & Away

Air Roswell Air Center (☎ 505-347-5703) is at the south end of Main. Mesa Air (☎ 505-347-5501) has six nonstop flights to and from Albuquerque every weekday, fewer on weekends. It also has two or three nonstops a day to Dallas/Ft Worth and one or two nonstops to Carlsbad and Hobbs. Connecting flights to other cities are available.

Bus The TNM&O/Greyhound Bus Depot (☎ 505-622-2510), 1100 N Virginia, has buses to Carlsbad ($15) and Albuquerque ($28) twice a day. There are also buses to Portales, Clovis, Las Cruces and Santa Fe. Buses to Texas go to Amarillo, Lubbock and El Paso.

Getting Around

Pecos Trails Transit (☎ 505-624-6766) has local buses throughout the city and to the airport.

Hertz (☎ 505-347-2211), Avis (☎ 505-347-2500) and National (☎ 505-347-2323) all have car rental offices at the airport.

AROUND ROSWELL
Bottomless Lakes State Park

Bottomless Lakes State Park (☎ 505-624-6058) is Roswell's most popular outdoor attraction. Seven lakes provide some relief from the summer heat with swimming, fishing, windsurfing, scuba diving, canoeing, walking, bird watching, picnicking and camping. A visitor center near the entrance provides information about which activities are permitted in which lake.

Day use is $3 per car, and camping is permitted in several places ($7 for tents, $11 or $13 with hookups). There are some showers. To get to the park, drive 10 miles east of Roswell on Hwy 380, then 5 miles south on Hwy 409.

Dexter National Fish Hatchery

The fish hatchery (☎ 505-734-5910) is 20 miles southeast of Roswell on Hwy 2 (take Hwy 285 southbound and look for signs). This hatchery is especially important for the study of rare and endangered South-western fish species. Visitors are welcome. The hatchery is next to Lake Van, where you can camp ($6 for tents, $10 for RVs with hookups).

Bitter Lake National Wildlife Refuge

The 38-square-mile Bitter Lake National Wildlife Refuge (☎ 505-622-6755) is particularly known for wintering water birds. The heart of the refuge is six artificial lakes totaling 1.2 sq miles. Tens of thousands of ducks, geese and sandhill cranes are found here from October to March, with mid-November to early December being peak times. The snow geese are particularly abundant and spectacular.

In the summer, various birds remain to nest, including the threatened snowy plover and the endangered least tern. Special protection for the tern means you probably won't get to see it, but there are many other species to observe. More than 300 have been recorded and a bird list is available. Also keep your eyes open for horned toads, snakes and other reptiles as well as deer, rabbits and coyotes.

The refuge is about 15 miles northeast of Roswell. Follow the signed roads from either Hwy 380 or 285/70. The refuge is open from one hour before sunrise to one hour after sunset. An 8½-mile self-guided auto tour is available, with plenty of stops and lookouts. The ranger station is open from 7:30 am to 4 pm Monday to Friday; a booth by the entrance has bird lists, maps and information at other times. Admission is free.

ARTESIA

Artesia is a crossroads town about halfway between Roswell and Carlsbad and halfway between Cloudcroft and Hobbs. During the late 1800s there were only a few buildings here, huddled around a spring in the middle of the dry Llano Estacado. Artesia came into being in 1903, when an artesian well was dug to irrigate the area. Twenty years later, another well yielded oil, and Artesia became an important agricultural and industrial town. During the cold war, Abo Elementary

School was built underground and can serve as a nuclear fallout shelter for the community. They say it's the first underground school in the USA.

Artesia (elevation 3400 feet) has a population of some 12,000 people. It is the home of New Mexico's largest petroleum refinery and the oil industry provides many jobs.

Orientation & Information

Artesia is the crossroads of the west-east Hwy 82 (Main St in town) and the north-south Hwy 285 (1st). Most businesses are on these streets.

The chamber of commerce (☎ 505-746-2744), 408 W Texas Ave, is open 9 am to 5 pm Monday to Friday. The library (☎ 505-746-4252) is at 306 W Richardson Ave. Local events are reported in the *Artesia Daily Press*. The post office (☎ 505-746-4412) is at 201 N 4th. The hospital (☎ 505-748-3333) is at 702 N 13th. The police (☎ 505-746-2703) are at 702 W Chisum Ave.

Artesia Historical Museum & Art Center

This museum (☎ 505-748-2390), 505 W Richardson Ave, is in a house built in 1904 and noted for the cobblestones used to

PLACES TO STAY
12 Budget Inn
13 Starlite Motel
14 Bill's RV Park
15 Odd Shop RV
     & Campground
16 Artesia Inn

PLACES TO EAT
7 La Fonda
10 K-Bob's Steak House

OTHER
1 Hospital
2 Bus Depot
3 Police Station
4 Chamber of Commerce
5 Post Office
6 Twin Cinema
8 Library
9 Artesia Historical Museum
    & Art Center
11 Abo Elementary School

Artesia

embellish the outside walls. Local artists have their work displayed in an annex, and there is an exhibit of local historical artifacts. Museum hours are from 8 am to 5 pm Tuesday to Saturday (except holidays). Admission is free.

Places to Stay

Campgrounds are quite basic, with many long-stay residents. Try *Ponderosa RV Park* (☎ 505-746-3209), 3204 W Main, *Odd Shop RV & Campground* (☎ 505-748-3779), 1502 S 1st, or *Bill's RV Park* (☎ 505-746-6184), 201 Hermosa Drive. This last seems the best. All allow tent camping, and have showers. Rates are $8 to $12. *Brantley Lake State Park* (see under Carlsbad) about 30 miles south also has camping.

The *Starlite Motel* (☎ 505-746-9834), 1018 S 1st, has simple but adequate rooms for $28 to $40. The best midpriced hotel is the *Artesia Inn* (☎ 505-746-9801, 800-682-4598), 1820 S 1st. It has a swimming pool and clean, comfortable rooms with refrigerators and coffeemakers. Rates are $30 to $40 single and $35 to $50 double. The *Budget Inn* (☎ 505-748-3377, fax 505-748-2958), 922 S 1st, is also in this price range.

The *Best Western Pecos Inn* (☎ 505-748-3324, 800-676-7481, fax 505-748-2868), 2209 W Main, is the best hotel in Artesia with 80 rooms, an indoor pool, a sauna, spa, restaurant and lounge. Many rooms have coffeemakers, wet bars, refrigerators and/or balconies. Rates are from $53 to $70.

Places to Eat

La Fonda (☎ 505-746-9411, 505-746-9377), 206 W Main, serves inexpensive Mexican food and is one of the best restaurants in town. Hours are from 11 am to 2 pm and 5 to 9 pm, though it may close on weekends.

The *Kwan Den* (☎ 505-746-9851) is in the Best Western Pecos Motel and serves Chinese and American breakfasts, lunch and dinners daily. *K-Bob's Steak House* (☎ 505-748-2208) is at 601 S 1st.

Entertainment

The *Twin Cinema* (☎ 505-746-4112), 418 W Main, shows movies at below-average prices.

Getting There & Away

The bus station (☎ 505-746-2276), 604 N 1st, has two buses a day to Carlsbad and two a day to Roswell and Albuquerque.

CARLSBAD

Carlsbad is an important destination for travelers in southeastern New Mexico because of its proximity to the world-famous Carlsbad Caverns, about 25 miles away. The caverns are described later; Carlsbad the city is described here.

Carlsbad is on the Pecos River, approximately 30 miles north of the Texas state line. Apache and Comanche Indians inhabited this dry area before the Europeans arrived. Several Spanish expeditions made exploratory trips along the Pecos in the 16th and 17th centuries. By the late 1800s, cowboys were driving huge herds of cattle along the Pecos River Valley; a local rancher, Charles B Eddy, founded the town in 1888. Originally named Eddy, it was renamed Carlsbad because local mineral springs reminded the inhabitants of the Karlsbad Spa in Bohemia. Carlsbad (population 30,000) is currently the Eddy County seat.

Ranching and the cultivation of cotton, alfalfa and vegetables were the base of the economy until the discovery of oil and potash (a mineral fertilizer). Carlsbad now produces 85% of the USA's potash. The proclamation of Carlsbad Caverns as a national monument in 1923 attracted a trickle of tourists, which soon became a flood – now hundreds of thousands of visitors come through every year. The most recent industry is the controversial WIPP project, in which radioactive waste is stored underground (see the sidebar Hazard, Boon or Both?).

The elevation is 3120 feet above sea level, and summer temperatures climb over 100°F fairly often, though nights are pleasant. Winters are cool but see little snowfall and only a few freezes. Annual precipitation is about 12 inches.

Orientation

The northern and eastern downtown areas of Carlsbad are bounded by the Pecos River. The main thoroughfare is Hwy 285, entering town from the northwest as Pierce St and then veering south to become Canal St, Carlsbad's main drag, which becomes S Canal south of Mermod and then National Parks Hwy at the south end of town.

Information

The chamber of commerce (☎ 505-887-6516, 800-221-1224) is at 302 S Canal. Hours are 8 am to 5 pm Monday to Friday; brochures are available from a stand after hours. The National Parks Information Center (☎ 505-785-2232, 505-885-8884), 3225 National Parks Highway, has information on both Carlsbad Caverns National Park and Guadalupe Mountains National Park, just across the state line in Texas. It is open from 8 am to 4:30 pm daily. The Lincoln National Forest Guadalupe Ranger Station (☎ 505-885-4181) is in the federal building at Halagueno and Fox. The library (☎ 505-885-6776) is opposite. The *Carlsbad Current-Argus* is the local daily. The post office (☎ 505-885-5717) is at 301 N Canyon. The medical center (☎ 505-887-4100) is at 2430 W Pierce. The police (☎ 505-885-2111) are at 405 S Halagueno St. Recycle at the drop-off containers on Park Drive south of Carlsbad Riverfront Park.

Living Desert State Park

This park (☎ 505-887-5516), on Skyline Rd (off Hwy 285 northwest of town), is the premier attraction in the town and definitely deserves a visit if you are interested in natural history. More zoo and botanical garden than park, it is spread out over the Ocotillo Hills on the northwestern outskirts of town and exhibits the wildlife of the Chihuahuan Desert. Well-marked trails wander through the park and take the visitor past wildlife enclosures and through natural-looking gardens. This is a great

---

Hazard, Boon or Both?

The Waste Isolation Pilot Plant (WIPP) is a controversial project to dispose of nuclear waste in underground salt beds near Carlsbad. First proposed in the 1970s, it has taken two decades of contentious debate and experiment for the project to be realized. The first containers of nuclear waste are scheduled to be delivered to the WIPP in the latter part of 1998.

Proponents point out that the project brings hundreds of jobs and strengthens Carlsbad's and New Mexico's economy by millions of dollars each year. Opponents of the project are concerned that a transportation accident could cause incalculable damage. The waste comes from all over the United States (especially from the Los Alamos area) and much of it has to travel thousands of miles to reach Carlsbad – how can it be transported absolutely safely over such long distances? And how long can it remain harmlessly buried?

The WIPP Visitor Center (☎ 505-234-7245, 800-336-9477), 4021 National Parks Hwy, was set up to explain the project, demonstrate how the waste is disposed and emphasize the project's safety. The visitor center is open from 7:30 am to 4:30 pm Monday to Friday. Tours of the plant are offered on Monday, Wednesday, Thursday and Friday mornings at 8:40 am; they last four hours and descend 2150 feet underground. Advance reservations are required (at least a week ahead is suggested) and participants must supply their own transportation to the plant, about 20 miles away. Long pants and closed shoes are required for everyone.

The other side of the coin is presented by Citizens for Alternatives to Radioactive Dumping (CARD, ☎ 505-266-2663), who publish a newsletter about the issues involved. ∎

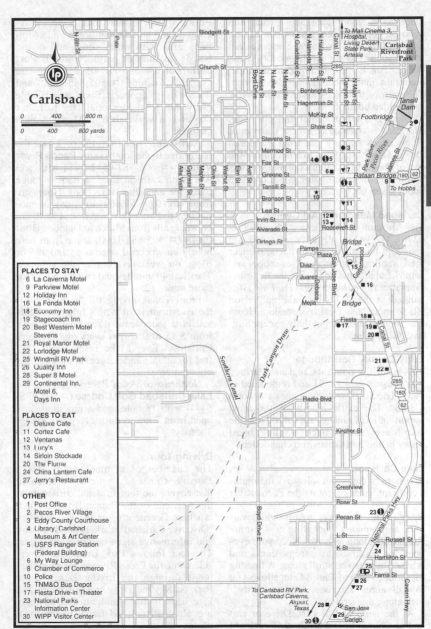

Carlsbad

| 0 | 400 | 800 m |
| 0 | 400 | 800 yards |

PLACES TO STAY
6 La Caverna Motel
9 Parkview Motel
12 Holiday Inn
16 La Fonda Motel
18 Economy Inn
19 Stagecoach Inn
20 Best Western Motel
   Stevens
21 Royal Manor Motel
22 Lorlodge Motel
25 Windmill RV Park
26 Quality Inn
28 Super 8 Motel
29 Continental Inn,
   Motel 6,
   Days Inn

PLACES TO EAT
7 Deluxe Cafe
11 Cortez Cafe
12 Ventanas
13 Lucy's
14 Sirloin Stockade
20 The Flume
24 China Lantern Cafe
27 Jerry's Restaurant

OTHER
1 Post Office
2 Pecos River Village
3 Eddy County Courthouse
4 Library, Carlsbad
   Museum & Art Center
5 USFS Ranger Station
   (Federal Building)
6 My Way Lounge
8 Chamber of Commerce
10 Police
15 TNM&O Bus Depot
17 Fiesta Drive-in Theater
23 National Parks
   Information Center
30 WIPP Visitor Center

place to see and learn about cacti and coyotes, gopher snakes and golden eagles, and wildlife with evocative Southwestern names such as agave, javelina, ocotillo and yucca. Black bear, pronghorn antelope, mountain lion and buffalo can also be seen. The view of the Pecos River Valley below is an added bonus.

There is a visitor center and gift shop. The park is open daily except Christmas. Hours are 8 am to 8 pm from Memorial Day to Labor Day, 9 am to 5 pm during the rest of the year (last admission is 1½ hours before closing). Admission is $3; children under seven get in free.

Carlsbad Museum & Art Center
The Museum & Art Center (☎ 505-887-0276), 418 W Fox, displays mastodon and cameloid bones, Apache artifacts, pioneer memorabilia, art from the Taos school and some local arts and crafts. See the large and dramatic *Jicarilla Apache Trading Post*, painted in the 1930s by LaVerne Nelson Black under New Deal sponsorship. Hours are from 10 am to 5 pm daily except Sunday. Admission is free.

Eddy County Courthouse
This historic building at Canal and Mermod was constructed in 1891 and remodeled in 1939. The Southwestern touches are worth a look: The cattle brands of the most important local ranches are carved into the door frames, and the interior ceilings boast heavy beams and ornate iron chandeliers.

Lake Carlsbad
A system of dams and spillways maintains a constant water height on the Pecos River for a 2-mile section north of the Bataan Bridge. This river-lake area provides various amusements, including a 4½-mile **Riverwalk** along its banks. Keep your eyes open for muskrats, fish, frogs, ducks and other critters as you stroll along. A floating footbridge south of Tansill Dam allows you to walk across the river. Anglers try their luck along this stretch.

At the north end of Park Drive or east end of Church St is **Carlsbad Riverfront**

Park, which offers picnicking, playgrounds and an adjacent beach and swimming area with water slides and diving boards (in summer only). Nearby is **Port Jefferson** (☎ 505-887-0512). Boats are available for hire (☎ 505-885-1600) and water-skiing is popular. Boats are available every day from Memorial Day to Labor Day and on weekends from March through October.

Across the river from the park (via the footbridge to the south) is the **Pecos River Village** (☎ 505-887-0512), 711 Muscatel Ave, with carnival rides, a narrow-gauge train ride and other attractions. Hours are from 5 to 10 pm Monday to Friday, Memorial Day to Labor Day, and from 1 to 10 pm on weekends from March to October. **Boat tours** (☎ 505-885-1600) leave from here hourly on weekend afternoons and at 5 or 6 pm on weekdays during the summer. They last 40 minutes and cost $3; $1.50 for those under 12.

From Thanksgiving till December 31, the riverfront is lit with Christmas lights and boat tours leave three times an hour from 5:45 to 9:15 pm every night, except Christmas Eve. Make reservations ($7; free for infants under three) at the chamber of commerce.

Northeast of Pecos River Village is the **Lake Carlsbad Golf Course** (☎ 505-885-5444) with 18 holes and a pro shop. It is open from 7 am to dusk every day except Tuesday.

Driving Tour
The chamber of commerce provides a *Discover Carlsbad Scenic Drive* brochure that covers the tour in detail. It begins at the west end of the Bataan Bridge, which is where Greene crosses the Pecos River. 'Discover Carlsbad' markers point the way and informative signs describe the sights. The tour follows Park Drive and Riverside along the Pecos River waterfront, then loops through the Living Desert State Park on Skyline Drive, takes Church and Pate back to town and finishes by driving along Pierce and Canal to the town center.

Places to Stay – Camping

Carlsbad RV Park & Campground (☎ 505-885-6333), 4301 National Parks Hwy, has more than 100 sites, a pool, laundry, playground and showers. Sites are $12 for tents or $16.50 with hookups. They are often full in summer. Also try *Windmill Grocery & RV Park* (☎ 505-885-9761), 3624 National Parks Hwy, with $15 sites. *Brantley Lake State Park* (☎ 505-457-2384), 12 miles north of Carlsbad and 5 miles east of Hwy 285, offers fishing, boating, picnicking, showers and camping. Day use is $3. Primitive tent sites are $6 or $7 and 50 sites with RV hookups are $11.

Places to Stay – Budget

Prices rise slightly in summer when it is hot, but the nearby national park and mild winters make this a year-round destination.

The following hotels offer simple but acceptable rooms in the $20s or lower $30s; they all have pools. *La Fonda Motel* (☎ 505-885-6242), 1522 S Canal, has quite good rooms with queen-size beds and refrigerators. The *Economy Inn* (☎ 505-885-4914), 1621 S Canal, has standard rooms and larger units with kitchenettes for a little more. The *La Caverna Motel* (☎ 505-885-4151), 223 S Canal, is centrally located. The *Royal Manor Motel* (☎ 505-885-3191), 2001 S Canal, has refrigerators in many rooms. The *Parkview Motel* (☎ 505-885-3117), 401 E Greene, has a playground and nice rooms with queen- and king-size beds and free in-room coffee. Most of these cheaper hotels offer weekly discounted rates.

The following hotels also have pools and charge in the mid-$30s or about $40 for a double in summer, from the $20s in winter. The *Stagecoach Inn* (☎/fax 505-887-1148), 1819 S Canal, offers a playground, children's pool, spa and a coin laundry. The *Lorlodge Motel* (☎ 505-887-1171, fax 505-887-6577), 2019 S Canal, has a small playground and microwaves and refrigerators in some rooms. The *Continental Inn* (☎ 505-887-0341, fax 505-885-1186), 3820 National Parks Hwy, has free coffee in its sizable rooms. The *Motel 6* (☎ 505-885-0011, fax 505-887-7861), 3824 National Parks Hwy, charges $32/38, less in winter.

Places to Stay – Middle

All the better hotels have pools, provide courtesy transportation to the bus depot or airport and have queen- and king-size beds. The *Super 8 Motel* (☎ 505-887-8888, fax 505-885-0126), 3817 National Parks Hwy, has a spa and provides breakfast and in-room coffee. Some rooms have a microwave and refrigerator, and there is a coin laundry. Rooms start at $46/50.

The *Quality Inn* (☎/fax 505-887-2861), 3706 National Parks Hwy, has a dining room and coffee shop, room service, a lounge with live entertainment and dancing, coin and valet laundries, a gift shop and attractively landscaped grounds with a spa. Rooms start at about $55/65 in summer, including breakfast. The similarly priced *Best Western Motel Stevens* (☎ 505-887-2851, 800-730-2851, fax 505-887-6338), 1829 S Canal, is by far the largest hotel in town, with more than 200 rooms, some with kitchenettes or microwave/refrigerator combos. There is a restaurant and lounge, game room, children's pool and spa. The slightly cheaper *Days Inn* (☎ 505-887-7800, fax 505-885-9433), 3910 National Parks Hwy, has an indoor pool and spa and includes continental breakfast.

The *Holiday Inn* (☎ 505-885-8500, fax 505-887-5999), 601 S Canal, is the only full-service hotel downtown. The hotel was renovated in 1993 and rates are about $75 to $90. There are good restaurants, room service, a lounge, playground, spa, sauna, exercise room and guest laundry.

Places to Eat

Those on a tight budget could try out the *Deluxe Cafe* (☎ 505-887-1304), 224 S Canal, open 5 am to 2 pm and featuring breakfast specials for $1.99 as well as a range of other inexpensive American and Mexican items. It's been here since 1951 and the interior looks about the same as it has for decades.

There are several homey and good Mexican restaurants. *Lucy's* (☎ 505-887-7714), 701 S Canal, is deservedly the most popular and is often packed with both locals and visitors. Reservations aren't a bad idea, especially on weekends. Apart from a great Mexican menu, Lucy's also features a steak bar and grill for dinner, and is Carlsbad's only Mexican restaurant selling alcohol. Most everything on the menu is well under $10. Hours are 11 am to 9:30 pm Monday to Saturday. Another good choice is the *Cortez Cafe* (☎ 505-885-4747), 506 S Canal, a smaller place that has been around since 1937 (a long time for southeastern New Mexico). It is open from 11 am to 2 pm and from 4:30 to 8 pm daily.

The *Sirloin Stockade* (☎ 505-887-7211), 710 S Canal, serves unpretentious steaks, seafood and other meals, mostly for under $10 and also features an inexpensive all-you-can-eat soup, salad and dessert bar. It is open from 11 am to 9 pm daily (10 pm on Fridays and Saturdays).

For Chinese dinners, try the *China Lantern Cafe* (☎ 505-885-3450), 3400 National Parks Hwy. This has been here since 1952, which is a good sign. Hours are 4:30 to 9 pm Tuesday to Saturday.

The better hotels all have good restaurants. The best in town is the *Flume* at the Best Western Motel Stevens. American food is served in an elegant but informal Western ambiance. Dinner entrées range from $8 to $17. The Flume is open daily from 5:30 am to 10 pm. The most elegant dinner choice is *Ventanas* in the Holiday Inn, with fine dining from 5:30 to 9:30 pm Tuesday to Saturday only.

Two 24-hour restaurants are *Jerry's* (☎ 505-885-6793), 3720 National Parks Hwy, and *Denny's* (☎ 505-885-5600), 810 W Pierce.

Entertainment

See the hotel lounges (above) for entertainment ideas. One of the liveliest bars in town is *My Way Lounge* (☎ 505-887-0212), 223 S Canal in front of La Caverna Motel. The wood-beam, rustic interior houses pool tables and a dance floor with live country & western and rock bands most nights of the week.

The *Fiesta Drive-in Theater* (☎ 505-885-4126), San Jose Blvd and Fiesta, has three screens, giving you the chance to experience a form of American entertainment that has almost disappeared: the drive-in movie. The concession stand offers a range of fast food (not just candy and popcorn), so you can eat here and make a night of it. For indoor movies, try the *Mall Cinema 3* (☎ 505-885-0777), 2322 W Pierce.

Visit the *Carlsbad Community Theater* (☎ 505-887-3157), on National Parks Hwy about 5 miles south of downtown, offering regular dramatic performances.

Getting There & Away

Air Carlsbad's City Airport (☎ 505-887-9008) is about 6 miles south of town. Mesa Air (☎ 505-885-0245) has four nonstop flights on weekdays and two on weekends to Albuquerque, with connections to other cities.

Bus The bus depot (☎ 505-887-1108), 1000 S Canyon, has TNM&O/Greyhound buses going to White's City, Hobbs, Roswell, Albuquerque and El Paso, Texas.

Getting Around

Hertz (☎ 505-887-1500) at the airport, and Enterprise (☎ 505-887-3039), 1724 S Canal, rent cars.

WHITE'S CITY

Named after Jim White, the first serious explorer of Carlsbad Caverns, this 'city' is just a Best Western 'resort' complex at the entrance to the national park. From White's City to Carlsbad Caverns is a 7-mile drive. Carlsbad is 21 miles north. There is a gas station.

Places to Stay & Eat

White's City RV Park has about 150 sites, many with RV hookups. Rates are $16 for up to six people per site, whether tenting or requiring hookups. There are showers, a laundry, a playground and pool and hot-tub privileges at the neighboring motels. The

Best Western Cavern Inn and the *Best Western Guadalupe Inn* have, between them, more than 100 large and acceptable rooms for about $75. You are paying for the convenience of staying near the park; rooms in Carlsbad are better and cheaper.

In the hotel complex there's a small grocery store, post office, gift shops and the Million Dollar Museum, which claims to have 30,000 Western items on display and charges visitors $2.50 to see them.

Fast Jack's serves fast food and the *Velvet Garden Restaurant & Saloon* has swinging Wild West-style doors to swagger (stagger?) through en route to a steak or seafood meal.

Granny's Opera House has old-fashioned melodrama (be prepared to cheer the heroine, boo the villain and throw your popcorn at the enemy) most nights during the summer.

Reservations for all these places are made at ☎ 505-785-2291 and are recommended in summer.

Getting There & Away

There are daily buses from Carlsbad or El Paso (Texas) to White's City with TNM&O. There is an airstrip at White's City for private aircraft. The motels have vans to pick you up at the airport or to take you to the caverns for a few dollars.

CARLSBAD CAVERNS NATIONAL PARK

Carlsbad Caverns has its skeptics. Who in their right mind would drive for hours across the desert just to see a cave? Once visitors see the caverns, however, even the most skeptical are impressed. This is one of the greatest cave systems in the world, and a visit is, without a doubt, a highlight of a journey through the Southwest.

The geological explanations for the cave system's existence are easy enough to understand and write about (see the sidebar below) but difficult to grasp in a realistic sense until you actually go there.

Indian people knew of the caves and left paintings near the entrance, but the steepness of the entrance precluded any

in-depth exploration until the early 1900s. Then, local cowboys discovered dung (guano) deposited in the cave mouth by the millions of bats inhabiting the cave. People began mining the guano, a valuable fertilizer.

One of the miners, Jim White, began venturing further into the cave and emerged with tales of huge rooms full of incredible geological formations. Slowly, word of his exploits filtered out and tourists began to visit the caverns. The earliest visitors were lowered into the cave in buckets, a far cry from today's system of elevators and walkways. In 1923, Carlsbad Caverns was proclaimed a national monument. It became a national park in 1930 and a World Heritage Site in 1995.

The park covers 73 sq miles and includes more than 80 caves; the visitor can see only a small fraction of the entire system. Even this fraction is huge by any standards. A two-mile subterranean walk from the cave mouth reaches an underground chamber called, with simple understatement, the Big Room. It is 1800 feet long and 255 feet high, and lies more than 800 feet below the surface. If you are pressed for time, you can descend by elevator, glimpse some of the underground highlights and return to the surface within a couple of hours. However, there is enough to keep you occupied for a couple of days or more.

The park's second attraction is the Mexican free-tail bat colony that roosts here from April to October. During the rest of the year the bats winter in Mexico. The colony once numbered several million, but pesticide use diminished the colony to about a quarter of a million. (Pesticides kill insects, bats eat insects and, after eating thousands of poisoned bugs, the bats themselves become poisoned.) Today, with some degree of control of pesticide use, the colony is recovering and population estimates range from 500,000 to a million bats.

There is a visitor center with information, a museum, a café, a gift shop and bookstore. Within the park you'll find a short nature trail, a 9-mile scenic drive and overnight backpacking.

Geology of Carlsbad Caverns National Park

Although once touted by geologists as a typical example of how most caves form, the caves in Carlsbad Caverns National Park actually have quite an unusual origin. Caves are normally created when rainwater, made slightly acidic by interaction with atmospheric carbon dioxide, dissolves limestone and widens fractures into long, low, conduit-shaped passages. In contrast, Carlsbad Caverns consists of large, interconnected rooms with high ceilings. These formed as hydrogen sulfide gas from adjacent oil deposits reacted with groundwater to form sulfuric acid, an extremely powerful dissolving agent that quickly (by geologic standards) scoured out huge volumes of bedrock. This occurred within the last 5 to 10 million years.

Another reason for these gigantic rooms is the nature of the rock that hosts the caves. Carlsbad Caverns lies in the Capitan Limestone of the Guadalupe Mountains. About 300 million years ago, the Capitan Limestone was a barrier reef that flourished in a shallow inland sea. Minerals crystallized out of the seawater, cementing the skeletons of the reef coral into thick rock layers that are massive enough to support the rooms, high ceilings and wide expanses of the caverns. Then the sea evaporated, leaving salt and gypsum deposits. Rainwater percolating through the exposed reef gradually dissolved some of the limestone, forming a few small caves.

Once the rooms were no longer submerged by groundwater, the rapid dissolution of the limestone ended and speleothems (cave formations) began to grow. Radiometric dating of large speleothems from the Big Room tells us that Carlsbad Cavern (the main tourist cave) was completely drained of water around 600,000 years ago. While they are found in numerous shapes and sizes, each speleothem is formed by the same basic process. As rainwater enters the cave, carbon dioxide gas escapes from the water, forcing calcium carbonate to crystallize. Stalactites (think *c* for ceiling) grow downward from drips hanging on the roof, while stalagmites (think *g* for ground) form upward when drips fall to the floor. Smaller formations include cave popcorn, cave pearls and helictites (small spiraling stalagmites). The numerous speleothems in Carlsbad Cavern attest to a humid climate in the past, but today, because of the hot, dry Southwestern climate, speleothems grow more slowly.   – Rhawn Denniston

Orientation & Information

The park entrance is immediately west of White's City. The main cavern and visitor center are 7 miles away along a winding mountain road lined with limestone cliffs in which cave entrances can be seen. Information is available at the National Parks Information Center in Carlsbad (☎ 505-785-2232) or at the visitor center in the park.

The park is open from dawn till dusk and admission is free. To enter the cavern, however, costs $6 for adults and $3 for children ages six to 15. (Golden Eagle Passes do not apply; Golden Age or Access Pass holders are eligible for a 50% discount). All cave entrance fees are collected at the visitor center, open from 8 am to 7 pm late May to mid-August and from 8 am to

5:30 pm the rest of the year. Ticket sales stop two to 3½ hours before the visitor center closes. With the entrance fee, you get a brochure with maps and park information. Everything is closed on Christmas.

If you want to try the 50-plus miles of hiking trails, topographic maps are available at the visitor center. A 1-mile nature trail starts outside the visitor center, and a 9½-mile scenic loop drive begins nearby – no trailers or large vehicles allowed. There is a picnic area.

Underground!

The main cavern is visited by either the Big Room or Natural Entrance Routes. Both are self-guided walking tours (see above for fees) and begin at the visitor center where you can rent an audio tour to follow at your own pace. The audio tour works automatically by electronic signals along the trail and provides educational commentary, music and sound effects. It is worth the additional $3 fee.

Underground temperatures are a constant 56°F, so a light sweater is appropriate. Smoking is not permitted anywhere underground. Food and drink are not allowed except in the **underground rest area**, which serves fast food, sandwiches and snacks. There are souvenirs (including postcards, which can receive special underground postmarks) and restrooms here. (The Park Service has considered closing the underground lunchroom because food particles attract creatures that don't belong in the cave system. Take care to keep all food in designated places.)

Pets are not allowed underground, but kennels (☎ 505-785-2281) are available at the surface for a small fee. Children's strollers are not allowed but much of the Big Room Route is accessible to wheelchairs. Touching any of the formations or stepping off the designated trails is prohibited.

Big Room Route This is the most popular tour. It begins with a 755-foot elevator descent from the visitor center to the underground rest area, followed by a 1-mile walk through the Big Room. The entire walk is paved and lit, and park rangers wander around to answer questions. The cavern and geological formations tower around you, and the views are splendid. This tour visits the best-known formations and sites and is a 'must' for park visitors. A shortcut allows you to take just half of the tour. The return is via the elevator. Tickets are sold at the visitor center from 8:30 am to 5 pm in summer, till 3:30 pm the rest of the year.

Natural Entrance Route This tour begins with a short walk from the visitor center to the main entrance of the cavern. From here, a steep trail hairpins down into the depths of the cave (wear good shoes for walking). It is an exciting 1-mile descent, passing through the huge Main Corridor and into a

number of smaller, scenic underground rooms. At the bottom, you reach the underground rest area where you can connect with the Big Room Route, thus making a 2-mile trip in all, or return immediately by elevator. Ticket sales stop at 3:30 pm in summer, 2 pm in winter. For visitors with the time and energy, the combined Natural Entrance/Big Room Routes are recommended.

Guided Tours The availability and variety of ranger- guided tours varies from year to year and you should call the park (☎ 505-785-2232, ext 429) to find out about current offerings and make the required advance reservations.

The **Kings Palace Guided Tour** leaves from the underground rest area and descends into the deepest part of the cavern open to the public, visiting four chambers that are off the self-guided routes described above. Rangers will turn off the lights on parts of the tour so you can experience the natural cave environment. The 1-mile tour takes 90 minutes, leaves several times a day and costs $5 ($2.50 for children and Golden Age Passport holders) in addition to the normal cavern admission fees. Children under four are not allowed.

For the adventurous, there are ranger-led **Wild Cave Tours** to some of the lesser-known areas. These tours leave from the visitor center and are not on paved trails. Participants may be required to wear hard hats and headlamps (furnished by the Park Service, but you need to provide four AA batteries). Be prepared to scramble, climb and get a little muddy. Some tours with candle lanterns give participants an idea of what it must have been like to be an early explorer. Reservations can be made up to six months in advance. Children and Golden Agers pay half price.

Tours are currently offered to Left Hand Tunnel (1½- to two-hour candlelit tour; $5; 9 am daily; 15 people maximum; no children under six), Lower Cave (two- to three-hour headlamp tour with long ladders; $15; 1 pm Monday to Friday; 12 people maximum; no children under 12), Hall of the

White Giants (three- to four-hour headlamp tour with tight crawls, climbs and ladders; $15; 1 pm on Saturday only; eight people maximum; no children under 12) and Spider Cave (similar to but dirtier than Hall of the White Giants; 1 pm on Sunday only).

Other Caves The above tours are all in or just off the main cavern. You can also visit **Slaughter Canyon Cave** (formerly New Cave), which is a 23-mile drive from the visitor center. This cave is not lit and is unpaved; it can be visited only on ranger-led tours. You must furnish your own flashlight and transportation. The tour is limited to 25 people and is fairly strenuous. Children under six are not permitted. Tour fees ($10 for adults) must be paid at the visitor center where you get directions for the 23-mile drive. From the parking lot it is a steep half-mile climb to the cave mouth followed by a 1¼-mile hike through the cave. The tour lasts about 2½ hours and is limited to 25 people. Tours leave at 10 am and 1 pm daily in summer and on weekends during the rest of the year.

The awe-inspiring and very beautiful **Lechuguilla Cave** was discovered in 1986. With a depth of 1593 feet and a length of about 60 miles it is the deepest and fourth largest cave in North America. Exploration is still continuing. See the March 1991 *National Geographic* magazine for superb photos. Note that visits to Lechuguilla are for experienced cavers with technical equipment only. Permits are required from the National Park Service, which allows very limited numbers of cavers to enter for exploration, surveys or scientific study.

Bat Watching
The colony of hundreds of thousands of Mexican free-tail bats inhabiting Carlsbad Cavern is a great attraction. The bats spend the day inside the cave (you can't see them) and come out at dusk. Rangers give interpretive lectures at the amphitheater by the cave's mouth while hundreds of visitors watch the bats emerge over a period of 30 minutes to two hours – quite a sight. The

time of emergence depends on the weather (storms force the bats to stay inside). The densest flights are in August and September when babies join parents. Flash photography is not permitted. The visitor center can usually predict fairly accurately what time the bat flight will occur. From October to April the bats are in Mexico.

Every year in August (usually the second Thursday), the Park Service has a Bat Flight Breakfast. This costs $6 and happens from 5 to 7 am. After breakfast, you get to watch the bats come swooping back into the cave. Call the park to find out the exact date. You can see the dawn arrival of the bats on other days too – the park is open, though the visitor center is closed till 8 am.

Places to Stay & Eat
There are no accommodations or car/RV overnighting within the park, although overnight backpacking trips into the desert backcountry are allowed by permit (which is free). Everything must be packed in, including water. Ask at the visitor center about trails. Meals are available at the visitor center and in the underground rest area.

GUADALUPE MOUNTAINS
This southeastern extension of the Sacramento Mountains continues through southeastern New Mexico and across into western Texas. The northern part of the range is in the Guadalupe District of New Mexico's Lincoln National Forest. South of the Texas state line, these mountains form the Guadalupe Mountains National Park. The eastern foothills of these mountains are in Carlsbad Caverns National Park.

The Guadalupe Mountains are remote and fairly dry. Camping and hiking are the main activities, and fishing and hunting are allowed in the national forest area. Parts of the Guadalupe Mountains are an exposed reef (the Capitan Reef) that was formed hundreds of million of years ago (see the Geology of Carlsbad Caverns sidebar earlier in this chapter). Today, geologists find numerous fossils of ancient sea creatures throughout the reef area.

Lincoln National Forest

The Guadalupe District of the Lincoln National Forest encompasses 445 sq miles and ranges in altitude from 3500 to 7600 feet, allowing for a varied wildlife population. The adjacent lands are under BLM supervision. There are few roads, however, and facilities are primitive.

The main attraction is **Sitting Bull Falls**, 50 miles from Carlsbad. There are waterfalls, swimming holes and a picnic area but no campground. The area is open from April to November. The falls are reached either by taking Hwy 285 north from Carlsbad for 12 miles and then heading west on Hwy 137 and 276, or by taking Hwy 62/180 south from Carlsbad for about 10 miles and taking Hwy 408 west to 137 and 276. These are mostly unpaved roads passable to cars most of the summer.

Hwy 137 (paved) also continues south to Rim Road 540 and Five Points Vista (viewpoint) on the way to the Guadalupe Mountains National Park. There is an RV Park (☎ 505-981-2439) and gas station at Queen, on Hwy 137 outside the national forest.

Dispersed camping is allowed throughout the national forest. Further information and maps are available in Carlsbad at the USFS Ranger Station or the BLM office.

Guadalupe Mountains National Park (Texas)

This national park, 55 miles south of Carlsbad and 110 miles east of El Paso, is in Texas, although the northern boundary is the New Mexican state line and the closest access is from New Mexico. If you've driven this far to see Carlsbad Caverns, you might want to see this national park as well.

The main activities are hiking and backpacking. Unlike many other Southwestern national parks, there is no scenic drive. The park is crossed in the far southeastern corner by Hwy 62/180, and there is a visitor center here. When I stopped by one foggy and slightly drizzly August day, I was the only visitor. If you consider the hordes of visitors thronging most national parks in August, you realize that this is a park for the seeker of remote wilderness. Guadalupe Mountains National Park is an island in the Chihuahuan Desert and contains Guadalupe Peak (8749 feet), the highest point in Texas.

The main visitor center (☎ 915-828-3251), Box 400, Salt Flat, TX 79847-9400, is open from 8 am to 4:30 pm (6 pm in the summer) and closed on Christmas. The center offers a small museum, a slide show, maps and books, and all the information you'll need. Admission to the park is free.

There is no food or lodging in the park, though there are two campgrounds. *Pines Springs Campground*, next to the visitor center, has water and restrooms but no showers. Campfires are prohibited. Camping is $7 a night, and the campground is rarely full except during some summer weekends. *Dog Canyon Campground*, at the far north of the park, can be reached via Hwy 137 from New Mexico, or along Hwy 408 from between Carlsbad and White's City; fill up with gas before the 60 mile one-way drive. This campground has similar services and occasionally fills with fall hunters.

The McKittrick Canyon Visitor Center is halfway between the New Mexican state line and the main visitor center, and has similar hours. It gives access to McKittrick Canyon, one of the most scenic hiking areas in the park. Both day and overnight hikes can be made from the canyon.

Both visitor centers and campgrounds give access to the 80 miles of hiking trails in the park. Backcountry camping is allowed in designated campsites with a permit, which can be obtained for free from the visitor centers. Water is available at some backcountry campsites – talk to rangers for details.

The nearest lodging is in White's City and Carlsbad (35 and 55 miles northeast) or in Van Horn, Texas, 75 miles south.

HOBBS

Hobbs is named after James Hobbs, a settler from Texas who built the first house here in 1907. Cattle ranching and the cultivation of alfalfa, cotton, grain and vegetables were economic mainstays until oil was discovered in 1928. Although cattle and agriculture are still important, Hobbs is now the center of New Mexico's largest oil field, and small oil pumps called pump-jacks or 'lufkins' can be seen working in the town.

Hobbs is 69 miles east of Carlsbad and 77 miles east of Artesia. The drive is through the flat ranch lands (formerly grasslands) of the Llano Estacado. This horizontal landscape is punctuated frequently by the seesaw-like pumpjacks, stolidly forcing oil to the surface. Texan pioneers, cattle ranches, oil fields – Hobbs is only 3 miles from the Texas state line and feels equally Texan and New Mexican.

With a population of 32,000, Hobbs is the largest town in Lea County (population 61,000).

Information

The chamber of commerce (☎ 505-397-3202), 400 N Marland Blvd, has information about Hobbs, as well as Lovington and Lea County. Hours are from 8 am to 5 pm Monday to Friday. The library (☎ 505-397-9328) is at 509 N Shipp Drive. The local newspaper is the *Hobbs News-Sun*. The post office (☎ 505-393-2912) is at 119 W Taylor. The Lea Regional Hospital (☎ 505-392-6581) is at 5419 Lovington Hwy. The police (☎ 505-397-9265) are at 301 N Dalmont.

Lea County Cowboy Hall of Fame & Western Heritage Center

The center (☎ 505-392-1275), 5317 Lovington Hwy, on the campus of New Mexico Junior College, honors prominent local ranchers and rodeo cowboys with commemorative plaques and displays of their personal memorabilia. There are also exhibits of local Indian culture, pioneer history and natural history. Hours are from 10 am to 5 pm Monday to Friday, noon to 5 pm on Saturday or by appointment (call ahead – they close during school holidays and at unpredictable times). Admission is free.

Thelma A Webber Southwest Heritage Room

The Heritage Room (☎ 505-392-6561 ext 315) is inside the Scarborough Memorial Library at the College of the Southwest, 6610 Lovington Hwy. Artifacts of local history ranging from Paleo-Indian through pioneering cowboy to early oil exploration are the focus of this small museum. Hours are 8 am to 9 pm from Monday to Thursday, 8 am to 5 pm on Friday and 9 am to 1 pm on Saturday during the school year. During the summer break, hours are 8 am to 5 pm Monday to Friday. The museum is closed on holidays. Admission is free.

Safari Ostrich Farms

Cattle ranching's newest competitor is ratite ranching, a small but growing industry in the Southwest. Ratites are flightless running birds with a flat breastbone and include the African ostrich, Australian emu and South American rhea, all of which can be seen at this farm. The Ostrich Farms (☎ 505-393-4920) are at 2700 Brand Drive, off Hwy 62/180 northeast of Hobbs. Tours are available.

Harry McAdams State Park

This park (☎ 505-392-5845), located off the Lovington Hwy 7 miles northwest of downtown, has a picnic area, children's playground and a small area museum in the visitor center. Day use is $3 per carload; overnight camping is $7 or $11 with hookups. Showers are available.

Confederate Air Force Museum

This collection of WWII aircraft in flying condition is in a hangar at the Lea County Airport on Carlsbad Hwy and can be toured by appointment at the chamber of commerce, though is often open for walk-in visitors.

Gliding

Hobbs' weather is ideal for soaring and gliding, and the town is the home of the National Soaring Foundation (☎ 505-392-6032) and the Soaring Society of America

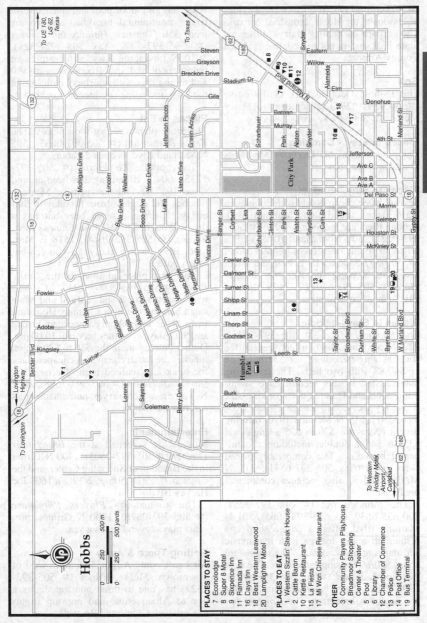

Hobbs

0   250   500 m
0   250   500 yards

To US 180,
US 62,
Texas

To Texas

To Lovington

Lovington Highway

To Western
Holiday Motel,
Airport,
Carlsbad

PLACES TO STAY
7   Econolodge
8   Super 8 Motel
9   Sixpence Inn
11 Ramada Inn
16 Days Inn
18 Best Western Leawood
20 Lamplighter Motel

PLACES TO EAT
1   Western Sizzlin Steak House
2   Cattle Baron
10 Kettle Restaurant
15 La Fiesta
17 Mi Won Chinese Restaurant

OTHER
3   Community Players Playhouse
4   Broadmoor Shopping
    Center & Theater
5   Pool
6   Library
12 Chamber of Commerce
13 Police
14 Post Office
19 Bus Terminal

(☎ 505-392-1177). You can take joy rides or lessons at the Hobbs Industrial Airpark. The airpark is behind Harry McAdams State Park and is not the commercial Lea County Airport.

Golf
The 18-hole Ocotillo Park Golf Course (☎ 505-397-9297) is adjacent to Harry McAdams State Park.

Places to Stay – Camping
Camping is available at *Harry McAdams State Park*; see above.

Places to Stay – Budget
Several basic cheap hotels with doubles in the $20s are found along Marland Blvd. Among them are the *Sixpence Inn* (☎ 505-393-0221), 509 N Marland Blvd, with a seasonal pool; the *Lamplighter Motel* (☎ 505-397-2406), 110 E Marland Blvd, also with a pool; and the *Western Holiday Motel* (☎ 505-393-6494), 2724 W Marland Blvd, and about five others.

Places to Stay – Middle
The *Super 8 Motel* (☎ 505-397-7511), 722 N Marland Blvd, offers free coffee and has singles/doubles for $31.88/35.88 or $40.88 with two beds. The remaining hotels listed in this section have swimming pools and feature queen- or king-size beds. Try the *Econo Lodge* (☎/fax 505-397-3591), 619 N Marland Blvd, offering decent rooms for $30 to $35 a single and $35 to $45 a double, including a continental breakfast. The comparably priced *Days Inn* (☎/fax 505-397-6541), 211 N Marland Blvd, also includes continental breakfast.

The *Ramada Inn* (☎ 505-397-3251, 800-635-6639, fax 505-393-3065), 501 N Marland Blvd, offers a coffee shop and restaurant, and a lounge with live music and dancing on weekends. The rooms are about $50/60 for singles/doubles. The *Best Western Leawood* (☎/fax 505-393-4101), 1301 E Broadway, has rooms in the $50s and includes breakfast. The *Comfort Inn* (☎/fax 505-392-2161), 5020 Lovington Hwy, has an indoor pool and spa, exercise room, continental breakfast and rooms from $50. The new *Holiday Inn Express* (☎ 505-392-8777, fax 505-392-9321), 3610 N Lovington Hwy, also features an indoor pool and spa. Rooms start at $60 and mini-suites with whirlpool baths are in the $80s, including continental breakfast.

Places to Eat
There are plenty of fast-food places. The *Kettle Restaurant* (☎ 505-397-0663), 505 N Marland Blvd, is open 24 hours.

The popular *La Fiesta* (☎ 505-397-1235), 604 E Broadway, has been around since 1957 serving inexpensive Mexican lunches and dinners from Monday to Saturday; it doesn't serve beer but has a drive-through. The *Mi Won Chinese Restaurant* (☎ 505-393-7644), 1518 E Marland Blvd, has a daily all-you-can-eat lunch buffet.

The best place in town is the *Cattle Baron* (☎ 505-393-2800), 1930 N Grimes, which serves steak and seafood and has a salad bar; there is also a lounge. Hours are from 11 am to 9:30 pm daily except Friday and Saturday, when they serve till 10:00 pm. Dinner entrées are in the $10 to $20 range; lunches are much cheaper. A cheaper place for steak and seafood is the *Western Sizzlin' Steak House* (☎ 505-393-7608), 2022 N Turner, which serves homemade rolls and has a salad bar.

Entertainment
Movies are screened at the *Broadmoor Theater* (☎ 505-397-2603), 1400 N Turner in the Broadmoor Shopping Center, and the *Cinema Three* (☎ 505-392-3988), 1609 Joe Harvey Blvd.

The *Community Players Playhouse* (☎ 505-393-0676), 1700 N Grimes, presents plays several times a year.

Getting There & Away
Air Lea County Airport is 5 miles west of downtown. Mesa Airlines (☎ 505-393-1327) has one to three nonstop flights a day to Albuquerque and nonstop flights to Carlsbad, Clovis and Roswell.

Bus The bus terminal (☎ 505-397-3535) is at 400 S Turner. TNM&O has one bus a day to Lovington, continuing into Texas, and two buses a day to Carlsbad, continuing to El Paso, Texas.

Getting Around

City Taxi (☎ 505-393-5151) gets you where you want. National (☎ 505-393-6424) at the airport and Enterprise (☎ 505-397-4334), 424 N Broadway, rent cars.

LOVINGTON

Although Hobbs is the largest and most important town in Lea County, Lovington, 22 miles northwest of Hobbs, is the county seat. The town is named after Robert Florence Love, around whose homestead the town was founded in 1908. Agriculture was Lovington's economic mainstay until 1950 when oil was found a few miles to the northeast. Now, oil and natural gas are Lovington's most important industries. The town has a population of 9500.

Orientation & Information

Hwy 18 (Main St) runs north-south and is the most important thoroughfare. Hwy 82 (Ave D) is the main east-west thoroughfare.

The chamber of commerce (☎ 505-396-5311) is at 1535 N Main. Hours are 9 am to noon and 1 to 5 pm Monday to Friday. The library (☎ 505-396-3144) is at 119 S Main. The post office (☎ 505-396-2300) is at 203 E Ave D. The police (☎ 505-396-2811) are at 213 S Love. The hospital (☎ 505-396-6611) is at 1600 N Main.

Lea County Historical Museum

The historical museum (☎ 505-396-4805) is housed in an old hotel at 103 S Love. Local pioneer artifacts are on display from 1 to 5 pm Monday to Friday.

Special Events

The Fourth of July is celebrated in Chaparral Park on S Commercial St, with entertainment all day, highlighted by the World's Greatest Lizard Race with dozens of reptilian racers competing for trophies. There are traditional fireworks in the evening.

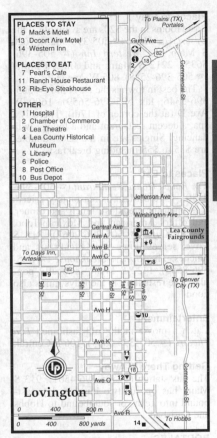

PLACES TO STAY
9   Mack's Motel
13 Desert Aire Motel
14 Western Inn

PLACES TO EAT
7   Pearl's Cafe
11 Ranch House Restaurant
12 Rib-Eye Steakhouse

OTHER
1   Hospital
2   Chamber of Commerce
3   Lea Theatre
4   Lea County Historical
    Museum
5   Library
6   Police
7   Post Office
10 Bus Depot

Lovington

The annual Lea County Fair & Rodeo (☎ 505-396-5344), one of the state's biggest county fairs and more than 60 years old, is held at the county fairgrounds during the second week in August. There's a top-notch PRCA rodeo as well as a huge variety of livestock and agricultural events ranging from swine judging and sheep shearing to a flower show. There are also parades, dances, a fiddlers contest, food booths, arts and crafts and much more.

The annual Southeastern New Mexico Arts & Crafts Show draws exhibitors from neighboring states during the first weekend in November.

Places to Stay

Basic rooms in the $20s are available at the *Desert Aire Motel* (☎ 505-396-3623), 1620 S Main, the *Western Inn* (☎ 505-396-3635), 2212 S Main, and *Mack's Motel* (☎ 505-396-2588), 805 W Ave D.

The best in town is the *Days Inn* (☎ 505-396-5346, fax 505-396-5659), 1600 W Ave D (at the corner of 17th). There is a spa, a decent restaurant and a lounge with dancing. Singles are in the $30s, doubles are $35 to $55 including breakfast.

Places to Eat

The *Ranch House Restaurant* (☎ 505-396-4130), 1318 S Main, is reasonably priced. It is open for breakfast, lunch and dinner, and offers American and Mexican food. *Pearl's Cafe* (☎ 505-396-2067), 318 S Love, serves home-style breakfasts and lunches. The *Rib-Eye Steakhouse* (☎ 505-396-8553), 1422 S Main, is locally popular. The restaurant in the Days Inn is also good.

Entertainment

Catch a movie at the old-fashioned *Lea Theatre* (☎ 505-396-5594), 106 E Central.

Getting There & Away

The bus station (☎ 505-396-4501), 913 S Main, has one or two buses a day eastbound into Texas or southbound to Hobbs and Carlsbad.

PORTALES

This pleasant college town (population: 12,000 friendly people and two or three old grouches) is the home of Eastern New Mexico University (ENMU). With almost 4000 students, the university contributes a great deal to the atmosphere and cultural life of the town. Several small museums are in and around Portales. The town lies at just over 4000 feet at the northern end of the Llano Estacado.

Because of the relatively deep water table, Portales was a very small town until the drilling of deep wells in the 1940s enabled agriculture to expand. Today, agriculture forms the base of the economy. Wheat, milo (a form of sorghum), corn, cotton and peanuts are the main crops. Portales produces more Valencia peanuts than anywhere in the world – peanut farming and peanut butter manufacturing are big business. Cattle ranching is also important, as is ENMU, which employs more than 500 people. Portales is also the Roosevelt County seat.

Orientation

Portales is 19 miles southwest of Clovis and 91 miles northeast of Roswell on Hwy 70 (this parallels the railway; there are no passenger services). Getting around can be confusing. Hwy 70 is a divided road downtown, running southwest to northeast on W 2nd and northeast to southwest on W 1st. Downtown streets run southwest to northeast, while avenues run southeast to northwest. Things get complicated away from the old downtown, where avenues change to run north-south and streets to east-west. Study the map.

Information

Tourist information is available from the Roosevelt Chamber of Commerce (☎ 505-356-8541), 200 E 7th, open from 9 am to 5 pm Monday to Friday. Information about ENMU is available on campus (☎ 505-562-1011). The *Portales News-Tribune* is the local daily newspaper. The library (☎ 505-356-3940) is at 218 S Ave B. The post office (☎ 505-356-4781) is at 116 W 1st (inside, check out *Buffalo Range*, a New Deal mural painted in 1938). The hospital (☎ 505-356-4411) is at 1700 S Ave O. The police (☎ 505-356-4404) are at 1700 N Boston Ave.

Eastern New Mexico University Museums

There are several museums on the campus that don't have fixed hours, so call ahead. **Roosevelt County Historical Museum** (☎ 505-562-2677, 505-562-2592) is on the southeast side of Hwy 70 near the ENMU (☎ 505-562-1011) administration buildings. It is open 8 am to 5 pm, Monday to Friday, plus weekends during the school

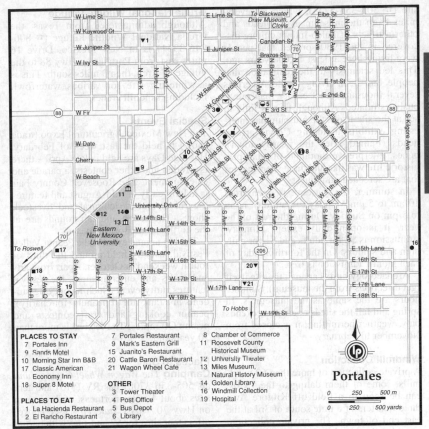

PLACES TO STAY
7   Portales Inn
9   Sands Motel
10 Morning Star Inn B&B
17 Classic American
    Economy Inn
18 Super 8 Motel

PLACES TO EAT
1   La Hacienda Restaurant
2   El Rancho Restaurant

7   Portales Restaurant
15 Juanito's Restaurant
20 Cattle Baron Restaurant
21 Wagon Wheel Cafe

OTHER
3   Tower Theater
5   Bus Depot
6   Library

8   Chamber of Commerce
11 Roosevelt County
    Historical Museum
12 University Theater
13 Miles Museum,
    Natural History Museum
14 Golden Library
16 Windmill Collection
19 Hospital

Portales

0   250   500 m
0   250   500 yards

year. The main focus is pioneer and early settlement history, though archaeology and Indian history are also represented. While you're nearby, take a look at the interesting New Deal murals in the administration building.

The **Jack Williamson Science Fiction Collection** is in the Golden Library (☎ 505-562-2624), south of the administration building. Williamson used to teach at ENMU and authored dozens of sci-fi novels and stories. His manuscripts and his letters to sci-fi writers Robert Heinlein and Ray Bradbury can be inspected

here. The library also has a New Deal mural.

The **Miles Museum** (☎ 505-562-2651) south of the library in Roosevelt Hall, has a geology display. Also in the same building is the **Natural History Museum** (☎ 505-562-2723), which focuses on local wildlife and is open 8 am to 5 pm on weekdays.

Blackwater Draw Museum & Site
The Blackwater Draw Museum (☎ 505-562-2202), on Hwy 70 about 7 miles northeast of downtown, is named after the important Blackwater Draw archaeological

site (☎ 505-356-5235), which is several miles from the museum. Arrowheads and other artifacts of Paleo-Indian culture discovered in the 1930s proved that people were living here at least 11,000 years ago. This led scientists to the realization that people had been living in the Americas several thousand years earlier than previously estimated. Although there's little to see at the site itself, the museum has interesting exhibits including Clovis arrowheads (named after the nearby town), bones, interpretive dioramas of what prehistoric life was like and three short movies that are screened on request.

In summer, the museum is open from 10 am to 5 pm Monday to Saturday, noon to 5 pm on Sunday. During the rest of the year, it is open daily except Monday. Admission is $2 for adults and $1 for children and seniors. On the fourth Sunday of each month admission is free.

Archaeology buffs can visit the site itself (get directions from the museum). Summer hours are the same as the museum's. In spring and fall the site is open on weekends only, weather permitting; it is closed from November to February.

Windmill Collection

A private collection of more than 60 windmills, some of them dating to the 1870s, can be seen in a field off Kilgore Ave, three-quarters of a mile south of 3rd at the east end of town. The private collection, owned and curated by Bill Dalley (☎ 505-356-6263), is the largest windmill collection in the USA.

Oasis State Park

This state park (☎ 505-356-5331), 1891 Oasis Rd, Portales, NM 88130, provides outdoor recreation for the residents of Portales and Clovis. There is a small lake (the oasis) for fishing, surrounded by cottonwood trees and sand dunes. Picnicking and camping (see Places to Stay) are available. Day use is $3 per car (free for bicycles). Get there by taking Hwy 70 2 miles northeast from Portales, then Hwy 467 north for about 6 miles.

Grulla National Wildlife Refuge

Although administered from Texas, the Grulla National Wildlife Refuge (☎ 806-946-3341) is in New Mexico. Drive 16 miles east from Portales on Hwy 88 to the village of Arch, then 3 miles south. This is a wintering site for various waterfowl, including sandhill cranes.

Special Events

The New Mexico Agricultural Expo (trade show) is held the last week of February. Heritage Days are held in late April – there is a rodeo and other contests, a parade and entertainment. The Roosevelt County Fair is held in early or mid-August and features a carnival and agricultural and livestock shows. The rodeo and fairgrounds are at the north end of Boston Ave.

The big annual event is the Peanut Valley Festival, usually held around the third or fourth weekend in October. Apart from arts and crafts and entertainment, the festival features nutty events such as burying students in a tank full of peanuts (for charity), peanut cooking and craft contests and peanut Olympics. The festival is more than 20 years old.

Places to Stay

Camping The *Wagon Wheel Campground* (☎ 505-356-3700) has RV ($13) and tent sites about 4 miles northeast of downtown on Hwy 70. *Oasis State Park* (see above) offers tent sites for $7 and sites with partial RV hookups are $11. There are showers. Each place has about 25 sites.

Hotels The *Sands Motel* (☎ 505-356-4424, 800-956-44234), 1130 W 1st, has a pool and queen- and king-size beds. Rates start at around $30, including breakfast at a neighboring McDonald's. The *Classic American Economy Inn* (☎ 505-356-6668, 800-901-9466), on Hwy 70 just west of ENMU, offers a pool and free coffee in rooms that have queen- or king-size beds. Rates are in the $30s.

The *Portales Inn* (☎ 505-359-1208), 218 W 3rd, has a restaurant. Standard singles/doubles start from $37/42. The *Super 8*

Motel (☎ 505-356-8518, fax 505-359-0431), 1805 W 2nd, has a spa and charges $45/49 or $52 with two beds, including in-room coffee.

B&Bs *Morning Star Inn B&B* (☎ 505-356-2994, MorningStarB&B@PDRPIP.com), 620 W 2nd, Portales, NM 88130, has three rooms sharing two baths and a two-room suite with private bath. Rates are $50 or $55 double with continental breakfast. There is a gift shop and TV lounge and smoking is not allowed.

Places to Eat
Early risers can try the following. *Mark's Eastern Grill* (☎ 505-359-0857), 1126 W 1st, is open daily from 5 am to 9 pm. The restaurant at the *Portales Inn* (☎ 505-359-1208), 218 W 3rd, is open from 6:30 am to 8 pm daily except Sunday when it closes at 2 pm.

The *Wagon Wheel Cafe* (☎ 505-356-5036), 521 W 17th, is small and unpretentious but has good homemade, country-style cooking and Mexican specials for lunch and dinner every day. *El Rancho* (☎ 505-359-0098), 101 N Chicago; *La Hacienda* (☎ 505-359-0280), 909 N Ave K; and *Juanito's* (☎ 505-359-1860), 813 S Ave C, all serve inexpensive Mexican lunches and dinners.

The fanciest place in town is the *Cattle Baron* (☎ 505-356-5587), 1600 S Ave D. This serves steak and seafood, has a lounge and is open from 11 am to 9:30 pm daily.

Entertainment
The College of Fine Arts at ENMU presents theater and symphony events several times a year. Call ENMU information (☎ 505-562-1011) or the *University Theater* (☎ 505-562-2710, 505-562-2711) for more details.

The *Tower Theater* (☎ 505-356-6081), 101 N Ave A, shows movies.

Getting There & Away
The nearest scheduled commercial air service is in Clovis. The private Portales Airport (☎ 505-478-2863) is west of town.

The bus depot (☎ 505-356-6914) is at 215 E 2nd. TNM&O has three daily buses to Clovis and Amarillo, Texas, and three daily buses to Roswell, Ruidoso, Alamogordo, Las Cruces and El Paso. There is also a daily bus traveling to both Santa Rosa and Albuquerque.

CLOVIS
Although Indians have roamed this area for millennia, there were no permanent Indian settlements here. This is the northern end of the desolate Llano Estacado; farther north the land merges into the high plains of northeastern New Mexico. Green Acres Lake, now in the middle of town, used to be a watering hole for cowboys herding cattle in the late 1800s.

Clovis was founded (comparatively recently) in 1906 to serve as a Santa Fe Railroad town. A railroad official's daughter who was studying French reportedly named the town after Clovis I (466 to 511 AD), the first Christian king of the Franks. The Blackwater Draw archaeological site (see under Portales, above) was discovered in the 1930s by a local, and the 'Clovis arrowheads' of the Paleo-Indians living in the area were named after the town.

Until the mid-20th century the town was more important as a railroad junction than as an agricultural center because of the dry soil. The Santa Fe Railroad (freight only) continues to be an economic mainstay, but the drilling of deep wells in the 1950s improved agriculture tremendously.

Clovis (population 34,000) is the seat of Curry County, which despite being the second smallest county in New Mexico, produces more wheat and sorghum than any other county in the state. Grain, alfalfa, corn and peanuts are important, as is livestock. Nearby Cannon Air Force Base is also economically vital and provides an estimated 10% of local jobs.

Orientation
Most motels are on Mabry Drive (Hwy 60/70/84), the main west-east street, which continues to Texas, 9 miles east. Prince Street (Hwy 70 southbound and Hwy 209

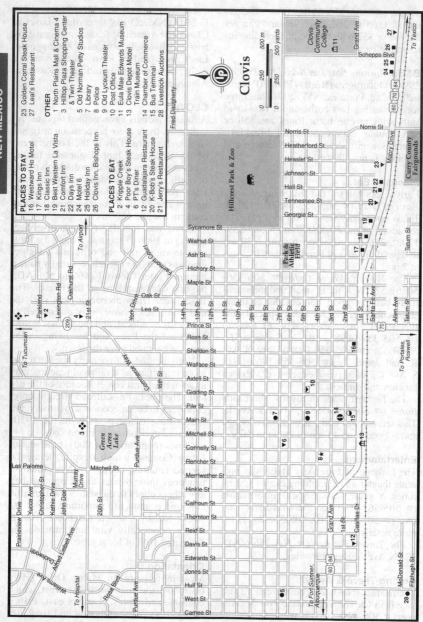

PLACES TO STAY
16 Westward Ho Motel
17 Kings Inn
18 Classic Inn
19 Best Western La Vista
21 Comfort Inn
22 Days Inn
24 Motel 6
25 Holiday Inn
26 Clovis Inn, Bishops Inn

PLACES TO EAT
4 Kripple Creek
6 Poor Boy's Steak House
6 PT's Diner
12 Guadalajara Restaurant
20 K-Bob's Steak House
21 Jerry's Restaurant

23 Golden Corral Steak House
27 Leal's Restaurant

OTHER
1 North Plains Mall & Cinema 4
3 Hilltop Plaza Shopping Center
   & Twin Theater
5 Old Norman Petty Studios
7 Library
8 Police
9 Old Lyceum Theater
10 Post Office
11 Eula Mae Edwards Museum
13 Clovis Depot Model
    Train Museum
14 Chamber of Commerce
15 Bus Terminal
28 Livestock Auctions

Clovis

northbound) is the major north-south street and Main Street is the most historic.

Information

The chamber of commerce (☎ 505-763-3435, fax 505-763-7266), 215 N Main, is open 9 am to 5 pm Monday to Friday. The library (☎ 505-769-7840) is at 701 N Main. The *Clovis News Journal* is the local newspaper. The post office (☎ 505-763-5556) is at 5th and Giddings. Clovis Recycling (☎ 505-769-2376, 505-762-0296) provides information about various drop-off sites in town. The hospital (☎ 505-769-2141) is at 2100 N Thomas. The police (☎ 505-769-1921) are at 300 Connelly.

Historic Buildings

Sections of Main are cobbled and have several interesting early buildings on the National Register of Historic Buildings. Some of this street looks like part of a 1940s Western movie set. The nine-story **Hotel Clovis**, topped by statues of Indian heads, is at 1st and Main, near the chamber of commerce. When built in 1931, it was New Mexico's tallest building and retained that status until 1953. It has been closed for some years and is available for sale. Want to buy a historic 100-room hotel? Renovation costs are estimated at $2 million. There are plans to turn it into a business center.

Built in 1919, the **Old Lyceum Theater** (☎ 505-763-6085), 411 N Main, was the site of regular performances until its closure in 1974. It has since been refurbished and has occasional performances. Tours of its ornate vaudeville interior are available on request; call or ask at the barbershop next door.

Up the street at 122 W 4th (a block west of Main) is a 1931 building, formerly the post office, then the county library and now an architect's office. The lobby houses a 4-by-9-foot oil mural of Clovis in the 1930s, painted under government New Deal sponsorship.

The town's oldest surviving house was built in 1907 and is at the Curry County Fairgrounds (☎ 505-763-6502) at 600 S Norris. The house contains a small museum

that is open during the annual county fair and by appointment at other times.

Norman Petty Studios

These recording studios are famous as the place where several early rock & roll artists made their names. Foremost among these was Buddy Holly, who recorded 'Peggy Sue' and other hits here in the 1950s, as well as Roy Orbison, Buddy Knox, Jimmy Gilmer and Roger Williams. Beatle Paul McCartney bought the rights to Buddy Holly's music in 1976 and was instrumental in renovating the old studio in 1986.

The old studio, 1313 W 7th, can be toured by appointment (call the chamber of commerce) and is open during the annual Clovis music festival. It is a minor mecca for fans of early rock & roll. The Petty family still operates a studio in Clovis.

Clovis Depot Model Train Museum

Housed in a train depot restored in 1950s period style, the model train museum (☎ 505-762-0066), 221 W 1st, has exhibits detailing the history of the British and Australian railway systems as well as US railroads. Hours are noon to 5 pm Wednesday to Sunday; admission is $3 ($1 for children); $7 per family.

Hillcrest Park & Zoo

Hillcrest Park has a swimming pool, gardens, picnic areas, tennis courts and the Municipal Golf Course (☎ 505-769-7871), 1220 Norris. It also houses Hillcrest Zoo (☎ 505-769-7873), with a petting zoo and about 500 animals. Hours are 9 am to 4 pm Tuesday to Sunday (5 pm in summer); admission is $1; 50¢ for six- to 18-year-olds.

Eula Mae Edwards Museum

This museum on the campus of the **Clovis Community College** (☎ 505-769-2811), 417 Schepps Blvd, has a small collection of prehistoric and Indian artifacts and hosts changing shows of local artists.

Livestock Auctions

Cattle are auctioned every Wednesday (☎ 505-762-4422), at 504 S Hull, drawing buyers from Texas, Kansas, Oklahoma and Arizona. In a good year about 70,000 head are sold for a total value of well over $30 million. Major horse auctions are held quarterly. Ranchers and cowboys, slow-moving cattle and fast-talking auctioneers – this is a good glimpse of the American West.

Ned Houck Park
Six miles north on Hwy 209, Ned Houck Park (☎ 505-389-5146) has fishing, archery, motorcycle dirt tracks and picnic grounds. It also has the **Pappy Thornton Farm Museum**, which displays turn-of-the-19th-century farm implements, a windmill and a ranch house.

Special Events
Pioneer Days occurs annually around the first weekend in June. It features a PRCA rodeo, a parade, a fiddlers contest, a chile cook-off, dancing and some athletic events including an outhouse race along Main.

The Music Festival, with its special emphasis on '50s rock & roll and tours of the old Norman Petty Studios, also features a balloon rally, a '50s classic car parade and, of course, dancing. This all happens around late August or early September.

Also around this time is the Curry County Fair, with livestock and agricultural exhibits, a tractor pull, food booths, square dancing and a carnival.

The Cannon Air Force Base (☎ 505-784-3311), 6 miles west of town, holds an open house in September.

Places to Stay – Camping
The *Campground of Clovis* (☎ 505-763-6360, fax 505-769-2202), 4707 W 7th, is 3½ miles west of downtown. Tent sites are $12.50; RV sites with hookups are $16. There are 52 sites and two camping cabins ($19), showers, a laundry room and a playground. *West Park Inn RV Park* (☎ 505-763-7218), 1500 W 7th, has 18 RV sites with hookups for $16.

In the past, overnight camping has been permitted at *Ned Houck Park* (see above). *Oasis State Park* (see under Portales, above) is 18 miles away (take Hwy 60/84

west for 3 miles, then Hwy 467 south for 13 miles to the signed access road).

Places to Stay – Budget
Clovis has the best hotel selection between Roswell and I-40.

The *Westward Ho Motel* (☎ 505-762-4451), 616 E 1st, is the closest to downtown and charges from $20 a single; rooms are basic but adequate. The reliable *Motel 6* (☎ 505-762-2995, fax 505-762-6342), 2620 Mabry Drive, charges $27/33 for singles/doubles and has a pool. Others with rooms beginning in the $20s include the *Kings Inn* (☎ 505-762-4486), 1320 Mabry Drive, and the *Classic Inn* (☎ 505-763-3439, 888-763-3439), 1400 Mabry Drive, which has a pool, a café next door, and some more expensive mini-suites with refrigerators and microwaves. The *Bishops Inn* (☎ 505-769-1953, 800-643-9239, fax 505-762-8304), 2920 Mabry Drive, with a pool and spa, has rooms starting around $30, including continental breakfast.

Places to Stay – Middle
Choose from the *Days Inn* (☎ 505-762-2971, fax 505-762-2735), 1720 Mabry Drive; *Comfort Inn* (☎ 505-762-4591, fax 505-763-6747), 1616 Mabry Drive; *Best Western La Vista* (☎ 505-762-3808, fax 505-762-1422), 1516 Mabry Drive; and *Clovis Inn* (☎ 505-762-5600, 800-535-3440), 2912 Mabry Drive. All have pools, pleasant rooms in the $30s and $40s, and include continental breakfast.

The best motel in town is the *Holiday Inn* (☎ 505-762-4491, fax 505-769-0564), 2700 Mabry Drive, with indoor and outdoor pools, sauna, spa, exercise room, restaurant and lounge bar. Rates are about $60.

Places to Eat
For breakfast, try *Kripple Creek* (☎ 505-762-7399), 2417 N Prince, which is open from 6 am to 11 pm daily and also serves sandwiches and Mexican food. Also try *Jerry's Restaurant* (☎ 505-762-2081), 1620 Mabry Drive, featuring inexpensive breakfasts; it's open 24 hours. *PT's Diner*

(☎ 505-762-8160), 217 W 7th, has 1950s memorabilia and serves a classic American diner menu.

Guadalajara (☎ 505-769-9965), 916 Casillas Drive, is open for lunch from 11 am to 2 pm Monday to Friday and for dinner from 5 to 9 pm Monday to Saturday – the restaurant has a nice Mexican ambiance. Also serving Mexican food, *Juanito's* (☎ 505-762-7822), 1608 Mabry Drive, is open from 11 am to 9 pm Tuesday to Saturday and 11 am to 2 pm on Sunday. *Leal's* (☎ 505-763-4075), 3100 Mabry Drive, is open from 10:30 am to 9 pm daily except Sunday when it closes at 8 pm. Leal's has been here since 1957 and is the town's fanciest Mexican restaurant; despite this status, most dishes are under $10.

For steak and seafood, try *K-Bob's Steak House* (☎ 505-763-4443), 1600 Mabry Drive, or the *Golden Corral Steak House* (☎ 505-762-7422), 2018 Mabry Drive. Both are fairly inexpensive, family-style restaurants. For a little more ambiance *Poor Boy's Steak House* (☎ 505-763-5222), 2115 N Prince, is your best bet. This restaurant has a good salad bar and is open daily from 11 am to 9 pm (10 pm on Friday and Saturday). It is considered Clovis' best restaurant; dinner entrées run in the $10 to $20 range.

Entertainment
The *North Plains Cinema 4* (☎ 505-763-7713), 2809 N Prince, and the *Hilltop Twin Theater* (☎ 505-763-7876), 21st and Main, both show movies.

Clovis City Limits (☎ 505-762-6485), 3800 Mabry Drive, is a bar that features country & western music and dancing – free dance lessons are available on Thursday nights.

Getting There & Away
Air Clovis Airport is 7 miles east of town on 21st. Mesa Airlines (☎ 505-389-1230) has three nonstop flights to Albuquerque Monday to Friday and one flight on Saturday and Sunday. There is a daily nonstop to Roswell.

Bus The bus terminal (☎ 505-762-4584) is at 121 E 2nd. TNM&O buses pass through on their run between Amarillo (Texas), Clovis, Portales, Roswell, Ruidoso, Alamogordo, Las Cruces and El Paso (Texas), three times a day in each direction. There is a daily bus to Santa Rosa and Albuquerque.

Getting Around
City Cab (☎ 505-762-6050) and WJR JPD Taxi (☎ 505-769-3900) can get you around. Avis (☎ 505-762-4084), at the airport, and Enterprise (☎ 505-763-9733), 500 E 1st, have car rentals.

FORT SUMNER
This village sprang up around old Fort Sumner and is in history books for two reasons: the disastrous Bosque Redondo Indian Reservation and Billy the Kid's last showdown with Sheriff Pat Garrett. The area is full of Indian and outlaw history.

The town of Fort Sumner (population about 1500) is the seat of small and sparsely populated De Baca County. It is on the Pecos River in the northern reaches of the Llano Estacado and has an economy based on agriculture and tourism.

Orientation
Hwy 60 (Sumner Ave) is the main thoroughfare and runs east-west through town; most places of interest lie along it. Hwy 84 to Santa Rosa leaves Sumner Ave northbound on 4th – this is the major north-south cross street. Fort Sumner is 84 miles north of Roswell, 45 miles southwest of Santa Rosa and 60 miles east of Clovis.

Information
The chamber of commerce (☎ 505-355-7705, 505-355-2462), is at 707 N 4th. Aficionados of outlaw history can contact their ilk through the Billy the Kid Outlaw Gang (☎ 505-355-9935, 505-355-2555), PO Box 1881, Taiban, NM 88134, 11 miles east of Fort Sumner. The library (☎ 505-355-2832) is at 300 W Sumner Ave. The De Baca General Hospital (☎ 505-355-2414) is at 500 N 10th. The post office

(☎ 505-355-2423) is at 622 N 5th. The Fort Sumner Sheriff's Office (☎ 505-355-2405) is in the courthouse at 514 Ave C.

Billy the Kid Museum

The Billy the Kid Museum (☎ 505-355-2380), 1601 E Sumner Ave, has more than 60,000 privately owned items on display. Obviously, there's more here than just a Billy the Kid exhibit – there are Indian artifacts and items from late-19th- and early-20th-century local life. Hours are from 8:30 am to 5 pm daily mid-May through September. In other months, Sunday hours are 11 am to 5 pm. The museum is closed Thanksgiving, Christmas and the first two weeks of January. Admission is $4; $2 for six- to 11-year-olds.

Fort Sumner State Monument

The state monument (☎ 505-355-2573) is 2 miles east of town on Hwy 60, then 4 miles south on Hwy 272. The original Fort Sumner was built here in 1862 as an outpost to fight the Apache tribe and the Confederate army around the time of the Civil War. After driving the Confederates south, the troops turned all their force on the Indians.

The battles that followed were cruel and bloody, involving broken treaties and several massacres. Many Apaches fled to Mexico; others were herded onto a desolate strip of land near the fort known as Bosque Redondo. The Navajos were soon forced to join the Apaches, walking the deadly 'Long Walk' from Canyon de Chelly, almost 400 miles to the west.

By the end of 1864, about 9000 Navajos and 500 Apaches had been incarcerated on the Bosque Redondo Reservation, where the federal government hoped to convert them to farmers. In 1868, General Sherman declared it a failure; the reservation was not sustainable because the land was harsh and unsuitable for intensive agriculture. After four years of starvation and deprivation, the surviving Indians were allowed to return to their homelands. About 3000 had died in these four years.

The fort was then purchased by Lucien Maxwell, one of the richest ranchers of the

period, who turned it into a palatial ranch. Maxwell literally owned most of New Mexico north of Fort Sumner and east of the Rockies – the largest spread ever owned by one individual in the United States. His son, Peter, inherited the ranch in 1875. Billy the Kid was visiting here on July 14, 1881, when he was shot and killed by Sheriff Pat Garrett.

Unfortunately, the original fort no longer stands, but a visitor center has interpretive exhibits and historical artifacts. The emphasis here is on Indian and pioneer history, explained by park rangers. Hours are 8:30 am to 5 pm except national holidays. Admission is $1 for adults and free for children. No camping is allowed.

Old Fort Sumner Museum

This museum is near the state monument. There is more local history here, with an emphasis on Billy the Kid, and a souvenir shop. Hours are 9 am to 5 pm daily, with extended summer hours, and admission is $3 ($2 for seven- to 14-year-olds).

Behind the museum are the graves of the Kid and Lucien Maxwell (see them for no charge). The Kid's tombstone is protected by an iron cage – 'souvenir hunters' keep stealing it.

De Baca County Courthouse

The courthouse (☎ 505-355-2601), 514 Ave C, was built in 1930. The 2nd floor has three walls of murals depicting *The Last Frontier*, painted by Russell Vernon Hunter in 1934 as part of President Franklin Roosevelt's New Deal domestic reforms. These murals can be viewed during business hours.

Sumner Lake State Park

The state park (☎ 505-355-2541), Box 125, Fort Sumner NM 88119, is located around an artificial lake formed by the damming of the Pecos River. The lake is locally popular for fishing, swimming, boating, waterskiing and watching beautiful sunsets. There is a picnic area, playground and campground here as well (see Places to Stay & Eat, below).

Admission is $3 per vehicle for day use. Get there by taking Hwy 84 north for 11 miles, then Hwy 203 west for 6 miles.

Special Events
Old Fort Days are held during the second weekend in June. They feature various athletic events, including a tombstone race in which contestants must negotiate an obstacle course while lugging an 80 lb tombstone. The purse for the winner is $1000. Other attractions are a rodeo, a parade, a mock gunfight, a barbecue and arts and crafts displays.

The De Baca County Fair is held in the last week in August. Call the chamber of commerce for details on both events.

Places to Stay & Eat
Camping is available at Sumner Lake State Park (see above), which charges $7 for camping, $11 for sites with partial hookups. There are 90 sites and showers. There is free camping (no water) near Bosque Redondo Lake, 2 miles south of the east end of town.

Two simple and fairly inexpensive motels are the *Coronado Motel* (☎ 505-355-2466), 309 W Sumner Ave, and the *Oasis Motel* (☎ 505-355-7414), 1700 E Sumner Ave. Some better rooms are available at the *Super 8 Motel* (☎/fax 505-355-7888), 1707 E Sumner Ave, with double rooms in the $40s. These last two are convenient for the Billy the Kid Museum.

Nearby, the best restaurant is *Sprouts Cafe* (☎ 505-355-7278), 1701 E Sumner Ave, open from 5 am to 8:30 pm. There is also *Fred's Restaurant & Lounge* (☎ 505-355-7500), at 1408 E Sumner Ave.

Getting There & Away
The Fort Sumner Bus Station (☎ 505-355-7745), 11th and Sumner Ave, has a daily TNM&O bus in each direction between Albuquerque and Clovis (continuing to Lubbock, Texas).

NEW MEXICO

Website Directory

GENERAL TRAVEL INFORMATION
Embassies & Visas
The US State Department's Visa Services webpage includes a list of embassy phone and fax numbers and addresses:
http://travel.state.gov/visa_services.html

National Parks & Public Lands
The National Park Service website has links to sites for every park and monument:
www.nps.gov

Bureau of Land Management:
www.nm.blm.gov

Public Lands Information Center:
www.publiclandsinfo.org/html/home.html

Disabled Travelers
Access-Able Travel Source:
www.access-able.com

Mobility International USA (MIUSA):
www.miusa.org

Disabled Sports USA offers recreational programs for the disabled:
www.nas.com/~dsusa

ACCOMMODATIONS
Hostels International/American Youth Hostels (HI/AYH):
www.hiayh.org

Kampgrounds of America (KOA):
www.KOAkampgrounds.com

Hotel Chains

Best Western	www.bestwestern.com
Budget Host	www.budgethost.com
Comfort Inn	www.comfortinn.com
Days Inn	www.daysinn.com
Econo Lodge	www.econolodge.com
Fairfield Inn by Marriott	www.fairfieldinn.com
Holiday Inn	www.holiday-inn.com
Howard Johnson	www.hojo.com
Ramada Inn	www.ramada.com
Quality Inn	www.qualityinn.com
Sleep Inn	www.sleepinn.com
Super 8 Motel	www.super8motels.com
Travelodge	www.travelodge.com

ARIZONA
Arizona Office of Tourism:
www.arizonaguide.com

Arizona Trail Association:
www.primenet.com/~aztrail/

Arcosanti
An architectural experiment in urban living:
www.arcosanti.org

Grand Canyon
Grand Canyon National Park home page:
www.thecanyon.com/nps

Grand Canyon Railway:
www.thetrain.com

When calling up websites, don't forget to precede the addresses given with **http://**

NEVADA

Nevada Commission on Tourism:
www.travelnevada.com

Las Vegas

Las Vegas Visitor Center:
www.lasvegas24hours.com

The Insider magazine:
www.insidervlv.com

What's On in Las Vegas magazine:
www.ilovevegas.com

NEW MEXICO

New Mexico Department of Tourism:
www.newmexico.org

Albuquerque

Albuquerque Convention & Visitors
Bureau:
www.abqcvb.org/

Angel Fire

Angel Fire Chamber of Commerce:
www.angelfirenm.com/visit

Red River

Red River Chamber of Commerce:
www.taoswebb.com/RedRiverInfo

Sante Fe

Santa Fe Convention & Visitors Bureau:
www.santafe.org

Museum of New Mexico:
www.nmculture.org

Taos

Taos Visitors Center and Chamber of
Commerce:
www.taoswebb.com/TAOS

Taos Ski Valley, Inc:
www.taoswebb.com/nmusa/skitaos/

UTAH

Utah Travel Council:
www.utah.com

Utah Ski & Snowboard Association:
www.skiutah.com

Brian Head

Brian Head Chamber of Commerce:
www.brianheadutah.com

Moab

Moab, Utah Home Page:
www.moab.net

Salt Lake City

Olympic Organizing Committee:
www.slc2002.org

When calling up websites, don't forget to precede the addresses given with **http://**

Index

ABBREVIATIONS

AZ – Arizona   CO – Colorado   NM – New Mexico   NV – Nevada   UT – Utah

MAPS

Albuquerque (NM)
  Area 746
  Central 734-735
  Metropolitan 724
  Old Town Area 726
Arches & Canyonlands National
  Parks (UT) 333
Arizona 376-377
  Central 501
  East-Central 588
  Northeastern 563
  Southeastern 672
  Southern 621
  Western 464
Artesia (NM) 946
Aztec (NM) 817

Beaver (UT) 268
Benson (AZ) 675
Bisbee Area (AZ) 685
Blanding (UT) 356
Brigham City (UT) 199
Bryce Canyon National Park
  (UT) 309
Bullhead City & Laughlin
  (AZ) 474-475

Capitol Reef National Park
  (UT) 322
Carlsbad (NM) 949
Cedar City (UT) 275
Chama (NM) 825
Clayton (NM) 878
Cloudcroft (NM) 925
Clovis (NM) 966
Colorado, Southwestern 701
Cottonwood (AZ) 518

Deming (NM) 902
Douglas (AZ) 690

Farmington (NM) 812-813
Flagstaff (AZ) 538-539
  Downtown 541
Flaming Gorge National
  Recreation Area (UT) 224

Gallup (NM) 848-849
Glen Canyon National
  Recreation Area (AZ) 458
Globe (AZ) 617
Grand Canyon & Lake Powell
  (AZ) 421
  Grand Canyon, Central
    (AZ) 423
  Grand Canyon Village
    (AZ) 426
Grants (NM) 842
Green River (UT) 329

Heber City (UT) 183
Hobbs (NM) 959
Holbrook (AZ) 568

Jerome (AZ) 515

Kanab (UT) 305
Kingman (AZ) 466

Lake Havasu City (AZ)
  480
Las Cruces (NM) 896-897
  Las Cruces Area 892
Las Vegas (NM) 863
Las Vegas (NV) 369
  Around Las Vegas 367
Logan (UT) 203
Lordsburg (NM) 915
Los Alamos (NM) 832
Lovington (NM) 961

Mesa (AZ) 396
Mesa Verde National Park
  (CO) 708
Moab (UT) 344
Monticello (UT) 354

New Mexico 718-719
  Northeastern 854
  Northwestern 809
  Southeastern 918
  Southwestern 881
Nogales (AZ) 667

Ogden (UT) 162-163

Page (AZ) 453
Panguitch (UT) 301
Park City (UT) 176
  Park City Area 172
Parker (AZ) 485
Payson (AZ) 591
Phoenix (AZ) 386-387
  Central 390
  Suburban 382
Pinetop-Lakeside (AZ) 598
Portales (NM) 963
Prescott (AZ) 506-507
Price (UT) 259
Provo (UT) 188
  Provo Center 191
Pueblos of New Mexico (NM)
  721

Raton (NM) 873
Richfield (UT) 254
Roosevelt (UT) 216
Roswell (NM) 941
Route 66
  AZ and NM 379
  LA to Chicago 378
Ruidoso Area (NM) 930

Safford (AZ) 612
Salt Lake City (UT) 127
  Downtown 130
  Metropolitan 138-139
  Orientation 121
Santa Fe & Taos (NM) 753
Santa Fe (NM) 756
  Downtown 758-759
Santa Fe Trail 754
Santa Rosa (NM) 856
Scottsdale (AZ) 393
Sedona (AZ) 524-525
  Uptown 531
Show Low (AZ) 595
Sierra Vista (AZ) 676
Silver City (NM) 907
Socorro (NM) 883

Southwest between 16 and 17
    Ancient Southwestern
        Cultures 19
    Geological Zones 28
    locator 15
Springerville-Eagar (AZ) 606
St George (UT) 283
    St George Area 281

Taos (NM) 790
    Taos Area 785
Tempe (AZ) 395
Tombstone (AZ) 681
Truth or Consequences (NM)
    887

Tucson (AZ) 626-627
    Downtown 629
    Metropolitan 623
    University of Arizona 631
Tucumcari (NM) 859

Utah 119
    Central 243
    Northeastern 213
    Northern 196-197
    Southeastern 327
    Southwestern 266
    Wasatch Mountains Region
        160
    Western 232

Vernal (UT) 219

Wickenburg (AZ) 503
Willcox (AZ) 693
Williams (AZ) 556
Winslow (AZ) 565

Yuma (AZ) 490-491

Zion National Park (UT) 295
Zuni Pueblo (NM) 846

TEXT

Map references are in **bold** type.

AAA 68, 113
Abbey, Edward 60, 326, 334
Abiquiu (NM) 829-830
accommodations 78-84
Acoma Pueblo (NM) 840-841
Agua Prieta (AZ) 690-691
Aguirre Springs National
    Recreation Area (NM) 901
air travel 101-107
    airlines 101
    airports 101
    regional 111
    tickets 102-104
Ajo (AZ) 661-662
Alamo Lake State Park (AZ) 488
Alamogordo (NM) 918-923, **921**
Albuquerque (NM) 723-745,
    724, 726, 734-735, 746
    accommodations 733-738
    activities 731-732
    children's activities 729
    entertainment 741-744
    history 723
    information 725
    orientation 725
    organized tours 732
    places to eat 738-741
    shopping 744
    spectator sports 744
    transportation 744-745
alcohol 86
    drinking laws 72, 86
    drinking laws, Arizona 380
    drinking laws, New Mexico
        722
    drinking laws, Utah 122
Algodones (Mexico) 493

Algodones Sand Dunes (AZ)
    493
Alpine (AZ) 609-610
Altamont (UT) 215
Anasazi Indians. See Ancestral
    Puebloan Culture
Ancestral Puebloan Culture
    19-20, 704-705
Ancho (NM) 924
Angel Fire (NM) 806-807
Angel Peak National Recreation
    Area (NM) 819
Antelope (NM) 879
Antelope Island State Park (UT)
    159-161
Antonito (CO) 824
Apache Indians 21, 25, 601-603,
    614-615
    history 601
    Jicarilla 21
    Mescaleros 21
Apache Lake (AZ) 619
Apache Trail (AZ) 618
archaeological sites
    Arizona 517, 520, 552-553,
        553-554, 605, 607, 616
    Colorado 704
    New Mexico 818, 821-822,
        835-836, 876
    Utah 318, 359
Arches National Park (UT) 332,
    336-337, **333**
Arcosanti (AZ) 521
area codes
    Arizona 379
    New Mexico 721
    Utah 121
Arizona 373-697, **376-377, 464,
    501, 563, 588, 621, 672**

recent history 375-378
    economy 378-379
Arizona-Sonora Desert (AZ) 36
Arizona-Sonora Desert Museum
    (AZ) 652-653
Arizona State University, 394
Arizona Trail 94
Arroyo Hondo (NM) 803
Artesia (NM) 945-947, **946**
Ash Fork (AZ) 561-562
ATMs 53
atom bomb 924
atomic research 831, 833
Aztec (NM) 817-819, **817**
Aztec Ruins National Monument
    (NM) 817-818

B&Bs 81
backpacking 91-95
    Arizona 429-433, 449-450,
        571, 582-583, 633-635,
        655-656, 679
    New Mexico 836
    Utah 214-215, 225, 229, 297-
        298, 311, 317, 324, 336,
        340-341
Baker Dam Reservoir (UT) 288
bald eagles 171, 299
Bandelier National Monument
    (NM) 835-836
bars 87
baseball 87-88, 497, 811
Basin and Range geologic
    province 27
basketball 87
baskets, use of 17
bats 956
Beale, Edward 463
Bear Lake (UT) 210-211

Bear Lake State Park (UT) 210
Beaver (UT) 267-269, **268**
Beaver Mountain Ski Area (UT) 209
Belen (NM) 750
Benson (AZ) 673-674, **675**
Bernalillo (NM) 747
Betatakin Pueblo (AZ) 582
Bicknell (UT) 318-320
bicycling 95-96, 115. *See also* mountain biking
    Arizona 434
    Utah 298
Billy the Kid 26, 717, 938, 970
Biosphere 2 (AZ) 653-654
bird watching 99
    Arizona 478, 489, 635-636, 663, 670, 678, 679, 686, 692, 695, 697
    New Mexico 858, 864, 875, 885, 894
    Utah 159, 170-171, 190, 198, 201, 207-208, 217, 237, 240, 262, 299, 309
Bisbee (AZ) 684-689, **685**
Bisti Badlands (NM) 816
Blanding (UT) 355-357, **356**
Bloomfield (NM) 819-820
Blue Hole (NM) 855
Bluewater Lake State Park (NM) 842
Bluff (UT) 360-362
Blumenschein, Ernest 784, 787
boating 96-97
    Arizona 472-473, 479, 598, 606-607, 608
    Utah 213, 226
Bonneville Salt Flats (UT) 233-234
books 57-60
border crossings
    Arizona 493, 666, 669, 686, 690-691
    New Mexico 905
Bosque del Apache National Wildlife Refuge (NM) 885
Bottomless Lakes State Park (NM) 945
Boulder (UT) 318
Boyce Thompson Southwestern Arboretum (AZ) 618
Brazos Canyon (NM) 828
Brian Head (UT) 272-273
Brian Head Ski Resort (UT) 272
Brigham City (UT) 196-200, **199**

Brigham Young University (UT) 189
Bryce Canyon National Park (UT) 308-312, **309**
Buckskin Mountain Colorado River State Park (AZ) 484
Buenos Aires National Wildlife Refuge Loop (AZ) 658-659
Buffalo Bill 237
Bullfrog Marina (AZ) 459-460
Bullhead City (AZ) 475-478, **474-475**
Bureau of Land Management (BLM) 70
Burr Trail (UT) 318
bus travel 107-108
    regional 111-112
business hours 73

Caballo Lake State Park (NM) 890
Cabeza Prieta National Wildlife Refuge (AZ) 498
cacti 36-39, 655
Caineville (UT) 325
Calf Creek Recreation Area (UT) 317
Callao (UT) 237
Cameron (AZ) 444-445
Camp Floyd/Stagecoach Inn State Park (UT) 236
Camp Verde (AZ) 520-522
camping 78-80
Canjilon (NM) 829
canoeing 97
Canyon de Chelly National Monument (AZ) 577-580
canyoneering 94-95
    Arizona 452
    Utah 316
Canyonlands National Park (UT) 337-343, **333**
The Canyons Ski Resort (UT) 173
Capitan (NM) 937
Capitol Reef National Park (UT) 321-324, **322**
car travel 82. *See also* driving laws
    AAA 68
    accidents 113
    cautions 112
    drive-aways 108-109
    driving permits 50
    major highways 107
    purchase 115
    rental 113-115

shipping vehicles 109
Carlsbad (NM) 947-952, **949**
Carlsbad Caverns National Park (NM) 953-956
Carrizozo (NM) 923-924
Carson National Forest (NM) 828-829
Carson, Kit 784, 787
Casa Grande (AZ) 657
Casa Grande Ruins National Monument (AZ) 657-658
Casa Malpais (AZ) 605
cash 52
casinos
    Arizona 380, 521, 590, 601, 615, 654
    Nevada 367-368
    New Mexico 742
    Utah 233
Cassidy, Butch 257, 267, 290, 299, 324
Castle Dale (UT) 262-264
Catalina State Park (AZ) 635
cattle drives 26
caves
    Arizona 469, 654, 674-675
    New Mexico 953-956
    Utah 187, 208-209, 231, 241, 306
Cedar Breaks National Monument (UT) 273-274
Cedar City (UT) 274-279, **275**
Cerrillos (NM) 749
Chaco Culture National Historical Park (NM) 821-822
Chama (NM) 824-828, **825**
Chambers (AZ) 571
Chemehuevi Indians 484
Chihuahua Desert 36-37
children
    travel tips 68, 105
chiles 891
Chimayo (NM) 781-782
Chinle (AZ) 577
Chiricahua Apache Indians 929
Chiricahua Mountains (AZ) 695-697
Chiricahua National Monument (AZ) 695-697
Chloride (AZ) 470-471
Chloride (NM) 890
Church of Latter-Day Saints (LDS). *See* Mormons
Cimarron (NM) 869-871
Cimarron Canyon State Park (NM) 871
cinemas 87

Circleville (UT) 299
City of Rocks State Park (NM) 905
Clayton (NM) 877-879, **878**
Clayton Lake State Park (NM) 879
Cleveland-Lloyd Dinosaur Quarry (UT) 262
Clifton (AZ) 610-611
climate 31-32
clothing 47
Cloudcroft (NM) 924-928, **925**
Clovis (NM) 965-969, **966**
Coalville (UT) 171
Cochise 375
Cochise Culture 880
Cochise Stronghold Recreation Area (AZ) 694
Cochiti Pueblo (NM) 748
Coconino National Forest (AZ) 521, 554
Cody, William F. See Buffalo Bill
Colorado 699-714, **701**
Columbus (NM) 905
Conchas Lake State Park (NM) 861
condors 447
Confederate Air Force Museum (NM) 958
Coral Pink Sand Dunes State Park (UT) 304
Corinne (UT) 201
Corona (NM) 924
Coronado National Memorial (AZ) 678-679
Coronado Trail Scenic Road (AZ) 608-609
Coronado, Francisco Vásquez de 21, 608, 621, 678, 723
Corrales (NM) 745-747
Cortez (CO) 700-703
Cosanti (AZ) 392
costs 53-54
    accommodations 53-54
    food 54
    transportation 53
Cottonwood (AZ) 517-520, **518**
Coyote Creek State Park (NM) 867-868
credit cards 52-53
crime 53
Crownpoint (NM) 851
cryptobiotic crust 335
Cuba (NM) 838 839
Cuchillo (NM) 890
cultural considerations 44, 74-75

Cumbres & Toltec Scenic Railroad (NM) 824-826
currency 51
customs 51, 106-107
cycling. See bicycling, mountain biking

dance 43-44
dangers & annoyances 70-72
Datil (NM) 886
Davis Dam (AZ) 472
Dead Horse Point State Park (UT) 337
debit cards 52-53
Deer Creek State Park (UT) 186
Deer Valley Resort (UT) 173
Delta (UT) 239-240
Deming (NM) 901-904, **902**
Dinosaur National Monument (UT) 228-230
disabled travelers 67
    air travel 104
Dixon (NM) 783
documents 48-50
Dolores (CO) 713-714
Domínguez, Francisco Atanasio 23
Dos Cabezas (AZ) 694
Douglas (AZ) 689-691, **690**
Dove Creek (CO) 707
drinking. See alcohol
drinks 86-87
driving laws 72
    Arizona 380
    New Mexico 721
    Utah 122
Duchesne (UT) 215-216
Duck Creek Village (UT) 279
Dulce (NM) 823

Eagar (AZ) 604-608, **606**
Eagle Nest (NM) 806
East Canyon State Park (UT) 171
ecology 33-35
economy 42
El Malpais National Monument (NM) 844-845
El Morro National Monument (NM) 845-846
El Porvenir (NM) 866
El Vado Lake State Park (NM) 828
electricity 61
Elephant Butte Lake State Park (NM) 889-890

Elk Meadows Ski & Summer Resort (UT) 269-270
email 56
embassies & consulates 50-51
emergencies 72
Enterprise (UT) 288
Enterprise Reservoir (UT) 288
entertainment 87-88
environmental issues 33-35, 613
    camping 92-93, 457
    dams 33-34
    nuclear waste 948
    tourism 270-271, 293, 310, 335, 424, 440, 709
    water use 33-35, 60, 377-378, 581
Ephraim (UT) 250-251
Escalante (UT) 313-314
Escalante Petrified Forest State Park (UT) 313-314
Escalante, Silvestre Vélez de 23
Española (NM) 779-781
ethnic groups 42-43
Eureka (UT) 238
exchange rates 51

Fairfield (UT) 236
Fairview (UT) 248-249
Farmington (NM) 809-816, **812-813**
fauna. See wildlife
faxes 56
Fenton Lake (NM) 838
Ferron (UT) 264
Ferron Canyon (UT) 264
Fillmore (UT) 246
first-aid kits 62
Fish Lake (UT) 321
fishing 97
    Arizona 434, 460, 472, 479, 598, 602, 606-607, 608, 615, 619
    Colorado 705
    New Mexico 763, 805, 826, 861, 868, 888
    Utah 210, 213-215, 223, 225-226, 244, 270, 279, 299, 302, 321
Fishlake National Forest (UT) 240, 246
Flagstaff (AZ) 536-551, **538-539, 541**
    accommodations 543-547
    activities 542-543
    entertainment 550
    history 536-537
    information 537

organized tours 543
orientation 537
places to eat 547-550
shopping 550
transportation 550-551
Flaming Gorge National
   Recreation Area (UT)
   223-228, **224**
flash floods 93
flora 35-40
Florence (AZ) 658
Folsom (NM) 876
Folsom Man 17, 876
food 82, 84-86
football 87
Forest Lakes (AZ) 593-594
Fort Pearce (UT) 289
Fort Sumner (NM) 969-971
Fort Union National Monument
   (NM) 867
fossils
   New Mexico 829, 879
   Utah 222, 228, 240, 262, 289
Fountain Green (UT) 245
Four Corners Monument Navajo
   Tribal Park (AZ) 580
Fredonia (AZ) 451
Fremont Indian State Park (UT)
   256
Fremont Indians (UT) 256
Frisco (UT) 242
Fruita (UT) 323-324
Fry Canyon (UT) 358

Gadsden Purchase 24, 375, 891
Gallinas Canyon (NM) 866
Gallup (NM) 847-853,
   848-849
Garden City (UT) 209-211
Garrett, Pat 26, 970
gay travelers 49, 66-67
genealogy 132
geography 27-28
geology 28-31
Georgia O'Keeffe Museum
   757-760
Geronimo 25, 622
ghost towns
   Arizona 502, 619, 674, 679,
      694
   New Mexico 890, 914, 924
   Utah 236, 238, 242, 290, 330
Gila Bend (AZ) 498-499
Gila Hot Springs (NM) 911
Gila National Forest (NM) 911
Gila River Arts & Crafts Center
   (AZ) 658

Glen Canyon Dam (AZ) 452,
   457, 459
Glen Canyon National
   Recreation Area **458**
   Arizona 457-461
   Utah 360
Glendale (UT) 304
Glenwood (NM) 913
gliding 958
Globe (AZ) 615-618, **617**
Goblin Valley State Park (UT)
   331
Gold Hill (UT) 238
Golden (NM) 749
Golden Spike National Historic
   Site (UT) 200-201
golf 100
Goosenecks State Park (UT)
   359
Goshute Indian Reservation
   (UT) 238
Goshute Indians 21
government 40-42
Grafton (UT) 290
Grand Canyon National Park
   (AZ) 420-438, 448-450,
   421, **423**, **426**
   accommodations 436-437,
      450
   activities 428-435, 449-450
   geology 430
   history 420-422
   information 422-428, 448
   North Rim 448-450
   organized tours 435-436, 450
   places to eat 437-438, 450
   South Rim 422-438
   transportation 438, 450
Grand Canyon Village (AZ)
   420-429
Grand Falls of the Little
   Colorado (AZ) 551
Grand Gulch Primitive Area
   (UT) 359
Grand Staircase-Escalante
   National Monument (UT)
   314-318
Granite Gap (NM) 914
Grants (NM) 841-844, **842**
Grantsville (UT) 235-236
Great Basin Desert 38-39
Great Basin National Park 240-
   241
Great Salt Lake (UT) 137
Green River (UT) 326-330, **329**
Green Valley (AZ) 662-664
Greer (AZ) 603-604

Guadalupe Mountains (NM)
   956-957
Guadalupe Mountains National
   Park (Texas) 957
Gunnison (UT) 252

Hachita (NM) 916
Hackberry (AZ) 470
Hall, Sharlot Mabrith 509
Halls Crossing Marina (AZ) 460
Hanksville (UT) 331
Harry McAdams State Park
   (NM) 958
Hashknife Posse 569
Hatch (NM) 891
Hatch (UT) 303
Havasu National Wildlife
   Refuge (AZ) 478
Havasupai Indian Reservation
   (AZ) 443-444
Hawley Lake (AZ) 602
health 62-65
   first-aid kit 62
   insurance 62
Heard Museum (AZ) 388
Heber City (UT) 182-185, **183**
Heber-Overgaard (AZ) 594
Helper (UT) 257-258
Henry Mountains (UT) 331-332
Heron Lake State Park (NM)
   828
hiking 91-95
   Arizona 316, 429-433, 443,
      449-450, 525-526, 553,
      571, 633-635, 655-656,
      696
   Colorado 711-712
   New Mexico 763, 926
   safety 93-94
   Utah 140, 214-215, 225, 296-
      297, 309-310, 316-317,
      324, 335-336, 339-340,
      341-342, 358, 362-363
Hillsboro (NM) 912
Hispanic people 43
history 17-27
hitchhiking 115
Hite Marina (AZ) 460
HIV/AIDS 65
   and visas 49
Hobbs (NM) 957-961, **959**
hockey 87
Hohokam Culture 18, 498
Holbrook (AZ) 567-570, **568**
Hole 'n the Rock (UT) 345
Hole-in-the-Rock Road (UT)
   317

holidays 73
Holly, Buddy 967
Homolovi Ruins State Park (AZ)
    564-565
Hoover Dam (AZ) 472
Hopi Indian Reservation (AZ)
    583-587
Hopi Indians 484, 583-584, 586
horseback riding 99
    Arizona 400, 439, 504, 543,
        636
    Utah 298
hostels 80
    membership 50, 80
hot springs
    Arizona 612
    New Mexico 864, 887-888,
        911
    Utah 198, 200, 256, 287, 289
hot-air ballooning 99
    Arizona 636
    Utah 174
House Rock Wildlife Area (AZ)
    446
houseboats 97
    Arizona 460-461, 481
Hovenweep National Monument
    (UT) 362-363
Hualapai Indian Reservation
    (AZ) 441-442
Hualapai Mountain Park (AZ)
    467
Hubbell Trading Post National
    Historic Site (AZ) 577
Humphreys Peak (AZ) 553
Huntington (UT) 262
Hurricane (UT) 289-290
Hyrum State Park (UT) 207

Ibapah (UT) 238
ice-skating 99
Indian reservations 43
    behavior on 44, 74
Indians. See Native Americans
    and names of individual tribes
Inn of the Mountain Gods (NM)
    929
insurance
    health 62
    travel 50
International Space Hall of Fame
    (NM) 919
Internet resources 56-57, 972-
    973
Isleta Pueblo (NM) 749

Jacob Lake (AZ) 446-448

jeep touring 100
Jemez Pueblo (NM) 837-838
Jemez Springs (NM) 836
Jerome (AZ) 514-517, 515
Jicarilla Apache Indian
    Reservation (NM) 822-823
Joes Valley Reservoir (UT) 263
Jornada del Muerto 22
Junction (UT) 299

kachinas 585-586
Kaibab National Forest (AZ)
    557, 559
Kaibab-Paiute Indian
    Reservation (AZ) 451
Kamas (UT) 212
Kanab (UT) 305-308, 305
Kanab Canyon (AZ) 451
Kanosh (UT) 246
Kartchner Caverns State Park
    (AZ) 674-675
kayaking 97
Kayenta (AZ) 580-581
Keet Seel Pueblo (AZ) 582
Kelly (NM) 886
Ketchum, Black Jack 877
Kimberly (UT) 256
Kingman (AZ) 465-469, 466
Kings Peak (UT) 214-215
Kingston (NM) 912
Kino, Eusebio 23
Kiowa National Grasslands
    (NM) 879
Kitt Peak National Optical
    Observatory (AZ) 660
Kodachrome Basin State Park
    (UT) 313

La Cienega (NM) 777
La Cueva (NM) 838
La Luz (NM) 923
La Paz County Park (AZ) 484
Laguna Pueblo (NM) 840
Lake Bonneville 31, 137
Lake Havasu City (AZ) 478-484,
    480
Lake Havasu State Park (AZ)
    481
Lake Mead National Recreation
    Area (AZ) 471-475
Lake Pleasant Regional Park
    (AZ) 399
Lake Powell (AZ)/(UT) 457-461
    ferry 461
Lake Roberts (NM) 910-911
language 46
    Navajo 572

Pueblo Indian 765
Las Cruces (NM) 891-900, 892,
    896-897
Las Trampas (NM) 782
Las Vegas (NM) 862-866, 863
Las Vegas (NV) 366-371, 367,
    369
    accommodations 368-370
    casinos 367-368
    entertainment 370-371
    history 366
    information 366-367
    orientation 366
    places to eat 370
    transportation 371
Laughlin (NV) 475-478, 474-
    475
laundry 62
lava tubes
    New Mexico 845
    Utah 247, 287
Lawrence, DH 803
Lawrence, Frieda 803
Leasburg Dam State Park (NM)
    901
Leeds (UT) 288
Lees Ferry (AZ) 446
legal matters 72-73
Lehi (UT) 194
Lehman Caves (UT) 241
lesbian travelers 66-67
Lincoln (NM) 938-939
Lincoln National Forest (NM)
    957
Lipan Apache Indians 929
Little Sahara Recreation Area
    (UT) 238-239
Loa (UT) 320-321
Logan (UT) 202-207, 203
Logan Canyon (UT) 208-209
London Bridge 478
Lordsburg (NM) 913-915, 915
Los Alamos (NM) 831-835, 832
Los Lunas (NM) 750
Los Ojos (NM) 828
Lovington (NM) 961-962, 961
Lowry Pueblo Ruins National
    Historic Landmark (CO)
    706-707
Luhan, Mabel Dodge 803, 830
Lukeville (AZ) 661
Lyman Lake State Park (AZ)
    608

Madera Canyon Recreation Area
    (AZ) 663
Madrid (NM) 749

Magdalena (NM) 885
Mancos (CO) 713
Manhattan Project 831-832
Manila (UT) 227
Manti (UT) 251-252
Manzano Mountains (NM) 750
Manzano Mountains State Park
    (NM) 750
maps
    hiking 92
    obtaining 47
Marble Canyon (AZ) 445-446
Martinez Lake (AZ) 489
Martinez, Maria 45, 778
Marysvale (UT) 256
Maxwell, Lucien 970
McClurg, Virginia 707
McDowell Mountain Regional
    Park (AZ) 399
McJunkin, George 876
Meadow (UT) 246
Mendon (UT) 207
Mercur (UT) 236
Mesa (AZ) 395-397, **396**
Mesa Verde National Park (CO)
    707-712, **708**
Mescalero Apache Indian
    Reservation (NM) 928-929
Mesilla (NM) 894, 899
Mesquite (NV) 287
Meteor Crater (AZ) 554
Mexican Hat (UT) 359-360
Mexican War 15, 24
Mexico 666-668, 669, 686,
    690-691
Midway (UT) 182-185
Milford (UT) 242
Mimbres pottery 19, 902, 908
Mineral Museum (NM) 882
Minersville State Park (UT) 267
missions
    Our Lady of Guadalupe (NM)
        846
    Salinas Pueblo Missions
        National Monument (NM)
        751
    San Agustin (NM) 749
    San Esteban del Rey (NM)
        841
    San Miguel (NM) 760
    San Xavier del Bac (AZ) 23,
        652
    Tumacacori (AZ) 23
Moab (UT) 343-353, **344**
    accommodations 348-351
    activities 346-347
    entertainment 353

information 345
places to eat 351-352
recent history 343
shopping 353
transportation 353
Mogollon (NM) 913
Mogollon Culture 18-19, 923
Mohave Indians 484
Mojave Desert 37-38
Moki Dugway (UT) 359
money 51-54
Monroe (UT) 255
Montezuma (NM) 864
Montezuma Castle National
    Monument (AZ) 520
Monticello (UT) 353-355, **354**
Monument Valley (UT) 359
Monument Valley Navajo Tribal
    Park (AZ) 581-582
Mora (NM) 867
Morenci (AZ) 610-611
Morgan (UT) 171
Moriarty (NM) 748
Mormon Miracle Pageant 251
Mormon Tabernacle Choir 129
Mormons
    history 118-120, 123, 124, 265
    polygamy 118, 305, 445
    religion 124-125
Moroni (UT) 245
Morphy Lake State Park (NM)
    867
mountain biking. See also
    bicycling
    Arizona 525, 542
    Colorado 705-706, 712
    Utah 272-273, 347
Mountainair (NM) 750
Mt Carmel Junction (UT) 304
Mt Graham (AZ) 613
Mt Lemmon (AZ) 635
Mt Pleasant (UT) 249
Muleshoe Ranch (AZ) 694
music 43-45

Naco (AZ) 686
Nambe Pueblo (NM) 778
national monuments
    Aztec Ruins (NM) 817-818
    Bandelier (NM) 835-836
    Canyon de Chelly (AZ)
        577-580
    Casa Grande Ruins (AZ)
        657-658
    Cedar Breaks (UT) 273-274
    Dinosaur (UT) 228-230
    El Malpais (NM) 844-845

El Morro (NM) 845-846
Fort Union (NM) 867
Grand Staircase-Escalante
    (UT) 314-318
Hovenweep (UT) 362-363
Montezuma Castle (AZ) 520
Natural Bridges (UT)
    357-358
Navajo (AZ) 582-583
Organ Pipe Cactus (AZ)
    660-661
Petroglyph (NM) 729
Pipe Spring (AZ) 451
Rainbow Bridge (AZ) 461
Salinas Pueblo Missions
    (NM) 751
Sunset Crater (AZ) 551-552
Timpanogos Cave (UT) 187
Tonto (AZ) 619
Tuzigoot (AZ) 517
Walnut Canyon (AZ) 553-554
White Sands (NM) 917-918
Wupatki (AZ) 552-553
National Park Service (NPS) 69
national parks
    Arches (UT) 332, 336-337
    Bryce Canyon (UT) 308,
        310-312
    Canyonlands (UT) 337-343
    Capitol Reef (UT) 321-324
    Carlsbad Caverns (NM)
        953-956
    Grand Canyon (AZ) 420,
        424-425, 427, 440, 448
    Great Basin 240-241
    Guadalupe Mountains (Texas)
        957
    Mesa Verde (CO) 707-712
    Petrified Forest (AZ) 570-571
    Saguaro (AZ) 654-656
    Zion (UT) 293-299
Native Americans
    arts 45, 760
    books about 58
    cultural events 573-574, 580,
        615, 657, 660, 786, 849,
        929
    dance 44, 585, 587, 638, 748,
        778
    early peoples 17-21, 704
    handicrafts 88-89, 732, 853
    music 44
    relocation of 24-25
Natural Bridges National
    Monument (UT) 357-358
Navajo Indian Reservation (AZ)
    571-583

accommodations 574, 576-577, 579, 580, 582, 583
information 573, 576, 578, 582
places to eat 576-577, 579, 580-581, 583
shopping 574, 575, 577, 579-580
special events 573-574
transportation 574-575
Navajo Indians 21, 571-573, 575, 577
Code Talkers 25, 572
history 571-573, 577
Long Walk 24, 573, 577, 584, 970
rug weaving 575, 851
Navajo Lake (UT) 279
Navajo National Monument (AZ) 582-583
Nephi (UT) 245-246
New Age 528
New Mexico 715-971, **718-719, 809, 854, 881, 918**
economy 719-721
recent history 717-719
pueblos 720, **721**
Newspaper Rock Park (UT) 353
newspapers 60
Nine Mile Canyon (UT) 217, 261
Nogales (AZ) 665-668, **667**
Norman Petty Studios (NM) 967
Oatman (AZ) 470

Ogden (UT) 161-169, **162-163**
accommodations 166-167
activities 165-166
entertainment 168-169
information 161-163
orientation 161
places to eat 167-168
transportation 169
OK Corral (AZ) 680
O'Keeffe, Georgia 757-760, 829, 830-831
Old Tucson Studios (AZ) 653
Oliver Lee State Park (NM) 923
Olympics. *See* Winter Olympic Games
Oñate, Juan de 22, 845
Ophir (UT) 236
Oppenheimer, J Robert 831-832
Orderville (UT) 304
Organ Pipe Cactus National Monument (AZ) 660-661
Osier (CO) 824

Otter Creek State Park (UT) 299
Overton (NV) 372

packrats 37
Page (AZ) 452-456, **453**
Paiute Indians 21, 265
Palisade State Park (UT) 251
Pancho Villa State Park (NM) 905
Panguitch (UT) 300-302, **301**
Panguitch Lake (UT) 302-303
Paragonah (UT) 271
Paria Canyon 316, 446
Park City (UT) 171-182, **172, 176**
accommodations 175-180
activities 173-175
entertainment 181-182
information 171-172
places to eat 180-181
shopping 182
transportation 182
Park City Mountain Resort (UT) 173
Park Valley (UT) 202
Parker (AZ) 484-486, **485**
Parker Dam (AZ) 484
Parowan (UT) 270-272
Parowan Gap petroglyphs (UT) 271
Pascua Yaqui Indian Reservation (AZ) 638, 654
passports 48
Patagonia (AZ) 668-671
Patagonia Lake State Park (AZ) 668
Patagonia-Sonoita Creek Preserve (AZ) 670
Payson (AZ) 589-593, **591**
Payson (UT) 244-245
Peach Springs (AZ) 470
Pearce (AZ) 694
Percha Dam State Park (NM) 890
Petrified Forest National Park (AZ) 570-571
Petroglyph National Monument (NM) 729
petroglyphs 20
Arizona 392, 498, 564, 567, 570, 656
Colorado 711
New Mexico 845, 923
Utah 217, 222, 229, 256, 271, 287, 323, 331, 346, 353
Phoenix (AZ) 381-419, **382, 386-387, 390**

accommodations 402-410
activities 399-401
children's activities 397
entertainment 415-416
history 381-383
information 384-388
organized tours 401
orientation 383-384
places to eat 410-415
shopping 417
spectator sports 416-417
transportation 418-419
photography 61
Picacho Peak State Park (AZ) 656-657
Picuris Pueblo (NM) 782-783
Pilar (NM) 783-784
Pine Valley (UT) 288
Pinetop-Lakeside (AZ) 597-601, **598**
Pinos Altos (NM) 908
Pipe Spring National Monument (AZ) 451
Pojoaque Pueblo (NM) 777-778
polygamy. *See* Mormons
Pony Express 237
Pony Express Trail (UT) 236-238
population 42-43
Portal (AZ) 697
Portales (NM) 962-965, **963**
postal services 54-55
pottery 837, 839-840
Powell, John Wesley 94, 223, 328, 420
powwows 277, 573
Gathering of Nations Powwow (NM) 732
Inter-Tribal Indian Ceremonial (NM) 850
Northern Ute Powwow (UT) 218
Wa:k Pow Wow (AZ) 637
Prescott (AZ) 505-514, **506-507**
Prescott National Forest (AZ) 508, 515
Price (UT) 258-261, **259**
Provo (UT) 187-194, **188, 191**
accommodations 190-192
entertainment 193
information 189
orientation 189
places to eat 192-193
transportation 194-194
Pueblo Revolt of 1680 23, 754
pueblos. *See* New Mexico
Puerto de Luna (NM) 855

Puerto Peñasco (Mexico) 661
Puffer Lake (UT) 270

Quail Creek State Park (UT)
    288-299
Quartzsite (AZ) 486-487
Quechan Indians 493
Quemado (NM) 886
Questa (NM) 803

radio stations 60
rafting. See river running
Rainbow Bridge National
    Monument (AZ) 461
Ramah (NM) 846
Ramsey Canyon Preserve (AZ)
    678
Raton (NM) 871-875, **873**
Raven Site (AZ) 605
Rayado (NM) 870
recycling 62
Red Fleet State Park (UT) 222
Red River (NM) 803
Red Rock Canyon (NV) 371
Red Rock State Park (NM) 848-
    849
religion 45-46
Reserve (NM) 913
Richfield (UT) 253-255, **254**
ristras 891
river running 96
    Arizona 433-434, 442, 521
    Colorado 706
    New Mexico 763, 791, 828
    Utah 220, 226, 230, 328, 339,
        346-347, 361
rock climbing 99
    Arizona 543, 635
    Utah 208, 298, 337, 339
Rock Hound State Park (NM)
    904
rockhounding 100, 202, 237,
    240-241
Rockport State Park (UT) 171
Rockville (UT) 290
rodeos 78, 87
    Arizona 510, 567, 573, 580,
        590, 615, 637, 660, 670,
        692
    New Mexico 810, 961
    Utah 200, 205, 216, 218, 235,
        260, 282, 304
Roosevelt (UT) 216-218, **216**
Roper Lake State Park (AZ) 612
Roswell (NM) 939-945, **941**
Route 66 378-379, 469, **378**,
    379

Ruidoso (NM) 929-937, **930**

Sabino Canyon (AZ) 634-635
Safford (AZ) 611-614, **612**
Saguaro National Park (AZ)
    654-656
Salina (UT) 252-253
Salome (AZ) 487-488
Salt Lake City (UT) 123-158,
    121, **127**, **130**, **138-139**
    accommodations 143-149
    activities 138-142
    children's activities 134-135
    entertainment 155-156
    history 123-124
    information 126-128
    organized tours 142
    orientation 124-126
    places to eat 149-155
    shopping 157
    spectator sports 156
    transportation 157-158
Salt Palace (UT) 126
Saltair (UT) 136
San Antonio (NM) 885
San Carlos Apache Indian
    Reservation (AZ) 614-615
San Carlos Lake (AZ) 615
San Felipe Pueblo (NM) 747
San Ildefonso Pueblo (NM) 778
San Juan Pueblo (NM) 779
San Luis (Mexico) 493
San Miguel (NM) 867
San Pedro Riparian National
    Conservation Area (AZ)
    679-680
San Rafael Desert (UT) 330-331
San Rafael Swell (UT) 330
Sandia Pueblo (NM) 745
Santa Ana Pueblo (NM) 747,
    839
Santa Clara Pueblo (NM) 778-
    779
Santa Fe (NM) 22, 752-776,
    753, **756**, **758-759**
    accommodations 765-770
    activities 762-764
    entertainment 773-775
    history 754-755
    information 755-757
    organized tours 764
    orientation 755
    places to eat 770-773
    shopping 775-776
    transportation 776
Santa Fe National Forest (NM)
    837, 866

Santa Fe Opera 762
Santa Fe Trail 24-25, **754**
Santa Rosa (NM) 855-857, **856**
Santa Rosa Lake State Park
    (NM) 856
Santo Domingo Pueblo (NM)
    748
Sapello (NM) 866
Sasabe (AZ) 659
scenic drives
    Arizona 429, 448-449, 526,
        578, 596, 608-609, 613,
        696
    New Mexico 802
    Utah 198, 207-208, 222-223,
        229, 244, 248, 297, 309,
        316-318, 323-324, 345-
        346, 359
Scofield State Park (UT) 258
Scottsdale (AZ) 392-394, **393**
scuba diving 855
Sedona (AZ) 522-536, **524-525**,
    531
    accommodations 527-533
    activities 525-527
    entertainment 536
    information 523
    organized tours 526
    orientation 523
    places to eat 533-536
    shopping 536
    transportation 536
Sego Canyon (UT) 330
sego lily 330
Seligman (AZ) 562
Seneca (AZ) 615
senior travelers 68
Shakespeare Ghost Town (NM)
    914
Shiprock (NM) 816
Shonto (AZ) 583
shopping 88-90
Shoshone Indians 21
Show Low (AZ) 594-597, **595**
Sierra Vista (AZ) 675-678, **676**
Silver City (NM) 905-910, **907**
Silver Reef (UT) 288
Sipapu (NM) 868
skiing, cross-country 98
    Arizona 434-435, 439, 555,
        558, 598, 602
    New Mexico 731, 763, 804
    Utah 141-142, 174, 186, 209,
        227, 244, 272
skiing, downhill 97-98
    Arizona 555, 558, 598, 602,
        636

New Mexico 731, 762, 789-790, 804, 806, 833, 868, 926, 931
Utah 141-142, 169-170, 173-174, 186, 209, 269-270, 272
Skyline Drive (UT) 248
Slickrock Trail (UT) 347
Smith, Joseph 124
Smokey Bear 937
Snow Canyon State Park (UT) 287
Snowbasin (UT) 169
snowboarding 97-98
Arizona 558, 602
New Mexico 868, 926
Utah 141-142, 169-170, 173, 270, 272
Snowflake (AZ) 594
Snowville (UT) 202
Socorro (NM) 880-885, **883**
Soleri, Paolo 392, 521
Sonoita (AZ) 668-671
Sonoita (Mexico) 661
Spanish Fork (UT) 194
special events 74-77
spectator sports 87-88
sporting events 77
Spring City (UT) 250
Springdale (UT) 290-293
Springer (NM) 868-869
Springerville (AZ) 604-608, **606**
Springville (UT) 194
St George (UT) 279-287, **281, 283**
accommodations 282-286
activities 282
entertainment 287
historic buildings 280
information 280
places to eat 286
transportation 287
St Johns (AZ) 608
Stagecoach Inn (UT) 236
Stansbury Mountains (UT) 236
stargazing 867
Arizona 540, 542
Utah 311
Starvation Lake State Park (UT) 215
Steiglitz, Alfred 830
Steinaker State Park (UT) 222
Steins (NM) 914
Steins Railroad Ghost Town (NM) 914
Storrie Lake State Park (NM) 864

Strawberry (AZ) 589
Strawberry Reservoir (UT) 212-214
student IDs 50
Sugarite Canyon State Park (NM) 872
Summerhaven (AZ) 635
Sundance Film Festival 175
Sundance Resort (UT) 186-187
Sunrise Ski Area (AZ) 602
Sunset Crater National Monument (AZ) 551-552
Supai (AZ) 443-444
Superior (AZ) 618
Superstition Wilderness (AZ) 620

Tabiona (UT) 215
Taliesin West (AZ) 392
Taos (NM) 784-802, **785, 790**
accommodations 792-797
activities 789-792
entertainment 800
history 784-785
information 786
orientation 785-786
places to eat 797-800
shopping 800-801
special events 792
transportation 801-802
Taos Pueblo (NM) 786
Taos Ski Valley (NM) 789
Taos Society of Artists 784
taxes 54
departure 110
taxis 116
Taylor (AZ) 594
Teasdale (UT) 318-320
telephone services 55. *See also* area codes
television 60
Tempe (AZ) 394-395, **395**
Tes Nez Iah (AZ) 580
Tesuque (NM) 776
Tesuque Pueblo (NM) 777
theater 87
Theodore Roosevelt Lake & Dam (AZ) 619
Thompson (UT) 330
Three Rivers Petroglyph National Recreation Area (NM) 923
Tierra Amarilla (NM) 828
Tijeras (NM) 749
time 61
Timpanogos Cave National Monument (UT) 187

tipping 54
Titan Missile Museum (AZ) 662-663
Tohono O'odham Indian Reservation (AZ) 659-660
Tohono O'odham Indians (AZ) 621-622, 637-638, 659-660
toilets 62
Toiyabe National Forest (NV) 372
Tombstone (AZ) 680-684, **681**
Tonto National Monument (AZ) 619
Tonto Natural Bridge State Park (AZ) 589
Tooele (UT) 234-235
Topock (AZ) 470
Torrey (UT) 318-320
Tortilla Flat (AZ) 619
tourist offices 48
tours, organized 109-110
train travel 108
regional 112
traveler's checks 52
Tremonton (UT) 200
Tres Piedras (NM) 829
Trinity Site (NM) 831, 924
Tropic (UT) 312-313
Truchas (NM) 782
Truth or Consequences (NM) 886-889, **887**
Truxton (AZ) 470
Tsaile (AZ) 580
Tuba City (AZ) 583
Tubac (AZ) 664-665
Tucson (AZ) 621-652, **623, 626-627, 629**
accommodations 638-643
activities 633-637
children's activities 630, 634
entertainment 648-650
history 623-624
information 625-628
organized tours 637
orientation 624-625
places to eat 643-648
shopping 650-651
spectator sports 650
transportation 651-652
Tucumcari (NM) 858-861, **859**
Tularosa (NM) 923
Tumacacori National Historical Park (AZ) 664
tumbleweeds 804
Tusayan (AZ) 438-441
Tuzigoot National Monument (AZ) 517

984　Index

UFOs 943
Uinta Mountains (UT) 214-215
Uintah & Ouray Indian
　Reservation (UT) 218
University of Arizona 630, **631**
University of New Mexico 728
US Forest Service (USFS) 69-70
Utah 117-363, **119**, **160**, **196-197**, **213**, **232**, **243**, **266**, **327**
　economy 120-121
　history 123-124
　recent history 118-120
　street layout 121-122
Utah Lake State Park (UT) 190
Utah Shakespearean Festival
　276
Utah Winter Sports Park 174
Ute Indians 21, 118
Ute Lake State Park (NM) 861

Valentine (AZ) 470
Valle (AZ) 441
Valle Vidal (NM) 871
Valley of Fire State Park (NV)
　372
Valley of Fires Recreation Area
　(NM) 923
Vaughn (NM) 857
Vega-Bray Observatory (AZ)
　674
Velarde (NM) 783
Vermilion Cliffs (AZ) 447
Vernal (UT) 218-222, **219**
Veyo (UT) 287
videos 61
Villa, Francisco 'Pancho' 905
Villanueva (NM) 867

Villanueva State Park (NM) 867
visas 48-50
　restrictions on 49
　work 77
Vulture City (AZ) 502

Wah Wah Mountains (UT) 241
Wahweap Marina (AZ) 459
Walnut Canyon National
　Monument (AZ) 553-554
Wasatch Mountain State Park
　(UT) 185
Waste Isolation Pilot Plant (NM)
　948
websites 56-57, 972-973
weights & measures 61
Wellington (UT) 261
Wellsville Mountains (UT) 207
Wenden (AZ) 488
Wendover (UT) 231-233
Wheeler Peak (UT) 241
Whipple Observatory (AZ) 663
White Mountain Apache Indian
　Reservation (AZ) 601-603
White Oaks (NM) 924
White Rock (NM) 835
White Sands National
　Monument (NM) 917-918
White Tank Mountain Regional
　Park (AZ) 399
White's City (NM) 952-953
White, Jim 953
Whiteriver (AZ) 601
whooping cranes 885
Wickenburg (AZ) 500-505, **503**
Wild Rivers National Recreation
　Area (NM) 803
wildlife 35-40

precautions 71-72, 310, 427
viewing, Arizona 447, 478,
　660, 678, 695
viewing, New Mexico 945,
　948, 956
viewing, Utah 208, 214, 223,
　238, 244, 248, 270, 309,
　314, 331
Willard (UT) 198
Willard Bay State Park (UT) 170
Willcox (AZ) 691-694, **693**
Williams (AZ) 555-561, **556**
Window Rock (AZ) 575-577
wineries
　Arizona 654, 666, 670
　New Mexico 730, 783, 867,
　　923
　Utah 345
Winslow (AZ) 564-567, **565**
Winston (NM) 890
Winter Olympic Games 89, 173-
　174
work 77
Wright, Frank Lloyd 392
Wupatki National Monument
　(AZ) 552-553

Young (AZ) 593
Young, Brigham 118, 131, 265,
　280
Yuba State Park (UT) 245
Yuma (AZ) 489-498, **490-491**

Zia Pueblo (NM) 839
Zion National Park (UT) 293-
　299, **295**
Zuni Pueblo (NM) 846-847, **846**

SIDEBARS

Ancestral Puebloan Settlement 704
Archaeology in Action 607
The Arizona Trail 94
The Bear Facts 937
Breaking Stereotypes of Pueblo Indians 720-721
Butch Cassidy 257
Cacti of the Southwest 38
Condors at Vermilion Cliffs 447
A Crash Course 113
Crossing the Border 669
Delivering Mail by Trusty Steed 237
The Desert as Muse 392
The Desert's Delicate Skin 335
Development on Mt Graham 613
DH Lawrence Memorial 803
Downtown Mall 893

Draining Lake Powell? 34
The Edible State Flower 330
Especially for Kids, Phoenix 397
Flaming Gorge Fishing Records 226
Flash Floods – A Deadly Danger in the Desert 93
Folsom Man 876
From Wildlife to Junk Food Junkies 310
Gas, Food, Lodging 82
Gearing Up for 2002 89
Geology of Carlsbad Caverns National Park 954
Geology of the Grand Canyon 430
Georgia O'Keeffe 830
The Grand Canyon in the 21st Century 424
Grand Canyon Overflights 440
Grand Falls of the Little Colorado 551
The Great Salt Lake 137

Hazard, Boon or Both? 948
The High Cost of Coal 581
Historic Restaurants 151
HIV & Entering the USA 49
In Search of the New Age 528
Kachinas 586
Kickin' Down Route 66 378-379
Kids' Stuff, Albuquerque 729
Kids' Stuff, Salt Lake City 134
Kids' Stuff, Tucson 634
Lake Powell Ferry 461
The Lincoln County War 938
Major League Baseball Spring Training:
    Cactus League 88
Marriage & Divorce 371
More in Maricopa 381
The Mormon Church 124
Mormon Genealogy 132
Native American Dance & Music 44
The Navajo Language 572
Navajo Weaving 575
New Mexican Indian Casinos 742
New Mexico Trivia 717
Not Quite FedEx 569
Note for Mesa Verde National Park Visitors 709
Packrats – Today's Pest, Yesterday's Historian 37

Paria Canyon-Vermilion Cliffs
    Wilderness Area 316
Park Etiquette 336
Petroglyphs 20
The Price of Popularity 293
Pueblo Languages 765
Ratite Farming 692
Respecting Ancient Sites 821
Rodeo: A Western Ritual 78
Rug Auction 851
Salt Palace Windmills & Tower 126
Sharlot Hall 509
Southern Utah – Being Loved to Death? 270
Speed Limit: 763 MPH 234
Storm Watch 427
The More the Merrier 445
Tourists from Afar 943
Tumbleweeds 804
Turquoise Trail 749
Utah Trivia 118
Vintage Vacation 687
Visiting Mexico 493
Visitors' Etiquette in Pueblos & on Reservations 74
Water Woes 425
Where the Buffalo Roam 159

THANKS

Kit Ashera, Philip Ashworth, Piotr Azia, S Barnett, Roger & Christine Beazley, Richard Beeson, Geoffrey Biddle, Hans Georg Bier, HJ Blumenthal, Manuela Braun, Heather Brossard, Geoff Budge, Chris Calvert, Buffy Carruthers, Claire Chadwick, Rick Clarkson, Michele DiNunzio & Veronica Cocco, Michael Collett, Ray & Sena Copson, Casey Corcoran, KE Curry, Yves De Cock, Lady Dollery, Miriam Fetzer, Joyce Friedman, Chris Gibb, Juliet Gill, Dennis Hahn, Brian Heeney, Nigel Henderson, Ursula Hilton-Jones, Melinda Jackson, Dick Kent, Jenny Kilb, Irving Kirsch, Vera Kramer, Bernard Lucien, Nicola & Eleonora Lugaresi, Rod Macmillan, Jeff Backer & Sally Martin, Rod McCallum, Peter McGulgan, Erik Moderegger, Polly Murray, Susan O'Hare, Marcos Gallego & Lorena Ortega, Dr & Mrs Steve Paley, John Palfrey, Uli Pfeiffer, Hope Riley, Thomas Rau & Andrea Rogge, Helen P Rouse, Ann H Sablosky, Larry W Sanchez, Tim Searle, Ann & Bill Stoughton, Mel Sutherland, Bill & Sue Tews, Doris Thibodeau, Muriel Toop, Bernard Van de Walle de Ghelcke, Kristine Van Dijck, Eileen Van Tyne, Joyce Walmsley, Rob & Delyn Williams, Barry Wiseman, A Woodrow, Ted Zelman

LONELY PLANET PRODUCTS

Lonely Planet is known worldwide for publishing practical, reliable and no-nonsense travel information in our guides and on our web site. The Lonely Planet list covers just about every accessible part of the world. Currently there are nine series: *travel guides, shoestring guides, walking guides, city guides, phrasebooks, audio packs, travel atlases, Journeys*–a unique collection of travel writing–and *Pisces Books* (diving and snorkeling guides.)

EUROPE

Amsterdam • Austria • Baltic States & Kaliningrad • Baltic States phrasebook • Britain • Central Europe on a shoestring • Central Europe phrasebook • Czech & Slovak Republics • Denmark • Dublin • Eastern Europe on a shoestring • Eastern Europe phrasebook • Finland • France • French phrasebook • Germany • German phrasebook • Greece • Greek phrasebook • Hungary • Iceland, Greenland & the Faroe Islands • Ireland • Italy • Italian phrasebook • Lisbon • London • Mediterranean Europe on a shoestring • Mediterranean Europe phrasebook • Paris • Poland • Portugal • Portugal travel atlas • Prague • Romania & Moldova • Russia, Ukraine & Belarus • Russian phrasebook • Scandinavian & Baltic Europe on a shoestring • Scandinavian Europe phrasebook • Slovenia • Spain • Spanish phrasebook • St Petersburg • Switzerland • Trekking in Greece • Trekking in Spain • Ukrainian phrasebook • Vienna • Walking in Britain • Walking in Italy • Walking in Switzerland • Western Europe on a shoestring • Western Europe phrasebook

NORTH AMERICA

Alaska • Backpacking in Alaska • Baja California • Bermuda • California & Nevada • Canada • Chicago • Deep South • Florida • Hawaii • Honolulu • Los Angeles • Mexico • Mexico City • Miami • New England • New Orleans • New York City • New York, New Jersey & Pennsylvania • Pacific Northwest USA • Rocky Mountains USA • San Francisco • Seattle • Southwest USA • USA phrasebook • Washington, DC & The Capital Region

CENTRAL AMERICA & THE CARIBBEAN

Bahamas, Turks & Caicos • Central America on a shoestring • Costa Rica • Cuba • Eastern Caribbean • Guatemala, Belize & Yucatán: La Ruta Maya • Jamaica • Panama

SOUTH AMERICA

Argentina, Uruguay & Paraguay • Bolivia • Brazil • Brazilian phrasebook • Buenos Aires • Chile & Easter Island • Chile travel atlas • Colombia • Ecuador & the Galápagos Islands • Latin American Spanish phrasebook • Peru • Quechua phrasebook • Rio de Janeiro • South America on a shoestring • Trekking in the Patagonian Andes • Venezuela

Travel Literature: Full Circle: A South American Journey

AFRICA

Arabic (Moroccan) phrasebook • Africa on a shoestring • Africa –The South • Cape Town • Cairo • Central Africa • East Africa • Egypt & the Sudan • Egypt travel atlas • Ethiopian (Amharic) phrasebook • Kenya • Kenya travel atlas • Malawi, Mozambique & Zambia • Morocco • North Africa • South Africa, Lesotho & Swaziland • South Africa travel atlas • Swahili phrasebook • Trekking in East Africa • Tunisia • West Africa • Zimbabwe, Botswana & Namibia • Zimbabwe, Botswana & Namibia travel atlas

Travel Literature: The Rainbird: A Central African Journey • Songs to an African Sunset: A Zimbabwean Story

ISLANDS OF THE INDIAN OCEAN

Madagascar & Comoros • Maldives & Islands of the East Indian Ocean • Mauritius, Réunion & Seychelles

Also Available: Brief Encounters • Travel with Children • Traveller's Tales

MAIL ORDER

Lonely Planet products are distributed worldwide. They are also available by mail order from Lonely Planet, so if you have difficulty finding a title please write to us. North American and South American residents should write to 150 Linden St, Oakland CA 94607, USA; European and African residents should write to 10A Spring Place, London NW5 3BH, UK; and residents of other countries to PO Box 617, Hawthorn, Victoria 3122, Australia.

NORTH-EAST ASIA

Beijing • Cantonese phrasebook • China • Hong Kong • Hong Kong, Macau & Canton • Japan • Japanese phrasebook • Japanese audio pack • Korea • Korean phrasebook • Mandarin phrasebook • Mongolia • Mongolian phrasebook • North-East Asia on a shoestring • Seoul • Taiwan • Tibet • Tibet phrasebook • Tokyo

Travel Literature: Lost Japan

MIDDLE EAST & CENTRAL ASIA

Arab Gulf States • Arabic (Egyptian) phrasebook • Cairo • Central Asia • Central Asia phrasebook • Iran • Israel & the Palestinian Territories • Israel & the Palestinian Territories travel atlas • Istanbul • Jerusalem • Jordan & Syria • Jordan, Syria & Lebanon travel atlas • Lebanon • Middle East • Turkey • Turkey travel atlas • Turkish phrasebook • Trekking in Turkey • Yemen

Travel Literature: The Gates of Damascus • Kingdom of the Film Stars: Journey into Jordan

INDIAN SUBCONTINENT

Bengali phrasebook • Bangladesh • Delhi • Goa • Hindi/Urdu phrasebook • India • India & Bangladesh travel atlas • Indian Himalaya • Karakoram Highway • Nepal • Nepali phrasebook • Pakistan • Rajasthan • Sri Lanka • Sri Lanka phrasebook • Trekking in the Indian Himalaya • Trekking in the Karakoram & Hindukush • Trekking in the Nepal Himalaya

Travel Literature: In Rajasthan • Shopping for Buddhas

SOUTH-EAST ASIA

Bali & Lombok • Bangkok • Burmese phrasebook • Cambodia • Ho Chi Minh • Indonesia • Indonesian phrasebook • Indonesian audio pack • Jakarta • Java • Laos • Lao phrasebook • Laos travel atlas • Malay phrasebook • Malaysia, Singapore & Brunei • Myanmar (Burma) • Philippines • Pilipino phrasebook • Singapore • South-East Asia on a shoestring • Thailand • Thailand's Islands & Beaches • Thai phrasebook • Thailand travel atlas • Thai audio pack • Thai Hill Tribes phrasebook • Vietnam • Vietnamese phrasebook • Vietnam travel atlas

ANTARCTICA

Antarctica

AUSTRALIA & THE PACIFIC

Australia • Australian phrasebook • Bushwalking in Australia • Bushwalking in Papua New Guinea • Fiji • Fijian phrasebook • Islands of Australia's Great Barrier Reef • Melbourne • Micronesia • New Caledonia • New South Wales & the ACT • New Zealand • Northern Territory • Outback Australia • Papua New Guinea • Papua New Guinea phrasebook • Queensland • Rarotonga & the Cook Islands • Samoa • Solomon Islands • South Australia • Sydney • Tahiti & French Polynesia • Tasmania • Tonga • Tramping in New Zealand • Vanuatu • Victoria • Western Australia

Travel Literature: Islands in the Clouds • Sean & David's Long Drive

THE LONELY PLANET STORY

Lonely Planet published its first book in 1973 in response to the numerous 'How did you do it?' questions Maureen and Tony Wheeler were asked after driving, bussing, hitching, sailing and railing their way from England to Australia.

Written at a kitchen table and hand collated, trimmed and stapled, *Across Asia on the Cheap* became an instant local best seller, inspiring thoughts of another book.

Eighteen months in South-East Asia resulted in their second guide, *South-East Asia on a shoestring*, which they put together in a backstreet Chinese hotel in Singapore in 1975. The 'yellow bible', as it quickly became known to backpackers around the world, soon became the guide to the region. It has sold well over half a million copies and is now in its 9th edition, still retaining its familiar yellow cover.

Today there are 350 titles, including travel guides, walking guides, language kits & phrasebooks, travel atlases, diving guides and travel literature. The company is the largest independent travel publisher in the world. Although Lonely Planet initially specialized in guides to Asia, today there are few corners of the globe that have not been covered.

The emphasis continues to be on travel for independent travelers. Tony and Maureen still travel for several months of each year and play an active part in the writing, updating and quality control of Lonely Planet's guides.

They have been joined by over 100 authors and 300 staff at our offices in Melbourne (Australia), Oakland (USA), London (UK) and Paris (France). Travelers themselves also make a valuable contribution to the guides through the feedback we receive in thousands of letters each year and on our website.

The people at Lonely Planet strongly believe that travelers can make a positive contribution to the countries they visit, both through their appreciation of the countries' culture, wildlife and natural features, and through the money they spend. In addition, the company makes a direct contribution to the countries and regions it covers. Since 1986 a percentage of the income from each book has been donated to ventures such as famine relief in Africa; aid projects in India; agricultural projects in Central America; Greenpeace's efforts to halt French nuclear testing in the Pacific; and Amnesty International.

'I hope we send people out with the right attitude about travel. You realize when you travel that there are so many different perspectives about the world, so we hope these books will make people more interested in what they see. Guidebooks can't really guide people. All you can do is point them in the right direction.'

– Tony Wheeler

LONELY PLANET PUBLICATIONS

Australia
PO Box 617, Hawthorn 3122, Victoria
☎ (03) 9819 1877 fax (03) 9819 6459
email talk2us@lonelyplanet.com.au

USA
150 Linden Street
Oakland, California 94607
☎ (510) 893 8555, TOLL FREE (800) 275 8555
fax (510) 893 8572
email info@lonelyplanet.com

UK
10A Spring Place,
London NW5 3BH
☎ (0171) 428 4800 fax (0171) 428 4828
email go@lonelyplanet.com.uk

France
1 rue du Dahomey, 75011 Paris
☎ 01 55 25 33 00 fax 01 55 25 33 01
email bip@lonelyplanet.fr

World Wide Web: www.lonelyplanet.com or *AOL keyword: lp*